P9-BJR-841

DATE DUE

DEMCO 38-296

American Educators'
Encyclopedia

American Educators' Encyclopedia

Edward L. Dejnozka and David E. Kapel

Revised Edition by David E. Kapel,
Charles S. Gifford, and
Marilyn B. Kapel

Greenwood Press
NEW YORK · WESTPORT, CONNECTICUT · LONDON

Library of Congress Cataloging-in-Publication Data

Dejnozka, Edward L.
    American educators' encyclopedia / Edward L. Dejnozka and David E.
Kapel.—Rev. ed. / by David E. Kapel, Charles S. Gifford, and
Marilyn B. Kapel.
      p. cm.
    Includes index.
    ISBN 0–313–25269–6 (lib. bdg. : alk. paper)
    1. Education—Dictionaries. I. Kapel, David E. II. Gifford,
Charles S. III. Kapel, Marilyn B. IV. Title.
LB15.D37 1991
370′.3—dc20   90–41510

British Library Catloguing in Publication Data is available.

Library of Congress Catalog Card Number: 90–41510
ISBN: 0–313–25269–6

First published in 1982

Greenwood Press, 88 Post Road West, Westport, CT 06881
An imprint of Greenwood Publishing Group, Inc.

Printed in the United States of America

The paper used in this book complies with the
Permanent Paper Standard issued by the National
Information Standards Organization (Z39.48–1984).

10 9 8 7 6 5 4 3 2 1

Copyright Acknowledgment

The authors gratefully acknowledge permission to quote from the following:

Reprinted by permission from G. Lester Anderson (ed), *Land-Grant Universities and Their
Continuing Challenge*, copyright 1976, Michigan State Univeristy Press.

This second edition is dedicated to Dr. Edward L. Dejnozka, a scholar, a teacher and an administrator. Dr. Dejnozka is sorely missed by the education profession. A unique and gentle person, he influenced the lives of all who were fortunate enough to know him.

Contents

Illustrations

Preface

American Educators' Encyclopedia has been written to provide school administrators, teachers, teacher educators, school board members, graduate students, librarians, parents, and others interested in American education with a ready (one-volume) reference book. The principal portion of this work consists of almost 2,000 entries (short articles) that are based on the names and terms frequently found in the literature of professional education. Another section, Appendixes, contains selected factual information that is presented largely in tabular form. We earnestly believe that the combination of entries and Appendix items will provide the reader, professional or lay person, with the basic information needed to understand each subject included.

The *Encyclopedia* is unique in at least one respect. Traditionally, encyclopedias, whether general or specific, are compiled by one or two editors whose job it is to review and compile articles that have been written by dozens of individuals. *American Educators' Encyclopedia* was not prepared in that fashion. In our case, we compiled a preliminary list of educational topics and, from it, selected those that we felt merited inclusion. We then authored entries, each averaging 100–200 words, covering the selected topics, this after referring to several related sources. In only a few instances did we prepare an entry based on but a single source.

Topical analysis of the entries indicated that they could be divided into 22 broad areas: Administration and Supervision; Art and Music Education; Audio-Visual Education and Library Science; Biographies (20th century); Business and Vocational Education; Child Growth and Development; Counseling and Guidance; Educational Measurement; Educational Organizations; Federal Programs and Legislation; Health, Physical Education, Recreation, and Dance; Higher Education; History and Philosophy of Education (including pre-20th century biographies); Mathematics and Science Education; Minority Education; Reading and Language Arts; School Finance and Business Administration; School Law; Social Studies; Special Education; Teaching and Learning; and Miscellaneous (a general category for topics that did not fit into any of the foregoing).

It was at this stage that we invited 22 authorities, one representing each of the 22 broad areas listed above, to review and validate our entries in their respective areas of expertise. This group of experts is identified elsewhere in this volume's front matter as the Board of Consulting Editors.

Consulting editors were asked to validate each entry assigned to them on the basis of three separate yet interrelated criteria. We posed the criteria in the interrogative:

1. Is the content factually correct?
2. Does the article cover the subject comprehensively?
3. Are the references relevant, well chosen, and reasonably current?

Additionally, our reviewers were invited to suggest other subjects that had not been included in our original list of topics.

Suggestions and criticisms received from the Board of Consulting Editors were studied. In most instances, modifications of our original entries were made to accommodate the advice of the experts.

The scope of *American Educators' Encyclopedia* is relatively broad, encompassing elementary, secondary, and higher education. In most instances, the entries have been prepared in the context of American education.

As indicated above, we prepared this book as a ready reference. We do not represent our entries to be definitive works. This would hardly have been possible given the fact that we were obliged to confine our material to one volume. Instead, the concise entries are intended to provide the professional and lay reader with enough basic information to be able to understand a given subject and, by using the references that follow each article, to know what additional sources to pursue to acquire further information.

We acknowledge our reliance upon and appreciation for the contributions of the authors cited in each article's reference section. Much of what we wrote is based on the works of these scholars and constitutes a distillation of what we perceived to be each subject's salient elements as presented by them. Without the original contributions made by these authors, preparation of *American Educators' Encyclopedia* would not have been possible.

E. L. D.
D. E. K.

Preface to the Second Edition

The decade of the 1980s saw vast changes in American society, its goals, and its educational aspirations. These changes were felt keenly in American education; most specifically by educators, the schools, and those involved in the schooling process. The first edition of the *American Educators' Encyclopedia* was published in 1982; consequently, the changes of the 1980s overlap, almost exactly, the time covered from the first publication of *American Educators' Encyclopedia* to this edition. The change, additions, and the updating and deletions found in this second edition reflect the changes in American education.

Over 200 items have been added to the text. The following are illustrative of the range of the new items: ACQUIRED IMMUNE DEFICIENCY SYNDROME (AIDS); AT-RISK STUDENTS; ATTENTION DEFICIT DISORDERS; BEST-EVIDENCE SYNTHESIS; CARNEGIE FORUM ON EDUCATION AND THE ECONOMY; CHOICE, SCHOOLS OF; various computer languages and statistical packages; COOPERATIVE LEARNING; DIRECT INSTRUCTION; INCLUSION PROCESS; INDUCTION PERIOD (INTO TEACHING); INTERACTIVE MODEL OF READING; LAUBACH LITERACY PROGRAM; MENTOR TEACHER; META-ANALYSIS; *MILLS v. DISTRICT OF COLUMBIA BOARD OF EDUCATION;* MINICOMPUTER; *A NATION AT RISK*; ODYSSEY OF THE MIND PROGRAM; PERSONAL COMPUTER (MICROCOMPUTER); RANDOM ACCESS MEMORY (RAM); READING LEVELS; SCHEMA THEORY; SEVERE AND PROFOUND DISORDERS; and TEACHER WARRANTY PROGRAM.

The authors have updated the entries retained from the first edition and have provided major additions to, and updating of, the original appendix. Rather than tempt fate and disrupt what has been extremely successful and useful to the users of the *American Educators' Encyclopedia*, the authors have kept the format and integrity of the original edition. As stated in the Preface to the first edition of this book, "We prepared this book as a ready reference." We have maintained that objective. We hope that readers, administrators, future teachers, students of education, parents, parent organizations, and all lay people interested in education will use the text as intended by the authors.

We would be remiss if we did not recognize and pay honor to the memory of Dr. Edward L. Dejnozka, the first coauthor of the 1982 *American Educators' Encyclopedia*. His foresight, leadership, writing skills, high standards, and original design made the first edition possible. He was a committed educator, scholar, teacher, and administrator. Even more important, he was a sensitive and humanistically oriented individual who cared for all, regardless of their station in life. He is sorely missed.

August 1990

D.E.K.
C.S.G.
M.B.K.

Acknowledgments

Hundreds of individuals assisted with the preparation of this reference work. They include the 22 consulting editors, identified elsewhere in this volume's front matter, whose willingness to contribute time and expertise we gratefully acknowledge. We are also indebted to the scores of nongovernmental and governmental representatives who willingly furnished us with current and voluminous information about their respective organizations. In addition, we want to express our appreciation to the authors and organizations who either helped us prepare or granted us permission to reprint several of the tables appearing in the Appendix section.

A number of reference librarians at Florida Atlantic University, the University of Louisville, and the University of Nebraska at Omaha provided us with invaluable assistance, frequently locating information that we had concluded was either unavailable or nonexistent. William Hafner, Sandra Mohl, Margaret Stone, and Linda Wiler, Reference Librarians of Florida Atlantic University, were of great help. Although all offered assistance, we especially want to recognize the many contributions provided by the tireless Margaret (Peggy) Stone of the Florida Atlantic University library staff. Her skills and generous contributions of time saved us countless hours of work and frequently unearthed invaluable reference leads.

Alice R. Morton, Archivist for the National Education Association, was equally generous with time, information, and documents. We quickly came to respect her enthusiasm for educational history, her encyclopedic memory, and the extensive library of educational documents that she has collected and organized during her lengthy tenure with NEA.

Cynthia Harris, Reference Editor for Greenwood Press, monitored the preparation of our manuscript. We acknowledge her timely suggestions and are especially appreciative of the decision-making latitude she extended to us.

Preliminary drafts of our numerous entries were typed by Barbara Case, Omaha; May Dejnozka, Boca Raton, Florida; Mary McCulloch, Louisville; and Deborah Schwab, also of Louisville. Final copies of the manuscript were typed by Barbara Ludt, Kathleen Meyer, Lorraine Murphy, and Kay Beach, all of southern Florida. We gratefully acknowledge this technical assistance.

May Dejnozka, above all others, devoted countless hours to varied tasks such as preliminary typing, assistance with correspondence, critical suggestions, and proofreading. Because of her contributions, we were spared much extra work; furthermore, her suggestions often served as well to improve the editorial quality of this volume.

Finally, we want to say thank you to the members of our two families for their encouragement and patience during the years that *American Educators' Encyclopedia* was in preparation.

E.L.D. and D.E.K.
May 1981.

Acknowledgments to the Second Edition

In order to revise a document, a sound original must be its base. During this revision process, we were constantly reminded of the contributions and services provided by the numerous individuals and organizations during the development of the original manuscript. Our gratitude to them is extended into yet another decade as we add others to the list who have made this revision possible.

Revising a text such as this includes the review of previously written material, the identification of current references for existing entries, and the recognition of the need for additional entries to assure the comprehensive and current nature for the second edition of the *American Educators' Encyclopedia*. Such tasks required the assistance of numerous colleagues representing the full spectrum of the field of American education. Rather than use a Board of Consulting Editors, as in the original edition, we called upon various colleagues to provide insight and expertise on entries within their professional specialties. We wish to recognize the institutions of these cooperative and helpful professionals: Glassboro State College, Louisiana State University in Baton Rouge, the Louisiana State University School of Medicine in New Orleans, Louisiana Tech University, the University of Georgia, the University of New Orleans, Temple University, National College of Education, St. Louis University, and the University of Texas.

In addition to our educational colleagues, librarians and their support staff at each of these institutions contributed generously to our research efforts. In this capacity, three additional institutions must be noted: the Library of Congress, the University of Nevada in Las Vegas, and Rutgers University.

Our writing efforts have required a support team to convert our scribbles to readable entries, to provide constant clerical support related to the numerous communications among the authors and their colleagues, and to proofread each "final" draft. For their assistance across the years and the miles, we gratefully recognize June Gifford, Dorothy Maguire, Patricia Peacock, and Betty Stearns. Finally we wish to acknowledge the many contributions, suggestions, and help extended to us by Ms. Teresa R. Metz, Senior Production Editor at Greenwood Publishing Group. Without her aid, the second edition would not have seen "the light of day."

D.E.K., C.S.G., and M.B.K.
August, 1990

Board of Consulting Editors for the First Edition

ROBERT CLAUSEN (Child Growth and Development), Professor of Education, New York University. Dr. Clausen holds three degrees: B.S., New Jersey State Teachers College at Newark; M.S., Indiana State Teachers College, Terre Haute; and Ed.D., Teachers College, Columbia University. Before joining the NYU faculty, he taught in the public schools of New Jersey; served on the faculties of the Agnes Russell Center, Teachers College, Columbia University, and the Laboratory School, Indiana State Teachers College; taught in the Scarsdale (N.Y.) Public Schools; and was Lecturer at Queens College (N.Y.). He was a contributor to the 1963 Yearbook of the Association for Student Teaching, *Curriculum for Today's Boys and Girls,* and is Past President of the New York State Association for Student Teaching. Professor Clausen directed NYU's Residence Center in Puerto Rico from 1963 to 1977.

VIRGIL A. CLIFT (Minority Education), Professor Emeritus of Education, New York University. Professor Clift earned the B.A. degree at Indiana University, the M.A. at Indiana State University, and the Ph.D. at Ohio State University. The Doctor of Humanities (Hon.) was conferred upon him by Indiana State University (1977). He received Indiana State University's Distinguished Alumni Award in 1976. Dr. Clift's professional background includes service as AID education advisor to the Kingdom of Libya; chairmanship of education departments at North Carolina Agricultural and Technical State University and Morgan State University; Fulbright Lecturer in Pakistan; and service as Distinguished Visiting Professor of Education, the University of Nebraska at Omaha. He was Senior Editor of the John Dewey Society's 16th Yearbook, *Negro Education in America* (1962), and Coeditor of the *Encyclopedia of Black America* (1981). The approximately 50 professional articles he has authored include annual contributions to the *World Topics Yearbook* since 1971.

WILLIAM W. COOLEY (Educational Measurement), Professor of Education, University of Pittsburgh, and Director of Evaluation Research, Learning Research and Development Center. Professor Cooley earned the B.S. degree at Lawrence University, the M.A. at the University of Minnesota, and the Ed.D. at Harvard University. Before assuming his present position, he directed Project TALENT for the American Institutes for Research. Dr. Cooley's principal publications are: coauthor, *Project TALENT One-Year Follow-Up Studies* (1966); coauthor, *Introduction to Statistical Procedures: With Computer Exercises* (1968); coauthor, *Multivariate Data Analysis* (1971); and coauthor, *Evaluation Research in Education* (1976). Articles authored by him have appeared in *Educational Research, Educational Psychologist,* and the *Journal of Applied Psychology Monograph.* Dr. Cooley serves on the AERA Council and Executive Board. In 1981, he was elected to the presidency of AERA. He is a fellow, American Association for the Advancement of Science; fellow, American Psychological Association; and fellow, Center for Advanced Study in Behavioral Sciences.

ROGER E. CROOKS (Audio-Visual Education and Library Science), Educational Specialist, U.S. Army Missile and Munitions School, Huntsville, Alabama. Before that he was Director, Educational Technology Center, University of Nebraska at Omaha. Degrees earned by Professor Crooks include the B.A., University of Texas at Austin; M.Ed., West Texas State University; and Ed.D., East Texas State University. He previously served on the staff of the Center for Educational Media and Technology, East Texas State University. An authority on Crowderian techniques of programmed instruction, his publication record includes articles concerned with subjects such as instructional media and information retrieval systems.

DONALD C. CUSHENBERY (Reading and Language Arts), Foundation Professor of Education, University of Nebraska at Omaha. Professor Cushenbery earned the B.S. degree at Fort Hays Kansas State College, the M.S. at Kansas State Teachers College (Emporia), and the Ed.D. at the University of Missouri-Columbia. Before joining the UNO faculty, he taught elementary school, held principalships in Kansas, and served as an Instructor at the University of Missouri. Dr. Cushenbery has worked as Visiting Professor of Reading at Ball State University, Sioux Falls College, and Augustana College. Reading texts that he has authored are: *Reading Improvement in the Elementary School* (1969); *Remedial Reading in the Secondary School* (1972); *Reading Improvement through Diagnosis, Remediation and Individualized Instruction* (1977); and *Guide to Meeting Reading Competency Requirements: Diagnosis and Correction of Reading Difficulties* (1981). He coauthored three additional books on reading: *Effective Reading Skills for the Slow Learners* (1972); *Reading and the Gifted Child* (1974); and *Reading Comprehension Skill Kits* (1980). Dr. Cushenbery has also written approximately 25 journal articles on various facets of reading instruction. In 1971, he was winner of the Great Teacher Award at the University of Nebraska at Omaha. In that same year, and again in 1975, he was elected one of the Outstanding Educators of America. In 1972, he served as one of 20 reading consultants to the U.S. Office of Education's Right to Read Program. Professor Cushenbery was elected to the presidency of the Nebraska Reading Council for academic year 1976–1977.

DONALD D. GEHRING (Higher Education), Associate Professor of Higher Education, University of Louisville. Professor Gehring earned the Bachelor of Science in Industrial Management at Georgia Institute of Technology; the M.Ed. at Emory University; and the Ed.D. at the University of Georgia. Before joining the UL faculty, he held several higher education positions including Director of Student Activities, Emory University, and Dean of Student Development, Mars Hill College. His major publications include *The College Student and the Court: Briefs of Selected Court Cases Involving Student/Institutional Relationships in Higher Education* (1977) and *The Schools and the Courts: Briefs of Selected Court Cases Involving Secondary and Elementary Schools* (1975). Dr. Gehring was elected 1980–81 President, Southern College Personnel Association, and has served on two committees of the Association of College and University Housing Officers.

SAMUEL GOLDMAN (Administration and Supervision), Dean, College of Human Resources and Professor of Rehabilitation Administration, Southern Illinois University-Carbondale. Before assuming his present post, Dean Goldman taught educational administration courses at the University of Chicago, Oklahoma State University, New York University, Syracuse University, and Ohio University. He held leadership positions at two of the aforementioned institutions: Chairman, Department of Educational Administration and Supervision, Syracuse University, and Dean, College of Education, Ohio University. Dr. Goldman has authored and coedited several books and monographs, including *Politics of Educational Administration* (Editor, 1963); *The School Principal* (1966) and *Integration and Separatism in Education* (Coeditor, 1970). In addition, he has authored numerous articles and research papers, most related to school leadership. Since 1965, he has served on approximately 20 boards and councils, including: Chairman, Executive Committee, National Conference of Professors of Educational Administration (1968–69); member, National Advisory Board, ERIC Clearinghouse in Management and Facilities (1970–72); President, University Council for Educational Administration (1971–72); member, Board of Directors, Appalachia Educational Laboratory (1972–79); and Vice-President, The Research and Development Association for Education (1977–78). Dr. Goldman has taught numerous seminars sponsored by the National Academy for School Executives and, in 1973, was cited as a Distinguished Professor by the National Academy. In 1980, he was awarded a citation by the Ohio Legislature for outstanding service to community.

ESIN KAYA-CARTON (Teaching and Learning), Professor of Educational Research, Hofstra University. A New York State certified psychologist, Professor Kaya-Carton holds the B.A. in Psychology, conferred by Barnard College, Columbia University; the M.A. in Educational Psychology, earned at Teachers College, Columbia University; and the Ph.D. in Psychology and Education, awarded by New York University. At Hofstra University, Professor Kaya-Carton heads the Ph.D. program in educational research and directs that institution's Bureau of Educational Evaluation. She was previously Chairperson of the Department of Educational Psychology at Hofstra. Before joining the Hofstra University faculty, Professor Kaya-Carton was affiliated with New York University's School of Education as Research Associate in the Experimental Teaching Center, later as Associate Professor of Educational Psychology. Since 1962, she has participated in research and evaluation projects for and with numerous agencies such as school districts, the U.S. Office of Education, Educational Testing Service, New York Urban League, and the Ford Foundation. Dr. Kaya-Carton has been an active consultant to school districts, a frequent leader of inservice programs, and has authored approximately 30 journal articles and papers on subjects such as the Dual Progress Plan, creativity, humor, attitudes toward education, and pupil evaluation.

LOU KLEINMAN (Miscellaneous), Professor of Education and Dean, School of Education and Allied Professions, University of Miami. Dean Kleinman earned the B.S. degree at New York University, the M.A. at Harvard University, and the Ed.D. at New York University. His professional experience includes teaching in New York and New Jersey schools, service as a Rutgers University Division Director, and an extensive tenure at New York University during which time he held several titles in the School of Education: Director of Educational Placement Services; Head of Teacher Education Section, Experimental Teaching Center; Director, Center for Field Research and School Services; Professor of Educational Administration; and Associate Dean. Articles authored by Dean Kleinman have appeared in *The Journal of Educational Sociology* and *The Journal of Teacher Education*. He is coauthor of *Grievances and their Resolution: Problems in School Personnel Administration* (1967). Dean Kleinman received the Distinguished Alumni Achievement Award, conferred by NYU's Education Alumni Association, and was recently elected to the presidency of the Florida Association of Colleges for Teacher Education.

GERARD L. KNIETER (Art and Music Education), Dean and Professor of Music, College of Fine and Applied Arts, The University of Akron. Dean Knieter earned the B.S. and M.A. degrees at New York University and the Ed.D. at Columbia University. He served on the music education faculties of San Jose State University (California), Duquesne University, and Temple University (where he was chairman of the department and head of the doctoral program) before assuming his present post. Dr. Knieter's most recent publications include: *The Teaching Process and Arts and Aesthetics* (1979); "Current Issues and Future Directions in Music Education" in Estelle R. Jorgensen (Editor), *McGill Symposium in School Music Administration and Supervision* (1979); and "Humanistic Dimensions of Aesthetic Education" in Arthur Motycka (Editor), *Music Education for Tomorrow's Society* (1976). He serves on the Board of Directors of the Theodore Presser Company and is Vice-President of the Initial

Teaching Alphabet Foundation. He has been a member of the Editorial Committee of the *Journal of Research in Music Education* and also served as editorial consultant to the *Journal of Aesthetic Education*. His previous service activities include service as advisor and consultant to school systems, state departments of education, universities, and professional associations.

RICHARD F. NEWTON (Social Studies), Associate Professor of Education and Director of Field Experiences (Secondary Education), Temple University. Dr. Newton holds the B.A., M.A., and Ph.D. degrees, each earned at Michigan State University. He taught in the elementary and secondary schools of Michigan and worked as Instructor at Michigan State University before assuming his present position. Books that Dr. Newton authored or edited are: *The Daily Newspaper in the American Classroom* (coauthor, 1974); *The Market System: Does It Work?* (Contributing Editor, 1974); and *Handbook of Teaching Materials in Family Finance Education* (1977). In addition, his several articles dealing with various facets of social studies have appeared in journals such as *School and Society*, *The Journal of Economic Education*, *Theory and Research in the Social Studies*, and *Teachers College Record*. Dr. Newton has served on the Board of Directors of the National Council for the Social Studies and numerous committees of that organization. He has been employed as a consultant to the U.S. Department of Education (Fulbright-Hays Program), the New York State Department of Education, colleges and universities, and school systems.

JOSEPH B. OXENDINE (Health, Physical Education, Recreation, and Dance), Professor and Dean, College of Health, Physical Education, Recreation, and Dance, Temple University. Dean Oxendine earned the A.B. at Catawba College and the Ed.M. and Ed.D. degrees at Boston University. In addition, he holds a (Hon.) Doctor of Science degree conferred by Catawba College. He taught in the public schools of Virginia before joining the Temple University faculty. Dr. Oxendine's publication record includes *Psychology of Motor Learning* (1968) and approximately 25 professional articles, published reports, and book chapters. In 1977, at the invitation of AAHPER, he conducted a nationwide study of general instruction programs (physical education) in all four-year U.S. institutions of higher education. His professional service record, dating to 1964, includes membership on the AAHPER panel that developed and published "Standards for College Physical Education Programs"; member, Recreation Committee, National Association for Retarded Children; Reviewer, Psychological and Social Sciences section, *The Journal of Gerontology;* member, Executive Committee, College Physical Education Council of the National Association for Sport and Physical Education; and President, Indian Rights Association.

FRANKLIN PARKER (History and Philosophy of Education; Selected Biographies), Benedum Professor of Education, West Virginia University. Professor Parker earned the A.B. degree at Berea College, Kentucky, the M.S. at the University of Illinois, and the Ed.D. at George Peabody College for Teachers of Vanderbilt University. Before coming to WVU in 1968, he taught at SUNY New Platz, University of Texas (Austin), and the University of Oklahoma. A prolific writer, bibliographer, and researcher, Professor Parker has authored an extensive number of books, published bibliographies, Phi Delta Kappa "fastbacks," pamphlets, book chapters, and journal articles. They include: *George Peabody: A Biography* (1971); *African Development and Education in Southern Rhodesia* (reprinted 1974); Coeditor, *American Dissertations on Foreign Education: A Bibliography with Abstracts* (15 volumes, 1971–81); Editor, *U.S. Higher Education: A Guide to Information Sources* (1980); and *Women's Education: A World View*, 2 volumes (1979 and 1981). Three PDK "fastbacks" that he has authored are: *The Battle of the Books: Kanawha County* (1975); *What Can We Learn From the Schools of China?* (1977); and *British Schools and Ours* (1979). He has also contributed on a fairly regular basis to encyclopedia yearbooks (e.g. *Americana, Collier's, Compton's,* and the *Reader's Digest Almanac and Yearbook*) and encyclopedias (e.g., *Academic American Encyclopedia, Encyclopedia of Education,* and *Encyclopedia of World Biography*). His articles have appeared as regular features in *School and Society, Comparative Education Review,* and the *Comparative and International Education Society Newsletter.* Professor Parker has studied and lectured widely abroad.

H. VAUGHN PHELPS (Educational Organizations), Superintendent of Schools, Westside Community Schools, Omaha, Nebraska. Superintendent Phelps holds a B.E. (Mechanical Engineering) degree from the University of Southern California and B.S., M.Ed., and Ed.D. degrees earned at the University of Nebraska. He served as Superintendent of Schools, Pleasanton, Nebraska, and Coordinator of Community Services, University of Nebraska, before assuming his present position. His organizational experience includes the presidency of the American Association of School Administrators and membership on several of its committees and commissions; presidency of the Associated Public School System; membership on the Science Education Advisory Board, National Science Foundation; and presidency of the Suburban School Superintendents. In his own state, he has been President of the Nebraska Association of School Administrators; Chairman, Nebraska Council of School Administrators; and Chairman, Nebraska Educational Television Council. He has twice been invited by the North Central Association to serve on school evaluation teams evaluating Department of Defense Dependent Schools in the European Theatre.

HAROLD S. RESNICK (Business and Vocational Education), Associate Professor, Career Development/Human Resource Development, Boston University. Dr. Resnick earned the B.S. degree at City College of the City of New York and the M.Ed. and Ed.D. degrees at Wayne State University. Before his appointment to the Boston University faculty, he taught industrial education subjects in the New York City and Detroit Public Schools, served as Associate Director of the Experienced Teacher Fellowship Program at Wayne State University, taught vocational and industrial education at Temple University, and was Associate Superintendent of the Minutemen Regional Technical School District, Lexington, Massachusetts. Professor Resnick has coauthored two books: *Metric Measure Simplified* (1974) and *Exploring Careers in Engineering and Manufacturing* (1976). Articles he has written have appeared in the *Journal of Industrial Teacher Education, Journal of Career Education, Journal of Vocational Education Research,* and other vocationally related publications. Dr. Resnick has provided training development and human resource consultant services to numerous agencies and organizations including the U.S. Department of Defense, Raytheon Data Systems Company, American Management Corporation, Philco-Ford Corporation, school systems, colleges, and universities. He recently completed a project for the Department of Defense Dependent Schools, the Vocational Development Training Program for School District Personnel (conducted in North and South Germany).

JEFFREY SCHILIT (Special Education), Professor and Chairperson, Department of Exceptional Student Education, Florida Atlantic University. Dr. Schilit earned the B.S. degree at California State College (Pa.); the M.Ed. at Pennsylvania State University; and the Ph.D. at Ohio State University. Before assuming his present position, he taught in the public schools of Ohio and served on the faculties of Duquesne University, the University of Alabama, and SUNY Buffalo. He has published approximately 35 papers, articles, curriculum guides, and bibliographies relating to various aspects of special education. His personal research has included investigations such as recreational skills of the mentally retarded; analysis of criminal justice personnel's understanding of the mentally retarded offender; and analysis of a transitional facility for preparing institutionalized retardates for community life.

JOHN SOKOL (Federal Legislation and Programs), Executive Director of Doctoral Studies, Seton Hall University. Dr. Sokol earned the B.S. in Engineering at the U.S. Naval Academy, and the M.A. and Ph.D. degrees at the University of California, Berkeley. Immediately before assuming his present position, he was Regional Commissioner of Education (Region 2) in the U.S. Office of Education. Dr. Sokol's professional experience also includes teaching service in the Berkeley, California Public Schools; Supervisor of Student Teachers, U.C. Berkeley; and, Professor of Education, Teachers College, Columbia University. In the U.S. Office of Education, he was Director of Educational Research and Assistant Regional Commissioner, Region 2, before becoming Regional Commissioner. He is author of *Computational Exercises in School Finance* (1966), *Developing A School District Budget* (1981), and various articles.

BETTE J. SOLDWEDEL (Counseling and Guidance), Interim Dean and Professor of Education, University of North Florida. Dr. Soldwedel holds the B.S. and M.S. degrees earned at Illinois State University, the Ed.D., earned at New York University, and the (Hon.) LL.D., conferred by Illinois State University. Before accepting appointment at the University of North Florida, she held a variety of educational positions: Instructor and Dean of Women, Eureka College; Assistant Professor and Director of Women's Residence Halls, Illinois State University; Associate Professor and Associate Dean of Students, Trenton State College; Professor and Department Chair, Guidance and Personnel Administration, NYU; and Director of Program Development for the U.S. Department of Labor's Job Corps. Among her major publications are the following: *Mastering the College Challenge* (1964); *Preparing for College: A Macmillan Guide for Parents* (1966); *Where Do I Go From Here?* (career guidance books for out-of-school youth, 1979); and, *Erasing Sex Bias* (1980). She edited the *National Quarterly Journal of the National Association for Women Deans, Administrators, and Counselors* (1968–72) and prepared 35 commercial filmstrips and teachers' guides on various counseling and guidance topics. She presently serves on the Editorial Board of the Journal of College Personnel.

FRANK X. SUTMAN (Mathematics and Science Education), Director of the Merit Center and Professor of Education, Temple University. Professor Sutman holds A.B. and A.M. degrees from Montclair State College and the Ed.D., earned at Teachers College, Columbia University. Before joining the Temple University faculty, he held teaching posts at SUNY Buffalo, Interamerican University of Puerto Rico, and William Patterson College. He has also served as Visiting Professor at Rutgers University, Hebrew University of Jerusalem, University of Mysore (India), and Huagzhou Institute of Science (People's Republic of China). Included among his more than 60 publications are: *Concepts in Chemistry* (Second Edition, 1967); "Hiding Behind Course Titles," *Journal of Research in Science Teaching* (1966); *A Darwinian Look at Science Education* (1972); and *Educating Personnel for Bilingual Settings* (1979).

FERDY J. TAGLE, JR. (School Finance and Business Administration), Deputy Superintendent of Schools, Brookline Public Schools, Massachusetts. Dr. Tagle earned the B.S. degree at State University of New York, Oswego, and had both the M.A. and Ed.D. degrees conferred by New York University. Previous leadership titles that he held before becoming Deputy Superintendent were Assistant Superintendent of Schools, North Rockland Central Schools, Stony Point, N.Y., and Assistant Superintendent for Administration and Finance, Brookline, Massachusetts. A widely recognized authority on school finance and business, Dr. Tagle has held important organizational leadership positions at the state, national, and international levels. In 1969–70, he served as President of the Massachusetts Association of School Business Officials.

User's Guide

The topics, or entries, in the *American Educators' Encyclopedia* are presented in strict alphabetical order. When entries contain two or more words, they are alphabetized as if they are one word. Biographical entries are alphabetized by family name and by given name when two or more individuals have the same last name (e.g. *Dewey, John* precedes *Dewey, Melvil*).

Several entries provide only cross-references to other entries. They appear in alphabetical order and are in the same bold-faced type as other entry titles. These cross-references are provided to help the reader locate information appearing under headings that do not accord exactly with the heading he or she has in mind. For example, a reader seeking information about "defamation of character" will not find a discussion under that heading but will be directed to the entries *Libel* and *Slander*. Each of the separate topics *Libel* and *Slander* contains information relating to character defamation.

A listing of "Abbreviations and Acronyms" is included in the front matter to facilitate location of topics when the reader knows only an abbreviation or acronym. For example, the list includes *MBO*, which is an abbreviation for *Management by Objectives*, and *PERT*, an acronym for *Program Evaluation and Review Technique*. Since abbreviations and acronyms are not usually used in topic headings, the list of "Abbreviations and Acronyms" should be consulted first. The list is limited to principal abbreviations and acronyms for items contained in the *American Educators' Encyclopedia*.

Additional cross-references appear at the end of several, although not all, entries. These direct the reader to other entries that overlap or are closely related to the topic under study. In some instances,

these additional cross-references also direct the reader to related appendixes. For example, at the close of the entry *National Education Association*, the reader is advised to see *American Teachers Association and National Teachers Association;* also, to see *Appendix XX: The Teacher of the Year*.

References listed at the end of each entry are short bibliographies. They are presented in alphabetical order, by author. When a work has two authors, both names are given, but due to space limitations, only the senior author's name is given, followed by "et al.," when there are three or more authors. The Post Office's abbreviations are used for states (e.g., *FL* for "Florida").

Biographical entries are limited to nonliving subjects. Dates of an individual's birth and death appear in parentheses following his or her name, for example, *Mort, Paul R*. (February 21, 1894–May 12, 1962).

Appendixes appear at the back of the book.

Much of the information describing organizations was gleaned from materials sent to us, at our request, by these groups. In many instances, these source materials consisted of promotion brochures and/or booklets that, although current, contained no publication date. The absence of publication date information is noted in each such instance.

Finally, several entries deal with specific legislation enacted by the federal government. References accompanying these entries usually include the original public law as reported in the *United States Statutes at Large*. The reader interested in amendments to the original laws is advised to check the annual legislative updates ("pocket parts") appearing in *U.S. Code Annotated*, published by West Publishing Company of St. Paul, Minnesota.

Abbreviations and Acronyms

AAC	Association of American Colleges	AECT	Association for Educational Communications and Technology
AACD	American Association for Counseling and Development	AEL	Appalachia Educational Laboratory
AACJC	American Association of Community and Junior Colleges	AERA	American Educational Research Association
AACTE	American Association of Colleges for Teacher Education	AFROTC	Air Force Reserve Officers Training Corps
AAGC	American Association for Gifted Children	AFT	American Federation of Teachers
AAHE	American Association for Higher Education	AGB	Association of Governing Boards of Universities and Colleges
AAHPERD	American Alliance for Health, Physical Education, Recreation, and Dance	AHEA	American Home Economics Association
		AHP	Association for Humanistic Psychology
AAMD	American Association on Mental Deficiency	AHPAT	Allied Health Professions Admission Test
AAP	Association of American Publishers, Inc.	AIAA	American Industrial Arts Association
AAPT	American Association of Physics Teachers	AIAW	Association for Intercollegiate Athletics for Women
AASA	American Association of School Administrators	AICS	Association of Independent Colleges and Schools
AASCU	American Association of State Colleges and Universities	AID	Agency for International Development
AASL	American Association of School Librarians	ALA	American Library Association
		ALISE	Association for Library and Information, Science Education
AAUP	American Association of University Professors	AMI	Association Montessori Internationale
A.B.	Bachelor of Arts	ANOVA	Analysis of Variance
ABE	Adult Basic Education	AOE	Association of Overseas Educators
ABPP	American Board of Professional Psychology, Inc.	APA	American Psychological Association
ACA	American Camping Association	APGA	American Personnel and Guidance Association
ACE	American Council on Education	AROTC	Army Reserve Officers Training Corps
ACEI	Association for Childhood Education International	ASBO	Association of School Business Officials of the United States and Canada
ACT	American College Tests		
ACTFL	American Council on the Teaching of Foreign Languages	ASCD	Association for Supervision and Curriculum Development
ADA	Average Daily Attendance	ASHA	American Speech-Language Hearing Association
ADAMHA	Alcohol, Drug Abuse, and Mental Health Administration		
		ASHE	Association for the Study of Higher Education
ADD	Attention Deficit Disorders		
ADE	Association of Departments of English	ASL	American Sign Language
		AST	Association for Student Teaching
ADFL	Association of Departments of Foreign Languages	ASTP	Army Specialized Training Program
		ATE	Association of Teacher Educators
ADM	Average Daily Membership	ATF	Australian Teachers' Federation

ATI	Aptitude-Treatment Interaction	CTF	Canadian Teachers' Federation
AVA	American Vocational Association	CTMM	California Test of Mental Maturity
B.A.	Bachelor of Arts	CWLA	Child Welfare League of America
BEOG	Basic Educational Opportunity Grant	CWSP	College Work Study Program
BFT	Biofeedback Training	DANTES	Defense Activity for Non-Traditional Education Support
B-G Test	Bender-Gestalt Test		
BIA	Bureau of Indian Affairs	DAT	Dental Aptitude Test
B.S.	Bachelor of Science	db	Decibel
BSA	Boy Scouts of America	DD	Developer/Demonstrator
BSCS	Biological Sciences Curriculum Study	DE	Department of Education
CA	Chronological Age	DE	Distributive Education
CA	Cooperating Administrator	DECA	Distributive Education Clubs of America
CACREP	Council for Accreditation of Counseling and Related Educational Programs	d.f.	Degrees of Freedom
		DI	Difficulty Index
		DISTAR	Direct Instruction System for Teaching Arithmetic and Reading
CAI	Computer Assisted Instruction	DPE	Delta Pi Epsilon
CAPE	Council for American Private Education	DPP	Dual Progress Plan
		DRA	Directed Reading Activity
CASC	Council for the Advancement of Small Colleges	DRT	Domain Referenced Test
		DRTA	Direct Reading Thinking Activity
CAT	California Achievement Test	DS	Differentiated Staffing
CBA	Chemical Bond Approach	DS	Discriminating Stimulus
CBC	Children's Book Council	DS	Down's Syndrome
CBE	Competency-Based Education	ECCP	Engineering Concepts Curriculum Project
CBE	Council for Basic Education		
CBTE	Competency-Based Teacher Education	ECOLA	Extending Concepts through Language Activities
CCC	Civilian Conservation Corps	ECS	Education Commission of the States
CCSSO	Council of Chief State School Officers	Ed.D.	Doctor of Education
		Ed.S.	Education Specialist
CEA	Canadian Education Association	E.E.G.	Electroencephalogram
CEC	Council for Exceptional Children	EEOC	Equal Employment Opportunity Commission
CEEB	College Entrance Examination Board		
CEFP	Council of Educational Facility Planners	EFL	Educational Facilities Laboratory
		EIS	Educational Institute of Scotland
CETA	Comprehensive Employment and Training Act	EMLAT	Modern Language Aptitude Test– Elementary
CEU	Continuing Education Unit	EPDA	Education Professions Development Act
CF	Cystic Fibrosis		
CFI	Camp Fire, Inc.	EPIE	Educational Products Information Exchange Institute
CHEMS	Chemical Education Material Study		
CICHE	Consortium for International Cooperation in Higher Education	EPL	Executive Professional Leadership
		ERIC	Educational Resources Information Center
CIJE	Current Index to Journals in Education		
		ERS	Educational Research Service
CLEP	College-Level Examination Program	ESCP	Earth Science Curriculum Project
COP	Career Opportunities Program	ESEA	Elementary and Secondary Education Act
COPES	Conceptually Oriented Program for Elementary Science		
		ESL	English as a Second Language
CoRT	Cognitive Research Thrust	ESP	Extrasensory Perception
COTA	Certified Occupational Therapy Assistant	ESS	Elementary Science Study
		ETS	Educational Testing Service
CP	Cerebral Palsy	ETV	Educational Television
CPEA	Cooperative Project in Educational Administration	EVS	Eye-Voice Span
		f	Frequency
CRL	Center for Research Libraries	FEC	Faculty Exchange Center
CSSO	Chief State School Officer		

FFA	Future Farmers of America	IIIR	Integrated Instructional Information Resource
FGP	Foster Grandparent Program	IPI	Individually Prescribed Instruction
FHA	Future Homemakers of America	IPM	Instructional Programming Model
FIE	Feuerstein's Instrumental Enrichment	IPS	Introductory Physical Science
FIPSE	Fund for the Improvement of Postsecondary Education	I.Q.	Intelligence Quotient
		I & R	Instruction and Research
FISLP	Federally Insured Student Loan Program	IRA	International Reading Association
		IRI	Informal Reading Inventory
FLES	Foreign Language in the Elementary School	ISD	Intermediate School District
		i.t.a.	Initial Teaching Alphabet
FORTRAN	FORmula TRANslator	ITBS	Iowa Tests of Basic Skills
FSA	Full-State Assumption	ITV	Instructional Television
FTA	Future Teachers of America	IYC	International Year of the Child
FTE	Full-Time Equivalent	JA	Junior Achievement
FWL	Far West Laboratory for Educational Research and Development	JCEE	Joint Council on Economic Education
		JROTC	Junior Reserve Officers Training Corps
GCMP	Greater Cleveland Mathematics Program		
		KDP	Kappa Delta Pi
GED	General Educational Development	K-R	Kuder-Richardson
GED	General Equivalancy Diploma	LAD	Language-Acquisition Device
GFE	Goal Free Evaluation	LAPS	Learning Activity Packets
GMAT	Graduate Management Admissions Test	LBDQ	Leader Behavior Description Questionnaire
GPA	Grade Point Average	LC	Library of Congress
GRE	Graduate Record Examination	LEA	Local Educational Agency
GSLP	Guaranteed Student Loan Program	LPN	Licensed Practical Nurse
GSUSA	Girl Scouts of the U.S.A.	LRE	Law-Related Education
HERO	Home Economics–Related Occupations	LRE	Least Restrictive Environment
		M.A.	Master of Arts
HEW	U.S. Department of Health, Education, and Welfare	MA	Mental Age
		MACOS	Man: A Course of Study
HHS	Department of Health and Human Services	MAT	Master of Arts in Teaching
		MAT	Miller Analogies Test
HPER	Health, Physical Education, and Recreation	MBD	Minimal Brain Dysfunction
		MBO	Management by Objectives
HPERD	Health, Physical Education, Recreation, and Dance	MCAT	Medical College Admissions Test
		McREL	Mid Continent Regional Educational Laboratory
IACE	Intergovernmental Advisory Council on Education	MD	Muscular Dystrophy
		MDTA	Manpower Development and Training Act
IACP	Industrial Arts Curriculum Project		
ICAI	Intelligent Computer-Assisted Instruction	M.Ed.	Master of Education
		MENC	Music Educators National Conference
ICET	International Council on Education for Teaching	MES	More Effective Schools
		MINNEMAST	Minnesota School Mathematics and Science Teaching Project
I/D/E/A	Institute for the Development of Educational Activities		
		MLA	Modern Language Association of America
I/E	Introversion/Extroversion		
IEA	International Association for the Evaluation of Educational Achievement	MLAT	Modern Language Aptitude Test
		MMPI	Minnesota Multiphasic Personality Inventory
IEP	Individual Education Plan		
IGE	Individually Guided Education	MPATI	Midwest Program on Airborne Television Instruction
IIC	Instructional Improvement Committee		
		MR	Mental Retardation
IIP	International Inter-visitation Program in Educational Administration	M.S.	Master of Science
		MS	Multiple Sclerosis

MSSC	Metropolitan School Study Council	NCAA	National Collegiate Athletic Association
MTS	Morale Tendency Score	NCATE	National Council for the Accreditation of Teacher Education
N	Number		
NAACP	National Association for the Advancement of Colored People	NCCPS	National Citizens Commission for the Public Schools
NABSE	National Alliance of Black School Educators, Inc.	NCDA	National Career Development Association
NABSS	National Alliance of Black School Superintendents	NCEA	National Catholic Educational Association
NABT	National Association of Biology Teachers	NCEA	National Community Education Association
NACIE	National Advisory Council on Indian Education	NCES	National Center for Education Statistics
NACTA	National Association of Colleges and Teachers of Agriculture	NCPEA	National Conference of Professors of Educational Administration
NAEA	National Art Education Association	NCREL	North Central Regional Educational Laboratory
NAEB	National Association of Educational Broadcasters	NCSS	National Council for the Social Studies
NAEOP	National Association of Educational Office Personnel	NCTE	National Council of Teachers of English
NAEP	National Assessment of Educational Progress	NCTEPS	National Commission on Teacher Education and Professional Standards
NAESP	National Association of Elementary School Principals		
NAYEYC	National Association for the Education of Young Children	NCTM	National Council of Teachers of Mathematics
NAIA	National Association of Intercollegiate Athletics	NDEA	National Defense Education Act
		NDN	National Diffusion Network
NAICU	National Association of Independent Colleges and Universities	NDSL	National Direct Student Loan
		NEA	National Education Association
NAIS	National Association of Independent Schools	NHS	National Honor Society
		NIE	National Institute of Education
NAPCAE	National Association for Public Continuing and Adult Education	NJCAA	National Junior College Athletic Association
NASBE	National Association of State Boards of Education	NP	Noun Phrase
		NPC	National Panhellenic Conference
NASC	National Association of Student Councils	NROTC	Naval Reserve Officers Training Corps
NASDTEC	National Association of State Directors of Teacher Education and Certification	NRTA	National Retired Teachers Association
		NSBA	National School Boards Association
NASE	National Academy for School Executives	NSCD	National School Development Council
NASSP	National Association of Secondary School Principals	NSF	National Science Foundation
NASULGC	National Association of State Universities and Land Grant Colleges	NSPRA	National School Public Relations Association
		NSSE	National Society for the Study of Education
NATA	National Association of Teachers' Agencies	NSSE	National Study of School Evaluation
National PTA	National Congress of Parents and Teachers	NSTA	National Science Teachers Association
NATTS	National Association of Trade and Technical Schools	NTA	National Teachers Association
		NTE	National Teacher Examinations
NAWDAC	National Association for Women Deans, Adminstrators, and Counselors	NTL	National Training Laboratories
		NUT	National Union of Teachers
NBCC	National Board for Certified Counselors	NWREL	Northwest Regional Educational Laboratory

NYC	Neighborhood Youth Corps		SAS	Statistical Analysis System
NZEI	New Zealand Educational Institute		SAT	Scholastic Aptitude Test
OCDQ	Organizational Climate Description Questionnaire		SCA	Speech Communication Association
OEO	Office of Economic Opportunity		SCAT	Cooperative School and College Ability Test
OERI	Office of Educational Research and Improvement (U.S.)		SCDE	School, College, Department of Education
OT	Occupational Therapy		SCF	Save the Children Federation
OTR	Occupational Therapist		SCII	Strong-Campbell Interest Inventory
PA	Parents Anonymous		SCIS	Science Curriculum Improvement Study
PAC	Parent Advisory Committee			
PBK	Phi Betta Kappa		SCP	Senior Companion Program
PBTE	Performance-Based Teacher Education		SCSS	SCSS Conversational System (software package)
PC	Personal Computer/microcomputer		SEA	State Educational Agency
PCAT	Pharmacy College Admissions Test		SEDL	Southwestern Educational Development Laboratory
PD	Professional Diploma			
PDK	Phi Delta Kappa		SEIL	Southeastern Educational Improvement Laboratory
PE	Physical Education			
PEA	Progressive Education Association		SEOG	Supplemental Educational Opportunity Grant
PEK	Phi Epsilon Kappa			
PERT	Program Evaluation and Review Technique		SES	Socioeconomic Status
Ph.D.	Doctor of Philosophy		SI	Systeme International d'Unites
PK	Psychokinesis		SIECUS	Sex Information and Education Council of the U.S.
PKP	Phi Kappa Phi			
POC	Professional Officer Course		SMSA	Standard Metropolitan Statistical Area
POS	Program of Study			
POSDCORB	Planning, Organizing, Staffing, Directing, Coordinating, Reporting, and Budgeting		SMSG	School Mathematics Study Group
			SOC	Servicemen's Opportunity Colleges
			SOI	Structure of Intellect
			SPC	Systemwide Program Committee
PPBS	Planning, Programming, Budgeting System		SPSS	Statistical Package for the Social Sciences
PPBES	Planning, Programming, Budgeting, Evaluation System		SQ3R	Survey, Question, Read, Recite, and Review
PPVT	Peabody Picture Vocabulary Test		S-R Theory	Stimulus-Response Theory
P.Q.	Perceptual Quotient		SRA	Science Research Associates
Project "PLAN"	Program for Learning in Accordance with Needs		SRT	Speech Reception Threshold
			SSR	Sustained Silent Reading
PSAT	Preliminary Scholastic Aptitute Test		SSSP	Secondary School Science Project
Psi	Symbol (Greek letter) for Study of Psychic Phenomena		STAD	Student Teams—Achievement Divisions
PSSC	Physical Science Study Committee		SVIB	Strong Vocational Interest Blank
PTA	Parent-Teacher Association		TA	Transactional Analysis
PUSH	People United to Save Humanity		T and I	Trade and Industrial Education
RAM	Random Access Memory (in computers)		TAT	Thematic Apperception Test
			TEFL	Teaching English as a Foreign Language
RBS	Research for Better Schools			
RET	Rational-Emotive Therapy		TESL	Teaching English as a Second Language
RIE	Resources in Education			
RIF	Reading Is Fundamental		TESOL	Teaching English to Speakers of Other Languages
RIF	Reduction in Force			
ROM	Read Only Memory (in computers)		TESS	(The) Educational Software Selector
RN	Registered Nurse		TGT	Teams-Games-Tournaments
R/REA	Rural/Regional Education Association		TIAA-CREF	Teachers Insurance and Annuity Association; College Retirement Equities Fund
RSVP	Retired Senior Volunteer Program			
s	Standard Deviation			
SAE	Student Action for Education		TLU	Teaching-Learning Units
SAPA	Science-A Process Approach		t.o.	Traditional Orthography

TOEFL	Test of English as a Foreign Language	VP	Verb Phrase
TSM	Time, Space, and Matter	VTR	Video Tape Recorder
TTT	Training of Teacher Trainers	WAIS	Wechsler Adult Intelligence Scale
UAA	Urban Affairs Association	WCOTP	World Conference of Organizations of the Teaching Profession
UCEA	University Council for Educational Administration	WEPU	Weighted Elementary Pupil Unit
UCSMP	University of Chicago School Mathematics Project	WICHE	Western Interstate Commission for Higher Education
UNESCO	United Nations Educational, Scientific and Cultural Organization	WISC	Wechsler Intelligence Scale for Children
UNICEF	United Nations International Children's Emergency Fund	WPPSI	Wechsler Preschool and Primary Scale of Intelligence
USAF I	U.S. Armed Forces Institute	$\bar{X}$	Mean
USOE	United States Office of Education	χ^2	Chi Square
USSA	United States Student Association	YMCA	Young Men's Christian Association
V-A-K-T	Visual-Auditory-Kinesthetic-Tactile	YM-YWHA	Young Men's/Young Women's Hebrew Association
VCR	Video Cassette Recorder	YWCA	Young Women's Christian Association
VISTA	Volunteers in Service to America		

ABACUS, a manipulative device used by mathematics educators to teach place values of numbers. It may also be used with older students as a calculating device. The simple abacus illustrated below consists of a frame within which parallel wires are enclosed. Beads or markers are placed on each wire. The extreme right wire represents *units*, the second from the right the *tens*, the third the *hundreds*, and so on. The beads appearing at the bottom of each wire indicate the *number* of units—tens, hundreds, and so on. In the illustration, the number 2,054 is depicted. (Note the treatment of zero.)

An open-end abacus contains no frame, thus making it possible for students to transfer beads from one wire to another.

The ancient Egyptians, Greeks, and Romans used different kinds of abaci for counting and computing.

References: Hunter Ballew, *Teaching Children Mathematics*, Columbus, OH: Charles E. Merrill Publishing Company, 1973; Rosalie Jensen, *Exploring Mathematical Concepts and Skills in the Elementary School*, Columbus, OH: Charles E. Merrill Publishing Company, 1973.

ABILITY, FINANCIAL—See FINANCIAL ABILITY

ABILITY GROUPING, a method of organizing children who have similarities as measured by tests or judgments or both. The formulations of these groupings may be based on: (1) intellectual or academic abilities, such as intelligence, or reading level; (2) psychomotor skills, such as skills with working with one's hands (e.g. carpentry, sewing), physical education (e.g. gymnastics), or related activities; (3) performing arts ability; and (4) characteristics unique to special student populations (e.g. the gifted or mentally retarded child).

There are many problems associated with classifying or identifying children in order to develop a homogeneous group according to an ability, trait, or characteristic. Testing, the nature of tests, and cultural/socioeconomic biases inherent in some tests constitute some of the problems. Another is the subjectivity involved in making judgments about individual children's abilities. (See HOMOGENEOUS AND HETEROGENEOUS GROUPING.)

References: Warren G. Findley and Miriam M. Bryan, *The Pros and Cons of Ability Grouping* (PDK Fastback 66), Bloomington, IN: The Phi Delta Kappa Educational Foundation, 1975; Larry W. Hughes and Gerald C. Ubben, *The Elementary Principal's Handbook: A Guide to Effective Action* (Third Edition), Boston: Allyn and Bacon, 1989.

ABINGTON SCHOOL DISTRICT v. SCHEMPP, a landmark legal decision relating to religious exercises (readings from the Bible and recitation of prayer) in the public schools. The U.S. Supreme Court, in 1963, ruled that the Abington School District in Pennsylvania, which required Bible reading even when students were excused from this

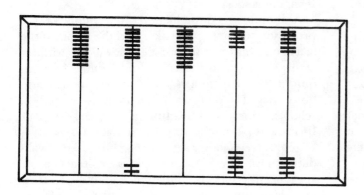

Abacus

exercise, violated the "Establishment Clause" of the Constitution's First Amendment; accordingly, such action was found to be unconstitutional. (See ESTABLISHMENT CLAUSE.)

References: Abington School District v. Schempp, 374 U.S. 203, 1963; David Fellman, *The Supreme Court and Education* (Third Edition), New York: Teachers College Press, 1976.

ABSENTEEISM—See ATTENDANCE, SCHOOL

ABSTRACTION, a mental process that enables an organism to identify and transfer the common characteristics or qualities of an object, situation, or experiences to another condition or sensory experience. The greater the differences in the conditions or experiences, the greater the degree of abstractive ability needed for successful transfer. Abstraction is used in certain concept attainment. Usually, abstract concepts, through symbols, are acquired by generalizations (i.e. similar or consistent responses) to separate and differing objects, situations, or experiences. Generally, school curricula are arranged in a way that permits the learner to move from the concrete to the abstract.

Abstractions have the following similar characteristics: (1) involve a mental process; (2) use symbols extensively; (3) require transfer to something else; (4) utilize common and/or similar characteristics derived from an object or experience; and (5) are heavily used in concept building and developments. They are found in thinking, learning, psychology, philosophy, mathematics, science, logic, art, music, and a large number of other human experiences. Psychologists are experimenting with the abstractive abilities of many animals; to date, man has been found to have the most sophisticated skills of abstraction.

References: Hubert G. Alexander, *Language and Thinking, A Philosophical Introduction,* Princeton, NJ: D. Van Nostrand Company, Inc., 1967; Stewart H. Hulse, et al., *Cognitive Processes in Animal Behavior,* Hillsdale, NJ: Lawrence Erlbaum Associates, Publishers, 1978; W. Edgar Vinacke, *The Psychology of Thinking* (Second Edition), New York: McGraw-Hill Book Company, 1974; P. C. Wason and P. N. Johnson-Laird, *Psychology of Reasoning,* Cambridge, MA: Harvard University Press, 1972.

ABSTRACTS, EDUCATIONAL, publications that summarize original documents dealing with an area of education. Abstracts include bibliographic entries, the summary of a particular document, and a subject index. They may include other information to help the reader as well.

There are many well-known educational abstract journals. Several are: *Children's Literature Abstracts; Child Development Abstracts and Bibliography; College Student Personnel Abstract; Completed Research in Health, Physical Education and Recreation; d(deafness) s(speech) h(hearing) Abstracts; Dissertation Abstracts; Education Administration Abstracts; ERIC—Resources in Education; Exceptional Child Education Abstracts; Language and Language Behavior Abstracts; Rehabilitation Literature;* and *Sociology of Education Abstracts.*

One of the most complete of the abstract journals is *ERIC—Resources in Education* (RIE), published monthly by the Office of Educational Research and Improvement. (See DISSERTATION ABSTRACTS INTERNATIONAL and ERIC.)

References: Harold Borko and Charles L. Bernier, *Abstracting Concepts and Methods,* New York: Academic Press, 1975; Wayne J. Krepel and Charles R. DuVall, *Education and Education-Related Serials: A Directory,* Littleton, CO: Libraries Unlimited, Inc., 1977; Eugene P. Sheehy, et al., *Guide to Reference Books* (Ninth Edition), Chicago: American Library Association, 1976; Marda Woodbury, *A Guide to Sources of Educational Information,* Washington, DC: Information Resources Press, 1976.

ACADEMIC DEAN—See DEAN, ACADEMIC

ACADEMIC FREEDOM, a right accorded to university professors (teachers and researchers) that embraces three distinct forms of freedom. They are: (1) the right to introduce controversial topics into the classroom as long as these are related to the subject under study; (2) freedom to pursue research and to publish research findings as part of one's academic duties; and (3) freedom to speak and to write as a citizen. These three guarantees are embodied in the American Association of University Professor's *Statement of Principles on Academic Freedom and Tenure,* a document adopted in 1940 and subsequently endorsed by over 60 professional associations.

Academic freedom includes the rights of the professor, teacher, or speaker and the rights of the learner or listener to pursue knowledge without external restrictions that would inhibit free inquiry. Such freedom is based upon the assumptions that: (1) there is value in knowledge; (2) schools, educational institutions, or speakers' platforms are places for the dissemination of knowledge; (3) free inquiry is the procedure used to validate knowledge; (4) the professor, teacher, or speaker has special competencies; and (5) individuals do not lose their rights as citizens (to exercise the freedom of speech) by virtue of being engaged in the pursuit of knowledge as teachers or as students.

References: Howard R. Bowen and Jack H. Schuster, American Professors: A National Resource Imperiled, New York: Oxford University Press, 1986; Richard D. Gatti and Daniel J. Gatti, Encyclopedic Dictionary of School Law, West Nyack, NY: Parker Publishing Company, Inc., 1975; Louis Joughin (Editor), Academic Freedom and Tenure: A Handbook of The American Association of University Professors, Madison, WI: University of Wisconsin Press, 1969; Paul H. Morrill and Emil R. Spees, The Academic Profession: Teaching in Higher Education, New York: Human Sciences Press, Inc., 1982.

ACADEMIC OFFICERS, higher education leaders responsible for recommending and implementing policies and procedures to meet or further the academic and instructional goals of an institution of higher education. Although a variety of academic administrative structures exist in colleges and universities (some rather simple, others complex, depending on the size and nature of the institution), there are several common positions/titles for academic officers. Among them are: President/Chancellor; Vice-President/Vice Chancellor/Provost for Academic Affairs/Dean of Faculty; Dean of a College or School; Dean of Professional School; Dean of Graduate School; Dean of Extension School/Continuing Education; Dean or Director of Summer School; and Director of Special Programs, Research, or a Center.

Academic officers usually come from the ranks of the professorship. Although academic officers may hold tenure as professors in a discipline or department, they do not hold tenure in the administrative position. Rather, they serve at the pleasure of the chief academic officer (president or chancellor) and the governing body of the institution (e.g. Board of Trustees). Administrators of student affairs, public relations, business affairs, planning and development, and athletics are generally not considered to be academic officers. (See BOARD OF TRUSTEES, COLLEGE AND UNIVERSITY; DEAN, ACADEMIC; and DEAN OF EDUCATION.)

References: Frederick E. Balderston, Managing Today's University, San Francisco: Jossey-Bass Publishers, 1974; Elwood B. Ehrle and John B. Bennett, Managing the Academic Enterprise, New York: American Council on Education, 1988; Edward Gross and Paul V. Grambsch, Changes in University Organization 1964–1971, New York: McGraw-Hill Book Company, 1974; Asa S. Knowles (Editor), Handbook of College and University Administration, New York: McGraw-Hill Book Company, 1970; Gary L. Riley and J. Victor Baldridge, Governing Academic Organizations, Berkeley, CA: McCutchan Publishing Corporation, 1977.

ACADEMIC PREPARATION FOR COLLEGE: WHAT STUDENTS NEED TO KNOW AND BE ABLE TO DO—See NATIONAL REFORM REPORTS (1980–86)

ACADEMIC QUARTER—See QUARTER, ACADEMIC

ACADEMIC RANK, title given to an individual who teaches and/or performs research at a college or university. The title (rank) denotes the individual's past training, experiences, and academic productivity (e.g. research, publications, teaching ability, contributions to the institution). In the early 1800s, only individuals who had endowments were called "professors." The title was so widely and freely bestowed on individuals during the later 1800s that, by 1900, as a reaction to the change, six universities (Columbia, Cornell, Chicago, Harvard, Michigan, and Wisconsin) had established the system for ranking of professors.

There are generally four ranks or levels: (1) instructor; (2) assistant professor; (3) associate professor; and (4) full professor. The instructor rank is normally the starting rank for those individuals who have not earned the highest terminal degree available in a particular discipline or are just starting a teaching/research career in higher education. There are no universal standards for the ranks; determining rank for a given individual is a function of the institution and/or the discipline.

Generally, faculty members move "through the ranks" to full professor via promotion. Recommendation for promotion usually comes from a faculty committee following an extensive review of the faculty member's achievements in the areas of teaching and/or research and/or service. For most professors, this process takes many years. Some professors remain at a particular rank throughout their teaching careers. At one time, when an individual was promoted from assistant to associate professor, he/she was simultaneously granted tenure. This perfunctory procedure is no longer being followed by many institutions.

References: Kenneth E. Eble, Professors as Teachers, San Francisco: Jossey-Bass Publishers, 1972; Herman Estrin and Delmer M. Goode, College and University Teaching, Dubuque, IA: Wm. C. Brown Company, Publishers, 1964; Richard D. Mandell, The Professor Game, Garden City, NY: Doubleday and Company, Inc., 1977.

ACADEMIC WORK AND EDUCATIONAL EX-CELLENCE—See NATIONAL REFORM RE-PORTS (1980–86)

ACADEMY, a term that has several meanings. In art, it is a building in which the arts are encouraged through instructional programs and exhibitions. A major function of the modern academy is to encourage artists through various types of funding support.

The first two modern fine arts academies were the Academia di Disegno, founded in Florence, Italy, 1563, and the Academy of St. Luke, founded in 1593, in Rome. Art academies are found in several major cities throughout the world, but two of the most influential are the Royal Academy of Arts in London (1768) and the Royal Academy of Painting and Sculpture in Paris (1648).

The original term dates back to ancient Greece, where the followers of Plato met in a park (northwest of Athens) during the 5th and 4th centuries B.C. The term not only was applied to the park (a place of study) but also to the school of Plato (learned society). Hence the second meaning of the term, namely a society of scholars or artists.

Academy is a term sometimes used to describe a school that has a special function or whose curriculum has a college-preparatory emphasis.
References: Horst de la Croix and Richard G. Tansey (Revised), *Gardner's Art Through the Ages* (Seventh Edition), New York: Harcourt Brace Jovanovich, Inc., 1980; Frederick Harlt, *Art: A History of Painting, Sculpture, Architecture* (Volume II), New York: Harry N. Abrams, Inc., Publishers, 1976; Nikolaus Pevsner, *Academies of Art, Past and Present,* Cambridge, England: Cambridge at the University Press, 1940.

ACADEMY FOR EDUCATIONAL DEVELOP-MENT—See EDUCATIONAL FACILITIES LABORATORY

A CAPPELLA, a term used in music that refers to music for voices alone (i.e. music that has no musical accompaniment). An Italian word that means "in the church style," *a cappella* originally referred to unaccompanied choral music. Today it is applied to all forms of music.
References: Willi Apel, *Harvard Dictionary of Music* (Second Edition, Revised and Enlarged), Cambridge, MA: The Belknap Press of Harvard University Press, 1970; J. A. Westrup and F. Harrison (Revised by Conrad Wilson), *The New College Encyclopedia of Music,* New York: W. W. Norton and Company, Inc., 1976.

ACCELERATION, the sometimes controversial practice of moving gifted learners through the curriculum at a relatively rapid rate. The practice, used at all educational levels, kindergarten through the university, permits the student to complete his/her academic studies in a time period shorter than that normally required of other students. Elimination of boredom, shorter time needed to absorb new information, and elimination of academic replication are often cited as arguments in support of acceleration. Opponents offer counter-arguments, one of them being that children who may be intellectually advanced are not advanced socially.

In 1963, Robert DeHaan reported that acceleration receives the most unequivocal support from research studies when compared with practices that either provide curriculum enrichment or standard curricula. In a study of mathematically talented youth, conducted recently at Johns Hopkins University, acceleration of up to four years was reported with no adverse effects on either personal adjustment or academic progress noted. (See ENRICHMENT PROGRAMS.)
References: Marsha M. Correl, *Teaching the Gifted and Talented* (PDK Fastback 119), Bloomington, IN: The Phi Delta Kappa Educational Foundation, 1978; Robert F. DeHaan, *Accelerated Learning Programs,* New York: The Center for Applied Research in Education, Inc., 1963; Daniel P. Keating, "Secondary-School Programs" in A. Harry Passow (Editor), *The Gifted and the Talented: Their Education and Development* (NSSE 78th Yearbook, Part I), Chicago: University of Chicago Press, 1979; Julian C. Stanley, "The Study and Facilitation of Talent for Mathematics" in A. Harry Passow (Editor), *The Gifted and the Talented: Their Education and Development* (NSSE 78th Yearbook, Part I), Chicago: University of Chicago Press, 1979; Julian C. Stanley, "Accelerating the Educational Progress of Intellectually Gifted Children" in Wayne Dennis and Margaret W. Dennis (Editors), *The Intellectually Gifted: An Overview,* New York: Grune and Stratton, 1976.

ACCOUNTABILITY, the demand for proof that an enterprise is meeting its stated purposes and goals. In education, the demand for accountability may come from students, teachers, parents, school administrators, school boards, governmental agencies, or the various publics served by the enterprise. Such demands may be directed at any or all individuals responsible for a classroom, a school program, a school building, or a school district. One primary outcome of such demands is the movement toward school-based evaluation, where the school becomes the unit of analysis for measuring effectiveness. Several approaches are being or have been used in the evaluation of such enterprises. They include two administrative models: the Planning-Programming-Budget System and Management by Objectives. Competency-Based Education is a school districtwide accountability approach used to assess the degree to which students have attained minimum proficiency in areas such as reading, language arts, or mathematics at specific grade levels and/or before receiving a high school diploma. Performance contracting, which received considerable attention in the 1960s, is yet another accountability vehicle that was tried in some school systems.

Many factors have led to the development of the accountability movement. They include the public's disenchantment with the schools, restricted availability of funds for schools, and governmental requirements.

Critics of educational accountability point to several issues that make it difficult to implement. These include political considerations, measurement-evaluation problems, and philosophical conflicts with this movement. In spite of these issues, educational accountability programs have begun to address issues, going beyond the standard factor of achievement to such things as student behavior and student/faculty attitudes. (See COMPETENCY-BASED EDUCATION; MANAGEMENT BY OBJECTIVES; PERFORMANCE CONTRACTING; and PLANNING, PROGRAMMING, BUDGETING, EVALUATION SYSTEM.)

References: Dale Parnell, *The Case for Competency-Based Education* (PDK Fastback 118), Bloomington, IN: The Phi Delta Kappa Educational Foundation, 1978; James W. Popham, *Educational Evaluation* (Second Edition), Englewood Cliffs, NJ: Prentice-Hall, Inc. 1988; Robert R. Spillane and Dorothy Levenson, *Management by Objectives in the Schools* (PDK Fastback 115), Bloomington, IN: The Phi Delta Kappa Educational Foundation, 1978; Beth Sulzer-Azaroff and G. Roy Mayer, *Achieving Educational Excellence: Using Behavioral Strategies*, New York: Holt, Rinehart and Winston, 1986; John W. Wick, *School-Based Evaluation*, Boston: Kluwer-Nijhoff Publishing, 1987).

ACCOUNTING—See SCHOOL ACCOUNTING

ACCREDITATION, an evaluation process that involves evaluating the quality level of an institution (e.g. elementary school, secondary school, college, or university), or programs sponsored by the institution, using predetermined standards. The practice of accreditation is fairly widespread in the United States, a fact that, in part at least, reflects the absence of a centralized federal ministry of education. Accreditation is normally carried out on a peer review basis by competent, nongovernmental agencies such as regional and/or local associations. Thus, it can be said to be a collegial activity conducted by institutions that have voluntarily organized to form and to support an accrediting association.

The specific functions of accreditation include: (1) certifying that an institution meets established standards; (2) identifying acceptable institutions for prospective students; (3) creating goals for self-improvement of weaker institutions; and (4) guiding institutions with respect to the acceptability of transfer credits.

Normally, the accreditation process involves: (1) establishment of standards by the accrediting association; (2) voluntary application for accreditation by an institution; (3) completion of a detailed self-study by the petitioning institution; (4) a field visit to the institution and evaluation carried out by a team of visitors chosen by the accrediting association; and (5) an accreditation decision that, if favorable, results in the inclusion of the institution in an official publication listing all approved institutions. (See ACCREDITING AGENCIES AND ASSOCIATIONS; NATIONAL COUNCIL FOR THE ACCREDITATION OF TEACHER EDUCATION; and NATIONAL STUDY OF SCHOOL EVALUATION.)

References: Melodie E. Christal and Dennis P. Jones, *A Common Language for Postsecondary Accreditation: Categories and Definitions for Data Collection*, Boulder, CO: National Center for Higher Education Systems, 1985; Division of Eligibility and Agency Evaluation, Bureau of Higher and Continuing Education, U.S. Office of Education, *Nationally Recognized Accrediting Agencies and Associations*, Washington, DC: The Division, November 1978; National Study of School Evaluation, *Evaluative Criteria for the Evaluation of Secondary Schools* (Sixth Edition), Falls Church, VA: National Study of School Evaluation, 1987.

ACCREDITING AGENCIES AND ASSOCIATIONS, organizations that prepare standards for educational institutions and subsequently apply those standards when evaluating individual institutions seeking accreditation. Most accrediting agencies are either state boards (or departments) of education, regional accrediting associations, or national institutional and specialized accrediting bodies. The earliest accrediting agencies were formed in the 19th century, primarily to facilitate effective articulation between secondary schools and institutions of higher education.

The six regional associations of colleges and universities in the United States (among the country's most prestigious accrediting groups) are: (1) New England Association of Schools and Colleges (formed in 1885); (2) Middle States Association of Colleges and Schools (1887); (3) North Central Association of Colleges and Schools (1895); (4) Southern Association of Colleges and Schools (1895); (5) Northwest Association of Schools and Colleges (1917); and (6) the Western Association of Schools and Colleges (1924).

The national institutional and specialized accrediting bodies include diverse agencies such as the American Medical Association, Society of American Foresters, American Board of Funeral Service Education, and the National Council for the Accreditation of Teacher Education. (See ACCREDITATION; NATIONAL COUNCIL FOR THE ACCREDITATION OF TEACHER EDUCATION; and NATIONAL STUDY OF SCHOOL EVALUATION. Also see APPENDIX XVIII: REGIONAL ACCREDITING ASSOCIATIONS.)

References: Division of Eligibility and Agency Evaluation, Bureau of Higher and Continuing Education, U.S. Office of Education, *Nationally Recognized Accrediting Agencies and Associations*, Washington, DC: The Division, November 1978; National Study of School Evaluation, *Evaluative Criteria for the Evaluation of Secondary Schools* (Sixth Edition), Falls Church, VA: National Study of School Evaluation, 1987.

ACCULTURATION, the process of adjusting or adapting to a culture. As they grow up, children learn (overtly and covertly) to adjust to the demands of the particular culture in which they happen to live. Likewise, people, as they move, may find themselves in another culture; they then must learn about the new culture and develop coping mechanisms that will enable them to adapt to the concepts, sentiments, institutions, dress, language patterns, and so forth that make up the new culture. Games and sports, language usage, values, ideals, food, fashions, hair styles, dancing, and attitudes are just a few of the elements affecting acculturation. Individuals who are members of racial, ethnic, religious, language, or social class groups different from the dominant society/ culture of a community are faced with the problems, stresses, and concerns of acculturation.

Although there are many subcultures and defined subgroups that exist in any society, schools are the major mechanisms used by the dominant society for acculturation.

Complete acculturation takes place when total assimilation into another culture has resulted. Multicultural education programs have been designed to allow for varying degrees of acculturation without destroying the viability, integrity, and identity of different cultural groups. (See MULTICULTURAL EDUCATION.)

References: Earnest V. Anderson and Walter B. Kolesnik (Editors), *Education and Acculturation in Modern Urban Society*, Detroit: University of Detroit Press, 1965; Dolores E. Cross, et al. (Editors), *Teaching in a Multicultural Society*, New York: The Free Press, 1977; Joe R. Feagin, *Racial and Ethnic Relations*, Englewood Cliffs, NJ: Prentice-Hall, Inc., 1978; Meyer Weinberg, *A Chance to Learn: The History of Race and Education in the United States*, Cambridge, England: Cambridge University Press, 1977.

ACHIEVEMENT, in the abstract, the reaching of a specific quantity or quality level by an individual. In education, pupil or student achievement can be divided into three categories: *cognitive*, or academic (e.g. reaching levels of competence in mathematics, English, social studies); *affective*, or development of personal-social adjustment (feelings, emotions, attitudes, etc.); and *psychomotor*, or development of motor skills (reaching specific levels of skills such as in physical education, shop, and sewing). Achievement and motivation are frequently interrelated. (See ACHIEVEMENT TESTS and MOTIVATION.)

References: J. Stanley Ahmann and Marvin Glock, *Evaluating Pupil Growth* (Fourth Edition), Boston: Allyn and Bacon, Inc., 1971; Janice T. Gibson and Louis A. Chandler, *Educational Psychology: Mastering Principles and Applications*, Boston: Allyn and Bacon, 1988; Norman A. Sprinthall and Richard B. Sprinthall, *Educational Psychology: A Developmental Approach* (Fourth Edition), New York: Random House, 1987.

ACHIEVEMENT AGE—See AGE-EQUIVALENT SCALES/SCORES

ACHIEVEMENT TESTS, instruments that measure what a student knows and/or can do. Inferences about how such knowledge was acquired are difficult to establish. Generally, the tests measure cumulative experiences from a variety of situations as well as serving as a terminal evaluation of individuals after a particular program or experience has been completed.

The distinction between aptitude and achievement tests cannot always be kept. Some achievement tests cover prior learning; others may be used as predictors of success in subsequent educational experiences. Achievement tests can: (1) facilitate learning by revealing weaknesses; (2) be used in determining individual needs; (3) be used in improving the instructional process; (4) aid in the formulation of educational goals; and (5) be used to determine the amount of content and skills being taught in a particular subject area.

There are many types of achievement tests: (1) general achievement batteries (e.g., California Achievement Test, Adult Basic Learning Examinations); (2) diagnostic tests (e.g. Stanford Diagnostic Reading Test, Stanford Diagnostic Arithmetic Test); (3) college admissions tests (e.g. Scholastic Aptitude Test, American College Test); and (4) subject matter tests (available in most subject areas at the elementary, high school, and college levels as well as in specific vocational areas). Buros's *Mental Measurement Yearbooks* and *Tests in Print* list all standard tests available. (See ACHIEVEMENT.)

References: Oscar K. Buros (Editor), *The Eighth Mental Measurements Yearbook* (Volumes I and II), Highland Park, NJ: The Gryphon Press, 1978; Oscar K. Buros (Editor), *Tests in Print II*, Highland Park, NJ: The Gryphon Press, 1974; Lee J. Cronbach, *Essentials of Psychological Testing* (Third Edition), New York: Harper and Row, Publishers, 1970.

ACOUSTICS, the study of sound. The emphasis of acoustics is on how well sound is heard, rather than on its production. Acoustics is important to educators because children who suffer from acoustic impedance may have hearing and speech difficulties and subsequent learning problems. Acoustical problems are also concerns in the construction of school buildings, banks, businesses, and theatres.

Acoustic signal levels are important to hearing and speech, for it is the signals that constitute the set of stimuli to which listeners must respond. Sound (made up of pure and complex tones) has varying frequencies, amplitudes, and durations. An acoustic spectrum, depicted on a graph, can illustrate the frequency components of a complex sound along with its amplitude. The ability to distinguish between the spectral characteristics of different sounds is extremely important in hearing and speech. Consequently, it is important to be able to identify acoustical problems.

Acoustic impedance, its identification, and its degree have become an important aspect of clinical audiologic test batteries and auditory evaluations. *Impedance* has been defined as resistance to motion (sound pressure wave). Acoustic impedance is usually measured under two conditions: *static* (the eardrum is at a normal resting position) and *dynamic* (the eardrum is under varying amounts of pressure).

References: James F. Curtis (Editor), *Processes and Disorders of Human Communications*, New York: Harper and Row, Publishers, 1978; B. P. Hildebrand and B. B. Brenden, *An Introduction to Acoustical Holography*, New York: Plenum Press, 1972; Jack Katz (Editor), *Handbook of Clinical Audiology*, Baltimore, MD: The Williams and Wilkins Company, 1978.

ACQUIRED IMMUNE DEFICIENCY SYNDROME (AIDS), a disease thought to be caused by a virus, such as Herpes 2, Human T. Cell Leukemia (HTLV), or other human immunodeficiency viruses (HIV). The virus damages the immune system, thus diminishing an individual's ability to fight diseases. The disease was first reported by the Centers for Disease Control (Atlanta, Georgia) in June of 1981. The centers for Disease Control estimate that there will be 250,000 cases of AIDS by 1991.

There may be 1 to 1.5 million people infected with HIV who do not show any signs of the illness and may never acquire full AIDS. AIDS, itself, is actually the final stage of the immune infection, with death caused by Pneumocystis pneumonia; a rare cancer—Kaposi's Sarcoma (KS); cryptococcus meningitis; and other such complications. Initially, AIDS was found in a few identifiable groups, such as homosexuals, intravenous (IV) drug users, and hemophiliacs. Now the disease can be found in all social strata and groups. It spreads primarily through intimate physical contact, exchange of body fluids, and shared needles. AZT is the only drug approved (1989) by the U.S. government that can delay the onset of the disease, and is used in treating those with AIDS.

The schools have been faced with two major problems: (1) children who have HIV (usually transmitted through the mother or through a blood transfusion) and attend school, and (2) AIDS Education programs for all children. Schools have recognized the need (and legal requirements) to allow HIV children to attend school and be in regular classrooms. As of May 1989, 28 states, plus the District of Columbia, have mandated educational programs on AIDS.

References: Don L. Bohl (Editor), *AIDS, the New Workplace Issues*, New York: American Management Association, 1988; Alan Cantwell, Jr., *AIDS: The Mystery and the Solution* (Second Edition), Los Angeles, CA: Aries Rising Press, 1986; Richard Liebmann-Smith, *The Question of*

AIDS, New York: The New York Academy of Sciences, 1985; William H. Masters, Virginia E. Johnson, and Robert C. Kolodny, *Crisis*, New York: Grove Press, 1988.

ACRYLIC PAINTS—See PLASTIC PAINTS and POLYMER PAINTS

ACTING OUT, a dramatic technique used in a language arts program to promote all types of expressions: feelings, speech, and hand and body movements (individual and/or group). Acting out can be performed by children of all ages, either as self-expression or as enactment of stories. From grades Kindergarten through 3, acting out is rather simplistic. With older children, it may take the form of dramatic play or choral reading.

There are many behavioral as well as cognitive purposes for acting out. Several are: (1) motivating and supporting shy children; (2) improving speech; (3) helping children to work together; (4) making learning fun; (5) furthering peer socialization; (6) developing understandings of the relationships of body and movement and speech; (7) channeling emotions; (8) developing speech patterns and various sounds; and (9) fostering creativity. (See LANGUAGE ARTS.)

References: Harry A. Greene and Walter T. Petty, *Developing Language Skills in the Elementary Schools* (Fifth Edition), Boston: Allyn and Bacon, Inc., 1975; John M. Kean and Carl Personke, *The Language Arts: Teaching and Learning in the Elementary School*, New York: St. Martin's Press, 1976; James Moffett and Betty Jane Wagner, *Student-Centered Language Arts and Reading, K-13*, Boston: Houghton Mifflin Company, 1976.

ACTION, an independent, volunteer, federal agency created by presidential executive order on July 1, 1971. The organization is divided into two major units: Domestic Operations and International Operations.

Domestic Operations consists of a national headquarters, 10 regional offices, and 47 state offices. VISTA volunteers (4,200), Foster Grandparents (15,000 volunteers), and RSVP (Retired Senior Volunteer Program, 220,000) are the major programs found in the Domestic Operations unit of ACTION.

International Operations is composed of a Washington headquarters and three regional subunits: Latin America; Africa; and North Africa, Near East, Asia, and the Pacific. The Peace Corps is the major program included in this operation (approximately 6,000 volunteers). (See VISTA.)

Reference: Michael P. Balzano, *Reorganizing the Federal Bureaucracy*, Washington, DC: American Enterprise Institute for Public Policy Research, 1977.

ACTION FOR EXCELLENCE—See NATIONAL REFORM REPORTS (1980–86)

ACTION RESEARCH, studies aimed at solving immediate problems arising as part of the operation of a school, a classroom, or an educational project. Its focus is on immediate application, not on theory development and/or broad generalizations. Since action research may be performed by teachers, administrators, and community project staff, as well as professional researchers, changes in behaviors and attitudes of those performing the research may be a by-product of such research. Consequently, action research has a significant inservice function, especially when performed by teachers.

Scientific rigor is not as important in action research as is finding a solution to an immediate problem. Although a variety of research methodologies may be used (survey, experimental, quasi-experimental, etc.), the case study approach is employed most often.

References: Ambrose Clegg, et al., *Triangulation: A Strategy for Formative Action Research on In-Service Education*, Kent, OH: Kent State University Teacher Corps, 1978; Stephen M. Corey, *Action Research to Improve School Practices*, New York: Teachers College, Columbia University, 1953; David E. Kapel, "Education Research on the Urban Scene," *Planning and Changing*, Summer 1973; George J. Mouly, "Research Methods" in Robert L. Ebel (Editor), *Encyclopedia of Educational Research* (Fourth Edition), New York: The Macmillan Company, 1969; Sandra Woodworth, *Ask Them: Action Research in Teaching Writing*, Durham, NH: University of New Hampshire, 1979.

ACT PROFICIENCY EXAMINATION PROGRAM—See AMERICAN COLLEGE TESTS

ACUITY, the ability of an individual to discriminate between two or more stimuli. Although there are many different acuities, visual and auditory discriminations are the two major types of interest to teachers.

Visual acuity includes: visibility; resolution; spatial-shape; vernier; motion; and stereoscoptics. *Auditory acuity* is concerned with the absolute threshold, or the loss of attenuation, of sound, differential frequencies, durations, and intensities. Acuity can also be a measure of touch (e.g. skin senses to vibrations, pressures, heat).

References: Edward C. Carterette and Morton P. Friedman, *Handbook of Perception*, New York: Academic Press, 1978; Melvin L. Rubin and Gordon L. Walls, *Fundamentals of Visual Science*, Springfield, IL: Charles C. Thomas, Publisher, 1969.

ADA, a high-level programming language (first published in 1980) developed for the United States Department of Defense. The language itself was actually written (under contract) by a French team of programmers headed by Dr. Jean Ichbiah. Ada has application beyond its initial military use; it has been used in standard business applications, in automobiles, and in microwave ovens, and has also been used in research found in many professional journals (including psychology, nursing, and education). Ada has many desirable software engineering characteristics, such as: structured programming, separation of specifications from implementation, reusability, portability, readability, efficiency. Ada programs are now available for use in microcomputers.

References: A. Nico Habermann and Dewayne E. Perry, *Ada for Experienced Programmers,* Reading, MA: Addison-Wesley Publishing Co., 1983; Edward Lieblein, "The Department of Defense Software Initiative—A Status Report," *Communications of the ACM,* Volume 29, Number 8, August 1986; Jean E. Sommot, "Why Ada Is Not Just Another Programming Language," *Communications of the ACM,* Volume 29, Number 8; August 1986.

ADAPTABILITY, ORGANIZATIONAL, a term that refers to the capacity of an organization (e.g. school system) to replace outmoded procedures and goals with new ones. Adaptation is considered to have taken place when a particular change (innovation) has been made throughout the entire organization.

Adaptability is an organizational response to environmental stimuli. Examples of such stimuli include financial variables such as level of expenditure, financial ability, and community demography.

Thomas Sergiovanni and Robert Starratt pointed out that organizations, like individuals, are in contact with their respective environments. That contact is effective as long as demands of the unit and its environment are essentially the same. When they are not, and adaptation needs to take place, changes in both the organization and its environment occur.

Studies of adaptability indicate that an institution's capacity to cope with changing situations is related, in part, to leadership capacity.

References: Richard O. Carlson, *Adoption of Educational Innovations,* Eugene, OR: Center for the Advanced Study of Educational Administration, University of Oregon, 1965; Donald H. Ross (Editor), *Administration for Adaptability* (Volumes I and III), New York: Metropolitan School Study Council, Teachers College, Columbia University, 1951; Thomas J. Sergiovanni and Robert J. Star-

ratt, *Supervision: Human Perspectives* (Second Edition), New York: McGraw-Hill Book Company, 1979; Ralph M. Stogdill, *Handbook of Leadership: A Survey of Theory and Research,* New York: The Free Press, 1974.

ADAPTED PHYSICAL EDUCATION, a physical education program that, although similar to regular physical education programs with respect to objectives, has been modified to accommodate the needs and abilities of exceptional children or adults. Arthur Daniels and Evelyn Davies defined it further to include "all facets of the regular physical education program but with selections and adaptations provided for the development of the capabilities of each individual" (p. 1).

Adapted physical education grew out of corrective physical education classes that, before World War I, focused on students with postural problems and were later broadened to accommodate students with physical handicaps. Most recently, with the emergence of the mainstreaming movement, adapted education has been serving all handicapped (physically and mentally) children and, where possible, providing them with all or part of their instruction in regular physical education classes.

References: Daniel D. Arnheim, et al., *Principles and Methods of Adapted Physical Education and Recreation* (Third Edition), St. Louis, MO: The C. V. Mosby Company, 1977; H. Harrison Clarke and David H. Clarke, *Developmental and Adapted Physical Education* (Second Edition), Englewood Cliffs, NJ: Prentice-Hall, Inc., 1978; Arthur S. Daniels and Evelyn A. Davies, *Adapted Physical Education* (Third Edition), New York: Harper and Row, Publishers, 1975; Hollis F. Fait, *Special Physical Education: Adapted, Corrective, Developmental* (Fourth Edition), Philadelphia: W. B. Saunders Company, 1978.

ADAPTIVE BEHAVIOR, that behavior needed to establish an equilibrium, or balance, for an individual between his/her inner world and the outer world (or environment). Adaptive behaviors can be manifested in different ways and are explained by many different models of human behavioral development (e.g. G. Stanley Hall, Arnold Gesell).

Jean Piaget explained adaptive behavior as human actions that consist of a continuous and perpetual mechanism of readjustment or equilibration, each of which is built upon its predecessor. The balancing of the process of *assimilation* (incorporation of the external world into the structures that have already been constructed within an individual) and *accommodation* (the readjustment of the structure to the external world) he defined as adaptation. The manifestation of adaptive behavior may be quite different for individuals; perceptions, past experiences, cognition, are only a few of the factors that influence adaptive behavior.

Adaptive behavior may be used by individuals to reestablish *homeostasis* (to maintain internal equilibria) in their biological system. Individuals may react specifically to balance overstimulation or understimulation in their systems. Under certain conditions, humans will eat particular foods to reestablish homeostasis within a certain body system. For example, in the summer it is not uncommon for athletes to crave salt to replace the salt they lost through activity. Eating of the salt is an example of adaptive behavior.

References: John Elliot (Editor), *Human Development and Cognitive Processes,* New York: Holt, Rinehart and Winston, Inc., 1971; George S. Klein, *Perception, Motives, and Personality,* New York: Alfred A. Knopf, 1970; Jean Piaget, *Biology and Knowledge,* Chicago: University of Chicago Press, 1971; Jean Piaget, *Six Psychological Studies,* New York: Random House, 1967; Kurt Schlesinger and Philip M. Graves, *Psychology: A Dynamic Science,* Dubuque, IA: Wm. C. Brown Company, Publishers, 1976.

AD HOC COMMITTEES, special committees created to complete a specified, nonrecurring type of work. Unlike standing (permanent) committees, ad hoc committees are given a prescribed period within which to complete a task or to prepare a report and are normally disbanded once their assignments have been completed. In education, ad hoc committees are appointed to facilitate the work of school boards, administrators, parent groups, professional organizations, and faculty groups.

References: H. Garrett, *Chairmanship of Committees,* New York: State Mutual Book and Periodic Service, Ltd., 1978; Henry M. Robert, *Robert's Rules of Order* (Newly Revised by Sarah C. Robert, et al.), Glenview, IL: Scott, Foresman and Company, 1970; John E. Tropman, et al., *Essentials of Committee Management,* Chicago: Nelson-Hall, Inc., 1979.

ADJUSTMENT, SOCIAL, one's interaction with his/her social environment while striving to meet personal needs and goals. At the same time, the social environment places the individual under pressures and constraints to behave in a certain manner. The degree of social adjustment achieved is determined by the point at which personal needs and social demands have been reconciled.

Adjustment is a two-way process; that is, an individual relates effectively with society, while the society provides the means through which an individual realizes his/her potential. At times, the individual may change and, at times, society may change. It is in the process of social adjustment that many personal psychological problems and issues arise. Motivation, achievement needs, dominance and deference needs, frustrations, conflicts, anxieties, defensive behaviors, learning, and acceptance-rejection are illustrative. In most societies, social adjustment is considered to be more important than physiological adjustment.

References: Abe Arkoff, *Adjustment and Mental Health,* New York: McGraw-Hill Book Company, 1968; Charles Costello, *Anxiety and Depression,* Montreal, Canada: McGill-Queen's University Press, 1976; Gardner Lindzey and Elliot Aronson (Editors), *Handbook of Social Psychology* (Second Edition), Cambridge, MA: Addison-Wesley Publishing Company, 1968; James M. Sawrey and Charles W. Telford, *Psychology of Adjustment* (Third Edition), Boston: Allyn and Bacon, Inc., 1971.

ADMINISTRATION BUILDING—See SCHOOL ADMINISTRATION CENTER

ADMINISTRATIVE TEAM, in education, usually "the administrative specialists who hold the title of deputy, associate, assistant, and district or area superintendent" (AASA, p. 11). In school districts of relatively small size, the definition may be broadened to include building principals. Tasks performed by the administrative team fall into six broad categories: (1) school-community relations; (2) curriculum and instruction; (3) pupil personnel; (4) staff personnel; (5) school plant management; and (6) business and finance.

Richard Gorton suggested that the administrative team has two principal objectives: "(1) to develop and present a unified front in collective bargaining with teachers and in the implementation of the master contract, and (2) to utilize collectively the talents and interests of individual administrators and supervisors to solve problems and improve education within the district." The latter objective is the one usually emphasized in the literature of educational administration.

In recent years, increased attention has been given to the concept of team management in education including aspects such as team training and team evaluation.

References: American Association of School Administrators, *Profiles of the Administrative Team,* Washington, DC: The Association, 1971; Roald F. Campbell, et al., *Introduction to Educational Administration* (Fifth Edition), Boston: Allyn and Bacon, Inc., 1977; Richard A. Gorton, *School Administration: Challenge and Opportunity for Leadership,* Dubuque, IA: Wm. C. Brown Company, Publishers, 1976.

ADMINISTRATIVE THEORY, an approach to the study of organizational behavior that employs sets of assumptions from which general laws or principles can be derived using logico-mathematical procedures. The assumptions (sometimes hypotheses) must be well verified. Theory can be formulated by: (1) collecting and systematically recording observations; (2) collecting and synthesizing the observations of others; (3) adapting theoretical models from other fields such as the social, behavioral, or physical sciences; and (4) logical deduction.

Theory was introduced to the field of educational administration (late 1950s) through the efforts of notable scholars such as Daniel E. Griffiths and Andrew W. Halpin. Since then, students of educational administration have used or developed numerous theories relating to motivation and organization. Social systems theory (Getzels and Guba) is one of the better known of these theories. (See GETZELS-GUBA MODEL.)

References: Daniel E. Griffiths, *Administrative Theory*, New York: Appleton-Century-Crofts, Inc., 1959; E. Mark Hanson, *Educational Administration and Organizational Behavior*, Boston: Allyn and Bacon, Inc., 1979; Andrew W. Halpin, "The Development of Theory in Educational Administration" in Andrew W. Halpin (Editor), *Administrative Theory in Education*, Chicago: Midwest Administration Center, 1958; Ronald W. Rebore, *Educational Administration: A Management Approach*, Englewood Cliffs, NJ: Prentice-Hall, Inc., 1985.

ADMISSIONS TESTING PROGRAMS, standardized tests taken by prospective undergraduate students as part of the admission processes required by many universities and colleges. Test scores are used in conjunction with other information to determine eligibility for admission to a particular institution. There is no set test or standard score used by all institutions. Rather, each institution establishes its own standards. Results of these tests, when used with other factors and information, have been shown to be relatively good predictors of success in college. (The best predictor is high school class rank.)

The two major test programs used in the United States are published by the College Entrance Examination Board (Scholastic Aptitude Test, Preliminary Scholastic Aptitude Test) and The University of Iowa (American College Testing Program). The SAT and PSAT are more commonly used in the East, while the ACT tends to be used more frequently in the Midwest and the South. In several European countries, school-leaving certificates (attesting to completion of 12 or 13 years of schooling) are used much as the high school diploma is used in the United States.

Graduate schools and many professional schools also require the completion of particular tests and the submission of scores as part of the admission process. The Graduate Record Examination is the standardized test used most widely at this level. Medical, law, and dental schools require tests unique to their specialties. (See AMERICAN COLLEGE TESTS; GRADUATE RECORD EXAMINATION; and SCHOLASTIC APTITUDE TEST.)

References: John A. Curry and Phyllis M. Schaen, "Admissions: An International Perspective" in Asa S. Knowles (Editor), *The International Encyclopedia of Higher Education* (Volume 2), San Francisco: Jossey-Bass Publishers, 1977; Julius Menacker, *From School to College: Articulation and Transfer*, Washington, DC: American Council on Education, 1975; Harlow G. Unger, *A Student's Guide to College Admissions*, New York: Facts on File Publications, 1986.

ADOLESCENCE, a chronological period (usually the teen years) in human development. It begins with the onset of physical and emotional processes leading to sexual and psychosexual maturity and is assumed to have ended when the individual is independent and socially productive.

Puberty, sometimes referred to as early adolescence, is the period when numerous physical (notably sexual and sexually related) changes take place. The first menstruation marks the beginning of puberty for girls; for boys, the signs are sexual potency and evidence of sperm in the semen. Secondary sex characteristics also appear: for boys, pubic and facial hair, stronger body build, and deeper voice; for girls, breast development, pubic hair, and subcutaneous fat. Although these physical changes normally occur between ages 10–13 for girls and a bit later for boys, physiologists report that the average age of puberty in Western countries has been changing, occurring three years earlier than was the case in 1880.

During later adolescence, the individual experiences conflicting emotions as the need for independence and status become stronger. Value orientations also change, including conformity to peer-group values and increased interest in the opposite sex. Intellectually, there is increased capability to do abstract thinking.

References: Gary S. Belkin and Jerry L. Gray, *Educational Psychology*, Dubuque, IA: Wm. C. Brown Company, Publishers, 1977; Lee J. Cronbach, *Educational Psychology*

(Third Edition), New York: Harcourt Brace Jovanovich, Inc., 1977; Janice T. Gibson and Louis A. Chandler, *Educational Psychology: Mastering Principles and Applications*, Boston: Allyn and Bacon, 1988; Mauritz Johnson (Editor), *Toward Adolescence: The Middle School Years* (NSSE 79th Yearbook, Part I), Chicago: University of Chicago Press, 1980; Norman A. Sprinthall and Richard C. Sprinthall, *Educational Psychology: A Developmental Approach* (Fourth Edition), New York: Random House, 1987.

ADULT BASIC EDUCATION (ABE), learning experiences or programs designed to provide two adult populations with the learning tools they require. The first population consists of adults who have never attended school, the second those who either had their schooling interrupted or seek to improve themselves for personal, occupational, or other reasons. The basic purpose of ABE is the elimination of adult illiteracy.

References: Combined Glossary: Terms and Definitions from the Handbooks of the State Educational Records and Reports Series, Washington, DC: National Center for Education Statistics, U.S. Department of Health, Education, and Welfare, 1974; Arthur P. Crabtree, "Adult Basic Education" in Lee C. Deighton (Editor), *The Encyclopedia of Education* (Volume 1), New York: The Macmillan Company and The Free Press, 1971.

ADULT EDUCATION, instruction and education offered to individuals who are no longer attending school or college and who voluntarily select such programs. Although there is confusion concerning what constitutes adult education, there appear to be some common characteristics: (1) the programs serve adults; (2) they may be offered by a variety of institutions, such as public schools, colleges, churches, technical institutions, cooperative extension services, governments, industry, or professional associations; (3) they may be offered in a variety of settings and environments; (4) academic credit may or may not be given; (5) diplomas or certificates may be earned; (6) programs have unique goals and thrusts; (7) participants may be males or females; (8) programs are found in almost every country of the world; and (9) most individuals pursuing adult education do so to meet their own educational, emotional, or psychological needs.

Adult education and *continuing education* are terms often used synonymously. Some view the differences as being philosophical. Others see continuing education as being staff training, career development, and lifelong while adult education is viewed as being more basic and consisting of programs such as adult basic education (reading, writing, arithmetic), high school-equivalency programs, citizenship education, and pre-employment training. (See CONTINUING EDUCATION.)

References: Stephen Brookfield, *Adult Learners, Adult Education and the Community*, New York: Teachers College Press, 1984; Alan Boyd Knox, *Helping Adults Learn*, San Francisco: Jossey Bass, 1986; Donald W. Mocker and George E. Spear, *Lifelong Learning: Formal, Nonformal, Informal, and Self-Directed*, Columbus, OH: The ERIC Clearinghouse on Adult, Career and Vocational Education, 1982.

AD VALOREM TAX, a form of property tax. A tax or duty is applied to a fixed (appraised) proportion of the value of the property (e.g. 22 percent) rather than on the property's total value. For American municipalities, it is the major source of income from taxes. Real estate taxes, a major source of revenue support for the public schools, are ad valorem taxes.

References: William S. Anderson (Editor), *Ballentine's Law Dictionary* (Third Edition), Rochester, NY: The Lawyer's Co-operative Publishing Company, 1969; Henry C. Black, *Black's Law Dictionary: Definitions of the Terms and Phrases of American and English Jurisprudence, Ancient and Modern* (Revised Fourth Edition), St. Paul, MN: West Publishing Company, 1968; Ernest H. Johnson, "Appraisal for Tax Assessments" in Edith J. Friedman (Editor), *Real Estate Encyclopedia*, Englewood Cliffs, NJ: Prentice-Hall, Inc., 1960; J. Edward Rountrey, et al., "Appraisal for Tax Purposes" in *Encyclopedia of Real Estate Appraising* (Third Edition), Englewood Cliffs, NJ: Prentice-Hall, Inc., 1978.

ADVANCED PLACEMENT PROGRAM, a national program developed to encourage high schools and colleges to work together. Its function is to stimulate the able learner and to reduce duplication of studies. The Advanced Placement Program reduces time waste (through duplication of courses offered at both the high school and college levels) for those high school students who take advanced placement courses in high school. Those meeting college-set criteria on the Advanced Placement Examination can receive college credit. The program is sponsored by the College Entrance Examination Board (CEEB).

Examinations in selected subjects are provided by the Advanced Placement Program. Individual colleges determine whether to grant credit for such courses and also establish the criterion score that must be reached before credit for a given subject can be given. Individual high schools design their own advanced placement courses. These offerings are influenced, to some extent, by the nature and content of the examination.

The Fund for the Advancement of Education supported two experiments that were forerunners to the Advanced Placement Program. These were the School and College Study of Admissions with Advanced Standing and the School and College Study of General Education. Out of these two experiments grew the Advanced Placement Program. CEEB began to administer the program in 1955. Advanced Placement is the only national program of its kind available to high school students.

Some high schools and individual colleges or universities have established programs in which students can earn college credit before high school graduation. They may be arranged as: college-taught special college courses; college-taught regular college courses (e.g. split-day programs); high school faculty-taught special college-level courses (e.g. Advanced Placement); and high school faculty-taught regular college-level courses.

References: College Entrance Examination Board, *Advanced Placement Course Description: Art*, Princeton, NJ: College Entrance Examination Board, 1979; College Entrance Examination Board, *The College Board Annual Report, 1987–88*, New York: The Board, 1988; Harlow G. Unger, *A Student's Guide to College Admissions*, New York: Facts on File Publications, 1986.

ADVANCED STANDING, an option offered by many colleges that permits students to be placed in courses beyond introductory or lower levels. Students who have taken advanced placement courses in high school and achieved a particular level (score) on an Advanced Placement Examination are frequently allowed to enroll in advanced college courses. The College Level Examination Program (CLEP), another testing program recognized by many institutions, is used for the same purpose. Credit for prior learning, transferring of course credits, or passing of specific placement examinations in a particular field of study are other techniques used to grant advanced standing.

In some colleges and universities, a student may use advanced standing to achieve early graduation (acceleration). In others, advanced standing serves an enrichment function, enabling students to develop more depth and/or breadth in a program without early graduation. (See ADVANCED PLACEMENT PROGRAM and COLLEGE LEVEL EXAMINATION PROGRAM.)

References: Carnegie Commission on Higher Education, *Continuity and Discontinuity*, New York: McGraw-Hill Book Company, 1973; College Entrance Examination Board, *The College Board Annual Report, 1987–88*, New York: The Board, 1988; Julius Menacker, *From School to College: Articulation and Transfer*, Washington, DC: American Council on Education, 1975.

ADVANCE ORGANIZERS, sets of ideas used by teachers to: (1) introduce students to new and meaningful materials and (2) help students recognize relevant ideas, concepts, or facts. Advance organizers give a student a general overview of materials and help to provide organizing elements for learning in advance of the actual body of material to be studied. They can be used to present high-order content concepts (subject) or high-order rules for hierarchical classification (process).

There are two major types of advance organizers: expository and comparative. The term *expository organizers* is used to describe those situations in which entirely unfamiliar material is presented for the first time. Such organizers include known and relevant knowledges about the subject, making it more plausible, cogent, and/or comprehensible. *Comparative organizers*, on the other hand, applies to those cases in which the material or subject area to be learned is not new. Such organizers point out similarities and differences between the familiar and the unfamiliar information or materials.

David P. Ausubel, in the 1960s, was a major contributor to the research in the development of such organizers.

References: David P. Ausubel, "The Use of Advance Organizers in the Learning and Retention of Meaningful Verbal Material," *Journal of Educational Psychology*, Volume 51, 1960; Janice T. Gibson and Louis A. Chandler, *Educational Psychology: Mastering Principles and Applications*, Allyn and Bacon, 1988; Joseph T. Lawton and Susan K. Wanska, "The Effects of Different Types of Advance Organizers on Classification Learning," *American Educational Research Journal*, Volume 16, No. 3, 1979.

ADVERSARY MODEL OF EVALUATION, an approach to program evaluation first popularized by Marilyn Kourilsky and Murray Levine, at UCLA, in 1973. However, Robert Stake and C. M. Gjerda (1971) originated the model before 1973 in an evaluation of an education program.

A program to be evaluated using the adversary model is assessed by two evaluators or two teams. One is "affirmative," the other "negative." Each evaluator or team is assigned to produce evidence and analyses that favor each established positive or negative stance about the program. That is, the team given the affirmative position collects and analyzes information and data that will produce a positive report. The negative team does the same thing, except that it is looking for negative information, data, and results. Both groups report their findings to each other and to a decision maker (an individual who must make the final decision concerning the program involved). In addition, both evaluators or teams may present their findings at a scheduled meeting where they must enumerate and defend contentions. They may be cross-examined by each other and by the decision maker. Ultimately, the decision maker synthesizes and makes decisions concerning the program from the information and reports supplied by the two groups and from the "debate." The program's basic assumptions are: (1) the decision maker will have better data as a result of competing analyses; (2) contending evaluators will be highly motivated; and (3) evaluators will not have to deal in their initial reports with conflicting conclusions as do most program evaluators.

A variation of the adversary model of evaluation approach may be used to evaluate two or more competing programs. Rather than having affirmative and negative evaluators or teams, each program evaluation is made by program advocates. Each must present his/her report to the other advocate and to the decision maker. The same procedures described above are then followed.

References: Marilyn Kourilsky, "An Adversary Model for Educational Evaluation," *Evaluation Comment*, June 1973; Murray Levine, "Scientific Method and the Adversary Model: Some Preliminary Suggestions," *Evaluation Comment*, June 1973; W. James Popham, *Educational Evaluation* (Second Edition), Englewood Cliffs, NJ: Prentice-Hall, Inc., 1988; Robert Stake and C. M. Gjerda, *An Evaluation of T City: The Twin City Institute for Talented Youth*, Urbana, IL: University of Illinois, 1971; Blaine R. Worthen and W. Todd Rogers, "Pitfalls and Potential of Adversary Evaluation," *Educational Leadership*, April 1980.

ADVISOR, ACADEMIC, that individual whose function it is to work with a student in planning the student's academic program. In some high schools, the academic advisor may be a faculty member, and in others, a student may be assigned to a trained school counselor whose specialty is academic planning and advising. Although the academic advisor may have to be involved in career or vocational counseling, crisis or personal counseling, testing and appraisal of skills and abilities, or other "related" counseling activities, he/she typically leaves these functions to specialized counselors. Instead, the counselor works with students in academically related areas such as course selec-

tion, seeking tutoring help, and program development.

In many colleges or universities, professors are assigned students, majoring in their particular fields, as advisees. Each semester these students are expected to see their advisors for academic guidance and to secure course approval for the following semester. In other institutions, students are assigned to "professional" academic advisors whose only task is to guide and advise students through an academic program. Advisees suspected of having major educational, psychological, or emotional problems are encouraged (by either their professors or the academic advisor) to see college counselors or other trained specialists. Peer advisors (students trained to serve as advisors to other students) are used in some colleges and universities.

References: Thomas J. Grites, *Academic Advising: Getting Us Through the Eighties,* Washington, DC: American Association for Higher Education, 1979; Howard C. Kramer and Robert E. Gardner, *Advising by Faculty,* Washington, DC: National Education Association, 1977; Merle M. Ohlsen, *Guidance Services in the Modern School* (Second Edition), New York: Harcourt Brace Jovanovich, Inc., 1974; B. Mark Schoenberg (Editor), *A Handbook and Guide for the College and University Counseling Center,* Westport, CT: Greenwood Press, 1978.

AEROBICS, an approach used in a physical fitness program that is intended to improve the cardiovascular system. Aerobics exercises can be carried on over a long period, because one is able to take in as much oxygen as needed. *Aerobics* means "with oxygen." Running long distances, playing handball and basketball, swimming, and riding bicycle are examples of aerobics exercises. Wind sprints or running up stairs are called *anaerobic activities*, because they are performed rapidly and function for a time without taking in oxygen (rather oxygen is drawn from oxygen compounds in the body). Once the body reaches oxygen debt, the exercise will stop involuntarily. Benefits of such intensive exercising include utilization of more oxygen during exercise, lower heart rate when not exercising, production of less lactic acid, and endurance increase.

References: Harold M. Barrow, *Man and His Movements,* Philadelphia: Lea and Febiger, 1971; Charles A. Bucher, *Foundations of Physical Education* (Eighth Edition), St. Louis, MO: The C. V. Mosby Company, 1979; Kenneth H. Cooper, *Aerobics,* New York: Bantam Books, Inc., 1968; Arthur Lessac, *Body Wisdom: The Use of Training of the Human Body,* New York: Drama Book Specialists, 1978.

AESTHETIC EDUCATION, a sometimes formal, sometimes informal process by which individuals are taught to: (1) recognize the difference between the arts and all other human activities and (2) develop their capacities for artistic expression. Regarding the latter focus, aesthetic programs seek to develop the learner's expressive potential by giving attention to creation, performance, and response.

Numerous and more specific goals have been identified for aesthetic education including: (1) the development of aesthetic taste and judgment; (2) learning about other cultures through the arts; (3) appreciating the uniqueness of each art (e.g. dance, music) as well as similarities among the arts; and (4) learning how to use art as a leisure time activity.

Aesthetic education is taught at all academic levels, primary grades through university, through discrete arts courses and/or interdisciplinary courses/programs.

References: Gerard L. Knieter, "Humanistic Dimensions of Aesthetic Education" in Arthur Motycka (Editor), *Music Education for Tomorrow's Society,* Jamestown, RI: GAMT Music Press, 1976; Gerard L. Knieter, "Music, the Arts, and Education" in Lee C. Deighton (Editor), *The Encyclopedia of Education* (Volume 6), New York: The Macmillan Company and The Free Press, 1971.

AFFECTIVE DOMAIN, one of three broad types of learning categorized by Benjamin Bloom and his associates. (The triad includes the affective, cognitive, and psychomotor domains.) The affective domain is comprised of behaviors and processes that reflect feelings, emotions, attitudes, beliefs, ideals, perceptions, values, interests, appreciations, and adjustments. David Krathwohl, Benjamin Bloom, and Bertram Masia, in 1964, developed a taxonomy of affective behavioral objectives that were arranged along a hierarchical continuum. They were: receiving (attending), 1.0; responding, 2.0; valuing, 3.0; organization, 4.0; and characterization, 5.0. According to these authors, an individual becomes sensitive to certain phenomena or stimuli (receiving, 1.0), perceives the behaviors to have worth (valuing, 3.0), and may, ultimately, organize these values, beliefs, and so on into a consistent system (characterization, 5.0). Although there is a tendency to divide the domains into discrete areas (e.g. cognitive, affective), there is a considerable amount of overlapping among them. (See COGNITIVE DOMAIN and PSYCHOMOTOR DOMAIN.)

References: Benjamin S. Bloom, *Handbook of Formative and Summative Evaluation of Student Learning,* New York:

McGraw-Hill Book Company, 1971; David R. Krathwohl, et al., *Taxonomy of Educational Objectives: The Classification of Educational Goals, Handbook #2. Affective Domain,* New York: David McKay Company, Inc., 1964; Thomas A. Ringness, *The Affective Domain in Education,* Boston: Little, Brown and Company, 1975.

AFFIRMATIVE ACTION, employment and promotion plans in which specific result-oriented procedures are developed to ensure equal opportunity employment and promotion opportunities for minorities (e.g. blacks, Spanish-Americans, native Americans) and women. Programs typically involve internal analysis to determine areas of deficiency with goals, timetables, plans of action, and training components thereafter developed to correct such deficiencies.

Other affirmative action plans involve recruitment of students. Here, too, the thrust is toward ensuring equal educational and training opportunity for minorities and women.

Although the most current federal effort in this area stems from the Civil Rights Act of 1964 (with the Equal Employment Opportunity Commission responsible for implementing the act), active employment of minorities in defense industries was ordered as early as 1941 by President Franklin Roosevelt (Executive Order #8802). Whether affirmative action programs are mandated by laws (federal or state) or developed in the private sector, they have in common the goal of providing equal opportunity.

References: Nathan Glaser, *Affirmative Discrimination: Ethnic Inequality and Public Policy,* New York: Basic Books, Inc., Publishers, 1975; Elaine Gruenfeld, *Promotion: Practices, Policies, and Affirmative Action,* Ithaca, NY: Cornell University, 1975; David H. Rosenbloom, *Federal Equal Employment Opportunity,* New York: Praeger Publishers, 1977.

AGE, CHRONOLOGICAL—See CHRONOLOGICAL AGE

AGE-EQUIVALENT SCALES/SCORES, measures describing an individual's test performance in relationship to what is expected of an average child at a particular age. An age-equivalent scale is based on what the "average" child from a specific age group scores on a particular test. For example, if the average 14-year-old earns a score of 40 on a particular test, 40 is converted to an age-equivalent score of 14. If a 10-year-old earns a score of 40 on that test, he/she has an age-equivalent score of 14; a 17-year-old scoring 40 on the same test is also said to have an age-equivalent score of 14.

Several problems have been reported relating to age-equivalent scales: measurement issues; misinterpretation of the scales or scores; and test problems. Because of these problems, authorities urge that age-equivalent scales/scores be used with care. *References:* Lewis R. Aiken, Jr., *Psychological Testing and Assessment* (Third Edition), Boston: Allyn and Bacon, Inc., 1978; William A. Angoff, "Scales, Norms, and Equivalent Scores" in Robert L. Thorndike (Editor), *Educational Measurement*, Washington, DC: American Council on Education, 1971; Lee J. Cronbach, *Essentials of Psychological Testing* (Fourth Edition), New York: Harper and Row, Publishers, 1984; Tom Kubiszyn and Gary Borich, *Educational Testing and Measurement: Classroom Application and Practice* (Second Edition), Glenview, IL: Scott Foresman and Company, 1987.

AGE-GRADE TABLES, special conversion tables usually included in teachers' or technical manuals of standardized tests. Age and grade equivalents often accompany the printouts of many test results. These can be used to help the teacher describe a raw score achieved by a student in terms of the score's equivalent age or grade level. Such tables generally include raw scores, standard scores, percentile scores, as well as age- and/or grade-equivalent scores.

Age scores may be expressed in terms of months (e.g. 60 months = 5 years) or in terms of years and months (e.g. 5 years 6 months, or 5.6). Grade scores are usually listed in terms of grade and month. The range within a given grade is 0.0 (September) to 0.9 (June). (The academic year begins in September and consists of 10 academic months.) Thus, 6.8 represents the sixth grade, eight month (May) equivalency and 7.2 represents seventh grade, second month (November) equivalency. The month designation depends on the test; therefore, the teacher's manual or technical manual needs to be reviewed. Many tests count September as 0.0 and October as 0.1 and so on; others may not.

Age and grade scores are based on the mean test scores achieved for a particular age or grade group. Monthly units are determined through the smoothing of a curve and other statistical/mathematical procedures. (See AGE-EQUIVALENT SCALES/SCORES and GRADE-EQUIVALENT SCALES.)
References: Lewis R. Aiken, Jr., *Psychological Testing and Assessment* (Third Edition), Boston: Allyn and Bacon, Inc., 1978; William A. Angoff, "Scales, Norms, and Equivalent Scores" in Robert L. Thorndike (Editor), *Educational Measurement*, Washington, DC: American Council on Education, 1971; Lee J. Cronbach, *Essentials of Psychological Testing* (Fourth Edition), New York: Harper and Row Publishers, 1984; Tom Kubiszyn and Gary Borich, *Educational Testing and Measurement: Classroom Application and Practice* (Second Edition), Glenview, IL: Scott Foresman and Company, 1987.

AGE, MENTAL—See MENTAL AGE

AGENCY FOR INTERNATIONAL DEVELOPMENT (AID), the agency within the United States Department of State responsible for U.S. foreign economic assistance programs that provide economic and human resource assistance to developing nations. The President of the United States was authorized, under the Foreign Assistance Act of 1961, to establish such an agency. On November 3, 1961, he issued Executive Order 10973 directing the Secretary of State to establish the Agency for International Development.

AID's central headquarters staff is in Washington, D.C. As of 1978–79, the agency had 70 overseas branches of sorts (41 missions, 10 AID offices, 10 AID sections in embassies, and 9 regional service/development offices). Its *developmental assistance programs* include: (1) Food, Nutrition, and Rural Development; (2) Population Planning and Health; (3) Education and Human Resources Development; and (4) Technical Assistance, Energy, Research, Reconstruction, and Selected Development Problems. AID also provides security support assistance designed to promote economic or political stability in areas of foreign policy interest. It also supports the following *specific programs*: Sahel Development (West Africa); American Schools and Hospitals Abroad; International Disaster Assistance; Reimbursable Development Program; Housing Guaranty Program; Food for Peace; Human Rights; Light Capital Technology; and Women in Development.
Reference: United States Government Manual, Washington, DC: Office of the Federal Register, National Archives and Record Service, General Services Administration, 1978.

AGNOSIAS, common types of interneurosensory learning disabilities that are reception and expression dysfunctions. Those afflicted lack the ability to identify, comprehend, or interpret objects through specific modality or sensory organs, such as seeing (*visual agnosia*), hearing (*auditory agnosia*), or touching (*tactile agnosia*) even though the information is received. *Form agnosia* is the inability of the individual to differentiate or discriminate geometric forms; *autotopagnosia* is a disability that prevents an individual from identifying body parts.

References: B. R. Gearheart, *Learning Disabilities: Educational Strategies,* St. Louis, MO: The C. V. Mosby Company, 1973; Kenneth W. Waugh and Wilma Jo Bush, *Diagnosing Learning Disorders,* Columbus, OH: Charles E. Merrill Publishing Company, 1971.

AGRAPHIA, a disorder of written language in which an individual cannot write a word, letter, or number because of an inability to relate the word, letter, or number image to the kinesthetic pattern (motor movements) needed to write each. This condition exists in the absence of a known paralysis.

In agraphia (also known as dysgraphia), the individual cannot start the motor movements (patterns) needed to copy a letter, a word, or a number even though he/she is able to read and to speak each one. Agraphia is a type of apraxia. (See APRAXIA.)

References: Tanis Bryan and James N. Bryan, *Understanding Learning Disabilities,* Port Washington, N.Y: Alfred Publishing Company, 1975; B. R. Gearheart (Editor), *Education of the Exceptional Child,* Scranton, PA: Intext Educational Publishers, 1972; Janet W. Lerner, *Children with Learning Disabilities* (Second Edition), Boston: Houghton Mifflin Company, 1976.

AGRICULTURAL EDUCATION, a specialized area of vocational education concerned specifically with agricultural science and production, farming, and ranching occupations. Although agriculture has been a major occupation in the United States since its founding, it wasn't until adoption of the First Morrill Act in 1862 that the science of agriculture in the United States was developed. The act established land-grant colleges and universities; they, in turn, established programs (degree, non-degree, extension services, continuing education, research) of practical education in agriculture as well as mechanic arts. Other acts such as Smith-Hughes (1917), George-Barden (1946), and Vocational Education (1963) supported agricultural education at the local school level.

Technological development, social changes, the rise of large farms, and the development of agribusinesses have changed agricultural education considerably since the 1920s. Its goals and objectives have been broadened to include study of business practices; political and community leadership; environmental issues; science and technology; training for agricultural occupations that are not involved in actual agricultural production per se; career awareness of the many agricultural occupations; continuing education; and human, emotional, and social development.

Agricultural education is not unique to the United States. An agricultural school was first opened in Bohemia in 1791. By the middle 1800s, many agricultural schools existed in Europe. Early agricultural education in the United States was encouraged and sponsored by agricultural societies such as the American Philosophical Society (1790s), Wenyaw Indigo Society (South Carolina, 1775), and the Kennebec Agricultural Society (Maine, 1807). Agricultural education has become a major educational commitment on the part of most states in the United States and the federal government. In most nations of the world, agricultural education is viewed as important and thus receives significant governmental support.

References: Charles A. Bennett, *History of Manual and Industrial Education,* Peoria, IL: Chas. A. Bennett Press, Inc., 1937; Harold Binkley and Carsie Hammonds, *Experience Programs for Learning Vocations in Agriculture,* Danville, IL: The Interstate Printers and Publishers, Inc., 1970; Harold Binkley and Rodney Tulloch, *Teaching Vocational Agriculture,* Danville, IL: The Interstate Printers and Publishers, Inc., 1980; Glenn Z. Stevens, *Agricultural Education,* New York: The Center for Applied Research in Education, Inc., 1967; Alfred C. True, *A History of Agricultural Education in the United States,* Washington, DC: U.S. Government Printing Office, 1929.

AGUILAR v. FELTON, a United States Supreme Court decision (July 1, 1985) that involved the sending of public school teachers and other professionals into private religious (parochial) schools to provide remedial education and clinical and guidance services. Six taxpayers (Yolanda Aguilar, et al.) initiated the action in the Eastern District Court of New York in 1978. They alleged that the New York City Title 1 program (of the Elementary and Secondary Education Act of 1965), which provided instruction on the premises of parochial schools, was unconstitutional. They felt that the use of such funds was a violation of the Establishment Clause of the First Amendment of the United States Constitution (the separation of church and state).

The Supreme Court ruled that the City of New York's use of federal funds to pay public employees to teach in parochial schools was a violation of the Establishment Clause and therefore was unconstitutional. Children in parochial schools could receive instruction as long as the instruction was not on the premises of the parochial school. (See ELEMENTARY AND SECONDARY EDUCATION ACT and ESTABLISHMENT CLAUSE.)

References: Aguilar v. Felton, *Supreme Court Reporter,* Volume 105, Number 18, July 1985; Eugene T. Conners,

Religion and the Schools: Significant Court Decisions in the 1980s, Bloomington, IN: Phi Delta Kappa, 1988.

AGUILLARD v. EDWARDS, (case ;85–1513), a United States Supreme Court ruling (June 19, 1987) that the Louisiana Balanced Treatment for Creation-Science and Evolution-Science in Public School Instruction Act was unconstitutional. The Court's action followed that of both the District and Circuit Courts—both declared the act unconstitutional, a violation of the Establishment Clause of the First Amendment.

The Supreme Court held that the act had no secular purpose and that its purpose was to promote a particular religious belief (creationism). The act prohibited the teaching of the theory of evolution in public schools unless accompanied by the teaching of the theory of "creation science." The act did not require the teaching of either. The supporters of the act claimed that the law protected "academic freedom." The Court rejected that position. The Court also held that the act was designed to promote the theory of creationism or prohibit the teaching of scientific theory (which is disdained by some groups). Seven justices of the Court supported the majority view, and two dissented. (See ESTABLISHMENT CLAUSE.)

Reference: Aguillard v. Edwards, *Supreme Court Reporter Interim Edition, Supreme Court of the United States, October Term, 1986*, St. Paul, MN: West Publishing Co., 1987.

AIDES—See PARAPROFESSIONALS IN EDUCATION

AIDS—See ACQUIRED IMMUNE DEFICIENCY SYNDROME

AIMS—See GOAL and OBJECTIVES

AIR FORCE RESERVE OFFICERS TRAINING CORPS (AFROTC), a program that permits young men and women to qualify for commissions in the Air Force while completing their college education. Two routes to commissioning are available: (1) the Four-Year Program and (2) the Two-Year Program. The *Four-Year* curriculum includes a General Military Course, completed during the freshman and sophomore years, and the more rigorous Professional Officer Course (POC), completed during the last two years of college. The *Two-Year* curriculum is limited to the Professional Officer Course. Admission to the first two years of the Four-Year Program is open to all college students. Those seeking admission to the POC must

be at least 17 years of age, pass an interview conducted by a board of Air Force officers, pass the Air Force physical examination, qualify on the Air Force Officer Qualifying Test, achieve well on SAT/ACT examinations, and have two years of college remaining.

The AFROTC curriculum includes "laboratory" experiences (e.g. drill and ceremonies) as well as regular classroom instruction. Visits to Air Force bases and flight instruction (for pilot candidates) are also a part of the program. POC students enlist in the Air Force Reserve and become eligible to receive a monthly, nontaxable allowance. Competitive scholarships are also available to Two-Year and Four-Year students.

Upon graduation from college, POC students are appointed second lieutenants and, depending on their programs (e.g. pilot, nursing, navigation), are obligated to complete four to six years of active service in the Air Force.

References: The Changing Profession: Information for Counseling on Air Force ROTC, Washington, DC: U.S. Government Printing Office, 1979; *What's New ... in Air Force ROTC* (ROTC 80-1), Washington, DC: U.S. Air Force Recruiting Service/Directorate of Advertising, 1980.

ALCOHOL, DRUG ABUSE, AND MENTAL HEALTH ADMINISTRATION (ADAMHA), an agency of the U.S. Public Health Service, Department of Health and Human Services, charged by Congress with preventing, controlling, and treating alcoholism, drug abuse, and mental-emotional illnesses. ADAMHA began to function in September 1973. The agency supports research through grants; support is also given to training projects and delivery programs. Additionally, it carries on research using agency-owned laboratory facilities.

ADAMHA's Division of Prevention, in cooperation with the National Institute on Alcohol Abuse and Alcoholism, supports a variety of alcohol-prevention programs with considerable attention given to the schools. The division also serves as a major data collection and distribution vehicle on alcoholism and alcohol abuse. A similar unit, operating cooperatively with the National Institute on Drug Abuse, is the Division of Resource Development. It sponsors training programs for drug rehabilitation workers, stresses drug prevention through special programs, and operates a National Clearinghouse for Drug Abuse Information. In cooperation with a third institute, the National Institute of Mental Health, numerous mental health service and research programs are carried out.

ALGORITHM   19

References: Alcohol, Drug Abuse, and Mental Health Administration, *ADAMHA: An Agency Serving People,* Rockville, MD: Public Health Service, U.S. Department of HEW, 1976; Public Law 93–282, *United States Statutes at Large,* 1974 (Volume 88, Part I), Washington, DC: U.S. Government Printing Office, 1976.

ALEXIA, inability to read, which is usually caused by brain damage. Alexia refers to the failure to acquire reading skills as well as to the loss (partial, complete) of reading ability through damage to the brain (e.g. cerebral stroke). There are three types of alexias: (1) *auditory,* difficulty distinguishing similar and dissimilar sounds and sounds within words, hence the phonic approach cannot be used to teach such an individual to read; (2) *visual,* difficulty differentiating or remembering printed words; and (3) *pure* or *word blindness,* inability to read, but other objects can be identified visually. (See AGNOSIAS.)

References: Janet W. Lerner, *Children with Learning Disabilities* (Second Edition), Boston: Houghton Mifflin Company, 1976; L. Nicolosi, et al., *Terminology of Communication Disorders,* Baltimore, MD: The Williams and Wilkins Company, 1978.

ALGORITHM, a means of communicating the way to do something, usually through the use of symbols or a distinctive pictorial design, or verbally. Algorithms can be used to help individuals solve problems; make decisions; perform tasks; understand rules, procedures, or regulations; and understand other complex items, tasks, or functions.

The value of algorithms is that one need only to read that part of the algorithm concerned with the task at hand and follow it, step by step, making decisions at particular points as specified. The language of the algorithm is usually simple although, in mathematics (where algorithms first started) and computer science, algorithms can appear to be quite complicated for those not familiar with them.

When an algorithm is developed, verbal content is reduced to a pictorial design that is sequential, logical, and precise. The algorithm focuses on a well-defined problem, flows in one direction, uses simplistic and edited language, and has a final outcome or solution. The following is an example of a format that illustrates the structure of an algorithm used in the performance of a task.

Algorithms are used in a variety of settings, ranging from industry, banks, and businesses to educational agencies as well as various disciplines such as mathematics and science. Algorithms in mathematics and science usually employ mathematical or scientific notations describing the way to achieve solution of a problem.

References: Richard Dorf, *Introduction to Computers and Computer Science* (Second Edition), San Francisco: Boyd and Fraser Publishing Company, 1977; Richard Haber-

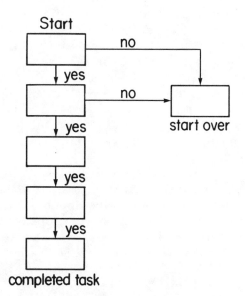

Sample Algorithm

man, *Mathematical Models, Mechanical Vibrations, Population Dynamics, and Traffic Flow,* Englewood Cliffs, NJ: Prentice-Hall, Inc., 1977; Ivan Horabin and Brian Lewis, *Algorithms,* Englewood Cliffs, NJ: Educational Technology Publications, 1978; Z. A. Melzak, *Mathematical Ideas, Modeling and Applications,* New York: John Wiley and Sons, 1976; J. F. Traub (Editor), *Algorithms and Complexity,* New York: Academic Press, 1976.

ALLIED HEALTH PROFESSIONS, those health-related professions/occupations that work together to provide patient care and/or health promotion. There is no common agreement as to whether physicians or dentists are included in this broad group, or whether those in the allied health professions provide the supportive services *under* the supervision (or guidance) of the physician or dentist. The preparation of allied health professionals are as varied as are the occupations; they range from short-term programs in noncollegiate settings to advanced graduate training. Some of the professions or fields are: nurse, midwife, medical assistant, hospital pharmacist, respiratory therapist, dental assistant, dietitian, environmental health technician, medical librarian, physical therapist, biomedical engineer, ultrasound technician, cyto-technologist, medical laboratory technician, physician's assistant. (See MEDICAL COLLEGE ADMISSIONS TEST.)
References: Christine H. McGuire, et al., *Handbook of Health Professions Education,* San Francisco, CA: Jossey-Bass Publishers, 1983; National Commission on Allied Health Education, *The Future of Allied Health Education,* San Francisco, CA: Jossey-Bass Publishers, 1980.

ALLIED HEALTH PROFESSIONS ADMISSION TEST (AHPAT)—See MEDICAL COLLEGE ADMISSIONS TEST

ALLITERATION, the recurrence of initial consonant sounds in successive words. Examples of alliteration follow: *s*oft *s*ilent *s*now; *w*hispering *w*ind; or *w*ild and *w*ooly. Poets refer to it as a "musical device" that contributes interest, color, or even humor to a piece of poetry. The use of alliteration adds to children's enjoyment of literature and creative writing as well as poetry.
References: Ruth K. Carlson, *Poetry for Today's Child,* Dansville, NY: The Instructor Publications, Inc., 1972; Mario Pei, *Glossary of Linguistic Terminology,* New York: Columbia University Press, 1966.

ALLPORT, GORDON W. (November 11, 1897–October 9, 1967), American psychologist whose principal research investigations were made in the field of personality. In his theory of "functional autonomy," he held that, to understand normal human behavior, one needs to examine the individual's current motives. This did much to dispel the former view, held by many of his peers, that adult motives evolve from childhood motives. In his writings, Allport stressed the idea that each individual personality is unique.

Included among his many writings are: *Personality: A Psychological Interpretation* (1937), *Nature of Personality* (1950), *Nature of Prejudice* (1954), and *Pattern and Growth of Personality* (1961).

Allport earned the B.A. (1919), M.A. (1921), and Ph.D. (1922) degrees at Harvard University (where he also spent the major portion of his teaching career). In 1937, he served as President of the American Psychological Association. For approximately 12 years (1937–49), Allport edited the *Journal of Abnormal and Social Psychology.*
References: James M. Ethridge and Barbara Kopala, *Contemporary Authors: A Bio-Bibliographical Guide to Current Authors and their Works* (Volumes 1–4, First Revision), Detroit: Gale Research Company, 1967; Forrest A. Kingsbury, "Allport, Gordon Willard" in Louis Shores (Editor), *Collier's Encyclopedia* (Volume 1), New York: Macmillan Educational Corporation, 1979; John F. Ohles, "Allport, Gordon Willard" in John F. Ohles (Editor), *Biographical Dictionary of American Educators* (Volume 1), Westport, CT: Greenwood Press, 1978.

ALLPORT-VERNON-LINDZEY SCALE, a measure of values along six dimensions. They are: (1) *theoretical,* dominant interest in truth and a critical rational approach; (2) *economic,* useful and practical values as stereotyped by the average businessman; (3) *aesthetic,* high value on form, harmony, grace, symmetry; (4) *social,* love of people, altruism; (5) *political,* personal power, influence not restricted to the field of politics; and (6) *religious,* mystical, unity of experience, comprehension of the cosmos.

The instrument's full title is *Study of Values: A Scale for Measuring the Dominant Interests in Personality.* The scale is published by the Houghton Mifflin Company. The initial tests were developed to test, empirically, Edward Spranger's six values (*Types of Men*). The tests were first published with P. E. Vernon in 1931 and later with Vernon and Gardner Lindzey (1951). They were designed initially for individuals with some college experience, but in 1968 norms were developed for grades 10, 11, and 12.

References: Oscar Buros (Editor), *The Seventh Mental Measurements Yearbook* (Volume 1), Highland Park, NJ: The Gryphon Press, 1972; Lee J. Cronbach, *Educational Psychology* (Third Edition), New York: Harcourt Brace Jovanovich, Inc., 1977; Joseph P. Ghougassian, *Gordon W. Allport's Ontopsychology of the Person,* New York: Philosophical Library, 1972.

ALTERNATE ROUTE (ALTERNATIVE CERTIFICATION), an approach used in more than 20 states (such as California, Georgia, New Jersey, and Louisiana) to attract primarily liberal arts and non teacher education graduates to the teaching profession. These programs vary from state to state. Some programs provide for state (or school-based) control of the limited pedagogical instruction provided the alternate route participants, sometimes called interns. Others provide for college control of the limited pedagogical instruction. The major commonalities across programs, however, are: (1) participants are usually liberal arts/science graduates; (2) participants immediately are placed in the classroom as teachers; (3) participants are hired on the first step of a teacher salary scale; (4) the first year of teaching counts towards tenure; (5) if successful after the first year (and completion of the pedagogical instruction), the participants receive the same teaching certificate as those who went through a regular collegial certification program.

Proponents have argued that the alternate route expands the teaching pool, has attracted minorities to teaching, and has provided a more controlled approach to emergency certification, and that liberal arts graduates have a sound academic base. Opponents have argued that the alternate route has undermined the quality and professionalism of teaching and places instructionally unprepared individuals immediately in the classroom. They argue that the program and the alternate route participants use children as instructional/teaching objects as participants learn how to survive in the classroom, research has not substantiated that the alternate route–trained teachers are more effective in the classroom than traditionally trained teachers, there can be reciprocity problems as an alternate route–trained teacher moves from one state to another, and finally, that recent changes in regularly certified teacher education programs require an academic base equal to, if not greater than, that of the liberal arts and science graduates. (Consequently, there is no longer a differential between the academic base of the alternate route participants and a regularly trained teacher.)

The alternate route is not new. School districts have used emergency certificates to place untrained teachers into classrooms where certified teachers are scarce. In the 1950s and 1960s, Master of Arts in Teaching (MAT) programs had the same function of attracting liberal arts and science graduates to the profession as does the alternate route program. The difference between many of the present alternate route programs and the MAT is that in the MAT, there was (1) collegial control of the program, (2) greater pedagogical instruction before placement in the classroom, (3) oftentimes higher GPA requirements because individuals were going into a graduate program, (4) closer supervision provided by the college as part of the program, and (5) master's degrees awarded at the end of the MAT program. (See MASTER OF ARTS IN TEACHING).

References: Association of Teacher Educators, *Alternatives, Yes. Lower Standards, No!* Reston, VA: The Association, 1989; Daniel Gursky, "Looking for a Shortcut," *Teacher Magazine*, December 1989, pp. 43–49; Theodore Krauss, *The Master of Arts in Teaching: An Idea Whose Time Has Come Again*, Washington, DC: Academy of Educational Development, Inc., 1988.

ALTERNATIVE CERTIFICATION—See ALTERNATE ROUTE

ALTERNATIVE EDUCATION, a generalized term used to describe educational/school programs that differ from traditional programs. Alternative education recognizes that there is no set educational or program design. It also recognizes that children, teachers, learning environments, and parents are unique; consequently, educational programs need to be designed to meet these differences. Alternative education includes nontraditional programs such as schools-within-schools, schools-without-walls, basic skills schools, special schools (e.g. for performing arts, aviation), and store front schools.

In alternative schools, instruction and curriculum are typically designed to accommodate individual students' needs, talents, and learning styles. As implied in the term *alternative*, alternative education provides an option or choice for the student and/or the parent. Not only is there a choice in the learning environment (physical structure, time periods, instructional modes), but in many alternative schools there is also a choice in the type of curriculum offered.

Alternative education is offered by public as well as private educational institutions.

References: Mario Fantini, "Alternatives and Choice in the Public Schools" in Allen B. Calvin (Editor), *Perspectives on Education,* Reading, MA: Addison-Wesley Publishing Company, 1977; John D. McNeil, *Curriculum: A Comprehensive Introduction,* Boston: Little, Brown and Company, 1977; Vernon Smith, et al., *Alternatives in Education,* Bloomington, IN: The Phi Delta Kappa Educational Foundation, 1976.

ALTRUISM, behaviors manifested by an individual that: (1) are voluntary; (2) benefit others; and (3) are performed without the individual's expecting an award. There does not appear to be an accepted and precise definition for altruism, although many psychologists accept these three characteristics of altruistic behaviors in lieu of a more precise definition.

Some psychologists have suggested that altruism cannot be defined, except by philosophers, because of the issues of reward (e.g. internal rewards); furthermore, that altruistic behaviors should be classified as prosocial behaviors (behaviors benefiting others while the benefits produced for the individuals involved may vary in degree).

Lawrence Kohlberg suggested that altruism changes as a function of the moral development of a child. According to him, altruism at Stage 1 in a child's development will be different from altruism at Stage 3. Still other psychologists have suggested that altruism is related to the social order of a society.

References: Daniel Bar-Tal, *Prosocial Behavior: Theory and Research,* New York: John Wiley and Sons, 1976; Garrett Hardin, *The Limits of Altruism,* Bloomington, IN: Indiana University Press, 1977; Lawrence Kohlberg, "From Is to Ought" in T. Mischel (Editor), *Cognitive Development and Epistemology,* New York: Academic Press, 1972; Ervin Staub, *Positive Social Behavior and Morality,* New York: Academic Press, 1978; Lauren Wispe (Editor), *Altruism, Sympathy, and Helping,* New York: Academic Press, 1978.

AMBIDEXTERITY, the equal and proficient use of both hands. At one time, authorities accepted the dominance of one part (right or left side) of the brain as causing handedness. Since there is significant interaction between both sides of the brain, many now believe that handedness is a function of genetic structure as well as learned behaviors.

Cases of true ambidexterity are rare. Some individuals considered to be ambidextrous are "hand-specific"; that is, they use the right hand for some particular activities and use the left hand for other particular activities.

Handedness is developmental in nature. Normally, children before the age of two shift from one hand to another. By two, most are either right or left handed; between two and one-half and three and one-half years of age they shift to being ambidextrous again. About four years of age, children begin to show a lifetime preference for right or left handedness.

An estimated 5 to 10 percent of the population in the United States is left handed. There are fewer cases of ambidexterity.

Reference: James W. Vander Zanden, *Human Development,* New York: Alfred A. Knopf, 1978.

AMBILINGUALISM, a form of bilingualism, the ability to speak two languages that are spoken in a particular country. For example, French and English are spoken in Canada; a person who has equal competency in both is considered to be ambilingual. Many countries have more than one national language. Belgium is one, Switzerland is another; many emerging Third World nations also have two or more recognized national languages. It is not uncommon to find ambilingual citizens in such countries. (See BILINGUAL-BICULTURAL EDUCATION.)

Reference: R. R. K. Hartmann and F. C. Stork (Editors), *Dictionary of Language and Linguistics,* New York: Halsted Press, 1976.

AMERICAN ALLIANCE FOR HEALTH, PHYSICAL EDUCATION, RECREATION, AND DANCE (AAHPERD), a voluntary organization made up of seven national associations. They are: (1) American Association for Leisure and Recreation; (2) American School and Community Safety Association; (3) Association for the Advancement of Health Education; (4) Association for Research, Administration and Professional Councils and Societies; (5) National Association for Girls and Women in Sport; (6) National Association for Sport and Physical Education; and (7) National Dance Association.

The AAHPERD was founded in 1885. Its 50,000 members are employed in more than 16,000 American school districts, over 2,000 colleges and universities, and more than 10,000 recreation units. Members are health and physical educators, coaches, athletic directors, and personnel from the fields of recreation, dance, safety, and leisure services. State and regional affiliates help to carry out the business of the organization. AAHPERD's main office is in Reston, Virginia. The association maintains numerous committees to provide leadership in relevant issues and publishes five journals: *Journal of Physical Education, Recreation, and Dance* (monthly), *Update* (9/year), *Health Education* (6/year), *Research Quarterly*, and *Leisure Today* (semiannual).

Reference: American Alliance for Health, Physical Education, Recreation, and Dance, *AAHPERD Facts: 1986–87*, Reston, VA: The Alliance, 1987.

AMERICAN ASSOCIATION FOR COUNSELING AND DEVELOPMENT (AACD), formerly the American Personnel and Guidance Association (APGA), a national organization of counseling and guidance professionals. AACD has more than 50,000 members in over 50 foreign countries, and is made up of four Regional Branch Assemblies, 56 state and international branches, 12 national divisions, and 2 affiliate organizations. The 14 groups are: American College Personnel Association (ACPA); Association for Counselor Education and Supervision (ACES); National Career Development Association (NCDA); Association for Humanistic Education and Development (AHEAD); American School Counselor Association (ASCA); American Rehabilitation Counseling Association (ARCA); Association for Measurement and Evaluation in Counseling and Development (AMECD); National Employment Counselors Association (NECA); Association for Multicultural Counseling and Development (AMCD); Association for Religious and Values Issues in Counseling (ARVIC); Association for Specialists in Group Work (ASGW); Public Offender Counselor Association (POCA); American Mental Health Counselor Association (AMHCA); and Military Educators and Counselors Association (MECA).

The association publishes the *Journal of Counseling and Development* (formerly *Personnel and Guidance Journal*), a newspaper, *Guidepost*, books, monographs, and pamphlets. In addition, AACA has been active in passing licensure legislation in 18 states in the United States. In 1981 an independent council was established by AACD for the accreditation of counseling education programs; the Council for Accreditation of Counseling and Related Educational Programs (CACREP) reviews and evaluates entry-level Master's Degree Programs in Community Counseling, Mental Health Counseling, School Counseling, and Student Affairs Practice in Higher Education. Accreditation can be earned for Counselor Education and Supervision Programs at the doctoral level. The National Board for Certified Counselors is another independent, nonprofit, voluntary, nongovernmental, related organization of AACD. The Association is headquartered in Alexandria, Virginia.

(See NATIONAL BOARD FOR CERTIFIED COUNSELORS.)

References: American Association for Counseling and Development, *Keep Pace with Your Profession! Join AACD*, Alexandria, VA: The Association, undated; Council for Accreditation of Counseling and Related Educational Programs, *Accreditation: Strengthening Credibility for the Profession*, Alexandria, VA: The Council, undated.

AMERICAN ASSOCIATION FOR GIFTED CHILDREN (AAGC), the first voluntary, nonprofit organization in the United States to serve the needs, exclusively, of gifted, talented, and creative children. The association was formed in 1946 by Dr. Ruth Strang and Pauline Williamson. AAGC gives particular attention to the growth and development of the gifted and talented in the area of the arts and humanities. Membership in the organization is open to interested lay and professional persons.

Included among the association's several goals is the revision and distribution of *Guideposts,* a series of bulletins directed to teachers, parents, administrators, and young people. *On Being Gifted,* a volume sponsored by AAGC, is the first book to be written about the education of the gifted and talented by the gifted and talented themselves.

AAGC's offices are in New York City.

References: American Association for Gifted Children, *The American Association for Gifted Children: Founded 1946,* New York: The Association, Undated Brochure; American Association for Gifted Children, *On Being Gifted,* New York: Walker and Company, 1978.

AMERICAN ASSOCIATION FOR HIGHER EDUCATION (AAHE), a national organization of academic administrators, researchers, professors, foundation officials, citizens, and governmental representatives who, as individuals (not as institutional representatives), seek to improve the overall quality of higher education. Current membership is approximately 6,400.

AAHE publishes the *AAHE Bulletin* and *Change Magazine* (jointly with Heldref Publications). Members get reduced rates for *ASHE/ERIC Research Reports* (published 10 times per year) and the *Journal of Higher Education* (published by the Ohio State University Press). *Current Issues in Higher Education* is published by AAHE from time to time. A national conference, conducted each spring, attracts some 2,000 participants. A conference on assessment (AAHE Assessment Forum) is held each year during the summer, while faculty workshops are held from time to time in a variety of locations throughout the United States.

AAHE is governed by a 19 member Board of Directors. The association's Executive Director and his staff, headquartered in Washington, D.C., carry out board policy.

References: American Association for Higher Education, *6 Reasons to Join*, Washington, DC: The Association, Undated Brochure; American Association for Higher Education, *Striving for Quality*, Washington, DC: The Association, Undated Brochure.

AMERICAN ASSOCIATION OF COLLEGES FOR TEACHER EDUCATION (AACTE),

a national professional organization consisting of over 716 collegiate institutions involved in the preparation of teachers. Institutional members appoint representatives from their respective faculties to participate in the business and professional affairs of the organization. State AACTE units exist in a majority of the states and territories. The association is dedicated to improving the effectiveness of the teaching profession and devotes much of its resources to enhancing the preservice and inservice preparation of teachers.

AACTE publishes the *Journal of Teacher Education* bimonthly, the *AACTE Bulletin* (a monthly newsletter), and various other publications of interest to teacher trainers. It also cosponsors the ERIC Clearinghouse on Teacher Education and plays an active role in NCATE (National Council for Accreditation of Teacher Education). The organization's headquarters staff is in Washington, DC. (See NATIONAL COUNCIL FOR THE ACCREDITATION OF TEACHER EDUCATION. Also see APPENDIX IX: PAST PRESIDENTS OF THE AMERICAN ASSOCIATION OF COLLEGES FOR TEACHER EDUCATION.)

References: American Association of Colleges for Teacher Education, *Directory 1989*, Washington, DC: The Association, 1989: American Association of Colleges for Teacher Education, *Quality Education Personnel: A Key to Human Services*, Washington, DC: The Association, Undated Brochure.

AMERICAN ASSOCIATION OF COMMUNITY AND JUNIOR COLLEGES (AACJC),

national organization devoted to promoting the sound growth of community and junior colleges (including technical colleges). Its scope is broad, representing the interests of trustees, administrators, and faculty members affiliated with two-year, postsecondary institutions. In 1980, institutional membership exceeded 900.

AACJC provides its members with numbers of services. It sponsors an annual convention plus workshops and assemblies. A governmental relations officer monitors federal legislative activity of interest to junior and community colleges. The association's office of data and research reports on trends/developments pertaining to two-year, postsecondary institutions. The President's Academy, composed of all chief administrative officers, makes professional development opportunities available to these administrators. Publications produced by AACJC include: (1) *Community and Junior College Journal*, published eight times a year; (2) *President's Memorandum*, a monthly newsletter; and (3) books/booklets dealing with timely subjects.

AACJC was organized in 1920. Its main offices are in Washington, D.C.

References: American Association of Community and Junior Colleges, *Individual and Community Development*, Washington, DC: The Association, 1980; American Association of Community and Junior Colleges, *What Have You Done for Us Lately?* (1979 Annual Report), Washington, DC: The Association, 1979.

AMERICAN ASSOCIATION ON MENTAL DEFICIENCY (AAMD),

a professional group that began in 1876 as the Association of Medical Officers of American Institutions for Idiots and Feeble-minded Persons. In 1906 it became the American Association for the Study of the Feeble-minded, and then in 1933 the organization changed its thrust. First, the group focused on the causes and conditions of "idiots and feeble-minded" individuals. The second change within the organization was much broader, the group began to focus on the nature of mental retardation and the thinking processes of the mentally retarded. The present focus is broader yet; the group promotes the general welfare, information, and standards of treatment for the mentally retarded while functioning as a facilitator for cooperation among individuals working with the mentally retarded.

Initial membership was limited to medical doctors (mostly administrators of institutions for the retarded); however, the present membership in AAMD includes educators, medical doctors, and psychologists, as well as administrators of institutions. There are approximately 10,000 members in the group. AAMD publishes two bimonthly journals, the *American Journal of Mental Deficiency* and *Mental Retardation*. The central office of AAMD is in Washington, D.C.

References: B. R. Gearhearst, and F. W. Litton, "The Trainable Retarded, a Foundation's Approach," (Second Edition), St. Louis, MO: C. V. Mosby, 1979.

AMERICAN ASSOCIATION OF PHYSICS TEACHERS (AAPT), a national organization whose objectives are "the advancement of the teaching of physics and the furtherance of appreciation of the role of physics in our culture" (*AAPT Directory,* p. ii). AAPT was organized in 1930.

Benefits and services to members include publication of several periodicals: *The Physics Teacher,* 9 issues a year; *American Journal of Physics,* 12 issues annually; the *AAPT Announcer,* an organizational newsletter published 4 times a year; and *Physics Today,* a 12-issue-a-year journal published by the American Institute of Physics. Additional benefits include books, pamphlets, slides, films, and so on developed to meet the needs of physics teachers; two national meetings a year; and numerous regional meetings held on an as-needed basis.

AAPT, since 1936, has awarded the Oersted Medal each year to individuals who have made notable contributions to the teaching of physics. The association also sponsors the annual Richtmyer Memorial and the Robert A. Millikan Lectures. Several distinguished service citations are also awarded each year.

AAPT's national office is in Stony Brook, N.Y.
References: American Association of Physics Teachers, *AAPT: A Shorter Path,* Stony Brook, NY: The Association, Undated Brochure; American Association of Physics Teachers, *Directory of Members: Constitution and Bylaws, Lists of Officers and Awards, Sections of the Association,* Stony Brook, NY: The Association, March 1976; American Association of Physics Teachers, *50 Years on Teaching Physics,* Stony Brook, NY: The Association, Undated Brochure.

AMERICAN ASSOCIATION OF SCHOOL ADMINISTRATORS (AASA), a national organization with membership open to professionals holding administrative positions in a public or private school system, a college or university, or an educational agency/organization or to individuals who teach education or educational administration at an institution of higher education. Total AASA membership currently approaches 20,000.

The organization was founded in 1865 as the National Association of School Superintendents. Between 1871 and 1969, it functioned as a department within the National Education Association.

AASA provides its members with numerous professional services: (1) *The School Administrator,* a monthly newsletter; (2) conventions and special meetings, including the Winter Convention and the Spring Conference; (3) other publications dealing with special topics in school administration; (4) professional development (inservice) activities, the most notable being the National Academy for School Executives; and (5) special communications prepared for specific groups of members (e.g. women administrators, professors, small-system superintendents). A membership roster, *Who's Who in Educational Administration,* appears every three years.

Headquartered in Arlington, Virginia, AASA works to implement several goals: (1) to provide relevant educational programs; (2) to attain legislation and policies that improve education; and (3) to achieve professional and economic well being for its members. (See NATIONAL ACADEMY FOR SCHOOL EXECUTIVES. Also see APPENDIX X: PAST PRESIDENTS OF THE AMERICAN ASSOCIATION OF SCHOOL ADMINISTRATORS.)
References: American Association of School Administrators, *10 AASA Membership Benefits,* Arlington, VA: The Association, Undated Brochure; American Association of School Administrators, *Annual Report,* Arlington, VA: The Association, 1980; American Association of School Administrators, *Your AASA in Nineteen Seventy-One–Seventy-Two* (Official Report), Washington, DC: The Association, 1972.

AMERICAN ASSOCIATION OF SCHOOL LIBRARIANS (AASL), one of 11 divisions making up the American Library Association. AASL serves to meet the unique professional needs of its 6,000 school (K–12) library media members. Major meetings are held concurrently with American Library Association conferences. A periodical, *School Media Quarterly,* serves as the official voice of the AASL. The AASL *Checklist of Materials,* revised annually, lists the relatively inexpensive publications prepared by the organization.

The work of the division is carried out by 40 committees, 7 regional directors, and an executive board. AASL's offices, shared with those of the American Library Association, are in Chicago. (See AMERICAN LIBRARY ASSOCIATION.)
References: American Association of School Librarians, *What AASL Does for YOU,* Chicago: The Association, Undated Mimeographed Flier; American Association of School Librarians, *Checklist of Materials,* Chicago: The Association, October 1979.

AMERICAN ASSOCIATION OF STATE COLLEGES AND UNIVERSITIES (AASCU), an organization of over 300 state colleges and universities located throughout the continental United

States, Guam, and the Virgin Islands. Organized in 1969, and with membership limited to publicly assisted four-year institutions, AASCU provides its members with numerous services. They include: (1) conferences and workshops; (2) analyses of federal legislation and programs; (3) general information services; (4) assistance with international programs; (5) an Academic Collective Bargaining Information Service; and (6) publications. Publications cover a wide variety of topics such as the student press, financial exigency plans, enrollment trends, and student due process. In addition to the 300-plus institutional members, AASCU includes over 30 state systems of higher education.

Organizational policies are established at AASCU's annual meeting. An elected board of directors meets four times each year. Committees and ad hoc task forces also help to carry out the work of the association. AASCU's offices are in Washington, D.C.

References: American Association of State Colleges and Universities, *American Association of State Colleges and Universities, '79,* Washington, DC: The Association, 1979; American Association of State Colleges and Universities, *Publications '79,* Washington, DC: The Association, 1979.

AMERICAN ASSOCIATION OF UNIVERSITY PROFESSORS (AAUP),

largest organization of its type in the United States devoted exclusively to the needs of teachers and researchers in colleges and universities. AAUP was formed in 1915. Its current membership exceeds 72,000, with members employed at more than 2,200 institutions of higher education. Much of AAUP's business is transacted by local chapters located on approximately 1,400 campuses.

Numbers of special committees, each assigned a letter of the alphabet for identification purposes, address the academic concerns of AAUP members. Committee A, which deals with academic freedom and tenure, was the first to be organized and remains one of the most preeminent in the association.

Throughout its history, AAUP has sought to set fair academic standards for the professoriate. Notable are those that fall within the purview of Committee A (e.g. academic due process, reappointment of nontenured faculty). From time to time, individual institutions are censured by AAUP for failing to correct unresolved issues and when mediation is resisted.

AAUP's main offices are in Washington, D.C.

References: American Association of University Professors, *Your Introduction to the American Association of University Professors,* Washington, DC: The Association, Undated Brochure; Walter P. Metzger, "Origins of the Association: An Anniversary Address," *AAUP Bulletin,* Summer 1965.

AMERICAN CAMPING ASSOCIATION (ACA),

a private, nonprofit organization serving the needs of camp directors/owners, camp staff members, educators, students, and others interested in camping. It is the sole national organization in the United States devoted exclusively to camping. Founded in 1910, ACA has a membership of 6,000 located in each of the 50 states.

The association's service activities include sponsorship of inservice training for camp leaders, providing advisory assistance to agencies/organizations concerning camping laws and regulations, informing the public about organized camping, and helping parents to select a camp. Periodicals published by ACA include 300 titles dealing with all aspects of camping leadership and a journal, *Camping Magazine,* which appears seven times annually. The *Parents' Guide to Accredited Camps,* published as an eighth issue of Camping Magazine, appears each January.

ACA, with main offices in Martinsville, Indiana, is the only accrediting organization for camps of all types.

References: American Camping Association, *ACA and You: Membership in the American Camping Association,* Martinsville, IN: The Association, 1980; American Camping Association, *Catalog of Selected Camping Publications,* Martinsville, IN: The Association, 1980.

AMERICAN COLLEGE TESTS (ACT),

standardized tests first published in 1959 by the American College Testing Program (Iowa City, Iowa). They are used by many colleges and universities as part of their undergraduate admissions testing program. ACT Assessment Program is the present title of the ACT tests. The Assessment Program includes: (1) the *Academic Tests* that cover four cognitive areas (English, mathematics, social studies, and natural science); (2) *ACT Interest Inventory Tests* that measure six areas; and (3) the *ACT Student Profile.* ACT also provides a research and reporting service. The Collegiate Assessment of Academic Proficiency (CAAP) is a new program offered by the American College Testing Program. The program is designed to assess general education foundational skills that are usually offered during the first two years of an undergraduate degree program. Reading, mathematics, writing, and critical thinking are the student learning outcomes measured by CAAP. Results can be used by institutions of higher education to assess institutional effectiveness, academic transfer knowledge, and program evaluations.

The tests are administered five times each year at various testing centers. Students pay for the tests and subsequently receive a report of scores. In addition, scores are sent to their respective high schools and to three colleges of their choice. The American College Testing Program also provides specialized tests for the granting of college credit and/or advanced college placement. Such exams are part of the ACT Proficiency Examination Program; included in the program are specialized tests in the following areas: history, anatomy and physiology; earth sciences; gerontology; English and English literature; business; accounting; finance; management; the criminal justice system; educational psychology; reading; education; nursing; and health care. (See ADMISSIONS TESTING PROGRAMS.)

References: Oscar K. Buros (Editor), *The Eighth Mental Measurements Yearbook* (Volume I), Highland Park, NJ: The Gryphon Press, 1978; Herbert S. Sacks, *Hurdles: The Admissions Dilemma in American Higher Education*, New York: Atheneum, 1978; Richard C. Sweetland, et al., *Tests, a Comprehensive Reference for Assessments in Psychology, Education and Business*, Kansas City, MO: Test Corporation of America, 1983.

AMERICAN COUNCIL ON EDUCATION (ACE), largest nongovernmental organization in the United States concerned with postsecondary education. Founded in 1918, ACE today consists of approximately 1,500 institutional members (institutions of higher education as well as national/regional associations). A 36-member Board of Directors and a permanent staff, in Washington, D.C., carry out much of the council's routine work. Institutional representatives are usually institutional presidents/chancellors or heads of postsecondary associations.

Five divisions within the council work to implement ACE's goals. They are: (1) *Division of Governmental Relations*, essentially a lobbying unit that represents higher education to the federal government; (2) *Division of Institutional Relations*, concerned with campus management and curriculum issues; (3) *Division of Policy Analysis and Research*, responsible for formulating ACE policy positions; (4) *Division of International Education Relations;* and (5) a communication unit, the *Division of External Relations.*

ACE publishes reports, studies, and research relating to higher education. Numerous periodicals are also available to members, the principal ones being *Educational Record,* a quarterly, and a weekly newsletter, *Higher Education and National Affairs.*
Reference: American Council on Education, *American Council on Education: Membership Information*, Washington, DC: The Council, Undated Brochure.

AMERICAN COUNCIL ON THE TEACHING OF FOREIGN LANGUAGES (ACTFL), a national membership organization devoted to foreign language teaching at all levels of instruction. ACTFL was organized in 1967. It works to provide practical assistance to teachers and administrators, frequently through linkages with scores of state, provincial, regional, and national organizations. Its membership currently approaches 10,000 foreign language educators.

The official journal of ACTFL is *Foreign Language Annals,* published six times annually. Relatively inexpensive materials of interest to foreign language instructors are available through the council's Materials Center. The organization's annual convention, the only such meeting devoted to foreign language education, is held in different parts of the country each year. The council's awards program consists of three specific awards: (1) the *Pimsleur Award,* dedicated to Paul Pimsleur, based on an outstanding research publication in the areas of foreign or second language instruction; (2) the *Steiner Award,* dedicated to Florence Steiner, awarded to one K–12 foreign language teacher and to one postsecondary teacher or administrator for distinguished teaching and service; and (3) the *Brooks Award,* dedicated to Nelson Brooks, awarded for excellence in the teaching of culture.

ACTFL's headquarters is in New York City.
References: American Council on the Teaching of Foreign Languages, *Out in Front and Right in Touch,* New York: The Council, Undated Brochure; American Council on the Teaching of Foreign Languages, *ACTFL Materials Center,* New York: The Council, Undated Publications List; *Foreign Language Annals* (Volume 12), New York: American Council on the Teaching of Foreign Languages, 1979.

AMERICAN EDUCATIONAL RESEARCH ASSOCIATION (AERA), an international professional organization whose principal concern is "the improvement of the educational process through the encouragement of scholarly inquiry related to education, the dissemination of research results, and their practical application" (*Membership For Your Discipline,* unpaginated). AERA's membership of 14,000 includes representatives from the fields of education, sociology, psychology, history, political science, anthropology, law, economics, philosophy, and statistics.

The association's annual meeting provides a forum in which prescreened reports and papers are presented. Other organizationally sponsored programs include research training sessions, topical conferences, and the Governmental/Professional Liaison Program through which educational research and development activities are monitored and reported.

AERA is divided into nine special-interest divisions: A, Administration; B, Curriculum and Objectives; C, Learning and Instruction; D, Measurement and Research Methodology; E, Counseling and Human Development; F, History and Historiography; G, Social Context of Education; H, School Evaluation and Program Development; and I, Education in the Professions.

Periodicals published by AERA are: *Educational Researcher,* a monthly journal; *Educational Evaluation and Policy Analysis,* published bimonthly; *American Educational Research Journal* (quarterly); *Journal of Educational Statistics* (quarterly); *Review of Educational Research* (quarterly); and *Review of Research in Education,* an annual. All AERA members receive *Educational Researcher* and any two of the other periodicals as part of their membership. Other AERA publications include: *Annual Meeting Abstracts, Encyclopedia of Educational Research, Review of Research in Education,* and the *Second Handbook of Research on Teaching.*

Each year, AERA makes annual awards to recognize those who have made outstanding contributions to educational research and development. The association, headquartered in Washington, D.C., also operates a placement service for the benefit of its members.

References: American Educational Research Association, *American Educational Research Association: A Membership For Your Discipline,* Washington, DC: The Association, Undated Brochure; American Educational Research Association, *American Educational Research Association: Publications,* Washington, DC: The Association, Undated Brochure.

AMERICAN EDUCATION WEEK, an annual observance designed to call attention to the needs and achievements of American schools. The observance is sponsored jointly by the National Education Association, the U.S. Department of Education, National PTA, National School Boards Association, the American Legion, and seven other organizations. National Education Week, which is held dur-

ing the first full week preceding Thanksgiving, is also supported by numbers of other organizations, private and governmental.

Reference: National Education Association, *NEA Handbook: 1988–89,* Washington, DC: The Association, 1988.

AMERICAN FEDERATION OF TEACHERS (AFT), a 600,000-member international labor union for teachers that is affiliated with the AFL-CIO. AFT's membership includes 80,000 professionals who work at the college/university level. The federation has approximately 2,000 locals (usually in school districts) scattered across the United States.

AFT was established in 1916 and, in that same year, chartered by the American Federation of Labor. The organization's highest governing body is the annual convention of delegates who represent the 2,000 (app.) locals. The delegates vote on significant issues and, every two years, elect the federation's president and 3 vice-presidents. Supervisors at the rank of principal or higher are not eligible for membership in AFT.

The Department of Organization and Field Services of AFT assists locals in collective bargaining elections and strike situations. Liaison with special constituencies, such as the Federation of Nurses and Health Professionals (FNHP), the Federation of State Employees (FSE) and the Standing Committee on Para-professionals and School-Related Personnel, are part of activities of the Department of Organization and Field Services.

In addition to promoting collective bargaining among teachers, AFT supports academic freedom as well as improved salaries, retirement programs, and fringe benefits for its members. Personal benefits offered by the AFT include: liability insurance, a Legal Defense Fund, and group insurance (health, term life, accident). AFT publishes several periodicals: *American Educator,* a quarterly professional journal; *American Teacher,* a monthly newspaper; *Action,* a weekly newsletter; *On Campus* for higher education members; *Healthwire,* a monthly for FNHP members; *Public Service Reporter,* a monthly for FSE members; paraprofessionals receive a quarterly titled *The Reporter.* AFT's central offices are in Washington, D.C.

References: American Federation of Teachers, *Facts about the American Federation of Teachers, AFL/CIO,* Washington, DC: The Federation, Undated Brochure; American Federation of Teachers; *Introducing the American Federation of Teachers, AFL/CIO,* Washington, DC: The Federation, Undated Brochure; American Federation of Teachers; *Today's Schools, Tomorrow's Challenges,* Washington, DC: The Federation, 1988.

AMERICAN HOME ECONOMICS ASSOCIA-TION (AHEA), national organization of home economists with a total membership in excess of 50,000 men and women. AHEA was founded in 1909; Ellen H. Richards was its first President. The association consists of a 28-member Board of Directors; an assembly of delegates (approximately 500); over 100 committees, councils, panels, and units; and 52 affiliated state associations, including Puerto Rico and the District of Columbia.

AHEA's work is carried out through four program areas: public policy, professional development, outreach, and research. The association is recognized by the Council on Post-Secondary Accreditation as the home economics accrediting unit for programs leading to the bachelor's degree. Additionally, it sponsors two periodicals: the *Journal of Home Economics,* published five times a year, and *AHEA Action,* a newspaper.

AHEA's national offices are in Washington, D.C.
Reference: American Home Economics Association, *A Force for Families,* Washington, DC: The Association, Undated Brochure.

AMERICAN INDUSTRIAL ARTS ASSOCIA-TION (AIAA), national organization concerned with the improvement of industrial arts curriculum and personnel. Established in 1939, AIAA is an affiliate of the National Education Association and serves as parent organization to the American Councils of Industrial Arts Teacher Education, Industrial Arts Supervisors, Elementary School Industrial Arts, Industrial Arts State Association Officers, and the American Industrial Arts College Student Association. Its numerous activities include: (1) publication of *Man Society Technology,* the official journal, eight times a year; (2) promoting educational programs funded by federal agencies; (3) publications and materials of interest to industrial arts educators; (4) sponsoring the "Industrial Arts Teacher of the Year" program; and (5) assisting state and local agencies to realize increased funding. The association's Accreditation and Evaluation Committee has prepared and published standards to be used when assessing the effectiveness of industrial arts programs.

AIAA's national office is in Washington, D.C.
References: Accreditation and Evaluation Committee, *Standards for Industrial Arts Programs and Professionals (Public and Private),* Washington, DC: American Industrial Arts Association, 1979; American Industrial Arts Association, *Directory of Colleges and Universities Offering Degrees in Industrial Arts,* Washington, DC: The Association, Spring 1977; American Industrial Arts Association,

For Special People, Washington, DC: The Association, Undated Brochure.

AMERICAN LIBRARY ASSOCIATION (ALA), the world's oldest and largest organization of professional librarians. Formed in 1876, ALA's membership of librarians, library trustees, authors, publishers, libraries, and others interested in librarianship has increased to over 35,000. The association works to promote quality libraries and librarianship service.

ALA provides its members with a large number of services. They include: (1) significant publications such as *Booklist* (a book guide to assist those who select books and media for public and school libraries), *Choice* (a similar guide for college and research libraries), and the *ALA Yearbook;* (2) awarding the Caldecott and Newberry medals each year; (3) accreditation of library education programs; (4) sponsorship of two (business and general) conferences each year; and (5) publication of *American Libraries,* a newsmagazine. ALA also sponsors National Library Week, works closely with legislators to encourage governmental support for libraries, and fights to preserve intellectual freedom through its Freedom to Read Foundation, the Intellectual Freedom Committee, and the Office for Intellectual Freedom.

The organization is divided into several divisions: (1) American Association of School Libraries; (2) American Library Trustee Association; (3) Association of College and Research Libraries; (4) Association for Library Service to Children; (5) Association of Specialized and Cooperative Library Agencies; (6) Library and Information Technology Association; (7) Library Administration and Management Association; (8) Public Library Association; (9) Reference and Adult Services Division; (10) Resources and Technical Services Division; and (11) the Young Adult Services Division. Many of the divisions publish their own journals and professional magazines. In addition, there are 15 "round tables," membership units that have interests falling outside the scope of the various divisions.

ALA's main office is in Chicago. (See AMERICAN ASSOCIATION OF SCHOOL LIBRARIANS; CALDECOTT MEDAL; CENSORSHIP; and NEWBERY MEDAL. Also see APPENDIXES IV and VIII: RANDOLPH CALDECOTT MEDAL AWARD WINNERS and JOHN NEWBERY MEDAL AWARD WINNERS.)
References: American Library Association, *Start A New Decade with a New Direction: ALA Can Show You the Way,*

Chicago: The Association, Undated Brochure; Filomena Simora, *The Bowker Annual of Library and Book Trade Information* (32nd edition), New York: R. R. Bowker Co., 1987.

AMERICAN PERSONNEL AND GUIDANCE ASSOCIATION (APGA)—See AMERICAN ASSOCIATION FOR COUNSELING AND DEVELOPMENT

AMERICAN PSYCHOLOGICAL ASSOCIATION (APA),

the major psychological organization in the United States. Membership exceeds 48,000. APA works to advance psychology as a science and as a profession. It does so by encouraging research, by maintaining high professional standards, and through dissemination of information using its 18 journals, a newspaper, and other publications.

APA consists of 36 separate divisions (e.g. General Psychology, Clinical Psychology, Educational Psychology, Hypnosis, Experimental Psychology). Each division elects its own officers, establishes its own membership requirements, and meets annually at the APA convention.

The organization provides three classes of membership: *Associate,* for those who have completed advanced graduate work; *member,* open to those holding a doctorate in the field; and *fellow,* a coveted status requiring divisional nomination and a record of distinguished professional achievement. APA's central office is in Washington, D.C.

Reference: American Psychological Association, *The American Psychological Association: 1979,* The Association, 1979.

AMERICAN PSYCHOLOGICAL ASSOCIATION: DIVISION 16,

also known as The Division of School Psychology of the American Psychological Association, one of the several divisions making up the APA. Division 16's objectives, as listed in its bylaws, "shall be: (a) to promote and maintain high STANDARDS of professional preparation and service within the specialty, (b) to increase effective and efficient PRACTICE of psychology within the schools, (c) to expand and disseminate appropriate scholarly KNOWLEDGE, (d) to provide opportunities for professional FELLOWSHIP, and (e) to engage in COLLABORATION and cooperation with individuals, groups, and organizations in the shared realization of these objectives" (unpaginated). The division works closely with APA and the Association for the Advancement of Psychology on numbers of matters including federal activities affecting education. Division 16 is represented on APA's governing body, the APA Council.

Division 16 members receive two publications: *The American Psychologist* (APA's journal) and *Monitor,* a monthly newsletter. They participate in APA conventions as well as special Division 16 workshops. Numerous publications addressed to school psychology are also made available. (See AMERICAN PSYCHOLOGICAL ASSOCIATION.)

References: American Psychological Association, Division 16, *School Psychology: Membership Brochure,* Washington, DC: The Association, Undated Brochure; Article I, *Bylaws, Division of School Psychology of the American Psychological Association,* Washington, D.C.: The Association, Undated.

AMERICAN SPEECH-LANGUAGE HEARING ASSOCIATION (ASHA),

a professional association of specialists in the fields of speech-language pathology and audiology. Included among its 30,000 members are individuals employed in both school and nonschool capacities. Founded in 1925, ASHA provides its membership with numerous services, including but not limited to: (1) advocacy and public information; (2) continuing education opportunities; (3) lobbying (reviewing federal or state legislation affecting the communicatively handicapped); and (4) publications. Periodicals published by ASHA are: *Asha,* a monthly professional journal; the *Journal of Speech and Hearing Research,* a research-oriented periodical; the *Journal of Speech and Hearing Disorders;* and *Language, Speech and Hearing Services in Schools.* ASHA's main offices are in Rockville, Maryland.

References: American Speech-Language Hearing Association, *American Speech-Language Hearing Association,* Rockville, MD: The Association, Undated Brochure; Nancy Yakes and Denise Akey (Editors), *Encyclopedia of Associations* (Volume I, Thirteenth Edition), Detroit: Gale Research Company, 1979.

AMERICAN VOCATIONAL ASSOCIATION (AVA),

a national organization of vocational education teachers, administrators, and counselors. AVA promotes research and legislation of interest to its members. It publishes the *American Vocational Journal.* Organized in 1925 and headquartered in Washington, D.C., AVA's membership presently exceeds 55,000. Twelve educational divisions within AVA facilitate the association's work: Agricultural, Business and Office, Distributive, Guidance, Health Occupations, Home Economics, Industrial Arts, Manpower, New and Related Services, Technical, Trade and Industrial, and Vocational Guidance.

References: Calfrey C. Calhoun and Alton F. Finch, *Vocational and Career Education: Concepts and Operations,* Belmont, CA: Wadsworth Publishing Company, Inc., 1976; Mary Wilson Pair (Editor), *Encyclopedia of Associations* (Twelfth Edition), Detroit: Gale Research Company, 1978.

AMERICA'S COMPETITIVE CHALLENGE: THE NEED FOR A NATIONAL RESPONSE—
See NATIONAL REFORM REPORTS (1980–86)

AMIDON PLAN, an instructional program formulated and demonstrated by Carl F. Hansen during his incumbency as the District of Columbia Superintendent of Schools. The plan carried the name of the Amidon School, the elementary school in which Hansen's ideas were carried out. The Amidon Plan received international attention during the early 1960s as a demonstration in basic education. Because its curriculum and methodology were perceived by many educators to be too narrowly organized around basic subjects, Hansen and his plan were subjected to considerable professional criticism. Both he and the program had supporters, however, especially among the laity.

The Amidon Plan stressed the basic subjects and used them as the building blocks leading to "intelligent behavior." The subjects were reading, writing, spelling, penmanship, speaking, grammar, mathematics, science, United States history, geography, health and physical education, music, and art. Teachers were expected to teach children directly (direct instruction) and in accordance with a predetermined schedule. Intraclass grouping was discouraged; instead, a track program was followed. Strict student discipline was encouraged. (See DIRECT INSTRUCTION.)

References: Carl F. Hansen, *The Amidon Elementary School: A Successful Demonstration in Basic Education,* Englewood Cliffs, NJ: Prentice-Hall, Inc., 1962 (Reprinted in 1977 by Greenwood Press, Westport, CT); F. Henry Johnson, "Amidon—A Return to Essentialism?" *The Education Digest,* November 1963.

AMPLIFICATION—See ELECTRONIC AMPLIFICATION

ANAEROBICS—See AEROBICS

ANALOGIES TEST ITEM, a type of test question that requires the respondent to associate meanings and to infer relationships. Two examples of relatively simple analogies items are: (1) black:white:: hot:____;· (2) April:____::August:Summer. In such items, the student must recognize a relationship between two terms (*opposites* and *months* in the seasons in the two examples given). Having inferred the relationship, he/she must demonstrate the correctness of the inference by providing a fourth term that can be associated with a related (and given) third term.

The analogies test item may be presented as a completion test item (as in the examples given above), as a multiple-choice item (the correct answer is chosen from several that the test constructor provides), or as a true-false test question (in which some answers are stated correctly, others incorrectly).

Analogies test items appear more frequently in standardized tests than in teacher-made tests, notably those designed to measure intelligence and aptitude.

References: D. G. Lewis, *Assessment in Education,* London, England: University of London Press Ltd., 1974; Arnold J. Lien, *Measurement and Evaluation of Learning* (Third Edition), Dubuque, IA: Wm. C. Brown Company, Publishers, 1976.

ANALYSIS OF VARIANCE (ANOVA), a statistical procedure by which two or more sets (groups) of data can be analyzed to determine whether there are significant differences between and among them. An *F*-ratio is used to determine the actual levels of differences. The procedure allows the effects of a particular factor or combination of factors to be measured and assessed.

There are many ANOVA designs. For example, a one-way analysis of variance may compare two or more groups using different treatments (experimental treatment, control, or no treatment group) on a selected criterion test (e.g. mathematics achievement). A two-way ANOVA may compare two or more groups using different treatments on a selected criterion test and further analyze sex differences. In such a two-way analysis, the first level is called Main Effect *A* (in this case treatment), and the second level, Main Effect *B* (sex). There is also an interaction ($A \times B$) possibility. If there is a significant interaction, it means that differences become a function of the subset or cell being analyzed (males under treatment 1, females under treatment 2, etc.) rather than being caused exclusively by either Main Effect *A* or *B*. The more levels (two-way, three-way, four-way, etc.), the more complex the analysis, and the more difficult it is to explain the main effects as well as the interactions. (See DEGREES OF FREEDOM; *F*-RATIO; and VARIANCE.)

References: L. R. Gay, *Educational Research: Competencies for Analysis and Application* (Third Edition), Columbus, OH: Merrill Publishing Company, 1987; William H. Hays, *Statistics* (Fourth Edition), New York: Holt, Rinehart and Winston, Inc., 1988; Harold O. Kiess, *Statistical Concepts for the Behavioral Sciences*, Boston: Allyn and Bacon, 1989.

ANALYTIC PHONICS—See PHONICS

ANDRAGOGY, a problem-centered approach for adult learning that takes learner's needs and interests into account. Several factors serve to distinguish *andragogy* (adult learning) from *pedagogy* (child learning). They include: (1) self-concept, with the adult less dependent on others; (2) experience; (3) readiness to learn; and (4) time perspective, andragogy being present-oriented while pedagogy is frequently future-oriented. John Ingalls cited seven steps that make up the andragogical process. They are: (1) establishing a learning climate; (2) providing for mutual planning; (3) identifying needs, interests, and values; (4) formulating objectives; (5) designing learning activities; (6) carrying out the learning activities; and (7) evaluation.

References: John D. Ingalls, *A Trainer's Guide to Andragogy* (Revised Edition), Washington, DC: Social and Rehabilitation Service, U.S. Department of Health, Education, and Welfare, April 1973; Malcolm S. Knowles, *Andragogy in Action*, San Francisco: Jossey-Bass Publishers, 1984.

ANECDOTAL RECORD, a written log containing specific accounts of a student's behavior. These accounts, prepared by the classroom teacher and covering an extended period, include entries such as descriptions of usual or unusual behavior, statements made by the student, or summaries of parent-teacher conferences. Anecdotes are dated; the setting for the incident is also indicated (e.g. classroom, corridor, playground). Incident descriptions are presented briefly and objectively. Once enough accounts have been collected, the teacher (frequently working with a counselor or school psychologist) uses them as a basis for interpreting the student's behavior and for planning intervention strategies.

Two concerns that have been expressed relative to anecdotal records are: (1) possible biased selection of incidents/events by the teacher, and (2) the possibility that such information in the cumulative folder can compound the misuse of information.

References: Richard C. Nelson, *Guidance and Counseling in the Elementary School*, New York: Holt, Rinehart and Winston, Inc., 1972; John J. Pietrofesa, et al., *Guidance: An Introduction*, Chicago: Rand McNally College Publishing Company, 1980; Bruce Shertzer and James D. Linden, *Fundamentals of Individual Appraisal: Assessment Techniques for Counselors*, Boston: Houghton Mifflin Company, 1979.

ANIMAL PSYCHOLOGY, a branch of psychology devoted to the study of animal behavior. Animal psychologists are primarily concerned with individual subjects. Much of their work is done with white rats, although some work with other animals such as monkeys and pigeons. In contrast, *ethology*, a form of animal psychology, is more interested in average behavior patterns of groups (species) of animals.

References: Donald A. Dewsbury, *Comparative Animal Behavior*, New York: McGraw-Hill Book Company, 1978; Irenaus Eibl-Eibesfeldt, *Ethology: The Biology of Behavior* (Second Edition), New York: Holt, Rinehart and Winston, Inc., 1975; H. Hediger, "Animal Psychology" in H. J. Eysenck, et al. (Editors), *Encyclopedia of Psychology*, New York: The Seabury Press, 1979.

ANTI-DISCRIMINATION LAWS, EMPLOYMENT, those laws passed by the various governments to outlaw discrimination in the employment of individuals. Over the years, numerous individuals have been either excluded from or not considered for employment because of sex, race, religion, ethnic origin, age, or physical handicap. These laws were passed to stop such practices.

On June 25, 1941, President Franklin Roosevelt issued Executive Order Number 8802, establishing a Committee on Fair Employment Practice in the Office of Production Management. Its purpose was to encourage full participation in the national defense program. Later, the Fair Employment Practice Commission was created.

It wasn't until 1964 (under the provisions of Title VII of the Civil Rights Act) that overt discrimination based on race, color, religion, sex, or national origin was outlawed. Revised Order Number 4 of the U.S. Department of Labor, dated December 4, 1971, led to the requiring of affirmative action plans of those firms receiving governmental contracts of $50,000 or more, plans designed to eliminate discriminatory practices in industry.

Most governmental units (federal, state, county, city) have passed anti-discrimination laws in the area of employment. These cover both public and private employment. Not only are there Constitutional provisions to prevent discrimination (Fifth and Fourteenth Amendments), but many federal laws have been passed for the express purpose of preventing employment discrimination. For example, the Equal Employment Opportunity Act of 1972 established the Equal Employment Opportunity Commission (EEOC). Age and pay discrimination in many occupations and businesses were outlawed by Congressional action with the passage of the Age Discrimination in Employment Act of 1967 (29 U.S. Code 623 et seq.) and the Equal Pay Act of 1963 (29 U.S. Code 1976 206) amending the Fair Labor Standards Act.

References: Clement Berwitz, *The Job Analysis Approach to Affirmative Action,* New York: John Wiley and Sons, 1975; *Equal Employment Opportunity: Court Cases,* Washington, DC: United States Office of Personnel Management, 1979; Louis C. Kesselman, *The Social Politics of FEPC,* Chapel Hill, NC: University of North Carolina Press, 1948; Richard A. Lester, *Reasoning about Discrimination: The Analysis of Professional and Executive Work in Federal Antibias Programs,* Princeton, NJ: Princeton University Press, 1980; *Shepard's Acts and Cases by Popular Names: Federal and State* (Volume 1, Second Edition), Colorado Springs, CO: Shepard's, Inc., 1979; Bette Ann Stead (Compiler), *Women in Management,* Englewood Cliffs, NJ: Prentice-Hall, Inc., 1978.

ANTISTRIKE LAWS, legislation that outlaws labor strikes by certain populations of workers. Such laws are usually designed to offset work stoppages in the public sector and impact on working groups such as federal employees, public school-teachers, and policemen. Steven Rynecki cited most of the arguments used to support and oppose the right of government workers to strike. Those *opposing* such a right voice arguments such as: (1) public employees represent the voter, thus to strike is to attack government; (2) the public suffers when public workers strike; (3) services provided by public employees are indispensible; and (4) politicians will yield to public sector demands rather than risk a strike. Those *supporting* the right to strike raise arguments such as: (1) not all governmental services are essential; (2) some private sector strikes are more disruptive than those in the public sector; (3) public employees will strike in spite of antistrike laws and policies; and (4) the right to strike is sometimes granted after all other administrative remedies have been exhausted (including impartial fact-finding).

In the 1960s and 1970s, strikes by teachers took place quite regularly, many involving large school systems such as New York, Chicago, San Francisco, Cleveland, and Detroit. In most cases, these work stoppages were illegal. Since 1970, some states (e.g. Pennsylvania, Hawaii, Oregon, Minnesota) have granted public employees the right to strike under certain conditions and/or restricted the use of injunctions where such strikes continue to be illegal. (See COLLECTIVE BARGAINING and TEACHER STRIKES.)

References: Jerome T. Barrett and Ira B. Lobel, "Public Sector Strikes—Legislative and Court Treatment," *Negotiations Management,* Volume VIII, No. 2, 1974; Richard G. Neal, *Avoiding and Controlling Teacher Strikes,* Washington, DC: Educational Service Bureau, Inc., 1971; Steven B. Rynecki, "Public Employee Strikes: Developing an Effective Management Strategy," *Negotiations Management,* Volume VIII, No. 9, 1975 (Reprinted from *Personnel News,* February 1975); "Strikes by AFT Locals, 1979–80," *American Teacher,* September 1980.

APHASIA, a general term denoting the loss of, or retardation in, the ability to understand or formulate language. An individual suffering from aphasia usually has difficulty in his/her ability to comprehend and manipulate words (speech, writing, or gestures). There are several subclassifications of aphasia. *Auditory aphasia* (word deafness, receptive aphasia) is the reduction or loss of the ability to comprehend the spoken word. *Developmental aphasia* (congenital aphasia) is caused by functional disorders such as brain dysfunction or brain damage. *Expressive aphasia* is a speech disorder describing an individual who knows what he/she wants to say but cannot remember the pattern of movements required for speech.

References: B. R. Gearheart (Editor), *Education of the Exceptional Child,* Scranton, PA: Intext Educational Publishers, 1972; B. R. Gearheart, *Learning Disabilities: Educational Strategies,* St. Louis, MO: The C. V. Mosby Company, 1973; Kenneth W. Waugh and Wilma Jo Bush, *Diagnosing Learning Disorders,* Columbus, OH: Charles E. Merrill Publishing Company, 1971.

APPERCEPTION, a form of information processing in which an individual evaluates new knowledges, sensations, concepts, and perceptions in terms of his/her past knowledges and experiences. Following evaluation, these become a part of the individual's total knowledge base (known as *apperception mass*). Stated differently, apperception is the process of discovering relationships and incorporating them into one's knowledge base.

The term *apperception* is not used as frequently in psychology today as it once was. It was considered by many 19th-century psychologists and educators to be an extremely high level of mental processing. James Baldwin, Johann Herbart, and Wilhelm Wundt were among those who included apperception in their approach to psychology and education.

References: James M. Baldwin, *Handbook of Psychology: Senses and Intellect* (Second Edition), New York: Henry Holt and Company, 1889; Charles De Garmo, *Apperception*, Boston: D. C. Heath and Company, 1903; Wilhelm Wundt, *Lectures on Human and Animal Psychology*, London, England: Swan Sonnenschein and Company, 1894.

APPRENTICESHIP, a training program designed to help young people, usually high school graduates, to learn a skilled trade. Such learning is of the on-the-job variety and takes place under the tutelage of a skilled craftsman. It is frequently supplemented by related classroom instruction. Apprenticeship training programs vary in length, ranging from one to five years. Sponsorship of such programs has traditionally taken one of three forms: (1) cosponsorship by management and labor; (2) sponsorship by management with the cooperation of a union; or (3) sponsorship by management alone. Apprentices are normally paid while they learn, starting at about half the rate paid to fully trained artisans and advancing to journeyman's scale upon completion of training.

In the recent past, Ben Burdetsky noted, several changes in apprenticeship training have been taking place. They include programs sponsored by community colleges, training centers operated jointly by employers and unions, increases in the number of female apprentices, and increased involvement by school systems.

The apprenticeship concept has been traced back to 13th-century England. For several hundred years, individual "masters" trained apprentices, normally for seven years, and during that time assumed responsibility for providing trainees with food, shelter, and clothing. The English apprenticeship model was adopted, with some variation, in several of the American colonies. (One notable modification required the master to see that the apprentice received a minimal education beyond technical instruction.)

The U.S. Department of Labor, in accordance with the National Apprenticeship Act of 1937, formulates and promotes standards for apprenticeship training. Similar legislation has been enacted by most of the states.

References: Ben Burdetsky, "New Directions in Apprenticeship Training," *Education Digest,* February 1978 (Originally Published in *Worklife,* August 1977); Employment and Training Administration, *Apprentice Training* (Revised), Washington, DC: U.S. Department of Labor, 1980; Employment and Training Administration, *The National Apprenticeship Program* (Revised), Washington, DC: U.S. Department of Labor, 1980; Huey B. Long, "Apprenticeship: Career Education Colonial Style," *Journal of Research and Development in Education,* Summer 1975; U.S. Department of Labor, *Apprenticeship: Selected References, 1974–1979,* Washington, DC: U.S. Government Printing Office, July 1979.

APRAXIA, the inability to perform a specific skill/act even though there is no known paralysis. Voluntary muscular movements are disrupted while the involuntary movements remain intact. Those with apraxia have difficulty articulating speech or formulating letters and words (*verbal* or *oral apraxia*). They may have difficulty with gestures, or they may have difficulty using tools in a purposeful way (*nonverbal apraxia*).

Individuals with apraxia that affects speech have problems of sequencing muscle movements (whether it be respiratory, laryngeal, or oral). Less severe cases of apraxia are called *dyspraxia*. Damage to Broca's area (anterior to the motor area of the left hemisphere) of the brain results in apraxia. In apraxia, neither muscle weakness nor spasticity is present.

References: Wendell Johnson, et al., *Diagnostic Methods in Speech Pathology,* New York: Harper and Row, Publishers, 1963; Lucille Nicolosi, et al., *Terminology of Communications Disorders,* Baltimore, MD: The Williams and Wilkins Company, 1978; Paul H. Skinner and Ralph L. Shelton, *Speech, Language, and Hearing: Normal Processes and Disorders,* Reading, MA: Addison-Wesley Publishing Company, 1978.

APTITUDE, the capacity (innate or acquired) of an individual to learn. Aptitude may refer to general learning potential or to capacity in a specific learning area. Mental ability (I.Q.) tests are commonly employed to measure general aptitude. There are also differential aptitude tests that divide general aptitude into component parts. Clerical, music, or mathematical tests are examples of specific aptitude tests. *Scholastic aptitude* should not be confused with *general intelligence*, nor should *scholastic aptitude* be confused with *academic achievement*. Although they are interrelated, these terms and concepts are not synonymous. Aptitude scores are used to predict how well an individual can achieve with appropriate training or education. Some authorities advise caution in the use of aptitude tests because all tests measure or reflect prior learning or experiences. Some children, for example, have not had the opportunity to acquire such prior learnings or experiences. (See APTITUDE TESTING.)

References: Harold W. Bernard, *Human Development in Western Culture* (Fifth Edition), Boston: Allyn and Bacon, Inc., 1978; Clinton Chase, *Measurement for Educational Evaluation* (Second Edition), Reading, MA: Addison-Wesley Publishing Company, 1978; Tom Kubiszyn and Gary Borich, *Education Testing and Measurement: Classroom Application and Practice* (Second Edition), Glenview, IL: Scott Foresman and Company, 1987.

APTITUDE TESTING, evaluation efforts intended to predict success in subsequent educational experiences or in some occupation. Instruments used may be classified as general intelligence tests, specific aptitude tests, and special aptitude tests.

Because many *intelligence tests* have been validated with tests that measure academic achievement, they are often classified as tests of scholastic aptitude. Commonly used general measures of intelligence include the Stanford-Binet Intelligence Scale, Otis Self-Administering Tests, Otis-Lennon Mental Ability Tests, California Test of Mental Maturity, SRA Tests of Educational Ability, Armed Forces Qualification Tests, and the Wechsler Adult Intelligence Scale (WAIS).

Tests for *specific aptitudes* provide a set of scores for different aptitudes rather than a single measure. These divide general intelligence into several independent factors, a recognition that intelligence is complex and includes elements that, at least, might be classified as academic, practical, mechanical, abstract, social, verbal, and numerical. The SRA Primary Mental Abilities Test (verbal meaning, numerical ability, abstract reasoning, clerical speed and accuracy, mechanical reasoning, space relations, language usage I: spelling, language usage II: grammar) is an example of such tests.

Special aptitude tests measure vision, hearing, motor dexterity, artistic talents, clerical, and mechanical aptitude. The following are representative special aptitude tests: Ortho-Rater (vision), Massachusetts Hearing Test (hearing), Crawford Small Parts Dexterity Test (motor dexterity), Minnesota Paper Form Board (spatial aptitude), Bennett Mechanical Comprehension Test (mechanical aptitude), Minnesota Clerical Test (clerical aptitude), Meier Art Judgment Test (artistic appreciation), Horn Art Aptitude Inventory (artistic production), Seashore Measures of Musical Talents (musical aptitudes), and the Torrance Tests of Creative Thinking (creativity).

Excellent sources and reviews of aptitude tests are found in Oscar Buros's *Mental Measurements Yearbooks* and *Tests in Print.* (See APTITUDE.)

References: Anne Anastasi, *Psychological Testing* (Third Edition), New York: Macmillan Publishing Company, Inc., 1968; Oscar K. Buros (Editor), *The Eighth Mental Measurements Yearbook* (Volumes I and II), Highland Park, NJ: The Gryphon Press, 1978; Oscar K. Buros (Editor), *Tests in Print II,* Highland Park, NJ: The Gryphon Press, 1974; Lee J. Cronbach, *Essentials of Psychological Testing* (Third Edition), New York: Harper and Row, Publishers, 1970.

APTITUDE-TREATMENT INTERACTION, a phrase used by educational researchers to describe differential relationships that exist between *treatment* (modes of instruction, programs, variables) and the *aptitude* (personalogical characteristics, pretreatment characteristics, intelligence, specific ability, etc.) of individuals. Research projects that focus on such interactions are called ATI studies. They are important because some students may be more successful with one instructional program, while other students may not. In addition, some students might be successful with alternative instructional programs, while others might not. ATI research does not emphasize individual differences per se but rather attempts to provide generalizations about treatment variables as related to the measurable characteristics of the individual.

References: Glenn Bract, "Experimental Factors Related to Aptitude—Treatment Interactions," *Review of Educational Research,* December 1970; Lee J. Cronbach and Richard E. Snow, *Aptitudes and Instructional Methods,* New York: Irvington Publishers, Inc., 1977.

AQUINAS, ST. THOMAS (1225-74), a Roman Catholic philosopher, theologian, and teacher who belonged to the Dominican order. Born near Aquino, Italy, St. Thomas Aquinas wrote 20 volumes during his lifetime, most concerned with philosophy and theology. He built much of his theological positions around the logic and arguments of Aristotle. As a result of his interest in Aristotle and his works, St. Thomas Aquinas was able to construct a complete rationale system of Christian Philosophy. One of his most important works was *Summa Contra Gentiles.*

Aquinas was also considered one of the most influential teachers of his day. He was affectionately called "The Angelic Doctor." His teaching began formally in 1252 when he went to Paris to teach as a bachelor. In 1256, he gave his inaugural lecture as master and eventually received his doctor's chair.

Pope John XXII, in 1323, canonized Aquinas, and, in 1567, Pope St. Pius V proclaimed him a "Doctor of the Universal Church." Saint Thomas

Aquinas was also proclaimed the patron of all Catholic universities, colleges, and schools.

References: G. G. Coulton, *Five Centuries of Religion* (Volume II), New York: Octagon Books, 1979; Herbert Thurston and Donald Attwater, *Butler's Lives of the Saints* (Volume 1, January, February, March), New York: P. J. Kennedy and Sons, 1962.

ARBITRATION, the settlement of disagreements between management and employees through the use of a third (ad hoc) party. Both parties meet with the arbitrator to present their arguments/data with the understanding that the arbitrator's decision, in most instances, will be a final and binding one. (Boards of education often resist binding arbitration because they cannot abrogate their ultimate responsibility for policymaking.)

The two principal types of arbitration are contract arbitration and grievance arbitration. *Contract arbitration,* seldom used in the United States except where the public interest is involved (e.g. utility companies), involves resolution of disputes over salaries and working conditions after the negotiating parties have failed to reach agreement. *Grievance arbitration,* which normally affects smaller numbers of people, addresses employee rights and is used as a last resort after all grievance procedures provided for in the organization's labor contract have been pursued without success. (See COLLECTIVE BARGAINING and MEDIATION.)

References: Tim Bornstein, *Arbitration: Last Stop on the Grievance Route,* Washington, DC: Labor-Management Relations Service, Inc., June 1974; W. D. Heisel, *New Questions and Answers on Public Employee Negotiation,* Chicago: International Personnel Management Association, 1973; Max S. Wortman, Jr. and C. Wilson Randle, *Collective Bargaining: Principles and Practices* (Second Edition), Boston: Houghton Mifflin Company, 1966.

ARCHITECTURAL BARRIERS, obstacles within or near buildings or facilities constructed in a manner that makes the buildings inaccessible to the physically handicapped. Public Law 90–480 provided that certain buildings financed with federal funds were to be designed "to insure that physically handicapped persons will have ready access to, and use of, such buildings" (p. 719). The law provided that design and construction standards to guarantee such access were to be developed: (1) by the Administrator of General Services in consultation with the Secretary of Health, Education, and Welfare (for public buildings); (2) by the Secretaries of Housing and Urban Development and HEW (for applicable residential structures); and

(3) by the Secretaries of Defense and HEW (for applicable facilities of the Department of Defense).

Public Law 94–142 extended this act's coverage to include the provision of centers on educational media and materials for the handicapped, these to encourage use of new technology and education programs for the handicapped.

References: Public Law 90–480, *United States Statutes at Large, 1968* (Volume 82), Washington, DC: U.S. Government Printing Office, 1969; Public Law 94–142, *United States Statutes at Large, 1975* (Volume 89), Washington, DC: U.S. Government Printing Office, 1977.

AREA STUDIES, a program of study and research that focuses on a specific section of the world. Area studies integrates the various disciplines of economics, sociology, anthropology, political science, geography, literature, psychology, biology, zoology, and other fields into an investigation of the past, present, and future of a particular geographic area of the world. The following are examples of the world's regions that might be included in area studies: Middle East, Southeast Asia and India, China, Far East, Latin America, Soviet Union, Europe, and North America. Area studies is an example of interdisciplinary research and study at both a theoretical and practical level. Since World War II, an increasing number of universities and colleges have offered programs and advanced degrees in area studies.

References: Wendell C. Bennett, *Area Studies in American Universities,* New York: Social Science Research Council, 1951; Commission on International Understanding, *Non-Western Studies in the Liberal Arts College,* Washington, DC: Association of American Colleges, 1964; Robert B. Hall, *Area Studies: With Special References to Their Implications for Research in the Social Sciences,* New York: Committee for World Area Research, 1949; Lucian W. Pyes (Editor), *Political Science and Area Studies: Rivals or Partners?,* Bloomington, IN: Indiana University Press, 1975; Charles Wagley, *Area Research and Training: A Conference Report on the Study of World Areas,* New York: Social Science Research Council, 1948.

AREA VOCATIONAL EDUCATION SCHOOL, as defined in the Vocational Education Amendments of 1968, is: "(A) a specialized high school used exclusively or principally for the provision of vocational education to persons who are available for study in preparation for entering the labor market, or (B) the department of a high school exclusively or principally used for providing vocational education in no less than five different occupational fields to persons who are available for study in preparation for entering the labor market, or (C) a technical or vocational school used exclusively or principally for the provision of vocational education to persons who have completed or left high school and who are available for study in preparation for entering the labor market, or (D) the department or division of a junior college or community college or university which provides vocational fields, under the supervision of the State Board, leading to immediate employment but not necessarily leading to a baccalaureate degree" (p. 1070). The legislative definition goes on to say that the school must be "available to all residents of the State designated and approved by the State Board, (p. 1070). (See VOCATIONAL EDUCATION; VOCATIONAL EDUCATION ACT OF 1963; and VOCATIONAL EDUCATION AMENDMENTS OF 1968.)

Reference: Public Law 90–576, *United States Statutes at Large, 1968* (Volume 82), Washington, DC: U.S. Government Printing Office, 1969.

ARITHMETIC MEAN—See MEAN

ARMY JUNIOR ROTC (JROTC), a high school-level military program made available to male and female secondary school students during the regular school year and as a regular part of the school's curriculum. Public and private high schools may offer such programs. A typical course extends over four years with instruction provided by selected Army officers and noncommissioned officers.

Instruction covers numerous topics, including but not limited to, organization, map reading, leadership, marksmanship, military history, hygiene and first aid, weapons and weapon safety, and drill. All uniforms, textbooks, and equipment are furnished free of charge. Participation in JROTC in no way obligates the student for any future military service. It may, however, strengthen the applications of those seeking Army Senior ROTC scholarships or admission to one of the military academies. (See ARMY RESERVE OFFICERS TRAINING CORPS.)

References: Army Junior ROTC: It's an Education in Itself (A Brochure), Washington, DC: U.S. Government Printing Office, April 1977; Department of the Army, "ROTC Status of Current/Projected Junior Programs" (Mimeographed), Washington, DC: The Department, Undated; United States Army Training and Doctrine Command, *Directory of ROTC/NDCC Units,* Fort Monroe, VA: The Command, 1979.

ARMY RESERVE OFFICERS TRAINING CORPS (AROTC), a program that prepares college students to become officers in the U.S. Army, the U.S. Army Reserve, and the Army National Guard. Two- and four-year programs are carried out in cooperation with participating colleges and universities. ROTC graduates receive their commissions at the time they earn their baccalaureate degrees.

Four-year programs consist of the Basic Course, a two-year program completed during the freshman and sophomore years of college, and the Advanced Course, open to eligible junior and senior students. These programs include, but are not limited to, course work in national defense, military history, leadership development, and tactics. Students enrolled in the Advanced Course attend a six-week Advanced Camp before the start of their senior year of study. Advanced Course students receive uniforms, military science textbooks, special pay for Advanced Camp participation, and a living allowance (in 1980) of up to $1,000 a year.

Two-year programs are available to students who have graduated from community or junior colleges. A camp experience is included in this program as well.

Competitive scholarships are available to eligible entering freshmen. Those receiving scholarships are obligated to serve four years on active duty following graduation from college. All other ROTC graduates must serve for three years. Those who have earned an accredited baccalaureate degree in nursing may apply for appointment to the Army Nurse Corps. (See AIR FORCE RESERVE OFFICERS TRAINING CORPS; ARMY JUNIOR ROTC; and NAVAL RESERVE OFFICERS TRAINING CORPS.)

References: Counselor's Reference, Army ROTC (A Brochure), Washington, DC: U.S. Government Printing Office, 1979; *Let Army ROTC Take Them Where They Want to Go* (A Brochure), Washington, DC: U.S. Government Printing Office, 1977; *The Army Nurse Corps Through Army ROTC,* Washington, DC: Department of the Army, Undated Brochure; *The Army ROTC Two-Year Program,* Washington, DC: Department of the Army, Undated Brochure.

ARMY SPECIALIZED TRAINING PROGRAM—See ASTP.

ART EDUCATION, a program of studies, K–12, that recognizes art as a distinctive discipline notwithstanding the fact that art education per se is a highly individualized process. Laura Chapman ascribed three purposes to art education: (1) to assure that the teaching of art includes two types of experience for children, *expression* and *response;* (2) to develop an awareness of society's artistic heritage; and (3) to demonstrate the role of art in society.

The National Art Education Association has indicated that the program of art education should include three principal components: (1) the *studio* component, which teaches basic art concepts and skills (e.g. technical aspects, expression); (2) the *art appreciation* component, with attention given to topics such as history, criticism, and aesthetics; and (3) the *advanced work* component, in which competency can be developed in at least one studio and/or appreciation area. The association's official policy advocates that art should be taught to all children, in a comprehensive program, by specially trained personnel who have adequate facilities and materials at their disposal.

At the college and university level, art education refers to training programs for prospective or practicing art teachers.

References: Laura H. Chapman, *Approaches to Art in Education,* New York: Harcourt Brace Jovanovich, Inc., 1978; William J. Ellena (Editor), *Curriculum Handbook for School Executives,* Arlington, VA: American Association of School Administrators, 1973; June K. McFee and Rogena M. Degge, *Art, Culture, and Environment: A Catalyst for Teaching,* Belmont, CA: Wadsworth Publishing Company, Inc., 1977; National Art Education Association Commission on Art Education, *Report of the NAEA Commission on Art Education,* Reston, VA: National Art Education Association, 1977.

ARTICULATION, PROGRAM, a general term used to describe program coordination between educational levels or units. Effective articulation exists when students may progress upwardly from one level or unit to another on a continuous and relatively uninterrupted basis. The achievement of integration and coordination of skills, attitudes, subject matter, goals, objectives, and experiences at the elementary level with those of the high school (to facilitate the future success of a student and his/her graduation from high school) exemplifies curriculum articulation. Another example is articulation of the high school program with that of colleges and universities. In this latter instance, articulation is achieved to the extent that students have the specific experiences in high school that will enhance their success in college. The two examples given illustrate *vertical* curriculum articulation.

Horizontal articulation refers to the integration of curriculum, teaching, and experiences across program elements at a particular level. For example, there may be curriculum articulation among mathematics, science, and social studies at the sixth-grade level.

Articulation of guidance and administrative procedures is also important and helps to tie together the various levels of education. When all areas are coordinated, the various program levels can be treated as a unified, logical, and efficient system.

References: B. Everard Blanchard, *A New System of Education,* Homewood, IL: ETC Publications, 1975; B. Everard Blanchard, *Behavioral Characteristics Peculiar to Articulation in American Educational Programs,* Dayton, OH: Educational Research Center, University of Dayton, 1972; Julius Menacker, *From School to College: Articulation and Transfer,* Washington, DC: American Council on Education, 1975; James L. Wattenbarger, "Improving Articulation," *New Directions in Community Colleges,* Summer 1974.

ARTICULATION, SPEECH, the speech sounds, in a connected discourse, that are made by vocalized or nonvocalized breath passing through the various parts of the mouth, throat, and jaws (such as the lips, tongue, velum, and pharynx). Articulation disorders (faulty speech, absence of speech) are caused by structural, physiological, or neurological problems in this part of the body. The production of incorrect standard speech sounds for no apparent reasons is referred to as a functional articulation disorder (e.g. psychological causation).

Functional articulation disorders may produce omissions, substitutions, distortions, and additions of speech sounds. They range in severity from very mild to extreme. The five major classifications of functional articulation problems are: (1) infantile preservation of sounds; (2) lisping; (3) lalling (mispronunciation of /r/ or /l/); (4) mispronunciation of other sounds; and (5) general oral inaccuracies. (See STUTTERING.)

References: Hugh H. Gregory, *Controversies About Stuttering Therapy,* Baltimore, MD: University Park Press, 1979; Lee E. Travis (Editor), *Handbook of Speech Pathology and Audiology,* Englewood Cliffs, NJ: Prentice-Hall, Inc., 1971; Haiganoosh Whitaker and Harry A. Whitaker (Editors), *Studies in Neurolinguistics* (Volume 2), New York: Academic Press, 1976; W. Dean Wolfe and Daniel J. Goulding (Editors), *Articulation and Learning,* Springfield, IL: Charles C. Thomas, Publisher, 1973.

ARTIFICIAL INTELLIGENCE, that part of the computer that enables it to make inferences and decisions, and to learn in a manner that is similar to the reasoning capabilities of humans. Artificial intelligence will enable computers to "converse" with people in natural language (such as English) rather than in computer language. Such computers will have speech capabilities (including understanding); artificial intelligence makes computers "smart." Fifth-generation computers are being developed to be "smart" computers.

Seymour Papert at Massachusetts Institute of Technology was one of the initial researchers in the field of artificial intelligence. Out of his research on LISP, which was developed for research in artificial intelligence, came LOGO—a problem-solving language that encourages the learner to program the computer, in which the computer becomes the tutee. (See LISP and LOGO.)

References: Neil Graham, *The Mind Tool, Computers and Their Impact on Society* (Fourth Edition), St. Paul, MN: West Publishing Co., 1986; Charles K. Kinzer, et al. (Editors), *Computer Strategies for Education*, Columbus, OH: Merrill Publishing Co., 1986; James Lockwood, et al., *Microcomputers for Educators*, Boston, MA: Little, Brown and Co., 1987; Paul F. Merrill, et al., *Computers in Education*, Englewood Cliffs, NJ: Prentice-Hall, Inc., 1986.

ARTS AND CRAFTS, a general area in art that includes decorative art, handmade articles, handicrafts, the nonmass production of furniture (chairs, cabinets, tables), metal work, weaving, pottery, basketry, clocks, wallpaper, prints, silverware, and jewelry.

Arts and crafts activities are included in most elementary school art curricula. They are also popular as part of the leisure time activities of many adults. There are extensive arts and crafts programs found in the United States; they range from hobbies to high levels of artistic production as an occupation.

The arts and crafts movement in art was started in England in the 1800s as an attempt to combat industrialism and mass production. It attempted to reintroduce the artistic creativity, skill, and quality of the medieval craftsman back into the industrial society. Each piece was carefully designed and artistically created by such craftsmen. Augustus Pugin, John Ruskin, Thomas Carlyle, and William Morris were leaders in the movement. They were motivated by what they saw were the declining social, moral, and aesthetic values of the society.

References: Isabelle Anscombe and Charlotte Gere, *Arts and Crafts in Britain and America*, New York: Rizzoli International Publications, Inc., 1978; Anthea Callen, *Women Artists of the Arts and Crafts Movement, 1870–1914,* New York: Pantheon Books, 1979; Lionel Lambourne, *Utopian Craftsmen: The Arts and Crafts Movement from the Cotswolds to Chicago*, Salt Lake City, UT: Peregrine Smith, 1980.

ART THERAPY, a therapeutic method that uses art as the method of communicating between patient and therapist. The patient uses pictorial images to express dreams, fears, conflicts, and so on. Unconscious feelings and thoughts can also be expressed in this manner. The patient is then encouraged to derive meaning from the drawings. Art therapy should only be practiced by highly trained therapists.

References: Edith Kramer, *Art Therapy in a Children's Community*, Springfield, IL: Charles C. Thomas, Publisher, 1958; Margaret Naumburg, *Dynamically Oriented Art Therapy*, New York: Grune and Stratton, 1966; Elinor Ulman and Penny Dachinger (Editors), *Art Therapy*, New York: Schocken Books, 1975.

ASSEMBLIES, or assembly programs, convocations of students that are scheduled in schools on a fairly regular basis. Assembly programs are considered to be an integral part of a school's total curriculum.

One writer on the subject (Addyse Lane-Palagyi) pointed out that assemblies serve seven purposes: (1) to unify the school, essentially fostering an esprit by bringing all or many of a school's students together and thus creating a "school atmosphere"; (2) to supplement classroom learning; (3) to inculcate common ideals, attitudes, and patriotism; (4) to develop a cultural awareness by having students view artistic performances; (5) to broaden students' interests; (6) to develop good audience habits; and (7) to develop self-expression. Before the widespread use of school intercom systems, assemblies were used as a medium for dissemination of information.

Assembly programs are frequently coordinated by a faculty advisor or a faculty assembly committee. Their responsibilities include scheduling of programs, assigning assembly dates to teachers, general supervision of assembly programs, and program evaluation.

References: Daniel R. Beach, "School Assemblies: The Lost Art," *NASSP Bulletin*, February 1979; Addyse Lane-Palagyi, *Successful School Assembly Programs*, West Nyack, NY: Parker Publishing Company, Inc., 1971.

ASSOCIATE'S DEGREES, academic degrees conferred upon completion of programs requiring less than four (usually two) years of college study. Most associate's degrees are awarded by junior or community colleges; numerous four-year colleges confer them as well. Among the more common degree designations (there are approximately 50) are the following: Associate in Arts, Associate in Science, and Associate in Applied Science.

The history of the associate's degree has been traced to Europe where, in 1865, the University of Durham began to award the Associate in Physical Science degree to students who completed a two-year program. In 1974–75, over 265,000 associate's degrees were awarded by American colleges and universities.

References: Asa S. Knowles (Editor), *Handbook of College and University Administration*, New York: McGraw-Hill Book Company, 1970; Janet A. Mitchell (Editor), *Higher Education Exchange: 78/79*, Princeton, NJ: Peterson's Guides and J. B. Lippincott Company, 1978; Robert Palinchak, *The Evolution of the Community College*, Metuchen, NJ: The Scarecrow Press, Inc., 1973.

ASSOCIATIONAL READING, a level of reading that requires the involvement of higher mental processes and in which the reader associates what he/she is reading with past experiences or future plans. The ability to make such associations is related to factors such as environment, motivation, and experience.

References: John J. De Boer and Martha Dallman, *The Teaching of Reading* (Third Edition), New York: Holt, Rinehart and Winston, Inc., 1970; Larry A. Harris and Carl B. Smith, *Reading Instruction: Diagnostic Teaching in the Classroom* (Third Edition), New York: Holt, Rinehart and Winston, Inc., 1980.

ASSOCIATION FOR CHILDHOOD EDUCATION INTERNATIONAL (ACEI), an organization of teachers, parents, school administrators, and university faculty members who have interest in the development of children (infancy through adolescence) in common. ACEI was formed in 1931 through merger of two formerly independent organizations, the International Kindergarten Union and the National Council of Primary Education. Its 15,000 members reside and work in each of the 50 states and in more than 70 countries.

The association has its headquarters in Washington, D.C. Services to members include two publications, each distributed five times a year: *Childhood Education,* a journal, and a newsletter. Numerous low-cost publications are also made available on a variety of subjects relating to early childhood education. The organization conducts an annual Study Conference that attracts a large number of participants.

Reference: Association for Childhood Education International, *Association for Childhood Education International,* Washington, DC: The Association, Undated Brochure.

ASSOCIATION FOR EDUCATIONAL COMMUNICATIONS AND TECHNOLOGY (AECT), a nonprofit professional association devoted to the interests of professionals involved with educational media and technology. Members are employed in a variety of settings including school systems, colleges and universities, libraries, museums, military establishments, businesses, and governmental agencies. Membership totals approximately 7,500.

AECT was established in 1923. Its principal function is instructional improvement with particular attention given to the professional development of members and improvement of the instructional tools they use.

Members are eligible to attend the organization's annual convention as well as workshops held before the convention. As part of their membership, they affiliate with one of AECT's eight divisions: (1) Information Systems; (2) Telecommunications; (3) Research and Theory; (4) Instructional Development; (5) International; (6) Industrial Training and Education; (7) Educational Media Management; and (8) Media Design and Production. Two monthly periodicals, *Instructional Innovator* and *ECT Newsletter,* are sent to each member. Two other periodicals/publications are available, both quarterlies. They are: the *Educational Communication and Technology Journal* and the *Journal of Instructional Development. Who's Who in the Media Field* (an annual) and numerous publications dealing with a variety of media topics are also published by AECT.

References: Association for Educational Communications and Technology, *AECT Changing the Shape of Instruction in the 80's,* Washington, DC: The Association, Undated Brochure; Association for Educational Communications and Technology, *AECT 1980–81 Publications,* Washington, DC: The Association, Undated Brochure.

ASSOCIATION FOR HUMANISTIC PSYCHOLOGY (AHP), founded in 1962, an organization composed of individuals interested in the humanistic development of the person, child, or adult. AHP is not made up exclusively of psychologists; many members are teachers, members of the clergy, social workers, or lay people.

AHP has developed regional organizations, or networks, as well as local groups. Its national headquarters is in San Francisco. A monthly newsletter and a quarterly, *Journal of Humanistic Psychology,* are published at national headquarters. From 1962 to 1969, the organization was called the American Association for Humanistic Psychology. It now has international affiliates, hence the name change. AHP sponsors many regional meetings and usually holds its national meeting in August of each year.

References: Denise S. Akey (Editor), *Encyclopedia of As-*

sociations (Fifteenth Edition), Detroit: Gale Research Company, 1980; George Leonard, "On AHP Membership," *Journal of Humanistic Psychology,* Winter 1981.

ASSOCIATION FOR INTERCOLLEGIATE ATHLETICS FOR WOMEN (AIAW),

a voluntary organization that serves as governing body for women's intercollegiate athletics in the United States. More than 900 institutions of higher education are members. Founded in 1971 as a unit within the National Association for Girls and Women in Sport of the American Alliance for Health, Physical Education, Recreation and Dance, AIAW established itself as a separate and independent organization in 1979. Institutional membership trebled in the decade following its founding.

The association administers a national championship program that comprises 39 national championships (6 open to all member institutions, 11 conducted within each of its three divisions). The 17 sports included in these championships are badminton, basketball, cross country, fencing, field hockey, golf, gymnastics, lacrosse, skiing, swimming and diving, synchronized swimming, fastpitch softball, slow-pitch softball, indoor track and field, outdoor track and field, tennis, and volleyball.

AIAW publications include the *AIAW Handbook,* the *National Championship Policy and Procedure Manual, AIAW Directory,* and *Regulations for Awarding Financial Aid to Student Athletes.* Numerous sports manuals have also been prepared by the association.

AIAW's headquarters office is in Washington, D.C.

References: National Championship Newsletter, Washington, DC: Association for Intercollegiate Athletics for Women, 1980; Untitled and Undated Fact Sheet, Washington, D.C.: Association for Intercollegiate Athletics for Women.

ASSOCIATION FOR LIBRARY AND INFORMATION SCIENCE EDUCATION (ALISE),

a professional organization composed of institutional and individual members dedicated to the advancement of education for the librarianship. The Association was formerly titled Association of American Library Schools. Institutions with library programs accredited by the ALA Committee on Accreditation may become institutional members. Programs not having ALA accreditation may become associate members. Individual membership is open to faculty, administrators, librarians, researchers and others. There are approximately 700 members in the Association. The Association publishes ALISE *Library and Information Science Education Statistical Report* and *Journal of Education for Library and Information Science.* State College, Pennsylvania, is the headquarters for ALISE. (See AMERICAN LIBRARY ASSOCIATION.)

Reference: Filomena Simora, *The Bowker Annual of Library and Book Trade Information* (32nd Edition), New York: R. R. Bowker Co., 1987.

ASSOCIATION FOR STUDENT TEACHING (AST),

a national organization of individuals who were interested in improving the quality of teacher education and had a particular interest in student teaching. AST was originally known as the National Association of Supervisors of Student Teaching. In 1970, its name was changed to Association of Teachers Educators (ATE). (See APPENDIX XII: PAST PRESIDENTS OF ASSOCIATION FOR STUDENT TEACHING (1921–69) AND ASSOCIATION OF TEACHER EDUCATORS (1970-PRESENT) and ASSOCIATION OF TEACHER EDUCATORS.)

Reference: Nancy Yakes and Denise Akey (Editors), *Encyclopedia of Associations* (Fourteenth Edition), Detroit: Gale Research Company, 1980.

ASSOCIATION FOR SUPERVISION AND CURRICULUM DEVELOPMENT (ASCD),

one of the largest professional education organizations in the United States. Classroom teachers, curriculum coordinators, supervisors, professors of education, and many other professionals involved in education make up its membership. Although a national organization (with headquarters in Washington, D.C.), ASCD has individual state units as well.

ASCD was founded in 1921 as the National Conference on Educational Methods. At one time, it was part of the National Education Association as the Department of Supervision and Curriculum Development.

Although the organization is interested in the improvement of education at all levels, its principal interest is in elementary and secondary education. ASCD publishes *Educational Leadership,* a professional journal, and a yearbook that usually focuses on a timely educational topic. It also publishes the newsletter, *News Exchange,* paperback booklets, monographs, videotapes, and other professional materials of interest to teachers and supervisors. (See APPENDIX XIII: PAST PRESIDENTS OF THE ASSOCIATION FOR SUPERVISION AND CURRICULUM DEVELOPMENT.)

References: Denise S. Akey (Editor), *Encyclopedia of Associations* (Fifteenth Edition), Detroit: Gale Research Company, 1980; Craig Colgate, Jr. and Patricia Broida, *National Trade and Professional Associations of the United States and Canada and Labor Unions* (Fifteenth Edition), Washington, DC: Columbia Books, Inc., Publishers, 1980.

ASSOCIATION FOR THE STUDY OF HIGHER EDUCATION (ASHE), a professional society that focuses on the study of higher education. The association stresses: (1) a broad scholarly study of higher education; (2) systematic inquiry; (3) the training and development of higher education researchers; and (4) the encouragement of graduate students' study of higher education. ASHE publishes the *Review of Higher Education, ASHE Notes* (a newsletter), and *Directory of ASHE Members and Higher Education Programs and Faculty* (biennial), and publishes with the ERIC Clearinghouse on Higher Education the series *ASHE-ERIC Higher Education Reports.* The association supports research by providing an Annual Research Achievement Award, Distinguished Dissertation Awards, a Committee on Graduate Student Activities, and a Committee on Curriculum, Learning, and Instruction. There is an 11-member Board of Directors, and its headquarters is located at Texas A&M University, College Station, Texas (although ASHE does have a small office in Washington, D.C.).

References: Association for the Study of Higher Education, *ASHE-ERIC Higher Education Reports, Complete Catalogue, 1981–86,* Washington, DC; The George Washington University, Undated; Association for the Study of Higher Education; *An Invitation to Membership; ASHE,* College Station, TX: The Association; Undated Brochure.

ASSOCIATION OF AMERICAN COLLEGES (AAC), an organization of postsecondary institutions that seeks to implement three principal purposes: "(1) to enhance and promote humane and liberating learning; (2) to strengthen member institutions as settings for humane and liberating learning; and (3) to extend the benefits of humane and liberating learning . . . through lifelong learning and continuing education" (*National Voice,* p. 1).

Membership in AAC is on an institutional basis and open to both public and private institutions of higher education. Individual colleges/schools within universities are also eligible for membership. Dues are variable, depending on enrollment size. A member institution's chief executive officer plus two other individuals chosen by him/her serve as institutional representatives.

AAC, whose national office is in Washington, D.C., serves its members in a variety of ways: (1) convening annual meetings; (2) sponsoring the National Fellows Program, which brings individuals from member institutions to AAC as staff members for 3–12 month periods; (3) presenting, annually, the Frederic W. Ness Award for the outstanding book contributing to liberal learning; and (4) publication of *Liberal Education,* a quarterly journal. Three AAC offices, which provide more specific types of assistance, are: (1) Office of Curriculum and Faculty Development; (2) Office of Institutional and Administrative Development; and, (3) Office of National Affairs. Member institutions may also receive special assistance with presidential searches, collective bargaining information, and the problem of improving the status of women in higher education.

References: Association of American Colleges, *AAC: The National Voice for Liberal Learning,* Washington, DC: The Association, 1979; Association of American Colleges, *National Fellows Program,* Washington, DC: The Association, Undated Brochure.

ASSOCIATION OF AMERICAN LIBRARY SCHOOLS—See ASSOCIATION FOR LIBRARY AND INFORMATION SCIENCE EDUCATION

ASSOCIATION OF AMERICAN PUBLISHERS, INC. (AAP), an organization consisting of approximately 350 publishing houses that serves as the major voice for the American publishing industry. Members' basic products include technical/scientific journals and books (hardcover and paperback) in the categories of school and college textbooks, general trade, reference, religious, technical, scientific, and medical. Some members produce maps, globes, charts, films and filmstrips, tapes, transparencies, and similar instructional materials.

General activities in which members have a common interest are referred to as "core activities." Standing committees give attention to "core" interests such as copyright, postal rates, freedom to read, and professional education for publishing. The organization's seven divisions (General Publishing Division; College Division; School Division; Technical, Scientific and Medical Division; Mass Paperback Division; Direct Marketing/Book Club Division; and International Division) elect their own chairpersons and pursue the specialized interests of division members.

AAP maintains offices in Washington, D.C., and New York. A full-time president serves as the organization's principal officer aided by an elected, 25-member board. AAP publishes both general and specialized reports as well as brochures of interest to the publishing industry.

References: Association of American Publishers, Inc., *An Introduction to Association of American Publishers, Inc.,* New York: The Association, Undated Booklet; Association of American Publishers, Inc., *1980 Publications List,* New York: The Association, 1980.

ASSOCIATION OF GOVERNING BOARDS OF UNIVERSITIES AND COLLEGES (AGB), a

nonprofit organization made up of governing, coordinating, and advisory boards of postsecondary education. AGB was founded in 1921 with membership limited to public university trustees. In 1964, membership was opened to members of both public and private governing boards.

Services provided to members and member institutions include conferences, workshops, and publications of interest to trustees. Regular publications include *AGB News Notes,* a monthly newsletter, and *AGB Reports,* a bimonthly journal. In addition, relatively inexpensive publications on a wide variety of governance-related subjects are produced. These are designed to fulfill the organization's principal objectives, including: (1) providing background information on critical issues; (2) achieving effective working relationships between trustees and administrators; and (3) improving interinstitutional understanding and communication.

AGB serves approximately 20,000 trustees and 1,300 colleges and universities. Its offices are in Washington, D.C.

References: Association of Governing Boards of Universities and Colleges, *AGB Statement of Purpose,* Washington, DC: The Association, 1980; Association of Governing Boards of Universities and Colleges, *AGB Members,* Washington, DC: The Association, 1979, Amended in 1980.

ASSOCIATION OF INDEPENDENT COLLEGES AND SCHOOLS (AICS), a national or-

ganization of private postsecondary institutions that are primarily engaged in the preparation of students for business careers. The AICS Accrediting Commission evaluates institutions that petition for accreditation. Petitioning schools/colleges must "be organized to train students . . . for business careers, have at least one residence program of instruction of not less than one academic year in length, and have been established for a period of at least two years" (p. 3). The Accrediting Commis-

sion, which is recognized as an official accrediting agency by the U.S. Department of Education, publishes an annual list of approved institutions. They are divided into three categories: (1) business schools; (2) junior colleges of business; and (3) senior colleges of business.

Over 500 institutions approved by AICS are presently operating in the continental United States, Guam, Puerto Rico, Costa Rica, and the Cayman Islands. AICS offices are in Washington, D.C.

Reference: The Accrediting Commission of the Association of Independent Colleges and Schools, *Directory of Institutions,* Washington, DC: The Association, 1980.

ASSOCIATION OF OVERSEAS EDUCATORS (AOE), a national organization of educators in-

terested in international education, serving foreign educators, and promoting world understanding. Organized in 1955, AOE also serves as a central organization for American educators who have had overseas educational experience as Fulbright-Hays teachers; Peace Corps teachers; Department of Defense, Department of Interior, and Department of State educators; consultants; and so on. Voting membership is available to Americans who have studied or worked abroad in some educational capacity. Institutional, associate, honorary, and student memberships are also available, the last three types not carrying the voting privilege.

AOE's national headquarters is at the American University, Washington, D.C.

Reference: Association of Overseas Educators, Inc., *Association of Overseas Educators, Inc.,* Washington, DC: The Association, Undated Brochure.

ASSOCIATION OF SCHOOL BUSINESS OFFICIALS OF THE UNITED STATES AND CANADA (ASBO), oldest and largest educational

management-oriented organization in North America. ASBO (the official abbreviation) was founded in 1910 as the National Association of School Accounting Officers. As it grew and its scope broadened, it underwent several name changes before assuming its present name in 1951.

ASBO's bylaws identify eight organizational objectives that include improving the performance of school business management personnel (20 specialties), promotion of research, and cooperation with other educational associations. Membership in the United States and Canada exceeds 5,000. Regular publications produced by ASBO include *School Business Affairs,* a monthly journal; its *Newsletter;*

and *Capitol Capsules*, a legislative bulletin. ASBO's central office is in Park Ridge, Illinois.

References: Association of School Business Officials of the United States and Canada, *School Business Affairs: Official Membership Directory*, Park Ridge, IL: The Association, 1979; George W. Grill and Wesley L. Brown, *ASBO—The First 50 Years: The Building of the School Business Management Profession*, Park Ridge, IL: The Association, 1960.

ASSOCIATION OF TEACHER EDUCATORS (ATE), founded in 1921, a national organization for individuals interested in, and concerned with, teaching and teacher education. In addition to the national structure, there are statewide ATE groups in most states. The organization's national headquarters is in Reston, Virginia. ATE was at one time known as the National Association of Supervisors of Student Teaching, later as the Association for Student Teaching (AST). It assumed its present name in 1970.

The organization holds an annual national meeting in February each year. It also conducts various summer workshops and miniclinics. ATE publishes newsletters, books and booklets, special reports, and monographs. Its major publication, *Action in Teacher Education*, is published quarterly. See APPENDIX XII: PAST PRESIDENTS OF ASSOCIATION FOR STUDENT TEACHING (1921-69) AND ASSOCIATION OF TEACHER EDUCATORS (1970–PRESENT); ASSOCIATION FOR STUDENT TEACHING.)

References: Denise S. Akey (Editor), *Encyclopedia of Associations* (Fifteenth Edition), Detroit: Gale Research Company, 1980; Craig Colgate, Jr. and Patricia Broida (Editors), *National Trade and Professional Associations of the United States and Canada and Labor Unions* (Fifteenth Edition), Washington, DC: Columbia Books, Inc., Publishers, 1980; *Quality Education Through Teacher Education*, Washington, DC: Association of Teacher Educators, Undated.

ASSOCIATIVE PROPERTY, a property, principle, or law used in the addition of natural numbers. The associative law, along with other similar laws, was reinstituted in the late 1950s with the advent of "modern arithmetic," primarily to enable elementary and secondary school children to conceptualize mathematics.

The associative property principle allows for the addition of three or more natural numbers. For example:

$$
\begin{array}{ll}
L & R \\
4 = a \quad (a + b) + c = a + (b + c) \\
6 = b \quad (4 + 6) + 10 = 4 + (6 + 10) \\
10 = c \quad 10 \;+\; 10 \;= 4 + 16 \\
\qquad\qquad 20 = 20
\end{array}
$$

Note that $(a + b)$ are associated on the L side of the sample equation and $(b + c)$ are associated on the R side. In either case, the sums of the associated numbers (those in parentheses) plus their respective remaining natural numbers equal each other. The associative property principle is used along with other mathematical properties in dealing with multiplication and other processes. For example, associative property explains the multiplication of several numbers: $(a \times b) \times c = a \times (b \times c)$. (See COMMUTATIVE PROPERTY and DISTRIBUTIVE PROPERTY.)

References: A. B. Evenson, *Modern Mathematics*, Chicago: Scott, Foresman and Company, 1962; William L. Schaaf, *Basic Concepts of Elementary Mathematics* (Third Edition), New York: John Wiley and Sons, 1969; C. W. Schminke, et al., *Teaching the Child Mathematics*, Hinsdale, IL: The Dryden Press, Inc., 1973.

ASSONANCE, the repetition of the same vowel sounds, although using different words. Assonance is sometimes used in puns, with similar sounding words being used but having different meanings.

The following is an example of assonance used in rhyming:

> "The Moon in June
> Shines on the Dune."

(See ALLITERATION.)

References: Joan I. Glazer and Gurney Williams III, *Introduction to Children's Literature*, New York: McGraw-Hill Book Company, 1979; Keith E. Nelson (Editor), *Children's Language* (Volume I), New York: Halsted Press, 1980; Robert B. Ruddell, *Reading-Language Instruction: Innovative Practices*, Englewood Cliffs, NJ: Prentice-Hall, Inc., 1974.

ASTIGMATISM, or blurred vision, an eye problem resulting from variations in the curvature of the cornea. This condition, a congenital one, keeps light rays from coming together in a clear and single focus. Symptoms include eyestrain and headaches. Common astigmatism can be corrected by special lenses that have been ground to neutralize the cornea's irregular curvature.

References: Edward Cotlier, "The Cornea" in Robert A. Moses (Editor), *Adler's Physiology of the Eye: Clinical Application* (Sixth Edition), St. Louis, MO: The C. V. Mosby Company, 1975; William H. Havener, *Synopsis of Ophthalmology* (Fifth Edition), St. Louis, MO: The C. V. Mosby Company, 1979; Harold Scheie and Daniel M. Albert, *Textbook of Ophthalmology* (Ninth Edition), Philadelphia: W. B. Saunders Company, 1977.

ASTP, *A*rmy *S*pecialized *T*raining *P*rogram, types of intensive training and education programs started by the U.S. Army during World War II. These college-level programs consisted of one or more 12-week terms. They included specialized training units in medicine, engineering, foreign languages, science, mathematics, and psychology. There were specific eligibility requirements for ASTP, as well as a prescribed procedure for placing qualified soldiers into a particular program (i.e. medicine, engineering). During its existence, ASTP offered 22 programs including aeronautical engineering, medicine, dentistry, veterinary medicine, personnel psychology, and languages (German, Italian, Japanese, Spanish, Russian and others).

ASTP had two levels: (1) *basic,* freshman-year college level to first half of sophomore year; and (2) *advanced,* second half sophomore to senior, and graduate level in some ASTP units. Many colleges and universities contracted with the United States government (Army, Navy, War Manpower Committee) for ASTP units.

References: Frederic D. Cheydleaur and Ethel A. Schenck, *From the ASTP Forward: Standardized Test Results in Foreign Languages at the University of Wisconsin, 1943–1949,* Madison, WI: Bulletin of the University of Wisconsin, 1950; *Essential Facts about the Army Specialized Training Program,* Washington, DC: U.S. Government Printing Office, 1943; "The Army Specialized Training Program," *Journal of the American Association of Collegiate Registrars,* July 1943.

ATAXIA, a type of cerebral palsy that results in inability to use and/or regulate muscles normally. Ataxia may occur in any area of the body. Often, it affects the muscles of the articulatory organs, causing articulation problems. Ataxia can cause impaired balance as well as lack of precision movement. Ataxia usually affects the quality of movement (i.e. the individual may have muscle movement facility but does not have normal control over the muscles). Movement may be clumsy, uncoordinated, unsteady; direction cannot be judged; or range cannot be judged. The cerebellum is the center for the coordination of movements in different parts of the central nervous system. Thus, ataxia can be attributed to the malfunction of the cerebellum.

References: Carlos Eyzaguirre and Salvatore J. Fidone, *Physiology of the Nervous System* (Second Edition), Chicago: Year Book Medical Publishers, Inc., 1975; Peter V. Karpovich and Wayne E. Sinning, *Physiology of Muscular Activity* (Seventh Edition), Philadelphia: W. B. Saunders Company, 1971; Lee Travis (Editor), *Handbook of Speech Pathology and Audiology,* Englewood Cliffs, NJ: Prentice-Hall, Inc., 1971.

ATHENIAN EDUCATION, a form of education introduced in the state of Athens during classical (Greek) times. Educational historians and physical educators consider it to be distinctive, because it was the first system of education concerned with the total (mental and physical) development of the individual. Athenian education, available to male students only, sought to prepare individuals whose attributes and abilities conformed to Athenian values. Specifically, the instructional program worked to develop men who possessed a strong ethical sense, knowledge, an appreciation of aesthetics, citizenship, loyalty (youths took the Athenian Oath), and physical prowess.

References: Carroll Atkinson and Eugene T. Maleska, *The Story of Education,* Philadelphia: Chilton Company—Book Division, 1962; Frederick A. G. Beck, *Greek Education,* London, England: Methuen and Company, Ltd., 1964; Wilham H. Freeman, *Physical Education in a Changing Society,* Boston: Houghton Mifflin Company, 1977.

ATHLETICS, organized and competitive sports of a vigorous nature that are carried out as one part of a total physical education program. Although athletic activities are conducted in high schools and colleges on an intramural basis, the term is most frequently used to denote sports activities that are interscholastic or intercollegiate. In recent years, women's athletics, aided by Title IX, have increased significantly in American secondary and postsecondary schools. (See TITLE IX.)

References: Charles A. Bucher, *Foundations of Physical Education* (Eighth Edition), St. Louis, MO: The C. V. Mosby Company, 1979; William H. Freeman, *Physical Education in a Changing Society,* Boston: Houghton Mifflin Company, 1977.

ATONY, lack of power under muscle contraction, the reduction of muscle tone or firmness, or the reduction of the natural elasticity of the muscular and fibrous tissue. Atony can lead to major problems including atrophy, fatigue, lack of control of muscles, and "back problems."

References: J. V. Basmajian, *Muscle Alive* (Fourth Edition), Baltimore, MD: The Williams and Wilkins Company, 1978; Peter V. Karpovich and Wayne E. Sinning, *Physiology of Muscular Activity* (Seventh Edition), Philadelphia: W. B. Saunders Company, 1971.

AT-RISK STUDENTS, those students in school, because of a variety of factors, who will not be able to make the transition to adulthood successfully. These students will either fail in school or be failed by the system. They may enter school unprepared for learning and formal education; their parent(s) may be indifferent to their educational, emotional or physical needs; they may be children of children (children of teenagers who are not prepared for parenting); they may have undiagnosed mental, emotional, or physical exceptionality that will interfere with learning; they may come from non-English-speaking families; they may suffer from racial/ethnic/gender/religious prejudice; they may come from impoverished homes and environments; or they may have a history of attending ineffective schools. These students will more often than not drop out of school before graduating, or they will leave school as functional illiterates. Because they will not benefit from the education provided them, they will become educationally disadvantaged.

Schools and communities have begun to recognize the plight of the at-risk student by establishing: early intervention programs (pre- and postnatal care, parenting education, and preschool programs), specialized curriculum, and the development of retention and reentry programs. Although urban areas will have a larger number of at-risk students, at-risk students may be found in suburban, rural, and affluent communities, too.

References: Committee for Economic Development, Research and Policy Committee, *Children in Need, Investment Strategies for the Educationally Disadvantaged*, New York: Committee for Economic Development, 1987; T.N. Kahl, "Students' Social Backgrounds" in Michael J. Dunkin (Editor), *The International Encyclopedia of Teaching and Teacher Education*, Oxford, England: Pergamon Press, 1987; Howard Rawlings, *The Evolving Reform Agenda*, Denver, CO: The Education Commission of the States, 1987.

ATROPHY, decrease in the size of, or the wasting away of muscles, usually through nonuse. Three major causes of atrophy are disease, malnutrition, and denervation. Atrophy may take several forms. *Malnutrition* usually causes a reduction in muscle fiber size and muscle fiber diameter. A general reduction in size of muscle fibers is caused through disease. *Denervation* causes small groups of fibers to decrease in size; degeneration of fiber structure also takes place.

References: J. V. Basmajian, *Muscle Alive* (Fourth Edition), Baltimore, MD: The Williams and Wilkins Company, 1978; George Kaldor and William J. Di Battista, *Aging in Muscle*, New York: Raven Press, 1978; Brian J. Sharkey, *Physiology of Fitness*, Champaign, IL: Human Kinetics Publishers, 1979.

ATTENDANCE AREA, also known as school attendance area, that geographical portion of a school district served by one school building. In districts with more than one school, it is not uncommon to find several, sometimes overlapping attendance areas, some serving elementary, others secondary students. The term *neighborhood school* is sometimes used as a synonym for attendance area. Recent court rulings requiring school districts to bring about racial balancing of students have brought about elimination or modification of the attendance area concept in numerous school districts. (See *BROWN v. BOARD OF EDUCATION OF TOPEKA* and RACIAL BALANCE.)

References: Commission on School District Reorganization, *School District Organization*, Washington, DC: American Association of School Administrators, 1958; Ralph B. Kimbrough and Michael Y. Nunnery, *Educational Administration: An Introduction*, New York: Macmillan Publishing Company, Inc., 1976.

ATTENDANCE REGISTER, or register of attendance, official record of student attendance maintained by the teacher, a document frequently used by states to determine how certain types of state aid are to be allocated. Registers indicate information such as: (1) names of all students, including entry and transfer dates; (2) days students were present, absent, tardy; and (3) personal information such as sex, date of birth, and home address of each student.

References: *Combined Glossary: Terms and Definitions from the Handbooks of the State Educational Records and Reports Series*, Washington, DC: National Center for Education Statistics, U.S. Department of Health, Education, and Welfare, 1974; Carter V. Good (Editor), *Dictionary of Education* (Third Edition), New York: McGraw-Hill Book Company, 1973.

ATTENDANCE, SCHOOL, a term indicating a student's physical presence at school. School officials take seriously the matter of pupils' attendance at school for at least two reasons. First, regularity of attendance is considered to be essential if effective learning is to take place. Second, pupil attendance (average daily attendance) data constitute the basis upon which states allocate financial aid to school districts. Low attendance rates translates into relatively lower dollar allocations.

Public schools currently average 180.0 school days a year. The average, in 1869–70, was 132.2 days; a century later (1971–72), it increased to 179.3 days. The schools are also enrolling larger ratios of children (5–17 years of age) than ever before. In 1870, only 55.0 percent of children in this age bracket were attending school. That figure has risen steadily since then: 70.0 percent in 1900,

90.0 percent in 1940, and now over 90.0 percent. Attendance rates of those enrolled have also been increasing: 82.0 percent in 1929–30, 90.0 percent in 1959–60, and 92.3 percent in 1975–76.

Student absenteeism varies from district to district. Nationally, approximately 8 percent of all students are absent on any given day. Considerably higher rates are being recorded in inner-city schools, with some individual urban schools reporting daily absentee rates of 30 to 40 percent.

Enforcement of attendance at school, Edith Abbott and Sophonisba Breckinridge pointed out, involves three types of action on the part of the school officials: (1) advising parents of their responsibility under the law; (2) appealing to the courts for assistance when parents wilfully refuse to perform this duty; and (3) enforcing discipline when parents are unable to have their children attend school regularly or to behave properly. (See AVERAGE DAILY ATTENDANCE and AVERAGE DAILY MEMBERSHIP.)

References: Edith Abbott and Sophonisba P. Breckinridge, *Truancy and Non-Attendance in the Chicago Schools,* New York: Arno Press and the New York Times, 1970; Chrissie Bamber, *Student and Teacher Absenteeism* (PDK Fastback 126), Bloomington, IN: The Phi Delta Kappa Educational Foundation, 1979; Mary A. Golladay, *The Condition of Education* (1976 Edition), Washington, DC: U.S. Government Printing Office, 1976; Paul L. Porwoll, *ERS Report: Student Absenteeism,* Arlington, VA: Educational Research Service, Inc., April 1978; National School Public Relations Association, *Suspensions and Expulsions: Current Trends in School Policies and Programs,* Arlington, VA: The Association, 1976.

ATTENTION DEFICIT DISORDER (ADD), a controversial diagnosis of an attention disorder in children. At one time the disorder was called Strauss Syndrome, Hyperactive Child Syndrome, Hyperkinetic Syndrome, or Minimal Brain Dysfunction (MBD). Initially it was believed that the syndrome was caused by damage to the brain. Presently it is felt that ADD is not always a function of brain damage. It is difficult to diagnose; no specific etiology has been found.

The American Psychiatric Association in their description of the diagnosis of attention deficit disorder (DSM-III criteria) provides for ADD with or without hyperactivity as well as an ADD, residual type. The residual type child once met the criteria with hyperactivity but no longer manifests hyperactivity. For the ADD with hyperactivity, the diagnostic criteria includes inattention, impulsivity, hyperactivity, occurs before age 7, lasts for at least six months, and is not due to schizophrenia, affec-

tive disorder, or severe or profound mental retardation. For ADD without hyperactivity, all of the criteria, except hyperactivity, hold. Younger children have more severe forms of ADD, while older children tend not to have such severe cases. Children between 8 and 10 years of age have the greatest number of incidents of ADD. Boys suffer more from the disorder than girls. (See MINIMAL BRAIN DYSFUNCTION).

References: American Psychiatric Assocation, *Diagnostic and Statistical Manual for Mental Disorders* (3rd edition), Washington, DC: The Association, 1980; Leon Oettenger, Jr. (Editor), *The Psychologist, the School, and the Child with MBD/LD,* New York: Grune and Stratton, Inc., 1978; Steven Schwartz and James H. Johnson, *Psychopathology of Childhood,* New York: Pergamon Press, 1985.

ATTENTION SPAN, the amount of time an individual concentrates on, or attends to, a particular activity. In recent years, attention research has focused on discrimination learning, neurophysiological factors, and information processing.

Attention spans can be influenced by many factors. Age is one. (Adults tend to have longer and better developed attention spans than do young children.) An individual's level of visual and auditory skill development is another. The ability to discriminate among stimuli, cues, and other psychological factors is also important in the development of attention spans. Motivation and interest are likewise important, as is individual mental ability.

Students who have certain types of psychological, physical, or learning problems frequently have relatively shorter attention spans, a fact that teachers must consider when planning and carrying out school activities.

References: W. K. Estes (Editor), *Attention and Memory,* Hillsdale, NJ: Lawrence Erlbaum Associates, Publishers, 1976; Paul G. Friedman, *Listening Processes: Attention, Understanding, Evaluation,* Washington, DC: National Education Association, 1978; Mercel Kinsbourne and Paula J. Caplan, *Children: Learning and Attention Problems,* Boston: Little, Brown and Company, 1979.

ATTENUATION, a term used in statistics to define the effects, due to errors of measurement, on the correlation of two measured variables. There are formulae available to "correct for attenuation." Included within the formulae are measures of reliability for the instruments (tests) used to assess each variable, as well as the coefficient of correlation calculated to determine the initial relationship between the two variables. The errors of measurement always suppress the coefficient of correlation; consequently, different conclusions may be produced when correlations are corrected for attenuation. With simple correlation, correcting for attenuation may not be important. However, when more complex correlations are used, correcting for attenuation is extremely important and should be done. This is particularly true when there are major differences between the reliabilities of the two measures. (See RELIABILITY.)

References: Joy Paul Guilford and B. Fruchter, *Fundamental Statistics in Psychology and Education* (Sixth Edition), New York: McGraw-Hill Book Company, 1977; Frederic M. Lord and M. R. Novick, *Statistical Theories of Mental Test Scores,* Reading, MA: Addison-Wesley Publishing Company, 1968.

ATTITUDE, a psychological construct or phenomenon that cannot be directly observed; rather, its existence is inferred. Although there is no set definition for attitude, there is considerable commonality among the various definitions that do exist in the literature. It is a predisposition to act, a state of readiness to act based on past experience, or a predisposition to act based on prior evaluations. It is *not* the act itself. Attitudes are learned; they are not innate. Attitudes are generally not transient; rather, they tend to be enduring and consistent. Attitudes consist of three elements: (1) emotions or affects; (2) cognition, beliefs, opinions; and (3) tendency to act.

The theoretical study of attitudes can include learning theory, behavioral theory, cognitive information processing, and component interaction. (See ATTITUDE SCALES.)

References: Lee Cronbach, *Educational Psychology* (Third Edition), New York: Harcourt Brace Jovanovich, Inc., 1977; William A. Mehrens and Irvin J. Lehmann, *Using Standardized Tests in Education,* New York: Longman, Inc., 1987; Jozef M. Nuttin, Jr., *The Illusion of Attitude Change,* New York: Academic Press, 1975; Ben Reich and Christin Adcock, *Values, Attitudes, and Behavior Change,* London, England: Methuen and Company, Ltd., 1976.

ATTITUDE SCALES, those measures that assess the feelings, negative or positive, of an individual toward some psychological object (e.g. a specific group, company policy). Usually, a total score is calculated that indicates the direction as well as the intensity of the attitude. One may, for example, have very strong positive or negative feelings about a particular nationality, racial group, or class of citizens.

Two major attitude scales are the Likert type and the Thurstone type. The *Likert-type scales* employ the following possible responses to a particular statement: strongly agree, agree, undecided, disagree, and strongly disagree. In a *Thurstone-type scale,* the respondent responds to those statements with which he/she agrees and does not respond to those with which he/she disagrees. In both scales, a total score is derived that is used to evaluate or assess the individual respondent's level of feeling. (See ATTITUDE.)

References: Anne Anastasi, *Psychological Testing* (Sixth Edition), New York: Macmillan Publishing Company, Inc., 1988; Allen L. Edwards, *Techniques of Attitude Scale Construction,* New York: Irvington Press, 1979; Tom Kubiszyn and Gary Borich, *Educational Testing and Measurement: Classroom Application and Practice* (Second Edition), Glenview, IL: Scott Foresman and Company, 1987; William A. Mehrens and Irvin J. Lehmann, *Using Standardized Tests in Education,* New York: Longman, Inc., 1987.

AUDING, hearing acts involving the human auditory system. Auding itself is responding to a feature or a set of events within the audible world. It includes the acoustic quality of pitch and loudness of sinusoidal waveforms, as well as taking the waves and turning them into electric impulses to be decoded by the brain. The elements of auding are hearing, listening, communication, and comprehension.

The auditory system in humans includes the external ear (acts as a megaphone), the middle ear (transmits energy from sound vibrations), and the inner ear (nerve fibers run to the base of the brain). (See AUDIOMETRY.)

References: A. V. Baru and T. A. Karaseva, *The Brain and Hearing: Hearing Disturbances Associated with Local Brain Lesions,* New York: Consultants Bureau, 1972; Thomas G. Giolas and Kenneth Randolph, *Basic Audiometry,* Lincoln, NE: Cliffs Notes, Inc., 1977; William Noble, *Assessment of Impaired Hearing,* New York: Academic Press, 1978.

AUDIOGRAM, a visual representation, on a graph, of the findings of a hearing (audiometric) test. Audiograms are constructed such that the vertical (ordinate) points are calibrated in dB-intensity (decibels) and the horizontal (abscissa) points are calibrated in Hertz-frequency. It is important that the scales used in the audiometric test are known, as the scales used in older tests were calibrated in dB's based on the ASA-1951 scale, while the newer tests use either the ANSI-1969 or ISO-1964 scales. When checking hearing changes, it is important that either the same scales be used or that the scales

Example of an Audiogram

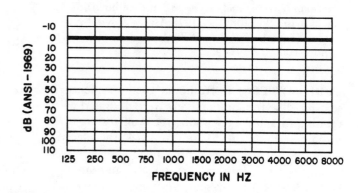

be assessed using the same zero reference level through appropriate conversions to the newer scales. Various symbols are used on an audiogram. Examples are: O, X, Δ, □, <, >.

An example of an audiogram ready to be completed appears above.
(See AUDIOMETERS and AUDIOMETRY.)

References: Jack Katz, *Handbook of Clinical Audiology* (Second Edition), Baltimore, MD: The Williams and Wilkins Company, 1978; Hayes A. Newby, *Audiology* (Fourth Edition), Englewood Cliffs, NJ: Prentice-Hall, Inc., 1979.

AUDIOLOGIST, a professional trained in the field of audiology and concerned with hearing as related to the daily communication demands faced by individuals. The audiologist does not treat individuals medically or surgically; the otologist does this. Two classifications of audiologists have developed in recent years: (1) the educational audiologist, and (2) the hearing clinician.

The *educational audiologist* specializes in the learning problems of children and works closely (usually in the schools) with parents, teachers, and administrators. The educational audiologist administers audiometric tests, diagnoses hearing loss, plans appropriate programs for the hearing impaired, counsels children and parents, conducts hearing conservation classes and programs, and studies the acoustical and amplification needs of a school.

The *hearing clinician* works with individuals of all ages in different settings. In the schools, the hearing clinician tests children, prepares diagnoses, and provides direct individualized therapy (speech and language development, auditory training, speech-

reading). Some hearing clinicians are employed by industry to work with industrial physicians, otologists, and other professionals to evaluate noise and hearing levels and to set up conservation-of-hearing programs related to coping with communications for the individual. (See AUDIOLOGY and OTOLOGIST.)

References: Hallowell Davis and S. Richard Silverman, *Hearing and Deafness* (Fourth Edition), New York: Holt, Rinehart and Winston, Inc., 1978; Jack Katz, *Handbook of Clinical Audiology* (Second Edition), Baltimore, MD: The Williams and Wilkins Company, 1978; Joseph Statloff, *Industrial Deafness,* New York: McGraw-Hill Book Company, 1957.

AUDIOLOGY, the science of hearing. Audiology is a broad field that includes medicine, psychology, electronics, sociology, physics and acoustics, and education as related to hearing. A major contribution of audiology has been the development of various hearing tests to identify hearing impairment. These tests have assisted neurologists and otologists in identifying individuals with hearing problems. Another major contribution of audiology has been the development of nonmedical rehabilitation programs for those with hearing problems.

Audiology courses/programs are usually offered by colleges of education or departments of speech, special education, and psychology. Departments of otolaryngology in schools of medicine may offer such courses as well. Audiology as a profession developed during World War II when the fields of speech pathology and otology were combined in the aural rehabilitation centers created by the United States military. (See OTOLOGIST.)

References: Jerome G. Alpiner, *Handbook of Adult Rehabilitative Audiology*, Baltimore, MD: The Williams and Wilkins Company, 1978; Hallowell Davis and S. Richard Silverman, *Hearing and Deafness* (Fourth Edition), Holt, Rinehart and Winston, Inc., 1978; Hayes A. Newby, *Audiology* (Fourth Edition), Englewood Cliffs, NJ: Prentice-Hall, Inc., 1979.

AUDIOMETERS, instruments used to measure hearing. The first audiometers were designed with a tuning fork and a telephone receiver (tuning fork audiometers) as their base. In 1914, the electric generator replaced the tuning fork. This was followed, in 1921, by the vacuum tube audiometer. From 1940 to the present, audiometers have become extremely sophisticated and are currently being developed for use with analog computers.

Puretone audiometry is assessed using instruments that measure air conduction and bone conduction. *Speech audiometry* is assessed by instruments designed to measure speech reception threshold (SRT) and speech discrimination. Audiometers range in size (depending on their purpose) from a small portable unit to a two-room audiological test suite. Many are designed to be used with both puretone and speech audiometry. (See AUDIOMETRY and SPEECH DISCRIMINATION SCORE.)

References: Thomas G. Giolas and Kenneth Randolph, *Basic Audiometry*, Lincoln, NE: Cliffs Notes, Inc., 1977; Aram Glorig (Editor), *Audiometry: Principles and Practices*, Baltimore, MD: The Williams and Wilkins Company, 1965.

AUDIOMETRY, the testing of hearing. There are many tests used to determine the cause of hearing loss as well as the degree of such loss. These range from voice, watch, and noisemaking tests to tuning forks (Weber's Tests, Rinne's Test, Schwabach's Test) as well as electronic instruments that can provide controlled sound intensity (air conduction, bone conduction, speech circuits, masking circuits, tone interrupter, pulsed tones, short-increment sensitivity ability).

Several examples of audiometric tests are: Lombard, Stenger, Doerfler-Stewart, Delayed-Feedback, Bekesy, and the psychogalvanic skin-resistance tests. These measure various functional hearing losses. (See AUDIOMETERS.)

References: Aram Glorig (Editor), *Audiometry: Principles and Practices*, Baltimore, MD: The Williams and Wilkins Company, 1965; William Noble, *Assessment of Impaired Hearing*, New York: Academic Press, 1978.

AUDIO-TUTORIAL INSTRUCTION, an instructional method, developed in the 1960s by botanist S. N. Postlethwait, that includes audiotapes prepared by the teacher. These tapes do not contain lectures per se; instead, they serve to direct individual students through a series of activities such as making observations, reading material in the library, conducting experiments, watching movies, and so on.

The overall course developed by Postlethwait consists of three elements: (1) the independent study session; (2) the general assembly session; and (3) the small assembly session. The *independent study* component is unscheduled. Here the student works alone using the tapes and does so at times chosen by him/her. Activities are pursued that have been prepared and presented in some sequential pattern by the instructor. In the *general assembly session,* all students are brought together periodically, more to get to know the person whose voice they hear on tape than to hear lectures. These sessions are used to give instructions, to provide orientation, and so on. In the *small assembly session,* small groups of students (eight to ten) meet to test each other and are called upon to deliver short, spontaneous lectures on topics chosen for them.

References: Robert B. Kozma, et al., *Instructional Techniques in Higher Education*, Englewood Cliffs, NJ: Educational Technology Publications, 1978; S. N. Postlethwait, et al., *The Audio-Tutorial Approach to Learning: Through Independent Study and Integrated Experiences* (Second Edition), Minneapolis, MN: Burgess Publishing Company, 1969.

AUDIT, CLASS, an option available to college students in which they register for, and attend, a class under special conditions. Auditing allows students to explore new areas of learning and to reinforce/improve upon external areas of interest or concern without the pressures and obligations of a regular class. Students who audit are usually not held responsible for class assignments and do not take tests. Auditors may participate in all other activities of the class. They do not receive a grade or academic credit, but the course is usually listed on their transcripts as an audited course. Generally, students who have audited a course cannot later take the course for credit. Some institutions charge reduced rates for audited courses. Permission of either the professor, advisor, dean, or other institutional official may be required before an individual can audit a course.

Reference: Asa S. Knowles (Editor), *The International Encyclopedia of Higher Education (Volume 1), San Francisco: Jossey-Bass Publishers, 1977.

AUDITING, an accounting procedure conducted for the purpose of verifying that a school district's or institution's business transactions were properly authorized and carried out in accordance with law. The procedure is a systematic one that is conducted on a regular basis (usually annual). Audits, Percy Burrup pointed out, are of three types: (1) *internal audits,* an ongoing monitoring procedure carried out by qualified personnel in the employ of the district or institution; (2) *state audits* that, if required by law, may be conducted on a regular basis (e.g. every three or four years); and (3) *external audits,* reviews carried out by qualified, outside individuals/agencies (normally certified public accountants), usually annually.

Auditing involves a comprehensive review of records and transactions. At the close of some audits (e.g. state, external), the professional auditors tender a written report of findings that may include both summaries of findings and recommendations for improvement of business practices.
References: Percy E. Burrup, *Financing Education in a Climate of Change* (Second Edition), Boston: Allyn and Bacon, Inc., 1977; John Greenhalgh, *Practitioner's Guide to School Business Management,* Boston: Allyn and Bacon, Inc., 1978; Stephen J. Knezevich and John G. Fowlkes, *Business Management of Local School Systems,* New York: Harper and Row, Publishers, 1960.

AUDITORY APHASIA—See APHASIA

AUDITORY DISCRIMINATION, the ability to detect speech sounds (identifying and sorting out consonant and vowel sounds). Not only should the individual be able to hear sounds, but she/he should be able to hear the differences among the intensity characteristics as well. This involves: specific sounds (words, syllables, nonsyllables, etc.), competing sounds, sounds of varying frequency, and varying pressure pattern consonants. Children with poor auditory discrimination will most likely have difficulty with language development as well as with articulation. These problems may lead to learning difficulties in school.

There are many auditory discrimination tests available. Several such tests are: Wepman Auditory Discrimination Test (three–five year age range); Buktenics Test of Nonverbal Auditory Discrimination (six–eight years); Kimmell and Wahl Screening Test for Auditory Perception (grades 2–6); Goldman-Fristoe-Woodcock Test of Auditory Dis-

crimination (three-year, eight-month–adult); The Pritchard-Fox Phoneme Auditory Discrimination Test (K and over); and the Lindamood Auditory Conceptualization Test (all ages). (See SPEECH-DISCRIMINATION SCORE.)
References: Oscar K. Buros (Editor), *The Seventh Mental Measurements Yearbook* (Volume II), Highland Park, NJ: The Gryphon Press, 1972; Emerald Dechant, *Diagnosis and Remediation of Reading Disability,* West Nyack, NY: Parker Publishing Company, Inc., 1968; John F. Savage and Jean F. Mooney, *Teaching Reading to Children with Special Needs,* Boston: Allyn and Bacon, Inc., 1979.

AUDITORY MEMORY SPAN, the length of time auditory or verbally presented materials are retained in memory. Memory span can be classified as being: (1) *immediate* (lasting a few seconds); *short term* (of intermediate duration); and *long term* (lasting for hours, days, or even years). It has been found that sensory memory of verbally presented materials, in the short run, tends to be more effective than the sensory memory of visually presented materials.

Auditory memory span is important in the classroom and is directly related to achievement. Techniques are available that will enhance and expand the auditory memory span. These include sound action (making up actions to go with the sound); mnemonics; silly sentences; oral drills; and games of all sorts. (See MNEMONIC DEVICE.)
References: Polly Behrmann, *Activities for Developing Auditory Perception,* San Rafael, CA: Academic Therapy Publications, 1975; Rita B. Eisenberg, *Auditory Competence in Early Life,* Baltimore, MD: University Park Press, 1976; Neil O'Connor and B. Hermelin, *Seeing and Hearing and Space and Time,* London, England: Academic Press, 1978.

AUDITORY TRAINERS—See ELECTRONIC AMPLIFICATION

AUDITORY TRAINING, a program designed to aid the hearing impaired to use what little hearing they do have. (Most individuals who are classified as deaf do have some residual hearing.) Before World War II, auditory training took place in schools for the deaf and focused on gross sounds. During World War II, auditory training evolved into a rehabilitation program to enable individuals to maximize residual hearing and to live normal, productive lives.

Auditory training usually centers around the use of an amplification aid. Thus, an individual receives training in how to wear and use such a device most effectively. The individual's speech-discrimination ability is assessed in order to prescribe the appropriate amplification aid. Individuals are also taught how to listen. Auditory training may include classes in speech reading and speech conservation as well as psychological counseling. Speechreading is the major focus of auditory training programs for individuals who are hearing impaired but for whom an amplification device is of little or no help. (See ELECTRONIC AMPLIFICATION).

References: Jack Katz, *Handbook of Clinical Audiology,* Baltimore, MD: The Williams and Wilkins Company, 1972; Hayes A. Newby, *Audiology* (Fourth Edition), Englewood Cliffs, NJ: Prentice-Hall, Inc., 1979.

AUGMENTED ROMAN ALPHABET—See INITIAL TEACHING ALPHABET

AURAL LEARNING, learning by means of listening. An individual is learning when he/she listens to verbal symbols with understanding (comprehension) and/or demonstrates an intent to learn from such symbols. Aural learning is the primary mode in oral language development in young children; it is also a major factor in reading readiness programs. In later life, a great deal of learning and skill development is acquired through aural learning.

School programs stress listening skills to promote aural learning. Language arts authorities note that there are many types of listening such as listening: (1) in social-situational cases; (2) for enjoyment; (3) critically; (4) very intently for understanding; and (5) for the acquisition of knowledge. (See AUDING.)

References: Nicholas Anastasiow, *Oral Language: Expression of Thought* (Updated Edition), Newark, DE: International Reading Association, 1979; Paul S. Anderson and Diane Lapp, *Language Skills in Elementary Education,* New York: Macmillan Publishing Company, Inc., 1979; Sidney Tiedt and Iris Tiedt, *Language Arts Activities for the Classroom,* Boston: Allyn and Bacon, Inc., 1978.

AURAL-ORAL APPROACH, or oralism, a multisensory method for teaching language and communication to the hearing impaired. This method makes use of whatever residual hearing the learner may have (aural) and supplements it with oral communication techniques such as speechreading, signing, and printing. (See TOTAL COMMUNICATION.)

References: James A. Pahz, et al., *Total Communication: The Meaning Behind the Movement to Expand Educational Opportunities for Deaf Children,* Springfield, IL: Charles C. Thomas, Publisher, 1978; Alice H. Streng, et al., *Lan-* *guage, Learning, and Deafness: Theory, Application, and Classroom Management,* New York: Grune and Stratton, 1978.

AUSTRALIAN TEACHERS' FEDERATION (ATF), a national organization of over 130,000 Australian teachers. ATF's principal aims are: (1) to provide cooperative activities for the professional benefit of its several affiliate organizations, and (2) to promote quality education (including funding increases from the federal government). The organization has eight affiliates: (1) Australian Capital Territory Teachers' Federation; (2) New South Wales Teachers' Federation; (3) Northern Territory Teachers' Federation; (4) Queensland Teachers' Union; (5) State School Teachers Union of Western Australia, Inc.; (6) Technical Teachers' Association of Victoria; (7) Victorian Secondary Teachers' Association; and (8) Victorian Teachers' Union. In addition, it has linkages with the South Australian Institute of Teachers and the Tasmanian Teachers' Federation.

ATF conducts an annual conference. An executive body consisting of the ATF president and the presidents (or presidents-elect) of the eight affiliated units meets five times a year to transact routine business and to consider items of importance to the organization. A general secretary, a research officer, and an assistant secretary constitute ATF's full-time secretariat. These staff members, headquartered in Canberra City, carry out ATF's day-to-day work. (See WORLD CONFEDERATION OF ORGANIZATIONS OF THE TEACHING PROFESSION.)

Reference: David Widdup, "Australian Teachers' Federation" (Unpublished Fact Sheet), Canberra City, Australia: Australian Teachers' Federation, 1980.

AUTHORITY, institutionalized power, specifically the capacity to move individuals in an organization toward realization of organizational goals. Authority is vested in an organization's leadership; in relatively large organizations, it is delegated to and shared with subordinates. Differences in organizational behavior normally take place as leaders (including school administrators) move from one role high in authority to another.

Subordinates respond to authority because those in supervisory positions hold positions with which power is associated.

John French and Bertram Raven identified five bases of social power: (1) *legitimate power,* reflecting the belief that a leader has the right, on the basis of his/her position, to make requests; (2) *expert power,* predicated on the assumption that the administrator is experienced and competent; (3) *referent power,* based on personal respect for the leader; (4) *reward power,* reflecting the belief that the superior can and will reward compliance; and (5) *coercive power,* reflecting the belief that a leader can and will punish noncompliance.

References: John R. P. French, Jr. and Bertram Raven, "The Bases of Social Power" in Patrick E. Connor (Editor), *Dimensions in Modern Management* (Second Edition), Boston: Houghton Mifflin Company, 1978; Daniel E. Griffiths, *Human Relations in School Administration,* New York: Appleton-Century-Crofts, Inc., 1956; Donald E. Orlosky, et al., *Educational Administration Today,* Columbus, OH: Charles E. Merrill Publishing Company, 1984; Thomas J. Sergiovanni and Fred D. Carver, *The New School Executive: A Theory of Administration* (Second Edition), New York: Harper and Row, Publishers, 1980.

AUTISM, one of several childhood disorders in which a child exhibits extreme withdrawal within himself/herself and has problems with all kinds of language. The causes of autism have not yet been isolated.

Autism manifests itself before the age of two or three; in most cases, it begins at birth. Some autistic babies scream a lot while others may be very placid and reserved. Autism can be identified from ages two to five, when children show aloofness, disinterest in the outside world, and have an unusual interest in a particular object. Autistic children respond to only certain sounds and have extreme difficulties with speech, talking, gestures, and voice. They also have problems with body movements and skill development. Autistic children are extremely aloof and withdraw from social situations. They also resist changes, have unusual fears (of harmless objects and not necessarily of objects that can hurt them), and lack knowledge of social conventions. They never lie. Autistic children cannot play with other children.

Autism requires the combined intervention efforts of doctors, teachers, parents, and brothers and sisters in special educational programs and therapy. Such intervention may not cure the problem, but it can help the autistic child to reduce the effects of the handicap.

References: Michael Fordham, *The Self and Autism,* London, England: William Heinemann Medical Books, Ltd., 1976; Eric Schopler and Robert J. Reichler (Editors), *Psychopathology and Child Development,* New York: Plenum Press, 1976; Lorna Wing, *Autistic Children,* New York: Brunner/Mazel, Inc., 1972; Lorna Wing (Editor), *Early Childhood Autism* (Second Edition), Oxford, England: Pergamon, 1976.

AUTOCRATIC LEADERSHIP, a style of leader behavior often contrasted with the more widely supported *democratic* style of administration and the *laissez-faire* leadership style. Leaders exhibiting autocratic behavior are characterized as individuals who establish plans and policies for the group they lead and who are not inclined to delegate. Albert Shuster and Don Stewart cited these additional manifestations of behavior: (1) little or no participation by staff in the decision-making process; (2) feelings and problems of the staff are either unknown or disregarded; (3) the group's social climate is ignored; and (4) orders are handed down and understandings disregarded. Ralph Stogdill's summary of research on democratic and autocratic leadership behavior concluded with the observation that productivity cannot be associated with either style. However, group members, when surveyed, report greater satisfaction with democratic leadership, particularly when group size is small. Conversely, he concluded, "members are better satisfied with autocratic leadership in large, task-oriented groups" (p. 370). (See DEMOCRATIC-AUTOCRATIC LEADERSHIP STYLES and DEMOCRATIC LEADERSHIP.)

References: E. Mark Hanson, *Educational Administration and Organizational Behavior,* Boston: Allyn and Bacon, Inc., 1979; Donald E. Orlosky, et al., *Educational Administration Today,* Columbus, OH: Charles E. Merrill Publishing Company, 1984; Albert H. Shuster and Don H. Stewart, *The Principal and the Autonomous Elementary School,* Columbus, OH: Charles E. Merrill Publishing Company, 1973; Charles L. Wood, Everett W. Nicholson, and Dale G. Findley, *The Secondary School Principal: Manager and Supervisor* (Second Edition), Boston: Allyn and Bacon, Inc., 1985.

AUTOMATED SPEECH, the synthesis of speech through machines. The battery operated artificial larynx, an electronic device that helps individuals who have had a laryngectomy, is one example of automated speech. Machines that speak are not a new interest; in 1779, a machine was developed that imitated the vowels *a, e, i, o, u.*

With the continued development and sophistication of computers, automatic voice readout devices attached to computers are being planned. When perfected, these will permit humans to listen to the computer rather than having to read printouts. This new development will create greater flexibility in the transmission of information. The digital coding of speech will enable humans to "converse" orally with the computer and vice versa. Continued research in this field will not only expand the entire field of communication but will provide sorely needed aid to the blind, the deaf, and those with speech disorders.

References: Gunner Fant (Editor), *Speech Communication, Speech Production and Synthesis by Rules* (Volumes 1, 2), New York: John Wiley and Sons, 1975; James L. Flanagan and Lawrence R. Rabiner, *Speech Synthesis,* Stroudsburg, PA: Dowden, Hutchinson and Ross, Inc., 1973; Allen Newell, et al., *Speech Understanding Systems,* Amsterdam, Holland: North-Holland Publishing, 1973; D. Raj Reddy, *Speech Recognition,* New York: Academic Press, 1975.

AUTOMATICITY, the development of automatic actions leading to the completion of a given task. The task, or skill, has achieved the level of automaticity when the individual performing it is no longer required to give that action conscious attention. In addition, she/he is able to do a very different process simultaneously. Most adults have reached a level of automaticity with walking. In fact, thinking of the subskills involved in the walking task could result in a loss of walking efficiency. This same concept can be illustrated with the process of reading. Attention to individual letters or sounds would negatively influence reading for understanding. The actual process of reading must reach a level of automaticity in order to allow the reader to devote conscious attention to ideas. Schools are responsible for developing automaticity in the basic skills necessary for more complicated learning.

References: Benjamin S. Bloom, "Automaticity: The Hands and Feet of Genius," *Educational Leadership,* Vol. 43, No. 5, February 1986; David LaBerge, "Unitization and Automaticity in Perception," *Nebraska Symposium on Motivation,* Vol. 92, 1980; S. Jay Samuel, "Some Essentials of Decoding," *Exceptional Education Quarterly,* Vol. 2, May 1984; Richard M. Shiffrin and Susan T. Dumais, "The Development of Automatism" in John R. Anderson (Editor), *Cognitive Skills and Their Acquisition,* Hillsdale, NJ: Lawrence Erlbaum Associates, 1981.

AUXILIARY PERSONNEL, staff members, professionals, as well as nonprofessionals, who render services that support or otherwise enhance an instructional program. Examples of auxiliary personnel working in the service of school districts are psychologists, speech therapists, audiologists, teacher aides, and cafeteria personnel. Some authorities (e.g. Carter Good) view the term *auxiliary personnel* more narrowly, limiting it to teacher assistants such as aides or paraprofessionals.

References: Carter V. Good (Editor), *Dictionary of Education* (Third Edition), New York: McGraw-Hill Book Company, 1973; Albert H. Shuster and Don H. Stewart, *The Principal and the Autonomous Elementary School,* Columbus, OH: Charles E. Merrill Publishing Company, 1973.

AUXILIARY SERVICES, in education, the support services provided by specialized personnel, certified and noncertified, for the purpose of enhancing the instructional program. Some auxiliary services are less directly related to instruction than others but are offered nevertheless for varying reasons (e.g. taxpayer request, state law).

Examples of auxiliary services provided by noncertified personnel are cafeteria services, transportation services, and custodial services. Illustrating auxiliary services normally rendered by certified personnel are health services, library services, social work, and speech therapy, along with instruction of a specialized nature taught by resource teachers (e.g. elementary school music, art, and physical education). (See AUXILIARY PERSONNEL.)

References: Oscar T. Jarvis, et al., *Public School Business Administration and Finance: Effective Policies and Practices,* West Nyack, NY: Parker Publishing Company, Inc., 1967; Lloyd E. McCleary and Stephen P. Hencley, *Secondary School Administration: Theoretical Bases of Professional Practice,* New York: Dodd, Mead and Company, 1965; Albert H. Shuster and Don H. Stewart, *The Principal and the Autonomous Elementary School,* Columbus, OH: Charles E. Merrill Publishing Company, 1973.

AVERAGE—See MEAN

AVERAGE DAILY ATTENDANCE, or ADA, an enrollment figure used for reporting district size. ADA is sometimes used to determine the amount of financial aid to be apportioned to a school district. The formula for determining ADA is:

$$\text{ADA} = \frac{\text{Total student days in attendance} \times 100}{\text{Total student days enrolled}}$$

Registers of attendance, maintained daily by classroom teachers, provide the preliminary data needed to compute a district's ADA. (See ATTENDANCE REGISTER; AVERAGE DAILY MEMBERSHIP; and FOUNDATION PROGRAMS.)

References: John E. Corbally, Jr., *School Finance,* Boston: Allyn and Bacon, Inc., 1962; Thomas J. Landers and Judith G. Myers, *Essentials of School Management,* Philadelphia: W. B. Saunders Company, 1977.

AVERAGE DAILY MEMBERSHIP, or ADM, a measure used to determine school district size. ADM is the measurement unit frequently employed when financial allocations are made to local school systems. Unlike average daily attendance (ADA), which reports the average number of students attending school each day, ADM indicates the number of students for whom physical accommodations need to be available. The formula for determining average daily membership is:

$$\text{ADM} = \frac{\text{Sum of the number of children present and number of children absent each day}}{\text{Number of days in the school year}}$$

(See AVERAGE DAILY ATTENDANCE and FOUNDATION PROGRAMS.)
References: Combined Glossary: Terms and Definitions from the Handbooks of the State Educational Records and Reports Series, Washington, DC: National Center for Education Statistics, U.S. Department of Health, Education, and Welfare, 1974; John E. Corbally, Jr., *School Finance,* Boston: Allyn and Bacon, Inc., 1962.

AXIOLOGY, in philosophy, the study of values. It is one of several major fields into which the study of philosophy has been divided. Others are: *ontology,* the study of what is real; *epistemology,* which is concerned with knowledge; and *logic,* or correct reasoning.

Axiology, itself, is further divided into two parts: (1) *ethics* (What is right conduct?), the study of values in the context of human behavior; and (2) *aesthetics* (What is beautiful?), a study that examines values in the context of beauty. (See EPISTEMOLOGY; LOGIC; and ONTOLOGY.)
References: George Kneller, *Introduction to the Philosophy of Education* (Second Edition), New York: John Wiley and Sons, 1971; Charles D. Marler, *Philosophy and Schooling,* Boston: Allyn and Bacon, Inc., 1975; Van Cleve Morris, *Philosophy and the American School,* Boston: Houghton Mifflin Company, 1961.

AXTELLE, GEORGE E. (November 28, 1893–August 1, 1974), educator and teacher of educational philosophy who won prominence as a pragmatic humanist philosopher, as an interpreter of John Dewey, and as an active civil libertarian. Axtelle helped to found the American Federation of Teachers. He coauthored *The Improvement of Practical Intelligence* (1940) and coedited *Teachers for Democracy* (1940), the fourth yearbook of the John Dewey Society.

Axtelle's preprofessorship experience included service as a public school administrator in Oregon (1920–24), Hawaii (1924–30), and California (1930–35). He earned his Ph.D. in 1935 from the University of California whereupon he began teaching educational philosophy at Northwestern University (where he remained until 1942). During World War II, he worked as a labor relations expert for the War Production Board (1942–45) and as Director of Employee Relations for the Office of Price Administration (1945–46). He served on the New York University faculty (1946–59) as Professor and Chairman of the Department of History and Philosophy. Following his retirement from NYU, he taught at Southern Illinois University (1959–68), where he developed The Center for Dewey Studies, and at United States International University (1968–74). During his career, Axtelle was a Fulbright Lecturer (Egypt). He also held the presidencies of the Philosophy of Education Society (1950) and the John Dewey Society (1961–63).
References: "Axtelle, Prof. George Edward," *Directory of American Scholars: A Biographical Directory* (Volume IV, Fourth Edition), New York: R. R. Bowker Company, 1964; Richard B. Morland, "Axtelle, George Edward" in John F. Ohles (Editor), *Biographical Dictionary of American Educators* (Volume 1), Westport, CT: Greenwood Press, 1978.

AZT—See ACQUIRED IMMUNE DEFICIENCY SYNDROME

BABBLING, a stage in speech development in which the infant utters and repeats monosyllabic sounds having no meaning. Early babbling is usually observed in the child's third or fourth month. An auditory feedback loop, sometimes referred to as the circular-reflex stage of repetition, is noted involving the baby's mouth and ears. The loop refers to related sensations experienced by the infant as sounds are uttered and then heard.

Early babbling sounds take the form of cooing and gurgling. Sound characteristics become different once the infant learns to sit up. In later months, another person may repeat the child's babbling sounds with the child repeating them in echolike fashion.

Lois Bloom and Margaret Lahey noted that research on babbling has taken two directions. One group of studies has attempted to relate babbling to later speech; other, and more recent, investigations have focused on vocalization alone, predicated on the belief that no exact relationship exists between babbling and later speech sounds. (See BABY TALK.)

References: Lois Bloom and Margaret Lahey, *Language Development and Language Disorders,* New York: John Wiley and Sons, 1978; Robert B. Johnston and Phyllis R. Magreb, *Developmental Disorders: Assessment, Treatment, Education,* Baltimore, MD: University Park Press, 1976.

BABY BOOM, a term referring to the relatively dramatic increase in the U.S. birth rate recorded during the 1940s and 1950s. Attributed, at least in part, to the prosperity experienced during and immediately following World War II, coupled with delayed marriages, the baby boom resulted in a significant increase in American school enrollments during these two decades and the early 1960s. The magnitude of the baby boom can be inferred from census data. These data show that the U.S. birth rate was 18.7 per 1,000 in 1935, 20.4 per 1,000 in 1945, and 25.0 per 1,000 in 1955. By 1975, the rate had decreased to 14.8 per 1,000. (See BIRTH RATE.)

References: Bureau of the Census, *Historical Statistics of the United States: Colonial Times to 1970* (Part I), Washington, DC: U.S. Department of Commerce, 1975; Bureau of the Census, *Statistical Abstract of the United States,* Washington, DC: U.S. Department of Commerce, 1979; Robert L. Church and Michael W. Sedlak, *Education in the United States: An Interpretative History,* New York: The Free Press, 1976.

BABY TALK (layman's term for early language development), language that usually develops between ages 20 to 40 months. Baby talk evolves from babbling (7–10 months) followed by consistent sound patterns (approximately ages 12 to 15 months). Such consistent patterns are first-word acquisitions of a child. After a receptive vocabulary has been developed, a child will begin uttering words, two at a time, about the age of 20 months. Baby talk is at its highest use at this time. Once prepositions, modifiers, and other elements of language are introduced, baby talk progresses very quickly to a precise and complex formal language.

The constant use of baby talk by older children may be a sign of learning, psychological, or mental problems. Authorities note that language impairment may exist and consequently recommend an in-depth analysis of the problem by a competent practitioner. (See BABBLING.)

References: Laura L. Lee, et al., *Interactive Language Development Teaching,* Evanston, IL: Northwestern University Press, 1975; Natalie Perry, *Teaching the Mentally Retarded Child* (Second Edition), New York: Columbia University Press, 1974; Martha E. Snell (Editor), *Systematic Instruction of the Moderately and Severely Handicapped,* Columbus, OH: Charles E. Merrill Publishing Company, 1978.

BACHELOR'S DEGREE, an academic diploma conferred upon completion of four (sometimes more) years of college/university study with a set number of credits earned by the student. Two principal degree categories are the Bachelor of Arts (B.A.) and the Bachelor of Science (B.S.). Frequently, the names of either or both are extended or embellished to include the student's specialty (e.g. Bachelor of Arts in Music, Bachelor of Science in Education) or to create specialized degrees (e.g. Bachelor of Music, Bachelor of Education). The typical bachelor's degree program includes a *major* field of study (e.g. English, social work), a *minor* field of study, and *electives.* Approximately 1,000,000 bachelor's degrees were awarded in the United States in 1979–80. (See ELECTIVE COURSES.)

References: Martin M. Frankel and Forrest W. Harrison, *Projections: Education Statistics to 1985–86,* Washington, DC: National Center for Education Statistics, 1977; Asa S. Knowles (Editor), *Handbook of College and University Administration,* New York: McGraw-Hill Book Company, 1970.

BACK-TO-THE-BASICS, a movement that developed in many sections of the country in the early 1970s. Some proponents of the movement feel that the schools are not teaching children to read, write, or do calculations. Others believe that there are too many frills offered by schools; consequently, children are not enrolling in basic courses or studying the "hard" disciplines. The movement originated and gained its greatest supporters outside the teaching profession.

The movement's supporters would have arithmetic, spelling, punctuation, reading, history, and penmanship offered at the elementary level. English, mathematics, history, civics, biology, chemistry, and physics would be offered at the secondary level. Courses such as art, music, physical education, driver education, modern mathematics, sociology, psychology, considered by many of the advocates of back-to-the-basics as frills, would be offered only after the basics or fundamental courses are taken. Many who support the movement are suspect of teaching methods such as inquiry, problem solving, and values clarification.

Reference: Ben Brodinsky, *Defining the Basics of American Education* (PDK Fastback 95), Bloomington, IN: The Phi Delta Kappa Educational Foundation, 1977.

BAGLEY, WILLIAM (March 15, 1874–July 1, 1946), teacher educator and educational psychologist whose criticism of progressive education pitted him, philosophically, against his contemporary, John Dewey. One of the founders of the essentialist movement, Bagley believed that schools should foster a respect for the value of knowledge for its own sake and teach those basic skills necessary for successful performance in adult society. He espoused rote learning, mastery of specific facts, and the teaching of selected aspects of our cultural heritage.

Before joining the faculty of Teachers College, Columbia University (where he served from 1917 to 1940), Bagley saw service as a rural schoolteacher, elementary school principal, superintendent, Vice President of the State Normal School in Montana, Superintendent at the State Normal and Training School, Oswego, New York, and Director of Education at the University of Illinois. A prolific writer, he authored numerous books dealing with diverse subjects such as classroom management, values, school discipline, and teaching. He also edited several professional publications including *School and Home Education,* the *Journal of the NEA,* and *School and Society.*

References: William W. Brickman, "Bagley, William Chandler" in John F. Ohles (Editor), *Biographical Dictionary of American Educators* (Volume 1), Westport, CT: Greenwood Press, 1978; Edell M. Hearn, "William Chandler Bagley: Teacher of Teachers," *Kappa Delta Pi Record,* October 1967; Isaac L. Kandel, *William Chandler Bagley,* New York: Teachers College, Columbia University, 1961.

BALLET, an international style of dance in which dancers, dressed in costume, perform on stage to musical accompaniment. It is sometimes referred to as theatrical dancing. This is usually done without singing or spoken words. Terminology for basic postures is in French.

The origin of this form of musical expression has been traced to the 15th century. It became a popular art form in western Europe, especially Italy, France, and England. Ballet became closely associated with opera and, as in the case of the minuet, actually served to introduce specific kinds of dance. Today, this art form is especially popular in the Soviet Union; its popularity in the United States, as in the rest of the world, is growing. This increased interest has prompted a growing number of children to study ballet, usually with private teachers.

References: Genevieve Guillot and Germaine Prudhommeau, *The Book of Ballet* (Translated by Katherine Carson), Englewood Cliffs, NJ: Prentice-Hall, Inc., 1976; Oleg Kerensky, *The World of Ballet,* New York: Coward-McCann, Inc., 1970; Lincoln Kirstein, "Ballet and Music" in Bruce Bohle (Editor), *The International Cyclopedia of Music and Musicians* (Tenth Edition), New York: Dodd, Mead and Company, 1975; Lincoln Kirsten, *Dance: A Short History of Classic Theatrical Dancing,* Westport, CT: Greenwood Press, 1970 (Originally published by G. P. Putnam's Sons, 1935).

BALL-STICK-BIRD, a method of teaching reading to severely retarded individuals. The fundamental premise of the system is that the story is the basic element of comprehension. Stories can be followed by children as young as age two—thus, the story serves as a cognitive organizer of both language and logic.

The system uses an oval (ball), a line (stick), and a *V* or angle (bird) to teach all the letters of the alphabet. After the first letter is learned, words can be constructed by adding a second letter. To accommodate the irregularity of the English language, *code approximation* is taught; the learner is asked to rely on context to figure out the sound of the letter(s). The emphasis is on context, thus concentrating on the story rather than the elements. Using code approximations for the elements enables the learner to understand passages without becoming confused by orthography. The system itself encompasses 10 books divided into two separate series. A teacher's manual accompanies each series.

References: EPIE Institute, "Brain-Compatible Teaching and Learning," *EPIEgram Materials,* Vol. 14, Number 5, February 1986; Renee Fuller, *Ball-Stick-Bird Reading System* (Volume 6–10), Stony Brook, NY: Ball-Stick-Bird Publication, 1975; Renee Fuller, "The Story as the Engram; Is It Fundamental to Thinking?" *The Journal of Mind and Behavior,* Volume 3, Number 2, Spring 1982; Renee Fuller, et al., Reading as Therapy in Patients with Severe IQ Deficits, *Journal of Clinical Child Psychology,* Volume 4, Number 1, Spring 1975.

BANK STREET WRITER, a software program designed to be used in the classroom. This word processor software has a clear and readable instructional program which is *menu-driven.* This means that the editing functions of the program are listed across the top of the screen. Pressing of a single key permits selection among the editing functions of the program. In addition to simple editing, the writer uses both upper- and lowercase letters. To aid the learner, words are not divided at the end of a line of text, as is the case with most programs. Lines of text being manipulated are highlighted on the screen so as to make them clearly visible.

Reference: Charles Temple and Jean Wallace Gillet, *Language Arts: Learning Theories and Teaching Practices,* Boston: Little, Brown and Co., 1984.

BARGAINING UNIT, a collective bargaining term referring to a group of employees who are represented by one union or are eligible to be represented by that union. Employees in such units generally have job interests and needs in common. In school systems, as in private industry, different groups of employees (e.g. teachers, custodians, bus drivers) may belong to different bargaining units. In such situations, especially where coalitions of unions do not exist, management negotiates separately with each union.

Teachers have the constitutional right to organize. In several states, where two or more unions seek to represent a given group of teachers, the school board may select one as the exclusive bargaining representative. The board is then expected to negotiate in good faith with the union chosen. Generally, however, a runoff election is held to choose the bargaining agent for each group of employees. In colleges and universities, faculty members generally choose their own bargaining unit through election.

In the United States, the major educational bargaining units are the National Education Association, American Federation of Teachers, and the American Association of University Professors. (See AMERICAN ASSOCIATION OF UNIVERSITY PROFESSORS; AMERICAN FEDERATION OF TEACHERS; COLLECTIVE BARGAINING; and NATIONAL EDUCATION ASSOCIATION.)

References: Thomas J. Flygare, *Collective Bargaining in the Public Schools* (PDK Fastback 99), Bloomington, IN: The Phi Delta Kappa Educational Foundation, 1977; W. D. Heisel, *New Questions and Answers on Public Employee Negotiations,* Chicago: International Personnel Management Association, 1973.

BAR GRAPH—See HISTOGRAM

BARNARD, HENRY (January 24, 1811–July 5, 1900), internationally noted education leader of the 19th century. As the first United States Commissioner of Education (1867–70), he did much to influence the future direction of the U.S. Office of Education. Barnard founded and edited the *American Journal of Education,* a highly regarded periodical that appeared between 1855 and 1882. Additionally, he authored numerous books and articles on education that covered a wide range of educational topics and interests.

Barnard's career included training in the law, service as a schoolteacher, delegate to the Connecticut General Assembly, work as Connecticut's first chief state school officer, and university administration (University of Wisconsin and St. John's College, Maryland).

Barnard was an early supporter of public education, believing that schools would temper social unrest and social change. He did much to promote the creation of common school districts throughout the United States. (See UNITED STATES COMMISSIONER OF EDUCATION and APPENDIX XXVI: UNITED STATES COMMISSIONERS OF EDUCATION.)

References: Ralph C. Jenkins and Gertrude C. Warner, *Henry Barnard: An Introduction,* Hartford, CT: Connecticut State Teachers Association, 1937; Richard E. Thursfield, *Henry Barnard's Journal of Education,* Baltimore, MD: Johns Hopkins Press, 1945; Donald R. Warren, "Barnard, Henry B." in John F. Ohles (Editor), *Biographical Dictionary of American Educators* (Volume I), Westport, CT: Greenwood Press, 1978.

BASAL READERS, reading textbooks prepared for separate elementary grade levels that, when adopted, constitute the basic tool (system) for the teaching of reading. Different publishers each have their own series of coordinated textbooks. These readers are developmental and are carefully controlled with respect to presentation of skill learnings, vocabulary, content, and sentence structure. The representative series includes a pre-primer, a primer, and approximately six graded readers. Teachers' manuals, which accompany each textbook, offer guidance to the teacher, usually on a lesson-by-lesson basis. Workbooks for students are also included in each series. Other reading books used concurrently for practice and/or enrichment purposes are referred to as *supplementary* readers.

Schools using the basal reader approach to reading instruction typically group students by reading ability (intraclass or interclass) and assign to each group the textbook(s) best suited to its reading level. (See SUPPLEMENTARY READERS.)
References: Estill Alexander, Jr., et al., *Teaching Reading,* Boston: Little, Brown and Company, 1979; Albert J. Harris and Edward R. Sipay, *How to Increase Reading Ability* (Eighth Edition), New York: Longman, Inc., 1985; Harry Singer and Dan Donlan, *Reading and Learning from Text* (Second Edition), Hillsadle, NJ: Lawrence Erlbaum Associates, Publishers, 1989.

BASELINE DATA, measures that are collected before the introduction of a treatment (e.g. instructional technique or mode). Baseline data are usually collected through the use of a pre-test. Differences between pre- and post-test results are then evaluated. Educational evaluations should use baseline data; this is particularly true where randomization of subjects or students is not possible. Baseline data may be collected using a single instrument (pre-test) or scores collected over time. For example, levels of achievement on a standardized test that ninth graders, in a particular community, have reached over a three-year period before a treatment is introduced may be used as baseline data.
Reference: Robert L. Thorndike, *Educational Measurement* (Second Edition), Washington, DC: American Council on Education, 1971.

BASIC, a high-level, general-purpose computer language that was designed to be interpreted (translated to machine language during the execution of the program) and interactive (allows input while the program is being run). Basic is much easier to use than FORTRAN (one of the original computer languages) and is used in mainframes, minicomputers, and microcomputers. BASIC is presently one of the major programs used in microcomputers—it comes as standard equipment in most. One reason for its popularity with the microcomputers is due to the fact that it takes little room in the "micros," while other languages take greater storage space.

BASIC stands for Beginners' All-purpose Symbolic Instruction Code. John G. Kemeny and Thomas E. Kurtz of Dartmouth College developed the language in 1964. (See COMPUTER LANGUAGE; FORTRAN; LOGO, and PASCAL.)
References: Charles K. Kinzer, et al. (Editors), *Computer Strategies for Education,* Columbus, OH: Merrill Publishing Co., 1986; Paul F. Merrill, et al., *Computers in Education,* Englewood Cliffs, NJ: Prentice-Hall, Inc., 1986.

BASIC EDUCATION, a term that refers to what some consider to be the essential elements of the school curriculum, usually fundamental subjects such as reading, mathematics, writing, science, history, foreign languages, and geography. These are the fields of study that serve as vehicles for the transmission of knowledge, past to present or present to future. Proponents of basic education argue that the overriding purpose of schools is to provide the learner with a concrete education; hence, they endorse an instructional program that stresses academics and academic excellence.

Since the time of the progressive education movement, the term *basic education* has been used, somewhat cynically, by that movement's critics to distinguish it from other curricular components such as driver education, social studies, industrial arts, and home economics.

More recently, as Ben Brodinsky pointed out, the term has taken on a broader meaning. Illustrating that breadth are three articles of conviction that Brodinsky believes all school boards need to consider as program basics: "(1) to equip all children with the skills, tools, and attitudes that will lay the basis for learning . . . ; (2) to develop [children's] capacities for thinking, working, creating, and gaining satisfaction out of life . . . ; [and] (3) encourage community participation in the education of the young" (pp. 39–40). (See BACK-TO-THE-BASICS.)
References: Ben Brodinsky, *Defining the Basics of American Education* (PDK Fastback 95), Bloomington, IN: The Phi Delta Kappa Educational Foundation, 1977; James S. Le Sure, *Guide to Pedaguese: A Handbook for Puzzled Parents,* New York: Harper and Row, Publishers, 1965; Edward W. Smith, et al., *The Educator's Encyclopedia,* Englewood Cliffs, NJ: Prentice-Hall, Inc., 1969.

BASIC EDUCATIONAL OPPORTUNITY GRANT (BEOG) PROGRAM, federal program introduced in 1973–74 to provide financial aid to qualified postsecondary students who are undergraduates and have not earned a bachelor's degree. Basic grants are made on the basis of financial need rather than scholarship. In 1980–81, awards ranged from $226 to $1,750 per student.

Assistance is available to students enrolled on at least a half-time basis (six semester hours) in undergraduate institutions as well as vocational, proprietary, and technical schools. Several million students receive BEOG monies each year. This is not a college-based program; instead, students apply directly to the federal government to establish eligibility.

References: Office of Evaluation and Dissemination, Department of Education, U.S. Department of Health, Education, and Welfare, *Annual Evaluation Report on Programs Administered by the U.S. Office of Education: Fiscal Year 1978,* Washington, DC: The Office, 1978; Public Law 92–318, Education Amendments of 1972, *United States Statutes at Large: 1972* (Volume 86), Washington, DC: U.S. Government Printing Office, 1973; Public Law 94–482, *United States Statutes at Large: 1976* (Volume 90, Part II), Washington, DC: U.S. Government Printing Office, 1978.

BASIC SIGHT VOCABULARY—See SIGHT VOCABULARY

BASIC SKILLS AND EDUCATIONAL PROFICIENCY PROGRAMS, a federal activity authorized by the Education Amendments of 1978. Its basic purpose is to assist public and private agencies as they work to improve the basic skills of children, youth, and adults.

Forerunner to this program was the Right to Read Program, a federal effort that concentrated on reading exclusively. The legislation creating the Basic Skills and Educational Proficiency Programs defined *basic skills* more broadly to include mathematics, reading, and oral and written communication.

The Basic Skills Program is a multidimensional one, comprising three major thrusts. Each, in turn, includes two or three rather carefully delimited areas of emphasis referred to as programs. The three thrusts and their respective component programs are: (1) *National Basic Skills Improvement* (made up of the Basic Skills Improvement in the Schools Program, which supports demonstration projects; the Parent Participation Program, which offers help to projects involving parent volunteers who provide out-of-school service with the basic skills; and the Out-of-School Basic Skills Improvement Program, which assists nonschool agencies providing basic skills assistance to youth and adults); (2) the *State Basic Skills* thrust (comprising the Formula Grant Program, a component program that assists states with the planning and implementation of basic skills improvement projects; and the State Leadership Program, whose purpose is to prepare individuals at the state level to demonstrate or carry out basic skills programs); and (3) the third thrust, known as the *Educational Proficiency* program (consisting of the Proficiency Standards Program, which involves establishment of basic standards for the basic skills and projects designed to help students achieve these standards; and the Achievement Testing Program, which seeks to help states and local educational agencies with basic skills measurement).

Reading is Fundamental, a program that supports the distribution of free books to schoolchildren, originally a part of Right to Read, was made a part of the Basic Skills and Educational Proficiency Program in 1978. (See READING IS FUNDAMENTAL and RIGHT TO READ.)

References: Basic Skills and Educational Proficiency, Washington, DC: U.S. Department of Health, Education, and Welfare, Undated Brochure; *Federal Register,* Volume 44, No. 83, April 27, 1979.

BATCH PROCESSING (in computing)—See STATISTICAL PACKAGE FOR THE SOCIAL SCIENCES

BATTERED-CHILD SYNDROME, a term coined in the early 1960s by University of Colorado pediatrician C. Henry Kempe. Kempe and his colleagues surveyed a limited number of hospitals to ascertain the nature and extent of cases involving children admitted who were suffering from nonaccidental injuries. A total of 302 cases were uncovered. In their report, they defined the battered-child syndrome as "a clinical condition in young children who have received serious physical abuse, generally from a parent or foster parent" (p. 17). They suggested that the syndrome "should be considered in any child exhibiting evidence of possible trauma (fracture of any bone, subdural hematoma, multiple soft tissue injuries, poor skin hygiene or malnutrition) or where there is a marked discrepancy between the clinical findings and the historical data as supplied by the parents" (p. 24). As part of their report, Kempe and his colleagues also commented on the then-prevailing reluctance of physicians to believe that evidences of this type could be attributed to parents. Physicians were urged to report all such cases to their local police authorities.

Recent advances in detecting the battered-child syndrome have been attributed to improvements in the field of pediatric radiology. (See CHILD ABUSE and CHILD ABUSE PREVENTION AND TREATMENT ACT.)

References: Ray E. Helfer and C. Henry Kempe (Editors), *The Battered Child* (Second Edition), Chicago: University of Chicago Press, 1974; C. Henry Kempe, et al., "The Battered Child Syndrome," *Journal of the American Medical Association,* July 7, 1962; Selwyn M. Smith, *The Battered Child Syndrome,* London, England: Butterworths, 1976; Selwyn M. Smith (Editor), *The Maltreatment of Children,* Lancaster, England: MTP Press Limited, 1978.

BATTERY—See TEST BATTERY

BATTLEDORE, a variant of the Hornbook, an early book of instruction. This lesson book became popular in the 1700s. It consisted of folded paper or cardboard, and marked the first time printed educational material was put in the hands of children. Unlike its predecessor, the Hornbook, the battledore contained no religious teachings. Instead, it consisted of the alphabet, numerals, an easy reading lesson, and simple woodcuts of animals. Use of the battledore continued into the nineteenth century. (See HORNBOOK.)

References: Charlotte S. Huck (Third Revised Edition), *Children's Literature in the Elementary School,* New York: Holt, Rinehart and Winston, 1979; Donna E. Norton, *Through the Eyes of Children: An Introduction to Children's Literature,* Columbus, Ohio: Charles E. Merrill Publishing Co., 1983.

BEDWETTING—See ENURESIS

BEHAVIORAL AGE—See DEVELOPMENTAL AGE

BEHAVIORAL COUNSELING, a counseling approach first endorsed in 1964 by John Krumboltz. The approach is based on the assumption that new behaviors can be learned and can replace old ones. The principal goal of this form of counseling is to help the client to behave differently. The counselor, acting as an interventionist, directs the counseling process by applying appropriate (scientific) learning principles and formulating strategies designed to meet the needs of the individual client.

N. Kenneth LaFleur indicated that behavioral counseling consists of four stages: (1) *assessment,* or determining what positive as well as negative things the client is doing presently; (2) *goal setting,* a step in which counselor and client together formulate attainable goals for counseling; (3) *technique implementation,* learning strategies developed and subscribed to by client and counselor; and (4) *evaluation-termination,* the stage devoted to assessment of client behaviors in the context of the previously established goals.

Behavioral counseling can be used with clients at all educational levels. E. L. Tolbert reported that it is especially popular with college-level students.

References: Gerald Corey, *Theory and Practice of Counseling and Psychotherapy,* Monterey, CA: Brooks/Cole Publishing Company, 1977; Ray E. Hosford and Louis A. de Visser, *Behavioral Approaches to Counseling: An Introduction,* Washington, DC: American Personnel and Guidance Association, 1974; N. Kenneth LaFleur, "Behavioral Views of Counseling" in Herbert M. Burke, Jr. and Buford Stefflre, *Theories of Counseling* (Third Edition), New York: McGraw-Hill Book Company, 1979; Bruce E. Shertzer and Shelley C. Stone, *Fundamentals of Counseling* (Second Edition), Boston: Houghton Mifflin Company, 1974.

BEHAVIORAL OBJECTIVES, specific statements, written in behavioral or performance terms, that express desired or anticipated learning outcomes. Behavior may be either *overt* (acts that are visible) or *covert* (acts that are not visible, such as mental), although some educators believe that behavior must be overt to be measured. Behavioral objectives can be used by classroom teachers to design and evaluate instruction. They may also be used in curriculum development and/or evaluation. When behavioral objectives are used, the typical model of instruction includes *instructional objectives* (behavioral objectives that are used for planning instruction) as its first element, followed by *preassessment* and *instructional procedures* and then *evaluation.*

Behavioral objectives should be written to include: (1) descriptions of observable behaviors; (2) the conditions under which the behaviors must exist and operate; and (3) the criteria to be used to determine whether the objective has been met. Behavioral objectives usually fall into one of three domains: cognitive, affective, or psychomotor. There are many types of behavioral objectives. Two principal types are: (1) *instructional,* which require the learner to define the elements of a well-written behavioral objective, and (2) *terminal,* requiring the learner to develop skill in writing terminal behavioral objectives. (See TAXONOMY.)

References: Richard W. Burns, *New Approaches to Behavioral Objectives* (Second Edition), Dubuque, IA: Wm. C. Brown Company, Publishers, 1977; Miriam B. Kapfer (Editor), *Behavioral Objectives: The Position of the Pendulum*, Englewood Cliffs, NJ: Educational Technology Publications, 1978; Robert J. Kible, et al., *Behavioral Objectives and Instruction*, Boston: Allyn and Bacon, Inc., 1970; Robert F. Mager, *Preparing Objectives for Programmed Instruction*, San Francisco: Fearon Publishers, Inc., 1962; Herbert D. Simons, "Behavioral Objectives: A False Hope for Education" in James R. Gress (Editor), *Curriculum: An Introduction to the Field*, Berkeley, CA: McCutchan Publishing Corporation, 1978.

BEHAVIOR MANAGEMENT, control over the behavior of an individual or individuals for the purpose of achieving a desired outcome or producing a behavioral change. Various techniques are available to control or "manage" an individual's behavior for different purposes (e.g. to reduce anxiety, jealousy, aggression, prejudices, or to improve learning). These may take the form of learning and teaching methods, medicines (drugs), modeling, human relations and interactions, affection, punishment, and psychology (e.g. behaviorism). Any one or more of these techniques may be employed.

Behavioral management is used by parents in the training and rearing of children, by teachers in the classroom, and by others who desire to shape the actions and attitudes of others. (See BEHAVIOR MODIFICATION.)

References: ABC Behavior Management Workbook, Van Nuys, CA: The Associates for Behavior Change, 1973; Daniel Duke (Editor), *Classroom Management* (NSSE 78th Yearbook, Part II), Chicago: University of Chicago Press, 1979; Robert L. Geiser, *Behavior Mod and the Managed Society*, Boston: Beacon Press, 1976; Judith M. Smith and Donald E. P. Smith, *Child Management,* Champaign, IL: Research Press Company, 1976; Dorothy Tennov, *Managing Children's Behavior*, Bridgeport, CT: University of Bridgeport, 1976.

BEHAVIOR MODIFICATION, the direct application of psychological learning and motivation theories to change the behavior of an individual. Reinforcement principles are used extensively in most behavior modification approaches.

Behavior modification had its origins in the area of psychology called behaviorism, with B. F. Skinner the major spokesman for behaviorism. Although the techniques of operant conditioning (as developed by B. F. Skinner) may be used in one model of behavioral modification, other tech-niques are used in other behavior modification models. Some of the techniques found in these other models are behavioral assessment, conditioning and counterconditioning, flooding (rapid exposure to conditioned stimulus), desensitization, aversive counterconditioning, operant conditioning, modeling, or cognition. Behavior modification techniques can be used in settings such as the classroom, clinics, the laboratory, or in social agencies. (See OPERANT BEHAVIOR and REINFORCEMENT.)

References: Michel Hersen, et al., *Progress in Behavior Modification* (Volume VI), New York: Academic Press, 1978; Albert Mehrabian, *Basic Behavior Modification*, New York: Harper and Row, Publishers, 1978; William L. Mikulas, *Behavior Modification*, New York: Harper and Row, Publishers, 1978; James Quina, *Effective Secondary Teaching: Going beyond the Bell Curve*, New York: Harper and Row Publishers, 1989; Norman A. Sprinthall and Richard C. Sprinthall, *Educational Psychology: A Developmental Approach* (Fourth Edition), New York: Random House, 1987.

BELL-SHAPED CURVE—See NORMAL DISTRIBUTION CURVE

BENDER-GESTALT TEST (B-G TEST), or simply the Bender Test, an individualized test used in a clinical setting. The instrument, a projective and nonprojective test for those aged four and over, has been used to measure maturation, psychological disturbances, intelligence, cortex injuries, the effects of convulsive therapy, and children with learning problems and to make early predictions of reading ability or problems.

The test originated with the study of gestalt psychology by Lauretta Bender at the Phipps Psychiatric Clinic, Johns Hopkins Hospital, in 1929-30. Dr. Bender adapted four of Max Wertheimer's figures into a group of nine figures to assess specific levels of behaviors found in gestalt psychology as well as in maturation. Dr. Bender's original subjects were psychotic, regressed, and defective schizophrenic patients. Her studies led to the publication of a monograph (1938) titled *A Visual Motor Gestalt Test and Its Clinical Use.* Since its publication, the Bender Test has become a widespread clinical tool. Test cards may be obtained from the American Ortho-psychiatric Association in New York City.

References: Joseph Gilbert, *Interpreting Psychological Test Data,* New York: Van Nostrand Reinhold Company, 1978; Elizabeth M. Koppitz, *The Bender-Gestalt Test for Young Children,* New York: Grune and Stratton, 1964; Alexander Tolor and Herbert C. Schulberg, *An Evalua-*

tion of the Bender-Gestalt Test, Springfield, IL: Charles C. Thomas, Publisher, 1963.

BENJAMIN, HAROLD

BENJAMIN, HAROLD (March 27, 1893–January 12, 1969), teacher educator and university administrator who won national attention after authoring the widely read satire *The Saber-Tooth Curriculum.* This frequently reprinted work appeared in 1930 under the pseudonym J. Abner Peddiwell.

Benjamin's career included professional service as teacher and administrator in Oregon, Assistant Professor of Education at the University of Oregon, Director of Student Teaching at Stanford University, Assistant Dean of the University of Minnesota's College of Education, Dean of Education at the University of Maryland, and as Professor at George Peabody College for Teachers (Nashville). This span of professional service extended from 1915 to 1958.

Franklin Parker reported that "Dr. Benjamin was proud of his military record and always insisted that it be included in his official biographical sketches" (p. 93). Other activities for which he is remembered are: (1) organizing and heading the International Education Relations Department, U.S. Office of Education; (2) membership on the U.S. delegation that drafted the UNESCO charter; (3) service on educational missions to Japan, Afghanistan, and South Korea (1946–55); and (4) many defenses of academic freedom.

Benjamin earned the Ph.D. degree at Stanford University (1927). He wrote *The Cultivation of Idiosyncrasy* (1949), *Higher Education in the American Republics* (1965), and other books including an autobiographical novel, *The Sage of Petaluma* (1965). He also edited *Democracy in the Administration of Higher Education* (1950), the 10th John Dewey Society Yearbook. (SEE SABER-TOOTH CURRICULUM.)

References: Erwin H. Goldenstein, "Benjamin, Harold Raymond Wayne" in John F. Ohles (Editor), *Biographical Dictionary of American Educators* (Volume 1), Westport, CT: Greenwood Press, 1978; Franklin Parker, "In Memoriam: Harold R. W. Benjamin, 1893–1969," *Kappa Delta Pi Record,* February 1969.

BEST-EVIDENCE SYNTHESIS

BEST-EVIDENCE SYNTHESIS, an approach used in the review of research in a particular area or topic in education. Only studies that have the highest internal and external validity and the strongest methodology are included. However, if high internal/external validity studies were never done, less rigorous research that meets selection criteria can be used; such research becomes the *best*

evidence available. The approach requires explicit a priori criteria for the selection of studies rather than the broad, if not exhaustive, standard used in other review approaches (such as meta-analysis). The best evidence principle is used quite extensively in courts when appropriate evidence in one case could not be as appropriate in another case because of better evidence being available.

Criteria for selecting the best evidence may include: minimum bias; external validity as an important and significant factor; set number of subjects, classes, and/or teachers to reduce unstable effects; utilization of a variety of methods when studies with high validities are unavailable; and direct or close relationship to the area under investigation. The approach and criteria were developed by Robert E. Slavin of Johns Hopkins University. (See META-ANALYSIS.)

References: R. E. Slavin, *Ability Grouping and Student Achievement in Elementary Schools: A Best-Evidence Synthesis* (Technical Report Number 1), Baltimore, MD: Center for Research in Elementary and Middle Schools, Johns Hopkins University, 1986; R. E. Slavin, Best-Evidence Synthesis: An Alternative to Meta-Analytic and Traditional Reviews, *Educational Research,* Volume 15, Number 9, 1986.

BETHEL PROJECT

BETHEL PROJECT, a summer training laboratory, held in Bethel, Maine, that was first started (1947) by the National Training Laboratories (NTL) and the Research Center for Group Dynamics. T-group (Training-group) learning is the major focus of the training laboratory. Such training focuses on: (1) how groups function; (2) the positive, neutral, and negative contributions of individuals; (3) decision-making processes; and (4) the facilitation of the maintenance of groups. In addition, individual sensitivity training and encounter training are provided.

The training laboratories are temporary residential communities in which individuals expand their knowledges and skills as well as experiment through direct interactions, participation, and living as part of a T-group. The T-group is usually made up of about 12 individuals and is relatively unstructured; the function is to make the T-group a productive organization.

The NTL Institute (formally the NTL-Institute for Applied Behavioral Science) is a nonprofit corporation associated with the NEA and is located in Arlington, Virginia. (See SENSITIVITY TRAINING and T-GROUP.)

References: Leland P. Bradford, et al., *T-Group Theory and Laboratory Method,* New York: John Wiley and Sons,

1964; Lee C. Deighton (Editor), *The Encyclopedia of Education* (Volume 6), New York: The Macmillan Company and The Free Press, 1971; Nancy Yakes, et al., *Encyclopedia of Associations* (Thirteenth Edition), Detroit: Gale Research Company, 1979.

BETHUNE, MARY M. (July 10, 1875–May 18, 1955), prominent black teacher who helped to establish Bethune-Cookman College, a Florida teacher training institution. Bethune-Cookman College resulted from the merger of the Cookman Institute and Bethune's own school, the Daytona Educational and Industrial School for Negro Girls, which she had established in 1904.

Mary Bethune was also a prominent political leader whose organizational talents were utilized by Presidents Hoover, Franklin Roosevelt, and Truman. During the Roosevelt administration, she was appointed to head the Office of Negro Affairs of the National Youth Administration, the first time an American black woman occupied a position of such importance.

Concurrent with her activities as political leader and school administrator, Bethune found time to play a leadership role in organizations such as the NAACP, National Urban League, the American Teachers Association, and the National Council of Negro Women (which she helped to found).

References: National Education Association, *The Legacy of Mary McLeod Bethune*, Washington, DC: The Association, 1974; Harry A. Ploski and Warren Marr II (Editors), *The Negro Almanac: A Reference Work on the Afro American* (Third Edition), New York: The Bellweather Company, 1976.

BIBLIOTHERAPY, an approach that uses reading to help children with emotional problems. Children read books whose characters have emotional problems similar to their own. These storybook characters approach and solve their problems; the children reading the stories are able to see how the problems are solved and thus gain insight into solving their own problems. The expectation is that children gain a better understanding of themselves and their behaviors through such reading.

It is important that teachers select the appropriate story to fit a particular child and his/her needs. It is not enough for the child to read the story. The teacher must guide the child through activities, questions, role playing, projects, and so on that will reinforce the story and enhance its therapeutic value. Bibliotherapy can be used for preventive purposes as well.

References: Mildred R. Donoghue, *The Child and the English Language Arts* (Third Edition), Dubuque, IA: Wm. C. Brown Company, Publishers, 1979; John F. Savage and Jean F. Mooney, *Teaching Reading to Children with Special Needs*, Boston: Allyn and Bacon, Inc., 1979.

BIDDING CYCLE, the steps in the purchasing process that need to be taken once a school district establishes a need for a service or item of equipment requiring purchase via competitive bidding. The steps, described by W. L. Schooler, a school business official, follow: (1) need for purchase is established; (2) appropriation and fund availability is determined; (3) bid specifications are prepared; (4) bidders are notified in accordance with state law; (5) bids are received and opened on date specified, checked for completeness, and evaluated; (6) awards are made; (7) purchase orders are prepared; (8) bid items are received; and (9) vendors are invited to assist with performance evaluation of their product. An Annual Bid Schedule should be developed, Schooler recommended, to facilitate future bids. Such schedules should include the date each item was bid, bid number, name of vendor selected, amount of award, and suggestions for future bidding.

Reference: William L. Schooler, "The Bidding Cycle and Vendor Assistance," *School Business Affairs*, March 1979.

BIDS—See COMPETITIVE BIDS

BILATERALITY, or bilateral symmetry, a term having to do with involvement of both sides of the body. It is also used to describe the right and left hemispheres of the brain as being duplicates of each other in terms of function and structure.

"Split-brain" research has indicated that the two hemispheres have specialized involvements. The left hemisphere is involved in verbal and mathematical functions, and the right hemisphere is involved in space, artistic functions, nonverbal images, and shapes. Research indicates that the two modes of consciousness do coexist within all individuals and that the two hemispheres' specializations complement each other. Research has also revealed that not only do the hemispheres have specializations, but they have the capability of performing some similar functions as well.

Considerable experimentation on the function and structure of the brain has been initiated since 1950. As a result, a body of knowledge about the brain, its function, and its structure is being developed.

References: Robert E. Ornstein, *The Psychology of Con-*

sciousness (Second Edition), New York: Harcourt Brace Jovanovich, Inc., 1977; Merlin C. Wittrock, *The Human Brain*, Englewood Cliffs, NJ: Prentice-Hall, Inc., 1977.

BILINGUAL-BICULTURAL EDUCATION, a program in which two languages are used in instruction that emphasizes the cultures of which the languages are a part. In American schools, English is one of the two languages used.

In years past, the American school curriculum was essentially monolingual and monocultural, reflecting the "melting-pot" theory, which held that all citizens should be assimilated into the American culture. Several factors have prompted a move away from that theory toward bilingual-bicultural education: (1) increasing recognition that the United States is a pluralistic (multicultural) society; (2) the fact that over 5,000,000 school children in the United States speak languages other than English; (3) data that show that many of these children are poor school performers; and (4) increased attention given to bilingual-bicultural education by the federal government, highlighted by the Bilingual Education Act of 1968.

At least three broad goals give direction to bilingual-bicultural education: (1) to foster positive self-concepts among children; (2) to facilitate learning; and (3) to help learners develop an understanding of differences in language, mores, and history among different cultural groups. (See BILINGUAL EDUCATION ACT; BILINGUAL INSTRUCTION; and, MULTICULTURAL EDUCATION.)

References: Jim Cummins and Merrill Swain, *Bilingualism in Education*, New York: Longman, Inc., 1986; Richardo L. Garcia, *Learning in Two Languages* (PDK Fastback 84), Bloomington, IN: The Phi Delta Kappa Educational Foundation, 1976; Pamela L. Tiedt and Iris M. Tiedt, *Multicultural Teaching: A Handbook of Activities, Information, and Resources* (Second Edition), Boston: Allyn and Bacon, Inc., 1986; Frances W. von Maltitz, *Living and Learning in Two Languages: Bilingual-Bicultural Education in the United States*, New York: McGraw-Hill Book Company, 1975.

BILINGUAL EDUCATION ACT (actually Title VII of the Elementary and Secondary Education Act of 1965, as amended in 1974), federal legislation that encourages establishment of educational programs that use bilingual educational practices, techniques, and methods. The act defines *program of bilingual education* to mean "a program of instruction, designed for children of limited English-speaking ability in elementary or secondary

schools, in which . . . there is instruction given in, and study of, English, and, to the extent necessary to allow a child to progress effectively through the educational system, the native language of the children of limited English-speaking ability, and such instruction is given with appreciation for the cultural heritage of such children, and, with respect to elementary school instruction, such instruction shall, to the extent necessary, be in all courses or subjects of study which will allow a child to progress effectively through the educational system" (pp. 504-5).

The act permits limited participation in such programs by English-speaking children, this for the purpose of acquiring appreciation of the cultural heritage of children with limited English-speaking ability.

The program is administered by the Office of Bilingual Education, U.S. Department of Education. (See *LAU v. NICHOLS* and NATIVE LANGUAGE.)

References: Jim Cummins and Merrill Swain, *Bilingualism in Education*, New York: Longman, Inc., 1986; Office of Planning, Budgeting and Evaluation, U.S. Office of Education, Department of H.E.W., *Annual Evaluation Report on Programs Administered by the U.S. Office of Education: Fiscal Year 1978*, Washington, DC: The Office, 1978; Carlos J. Ovando and Virginia P. Collier, *Bilingual and ESL Classrooms*, New York: McGraw-Hill Book Co., 1985; Public Law 93-380, "Amendments to the Elementary and Secondary Education Act of 1965," *United States Statutes at Large* (Volume 88, Part I), Washington, DC: U.S. Government Printing Office, 1976.

BILINGUAL INSTRUCTION, a form of language teaching that, in most American schools, involves using the non-English-speaking student's native language as a bridge until he/she is able to move into a program in which English is the exclusive language of instruction. Concurrently, the student is exposed to the English language.

Ricardo Garcia indicated that there are two principal ways of teaching English to those classified as linguistic minority students. The first, known as the *native language method*, involves teaching of reading and writing (by bilingual teachers) in the student's native language. Transfer to English is made after native language skills are mastered. The second method, *English as a second language* (ESL), involves the assignment of students to regular, English-speaking classes. During parts of the school day, the student receives intensive English instruction taught by a resource teacher often working in a setting other than the child's regular classroom. Both methods have advantages and disadvantages. Research data indicate no superiority of one method over the other. (See BILINGUAL-BICULTURAL EDUCATION and ENGLISH AS A SECOND LANGUAGE.)

References: Jim Cummins and Merrill Swain, *Bilingualism in Education*, New York: Longman, Inc., 1986; Ricardo L. Garcia, *Learning in Two Languages* (PDK Fastback 84), Bloomington, IN: The Phi Delta Kappa Educational Foundation, 1976; Carlos J. Ovando and Virginia P. Collier, *Bilingual and ESL Classrooms*, New York: McGraw-Hill Book Co., 1985.

BINARY OPERATIONS, the function of a system in either one of two states (e.g. "on" or "off"). In mathematics, it is a function (addition, subtraction, etc.) within the binary number system. The binary number system uses only two symbols: 0 and 1. Because there are only two symbols used, the base of the binary system is 2, e.g. 2^0, 2^1, 2^2, 2^3, and so on ($2^0 = 1$, $2^1 = 1$, $2^2 = 4$, $2^3 = 8$, $2^4 = 16$, and so on).

The binary number 1011 can be converted to its decimal equivalent as follows:

Start binary place value always to the right

$\underline{1}(2^0) + \underline{1}(2^1) + \underline{0}(2^2) + \underline{1}(2^3)$
$1(1) + 1(2) + 0(4) + 1(8) =$
$1 + 2 + 0 + 8 = 11$

Other examples:

From ——————(Conversion)——————→To

Binary Value	$2^0=1$	$2^1=2$	$2^2=4$	$2^3=8$	$2^4=16$	Decimal Value
1101	1	0	1	1		13
101	1	0	1			5
1000	0	0	0	1		8
11010	0	1	0	1	1	26

Because there are only two symbols (0, 1), the binary system is useful in computers.

References: Assistant Masters Association, *Teaching of Mathematics in Secondary Schools* (Second Edition), Cambridge, England: Cambridge University Press, 1974; B. Kechen, *Binary Time Series*, New York: Marcel Dekker, Inc., 1980; C. W. S. Schminke, et al., *Teaching the Child Mathematics* (Second Edition), New York: Holt, Rinehart and Winston, Inc., 1978; Robert G. Underhill, *Teaching Elementary School Mathematics* (Second Edition), Columbus, OH: Charles E. Merrill Publishing Co., 1977.

BINET, ALFRED (July 8, 1857–October 18, 1911), French psychologist who, along with Théodore Simon, developed the first useful test of children's intelligence in 1905. Binet had been asked by the French government to devise a test that could identify children who were mentally retarded and would be unable to benefit from a normal school program. Binet and Simon developed a scale of 30 items that they titled the "New Methods for Diagnosing Idiocy, Imbecility, and Moronity." The scale described criteria that allowed physicians and psychologists to identify these three levels of retardation.

Binet felt that intelligence was a complex trait. For this reason, his test included vocabulary, understanding of social situations, and verbal and pictorial problems. The Binet test was individually administered. Lewis Terman, in 1916, adapted the Binet-Simon to the American learner and later revised it in 1937. The new test was titled the Stanford-Binet Test.

Binet was born in Nice, France. His father was a physician and his mother an artist. Although a licensed lawyer, he never practiced law. He became an experimental psychologist as well as an experimental pedagogue. Between 1905 and his death in 1911, he produced four plays in Paris in addition to his work as a psychologist. (See TERMAN, LEWIS.)

References: Lewis M. Terman, *The Measurement of Intelligence*, Boston: Houghton Mifflin Company, 1916; Theta H. Wolf, *Alfred Binet*, Chicago: University of Chicago Press, 1973.

BINOCULAR VISION, integrating into a single image the information received simultaneously through both eyes when looking at the same object. Binocular difficulties are produced when the two eyes do not function together.

There are three general binocular problems. The first, the lack of coordination between the two eyes, is called *strabismus*. Second, when the lenses of the eyes cannot fuse images, *inadequate fusion* results. Finally, *aniseikonia* occurs when the ocular image of the same object is fixated by the eyes as unequal sizes or shapes. Problems with binocular vision frequently contribute to reading problems and other learning disorders.

References: Janet W. Lerner, *Children with Learning Disabilities* (Second Edition), Boston: Houghton Mifflin Company, 1976; Kenneth W. Waugh and Wilma Jo Bush, *Diagnosing Learning Disorders*, Columbus, OH: Charles E. Merrill Publishing Company, 1971.

BIOFEEDBACK, knowledge of the state of a bodily process (e.g. heart beat, brain wave, temperature, muscles), usually provided by an external sensor. The function of this information (feedback) is to help the individual influence physiological responses of two kinds: those not usually under voluntary control, and those formerly regulated but not now controlled responses. Through biofeedback training (BFT), an individual can learn to control the "inner self."

Biofeedback is a form of machine-mind communication. Its origins are found in medical and biological research. Thermometers and EKG and EEG machines are three instruments frequently used as external devices to supply information. Other machines are also available to monitor organs or bodily processes. Numbers, sounds, and colors are used in reporting biofeedback data to individuals, but it takes training to be able to utilize the biofeedback information appropriately.
References: Edward B. Blanchard and Leonard H. Epstein, *A Biofeedback Primer*, Reading, MA: Addison-Wesley Publishing Company, 1978; Barbara B. Brown, *New Mind, New Body*, New York: Harper and Row, Publishers, 1974; Marvin Karlins and Lewis M. Andrews, *Biofeedback: Turning on the Power of Your Mind*, Philadelphia: J. B. Lippincott Company, 1972; Gary E. Schwartz and Jackson Beatty (Editors), *Biofeedback: Theory and Research*, New York: Academic Press, 1977; David Shapiro, et al., *Biofeedback and Self Control*, Chicago: Aldine Publishing Company, 1973.

BIOLOGICAL SCIENCES CURRICULUM STUDY (BSCS), a curriculum project aimed at improving the teaching of biology at all levels of education. BSCS was undertaken in 1958 by the American Institute of the Biological Sciences with major funding support provided by the National Science Foundation.

One of the project's first undertakings was the preparation of three introductory biology textbooks. (The Blue text had a molecular-chemical emphasis; the Green version emphasized ecology; and the Yellow had a more traditional broad-base emphasis.) These, directed at the high school student, were authored by three teams of writers working during the summers of 1960–62. The texts: (1) stressed understanding and appreciation of scientific inquiry; (2) were supplemented by a variety of instructional materials that included laboratory books, charts, teacher manuals, and an array of nonprint items; and (3) were designed to satisfy a common set of aims. The titles of these texts, several editions of which have appeared since initial publication, are: Blue version, *Biological Science: Molecules to Man;* Green version, *High School Biology;* and the Yellow version, *Biological Science: An Inquiry Into Life.* Research evidence indicates that students exposed to the BSCS program fared better on biology achievement tests than did those taught using more traditional approaches.

BSCS has produced numbers of other biology materials, some aimed at elementary school, middle school, advanced high school, and college students, others at the special education child.
References: David P. Ausubel, "An Evaluation of the BSCS Approach to High School Biology," *The American Biology Teacher*, March 1966; BSCS, *Biological Science: An Inquiry Into Life*, New York: Holt, Rinehart and Winston, Inc., 1966; BSCS, *Biological Science: Molecules to Man*, Boston: Houghton Mifflin Company, 1968; BSCS, *High School Biology*, Chicago: Rand McNally and Company, 1968; Alfred T. Collette, *Science Teaching in the Secondary School: A Guide for Modernizing Instruction*, Boston: Allyn and Bacon, Inc., 1973; J. David Lockard (Editor), *Science and Mathematics Curricular Developments Internationally, 1956–1974*, College Park, MD: Science Teaching Center, University of Maryland (Joint Project with the Commission on Science Education, American Association for the Advancement of Science).

BIRTH RATE, the number of live births recorded for a given population during a specific period. Usually, it is the number of births per 1,000 population at midyear, a measure known as the crude birth rate. Between 1955 and 1957, the crude birth rate in the United States was 25 to 27 per 1,000; in 1973, it decreased to 15 births per 1,000. Between 1965 and 1974, the world birth rate dropped significantly, although there are many countries where the rate has continued to increase.

The formula for determining *crude birth rate* is:

$$\frac{\text{Number of live births during the year}}{\text{Average or midyear population}} \times 1{,}000$$

A second measure of birth rate, the *category-specific birth rate,* generally refers to women in a specific category. The formula for computing a *category-specific birth rate,* using the professional women category as an example, is:

$$\frac{\text{Births during the year to professional women}}{\substack{\text{Average or midyear number of women aged} \\ \text{30–35 in the population}}} \times 1{,}000$$

Birth rates have a significant effect upon the entire society. Significant changes in either direction will ultimately affect schools, business, industrial production, employment, demand for goods and services, retirement funds, food production, demand for food, tax bases for various governmental structures, and so on. (See BABY BOOM.)

References: Michael R. Greenberg, et al., *Local Population and Employment Projection Techniques*, New Brunswick, NJ: The Center for Urban Policy Research, 1978; Tomas Frejka, *The Future of Population Growth*, New York: John Wiley and Sons, 1973; Judah Matras, *Introduction to Population*, Englewood Cliffs, NJ: Prentice-Hall, Inc., 1977; *World Population Growth and Response, 1965–1975*, Washington, DC: Population Reference Bureau, Inc., 1976.

BIRTH SURVIVAL METHOD OF PREDICTING POPULATION—See PREDICTING PUPIL POPULATIONS

BLACK COLLEGES, those institutions of higher education initially established for the education and training of black Americans. Lincoln University (Chester, Pa.), Wilberforce University (Towawa Springs, Ohio), and Cheyney State College (Cheyney, Pa.) were established for this purpose before the Civil War and several similar and distinguished institutions were founded immediately after the Civil War: Atlanta University (Atlanta, Ga.); Howard University (Washington, D.C.); Fisk University (Nashville, Tenn.); and Hampton Institute (Hampton, Va.). A majority of black colleges and universities are located in the southern states of the United States.

Many of the older black colleges and universities were started by religious groups. By the 1890s, there were several state supported black colleges in existence. In 1900, a total of 35 public and private black colleges were operating. By 1976, there were 106 traditionally black institutions of higher education in the United States of which 16 were two-year institutions. Today, all public black colleges are under a mandate to integrate their student bodies. Although integrated, many continue to have a majority of blacks in their student population.

Most universities in the United States have integrated student bodies; yet 40 percent of blacks who attended college in 1975 chose to enroll in predominantly black colleges. (See UNITED NEGRO COLLEGE FUND.)

References: Black Colleges in the South, Atlanta, GA: Southern Association of Colleges and Schools, 1971; Alan Pifer, *Higher Education of Blacks in the United States*, New York: Carnegie Corporation of New York, 1973; Charles V. Willie and Ronald R. Edmonds (Editors), *Black Colleges in America*, New York: Teachers College Press, 1978.

BLACK EDUCATION, a broad term used to cover the history and present status of education specifically designed for blacks in the United States. Black education had its beginnings during the American colonial period. Before the Civil War, education for blacks was limited. In the North, it was provided by religious groups; in the South, it was almost nonexistent because of the "Black Codes." Public elementary education became available to blacks in the North in the early 1800s (e.g. Philadelphia, 1822). It wasn't until the post-Civil War period that public education for black Americans was available universally (the level of education provided varied from one state to another).

The *Plessy v. Ferguson* Supreme Court decision of 1896, which held that separate but equal schools were constitutional, virtually institutionalized dual systems of education in the southern and some northern states. The famous *Brown v. Board of Education of Topeka* decision, rendered by the U.S. Supreme Court in 1954, declared racially separate schools to be unconstitutional. Since then, black education has undergone considerable change, especially with respect to the increased ratio of black children attending desegregated schools in the South.

The National Center for Education Statistics recently reported that "(r)acial isolation of black students has increased only in the Northeast region since 1970. In the South, where the largest number of black students attend school, less than one-fourth attend schools that are racially isolated" (p. 57).

At the higher education level, NCES reported that "(i)n 1977, the college enrollment rate of blacks approximated that of whites . . . [however], data on degrees awarded to racial/ethnic groups show that . . . blacks are underrepresented at all degree levels" (p. 213). At the college and university level, large percentages of blacks continue to attend predominately black institutions. (See BLACK COLLEGES; *BROWN v. BOARD OF EDUCATION OF TOPEKA:* and *PLESSY v. FERGUSON.*)

References: Nancy B. Dearman and Valena W. Plisko, *The Condition of Education: 1979 Edition*, Washington, DC: National Center for Education Statistics, U.S. Department of Health, Education, and Welfare, 1979; Vincent P. Franklin and James D. Anderson (Editors), *New Perspectives on Black Educational History*, Boston: G. K. Hall and Company, 1978; Carleton Mabee, *Black Education in New York State*, Syracuse, NY: Syracuse University Press, 1979; Thomas Sowell, *Black Education: Myths and Tragedies*, New York: McKay Book Company, 1972.

BLACK ENGLISH, or black dialect, or black English vernacular, a nonstandard English sometimes used by black Americans. Black English is a resultant of the linguistic-cultural African heritage of black Americans. There are specific Afro-American meanings, interpretations, and gestures that, when used with European-American speech, result in a unique and viable language.

Black English has its own linguistic structure (i.e. sound, syntactical, and semantic) and consequently is one of many recognized nonstandard languages spoken in the United States. Examples of black English are: "My mother, she work there," "Here go a boy," "It's a lamp on the floor," "I here." Black English tends to contract sentences, so it takes fewer words to express an idea or meaning than required in standard English.
References: Jean Berko Gleason (Editor), *The Development of Language*, Columbus, OH: Charles E. Merrill Publishing Company, 1985; William Labov, "Recognizing Black English in the Classroom" in J. Chambers (Editor), *Black English: Educational Equity and the Law*, Ann Arbor, MI: Karoma Publishers, 1983; Judith Wells Lindfors, *Children's Language and Learning* (Second Edition), Englewood Cliffs, NJ: Prentice-Hall, Inc., 1987; Geneva Smitherman, *Talkin and Testifying*, Boston: Houghton Mifflin Company, 1977; Geneva Smitherman "What Go Round Come Round: King in Perspective" in C. K. Brooks (Editor), *Tapping Potential: English and Language Arts for the Black Learner*, Urbana, IL: National Council of Teachers of English, 1985; Pamela L. Tiedt and Iris M. Tiedt, *Multicultural Teaching: A Handbook of Activities, Information, and Resource* (Second Edition), Boston: Allyn and Bacon, Inc., 1986.

BLACK ENGLISH VERNACULAR—See BLACK ENGLISH and VERNACULAR LEARNING

BLACK HISTORY MONTH, previously known as Black Expressions Week, Black History Week, or by its original name, Negro History Week, an annual observance sponsored by schools and other organizations for the purpose of recognizing the achievements of Afro-Americans. The observance takes place each February. The first such celebration (Negro History Week) took place in 1926.

In 1915, Dr. Carter G. Woodson, a pioneer in the field of Afro-American history (and the son of slave parents) helped to found the Association for the Study of Negro Life and History. The organization's purpose was to collect data and to publish information about the Negro and, through such information, to bring about harmony between Negroes and whites. In addition, he helped to found the *Journal of Negro History* (1916), later the *Negro History Bulletin* (1937). Creation of the association, publication of the two journals, and observance of Negro History Week all emphasized the cultural and social accomplishments of Afro-Americans and served to bring about realization of Woodson's basic goal: instillation of cultural pride within Afro-Americans.

Black History Month is observed in elementary and secondary schools, institutions of higher education, churches, and other similar organizations.
References: Otey M. Scruggs, "Carter G. Woodson, The Negro History Movement, and Africa," *Pan African Journal*, Spring 1974; Carter G. Woodson, "Negro History Week," *Journal of Negro History*, April 1926; Alfred Young, "The Historical Origin and Significance of National Afro-American (Black) History Month Observance," *Negro History Bulletin*, January–February–March 1980.

BLACK STUDIES, sometimes titled Afro-American Studies, a circumscribed program of studies that serves various purposes. In some American school districts and universities, it is included in the curriculum as a vehicle for changing the image of Afro-Americans by noting the contributions people of African origin have made to the development of the United States. In other instances, still different reasons are offered (e.g. to provide black students with psychological identity, to foster improved racial understanding, or to present a systematic study of black people).

The teaching of Black Studies was introduced in many schools and colleges as the result of student demands fomented during the period of student activism (1960s). Programs, courses, and/or units dealing with this subject are now to be found at all school levels. Curricula vary. They may include any or all of the following study foci: black history, black self-concept, famous black people, African geography, black literature, black art and music, and languages (e.g. Swahili).

Numerous questions concerning Black Studies are still being studied and debated by educators, including these two: (1) Are Black Studies courses best taught by black teachers? (2) Should such study be made a separate curriculum component or should it be integrated into existing curricula?
References: Nick Aaron Ford, *Black Studies: Threat or Challenge*, Port Washington, NY: Kennikat Press, Inc., 1973; Raymond H. Giles, Jr., *Black Studies Programs in Public Schools*, New York: Praeger Publishers, 1974; Clifford D. Watson, *Pride: A Handbook of Black Studies Techniques for the Classroom Teacher*, Stevensville, MI: Educational Service, Inc., 1971.

BLEND, the fusion (combining) of two or more consonants in a word without either sound losing its identity. Examples are "bl," "cr," and "rk." When three consonants are brought together they are known as trigraphs (e.g. "str," "spl," and "scr"). Blends may appear at the beginning, in the middle, or at the end of a word. The study of blends is an important component of phonics instruction.
References: Lois A. Bader, *Reading Diagnosis and Remediation in Classroom and Clinic,* New York: Macmillan Publishing Company, Inc., 1980; Patrick Groff, *Phonics: Why and How,* Morristown, NJ: General Learning Press, 1977.

BLINDNESS, visual acuity in the better eye, with correction of 20/200 or less, or a defect in the visual field so the widest diameter of vision subtends an angle no greater than 20°. The problem with such a definition is that: (1) it is based on physiological terms; (2) rather than being scientifically developed, it reflects the opinion of experts; and (3) it was not created for children. In fact, there is no universally accepted definition of blindness except in cases of absolute blindness (no light perception).

Some authorities prefer to use the term *visually impaired;* however, individuals who may be classified as visually impaired have differing levels of vision. Some educators use the term *educational blindness,* which has been defined as an inability to profit from printed material, even with magnification. The majority of blind children have been impaired since birth, with one-third having no useful vision (prenatally induced). Heredity plays a major role in blindness in children. Many blind children have other handicaps as well. Blindness at any age can be caused by illness or accidents.

Increasing numbers of schools have developed special programs for children with visual impairments. Such children are placed in regular classrooms (mainstreamed) for part of, or for the entire day. These programs have enabled blind children to participate in almost all activities in which nonvisually impaired individuals participate. (See VISUAL IMPAIRMENT.)
References: Thomas J. Carroll, *Blindness,* Boston: Little, Brown and Company, 1961; James E. Jan, et al., *Visual Impairment in Children and Adolescents,* New York: Grune and Stratton, 1977; David H. Warren, *Blindness and Early Childhood Development,* New York: American Foundation for the Blind, Inc., 1977.

BLOCK GRANTS, sometimes referred to as "bloc" grants, federal allocations of money that the grantee (e.g. state, municipality) may spend as it best sees fit so long as the intent of the legislation authorizing the grant is satisfied. The actual amount of each block grant is determined using some predetermined formula (e.g. population, number of employed persons). Preliminary to actual distribution of block grants, each state is normally expected to submit, and to have approved, a state plan that details how block grant monies are to be spent.

Block grants are unique in at least two respects. First, although programs are funded using federal money, the authority to spend is made at the local level. Second, the grantee enjoys considerable decision-making flexibility.

In recent years, the block-grant mechanism has been used to support programs such as The Comprehensive Employment and Training Act (CETA) and special programs for senior citizens.
References: Annual Register of Grant Support, 1979-80 (Thirteenth Edition), Chicago: Marquis Who's Who, 1979; Virginia P. White, *Grants: How to Find Out About Them and What to Do Next,* New York: Plenum Press, 1975.

BLOCK PRINT, a method of printing (impressing) a picture or words on material from a block (the ink carrier) on which the picture or words are carved. Although any material (e.g. cork, rubber, tile, pine wood, sponges) can be used as the block, the most popular blocks are made of linoleum. Linoleum is easy to carve and holds up well under many printings. The most popular materials on which pictures and/or words are printed are paper and fabrics.

Block printing is an old craft. (Books were first printed by block prints.) Today, block printing is a very popular craft activity found in many elementary and secondary art programs. It requires only a few tools: gouges, knives, inks, and brayers (to spread the inks). Block printing, as a school or leisure activity, is relatively inexpensive and allows for a great deal of creativity on the part of those who carve and print the blocks.
References: Janet D. Erickson, *Block Printing on Textiles,* New York: Watson-Guptill, 1961; Gaston Petit and Amadio Arboleda, *Evolving Techniques in Japanese Woodblock Prints,* Tokyo, Japan: Kodansha International, 1977.

BLOOM'S TAXONOMY—See TAXONOMY

BOARD OF EDUCATION, LOCAL, governing board of a local school district. School boards derive their authority from, and work as agents of, the state. They constitute the legislative arm of the local school system, establishing policies to guide the superintendent and other professional staff members in carrying out day-to-day school operations. Specific responsibilities of the local school board include the hiring of a superintendent (or chief administrator), approving the budget recommended by the superintendent, approving the school calendar, adopting salary schedules for teachers and other employees, acting on the superintendent's recommendations concerning hiring and termination of employees, and engaging in contracts in behalf of the district. Fiscally independent boards also have the authority to levy taxes, subject to state law.

Most school board members are elected. The sizes of school boards vary, generally not exceeding nine members. (See FISCAL INDEPENDENCE.)

References: Roald F. Campbell, et al., *The Organization and Control of American Schools* (Fourth Edition), Columbus, OH: Charles E. Merrill Publishing Company, 1980; Keith Goldhammer, *The School Board*, New York: The Center for Applied Research in Education, Inc., 1967; Samuel Goldman, "School Board Relations: Control of the Schools" in Lee C. Deighton (Editor), *The Encyclopedia of Education* (Volume 8), New York: The Macmillan Company and The Free Press, 1971; Ronald W. Rebore, *Educational Administration: A Management Approach*, Englewood Cliffs, NJ: Prentice-Hall, Inc., 1985; Jon Wiles and Joseph Bondi, *The School Board Primer*, Boston: Allyn and Bacon, Inc., 1985.

BOARD OF EDUCATION MEMBERSHIP, service as a member of a local school board. *Qualifications* for membership vary from state to state and, where they exist, tend to be minimal. Examples of such qualifications include being a qualified voter in the school district, taxpayer status, having completed a certain minimum education (e.g. completion of elementary school), being of good character, being a parent, or being a certain age. Desired *qualities* identified by some authorities include, but are not limited to, interest in children, open-mindedness, maturity, success in one's chosen occupation, ability to make decisions, having time to devote to boardmanship, frankness, proven leadership ability in the community, and integrity.

Members are selected or elected depending upon state laws. The large majority (over 90 percent) of school board members are elected for fixed terms (e.g. four years); appointive boards tend to be found in large city school systems and certain southern states. In most states, elected members are chosen on a nonpartisan basis. In some communities a "caucus" body, broadly representative of the community, is used to identify, encourage, and support promising candidates. Community issues frequently influence the outcome of school board elections.

The social composition of board members has been studied by several investigators. Most report that members are among the more successful residents of their communities and tend to be businessmen or professionals. In a 1974 study, the National School Boards Association found that approximately 88 percent of the nation's school board members were men. In a 1979 survey by the same organization, the ratio of males was reported to be 72 percent. That same study found that 90 percent of the members surveyed were Anglo-American (i.e. nonminority), almost 70 percent were 40 years of age or older, and approximately 60 percent had annual incomes of $30,000 or more.

References: Commission on the Role of Women in Educational Governance, *Women on School Boards* (Report No. 1974-1), Evanston, IL: National School Boards Association, 1974; Arthur W. Foshay (Editor), *The Rand McNally Handbook of Education*, Chicago: Rand McNally and Company, 1963; Charles E. Reeves, *School Boards: Their Status, Functions and Activities*, Westport, CT: Greenwood Press, 1969 (Originally published in 1954 by Prentice-Hall, Inc.); Kenneth E. Underwood, et al., "Portrait of the American School Board Member," *The American School Board Journal*, January 1980; Freeman H. Vaughn, "School Boards: Selection of Members" in Lee C. Deighton (Editor), *The Encyclopedia of Education* (Volume 8), New York: The Macmillan Company and The Free Press, 1971.

BOARD OF EDUCATION STANDING COMMITTEES, permanent committees made up of one or more school board members who carry out specific duties assigned to them by the total board of education. The practice of using standing committees dates back to the early 19th century when, before school superintendencies were created, local boards were responsible for both administrative as well as policy affairs of the district. At the turn of the century, even after full-time superintendents had been appointed, the sizes of some school boards remained unusually large (some city districts actually had hundreds of board members). Standing committees were seen as a necessary vehicle for the involvement of these many board members in the affairs of their respective school systems.

Educational literature today almost universally recommends against the use of school board standing committees. Some arguments offered in support of this position follow: (1) the practice tends to divide the board into smaller ones; (2) standing committees are more likely to assume administrative duties than is a board that operates as a committee of the whole; (3) the work of standing committees is sometimes overlapping; and (4) the practice compounds the task of having the board operate as a coordinated unit.

In spite of those recommendations, standing committees continue to be used by all types of boards but especially so in city school districts and those with large enrollments. A 1975 National School Boards Association survey revealed that 52 percent of the districts sampled reported using them. Although the kinds of standing committees vary from one school district to the next, some are common to several districts. These include finance committees, executive committees, personnel committees, buildings and grounds committees, and committees on rules and regulations. Those who support the use of standing committees point to them as timesaving vehicles and groups that are able to examine critical issues in depth. (See AD HOC COMMITTEES.)

References: California School Boards Association, *Boardsmanship: A Guide for the School Board Member* (Third Edition), Sacramento, CA: The Association, 1967; National School Board Association, *School Board Meetings* (Research Report Number 1976–2), Evanston, IL: The Association, 1976; Charles E. Reeves, *School Boards: Their Status, Functions and Activities,* Westport, CT: Greenwood Press, 1969 (Reprint of a Prentice-Hall Book published in 1954).

BOARD OF EDUCATION, STATE, the body responsible for supervising the schools of a state or possession. State boards of education operate within legal frameworks established by state constitutions and statutes. They generally concern themselves with elementary and secondary education, although some have higher education oversight responsibility as well. Separate state boards for vocational education or higher education coexist with state boards of education in several states.

The principal functions of the state board of education include: (1) appointment of the chief state school officer (in 28 states); (2) adoption of a budget and personnel policies for the state department of education; (3) representing the state in educational matters involving the federal government; and (4) formulation of policies or recommendations designed to improve education in the state.

Three principal methods of selecting board members are used: (1) gubernatorial appointment; (2) election; or (3) ex officio membership (e.g. governor, chief state school officer). Board sizes range from 3 to 24 members, the average being 5 to 7. Most members serve 4- or 6-year terms with term lengths ranging from 2 to 15 years.

References: Sam Harris, *State Departments of Education, State Boards of Education, and Chief State School Officers,* Washington, DC: U.S. Government Printing Office, 1973; Thomas J. Landers and Judith G. Myers, *Essentials of School Management,* Philadelphia: W. B. Saunders Company, 1977.

BOARD OF TRUSTEES, COLLEGE AND UNIVERSITY, an institution of higher education's governing body. Boards of trustees have as their primary responsibility the establishment of policies under which the institution is to be governed. Additionally, trustees, in close consultation with their administrators, set long-range goals for the college/university and also deal with strategic long-term planning (including budgeting and investment of endowment or other reserve funds).

Most of the day-to-day work of carrying out established policies is delegated to the institution's president and, through him/her, to other administrators. The board of trustees is responsible for appointing the president and must also delineate, as specifically as possible, the powers and duties of the administration vs. the decision-making prerogatives it wishes to retain.

Trustees are selected for membership in four principal ways: (1) election; (2) appointment; (3) cooptation; and (4) ex officio selection. The status of the institution (private vs. public) frequently influences the selection process. Trustees are organized in accordance with bylaws or some similar governing document. Organizational structure includes officers (e.g. chairperson, vice-chairperson) and, frequently, working committees.

References: Association of Governing Boards of Universities and Colleges, *Financial Responsibilities of Governing Boards of Colleges and Universities,* Washington, DC: The Association, 1980; Louis H. Heilbron, *The College and University Trustee,* San Francisco: Jossey-Bass Publishers, 1973; Orley R. Herron, Jr., *The Role of the Trustee,* Scranton, PA: International Textbook Company, 1969.

BOBBITT, JOHN FRANKLIN (February 16, 1876–March 7, 1956), a professor of educational administration with a specialty in curriculum and curriculum development. He spent most of his professional career at the University of Chicago

(1904–1941). Between 1902 and 1907, Dr. Bobbitt taught in the Philippines, where he served on a committee to develop a curriculum for the Philippine schools. He was also involved in curriculum planning surveys in the cities of Cleveland (1915), Denver (1916), and San Antonio (1915).

The principle that curriculum should prepare the learner for those activities that make up an individual's life was the center of Bobbitt's approach to curriculum and curriculum development. Consequently, job analysis (through scientific analysis) and the identification of specific mechanical skills or behaviors played a major role in Bobbitt's curriculum development. His approach was based on the theory of social utility. Bobbitt and W. W. Charters utilized the job analysis approach to curriculum development; Bobbitt used the discover, through analysis, approach to identify curriculum objectives, while W. W. Charters started from a philosophical base and then used job analysis to develop the curriculum objectives.

Bobbitt wrote extensively in the area of curriculum. He authored: *The Curriculum* (1918), *How to Make a Curriculum* (1924), and *The Curriculum of Modern Education* (1941). (See CHARTERS, WERRETT WALLACE; MASTERY LEARNING; and SOCIAL UTILITY.)

References: John Franklin Bobbitt, *The Curriculum*, Boston: Houghton-Mifflin, 1918; John Franklin Bobbitt, *How to Make a Curriculum*, Boston: Houghton-Mifflin, 1924; James B. MacDonald and Dwight Clark, "Critical Value Questions and the Analysis of Objectives and Curriculum" in Robert M. W. Travers (Editor), *Second Handbook of Research in Teaching*, Chicago: Rand McNally and Co., 1973; Daniel Tanner and Laurel Tanner, *Curriculum Development Theory into Practice* (Second Edition), New York: Macmillan Publishing Co., 1980.

BODE, BOYD H. (October 4, 1873–March 29, 1953), noted philosopher and educator whose writings helped to influence the philosophical direction of American education during the first half of the 20th century. Bode's philosophical orientation closely approximated that of John Dewey. His principal writings included: *Fundamentals of Education* (1921); *Democracy as a Way of Life* (1937); and *How We Learn* (1940). His *Progressive Education at the Crossroads* (1938) was an incisive criticism of child-centered progressivism and an advocacy of education for democracy emphasizing use of the method of intelligence and comparison of conflicting world views.

Bode earned his Ph.D. at Cornell University. His teaching experience included service as Professor of Philosophy, University of Illinois (1909–21), and, from 1921–44, as Professor of Education and Head of the Department of Principles and Practices of Education, Ohio State University. He later taught at the Graduate Institute for Education, Cairo, Egypt, the University of Tennessee, and the University of British Columbia for short periods.

References: Ernest E. Bayles, "Bode, Boyd Henry" in John F. Ohles (Editor), *Biographical Dictionary of American Educators* (Volume 1), Westport, CT: Greenwood Press, 1978; "Bode, Boyd Henry" in *Who Was Who in America* (Volume 3), Chicago: The A. N. Marquis Company, 1963.

BODILY-KINESTHETIC INTELLIGENCE, one of the seven biologically based intelligences found in all humans. It is part of the Multiple Intelligence Theory (MI Theory). Control of bodily movement is achieved by part of the motor cortex. Regardless of culture or social environment, children follow a board development schedule of body movement, thus giving this intellect a biological rather than a learned base. The fact that some are "natural athletes" without formal instruction or experiences further supports the biological base of this intellect. It is in sports that bodily kinesthetic intelligence is most apparent and is the primary source of intelligence for problem solving. However, all those involved in playing sports must use a variety of intelligences while playing the sport—bodily kinesthetic intelligence does not function along. (See INTELLIGENCE; INTERPERSONAL INTELLIGENCE; INTRAPERSONAL INTELLIGENCE; LINGUISTIC INTELLIGENCE; LOGICAL-MATHEMATICAL INTELLIGENCE; MULTIPLE INTELLIGENCE THEORY; MUSICAL INTELLIGENCE; and SPATIAL INTELLIGENCE.)

References: Howard Gardner, *Frames of Mind*. New York: Basic Books, 1976; Joseph Walter and Howard Gardner, "The Development and Education of Intelligence" in F. R. Link (Editor), *Essays on the Intellect*, Alexandria, VA: Association for Supervision and Curriculum Development, 1986.

BODY LANGUAGE—See KINESICS and NONVERBAL COMMUNICATIONS

BOND, SCHOOL—See SCHOOL BOND

BOOK FAIR, or book festival, a local school or community project in which books are displayed for the purpose of stimulating interest in them, usually among young people. Book fairs are often conducted in conjunction with National Children's Book Week, an annual observance sponsored by the Children's Book Council.

Book fairs vary with respect to scope and type. A common approach is one in which new books are placed on display by a local sponsor (e.g. PTA) working cooperatively with a local bookseller. Books are sold and proceeds from sales are then used to support some educational project. Other types may feature paperback books only or may be limited to the exchange (or sale) of used books. Fairs may be conducted in schools, libraries, or houses of worship. Related activities such as puppet shows, storytelling, displaying of posters and book jackets, or talks by authors are sometimes scheduled to complement the displaying of books. (See CHILDREN'S BOOK COUNCIL and NATIONAL CHILDREN'S BOOK WEEK.)

References: John J. DeBoer and Martha Dallman, *The Teaching of Reading* (Third Edition), New York: Holt, Rinehart and Winston, Inc., 1970; Carol Kline, "Planning Problem-Free Book Fairs," *School Library Journal,* February 1977; Nancy Polette and Marjorie Hamlin, *Reading Guidance in a Media Age,* Metuchen, NJ: The Scarecrow Press, Inc., 1975.

BOOKMOBILE, a vehicle that functions as a mobile branch of a library, making books and magazines available to borrowers. Such vehicles are generally of two types: (1) the tractor-trailer, capable of carrying 5,000–7,000 books and that, once detached from its trailer, may be left parked in one area for a fixed period, and (2) the smaller, van-type of vehicle that carries fewer books (1,500–4,000 volumes) and that normally visits several stations on any given day. Bookmobiles may be used to make lender service available to patrons who do not enjoy library service in their localities, as a temporary replacement for a library, or as a supplement designed to encourage increased lender usage. Bookmobiles are sometimes called upon to service schools, notably those lacking a school library of their own.

A study of bookmobile costs, conducted in Pennsylvania (Teh-wei Hu, et al.), revealed that, on average, 46 percent of the books checked out were adult fiction and 36 percent, juvenile. Twenty percent of the books borrowed were never read. Patrons (88 percent were women, a statistic explained by the fact that bookmobile service is generally provided during working hours) reported a very high degree of satisfaction with services received.

References: Eleanor F. Brown, *Modern Branch Libraries and Libraries in Systems,* Metuchen, NJ: The Scarecrow Press, Inc., 1970; Eleanor F. Brown, *Bookmobiles and Bookmobile Service,* Metuchen, NJ: The Scarecrow Press, Inc., 1967; Teh-wei Hu, et al., *A Benefit-Cost Analysis of Alternative Library Delivery Systems,* Westport, CT: Greenwood Press, 1975.

BOOK TALKS, oral presentations (usually by librarians) to groups of students or parents. Book talks to students serve several purposes. Three of the major ones are: (1) to generate the idea of reading for pleasure; (2) to expose students to new reading fields; and (3) to familiarize students with the library, its holdings, and its personnel. The overriding objective is promotion of interest in reading.

Book talks to parents serve essentially the same purposes. In addition, they can be used to encourage family reading at home and to assist parents with child-rearing problems.

Some talks feature one book. In such cases, plot segments are included, along with the introduction of some characters, to stimulate interest in the volume. Other talks are broader in scope, covering a particular subject or theme.

References: Margaret Edwards, *The Fair Garden and the Swarm of Beasts,* New York: Hawthorn Books, Inc., 1969; Dorothy A. McGinnis (Editor), *Oral Presentations and the Librarian,* Syracuse, NY: Syracuse University Press, 1971; Nancy Polette and Marjorie Hamlin, *Reading Guidance in a Media Age,* Metuchen, NJ: The Scarecrow Press, Inc., 1975.

BOSTON LATIN SCHOOL—See LATIN GRAMMAR SCHOOL

BOTTOM-UP MODEL OF READING, a theory of the reading process that utilizes a part-to-whole approach. Visual perception is the first step in this process. The reader then proceeds in steps to letter recognition, decoding, word recognition, and finally to syntactic and semantic rules. Information gained at one level is a prerequisite to moving to the next higher level. The model emphasizes decoding mastery prior to meaning. Skill in phonics gives the reader a way to name a word; she/he then searches semantic memory to give the decoded word meaning. Bottom-up theorists believe that a child's broad experience with spoken language provides the connection between the decoding process and the meaning. They advocate teaching of sound-symbol correspondence (phonics) prior to emphasizing meaning. Accuracy in oral reading is crucial.

References: Patrick J. Finn, *Helping Children Learn to Read,*

New York: Random House, 1985; Lenore H. Ringler and Carol K. Weber, *A Language-Thinking Approach to Reading Diagnosis and Teaching*, New York: Harcourt Brace Jovanovich, Publishers, 1984.

BOY SCOUTS OF AMERICA (BSA),

national organization for boys founded in 1910 and chartered by Congress in 1916. Scouting for boys began in England (1907), largely due to the writings and efforts of Lord Baden-Powell. Many of his program ideas were incorporated into BSA.

The organization was designed to build desirable qualities of character, to teach citizenship, and to develop fitness in boys and young men. The BSA is divided into three subunits: *Cub Scouting*, for boys 7–10; *Scouting*, for boys 11–17; and *Explorers*, for young men and women 15–20. As of December 31, 1978, membership in these subunits was: Cub Scouts, 1,787,791; Scouts, 1,123,316; and Explorers, 392,162. Local Cub Packs, Scout Troops, and Explorer Posts/Ships, staffed by volunteer adult leaders, numbered 134,171. BSA publications include *Boys' Life, Scouting,* and *Exploring.* BSA's main offices are in North Brunswick, New Jersey.

Reference: Public Relations Division, Boy Scouts of America, *Fact Sheets:* "BSA at a Glance," "Historical Highlights," and "Scouting Around the World," Undated Brochures.

BOYS TOWN,

a home for homeless, abandoned, or neglected boys founded by Father Edward J. Flanagan. Through its residential program, Boys Town has accommodated over 14,000 boys since Father Flanagan opened his first home for boys in 1917.

The institution's present campus of 1,400 acres includes 65 buildings, a 1,000 acre farm, a middle school, a high school, and a Vocational Career Center. Its residential population consists of approximately 400 boys of all races and creeds. Boys live in campus homes with 8–9 other boys. Each home is supervised by a husband-wife team known as family-teachers.

In recent years, Boys Town has become a multiservice organization. Physically, socially, and emotionally maladjusted boys and girls are now also being helped through new programs such as the Boys Town Institute for Communication Disorders in Children (established 1972) and the Boys Town Center for the Study of Youth Development (also founded in 1972).

Boys Town, located in Omaha, Nebraska, is administered by a 21-member Board of Directors and a residential director. Most of the institution's programs are supported through contributions made by individual contributors. (See FLANAGAN, EDWARD J.)

References: Boys Town: Memories and Dreams, Boys Town, NE: Father Flanagan's Boys Home, Undated Brochure; *Facts About Boys Town,* Boys Town, NE: Father Flanagan's Boys Home, Undated Brochure; Fulton Oursler and Will Oursler, *Father Flanagan of Boys Town,* Garden City, NY: Doubleday and Company, Inc., 1949; Clifford Stevens, *Boys Town: Father Flanagan's Dream,* Boys Town, NE: Boys Town Publications (Originally published as *Father Flanagan: Builder of Boys* by P. J. Kennedy and Sons, 1967).

BRAILLE,

a touch system of reading and writing for the blind, developed by Louis Braille, consisting of embossed dots that form 34 basic characters. It is a phonetic alphabet system, originally designed as a secret code for the French military. Joel W. Smith, at the Perkins Institution in the United States (in the late 1800s), adapted the Braille system for American use. He used the Braille cell (6 dots), retained 12 of Braille's letter symbols, and redistributed all of the other symbols. His alphabet, based on letter occurrence, was called the modified, later the American Braille. It wasn't until 1932 that a standard Braille was accepted (Standard English Braille). The Braille code is made up of 63 characters that can be used singly or in combination (260). Examples of Braille are illustrated below.

There are many Braille aids available today, including slate and stylus, mechanical writers, and typewriters.

References: Randall K. Harley, et al., *The Teaching of Braille Reading,* Springfield, IL: Charles C. Thomas, Publisher, 1979; J. Alvin Kugelmass, *Louis Braille,* New York: Julian Messner, Inc., 1951; Berthold Lowenfeld, et al., *Blind Children Learn to Read,* Springfield, IL: Charles C. Thomas, Publisher, 1969.

Example of Braille

BRAIN DAMAGE, any injury to the soft nerve tissues that are a part of the central nervous system and that are enclosed within the skull (known as the brain). Psychologists Heinz Werner and Alfred A. Strauss, through their research, developed a new category of exceptional children known as *brain injured*. Their work led to the theory that brain injuries may be exogenous (not due to an inherited trait or characteristic). Injuries to the brain could occur before, during, and after birth.

There are many terms used to indicate brain damage, including brain-injured, Strauss Syndrome, neurophrenia, neurological impairment, brain dysfunction, and hyperkinetic syndrome. Brain damage can be either major or severe; it can be minimal (minor) or mild. Cerebral palsies, epilepsies, autism, mental subnormalities, and severe aphasia are examples of major damage. Impairment of fine motor coordination, deviations in impulse control, deviations in attention, and intellectual deficits may be products of minimal brain damage. Many psychologists and educators object to the term *minimal brain damage,* because it is not an easily identifiable problem nor is the term universally defined or accepted.

Reference: Janet W. Lerner, *Children with Learning Disabilities,* Boston: Houghton Mifflin Company, 1976.

BRAINSTORMING, a form of group discussion that emphasizes creative or imaginative thinking. This method was developed and named by an advertising executive, Alex Osborn. It involves bringing a group of people together. A problem is posed; creative (even daring) ideas for its resolution are solicited. All ideas are accepted without criticism, reaction, or discussion. The method is essentially designed to promote ideas for eventual discussion by others.

References: Ernest G. Bormann, *Discussion and Group Methods: Theory and Practice* (Second Edition), New York: Harper and Row, Publishers, 1975; Alexander F. Osborn, *Applied Imagination: Principles and Procedures of Creative Problem-Solving,* New York: Scribner's, 1963; David Potter and Martin P. Andersen, *Discussion in Small Groups: A Guide to Effective Practice* (Third Edition), Belmont, CA: Wadsworth Publishing Company, Inc., 1976.

BRANCHING PROGRAMMING, a format used in many programmed instruction materials in which the student's response is used to control the programmed materials presented. Unlike linear programming, where the order of frames is predetermined, the order of presentation of frames in branching is determined by the nature of the student's response. (See illustration below.)

Branching allows for sequencing that might be: (1) forward in a particular order based on a particular sequence determined by the level of accomplishment of the student; (2) backward in a particular order, again determined by the student (this might be for review or reinforcement purposes); or (3) other combinations of programming. Differential psychology is the basis for the branching approach to programmed instruction, an approach first suggested by Norman Crowder in 1961. (See LINEAR PROGRAMMING and PROGRAMMED INSTRUCTION.)

References: Allen D. Calvin, *Programmed Instruction: Bold New Venture,* Bloomington, IN: Indiana University Press, 1969; Denny G. Langdon (Editor), *Programmed Instruction,* Englewood Cliffs, NJ: Educational Technology Publications, 1978; Stuart Margulies and Lewis D. Eigen, *Applied Programmed Instruction,* New York: John Wiley and Sons, 1962.

BRIGGS, THOMAS H. (January 25, 1877–August 12, 1971), noted teacher educator and authority on

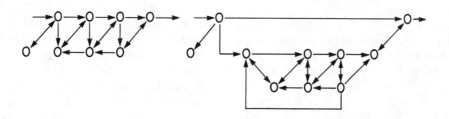

Two Examples of Branching
(There are many different designs)

curriculum, supervision, and the American junior high school. During most of his career, he was a member of the Teachers College, Columbia University faculty (1912–42).

Briggs earned the A.B. degree from Wake Forest College (1896) and the Ph.D. (1914) from Columbia University. He began high school teaching in Elizabeth City, North Carolina (1896), and, following short tenures at J. B. Stetson University and Chicago's Princeton-Yale Academy, joined the Eastern Illinois State Normal School faculty (1901) where he served for ten years.

In addition to writing and coauthoring books in the fields of reading, grammar, and English, he wrote *The Junior High School* (1920), *Curriculum Problems* (1926), *Secondary Education* (1933), and *Pragmatism and Pedagogy* (1940). He also edited secondary school textbooks, conducted school surveys, and made contributions to national organizations such as the National Education Association, National Association of Secondary School Principals (Director of Consumer Education Study, 1942–45), and the Council for the Advancement of Secondary Education (Board Chairman, 1951).

References: Jacques Cattell and E. E. Ross (Editors), *Leaders in Education: A Biographical Directory* (Third Edition), Lancaster, PA: The Science Press, 1948; Harold J. McKenna, "Briggs, Thomas Henry" in John F. Ohles (Editor), *Biographical Dictionary of American Educators* (Volume 1), Westport, CT: Greenwood Press, 1978.

BRITISH EDUCATION INDEX, a cumulative index listing significant educational articles appearing in selected British educational periodicals. Currently, over 200 such periodicals (all published in the English language) are indexed on a regular basis. Entries may be found subsuming any (or all) of three classifications: (1) "Subject Index"; (2) "Subject List of Articles"; and (3) "Author Index." Yet another section, "List of Titles of Periodicals and Publishers," provides the titles and addresses of all periodicals indexed.

References: Eugene P. Sheehy, *Guide to Reference Books* (Ninth Edition), Chicago, American Library Association, 1976; Robert Vickers (Editor), *British Education Index* (Volume 15), London, England: Bibliographic Services Division, The British Library, 1979.

BRITISH INFANT SCHOOL, a general term that has been applied to those British primary schools that stress informal education. The infant schools accommodate children from ages five to seven or eight. Piagetian psychology is the base for most of the educational programs found in the British Infant Schools. Some of the characteristics of the Infant Schools are: an integrated day; activities not based on a prescribed time allotment but rather utilizing learning centers; groups formed vertically with children of all ages belonging to a group, rather than children grouped according to ability, age or some other category; thought process orientation (inductive reasoning, problem solving); play activities as a central theme; and child-centered activities with children being trusted to make decisions.

The British Infant School has been a major influence on American open education programs. The British Infant School became a major force in education after the Plowden Report was published in 1967. This report was a government financed study of early childhood education in Wales and England. (See OPEN EDUCATION and PLOWDEN REPORT.)

References: Ellis D. Evans, *Contemporary Influences in Early Childhood Education* (Second Edition), New York: Holt, Rinehart and Winston, Inc., 1975; Raymond S. Moore, et al., *Schools Can Wait*, Provo, UT: Brigham Young University Press, 1979; Lady Bridget Plowden (Chairperson), *Children and Their Primary Schools: A Report to the Central Advisory Council for Education in England* (Volume 1), London, England: Her Majesty's Stationery Office, 1967.

BROWN v. BOARD OF EDUCATION OF TOPEKA, the U.S. Supreme Court decision which held that the Fourteenth Amendment of the U.S. Constitution forbids states to impose segregation of the races in the public schools. The decision was rendered in 1954.

Actually, four separate cases from Kansas, South Carolina, Virginia, and Delaware (*Brown v. Board of Education of Topeka*, 98 F. Supp. 797, 1951; *Briggs v. Elliot*, 103 F. Supp. 920, 1952; *Gebbart v. Belton*, 33 Del. Ch. 144, 1952; *Davis v. County School Board*, 103 F. Supp. 337, 1952) were consolidated into one case and heard by the U.S. Supreme Court. The decision relating to the four cases was handed down in *Brown v. Board of Education of Topeka*, 347 U.S. 483, 493, 1954. Sometimes known as Brown I, it held: "In the field of public education the doctrine of 'separate but equal' has no place. Separate educational facilities are inherently unequal."

Brown II (*Brown v. Board of Education of Topeka*, 349 U.S. 294, 1955) held that local school authorities have the primary responsibility for implementing Brown I. The Supreme Court further stated that a "prompt and reasonable start" toward full implementation was to be made. It also held that this implementation must be made "with all deliberate speed." (See DE FACTO SEGREGATION and DE JURE SEGREGATION.)

References: Clifford P. Hooker (Editor), *The Courts and Education* (NSSE 77th Yearbook, Part I), Chicago: University of Chicago Press, 1978; Perry A. Zirkel (Editor), *A Digest of Supreme Court Decisions Affecting Education,* Bloomington, IN: Phi Delta Kappa, 1978.

BUCKLEY AMENDMENT, popular designation for the Family Educational Rights and Privacy Act that was passed by Congress as a rider to the Education Amendments of 1974. The amendment, named for Senator James Buckley who introduced it, provided that federal funds are to be denied to any school system or institution of higher learning that refuses to show the contents of a student's record to his/her parents or, in the case of students 18 years or older, to the students themselves. The law, in addition to using federal funding as leverage for enforcement, is significant for having established two principles: (1) that parents (until the student becomes 18 years of age) have the right to see their own children's records, and (2) parents may not examine the records of any other student.

At least six parts of the amendment and HEW's implementing regulations are important for school officials to remember: (1) parents of a student (or the 18-year-old) must be shown the records no more than 45 days after requesting to see them; (2) any item in the records may be subject to a validity challenge; (3) items inserted before January 1, 1975, need not be shown; (4) a student may waive his/her right to see confidential letters such as letters of recommendation; (5) the right of a school to release personal information about a student to a third party is restricted; and (6) students and parents are to be notified of their rights as regards access to records. (See CUMULATIVE RECORD.)

References: Family Educational Rights and Privacy Act, *United States Statutes at Large* (Volume 88, Part I), Washington, DC: U.S. Government Printing Office, 1974; Thomas J. Flygare, *The Legal Rights of Students* (PDK Fastback 59), Bloomington, IN: The Phi Delta Kappa Educational Foundation, 1975; William A. Kaplin, *The Law of Higher Education: Legal Implications of Administrative Decision Making,* San Francisco: Jossey-Bass Publishers, 1978.

BUDGET—See SCHOOL BUDGET

BULLETIN BOARD, or tackboard, fixed or movable surface to which display items may be tacked or stapled. The material of which bulletin boards are most frequently constructed is cork.

The bulletin board is one of the least expensive of all the teaching resources available to the teacher. It can be used to fulfill any of a number of instructional purposes, including these: (1) to stimulate student interest (e.g. a display depicting some newsworthy event); (2) to permit an entire class to view a single copy of some instructional material; (3) to call attention to a particular event (e.g. holiday celebration); (4) to add to the attractiveness of a classroom; and (5) to introduce or culminate a unit. Most authorities agree that students should be encouraged to plan and to create bulletin board displays.

References: Melville K. Bowers, *Easy Bulletin Boards* (Number 2), Metuchen, NJ: The Scarecrow Press, Inc., 1974; James W. Brown, et al., *AV Instruction: Technology, Media, and Methods* (Fifth Edition), New York: McGraw-Hill Book Company, 1977; Robert V. Bullough, Sr., *Creating Instructional Materials* (Second Edition), Columbus, OH: Charles E. Merrill Publishing Company, 1978; Carleton W. H. Erickson and David H. Curl, *Fundamentals of Teaching with Audiovisual Technology* (Second Edition), New York: The Macmillan Company, 1972.

BUREAUCRACY, normally a civil service organization charged with governance or carrying out of governance-related tasks. Bureaucracies gained prominence following the decline of 19th-century social systems that had aristocratic privilege as their keystone.

A German scholar, Max Weber (1864–1920), pioneered in research dealing with bureaucracies. His characterization of a bureaucracy included the following elements: (1) fixed and official jurisdictional areas of responsibility assigned to officials; (2) responsibilities (activities) carried out in accordance with a widely understood system of rules or regulations; (3) rational-legal authority granted to officials for discharging their respective duties; (4) employment of individuals on the basis of generally regulated qualifications as opposed to social ties; and (5) a hierarchical system of superior-subordinate relationships with authority flowing from top down. Officials in a bureaucracy, Weber noted, are normally career employees who, to the limits of their respective abilities, can realize upward mobility within the organization. Corresponding increases of an economic and social esteem nature generally accompany each promotion.

The term *bureaucracy* has been popularized and is often pejoratively used to describe organizations that are inefficient, slow, and nonresponsive.

References: H. H. Gerth and C. Wright Mills (Translators and Editors), *From Max Weber: Essays in Sociology,* New York: Oxford University Press (A Galaxy Book), 1965; Michael Pusey, *Dynamics of Bureaucracy: A Case Analysis in Education,* Sydney, Australia: John Wiley and Sons Australasia Pty. Ltd., 1976; Robert Townsend, *Up the Organization,* New York: Alfred A. Knopf, 1970.

BUREAU OF INDIAN AFFAIRS (BIA), a unit within the U.S. Department of Interior that was organized for the purpose of helping Indians and Native Alaskans to develop to their fullest. When first created in 1824, BIA was assigned to the War Department; when actually established (in 1849), it was transferred to the Department of Interior.

BIA's principal objectives include helping Indians and Native Alaskans: (1) to manage their own affairs, and (2) to develop their resources and individual potentialities. Many of BIA's activities are directly or indirectly related to education: (1) making educational opportunities available to children and adults in public or BIA schools; (2) helping Indians and Native Alaskans to create and manage their own school systems; and (3) providing social service, community development, and similar support services. Much of BIA's work is carried out by Area Offices, virtually all of which are in western states.

In the late 1970s, there were slightly more than 200,000 American Indian children of school age. Of that number, approximately two-thirds were enrolled in public schools. BIA schools (193) were serving almost 50,000 Indian children who resided in regions where public schools were not available.

BIA is but one of several federal agencies providing services to Indians and Native Alaskans.

References: Barry Klein (Editor), *Reference Encyclopedia of the American Indian* (Third Edition, Volume I) Rye, NY: Todd Publications, 1978; Office of Education, Department of HEW, *A Brief History of the Federal Responsibility to the American Indian,* Washington, DC: U.S. Government Printing Office, 1979; Office of the Federal Register, National Archives and Records Service, General Services Administration, *United States Government Manual, 1978/79,* Washington, DC: U.S. Government Printing Office, 1978.

BUROS, OSCAR KRISEN (June 14, 1905–March 19, 1978), an educational psychologist and statistician. He was an expert in educational measurement and testing and wrote extensively in the field.

Buros was editor of the *Mental Measurements Yearbooks* (through the Eighth Edition), *Tests in Print* (I, II), *Personality Tests and Reviews* (I, II), and many other authoritative volumes. The *Eighth Mental Measurements Yearbook* was his 24th major publication.

Buros was a high school teacher before accepting teaching positions at Teachers College, Columbia University (1929–30) and Rutgers University (1932–65). His professional activities included the establishment of the Institute of Mental Measurements as well as serving as its Director. He was Associate Director of the evaluation staff of the Eight-Year Study, did extensive consulting with developing nations in Africa as well as in the United States, and served as President of the Gryphon Press. (See EIGHT-YEAR STUDY and TESTS IN PRINT.)

References: Oscar K. Buros (Editor), *The Eighth Mental Measurements Yearbook* (Volumes I and II), Highland Park, NJ: The Gryphon Press, 1978; Jacques Cattell, *American Men and Women of Science: The Social and Behavioral Sciences* (Twelfth Edition), New York: Jacques Cattell Press and R. R. Bowker Company, 1973.

BUSINESS EDUCATION, a component of the secondary school curriculum that provides students with information and skills about the world of business. The typical business education curriculum is made up of two parts, vocational business education and general business education. *Vocational business education* consists of those skill courses that lead to employment in the business field upon graduation. They include clerical and general office work, bookkeeping-accounting, secretarial work (including typing, word processing, and stenography), business management, and distributive education. *General business education* offerings seek to develop economic understanding. They are aimed at all students, not just those preparing for a business occupation. General business education provides consumer education and information about our economic system. Selected business courses (e.g. typing) are available to nonmajors seeking to acquire specialized skills for personal use.

At the college and university level, business education refers to training programs for prospective or practicing business education teachers.

In increasing numbers, two-year community colleges offer business education programs, vocational and general.

References: Gladys Bahr and F. Kendrick Bangs (Editors), *Foundations of Education for Business* (National Business Education Yearbook, No. 13), Reston, VA: National Business Education Association, 1975; Leroy Brendel and Herbert Yengel, *Changing Methods of Teaching Business Subjects* (National Business Education Yearbook, No. 10), Washington, DC: National Business Education Association, 1972; Lloyd V. Douglas, et al., *Teaching Business Subjects* (Third Edition), Englewood Cliffs, NJ: Prentice-Hall, Inc., 1973.

BUSING, a means of transporting children to and from school or school-related activities. The use of buses to transport children is not new. For years children in many rural communities have been bused from their homes to attend centrally located schools. With the movement to consolidate schools and school districts during the 1940s and 1950s, geographic attendance areas grew in size, thus requiring the use of buses to enable children in those extended areas to attend such consolidated schools.

Busing has also been a means of desegregating student populations, particularly in large urban school districts. It wasn't until April 20, 1971, that the United States Supreme Court ruled that tactual desegregation would require transporting children to new schools, many out of their neighborhood (*Swann v. Charlotte-Mecklenburg Board of Education*, 402 U.S. 1, 1971). Busing plans, for desegregation purposes, have been ordered by the courts in many areas of the country. Pontiac, Michigan; Nashville, Tennessee; Omaha, Nebraska; and Boston, Massachusetts, are just a few of the cities that have been involved in court-ordered busing. Although busing for desegregation purposes accounts for only a small percentage of those children bused daily to school in the United States, the issue has generated a considerable amount of debate.

References: Judith Bentley, *Busing: The Continuing Controversy*, New York: Franklin Watts, 1982; Judith F. Buncher, *The School Busing Controversy: 1970–75*, New York: Facts on File, 1975; J. Dennis Lord, *Spatial Perspectives on School Desegregation and Busing*, Washington, DC: Association of American Geographers, 1977; Nicolaus Mills (Editor), *Busing USA*, New York: Teachers College Press, 1979; Gary Orfield, *Must We Bus?* Washington, DC: The Brookings Institution, 1978.

BUTLER, NICHOLAS MURRAY (April 2, 1862–December 7, 1947), a leading scholar, college administrator, and philosopher. Dr. Butler was the first Dean of Columbia University's Faculty of Philosophy (1890). He became the 12th President of Columbia University in 1901 and retained that position until 1945.

Dr. Butler played a leading role in education. In 1889, he helped establish the New York College for the Training of Teachers and was named its President; approximately a decade later, it became part of Columbia University and was named Teachers College. As part of Columbia University, Teachers College attracted many great scholars and philosophers of education (John Dewey, William Kilpatrick, E. L. Thorndike, and others), making it one of the leading institutions of its day. In addition, Dr. Butler participated in the creation of the College Entrance Examination Board. He played a major role in the writing (in 1894) of the Committee of Ten (NEA) report that influenced high school curriculum in the United States. In toto, he had 3,000 books, articles, essays, reports, and speeches published.

Dr. Butler was also a leader in national and international affairs. He was a candidate for U.S. Vice-President in 1912, wrote on foreign affairs, helped to establish the Carnegie Endowment for International Peace, supported the Kellogg-Briand Peace Pact, and won the Nobel Peace Prize in 1931. (See COLLEGE BOARD and COMMITTEE OF TEN.)

References: John William Burgess, *Reminiscences of an American Scholar*, New York: Columbia University Press, 1934; Nicholas M. Butler, *Education in the United States,* New York: Johnson Reprint Corporation, 1968; Nicholas M. Butler, *The Meaning of Education,* New York: The Macmillan Company, 1905; Nicholas M. Butler, *Why War?*, New York: Scribner's, 1940; Albert Marrin, *Nicholas Murray Butler,* Boston: Twayne Publishers, 1976.

BUZZ GROUPS, small units (four to seven members) into which a class or other larger group is divided for the purpose of discussing specific topics. The buzz group fulfills several instructional purposes: (1) permits students (participants) to solve problems collaboratively; (2) facilitates integration of subject material; and (3) provides a forum for peer teaching-learning. Decisions or other results arrived at by the buzz group are reported back to the larger group. Meetings of buzz groups are called buzz sessions.

Reference: William H. Bergquist and Steven R. Phillips, *A Handbook for Faculty Development*, Washington, DC: The Council for the Advancement of Small Colleges, 1975.

CALDECOTT MEDAL, named in honor of the British picture book artist Randolph Caldecott, is awarded each year for the best American children's picture book published in the preceding year. The medal was introduced in 1938, at the suggestion of Frederic G. Melcher, and awarded to Dorothy P. Lathrop for her illustrations in *Animals of the Bible*. Winners of each year's medal are selected by committees of children's librarians who are affiliated with the American Library Association. (See APPENDIX IV: RANDOLPH CALDECOTT MEDAL AWARD WINNERS.)

References: Mary Hill Arbuthnot, et al., *Children and Books* (Fourth Edition), Chicago: Scott, Foresman and Company, 1972; Charlotte S. Huck and Doris A. Young, *Children's Literature in the Elementary School* (Third Edition), New York: Holt, Rinehart and Winston, Inc., 1976.

CALIFORNIA ACHIEVEMENT TESTS (CAT) a battery of tests that measure knowledge of content and educational skills that are basic to learning. The CAT focuses on the ability to understand the meaning of content materials, problem solving, and performance in reading, mathematics, and language. Scores are available for: *reading*— vocabulary, comprehension, total; *mathematics*— computation, concepts and problem solving, total; and *language*—mechanics, auding (grades 1.5–2), usage and structure, spelling, total. There are five levels of the California Achievement Tests. The appropriate grades per level are: grades 1.5–2, Level 1; grades 2–4, Level 2; grades 4–6, Level 3; grades 6–9, Level 4; and grades 9–12, Level 5.

Reference: Oscar K. Buros (Editor), *The Seventh Mental Measurements Yearbook* (Volume I), Highland Park, NJ: The Gryphon Press, 1972; Ernest W. Tiegs and Willis W. Clark, *California Achievement Tests, 1970 Edition,* Monterey, CA: CTB/McGraw-Hill, Inc., 1970.

CALIFORNIA TEST OF MENTAL MATURITY (CTMM), an omnibus group test of mental ability. The short form of the test is titled the California Short-Form Test of Mental Maturity. The test's two forms each have levels that are appropriate for grades Kindergarten to 16 and for adults. The *long form* provides eight scores: (1) logical reasoning; (2) spatial relationships; (3) numerical reasoning; (4) verbal concepts; (5) mem-

ory; (6) language total; (7) nonlanguage total; and (8) a total score. There are six test levels numbered 0–5. Each level covers a particular grade range (e.g. Level 0, grades kindergarten–1.0; Level 3, grades 7–9). Hand-scored as well as machine-scored tests are available. The *short form* produces seven scores: (1) logical reasoning; (2) numerical reasoning; (3) verbal concepts; (4) memory; (5) language total; (6) nonlanguage total; and (7) total score. Hand-scored and machine-scored tests are also available for the short form.

Both tests produce a deviation I.Q. score. This permits comparison with the Stanford-Binet Tests. The CTMM was first published in 1936. There has been some criticism of the instrument over technical issues; overinterpretation of the scores should be watched. (See INTELLIGENCE TESTS and STANFORD-BINET TEST.)

Reference: Oscar K. Buros (Editor), *The Seventh Mental Measurements Yearbook* (Volume I), Highland Park, NJ: The Gryphon Press, 1972.

CAMP FIRE, INC. (CFI), a multiprogram, multiservice organization serving young people, birth to 21 years of age. Founded (in 1910) by Dr. Luther Gulick, a prominent physical educator, and his wife as the Camp Fire Girls, Inc., the organization assumed its present name in 1979. The name change reflects the fact that CFI now serves both boys and girls.

Camp Fire, Inc., operates three major programs: (1) Club Programs; (2) Outdoor Programs; and (3) Response Programs. *Club Programs* operate on a year-round, small group basis under adult supervision. Members progress through four program levels: Blue Birds; Adventurers; Discovery; and Horizon. *Outdoor Programs* feature activities such as day camping, trips, and group camping. *Response Programs,* developed by individual councils, include diverse activities such as day care centers, delinquency-prevention projects, and tutorial-reading programs.

Headquartered in Kansas City, CFI claims over 750,000 members (adults and youth). Its councils (almost 350) serve youth in 35,000 communities. A 40 member National Board of Directors gives direction to the organization and oversees its full-time professional staff. A publication for CFI leaders, *Leadership Magazine,* appears quarterly.

References: Camp Fire Girls, Inc., *Fact Sheet-1979*, Kansas City, MO: Camp Fire Girls, Inc., 1979; "Camp Fire Girls" in Peter Romanofsky (Editor), *Social Service Organizations* (Volume 1), Westport, CT: Greenwood Press, 1978.

CANADIAN EDUCATION ASSOCIATION (CEA),

or L'Association Canadienne d'Education, national professional organization of individuals working in, or desirous of contributing to, the improvement of Canadian public education. CEA serves as a clearinghouse for educational information. Organized in 1892, it brings together educational leaders working at several different levels: administrators, trustees, organizational leaders, and teacher educators. Sources of funding include school boards, individual memberships, and grants from provincial departments of education.

A 30-member board of directors (including each of the 10 deputy ministers of education) oversees the work of the organization. CEA produces four regular periodicals: *Education Canada,* a quarterly; *CEA Newsletter,* published nine times each year; the *Bulletin,* also published nine times annually and prepared for the benefit of francophone members; and *News Bulletin,* issued fortnightly during the school year. The association also publishes reports on a variety of school-related subjects. CEA serves as the coordinating office for teacher exchange programs with the United States and Great Britain. The organization's annual conference attracts approximately 1,000 members. CEA's main office is in Toronto, Ontario.

References: Canadian Education Association, "The Canadian Education Association," *CEA Handbook*, Toronto, Canada: The Association, 1980; Margaret Gayfer, *An Overview of Canadian Education* (Second Edition), Toronto, Canada: Canadian Education Association, 1978.

CANADIAN EDUCATION INDEX,

the Canadian counterpart to the *American Education Index. Canadian Education Index* lists educational articles appearing in approximately 160 Canadian periodicals and newsletters. Indexes are published five times each year.

Reference: Bill Katz and Berry G. Richards, *Magazines for Libraries* (Third Edition), New York: R. R. Bowker Company, 1978.

CANADIAN TEACHERS' FEDERATION (CTF),

also known as Fédération Canadienne Des Enseignants, a national organization of Canadian teachers, founded in 1920, that works closely with its 14 provincial and territorial component units. CTF's membership roll includes almost a quarter-million members. Its five largest component units, presented in order of membership size, are: Ontario Teachers' Federation; British Columbia Teachers' Federation; Alberta Teachers' Association; Manitoba Teachers' Society; and the Nova Scotia Teachers' Union.

The activities of the federation are directed by a representative legislative body that meets once annually. Implementing the organization's policies are a Board of Directors, an Executive Committee, and CTF's President. Recent activities carried out by CTF address issues such as teacher welfare, teacher education, teachers' pensions, economics of education, and improvement of educational quality. The CTF Resource Centre contains more than 250,000 documents that are available to help committees and provincial/territorial units in the course of their work. In addition, two special commissions (French Language Commission and Commission on French as a Second Language) tender recommendations designed to improve the education of Canada's English-speaking and francophone students. CTF's central offices are in Ottawa.

Reference: Canadian Teachers' Federation, *Canadian Teachers' Federation*, Ottawa, Canada: The Federation, 1979.

CANONICAL CORRELATION,

a multivariate statistical-analysis procedure used to assess the interrelationships between two sets of measurements. These measurements must be made on the same subjects or students.

The canonical correlation procedure produces canonical variates (factors) and a Canonical R (correlations) for each variate. The variates identify, through weights, those measures in each set that contribute most heavily to the correlated elements. Since the statistical procedure is based on producing the strongest relationships in order of importance, the first canonical variate will be the strongest and have the largest Canonical Correlation (R). The Canonical R measures the actual relationship; the larger the number, the stronger the relationship. The Canonical R can never exceed 1.00. The canonical correlation was first developed in 1935 by Harold Hotelling, a famous educational statistician.

References: Walter R. Borg and Meredith D. Gall, *Educational Research: An Introduction* (Fifth Edition), New York: Longman, Inc., 1989; William M. Hays, *Statistics* (Fourth Edition), New York: Holt, Rinehart and Winston, Inc., 1988; Fred N. Kerlinger, *Foundations of Be-*

havioral Research (Third Edition), New York: Holt, Rinehart and Winston, Inc., 1986.

CAPACITY LEVEL—See EXPECTANCY LEVEL

CAPITAL OUTLAY, expenditures that a school district makes for land, equipment, and school buildings. Such expenditures increase the school system's nonmoney assets. (See SCHOOL BUDGET.)

References: I. Carl Candoli, et al., *School Business Administration: A Planning Approach*, Boston: Allyn and Bacon, Inc., 1978; Paul L. Reason and Alpheus L. White, *Financial Accounting for Local and State School Systems*, Washington, DC: U.S. Office of Education, 1957.

CAPITATION GRANT, an allocation of money to an institution or to a governmental agency on the basis of head count or number of persons to be served. Most capitation grants are made to institutions of higher education or training organizations with enrollment determining the exact amount of money to be apportioned to each.

References: Annual Register of Grant Support, 1979–80 (Thirteenth Edition), Chicago: Marquis Who's Who, 1979; Asa S. Knowles (Editor), *The International Encyclopedia of Higher Education* (Volume 1), San Francisco: Jossey-Bass Publishers, 1977; Virginia P. White, *Grants: How to Find Out About Them and What to Do Next*, New York: Plenum Press, 1975.

CARD CATALOGUE, repository for single cards containing information on each book or other reference item available in a library. Cards are of uniform size and are stored on their edges in a special cabinet containing drawers that are normally organized vertically. Each card contains a class or call number to facilitate book location as well as related information such as title, author, publisher, and publication date. The earliest known card catalogue was prepared by the Abbe Rosier (1775). It contained handwritten slips of paper that were filed in shallow trays.

References: Leonard M. Harrod, *The Librarians' Glossary and Reference Book* (Third Edition), New York: Seminar Press, 1971; Thomas Landau, *Encyclopedia of Librarianship* (Second Revised Edition), New York: Hafner Publishing Company, 1961; Pauline A. Seely, *ALA Rules for Filing Catalog Cards* (Second Edition); Chicago: American Library Association, 1968.

CARDINAL PRINCIPLES OF SECONDARY EDUCATION, a statement of objectives for American secondary schools published in 1918 by the Commission on the Reorganization of Secondary Education. The commission, created by the National Education Association, identified seven objectives that did much to influence high school curricula. The Seven Cardinal Principles were: (1) health; (2) command of fundamental processes; (3) worthy home membership; (4) vocation; (5) citizenship; (6) worthy use of leisure; and (7) ethical character.

References: Commission on the Reorganization of Secondary Education, NEA, *Cardinal Principles of Secondary Education*, Washington, DC: Government Printing Office Bulletin No. 35, 1918; National Education Association, "The Seven Cardinal Principles Revisited," *Today's Education*, September–October 1976; Donald F. Popham, *Foundations of Secondary Education: Historical, Comparative, and Curricular*, Minneapolis, MN: Burgess Publishing Company, 1969; William Van Til, *Secondary Education: School and Community*, Boston: Houghton Mifflin Company, 1978.

CAREER-BOUND SUPERINTENDENTS—See PLACE-BOUND AND CAREER-BOUND SUPERINTENDENTS

CAREER EDUCATION, a major redirection in education suggested by U.S. Commissioner of Education Sidney P. Marland to refocus itself toward the world of work. Career education includes: (1) career awareness and the awareness of the world of work; (2) in-depth exploration of occupational clusters; (3) career preparation; (4) knowledge and understanding of the economic system of the United States; and (5) career specialization. Career education extends from early childhood through an individual's working life.

There is no universal definition of career education; states have differing ones. The most common is the Oregon Conceptual Model (Awareness, K–6; Exploration, 7–10; Preparation, 11–12; Specialization, posthigh school–adult). Career education, not to be considered another term for vocational education, extends through all subject areas and all educational levels by merging the academic world with the world of work. This merger, or integration, is intended to foster economic independence, appreciation for the dignity of work, and the production of personal satisfaction.

References: Rupert Evans, et al., *Career Education in the Middle/Junior High School*, Salt Lake City, UT: Olympus Publishing Company, 1973; Jack W. Fuller and Terry O. Wheaton (Editors), *Career Education: A Lifelong Process*, Chicago: Nelson-Hall, Inc., 1979; David C. Gardner and

Sue Allen Warren, *Careers and Disabilities: A Career Education Approach*, Stamford, CT: Greylock Publishers, 1978; Kenneth B. Hoyt, *Career Education: Where It Is and Where It Is Going*, Salt Lake City, UT: Olympus Publishing Company, 1981; David L. Jesser, *Career Education: A Priority of the Chief State School Officers*, Salt Lake City, UT: Olympus Publishing Company, 1976.

CAREER GUIDANCE, a guidance program that focuses on an individual's occupational development throughout his/her working life. It includes more than vocational selection, covering personal and educational guidance as well.

Career guidance is usually provided by professionally trained counselors able to help an individual to: (1) assess his/her assets and liabilities; (2) understand the demands, needs, and opportunities of the world of work; (3) make plans for the short and long run that are realistic and appropriate for the interests and skills of the individual; (4) plan and secure appropriate training and education; (5) make contacts in the world of work; and (6) acquire information on the availability of employment. Such guidance includes testing (skills, interests); psychological guidance and support; follow-up and evaluation; awareness of new and future industrial, business, and vocational trends; awareness of market and industrial conditions; knowledge of various career choice theories; and understanding of personal and psychological human needs.

Career guidance is provided in many high schools in the United States. Currently, career awareness is being developed formally, through career education, in the elementary schools. Job service and other agencies also provide career guidance for individuals. (See CAREER EDUCATION.)
References: Henry Barow (Editor), *Career Guidance for a New Age*, Boston: Houghton Mifflin Company, 1973; Charles A. Harkness, *Career Counseling*, Springfield, IL: Charles C. Thomas, Publisher, 1976; Edwin Herr and Stanley Cramer, *Career Guidance through the Life Span*, Boston: Little, Brown and Company, 1979; H. H. London, *Principles and Techniques of Vocational Guidance*, Columbus, OH: Charles E. Merrill Publishing Company, 1973; Samuel H. Osipow, Theories of Career Development (Second Edition), New York: Appleton-Century-Crofts, Inc., 1973; Richard Rehberg and Laurence Hotchkiss, "Career Counseling in Contemporary U.S. High Schools" in David C. Berliner (Editor), *Review of Research in Education #7*, Washington, DC: American Educational Research Association, 1979; Stephen G. Weinrach, *Career Counseling*, New York: McGraw-Hill Book Company, 1979.

CAREER LADDERS FOR TEACHERS, a plan that coordinates teacher certification and evaluation with career development. Between 1983–86, varied forms of career ladder programs have been implemented in 15 states; during that same period, 7 additional states have enacted legislation for programs. Plans vary from state to state; however, a common goal is to provide an incentive to exemplary teachers to remain in the teaching profession. Some states have developed criteria for implementation of programs, while others have allowed complete local autonomy. Tennessee adopted a five-rung ladder: Probationary, Apprentice, Career I, Career II, and Career III. Teachers move up the ladder based on test results and observation. Charlotte-Mecklenburg, North Carolina, has a three-level career ladder based on classroom, faculty, and professional performance. Expectations in all three categories are made available to teachers, and decisions are made as a result of observation and other data. (See MENTOR TEACHER.)
References: Russel L. French, "Commentary: 'Misconceptions' in Critique of Career Ladders," *Education Week*, Volume 14, 1986; Carol Furtwengler, "Tennessee's Career Ladder Plan: They Said It Couldn't Be Done!" *Educational Leadership*, November 1985; Philip C. Schlechty, "Evaluation Procedures in the Charlotte-Mecklenburg Career Ladder Plan," *Educational Leadership*, November 1985.

CAREER OPPORTUNITIES PROGRAM (COP), a federally funded program that provided education and experiences for paraprofessional teacher aides in low income (urban, rural) areas. Its purpose was to foster their advancement within the field of education, ultimately to the status of certified teacher. The program was authorized by the Education Professions Development Act (1967), a component of the War on Poverty. It was first funded in 1970 and lasted until 1977.

COP was a small program that served approximately 15,000 participants. Parents and residents from low-income areas became teacher aides in their home communities with many earning college degrees and teacher certification.
References: David E. Kapel, "Career Ladders and Lattice," *Education and Urban Society*, August 1970; George R. Kaplan, *From Aide to Teacher*, Washington, DC: U.S. Department of Health, Education, and Welfare, 1977; Public Law 90–35, *United States Statutes at Large, 1967* (Volume 81), Washington, DC: U.S. Government Printing Office, 1968.

CARNEGIE CORPORATION OF NEW YORK, a philanthropic foundation created in 1911 by steel magnate Andrew Carnegie. Since its founding, the foundation has awarded grants exceeding $500,000,000.

Early grants were directed toward establishment of free public libraries, a subject in which Carnegie was vitally interested. The organization is presently working to improve education at all levels; higher education, early childhood education, and elementary-secondary education. Additionally, its public affairs program supports social justice and equal opportunity efforts. The corporation's Commonwealth Program underwrites projects that focus on communication improvement and leadership development in the Caribbean, southern Africa, and the South Pacific.

The corporation's capital fund is valued at almost $300,000,000. Approximately $12,000,000 of this amount is committed each year. (See CARNEGIE FOUNDATION FOR THE ADVANCEMENT OF TEACHING.)

References: Carnegie Corporation of New York, *General Information,* New York: The Corporation, Undated Booklet; Carnegie Corporation of New York, *List of Grants: 1977,* New York: The Corporation, 1977.

CARNEGIE FORUM ON EDUCATION AND THE ECONOMY, a program established in 1985 by the Carnegie Corporation of New York. A 10-year agenda was defined to study the relationship between economic growth and the education of the people who will contribute to that growth. On the recommendation of its Advisory Council, the Carnegie Forum established a Task Force on Teaching as a Profession. The task force was composed of members of the Advisory Council plus outstanding individuals in the fields of business, education, journalism, public service, and science. Recognizing the important role assumed by teachers in the educational process, the president of the Carnegie Corporation directed the task force to report findings and recommendations on that subject at the first annual meeting of the forum (1986). The report was entitled *A Nation Prepared: Teachers for the 21st Century.* That report was the first in a series of recommendations on American education. (See NATIONAL CENTER ON EDUCATION AND THE ECONOMY and *(A) NATION PREPARED: TEACHERS FOR THE 21ST CENTURY.*)

References: Carnegie Forum on Education and the Economy, *A Nation Prepared: Teachers for the 21st Century,* New York: Carnegie Corporation of New York, 1986.

CARNEGIE FOUNDATION FOR THE ADVANCEMENT OF TEACHING, established in 1905 by Andrew Carnegie. Originally, the principal role to be played by the foundation was the provision of pensions for American and Canadian college teachers. In 1918, after it was determined that the assets of the foundation were insufficient to support this major effort, the Carnegie Corporation and the Carnegie Foundation jointly established the Teachers Insurance and Annuity Association, an independent retirement company that provides pensions for college professors. The cosponsors subsequently contributed in excess of $17,000,000 to TIAA. This amount was allocated over the three-plus decades following TIAA's creation.

In recent years, the foundation has had the study of higher education as its principal focus. The Carnegie Commission on Higher Education, which sponsored or produced policy reports between 1967 and 1973, was one of its better-known efforts. (See CARNEGIE CORPORATION OF NEW YORK and TIAA-CREF.)

References: Carnegie Corporation of New York: *General Information,* New York: The Corporation, Undated Booklet; Marianna O. Lewis (Editor), *The Foundation Directory* (Sixth Edition), New York: The Foundation Center, 1977.

CARNEGIE REPORT—See *(A) NATION PREPARED: TEACHERS FOR THE 21ST CENTURY*

CARNEGIE UNIT, a measure of academic credit used to determine a student's eligibility for graduation from high school. The Carnegie Unit is a measure of study time representing 120 hours of classwork completed in one year. For example, a course scheduled to meet 5 times a week, 40 minutes a day, over a period of 36 weeks yields one Carnegie Unit. Variations in the number of sessions per week or the number of minutes in a period are permitted to accommodate special types of classes (e.g. science laboratories). Most four-year high schools mandate completion of at least 16 Carnegie Units for graduation, including required courses such as English or American History.

The Carnegie Unit originated at the turn of the 20th century, the product of the Committee on College Entrance Requirements. In recent years, it has been subject to some criticism as a rigid and anachronistic system that no longer assures quality of learning. (See COMMITTEE ON COLLEGE ENTRANCE REQUIREMENTS.)

References: John Dettre, "The Carnegie Unit: A Doubtful Practice," *NASSP Bulletin*, November 1975; Arthur W. Foshay (Editor), *The Rand McNally Handbook of Education*, Chicago: Rand McNally and Company, 1963; Kenneth Hovet, "What Are the High Schools Teaching?" in the 1956 Yearbook, *What Shall the High Schools Teach?* Washington, DC: Association for Supervision and Curriculum Development, 1956; Charles L. Wood, Everett W. Nicholson, and Dale G. Findley, *The Secondary School Principal: Manager and Supervisor* (Second Edition), Boston: Allyn and Bacon, Inc., 1985.

CARREL, sometimes referred to as a study carrel or individual study carrel, a partitioned or enclosed area in which a student works on an individual basis. Generally located in libraries, carrels afford privacy and eliminate sound/visual distractions that would normally disturb or interrupt other students. Users of carrels work with several types of materials including books, records, teaching machines, tapes, slide projectors, and radios.

Carrels are partitioned off on three sides. They may be structurally simple or complex. *Simple carrels* (also known as dry carrels) normally consist of a surface (desk) area on which students may write or work with a shelf or two available for temporary storage of books and equipment. Many are portable. *Complex carrels,* also known as wet carrels, include electrical outlets to permit use of audiovisual equipment. Some of the most sophisticated types even provide connections to a central storage bank, a feature that permits the user to signal the kind of program needed, thus sparing him/her the task of carrying equipment to and from the carrel.
References: Ralph E. Ellsworth and Hobart D. Wagener, "A New Concept for a School Library" in Pearl L. Ward and Robert Beacon (Editors), *The School Media Center: A Book of Readings*, Metuchen, NJ: The Scarecrow Press, Inc., 1973; Derick Unwin and Ray McAleese, *Encyclopedia of Educational Media Communications and Technology*, Westport, CT: Greenwood Press, 1978.

CASE CONFERENCE, a meeting in which two or more professionals discuss, evaluate, and plan strategies for a client. In schools, the client is invariably a student. Participating professionals may include one or more teachers, a nurse-teacher, a counselor, a speech therapist, a school psychologist, and so on. The case conference is a formal meeting, one in which behavioral outcomes are specified for the student under study and in which consensus is reached with respect to strategies needed to help the student achieve the outcomes specified.

A case conference model developed by Michael Tracy and Fred Kladder involves these steps: (1) referral of the client needing assistance; (2) appointing of the case conference committee (professionals); (3) collecting information about the client; (4) sharing of the information; (5) developing an individual educational plan for the client; (6) deciding on placement; and (7) review. The student's parents, a school administrator, or others concerned with the student's educational progress take case conference committee suggestions under advisement and are normally the individuals whose approval and support are enlisted.
References: Bruce Shertzer and James D. Linden, *Fundamentals of Individual Appraisal: Assessment Techniques for Counselors*, Boston: Houghton Mifflin Company, 1979; Michael I. Tracy, et al., *Case Conference: A Simulation and Source Book*, Indianapolis, IN: Indiana Department of Public Instruction and the Indiana University Developmental Training Center, 1976.

CASE STUDY, an investigatory method used to study individuals, groups, or institutions. Detailed written descriptions are prepared by the investigator (e.g. counselor, psychologist) that: (1) describe the subject under study; (2) report behavior patterns and the physical/psychological characteristics that may be related to the behaviors observed; and (3) suggest factors (characteristics) that appear to relate causally to the behavior pattern noted. Background information about individual subjects (e.g. students) may include such information as family history, record of grades, attendance, health history, interests, and comments by other professionals.

In 1937, Gordon Allport suggested that effective case studies "fall into three sections: (a) a description of the present status, (b) an account of past influences and successive stages of development, and (c) an indication of future trends" (p. 394). Another authority, Tyrus Hillway, cautioned that a weakness of the method, especially when cause-and-effect relations are proffered, is its subjectivity. He indicated that case study conclusions are acceptable "only when: (1) the same causes produce the same effect... in a sufficient number of cases, or (2) corrective remedies applied... prove effective, or (3) both" (p. 47).
References: Gordon W. Allport, *Personality, A Psychological Interpretation*, New York: H. Holt and Company, 1937; Lee J. Cronbach, *Educational Psychology* (Third Edition), New York: Harcourt Brace Jovanovich, Inc., 1977; Tyrus Hillway, *Handbook of Educational Research: A Guide to Methods and Materials*, Boston: Houghton Mifflin Company, 1969.

CATEGORICAL AID, one of three types of appropriations for purposes such as education. Categorical aid includes monies for categories of activity that have been specifically earmarked by Congress, a state legislature, or other higher jurisdiction. The remaining two types of aid are *block grants* and *general aid.*

Notwithstanding the limitations and problems associated with it, school officials have been willing to accept categorical aid. Perhaps the most compelling reason for doing so is the fact that the likelihood of schools receiving significant general (and usually unfettered) aid is quite remote.

Specific arguments against categorical aid are: (1) it gives too much power and control to the federal government; (2) it sometimes produces curricular imbalances at the school district level; (3) the red tape and report writing it requires; and (4) the likelihood that programs supported by categorical aid may become relatively permanent. The single specific advantage associated with categorical aid is that it can cause states and school districts to move in prescribed directions. (See BLOCK GRANTS.)

References: Joel S. Berke and Robert J. Goettel, "The Role of Categorical Programs in the Post-Rodriquez Period" in John Pincus (Editor), *School Finance in Transition: The Courts and Educational Reform,* Cambridge, MA: Ballinger Publishing Company, 1974; Percy E. Burrup, *Financing Education in a Climate of Change* (Second Edition), Boston: Allyn and Bacon, Inc., 1977; Jerome T. Murphy, *State Education Agencies and Discretionary Funds,* Lexington, MA: Lexington Books, 1974.

CATHARSIS, the healthful "talking out" of one's ideas/problems. The theory of catharsis holds that one can deal with repressed ideas and problems to the extent that they are brought into consciousness. Another implication is that catharsis, by being channeled in this manner, relieves tension, anxiety, and aggressive energy and thus helps to make the individual more passive.

References: Shervert H. Frazier, et al., *A Psychiatric Glossary: The Meaning of Terms Frequently Used in Psychiatry* (Fourth Edition), New York: Basic Books, Inc., Publishers, 1975; Michael P. Nicholas and Melvin Zax, *Catharsis in Psychotherapy,* New York: Gardner Press, Inc., 1977.

CATHOLIC SCHOOLS, the largest group of parochial schools operating in the United States. Affiliated with the Roman Catholic Church, Catholic schools are of four basic types: (1)*single-parish schools,* those elementary and secondary schools operated by a local parish; (2)*interparish schools,* op-erated by several parishes; (3) *diocesan schools;* and (4) *private schools,* those operated by a particular religious community (usually academies and college preparatory institutions). In 1978-79, approximately 90 percent of the Catholic elementary schools were administered by local parishes, while 70 percent of the secondary schools were either diocesan or privately operated.

The National Catholic Educational Association reported that U.S. Catholic schools, in 1978-79, enrolled 3,274,000 elementary and secondary school students. They were attending 9,850 schools, of which 8,159 were elementary schools. In the same year, the full-time teaching staff of these schools consisted of 147,948 faculty members of whom 102,497 were lay teachers, 39,069 sisters, and 6,382 male religious. Trends covering the last five to ten years indicate that enrollment and numbers of schools are decreasing and the size of the lay staff is increasing.

The 1978-79 Catholic school enrollment of 3,274,000 represented approximately 7 percent of the nation's total K-12 enrollment. In 1965-66, 87 percent of all students attending private (parochial and nondenominational) schools were enrolled in Catholic schools. In 1978-79, that ratio dropped to 64 percent. (See CHRISTIAN SCHOOLS; NONPUBLIC SCHOOLS; PAROCHIAL SCHOOLS; and YESHIVA.)

References: A Statistical Report on U.S. Catholic Schools, 1979-80 (An Excerpt from *Catholic Schools in America,* 1980), Washington, DC: National Catholic Educational Association, 1980; *Catholic Schools in America* (1980 Edition), Englewood, CO: Fisher Publishing Company (in cooperation with the National Catholic Educational Association), 1980; Otto F. Kraushaar, *Private Schools: From the Puritans to the Present* (PDK Fastback 78), Bloomington, IN: The Phi Delta Kappa Educational Foundation, 1976; James M. Lee (Editor), *Catholic Education in the Western World,* Notre Dame, IN: University of Notre Dame Press, 1967.

CAUSAL-COMPARATIVE RESEARCH—See CAUSALITY

CAUSALITY, a research term used to describe a relationship between/among variables such that a change in one, in cause-and-effect fashion, produces a change in the other(s). For example, when reductions in automobile speed limits can be shown to produce reductions in automobile accidents, causality between the *speed* and *accident rate* variables can be said to have been established.

Causality can be inferred from either experimental or nonexperimental studies. In the *experi-*

mental method, the researcher controls all factors except one, the independent variable that is manipulated with the consequent effect of that manipulation then studied. The second approach, the *causal-comparative method* (also known as ex post facto research), attempts to ascertain the causes of noted effects after-the-fact (or working from the effects backward). Sociologists who note and study crime-rate differences between two otherwise similar communities are using the causal-comparative method, inferring what they believe to be the factor(s) producing such differences.

The fact that variables are correlated does not in and of itself indicate that their relationship is causal.

References: Jean R. Dyer, *Understanding and Evaluating Educational Research,* Reading, MA: Addison-Wesley Publishing Company, 1979; Fred N. Kerlinger, *Foundations of Behavioral Research* (Third Edition), New York: Holt, Rinehart and Winston, Inc., 1986; Emil J. Posavac and Raymond J. Carey, *Program Evaluation: Methods and Case Studies* (Third Edition), Englewood Cliffs, NJ: Prentice-Hall, 1989.

CEILING, BUDGET—See TAX AND EXPENDITURE LIMITATIONS

CENSORSHIP, efforts by individuals, groups, or governments to keep individuals from hearing, seeing, or reading information presumed to be harmful to public morality or to government. Those exercising censorship have offered moral, religious, and other rationale in defense of their actions.

Library books and textbooks used in the schools are frequent targets of censors. Works such as *The Scarlet Letter, The Good Earth,* and *The Catcher in the Rye* are among the hundreds of library books that individuals or pressure groups have sought to ban from the shelves of school libraries. Similarly, censors have exerted pressure at the state level (in states with state textbook adoption laws) and the local school district level (in all other states) to keep "undesirable" books from being used by school children.

Numerous national organizations have worked to preserve intellectual freedom when censors' charges are believed to be without foundation. Several have developed suggested policies/procedures for school districts to follow when subjected to censorship attempts. These organizations include the American Library Association, the National Council of Teachers of English, the National Education Association, and the American Association of University Professors.

References: James E. Davis (Editor), *Dealing with Censorship,* Urbana, IL: National Council of Teachers of English, 1979; Edward De Grazia, *Censorship Landmarks,* New York: R. R. Bowker Company, 1969; Felice F. Lewis, *Literature, Obscenity, and Law,* Carbondale, IL: Southern Illinois University Press, 1976.

CENSUS—See SCHOOL CENSUS

CENTER FOR DEATH EDUCATION AND RESEARCH, a nonprofit organization that seeks "to bring recent and relevant ideas, information, and insights concerning the important subject of death to as wide an audience as possible" (unpaginated booklet). Established in 1969, it is an integral part of the Department of Sociology, University of Minnesota.

The center sponsors original research dealing with attitudes toward death and bereavement. Information relating to death and dying is collected and disseminated to laymen and professionals. The center's audio tapes (e.g. Death and the Family, Talking to Children About Death, Adolescent Suicide) are available for sale. Video cassettes (e.g. Grief, Death and the Child) are available on a rental basis. Additionally, the center: (1) offers undergraduate and graduate classes dealing with death, grief, and bereavement; (2) provides speakers; and (3) sponsors symposia. The *Bibliography on Death, Grief and Bereavement* (Arno Press), containing almost 4,000 references, was compiled by the center. Local and national advisory boards help give direction to the center's activities.

Reference: Center for Death Education and Research, *Center for Death Education and Research,* Minneapolis, MN: University of Minnesota, Undated Booklet.

CENTER FOR RESEARCH LIBRARIES (CRL), a nonprofit organization operated by member institutions. CRL was founded in 1949 by ten universities (with help from the Carnegie and Rockefeller Foundations) and named the Midwest Interlibrary Center. It assumed its present name in 1965. Currently, over 180 members and associate members make up CRL.

The purpose of the center is to make infrequently used research materials available to scholars. The present library collection consists of over 3,000,000 volumes that readers may borrow for unlimited periods of time. Book requests, processed through the reader's local interlibrary loan department, may be transmitted using the Tymshare computer network, telephone, or collect teletype. Loans are made to libraries, not to individuals.

Subject matter fields represented in the CRL collection include literature, social sciences, fine arts, physical sciences, medicine, technology, Africana, railroading, and meteorology. Types of materials available are: (1) microform and facsimile copies of archival records; (2) over 600,000 foreign dissertations; (3) government documents (foreign, federal, and state); (4) journals (over 14,000 subscriptions are held); (5) monographs; (6) newspapers (including backfiles); and (7) one of the largest collections of North American university and college catalogs. CRL is in Chicago.

References: Center for Research Libraries, *Research Materials Available from the Center for Research Libraries,* Chicago: The Center, 1980; Anthony T. Kruzas and Linda V. Sullivan, *Encyclopedia of Information Systems and Services* (Third Edition), Detroit: Gale Research Company, 1978.

CENTILE—See PERCENTILE

CENTRAL DEAFNESS, or word deafness, a term used to describe speech and language defects that are similar to the defects of hearing impaired or deaf children. However, the defects of central deafness are caused by brain injury or damage to the auditory nerve pathways. In short, the brain does not function as it should. Literally, central deafness is not deafness, since it is possible for the individual to have his/her hearing mechanism operate properly and still not be able to understand what is being heard. With very small children, it is difficult to distinguish between an actual hearing loss and the inability of the brain to function appropriately. (See AGNOSIAS and APHASIA.)

References: A. V. Baru and T. A. Karaseva, *The Brain and Hearing,* New York: Consultants Bureau, 1972; Hallowell Davis and S. Richard Silverman, *Hearing and Deafness* (Fourth Edition), New York: Holt, Rinehart and Winston, Inc., 1978; A. Bruce Graham (Editor), *Sensorineural Hearing Process and Disorders,* Boston: Little, Brown and Company, 1967; Alice Streng, et al., *Hearing Therapy for Children* (Second Edition), New York: Grune and Stratton, 1958.

CENTRALIZATION—See DECENTRALIZATION

CENTRAL PROCESSING UNIT—See MICROPROCESSOR

CENTRAL TENDENCY MEASURES, procedures used to summarize a distribution of scores such that a specific measure could describe all the scores. There are three generally used measures of central tendency: mode, median, and mean.

A *mode* (M_o) is the most frequent score in a group of scores. In the following distribution of scores, 6, 6, 7, 7, 7, 7, 8, 8, 9, 10, 11, the number 7 is the mode. There were four scores of 7, the most frequent score.

Median (M_{dm}) is the point above and below which 50 percent of the scores fall. In the following distribution of scores, 2, 3, 3, 5, 8, 10, 11, 12, 12, 20, 21, the number 10 is the median score. In the following distribution of scores, 3, 3, 5, 8, 10, 11, 12, 12, 20, 21, the number 10.5 is the median.

The arithmetic average, or *mean* ($\bar{X}$, μ, M), is calculated by adding all the scores in a distribution and dividing by the number of scores. For the following distribution, 2, 3, 3, 5, 8, 10, 11, 12, 12, 20, 21, 22, the mean ($\bar{X}$) is 10.75. (See MEAN; MEDIAN; and MODE.)

References: Emanuel J. Mason and William J. Bramble, *Understanding and Conducting Research/Applications in Education and the Behavioral Sciences,* New York: McGraw-Hill Book Company, 1978; Bruce W. Tuckman, *Conducting Educational Research* (Second Edition), New York: Harcourt Brace Jovanovich, Inc., 1978.

CEREBRAL DOMINANCE, a state in which either the left or right hemisphere of the brain has a predominant function over a particular task. Research has indicated that right-handed people have a predominant left hemisphere. The cerebral dominance of left-handed individuals is not as clear-cut, however; some are left-hemisphere dominant and others are dominant in the right.

A specific hemispheric dominance for language and other functions has not been firmly established. It does appear that lesions in a particular hemisphere will cause apraxia, aphasia, and other disorders. (See AMBIDEXTERITY; APHASIA; and APRAXIA.)

References: Arthur L. Benton, *Right-Left Discrimination and Finger Localization,* New York: Harper and Brothers, 1959; M. Kinsbourne, "Cerebral Dominance: Learning and Cognition" in H. R. Myklebust (Editor), *Progress in Learning Disabilities* (Volume III), New York: Grune and Stratton, 1975.

CEREBRAL PALSY (CP), a descriptive term that covers the neuromotor component of the "brain-damage syndrome." Paralysis of the limbs, involuntary movement, incoordination, weakness, and functional deviation of the motor system resulting from a nonprogressive brain lesion are symptoms of cerebral palsy. Children who have progressive brain lesions cannot be considered to have cerebral palsy until the lesion becomes nonprogressive.

Because brain lesions cause CP, other problems such as mental deficiency, seizures, and sensory and emotional disturbances can exist concurrently. Treatment may include differing modalities such as surgery, physical and speech therapy, braces, and drugs. As of 1980, CP has been noncurable and nonfatal. Its effects can be reduced through therapy. (See BRAIN DAMAGE.)

References: William M. Cruikshank (Editor), *Cerebral Palsy: A Developmental Disability* (Third Edition), Syracuse, NY: Syracuse University Press, 1976; D. P. Hallihan and J. M. Kauffman, *Exceptional Children*, Englewood Cliffs, NJ: Prentice-Hall, Inc., 1978; Sidney Keats, *Cerebral Palsy*, Springfield, IL: Charles C. Thomas, Publisher, 1977; Sophie Levitt, *Physiotherapy in Cerebral Palsy*, Springfield, IL: Charles C. Thomas, Publisher, 1962; Mariana Newton, *Cerebral Palsy: Speech, Hearing, and Language Problems*, Lincoln, NE: Cliffs Notes, Inc., 1977.

CERTIFICATION, also referred to as teacher certification, the practice (required in all states) of licensing educational professionals. Eligibility for certification as a teacher requires fulfillment of up to three broad sets of requirements: (1) citizenship, health, age and moral requirements; (2) completion of a bachelor's degree, including prescribed courses, or a total, approved teacher training program; and (3) completion of specific courses (e.g. state history), a requirement imposed by a minority of the states. Certification for specialized positions such as principal, school psychologist, guidance counselor, and so on requires a prescribed amount of graduate level study and, usually, successful teaching experience.

In states using the approved program route to certification, a written statement attesting to successful completion of a state-approved or nationally accredited program qualifies applicants for licensure; in other states, a review (by state education certification officials) of transcripts is required. Passing of a teacher competency examination has, in recent years, been made an additional requirement in an increasing number of states. (See ACCREDITING AGENCIES AND ASSOCIATIONS; NATIONAL ASSOCIATION OF STATE DIRECTORS OF TEACHER EDUCATION AND CERTIFICATION; and NATION-

AL COUNCIL FOR THE ACCREDITATION OF TEACHER EDUCATION.)

References: Mary Paxton Burks, *Requirements for Certification for Elementary Schools, Secondary Schools, Junior Colleges* (51st Edition), Chicago: The University of Chicago Press, 1987; William P. Gorth and Michael L. Chernoff (Editors), *Testing for Teacher Certification*, Hillsdale, NJ: Lawrence Erlbaum Associates, Publishers, 1986; Betty Levitov (Editor), *Licensing and Accreditation in Education: The Law and the State Interest*, Lincoln, NE: University of Nebraska Printing and Duplicating Service, 1976; Study Commission on Undergraduate Education and the Education of Teachers, *Teacher Education in the United States: The Responsibility Gap*, Lincoln, NE: University of Nebraska Press, 1976.

CHAINING, a term used in operant behavior psychology that describes behavior in a temporal sequence such that the responses to one stimulus are followed by other stimuli that reinforce the response and facilitate subsequent responses. An example of a chain is illustrated on page 93.

In this chain, R_1 provides part of or the entire stimulus (S_2) for R_2 and so on. Thus, S_2 has an eliciting or discriminative stimulus function for R_2 and may reinforce response R_1. When responses are similar, the chain is called *homogenous*. If the responses are quite different (walking to a counter, moving a tray, tasting a piece of food), the chain is called *heterogeneous*. Chaining is used extensively in some forms of programmed learning and instruction. (See PROGRAMMED INSTRUCTION.)

References: Charles Catania (Editor), *Contemporary Research in Operant Behavior*, Glenview, IL: Scott, Foresman and Company, 1968; P. B. Dews (Editor), *Festschrift for B. F. Skinner*, New York: Appleton-Century-Crofts, Inc., 1970; Werner K. Honig and J. E. R. Staddon (Editors), *Handbook of Operant Behavior*, Englewood Cliffs, NJ: Prentice-Hall, Inc., 1977.

CHAIRPERSON—See DEPARTMENT CHAIRPERSON

CHALLENGE GRANT—See MATCHING GRANT

CHAMBER MUSIC, secular music for small ensembles of solo instruments. Unlike orchestras, where several instruments of the same kind may be included, chamber music usually has one of each instrument represented in the performing group. Where three instruments (players) are involved (e.g. violin, viola, bass), the ensemble is known as a trio. Different names are used to indicate the

Chaining Example

$$S_1 \rightarrow R_1 \rightarrow S_2 \rightarrow R_2 \rightarrow S_3 \rightarrow R_3$$

number of players: quartet (four), quintet (five), sextet (six), septet (seven), and octet (eight).

Through the 19th century, chamber music was performed almost exclusively by amateur musicians, usually in private music rooms for the enjoyment of the players. Beethoven and some of his successors then began to write quartets and other pieces for chamber music that, because of their technical difficulty, had the effect of limiting many performers to professional musicians. Bartok and Schoenberg have been among the greatest creators of chamber music in the 20th century.

References: Willi Apel, *Harvard Dictionary of Music* (Second Edition, Revised and Enlarged), Cambridge, MA: The Belknap Press of Harvard University Press, 1970; Michael Tilmouth, "Chamber Music" in Stanley Sadie (Editor), *The New Grove Dictionary of Music and Musicians* (Volume 4), London, England: Macmillan Publishers Limited, 1980; Sherman Van Solkema, "Chamber Music" in Bruce Bohle (Editor), *The International Cyclopedia of Music and Musicians* (Tenth Edition), New York: Dodd, Mead and Company, 1975.

CHANGE AGENT, a person, group, or agency used by an organization for the purpose of bringing about some form of personal or institutional change. Such agents normally come from outside the organization, frequently working in a consultative capacity. Nevertheless, as some students of organizational change have pointed out, change agents may also be found within the organization, some having been employed specifically to produce change.

Ronald Havelock sees change agents performing four frequently overlapping kinds of service: (1) catalyzing change by disrupting the status quo; (2) offering solutions to problems; (3) facilitating change by providing resource help; and (4) matching resource people, in and out of the organization, with problems to be solved.

In his systems theory of organizational change, Daniel Griffiths offered some propositions that identify the chief administrator of an open system (e.g. school district) as a change agent. Conditioning the likelihood of change in the system, he suggested, are considerations such as: (1) whether the leader is from outside the system ("outsiders" are seen as having greater change potential); and (2) the chief administrator's length of tenure (years of service in office and number of organizational innovations are proposed as being inversely related).

References: Warren G. Bennis, et al. (Editors), *The Planning of Change: Readings in the Applied Behavorial Sciences,* New York: Holt, Rinehart and Winston, Inc., 1962; David S. Bushnell and Donald Rappaport (Editors), *Planned Change in Education: A Systems Approach,* New York: Harcourt Brace Jovanovich, Inc., 1971; Wendell L. French and Cecil H. Bell, Jr., *Organization Development: Behavioral Science Interventions for Organization Improvement* (Second Edition), Englewood Cliffs, NJ: Prentice-Hall, Inc., 1978; Daniel E. Griffiths, "Administrative Theory and Change in Organizations" in Matthew B. Miles (Editor), *Innovation in Education,* New York: Bureau of Publications, Teachers College Press, 1964; Ronald G. Havelock, *The Change Agent's Guide to Innovation in Education,* Englewood Cliffs, NJ: Educational Technology, 1973.

CHANGE ORDER, a request to modify the plans of a building (including a school) during the course of its construction. Change orders are most frequently prompted by a need to correct an architectural error or by a desire to improve upon a building's original design. Costs for such changes depend on several factors: (1) the extent to which construction has progressed; (2) the number of change orders processed; and, (3) the nature of the change(s) requested. Authorities advise that change orders be prepared on a standard form; that the forms be numbered consecutively and attached to the construction contract; and, finally, that they be signed by the contractor, the architect, and an official of the contracting institution (e.g. school district).

Change orders are sometimes used at the outset of a project for the purpose of negotiating a lower construction cost. This is a procedure sometimes employed when the lowest bid exceeds the appropriation. Ethics would require solicitation of the same change order quotation from the three lowest bidders to see if there would be any change in ranking of the low bidder. Should this occur, authorities suggest it would be prudent to rebid the project with the change orders deleted from the rebid documents.

References: Sam F. Brewster, *Campus Planning and Construction: Physical Facilities for Universities and Colleges,* Washington, DC: The Association of Physical Plant Administrators of Universities and Colleges, 1976; Basil Castoldi, *Educational Facilities: Planning, Remodeling, and Management,* Boston: Allyn and Bacon, Inc., 1977.

CHANT, music that is ritualistic and generally monophonic (i.e. consisting of a single melodic line, frequently repeated). The term is also used in connection with unaccompanied liturgical music sung in Christian churches. Numbers of Eastern and Western cultures had and/or have their own chants (e.g. Indian tribes of North America). The term *Anglican chant* refers to Anglican church music used for the singing of the psalms and canticles.

References: Willi Apel, *Harvard Dictionary of Music* (Second Edition, Revised and Enlarged), Cambridge, MA: The Belknap Press of Harvard University Press, 1970; Marion Bauer, "Chant" in Bruce Bohle (Editor), *The International Cyclopedia of Music and Musicians* (Tenth Edition), New York: Dodd, Mead and Company, 1975; J. A. Westrup and F. L. Harrison (Revised by Conrad Wilson), *The New College Encyclopedia of Music,* New York: W. W. Norton and Company, Inc., 1976.

CHAPBOOK, an inexpensive book first printed in England during the 1500s and even earlier in France. The label originated with the pedlar, who was called a chapman. He carried these inexpensive books with him as he peddled his wares. The word *chap* comes from an Old English word meaning *trade.* In addition to purchasing from chapmen, customers could go directly to printers to select their texts. Published to capture the business of the common person, they recorded in print tales passed down through the Middle Ages by storytellers. The earliest known printed version of *Tom Thumb* can be found in a chapbook dated 1621. At a time greatly influenced by the strict Puritan moral code, chapbooks brought to the people stories of adventure, humor, and fantasy. Chapbooks were enjoyed in both England and the United States until the early 1800s, when their popularity declined. They served as a forerunner to many children's books, Western stories, and even comic books.

References: John Ashton, *Chapbooks of the Eighteenth Century,* London: Chatto and Windus, 1982; Joan T. Glazer and Gurney Williams III, *Introduction to Children's Literature,* New York: McGraw-Hill Book Company, 1979; Donna E. Norton, *Through the Eyes of Children: An Introduction to Children's Literature,* Columbus, OH: Charles E. Merrill Publishing Company, 1983.

CHAPTER 1—See EDUCATION CONSOLIDATION IMPROVEMENT ACT

CHAPTER 2—See EDUCATION CONSOLIDATION IMPROVEMENT ACT

CHARISMATIC LEADERSHIP, or charismatic authority, a personal quality, ascribed by the leader's followers, that distinguishes ordinary leaders from those perceived to have unusual powers or qualities. Max Weber, one of the first to write about charismatic authority, described the charismatic leader as one possessing "a certain quality of an individual personality by virtue of which he is set apart from ordinary men and treated as endowed with supernatural, superhuman, or at least specifically exceptional powers or qualities" (Eisenstadt, p. 48). A later writer on charisma, psychoanalyst Irvine Schiffer, argued that Weber's definition is limited. He offered the view that the charismatic image is created "by a mass of people evolving a process from within themselves, thence projecting it outwards onto a suitable chosen object" (p. 19). Whatever the definition, it is clear that numbers of charismatic leaders have emerged throughout history (e.g. Christ, Hitler, Churchill, and M. L. King). Each possessed a mystique that made him attractive to and popular with his respective constituency.

Studies of charismatic leadership in organizations have been undertaken since the appearance of Weber's first book on the subject. For example, using a "Charismatic Leadership Inventory," Lowell Scott studied selected Kentucky superintendents and found that those with longer tenure tended to earn higher CAS (charisma) scores.

References: S. N. Eisenstadt (Editor), *Max Weber on Charisma and Institution Building: Selected Papers,* Chicago: University of Chicago Press, 1968; Irvine Schiffer, *Charisma: A Psychoanalytic Look at Mass Society,* Toronto, Canada: University of Toronto Press, 1973; Lowell K. Scott, "Charismatic Authority in the Rational Organization," *Educational Administration Quarterly,* Spring 1978; Max Weber, *The Theory of Social and Economic Organization* (Translated by A. M. Henderson and Talcott Parsons), Glencoe, IL: The Free Press, 1947.

CHARLES W. HUNT LECTURES, a lecture series sponsored by the American Association of Colleges for Teacher Education. Named in honor of AACTE's former Secretary-Treasurer, Charles W. Hunt, the series was officially established when Laurence D. Haskew, on February 10, 1960, delivered the first Charles W. Hunt Lecture. Succeeding lectures have been delivered at the beginning of the association's annual meetings. Since 1960, prominent persons such as James B. Conant, Lindley P. Styles, and Florence B. Stratemeyer have been invited to participate in the lecture series. (See AMERICAN ASSOCIATION OF COLLEGES FOR TEACHER EDUCATION.)

Reference: American Association of Colleges for Teacher Education, *A Decade of Thought on Teacher Education: The Charles W. Hunt Lectures,* Washington, DC: The Association, 1969.

CHARTERS, WERRETT WALLACE (October 24, 1875–March 8, 1952), a Canadian-born educator who held many educational professorships in several of the most significant universities in the United States from 1904 until 1947. He taught at the University of Missouri (1910–17), University of Illinois (1917–19), Carnegie Institute of Technology (1919–23), University of Pittsburgh (1924–25), University of Chicago (1925–28), and Ohio State University (1928–47).

Although he wrote extensively in the area of education, teacher education, and curriculum, he was considered a leader in the field of radio and motion pictures as related to teaching and education. Like Franklin Bobbitt, Charters utilized the job analysis as a base for the development of specific training programs (especially in vocational preparation programs). His texts, *Curriculum Construction* (1923) and *Basic Materials for a Pharmaceutical Curriculum* (1927), reflect his job analysis approach to curriculum development. The Commonwealth Teacher Training Study (1929) was a national teacher preparation study that he directed. (See BOBBITT, JOHN FRANKLIN and SOCIAL UTILITY.)

References: W. W. Charters, et al., *Basic Materials for a Pharmaceutical Curriculum,* New York: McGraw-Hill Book Co., Inc., 1927; W. W. Charters, *Curriculum Construction,* New York: Macmillan Co., 1923; Adolphe E. Meyer, *An Educational History of the American People,* New York: McGraw-Hill Book Co., Inc., 1957; John F. Ohles (Editor), *Biographical Dictionary of American Educators,* Westport, CT: Greenwood Press, 1978.

CHAUTAUQUA MOVEMENT, an early system of adult education that originated (1874) in Chautauqua, New York. It originally consisted of short, instructional meetings conducted in a camplike setting. First introduced as a vehicle for training Sunday school teachers, the movement expanded into one consisting of numerous offerings that appealed to the 19th-century American's thirst for self-instruction. The broadened program

included correspondence courses, concerts, special lectures, and various types of entertainment. A variation, the traveling Chautauqua, was later introduced that took those programs into small communities, particularly those in the American midwest.

In 1878, reading circles were inaugurated that featured a four-year guided reading program and attracted over 8,000 circle members. That number increased dramatically in the decade that followed.

As time went by, "independent" Chautauquas were established in different parts of the country. Tents frequently were used for meetings. Following World War I, the popularity of the Chautaqua movement declined, a fact partly attributable to the arrival of radio in America.

Reference: Joseph E. Gould, *The Chautauqua Movement: An Episode in the Continuing American Revolution,* Albany, NY: State University of New York Press, 1972.

CHEEVER, EZEKIEL (January 25, 1614–August 21, 1708), one of the leading educators during the American colonial period. He was for many years employed as master at the Boston Latin School. It was there that he culminated his educational career, a career that made him the best known grammar school master in his time.

Cheever was born in England and educated at Cambridge University. At 23, he emigrated to Boston. Shortly thereafter, he moved again to accept a teaching position in the New Haven Grammar School, a position he held for 12 years. This appointment was followed by 11 years of service at Ipswich, Massachusetts, and 9 additional years as master of the Charlestown Grammar School. In 1670, at 55 years of age, he became master of the Boston Latin School, a post he held for 38 years. His book, *Accidence, A Short Introduction to the Latin Tongue,* was a standard textbook for well over a century. (See LATIN GRAMMAR SCHOOL.)

References: Elmwood P. Cubberly, *Readings in Public Education in the United States: A Collection of Sources and Readings to Illustrate the History of Educational Practice and Progress in the United States,* Boston: Houghton Mifflin Company, 1934 (Reprinted in 1970 by Greenwood Press); John F. Ohles, "Cheever, Ezekiel" in John F. Ohles (Editor), *Biographical Dictionary of American Educators* (Volume 1), Westport, CT: Greenwood Press, 1978.

CHEMICAL BOND APPROACH (CBA), a curriculum project carried out by the Chemical Bond Approach Committee (1958–65) that sought to revitalize the teaching of high school chemistry. The decision to prepare a new chemistry course grew out of two meetings of high school and college teachers, these held in 1957 and 1958. Project headquarters were established at Earlham College, Richmond, Indiana, in 1958.

A five-part text, the heart of CBA, was prepared, field tested, and revised between 1958 and 1963. It was published commercially in 1963 under the title, *Chemical Systems.* Supplementing the text are materials such as laboratory books, tests, and teacher manuals. The text's central theme, reflected in the project's title, is that there is a structure within each chemical system that changes during a chemical reaction. Much attention is given to experimentation and assisting the student to think about chemical reactions.

References: Chemical Bond Approach Committee, *Chemical Systems,* New York: McGraw-Hill Book Company, 1963; Richard E. Haney, *The Changing Curriculum: Science,* Washington, DC: Association for Supervision and Curriculum Development, NEA, 1966; Paul D. Hurd, *New Directions in Teaching Secondary School Science,* Chicago: Rand McNally and Company, 1969; Arthur H. Livermore and Frederick L. Ferris, Jr., "The Chemical Bond Approach Course in the Classroom," *Science,* December 7, 1962; J. David Lockard (Editor), *Science and Mathematics Curricular Developments Internationally, 1956–1974,* College Park, MD: Science Teaching Center, University of Maryland (Joint Project with the Commission on Science Education, American Association for the Advancement of Science), 1974.

CHEMICAL EDUCATION MATERIAL STUDY (CHEMS), a program begun in 1959 to improve the high school chemistry curriculum. It sought to increase the supply and to improve the content of materials available to teachers of chemistry as well as to deemphasize descriptive chemistry teaching in favor of increased experimentation. CHEMS, initiated by a committee of the American Chemical Society, was funded by the National Science Foundation. Two centers were established to carry out the project, one at the University of California, Berkeley, the other at Harvey Mudd College, Claremont, California.

A writing committee prepared preliminary tests and accompanying laboratory experiments in 1960. These were subsequently field tested, revised, and finally published (by W. H. Freeman and Company) in 1963. The CHEMS Committee completed its work in 1963. In 1966, proposals from various publishers to revise and publish various parts of the program were granted.

Although CHEMS has been criticized by some chemistry educators for different reasons, the material has been widely used, in part or in toto, in the United States and numbers of foreign countries.

References: Alfred T. Collette, *Science Teaching in the Secondary School: A Guide for Modernizing Instruction,* Boston: Allyn and Bacon, Inc., 1973; J. David Lockard (Editor), *Science and Mathematics Curricular Developments Internationally, 1956–1974,* College Park, MD: Science Teaching Center, University of Maryland (Joint Project with the Commission on Science Education, American Association for the Advancement of Science), 1974; Richard J. Merrill and David W. Ridgway, *The CHEM Study Story,* San Francisco: W. H. Freeman and Company, 1969.

CHEMOTHERAPY (CHILD SEDATION), the use of chemical drugs to treat several forms of childhood behavior disorders (learning, behavior, and convulsive). Drugs are sometimes used when a child is in either a depressed or very active state.

Some drugs are used to stimulate the child. These include the monoamine oxidose inhibitors, a family of drugs used to stimulate individuals. Such drugs will allow the brain to receive more signals, thus enabling the child to respond to more stimuli.

Tranquilizers, such as cinanserin and methysergide, reduce the amount of chemical transmitter substances in the brain. They are used to reduce activity, especially when a child is in a very hyperactive state.

The drugs in chemotherapy are used as medication in the management of disorders. The following is a partial list of disorders that may be treated by chemotherapy: grand mal, petit mal, myoclonic convulsions, several mental retardation disorders, cerebral palsy, childhood psychosis, and enuresis. The use of chemotherapy for classroom purposes has generated considerable professional controversy.

References: James T. Bosco and Stanley S. Robin (Editors), *The Hyperactive Child and Stimulant Drugs,* Chicago: University of Chicago Press, 1977; Kenneth D. Gadow, *Children on Medication,* Reston, VA: The Council for Exceptional Children, 1979; Jerome Kagan and Ernest Havemann, *Psychology: An Introduction* (Second Edition), New York: Harcourt Brace Jovanovich, Inc., 1972; John Taylor, *The Shape of Minds to Come,* New York: Weybright and Talley, 1971.

CHICANO EDUCATION, programs designed for children and adults of Spanish-Mexican antecedents. Recommended programs include: (1) bilingual instruction (based on the actual language spoken in the home); (2) cultural awareness and acceptance; (3) culturally identifiable and honest

curriculum that is built upon the social-cultural base of the children or community; (4) opportunities to learn and accept the viability of the Spanish-Mexican heritage, society, literature, and background (including the contributions made by Chicanos to all of society, not just the United States); and (5) expansion of educational opportunities. Chicano education is not just ethnic or multicultural education; rather, it is the alteration of the entire school curriculum to meet the needs of the Chicano population.

There is no strict definition of Chicano education, for the Spanish-Mexican-American population is diverse. For example, although most Chicanos live in the Southwest, significant language and cultural differences exist within this one region.

Many authorities have suggested that the term *Chicano education* is too restrictive and should be broadened to include other major Spanish-speaking populations in the United States as well (e.g. Cubans, Puerto Ricans, South and Central Americans, and those from Spain). They point out that although each group is unique, members cope with many of the same educational problems and concerns. Therefore, they conclude, the basic structure and design of Chicano education would be appropriate for all Hispanic-Americans. (See MULTICULTURAL EDUCATION.)

References: Thomas P. Carter, *Mexican-Americans in School: A History of Educational Neglect*, New York: College Entrance Examination Board, 1970; Henry Sioux Johnson and William J. Hernandez-M., *Educating the Mexican American*, Valley Forge, PA: Judson Press, 1970; Earl J. Ogletree and David Garcia, *Education of the Spanish-Speaking Urban Child*, Springfield, IL: Charles C. Thomas, Publisher, 1975; *Parameters of Institutional Change: Chicano Experiences in Education*, Hayward, CA: Southwest Network for Chicanos, 1974.

CHIEF STATE SCHOOL OFFICER (CSSO), the highest ranking educational officer in the state. In some states (or possessions), the CSSO is known as the commissioner of education; in others, as the state superintendent of public instruction. CSSOs serve as executive officers to state boards of education and concurrently administer their respective state departments of education. They are selected in one of three ways: (1) *popular election*, with some chosen on a partisan ballot; (2) *appointment by the state board of education*, the method favored by increasing numbers of states; and (3) *appointment by the governor*. In 1920, approximately 70 percent of all CSSOs were elected; by 1975, only 40 percent

were. The tenure of service for CSSOs in states having fixed terms of office ranges from one to five years; four year terms are most common. Duties of the CSSOs are frequently regulatory, with much of their authority derived from legislatures and the courts. Of late, these administrators have also been active as state planners and as promulgators of research. (See BOARD OF EDUCATION, STATE; COUNCIL OF CHIEF STATE SCHOOL OFFICERS; and STATE DEPARTMENT OF EDUCATION.)

References: Council of Chief State School Officers and the Education Commission of the States, *Fifty Education Chiefs*, Denver, CO: Education Commission of the States, 1976; Thomas J. Landers and Judith G. Myers, *Essentials of School Management*, Philadelphia: W. B. Saunders Company, 1977; Leroy J. Peterson, et al., *The Law and Public School Operation* (Second Edition), New York: Harper and Row, Publishers, 1978.

CHILD ABUSE, defined in federal legislation as "the physical or mental injury, sexual abuse, negligent treatment, or maltreatment of a child under the age of eighteen by a person who is responsible for the child's welfare under circumstances which indicate that the child's health or welfare is harmed or threatened thereby" (p. 5). This legislative definition notwithstanding, authorities on the subject have yet to agree on a common definition of child abuse, pointing out that state statutes each define it differently as do professionals and researchers who employ varying criteria.

Basically, injuries to children are of two types: (1) those reflecting specific actions committed by adults (*abuse*), and (2) those involving failure to act (*negligence*). The former category includes physical, sexual, verbal, and similar forms of abuse; the latter consists of physical and emotional neglect. Authorities are in general agreement that instances of neglect outnumber those of abuse. Reliable statistics indicating the incidence of child abuse are not available. The literature on the subject indicates that most of the far-ranging estimates offered by experts are probably underestimates.

Since 1961, all states have enacted laws requiring physicians to report all cases where wilfully inflicted injuries to children are suspected. A majority of states also involve teachers in cases of child abuse or neglect, requiring them to report all suspected cases. (See BATTERED CHILD SYNDROME and CHILD ABUSE PREVENTION AND TREATMENT ACT.)

References: Lynn Fossum and Lauralee Sorensen, "The Schools See It First: Child Abuse/Neglect," *Phi Delta Kappan,* December 1980; Christine C. Herbruck, *Breaking the Cycle of Child Abuse,* Minneapolis, MN: Winston Press, Inc., 1979; Wayne C. Huey and Theodore P. Remley, Jr., *Ethical and Legal Issues in School Counseling,* Alexandria, VA: American School Counselor Association, 1988; Office of Child Development, *Child Abuse and Neglect: The Problem and Its Management* (Volumes 1 and 2), Washington, DC: U.S. Department of Health, Education, and Welfare, 1976; Public Law 93–247, *United States Statutes at Large, 1974* (Volume 88, Part I), Washington, DC: U.S. Government Printing Office, 1976.

CHILD ABUSE PREVENTION AND TREATMENT ACT (Public Law 93-247), legislation enacted by Congress in 1974. The act directed the Secretary of Health, Education, and Welfare to create a National Center on Child Abuse and Neglect and charged the center with responsibility for: (1) compiling child abuse and neglect research data; (2) serving as a clearinghouse on child abuse programs; (3) compiling and publishing training materials; (4) providing technical assistance; (5) conducting research; and (6) studying the incidence and severity of child abuse. Additionally, the act offered a definition of "child abuse and neglect" and authorized the Secretary to award grants or to contract with agencies/organizations "for demonstration programs and projects designed to prevent, identify, and treat child abuse and neglect" (p. 5). (See CHILD ABUSE.)
Reference: Public Law 93–247, *United States Statutes at Large, 1974* (Volume 88, Part I), Washington, DC: U. S. Government Printing Office, 1976.

CHILD ACCOUNTING—See PUPIL ACCOUNTING

CHILD ADVOCATES, individuals, programs, or groups that support, represent, or protect children against abuse, neglect, or exploitation. Because children are in a dependent state, their legal "rights" as individuals and citizens are often denied them. Child advocates attempt to ensure that children are not taken advantage of by either parents or institutions. Most advocates come from private organizations; however, some state and federal laws require the appointment of child advocates when conditions warrant.

Advocates are concerned about children in almost all aspects of a society (i.e. dealing with child abuse in the home; providing appropriate representation in legal proceedings; monitoring educational opportunities; providing appropriate health care; dealing with the rights of institutionalized children; protecting the rights of retarded or exceptional children; or protecting the rights of children in courts, hospitals, and foster homes).

There are many private organizations that will assume the role of child advocate. The following are only a few such organizations: Youth Advocates, Inc.: American Civil Liberties Union (Child Advocacy Project); Berkeley Youth Alternatives; Center for Public Representation (Juvenile Justice Project); Children's Hospital National Medical Center (Child Health Advocacy Program); Food Research and Action Center; Michigan Coalition of Runaway Services; and Save the Children Federation.
References: Mary L. Bundy and Rebecca G. Whaley (Editors), *The National Children's Directory,* College Park, MD: Urban Information Interpreters, Inc., 1977; *Directory for the Child Care Advocate,* Washington, DC: Day Care and Child Development Council of America, Inc., Undated; George G. Newman (Editor), *Children in the Courts: The Question of Representation,* Ann Arbor, MI: Institute of Continuing Legal Education, 1967; Marsden Wagner and Mary Wagner, *The Danish National Child-Care System,* Boulder, CO: Westview Press, 1976.

CHILD BENEFIT THEORY, a legal concept that has specific application to church-state separation in education. In ruling on several significant cases involving use of tax money to provide certain services to children enrolled in parochial schools, the U.S. Supreme Court has emphasized that governmental units may not use public funds to support a religion. The Court has also ruled, however, that aid to students attending parochial schools (e.g. bus transportation, loan of textbooks) is legal. This doctrine, which holds that aid to children does not constitute aid to religious schools, is known as the child benefit theory.
References: William R. Hazard, *Education and the Law: Cases and Materials on Public Schools* (Second Edition), New York: The Free Press (Macmillan), 1978; E. Edmund Reutter, Jr. and Robert R. Hamilton, *The Law of Public Education* (Second Edition), Mineola, NY: The Foundation Press, Inc., 1976.

CHILD-CARE CENTER—See DAY CARE

CHILD-CENTERED CURRICULUM, a curriculum in which the entire school program revolves around the child. In such programs, the needs and interests of teachers, parents, and administrators are all subordinated to the needs and interests of children. Curriculum content is viewed as a vehicle and not an end in and of itself. The child-centered curriculum, closely related to the whole-child concept of instruction, was endorsed by progressivists such as John Dewey, Francis Parker, Granville Hall, Harold Rugg, and Arthur Jersild. Its supporters defend it as a viable curriculum on the grounds that it has its base in how children grow and develop.

References: Robin Barrow and Geoffrey Milburn, *A Critical Dictionary of Educational Concepts*, New York: St. Martin's Press, 1986; Alexander Frazier, "Curriculum Making for Children: Elements and Issues" in Alexander Frazier (Editor), *A Curriculum for Children*, Washington, DC: Association for Supervision and Curriculum Development, NEA, 1969; Michael Schiro, *Curriculum for Better Schools: The Great Ideological Debate*, Englewood Cliffs, NJ: Educational Technology Publications, 1978.

CHILD DEVELOPMENT, a field of study that David Ausubel and Edmund Sullivan defined as "that branch of knowledge concerned with the nature and regulation of significant structural, functional and behavioral changes occurring in children as they advance in age and maturity" (p. 2). Childhood, these same authors pointed out, is one of four age periods into which the field of human development has been divided. The four periods are childhood, adolescence, maturity, and senescence. The childhood period has been further subdivided for purposes of study. Its subclassifications are: (1) *prenatal,* the period between conception and birth; (2) *neonatal,* birth to approximately four weeks; (3) *infancy,* four weeks to two years; (4) *preschool,* ages two to six; (5) *middle childhood,* ages six to nine; and (6) *preadolescence,* age nine to adolescence.

Among the developmental variables studied by students of child development are personality, perceptions, self-concepts, linguistic development, cognitive development, and physical growth. Also considered are topics such as parent-child relations, the child in school, peer relations, family influences, and the impact of culture.

Numerous theories of child development have been formulated as a part of developmental psychology. They include the theories of Jean Piaget, Kurt Lewin, Heinz Werner, and Sigmund Freud as well as those of Stimulus-Response (S-R) psychologists such as B. F. Skinner and John Watson.

References: David P. Ausubel and Edmund V. Sullivan, *Theory and Problems of Child Development* (Second Edition), New York: Grune and Stratton, 1970; Carol Seefeldt and Nita Barbour, *Early Childhood Education: An Introduction,* Columbus, OH: Charles E. Merrill Publishing Company, 1986.

CHILD FIND, an annual census conducted by states and local educational agencies for the purpose of locating and evaluating handicapped children, birth to age 18, residing in their respective jurisdictions. This child identification program is required by Public Law 94-142, The Education of all Handicapped Children Act. Child Find serves two purposes: (1) to find handicapped children who are not being served by the schools, and (2) to identify handicapped children who are being served inadequately. (See PUBLIC LAW 94-142.)

References: Pennsylvania Association for Retarded Children, Inc., *Take Steps for Your Child's Right to Education,* Harrisburg, PA: The Association, Undated Brochure; H. Rutherford Turnbull and Ann Turnbull, *Free Appropriate Public Education: Law and Implementation,* Denver, CO: Love Publishing Company, 1978; Public Law 94-142, *United States Statutes at Large, 1975* (Volume 89), Washington, DC: U.S. Government Printing Office, 1977.

CHILD NUTRITION ACT, federal legislation, enacted in 1966 and amended twice in the 1970s, that was designed "to safeguard the health and well-being of the Nation's children, and to encourage the domestic consumption of agricultural and other foods, by assisting States, through grants-in-aid and other means, to meet more effectively the nutritional needs of our children" (Public Law 89-642, p. 885). The legislation provided funds to encourage milk consumption by children attending nonprofit schools, child-care centers, nursery schools, settlement houses, summer camps, and similar nonprofit institutions. Provision was also made for a pilot breakfast program in schools. These programs, which have economically poor children as their target, were made the responsibility of the Secretary of Agriculture.

The act was expanded and extended in 1970 and again in 1977.

References: Public Law 89-642, *United States Statutes at Large, 1966* (Volume 80, Part I), Washington, DC: U.S. Government Printing Office, 1967; Public Law 91-248 and Public Law 91-295, *United States Statutes at Large, 1970-1971* (Volume 84, Part I), Washington, DC: U.S. Government Printing Office, 1971.

CHILD PSYCHOLOGY, the field of psychology concerned with the study, description, and prediction of human growth as well as the development, behavior, and behavioral changes of young children and adolescents. Human growth, human development, behavioral patterns, maturation, and the relationship of heredity and environment to development are studied. Laws and theories relating to children and adolescents are developed, studied, and tested.

It is not uncommon for an introductory child psychology course (college level) to include topics such as prenatal development; genetic theories; physical, motor, and behavioral development of infants and toddlers; physical growth; behaviors; and personality, social, language, and cognitive development of preschool children. Older children are also studied with attention given to topics such as vocational interest, psychosexual development, intelligence, learning theories, social development, and academic achievement. (See EDUCATIONAL PSYCHOLOGY and PSYCHOLOGY.)

References: Sidney W. Bijou, *Child Development: The Basic Stage of Early Childhood,* Englewood Cliffs, NJ: Prentice-Hall, Inc., 1976; Dorothy H. Cohen and Virginia Stern, *Observing and Recording the Behavior of Young Children,* New York: Teachers College Press, 1978; Margaret C. Donaldson, *Children's Minds,* New York: W. W. Norton and Company, Inc., 1979; Langdon E. Longstreth, *Psychological Development of the Child,* New York: Ronald Press Company, 1974; Jean Piaget and Barbel Inhelder, *The Psychology of the Child,* New York: Basic Books, Inc., Publishers, 1969.

CHILDREN'S BOOK CLUBS, organizations whose members purchase juvenile books on a regular basis and, usually, at a reduced rate. One author (Nancy Larrick) estimated that over 22 million Americans regularly buy books through children's book clubs.

Two types of clubs are available to children. The *hardcover* book clubs mail books of their choosing to members on a regular basis. Among the better known clubs of this type are: (1) Grow-With-Me Book Club; (2) Junior Literary Guild; (3) I Can Read Book Club; (4) Parents' Magazine Read Aloud and Easy Reading Program; and (5) Weekly Reader Children's Book Club. *Paperback* book clubs distribute relatively inexpensive books produced by many publishers. Children place orders with their teachers or librarians, selecting titles from annotated lists made available by the club. Some of the largest paperback book clubs are: (1) Firefly Book Club; 2) Scholastic Book Clubs; (3) Young Readers Press, Inc.; and (4) Xerox Paperback Book Clubs.

References: Nancy Larrick, *A Parent's Guide to Children's Reading* (Fourth Edition), Garden City, NY: Doubleday and Company, Inc., 1975; George D. Spache, *Good Reading for Poor Readers* (Ninth Edition), Champaign, IL: Garrard Publishing Company, 1974.

CHILDREN'S BOOK COUNCIL (CBC), a nonprofit organization that promotes and encourages the reading of books by children. Its members are publishers of trade books for children. CBC sponsors National Children's Book Week, held every year in November. The council has established a center for the examination of children's books. In addition, the Children's Book Council, along with other organizations, has developed a book program that is discipline specific. The council publishes a calendar, information sheets, bibliographies, brochures, and other printed materials related to the encouragement of the use of good books by children. CBC's headquarters is in New York City.

The council, formed in 1945 and incorporated 12 years later, neither publishes nor reviews children's books. It works closely with other national organizations, however, such as the American Library Association, National Council of Teachers of English, International Reading Association, and the Association for Childhood Education International. (See NATIONAL CHILDREN'S BOOK WEEK.)

References: The Children's Book Council, Inc., *The Children's Book Council, Inc,* New York: The Council, Undated Brochure; Mary Wilson Pair, *Encyclopedia of Associations* (Twelfth Edition), Detroit: Gale Research Company, 1978.

CHILDREN'S BOOK WEEK—See NATIONAL CHILDREN'S BOOK WEEK

CHILDREN'S LITERATURE, published reading material, usually of good quality, that has been written for children. Such literature is usually prepared by writers who specialize in this particular reader market, and it enjoys considerable popularity with young readers. In schools, the books used for literature programs are of two types: (1) *trade books* (also available in bookstores) that generally contain one or more stories and are designed to entertain the reader, and (2) *trade texts,* works designed for school use and that, like textbooks, have controlled vocabulary.

Few books were written for children before the 19th century. Early books of this type were moralistic and frequently authored by women. Folk and fairy tales, such as those written by the Grimm brothers and Hans Christian Andersen, were popular in the 1800s as were adventure and animal stories. About this time, increased attention was being given to illustrations in children's books.

In the 20th century, publication of children's books became a big business. In 1970 alone, for example, over 2,500 juvenile titles appeared.

"Children's Literature" is also the title given to a course offered in teacher training institutions and typically required of those preparing for careers as elementary school teachers. (See CALDECOTT MEDAL and NEWBERY MEDAL; also see APPENDIXES IV and VIII: RALPH CALDECOTT MEDAL AWARD WINNERS and JOHN NEWBERY MEDAL AWARD WINNERS.)

References: Charlotte S. Huck, Susan Hepler, and Janet Hickman, *Children's Literature in the Elementary School* (Fourth Edition), New York: Holt, Rinehart and Winston, 1987; Donna E. Norton, *Through the Eyes of a Child: An Introduction to Children's Literature*, Columbus, OH: Charles E. Merrill Publishing Company, 1983.

CHILD WELFARE, those welfare services that have a specialized focus on children. It is a broad field of services that includes: (1) *supportive services,* such as family service, child-guidance service, protection; (2) *supplementary services,* such as day care, homemaking, health care; and (3) *substitute service,* such as foster family care, adoption, placing children in appropriate institutions. Most of the services are provided by social workers who are trained in the field of child welfare. These individuals are employed by both public and private welfare agencies.

There are several agencies concerned primarily with child welfare. The Child Welfare League of America, Save the Children Federation, and the Social Legislation Information Service are a few of the national organizations devoted to this cause. Every state or city has a local organization specifically concerned with child welfare, these in addition to the governmental agencies having legal mandate for child welfare. (See CHILD WELFARE LEAGUE OF AMERICA and SAVE THE CHILDREN FEDERATION.)

References: Stevanne Auerbach and James A. Rivaldo, *Rationale for Child Care Services: Programs and Politics,* New York: Human Sciences Press, Inc., 1975; Mary L. Bundy and Rebecca G. Whaley (Editors), *The National Children's Directory,* College Park, MD: Urban Information Interpreters, Inc., 1977; Joan Laird and Ann Hartman (Editors), *A Handbook of Child Welfare: Content, Knowledge and Practice,* London: Collier Macmillan Publishers, 1985.

CHILD WELFARE LEAGUE OF AMERICA (CWLA), a national voluntary agency, founded in 1920 for the protection and welfare of children and youth. The league sets standards for adoption, child protective services, and homemaking services for children. It functions as a voluntary accrediting agency for child care facilities. The league has also been involved in research on foster care and other child-welfare activities and in administering special projects. The CWLA maintains a 3,000-volume reference library as well. Its main offices are located in New York City.

References: Child Welfare League of America, *Standards for Child Protective Service,* New York: Child Welfare League of America, Inc., 1960; Lela B. Costen, *Child Welfare: Policies and Practice,* New York: McGraw-Hill Book Company, 1972; Peter Romanofsky (Editor), *Social Service Organizations* (Volume 1), Westport, CT: Greenwood Press, 1978; Jack C. Westman, *Child Advocacy,* New York: The Free Press, 1979.

CHI SQUARE TEST(χ^2), a statistical test used in educational research to test whether there are significant differences between or among categories of data. This method compares results *obtained* with those *expected.* The procedure includes the construction of a contingency table, the determination of expected frequencies, the calculation of a chi square ratio, and the use of a chi square distribution table. The numbers in the contingency table represent counts, or frequencies (nonparametric data). The following is an example of a 2×2 contingency table (two variables on each axis):

Chi-Square Contingency Table

	Blue Eyes	Brown Eyes	Total
Boys	6	36	42
Girls	9	29	38
Total	15	65	80

In this example, the proportion of blue- and brown-eyed boys and girls is about equal. Consequently, the chi square ratio does not reach a level of statistical significance.

References: Walter R. Borg and Meredith D. Gall, *Educational Research: An Introduction* (Fifth Edition), New York: Longman, Inc., 1989; Harold O. Kiess, *Statistical Concepts for the Behavioral Sciences*, Boston: Allyn and Bacon, 1989.

CHOICE, SCHOOLS OF, a term used for schools where the student enrollment is a function of parental selection. Parents within a school district may select any school within that district to enroll their children. Such selection is usually based on the "quality" reputation of the school, high student achievement and success, school curriculum, or other educational factors or considerations. Some states permit choice of schools between school districts.

The purpose of choice is not only to allow individual parental decisions concerning school enrollment; it is seen by some educational policymakers as a means of improving school programs and raising student achievements, for schools with weak programs would not attract students and would subsequently loose enrollment and support. Therefore, such schools would be forced to improve their programs in order to attract students; the schools would have to be more responsive to the demands of parents for higher student achievement and greater parental involvement. Critics have raised questions about funding, transportation, availability of spaces in choice schools, availability of information on which parents can make such decisions, teacher training and teacher selection, and racial balances, especially in urban school districts and/or with interdistrict choice program.

Choice is not a new concept. Magnet schools, alternative schools, schools within-a-school, and schools without walls are all varying degrees of choice. A major difference is that choice tends to be either statewide or district-wide and is open to all parents; these other choices are limited in terms of number of schools available or are limited in terms of the types of programs being offered. Private school education has always been an option for parents—but at considerable expense. The voucher system is another form of choice, but it is usually available for use in both the public and private school sectors.

In some form or another, choice exists in 40 out of the 50 states, and is presently expanding. In 1989, choice had become part of the national educational policy of President George Bush. The state of Minnesota, in 1989, had three choice programs and was one of the leaders of interdistrict choice programming. (See ALTERNATIVE EDUCATION; MAGNET SCHOOL; SCHOOLS-WITHIN-A-SCHOOL; SCHOOLS WITHOUT WALLS; and VOUCHERS.)

References: Frank J. Esposito, *Public School Choice: National Trends and Initiatives*, Trenton, NJ: New Jersey State Department of Education, 1988; National Governors Association, *Time and Results: The Governors' 1991 Report on Education*, Washington, DC: National Governors Association, 1986; Mary Jane Raywid, "Excellence and Choice: Friends or Foes?" *The Urban Review*, Volume 19, Number 1, 1987.

CHOIR, in music, a body of church singers. Comparable secular groups of singers are referred to as a chorus. (Choruses are organized in many elementary and secondary schools and in most institutions of higher education.) The term *choir* is also used to identify various groups of instruments within the orchestra (e.g. string choir, brass choir).

References: Willi Apel, *Harvard Dictionary of Music* (Second Edition, Revised and Enlarged), Cambridge, MA: The Belknap Press of Harvard University Press, 1970; Bruce Bohle (Editor), *The International Cyclopedia of Music and Musicians* (Tenth Edition), New York: Dodd, Mead and Company, 1975.

CHORAL SPEAKING, a general term used to describe oral communication by a group. Other names used for choral speaking include group speaking, speech chorus, choric speech, and voice choir. Although choral speaking may be interpreted broadly to include group communication activities such as recitation of the Pledge of Allegiance or a congregation's recitation of prayer, its narrower (and more common) meaning refers to performance by a voice choir.

The voice choir consists of a group of people who, under the direction of a "choir director," recite poetry or free verse together for their own enjoyment as well as that of an audience. Specific lines may be assigned to small groups within the chorus, these organized on the basis of voice qualities: light, medium, and dark. *Light* voices are high in pitch and have little resonance; *dark* voices, in contrast, are low in pitch and rich in resonance. *Medium* voices fall in between these two.

References: Martha Dallman, *Teaching the Language Arts in the Elementary School* (Third Edition), Dubuque, IA: Wm. C. Brown Company, Publishers, 1976; Mildred R. Donoghue, *The Child and the English Language Arts* (Third Edition), Dubuque, IA: Wm. C. Brown Company, Publishers, 1979; E. Kingsley Povenmire, *Choral Speaking and the Voice Choir,* New York: A. S. Barnes and Company, 1975.

CHORD, in music, the sounding of three or more notes at the same time. The simplest chord is the triad, made up of two thirds. Its bottom note is called the *root,* the middle note (a third above the root) the *third,* and the last note (a fifth above the root), the *fifth.*

The classification of chords and their relation to each other is studied in the musical field known as harmony. It is a complex subject that musicians, composers, and arrangers must know to be musically literate.

References: Christine Ammer, *Harper's Dictionary of Music,* New York: Harper and Row, Publishers, 1972; Willi Apel, *Harvard Dictionary of Music* (Second Edition, Revised and Enlarged), Cambridge, MA: The Belknap Press of Harvard University Press, 1970.

CHRISTIAN SCHOOLS, private Protestant fundamentalist schools (elementary and secondary) whose programs are based upon basic belief in the authority and centrality of: (1) the Bible as the final revelation of God, and (2) Jesus Christ. Thomas Smith, a writer on the subject of Christian schools, ascribed numerous goals to them including the following: (1) to win boys and girls to Christ; (2) to bring education back to Bible principles; (3) to complement the home; and (4) to save children from an ungodly society.

Although exact enrollment statistics for Christian schools are difficult to obtain, it has been reported that, in the late 1970s and early 1980s, they constituted the fastest growing educational movement in the United States. The four major fundamentalist school organizations to which Christian schools belong are the American Association of Christian Schools, Association of Christian Schools International, National Association of Christian Schools, and Christian Schools International. Collective enrollments in member schools increased by almost 120 percent between 1971 and 1977. Some critics charge that these schools were frequently created to escape the impact of legislation and court rulings mandating racial integration of the schools.

Christian schools provide an academic program that emphasizes and/or strives to achieve fundamental skills, good study habits, independent study, and appreciation of the arts. Advocates claim their programs and discipline relative to public schools, are more stringent.

References: Paul A. Kienel, *Reasons for Sending Your Child to a Christian School,* La Habra, CA: P. K. Books, 1978; Paul A. Kienel (Editor), *The Philosophy of Christian School Education,* Whittier, CA: Western Association of Christian Schools, Undated; Virginia D. Nordin and William L. Turner, "More Than Segregation Academies: The Growing Protestant Fundamentalist Schools," *Phi Delta Kappan,* February 1980; Thomas L. Smith, *What Every Parent Should Know About Christian Education*, Murfreesboro, TN: The Christian Educator Publications, 1976.

CHROMATIC SCALE, a musical scale built on semitones, or half-steps. The scale consists of 12 such semitones. Accidentals (sharps, flats, and naturals) are used to indicate chromatics. The earliest use of the chromatic scale in Western civilization has been traced to the chromatic tetrachord music of Greece.

References: Willi Apel, *Harvard Dictionary of Music* (Second Edition, Revised and Enlarged), Cambridge, MA: The Belknap Press of Harvard University Press, 1970; Bruce Bohle (Editor), *The International Cyclopedia of Music and Musicians* (Tenth Edition), New York: Dodd, Mead and Company, 1975; J. A. Westrup and F. L. Harrison (Revised by Conrad Wilson), *The New College Encyclopedia of Music,* New York: W. W. Norton and Company, Inc., 1976.

CHRONOLOGICAL AGE (CA), the exact age of a person expressed in years and/or months. Chronological age is one of the two major measures used in calculating Intelligence Quotient (I.Q.) scores. The other is mental age. (See IN-TELLIGENCE QUOTIENT and MENTAL AGE.)

Reference: Anne Anastasi, *Psychological Testing* (Sixth Edition), New York: Macmillan Publishing Company, Inc., 1988.

CHURCH-STATE RELATIONS IN EDUCA-TION, those educational interactions between the public and religious schools/agencies that have been forged as a result of tradition, legal restrictions, and court decisions. The First and Fourteenth Amendments to the U.S. Constitution have restricted Congressional and state control over religious schools. There are many other restrictions placed on the state, the specific nature of these depending on state statutes.

Regardless of the Constitutional and other legal restrictions, states do have limited interactions, as well as very limited control, over religious schools. By and large, public funds cannot be used to aid children who attend religious schools; however, under the "Child Benefit Theory" (*Cochran v.*

Louisiana State Board of Education, 281 U.S. 370, 1930) public funds can be used under restricted conditions (e.g. purchase of secular textbooks). Church-state relations covers many areas besides direct funding (e.g. Bible reading in the public school, school attendance, prayers in the public schools, released time, shared time, sex education, vaccination and other health requirements, building codes, teacher certification, busing and transportation, and testing and diagnostic service). The matter of interactions, relationships, requirements, state restrictions, and state participations that affect church-state relations in education are constantly being challenged in the courts with the result that these church-state relationships are being modified regularly. (See CHILD BENEFIT THEORY and SHARED TIME.)

References: Richard D. Gatti and Daniel J. Gatti, *Encyclopedic Dictionary of School Law,* West Nyack, NY: Parker Publishing Company, Inc., 1975; William R. Hazard, *Education and the Law* (Second Edition), New York: The Free Press, 1978; Leroy J. Peterson, et al., *The Law and Public School Operation* (Second Edition), New York: Harper and Row, Publishers, 1978; Perry A. Zirkel (Editor), *A Digest of Supreme Court Decisions Affecting Education,* Bloomington, IN: Phi Delta Kappa, 1978.

CITIZENS' COMMITTEES, in education, groups of laymen constituted for the purpose of providing advisory assistance to administrators, teachers, and/or governing boards. These bodies, although formally organized, are normally ad hoc, lack formal authority, and are made up of people who serve voluntarily and without compensation. Their functions are usually prescribed for them. Committee members may be selected because of their expertise in a certain area or because of demonstrated interest in education or a certain aspect of education. Citizens' committees have been organized to offer advice on matters such as school site selection, budget, certain aspects of the curriculum (e.g. sex education), pupil transportation, school building construction, and library book selection.

Roald Campbell and associates cited six purposes served by citizen participation in school affairs. They are: (1) to increase public understanding and support for the schools; (2) to provide citizens with certain types of instruction; (3) to co-opt potential opponents (i.e. inviting critics to offer help with the expectation that their criticism will be softened once they have been made aware of the facts); (4) to seek advice; (5) to increase the amount

of human and material resources available to the schools (e.g. having committee members serve as school aides); and (6) to monitor the performance of the schools.

References: Roald F. Campbell, et al., *The Organization and Control of American Schools* (Fourth Edition), Columbus, OH: Charles E. Merrill Publishing Company, 1980; Beverly D. Chinn, "Public School Advisory Committees: Characteristics, Contributions, and Perceptions of Role and Functions," Unpublished Doctoral Dissertation, Florida Atlantic University, 1975; David B. Dreiman, *How to Get Better Schools: A Tested Program,* New York: Harper and Brothers, 1956; Albert J. Riendeau, *The Role of the Advisory Committee in Occupational Education in the Junior College,* Washington, DC: American Association of Junior Colleges, 1967.

CITIZENSHIP EDUCATION, the study of citizens' rights, responsibilities, and tasks normally associated with groups to which the individual belongs. Examples of such groups are families, neighborhood organizations, schools, and governments at all levels. Former Secretary of HEW David Mathews offered three definitions of citizenship education that, collectively, accord with the definition offered above: (1) acquiring the knowledge necessary to function effectively as a citizen; (2) having a belief in citizenship; and (3) understanding of one's relationship to government.

School systems, in recent years, have been strengthening (reviving) civic education as a part of the social studies, a move at least partly attributable to national surveys (e.g. National Assessment of Educational Progress) that indicate that sizeable numbers of school children know little about their governments and how they operate.

The Basic Citizenship Competencies Project identified seven citizenship competencies considered to be fundamental to citizenship education. They are: (1) acquiring and using information; (2) assessing involvement (i.e. determining one's personal stake in political issues); (3) making decisions; (4) making judgments; (5) communicating; (6) cooperating (as a member of a group); and (7) promoting interests (i.e. learning how to work with and within institutions to promote/project one's interests).

References: John Chaffee, Jr. (Editorial Coordinator), *Education and Citizenship: A Conference Report,* Denver, CO: Office of Education, U.S. Department of Health, Education, and Welfare, 1976; *Educational Leadership,* October 1980 (Theme Issue); Le Ann Meyer, *The Citizenship Education Issue: Problems and Programs* (Report No. 123), Denver, CO: Education Commission of the States,

February 1979; Richard C. Remy, *Citizenship and Consumer Education: Key Assumptions and Basic Competencies* (PDK Fastback 144), Bloomington, IN: The Phi Delta Kappa Educational Foundation, 1980; Richard C. Remy, *Handbook of Basic Citizenship Competencies: Guidelines for Comparing Materials, Assessing Instruction and Setting Goals,* Alexandria, VA: Association for Supervision and Curriculum Development, 1979.

CIVILIAN CONSERVATION CORPS (CCC), quasi-military camps for unemployed youth organized and funded by The New Deal Administration of President Franklin Roosevelt. These camps were organized in 1933 to combat youth unemployment resulting from the Great Depression, and they lasted until 1942. Although basic education courses were offered in the CCC camps, the main educational thrust was the learning of skills useful to the filling of public service jobs in the conservation of natural resources.

More than 2,500,000 Americans participated in the CCC camps; yet many more than these youths benefited. Projects to combat soil erosion and work on reforestation benefited farmers. Businessmen had contracts to supply materials and equipment to the camps. The families of those enrolled in the camps also benefited by receiving monthly allotment checks.

The concept of the CCC camps did not originate with the Roosevelt Administration. Small-scale camps were already in existence in the states of California and Washington. These were state and Forest Service cooperative ventures. The governments of Bulgaria, Netherlands, Norway, Sweden, Denmark, Austria, and Germany had also instituted conservation camps for the unemployed by 1932. However, it was President Roosevelt, with his love for conservation, who developed and implemented the concept on a large scale across the United States.

References: Frank E. Hill, *The School in the Camps: The Educational Program of the Civilian Conservation Corps,* New York: American Association for Adult Education, 1942; John A. Salmond, *The Civilian Conservation Corps, 1933-1942: A New Deal Case Study,* Durham, NC: Duke University Press, 1967.

CIVIL RIGHTS, rights to personal liberty granted by the Constitution that apply to individuals as well as to groups. (Examples are the right to due process, privacy, free speech, etc.) A recent Phi Delta Kappa report noted that "human rights become civil rights when they are enforced through judicial (legal) or administrative action" (p. 3). It also made

the point that human rights "accord each person full dignity, respect, and value, simply because he is human" (p. 3).

In the United States, concern for civil rights took on revolutionary characteristics in the 1950s and 1960s when the black civil rights movement sought to free black citizens from the yoke of racial discrimination. Numerous events served to reinforce that early movement. They included the *Brown* decision (1954) rendered by the Supreme Court, increased militancy by blacks, and effective leadership by well-known individuals such as Dr. Martin Luther King. The civil rights movement resulted in significant judicial, executive, and legislative reforms that granted black citizens increased equality of opportunity and equal justice before the law.

The successes recorded by the black civil rights movement led to similar protest drives by Indian, homosexual, women's, and other organized groups desirous of achieving their own civil rights. In varying ways, each of these movements impacted on the schools, influencing curricula, instructional materials, due process procedures, and the like. Sometimes less heralded, nevertheless equally successful demands for full civil rights treatment were registered by handicapped persons, teachers, and students. They, too, necessitated both procedural and instructional reforms in the schools (See *BROWN v. BOARD OF EDUCATION OF TOPEKA.*)

References: Joan M. Burke, *Civil Rights: A Current Guide to the People, Organizations, and Events* (Second Edition), New York: R. R. Bowker Company, 1974; Editorial Research Reports, *The Rights Revolution,* Washington, DC: Congressional Quarterly, Inc., 1978; Hoyt Gimlin, *The Rights Revolution: Timely Reports to Keep Journalists, Scholars and the Public Abreast of Developing Issues, Events and Trends,* Washington, DC: Congressional Quarterly, Inc., 1978; Phi Delta Kappa Teacher Education Project on Human Rights, *A Guide for Improving Public School Practices in Human Rights,* Bloomington, IN: Phi Delta Kappa, 1975.

CIVIL RIGHTS ACT OF 1964, federal legislation enacted to eliminate racial or ethnic segregation in the United States. The act consisted of 11 titles, several of which had direct implication for public education. Titles I, II, and III guaranteed voting rights, provided injuncture relief against discrimination in places of public accommodation, and provided for the desegregation of public facilities, respectively. Title IV provided for the desegregation of public education; Title V amended certain procedures for the Commission on Civil Rights;

Title VI provided for nondiscrimination in federally assisted programs; and Title VII assured equal employment opportunity. The Equal Employment Opportunity Act of 1972 (P.L. 92–261) amended certain sections of the Civil Rights Act of 1964.

References: Beryl A. Radin, *Implementation, Change, and the Federal Bureaucracy: School Desegregation Policy in H.E.W., 1964–1968,* New York: Teachers College Press, 1977; Public Law 88–352, *United States Statutes at Large, 1964* (Volume 78), Wasington, DC: U.S. Government Printing Office, 1965.

CIVIL RIGHTS COMMISSION, a unit within the executive branch of the federal government, created in 1957 and charged with three principal responsibilities. As enumerated in Public Law 85–315 (Civil Rights Act of 1957), the commission is expected to: "(1) investigate allegations . . . that certain citizens of the United States are being deprived of their right to vote and have that vote counted by reason of their color, race, religion, or natural origin . . . ; (2) study and collect information concerning legal developments constituting a denial of equal protection of the laws under the Constitution; and, (3) appraise the laws and policies of the Federal Government with respect to equal protection of the laws under the Constitution" (p. 635).

The commission's six members, appointed by the President with the advice and consent of the Senate, have been granted several powers including the right to subpoena witnesses, to hire a full-time staff director, and to use advisory committees.

The Civil Rights Act of 1964 broadened the duties of the commission to include investigation of civil rights in areas such as education, housing, employment, transportation, use of public facilities, or the administration of justice.

References: Public Law 85–315, *United States Statutes at Large, 1957* (Volume 71), Washington, DC: U.S. Government Printing Office, 1958; Public Law 88–352, *United States Statutes at Large, 1964* (Volume 78), Washington, DC: U.S. Government Printing Office, 1965.

CLASSICAL CONDITIONING, a school of psychology within the general field of behavioristic psychology. Classical conditioning's historical antecedents are found in the experiments of Russian physiologist Ivan Michaelovich Sechenov (1829–1905) and Ivan Petrovich Pavlov (1849–1936). The base of classicial conditioning is the conditioned reflex, or respondent conditioning through the pairing of a conditioned stimulus with an uncon-

ditioned stimulus to produce a conditioned response. Stimulus-response bonds (S-R) and S-R chaining are studied in classical conditioning. J. B. Watson, E. C. Tolman, and C. L. Hull are among those who have made major contributions to the classical conditioning school of psychology. (See CONDITIONED RESPONSE and PAVLOV, IVAN P.)

References: Abraham Black and William Prokasy (Editors), *Classical Conditioning II,* New York: Appleton-Century-Crofts, Inc., 1972; B. R. Hergenhahn, *An Introduction to Theories of Learning* (Third Edition), Englewood Cliffs, NJ: Prentice-Hall, Inc., 1988; Gregory A. Kimble, *Foundations of Conditioning and Learning,* New York: Appleton-Century-Crofts, Inc., 1967; William Prokasy, *Classical Conditioning: A Symposium,* New York: Appleton-Century-Crofts, Inc., 1965.

CLASSICAL EDUCATION, a form of education that had its origins during the 1400s to the 1700s in Western Europe. In recent years, it has come to mean education in the general areas of liberal arts, general education, or humanities. Subjects such as literature, art, philosophy, history, music, foreign language (especially Latin and Greek), logic, oratory, poetry, drama, ethics, are all part of the classical heritage. Classical education emphasizes the contributions made to society by the great writers, originally the classical authors of Greece and Rome, although more modern writers have also been included in the programs.

The Great Books Programs of the University of Chicago and St. Johns College are examples of programs more classically oriented than the traditional programs found in most other universities. (See GENERAL EDUCATION.)

References: Sidney G. Ashmore, *The Classics and Modern Training,* New York: G. P. Putnam's Sons, 1905; Donald N. Bigelow (Editor), *The Liberal Arts and Teacher Education,* Lincoln, NE: University of Nebraska Press, 1971; T. S. Eliot, *The Classics and the Man of Letters,* New York: Haskell House Publishers, Ltd., 1974; Robert M. Hutchins, *Great Books,* New York: Simon and Schuster, 1954; The Four School Study Commission, *16–20: The Liberal Education of an Age Group,* New York: College Entrance Examination Board, 1970.

CLASSICAL LANGUAGES, those languages that were used by the ancients. Latin and Greek are the two major classical languages. One of the reasons given for teaching classical languages today is to enable an individual to study the works of the ancient scholars and authors. Another reason, commonly invoked in years past, was to train the mind.

Classical languages were the only foreign languages taught in most schools until the 19th century. They were originally taught through the systematic study of grammar and syntax. It wasn't until the early 1900s that other methods, such as the direct method, were used. (See DIRECT METHODS and GRAMMAR TRANSLATION METHOD.)

References: Howard B. Altman (Editor), *Foreign Language Learning: Meeting Individual Needs,* Elmsford, NY: Pergamon Press, Inc., 1979; Jermaine D. Arendt, et al. (Editors), *Foreign Language Learning, Today and Tomorrow,* Elmsford, NY: Pergamon Press, Inc., 1979; Wilga M. Rivers, *Teaching Foreign-Language Skills,* Chicago: University of Chicago Press, 1968.

CLASSICAL ORGANIZATION THEORY—See ORGANIZATIONAL BEHAVIOR

CLASSIFIED PERSONNEL, also known as noncertified or noneducational personnel, school system employees whose services, although noninstructional in nature, nevertheless support the instructional program. The services rendered by classified personnel include diverse activities such as plant, food, clerical, business, and health services. One group of school personnel authorities (Ben Harris and associates) divide noninstructional services into two broad categories. The first, *special pupil support,* includes employees whose principal duties involve food serving, home visiting, physical examining, disciplining, hall monitoring, bus loading, and playground directing. The second category, *noninstructional support,* consists of persons who do tax collecting, budgeting, purchasing, bookkeeping, and cleaning. One of the fastest growing groups of noncertificated employees are paraprofessionals or aides.

Rules and regulations governing classified personnel exist in most school districts. These normally include topics such as written job descriptions, descriptions of recruitment procedures, wage scales (including the requisite classification system that places noncertificated positions hierarchically), fringe benefits, evaluation procedures, promotion opportunities, grounds for termination, and grievance procedures.

References: Ben M. Harris, et al., *Personnel Administration in Education: Leadership for Instructional Improvement,* Boston: Allyn and Bacon, Inc., 1979; Emery Stoops, et al., *Handbook of Educational Administration: A Guide for the Practitioner,* Boston: Allyn and Bacon, Inc., 1975.

CLASS RANK, or class standing, the relative position of a student in his/her graduating class based on grade-point average (usually cumulative). It may be expressed in one of two ways: (1) as a particular position (e.g., ranks 40th in a class of 112), or (2) as a statistical centile (e.g. upper quarter of his/her class). Class rank is one of the criteria used by colleges and universities to determine an applicant's eligibility for admission.

References: *Barron's Profiles of American Colleges* (Volume I, Eleventh Edition), Woodbury, NY: Barron's Educational Series, Inc., 1978; Maureen Matheson (Editor), *The College Handbook, 1979–80,* New York: College Entrance Examination Board, 1979; Harlow G. Unger, *A Student's Guide to College Admissions,* New York: Facts on File Publications, 1986; R. Fred Zuker and Karen C. Hegener, *Peterson's Guide to College Admissions: How to Put the Odds on Your Side,* New York: Monarch Press, 1977.

CLASSROOM MANAGEMENT, a broad term meaning the organization of a classroom such that instruction will be effective and efficient. Classroom management includes the ability of the teacher to deal effectively with a wide range of student abilities. It involves helping students to become responsible for themselves; helping them to work cooperatively; helping them to work on assignments as independently as possible; motivating students to want to learn; altering the negative behavior of disruptive children; providing positive, reasonable, sensitive, and effective discipline; and utilizing appropriate and varied learning/teaching strategies. It is the utilization, in an organized and planned way, of all management elements appropriate for the classroom. Although "classroom discipline" is sometimes used as a synonym, classroom management clearly involves more than this single element.

There is no set procedure for establishing effective classroom management inasmuch as classes, students, times, and environments are different and do change. However, knowledge of, and the ability to apply varied teaching techniques, activities and materials, the theory of classroom management; student behavior; modeling behaviors; theories of learning; the needs of children; incentives; individual differences; and group dynamics are a few of the elements that foster good classroom management.

References: James S. Cangelosi, *Classroom Management Strategies: Gaining and Maintaining Students' Cooperation,* New York: Longman, Inc., 1988; Earl J. Montague, *Fundamentals of Secondary Classroom Instruction,* Columbus, OH: Merrill Publishing Company, 1987; James Quina, *Effective Secondary Teaching: Going beyond the Bell Curve,* New York: Harper and Row Publishers, 1989.

CLASSROOM OBSERVATION—See EVALU-ATION, TEACHER and OBSERVATIONAL TECHNIQUES

CLASS SIZE, the number of pupils who meet regularly for all or a definite fraction of a school day with one particular teacher. From 1934 to 1964, class size in public schools decreased from a then acceptable 40 pupils per teacher to approximately 30:1 and 25:1 in the elementary and secondary school, respectively. The "baby boom" of the 1960s altered the decrease, but the decline in the birth rate of the 1970s again decreased average class sizes in schools.

There is considerable debate over class size. The research yields mixed results about whether there is an optimum class size for learning. One study, a review of research results compiled by Dr. G. Glass of the University of Colorado (1979), indicated that there is a point where the learning curve increases significantly, but that this point is where the class size is rather low. Further, he reported, there is little significant change with classes having enrollments above 20. Class size is not only important for program planning and development, but it is an important factor influencing school building design as well as school funding. Some state and federal agencies have placed limits on the size of classes in certain programs and in some formula funding. (See NUMERICAL STAFFING ADEQUACY and PUPIL-TEACHER RATIO.)
References: Class Size: A Summary of Research, Arlington, VA: Educational Research Service, Inc., 1978; W. D. McClurkin, *School Building Planning,* New York: The Macmillan Company, 1964; Herbert J. Walberg (Editor), *Educational Environments and Effects,* Berkeley, CA: McCutchan Publishing Corporation, 1979.

CLEARING HOUSES—See ERIC

CLEF, symbols appearing at the beginning of a musical stave. These symbols are important because they give pitch-meaning to the notes that follow them. The G (treble) clef, depicted as 𝄞 , is placed on the second line of the stave and is the clef commonly used today in vocal scores. The F (bass) clef, drawn as 𝄢 , is placed on the fourth line of the staff. In keyboard music, the G clef is normally used in conjunction with music for the right hand, the F clef for the left.
References: Bruce Bohle (Editor), *The International Cyclopedia of Music and Musicians* (Tenth Edition), New York: Dodd, Mead and Company, 1975; Hugo Riemann, *Dictionary of Music,* New York: Da Capo Press,

1970; J. A. Westrup and F. L. Harrison (Revised by Conrad Wilson), *The New College Encyclopedia of Music,* New York: W. W. Norton and Company, Inc., 1976.

CLEFT PALATE, a birth defect characterized by an opening in the roof of the mouth. The condition may be accompanied by a slit, or opening in the lip (cleft lip). Authorities classify cleft palate cases into one of four categories: (1) cleft of soft palate; (2) cleft of hard and soft palate; (3) cleft of both palates with opening extending to one side of the lip; and (4) cleft of both palates with openings extending to both sides of the lip.

Recent estimates place the incidence of cleft palate at 1:700. The exact cause of the condition, more prevalent among boys than girls, has yet to be determined.

Cleft palate results in nasal speech and articulatory disorders. Intelligibility is variable, depending on the nature of the defect. Researchers indicate that cleft palate children tend to speak later than other children; some learning loss may also be present.

Cleft palate habilitation is possible with surgery and use of special speech appliances (prosthetic devices). Teams of specialists (dentists, speech pathologists, surgeons, etc.) have often experienced success in helping cleft palate children.
References: D. C. Spriestersbach and Dorothy Sherman (Editors), *Cleft Palate and Communication,* New York: Academic Press, 1968; Charles Van Riper, *Speech Corrections* (Sixth Edition), Englewood Cliffs, NJ: Prentice-Hall, Inc., 1978; Harold Westlake and David Rutherford, *Cleft Palate,* Englewood Cliffs, NJ: Prentice-Hall, Inc., 1966.

CLEP—See COLLEGE-LEVEL EXAMINATION PROGRAM

CLERK-OF-THE-WORKS, an employee of an institution (e.g. school system) who supervises building construction projects. The clerk's responsibility is to see that design irregularities do not take place and that materials used by building contractors conform to contract specifications. Because the clerk-of-the-works is in daily contact with the superintendent of construction and other technicians, it is recommended that he/she be knowledgeable about construction method; furthermore, he/she needs to be very familiar with the plans and specifications of the project he/she is supervising.

The clerk-of-the-works, as indicated above, is the owner's or institution's (e.g. school system) inde-

pendent representative on the project. This individual is sometimes placed on the architect's payroll to avoid local civil service requirements. Regardless of the payroll assignment, he/she is (should be) responsible to the owner or institution.
References: Sam F. Brewster, *Campus Planning and Construction: Physical Facilities for Universities and Colleges,* Washington, DC: The Association of Physical Plant Administrators of Universities and Colleges, 1976; Basil Castoldi, *Educational Facilities: Planning, Remodeling, and Management,* Boston: Allyn and Bacon, Inc., 1977.

CLEVELAND BOARD OF EDUCATION v. LAFLEUR, a lawsuit argued before the U.S. Supreme Court (1974) that challenged the legality of regulations requiring pregnant teachers to take unpaid maternity leaves for several months preceding and following childbirth. Such uniform cutoff dates, the Court ruled, were unnecessarily restrictive in the sense that they violated the teacher's fundamental right to marriage and procreation.

While declaring mandatory cutoff dates to be unconstitutional, the Court did not deny a school district's right to: (1) require advance notice of those planning to take maternity leave, and (2) require a doctor's medical certificate before returning to work.
References: Cleveland Board of Education v. LaFleur, 414 U.S. 632, 94 S.Ct., 1974; EEOC Guidelines, 44 *Federal Register,* March 9, 1979 (p. 13278); *General Electric Co. v. Gilbert,* 429 U.S. 125, 97 S.Ct. 401, 50 L.Ed. 2d 343 (1976); Frank R. Kemerer and Kenneth L. Deutsch, *Constitutional Rights and Student Life: Value Conflict in Law and Education,* St. Paul, MN: West Publishing Company, 1979; E. Edmund Reutter, Jr., *The Law of Public Education* (Second Edition), Mineola, NY: The Foundation Press, Inc., 1976.

CLIENT-CENTERED COUNSELING, an approach to counseling whose origin is attributed to Carl Rogers. A form of humanistic therapy, the client-centered approach is predicated on the assumption that individuals are in the process of growing and seek to actualize their own potential; furthermore, that individuals are basically good and capable of making decisions affecting their own lives. When working with a client, the counselor does not make decisions for him/her. Instead, in a nondirective manner, the counselor plays an empathetic role that leads to establishment of an accepting, supportive, and safe *relationship* with the client. Once this climate has been established, the counselor, as humane facilitator, helps the client to face reality with major responsibility for the direction of therapy resting with the client.
References: Herbert M. Burks, Jr., and Buford Stefflre, *Theories of Counseling* (Third Edition), New York: McGraw-Hill Book Company, 1979; Gerald Corey, *Theory and Practice of Counseling and Psychotherapy,* Monterey, CA: Brooks/Cole Publishing Company, 1977; E. L. Tolbert, *An Introduction to Guidance,* Boston: Little, Brown and Company, 1978.

CLINICAL SUPERVISION, a specific type of supervision whose development is attributed to Morris L. Cogan. According to Cogan, *general supervision* and *clinical supervision* are terms that have distinct meanings. The former refers to all out-of-classroom supervisory activities such as curriculum development, creation of new report cards, and so on. Clinical supervision, on the other hand, has an intraclassroom focus with emphasis placed upon teacher growth. The overriding purpose of clinical supervision is the improvement of the teacher's classroom performance. The most important data used to help realize this purpose are drawn from the supervisor's observations of classroom activities.

The carrying out of clinical supervision involves five stages, these sometimes referred to as "the cycle of clinical supervision." They are: (1) *preobservation conference* between teacher and supervisor; (2) *observation(s)* by the supervisor; (3) *analysis and strategy,* a step that requires the supervisor to assess observations made, to infer patterns from his/her observations, and to propose strategies for conferring with the teacher; (4) *supervisory conference* between teacher and supervisor, at which time the teacher receives feedback (with considerable positive support); and (5) *postconference analysis,* a self-audit in which the supervisor attempts to evaluate his/her own supervisory role.
References: Morris L. Cogan, *Clinical Supervision,* Boston: Houghton Mifflin Company, 1973; Morris L. Cogan, "Rationale for Clinical Supervision," *Journal of Research and Development in Education,* Winter 1976; Robert Goldhammer, et al., *Clinical Supervision: Special Methods for the Supervision of Teachers* (Second Edition), New York: Holt, Rinehart and Winston, Inc., 1980; Larry W. Hughes and Gerald C. Ubben, *The Elementary Principal's Handbook: A Guide to Effective Action* (Third Edition), Boston: Allyn and Bacon, 1989; Charles A. Reavis, *Teacher Improvement Through Clinical Supervision* (PDK Fastback 111), Bloomington, IN: The Phi Delta Kappa Educational Foundation, 1978.

CLIQUE, a term referring to a self-contained group of individuals within a larger group.

Sociological theorists suggest that subsets of people (cliques) separate themselves from the rest of a group voluntarily, exhibit high levels of personal interaction and consensus, and are frequently goal oriented.

In schools, cliques are formed on the basis of factors such as interests, age, sex, values, intelligence, and socioeconomic status. Research suggests that cliques within a large group (e.g. classroom, grade level, school) are ordered hierarchically. In school groups, such rankings frequently reflect *popularity* and *power*. (See SOCIOGRAM.)

References: Maureen T. Hallinan, *The Structure of Positive Sentiment,* New York: Elsevier Scientific Publishing Company, 1974; Thomas F. Hoult, *Dictionary of Modern Sociology,* Totowa, NJ: Littlefield, Adams and Company, 1969.

CLOSURE, MATHEMATICAL, a principle in mathematics that describes a particular operation of a set of natural numbers. If one were to add or multiply two natural numbers found in a set, and the sum or product were to be a natural number found in the same set, then the operations could be considered closed. For example, in the set $\{1, 2, 3, 4, 5\}$, the addition of $2 + 3$ or $3 + 2$ is closed, because 5 is in the set; so is $1 + 4$ or $4 + 1$, 1×2 or 2×1, 1×3 or 3×1. So is 2×2; but 2×3 or 3×2 is not closed, because 6 is outside the set.

Subtraction is not a closed operation, even if the natural numbers are to be found in the set. For example, in the set $\{1, 2, 3, 4, 5\}$, $5 - 4$ is in the set $(=1)$, but $4 - 5$ is not and negative values have no meaning for natural numbers.

Natural numbers form a sequence of consecutive numbers such that any number is always less than al the numbers ahead of it. The numbers $\{7, 8, 9, 10\}$ or $\{1000, 1001, 1002\}$ are examples of a set of natural numbers.

References: A. B. Evenson, *Modern Mathematics,* Chicago: Scott, Foresman and Company, 1962; L. Clark Lay, *The Study of Arithmetic,* New York: The Macmillan Company, 1966; Jack D. Wilson, *Elementary Mathematics: A Modern Approach,* New York: McGraw-Hill Book Company, 1967.

CLOSURE, PSYCHOLOGICAL, in gestalt psychology, a drive to seek completion of an experience, a desire, a perception, or a need. All individuals have a desire and need for closure. Although an individual can exist in some state of incompleteness, an inordinately excessive drive for closure can create psychological problems of human be-

havior. Obsession or compulsion may be a product of such need. Other problems may develop when an individual fails to spend enough time on an experience to develop closure or when he/she does not allow relationships to develop that foster attainment of closure.

References: Erving Polster and Miriam Polster, *Gestalt Therapy Integrated,* New York: Brunner/Mazel, Inc., 1973; Daniel Rosenblatt, *Opening Doors: What Happens in Gestalt Therapy,* New York: Harper and Row, Publishers, 1975; Edward W. Smith (Editor), *The Growing Edge of Gestalt Therapy,* New York: Brunner/Mazel, Inc., 1976; John O. Stevens (Editor), *Gestalt Is,* Moab, UT: Real People Press, 1975.

CLOZE PROCEDURE, a reading technique used to measure a student's language ability. Students are instructed to read a passage consisting of approximately 250 words. The passage's first and final sentences are usually left intact. In the other sentences, every Nth (usually fifth) word is deleted. In place of the omitted words, lines of equal length are inserted. Students are then asked to infer the missing words from context and to fill in the blanks with the correct words. Varying frequencies of omissions (e.g. every seventh, tenth word) may be used. The Cloze procedure is employed in reading research to determine a student's approximate reading level or to select appropriate reading materials. The Cloze technique was derived from the gestalt concept of closure.

References: Eldon E. Ekwall, *Diagnosis and Remediation of the Disabled Reader,* Boston: Allyn and Bacon, Inc., 1976; Harry Singer and Dan Donlan, *Reading and Learning from Text* (Second Edition), Hillsdale, NJ: Lawrence Erlbaum Associates, Publishers, 1989; Robert M. Wilson and Craig J. Cleland, *Diagnostic and Remedial Reading for Classroom and Clinic* (Sixth Edition), Columbus, OH: Merrill Publishing Company, 1989.

CLUES (READING), stimuli that suggest meaning to a reader. In reading, there are many clues that will aid a reader in acquiring meaning from printed material. Meaning can be inferred from clues in a title that suggests a plot, from trends in a story, or from characters found in the story. There are many types of clues: content, context, experience, phonetic, word structure, word recognition, and so on. These clues aid in the reading process; their use should be encouraged in the teaching of reading to children.

References: Dolores Durkin, *Teaching Them to Read* (Third Edition), Boston: Allyn and Bacon, Inc., 1978; Charles T. Mangrum II and Harry W. Forgan, *Developing Competencies in Teaching Reading,* Columbus, OH:

Charles E. Merrill Publishing Company, 1979; Wayne Otto, et al., *How to Teach Reading*, Reading, MA: Addison-Wesley Publishing Company, 1979.

CLUSTER SAMPLING—See SAMPLING

COACH, ATHLETIC, an instructor in one or more sports. This position is most commonly found at the high school and college levels where extramural programs are routinely made available to qualified students.

Don Emery pointed out that the success of coaches reflects behaviors/achievements in four broad activity areas: (1) the coaching and teaching methods/techniques employed; (2) the coach as a person, including personal characteristics, education, and training; (3) ability to organize and administer effectively; and (4) public relations practices.

Coaches, especially those working in smaller institutions, are often given assignments that include both teaching and coaching responsibilities. The number of varsity sports included in a school's athletic program is also a function of institutional size. Among the more common sports requiring the services of a coach are football, basketball, baseball, golf, swimming, tennis, volley ball, gymnastics, and soccer. In recent years, primarily as the result of federal legislation requiring equity for female students, the number and prominence of women coaches has been increasing steadily throughout the United States. (See TITLE IX.)

References: Jay J. Coakley, *Sport in Society: Issues and Controversies*, St. Louis, MO: The C. V. Mosby Company, 1978; Don B. Emery, "Scoring the Factors in Successful High School Coaching" in John D. Massengale (Editor), *The Principles and Problems of Coaching*, Springfield, IL: Charles C. Thomas, Publisher, 1975; Patsy Neal, *Coaching Methods for Women* (Second Edition), Reading, MA: Addison-Wesley Publishing Company, 1978; Ralph J. Sabock, *The Coach* (Second Edition), Philadelphia: W. B. Saunders Company, 1979.

COCHRAN v. LOUISIANA BOARD OF EDUCATION, a significant lawsuit argued before the U.S. Supreme Court. In Louisiana, a school district purchased textbooks for the teaching of secular subjects and made these available to parochial school students free of charge. Opponents argued that it was unconstitutional for taxpayers' money to be used for this purpose. The Court (in 1930) ruled unanimously that this violated neither the First nor the Fourteenth Amendments, and thus this practice was not construed to be unconstitu-

tional. The Court pointed out, furthermore, that beneficiaries of such purchases were the students and not the parochial schools in which they were enrolled. This distinction gave rise to the oft-cited "child benefit theory." (See CHILD BENEFIT THEORY and PAROCHIAD.)

References: Cochran v. Louisiana State Board of Education, Supreme Court of the United States, 1930, 281 U.S. 370; Earl Hoffman, "Milestones on the Road to Parochiad," *NSSP Bulletin,* December 1974; Dale E. Twomley, *Parochiad and the Courts,* Berrien Springs, MI: Andrews University Press, 1979.

COCURRICULAR ACTIVITIES—See EXTRACLASS ACTIVITIES

CODE OF ETHICS OF THE EDUCATION PROFESSION, a document developed by the National Education Association for the purpose of guiding the professional behavior of its membership as well as all other professionals working in education. The initial national code was adopted in 1929; several revisions have been made since then. The current code consists of a Preamble and two "principles": Principle I, *Commitment to the Student,* and Principle II, *Commitment to the Profession.* Several specific guidelines subsume each.

NEA's Professional Ethics Committee works closely with the ethics committees of state and local units in helping to interpret the code's contents. The code's enforcement has posed problems, some attributable to the teaching profession's relatively apathetic stance on this subject and some to the fact that many states have legislated procedures for dealing with unprofessional behavior. When enforcement action is required by NEA, the matter is referred to the organization's Commission on Professional Rights and Responsibilities.

The NEA code has been adopted by many states and local school districts as a guide for their respective professional employees. (See APPENDIX I: CODE OF ETHICS OF THE EDUCATION PROFESSION.)

References: National Education Association, *NEA Handbook, 1977-78,* Washington, DC: The Association, 1977; Robert W. Richey, *Planning for Teaching: An Introduction to Education* (Sixth Edition), New York: McGraw-Hill Book Company, 1979.

COEDUCATION, education for boys and girls that takes place concurrently and in the same school and/or in the same classroom. For education to be truly coeducational, boys and girls must be admitted to the programs on equal terms.

Although many early academies were coeducational, Oberlin was the first coeducational college to be established in the United States. It admitted women to its program from the college's inception in 1833. It wasn't until the latter half of the 19th century that women were admitted, to any great extent, to other institutions of higher learning.

Coeducation for children is not new. Plato argued for boys and girls being educated together in *The Republic* and coeducation occasionally occurred during the Reformation in Europe.

In the United States, the common school of the 1830s, 1840s, and 1850s fostered coeducation. From the beginning, one of its goals was to provide free elementary education for every white child. Two common school reformers, Henry Barnard of Connecticut (1850s) and Horace Mann of Massachusetts (1830s), laid the base for free public education for both boys and girls in the United States. Coeducation in American secondary schools also became common in the 19th century.

References: Robert L. Church, *Education in the United States,* New York: The Free Press, 1976; Adolphe E. Meyer, *An Educational History of the Western World* (Second Edition), New York: McGraw-Hill Book Company, 1972; David A. Welton, *Realms of Teaching,* Chicago: Rand McNally College Publishing Company, 1979.

COFFMAN, LOTUS DELTA (January 7, 1875–September 22, 1938), educator who gained prominence as President of the University of Minnesota (1920–38) and as a leader of the American Council on Education (ACE). During his years as Minnesota President, he introduced numerous educational innovations that attracted world interest. He was active in the ACE since its inception, twice serving as the council's elected Chairman (1922–23 and 1935–36).

Coffman was also a prolific writer. His better known works included *Reading in Public Schools* (1908) and *How to Teach Arithmetic* (1913), both of which he coauthored, as well as *The Social Composition of the Teaching Population* (1911) and *The State University: Its Work and Problems* (1934). A complete bibliography of his writings (143 entries) appears at the close of Malcolm Willey's memorial tribute to him.

Coffman earned the A.B. and A.M. degrees at Indiana University and the Ph.D. at Columbia University. As an undergraduate, he also attended Indiana State Normal School (now, Indiana State University), an institution whose Coffman Distinguished Professorship carries his name.

Coffman's career included service as a teacher, public school administrator, and Director of Teacher Training (Illinois State College). He taught education at Columbia University (1909–11), the University of Illinois (1912–15), and the University of Minnesota where he also held the education deanship. A leader in professional organizations other than ACE, Coffman served as President, National Society of College Teachers of Education (1917–18); Chairman, Educational Policies Commission (1935–38); and President, National Association of State Universities (1930).

References: Lawrence B. Smelser, "Coffman, Lotus Delta" in John F. Ohles (Editor), *Biographical Dictionary of American Educators* (Volume 1), Westport, CT: Greenwood Press, 1978; "Coffman, Lotus Delta" in *Who Was Who in America* (Volume 1), Chicago: The A. N. Marquis Company, 1962; Malcolm M. Willey, "Lotus Delta Coffman: Educational Statesman, 1875–1938," *The Educational Record,* January 1939.

COGNITION, a term not easily defined or one whose meaning is not universally accepted. Cognition is defined according to the "school" of psychology from which it stems. Many cognitive psychologists would restrict the definition to the higher mental processes such as knowledge, intelligence, thinking, acquisition of new meaning, generating plans and strategies, reasoning, and problem solving. Many behaviorists, on the other hand, would restrict the term to conditioning, rote verbal learning, and other procedures or processes consistent with their approach to learning. Still other schools have their specific and varied definitions. It generally means the gaining of knowledge.

Numerous factors influence cognition. These include organized motor movements, perceptions, social-communication use of language, attitudes, emotions, and environment. Each, it could be argued, constitutes a part of the definition. John Flavell suggested that "man is cognitive" and carries out a variety of mental operations to achieve a variety of mental products. These operations, too, can be said to make up cognition.

References: Gery D'Ydewalle and Willy Lens (Editors), *Cognition in Human Motivation and Learning,* Hillside, NJ: Lawrence Erlbaum Associates, Publishers, 1981; John H. Flavell, *Cognitive Development,* Englewood Cliffs, NJ: Prentice-Hall, Inc., 1977; John B. Kirby and T. B. Biggs (Editors), *Cognition-Development and Instruction,* New York: Academic Press, 1980; Norman A. Sprinthall and Richard C. Sprinthall, *Educational Psychology: A Developmental Approach* (Fourth Edition), New York: Random House, 1987.

COGNITIVE DOMAIN, a broad classification of behaviors and objectives that emphasizes or deals with acquisition of knowledge, intellectual abilities, intellectual skills, problem solving, and similar intellectual learnings.

Benjamin Bloom and associates, in 1956, developed a taxonomy of educational cognitive domain objectives. These objectives were divided into broad areas of: Knowledge, 1.00; Comprehension, 2.00; Application, 3.00; Analysis, 4.00; Synthesis, 5.00; and Evaluation, 6.00. Joy P. Guilford's "Structure of the Intellect" model contributed to the educational formulation of the cognitive domain. Raymond Cattell, E. Paul Torrance, Philip Vernon and other educational psychologists also helped to define the domain. (See TAXONOMY.)

References: Benjamin S. Bloom, et al., *Taxonomy of Educational Objectives (Handbook I): Cognitive Domain,* New York: David McKay Company, Inc., 1956; Joy P. Guilford, *Nature of Human Intelligence,* New York: McGraw-Hill Book Company, 1968; Philip E. Vernon, *Intelligence: Heredity and Environment,* San Francisco: W. H. Freeman and Company, 1979.

COGNITIVE MAPPING, learning through meaningful cognitive behavior (i.e. using signs or *patterns of stimuli* to reach a goal) rather than through conditioned movement per se. First proposed by Edward C. Tolman, a cognitive learning theorist, in 1930, cognitive mapping leads to goal achievement and assumes latent learning, field expectancies, motivation, and understanding (rather than learning through conditioning). He found that rats not previously rewarded had learned more from their maze than would be indicated by their behavior before rewards had been given. The rats had fewer errors in running the maze once reward had been introduced as a result of their previous experiences in it. The rats, he concluded, had formed cognitive maps through exploration and observation; they had used environmental cues to develop these cognitive maps.

In humans, cognitive maps are developed by utilizing cues, knowledges of an environment, and cognitive patterning to facilitate the reaching of a goal. Such cues, knowledges, and stimuli are organized into patterns in the brain (cognitive maps) that, in turn, lead to learning (goal realization).

References: Frank Restle, *Learning Animal Behavior and Human Cognition,* New York: McGraw-Hill Book Company, 1975; William S. Sahakian, *Psychology of Learning,* Chicago: Markham Publishing Company, 1970; John A. R. Wilson, et al., *Psychological Foundations of Learning and Teaching* (Second Edition), New York: McGraw-Hill Book Company, 1974.

COGNITIVE RESEARCH TRUST (CoRT), an instructional program on thinking skills developed by Edward deBono. This curriculum is built on the theory that thinking is a skill that can be taught directly. There are 60 CoRT lessons beginning with the PMI. The PMI is a scanning tool that requests students to analyze *P*lus (good points), *M*inus (bad points), and *I*nteresting (worthy of special note but not necessarily good or bad) aspects of a given problem prior to formulating a solution or opinion to the given concept. CoRT includes many operating tools such as PMI to aid teaching of thinking skills. DeBono believes the middle grade (ages 9 to 11) to be best suited to the teaching of thinking. Children at this age have sufficient verbal knowledge and experience to use with the thinking tools.

References: DeBono, Edward, "The Direct Teaching of Thinking as a Skill," *Phi Delta Kappan,* June 1983; deBono, Edward, *CoRT Thinking Program,* Elmsford, NY: Pergamon, Inc., undated.

COGNITIVE STYLE, a consistent approach used by an individual to organize and process information. The style influences his/her approach to tasks that involve thinking and problem solving. It is developed as the result of rules and strategies that the individual uses when adapting to new information.

Cognitive style reflects the cognitive developmental state that one is in. Jean Piaget suggested that there are four stages of cognitive development: (1) *sensorimotor* (birth–1½/2 years); (2) *preoperational* (1½/2–6/7 years); (3) *concrete operational* (6/7–11/12 years); and (4) *formal operational* (11/12–adult). Ruth Ault proposed that the stages of cognitive development are perception, memory, generation and testing of hypothesis, and evaluation. These four, she suggested, occur at all ages, but they develop more extensively as one gets older. Herman Witkin's contribution to understanding of cognitive style is known as the field independence/dependence approach. According to Witkin, a field-independent individual can separate cognitive information into parts, while a field-dependent person cannot do so as easily.

Cognitive style may include the integration, hierarchic integration, subordination, coordination, regulation, conflict, and equilibration of cognitive information. Cognitive style is internal to the individual; it should not be confused with the outward manifestation of overt behavior. (See COGNITION.)

References: Ruth Ault, *Children! Cognitive Development,* New York: Oxford University Press, 1977; Kenneth M. Goldstein and Sheldon Blackman, *Cognitive Style: Five*

Approaches and Relevant Research, New York: John Wiley and Sons, 1978; Jean Piaget, *The Development of Thought: Equilibrium of Cognitive Structure,* New York: The Viking Press, 1977; Linda Siegal and Charles J. Brainerd, *Alternatives to Piaget,* New York: Academic Press, 1978; Herman A. Witkin, *Cognitive Styles in Personal and Cultural Adaptation,* Worcester, MA: Clark University Press, 1977.

COGNITIVE THEORY IN FOREIGN-LANGUAGE ACQUISITION, a theory that holds that all people are born with the *ability* to learn a first (their native) language. This mental ability, along with other mental abilities, is developed as the individual matures. According to the theory, learning a first language is a complex mental process; language learning is not achieved by imitation, practice, and reinforcement only. This ability is *not* a predisposition to language acquisition as believed by those who hold to the nativistic theory. (See NATIVISTIC THEORY.)

References: Kenneth Chastain, *Developing Second-Language Skills: Theory to Practice* (Third Edition), Chicago: Rand McNally College Publishing Company, 1976; A. J. VanEssen, et al., *The Context of Foreign-Language Learning,* Assen, The Netherlands: Van Gorcum and Company V. V., 1975.

COHESION COMPREHENSION, a reading skill that enables the individual to link sentences together to enhance understanding. Authors use a variety of cohesive devices that are both semantic and syntactic—i.e., conjunctions, pronouns, and repetitions. Successful interpretation of one idea depends on accurate understanding of a preceding one. The links establishing cohesion are labelled *ties*; an instance of cohesion is a *cohesion tie.* Such ties can be found within or between sentences. Most cohesion ties found in school texts are anaphoric (related back) in nature. Cataphoric (related forward) ties are less common within school materials; however, the phenomena can occur in literary introductions where meaning is unclear until further on in the passage.

Since cohesion is a text-related phenomenon, teachers should study reading assignments in order to predict and allay problem areas where comprehension might break down because of confusing cohesion relationships. A common area of breakdown is between main clauses; a quick study of such clauses can enable the teacher to intervene with information to reinforce the cohesive ties necessary to comprehension.

References: J. W. Irwin, *Teaching Reading Comprehension Processes,* Englewood Cliffs, NJ: Prentice-Hall, 1986; J. W. Irwin (Editor), *Understanding and Teaching: Cohesion Comprehension,* Newark, DE: International Reading Association, 1986; W. Kintsch and T. A. Van Dijk, "Toward a Model of Text Comprehension and Production," *Psychological Review,* 85, 1978; H. Riesser, "On the Development of Text Grammars" in W. V. Dressler (Editor), *Current Trends in Textlinguistics,* New York: Walter de Gruyter, 1978.

COHESIVENESS—See GROUP COHESIVENESS

COLEMAN REPORT, popular title for the study, *Equality of Educational Opportunity,* published in 1966 by James S. Coleman, Johns Hopkins University sociologist, and his associates. The study, which included data on 600,000 children, was carried out in accordance with legislative mandate (Section 402, Title IV, Civil Rights Act of 1964) that sought information "concerning the lack of availability of equal educational opportunities for individuals by reason of race, color, religion, or national origin in public educational institutions at all levels" (p. 247).

The study's major findings included the fact that: (1) most American children were then attending largely segregated schools; (2) school factors, including facilities, had little relationship to student achievement; and (3) children from disadvantaged backgrounds, regardless of race, learned more when attending schools with children of advantaged backgrounds.

The study was subsequently criticized by numbers of scholars, primarily on the basis of the manner in which data were collected, treated, and interpreted.

References: Elchanan Cohn, *The Economics of Education* (Revised Edition), Cambridge, MA: Ballinger Publishing Company, 1979; James S. Coleman, et al., *Equality of Educational Opportunity,* Washington, DC: U.S. Government Printing Office, 1966; Public Law 88-352, *United States Statutes at Large* (Volume 78), Washington, DC: U.S. Government Printing Office, 1965.

COLLAGE, an art technique that involves fastening (gluing) cut-out materials such as paper, cloth, and wood to a base such as paper or a mounting board. The result is a posterlike product having an aesthetic character of its own. Creating a collage entails three steps: (1) *selecting* materials to be used; (2) *arranging* the materials; and (3) *pasting* (fastening) them.

References: Leslie A. Baker, *The Art Teacher's Resource Book,* Reston, VA: Reston Publishing Company, Inc., 1979; Chandler Montgomery, *Art for Teachers of Children: Foundations of Aesthetic Experience,* Columbus, OH: Charles E. Merrill Publishing Company, 1968.

COLLECTIVE BARGAINING, a labor relations term for bilateral decision making (negotiations) about working conditions. Such negotiations involve representatives of workers and representatives of the employers who come together for the purpose of reaching agreement.

Section 8 (d) of the Taft-Hartley Act provides a legal and more expansive definition of collective bargaining. It reads: "to bargain collectively is the performance of the mutual obligation of the employer and the representative of the employees to meet at reasonable times and confer in good faith with respect to wages, hours, and other terms and conditions of employment, or the negotiations of an agreement, or any question arising thereunder, and the execution of a written contract incorporating any agreement reached if requested by either party, but such obligation does not compel either party to agree to a proposal or require the making of a concession" (p. 142).

The major labor organizations representing educators are the National Education Association (approximately 1.8 million members) and the American Federation of Teachers (about 520,000 members). In recent years, both have been actively involved in collective bargaining activities in American school districts and institutions of higher learning. (See AMERICAN FEDERATION OF TEACHERS and NATIONAL EDUCATION ASSOCIATION.)

References: Thomas J. Flygare, *Collective Bargaining in the Public Schools* (PDK Fastback 99), Bloomington, IN: The Phi Delta Kappa Educational Foundation, 1977; Labor-Management Relations Act (Amended), *United States Statutes at Large, 1947* (Part I), Washington, DC: U.S. Government Printing Office, 1948; Frank W. Lutz and William E. Caldwell, "Collective Bargaining and the Principal" in Donald A. Erickson and Theodore L. Reller (Editors), *The Principal in Metropolitan Schools*, Berkeley, CA: McCutchan Publishing Corporation, 1978; Robert C. O'Reilly, *Understanding Collective Bargaining in Education: Negotiations, Contracts and Disputes Between Teachers and Boards*, Metuchen, NJ: The Scarecrow Press, Inc., 1978; Virginia Richardson-Koehler, et al., *Educators' Handbook: A Research Perspective*, New York: Longman, Inc., 1987; Max S. Wortman, Jr. and C. Wilson Randle, *Collective Bargaining: Principles and Practices* (Second Edition), Boston: Houghton Mifflin Company, 1966.

COLLEGE AND UNIVERSITY PRESIDENT— See PRESIDENT, COLLEGE AND UNIVERSITY

COLLEGE: A REPORT ON UNDERGRADUATE EDUCATION IN AMERICA— See NATIONAL REFORM REPORTS (1980–86)

COLLEGE BOARD, or College Entrance Examination Board, a nonprofit association of more than 2,400 colleges, universities, secondary schools, education associations, and agencies that offers services to secondary and postsecondary school students. The board was founded in 1900 to provide assistance and research information to students moving from high school to college.

Some of the better known products/services offered by the College Board include: (1) the Scholastic Aptitude Test (SAT), a college admissions examination; (2) the Preliminary Scholastic Aptitude Test/National Merit Scholarship Qualifying Test, used to help high school juniors apply and qualify for National Merit scholarships and to assist high schools with the task of guiding students; (3) the College Level Examination Program (CLEP), tests used for advanced placement at the college level; and (4) the College Scholarship Service, which helps students apply for financial aid. The *College Handbook,* a directory of more than 2,800 two- and four-year colleges, is published regularly.

The College Board's main offices are in New York City. Six regional offices are scattered throughout the continental United States; a Latin American office is located in Puerto Rico. (See COLLEGE-LEVEL EXAMINATION PROGRAM; NATIONAL MERIT SCHOLARSHIP; and SCHOLASTIC APTITUDE TEST.)

Reference: College Entrance Examination Board, *The College Board Annual Report, 1987–1988,* New York: The Board, 1988.

COLLEGE CREDIT, a record-keeping procedure used by postsecondary educational institutions for accounting, certifying, and, at times, credentialing those students who have successfully completed a specific course(s). Credit implies that learning and the acquisition of specific knowledges have taken place. Traditionally, college credit takes the form of semester hours, these usually based on several factors: actual time in the classroom (one semester hour awarded for about 15 clock hours per 15-week semester of classroom instruction); level of the course work (undergraduate, graduate); nature of the course (traditional classroom, laboratory, field-based, etc.); and place in a specific curriculum (e.g. lower-level undergraduate, upper-level undergraduate). Colleges and universities using the quarter rather than the semester calendar award quarter hours of credit for courses completed. Three quarter hours are equivalent to two semester hours.

Most colleges and universities require the completion of a specific number of credit awarding courses and experiences in a specific sequence before awarding a degree. Generally, this involves completion of approximately 60 semester hours for an associate degree, 110 to 135 semester hours for an undergraduate (B.A. or B.S.) degree, an additional 30–40 graduate semester hours for a masters degree, and 70–100 total graduate semester hours for a doctoral degree. Many institutions grant college credit for work experience, credit earned at other institutions, through testing under selected conditions, or through life experiences.

Quality points are used in determining grade-point averages, "honors," eligibility for graduation, as well as admission standards for entrance into a graduate program. (Quality points reflect grades earned in a course as well as semester hours earned.) With the advent of "reforms" such as mini-college courses, recognition of student centered learning, external degree programs, and testing for credit, the awarding of college credit is changing. (See COLLEGE-LEVEL EXAMINATION PROGRAM; QUARTER, ACADEMIC; and SEMESTER.)

References: John K. Folger, et al., *Human Resources and Higher Education*, New York: Russell Sage Foundation, 1970; Michael Marien, *Beyond the Carnegie Commission: A Policy Study Guide to Space/Time, Credit-Preference Higher Education*, Syracuse, NY: Educational Policy Research Center, 1972; Peter Meger, *Awarding College Credit for Non-College Learning*, San Francisco: Jossey-Bass Publishers, 1975; Francis C. Rosecrance, *The American College and Its Teachers*, New York: The Macmillan Company, 1962; Dyckman W. Vermilye (Editor), *Learner-Centered Reform*, San Francisco: Jossey-Bass Publishers, 1975.

COLLEGE ENTRANCE EXAMINATION BOARD—See COLLEGE BOARD

COLLEGE-LEVEL EXAMINATION PROGRAM (CLEP), a program that permits traditional and nontraditional students to earn college credit by examination. CLEP was originally designed to evaluate individuals who had acquired different types of knowledge via various postsecondary experiences (e.g. correspondence courses, on-the-job training). The program now accommodates large numbers of precollege students desirous of entering college with advanced standing. Many commonly receive credit for one year of college. Over 1,700 colleges and universities offer college credit on the basis of CLEP scores.

CLEP, a service of the College Entrance Examination Board, sponsors two types of examinations. *General examinations* are available in 5 liberal arts subject areas (English composition, mathematics, natural sciences, social sciences, and humanities). *Subject examinations* may be taken in any of 50 different subjects or areas. They are available in the fields of business, dental auxiliary education, education, humanities, literature, mathematics, medical technology, modern languages (French, German, and Spanish), nursing, sciences, and social sciences. CLEP examinations, developed by rotating committees of higher education faculty in cooperation with the Educational Testing Service, are administered monthly in approximately 1,000 test centers.

References: College Entrance Examination Board, *The College Board Annual Report, 1987–88*, New York: The Board, 1988; Richard C. Sweetland, et al., *Tests, A Comprehensive Reference for Assessments in Psychology, Education and Business*, Kansas City, MO: Test Corporation of America, 1983.

COLLEGE OF EDUCATION, or school of education, a degree-granting teacher training institution that offers preservice and inservice professional instruction in the field of education. Nondegree programs leading to certification are also usually offered. Other educational professionals (e.g. principals, counselors, supervisors) are trained in such institutions as well. A large number of colleges of education offer professional courses at both the undergraduate and graduate levels. Degrees conferred may be the B.A. or B.S. in Education; M.A. or M.S.; Ed.S.; and/or Ed.D. or Ph.D.

Colleges of education evolved from the normal schools that were prevalent during the 19th century. In the late 1800s and early 1900s, education emerged as a separate discipline in many colleges and universities. Separate teachers colleges (e.g. Teachers College, Columbia, 1887) were created on some campuses by 1900.

Colleges/schools of education are currently an integral part of many universities although a small number, such as National College of Education, are independent institutions. In smaller institutions of higher education, the primary professional education unit is called a department of education. The abbreviation "SCDE" is a collective term used to describe all *s*chools, *c*olleges, and *d*epartments of *e*ducation. Egon Guba and David Clark, in 1978, reported that there were 1,367 SCDEs in the United States located in approximately 72 percent of all four-year colleges and universities. In 1981, the American Association of Colleges for Teacher Education reported that of its 774 member institutions, 509 were accredited by the National Council for Teacher Education. Collectively, these 774 institutions conferred 217,136 education degrees, of which 120,629 were undergraduate. (See EDUCATIONAL INSTITUTION; NATIONAL COUNCIL FOR THE ACCREDITATION OF TEACHER EDUCATION; NORMAL SCHOOLS; PROFESSORSHIP IN EDUCATION; TEACHER; and TEACHER EDUCATION.)

References: AACTE Briefs, March 1981; John S. Brubacher and Willis Rudy, *Higher Education in Transition* (Third Revised Edition), New York: Harper and Row, Publishers, 1976; Charles W. Case and William A. Matthes (Editors), *Colleges of Education: Perspectives on Their Future,* Berkeley, CA: McCutchan Publishing Corporation, 1985; Egon G. Guba and David L. Clark, "Are Schools of Education Languishing?" *New York University Education Quarterly,* Winter 1978; Robert B. Howsam, et al., *Educating a Profession,* Washington, DC: American Association of Colleges for Teacher Education, 1976.

COLLEGE WORK-STUDY PROGRAM (CWSP), a federally funded student financial aid program originally authorized by the Economic Opportunity Act of 1964 as an antipoverty measure. The program's regulations/provisions were subsequently modified in 1968, 1972, and 1976. College work-study makes meaningful work opportunities available to students who have demonstrated financial need. Wages are paid on an hourly basis to students employed by the college or those engaged in non-profit, off-campus work. The federal government provides 80 percent of the wages; the remaining 20 percent is furnished by the college or off-campus employer.

References: Cathy A. Chance, *Florida Atlantic University Student Employment Manual,* Boca Raton, FL: Office of Student Employment, Florida Atlantic University, January 1980; Chester E. Finn, Jr., *Scholars, Dollars, and Bureaucrats,* Washington, DC: The Brookings Institution, 1978; Public Law 88-452, *United States Statutes at Large, 1964* (Volume 78), Washington, DC: U.S. Government Printing Office, 1965; Public Law 90-575, *United States Statutes at Large, 1968* (Volume 82), Washington, DC: U.S. Government Printing Office, 1969; Public Law 93-318, *United States Statutes at Large, 1972* (Volume 86), Washington, DC: U.S. Government Printing Office, 1973; Public Law 94-482, *United States Statutes at Large, 1976* (Volume 90, Part 2), Washington, DC: U.S. Government Printing Office, 1978.

COLLOQUIUM, a session (presentation) or a series of sessions that focus on a particular topic or area. In higher education, colloquia are sometimes conducted to permit graduate students to report and evaluate research on a specific topic. In other colloquia, professors or visiting scholars report on research or on a specific subject. Participants normally come well prepared, having done considerable study on the material to be presented.

Colloquia predate the invention of printing, the period when the oral method of teaching was the only mode of instruction. Later, Latin textbooks, in dialogue form, were known as colloquia. Colloquia were a popular method of instruction used during the Renaissance and post-Renaissance periods. The seminar method has its origin in the colloquium. (See SEMINAR METHOD.)

References: John S. Diekhoff, *The Domain of the Faculty in our Expanding Colleges,* New York: Harper and Brothers, 1956; Asa S. Knowles (Editor), *The International Encyclopedia of Higher Education* (Volume 1), San Francisco: Jossey-Bass Publishers, 1977; Paul Monroe (Editor), *A Cyclopedia of Education,* New York: The Macmillan Company, 1911.

COLOR, hue discrimination (radiant energy) as seen by the eye. This is produced by wavelengths of light reflected by an object and transmitted to the eye. An object will absorb certain wavelengths and reflect others; this is determined by its surface. The reflected light is seen as the color of the object. Pure white reflects all light; black reflects none.

Daylight contains all the wavelengths of color (violet, blue-violet, blue, green-blue, green, yellow-green, yellow, orange-yellow, orange, red-orange, red, and red-violet). The *primary colors* are red, blue, and yellow, and the *secondary colors,* a product of two primary colors, are green, violet, and orange. Green is made up of blue and yellow, violet of blue and red, and orange of red and yellow. A mixture of three colors is called a *tertiary color.*

Each color in the spectrum of daylight absorbs certain wavelengths and has an opposite color that reflects those wavelengths. These colors are called *complementary colors.* The following colors are complementary: red/green; red-violet/yellow-green; violet/yellow; blue-violet/orange-yellow; blue/orange; red-orange/green-blue. In a *color circle* (or *color wheel*) of all the colors in daylight, the complementary colors are located opposite each other.

The study of color includes physics, physiology, and even psychology (color has many effects on humans). Color is used in all fields of endeavor and thus is not just important in art. (See COLOR PSYCHOLOGY.)

References: Faber Birren, *Color Perception in Art,* New York: Van Nostrand Reinhold Company, 1976; Dean B. Judd and Gunter Wyszecki, *Color in Business, Science and Industry,* New York: John Wiley and Sons, 1975; Harald Küppers, *Color: Origin, Systems, Uses,* London, England: Van Nostrand Reinhold Company, 1973; Margaret Walch, *The Color Source Book,* New York: Scribner's, 1979.

COLOR BLINDNESS, the inability of an individual's visual system to use information contained in the wavelengths or quanta emitted by an object or light source. *Quanta* are packets of energy found in a stream or beam of light.

Specific colors correspond to specific wavelengths of the spectrum. Individuals with normal color vision can discriminate between and among sets of wavelengths (colors); a totally color blind person can not. There are, however, differing degrees of color blindness. Color blindness can be caused either by a disease or by genetic factors.

References: Color Vision, Washington, DC: National Academy of Sciences, 1973; Tom N. Cornsweet, *Visual Perception,* New York: Academic Press, 1970; Ralph M. Evans, *The Perception of Color,* New York: John Wiley and Sons, 1974; Richard C. Teevan and Robert C. Birney, *Color Vision,* Princeton, NJ: D. Van Nostrand Company, Inc., 1961.

COLOR LIFT, or picture lift, a process for transferring pictures from a clay-coated paper to a transparency that may then be used for overhead projection. (Not all papers are clay coated.) Color photographs appearing in most magazines can be "lifted" by affixing a special acetate sheet to the picture chosen for transfer. Both, under pressure, are usually inserted into a hot press, although other transfer processes may also be used. Acetate and picture are then separated by placing them into water to which a detergent has been added. Once washed and permitted to dry, the acetate sheet is sprayed with a special, clear coating to accent the colors and to preserve the transparency.

Because the process involves direct "lifting" of the picture, enlargements of the original image cannot be made. Also, inasmuch as the process physically "lifts" the ink from paper to transparency, only expendable pictures should be used.

References: James W. Brown, et al., *AV Instruction: Technology, Media, and Methods* (Fifth Edition), New York: McGraw-Hill Book Company, 1977; John R. Bullard and Calvin E. Mether, *Audiovisual Fundamentals: Basic Equipment Operation, Simple Materials Production* (Second Edition), Dubuque, IA: Wm. C. Brown Company, Publishers, 1979; Ed Minor and Harvey R. Frye, *Techniques for Producing Visual Instructional Media* (Second Edition), New York: McGraw-Hill Book Company, 1977; Walter A. Wittich and Charles F. Schuller, *Audiovisual Materials: Their Nature and Use* (Third Edition), New York: Harper and Brothers, 1962.

COLOR PHONICS SYSTEM, a remedial reading approach that uses color coding as a means of teaching letter sounds to dyslexic readers. Teachers employing this system begin by using phonetically regular words, short sentences, and short vowels. Vowels are printed in red. Words are broken up into syllables. Clear vocalization and auditory sequences are used in blending phonemes. Spelling rules are introduced. Ultimately, black vowels are used to replace the color-coded vowels.

The program can also be used with other remedial reading programs. It should not be used with color blind or brain injured (color agnosia) children, however. (See DYSLEXIA.)

References: Color Phonics System, Cambridge, MA: Educators Publishing Service (Undated); Emerald V. Dechant, *Diagnosis and Remediation of Reading Disability* (Second Edition), Englewood Cliffs, NJ: Prentice-Hall, Inc., 1981.

COLOR PRINTS, products of a printmaking process in which two or more colors are used. Usually, a separate plate or block is used to impress each major color on the material receiving the print. Color variations are made by overprinting two or more colors in the same space. The actual design can be carved or etched on various blocks, stones, or metals; silk-screen stencils can also be used. These surfaces are inked and then printed on a material such as paper or fabric. Color prints are normally limited to four major colors, plus overprinting. Limited color printing is taught as part of many elementary and secondary art curricula. (See BLOCK PRINT; ETCHING; and SILK SCREEN.)

References: Margaret Bartran, *A Guide to Color Reproductions* (Second Edition), Metuchen, NJ: The Scarecrow Press, Inc., 1971; Jack H. Coote, *Color Prints,* New York: Focal Press, Inc., 1973; Richard D. Lane, *Images from the Floating World: The Japanese Print,* New York: G. P. Putnam and Sons, 1978.

COLOR PSYCHOLOGY, a specialized field of study devoted to the influence of color on man's activity. Color changes in the environment, some research has shown, can produce certain physiological responses. They, in turn, are capable of affecting the individual's psychological status, producing emotional changes. Some research also indicates that specific colors are frequently associated with specific moods (e.g. red with excitement, hostility, stimulation; black with melancholy behavior; blue with serenity, peacefulness). In spite of these different findings, investigators have yet to establish a consistent relationship between color and behavior.

In 1947, Max Luscher developed the Luscher Color Test: the "quick" test, which uses eight colors, and the "full" test. It has been found that well-adjusted test takers normally select the primary colors as their first choices. Auxiliary colors (violet, brown, gray, and black), when chosen, normally suggest negative attitudes toward life.

References: Robert M. Goldenson, *The Encyclopedia of Human Behavior: Psychology, Psychiatry, and Mental Health* (Volume I), Garden City, NY: Doubleday and Company, Inc., 1970; Katinka Matson, *The Psychology Today Omnibook of Personal Development,* New York: William Morrow and Company, Inc., 1977; Ian Scott (Translator and Editor), *The Luscher Color Test,* New York: Pocket Books, 1971.

COMENIUS, JAN AMOS (KOMENSKY) (1592–1670), an educational reformer who was born in southeastern Moravia (Czechoslovakia). Comenius's father was a member of the Unity of Brethren, a Protestant religious group living in Moravia, and Comenius was raised according to the rules of that group. At 12 years of age, Comenius lost his father, mother, and two sisters to the plague. At 16, he was sent to the grammar school of Prerov where he was encouraged to study. Comenius later attended the University of Heidelberg and, at the age of 24, was ordained a minister. He preached to his congregation in both Czech and German and taught many practical arts to children. As a result of the religious wars of that time, Comenius was forced to flee, living in various places in Moravia, Bohemia, Poland, England, Sweden, Hungary, and Holland.

As a result of his travels, Comenius had considerable influence on education. He felt that education, as taught in the 1600s, was obsolete and deplorable. He wrote extensively on the need for educational reform (*Great Didactic, Ipera Didactic Omnia,* and *Traditio Lampadis*). *Janua Linguarum Reserata, The Gate of Languages Unlocked,* was a Latin handbook that did not focus on grammar; rather, it gave descriptions of useful things to know. It was written originally in Czech and Latin. His *Orbis Sensualium Pictus,* or the *Visible World in Pictures,* was based on the assumption that children could learn any language if there were pictures to accompany words. These two texts made Comenius internationally known. Although Comenius was a

highly productive writer, most of his manuscripts were not published until 1966.

References: Vratislav Busek (Editor), *Comenius,* New York: Czechoslovak Society of Arts and Sciences in America, Inc., 1972; C. H. Dobinson (Editor), *Comenius and Contemporary Education,* Hamburg, Germany: UNESCO Institute for Education, 1970; Wilhelmus Road, *Comenius and the Low Countries,* Amsterdam, Holland: Van Gendt and Company, 1970; Robert F. Young, *Comenius in England,* New York: Arno Press and the New York Times, 1971.

COMMISSIONER OF EDUCATION—See CHIEF STATE SCHOOL OFFICER

COMMISSION ON ACADEMIC FREEDOM AND PRE-COLLEGE EDUCATION, a commission created in 1985 by the American Association of University Professors. The commission was established to aid schools (elementary and secondary) in combating censorship being imposed from outside. The American Association of University Professors felt that censorship at the elementary and/or secondary levels would affect higher education indirectly if not directly. The association also felt that schools could benefit from external support. The commission issued a report titled *Liberty and Learning in the Schools, Higher Education's Concerns* (1985). The report described academic freedom in the schools (K–12), the history of censorship at that level, effects on instructional materials, and the subsequent effects on higher education. The report listed 15 recommendations in the following areas: recommendations for colleges and universities, the academic disciplines, and individual faculty members. (See CENSORSHIP).

References: Lee Burres, "Censorship in School Libraries," *Yearbook of the American Library Association,* Volume 8, 1983; Commission on Academic Freedom and Pre-College Education, *Liberty and Learning in the Schools, Higher Education's Concerns,* Washington, DC: American Association of University Professors, 1986; Sissy Kegley and Gen Guerrero, *Censorship in the South. A Report of Four States, 1980–85,* Atlanta, GA: American Civil Liberties Union, 1986.

COMMITTEE OF FIFTEEN, one of three historically significant study committees appointed by the National Education Association. (The others were the Committee of Ten on Secondary School Studies and the Committee on College Entrance Requirements.) Also known as the Committee of Fifteen on Elementary Studies, this group (appointed in 1893) tendered a report in 1895 that supported the concept of the eight-year elementary school and essentially reinforced the importance of grammar, literature, arithmetic, geography, and history as excellent mind-training subjects. Grammar emerged as the most important of the elementary school subjects, or common branches. The committee also recommended that the common branches be taught as separate subjects rather than being correlated. Improved articulation between the elementary and secondary school was urged. (See COMMON BRANCHES; COMMITTEE ON COLLEGE ENTRANCE REQUIREMENTS; and COMMITTEE OF TEN.)

References: Elwood P. Cubberly, *Public Education in the United States: A Study and Interpretation of American Educational History* (Revised and Enlarged Edition), Cambridge, MA: The Riverside Press, 1962; William T. Harris, et al., *Report of the Committee of Fifteen on Elementary Education,* New York: Arno Press, 1969 (Reprint of 1895 Edition); National Education Association, "Report of the Committee of Fifteen," *Educational Review,* March 1895; Daniel Tanner and Laurel N. Tanner, *Curriculum Development: Theory Into Practice,* New York: Macmillan Publishing Company, Inc., 1975.

COMMITTEE OF TEN, one of three study committees appointed by the National Education Association to study various aspects of school programs. Between 1888 and 1891, Harvard University President Charles W. Eliot agitated for educational reform in American schools. Largely due to his agitation, the three NEA committees were formed. They were: (1) Committee of Ten, appointed in 1891 to study and report on secondary school studies; (2) Committee of Fifteen (appointed in 1893), which studied elementary education; and (3) the Committee on College Entrance Requirements, appointed in 1895.

President Eliot chaired the Committee of Ten on Secondary School Studies. The committee's report, published in 1894, identified and discussed nine subjects that served to standardize and give direction to the American secondary school curriculum. They were: (1) Latin; (2) Greek; (3) English; (4) other modern languages; (5) mathematics; (6) physics, astronomy, and chemistry; (7) natural history (biology, zoology, and physiology); (8) history, civil government, and political economy; and (9) geography. Significantly, subjects such as art and music were not included. Although the committee stressed that the secondary school should accommodate the needs of noncollege-bound as well as college-bound students, it paradoxically insisted that "every subject which is taught at all in a secondary school should be taught in the same way and to the same extent to every pupil so long as he pursues it." Also recommended was a four-track system, two superior and two relatively inferior. (See COMMITTEE ON COLLEGE ENTRANCE REQUIREMENTS and COMMITTEE OF FIFTEEN.)

References: Elwood P. Cubberly, *Public Education in the United States: A Study and Interpretation of American Educational History* (Revised and Enlarged Edition), Cambridge, MA: The Riverside Press, 1962; Carl H. Gross and Charles C. Chandler, *The History of American Education Through Readings,* Boston: D. C. Heath and Company, 1964; National Education Association, *Report of the Committee of Ten on Secondary School Studies,* New York: Arno Press, 1969 (Reprint of 1893 Edition); Daniel Tanner and Laurel N. Tanner, *Curriculum Development: Theory Into Practice,* New York: Macmillan Publishing Company, Inc., 1975.

COMMITTEE ON COLLEGE ENTRANCE REQUIREMENTS, one of three significant study committees appointed by the National Education Association. Formed in 1895 and chaired by Chicago's superintendent of high schools, this committee formulated recommendations that influenced the high school curriculum for years to come. The nature of that influence could be characterized as being academically traditional, a not surprising fact given the subject matter orientation of the committee's members.

The principal recommendation contained in the committee report, published in 1899, was the standardization of college entrance admission requirements based on units of high school work completed. This admissions approach was to replace the several college entrance examinations that were then in use. The committee proposed successful completion of four units of foreign language, two of English, two of mathematics, and one each of science and history, these in addition to approved electives. Also recommended was a move away from the 8-4 school organization plan to the 6-6 plan. (See COMMITTEE OF FIFTEEN; COMMITTEE OF TEN; and ORGANIZATIONAL PLANS.)

References: Elwood P. Cubberly, *Public Education in the United States: A Study and Interpretation of American Educational History* (Revised and Enlarged Edition), Cambridge, MA: The Riverside Press, 1962; Daniel Tanner and Laurel N. Tanner, *Curriculum Development: Theory Into Practice,* New York: Macmillan Publishing Company, Inc., 1975; Robert S. Zais, *Curriculum: Principles and Foundations,* New York: Harper and Row, Publishers, 1976.

COMMITTEE ON ECONOMY OF TIME—See SOCIAL UTILITY

COMMON BRANCHES, or common branch subjects, a term used years ago to describe the major components of the elementary (common) school curriculum. In 1936, Section 116 of the New York State *Regulations of the Commissioner of Education* defined *common branch subjects* to mean any or all of the subjects usually included in the daily program of an elementary school classroom such as arithmetic, civics, drawing, elementary science, English language, geography, history, hygiene, physical activities, practical arts, singing, writing, and other similar subjects. The term is seldom, if ever, used in the curriculum sense today.

New York State, until September 1, 1966, referred to its elementary school teaching credential as a common branches certificate.

Reference: Section 116, *Regulations of the Commissioner of Education*, Albany, NY: The State Education Department (Adopted 1936).

COMMON SCHOOL DISTRICT, a basic administrative unit (school district) that possesses any or all of the following characteristics: (1) the unit (district) is small; (2) the unit is located in a rural area; (3) the unit's boundaries are not coterminous with those of any other governmental unit; and (4) the unit operates an elementary school program only (although some common schools do serve all students, K–12). Some common school districts are nonoperating districts.

The term *common school district* is sometimes used generically and as a synonym for *common school.* This practice notwithstanding, the two terms each have specific meanings. (See COMMON SCHOOLS; LATIN GRAMMAR SCHOOL; and NONOPERATING DISTRICTS.)

References: Commission on School District Reorganization, *School District Organization*, Washington, DC: American Association of School Administrators, 1958; Robert W. Richey, *Planning for Teaching: An Introduction to Education*, New York: McGraw-Hill Book Company, 1968.

COMMON SCHOOLS, forerunners of the modern public schools, established in the 1830s in the United States. These schools were tax supported. They provided a free, basic, common, foundational education program for all children, grades 1–8. Horace Mann, Superintendent of Schools for Massachusetts (1837–48), was a prime mover for the establishment of common schools. It

was the increasing urbanization and industrialization of the United States by the 1830s that facilitated the development of the common school movement as well as what is sometimes called the common school revival (reform of education along state lines, a common curriculum, and the extension of education through free public schools).

The idea of a common public education did not originate with Horace Mann. In 1789, an article appeared in *The Massachusetts Magazine* titled "Essay on the Importance of Studying the English Language Grammatically." It argued for an expanded common school curriculum (beyond the Latin School) and public grammar schools. (See MANN, HORACE.)

References: Frederick M. Binder, *The Age of the Common School, 1830–1865*, New York: John Wiley and Sons, 1974; B. A. Hinsdale, *Horace Mann and the Common School Revival in the United States*, New York: Scribner's, 1898; Bruce R. Joyce and Greta G. Morine, *Creating the School*, Boston: Little, Brown and Company, 1976; Horace Mann, *Lectures on Education*, New York: Arno Press and the New York Times, 1969.

COMMUNICATION, a word derived from the Latin, *communico*, which means "to share." The literature of communication is replete with definitions of this social process, many taking the form of communication models. One study of mass media describes the process this way:

> Who
> Says What
> In Which Channel
> To Whom
> With What Effect?

Other models include these elements: (1) the communication *source* (transmitter); (2) the *encoder* (the form in which a message is transmitted); (3) the *message;* (4) the *channel;* and (5) the *receiver.*

In organizations, communication is an element of administrative process. Hierarchically speaking, it is multidirectional: upward, downward, and horizontal. Formal communication systems exist in organizations as do informal systems, the latter based on members' personal and social relationships. (See COMMUNICATION CHANNEL; COMMUNICATION THEORY; NONVERBAL COMMUNICATIONS; and VERBAL COMMUNICATION.)

References: Russell T. Gregg, "The Administrative Process" in Roald F. Campbell and Russell T. Gregg (Editors), *Administrative Behavior in Education*, New York: Harper and Brothers, 1957; Richard C. Huseman, et al.,

Interpersonal Communication in Organizations: A Perceptual Approach, Boston: Holbrook Press, Inc., 1976.

COMMUNICATION CHANNEL,

COMMUNICATION CHANNEL, the means by which messages are communicated. Television, motion pictures, newspapers, and books are all technological channels, these employed by transmitters of information desirous of reaching large (mass) audiences.

In human communication, Michael Nolan pointed out, there are four channel categories that, like the technological channels, facilitate message transmission (verbal as well as nonverbal). They are: (1) *voice,* which includes not only the transmission of verbal information but also "paralanguage" characteristics such as pitch, laughing, and rate; (2) *body,* or body language, in which emotions are indicated through use of different body parts, especially the face; (3) *objects,* such as uniforms, insignia, and cosmetics, which serve to communicate information; and (4) *environment* (e.g. the physical environment we create for ourselves and the manner in which we make use of time). (See COMMUNICATION; NONVERBAL COMMUNICATIONS; and VERBAL COMMUNICATION.)

References: William E. Francois, *Introduction to Mass Communications and Mass Media,* Columbus, OH: Grid, Inc., 1977; Michael J. Nolan, "The Relationship Between Verbal and Nonverbal Communication" in Gerhard J. Hanneman and William J. McEwen (Editors), *Communication and Behavior,* Reading, MA: Addison-Wesley Publishing Company, 1975.

COMMUNICATION THEORY, or information theory, concerned with the quantitative measure of information and how it is transmitted. It deals with: (1) the *amount of information* contained in a message, no matter what the source; (2) the *rate* at which the message is transmitted over or through a means of communication; and (3) the *understanding* of the message. Communication theory involves not only psychology but the various forms of transmission as well (e.g. human, electronic, mechanical, simulation, games, symbolic logic, systems development and engineering, feedback systems, signals, random noise, prediction). Communication theory is a highly technical, scientific, and mathematical field of study.

References: A. V. Balakrishnan, et al., *Communication Theory,* New York: McGraw-Hill Book Company, 1968; Charles D. Flagle, et al., *Operations Research and Systems Engineering,* Baltimore, MD: The John Hopkins Press, 1960; Judith Nelson, *Communication Theory and Social Work Practice,* Chicago: University of Chicago Press, 1980.

COMMUNITY ACTION PROGRAM, organized effort designed to encourage urban and rural communities to use their resources for the purpose of combating poverty. Title II of the 1964 Economic Opportunity Act, one of several War on Poverty efforts, authorized federal support of community action programs. In this act, a *community action program* was defined as one "(1) which mobilizes and utilizes resources, public or private, of any urban or rural, or combined urban and rural, geographical area (referred to in this part as a 'community'), including but not limited to a State, metropolitan area, county, city, town, multicity unit, or multicounty unit in an attack on poverty; (2) which provides services, assistance, and other activities of sufficient scope and size to give promise of progress toward elimination of poverty or . . . causes of poverty; (3) which is developed, conducted, and administered with the maximum feasible participation of residents of the areas and members of the groups served; and (4) which is conducted, administered, or coordinated by a public or private nonprofit agency (other than a political party), or a combination thereof" (p. 516). (See ECONOMIC OPPORTUNITY ACT and OFFICE OF ECONOMIC OPPORTUNITY.)

Reference: Public Law 88-452, *United States Statutes at Large, 1964* (Volume 78), Washington, DC: U.S. Government Printing Office, 1965.

COMMUNITY COLLEGE, a two-year postsecondary institution of higher education that is publicly supported and usually serves a particular community or region. The first public junior colleges were established in the early 1900s. Many began as extensions (grades 13 and 14) of existing high schools and later began to operate as separate institutions with their own governing boards. There are three basic types of two-year institutions: (1) the *community college,* which offers a comprehensive curriculum; (2) the private *junior college;* and (3) *technical colleges* (e.g. colleges of aeronautics, agriculture).

The comprehensive community college offers a broad spectrum of curricula. They comprise: (1) *transfer programs,* which include basic courses for students planning to complete a baccalaureate degree at a four-year institution; (2) *occupational programs;* (3) *adult and continuing education programs,* primarily for part-time students who may not be interested in a degree; and (4) *remedial programs.* Some programs lead to certificates or the associate degree; others do not. Courses are taught by regular full-time faculty and, in some cases, a large adjunct faculty as well.

Community colleges grew rapidly in the United States following World War II. In the 1960s, one new community college opened each week. Between 1968 and 1978, 250 new ones were created, with many attracting a growing number of women, older students, and minority students. In 1978–79, there were 928 publicly controlled two-year institutions operating in the United States with a combined enrollment approaching 4,000,000 students. (See ASSOCIATE'S DEGREES and JUNIOR COLLEGE.)

References: Arthur M. Cohen and John Lombardi, "Can the Community Colleges Survive Success?" *Change,* November–December 1979; Maurice R. Duperre, "Short-Cycle Education" in Asa S. Knowles (Editor), *The International Encyclopedia of Higher Education* (Volume 8), San Francisco: Jossey-Bass Publishers, 1977; Howard B. London, *The Culture of A Community College,* New York: Praeger Publishers, 1978; Charles R. Monroe, *Profile of the Community College.* San Francisco: Jossey-Bass Publishers, 1972; Andrew J. Pepin, *Fall Enrollment in Higher Education, 1977: Final Report,* Washington, DC: National Center for Education Statistics, U.S. Department of HEW, 1979; Arthur Podolsky and Carolyn R. Smith, *Education Directory, Colleges and Universities: 1977–78,* Washington, DC: National Center for Education Statistics, U.S. Department of HEW, 1979.

COMMUNITY EDUCATION, a manifestation of the lifelong education concept, a process that brings together the physical and human resources of a community to make diverse educational opportunities available to community residents. Typical programs are administered by a community education director. Working closely with a community education council, this school official oversees activities most often available during non-school periods. Programs are usually carried out in local school buildings.

Interest in the community school movement was sparked by a Mott Foundation grant made to the Flint, Michigan, schools. The Flint project led to the creation of regional university centers where training of community school leaders and dissemination activities take place.

In recent years, some states and the federal government have made financial aid available to school districts sponsoring community school programs. (See COMMUNITY SCHOOLS AND COMPREHENSIVE EDUCATION ACT OF 1978; LIFELONG EDUCATION; and MOTT FOUNDATION.)

References: James D. Logsdon and V. M. Kerensky (Guest Editors), *NASSP Bulletin,* November 1975; Maurice F. Seay and Associates, *Community Education: A Developing Concept,* Midland, MI: Pendell Publishing Company, 1974.

COMMUNITY SCHOOLS AND COMPREHENSIVE EDUCATION ACT OF 1978, actually Title VIII of the Education Amendments of 1978, enacted by Congress to: "provide . . . educational, recreational, cultural and other related community and health services, in accordance with the needs, interests, and concerns of the community through the expansion of community education programs" (pp. 2284–85). The act also seeks to stimulate research and development in community education.

Funds authorized by the act are allotted to the states as well as local educational agencies. The act requires each state to prepare a state plan, one that: (1) sets aside at least 80 percent of the amounts received for distribution among local educational agencies, and (2) is designed to serve all age groups within the community. Funds are also provided: (1) to help institutions of higher education that offer community education training programs; and (2) for the National Institute of Education to carry out community education research. (See COMMUNITY EDUCATION.)

Reference: Public Law 95-561, *United States Code: Congressional and Administrative News, 95th Congress, Second Session* (Volume 2), St. Paul, MN: West Publishing Company, 1978.

COMMUTATIVE PROPERTY, a mathematical property of natural numbers that allows the numbers to be exchanged (commuted) without affecting the sum or product. Commutative property can be used in addition and multiplication. Learning about the commutative property aids children with the conceptualization of mathematical processes. Some examples showing the commutative property follow:

In addition

2 + 4 can be commuted to 4 + 2

$$\begin{array}{ccc} 2 & 4 & 10 \\ + \text{ can be commuted to } + & \text{ can be commuted to } + \\ 4 & 10 & 2 \\ + & + & + \\ 10 & 2 & 4 \\ \hline \end{array}$$

In multiplication

4 × 6 can be commuted to 6 × 4

$$\begin{array}{cc} 4 & \text{ can be commuted to } 6 \\ \times 6 & \times 4 \end{array}$$

(See ASSOCIATIVE PROPERTY AND DISTRIBUTIVE PROPERTY.)

References: Edward G. Begle, *The Mathematics of the Elementary School,* New York: McGraw-Hill Book Company, 1975; Albert B. Bennett, Jr. and Leonard T. Nelson, *Mathematics: An Informal Approach,* Boston: Allyn and Bacon, Inc., 1979; William L. Schaaf, *Basic Concepts of Elementary Mathematics* (Third Edition), New York: John Wiley and Sons, 1969; W. Henry Spragens, *Mathematics for Elementary Teachers,* Boston: Allyn and Bacon, Inc., 1972.

COMMUTER STUDENT—See RESIDENTIAL STUDENT

COMPARATIVE EDUCATION, a component of educational foundations in which similarities and differences among the world's educational systems are studied. Before 1945, comparative education was generally limited to the collection of descriptions and data concerning school systems in different countries. More recently, spurred by the United Nations and similar international bodies, the field has become concerned with analysis of such data in the context of a country's (or region's) social, economic, and political development. The goals of comparative education include: (1) increasing understanding of education in a particular country or region; (2) providing information for use by educational practitioners and planners; and (3) improving international understanding.

References: George Z. F. Bereday, *Comparative Method in Education,* New York: Holt, Rinehart and Winston, Inc., 1966; Max A. Eckstein and Harold J. Noah, *Scientific Investigations in Comparative Education,* New York: The Macmillan Company, 1969; Torsten Husen, *The Learning Society,* London, England: Methuen and Company, Ltd., 1974.

COMPARATIVE PSYCHOLOGY, a branch of psychology devoted to studying and comparing behaviors of different animal species, races of man, or different developmental stages of man (the latter sometimes called developmental psychology). It is principally concerned with nonhuman subjects whose behavior and problems are then compared with human conduct. Comparative psychologists study topics such as the use of drugs and their effects upon behavior; nutrition; genetics; and memory. Although the interests of animal psychology and comparative psychology frequently overlap, the two fields are separate and discrete.

References: Donald A. Dewsbury, *Comparative Animal Behavior,* New York: McGraw-Hill Book Company, 1978; Robert A. Hinde, *Animal Behavior: A Synthesis of Ethology and Comparative Psychology* (Second Edition), New York: McGraw-Hill Book Company, 1970; H. C. Holland, "Comparative Psychology" in H. J. Eysenck, et al. (Editors), *Encyclopedia of Psychology,* New York: The Seabury Press, 1979.

COMPENSATION, MATHEMATICAL, a procedure used in addition where a number is subtracted from a number and then added to another number to make addition easier. For example, 24 + 18 + 6 + 17 could be altered through compensation as follows: 4 could be taken away from 24 and added to 18, thus [24 − 4] = 20 + (18 + 4) = 20 + 22 = 42; and 3 could be taken away from 6 and added to 17, thus [6 − 3] = 3 + (17 + 3) = 3 + 20 = 23; then 42 + 23 could be added together to give a final sum of 65.

References: Wilbur H. Dutton, et al., *Arithmetic for Teachers* (Second Edition), Englewood Cliffs, NJ: Prentice-Hall, Inc., 1970; Rosalie Jensen, *Exploring Mathematical Concepts and Skills in the Elementary School,* Columbus, OH: Charles E. Merrill Publishing Company, 1973; Helene Sherman, *Common Elements in New Mathematics Programs,* New York: Teachers College Press, 1972.

COMPENSATION, PSYCHOLOGICAL, the development of an alternative goal, motive, or skill to make up for a weakness or limitation. For example, an individual who is physically small and weak may excel academically as compensation for not being able to excel in athletics.

A special case of compensation is "overcompensation." Here an individual strives to excel in the same area as his/her weakness. A physically weak child may "overcompensate" by spending long hours developing him/herself physically. There are times when the compensatory activity becomes a highly desirable goal; however, there is also the danger the activity will remain secondary and consciously cause psychological problems.

In instances of physiological injuries, compensation is related to the recovery of an injured or lost function. Often this is achieved through the use of what is left of the organ, or other organs take over the task. Research on the brain and the central nervous system has indicated that such changes are related to physiological compensation.

References: Ezras A. Asratian, *Compensatory Adaptations Reflex Activity and the Brain,* Oxford, England: Pergamon Press, 1965; James Geiwitz, *Looking at Ourselves,* Boston: Little, Brown and Company, 1976; Kenneth U. Gutsch and Larry L. Thornton, *Insights into Human Development: Commentaries,* Jackson, MS: University Press of Mississippi, 1978; Kurt Schlesinger and Philip M. Groves, *Psy-*

chology: A Dynamic Science, Dubuque, IA: Wm. C. Brown Company, Publishers, 1976.

COMPENSATORY EDUCATION, educational programs designed to help children compensate for the negative effects that social and economic deterrents have had on their academic and social growth. These programs were prompted by the fact that a great majority of children from low-income and poverty areas (rural as well as urban) were achieving poorly in school. The federal government, in the 1960s, instituted many compensatory education programs designed to reduce the handicaps that many children had who came from such environments. The programs tended to focus on basic skill development; however, many included other foci as well, including enrichment and attitude change activities.

Under the direction of the Office of Economic Opportunity (OEO), Head Start Programs for preschool children were started (1965). (Head Start became a part of the Department of Health, Education, and Welfare in 1969.) Job Corps, Upward Bound, and the Neighborhood Youth Corps were other of OEO's programs, these designed for older youth. Title I of the Elementary and Secondary Education Act of 1965 provided funds for compensatory education in the schools. Follow Through Projects were designed for low income children in the primary grades. Compensatory education funds have been spent for special programs, texts, equipment, and to provide sundry educational opportunities. By 1979, over 6,000,000 low income children had received a variety of services through such compensatory education programs.

Research results seeking to ascertain the effectiveness of compensatory programs show mixed results. Part of the problem has been the changing and shifting goals of such programs.

References: Robert J. Havighurst and Daniel V. Levine, *Education in Metropolitan Areas* (Second Edition), Boston: Allyn and Bacon, Inc., 1971; Robert J. Havighurst and Daniel V. Levine, *Society and Education* (Fifth Edition), Boston: Allyn and Bacon, Inc., 1979; Johanna K. Lemlech, *Handbook for Successful Urban Teaching*, New York: Harper and Row, Publishers, 1977.

COMPETENCY-BASED EDUCATION (CBE), an approach to instruction that assumes each learner will reach specific minimum levels of achievement or competency. Minimum basic competencies are of three types: (1) those that should be reached grade by grade, or course by course; (2) those one

must reach before graduating from high school; and (3) a combination of 1 and 2.

To determine whether an individual reaches the required level of achievement or competency in a given area, a standard competency test is administered. These tests are generally administered school systemwide, either by grade or at a certain point before graduation. Minimum competency testing frequently focuses on "survival skills" in selected areas such as reading, language arts, mathematics, and citizenship.

Although the competency-based education movement of the 1970s focused generally on minimum "survival skill" standards and are a consequence of the school system accountability movement, competency testing is not new in American education. Such competency tests existed in the Boston Public Schools (1840s), in New York (Regents Examination, 1900s), and in Philadelphia (Central High School's rhetoric tests, 1940s). (See COMPETENCY-BASED TEACHER EDUCATION and SURVIVAL SKILLS TESTS.)

References: Leo H. Bradley, *Complete Guide to Competency-Based Education*, Englewood Cliffs, NJ: Prentice-Hall, 1987; Walt Haney and George Madaus, "Making Sense of the Competency Testing Movement," *Harvard Educational Review*, November 1978; Dale Parnell, *The Case for Competency Based Education* (PDK Fastback 118), Bloomington, IN: The Phi Delta Kappa Educational Foundation, 1978.

COMPETENCY-BASED TEACHER EDUCATION (CBTE), also known as performance-based teacher education (PBTE), a sometimes controversial system designed to train teachers and to test them on the basis of ability (competency) to exhibit specific, predetermined, and desirable teaching behaviors. Where traditional teacher education programs require trainees to complete a specified program of studies, CBTE's accountability element emphasizes demonstrated performance. The goals that CBTE trainees must meet are generally stated in behavioral terms. This approach to teacher education is strongly supported by those demanding increased accountability in the field of teacher education.

References: W. Robert Houston and Robert B. Howsam (Editors), *Competency-Based Teacher Education: Progress, Problems, and Prospects,* Chicago: Science Research Associates, Inc., 1972; W. Robert Houston (Editor), *Competency Assessment, Research, and Evaluation: A Report of a National Conference,* Syracuse, NY: National Dissemination Center for Performance-Based Education, 1974.

COMPETITIVE BIDS, formal and sealed offers, tendered by suppliers, to provide specified goods or services to prospective purchasers. In school districts, the purchaser is usually the board of education. Such bids are submitted by vendors in accordance with specifications prepared by the school staff. Bids may be submitted for one or a group of items/services. Certified checks or bonds (usually 5–10 percent of the bid) are normally expected to accompany the bid to demonstrate the supplier's good faith.

Bids received by a board of education are opened publicly at a previously announced time. The successful supplier need not be the lowest bidder; however, he/she is expected to be the lowest responsible bidder. Samples submitted with each bid normally become the property of the school board. All good faith checks/bonds, however, except those of the successful bidder, are returned.

State laws require competitive bidding for contracts exceeding a specified sum of money. These laws serve at least three purposes: (1) securing a fair price for the taxpayer; (2) preventing collusion between buyer and seller; and (3) ensuring quality work or service. (See BIDDING CYCLE.)
References: John Greenhalgh, *Practitioner's Guide to School Business Management,* Boston: Allyn and Bacon, Inc., 1978; Stephen J. Knezevich and John G. Fowlkes, *Business Management of Local School Systems,* New York: Harper and Brothers, 1960; E. Edmund Reutter, Jr. and Robert R. Hamilton, *The Law of Public Education* (Second Edition), Mineola, NY: The Foundation Press, Inc., 1976.

COMPLETION TEST, an examination that requires the student to provide a missing word or phrase on the basis of a question, an incomplete sentence, or a word association stimulus. Although the respondent must furnish the correct answer, the completion test is often classified as an objective test. Sometimes referred to as a "fill-in-the-blank" type of test, the instrument relies heavily on student recall.

Both advantages and weaknesses can be associated with this particular type of test. Some of the major advantages include: (1) relative ease of construction (although care must be taken to delimit the question so that it leads to one answer); (2) the probability of respondent guessing is reduced; and (3) it encourages more intensive study by the student than would other types of objective tests. Weaknesses include: (1) the test does not lend itself to machine scoring; (2) higher order mental pro-

cesses cannot be tested readily; and (3) examinations that result in testing of unrelated facts.
References: Tom Kubiszyn and Gary Borich, *Educational Testing and Measurement: Classroom Application and Practice* (Second Edition), Glenview, IL: Scott Foresman and Company, 1987; Jon C. Marshall and Loyde W. Hales, *Classroom Test Construction,* Reading, MA: Addison-Wesley Publishing Company, 1971; Fred M. Smith and Sam Adams, *Educational Measurement for the Classroom Teacher* (Second Edition), New York: Harper and Row, Publishers, 1972.

COMPLEX ORGANIZATION, a social unit, structured along bureaucratic lines, that exists to implement specific goals. The complex organization is at the same time a formal and an informal structure. Its *formal* characteristics include elements such as individuals performing prescribed roles, a system of superior-subordinate relationships, and coordination to ensure that all members of the organization are working to carry out specific goals. The *informal* groupings, although not evident officially, consist of primary-group affiliations that help to meet the social and psychological needs of the organization's members.

The school is a complex organization, one whose operation is made particularly difficult given the fact that it has a human product and serves numbers of client groups (i.e. parents, teachers, legislators, taxpayers). (See INFORMAL ORGANIZATION and ORGANIZATION.)
References: Amitai Etzioni (Editor), *Complex Organizations: A Sociological Reader,* New York: Holt, Rinehart and Winston, Inc., 1964; Lawrence Hrebiniak, *Complex Organizations,* St. Paul, MN: West Publishing Company, 1978; Robert G. Owens, *Organizational Behavior in Schools,* Englewood Cliffs, NJ: Prentice-Hall, Inc., 1970.

COMPOSITION, in language study, a form of written communication that is taught at virtually all levels of education. Ideas are chosen and presented by the writer in a form deemed to be correct. Authorities suggest that the classroom teacher can contribute to the development of students' composition ability by creating a climate in which creative ideas are encouraged, respected, and responded to. When evaluating written composition, some argue, correctness of expression (skills) should be subordinated to the quality or value of the idea (content) being presented. Rich personal experiences are recognized as being a significant factor motivating the writing of compositions.

Composition is taught and learned in stages. Young children, able to speak readily but possessing little or no writing skill, are encouraged to dictate their ideas to the teacher who writes them down. This material is then copied by the child(ren). The mechanics of writing (e.g. paragraph structure, opening and closing sentences) are taught formally to older children.

Mildred Donoghue listed numerous factors that affect children's writing performance, these reflecting the literature and research related to written composition. They include, but are not limited to: (1) intellectual capacity; (2) reading achievement; (3) grade level and/or chronological age; (4) sex; and (5) oral language proficiency.
References: Mildred R. Donoghue, *The Child and the English Language Arts* (Third Edition), Dubuque, IA: Wm. C. Brown Company, Publishers, 1979; Donna M. Johnson and Duane H. Roen, *Richness in Writing: Empowering ESL Students*, New York: Longman, Inc., 1989; Harry Singer and Dan Donlan, *Reading and Learning from Text* (Second Edition), Hillsdale, NJ: Lawrence Erlbaum Associates, Publishers, 1989.

COMPREHENSION, understanding the meaning of a message whether the message is written, spoken, visual, abstract, or nonverbal. Comprehension is an intellectual ability that is more complex than just knowledge or memory acquisition. It exists at differing levels; different orders of processing knowledge and intellectual materials are involved.

Comprehension is difficult to measure. Normally, this is done by presenting the individual with a situation in which judgment of consequent behavior is made. Answering questions, following directions, paraphrasing, measuring specific reactions, assessing social situations, understanding sentences, and testing of memory are but a few methods used to measure comprehension. (See PERCEPTIONS.)
References: Richard C. Anderson, et al. (Editors), *Schooling and the Acquisition of Knowledge*, Hillsdale, NJ: Lawrence Erlbaum Associates, Publishers, 1977; Joel R. Davitz and Samuel Ball, *Psychology of the Educational Process*, New York: McGraw-Hill Book Company, 1970; John R. Wilson, et al., *Psychological Foundations of Learning and Teaching* (Second Edition), New York: McGraw-Hill Book Company, 1974.

COMPREHENSION, READING—See READING COMPREHENSION

COMPREHENSIVE EMPLOYMENT AND TRAINING ACT (CETA), federal legislation enacted in 1973 that authorized creation of community-level programs to make training and job opportunities available to the unemployed, the disadvantaged, and the underemployed. Block grants are awarded to states, counties, and combinations of local units to operate programs that are based on local needs. CETA is administered by the Office of Comprehensive Employment Development Programs, U.S. Department of Labor. (See SUMMER YOUTH EMPLOYMENT PROGRAM.)
References: Office of Federal Register, National Archives and Records Service, General Services Administration, *United States Government Manual, 1978/79,* Washington, DC: U.S. Government Printing Office, 1978; Public Law 93-203, *United States Statutes at Large, 1973* (Volume 87), Washington, DC: U.S. Government Printing Office, 1974.

COMPREHENSIVE EXAMINATIONS, written and/or oral examinations, usually taken by graduate students to assess breadth of understanding in a field of knowledge (major/minor). These examinations are normally administered near the end of a student's program but are not considered final examinations. Successful completion of such examinations usually takes place before a graduate student's writing of a master's thesis or doctoral dissertation. Universities have different requirements and types of comprehensive examinations. Some refer to such examinations as "preliminary examinations" and use them as a condition for admission to candidacy.
References: *Iowa State University Bulletin, Graduate College Catalog, 1977/79; Asa S. Knowles (Editor), The International Encyclopedia of Higher Education* (Volume 1), San Francisco: Jossey-Bass Publishers, 1977; *The University of Iowa Bulletin, General Catalog, 76/78; University of Nebraska, Lincoln, 1979-81 Graduate Studies,* 1979.

COMPREHENSIVE HIGH SCHOOL, unitary secondary school that enrolls all youth in a given district or area and offers them a comprehensive curriculum that includes vocational, general, and precollege programs. This organizational template, for years almost uniquely American, contrasts markedly with the specialized high school models found in most other countries of the world.

The comprehensive high school emerged in the early part of the 20th century. Since then numerous individuals and commissions have proffered recommendations designed to make it a more viable educational institution. Among them were: (1) the Commission on the Reorganization of Secondary Education (1918), which drafted the Seven Cardinal Principles of Secondary Education; (2) James

B. Conant, author of *The American High School Today* (1959); (3) the National Commission on the Reform of Secondary Education (1973), a study team sponsored by the Kettering Foundation; and (4) B. Frank Brown, author-educator. (See CARDINAL PRINCIPLES OF SECONDARY EDUCATION; CONANT REPORT; and NATIONAL COMMISSION ON THE REFORM OF SECONDARY EDUCATION.)

References: B. Frank Brown, *New Directions for the Comprehensive High School,* West Nyack, NY: Parker Publishing Company, Inc., 1972; James B. Conant, *The American High School Today: A First Report to Interested Citizens,* New York: McGraw-Hill Book Company, 1959; James B. Conant, *The Comprehensive High School: A Second Report to Interested Citizens,* New York: McGraw-Hill Book Company, 1967; Daniel Tanner, "Splitting Up the School System: Are Comprehensive High Schools Doomed?" *Phi Delta Kappan,* October 1979.

COMPULSORY EDUCATION, a series of state laws that require parents to send children to school and require the establishment of educational facilities (including teachers to provide the education for the children). Initially, compulsory education laws, as passed in the Massachusetts Bay Colony between 1642 and 1701, established minimal standards for the education of children, and the establishment of schools. In 1852, the State of Massachusetts passed the first compulsory education law that required parents to send their children to public school for a minimum of 12 weeks. By 1918, all states had passed compulsory attendance laws, although they were not enforced until 1930. In the 1920s, court decisions invalidated the requirement that children must attend only public schools. In most states, compulsory education requires children between the ages of 8 and 13–16 to attend school. (See *OREGON* CASE.)

References: Michael S. Katz, *A History of Compulsory Education Laws* (PDK Fastback 75), Bloomington, IN: The Phi Delta Kappa Educational Foundation, 1976; James E. McClellan (Editor), *Toward an Effective Critique of American Education,* Philadelphia: J. B. Lippincott Company, 1968; Perry A. Zirkel (Editor), *A Digest of Supreme Court Decisions Affecting Education,* Bloomington, IN: Phi Delta Kappa, 1978.

COMPUTER-ASSISTED INSTRUCTION (CAI), the presentation of instructional material through the use of electronic computers. Programs for a particular subject area are placed in a computer. A student will sit at a display terminal of some type (e.g. graphic, typewriter, printer) and respond to specific program elements or frames. Generally, the student will respond overtly to the stimuli displayed. Depending on the nature of the program, the student's response will be acknowledged either by moving him/her forward in the program, having the student react again to the stimuli, or presentation of alternate materials.

Computer-assisted and *intelligent computer-assisted* instruction are based on the reaction of the students to elements in a particular program, while *computer-based* instruction primarily manipulates the direction of the instruction. Computer-based instruction has more of a direct guidance function, one that might include CAI as an operational mode of instruction. When extended to a higher level of computer use, such learning is often referred to as Computer-Managed Learning (CML), which occurs when the computer also produces statistical reports on student performance or system utilization. Computer-assisted instruction has its origin in programmed instruction. (See *INTELLIGENT COMPUTER-ASSISTED INSTRUCTION* and *PROGRAMMED INSTRUCTION.*)

References: Christopher Dean and Quentin Whitlock, *A Handbook of Computer-Based Training,* New York: Nichols Publishing, 1988; Neil Graham, *The Mind Tool, Computers and Their Impact on Society* (Fourth Edition), St. Paul, MN: West Publishing Co., 1986; Robert E. Hoye and Anastasia C. Wang, *Index to Computer Based Learning,* Englewood Cliffs, NJ: Educational Technology Publications, 1973; Roger Williams and Colin Maclean, *Computing in Schools,* Edinburgh, England: Holmes McDougall Ltd., 1985.

COMPUTER GAMES, a form of software for microcomputers. There are three basic types of games. The first type is known as the video-game. This is the "shoot-em" type found in game rooms. Video games have excellent graphics and very fast action. Early examples of video games are *Space Invaders, Pac Man,* and *Donkey Kong.* Adventure games form the second category. These are long-playing word games that do not always have graphics. The players must make careful decisions; some are very complex. The third type of computer game is the educational game. Some use simulation while others foster creativity. They represent an enjoyable means of learning.

References: Grace Murray Hopper and Steven L. Mandell, *Understanding Computers,* St. Paul, MN: West Publishing Company, 1984; Alan M. Lesgold, "A Rationale for Computer-Based Reading Instruction" in Alex Cherry Wilkinson (Editor), *Classroom Computers and Cognitive Science,* New York: Academic Press, 1983; David R. Sullivan, et al., *Computing Today: Microcomputer Con-*

cepts and Applications, Boston: Houghton Mifflin Company, 1985.

COMPUTER LANGUAGE,

a specific set of notations used to encode computer programs. Computer languages have certain strengths: (1) they may be compiled separately; (2) they provide internal subroutines, types of argument—transmission; (3) they support information modules (e.g. how global data are dealt with); and so on. Computer languages, computer programs, assembly language, and machine language are all part of the "software" of the computer, and the printer, electronic structure, and so on are considered part of the "hardware."

The names of the most common computer languages are: FORTRAN IV (scientific), COBOL (business), APL (mathematics), BASIC (engineering), RPG II (small report writing), PL/I (multipurpose), and ALGOL (scientific). There is an entire field of science and study developing around the computer, computer languages and programs, computer logic, and software (sometimes called information science). (See *ADA; BASIC; COMPUTER PROGRAM; HARDWARE, COMPUTER; INFORMATION SCIENCE; LISP; LOGO; PASCAL;* and *SOFTWARE, COMPUTER.*)

References: Maurice H. Halstead, *Elements of Software Science*, New York: Elsevier North-Holland Publishing, 1977; Glenford J. Myers, *Composite/Structured Design*, New York: Van Nostrand Reinhold Company, 1978.

COMPUTER LITERACY,

a term of the computer age, the goal of which is in dispute. Some experts define computer literacy as knowing a programming language and being able to program; others state that literacy only requires an individual to be able to use and respond to packaged software. E. M. Poler (1982) suggested looking at computer literacy in a more flexible manner. An individual would be computer literate when she/he can interact with the computer as necessary in specific disciplines. In teaching computer literacy, emphasis should be on the utilization of the computer as a tool; understanding its structure as a machine is unnecessary.

References: James Lockard, et al., *Microcomputers for Educators*, Boston, MA: Little, Brown and Company, 1987; E. M. Poler, "Computer Literacy: Different Strokes for Different Folks," *New York Times*, Summer Survey of Education, August 21, 1982; Alex Cherry Wilkinson and Janice Patterson, "Issues at the Interface of Theory and Practice" in Alex Cherry Wilkinson (Editor), *Classroom Computers and Cognitive Science*, New York: Academic Press, 1983.

COMPUTER PROGRAM,

a series of notations (letters, numbers, or symbols) that has structure, function(s), logic, context, and notations used to control the operation of an electronic computer. There are many types of computer programs; each has standard symbols, rules, and formats. Computer programs enable computer programmers (those who write programs as a profession), businessmen, and others to take advantage of the speed, logic, and accuracy of the modern computer.

Businessmen and school administrators employ computer programs for purposes such as accounting, inventories, and school schedules. Researchers may write computer programs to enable them to do complex data analyses. Programs are the means, through symbols, by which an individual can direct the computer to perform certain functions, and the means by which an individual can put information in or retrieve data from the memory of a computer. (See COMPUTER LANGUAGE.)

References: Glenford J. Myers, *Composite/Structured Design*, New York: Van Nostrand Reinhold Company, 1978; Lawrence J. Prince and David F. Nyman, *Introduction to Computers and Computer Programming*, Englewood Cliffs, NJ: Prentice-Hall, Inc., 1972.

CONANT, JAMES B.

(March 26, 1893–February 11, 1978), distinguished eductor, chemist, and diplomat. Conant spent virtually all of his academic years at Harvard University (1919–53). From 1933 to 1953, he was that institution's President. He later served as United States High Commissioner to West Germany (1953–55) and Ambassador to West Germany (1955–57).

Although a teacher of chemistry, Conant became well known to school people and the country's laity for his studies of American public education. Three of these widely read reports were *The American High School Today* (1959), *The Education of American Teachers* (1963), and *The Comprehensive High School* (1967). Included among the other books he authored were *Understanding Science* (1947), *Education in a Divided World* (1948), *Slums and Suburbs* (1961), and *Shaping Educational Policy* (1964). He also coauthored a high school chemistry text (with N. H. Black, 1920) and edited *Harvard Case Histories in Experimental Science* (1957).

Conant earned two degrees at Harvard University (A.B. in 1913 and Ph.D. in 1916). He served in the U.S. Army during World War I. From 1941 to 1946, he was a member of the Educational Policies

Commission. Other of his service activities included chairmanship of the National Science Foundation (1951) and membership on the Carnegie Foundation for the Advancement of Teaching. (See CONANT REPORT.)

References: Norman J. Bauer, "Conant, James Bryant" in John F. Ohles (Editor), *Biographical Dictionary of American Educators* (Volume 1), Westport, CT: Greenwood Press, 1978; James B. Conant, *My Several Lives: Memoirs of a Social Inventor,* New York: Harper and Row, Publishers, 1970; Charles Moritz (Editor), *Current Biography Yearbook 1978,* New York: The M. W. Wilson Company, 1978; *Who's Who in America, 1978–79* (Volume 1, Fortieth Edition), Chicago: Marquis Who's Who, 1978.

CONANT REPORT, a study of the American comprehensive high school completed in 1958 by James B. Conant. The study was supported by a grant from the Carnegie Corporation of New York. Conant, former President of Harvard University, together with a special staff, made numerous observations and recommendations after evaluating 103 high schools in 26 states.

Conant suggested that the comprehensive high school should offer: (1) a general education for all students; (2) elective courses for those planning to enter the world of work upon graduation; and (3) special (including advanced) courses for college-bound youth. He found only eight of the schools sampled fulfilling these three objectives.

Conant recommended closing small high schools (those graduating fewer then 100) through district reorganization. His report also called for improved school-community relations, one guidance counselor for every 250–300 students, more individualization of instruction, and increased attention to slow learners as well as to the academically talented. (See COMPREHENSIVE HIGH SCHOOL.)

References: James B. Conant, *The American High School Today: A First Report to Interested Citizens,* New York: McGraw-Hill Book Company, 1959; A. Harry Passow, *American Secondary Education: The Conant Influence,* Reston, VA: National Association of Secondary School Principals, 1977.

CONCEPTUALLY ORIENTED PROGRAM FOR ELEMENTARY SCIENCE (COPES), a project initiated at New York University (1965) that resulted in the development of a new, K–6 elementary science curriculum. The curriculum was built around a framework of specific conceptual schemes, each of which is taught concurrently and presented sequentially throughout the elementary grades. The five basic (conceptual) concepts are titled: (1) the *Structural Units of the Universe;* (2)

Interaction and Change; (3) *Conservation of Energy;* (4) *Degradation of Energy;* and, (5) the *Statistical View of Nature.* COPES seeks to develop scientific literacy and also, through the use of activities of an exploratory and nonreading nature, to foster the basic skills of science.

Materials consist of manuals for teachers, tests, and newsletters. All are directed at the teacher; no materials for students are included.

Funding to support COPES came initially from the U.S. Office of Education, later from the National Science Foundation.

References: Glenn O. Blough and Julius Schwartz, *Elementary School Science and How to Teach It* (Fifth Edition), New York: Holt, Rinehart and Winston, Inc., 1974; Howard J. Hausman, *Choosing a Science Program for the Elementary School* (Occasional Papers No. 24), Washington, DC: Council for Basic Education, October 1976; J. David Lockard (Editor), *Science and Mathematics Curricular Developments Internationally, 1956–1974,* College Park, MD: Science Teaching Center, University of Maryland (Joint Project with the Commission on Science Education, American Association for the Advancement of Science), 1974; Nathan S. Washton, *Teaching Science in Elementary and Middle Schools,* New York: David McKay Company, Inc., 1974.

CONCILIATION, a general term for attempts to resolve disagreements between the two sides in a dispute. Neutral third parties are used to clarify issues for the disputants. Except for some minor differences, *conciliation* is a synonym for *mediation.* (See COLLECTIVE BARGAINING and MEDIATION.)

References: Carl Heyel (Editor), *The Encyclopedia of Management* (Second Edition), New York: Van Nostrand Reinhold Company, 1973; Hano Johannsen and G. Terry Page, *International Dictionary of Management: A Practical Guide,* London, England: Kogan Page Ltd., 1977; Katherine Seide (Editor), *A Dictionary of Arbitration and its Terms: Labor, Commercial, International,* Dobbs Ferry, NY: Oceana Publications, Inc. (For the Eastman Library of the American Arbitration Association), 1970.

CONDEMNATION OF PROPERTY—See EMINENT DOMAIN

CONDITIONED RESPONSE, in classical conditioning, that response from an organism that results from the pairing of a *conditioned stimulus* (a neutral stimulus) with an *unconditioned stimulus* (a stimulus that is given independence from the organism). After a sufficient number of repeated and identical pairings, the conditioned stimulus will eventually produce the same response without the unconditioned stimulus being present. For example, in establishing a conditioned response in a rat, a psychologist rings a bell (conditioned stimulus) and then drops food (unconditioned stimulus) to the hungry rat; the food will increase salivation. After the pairing of the bell and food has been completed a number of times, the bell alone will cause salivation. When this happens, the resulting salivation is the conditioned response. (See CLASSICAL CONDITIONING; CONDITIONED STIMULUS; and INSTRUMENTAL CONDITIONING.

References: C. B. Ferster, et al., *Behavior Principles* (Second Edition), Englewood Cliffs, NJ: Prentice-Hall, Inc., 1975; B. R. Hergenhahn, *An Introduction to Theories of Learning* (Third Edition), Englewood Cliffs, NJ: Prentice-Hall, Inc., 1988; Gregory A. Kimble, *Foundations of Conditioning and Learning*, New York: Appleton-Century-Crofts, Inc., 1967; Donald L. King, *Conditioning: An Image Approach*, New York: Gardner Press, Inc., 1979.

CONDITIONED STIMULUS, in classical conditioning, that stimulus that starts out as a neutral one. When paired with an unconditioned stimulus, however, it elicits a particular response and, consequently, over time, can produce the particular conditioned response without the unconditioned stimulus being present. For example, when a psychologist initially rings a bell before dropping food, the bell would probably not start salivation in a hungry animal. After pairing the bell with food, over several trials, with resulting salivation, the bell becomes a conditioned stimulus when it causes salivation without the presence of food. (See CONDITIONED RESPONSE and CLASSICAL CONDITIONING.)

References: C. B. Ferster, et al., *Behavior Principles* (Second Edition), Englewood Cliffs, NJ: Prentice-Hall, Inc., 1975; B. R. Hergenhahn, *An Introduction to Theories of Learning* (Third Edition), Englewood Cliffs, NJ: Prentice-Hall, Inc., 1988; Howard Rachlin, *Introduction to Modern Behaviorism* (Second Edition), San Francisco: W. H. Freeman and Company, 1976.

CONFIGURATION—See WORD CONFIGURATION

CONFLICT MANAGEMENT, a perception of leadership that challenges the traditional view that conflict in organization is disruptive and reflects negatively on the skills of the organization's leader. Students of conflict management hold that conflict situations can be constructive, creative forces that permit the leader to institute change and to demonstrate innovative leader behavior even as he/she works to keep the conflict situation contained.

Potential for conflict exists in all organizations in varying degrees. It can take place between individuals, between an individual and a group, between groups, between groups and an organization, or between organizations. Louis Pondy identified five stages in a conflict situation: (1) *latent* conflict; (2) *perceived* conflict, where the parties involved are cognitively aware of conflict conditions; (3) *felt* conflict, in which the conflict situation produces emotional feelings; (4) *manifest* conflict, in which the parties demonstrate conflict behavior; and (5) *aftermath*, which Pondy described as the legacy of a conflict episode.

References: Andrew J. DuBrin, *Fundamentals of Organizational Behavior: An Applied Perspective,* New York: Pergamon Press, Inc., 1974; E. Mark Hanson, *Educational Administration and Organizational Behavior,* Boston: Allyn and Bacon, Inc., 1979; Louis R. Pondy, "Organizational Conflict: Concepts and Models," *Administrative Science Quarterly,* September 1967; Thomas J. Sergiovanni and Fred D. Carver, *The New School Executive: A Theory of Administration* (Second Edition), New York: Harper and Row, Publishers, 1980.

CONGENITAL DISORDERS, those disorders, defects, or anomalies caused by familial and hereditary tendencies or factors. In the case of congenital disorders of the heart, for example, German measles contracted by the mother during the first two or three months of pregnancy can be the cause of the disorder. Chromosomal structure and the genetic mechanisms of humans are being studied, along with better prenatal care, in an attempt to reduce congenital disorders. Congenital disorders include cataracts; deafness; absence of limbs, fingers, toes; dislocations; hepatic fibrosis; or total color blindness. Multiple disorders may also occur.

References: Richard M. Goodman and Robert J. Gorlin, *Atlas of the Faces in Genetic Disorders* (Second Edition), St. Louis, MO: The C. V. Mosby Company, 1977; Dwight T. Janerich, et al. (Editors), *Congenital Defects: New Directions in Research,* New York: Academic Press, 1974; Max Levitan and Ashley Montagu, *Textbook of Human Genetics* (Second Edition), New York: Oxford University Press, 1977.

CONNOTATIVE MEANING—See DENOTATION

CONSERVATION EDUCATION, a broad term for those experiences and courses offered in the elementary, high schools, and colleges that develop concepts, knowledge, attitudes, skills, and behaviors that produce better understanding of the relationship of humans to the land and the land to humans. One major purpose of conservation education is to improve the physical environment; another, leading to realization of such improvement, is development of understandings.

A major problem with the definition is that conservation education is *not* a separate discipline. In the elementary school, it may be taught as part of outdoor education, recreation, or environmental education. At the secondary school level, units in science, social studies, outdoor education, recreation, sports, literature, and mathematics may also touch on conservation.

At the college level, conservation education is more vocational in orientation with emphasis placed on natural resource management. Soil conservation, forestry, freshwater management, and watershed management are just a few of the vocational areas included.

References: John W. Brainerd, *Nature Study for Conservation,* New York: The Macmillan Company, 1971; Henry Clepper (Editor), *Careers in Conservation,* New York: John Wiley and Sons, 1979; Julian W. Smith, et al., *Outdoor Education* (Second Edition), Englewood Cliffs, NJ: Prentice-Hall, Inc., 1972.

CONSERVATORY, a school that specializes in the practical and theoretical teaching of music. The term comes from the Italian, dating back to "conservatorios." These were orphanages designed to "conserve" children. Their educational programs frequently stressed music.

The conservatory is primarily concerned with developing performers and, to some degree, composers. Conductors (performers too) are also trained in conservatories. These schools teach the necessary theoretical subjects as well.

References: Willi Apel, *Harvard Dictionary of Music* (Second Edition, Revised and Enlarged), Cambridge, MA: The Belknap Press of Harvard University Press, 1970; J. A. Westrup and F. L. Harrison (Revised by Conrad Wilson), *The New College Encyclopedia of Music,* New York: W. W. Norton and Company, Inc., 1976.

CONSIDERATION—See LEADER BEHAVIOR DESCRIPTION QUESTIONNAIRE

CONSOLIDATION, an organizational term used in education to describe the merging of two or more schools or school districts. Consolidated schools are sometimes referred to as centralized schools.

Considerable school and school district consolidation (reorganization) took place in the United States between 1959 and 1977. The National Center for Education Statistics, in 1979, reported that "(t)wenty years ago there were 120,953 public schools organized into 47,594 school districts. In 1977, the number of schools and school districts had been reduced to 87,315 and 16,112 respectively" (p. 48). Much of the consolidation movement in America can be attributed to a massive (and often politically unpopular) effort, carried out by many state legislatures, to eliminate small, educationally inefficient, and fiscally poor school districts.

References: Roald F. Campbell, et al., *The Organization and Control of American Schools* (Fourth Edition), Columbus, OH: Charles E. Merrill Publishing Company, 1980; Commission on School District Reorganization, *School District Organization,* Washington, DC: American Association of School Administrators, 1958; Nancy B. Dearman and Valena W. Plisko, *The Condition of Education* (Statistical Report), Washington, DC: National Center for Education Statistics, U.S. Department of HEW, 1979; Carter V. Good (Editor), *Dictionary of Education* (Third Edition), New York: McGraw-Hill Book Company, 1973.

CONSORTIUM, EDUCATIONAL, a form of voluntary interinstitutional cooperation, with a formal administrative structure, in which three or more institutions participate for the purpose of carrying out one or more educational programs. Each participating institution contributes to the support of the consortium. One of the first consortia to be established in the United States involved the Claremont Colleges of Southern California. That interinstitutional arrangement began with the sharing of a library. In 1975, Franklin Patterson reported, there were 106 multipurpose, higher education consortia operating in the United States. Literally thousands of less-structured linkage arrangements exist today, these loosely (some say, incorrectly) referred to as consortia as well.

References: Asa S. Knowles (Editor), *Handbook of College and University Administration,* New York: McGraw-Hill Book Company, 1970; Franklin Patterson, *Colleges in Consort: Institutional Cooperation Through Consortia,* San Francisco: Jossey-Bass Publishers, 1974; Franklin Patterson, "Consortia in the United States" in Asa S. Knowles (Editor), *The International Encyclopedia of Higher Education* (Volume 3), San Francisco: Jossey-Bass Publishers, 1977.

CONSORTIUM FOR INTERNATIONAL COOPERATION IN HIGHER EDUCATION (CICHE)—See INTERNATIONAL COUNCIL ON EDUCATION FOR TEACHING

CONSTITUTIONAL TYPES, categories of physical or body build. William Sheldon, one of several researchers to have investigated human body-build characteristics, studied photographs of male college students and proposed a tridimensional system for classifying body types. The dimensions he introduced are endomorphy, mesomorphy, and ectomorphy.

Endomorphic (or fat) types tend to have round-shaped bodies, are broad-hipped, and short-legged. *Mesomorphics* possess a body structure with good muscle and bone development. *Ectomorphic* individuals tend to be thin, have tall slender bodies, and are small-muscled.

Sheldon attempted to relate constitutional types to specific personality traits, an effort that was subjected to considerable criticism.

References: Morris E. Eson, *Psychological Foundations of Education* (Second Edition), New York: Holt, Rinehart and Winston, Inc., 1972; William H. Sheldon, "Constitutional Factors in Personality" in Joseph M. Hunt (Editor), *Personality and the Behavior Disorders* (Volume I), New York: Ronald Press Company, 1944; William H. Sheldon, *Atlas of Men: A Guide for Somatotyping the Adult Male at All Ages,* New York: Harper and Brothers, 1954.

CONSTRUCT VALIDITY—See VALIDITY

CONSULTANTS, EDUCATIONAL, experts hired by schools, colleges, corporations, industries, or educational agencies to provide specialized help, advice, planning, or presentations to solve one or more educational problems. The range of services they provide is extensive. Consultants may help to design a school building or a curriculum. They may help set up a school management system or find problems within an existing one. They may work with teachers in the classroom or provide in-service education. Consultants are hired for a short period, usually one, two, or more days or, at most, several months. They are usually paid a specified, agreed-upon amount and are not considered employees.

Another kind of educational consultant is concerned directly with student personnel. This consultant works with and helps administrators, teachers, parents, and children to facilitate each child's potential through knowledge of the total milieu or life space confronting each child. Such a consultant, usually employed on a long-term basis, is a resource and catalytic agent for the professional staff and children.

References: Duane Brown, et al., *Consultation: Strategy for Improving Education* (New Edition), Boston: Allyn and Bacon, Inc., 1979; Don Dinkmeyer and Jon Carlson,

Consulting, Columbus, OH: Charles E. Merrill Publishing Company, 1973; Paul Wassemen and Janice McLean (Editors), *Consultants and Consulting Organizations Directory* (Third Edition), Detroit: Gale Research Company, 1976.

CONSUMER AND HOMEMAKING HOME ECONOMICS—See FAMILY RESOURCES EDUCATION

CONSUMER EDUCATION, programs or units found in mathematics, social studies, home economics, and other fields of study that focus on how one spends money for goods and services, whether directly or indirectly. The major goals of consumer education are: (1) to make individuals aware of their role in the economy; (2) to learn how the economy functions; (3) to know how to make appropriate consumer decisions; and (4) to learn how to manage and maximize finances used to purchase or secure goods and services. Consumer education, sometimes as a unit of study, sometimes as a course, is found included in the curricula of many elementary schools, secondary schools, and colleges.

Schools are not the only source of consumer education. The United States government, for example, has established a Consumer Protection Agency that is involved in consumer education. Many states have similar agencies.

The following are a few of the topics studied as part of consumer education: money management; credit; food, clothing, and other item purchases; taxes; savings and investments; consumer protection; consumer laws; home buying; and transportation. (See HOME ECONOMICS.)

References: E. Scott Maynes, *Decision-making for Consumers: An Introduction to Consumer Economics*, New York: Macmillan Publishing Company, Inc., 1976; Wilbur O. Maedke, et al., *Consumer Education*, Encino, CA: Glencoe Publishing Company, 1979; Archie W. Troelstrup and E. Carl Hall, *The Consumer in American Society* (Sixth Edition), New York: McGraw-Hill Book Company, 1978; Farren Webb, *Teaching Consumer Skills and How to Survive in America*, Denver, CO: Center for Teaching International Relations, 1980.

CONTENT ANALYSIS, a technique used to evaluate a passage, book, test, or program in terms of a particular category or classification. Content analysis is used to ascertain the readability of a text or passage. It can be used to determine whether certain valuing terms are used in printed materials. The misrepresentation of selected ethnic, sex, or racial groups in television scheduling can be established through content analysis of television programs. Analysis of responses to an open-ended questionnaire can be tabulated through a content analysis of the types of answers elicited. Since the goal of the content analysis determines the nature of the analysis, there is no specific or set procedure to follow other than determining the categories to be studied.

References: Scarvia B. Anderson, et al., *Encyclopedia of Educational Evaluation,* San Francisco: Jossey-Bass Publishers, 1975; J. William Asher, *Educational Research and Evaluation Methods,* Boston: Little, Brown and Company, 1976.

CONTENT VALIDITY—See VALIDITY

CONTINGENCY LEADERSHIP THEORY, a basis for examining leadership that holds that both *task-oriented* and *relations-oriented* leaders can be effective providing that situations exist that are supportive of their respective leadership styles.

Fred Fiedler, a pioneer in the field of contingency management theory, examined the relationships between each of these styles and each of three situational characteristics of an organization. The three situational dimensions were: (1) *leader-members relationship* (good vs. bad); (2) *task structure* (high vs. low); and (3) the *leader's power position* (strong vs. weak). The investigator concluded that both styles were effective assuming the situational "match" was right. More specifically, the task-oriented leader was found to operate best when situations are either very favorable or very unfavorable. (Favorableness was used to mean the extent to which the situation permits the leader to influence the group toward organizational goals.) The human-relations style leader, on the other hand, was found to be most effective in group situations falling within the intermediate range of favorableness.

References: Fred E. Fiedler, *A Theory of Leadership Effectiveness,* New York: McGraw-Hill Book Company, 1967; E. Mark Hanson, "School Management and Contingency Theory: An Emerging Perspective," *Educational Administrative Quarterly,* Spring 1979; Thomas J. Sergiovanni and Robert J. Starratt, *Supervision: Human Perspectives* (Second Edition), New York: McGraw-Hill Book Company, 1979.

CONTINUING EDUCATION, educational and training programs for adult learners. Continuing education grew out of the adult education movement. Unlike early adult education programs that

had relatively restricted foci (citizenship training, high school education, remedial education), continuing education has the much broader connotation of lifelong learning as its base.

Continuing education began to develop significantly and to expand in the late 1960s as a recognition of the need: (1) for providing education for disadvantaged adults; (2) to respond to the increasing technological sophistication of the society; (3) for skill renovation; (4) for self-realization on the part of adults; (5) for personal, family, civic, and social competencies; and (6) to satisfy avocational and cultural needs.

Continuing education takes many forms. Offerings may range from formal degree programs to workshops, seminars, correspondence courses, on-campus and off-campus courses, and various nontraditional experiences. Many colleges and universities have continuing-education divisions (e.g. College of Continuing Studies) that sponsor programs ranging from one- or two-day experiences to semester-long and year-long courses. Many plan programs jointly with business groups and/or labor unions. College credit or continuing education units (CEUs) may be awarded. (See CONTINUING EDUCATION UNIT.)

References: Peter Jarvis, *Adult and Continuing Education,* New York: Nichols Publishing, 1983; Malcolm Knowles, *The Adult Learner: A Neglected Species,* Houston, TX: Gulf Publishing, 1973; A. A. Liveright, *A Study of Adult Education in the United States,* Boston: Center for the Study of Liberal Education, Boston University, 1968; Dyckman W. Vermilye, *Lifelong Learners: A New Clientele for Higher Education,* San Francisco: Jossey-Bass Publishers, 1974.

CONTINUING EDUCATION UNIT (CEU), a standard measure of educational achievement used by many colleges and universities offering adult- or continuing-education courses and by an increasing number of professional associations. Not to be confused with *academic credits,* which are accumulated to fulfill degree requirements, CEUs simply attest to clock-hour completion of special offerings such as workshops, inservice programs, institutes, and occupational seminars. One CEU is usually granted for every ten contact hours of work completed. CEUs are used to renew certain vocational licenses and as a basis for recording inservice work completed. A National Task Force on the Continuing Education Unit (1968–74), formed by the National University Extension Association, The American Association of Collegiate Registrars and Admission Officers, U.S. Office of Education, and U.S. Civil Service Commission, defined the

CEU. (See CONTINUING EDUCATION.)

References: Council on the Continuing Education Unit, *The Continuing Education Unit: Criteria and Guidelines,* Silver Spring, MD: The Council, 1979; Carl Hadsell, "A CEU Record-Keeping Solution," *College and University,* Summer 1977; Beverly T. Watkins, "Continuing Education Unit Gains as Measures of Non-Credit Study," *The Chronicle of Higher Education,* July 9, 1979.

CONTINUOUS PROGRESS PLAN—See NON-GRADED SCHOOL

CONTRACT, an agreement involving two or more parties. Contracts are expressed (usually in writing) in terms that are understandable and with which all parties involved concur. Terms are binding on all who are parties to the agreement. Supporting the contract is some consideration (i.e. something of value that one party gives or promises in exchange for some act or promise made by another party).

Most expenditures made by a school district are covered by contract. Included are professional services rendered by administrators and teachers, school construction, and school supplies or equipment. (Contracts for teachers' salaries are usually not reduced to individual contracts, but rather are implied by virtue of official appointment and acceptance through employment.) The school district's authority to engage in contracts is granted (and limited) by state law. (See CONTRACT, TEACHER.)

References: Daniel J. Gatti and Richard D. Gatti, *The Teacher and the Law,* West Nyack, NY: Parker Publishing Company, Inc., 1972; Leroy J. Peterson, et al., *The Law and Public School Operation* (Second Edition), New York: Harper and Row, Publishers, 1978.

CONTRACT, TEACHER, an agreement between a teacher and a school board for teaching services to be rendered. Although minimum requirements for teaching are governed by state and federal laws, school districts may impose additional training, experience, or similar requirements that do not violate the teacher's constitutional rights. One authority (William Hazard) pointed out that contracts between teachers and school boards include these elements: (1) *mutual assent* (board makes an offer that the teacher accepts); (2) *competent parties* (both parties are legally qualified to engage in contract); (3) *consideration* (salary agreed to); (4) *legal bargain* (understanding that the agreement is not forbidden by law); and (5) *form* required by law.

Local regulations (e.g. school board policies and regulations) and state laws are a part of the con-

tract. Should the two be at variance, state law takes precedence. The automatic inclusion of such regulations and laws applies to tenured as well as probationary teachers. Voidable (defective) contracts often involve irregularities such as: (1) contracts made with individual board members rather than the whole board; (2) contracts signed by uncertified teachers; or (3) contracts approved at other than official school board meetings.

Annual contracts are issued for one year. *Continuing contracts* specify that the teacher is automatically reemployed for another year unless advised otherwise by a specific date. Permanent status (tenure) is granted following successful completion of a probationary period (usually three to five yars). Employment is continuous for tenured teachers; dismissal is possible only after good cause has been established. (See CONTRACT and TENURE.)

References: William R. Hazard, *Education and the Law* (Second Edition), New York: The Free Press, 1978; Leroy J. Peterson, et al., *The Law and Public School Operation* (Second Edition), New York: Harper and Row, Publishers, 1978; Robert W. Richey, *Planning for Teaching: An Introduction to Teaching* (Sixth Edition), New York: McGraw-Hill Book Company, 1979.

CONTROL, ADMINISTRATIVE, the sum of those forces and factors that permit some individuals (e.g. managers) to influence or to exert control over others (e.g. subordinates). Fred Fiedler pointed out that the leader's capacity to control is influenced by three factors: (1) his/her relationships with group members; (2) the degree to which tasks (i.e. job analyses) are delineated clearly; and (3) the power of the leader (e.g. his/her ability to reward/punish).

Thomas Sergiovanni and Fred Carver cited three control strategies followed by leaders, including school executives. They are: (1) *coercive,* procedures employed for the purpose of stimulating individuals to work toward implementation of institutional goals (some of which can result in morale loss); (2) *utilitarian,* motivation of individuals using material gains as an inducement to behave in a particular fashion; and (3) *normative,* a strategy that prompts group members to perform in certain ways because such ways are recognized as being basically sound and defensible.

Control pervades all types of organizations. Some of it, as the preceding discussion implies, is extralegal. Other forms of control (e.g. the body of law governing education in a given state) are essentially legal in character and origin.

References: Roald F. Campbell, et al., *The Organization*

and Control of American Schools (Fourth Edition), Columbus, OH: Charles E. Merrill Publishing Company, 1980; Allan R. Cohen, et al., *Effective Behavior in Organizations: Learning From the Interplay of Cases, Concepts, and Student Experiences* (Revised Edition), Homewood, IL: Richard D. Irwin, Inc., 1980; Fred E. Fiedler, "Engineer the Job to Fit the Manager," *Harvard Business Review*, September–October 1965; Thomas J. Sergiovanni and Fred D. Carver, *The New School Executive: A Theory of Administration* (Second Edition), New York: Harper and Row, Publishers, 1980.

CONTROL GROUP, in experimental and quasi-experimental educational research, that group not subject to experimental treatment but otherwise similar to the experimental group in its makeup. For example, in a study of the effects of a particular drug, the experimental group receives the drug and the control group receives a placebo (a neutral substance having no effect). Subsequently, the effects of the drug on the experimental group are compared to the effects of the placebo on the control group. Effects (differences) noted are then attributed to the drug.

The procedures used in forming or selecting a control group should be exactly the same as those used in developing an experimental group. Thus, the control and experimental groups will be similar to each other except that one receives a treatment and the other does not. In certain experimental designs, more than one control group can be used. (See EXPERIMENTAL DESIGN and QUASI-EXPERIMENTAL DESIGN.)

References: Walter R. Borg and Meredith D. Gall, *Educational Research: An Introduction* (Fifth Edition), New York: Longman, Inc., 1989; George K. Cunningham, *Educational and Psychological Measurement*, New York: Macmillan Publishing Company, 1986; L. R. Gay, *Educational Research: Competencies for Analysis and Application* (Third Edition), Columbus, OH: Merrill Publishing Company, 1987; Harold O. Kiess, *Statistical Concepts for the Behavioral Sciences*, Boston: Allyn and Bacon, 1989; Emil J. Posavac and Raymond J. Carey, *Program Evaluation: Methods and Case Studies* (Third Edition), Englewood Cliffs, NJ: Prentice-Hall, 1989.

CONTROLLED READING, the pacing (level and/or speed) of an individual during reading instruction in order to maximize the reading process. The child is normally paced at a level selected to preclude boredom, overtaxation, or confusion.

Types and levels of materials used in the classroom constitute one general way to pace reading. Pacing may also be accomplished by using mechanical devices. Such machines not only control what the reader sees but the rate at which it is being shown. Tachistoscopes and films are two aids to mechanical pacing and controlled reading. (See TACHISTOSCOPE.)

References: Dolores Durkin, *Teaching Them to Read* (Third Edition), Boston: Allyn and Bacon, Inc., 1978; Richard J. Smith, et al., *The School Reading Program*, Boston: Houghton Mifflin Company, 1978.

CONTROL THEORY, a theory of human behavior developed by William Glasser. Control theory is almost the opposite of conditioning response theory. The theory focuses on what human beings need to be satisfied; it is about working in the classroom to provide current need satisfaction. According to control theory, human behavior attempts to satisfy the following basic needs: survival and reproduction, belonging and love, gaining power, freedom, and fun. Since students attempt to fulfill needs that are unsatisfied, schools should be designed to recognize and capitalize on the need for satisfaction. Students (according to control theory) do what is most satisfying to them. Situations or other individuals do not cause a behavioral response; rather, behavior arises from within (the opposite of traditional conditioning response theory). As Glasser states in his book *Control Theory in the Classroom*, "A good school could be defined as a place where almost all students believe that if they do some work, they will be able to satisfy their needs enough so that it makes sense to keep working" (p. 15). The learning-team approach, or model, is central to enabling schools, especially secondary schools, to be an environment where students can meet needs, be motivated, and will work. (See COOPERATIVE LEARNING and INSTRUMENTAL CONDITIONING.)

References: William Glasser, *Control Theory*, New York: Harper and Row, 1985; William Glasser, *Control Theory in the Classroom*, New York: Harper and Row, 1986.

CONVERGENT THINKING, the process by which one focuses on a particular answer or response. Convergent thinking (production) is one of five operational elements found in J. P. Guilford's model of the structure of intelligence. Where *divergent* thinking focuses on the production of many responses, *convergent* thinking focuses on a single response. Most intelligence tests require convergent thinking, as do most single response tests. A few creativity tests, on the other hand, require the individual to give as many responses as possible to a particular test item or stimulus.

References: Robin Barrow and Geoffrey Milburn, *A Crit-*

ical Dictionary of Educational Concepts, New York: St. Martin's Press, 1986; Joy P. Guilford, "Intelligence: 1965 Model," *American Psychologist*, Volume 21, 1966; W. Edgar Vinacke, *The Psychology of Thinking* (Second Edition), New York: McGraw-Hill Book Company, 1974.

CONVULSIVE DISORDERS, those disorders that cause seizures, convulsions, or spasms. Convulsive disorders may cause the legs, body, or head to contract violently. These contractions are involuntary. Some convulsive disorders may cause unconsciousness without the manifestation of muscular contractions. Convulsive disorders are attributed to a disruption of electrical impulses in the brain.
References: D. P. Hallihan and J. M. Kauffman, *Exceptional Children*, Englewood Cliffs, NJ: Prentice-Hall, Inc., 1978; Patricia I. Myers and Donald D. Hammill, *Methods for Learning Disorders* (Second Edition), New York: John Wiley and Sons, 1976.

COOPERATING ADMINISTRATOR (CA), in education, the practicing school leader responsible for supervising the field work of an educational administration intern. CAs are chosen because they have proven themselves to be able and successful educational administrators who possess the attitudes and qualities necessary to guide administrators-in-training. CAs may be building principals, superintendents, central office administrators, directors, or university administrators. (See INTERNSHIP.)
References: Roald F. Campbell, et al., *Introduction to Educational Administration* (Fifth Edition), Boston: Allyn and Bacon, Inc., 1977; Stephen B. Hencley (Editor), *The Internship in Administrative Preparation*, Columbus, OH: The University Council for Educational Administration, 1963; Van Miller, *The Public Administration of American School Systems*, New York: The Macmillan Company, 1965.

COOPERATING TEACHER, the regular (practicing) teacher responsible for supervising the work of a student teacher. The cooperating teacher, also known as the *critic* teacher or *supervising* teacher, is expected to guide the student teacher through a series of experiences that will prepare him/her to assume the full responsibility of teaching. Normally chosen by virtue of successful teaching experience, the cooperating teacher performs several duties: (1) serves as a role model for the student teacher; (2) organizes the program of experiences for the student; (3) inducts the student teacher into classroom and school activities; (4) provides the student teacher with practical guidance; and (5) reviews the student teacher's progress with the college/university supervisor.

(See STUDENT TEACHING.)
References: William A. Bennie, *Supervising Clinical Experiences in the Classroom*, New York: Harper and Row, Publishers, 1972; Betty D. Roe, Elinor P. Ross, and Paul C. Burns, *Student Teaching and Field Experiences Handbook*, Columbus, OH: Charles E. Merrill Publishing Company, 1984.

COOPERATIVE EXTENSION—See EXTENSION PROGRAMS

COOPERATIVE LEARNING, approaches to classroom learning and instruction that were developed in the 1970s. The approaches have been shown to have positive effects on achievement, individual support, peer support, group mixing and interaction, motivation, and self-esteem for both high and low achievers. Cooperative learning is a form of small-group instruction that can be integrated into regular classrooms. Students can either work on a project *as a group* or can work independently on a project *within a group*. Cooperative learning may be considered a supplement or an option to the traditional competitive approach used in most classrooms.

There are several Cooperative Learning programs: Learning Together, Group Investigation, Team Assisted Individualization, and Learning-Teams. Stallings and Stipek (1986) reported that Teams-Games-Tournaments, Student Teams and Achievement Division, and Jigsaw, three design approaches to small group instruction, have been found to have varying positive effects on achievement and learning with different student groups. The Johnson and Johnson model of cooperative learning is less competitive than the Slavin approach. (See CONTROL THEORY.)
References: William Glasser, *Control Theory in the Classroom*, New York: Harper and Row, 1986; D. W. Johnson and R. T. Johnson, *Learning Together and Alone: Cooperative, Competitive, and Individualistic Learning*, Englewood Cliffs, NJ: Prentice-Hall, 1987; Robert E. Slavin, *Cooperative Learning*, New York: Longman Publishing Co., 1983; Jane Stallings and Deborah Stipek, "Research on Early Childhood and Elementary School Teaching Programs" in Merlin C. Wittrock (Editor), *Handbook of Research on Teaching* (Third Edition), New York: Macmillan Publishing Co., 1986.

COOPERATIVE PROJECT IN EDUCATIONAL ADMINISTRATION (CPEA), a concerted and significant effort to improve the preparation programs of educational administrators. Financed by the W. K. Kellogg Foundation and initiated in the early 1950s, the project sought to fulfill five major purposes: (1) to improve the preservice and inservice training programs for school administrators; (2) to foster greater sensitivity to social problems by using an interdisciplinary (notably the social sciences) approach; (3) to disseminate research findings to school administrators; (4) to discover new knowledge about education and educational administration; and (5) to foster cooperation and improved communication among universities within a region and between these institutions and other organizations/agencies interested in educational administration.

At first, eight regional centers were established on American university campuses. These were located at Teachers College, Columbia University; University of Chicago; George Peabody College for Teachers; University of Texas; Ohio State University; University of Oregon; Harvard University; and Stanford University. A Canadian project, introduced later at the University of Alberta, had the effect of making CPEA an international project.

CPEA was originally funded for five years; subsequent extensions were granted. Many of the activities that had their beginnings in CPEA continue to influence current preparation programs.

References: George F. Faber and Gilbert F. Shearron, *Elementary School Administration: Theory and Practice,* New York: Holt, Rinehart and Winston, Inc., 1970; Hollis A. Moore, Jr., *Studies in School Administration,* Washington, DC: American Association of School Administrators, 1957; *Toward Improved School Administration: A Decade of Professional Effort to Heighten Administrative Understanding and Skills,* Battle Creek, MI: W. K. Kellogg Foundation, 1961.

COOPERATIVE STUDY OF SECONDARY SCHOOL STANDARDS—See NATIONAL STUDY OF SCHOOL EVALUATION

COOPERATIVE VOCATIONAL EDUCATION, an on-the-job program of study for which participating secondary school students receive academic credit. Selected students, normally those working in some field of vocational education, are assigned to work with a local employer. They perform work that is occupationally related to their respective programs of study. On a scheduled basis, part of the school day/week is devoted to working with the employer and part is spent at school. At least half of the students' work is spent working in the field.

References: E. F. Mitchell, *Cooperative Vocational Education: Principles, Methods, and Problems,* Boston: Allyn and Bacon, Inc., 1977; Dennis C. Nystrom, et al., *Instructional*

Methods in Occupational Education, Indianapolis, IN: Bobbs-Merrill Educational Publishing, 1977.

COORDINATING, an element of administrative process that, if successfully implemented, results in what Russell Gregg described as "unifying the contributions of people, materials, and other resources toward the achievement of a recognized purpose" (p. 307). In a formal organization, coordinating involves three principal activities: (1) developing institutional goals/purposes; (2) affecting an effective division of labor such that specific and carefully predetermined responsibilities are assigned to each employee; and (3) fostering a willingness among employees to carry out the duties assigned to them. Planning, communication, and leader personality are among the organizational climate factors that, if effective, serve to maximize coordinating.

References: Russell T. Gregg, "The Administrative Process" in Roald F. Campbell and Russell T. Gregg (Editors), *Administrative Behavior in Education,* New York: Harper and Brothers, 1957; Jesse B. Sears, *The Nature of the Administrative Process: With Special Reference to Public School Administration,* New York: McGraw-Hill Book Company, 1950; Herbert A. Simon, *Administrative Behavior: A Study of Decision-Making Processes in Administrative Organization* (Second Edition), New York: The Macmillan Company, 1961.

COPYBOOKS, books formerly used in elementary schools for the teaching of penmanship. They contained handwriting samples that the student was expected to imitate. The earliest copybooks, John Nietz reported, "were either like a bound and lined tablet with covers, or merely a bound tablet with empty lines and printed model script at the top of each page" (p. 319).

Copybooks were used in the United States from approximately 1785 through the early part of the 20th century. The first known American copybook was Isaiah Thomas's *The Writing Scholar's Assistant* (1785). A series of copybooks produced by Platt Roger Spencer (beginning in 1848) incorporated some of the work/methods contained in previously published copybooks and included a method for use with the steel pen (invented in the early 1800s). They were used until the turn of the century along with numerous others that large publishing houses had begun to distribute. Among the latest copybooks to be produced in America were those authored by A. N. Palmer, C. P. Zaner, and E. W. Blosser. (See PALMER, AUSTIN N. and PALMER METHOD.)

References: Charles Carpenter, *History of American*

Schoolbooks, Philadelphia: University of Pennsylvania Press, 1963; John A. Nietz, *Old Textbooks,* Pittsburgh, PA: University of Pittsburgh Press, 1961.

COPYRIGHT, five exclusive rights granted to the creators of certain literary and art works. These are the right: (1) to reproduce the copyrighted work in copies or phonorecords; (2) to prepare derivative works based upon the copyrighted work; (3) to distribute copies of phonorecords through sale, rental, lease, or lending; (4) to perform the copyrighted work publicly; and (5) to display the copyrighted work publicly. The protection of copyright can be granted to cover literary works; musical works (including words); dramatic works; pantomimes and choreographic works; pictorial, graphic, and sculptural works; motion pictures and other audiovisual works; and sound recordings.

Before 1978, copyright protection remained in effect for 28 years and could be renewed for another 28 years. On January 1, 1978, the Copyright Act of 1976 became operative. It provided that works copyrighted after January 1, 1978 are to be protected for the life of the author plus 50 years or, in the case of "works for hire" (e.g. textbooks), such protection shall run for 100 years from creation or 75 years from publication, whichever is shorter. The new act also provided that limited copyright protection is secured automatically when the work is fixed in a copy or phonorecord for the first time. For fuller protection, works should be registered with the U.S. Copyright Office, Library of Congress, Washington, D.C. 20559. This procedure involves: (1) completion of an application form obtainable from the Copyright Office; (2) fee payment of $10; and (3) deposit of one or two copies of the work, depending on its nature.

So-called fair-use criteria make it possible for individuals, including teachers, to make *limited use* of copyrighted materials. They include specific limitations on library photocopying. (See LIBRARY OF CONGRESS.)

References: Copyright Office, Library of Congress, *The Nuts and Bolts of Copyright* (Circular R1), Washington, DC: The Office, January 1980; Alan Latman, *The Copyright Law: Howell's Copyright Law Revised and the 1976 Act* (Fifth Edition), Washington, DC: The Bureau of National Affairs, Inc., 1979; *The New Copyright Law,* Glenview, IL: Scott, Foresman and Company, 1979.

CORE PROGRAM, initially a progressive education program developed in the 1930s in the United States. When first introduced, the term *core* was used both to describe an integrated curriculum as well as an administrative class-period arrangement. Content (based on needs or interests of students) within a designated period (usually one-third or two-thirds of a day in the secondary school) was developed by a team of teachers, often with the help of the students themselves. In the 1940s, core evolved into "blocks of time" with the integration of subject matter (e.g. English-social studies, mathematics-science) taught during a two- or three-class period. Teachers attempted to correlate subject matter. Core programs also developed that focused on general education that was common for all children. The core movement lasted until the 1950s, but it was never universally accepted in the schools.

At the college level, core programs are those courses, course areas, or experiences required of all students enrolled in a program. The general education courses required for graduation can be considered core courses, and within a specialty, there can be courses that all students must have that can be considered part of the specialty core. (See DUAL PROGRESS PLAN.)

References: James R. Gress and David E. Purpel, *Curriculum: An Introduction to the Field,* Berkeley, CA: McCutchan Publishing Corporation, 1978; J. Galen Saylor and William M. Alexander, *Curriculum Planning for Modern Schools,* New York: Holt, Rinehart and Winston, Inc., 1966; Daniel Tanner and Laurel N. Tanner, *Curriculum Development,* New York: Macmillan Publishing Company, Inc., 1975.

CORPORAL PUNISHMENT, physical punishment applied to the body and producing pain (e.g. whipping, spanking). In years past, this form of discipline was used commonly in schools, presumably because it reinforced the notion that children needed to learn to be subservient to authority. More recently, corporal punishment has lost favor among educators for both pedagogical and psychological reasons.

The practice of corporal punishment in the schools is sometimes governed by the states, more often by individual board of education policies. New Jersey and Georgia, for example, are states that expressly forbid corporal punishment by teachers. Some states have enacted legislation that permits it; many are "silent" on the matter. School board policies are generally more specific on the subject, indicating whether or not the practice is to be allowed. In districts where corporal punishment is permitted, policies often place limits on the kind of punishment to be administered or they may prescribe who (e.g. building principal) is to do the punishing.

The courts have held that corporal punishment may be used in school districts that permit the practice as long as the punishment is reasonable, not excessive, is administered without malice, and the reason for it is understood by the child.

References: Richard D. Gatti and Daniel J. Gatti, *Encyclopedic Dictionary of School Law,* West Nyack, NY: Parker Publishing Company, Inc., 1975; William R. Hazard, *Education and the Law: Cases and Materials on Public Schools* (Second Edition), New York: The Macmillan Company and The Free Press, 1978; Irwin A. Hyman and James H. Wise (Editors), *Corporal Punishment in American Education: Readings in History, Practice, and Alternatives,* Philadelphia: Temple University Press, 1979; Adah Mauer, *Paddles Away: A Psychological Study of Physical Punishment in Schools,* Palo Alto, CA: R and E Research Associates, 1981.

CORRECTED PROMOTION METHOD OF PREDICTING POPULATION—See PREDICTING PUPIL POPULATION

CORRECTED-TEST METHOD, an approach to the teaching of spelling that some researchers contend is the most effective method of teaching this subject. Two basic steps are involved: (1) the teacher administers a test using spelling words that students have not previously studied; and (2) self-correction of the test by students who use a master list of words for this purpose. All misspelled words are then written correctly by the student. One investigator (Robert Hillerich) concluded that the corrected-test method, which provides immediate and positive feedback, accounts for 95 percent of all spelling learning. (See SPELLING.)

References: Robert L. Hillerich, "Let's Teach Spelling-Not Phonetic Misspelling," *Language Arts,* March 1977; Donna E. Norton, *The Effective Teaching of Language Arts,* Columbus, OH: Charles E. Merrill Publishing Company, 1980.

CORRECTIVE READING—See REMEDIAL READING

CORRELATED STUDIES—See INTEGRATED STUDIES

CORRELATION (r), a statistic that indicates the relationship of two or more characteristics of a group of individuals. For example, the relationship between intelligence (I.Q.) and reading achievement can be expressed in terms of a correlation coefficient. There are several correlations that can be calculated. Most will range from -1.00 to $+1.00$, with zero indicating no relationship. A $+1.00$ indicates that (within a set of scores for a group) as one score for an individual goes up in magnitude, so does a score increase in another set, at the same level of magnitude, for the same individual. A -1.00 indicates that as one set of scores increases in magnitude, the other set decreases at the same level of magnitude for the same group.

The most commonly used correlations are the Pearson product-moment correlation and the Spearman rank-order correlation (Rho). Other correlations include: biserial, point biserial, phi (ϕ), tetrachoric, and coefficient of contingency. These measure the relationship of two variables. In addition, there are partial correlations (known as first order, second order, etc.) that nullify the effects of a third (first order) or third and fourth variable (second order), and so forth on the two primary variables to be correlated. Multiple correlations and canonical correlations measure the relationships of more than two variables.

Correlation may also be used for other statistical purposes such as prediction analysis. (See CANONICAL CORRELATION.)

References: L. R. Gay, *Educational Research: Competencies for Analysis and Application* (Third Edition), Columbus, OH: Merrill Publishing Company, 1987; William M. Hays, *Statistics* (Fourth Edition), New York: Holt, Rinehart and Winston, Inc., 1988.

CORRELATION, SUBJECT, a curriculum pattern in which two or more subject areas are taught together or analyzed by learners to determine their natural relationship to each other. For example, career education can be taught in English, social studies, science, mathematics or other subject areas; or medieval history and medieval English literature are sometimes taught simultaneously. Other examples are when a particular physics area is used in teaching algebra, or when teachers of English and social studies use parallel themes or related materials in their separate classes. The purpose of subject correlation is to help the learner discover the relationships that exist between or among subjects. Although the correlation of subject matter crosses disciplines or departments, there usually is no attempt to have a major redesign of the subject curriculum or to departmentalize subjects.

References: Louis Rubin, (Editor), *Curriculum Handbook,* Boston: Allyn and Bacon, Inc., 1977; Daniel Tanner and Laurel N. Tanner, *Curriculum Development,* New York: Macmillan Publishing Company, Inc., 1975.

CORRESPONDENCE, ONE-TO-ONE—See ONE-TO-ONE CORRESPONDENCE

CORRESPONDENCE SCHOOL, an educational institution that offers courses through the mails. Such institutions may be proprietary (private) schools or colleges/universities offering courses and programs as part of their extension activities.

Instruction via correspondence was introduced in the United States (1892) by William R. Harper, the founding President of the University of Chicago. Recent estimates place the number of American correspondence schools at more than 900 with a combined enrollment exceeding 5,000,000 students.

References: Ossian Mackenzie, et al., *Correspondence Instruction in the United States: A Study of What It Is, How It Functions, and What Its Potential May Be,* New York: McGraw-Hill Book Company, 1968; National University Extension Association, *Guide to Independent Study Through Correspondence Instruction: 1975–1977,* Washington, DC: The Association, 1975; Frances C. Thomson (Editor), *The New York Times Guide to Continuing Education in America,* New York: Quadrangle Books, 1972.

COSMOPOLITANS—See GOULDNER MODEL

COST EFFECTIVENESS, a result of analyses that are made for the purpose of determining the extent to which resources allocated to a specific objective actually contribute to realization of that objective. This form of analysis, frequently reported in dollars and cents terms, is a device that makes it possible to compare a particular approach to goal realization with alternative approaches. It implies, Terry Geske indicated, "that the preferred alternative(s) will be selected on the basis of efficiency criteria" (p. 453). (See MANAGEMENT BY OBJECTIVES and ZERO-BASE BUDGETING.)

References: Combined Glossary: Terms and Definitions from the Handbooks of the State Educational Records and Reports Series, Washington, DC: National Center for Education Statistics, U.S. Department of Health, Education, and Welfare, 1974; Terry G. Geske, "Some Observations on Cost-Effectiveness Analysis in Education," *Journal of Education Finance,* Spring 1979; Joint Committee on Standards for Educational Evaluation, *Standards for Evaluations of Educational Programs, Projects, and Materials,* New York: McGraw-Hill Book Company, 1981.

COTTAGE SYSTEM, a housing arrangement for residents of training schools, corrections/custodial institutions, or similar juvenile facilities. Small groups of residents, ranging from 6 to 40, occupy a "home," or "cottage," which is usually located on the institution's campus and which is supervised by resident adults known as cottage "parents." (Boys Town refers to the husband-wife teams as "family teachers.") The purpose of the cottage system is to replace the cold, large dormitories with smaller living units that provide a more personalized environment and a substitute family of sorts. The individual resident learns to live and to identify with a primary group, his/her cottage peers. Social workers and other human services specialists are usually available to provide specialized assistance/treatment.

The first cottage systems in the United States were founded in Massachusetts (1854) and Ohio (1858). Forerunners to the system were "houses of refuge" (reformatories), special school and housing facilities established in the early 1800s, which served to separate institutionalized children from the adult inmates with whom they had previously been incarcerated.

Variations of the cottage system are currently used in numerous residential institutions for the young. Also, the system is now being used with selected adult populations. (See BOYS TOWN.)

References: Harry E. Allen and Clifford E. Simonsen, *Corrections in America: An Introduction* (Second Edition), Encino, CA: Glencoe Publishing Company, Inc., 1978; Clemens Bartollas and Stuart J. Miller, *The Juvenile Offender: Control, Correction, and Treatment,* Boston: Holbrook Press, Inc., 1978; *Facts About Boys Town,* Boys Town, NE: Boys Town, Undated Brochure; Howard W. Polsky, *Cottage Six: The Social System of Delinquent Boys in Residential Treatment,* New York: John Wiley and Sons, 1967.

COUNCIL FOR ACCREDITATION OF COUNSELING AND RELATED EDUCATIONAL PROGRAMS (CACREP)—See AMERICAN ASSOCIATION FOR COUNSELING AND DEVELOPMENT

COUNCIL FOR AMERICAN PRIVATE EDUCATION (CAPE), a council composed of 15 national private school associations that represent 75 percent of the students enrolled in private schools in the United States (about 4.2 million students). Members of the council operate 15,000 nonprofit private elementary and/or secondary schools.

CAPE was formed in 1971 with the following functions:

1. Represent private school interests in the U.S. Congress;
2. Increase access to private schools for all families;

3. Participate in national discussions about school improvement;

4. Participate in relevant court cases or actions;

5. Foster communications between members of the organization;

6. Foster communication between private education and governmental organizations, media, and the public; and

7. Engage in research in private education.

Fifteen organizations compose CAPE. These include Lutheran, Episcopal, Catholic, Jewish, Friends, Christian, Seventh-Day Adventist, military, and independent schools. CAPE publishes a monthly newsletter (*Outlook*), a two-page letter (*Capeletter*) on a need-to-know basis. The council started in 1983–84 to administer the Exemplary Private School Recognition Project for the United States Department of Education. The program's function is to recognize exemplary private schools in order to promote what constitutes an exemplary school and to facilitate school improvement on a national basis. The council has published reports listing such private schools (Exemplary Schools 1985, Exemplary Schools 1986).

CAPE is governed by a nineteen member Board of Directors and has an Executive Director. The national officer of CAPE is located in Washington, D.C. (See SCHOOL RECOGNITION PROGRAMS.)

References: James Howard, *Exemplary Schools, 1985, Exemplary Private School Recognition Project 1984–85*, Washington, DC: Council for American Private Education, 1985; James Howard, *Exemplary Schools, 1986, Private Elementary School Recognition Program 1985–86*, Washington, DC: Council for American Private Education, 1986; *Council for American Private Education, Voice of the Nation's Private Schools*, Washington, DC: Council for American Private Education, undated.

COUNCIL FOR BASIC EDUCATION (CBE), an organization whose principal goal is the strengthening of teaching and learning in American schools. The council was formed in 1956 by a group of charter members that included Sidney J. Harris, Mark Van Doren, and Alfred A. Knopf. Its current membership includes approximately 5,000 laymen and some educators. CBE subscribes to the view that all students, the severely retarded excepted, should "receive instruction in the basic intellectual disciplines, especially English,... mathematics, science, history, geography, government, foreign language, and the arts" (*CBE, What It Is,* p. 1).

Through its information-service program, CBE works to raise academic standards at the local community level. The council publishes the *CBE Bulletin* ten times annually. Additionally, numerous studies are published that relate to basic education. Since its formation, the council, headquartered in Washington, D.C., has called for strengthening of reading instruction in the schools and the reform of teacher education programs.

References: Council for Basic Education, *CBE: What It Is and What It Does to Strengthen and Improve American Schools,* Washington, DC: The Council, Undated Leaflet; Mary Wilson Pair (Editor), *Encyclopedia of Associations* (Twelfth Edition), Detroit: Gale Research Company, 1978.

COUNCIL FOR EXCEPTIONAL CHILDREN (CEC), an organization made up of 65,000 educators, parents, and others interested in helping exceptional children and youth. CEC consists of 986 local chapters, these located in 53 states and Canadian provinces. Its headquarters is in Reston, Virginia.

Within the organization, several interest groups or divisions carry out special programs. They are: Council of Administrators of Special Education; Council for Children with Behavioral Disorders; Division on Mental Retardation; Division for Children with Learning Disabilities; Division for Early Childhood; Teacher Education Division; Association for the Gifted; Division on the Physically Handicapped, Homebound, and Hospitalized; Division for the Visually Handicapped: Partially Seeing and Blind; Council for Educational Diagnostic Services; Division for Children with Communication Disorders; and the Division on Career Development.

References: Council for Exceptional Children, *CEC Divisions*, Reston, VA: The Council, Undated Brochure; Council for Exceptional Children, *Press Release*, Reston, VA: The Council, Undated Mimeograph Release; William L. Heward and Michael D. Orlansky, *Exceptional Children: An Introductory Survey of Special Education*, Columbus, OH: Merrill Publishing Company, 1988.

COUNCIL FOR THE ADVANCEMENT OF SMALL COLLEGES (CASC), national organization of small, nonprofit, independent colleges of liberal arts and sciences. Founded in 1955, CASC limits membership to institutions that: (1) enroll fewer than 2,000 students; (2) offer half of their coursework in general education; (3) offer at least five areas of study in arts and sciences; (4) have been in operation at least three years; and (5) hold at least *candidate* accreditation status in a regional accrediting association. More than 225 colleges belong to the council.

CASC makes numerous services available to member institutions. They include: (1) an annual, four-day institute, a work session built around a preselected theme; (2) research and development activities; (3) faculty and administrator development services; (4) assistance to developing institutions; and (5) publications that include a quarterly newsletter as well as books and monographs. In recent years, CASC has created a National Consulting Network that provides resource help to member institutions.

CASC's activities are supported out of dues received as well as donations from foundations and corporations. An elected 17-member Board of Directors governs the council. The organization's main office is in Washington, D.C.

References: Council for the Advancement of Small Colleges, *Twenty-Four Years of Serving the Nation's Small Independent Colleges,* Washington, DC: The Council, 1979; Council for the Advancement of Small Colleges, *National Consulting Network for Liberal Arts Colleges,* Washington, DC: The Council, Undated Brochure.

COUNCIL OF CHIEF STATE SCHOOL OFFICERS (CCSSO), an organization whose membership is made up of the 50 state superintendents and commissioners of education. The council also includes the chief educational officers from seven extrastate jurisdictions (Puerto Rico, Virgin Islands, Guam, American Samoa, Trust Territory of the Pacific, Canal Zone, and the Northern Mariana Islands). The organization has been functioning as an independent national council since 1927.

CCSSO serves as a clearinghouse for its members, seeks to reach members' consensus on significant educational issues, communicates such consensus to governmental officials, and sponsors professional growth activities for members and their staffs. The day-to-day work of the council is performed by an Executive Secretary working under the direction of a Board of Directors. Headquartered in Washington, D.C., the council derives some of its financing from state sources, some from special grants.

References: Council of Chief State School Officers, *1979 Policy Statements,* Washington, DC: The Council, 1979; Council of Chief State School Officers, *Council of Chief State School Officers,* Washington, DC: The Council, 1978.

COUNCIL OF EDUCATIONAL FACILITY PLANNERS, INTERNATIONAL (CEFP), an organization consisting of group and individual members who are involved in the planning, designing, constructing, maintaining, or equipping of school facilities. Included in the membership are architects, consultants, engineers, educational administrators, industrial organizations, and students. Organized in 1921 as the National Council on Schoolhouse Construction, CEFP assumed its present name in 1969. Two years later, the word *international* was added to its title, this to reflect the council's expanded activities. A "Planner of the Year" award is made each year to the planner who has done most to influence facility planning. CEFP's offices are located in Columbus, Ohio.

References: Denise S. Akey (Editor), *Encyclopedia of Associations* (Fifteenth Edition), Detroit: Gale Research Company, 1980; *Guide for Planning Educational Facilities,* Columbus, OH: Council of Educational Facility Planners, International, 1976.

COUNCIL OF SCHOOL ATTORNEYS—See NATIONAL SCHOOL BOARDS ASSOCIATION

COUNCIL OF SCHOOL BOARD NEGOTIATORS—See NATIONAL SCHOOL BOARDS ASSOCIATION

COUNCIL OF URBAN BOARDS OF EDUCATION—See NATIONAL SCHOOL BOARDS ASSOCIATION

COUNSELING—See GUIDANCE AND COUNSELING

COUNSELOR—See GUIDANCE COUNSELOR

COUNTS, GEORGE SYLVESTER (December 9, 1889–November 10, 1974), an educational reformer of the 1930s, 1940s, and 1950s who advocated the acceptance of democratic and egalitarian values for the teaching profession. He saw a close relationship between group life and education and a close relationship between the environment (including practices, laws, traditions, culture) and education. He advocated social planning and social engineering. Although he taught at many universities, he spent most of his teaching career at Teachers College, Columbia University (1927–56). Counts was active in politics and in liberal movements. He was very active in the teaching profession and was President of the American Federation of Teachers from 1939 to 1942.

Some of his better known articles and books are: "The Place of the School in the Social Order"

(1926); *The Social Composition of Boards of Education* (1927); "Who Shall Make the Curriculum" (1927); *Dare the School Build a New Social Order* (1932); "Dare Progressive Education Be Progressive" (1932); *The Schools Can Teach Democracy* (1939); *Education and American Civilization* (1952); *Education and the Foundations of Human Freedom* (1962); "Should the Teacher Always Be Neutral?" (1969). From 1936 to 1942, he edited *Social Frontiers*, an Educational Policies Commission periodical.

References: Ralph E. Ackerman, "Counts, George Sylvester" in John F. Ohles (Editor), *Biographical Dictionary of American Educators* (Volume 1), Westport, CT: Greenwood Press, 1978; George S. Counts, "A Humble Autobiography" in Robert J. Havighurst, *Leaders in American Education* (NSSE 70th Yearbook, Part II), Chicago: University of Chicago Press, 1971; Gerald L. Gutek, *The Educational Theory of George S. Counts*, Columbus, OH: Ohio State Press, 1970.

COUNTY HOME AGENT—See HOME DEMONSTRATION AGENT

COURSE OF STUDY, a detailed instructional outline designed to guide the teacher who is assigned to teach a given subject to a particular group of students. Although there is no standard format for a course of study, this document normally includes items such as a statement of course objectives, student requirements (including prerequisites), anticipated outcomes, a listing of topical units, instructional methodology, recommended/required readings, and evaluation techniques to be employed.

Unlike lesson plans, which are typically prepared by teachers for their own use, courses of study are often prepared by groups of teachers and supervisors and, in many instances, are subject to approval by a higher level of authority (e.g. administrators, boards of education, college curriculum committees). Such reviews help to ensure that: (1) each outline conforms to local requirements; (2) resources are available to support the instructional plans prepared; and (3) the proposed course can be articulated with other courses, existing or proposed.

References: John Dewey, "Course of Study" in Paul Monroe (Editor), *A Cyclopedia of Education* (Volume 2), New York: The Macmillan Company, 1911 (Republished by Gale Research Company, Detroit, 1968); Carter V. Good (Editor), *Dictionary of Education* (Third Edition), New York: McGraw-Hill Book Company, 1973; Asa S. Knowles (Editor), *Handbook of College and University Administration*, New York: McGraw-Hill Book Company, 1970; Albert J. Pantler, Jr., *Shop and Laboratory Instructor's Handbook: A Guide to Improving Instruction*, Boston: Allyn and Bacon, Inc., 1978.

CREATIVE DRAMATICS, or creative drama, a language experience that permits one or more learners to express their own ideas and feelings in a manner of their own choosing. Unlike scripted plays, in which participants memorize and express the ideas of the play's author, creative dramatics involves spontaneous dialogue. This form of dramatics is natural among young children who, when at free play, are often observed "playing house," "playing school," and so on.

Authorities suggest that classroom creative dramatics is best carried out without an audience and in a manner that permits all children, regardless of talent, to participate. Puppetry, pantomime, dramatic play, and the dramatization of stories are examples of activities that can be used with creative dramatics.

References: Paul S. Anderson and Diane Lapp, *Language Skills in Elementary Education* (Third Edition), New York: Macmillan Publishing Company, Inc., 1979; Nancy E. Briggs and Joseph A. Wagner, *Children's Literature Through Storytelling and Drama* (Second Edition), Dubuque, IA: Wm. C. Brown Company, Publishers, 1979; Mildred R. Donoghue, *The Child and the English Language Arts* (Third Edition), Dubuque, IA: Wm. C. Brown Company, Publishers, 1979; John M. Kean and Carol Personke, *The Language Arts: Teaching and Learning in the Elementary School,* New York: St. Martin's Press, 1976.

CREATIVE WRITING, that part of the expressional arts in which individuals communicate, through the written word, their ideas and perceptions. Creative writing requires novel descriptions of the real world. It is a mix of reality, imagination, and originality. Creative writing includes: originality of ideas; originality of phrase and organization of thought; unique patterns of words and their meaning; development of unusual pictures through words; the creation of ideas; and creation of unique relationships. Novels, stories, books, and poems are all examples of creative writing. Creative writing is part of the language arts program, early primary grades through college.

References: Lucy M. Calkins, *The Art of Teaching Writing*, Portsmouth, NH: Heinemann Educational Books, Inc., 1986; Jean Berko Gleason (Editor), *The Development of Language*, Columbus, OH: Charles E. Merrill Publishing Company, 1985; Dorothy Grant Hennings, *Communication in Action: Teaching the Language Arts* (Third Edition), Boston: Houghton Mifflin Company, 1986.

CREATIVITY, a complex mental process used to solve problems through novel solutions. It involves the putting together of new, different, and unique ideas, responses, forms, shapes, sounds, colors, approaches, or relationships that usually have implications elsewhere. Most authorities agree that it is easier to identify the product of creativity (e.g. story, picture, poem, invention) than to define the process of creativity. Psychologists J. W. Getzels, P. W. Jackson, J. P. Guilford, and E. Paul Torrance have done extensive research in the areas of the identification of creative thinking and creative behavior. Torrance has done extensive research and writing in the area of creativity and its development in children in the classroom.

References: Gary A. Davis and Sylvia B. Rimm, *Education of the Gifted and Talented,* (Second Edition), Englewood Cliffs, NJ: Prentice-Hall, Inc., 1989; Gary A. Davis and Joseph A. Scott, *Training Creative Thinking,* New York: Holt, Rinehart and Winston, Inc., 1971; Joe Khatena, *The Creatively Gifted Child: Suggestions for Parents and Teachers,* New York: Vantage Press, 1978; E. Paul Torrance, *Creativity in the Classroom,* Washington, DC: National Education Association, 1977; E. Paul Torrance, *Education and the Creative Potential,* Minneapolis, MN: University of Minnesota Press, 1963.

CREDENTIALING, the issuing of documents that attest that an individual has successfully fulfilled the requisites of the particular credential conferred. There are three principal credentials categories: (1) *licenses,* certificates issued by a governmental agency that grant their holders the right to practice or to engage in some specific activity (e.g. to practice barbering); (2) *professional* (or occupational) *certificates,* issued by a professional/occupational organization attesting to the holder's eligibility to practice in some specified field; and (3) *diplomas,* including academic degrees, issued by an educational institution.

Credentialing involves the establishment of standards, the use of those standards to determine an applicant's eligibility for credentialing, issuance of the credential, and, if needed, reissuance or extension of the document at prescribed intervals of time. Credentials are issued to protect consumers from incompetent or less than qualified practitioners. (See CONTINUING EDUCATION UNIT.)

References: Randall Collins, *The Credential Society,* New York: Academic Press, 1979; Jerry W. Miller and Olive Mills (Editors), *Credentialing Educational Accomplishment: Report and Recommendations of the Task Force on Educational Credit and Credentials,* Washington, DC: American Council on Education, 1978.

CREDIT HOUR, or student credit hour, a unit used by institutions of higher education to measure/record academic work successfully completed by students. A specific number of credit hours is assigned to each course, this reflecting the number of clock hours spent in class each week and the number of weeks in the academic term. The most common units are *semester hours* (for colleges and universities whose academic year is divided into semesters) and *quarter hours* (for institutions whose year is divided into academic quarters). Institutions on the trimester plan normally employ the semester hour system. When converting from semester hours to quarter hours, or vice-versa, the formula three quarter hours = two semester hours is followed.

Graduation requirements specify the number of credit hours to be completed for a given academic degree (e.g. 125 semester hours for a bachelor's degree, 64 semester hours for an associate's degree).

References: William E. Hopke (Editor), *Dictionary of Personnel and Guidance Terms: Including Professional Agencies and Associations,* Chicago: J. G. Ferguson Publishing Company, 1968; Asa S. Knowles (Editor), *The International Encyclopedia of Higher Education* (Volume I), San Francisco: Jossey-Bass Publishers, 1977; Ernest A. Vargas, "The Credit Hour: An Anachronism" in James W. Johnston, et al., *Proceedings of the Second National Conference on Research and Technology in College and University Teaching,* Gainesville, FL: J. W. Johnston, Department of Psychology, University of Florida, 1975.

CREDIT UNION, TEACHERS, a cooperative association of teacher shareholders that functions as a banking type of organization. Each shareholder has only one vote, regardless of the number of shares owned. Members may also borrow from the credit union. Although functioning as depositories for money and as organizations to lend money, credit unions are restricted in many states from doing business with the general public because their charters (either state or federal) restrict them to serving a particular group. Teacher credit unions usually serve educators.

Credit unions originated in Germany in the 1840s and 1850s. Massachusetts passed the first state credit union law in 1909. The first Federal Credit Union Act was passed in 1934. Under state and federal laws, credit unions are highly controlled with respect to structure, restrictions on membership, par value of shares, voting rights, governance, deposits, type of loans, investments, and so on. The National Credit Union Administration is the federal agency responsible for chartering, supervising, examining, and insuring federal credit unions. Generally, at the state level, agencies responsible for commercial banks are also responsible for state credit unions. By the end of 1976, credit unions, including teacher credit unions, had total assets of 44.8 billion dollars with a membership of 33,600,000 in over 22,000 credit unions.

References: John T. Croteau, *The Economics of the Credit Union,* Detroit: Wayne State University Press, 1963; Donald J. Melvin, et al., *Credit Unions and the Credit Union Industry,* New York: The New York Institute of Finance, 1977; J. Carroll Moody and Gilbert C. Fite, *The Credit Union Movement,* Lincoln, NE: University of Nebraska Press, 1971.

CRETINISM, a term associated with particular types of dwarfism and mental deterioration. There are three general classifications: *sporadic cretinism,* including isolated cases of congenital thyroid aplasia, idiotic myroedemateuse, congenital myxedema, angeborne myxidiotie, and congenital athyroidism; *endemic cretinism,* involving an unusually large number of cases found in a particular geographic area, sometimes caused by thyroid deficiency (endemic goiters); and *acquired hypothyroidism and athyroidism,* changes and/or loss of thyroid functions caused by postinfections (e.g. measles), trauma, degenerative infantile myxedema, or juvenile myxedema. Iodized salt and medication can prevent many cases of cretinism. Cretinism has all but vanished as a result of improved nutrition, medicine, and early treatment.

The characteristics of cretins are uniform: (1) adult is a dwarf (about three feet tall); (2) head is large, round, skull appears heavy; (3) black wiry hair; (4) ears are large and flabby; (5) neck is short and broad; and (6) movements are slow and awkward. Mental development is a function of how much the thyroid is operating and when cretinism first occurred.

References: Clemens E. Benda, *Mongolism and Cretinism,* New York: Grune and Stratton, 1946; Lloyd M. Dunn (Editor), *Exceptional Children in the Schools,* New York: Holt, Rinehart and Winston, Inc., 1963; Diane E. Papalia and Sally W. Olds, *Human Development,* New York: McGraw-Hill Book Company, 1978.

CRITERION, in education a set standard by which the presence or absence of the quality of behavior can be measured. For example, an acquisition of knowledge standard (reading level, number of correct answers) is established; subsequently, students are assessed to determine whether or not they meet that standard. Or criteria may be set for psychomotor skills. In such cases, the height jumped by a person, the weight lifted, the distance a ball is thrown, and so on can be assessed against a predetermined criterion. Success or failure is based on whether or not an individual meets the preset standard. In most cases, the criterion is the minimum goal to be attained or reached by an individual or group.

There are numbers of problems associated with setting criteria to assess learning. They include diverse considerations such as measurement problems, decisions concerning the setting of a criterion, instruments used, as well as basic philosophical issues concerning individual criteria. (See CRITERION-REFERENCED TEST and NORM-REFERENCED TESTS.)

References: Anne Anastasi, *Psychological Testing* (Sixth Edition), New York: Macmillan Publishing Company, 1988; W. James Popham, *Educational Evaluation* (Second Edition), Englewood Cliffs, NJ: Prentice-Hall, 1988; Raymond Sumner and T. S. Robertson, *Criterion Referenced Measurement and Criterion Referenced Tests,* Windsor, England: National Foundation for Educational Research, 1977.

CRITERION-REFERENCED TEST, examination in which level is used to evaluate an individual's performance. The standard or criterion may be: (1) set within a highly restricted behavior domain (e.g. ability to add and subtract complex fractions); (2) expressed in terms of specific behavioral objectives; (3) a level of learner proficiency (the learner reaches a specific level of "quality"); or (4) a set of broad, long-range goals. The first three standard areas can be measured more precisely than can the long-range goals.

The focus of criterion-referenced tests is on performance of the individual as measured against a standard or criterion rather than performance evaluated against others taking the same test. Evaluations are made in terms of specific achievements or proficiencies as demonstrated on a test or measurement instrument. Considerable concern has been expressed about the construction and content, validation (validity and reliability), measurement properties, and uses of criterion-referenced tests. The debate over criterion-referenced tests, their properties, and their use as opposed to norm-referenced tests has raged since 1963 when Robert Glaser delineated differences between them. (See NORM-REFERENCED TESTS.)

References: Tom Kubiszyn and Gary Borich, *Educational*

Testing and Measurement: Classroom Application and Practice (Second Edition), Glenview, IL: Scott Foresman and Company, 1987; William A. Mehrens and Irvin J. Lehmann, *Using Standardization Tests in Education*, New York: Longman Inc., 1987; W. James Popham, *Educational Evaluation* (Second Edition), Englewood Cliffs, NJ: Prentice-Hall, Inc., 1988.

CRITICAL-INCIDENT TECHNIQUE, a systematic procedure used in job analysis, personnel selection, and personnel classification. The technique was first developed by John C. Flanagan. Specific descriptions of satisfactory and unsatisfactory employees are collected (usually over a limited period). Common characteristics are then abstracted, sorted, and studied. These data allow personnel officials and/or psychologists to specify worker requirements for success in given jobs. The data also allow for the identification of other variables to be measured and possible instruments (tests) that can be used in such measurement.
References: Lee J. Cronbach, *Essentials of Psychological Testing* (Third Edition), New York: Harper and Row, Publishers, 1970; John C. Flanagan, "The Critical Incident Technique," *Psychological Bulletin,* Volume 51, 1954.

CRITICAL THINKING, the ability to judge and evaluate information and/or evidence, drawing conclusions that are objective and logical. A critical thinker is one who is able to identify and/or know premises, assumptions, hypotheses, appropriate theory, the quality (e.g. nonambiguous, ambiguous) of statements, false arguments, generalizations, the reliability of observations, and other factors that contribute to or detract from the process of critical thinking. A critical thinker is skilled in deductive and other forms of logic; he/she is also objective.

Critical thinking is an important part of a school curriculum and is often developed formally in the elementary schools. It is an especially significant part of programs in English (language arts), mathematics, social science, and science programs.
References: Barry F. Anderson, *Cognitive Psychology: The Study of Knowing, Learning, and Thinking*, New York: Academic Press, 1975; Barry K. Beyer, *Practical Strategies for the Teaching of Thinking*, Boston: Allyn and Bacon, Inc., 1987; Edward DeBono, *Practical Thinking: Four Ways to be Right, Five Ways to be Wrong*, Harmondsworth, England: Penguin Ltd., 1976; John Dewey, *How We Think*, Boston: D. C. Heath and Company, 1933; Rainer H. Kluwe and Hans Spada, *Developmental Models of Thinking*, New York: Academic Press, 1980.

CRITIC TEACHER—See COOPERATING TEACHER

CROSS-AGE TUTORING—See PEER TUTORING

CROSS-CULTURAL EDUCATION, educational programs that deal with the similarities and differences existing between or among cultures. These cultures may be found in the same country (e.g. urban, mountain) or in different countries (e.g. Japan, the United States). Characteristics of people, as well as their cultures, are studied with attention given to such factors as history, social structure and sociology, economics, patterns of behavior, anthropology, values, customs, the adaptive processes of the society, maturation, and self-actualization. The universal characteristics of people, as well as their differences, are studied in depth to help students understand their own as well as other cultures. Many of the World Culture courses introduced in American junior and senior high schools in the late 1950s and early 1960s were examples of cross-cultural education.
References: Douglas Heath, *Maturity and Competence: A Transcultural View,* New York: Gardner Press, Inc., 1977; Raoul Naroll and Ronald Cohen, *A Handbook of Method in Cultural Anthropology,* New York: The Natural History Press, 1970; Wendell H. Oswalt, *Other People, Other Customs,* New York: Holt, Rinehart and Winston, Inc., 1972.

CUBBERLY, ELWOOD P. (June 6, 1868–September 14, 1941), noted educational historian and the individual considered by many to be the father of educational administration. Cubberly earned his graduate degrees at Columbia University. He was Superintendent of Schools in San Diego from 1896 to 1898. Cubberly Left the superintendency to join the Stanford University faculty as Professor of Education, a post he held for the remainder of his career. He also served as Dean of Stanford's School of Education from 1917 to 1933.

Cubberly's *Public Education in the United States*, a somewhat controversial book published in 1919 by the Houghton Mifflin Company, was read widely in the field of education. Most of Cubberly's books, of which he wrote many, were studies in school administration.
References: Lawrence A. Cremin, *The Wonderful World of Elwood Patterson Cubberly*, New York: Bureau of Publications, Teachers College, Columbia University, 1965; Alan H. Eder, "Elwood Patterson Cubberly" in John F. Ohles (Editor), *Biographical Dictionary of American*

Educators (Volume 1), Westport, CT: Greenwood Press, 1978; Jesse B. Sears and Adin D. Henderson, *Cubberly at Stanford,* Stanford, CA: Stanford University Press, 1957.

CUISENAIRE NUMBER-IN-COLOR PLAN, a visual physical model of the base 10 number system, used in the primary grades to aid children in learning the number system. Georges Cuisenaire cut rods from wood (known as Cuisenaire rods) that were of different but related lengths (1 to 10 centimeters). He colored each rod length differently to teach children the number system visually as well as physically. In 1953, Caleb Gattegno of England observed Cuisenaire, saw the success he was experiencing, and along with Cuisenaire introduced the procedure to England.

The rods are colored as follows: white—1 cm; red—2 cm; light green—3 cm; purple—4 cm; yellow—5 cm; dark green—6 cm; black—7 cm; brown—8 cm; blue—9 cm; and orange—10 cm. The basis of the system is discovery of number concepts and relationships through manipulation of the rods.

References: Eileen M. Churchill, *Counting and Measuring,* Toronto, Canada: University of Toronto, 1961; Clyde G. Corle, *Teaching Mathematics in the Elementary School,* New York: Ronald Press Company, 1964; Cuisenaire Company of America, Inc., *An Introduction to Cuisenaire Rods,* New Rochelle, NY: Cuisenaire Company of America, Inc., 1980; M. Vere DeVault, *Improving Mathematics Programs,* Columbus, OH: Charles E. Merrill Books, Inc., 1961; Louis Rubin, *Curriculum Handbook,* Boston: Allyn and Bacon, Inc., 1977.

CULTURAL IMPERATIVES AND CULTURAL ELECTIVES, terms used to distinguish the two curriculum blocks making up the Dual Progress Plan (DPP). (DPP is a form of departmentalization developed for use in the elementary school.) The author of the DPP, George D. Stoddard, divided the curriculum into two components: the "cultural imperatives" and the "cultural electives." The former consists of language arts-social studies. According to Stoddard, proficiency in these areas, especially written and oral communication, is essential to successful assimilation into adult society. These are the skills demanded by our culture; hence it is argued that these should be viewed by the school as imperatives.

Mathematics, science, and the arts, on the other hand, are referred to as the "cultural electives." A rudimentary knowledge of these skills, DPP proponents concede, is essential; however, only those contemplating careers in scientific fields or the humanities need master these subjects on an advanced level. (See DUAL PROGRESS PLAN.)

References: Glen Heathers, *Organizing Schools Through the Dual Progress Plan,* Danville, IL: The Interstate Printers and Publishers, Inc., 1967; George D. Stoddard, *The Dual Progress Plan,* New York: Harper and Row Publishers, 1961.

CULTURAL LITERACY, a term popularized by E. D. Hirsch, Jr., to include basic (core) knowledge needed by an individual to be successful in the modern world. This core knowledge spans all classes of human beings and represents the major areas of human interaction. In order to be a competent, contributing member of society, there is a background of information that each individual must possess. Since communication is central to human productivity, it must be built around common backgrounds of knowledge. Hirsch contends that it is the lack of broad background knowledge that is reflected in the illiteracy of our young men and women. To counteract this cultural illiteracy, Hirsch suggests a revamping of materials used in the schools. Materials should reflect the core information—cultural literacy must be made a priority of schooling in America. Hirsch concludes his text with a compilation of terms entitled "What Literate Americans Know."

Alan Purves suggests that cultural literacy may be defined in terms of those knowledges, skills, and values necessary to promote: communication (among individuals); the acceptance and valuing of norms, mores, and customs; and personal independence that stems from the ability to move easily within the culture (or society) because of the base acquired by being culturally literate. General education programs, in schools and in colleges and universities, often have the function of providing, in a formal structure, the base to make a student culturally literate. (See GENERAL EDUCATION.)

References: E. D. Hirsch, Jr., *Cultural Literacy,* Boston, MA: Houghton Mifflin Co., 1987; Alan C. Purves, "General Education and the Search for a Common Culture" in Ian Westbury and Alan C. Purves (Editors), *Cultural Literacy and the Idea of General Education,* Chicago: National Society for the Study of Education, 1988.

CULTURALLY DEPRIVED, or culturally disadvantaged, a term used initially in the 1960s to describe a person who came from a disadvantaged or deprived environment. Typically, such individuals belong to the relatively low socioeconomic strata of society and generally have family incomes at or below the poverty level. Since all cultures possess positive and negative characteristics, and people in one culture could likely be considered as being disadvantaged in another, the term has little real meaning except as an anthropological description or in cross-cultural studies.

Children and adults may be educationally disadvantaged (i.e. not having the educational background, experiences, basic skills, and training to compete successfully in the general society, consequently being at a disadvantage). Children and adults may also be socially disadvantaged such that their social class affects them adversely as they participate in the larger, or dominant society. By 1980, the term *disadvantaged* came to be all-inclusive, describing an adult or child who is socially, economically, and educationally at a disadvantage in a school or social environment.

A disadvantaged person may have nonstandard language as his/her only language base, poor health, dietary problems, learning problems, family problems, money problems, social problems, and/or school adjustment problems, any of which may affect success in school or in the environment. Not all disadvantaged children or adults have all these problems. Most children and adults from disadvantaged environments are able to cope successfully in school and in the larger society.

Headstart and Follow-Through are illustrative of the several United States federal projects designed to aid the disadvantaged child. (See FOLLOW-THROUGH PROGRAM and OPERATION HEADSTART.)
References: Cornelius L. Grove, *Communications Across Cultures: A Report on Cross-Cultural Research*, Washington, DC: National Education Association, 1978; Open University, *Sorting Them Out: Two Essays on Social Differentiation*, Bletchley, England: Open University Press, 1972; Frank Riessman, *The Culturally Deprived Child*, New York: Harper and Row, Publishers, 1962; Edward Zigler and Jeanette Valentine (Editors), *Project Headstart: A Legacy of the War on Poverty*, New York: The Free Press, 1979.

CULTURE-FAIR TESTS, examinations made up of items that reflect similar influences from various cultures. Thus, prior experiences in different cultural settings would be common and hence not affect test results either negatively or positively.

Culture-fair tests are built on the assumption that there is no content culturally independent and that it is "fair" to test comparable effects of culture. Test exercises reflect material taught explicitly in all cultures. Mastery, then, is not a function of a lack of cultural experiences since all students,

theoretically, have had such experiences. Anne Anastasi, authority on testing, feels that the making of culturally fair (or free) tests yields results that have little testing value given the impact particular cultures have on unique content and/or experiences. (See CULTURE-FREE TESTS.)
References: Anne Anastasi, "Some Implications of Cultural Factors for Test Construction" in *Proceedings of the 1949 Invitational Conference on Testing Problems*, Princeton, NJ: Educational Testing Service, 1949; William A. Mehrens and Irvin J. Lehmann, *Using Standardized Tests in Education*, New York: Longman Inc., 1987.

CULTURE-FREE TESTS, examinations whose content and procedures are free of cultural influences. The motivation behind a culture-free test is to reduce either the positive or negative effects (on testing) that an individual from one culture accrues by being from that culture.

The Army Examination Beta, a test developed for testing foreign-speaking and illiterate soldiers in World War I, was one of the first attempts to develop a culture-free test. Neither the examiner nor those being examined used a language; instead, gestures, pantomime, and demonstrations were employed. The examinees used lines or simple remarks as responses.

There is general recognition that it is almost impossible to develop a culture-free test because content that is completely free of cultural influences is extremely difficult to isolate. Additionally, the interaction of procedure, content, and the individual makes the task of developing a cultural-free test more difficult, some say almost impossible. (See CULTURE-FAIR TESTS.)
References: Anne Anastasi, *Psychological Testing* (Sixth Edition), New York: Macmillan Publishing Company, Inc., 1988; Arthur Jensen, *Bias in Mental Testing*, New York: The Free Press, 1980.

CULTURE SHOCK, a term attributed to anthropologist Kalervo Oberg that refers to the feeling of disorientation and helplessness that sometimes results when a person from one culture is exposed to another culture. One writer on the subject (George Foster) believes that culture shock covers four stages: (1) euphoria over being placed in new surroundings; (2) the crisis period, when the individual feels that everyone is indifferent to him and then becomes cynical; (3) the recovery stage that takes place when the alien culture's mores and cues become familiar; and (4) recovery, with few or no anxieties. He suggested that culture shock may last six months or more.

In the early 1970s, Kenneth Kron studied a group of white Kentucky teachers who had been transferred to inner-city schools (to achieve racial balance) and found that several did experience culture shock, exhibiting such reactions as frustration, hysteria, depression, and exhaustion. On the basis of his study, he recommended three activities that might serve to achieve culture shock reduction among teachers: (1) using volunteer teachers for inner-city work; (2) making teachers aware of culture shock before transfer; and (3) carrying out inservice programs to acquaint teachers with inner-city schools and children.

References: George M. Foster, *Traditional Cultures and the Impact on Technological Change,* New York: Harper and Row, Publishers, 1962; Kenneth N. Kron, *Culture Shock and the Transfer Teacher,* Lexington, KY: Bureau of School Service, College of Education, University of Kentucky, 1972.

CUMULATION, PRINCIPLE OF, a principle of learning in which simpler material is presented (learned) first, followed by more complex learning that builds upon what has already been learned. Thus, one "cumulates," or brings forward, what he/she has learned when attempting to master more complex knowledges or skills. The cumulation principle is used in teaching subjects such as mathematics and foreign languages.

References: Jermaine D. Arendt, et al. (Editors), *Foreign Language Learning,* New York: Pergamon Press, 1979; Frank M. Grittner (Editor), *Learning a Second Language* (NSSE 79th Yearbook, Part II), Chicago: University of Chicago Press, 1980; Raymond R. Renard and Jean-Jacques Van Vlasselaer, *Foreign Language Teaching with an Integrated Methodology,* Paris, France: Didier Publishing Company, 1976.

CUMULATIVE RECORD, a student personnel form on which school teachers and other officials record significant information about an individual child. These records are maintained throughout the pupil's stay in a given school or school district. The typical card contains six categories of information: (1) biographical; (2) health; (3) standardized tests; (4) attendance; (5) comments of teachers; and (6) miscellaneous. Of late, the courts, organized parent groups, and public interest bodies have been challenging the tradition of treating cumulative records as confidential information available only to school personnel. (See BUCKLEY AMENDMENT.)

References: Kelly Frels and Ann R. Robertson, "Privacy" in Clifford P. Hooker (Editor), *The Courts and Education* (NSSE 77th Yearbook, Part I), Chicago: University of Chicago Press, 1978; Frank W. Miller, et al., *Guidance Principles and Services* (Third Edition), Columbus, OH: Charles E. Merrill Publishing Company, 1978.

CURIOSITY, a psychological term used to describe the motive behind a behavior that seeks to investigate and possibly manipulate the environment. Curiosity is a motivational condition, one that has helped humans to explore and to explain the unknown.

There are many behaviors manifested by people to satisfy their curiosity. They will ask questions, read books, or explore different environments. Sometimes the behavior will be physical, such as feeling or touching, or the behavior will be mental such as reading or scanning one's surroundings.

Curiosity in children is quite natural; its fostering in the classroom is normally encouraged. Curiosity can be a strong motivational factor in exploring science and other school subjects in which interest exists or is aroused.

References: Wallace H. Maw and Ethel W. Maw, *Personal and Social Variables Differentiating Children with High and Low Curiosity,* Newark, DE: University of Delaware, 1965; E. J. Peill, *Invention and Discovery of Reality,* London, England: John Wiley and Sons, 1975; Kurt Schlesinger, et al., *Psychology: A Dynamic Science,* Dubuque, IA: Wm. C. Brown Company, Publishers, 1976.

CURRENT EVENTS, or current affairs, a social studies activity that involves the discussion, study, and evaluation of significant contemporary happenings at local, state, national, and international levels. Several purposes give direction to current events instruction, the notable ones being: (1) to promote interest in world affairs; (2) to develop such specific skills as reading, map reading, and use of newspapers and other news sources; (3) to encourage study and analysis of issues before taking a personal stand; and (4) to distinguish significant from insignificant news happenings.

A variety of teaching strategies can be used in the teaching of current events. Sidney Tiedt and Iris Tiedt suggested six: (1) student reporting of daily news events; (2) using simulated press conferences as a way to elicit information; (3) keeping a current events scrapbook; (4) studying people who are in the news; (5) making use of newspaper photographs; and (6) recording of news on a class-made time-line. Other techniques include use of news maps, bulletin boards, and general class discussions.

Current events can be taught at all grade levels. *References:* John Jarolimek, *Social Studies in Elementary Education* (Fourth Edition), New York: The Macmillan Company, 1971; John U. Michaelis, *Social Studies for Children in a Democracy: Recent Trends and Developments* (Sixth Edition), Englewood Cliffs, NJ: Prentice-Hall, Inc., 1976; Sidney W. Tiedt and Iris M. Tiedt, *Imaginative Social Studies Activities for the Elementary School*, Englewood Cliffs, NJ: Teachers Practical Press, Inc., 1964.

CURRENT INDEX TO JOURNALS IN EDUCATION (CIJE), a monthly guide to journals in the field of education. Published by the Oryx Press, it covers approximately 800 periodicals. Separate subject and author listings facilitate the researching of articles. Indexes are cumulated every six months, January–June and July–December. CIJE is one of several references published as part of ERIC. (See ERIC.)
References: Current Index to Journals in Education (Volume 20), Phoenix, AZ: Oryx Press, 1988; Eugene P. Sheehy, et al., *Guide to Reference Books* (Ninth Edition), Chicago: American Library Association, 1976.

CURRICULUM, a complex term that has no agreed upon definition. Some educators define it as comprising all planned experiences in school that are the results of what teachers do. Others expand the definition to include all experiences that a learner has in a school, whether or not planned, to reach the institution's broad goals and objectives. Such experiences may consist of a pattern of courses, guidance, specific instruction, physical activities, opportunities for experiences, testing and evaluation, modes of interactions, or any or all of these. Curriculum, authorities suggest, should be rational, complete, have goals and objectives, reflect planning, relate to instruction and learning theories, consider the learner, have criteria for evaluation, be capable of being evaluated, and reflect a sound educational philosophy. As the foregoing discussion indicates, curriculum is more than just a program of studies or a set sequence of courses to be followed by the student.
References: James A. Beane, Conrad F. Toepfer, Jr., and Samuel J. Alessi, Jr., *Curriculum Planning and Development*, Boston: Allyn and Bacon, Inc., 1986; Allan A. Glatthorn, *Curriculum Leadership*, Glenview, IL: Scott, Foresman and Company, 1987.

CURRICULUM COORDINATOR, full-time supervisor responsible for curriculum improvement in a school or school district. Some other titles used to designate officials carrying out this function are "assistant superintendent for instruction," "curriculum director," "curriculum consultant," or "curriculum supervisor." The number of curriculum coordinators employed by a school district normally depends on district size.

The duties performed by curriculum coordinators are variable. They include activities such as the following: (1) helping to determine curricular goals and priorities; (2) coordinating the work of faculty groups engaged in curriculum planning; (3) monitoring and disseminating research activities taking place in and out of the district; (4) working with building principals to improve school programs; and (5) supervising the activities of program specialists working in specific areas of instruction.
References: Kathryn V. Feyereisen, et al., *Supervision and Curriculum Renewal: A Systems Approach*, New York: Appleton-Century-Crofts, Inc., 1970; Albert I. Oliver, *Curriculum Improvement: A Guide to Problems, Principles, and Process* (Second Edition), New York: Harper and Row, Publishers, 1977; Edward Pajak, *The Central Office Supervisor of Curriculum and Instruction*, Boston: Allyn and Bacon, Inc., 1989.

CURRICULUM COUNCIL, an advisory body organized to facilitate curriculum change and improvement. Individuals serving on such councils usually represent various interest groups (e.g. parents, teachers, administrators, students) that are affected by school curriculum. Councils may be school districtwide, may focus on a cluster of schools, or may focus on but one school. Some are restricted to one area of the curriculum, such as elementary language arts, middle school mathematics, music, or physical education.

Curriculum councils generally make recommendations to school administrators responsible for overseeing curriculum, or to school boards. Some are involved in curriculum evaluation; others play but a limited research role. There is no set design or structure for such councils. Some are made up primarily of professional educators; others are a mix of professionals and nonprofessionals; still others are primarily composed of nonprofessionals. Those in the last group often have at least one professional member who is knowledgeable in the curriculum area.
References: Jack R. Frymier and Horace C. Hawn, *Curriculum Improvement for Better Schools*, Worthington, OH: Charles A. Jones Publishing Company, 1970; James R. Gress and David E. Purpel, *Curriculum: An Introduction to the Field*, Berkeley, CA: McCutchan Publishing Corporation, 1978.

CURRICULUM, ELEMENTARY SCHOOL, those activities, programs, and experiences that have been planned and structured for children in grades K through 6. Although some school districts have included several of the upper elementary grades (4, 5, or 6) as middleschool grades, K–6 are generally considered the elementary grades. It is during this period of a child's education that the foundation for formal learning and education is developed. Subject areas making up the elementary curriculum include language arts, reading, social studies, science, mathematics, physical education, health, and fine arts. All areas of the affective, psychomotor, and cognitive domains of the child are developed. (See AFFECTIVE DOMAIN; COGNITIVE DOMAIN; and PSYCHOMOTOR DOMAIN.)

References: Ruth C. Cook and Ronald C. Doll, *The Elementary School Curriculum*, Boston: Allyn and Bacon, Inc., 1973; Daisy M. Jones, *Curriculum Targets in the Elementary School*, Englewood Cliffs, NJ: Prentice-Hall, Inc., 1977; Walter T. Petty (Editor), *Curriculum for the Modern Elementary School*, Chicago: Rand McNally College Publishing Company, 1976; William B. Ragan and Gene D. Shepherd, *Modern Elementary Curriculum* (Fourth Edition), New York: Holt, Rinehart and Winston, Inc., 1971.

CURRICULUM, MIDDLE SCHOOL, those activities, programs, and experiences that have been structured and designed for students in grades designated by a school district as belonging in either "middle school," "intermediate school," or "junior high school." In some districts, such designations consist of grades 4–5–6–7–8; in others, only grades 5–6–7–8 or grades 7–8–9 are included.

The foci of the middle school curriculum are many. The curriculum is structured to provide programs for the early and preadolescent. It allows for exploration; provides for individualization; is child/student centered; allows for limited specialization; and provides an atmosphere for cognitive, psychological, and physical development. Although there appears to be some similarity between actual offerings in the middle school and those offered in high schools, the depth, the content, the emphases, and the actual modes of instruction may be quite different. The middle school curriculum includes offerings in language arts, reading, mathematics, science, social studies, music, arts, physical education, health, foreign language, business education, homemaking, and vocational education. The depth and breadth of the offerings become a function of the grade(s) in which they are offered. There is also significant emphasis on guidance and individual self-development in the middle school curriculum. (See CURRICULUM; MIDDLE SCHOOL; and SECONDARY SCHOOL.)

References: Allan A. Glatthorn, *Curriculum Leadership*, Glenview, IL: Scott, Foresman and Company, 1987; Sylvester Kohut, Jr., *The Middle School: A Bridge between Elementary and High Schools* (Second Edition), Washington, DC: National Education Association, 1988.

CURRICULUM, PRESCHOOL AND KINDERGARTEN, those activities and programs found in preschools (ages 3–4) and Kindergartens (ages 5 or 6). Although there is no common set of experiences (curriculum) established for *preschools*, there are commonly accepted emphases such as socialization, physical health needs, fantasy and nonfantasy play, self-expression, discrimination skills, free-play environment, development of positive self-images, and, in some cases, compensatory programs for disadvantaged children. These emphases have been heavily influenced by psychologists and child development specialists.

Kindergarten curricula are more structured than those found in preschool programs; nevertheless, there is no common program found throughout the United States. In fact, some school districts still offer no Kindergarten program at all. Broad program areas included in most Kindergarten programs are socialization, aesthetic development (art, music, literature), sensory-motor development, language development, self-care, free play, self-development, and academic readiness (reading, number skills, other subject matter content).

References: Ellis D. Evans, *Contemporary Influences in Early Childhood Education*, New York: Holt, Rinehart and Winston, Inc., 1971; Katherine H. Read, *The Nursery School*, Philadelphia: W. B. Saunders Company, 1971; Bernard Spodek and Herbert T. Walberg, *Early Childhood Education*, Berkeley, CA: McCutchan Publishing Corporation, 1977.

CURRICULUM, SECONDARY SCHOOL, those activities, programs, and experiences that have been structured and designed for grades 7–12. In many school districts, grades 7, 8, and sometimes 9 are considered to be either junior high or middle-school grades. However, secondary school curriculum has traditionally included grades 7 and 8 in addition to grades 9–12. In many cases, the secondary school is the last formal educational experience a student will have; therefore, the secondary school curriculum is varied and has many foci (e.g. college preparation, vocational preparation, self-development, socialization, talent development, and citizen development). Students typically pursue a specialized curriculum (e.g. college preparation, vocational training). Such program variety is less likely to be found in small high schools.

Secondary curricula are usually divided by departmental offerings. They traditionally have been: business and distributive education, English and communications, fine arts, foreign languages, home economics, industrial arts, mathematics, science, social studies, health and physical education, and vocational and technical education. Vocational and technical education programs are also offered in separate specialized schools. (See CURRICULUM, MIDDLE SCHOOL.)

References: Weldon Beckner and Joe D. Cornett, *The Secondary School Curriculum,* Scranton, PA: Intext Educational Publishers, 1972; Kenneth H. Hoover, *Learning and Teaching in the Secondary School* (Third Edition), Boston: Allyn and Bacon, Inc., 1972; Kenneth H. Hoover, *Secondary/Middle School Teaching,* Boston: Allyn and Bacon, Inc., 1977; J. Lloyd Trump and Delmas F. Miller, *Secondary School Curriculum Improvement: Meeting Challenges of the Times,* Boston: Allyn and Bacon, Inc., 1979.

CURSIVE WRITING, traditional form of handwriting used in our culture. Unlike manuscript writing, in which individual letters are separated from each other, cursive writing involves the connecting of letters and the placing of them on a slant. Words are written in a flowing and sustained motion (e.g. *dog*, *many*). The pencil or pen is lifted at the end of the word.

Cursive writing is generally taught to elementary school students after they have mastered the simpler manuscript form of handwriting, usually in the second or third grade. Four to six weeks of instruction is required to help the student transfer from the manuscript to the cursive system. (See MANUSCRIPT WRITING.)

References: Martha Dallman, *Teaching the Language Arts in the Elementary School* (Third Edition), Dubuque, IA: Wm. C. Brown Company, Publishers, 1976; Mildred R. Donoghue, *The Child and the English Language Arts* (Third Edition), Dubuque, IA: Wm. C. Brown Company, Publishers, 1979.

CYBERNETICS, the science of communication and control in man and machines. The term was first used by Norbert Wiener in 1948. Through the study of the brain and the central nervous system, and mechanical and electrical systems, cybernetics permits better understanding of and insight into human functioning. Systems theories have been developed, information-processing machines (computers) created, and organizational structures (model building) constructed as part of cybernetics. Many fields have been affected by cybernetics (e.g. biology, medicine, teaching, industry, business). The development of artificial intelligence through use of computer and programming is an attempt to emulate the working of the human brain, an effort intended to bring about a better understanding of how the brain operates.

References: Peter Calow, *Biological Machines,* London, England: William Clowes and Sons, Ltd., 1976; Harold E. Holt, *Cybernetics and the Image of Man,* Nashville, TN: Abingdon Press, 1968; Michael A. Orbit, *The Metaphorical Brain,* New York: Wiley-Interscience, 1972; Gordon Pask, *The Cybernetics of Human Learning and Performance,* London, England: Hutchinson and Company, 1975.

CYSTIC FIBROSIS (CF), more formally cystic fibrosis of the pancreas, a congenital and chronic childhood disease involving the exocrine glands. It is estimated that of the babies afflicted with cystic fibrosis, approximately one-half will not survive beyond the age of 14. In spite of these statistics and the fact that the disease has no known cure, the life spans of cystic fibrosis children have been increased somewhat by modern medicine. Nevertheless, most will not reach adulthood.

CF is a genetic disorder. The gene carrying this hereditary disease is recessive. This means that: (1) both parents must be carriers of the disease for it to appear in a child, and (2) the probability of their newborn child being afflicted is 1:4. Interestingly, cystic fibrosis is almost exclusively limited to Caucasians.

The disease takes many forms and progresses at an irregular rate. Symptoms include blockages of the pancreatic ducts by mucus, resulting in failure of the body to break down and absorb fat and protein. Poor weight gain and, eventually, retarded physical development results. Mucus also causes lung malfunctioning. Other symptoms include coughing, extremely foul stool and gas odors, and excessive loss of salt in the sweat. (Foul bowel movements and the discovery that children "taste" salty are two symptoms that first become apparent to parents.) These extreme and, in many cases, clearly evident symptoms frequently cause the afflicted child to limit social interaction with other children.

Various measures are taken to treat cystic fibrosis, including: (1) dietary therapy (including protein and fat); (2) administration of pancreatin; (3) treatment of respiratory infections using antibiotics; (4) aerosol therapy; and (5) especially in hot weather, increased consumption of salt and water.

References: Paul Quinton, *Current Research in Cystic Fibrosis: Fact Sheet for Young Adults and Adults with Cystic Fibrosis,* Atlanta, GA: Cystic Fibrosis Foundation, March 1975; Georgia Travis, *Chronic Illness in Children: Its Impact on Child and Family,* Stanford, CA: Stanford University Press, 1976; Edward Wasserman and Lawrence B. Slobody, *Survey of Clinical Pediatrics* (Sixth Edition), New York: McGraw-Hill Book Company, 1974.

DALCROZE METHOD, a method of teaching music, named for its developer, Emile Jacques-Dalcroze. Dalcroze based his method on premises such as these: (1) that the skills and understandings of musicianship are based on active musical experience; (2) that music should be taught sequentially, with rhythm an important early experience; and (3) that ear training and rhythmic movement should precede instrumental study.

The Dalcroze method comprises three principal areas of study: eurhythmics, solfege, and improvisation. *Eurhythmics*, or rhythmic movement, is designed to help students "feel" music through bodily movement. *Solfege* includes those activities intended to help students to read music at first sight. *Improvisation* consists of those activities that enable students to invent, or to create, music. (See JACQUES-DALCROZE, EMILE.)

References: Arthur F. Becknell, "A History of the Development of Dalcroze Eurhythmics in the United States and its Influence on the Public School Music Program," Unpublished Doctoral Dissertation: University of Michigan, 1970; Elsa Findlay, *Rhythm and Movement: Applications of Dalcroze Eurhythmics*, Evanston, IL: Summy-Birchard, 1971; Emile Jacques-Dalcroze, "Dalcroze Explains his Method," *Literary Digest*, September 1923; Beth Landis and Polly Carder, *The Eclectic Curriculum in American Music Education: Contributions of Dalcroze, Kodaly, and Orff*, Washington, DC: Music Educators National Conference, 1972.

DALCROZE SCHOOL OF MUSIC, located in New York City, the only Dalcroze teacher training school in the Americas authorized by Dr. Emile Jacques Dalcroze. Five departments offer musical education of different types to students of all ages: (1) the Dalcroze Teachers Training Course, a three- to four-year curriculum leading to the Dalcroze Teachers Certificate; (2) classes for adults desirous of improving their musicianship; (3) special courses for teachers working in public and private schools; (4) courses for children (rhythm, solfege, and improvisation) ages 3.5 years and older; and (5) instrumental courses, private and ensemble. Two types of teachers' certificates are conferred by the school: (1) the *Dalcroze Teachers Certificate*, a diploma, and (2) the *Elementary Certificate*, a special certificate that permits its holders to use Dalcroze methodology and principles in their work. Requirements for the two certificates are

standard throughout the world. (See DALCROZE METHOD and JACQUES-DALCROZE, EMILE.)
Reference: Dalcroze School of Music, *Dalcroze School of Music, 1980–1981*, New York: The School, 1980.

DALTON PLAN, an instructional plan that features study contracts with students. Named after Dalton, Massachusetts, the district in which it was introduced (1920), the original Dalton Plan had two principal components. The first was an individualized program of instruction. Each intermediate grade student signed a contract that projected, for one month, the school work he/she was to complete. The contract listed numerous daily assignments, or "problems," in academic subjects that, when completed, were recorded on a chart by the student. The plan's second part, devoted to the physical and social development of students, involved whole-group instruction. Many variations of the Dalton Plan were later introduced throughout the country with the contract concept central to most.
References: Henry J. Otto, *Elementary School Organization and Administration* (Third Edition), New York: Appleton-Century-Crofts, Inc., 1954; Helen H. Parkhurst, *Education on the Dalton Plan*, New York: E. P. Dutton and Company, 1929.

DAME SCHOOL, an informal private school found in colonial New England. Young children were taught the alphabet, reading and arithmetic, the hornbook, and other elemental subjects by a woman in her own home. Young boys frequently learned to read in dame schools, then went on to enroll in town schools that often set ability to read as a condition for admission. Tuition fees were collected by the women operating dame schools.

The dame school idea was first practiced in England, later introduced in the colonies. Educational historians believe these early neighborhood schools were most numerous in the 17th century.
References: Newton Edwards and Herman G. Rickey, *The School in the American Social Order* (Second Edition), Boston: Houghton Mifflin Company, 1963; Edgar W. Knight, *Education in the United States* (Third Revised Edition), Westport, CT: Greenwood Press, 1969 (Reprinted).

DANCE, a form of expressive and/or rhythmic motor activity performed with or without music. These movements are not necessarily a means to an end, as is the case in sports where rhythm movements have an expressed purpose (e.g., kicking the ball). Dance can express an individual's feelings; it can be used as a means of nonverbal communication; and it can be used to develop motor skills, awareness, alertness, fitness, coordination of mind and muscles, respect for rules, techniques, strategies, vocabulary (related to dance), values, socialization, cooperation, theory, and other outcomes.

Dance is normally an integral part of the physical education programs in elementary schools. At the secondary and college levels, it is often offered as a separate program. Dance can also be integrated into the curricula of various other disciplines.

References: Erna Caplow-Lindner, et al., *Therapeutic Dance/Movement: Expressive Activities for Older Adults,* New York: Human Sciences Press, 1979; Barbara Mettler, *Creative Dance in Kindergarten,* Tucson, AZ: Mettler Studios, 1976; Joan Russell, *Creative Dance in the Primary School* (Second Edition), London, England: MacDonald and Evans, 1975; Joan Russell, *Creative Dance in the Secondary School,* London, England: MacDonald and Evans, 1969; Rudolf von Laban, *The Language of Movement,* Boston: Plays, Inc., 1974.

DARTMOUTH COLLEGE CASE, landmark lawsuit involving Dartmouth College. Dartmouth, a private institution of higher education, was chartered in 1769 when New Hampshire was still a colony. After New Hampshire became a state (1788), laws were passed by the new state's legislature including one that revised the status, membership selection procedures, and board size of the college's Board of Trustees. This legislation was challenged and, in 1819, the U.S. Supreme Court ruled that the state lacked the authority to revoke the charter (essentially a contract) of a private college.

References: Newton Edwards, *The Courts and the Public Schools: The Legal Basis of School Organization and Administration* (Third Edition), Chicago: University of Chicago Press, 1971; *Trustees of Dartmouth College v. Woodward,* 4 Wheaton (U.S.) 518, 4 L.Ed. 629 (N.H. 1819).

DATA (plural for datum), elements of information that can be used to describe organisms, events, or phenomena. Data can be classified into two broad categories: qualitative and quantitative. *Qualitative* data supply information on attributes such as hating, loving, and honesty, and *quantitative* information describes concrete specifics such as speed, categories, grades, or numbers. Qualitative information can be altered through appropriate

data-collecting instruments and changed into quantitative data.

Quantitative data are collected by instruments using various scales. Such scales are: (1) *nominal,* those in which data are placed in a specific category and in which there are no intervals between each category (e.g. dog, cat, cow, male, and female); (2) *ordinal,* those involving ranking of information with no equal intervals between ranks (thus the rank of the first may be very close to the second, but the third may be very far away from the rank of the second); (3) *interval,* in which there are equal distances between each score, but there is no absolute zero, thus preventing direct comparisons (e.g. a person with an I.Q. of 100 is not twice as smart as a person with an I.Q. of 50); and (4) *ratio,* scales in which there are equal intervals and there is an absolute zero (e.g. a person who is six feet tall is twice the height of a three-foot-tall person).

Most educational test data are either nominal, ordinal, or interval in nature. Ratio data are the most accurate, but are seldom possible in education.

References: Robert L. Baker and Richard E. Schutz (Editors), *Instructional Product Research,* New York: American Book Company, 1972; L. R. Gay, *Educational Research: Competencies for Analysis and Application* (Third Edition), Columbus, OH: Charles E. Merrill Publishing Company, 1987; Melvin R. Novick and Paul H. Jackson, *Statistical Methods for Educational and Psychological Research,* New York: McGraw-Hill Book Company, 1974.

DATA BANK, a collection of data in a particular field, a particular subject area, or a collection of data from/about a specific group of individuals. For example, facts and records on professional baseball players may be stored in a single data bank. Production records in a particular industry may comprise another such bank. School achievement records of children could be in yet another data bank. The United States Internal Revenue Service maintains many data banks, as do the Commerce Department, the Department of Education, the United States Census Bureau, and various other state and local agencies. Educational agencies, at all levels, have also developed these banks for particular purposes.

Data banks have been referred to as collections of data bases. Sometimes, data bases are called a collection of data banks. Regardless, the strength of a data bank reflects the ease of data retrieval and analysis as well as the validity of the data per se; therefore, it is important that the storage and retrieval system used be well designed, operative, and usable. Computer systems have made the collection of large amounts of data feasible and cost efficient.

In industry, the development of computers and storage facilities has led to the development of data banks that, in turn, have created a new approach to management: data-based management or database organization. Two educational research efforts, Project TALENT and the National Assessment of Education Progress, have developed large data banks that have been used by educational researchers engaged in significant studies and formulation of educational policy decisions. (See NATIONAL ASSESSMENT OF EDUCATIONAL PROGRESS and PROJECT TALENT.)

References: J. D. Lomax, *Data Dictionary Systems,* Manchester, England: The National Computing Center, 1977; James Marten, *Computer Data-Base Organization,* Englewood Cliffs, NJ: Prentice-Hall, Inc., 1977; Charles J. Sippl and Robert Bullen, *Computers at Large,* Indianapolis, IN: The Bobbs-Merrill Company, Inc., 1976.

DATA PROCESSING IN EDUCATION, a procedure used to collect, store, and retrieve information that can be used by school personnel for specific purposes. The advent of the electronic computer has enabled those in education to have access to large amounts of data and to utilize such data effectively. There are many purposes for collecting data. Equipment management, student personnel management, staff file information, computer-based instruction, enrollment planning and projection, and financial projections are but a few functions served through data processing.

The unit of information is important. Students, teachers, classrooms, tax rateables, population sectors, school systems, and so on each constitutes a unit of information. The nature of such units is determined by the projected use of the information to be gathered. Most larger school districts have a system of data processing. Data processing personnel may be housed in a central office (near computers or computer terminals) or in schools large enough to warrant having such specialists.

Data processing is a part of a larger information system that requires that the data be collected in a compatible form (e.g. cards, tapes, disks, or direct access through terminals) to facilitate processing. (See COMPUTER-ASSISTED INSTRUCTION and DATA BANK.)

References: O. Lecarme and R. Lewis, *Computers in Education: Proceedings of the IFIP 2nd World Conference,* Amsterdam, Holland: Elsevier North-Holland, Inc., 1975; Charles Mosmann (Editor), *Statewide Computing Systems,* New York: Marcel Dekker, Inc., 1974.

DAY CARE, an all-day program housed in a facility (center) that operates five days a week, from 8 to 12 hours a day, for children from two to five years of age. Some day care centers include infant care as well.

Day care is not a new type of program. One of the first in the United States was established in 1838. Early programs tended to be used during times of war when large numbers of women went to work. Until the 1960s, there were few day care centers operating to accommodate working mothers. Those that were in existence did little except act as "baby sitters."

Today, many centers sponsor comprehensive programs that provide child development services, nutrition and feeding, and formal instruction. They follow planned schedules and offer a curriculum that includes activities such as housekeeping, art, sand and water play, storytelling, and number games. Equipment and instructional material is available that serves to help each child to develop physically, emotionally, socially, and intellectually. After-school programs are offered in many cases for children of school age.

Day care centers can be found operating in diverse locations such as private homes, factories, cooperative centers, private centers, university campuses, and social agency centers. In many states, day care centers must be licensed by the state; many employ trained teachers and aides. (See BRITISH INFANT SCHOOL; INFANT EDUCATION; and PRE-SCHOOL.)

References: Stevanne Auerbach (Editor), *Creative Centers and Homes* (Volume III), New York: Human Sciences Press, 1978; E. Belle Evans, et al., *Day Care,* Boston: Beacon Press, 1971; Beatrice M. Glickman and Nasha B. Springer, *Who Cares for the Baby? Choices in Child Care,* New York: Schocken Books, 1978; Bryna Siegel-Gorelick, *The Working Parents' Guide to Child Care,* Boston: Little, Brown and Company, Inc., 1983.

DEAF-BLIND, exceptional individuals who have auditory and visual handicaps that cause severe communication, developmental, and educational problems. Deaf-blind children are classified as being multihandicapped and are usually enrolled in special education programs. In some cases, such individuals have some usable vision, some usable hearing, or some of both. One of the primary objectives of the special educational programs for such people is to develop existing visual and hearing skills to the highest possible level. Some deaf-blind individuals have severe mental and emotional handicaps as well.

Deaf-blindness may be caused by many factors. The 1963–65 rubella epidemic, a major contributing factor, caused the birth of 5,000 deaf-blind children in the United States.

References: A Manual for Assessment and Training of Severely Multiply Handicapped Deaf-Blind Students, Southbury, CT: Southbury Training School, 1976; Marvin Efron and Beth Reilly DuBoff, *A Vision Guide for Teachers of Deaf-Blind Children,* Raleigh, NC: North Carolina Department of Public Instruction, 1975; Lee D. Hagmeier (Editor), *Prevocational Stepping-Stones for Deaf-Blind Persons,* Seattle, WA: Northwest Center for Deaf-Blind Children, 1975.

DEAFNESS, or hearing impairment, a general classification for those whose sense of hearing is nonfunctional to the extent that it interferes with daily functioning. There have been many subclassifications of deafness: *congenitally deaf,* those born without hearing; *adventitiously deaf,* those born with hearing but who became deaf through accident or illness; *exogenous deaf,* deafness caused by hereditary factors; *sensory-neural deafness,* hearing loss caused by trauma, maldevelopment, or disease affecting the middle ear; *central deafness,* auditory impairment caused by lack of normal functioning of the auditory pathways from the inner ear to the brain; and *presbycusia,* natural loss of hearing due to age.

In very young children, *deafness* can be defined as the loss of hearing that precludes the normal development of speech (the loss is at birth or before two or three years of age). *Partial hearing* or *hard of hearing* can be defined as the loss of hearing that is not sufficient to preclude the development of speech. (See HEARING LOSS.)

References: William I. Gardner, *Learning and Behavior Characteristics of Exceptional Children and Youth,* Boston: Allyn and Bacon, Inc., 1977; Orval G. Johnson and James W. Bommarito, *Tests and Measurements in Child Development: A Handbook,* San Francisco: Jossey-Bass Publishers, 1971; Helmer R. Myklebust, *The Psychology of Deafness* (Second Edition), New York: Grune and Stratton, 1964.

DEAN, ACADEMIC, in colleges and universities, the academic officer responsible for administering a school or a college. The title *academic dean* is generic and may be used to describe a number of positions carrying specific titles such as dean of the college, dean of instruction, and dean of liberal arts. Job analyses for academic deans tend to vary, with differences influenced by factors such as institutional size, the mission of the college/university, institutional status (e.g. private vs. public), and type of unit. Nevertheless, the deanship typically includes duties such as: (1) formulating personnel recommendations (e.g. appointment, salary, promotion); (2) overseeing annual evaluations of faculty; (3) supervising student advisement activities; (4) budget supervision; (5) working with department heads; (6) committee work; (7) orientation of new faculty; and (8) approving part-time faculty appointments.

Academic deans normally hold academic rank in their respective units, have had higher education teaching experience, and usually hold the doctoral degree. Tenure, when accorded, is normally extended to the incumbent as a member of the professoriate rather than as an administrator.

References: Arthur J. Dibden (Editor), *The Academic Deanship in American Colleges and Universities,* Carbondale, IL: Southern Illinois University Press, 1968; Elwood B. Ehrle and John B. Bennett, *Managing the Academic Enterprise,* New York: American Council on Education, 1988; John W. Gould, *The Academic Deanship,* New York: Bureau of Publications, Teachers College, Columbia University, 1964; Allan Tucker and Robert A. Bryan, *The Academic Dean: Dove, Dragon, and Diplomat,* New York: American Council on Education, 1988.

DEAN, HIGH SCHOOL, the professional (usually a trained guidance counselor) responsible for the general administration of student personnel services in a high school. Social, educational, vocational, and other guidance (including discipline) services are generally a part of his/her responsibilities. The scope and extent of each dean's tasks are determined by individual school districts and/or the administrative structure of the high school.

Reference: C. M. Charles, et al., *Schooling, Teaching, and Learning: American Education,* St. Louis, MO: C. V. Mosby Company, 1978.

DEAN OF EDUCATION, academic officer responsible for the management of a school or college of education. The dean's principal responsibilities include curriculum oversight, recruitment and evaluation of faculty, outreach activities with client school systems, budget management, resource allocation, and contacts with students.

He/she represents the professional school or college at meetings with other higher institution administrators and, usually, at selected national meetings (e.g. annual meeting of the American Association of Colleges of Teacher Education).

The deanship is a nontenured position. The specific title accorded the education dean varies, usually reflecting the local unit's organizational structure. Specific titles include: Dean of Education; Dean, College/School of Education; Dean, Teachers College; Dean, Graduate College/School of Education; or Dean of Professional Studies.

The Dean of Education normally holds professorial rank in one of the college's/school's academic departments and, depending on local needs and practices, may also do some teaching. Names, titles, and office addresses of most deans of education appear in the annual *Directory*, published by the American Association of Colleges of Teacher Education. (See COLLEGE OF EDUCATION.)
References: Edward L. Dejnozka, "The Dean of Education: A Study of Selected Role Norms," *Journal of Teacher Education*, September–October 1978; Daniel E. Griffiths and Donald McCarty (Editors), *The Dilemma of the Deanship*, Danville, IL: The Interstate Printers and Publishers, Inc., 1980; David E. Kapel and Edward L. Dejnozka, "The Education Deanship: A Further Analysis," *Research in Higher Education*, Volume 10, No. 2, 1979.

DEATH EDUCATION, units of study and courses ranging from discussions to formal study of death and dying. Such programs seek to achieve two principal aims: (1) providing factual information about death, and (2) encouraging individuals to express their feelings/fears related to death, thereby increasing their own zest for living. Programs that include both lectures and discussion opportunities facilitate realization of these aims.

Authorities urge that death education be made a part of all school curricula, Kindergarten through college. For young children, the program's aims may be satisfied by incidental instruction such as observing the life cycles of fish and small animals kept in the classroom, current events discussions following the death of prominent persons, and discussions prompted by a death in the family of a class member. Daniel Leviton, a college teacher of death education, classifies his subject matter under three headings: (1) education concerning death and dying; (2) the bereavement process; and (3) suicide and suicide prevention.
References: Early A. Grollman (Editor), *Explaining Death to Children*, Boston: Beacon Press, 1967; Donald P. Irish,

"Death Education: Preparation for Living" in Betty R. Green and Donald P. Irish (Editors), *Death Education: Preparation for Living*, Cambridge, MA: Schenkman Publishing Company, 1971; Daniel Leviton, "The Role of the Schools in Providing Death Education" in Betty R. Green and Donald P. Irish (Editors), *Death Education: Preparation for Living*, Cambridge, MA: Schenkman Publishing Company, 1971; Olle J. Z. Sahler (Editor), *The Child and Death*, St. Louis, MO: The C. V. Mosby Company, 1978.

DEBATE, a discussion procedure in which both sides of an issue (proposition) are presented by two individual debaters or two teams of debaters. Its purpose is to have pro and con arguments presented in an objective manner and for the benefit of listeners or readers. Issues are presented in the form of propositions requiring action (e.g. "*Resolved*, That the legal drinking age should be lowered to 18"). In debating, the team supporting the affirmative position has the burden of proof; the negative (opposing) team normally defends the status quo. Moderators are used to introduce the debaters and, in the absence of timekeepers, are responsible for seeing that individual team members do not exceed the time limits agreed to before the start of the debate. Presentations follow a particular order: first speaker pro, first speaker con, second speaker pro, and so on. After each debater has made his/her presentation, the same order is followed for presentation of rebuttal statements.

In schools, the debate procedure is most frequently used as a language experience or as a means for presenting significant social studies issues. Supporters of the debate as an instructional method indicate that it serves to crystallize an issue, presents both sides objectively, and stimulates interest. Critics cite this method's several weaknesses, key among them being the facts that (1) it involves but a limited number of students, and (2) it stresses "black or white" thinking, with little opportunity for "gray." (See FORENSICS.)
References: Leonard H. Clark and Irving S. Starr, *Secondary School Teaching Methods* (Third Edition), New York: Macmillan Publishing Company, Inc., 1976; Kenneth H. Hoover, *The Professional Teacher's Handbook: A Guide for Improving Instruction in Today's Middle and Secondary Schools* (Abridged Second Edition), Boston: Allyn and Bacon, Inc., 1976; Wayne N. Thompson, *Modern Argumentation and Debate: Principles and Practices*, New York: Harper and Row, Publishers, 1971.

DEBT SERVICE, a budgetary term that refers to those expenditures made by an institution (e.g.

school district) to reduce its long-term indebtedness. It includes payments for principal and interest as well as service charges and similar expenses that are directly related to the retirement of loans. Debt service typically includes indebtedness incurred as the result of land or equipment purchases or the cost of building construction. (See SCHOOL BUDGET.)

References: John E. Corbally, Jr., *School Finance,* Boston: Allyn and Bacon, Inc., 1962; Stephen J. Knezevich and John Guy Fowlkes, *Business Management of Local School Systems,* New York: Harper and Brothers, 1960; Paul L. Reason and Alpheus L. White, *Financial Accounting for Local and State School Systems,* Washington, DC: U.S. Office of Education, 1957.

DECENTRALIZATION, an organizational effort to bring authority for control and management to local (grass roots) levels. E. Mark Hanson defined decentralization "as the delegation of authority over specific decisions to a subunit" (p. 33). Contrasting *decentralization* with its antonym, *centralization,* and relating this pair of terms to education, he observed: "If decision-making authority is concentrated in the hands of the chief school officer, then the organization is said to be centralized; but if such authority is delegated down the ranks of the hierarchy, then decentralization has taken place" (p. 33).

In education, much of the literature dealing with decentralization is presented in the context of school district size. Large systems, notably urban systems with inordinately large enrollments, continue to seek ways to decentralize decision-making authority while retaining overall control at the central office level. New York City, for example, passed a decentralization law in 1969 that created 31 community school boards and assigned limited operating control to each.

Edgar Morphet and associates argued that decentralization should be instituted when the grass roots locus is likely to improve decision-making efficiency. They suggested: "Those things should be decentralized and carried out on a local level which require decisions relating particularly to local needs and which, if done centrally, would prevent or limit desirable initiative and handicap the development of effective local leadership and responsibility" (p. 27).

References: Roald F. Campbell, et al., *The Organization and Control of American Schools* (Fourth Edition), Columbus, OH: Charles E. Merrill Publishing Company, 1980; E. Mark Hanson, *Educational Administration and Organizational Behavior,* Boston: Allyn and Bacon, Inc., 1979; Ralph M. Kimbrough and Michael Y. Nunnery, *Educational Administration: An Introduction,* New York: Macmillan Publishing Company, Inc., 1976; Edgar L. Morphet, et al., *Educational Organization and Administration: Concepts, Practices and Issues,* Englewood Cliffs, NJ: Prentice-Hall, Inc., 1967.

DECIBEL (db), a unit of measure of sound intensity. A decibel is a ratio unit that measures the extent to which the intensity of one sound is different from that of another. A decibel is one-tenth of a bel. A *bel* is a measure that indicates that one sound is ten times greater (or less) than another. Because a logarithmic scale is used, the difference between 10 decibels at the lower end of the scale is much less than 10 decibels at the upper end of the scale. The decibel range for *whispering* is 30 db–20 db; for *conversation,* 68 db–50 db; for *loud sounds,* 100 db–80 db; *very loud,* 110 db–100 db; *discomfort* and *pain,* 110 db and greater.

References: William I. Gardner, *Learning and Behavior Characteristics of Exceptional Children and Youth,* Boston: Allyn and Bacon, Inc., 1977; Helmer R. Myklebust, *The Psychology of Deafness* (Second Edition), New York: Grune and Stratton, 1964.

DECILE, a division of a frequency of scores, observations, cases, or items such that each division contains one-tenth of the scores, observations, and so forth. Since each decile breaks a distribution into ten equal parts, there are only nine points (deciles):

Distribution	1-10	11 - 20	21 - 30	. . . . . .	80	81 - 90	91 - 100
Decile	D_1	D_2	D_3	. . . . . .	D_8	D_9	
Percentile	10th	20th	30th		80th	90th	

Decile

References: Max D. Englehart, *Methods of Educational Research,* Chicago: Rand McNally and Company, 1972; Bruce W. Tuckman, *Conducting Educational Research,* New York: Harcourt Brace Jovanovich, Inc., 1972; Bernard Ostle and Richard W. Menseng, *Statistics in Research* (Third Edition), Ames, IA: The Iowa State University Press, 1975.

DECISION MAKING, a key element of the administrative process that includes not only the act of making decisions but their implementation as well. Daniel Griffiths, well-known theorist in educational administration, identified six steps that, collectively, make up decision making: (1) recognizing, defining, and limiting the problem; (2) analyzing and evaluating the problem; (3) establishing criteria by which possible solutions to the problems are to be evaluated; (4) collecting data; (5) formulating and selecting the preferred solution(s); and (6) implementing the solution preferred. Other students of decision making have identified somewhat different numbers of steps; generally, however, they accord with Griffiths's sequencing.

The decision-making literature of educational administration has been influenced by the writings of noneducators such as Chester Barnard and Herbert Simon. In recent years, researchers in and out of education have been developing decision-making models to help make decision making more scientific, hence offering greater opportunity for compiling research evidence that may suggest effective and/or ineffective administrative practice.

References: Chester I. Barnard, *The Functions of the Executive,* Cambridge, MA: Harvard University Press, 1938; Richard A. Gorton, *School Administration and Supervision: Important Issues, Concepts, and Case Studies* (Second Edition), Dubuque, IA: Wm. C. Brown Company, Publishers, 1980; Daniel E. Griffiths, *Administrative Theory,* New York: Appleton-Century-Crofts, Inc., 1959; Thomas J. Sergiovanni, et al., *Educational Governance and Administration,* Englewood Cliffs, NJ: Prentice-Hall, Inc., 1980; Herbert A. Simon, *Administrative Behavior: A Study of Decision-Making Processes in Administrative Organization* (Second Edition), New York: The Macmillan Company, 1962.

DECLARATION OF THE RIGHTS OF THE CHILD, a document unanimously adopted by the General Assembly of the United Nations on November 20, 1959. The Declaration consists of a Preamble and ten Principles that address concerns such as the child's right to a name and nationality, adequate housing and health, special care if handicapped, and education. The Declaration was adopted by 70 votes to 0, with 2 abstentions.

A forerunner to the *Declaration of the Rights of the Child,* known as the *Declaration of Geneva,* was adopted by the League of Nations on September 26, 1924. It, too, enumerated the rights of the child. (See APPENDIX II: DECLARATION OF THE RIGHTS OF THE CHILD.)

References: David C. Coyle, *The United Nations and How It Works* (Revised Edition), New York: Columbia University Press, 1969; *Yearbook of the United Nations,* New York, 1959.

DECODING, a skill enabling a reader to identify words through a letter-sound relationship or a grapheme-phoneme correspondence. Decoding in and of itself does not imply the comprehension, understanding, or meaning of the word being decoded.

Supporters of the linguistic approach to reading regard decoding as a legitimate activity in the development of reading skills. (See GRAPHEME and PHONEME.)

References: Aaron S. Carton, *Orientation to Reading,* Rowley, MA: Newbury House Publishers, Inc., 1976; William Kottmeyer, *Decoding and Meaning,* New York: McGraw-Hill Book Company, 1974; Christopher Walker, *Teaching Prereading Skills,* London, England: Ward Lock Educational, 1975.

DEDUCTIVE APPROACH, an approach in logic or reasoning that goes from the general to the more specific. Examples of deductive reasoning are Aristotle's syllogisms. They start with two premises (major, minor) that form the base for a conclusion, for example, all humans drink liquids (major), all children are human (minor), therefore all children drink liquids (conclusion).

Children in classrooms can be and are encouraged to use deductive reasoning. When they collect information and form the information into premises, and then use the information to substantiate their conclusions (solve problems), they have employed the deductive approach. (See INDUCTIVE APPROACH.)

References: Ralph E. Martin, Jr., George H. Wood, and Edward W. Stevens, Jr., *An Introduction to Teaching: A Question of Commitment,* Boston: Allyn and Bacon, Inc., 1988; Debold B. Van Dalen and William T. Meyer, *Understanding Educational Research* (Fourth Edition), New York: McGraw-Hill Book Company, 1979.

DE FACTO SEGREGATION, the physical separation or isolation of children belonging to one ethnic, racial, or identifiable group as a result of factors *not* directly attributable to governmental mandates (e.g. rules, policies, laws). Frequently, social, economic, or housing conditions produce enrollment imbalances wherein children from one group are either overrepresented or underrepresented in a school population or in a particular school building. (See DE JURE SEGREGATION.)

References: Kern Alexander, et al., *Public School Law: Cases and Materials,* St. Paul, MN: West Publishing Company, 1969; E. Edmund Reutter, Jr. and Robert R. Hamilton, *The Law of Public Education* (Second Edition), Mineola, NY: The Foundation Press, Inc., 1976.

DEFAMATION OF CHARACTER—See LIBEL and SLANDER

DEFENSE ACTIVITY FOR NON-TRADITIONAL EDUCATION SUPPORT (DANTES), an educational activity that provides support to the voluntary education programs of all U.S. military service personnel. DANTES, headquartered in Pensacola, Florida, and formally administered for the several military services by the Navy, was created in 1974, replacing the U.S. Armed Forces Institute (USAFI).

One of its activities involves coordination of the DANTES Independent Study Support System, a program that makes over 7,000 independent study courses (offered by accredited colleges and universities) available to service personnel interested in working toward a college degree. DANTES also: (1) administers a series of examination programs (e.g. ACT, GED, SAT); (2) maintains an examination recording and reporting system, including USAFI transcripts; (3) administers certification examinations in cooperation with a number of certification organizations (e.g. American Association of Medical Assistants, the Institute for Certification of Computer Professionals); (4) serves as the Defense Department's representative for the contract that operates SOC (Servicemen's Opportunity Colleges); and (5) engages in developmental activities of a liaison nature for the purpose of maximizing nontraditional educational opportunities for service personnel, including those on duty in isolated regions of the world where formal educational programs are not available. (See SERVICEMEN'S OPPORTUNITY COLLEGES.)

References: Independent Study Catalog, Pensacola, FL: Defense Activity for Non-Traditional Education Support, March 1980; *The Mission and Activities of DANTES,* Pensacola, FL: Defense Activity for Non-Traditional Education Support (Brochure), 1980.

DEFICIT, a broad term used in education that has many meanings. The difference between what is expected of a child and what he/she achieves is called a deficit. The degree of deficit is often used to characterize children with learning problems. Deficit can also be used with children who have psychological problems that lead to a deficit in achievement. Deficit may also be used to describe a physical problem. For example, a child may have a sensory deficit (e.g. hearing impaired, visually handicapped). Not all children who have a deficit can be classified as learning disabled, mentally retarded, physically handicapped, nor do they fall within any of the other exceptional child classifications. Some may be underachieving because of poor backgrounds, home problems, lack of motivation, or other like reasons.

When used as a financial term, deficit indicates overspending and means the difference between monies budgeted and the amount actually spent.

References: Maynard C. Reynolds and Jack W. Birch, *Teaching Exceptional Children in all America's Schools,* Reston, VA: The Council for Exceptional Children, 1977; David A. Sabatino and Ted L. Miller (Editors), *Describing Learner Characteristics of Handicapped Children and Youth,* New York: Grune and Stratton, 1979; Edward Zigler and Jeanette Valentine, *Project Head Start,* New York: The Free Press, 1979.

DEGREE MILL, or diploma mill, a derogating term for degree-granting organizations that Robert Reid defined as "certain institutions calling themselves colleges or universities which confer 'quick-way,' usually mail-order, degrees on payment of a fee" (p. 4). Such institutions, Reid pointed out, grant degrees at all levels and fail to require the investment of time, effort, and thought normally associated with bona fide academic degrees.

Diploma mills have been described as having the following common characteristics: (1) untrained, sometimes nonexistent faculties; (2) drastic telescoping of curricula and study time requirements; (3) purported instruction by correspondence; (4) unqualified students; (5) exaggerated catalog descriptions; (6) exaggerated and often fallacious advertising; (7) nonexistent campuses; and (8) unqualified and unethical officers.

The legitimate academic community has persistently sought to eliminate degree mills, often with the assistance of federal agencies (including the U.S. Postal Service), the National Education As-

sociation, state legislatures and state education agencies, and the American Council on Education.
References: Walter C. Eells, *Degrees in Higher Education,* New York: The Center for Applied Research in Education, Inc., 1963; Robert H. Reid, *American Degree Mills: A Study of their Operations and of Existing and Potential Ways to Control Them,* Washington, DC: American Council on Education, 1959.

DEGREES OF FREEDOM (d.f.), a concept used in statistical formulae. Developed in "small-sample statistics," it indicates the number of ways that data can vary, hence the term *freedom:* freedom to vary.

For example, if there are six numbers with a fixed sum of 100, then five could be varied arbitrarily while a sixth number would be set by the sum of the other five in order to keep the fixed sum of 100. In this illustration, the degree of freedom would be five (N − 1) because five numbers could be varied within the restrictions of keeping a fixed sum. Degrees of freedom is related to: independence of sampling; restrictions; and mathematics of the "law of chance." Researchers use d.f. to determine the probability of an event occurring by chance.
References: L. R. Gay, *Educational Research: Competencies for Analysis and Application* (Third Edition), Columbus, OH: Merrill Publishing Company, 1987; David S. Moore and George P. McCabe, *Introduction to the Practice of Statistics,* New York: W. H. Freeman and Company, 1989.

DEGREES, ACADEMIC, titles bestowed by a college or university that attest to satisfactory completion of specific courses of study. The four types of degrees conferred are: (1) *associate degree,* usually granted by a community or junior college (sometimes by four-year institutions) following two years of study; (2) *baccalaureate degree,* normally conferred upon completion of a four-year program of study; (3) *master's degree,* a graduate degree requiring one, sometimes two, years of study; and (4) the *doctor's degree,* the most advanced graduate degree that, depending upon course of study, requires from three to seven years of postbaccalaureate study. (See ASSOCIATE'S DEGREES; BACHELOR'S DEGREE; DOCTOR'S DEGREE; EDUCATIONAL SPECIALIST; and MASTER'S DEGREE.)
References: Asa S. Knowles (Editor), *Handbook of College and University Administration,* New York: McGraw-Hill Book Company, 1970; Asa S. Knowles (Editor), *The International Encyclopedia of Higher Education,* San Francisco: Jossey-Bass Publishers, 1977; Janet A. Mitchell,

Higher Education Exchange: 78-79, Princeton, NJ: J. B. Lippincott Company, 1978.

DEINSTITUTIONALIZATION, a movement (which gained momentum in the 1960s and 1970s) to reduce the number of exceptional persons confined to residential institutions. These institutions provide full-time care away from the home. They include residential schools such as those for the hearing impaired, the visually impaired, and the mentally retarded. The deinstitutionalization movement and mainstreaming gained popularity about the same time.

Alternatives to institutionalization, sometimes referred to as normalization strategies, are being developed to meet the needs of individuals who, until the recent past, had been committed perfunctorily. They include the development of halfway houses that provide needed care in the local community and the use of smaller facilities located closer to the individual's home. (See HALFWAY HOUSE; LEAST RESTRICTIVE ENVIRONMENT; RESIDENTIAL SCHOOL; and SPECIAL EDUCATION PLACEMENT CASCADE.)
References: Daniel P. Hallahan and James M. Kauffman, *Exceptional Children: Introduction to Special Education,* Englewood Cliffs, NJ: Prentice-Hall, Inc., 1978; R. C. Scheerenberger, "Deinstitutionalization in Perspective" in James Paul, et al. (Editors), *Deinstitutionalization,* Syracuse, NY: Syracuse University Press, 1977; Robert M. Smith and John T. Neisworth, *The Exceptional Child: A Functional Approach,* New York: McGraw-Hill Book Company, 1975.

DE JURE SEGREGATION, a legal term characterizing intentional (deliberate) separation of students on the basis of race or ethnic origin. In 1954, the United States Supreme Court rejected the "separate but equal" doctrine and adjudged such segregation to be unconstitutional. (See DE FACTO SEGREGATION and *BROWN v. BOARD OF EDUCATION OF TOPEKA.)*
References: Brown v. Board of Education of Topeka, 347 U.S. 483, 74 S.Ct. 686, 98 L.Ed. 873 (1954) (Case No. 85); *Brown v. Board of Education of Topeka,* 349 U.S. 294, 75 S.Ct. 753, 99 L.Ed. 1083 (1955) (Case No. 86); Leroy J. Peterson, et al., *The Law and Public School Operation* (Second Edition), New York: Harper and Row, Publishers, 1978; E. Edmund Reutter, Jr. and Robert R. Hamilton, *The Law of Public Education* (Second Edition), Mineola, NY: The Foundation Press, Inc., 1976.

DELAYED GRATIFICATION—See GRATIFICATION, DELAY OF

DELAYED SPEECH, or delayed language, sometimes called maturational lag, a form of language disorder. In delayed speech, normal sequences of language development, understanding, and use are: (1) started later than expected; (2) developed slower than expected; or (3) started later with language usage, understanding, and development not progressing at a normal rate.

There are many reasons for delayed speech such as emotional problems, mental retardation, deafness, congenital aphasia, acquired aphasia, autism, and minimal brain dysfunction. Children with delayed speech do have a language handicap. Since there are several possible causes for the handicap, authorities urge teachers and speech pathologists to be careful in the diagnosis and treatment of the speech disorder.

References: Lois Bloom and Margaret Lahey, *Language Development and Language Disorders,* New York: John Wiley and Sons, 1978; Keith E. Nelson (Editor), *Children's Language,* New York: Gardner Press, Inc., 1978; William H. Perkins, *Speech Pathology: An Applied Behavioral Science* (Second Edition), St. Louis, MO: The C. V. Mosby Company, 1977.

DELEGATION, in formal organizations, the conferring of specified authority by a superior to a subordinate. Operationally, the subordinates to whom authority has been delegated are expected to use their own judgment in carrying out tasks or solving problems that fall within the purview of their duties. Final responsibility for the manner in which this judgment is carried out, however, remains with the supervisor who did the delegating. The amount of delegation that takes place in an organization is usually related to organization size and complexity. Critics of delegation contend that its wide usage produces organizational rigidity and serves to restrain the creative potential of the organization's members.

Uncertainty about when to delegate and/or anxiety about relinquishing duties keeps some administrators from delegating to their own subordinates.

References: Wallazz B. Eaton, "Democratic Organization: Myth or Reality," *Bulletin of National Association of Secondary School Principals,* October 1961; Richard A. Gorton, *School Administration: Challenge and Opportunity for Leadership,* Dubuque, IA: Wm. C. Brown Company, Publishers, 1977.

DELPHI TECHNIQUE, originally a prediction technique. Today, it is an approach used to arrive at a level of agreement and not just for prediction purposes. The technique is systematic and requires individuals, in isolation, to respond to a group of statements (usually by mail). Several rounds of statements are presented. In the first round, participants are requested to respond to statements, problems, or goals. Each respondent is then given a controlled summary indicating how other participants responded. They are then asked to revise their own opinions or ratings; subsequently, they are again given a controlled summary. These steps are repeated until a general consensus of opinion is developed. The approach was developed by the RAND Corporation in 1969.

References: Harold A. Linstone and Murray Turoff (Editors), *The Delphi Method: Techniques and Applications,* Reading, MA: Addison-Wesley Publishing Company, 1975; Weldon F. Zenger and Sharon K. Zenger, *Curriculum Development: At the Local Level,* Saratoga, CA: R and E Publishers, 1986.

DELTA PI EPSILON (DPE), graduate fraternity in business education. The organization's first chapter was founded in 1936 at New York University. By 1976, the fraternity had 75 active chapters and a total membership of 19,000. DPE's headquarters is located on the campus of Gustavus Adolphus College, St. Peter, Minnesota. Two of the fraternity's better known publications are *Business Education Index* and a research quarterly, *Delta Pi Epsilon Journal.*

Reference: John Robson (Editor), *Baird's Manual of American College Fraternities* (Nineteenth Edition), Menasha, WI: Baird's Manual Foundation, Inc., 1977.

DEMOCRATIC-AUTOCRATIC LEADERSHIP STYLES, distinctive and contrasting forms of leader behavior. The terms *democratic leadership* and *autocratic leadership,* along with *laissez-faire leadership,* were made popular as the result of research findings reported by Kurt Lewin, Ronald Lippitt, and Ralph White. They represent points on a continuum, with effectiveness depending on the situation.

As part of their study, completed in 1938 at the University of Iowa, the investigators organized young boys into hobby clubs. Each club consisted of five boys, led by adults who, by design, exhibited different leadership styles. Trained observers found that the groups responded differently to each of the three leadership styles noted above.

Boys experiencing *democratic leadership* responded well to their leadership. Morale, work quality and similar factors were high. *Autocratic leadership* resulted in high productivity. However, it also precipitated resistance, lower morale, and greater dependency. The last style, *laissez-faire* (middle position), appeared to produce indecision, frustration, and relatively poorer work. (See AUTOCRATIC LEADERSHIP and DEMOCRATIC LEADERSHIP.)

References: Kurt Lewin, et al., "Patterns of Aggressive Behavior in Experimentally Created 'Social Climates,' " *Journal of Social Psychology*, Volume X, 1939; Donald E. Orlosky, et al., *Educational Administration Today*, Columbus, OH: Charles E. Merrill Publishing Company, 1984; Charles L. Wood, Everett W. Nicholson, and Dale G. Findley, *The Secondary School Principal: Manager and Supervisor* (Second Edition), Boston: Allyn and Bacon, Inc., 1985.

DEMOCRATIC LEADERSHIP, a characterization of leadership that involves behavioral elements such as group decision making and the recognition of group authority. The democratic school administrator makes frequent use of committees and advisory bodies on which faculty members, parents, and/or students may serve. An assumption underlying such participatory management is the notion that *those who share, care*.

The idea of democratic administration began to be widely promoted among school administrators in the 1930s. Conversely, autocratic leadership was increasingly criticized as a leadership style that had little place in the schools if only because it was alien to the concept of democracy.

In 1939, Kurt Lewin and his colleagues reported on their study of autocratic, democratic, and laissez-faire leadership styles.

After reviewing the research evidence dealing with democratic vs. autocratic supervision, Ralph Stogdill concluded that neither appears to have an advantage with respect to productivity. However, he added, satisfaction of group members is associated with the democratic leadership style. (See AUTOCRATIC LEADERSHIP and DEMOCRATIC-AUTOCRATIC LEADERSHIP STYLES.)

References: Ralph B. Kimbrough and Michael Y. Nunnery, *Educational Administration: An Introduction*, New York: Macmillan Publishing Company, Inc., 1976; Kurt Lewin, et al., "Patterns of Aggressive Behavior in Experimentally Created 'Social Climates,' " *Journal of Social Psychology*, Volume X, 1939; Ralph M. Stogdill, *Handbook of Leadership: A Survey of Theory and Research*, New York: The Free Press, 1974; Charles L. Wood, Everett W. Nicholson, and Dale G. Findley, *The Secondary School Prin-*

cipal: Manager and Supervisor (Second Edition), Boston: Allyn and Bacon, Inc., 1985.

DEMOGRAPHY, a study of the changes and distribution of populations over time. Included are the areas of fertility, mortality, marriage, migration, and social mobility. Demography is a highly mathematical and statistical field of study, for its purpose is to describe trends as well as the present. Census data are used in the discipline of demography. This fact makes it extremely important in education for the planning of new schools, the closing of others, making changes in school curriculum as a function of changes in society or changes in the population served, funding and taxing for school support, transportation routes, and changes in the needs of business and industry.

References: Bernard Benjamin, *Demographic Analysis,* New York: Praeger Publishers, 1969; Donald J. Bogue, *Principles of Demography*, New York: John Wiley and Sons, 1969.

DENASALITY—See NASAL

DENOTATION, a reading term that refers to the *literal* or *actual meaning* of a word. For example, the word *fat* means too much fatty tissue. This definition is the denotative meaning of the word. In contrast, the cultural, social, or personal negative value placed on the word *fat* is its *connotative meaning.*

References: Dolores Durkin, *Teaching Young Children to Read* (Third Edition), Boston: Allyn and Bacon, Inc., 1980; Dianne Lapp and James Flood, *Teaching Reading to Every Child*, New York: Macmillan Publishing Company, Inc., 1978; Walter T. Petty and Julie M. Jensen, *Developing Children's Language*, Boston: Allyn and Bacon, Inc., 1980; Harry Singer and Dan Donlan, *Reading and Learning from Text*, Boston: Little, Brown and Company, 1980.

DENTAL APTITUDE TEST—See MEDICAL COLLEGE ADMISSIONS TEST

DEONTOLOGY, the study of duty or obligation. It is a science or theory of ethics that distinguishes duty from the traditional philosophical considerations of rightness vs. wrongness. The deontologist reasons that one does something out of a sense of duty or obligation rather than for reasons of morality. One of the first to have used the term was Jeremy Bentham. The philosophies of Immanuel Kant and David (William) Ross were deontological in approach.

Deontology is the opposite of axiological ethics. (See AXIOLOGY and ETHICS.)

References: Héctor-Neri Castoñeda, *Thinking and Doing: The Philosophical Foundations of Institutions,* Dordrecht, Holland: D. Reidel Publishing Company, 1975; James H. Hyslop, "Deontology" in James Hastings (Editor), *Encyclopedia of Religion and Ethics* (Volume IV), New York: Scribner's, 1924; Ralph G. Ross, *Obligation,* Ann Arbor, MI: University of Michigan Press, 1970; Georg Henrik von Wright, *An Essay in Deontic Logic and the General Theory of Action,* Amsterdam, Holland: North-Holland Publishing, 1968; George B. Wall, *Introduction to Ethics,* Columbus, OH: Charles E. Merrill Publishing Company, 1974.

DEPARTMENTALIZATION, a method of organizing the school, college, or university and its respective curricula into different subject areas (e.g. mathematics, English, physical education, art, music, social studies, and home economics) with teachers who are subject specialists assigned to each. In elementary and secondary schools, departments usually cross grade levels (e.g. teachers assigned to the art department will teach art to students from several grades).

Departmentalization began as a means of developing teacher specialization since teachers trained in the early 1900s often did not have the competencies to teach several subjects. As mass education developed and more subjects were added to the curriculum to meet the needs of high school and junior high school students, the popularity of departmentalization increased. Departmentalization by subject area is found most commonly in high schools and institutions of higher education. In fewer cases is departmentalization found in the elementary schools. (See CORE PROGRAM and DUAL PROGRESS PLAN.)

References: Rudyard K. Bent and Adolph Unrich, *Secondary School Curriculum,* Lexington, MA: D. C. Heath and Company, 1969; John H. Hansen and Arthur C. Hearn, *The Middle School Program,* Chicago: Rand McNally and Company, 1971; William Van Til, *Education: A Beginning* (Second Edition), Boston: Houghton Mifflin Company, 1974.

DEPARTMENT CHAIRPERSON, also known as department head or department chair, leader of a secondary school, college, or university academic department. The specific duties associated with this position, although variable, generally subsume three basic forms of responsibility: (1) personnel supervision; (2) curriculum development; and (3) services administration. Department chairpersons are concurrently leaders of their respective departments, members of an administrative team (which includes all other chairs and the principal or college dean), and subordinates of the principal or college dean. Some are appointed by their school's chief administrator, others (particularly those serving in institutions of higher education) are likely to be elected and/or recommended by departmental faculty members. In some cases, chairs serve for a fixed period (e.g. three-year terms); in others, the appointment is continuous. In most instances, chairs also do some teaching.

Thomas Sergiovanni identified a lengthy list of criteria that should be considered when assessing a secondary school chairperson's behavior. Examples follow: (1) chair has confidence and trust in teachers; (2) seeks teachers' ideas and opinions; (3) respects the competencies and abilities of individuals; and (4) encourages teachers to share information with others.

Some research indicates that chairs, especially in colleges and universities, may occasionally encounter difficulty in reconciling their roles as advocates for faculty members with their obligations to their own immediate superiors. Other research indicates that the role of the chair varies with type of department.

References: Michael G. Callahan, *The Effective School Department Head,* West Nyack, NY: Parker Publishing Company, Inc., 1971; David E. Kapel and Edward L. Dejnozka, "The Education Deanship: A Further Analysis," *Research in Higher Education,* Volume 10, No. 2, 1979; Thomas J. Sergiovanni, *Handbook for Effective Department Leadership: Concepts and Practices in Today's Secondary Schools,* Boston: Allyn and Bacon, Inc., 1977; John C. Smart and Charles F. Elton, "Administrative Roles of Department Chairmen" in John C. Smart and James R. Montgomery (Editors), *Examining Departmental Management,* San Francisco: Jossey-Bass Publishers, 1976.

DEPENDENTS' SCHOOLS, elementary and secondary schools that provide K–12 education for eligible minor dependents of U.S. military and civilian personnel who are stationed overseas. Responsibility for maintaining these schools was, until recently, vested in the U.S. Department of Defense. In 1981, it was under transition into the newly created Department of Education.

The dependents' schools were recently organized into a formal system per mandate of Congress (Public Law 95–561). The system, staffed primarily by civilians, serves almost 140,000 students in 23 countries. Another 2,600 students are enrolled in tuition-fee schools where dependents' schools do not exist. As part of the new system, considerable decentralization of authority (to the school principals) has been taking place and a coordinated, systematic curriculum is in the process of being developed.

The Office of Dependents Schools has a central office staff headquartered in Alexandria, Virginia, with six regional offices: Atlantic; Germany, North; Germany, South; Mediterranean; Pacific; and Panama.

References: Five-Year Curriculum Development Plan, Washington, DC: Department of Defense Dependents Schools, September 24, 1979; *Report to the Congress on the Organization of the Dependents' Education System*, Washington, DC: Department of Defense Dependents Schools, Undated: *Summary of Programs*, Washington, DC: Department of Defense Dependents Schools, April 1980.

DERIVED SCORES, scores that are based on the performance of a particular sample that is used as a norm. Age-equivalent and grade-equivalent scores are derived scores, as are standard scores. When a raw score is expressed in relative terms for a normative group, the normative term used is a derived score. For example, if a raw score (68) on a test is converted to a grade-equivalent score (3.6), the raw score will be the average score for a child in the third grade, sixth month; the grade-equivalent score, in this illustration, is the derived score. (See AGE-EQUIVALENT SCALES/SCORES and GRADE-EQUIVALENT SCALES.)

References: Anne Anastasi, *Psychological Testing* (Sixth Edition), New York: Macmillan Publishing Company, 1988; George K. Cunningham, *Educational and Psychological Measurement*, New York: Macmillan Publishing Company, 1986.

DESCHOOLING, a philosophical idea developed by some critics of current, institutionalized education to discontinue existing school systems and to supplant them with alternative approaches that: (1) are more imaginative and humanistic, and (2) provide free choice for the learner. Ivan Illich, one of the critics, bemoaned the fact that schools teach students to become overly dependent on their teachers, the system, and other institutions. He proposed greater freedom of educational choice for individuals as an alternative. John Holt, another supporter of deschooling, has echoed this sentiment: "We must look beyond the question of reforming schools and at the larger question of schools and schooling itself.... Are they the best means of doing it? What might be other or better ways?" (p. 5).

The concept of deschooling is consonant with many of the educational ideas propounded earlier by Emerson and Rousseau. Much of the recent interest in the concept is attributable to dissatisfaction with current education, particularly its re-

ported failure to reach poor minority children. (See ALTERNATIVE EDUCATION.)

References: George Henderson, *Introduction to American Education: A Human Relations Approach*, Norman, OK: University of Oklahoma Press, 1978; John Holt, *Freedom and Beyond*, New York: E. P. Dutton, 1972; Ivan Illich, *Deschooling Society*, New York: Harper and Row, Publishers, 1974.

DESEGREGATION, a term used to describe the bringing together of different groups (racial, religious, social class, ethnic) where previously they had been separated, sometimes as the result of deliberate segregation.

In the famous *Brown v. Board of Education of Topeka* decisions of 1954 and 1955, the U.S. Supreme Court ruled that separate educational facilities are inherently unequal and instructed school districts with racially segregated schools to desegregate them with all deliberate speed. Various techniques have been used to bring about racial desegregation of the schools. Magnet schools, school pairing, and busing are illustrative. Still, principally as a result of housing patterns, many schools remain racially segregated.

Desegregation should not be confused with integration. Integration is extremely difficult to achieve for it seeks to bring about moral and social interaction of groups based on freedom and equity; it is not physical per se. Desegregation, on the other hand, seeks to bring groups together physically. Integration begins with desegregation and moves beyond that point. (See *BROWN v. BOARD OF EDUCATION OF TOPEKA;* BUSING; MAGNET SCHOOL; and PRINCETON PLAN.)

References: Harold B. Gerard and Norman Miller, *School Desegregation*, New York: Plenum Press, 1975; Norene Harris, et al., *The Integration of American Schools*, Boston: Allyn and Bacon, Inc., 1975; Anna Holden, *The Bus Stops Here*, New York: Agathon Press, Inc., 1974; Willis D. Hawley (Editor), *Effective School Desegregation: Equity, Quality, and Feasibility*, Beverly Hills, CA: Sage Publications, 1981; Clifford P. Hooker, "Issues in School Desegregation Litigation" in Clifford P. Hooker (Editor), *The Courts and Education* (NSSE 77th Yearbook, Part I), Chicago: University of Chicago Press, 1978.

DETENTION, a form of discipline (punishment) used in school. It involves keeping students under supervision for an extra period, usually after class or at the end of the regular school day, and often in a particular place such as a classroom or detention hall. Students are normally expected to do schoolwork during the detention period. Detentions are usually used as punishment for minor disciplinary infractions.

Although not as prevalent in today's schools as in former ones, detention rooms or detention halls can still be found in some schools. Authorities do not consider the use of detentions to be consonant with positive classroom management and discipline.

References: William C. Bagley, *School Discipline,* New York: The Macmillan Company, 1976; Daniel L. Duke and Adrienne M. Meckel, *Managing Student Behavior Problems,* New York: Teachers College Press, 1980; Clifford H. Sweat, et al., *Discipline in the Junior High/Middle School,* Danville, IL: The Interstate Printers and Publishers, Inc., 1976; Elizabeth H. Weiner (Editor), *Discipline in the Classroom* (Second Edition), Washington, DC: National Education Association, 1980.

DETROIT CASE—See *MILLIKEN v. BRADLEY*

DETROIT X-Y-Z PLAN, a homogeneous grouping plan developed for the Detroit Public Schools by Dr. Charles Berry in 1919. The plan placed elementary school children into one of three groups based on intelligence and achievement tests. Those in the "X" group were children who scored in the top 20 percent of the class. The next 60 percent of the children were placed in the "Y" group. Those in the lowest 20 percent were assigned to the "Z" group. (See ABILITY GROUPING.)

References: Warren G. Findley and Miriam M. Bryan, *Ability Grouping: 1970 Status, Impact and Alternatives,* Athens, GA: Center for Educational Improvement, University of Georgia, 1971; Anne Morgenstern, *Grouping in the Elementary School,* New York: Pitman Publishing Corporation, 1966; Herbert H. Ryan, *Ability Grouping in the Junior High School,* New York: Harcourt, Brace and Company, 1927; Alfred Yates, *Grouping in Education,* New York: John Wiley and Sons, 1966.

DEVELOPING INSTITUTION, a college or university (public or private) that, for financial or other reasons, is struggling for survival and that is not in the academic mainstream of higher education. Title III of Public Law 89-329, otherwise known as the Higher Education Act of 1965, defined a developing institution as one that: (1) admits graduates of secondary schools; (2) offers two-and/or four-year degree programs; (3) is accredited by a nationally recognized accrediting agency; (4) has been established (in accordance with the foregoing) for at least five years; (5) is

making an effort to improve its teaching and administrative staffs as well as its student services; (6) "is, for financial or other reasons, struggling for survival and is isolated from the main currents of academic life" (p. 1229); (7) meets such other requirements as the Commissioner of Education may want to impose; and (8) does not prepare persons for the ministry or related fields. The act, through provision of grants, authorized activities such as faculty or student exchanges, faculty and administration improvement programs, the introduction of new curricula, and cooperative programs involving joint use of facilities. Fellowships were also made available to encourage able graduate students and other qualified persons to teach at developing institutions.

Between 1976 and 1977, an estimated $700,000,000 was awarded to approximately 800 institutions under the provisions of the act. Congressional criticism of the program was voiced in 1979 for several reasons, a principal one being that none of the participating institutions had graduated from Title III.

References: Lorenzo Middleton, "U.S. Program for Developing Colleges is Subject to Two Major Investigations," *The Chronicle of Higher Education,* October 29, 1979; Public Law 89-329, *United States Statutes at Large: 1965* (Volume 79), Washington, DC: U.S. Government Printing Office, 1966.

DEVELOPMENTAL AGE, or behavioral age, the level of behavioral maturity reached by a child. It is also the normative behavior expected at a given age level. Although related to physical maturity and chronological age, developmental age may not always be correlative with them. For example, a child may be six years old but is functioning at the developmental level equivalent to that of a typical five-year-old. Also, it is not based on any particular area of behavior. Developmental age is considered by some to be a better measure than chronological age as an entrance criterion for selected activities such as starting school.

Francis Ilg, Arnold Gesell, and others have done a considerable amount of research in this area at the Gesell Institute, Yale University. They found that two, five, and ten are developmental ages where there is considerable equilibrium in the child. That is, the child has little difficulty either internally or externally; he/she is not as withdrawn and as afraid of strangers as at other developmental ages and is outgoing and amiably adjusted.

References: Arnold L. Gesell, et al., *Child Development,*

New York: Harper and Row, Publishers, 1949; Arnold L. Gesell, et al., *The Child from Five to Ten* (Revised Edition), New York: Harper and Row, Publishers, 1977; Francis L. Ilg and Louise B. Ames, *Child Behavior,* New York: Harper and Row, Publishers, 1966; Francis L. Ilg and Louise B. Ames, *School Readiness* (New Edition), New York: Harper and Row, Publishers, 1972.

DEVELOPMENTAL APHASIA—See APHASIA

DEVELOPMENTAL READING, a systematic program in which each individual maximizes his/her abilities and skills to approach the limit of his/her ability to learn to read. The program requires that a master plan be developed. This plan must include specific objectives; instructional modes, materials, and sundry learning experiences must also be indicated. Articulation of experiences and the coordination of instruction is necessary to develop a viable developmental reading plan.

Because the goals of such plans are addressed to individual learners, the emphasis of specific plans may not be the same for any two readers. The overall plan may include the following instructional elements: *developmental,* sequential development of reading skills; *corrective,* provides diagnosis and corrective teaching; *accelerated,* enrichment and challenge for able students; *adapted,* for slow learners; and *remedial,* for those with reading disabilities. (See REMEDIAL READING.)
References: Albert J. Harris and Edward R. Sipay, *How to Increase Reading Ability* (Eighth Edition), New York: Longman, Inc., 1985; Harry Singer and Dan Donlan, *Reading and Learning from Text* (Second Edition), Hillsdale, NJ: Lawrence Erlbaum Associates, Publishers, 1989.

DEVELOPMENTAL TASKS, those tasks or behaviors that are appropriate for a particular developmental stage of a child or learner. These were defined by Robert Havighurst as those tasks that arise at a certain period of development such that successful completion hopefully leads to happiness and further success with later tasks; failure leads to unhappiness and later difficulties. Developmental tasks have their base in the developmental principles of Havighurst, Jean Piaget, Lawrence Kohlberg, and other psychologists.

Since developmental psychology is based on a sequence of maturation, developmental tasks are also sequential and have various levels of difficulty and complexity. Developmental tasks should help a learner progress from one level of development to another. For example, those tasks or behaviors that a child performs while in Stage I (sensory-motor intelligence, birth to two years) are less complex when compared to activities faced by a more mature child in Stage IV.
References: Henry Dupont, *Educating Emotionally Disturbed Children* (Second Edition), New York: Holt, Rinehart and Winston, Inc., 1975; Robert J. Havighurst, *Developmental Tasks and Education* (Third Edition), New York: Longman, Inc., 1972; Lester Mann and David A. Sabatino (Editors), *The Third Review of Special Education,* New York: Grune and Stratton, 1976; George T. Mouly, *Psychology for Effective Teaching,* New York: Holt, Rinehart and Winston, Inc., 1973; David A. Sabatino and Ted L. Miller (Editors), *Describing Learner Characteristics of Handicapped Children and Youth,* New York: Grune and Stratton, 1979.

DEVELOPMENTAL THEORIES, theories that hold that individuals pass through various stages of development. Each stage has particular characteristics that are considered to be *normal* and *expected.* These theories are rarely predicated on chronological age per se. Rather, they are based on maturation and/or experience and tend to be hierarchical in nature. Most have evolved as products of prior research and observations.

The theories developed by Jean Piaget, Lawrence Kohlberg, and John Dewey are examples of developmental theories. (See DEVELOPMENTAL AGE; DEWEY, JOHN B.; MORAL DEVELOPMENT; and PIAGET, JEAN.)
References: Elizabeth B. Hurlock, *Child Development* (Sixth Edition), New York: McGraw-Hill Book Company, 1978; Paul H. Mussen, et al., *Child Development and Personality* (Fourth Edition), New York: Harper and Row, Publishers, 1974; Jean Piaget, *The Origins of Intelligence in Children,* New York: International Universities Press, 1962; Edna K. Shapiro and Evelyn Weber (Editors), *Cognitive and Affective Growth: Developmental Interaction,* Hillsdale, NJ: Lawrence Erlbaum Associates, Publishers, 1981.

DEVELOPMENT OFFICE, an administrative office in a college or university that is responsible for institutional fund-raising. The individual in charge of this office is commonly referred to as a development officer. Given the increasingly significant role played by development officers, many have been given status titles (e.g., vice-president) to indicate the relative importance ascribed to this particular activity.

Jack R. Bohlen enumerated several functions associated with the development office. They include: fund-raising, annual giving, capital appeals, deferred giving, foundation development, and corporation support. To implement these functions successfully, Richard Cheshire suggested, requires development officers to possess four skills: (1) education; (2) organization; (3) communication; and (4) marketing.

References: Jack R. Bohlen, "The Development Office—Organization, Policies, and Standards" in Asa S. Knowles (Editor), *Handbook of College and University Administration: General*, New York: McGraw-Hill Book Company, 1970; Richard D. Cheshire, "The State of the Art" in A. Westley Rowland (Editor), *Handbook of Institutional Advancement*, San Francisco: Jossey-Bass Publishers, 1977; Eugene M. Repucci, Jr., "Development, College and University" in Asa S. Knowles (Editor), *The International Encyclopedia of Higher Education* (Volume 4), San Francisco: Jossey-Bass Publishers, 1977.

DEVIATION, a term having many meanings, depending on context and subject. In statistics, deviation is the distance between (or from) one point and another. For example, the distance (difference) of a score below or above a mean is the "deviation from the mean." In sociology, the term was at one time used to describe behavior that was abnormal (i.e. not consistent with the norms of society). Behaviors that broke socially acceptable rules (e.g. homosexual behavior, mental disorders, alcoholism, certain crimes) were judged in absolute terms. Today, deviant behavior is more difficult to define because of changes in normative rules.

Deviance can occur in: intellectual ability, motor skills, personality, sensory skills, attitudes, or in any combination of these. Exceptional children normally suffer from a particular deviance from the norm.

References: H. Taylor Buckner, *Deviance, Reality, and Change*, New York: Random House, Inc., 1971; Marshall B. Clinard, *Sociology of Deviant Behavior* (Fourth Edition), New York: Holt, Rinehart and Winston, Inc., 1974; Jonathan L. Freedman and Anthony N. Doob, *Deviancy: The Psychology of Being Different*, New York: Academic Press, 1968; Charles W. Telford and James M. Sawrey, *The Exceptional Individual*, Englewood Cliffs, NJ: Prentice-Hall, Inc., 1972.

DEVIATION I.Q., a standard score that is based on a mean of 100 and a standard deviation that is approximately 16. Deviation I.Q. scores use the measures (mean, standard deviation) of the Stanford-Binet I.Q. test score distributions as their base.

Many distributions of scores of new intelligence tests do not have means of 100 (they may be 60, 90, 130) and standard deviations of 16. To compare scores from one test with those of other tests, the scores are converted to a standard score (mean = 100, s.d. = 16). This conversion, called a deviation I.Q., allows for interpretation by comparing results and levels with other tests. Deviation I.Q. scores are not intelligence test scores as such; rather, they are calculated as standard scores. However, the initial score, before standard score conversion, is derived from an intelligence test, hence the term *deviation I.Q.* (See STANDARD DEVIATION and STANDARD SCORES.)

References: Anne Anastasi, *Psychological Testing* (Sixth Edition), New York: Macmillan Publishing Company, Inc., 1988; Lee J. Cronbach, *Essentials of Psychological Testing* (Fourth Edition), New York: Harper and Row, Publishers, 1984.

DEWEY DECIMAL CLASSIFICATION, a library classification system used in most American school and public libraries. It was first published in 1876 by Melvil Dewey, its creator, and has been revised numbers of times since then. The system was adopted widely, primarily because of its simplicity.

The Dewey Decimal Classification system arranges all knowledge into ten broad classifications, or "classes." One-digit numbers, beginning with "0," are assigned to each class. They are: 0, General Works; 1, Philosophy (including psychology); 2, Religion; 3, Social Sciences; 4, Philology; 5, Natural (Pure) Sciences; 6, Useful Arts (including medicine, agriculture, business and industry); 7, Fine Arts; 8, Literature; and 9, History (including geography and biography).

Each class is divided into ten subclasses known as "divisions." The divisions, in turn, are subdivided into ten "sections." Thus, the basic classification system actually consists of three-digit whole numbers each of which has a very specific meaning (e.g. 630, agriculture; 632, plant diseases and pests; 636, production of livestock and domestic animals). Decimals may be added, ad infinitum, to each three-digit number to refine classifications further (e.g. 631.586, dry farming).

Although the Library of Congress Classification system is used in many university and other large libraries, the Dewey Decimal Classification system is the one most widely used in the world. (See DEWEY, MELVIL and LIBRARY OF CONGRESS CLASSIFICATION.)

References: Benjamin A. Custer, "Dewey Decimal

Classification" in Allen Kent and Harold Lancour (Editors), *Encyclopedia of Library and Information Science* (Volume 7), New York: Marcel Dekker, Inc., 1972; Thomas Landau (Editor), *Encyclopedia of Librarianship* (Second Revised Edition), New York: Hafner Publishing Company, 1961.

DEWEY, JOHN B. (October 20, 1859–June 2, 1952), prominent educator, philosopher, and psychologist. Before joining the University of Chicago faculty as Chairman of its Philosophy and Education Department (1894–1904), Dewey taught at the Universities of Michigan and Minnesota. He became Professor of Philosophy at Columbia University (1904) and remained there until his retirement in 1930.

Dewey was perhaps best known as the articulate proponent of progressive education. He was also a preeminent philosopher. His writings and teachings did much to shape the direction of American public education during the first half of the 20th century.

Among his better known works were: *How We Think* (1910); *Democracy and Education* (1916); *Experience and Nature* (1925); *Art as Experience* (1934); and *The Quest for Certainty* (1939).

An activist as well as a scholar, Dewey was involved in numbers of other efforts: founder of the New School for Social Research; an organizer of the first teacher union in New York City; President of the American Psychological Association (1899–1900) and the American Philosophical Society (1905–6); and honorary Vice-President of the New York State Liberal Party. The John Dewey Society, a professional education organization, was named in his honor.

References: George Dykhuizen, *The Life and Mind of John Dewey*, Carbondale, IL: Southern Illinois University Press, 1973; Jerome E. Leavitt, "Dewey, John B." in John F. Ohles (Editor), *Biographical Dictionary of American Educators* (Volume 1), Westport, CT: Greenwood Press, 1978; Adolphe E. Meyer, *Grandmasters of Educational Thought*, New York: McGraw-Hill Book Company, 1975.

DEWEY, MELVIL (December 10, 1851–December 26, 1931), an American, creator of the decimal classification system for libraries that continues to bear his name. Dewey graduated from Amherst College in 1874. While a student, he worked in the college's library and remained there after graduation, quickly becoming its Acting Director.

After studying his institution's library, and following numbers of visits to other libraries, he determined to develop an efficient, standardized system for classifying library holdings. This became known as The Decimal Classification System, developed by Dewey with the assistance of Amherst faculty members and with the endorsement of the Amherst Library Committee. It was described in his publication *A Classification and Subject Index for Cataloging and Arranging the Books and Pamphlets of a Library* (1876).

Dewey left Amherst in 1876 and helped found the American Library Association in the same year. He served as ALA's Secretary for 14 years, then became its President.

Dewey served as Librarian of Columbia College (Columbia University) from 1883 to 1889. He moved the school to Albany, N.Y., following a disagreement with Columbia's trustees, renaming it the New York State Library School. He later became State Librarian in New York. Toward the end of his career, he promoted traveling libraries to serve small communities and worked to give female librarians full and equal status within the library profession. (See DEWEY DECIMAL CLASSIFICATION.)

References: Winifred B. Linderman, "Dewey, Melvil" in Allen Kent and Harold Lancour (Editors), *Encyclopedia of Library and Information Science* (Volume 7), New York: Marcel Dekker, Inc., 1972; Fremont Rider, *Melvil Dewey*, Chicago: American Library Association, 1944.

DEXTRALITY—See SINISTRAL

DIACRITICAL MARKS, or diacritic marks, keys used to indicate how a word is to be pronounced. They are most frequently found in dictionaries but may vary from one dictionary to the next. The teaching of diacritical marks is normally taught as part of the language arts dictionary skills. A few examples of diacritical marks follow: ā, as in day; ä, as in art; and, yə, as in ammunition.

Reference: Paul S. Anderson and Diane Lapp, *Language Skills in Elementary Education* (Third Edition), New York: Macmillan Publishing Company, Inc., 1979.

DIAGNOSTIC-PRESCRIPTIVE TEACHING, a teaching approach that includes the assessing of a learning and/or behavioral problem as well as a defined and planned approach to its solution. It is an individualized approach, based on the individual and unique needs of the learner.

Both formal (e.g. psychological assessments, educational tests, school histories) and informal (e.g. observations, teacher opinions) methods of evaluation and assessment are used as part of the *diagnostic segment* of the approach. The *prescription* depends on the diagnosis. Resources, physical arrangements of the classroom, teacher skills, and other factors likely to affect the educational/learning program are considered when individual prescriptions are developed. Various teaching methods (behavior modification, mastery teaching, etc.) may be used as part of the prescriptive segment. Often, teachers, parents, school psychologists, resource teachers, and other professionals are involved in the development and implementation of teaching prescriptions.

Diagnostic-prescriptive teaching is used extensively, though not exclusively, with exceptional children. (See INDIVIDUAL EDUCATION PLAN and INDIVIDUALLY PRESCRIBED INSTRUCTION.)

References: Albert J. Harris and Edward R. Sipay, *How to Increase Reading Ability* (Eighth Edition), New York: Longman, Inc., 1985; John Jarolimek and Clifford D. Foster, *Teaching and Learning in the Elementary School* (Third Edition), New York: Macmillan Publishing Company, 1985; Colleen J. Mandell and Edward Fiscus, *Understanding Exceptional People*, St. Paul, MN: West Publishing Company, 1981; John Stellern, et al., *Introduction to Diagnostic-Prescriptive Teaching and Programming*, Glen Ridge, NJ: Exceptional Press, 1976.

DIAGNOSTIC TESTS, instruments used in education that identify an individual's particular strengths and weaknesses. They enable the teacher to isolate areas of need and to develop whatever program of remediation the learner may require.

There are many problems associated with diagnostic tests. For example, some are not reliable; some are too short. These test scores should not be seen as constituting the sole measures of a child's strength or weakness; rather, they should be considered along with other factors when developing a program for him/her. The most common diagnostic tests found in schools are those used in reading and arithmetic (e.g. Stanford Diagnostic Reading Test, Stanford Diagnostic Arithmetic Test).

References: Anne Anastasi, *Psychological Testing* (Sixth Edition), New York: Macmillan Publishing Company, Inc., 1988; Lee J. Cronbach, *Essentials of Psychological Testing* (Fourth Edition), New York: Harper and Row, Publishers, 1984; William A. Mehrens and Irvin J. Lehmann, *Using Standardized Tests in Education*, New York: Longman Inc., 1987.

DIAGRAMMING SENTENCES, a teaching technique employed by some teachers of grammar, especially during the early decades of the 20th century. The technique utilizes diagrams that indicate, visually, the parts of a sentence and their syntactic relationships. An example, using *traditional diagramming,* appears below for the sentence: "The girl threw the ball into the street": Another approach makes use of so-called branching tree diagrams.

Research shows that diagramming, when taught to children, does little to improve either their writing skills or their understanding of syntax. It also reveals that diagramming was originally used to teach Latin and was later employed as an aid to English instruction.

References: John F. Savage, *Effective Communication: Language Arts Instruction in the Elementary School,* Chicago: Science Research Associates, Inc., 1977; J. Stephen Sherwin, *Four Problems in Teaching English: A Critique of Research,* Scranton, PA: International Textbook Company (For the National Council of Teachers of English), 1969.

DIAL-ACCESS SYSTEM, or direct-access, a system developed for computers to allow an individual, using the central processing unit, to enter data, to change records, or to make use of specific data stored on tapes, drums, magnetic cards, or magnetic disks. Direct-access allows for the updat-

Diagramming Sentences

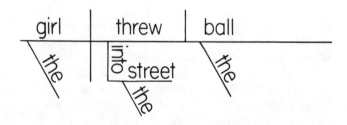

ing of records as soon as a transaction is recorded in the computer. Many stores now use a form of direct-access at checkout counters, where a transaction is recorded and automatic inventory updating occurs at the same time. Presently, some computer systems use telephones and telephone lines to enable an individual to enter a computer system from terminals that are not near the main computers (many times the terminals are hundreds of miles away).

Some colleges use a dial-access system in which lectures are stored on either an audio-tape or video-tape. A student sits at a display (or source of sound), dials a specific identification number, and the appropriate lecture is played for him/her. Although computers may not be used in such systems, the approach is cited here as an example of a dial-access system through which information stored in one place is quickly and efficiently utilized in another through electronic means. Dial-access has facilitated the development of computer-based and computer-assisted instruction.

References: John A. Brown, *Computers and Automation* (Revised Edition), New York: Arco Publishing Company, 1974; J. E. Kemp, *Planning and Producing Audiovisual Materials* (Fourth Edition), New York: Thomas Y. Crowell, 1980; Walter A. Wittich and Charles F. Schuller, *Instructural Technology: Its Nature and Use* (Fifth Edition), New York: Harper and Row, Publishers, 1973.

DIALECTIC METHOD, a teaching approach based on the clarification of ideas, complex concepts, or ambiguities through logical discussions or logical arguments among those in the classroom. In dialectical thinking, higher level concepts develop from contradictory concepts, notations, or thoughts that the method seeks to reconcile.

The dialectic method has its base in the works of Socrates, Kant, and, later, Hegel.

References: Geoffrey R. G. Mure, *Idealist Epilogue,* Oxford, England: Clarendon Press, 1978; Klaus F. Riegel, *Foundations of Dialectical Psychology,* New York: Academic Press, 1979; Nicholas Rescher, *Dialectics: A Controversy-Oriented Approach to the Theory of Knowledge,* Albany, NY: State University of New York Press, 1977.

DIATONIC SCALE—See SCALE, MUSICAL

DIFFERENTIAL APTITUDE TESTS—See APTITUDE TESTING

DIFFERENTIAL REINFORCEMENT—See REINFORCEMENT

DIFFERENTIATED CURRICULUM, a program of instruction that has been prepared to meet the unique needs of special students. The National Center for Education Statistics lists seven categories that subsume the term *differentiated curriculum.* They are: (1) bilingual education; (2) education for the disadvantaged; (3) education for the gifted; (4) education for the handicapped; (5) migrant education; (6) urban education; and (7) other differentiated curriculum.

References: Yeuell Y. Harris and Ivan N. Seibert (Editors), *The State Education Agency* (State Educational Records and Reports Series: Handbook VII), Washington, DC: National Center for Education Statistics, U.S. Department of Health, Education, and Welfare, 1975; John F. Putnam and W. Dale Chismore (Editors), *Standard Terminology for Curriculum and Instruction in Local and State School Systems* (State Educational Records and Reports Series: Handbook VI), Washington, DC: National Center for Education Statistics, U.S. Department of Health, Education, and Welfare, 1970.

DIFFERENTIATED STAFFING (DS), an organizational model for staff (school personnel) utilization that includes different levels of teaching talent and varying levels of instructional responsibility. Differentiated staffing plans were popularized in the 1950s and 1960s when J. Lloyd Trump's staff utilization and team teaching studies, sponsored by the National Association of Secondary School Principals, were receiving international attention.

Numbers of DS models have been developed. Most involve instructional teams consisting of professionals and paraprofessionals, some including as many as nine people. Common to many DS teams are generic titles such as: (1) *master teacher,* the senior member of the team and its conceptualizer; (2) *regular teacher(s),* capable of doing large or small group teaching; (3) *student teacher;* and (4) *teacher aide.* Working conditions, including salary ranges, vary for each job title. (See TEAM TEACHING.)

References: Richard A. Dempsey and Rodney P. Smith, Jr., *Differentiated Staffing,* Englewood Cliffs, NJ: Prentice-Hall, Inc., 1972; James Lewis, Jr., *Differentiating the Teaching Staff,* West Nyack, NY: Parker Publishing Company, Inc., 1971; Ian Templeton, *Differentiated Staffing: School Leadership Digest,* Arlington, VA: National Association of Elementary School Principals, 1974.

DIFFICULTY INDEX (DI), a measure used to indicate the degree to which respondents answered a particular question correctly. The higher the difficulty index, the greater is the number of students who answered the item correctly. The range of a difficulty index is 0 to 100, with 0 indicating that no one answered an item correctly, 75 indicating that 75 percent of the respondents had the correct answer, and 100 meaning that 100 percent of all respondents answered correctly.

Difficulty index is often used to assess individual items in a test. Questions can be raised about the values of a test item when an extremely large number of test takers cannot answer it correctly (D.I. $\leq$ 10) or when a large number do answer it correctly (D.I. $\geq$ 90). The point of rejection of an item depends on the test's or item's purpose; there is no set level as such. It is important to keep in mind that difficulty index is employed to help assess a test or a test item, not the individuals taking it.

References: H. H. Remmers, et al., *A Practical Introduction to Measurement and Evaluation* (Second Edition), New York: Harper and Row, Publishers, 1965; Julian Stanley and Kenneth D. Hopkins, *Educational Psychological Measurement and Evaluation*, Englewood Cliffs, NJ: Prentice-Hall, Inc., 1972; Gerald Wallace and Stephen C. Larsen, *Educational Assessment of Learning Problems: Testing for Teaching*, Boston: Allyn and Bacon, Inc., 1978.

DIGRAPH, two letters placed together to represent a single sound. Digraphs are of two types, vowel and consonant. Letter combinations such as *ai, ea,* and *ie* are illustrative of *vowel digraphs; gh, ch,* and *ck* are examples of *consonant digraphs.*

References: Estill Alexander, Jr., et al., *Teaching Reading,* Boston: Little, Brown and Company, 1979; Delwyn G. Schubert, *A Dictionary of Terms and Concepts in Reading* (Second Edition), Springfield, IL: Charles C Thomas, Publisher, 1964.

DIORAMA, three-dimensional scene that presents a lifelike tableau. Dioramas are frequently found in museums where mounted birds and animals are presented in settings closely resembling their native habitat. Imaginative use of background and terrain materials contribute to the realism of the display.

In schools, dioramas are normally miniaturized. Shoeboxes or similar small boxes can be used as stages within which the diorama is enclosed. Scenes painted on oak tag provide the background. Miniaturized three-dimensional figures (e.g. people, animals, buildings) are placed in the middle or foreground. Terrain may be depicted as flat or rolling, the latter effect produced by using such materials as soil, plaster of paris, or clay. Examples of diorama scenes are an Indian village, a battle, or a railroad station.

References: James W. Brown, et al., *AV Instruction: Technology, Media, and Methods* (Fifth Edition), New York: McGraw-Hill Book Company, 1977; Robert V. Bullough, Sr., *Creating Instructional Materials* (Second Edition), Columbus, OH: Charles E. Merrill Publishing Company, 1978; John Harrell, *Basic Media in Education,* Winona, MN: St. Mary's College Press, 1974.

DIPLOMA MILL—See DEGREE MILL

DIPLOMATE IN PROFESSIONAL PSYCHOL-OGY, a psychologist who, by virtue of advanced training, experience, and ability has earned a special diploma conferred by the American Board of Professional Psychology, Inc. (ABPP). Established in 1947 (and originally known as the American Board of Examiners in Professional Psychology), ABPP awards diplomas in four professional specialities: (1) Clinical Psychology; (2) Counseling Psychology; (3) Industrial and Organizational Psychology; and (4) School Psychology.

Diplomate applications are accepted from individuals who meet carefully prescribed criteria, including but not limited to the following: (1) a doctorate in psychology, conferred by a recognized institution of higher education: (2) completion of an 1,800-hour internship (required for all specialities except Industrial and Organizational Psychology); (3) completion of five years of acceptable experience, four of which must be postdoctoral; (4) active engagement in professional work; (5) evidence of continuing education in psychology; and (6) membership in the American Psychological Association.

Applicants who meet these preliminary criteria are then asked to submit credentials for review. Once these have been approved, the applicant becomes a *candidate* for the diploma. He/she must subsequently submit work samples for review and approval by a regional board. Finally, the candidate must pass an ABPP examination administered by a committee of examiners and taking up to four hours to complete.

In 1980, there were approximately 2,600 diplomates in psychology.

Reference: American Board of Professional Psychology, Inc., *Policies and Procedures for the Creation of Diplomates in Professional Psychology,* Washington, DC: The Board, 1979.

DIPTHONG, a letter combination that represents a sound made when two vowels are slurred or blended together. Among the most important dipthongs encountered and used by teachers of reading are the *oi* sound (as in s*oi*l or b*oy*) and the *ou* sound (as in r*ou*nd or c*ow*). Other fairly common dipthongs are: $\overline{oo}$, as in sp*oo*n; $\breve{oo}$, as in g*oo*d; ay, as in pr*ay*; y, as in m*y*; *ōw*, as in t*ow*; au, as in f*au*lt; and, aw, as in dr*aw*. Dipthongs are sometimes referred to as vowel blends.

References: Frank B. May and Susan B. Eliot, *To Help Children Read: Mastery Performance Modules for Teachers in Training* (Second Edition), Columbus, OH: Charles E. Merrill Publishing Company, 1978; Florence G. Roswell and Gladys Natchez, *Reading Disability: A Human Approach to Learning* (Third Edition), New York: Basic Books, Inc., Publishers, 1977.

DIRECT ACCESS—See DIAL-ACCESS SYSTEM

DIRECTED READING ACTIVITY (DRA), a lesson plan format used by many basal reading series. The following sections are included: (1) readiness to read the story—this introductory phase is designed to provide important background information, develop new concepts necessary to understanding, and present a purpose for reading; (2) guided silent reading; (3) discussion and interpretation; (4) skill development and practice, which provide further activity with vocabulary, decoding strategies, study skills, and comprehension; (5) follow-up activities, which are usually independently performed—they can include workbook pages, additional reading, art, music, and/or writing activities. Teacher's guide books that accompany basal readers provide step-by-step directions to operationalize the DRA. One benefit of the directed reading activity is that it provides for differences in abilities and backgrounds.

References: Betty S. Heathington, "Basal Readers," in J. Estill Alexander (Editor), *Teaching Reading*, Boston: Little, Brown and Company, 1983; Barbara E. R. Swaby, *Teaching and Learning Reading: A Pragmatic Approach*, Boston: Little, Brown and Company, 1984.

DIRECT INSTRUCTION, a structured teaching strategy that increases teacher effectiveness. The strategy mandates high levels of student involvement within teacher-directed classrooms. Materials are carefully sequenced to meet the instructional goals. The teacher chooses materials appropriate to the student's ability level and paces the learning activities accordingly. Direct instruction generally includes the following: (1) explicit explanations of materials to be used, skills to be mastered, and objectives to be met, (2) teacher modeling of expected activity, (3) student practice with immediate feedback, and (4) task analysis to insure appropriate levels of instruction. Many commercial materials have been developed around the direct instruction strategy (e.g., DISTAR). Frequently, such material includes a specific script for the instructor to follow. Such a script controls the instructional interaction. (See DISTAR PROGRAM.)

References: D. Carnine and J. Silbert, *Direct Instruction Reading*, Columbus, OH: Merrill, 1979; M. Condon and M. Kapel, "Case Study of a Changing Reading Program and the Role of Teacher Effectiveness" in J. V. Hoffman (Editor), *Effective Teaching of Reading: Research and Practice*, Newark, DE: International Reading Association, 1986.

DIRECTIONALITY, a form of laterality (cerebral hemisphere dominance) that is concerned with motor movements and balance. Directionality involves movements from right to left (or left to right), up from down (or down from up), and rear from front (or front from rear).

At one time, problems with directionality were thought to be linked with reading problems or learning disabilities. Therefore, exercises designed to improve directionality were used with children who had learning or reading problems. There is little evidence available to indicate that reading abilities were enhanced as a result of such exercises. (See LATERALITY.)

References: Patricia H. Gillespie and Lowell Johnson, *Teaching Reading to the Mildly Retarded Child*, Columbus, OH: Charles E. Merrill Publishing Company, 1974; Wineva Grzynkowicz, *Basic Education for Children with Learning Disabilities*, Springfield, IL: Charles C. Thomas, Publisher, 1979; J. Jeffries McWhirter, *The Learning Disabled Child: A School and Family Concern*, Champaign, IL: Research Press Company, 1977; Emmett Velten and Carlene T. Sampson, *Rx for Learning Disability*, Chicago: Nelson-Hall, Inc., 1978.

DIRECT METHODS, also known as natural or reformed methods, the various methods used in foreign-language instruction that stress the learning of a foreign language under conditions as natural as possible. That is, students learn the foreign language in much the same manner as they learn their "native language." Stress is placed on oral language and not grammar. Rather than being studied through a list of rules, grammar is learned indirectly through language usage. In many classes, the native language is not used at all; the foreign language is the sole means of communication. Many visual aids are used (e.g. pictures, objects).

Direct methods were developed in the late 1800s. Although many schools are not completely committed to them, some elements of direct methods are found in most foreign language instructional programs. (See GRAMMAR TRANSLATION METHOD.)

References: Wilga M. Rivers, *Teaching Foreign-Language Skills,* Chicago: University of Chicago Press, 1968; David Webb, *Teaching Modern Languages,* London, England: David and Charles, Inc., 1974.

DIRECTOR OF PUPIL PERSONNEL SERVICES, or director of student services, the individual responsible for coordinating a school or school district's program of pupil personnel services. Tasks normally associated with this leadership position include administration of guidance services; attendance; educational, career, and personal-social counseling; social-work programs; coordination of testing programs and student referrals; health services; working with school administrators; preparing budgets for personnel services; helping to formulate program and personnel policies; and articulation with such groups as parents, teachers, and community social service agencies. Some authorities contend that directors of pupil personnel services should: (1) be trained in the field of guidance; (2) possess experience in at least one of the positions included in the personnel program; (3) give evidence of personal and professional maturity; and (4) have some leadership (administrative) training.

References: Howard L. Blanchard, *Organization and Administration of Pupil Personnel Services,* Springfield, IL: Charles C. Thomas, Publisher, 1974; Edward C. Glanz, *Guidance: Foundations, Principles, and Techniques* (Second Edition), Boston: Allyn and Bacon, Inc., 1974; Merle Ohlsen, *Guidance Services in the Modern School* (Second Edition), New York: Harcourt Brace Jovanovich, Inc., 1974.

DIRECTOR OF STUDENT SERVICES—See DIRECTOR OF PUPIL PERSONNEL SERVICES

DIRECT READING THINKING ACTIVITY (DRTA), a lesson plan format used in conjunction with basal readers and content area materials. It can be employed on either a group or individual basis. Originally suggested by Stauffer (1969) as a means of guiding the reader to declare his/her own reason for reading in order to activate and shape understanding, it generally follows a four-step process: (1) Readers are guided in identification of the purpose for reading the selection. This is achieved through guided discussion that draws on student background. (2) The rate of reading necessary to the type of material and established purpose is determined. For example, it may be necessary to skim for a main idea rather than to read in depth. (3) The passage is read silently to relate the print to purposes that were set and hypotheses that were put forth. (4) Comprehension is furthered as the instructor guides the sharing of information as it relates to previously established purposes for the reading.

References: Frank J. Guzzak, *Diagnostic Reading Instruction,* New York: Harper and Row Publishers, 1985; Russell G. Stauffer, *Directing Reading Maturity as a Cognitive Process,* New York: Harper and Row, 1969.

DISCIPLINE, CLASSROOM, a process that maximizes the learning environment through classroom management on the part of teachers and self-control on the part of students. There is no single acceptable definition of discipline. Some definitions center on control of student behaviors by teachers and others view discipline as coming internally from students. The ultimate goal of classroom discipline is to create a learning environment that is effective, efficient, and positive.

Many factors influence the types of classroom discipline being used. Teacher's personality, teaching style, philosophy, subject matter, region of the country, regulations, laws, student needs, student behaviors, student learning style, student attitudes, teacher attitudes, parental attitudes and support are but a few of the factors. (See CLASSROOM MANAGEMENT.)

References: Greg H. Frith, *Behavior Management in the Schools: A Primer for Parents,* Springfield, IL: Charles C. Thomas Publisher, 1985; Fredric H. Jones, *Positive Classroom Discipline,* New York: McGraw-Hill Book Company, 1987; James Quina, *Effective Secondary Teaching: Going beyond the Bell Curve,* New York: Harper and Row Publishers, 1989; Howard Seeman, *Preventing Classroom Discipline Problems,* Lancaster, PA: Technomic Publishing Company, Inc., 1988.

DISCIPLINE, MENTAL, simplistically the training of the mind in a specific area or for a specific purpose. In years past, certain academic subjects were believed to help in training such that, after studying a subject, one would have improved mental powers. Mathematics, for example, was a subject that was supposed to improve one's ability to reason, regardless of the situation. Other subjects were believed to improve one's ability to think. Research has not yet been able to establish a relationship between areas of study and mental discipline per se.

References: David Pears, *Questions in the Philosophy of Mind,* New York: Barnes and Noble, 1975; William G. Perry, Jr., *Forms of Intellectual and Ethical Development in the College Years,* New York: Holt, Rinehart and Winston, Inc., 1970; Karl R. Popper and John C. Eccles, *The Self and Its Brain,* London, England: Springer International, 1977.

DISCIPLINE, SUBJECT, a general term used for a broad area of study, curriculum, or body of organized knowledge. Discipline refers to the basic and philosophical areas and principles of subject matter rather than to a specific course. For example, mathematics is today recognized as a discipline, English as another, and foreign language and science as still others. Classically, the definition included only three broad areas of study: (1) humanities (e.g. history, English); (2) social sciences (e.g. psychology, sociology); and (3) the natural sciences (e.g. mathematics, chemistry). It is not always easy to classify a particular subject into one of the three areas for a subject, such as geography, may qualify for inclusion in more than one area.

Some courses or programs may be made up of elements from two or more disciplines. They are classified as being interdisciplinary.

References: Edward Quinn, et al. (Editors), *Interdiscipline,* New York: The Free Press, 1972; Daniel Tanner and Laurel N. Tanner, *Curriculum Development,* New York: Macmillan Publishing Company, Inc., 1975.

DISCOURSE, refers to all exchange in the medium of language; as such, it involves both written and oral modes of communication. Individuals send and receive communications both in writing and orally—hence discourse involves a four-way interaction. A single instance of discourse has a sender, a receiver, and a message, all bound by a unifying purpose. For example, the message could be delivered via letter, play, conversation, advertisement, poem, etc. It is necessary that the learner be provided an opportunity to practice all roles and forms of discourse. Goals of discourse should hold students accountable to sending and receiving information effectively in both oral and written forms of communication.

References: James Moffett, *Teaching the Universe of Discourse,* Boston: Houghton Mifflin Company, 1968; James Moffett and Betty Jane Wagner, *Student-Centered Language Arts and Reading K–13: A Handbook for Teachers* (Third Edition), Boston: Houghton Mifflin Company, 1983.

DISCOVERY METHOD, an instructional approach that encourages the student to discover some concept or principle by using his/her own mental processes. The specific cognitive processes associated with the discovery method are observing, classifying, measuring, predicting, describing, and inferring. School curricula and/or special project materials in some schools are designed to promote this particular learning method.

An early exponent of the discovery method, Psychologist Jerome S. Bruner, defined it as "a matter of rearranging or transforming evidence in such a way that one is enabled to go beyond the evidence so reassembled to additional new insights" (p. 22). He offered four benefits to be derived from learning by discovery: (1) *intellectual potency,* or developing the mind by using it; (2) *intrinsic motives,* the personal satisfaction that grows out of the successful learning by discovery experience; (3) *learning the heuristics of discovery;* and (4) *conservation of memory,* or the improvement of recall.

References: Joseph Abruscato, *Teaching Children Science* (Second Edition), Englewood Cliffs, NJ: Prentice-Hall, 1988; Jerome S. Bruner, "The Act of Discovery," *Harvard Educational Review,* Winter 1961; Leonard H. Clark and Irving S. Starr, *Secondary and Middle School Teaching Methods,* New York: Macmillan Publishing Company, 1986; John Jarolimek and Clifford D. Foster, *Teaching and Learning in the Elementary School* (Third Edition), New York: Macmillan Publishing Company, 1985.

DISCREPANCY EVALUATION MODEL, a method used to assess specific educational programs. First proposed by Malcolm Provus (in 1971), the model provides ongoing (formative) and final (summative) evaluation information. During a program's ongoing phases, actual conditions and events are compared periodically with what is expected (program standards). The results (discrepancies) are then studied. Those in charge of the program may decide to alter the structure of the program, change performances, change the program standards, do all three, keep the program as designed, or terminate it.

Program standards are derived from three sources: (1) the stated objectives and goals of the program; (2) the values of the program staff; and (3) the values and objectives of the client population being served. Discrepancy evaluation consists of five stages: (1) Design Adequacy; (2) Installation Fidelity; (3) Process Adjustment; (4) Product Assessment; and (5) Cost Benefit (the last being optional). A feedback loop between each stage and Stage I (where the program standards are de-

veloped) constitutes a major part of the model.
References: W. James Popham, *Educational Evaluation* (Second Edition), Englewood Cliffs, NJ: Prentice-Hall, Inc., 1988; Malcolm Provus, *Discrepancy Evaluation*, Berkeley, CA: McCutchan Publishing Corporation, 1971.

DISCRIMINATION, a term that has several meanings. In psychology, discrimination is the ability to make choices, respond differently, or see differences among various stimuli (e.g. sound, color, depth, forms, texture, smell, size). The inability to distinguish among stimuli can lead to many educational/learning problems. For example, some speech problems are produced by poor auditory (sound) discrimination, and some learning problems are caused by poor visual discrimination.

Discrimination, as a sociological term, usually has a negative meaning, especially when an individual or group receives or doles out unequal, unfair, or unjust treatment because of one's race, religion, social class, ethnic identification, sex, age, and so on. Such discrimination can occur in diverse areas such as education, social groups, employment, and housing.

Finally, the term has a special meaning when used in the context of testing. A desirable characteristic of a test (or test item) is that it distinguishes (discriminates) among those who take the test. That is, the test is designed to identify various levels of achievement, ability, aptitude, and so on. However, if a test is constructed such that individuals from certain populations or groups are placed in an unfair position, and individuals from other populations or groups have an advantage based on group or population membership, the test is said to discriminate unfairly. Such test discrimination is clearly undesirable. It has been alleged by some critics that some standardized achievement tests discriminate unfairly because they were constructed for, and normed, using middle socioeconomic children. In such cases, the critics argue, low socioeconomic children residing in depressed areas are placed at a relative disadvantage. (See AUDITORY DISCRIMINATION and VISUAL DISCRIMINATION.)
References: Barry D. Adams, *The Survival of Domination: Inferiorization and Everyday Life,* New York: Elsevier-North Holland, Inc., 1978; Harvey L. Gochros and Jean S. Gochros (Editors), *The Sexually Oppressed,* New York: Association Press, 1977; Donald L. Rampp, *Auditory Processing and Learning Disabilities,* Lincoln, NE: Cliffs Notes, Inc., 1980; Meyer Weinberg, *A Chance to Learn: The History of Race and Education in the United States,* New York: Cambridge University Press, 1977.

DISCRIMINATION INDEX, a measure used in test development that indicates the extent to which a test item can distinguish between individuals who have the ability being measured and those who do not. If those who have the ability being tested respond to an item correctly more often than those who do not, the item is said to have a positive index. If the reverse is true, the index is considered to be negative. The index ranges from +1.00 to −1.00. A +1.00 test item index indicates that all those with the ability being tested responded correctly, and those without the ability responded incorrectly. A "0" index means that about the same number of those with ability and those without ability responded correctly. A −1.00 indicates that those without the ability being tested answered correctly and those with the ability being tested answered incorrectly. It is rare to have discrimination indexes of either +1.00 or −1.00. Although there is no ideal index (this depends on the item and purpose of the test), a +0.20 is considered to be an acceptable level of discrimination for most test items.
References: Tom Kubiszyn and Gary Borich, *Educational Testing and Measurement: Classroom Application and Practice* (Second Edition), Glenview, IL: Scott Foresman and Company, 1987; Gilbert Sax, *Principles of Educational and Psychological Measurement and Evaluation* (Third Edition), Belmont, CA: Wadsworth Publishing Company, 1989.

DISCRIMINATIVE STIMULUS, a particular stimulus in operant conditioning that can determine whether a voluntary response occurs or does not occur. For example, an animal is taught to ring a bell (voluntary response), and the animal receives food (reinforcement) after ringing the bell. Then one of two objects is placed next to the animal. Whenever object #1 is near, the bell can not be rung (and consequently the animal is not fed); when object #2 is near, the bell can be rung (and consequently the animal is fed). Soon the animal learns that object #1 means no ringing and no food, and that object #2 means the opposite. The animal stops trying to ring the bell whenever object #1 is placed near and will ring the bell whenever object #2 replaces object #1. Thus, the animal learns that object #2 is a positive discriminative stimulus (DS+), because it provides information that the bell can be rung and will be reinforced. Object #1, on the other hand, is a negative discriminative stimulus (DS−), because it provides information that the bell will not ring and therefore there will be no reinforcement. The paradigm appearing below illustrates the discriminative stimulus. (See LEARNING, DISCRIMINATION and OPERANT BEHAVIOR.)

References: Werner K. Honig and T. E. R. Staddon (Editors), *Handbook of Operant Behavior,* Englewood Cliffs, NJ: Prentice-Hall, Inc., 1977; T. William Moore, et al., *Conditioning and Instrumental Learning* (Second Edition), New York: McGraw-Hill Book Company, 1978; Barry Schwartz, *Psychology of Learning and Behavior,* New York: W. W. Norton and Company, Inc., 1978.

DISCUSSION METHOD, purposeful conversation in which several individuals participate. A commonly employed instructional method, discussion serves several purposes: (1) to encourage analysis; (2) to introduce varying interpretations; and (3) to arrive at some general conclusion or agreement. Profitable classroom discussions are those in which the teacher (or other discussion leader) is open-minded and does not impose his/her ideas. Furthermore, they require participation by as many students as possible. Effective discussion results in the emergence of new skills, concepts, and understandings, these arrived at through reflective thinking.

Discussions may involve a whole class or small groups into which the class has been divided. Small-group discussions normally require the selection of discussion leaders and recorders, the latter responsible for summarizing and reporting discussion results to the class as a whole.

References: Leonard H. Clark and Irving S. Starr, *Secondary School Teaching Methods* (Third Edition), New York: Macmillan Publishing Company, Inc., 1976; Kenneth H. Hoover, *The Professional Teacher's Handbook: A Guide for Improving Instruction in Today's Middle and Secondary Schools* (Abridged Second Edition), Boston: Allyn and Bacon, Inc., 1976; J. Lloyd Trump and Delmas F. Miller, *Secondary School Curriculum Improvement: Meeting Challenges of the Times* (Third Edition), Boston: Allyn and Bacon, Inc., 1979.

DISPERSION, a measure used in statistics that indicates the degree to which a set of scores are distributed, or their degree of variability. Standard deviation, variance, average deviation, semi-

interquartile range, and total range are all measures of dispersion. Knowledge of score dispersions helps to give meaning to the scores. For example, one class of students may have a set of test scores with a mean of 75 and a range of scores from 5 to 150; another class of students may have a set of scores on the same test with a mean of 75 and a range of scores from 50 to 100. It is clear that the students in the first class were not as homogeneous, in terms of scores, as were those in the second class notwithstanding the fact that their group means were the same.

References: Carol Taylor Fitz-Gibbon and Lynn Lyons Morris, *How to Calculate Statistics,* Beverly Hills, CA: Sage Publications, Inc., 1978; Joy P. Guilford and Benjamin Fruchter, *Fundamental Statistics in Psychology and Education* (Sixth Edition), New York: McGraw-Hill Book Company, 1978; Albert K. Kurtz and Samuel T. Mayo, *Statistical Methods in Education and Psychology,* New York: Springer-Verlag, 1979.

DISRUPTIVE BEHAVIOR, student behavior of an atypical nature that creates role conflicts in the classroom. Such conflicts may affect student-student or teacher-student relationships. According to Edward Ladd, student behavior that is sometimes viewed as being disruptive by school officials includes: (1) verbal expressions (e.g. obscenity); (2) participation in organizations considered to be potentially disruptive; (3) overt interruption of school activities; and (4) presentation of self in ways calculated to be disruptive (e.g. indecent dress). Ladd cautioned the school administrator not to define disruptive behavior too narrowly and reminded him/her that the official is obligated to control disruptive behavior only "as is: (1) necessary and reasonable . . . in furtherance of the school's legitimate concerns, and, (2) not protected from his (her) control by the student's legal rights" (p. 3).

Jean Davis identified several methods for dealing with disruptive behavior in the classroom: (1) the *teacher-dominant* approach, with teacher demanding specific rules of behavior and students complying; (2) the *analytic* approach, a method requiring the teacher to analyze a student's behavior and to discuss this with the student; (3) the *behavioristic* approach, one in which rewards or

Discriminative Stimulus

DS+ ⟶ Response ⟶ Reinforcement ⟶ Unconditional Response
DC- ⫸ Response ⫸ Reinforcement ⫸ Unconditional Response

punishments are used to elicit specific kinds of performance; (4) the *student-centered* approach, an approach granting maximum freedom to the student; and (5) the *teacher-student interaction* approach that requires both teacher and student to work together to produce desirable behavior. (See DISCIPLINE, CLASSROOM.)

References: Fredric H. Jones, *Positive Classroom Discipline*, New York: McGraw-Hill Book Company, 1987; Howard Seeman, *Preventing Classroom Discipline Problems*, Lancaster, PA: Technomic Publishing Company, Inc., 1988.

DISSERTATION, a scholarly paper, completed by a candidate for an advanced degree, that: (1) is prepared under the direction of a faculty committee; (2) requires in-depth knowledge of a particular subject; (3) is normally based on independent research; and (4) reflects a high level of scholarship as well as a demonstrated knowledge of research methodology. Dissertations are required of virtually all students pursuing the Ph.D., Ed.D., and similar advanced doctorates. They are less frequently required of master's degree students.

Individual institutions of higher education establish their own operational definitions of "dissertation." Some examples follow: (1) *Ohio State University*, "a definite contribution to knowledge of importance sufficient to warrant its publication" (p. 50); (2) *New York University*, "must show ability to follow approved methods of scholarly investigation and give evidence of exhaustive study of a special field. It should either add to the knowledge of the subject or represent a new and significant interpretation" (pp. 17 and 18); and (3) *Princeton University*, "must show that the candidate has technical mastery of the field and is capable of independent research. This study must enlarge or modify what was previously known or present a significant new interpretation of known materials" (p. 15).

References: James E. Mauch and Jack W. Birch, *Guide to the Successful Thesis and Dissertation*, New York: Marcel Dekker, Inc., 1983; *New York University Bulletin, 1978–79: Graduate School of Arts and Science*, New York: New York University, April 10, 1978; *Ohio State University Bulletin: Graduate School, 1976–78, Book 2*, Columbus, OH: Ohio State University, April 2, 1976; *Princeton University Graduate School Announcement, 1977–78*, Princeton, NJ: Princeton University (Undated).

DISSERTATION ABSTRACTS INTERNATIONAL, a monthly compilation of doctoral dissertation abstracts that have been submitted to University Microfilms, Ann Arbor, Michigan, by cooperating institutions in the United States, Canada, and Europe. A name change, from *Dissertation Abstracts* to *Dissertation Abstracts International*, was made in 1969 to reflect the inclusion of abstracts received from some European universities. (Previously, *Dissertation Abstracts* covered only U.S. and Canadian institutions.) *Dissertation Abstracts* was first published in 1938.

The compilation appears in two separately bound sections (Section A, the humanities and the social sciences; Section B, the sciences and engineering). Abstracts of dissertations completed in the field of education are included in Section A. Subsuming education are numbers of more specific headings such as administration, audiovisual, history, programmed instruction, and teacher training.

Dissertations submitted to University Microfilms are microfilmed and are available for purchase.

In 1973, Xerox University Microfilms published *Comprehensive Dissertation Index, 1861–1972*, a 37-volume summary of over 400,000 dissertations. This basic index is supplemented annually.

References: Eugene P. Sheehy, et al., *Guide to Reference Books* (Ninth Edition), Chicago: American Library Association, 1976; University Microfilms International, *Dissertation Abstracts International*, Ann Arbor, MI: Xerox University International, 1980; Xerox University Microfilms, *Comprehensive Dissertation Index, 1861–1972*, Ann Arbor, MI: Xerox University Microfilms, 1973.

DISTANCE, SOCIAL, in sociology, the way in which relationships among social classes are described. For example, the further away a group is from another group as measured on social-distance scales, the less is the interaction between them. In a segregated society, social distance between the separated groups is usually great (e.g. there is little socializing and intermarriage between members of each group; frequently, considerable hostility exists). Several factors contribute to social distance including history, laws, housing patterns, geographic space, education, fear, family background and mores, experiences, and limited opportunities.

There are two ways to measure social distance. One is to observe the interactions of the groups (e.g. noting actual housing patterns or marriage practices). Another, a more personalized approach, involves asking individuals to rank various groups in terms of whether they want to develop social relationships (e.g. marriage, housing, working together) with members of these other groups.

Evidence exists to show that social distance exists among children as well as adults.

References: Arthur Britton, *The Privatised World,* London, England: Routledge and Kegan Paul, 1977; Ceri Peach (Editor), *Urban Social Segregation,* London, England: Longman Group, Ltd., 1975; P. Stringer and D. Bannister (Editors), *Constructs of Sociality and Individuality,* London, England: Academic Press, 1979; Robert M. Thomas, *Social Differences in the Classroom,* New York: David McKay Company, Inc., 1965.

DISTAR PROGRAM, or Distar Instructional System, a reading, language, and arithmetic program that is highly structured. The major elements of the program include tasks that are structured for teachers and students, controlled practice, and sequencing of skills to ensure mastery. Prescribed teacher actions and statements are described fully. Exact words, signalling for response, and other teacher behaviors are spelled out. DISTAR uses a mastery based learning approach.

The Distar Reading Program was developed by Siegfried Engelmann and Elaine Bruner under a United States Office of Education grant. Its full title, from which the acronym DISTAR is derived, is *Direct Instruction System for Teaching Arithmetic and Reading.* The program is made up of a series of kits: Reading I, II, and III; Language I, II, and III; Arithmetic I, II, and III; master tests; activity kits; library series; strategy games; profile folders; and teacher training programs. Grade levels at which DISTAR is directed range from pre-school through grade 3. The program has been published by Science Research Associates since 1969. (See MASTERY LEARNING.)

Reference: Siegfried Engelmann and Elaine C. Bruner, *Distar Reading,* Chicago: Science Research Associates, Inc., 1977.

DISTRACTORS, in test item construction, the incorrect choices in a multiple-choice or matching test item. Distractors are also referred to as alternatives, decoys, foils, or misleads. Testing authorities recommend that distractors should be reasonable and plausible such that individuals not having knowledge about a subject will select them, and those having the knowledge will select the correct response.

For example, a, c, d, and e are all distractors in the following multiple-choice test item: Which university basketball team won the 1980 NCAA basketball championship? a.) UCLA; b.) University of Louisville; c.) St. Johns University; d.) University of Kentucky; or e.) Indiana University.

References: William L. Goodwin and Laura A. Driscoll, *Handbook for Measurement and Evaluation in Early Childhood Education,* San Francisco: Jossey-Bass Publishers, 1980; Tom Kubiszyn and Gary Borich, *Educational Testing and Measurement: Classroom Application and Practice* (Second Edition), Glenview, IL: Scott Foresman and Company, 1987; Victor H. Noll and Dale P. Scannell, *Introduction to Educational Measurement* (Third Edition), Boston: Houghton Mifflin Company, 1972.

DISTRIBUTIVE EDUCATION (DE), vocational education for retail selling. The field of distributive education, a program now available to large numbers of high school students and adults, was for all intents and purposes initiated by enactment of the George-Deen Act in 1936. That legislation, essentially an amendment to the Smith Hughes Act, authorized appropriation of $1,200,000 to pay salaries of certain persons engaged in the teaching of distributive occupational subjects. Succeeding federal legislation did much to expand distributive education and to authorize training programs for the preparation of distributive education teachers.

Distributive education programs revolve around product and service areas of marketing activity. They feature instruction in merchandising, marketing, and management. Much of the program is "cooperative," an arrangement that permits students to study in school and to gain practical work experience in the business community. It is common practice in many secondary schools for distributive education students to operate and maintain the "school store" as their cooperative education experience. (See COOPERATIVE VOCATIONAL EDUCATION.)

References: Willard R. Daggett, *The Dynamics of Work,* Cincinnati, OH: South-Western Publishing Company, 1984; Roy W. Roberts, *Vocational and Practical Arts Education: History Development, and Principles* (Third Edition), New York: Harper and Row, Publishers, 1971.

DISTRIBUTIVE EDUCATION CLUBS OF AMERICA (DECA), a national organization made up of vocational distributive education students (high school and postsecondary). Local chapters and chartered state associations carry out much of the organization's work. The club was founded in 1948 with 17 states included as charter members. Membership recently reached 185,000. DECA's structure includes a student organization and an adult organization.

Local chapters organize and carry out their own programs. Activities are diverse, including tours, clinics, banquets, and socials. Some DECA chapters operate school stores with part of their profits used to support the local unit.

DECA publishes *Distributor*, a quarterly, and *Newsletter*, a monthly. Its main offices are located in Reston, Virginia. (See DISTRIBUTIVE EDUCATION.)

References: Estelle L. Popham, et al., *A Teaching-Learning System for Business Education*, New York: McGraw-Hill Book Company, 1975; Roy W. Roberts, *Vocational and Practical Arts Education: History, Development, and Principles* (Third Edition), New York: Harper and Row, Publishers, 1971.

DISTRIBUTIVE PROPERTY, a concept taught in conjunction with the teaching of the multiplication of a series of natural numbers. Distributive property, another of the "modern mathematical" laws that became a part of the mathematics curriculum in the late 1950s, is taught to help children conceptualize the process of multiplication. Distributive property explains the process of multiplication over addition. For example:

$$a(b + c) = (a \times b) + (a \times c)$$
$$4(6 + 7) = (4 \times 6) + (4 \times 7)$$
$$= 24 + 28$$
$$= 52$$

In a complex multiplication problem several approaches can be used to find a solution with approach determined by the properties used.

$$4(6 + 7) + 5 (6 + 7 + 3) =$$
$$(4 \times 6) + (4 \times 7) + (5 \times 6) + 5 (7 + 3) =$$
$$24 + 28 + 30 + 50 =$$
$$52 + 30 + 50 =$$
$$52 + 80 =$$
$$132$$
or
$$4 \times 13 + 5 \times 16 =$$
$$4 (6 + 7) + 5 (6 + 7 + 3)$$
$$\vdots$$
$$\vdots$$

The last examples given include the distributive properties as well as the associative and commutative properties. (See ASSOCIATIVE PROPERTY and COMMUTATIVE PROPERTY.)

References: A. B. Evenson, *Modern Mathematics*, Chicago: Scott, Foresman and Company, 1962; Seymour Hayden, *Introductory Mathematics*, New York: Dodd, Mead and Company, 1967; William L. Schaaf, *Basic Concepts of Elementary Mathematics*, New York: John Wiley and Sons, 1969.

DIVERGENT THINKING, an element in J. P. Guilford's theoretical model for the structure of intellect. It is an intellectual process or operation that is performed by humans. When a person is being creative, is thinking of new and/or unique ideas, or is envisioning new and varied roles for an object(s), the person is described as doing divergent thinking. Individuals who develop or propose alternative solutions to problems are demonstrating divergent thinking. To some extent, divergent thinking is the opposite of convergent thinking. (See CONVERGENT THINKING.)

References: Richard C. Anderson, et al., *Schooling and the Acquisition of Knowledge*, Hillsdale, NJ: Lawrence Erlbaum Associates, Publishers, 1977; Joy P. Guilford, *Intelligence, Creativity and Their Educational Implications*, Los Angeles: Knapp Press, 1968; George T. Mouly, *Psychology for Effective Teaching* (Third Edition), New York: Holt, Rinehart and Winston, Inc., 1973; Harold F. O'Neil, Jr. and Charles D. Spielberger, *Cognitive and Affective Learning Strategies*, New York: Academic Press, 1979; Glen E. Snelbecker, *Learning Theory, Instructional Theory, and Psychoeducational Design*, New York: McGraw-Hill Book Company, 1974.

DOCTOR'S DEGREE, the most advanced academic degree conferred by an institution of higher education. Most doctor's degrees require at least three years of postbaccalaureate study. They are of two types: the *research* degree and the *professional* degree. The former type includes the Doctor of Philosophy, first conferred in the United States by Yale University (1861), which includes among its requirements the writing of a dissertation in some area of unexplored knowledge. The *professional* category includes degrees such as the Doctor of Medicine, Doctor of Pharmacy, and the Doctor of Veterinary Medicine.

The Doctor of Education degree, categorized as a research degree, was first offered by Harvard University in 1920. A forerunner to it, the Doctor of Pedagogy, was introduced by New York University in 1891.

A total of 32,750 doctoral degrees were conferred in 1980 by American universities.

References: Nancy B. Dearman and Valena W. Plisko, *The Condition of Education* (1980 Edition), Washington, DC: National Center for Education Statistics, U.S. Department of Education, 1980; Walter C. Eells and Harold A. Haswell, *Academic Degrees Earned and Honorary Degrees Conferred by Institutions of Higher Education in the United States*, Washington, DC: Office of Education, U. S. Department of HEW, 1960 (Reprinted in 1970 by Gale Research Company, Detroit); Stephen H. Spurr,

Academic Degree Structures: Innovative Approaches, New York: McGraw-Hill Book Company, 1970.

DOGMATISM, a mode of thought characterized as closed-mindedness, that influences how one relates to ideas, people, or authority.

Psychologist Milton Rokeach and his colleagues (developers of the Rokeach or Dogmatism Scale) concluded that each living being acts in accordance with a personal belief-disbelief system, in effect a point falling somewhere along an "open-closed" continuum. The more "open" one's belief system, the greater is the likelihood that the individual will act on the intrinsic merits of new information received. Conversely, the more "closed" the belief system, the more likely it is that information received will be confused with such outside factors as personal emotions, expectations, or prejudices. (See ROKEACH SCALE.)

References: Milton Rokeach, *The Open and Closed Mind,* New York: Basic Books, Inc., Publishers, 1960; H. D. Schmidt, et al., "Dogmatism" in H. J. Eysenck, et al. (Editors), *Encyclopedia of Psychology* (Volume 1), New York: Herder and Herder, 1972.

DOGMATISM SCALE—See ROKEACH SCALE

DOLCH WORD LIST—See WORD LISTS

DOMAIN-REFERENCED TESTS (DRT), examinations made up of items randomly selected from a pool of items representing a well-defined set or class of tasks (known as domain). Domain-referenced tests are a specific set of criterion-referenced tests, hence have the same basic usage as criterion tests. However, the evaluation of DRT results is more specific and exact.

For example, a student correctly responds to 80 out of 100 addition problems randomly selected from a basic fourth grade list of addition problems (the domain is fourth grade addition problems). The interpretation is that the student can solve 80 percent of fourth grade addition problems. This example includes the basic characteristics of DRT: (1) a subset of knowledges, skills, understandings; (2) the behavior expected of the student was described; (3) a large number of items was generated; and (4) the items were selected randomly from a pool of items that represent the domain.

Domain-referenced tests have several major advantages. Most important, they allow for a specific interpretation of an examinee's ability to function in a defined area. In addition, DRT reliability can be determined through its internal consistency, and its content validity can be assessed through logical analysis, procedures for item generation, and each specific test item. DRT is limited by misconceptions of the nature of the tests (e.g. it cannot be used to assess attitudes), problems of test development, and domain definitions/limitations.

References: Wells Hively (Editor), *Domain Referenced Testing,* Englewood Cliffs, NJ: Educational Technology Publications, 1974; Jason Millman, "Criterion-Referenced Measurement" in W. James Popham (Editor), *Evaluation in Education,* Berkeley, CA: McCutchan Publishing Corporation, 1974; W. James Popham, *Educational Evaluation* (Second Edition), Englewood Cliffs, NJ: Prentice-Hall, 1988.

DOMAN-DELACATO METHOD—See PATTERNING

DORMITORIES, institutional housing facilities in which college, university, and private school students reside while attending school. On some campuses, dormitories are referred to as "residence halls." There are many types of dormitories. Some are equipped with eating facilities, others are not. Most dormitories have study facilities, common meeting and social rooms, and are designed to provide a positive living-learning environment. College and university dormitories were, until the 1960s, segregated by sex. Now there are many different coeducational arrangements that permit students of both sexes to occupy a single dormitory (e.g. every other floor is restricted to either males or females). In most schools, colleges, and universities, costs charged for dormitories are in addition to the cost of tuition.

On small campuses, dormitories normally house between 100 and 200 students. Larger institutions may have multistory buildings housing in excess of 1,000 students. Dormitories are usually staffed by older and mature males and females, often graduate students (many of whom are trained counselors). (See RESIDENTIAL STUDENT.)

References: John T. Agria, *College Housing,* Washington, DC: American Enterprise Institute for Public Policy Research, 1972; Arthur W. Chickering, *Commuting Versus Resident Students,* San Francisco: Jossey-Bass Publishers, 1974; Harold C. Riker and Frank G. Lopez, *College Students Live Here,* New York: Educational Facilities Laboratories, 1961.

DOUBLE SESSIONS, division of the school day into two separate parts (sessions) with two groups of students occupying a single room or building. For example, a high school on double session may schedule freshmen and sophomore students to attend classes during the morning session and require juniors and seniors to attend during the afternoon session. Double sessioning is usually used when the number of students to be accommodated exceeds the school building's student capacity.

Reference: Combined Glossary: Terms and Definitions from the Handbooks of the State Educational Records and Reports Series, Washington, DC: National Center for Education Statistics, U.S. Department of Health, Education, and Welfare, 1974.

DOWN'S SYNDROME (DS), or mongolism, a genetically linked mental retardation syndrome resulting from chromosomal abnormality. The British physician, J. Langdon Down, identified the syndrome in 1866. He named those afflicted with it "mongoloids," because the thick folds in the corners of their eyes gave them a Mongolian appearance. More recently, the contraction "Dowsyn" has come into use as a substitute for Down's Syndrome.

The exact cause of Down's Syndrome has been linked to an extra chromosome in the individual, 47 instead of 46. Evidence exists to show that incidence of the syndrome increases with the biological age of the mother. In years past, DS children had relatively short life expectancies but improved prenatal and postnatal care has extended them considerably.

Down's Syndrome children are often born before the expected delivery date, are usually short, have distinctive facial features (e.g. flat nose; larger tongue), and have broad hands with short fingers. Their intelligence levels tend to be low, ranging from very severely retarded to near normal.

References: William H. Berdine and A. Edward Blackhurst (Editors), *An Introduction to Special Education* (Second Edition), Boston: Little, Brown and Company, 1985; Ann Gath, *Down's Syndrome and the Family: The Early Years,* London, England: Academic Press, 1978; Christof Wunderlich, *The Mongoloid Child: Recognition and Care* (Translated from the German by Royal L. Tinsley, Jr., et al.), Tucson, AZ: The University of Arizona Press, 1977.

DRAFTING, the precision drawing of plans, blueprints, industrial drawings, or designs, usually for architects, engineers, various industries, or builders. Draftsmen, those who do the actual drawing, use mechanical drawing techniques and procedures in developing such drawings. Since there are accepted mechanical drawing standards and conventions (e.g. scales, systems of projections, notations, lettering systems, symbols), engineers or builders can build what is drawn by the draftsman with little difficulty and with a high degree of accuracy.

Draftsmen usually use various mechanical devices when creating a drawing. These include T-squares, compasses, protractors, drafting machines, rulers, French curves, and straight edges. (The term *mechanical drawing* reflects the fact that mechanical devices are used in the development of drawings. This distinguishes it from freehand drawing done by most artists.)

Drafting and mechanical drawing are included in most industrial arts and vocational education curricula. Advanced drafting programs are offered in many high schools, vocational schools, and postsecondary trade schools.

References: James A. Dunn, et al., *Career Education: A Curriculum Design and Instructional Objectives Catalog,* Palo Alto, CA: The American Institute for Research in the Behavioral Sciences, 1974; Jay Helsel and Byron Urbanick, *Mechanical Drawing* (Ninth Edition), New York: McGraw-Hill Book Company, 1980; Warren L. Luzadder, *Fundamentals of Engineering Drawings for Design, Product Development, and Numerical Control* (Seventh Edition), Englewood Cliffs, NJ: Prentice-Hall, Inc., 1977; Wilbur R. Miller, *Drafting,* Bloomington, IL: McKnight and McKnight Publishing Company, 1978; G. Harold Silvius and Ralph C. Bohn, *Planning and Organizing Instruction* (Second Edition), Bloomington, IL: McKnight and McKnight Publishing Company, 1976; John E. Traister, *Electrical-Electronic Drafting and Design,* Reston, VA: Reston Publishing Company, 1979.

DRAMATICS—See CREATIVE DRAMATICS

DRESS POLICY, or dress codes, guidelines set forth by a board of education or other policymaking body that prescribe or proscribe dress and/or appearance for students or teachers. In the middle 1960s, numerous lawsuits were initiated that challenged the right of a board or its administration to enforce dress codes. Most frequently challenged have been those policies that regulate both student dress and hair styles.

Insofar as student dress policies are concerned, the courts have not been uniform in their treatment of such cases. The U.S. Supreme Court has refused to hear appeals from lower courts, thereby leaving resolution of such cases to these courts. Some lower courts have ruled in favor of students on First, Ninth, or Fourteenth Amendment grounds; some have decided on the basis of safety or due process; others have made determinations based on the reasonableness of such policies. Hairstyle (head or face) rulings have been as varied as those relating to dress.

Policies and regulations governing dress and appearance of teachers increased in the 1970s. They dealt with issues such as wearing of beards, hair length, and the requiring of male teachers to wear neckties. Here, too, the courts have rendered a wide variety of decisions. It has been observed that the number of such cases (for teachers as well as students) has been decreasing as society has become more accepting of nontraditional (i.e. longer) hair styles and informal dress.

References: Leroy J. Peterson, et al., *The Law and Public School Operation* (Second Edition), New York: Harper and Row, Publishers, 1978; E. Edmund Reutter, Jr., *The Courts and Student Conduct,* Topeka, KS: National Organization on Legal Problems of Education, 1975.

DRILL, a teaching technique, usually individualized, that involves repetition of an activity for the purpose of reinforcing what has already been learned, perfecting a skill (e.g. violin playing), or increasing one's understanding of a subject. Commonly referred to as *practice,* drill takes place after the learner has developed a preliminary understanding of the skill to be achieved. Its effectiveness is increased to the extent that he/she is motivated to practice. Given the boredom that normally accompanies this technique, authorities recommend that drill take place each day but that it be limited to relatively short practice periods (e.g. 15 to 30 minutes).

References: Leonard H. Clark and Irving S. Starr, *Secondary School Teaching Methods* (Third Edition), New York: Macmillan Publishing Company, Inc., 1976; Kenneth H. Hoover, *The Professional Teacher's Handbook: A Guide for Improving Instruction in Today's Middle and Secondary Schools* (Abridged Second Edition), Boston: Allyn and Bacon, Inc., 1976.

DRIVER EDUCATION, usually a separate course of traffic-safety education that seeks to prepare safe automobile drivers. Most driver education courses offered in high schools are divided into two parts: (1) classroom instruction, and (2) laboratory and practice driving. Driver education is an elective, or cocurricular course taken at the option of students. It is supported and funded by schools as well as insurance groups, safety councils, and automobile dealer organizations. Many insurance companies make reduced premium rates available to teenage drivers who have successfully completed a driver education course. In many states, driver education teachers must be certified in the field of driver education.

Areas covered in driver education include: knowledge about a car, maintaining a car, mechanics of a car, legal problems and obligations in driving, defensive driving in all environments (e.g. city, highway, mountains) and under all conditions (snow, rain, etc.), emergencies, traffic laws, accident procedures and legal obligations, insurance, drugs and alcohol, pedestrian safety, the psychology of driving, and actual hands-on driving. Although most driver education courses are found in the schools, many states have a point system for traffic violations and require experienced drivers to take special driver education courses when they accumulate a set number of violation points. (See SAFETY EDUCATION.)

References: Maxwell Halsey, et al., *Let's Drive Right,* Glenview, IL: Scott, Foresman and Company, 1972; Louis Rubin, *Curriculum Handbook,* Boston: Allyn and Bacon, Inc., 1977.

DROP-ADD, the procedure followed by college and university students to change their class or course schedules. Students typically complete a form (drop-add form) and, depending on local regulations and restrictions, may have to pay a fee for requesting such change(s). In some colleges, students may "drop" a class or course up to the time of the final examination and pay no fee. In others, a fee is charged should the request come after a certain published date. In still others, no changes may be made after a certain published date. The drop-add procedure makes three options available to the student: (1) "dropping" a course and "adding" another to his/her schedule; (2) "dropping" a course and "adding" none; or (3) expanding his/her schedule by "adding" one or more courses.

References: *University of Arizona General Catalog, 1979–80, 1980–81; University of Kentucky Bulletin, 1979–80; Western Kentucky University Bulletin, 1979.*

DROPOUTS, a term used to describe individuals who leave an activity, a course, a program, or a school before completing its requirements and who do so voluntarily. For example, a boy who leaves school before graduation for other than legitimate reasons (e.g. family moving away), and is not expelled or suspended, is considered a dropout. Dropouts come from all socioeconomic levels as well as all racial and ethnic groups. They are found in all regions of the country, include boys and girls, represent all intellectual levels, and are found at all age levels.

There are many reasons why individuals drop out of an activity, course, program, or school. Nonsuccess, poor educational background, low intelligence, not meeting personal needs, boredom, activity not challenging, personality, emotional and adjustment problems, home environment, need to be involved in other activities (e.g. work) at the same time, illness and other physical problems, low expectations, marriage, low attainment, and expectations of parents are but a few of the reasons given by individuals who leave before completion. Many times there are a combination of reasons that lead a person to become a dropout.

School dropouts are found at the high school and college levels. In high school, the student may drop out of school once he/she has passed the state compulsory attendance age. Bureau of the Census data indicate that the high school dropout rate for all students has stabilized in recent years, yet remains higher for black youth than white.

References: Andrew Hahn and Jacqueline Danzberger, *Dropouts in America,* Washington, DC: Institute for Educational Leadership, 1987; Oscar G. Mink and Bernard A. Kaplan, *America's Problem Youth,* Scranton, PA: International Textbook Company, 1970; Nancy C. Myll, *The Dropout Prevention Handbook: A Guide for Administrators, Counselors, and Teachers,* West Nyack, NY: Parker Publishing Co., 1988.

DRUG, a medicine or a substance used in making medicine that, when used illegally, has come to be used loosely as a synonym for "narcotics." The fact that use of drugs can alter perceptions of self and environment has prompted man, throughout history, to seek them out for other than medicinal purposes, specifically pleasure and/or escape. In recent years, drugs have come to be a major concern of educators owing to their widespread use and abuse by young people.

Harold Cornacchia and associates pointed out that frequently abused drugs fall into five broad classifications. They are: (1) the *central nervous system stimulant drugs,* such as amphetamines, cocaine, and even the minor stimulants, nicotine and caffeine; (2) the *central nervous system depressant drugs,* including alcohol, barbituates, and inhalants; (3) *psychedelic drugs,* also known as hallucinogenics, which include LSD and marijuana; (4) *narcotic drugs,* such as opium, heroin, and other opium derivations; and (5) *nonprescription* (*over-the-counter*) *drugs,* such as aspirin, antihistamines, cough medicines, diet pills, and sleeping pills. (See DRUG ABUSE and DRUG-ABUSE EDUCATION.)

References: Harold J. Cornacchia, *Drugs in the Classroom: A Conceptual Model for School Programs* (Second Edition), St. Louis, MO: The C. V. Mosby Company, 1978; Bill C. Wallace, *Education and the Drug Scene,* Lincoln, NE: Professional Educators Publications, Inc., 1974.

DRUG ABUSE, a largely subjective term that has several (including moralistic) definitions. Contributing to the difficulty of achieving a single, commonly accepted definition for the term is the emotionalism that the terms *drugs* and *drug abuse* have been generating in recent years. Some health educators (e.g. Bill Wallace) caution educators not to become involved with the "goodness" and "badness" arguments relating to use of drugs but to use their energies, instead, to become informed about the various drugs and the people who use them.

Harold Cornacchia and associates defined *drug abuse* as "the illegal self-administration of drugs, narcotics, chemicals, and other substances to the possible detriment of the individual, of society, or of both" (p. 34). Others, such as David Smith and John Luce, offered a more personalistic definition, referring to drug abuse as the point where it interferes with an individual's health, his/her economic adjustment, or his/her social adjustment. (See DRUG and DRUG-ABUSE EDUCATION.)

References: Harold J. Cornacchia, et al., *Drugs in the Classroom: A Conceptual Model for School Programs* (Second Edition), St. Louis, MO: The C. V. Mosby Company, 1978; Delbert S. Elliott, *Explaining Delinquency and Drug Abuse,* Beverly Hills, CA: Sage Publications, 1984; Bill C. Wallace, *Education and the Drug Scene,* Lincoln, NE: Professional Educators Publications, Inc., 1974.

DRUG-ABUSE EDUCATION, a general term used to describe the various programs being carried out in schools and other agencies for the purpose of having students develop an awareness of drugs as well as the inner strengths/resources necessary to make correct decisions during times of stress or conflict. The Drug Abuse Council has identified seven goals for K–12 drug-abuse education programs. They are: "(1) to increase an individual's knowledge about drugs; (2) to affect an individual's attitude toward personal consumption of drugs; (3) to alter an individual's drug abuse behavior; (4) to increase an individual's participation in alternatives; (5) to classify an individual's values; (6) to improve an individual's decision-making skills; and, (7) to improve an individual's self-concept" (Bushey, p. 2).

These goals notwithstanding, there is no general agreement regarding the best kind of drug education program, primarily because none has proven successful to date. Roger Aubrey pointed out that scare programs, integrated programs, use of addicts, or use of several newer approaches have yet to demonstrate effectiveness.

References: L. Annette Abrams, et al. (Editors), *Accountability in Drug Education: A Model for Evaluation*, Washington, DC: The Drug Abuse Council, Inc., 1973; Roger F. Aubrey, *The Counselor and Drug Abuse Programs*, Boston: Houghton Mifflin Company, 1973; Harold J. Cornacchia, et al., *Drugs in the Classroom: A Conceptual Model for School Programs*, St. Louis, MO: The C. V. Mosby Company, 1978; John Eddy, *The Teacher and the Drug Scene* (PDK Fastback 26), Bloomington, IN: The Phi Delta Kappa Educational Foundation, 1973; Delbert S. Elliott, *Explaining Delinquency and Drug Abuse*, Beverly Hills, CA: Sage Publications, 1984.

DRY CARREL—See CARREL

DRY MOUNT—See MATERIALS PRESERVATION

DUAL PROGRESS PLAN (DPP), a form of departmentalization in the elementary school. The plan was proposed in 1956 by George D. Stoddard as a way to permit students, in certain subject fields, to progress as rapidly or as slowly as their abilities allow.

DPP divides the curriculum into two principal parts: *cultural imperatives* (essential for successful functioning in modern society), and *cultural electives* (those areas not as essential). The plan requires employment of core teachers (language arts-social studies), subject-matter specialists, and use of ability grouping.

DPP was implemented in the Long Beach, New York, and Ossining, New York, school systems as part of a demonstration project funded by the Ford Foundation. (See CULTURAL IMPERATIVES and CULTURAL ELECTIVES.)
References: Glen Heathers, *Organizing Schools Through the Dual Progress Plan: Tryouts of A New Plan for Elementary and Middle Schools*, Danville, IL: The Interstate Printers and Publishers, Inc., 1967; George D. Stoddard, *The Dual Progress Plan*, New York: Harper and Row, Publishers, 1961.

DUAL SUPERVISION—See UNITY OF COMMAND

DU BOIS, WILLIAM E. B. (February 23, 1868–August 27, 1963), black social scientist who, for reasons of scholarship and intellectual ability, came to be known as the dean of Negro intellectuals. A founder of the National Association for the Advancement of Colored People and a teacher of economics at Atlanta University, he debated regularly with Booker T. Washington regarding the kind of education the American Negro should receive. Washington held out for vocational skill development; Du Bois championed liberal arts and humanities training, primarily to help the black to study and cultivate his own culture. Du Bois wanted not only economic equality but civil and political equality for blacks as well.

While at Atlanta University, where he taught economics, history, and sociology, Du Bois founded *Phylon*, a quarterly devoted to the Negro in America. He was the editor of the NAACP's official organ, *Crisis*, from 1910 to 1932, and served as head of the NAACP's research department between 1944 and 1948. During his lifetime, Du Bois authored several books dealing with slavery, the problems of black Americans, and racial problems. He was concerned about the liberation of African colonies and, in 1900, at the first Pan-African Conference in London, advocated their independence. He wrote many books and articles, among them "The Suppression of the African Slave-Trade to America" in the *Harvard Historical Series* (1896), *The Philadelphia Negro* (1899), *Atlanta University Studies* (1897–1911), *The Souls of Black Folk* (1903), *The World and Africa* (1948), and *In Battle for Peace* (1952). He died in Ghana where he had gone, at age 93, to edit *Encyclopedia Africana*.

Du Bois earned a baccalaureate at Fisk University and the Ph.D. at Harvard. Two years before his death, he joined the Communist Party, a move that added to his already established reputation as a controversial figure.
References: Russell L. Adams, *Great Negroes Past and Present*, Chicago: Afro-Am Publishing Company, 1964; Herbert Aptheker (Editor), *Prayers for Dark People*, Amherst, MA: University of Massachusetts Press, 1980; Paul C. Partington, *W. E. B. Du Bois: A Bibliography of His Published Writings*, Whittier, CA: P. C. Partington, 1979; Harry A. Ploski and Warren Marr II, *The Negro Almanac: A Reference Work on the Afro-American* (Third Edition), New York: The Bellwether Company, 1976.

DUE PROCESS, procedural rights for students and teachers designed to ensure fundamental fairness when decisions of a personal rights nature are made. Although the courts have been reluctant to prescribe specific due process procedures, they are in general agreement that due process should include notice and hearing. *Notice* requires notification of a decision affecting a party; *hearing* assures the right of the party to be heard (rebuttal) on such personal rights matters as suspension, expulsion, or termination. Additionally, the party affected must be acquainted with all relevant evidence and provided with fair-play safeguards such as representation by legal counsel, the right to confront and cross-examine witnesses, and access to stenographic transcripts of the proceedings.

The nature and extent of due process rights for teachers depend on their employment status.

Due process procedures are derived from the Fifth Amendment and the Due Process Clause of the Fourteenth Amendment to the U.S. Constitution. The latter reads: "nor shall any State deprive any person of life, liberty or property, without due process of law."

References: Thomas Flygare, *The Legal Rights of Students* (PDK Fastback 59), Bloomington, IN: The Phi Delta Kappa Educational Foundation, 1975; Thomas Flygare, *The Legal Rights of Teachers* (PDK Fastback 83), Bloomington, IN: The Phi Delta Kappa Educational Foundation, 1976; Richard D. Gatti and Daniel J. Gatti, *Encyclopedic Dictionary of School Law,* West Nyack, NY: Parker Publishing Company, Inc., 1975; Patricia A. Hollander, *Legal Handbook for Educators,* Boulder, CO: Westview Press, 1978.

DUPLICATOR—See SPIRIT DUPLICATION

DWARFISM—See CRETINISM

DYSFLUENCY—See STUTTERING

DYSGRAPHIA, inability to write, probably due to a neurological disorder. Although some dysgraphics write fairly legibly, their writing is disordered. The disordered writing may take many forms, including: (1) poor formation of complete, individual letters; (2) inability to combine letters to form meaningful words; (3) telescoping of letters; (4) letter reversals (e.g. "d" for "b"); (5) up and down writing, giving it a roller-coaster-like appearance; and (7) generally poor penmanship. Dysgraphia is frequently, although not always, related to dyslexia. To date, it is not medically treatable but careful instruction can help to overcome its extreme manifestations. (See DYSLEXIA.)

References: R. M. N. Crosby, *The Waysiders: Reading and the Dyslexic Child,* New York: The John Day Company, 1976; George Kaluger and Clifford J. Kolson, *Reading and Learning Disabilities,* Columbus, OH: Charles E. Merrill Publishing Company, 1969.

DYSLEXIA, the inability to master reading at a normal age level that is not caused by a general disorder (mental retardation), major brain injury, or major emotional disturbance. Dyslexia may be caused by any number of factors and should be considered a general term describing a reading condition. Some causes of dyslexia are: lack of proper stimulation for language acquisition; emotional deprivations caused by an abnormal family environment; social-cultural or educational deprivation; minimal brain dysfunction; limited ability; and lack of mental and/or physical maturation.

A dyslexic child may: (1) have poor perceptual-motor coordination; (2) have poor intermodal integration; (3) reverse letters or words; (4) have faulty serial ordering and temporal differentiation, or (5) may have great difficulty with sound segmentation. A dyslexic child may manifest any number of the above problems. Elena Boder, M.D., classified dyslexic readers as auditory, visual, or auditory-visual dyslexic.

A major source of confusion with the term *dyslexia* is its basic definition; teachers, psychologists, and physicians define the term as it relates to their respective fields of interest. Another major concern with the term stems from problems of determining what is a normal age level in reading. A third problem is identifying the basic symptoms. (See MIRROR READING and STREPHOSYMBOLIA.)

References: Elena Boder, "Development Dyslexia: A Diagnostic Screening Procedure Based on Three Characteristic Patterns of Reading and Spelling," *Claremont Reading Conference,* 1968; Elena Boder, "Developmental Dyslexia," *Journal of School Health,* Volume 40, 1970; Eleanor J. Gibson and Harry Levin, *The Psychology of Reading,* Cambridge, MA: The MIT Press, 1975; Emerald V. Dechant and Henry P. Smith, *Psychology in Teaching Reading* (Second Edition), Englewood Cliffs, NJ: Prentice-Hall, Inc., 1977; National Institute of Mental Health, *Caring About Kids: Dyslexia,* Rockville, MD: The Institute, 1978.

EARLY ADMISSIONS—See ROLLING ADMISSIONS

EARLY CHILDHOOD EDUCATION, generally considered to be that formal level of education provided for young children, pre-school through and including Kindergarten. (Some authorities include grades 1–3 as part of Early Childhood Education.) Although education for young children has always been important in most societies, Johann Pestalozzi (1746–1827) and Friedrich Froebel (1792–1852) are credited with starting formal education for young children with the advent of the Kindergarten.

Maria Montessori (1870–1952) and Margaret McMillan (1860–1931) are reported to have started the first nursery schools. Day Care centers were established during World War II to accommodate working mothers. During the 1960s, more formal cognitive development programs for the two- to five-year-olds (pre-school) were generated. Early childhood education has been heavily influenced by child psychologists and child development experts, particularly Jean Piaget, Urie Bronfenbrenner, and Arnold Gesell. (See FROEBEL, FRIEDRICH W.; MONTESSORI, MARIA; PIAGET, JEAN; and PESTALOZZI, JOHANN HEINRICH.)

References: Millie C. Almy, *The Early Childhood Educator,* New York: McGraw-Hill Book Company, 1975; Carol Seefeldt and Nita Barbour, *Early Childhood Education: An Introduction,* Columbus, OH: Charles E. Merrill Publishing Company, 1986; Bernard Spodek and Herbert J. Walberg (Editors), *Early Childhood Education: Issues and Insights,* Berkeley, CA: McCutchan Publishing Corporation, 1977.

EARTH SCIENCE CURRICULUM PROJECT (ESCP), a project organized by the American Geological Institute and funded in 1962 by the National Science Foundation. It was instituted to achieve two ends: (1) preparation of new materials for a one-year, secondary school earth science course, and (2) improving the education of earth science teachers. The project developed an innovative course, *Investigating the Earth,* designed for students in grades 7–10. A textbook carrying the same title was published in 1964 (revised and published by the Houghton Mifflin Company in 1967) along with supplementary materials that included a teacher's guide, field study guides, laboratory books, filmstrips, and tests. The ESCP course was experience centered and stressed student inquiry. Inservice institutes for teachers were also supported by the project.

Various efforts were made to evaluate the effectiveness of the ESCP course, most concluding that students who completed it achieved better on formal tests than did their non-ESCP counterparts, were better thinkers, and were more likely to do better in college geology courses.

National Science Foundation funding of the project was phased out in 1970. ESCP subsequently became part of the American Geological Institute's Earth Science Education Program.

References: Alfred T. Collette, *Science Teaching in the Secondary School: A Guide for Modernizing Instruction,* Boston: Allyn and Bacon, Inc., 1973; Richard E. Haney, *The Changing Curriculum: Science,* Washington, DC: Association for Supervision and Curriculum Development, NEA, 1966; J. David Lockard (Editor), *Science and Mathematics Curricular Developments Internationally, 1956–1974,* College Park, MD: Science Teaching Center, University of Maryland (Joint Project with the Commission on Science Education, American Association for the Advancement of Science), 1974; John F. Thompson, et al., "Evaluation of NSF Funded ESCP Inservice Institutes," *Journal of Geological Education,* November 1973.

ECLECTIC READING METHOD, a system of reading instruction in which the teacher employs the best elements of several reading approaches. Most eclectic programs make use of a basal reader that is supplemented by teacher-selected materials such as workbooks, fiction, and study-skill manuals. One authority (John Manning) suggested that effective eclectic teaching of reading takes place when the teacher: (1) understands diagnosis of pupil deficiencies as developmental method; (2) employs systematic oral reading for diagnosis purposes; (3) utilizes instructional materials designed to teach specific skills; and (4) employs materials to intensify practice in specific reading areas.

References: Eldon E. Ekwall and James L. Shanker, *Teaching Reading in the Elementary School* (Second Edition), Columbus, OH: Merrill Publishing Company, 1989; John C. Manning, "Eclectic Reading Instruction for Primary Grade Success" in Althea Beery, et al. (Editors), *Elementary Reading Instruction: Selected Materials* (Second Edition), Boston: Allyn and Bacon, Inc., 1974; Barbara

D. Stoodt, *Reading Instruction* (Second Edition), New York: Harper and Row, Publishers, 1989.

ECONOMIC OPPORTUNITY ACT, federal legislation enacted in 1964 that was a part of the War on Poverty and that had minorities and the poor as its principal targets. This legislation was comprehensive. It established two well-known service organizations: Job Corps and Volunteers in Service to America (VISTA). Work training programs were established "to provide useful work experience opportunities for unemployed young men and young women, through participation in state and community work-training programs" (U.S. Statutes, p. 512). Work study programs were also established to make part-time employment opportunities available to college students from low income families. Community action programs were also authorized. They were created "to provide stimulation and incentive for urban and rural communities to mobilize their resources to combat poverty through community action programs" (U.S. Statutes, p. 516). Other provisions of the Economic Opportunity Act included support for adult basic education programs, special programs for migrant and low-income rural families, employment and investment incentives, and work-experience programs.

This legislation was eventually replaced by CETA, the Comprehensive Employment and Training Act. (See COMPREHENSIVE EMPLOYMENT AND TRAINING ACT and OFFICE OF ECONOMIC OPPORTUNITY.)
References: Garth Mangum and David Snedeker, *Manpower Planning for Local Labor Markets*, Salt Lake City, UT: Olympus Publishing Company, 1974; National Advisory Council on Economic Opportunity, *Seventh Annual Report*, Washington, DC: The Council, June 1974; Public Law 88-452, *United States Statutes at Large, 1964* (Volume 78), Washington, DC: U.S. Government Printing Office, 1965.

ECONOMICS OF EDUCATION, a field of study in education that deals broadly with education and finances. This subject's content embraces three areas of concern, expressed here as questions: (1) In what way does a society utilize its resources to produce different kinds of education and/or training (primarily schooling)? (2) How is education distributed among various populations and individuals? and (3) What kinds of educational activities should a society support?
References: Charles S. Benson, *The Economics of Public Education* (Second Edition), Boston: Houghton Mifflin

Company, 1968; Elchanan Cohn, *The Economics of Education* (Revised Edition), Cambridge, MA: Ballinger Publishing Company, 1979.

ECTOMORPHY—See CONSTITUTIONAL TYPES

EDUCATING AMERICANS FOR THE 21ST CENTURY: A REPORT TO THE AMERICAN PEOPLE AND THE NATIONAL SCIENCE BOARD—See NATIONAL REFORM REPORTS (1980–86)

EDUCABLE RETARDATION—See MENTAL RETARDATION

EDUCATION ABSTRACTS: UNESCO, reference books published by the United Nations Educational Scientific and Cultural Organization, Paris, France. They were published on a generally irregular basis from 1949 to 1964. *Education Abstracts,* when first published, were annotated guides that appeared ten times each year. Starting with Volume 6, reports were presented about various countries, these in the context of some preselected topic (e.g. agricultural education). UNESCO's *Education Abstracts* ceased publication with Volume XVI, No. 4, 1964.
References: John W. Best, *Research in Education* (Third Edition), Englewood Cliffs, NJ: Prentice-Hall, Inc., 1977; *Education Abstracts: Agricultural Education* (Part II), Paris, France: UNESCO, Volume XVI, No. 4, 1964; Eugene P. Sheehy, *Guide to Reference Books* (Ninth Edition), Chicago: American Library Association, 1976.

EDUCATIONAL EQUITY, providing every student with equality of educational opportunity regardless of his/her race, national origin, color, gender, or socioeconomic status. Data indicate that student achievement is frequently related to these demographic variables. The goal of educational equity is to reduce, eventually eliminate these correlations.
Reference: National Institute of Education, *Teaching and Learning Research Grants Announcement: Fiscal Years 1981, 1982, 1983, 1984,* Washington, DC: U.S. Department of Education, August 1980.

EDUCATIONAL FACILITIES LABORATORY (EFL), until recently an independent foundation working to: (1) help educational institutions resolve their physical problems; (2) encourage research and experimentation dealing with school plant and other physical planning; and (3) disseminate information relating to educational facilities. EFL was created in 1958 by the Ford Foundation and, during the first 12 years of its existence, received 100 percent of its financial support from it. In 1979, steps were taken to merge EFL with the Academy for Educational Development. The merger provided that EFL would become a division of the Academy but retain its original name.

EFL has been involved in planning and facilities activities at all educational levels, pre-school through postgraduate. They have included projects such as planning of special instructional facilities, finding alternate ways to finance school buildings, building conversions, student housing, planning facilities for the handicapped, and even planning education for new towns. In the recent past, it has been actively involved in the promotion of energy management. EFL has also published numbers of books, reports, and pamphlets on various topics relating to educational facilities. The division's main office is in New York City.

References: Academy for Educational Development, *Academy Publications*, Washington, DC: The Academy, Undated Booklet; Academy for Educational Development, *EFL and Educational Facilities Planning*, Washington, DC: The Academy, Mimeographed Newsletter, January 1980; Academy for Educational Development, *EFL and Energy Management*, Washington, DC: The Academy, Mimeographed Newsletter, January 1980; *Academy News*, July 1979.

EDUCATIONAL GERONTOLOGY—See GERONTOLOGY

EDUCATIONAL INSTITUTE OF SCOTLAND (EIS), one of the oldest teachers' organizations in the world (established 1847). EIS is a national body. It consists of 37 local associations, each represented (on a proportional representation basis) on a Central Council that has a combined membership of 165. Divisional councils (regional units) facilitate work that does not have a national purview. These intermediate bodies are not represented on the Central Council.

EIS conducts its annual general meeting each June. More routine matters of concern to the institute are carried out by the council during its September, November, February, and April meetings. Six standing committees carry out specific activities for the institute (e.g. salaries). Membership includes public as well as Catholic teachers, the latter organized into three Catholic teachers' districts that are represented on the institute's council.

Members of EIS concurrently belong to one of four sections: (1) Primary Education; (2) Secondary Education; (3) Special Education; or (4) Remedial Education. In addition, five National Sections (e.g. Nursery Teachers' and Psychologists') were created recently to meet the unique needs of specialized personnel.

EIS was granted a Royal Charter in 1851. This was amended recently to grant the organization trade union status.

EIS's main office is in Edinburgh. (See WORLD CONFEDERATION OF ORGANIZATIONS OF THE TEACHING PROFESSION.)

References: Educational Institute of Scotland, *Organization of the EIS* (Organization of EIS, No. 1.2), Edinburgh, Scotland: The Institute, Undated Bulletin; Educational Institute of Scotland, *The History of the Institute* (Organization of EIS, No. 1.1), Edinburgh, Scotland: The Institute, Undated Bulletin.

EDUCATIONAL INSTITUTION, an organization or establishment whose principal purpose is the offering of instruction. A functional definition of this term appears in Section 901, Title IX, Public Law 92-318: "(A)n educational institution means any public or private preschool, elementary, or secondary school, or any institution of vocational, professional, or higher education, except that in the case of an educational institution composed of more than one school, college, or department which are administratively separate units, such term means each such school, college, or department" (p. 374). A more general definition is offered by the National Center for Educational Statistics: "a public, private, or proprietary organization or establishment devoted to the promotion, development, and attainment of learning at one or more levels of instruction, and embracing such designations as school, college, institute, or university" (p. 175).

References: W. Dale Chismore and Quentin M. Hill, *A Classification of Educational Subject Matter* (State Educational Records and Reports Series: Handbook XI), Washington, DC: National Center for Education Statistics, U.S. Department of Health, Education, and Welfare, 1978; Public Law 92-318, *United States Statutes at Large, 1972* (Volume 86), Washington, DC: U.S. Government Printing Office, 1973.

EDUCATIONAL LEARNING BLOCK—See LEARNING BLOCK

EDUCATIONALLY DISADVANTAGED—See CULTURALLY DEPRIVED

EDUCATIONAL MALPRACTICE—See *PETER DOE v. SAN FRANCISCO UNIFIED SCHOOL DISTRICT*

EDUCATIONAL PARK, sometimes called a consolidated campus, a single school site accommodating children of all ages and all grade levels. These sites are rather large, for there may be several school buildings and other school facilities constructed on them. Educational parks have been proposed as a solution to school segregation since school attendance areas are broad, usually one in a school district.

There are several problems associated with educational parks. Because the sites have to be quite large, there is the problem of obtaining available land. Another issue is the age range of children converging on such a site; 6-year-olds attend the same campus as 18-year-olds. Transportation flow is yet another problem. Finally, desegregation may take place at the site, but integration within each unit may not occur of itself.

Variations of the educational park concept have been implemented. One, an educational and cultural park, has been developed in West Philadelphia, Pennsylvania, where a public high school, university, and science and technology center have been built in the same large complex.

References: AASA Commission on School Buildings, *Schools for America*, Washington, DC: American Association of School Administrators, 1967; Nicholaus L. Engelhardt, *Complete Guide for Planning New Schools*, West Nyack, NY: Parker Publishing Company, Inc., 1970.

EDUCATIONAL POLICIES COMMISSION, a study group sponsored by the National Education Association and the American Association of School Administrators that, in 1938, published a statement of aims for American education. This significant goals document called for a reevaluation of the purposes of school. The commission was influenced by the progressive education movement. Not surprisingly, its report placed considerable emphasis on the development of the individual in society.

The commission's report consisted of four broad goal statements. The first, *The Objectives of Self-Realization,* included as objectives the inquiring mind, speech, reading, writing, number, sight and hearing skills, health knowledge and habits, public health, recreation, intellectual and aesthetic interests, and character. The second, *The Objectives of Human Relationship,* had these objectives: respect for humanity, friendships, cooperation, courtesy,

appreciation and conservation of the home, homemaking, and democracy in the home. The third broad goal, *The Objectives of Economic Efficiency,* consisted of objectives relating to work, occupational information and choice, occupational efficiency and adjustment, occupational appreciation, personal economics, consumer judgment and protection, and efficiency in buying. The final goal statement, *The Objectives of Civic Responsibility,* addressed these specific objectives: social justice, social activity, social understanding, critical judgment, tolerance, conservation, social applications of science, world citizenship, law observance, economic literacy, political citizenship, and devotion to democracy.

The commission is no longer in existence.

Reference: Educational Policies Commission, *The Purposes of Education in American Democracy,* Washington, DC: The Commission, 1938.

EDUCATIONAL PRODUCTS INFORMATION EXCHANGE INSTITUTE (EPIE), a consumer information organization. EPIE was chartered initially in 1967 and then permanently in 1975 by the Regents of the University of the State of New York. It is a nonprofit organization and is supported through memberships (about 3,500), subscriptions ("EPIEgrams"), workshops, and grants. EPIE services primarily school districts and state education agencies.

EPIE and the newly established Software Evaluation Office was located on the C. W. Post campus of Long Island University; it is located (1990) in South Hampton, New York, with the following mailing address: P.O. Box 839, Water Mill, NY, 11976. The Software Evaluation Office maintains an electronically accessible database on educational software—called TESS (The Educational Software Selector.) In addition, EPIE has created a system that permits schools to locate appropriate computer and video software, textbooks, and other teaching materials that are congruent with curriculum objectives and tests; this system is titled Integrated Instructional Information Resource (IIIR). (See SOFTWARE.)

References: Brenda Branen-Broadbent and R. Kent Wood (Editors), *Educational Media and Technology Yearbook,* Volume 15, Englewood, CO: Libraries Unlimited, Inc., 1989; Educational Products Information Exchange Institute, *Selector's Guide for Elementary School/Junior High School Science Programs* (EPIE Report Number 77) New York: EPIE Institute, 1977; Educational Products Information Exchange Institute, *Education Newsletter,* Long Island University, Volume 15, Number 2, Winter 1988.

EDUCATIONAL PROGRAM—See PROGRAM, EDUCATIONAL

EDUCATIONAL PSYCHOLOGY, the study of psychology as it applies to educational/instructional practices. Educational psychology combines both education and psychology. It focuses on the improvement of the learning/instructional environment by studying individuals (learners and teachers) in the classroom/school. Educational psychologists apply existing psychological theories, concepts, and principles; they also develop new ones. There are many elements of general psychology that are used in the school/educational setting including human development, sensations, perceptions, attitudes, problem solving, personality, adjustment, learning theory, measurement, evaluation, assessment, interests, motivation, instructional technology, mental health, learning-models, and behavior modification. (See BEHAVIOR MODIFICATION; PERSONALITY; and PSYCHOLOGY.)

References: Robert C. Craig, et al., *Contemporary Educational Psychology: Concepts, Issues, Applications*, New York: John Wiley and Sons, 1975; Janice T. Gibson and Louis A. Chandler, *Educational Psychology: Mastering Principles and Applications*, Boston: Allyn and Bacon, 1988; Robert Glaser (Editor), *Advances in Instructional Psychology*, Hillsdale, NJ: Lawrence Erlbaum Associates, Publishers, 1978.

EDUCATIONAL RESEARCH SERVICE (ERS), a nonprofit agency, established in 1973, that carries out research in the areas of educational management and policy. Seven management organizations sponsor ERS and account for approximately 10 percent of its budget. They are: (1) American Association of School Administrators; (2) American Association of School Personnel Administrators; (3) Council of Chief State School Officers; (4) National Association of Elementary School Principals; (5) National Association of Secondary School Principals; (6) National School Boards Association; and (7) National School Public Relations Association. Over 2,500 school systems and educational agencies subscribe to ERS and collectively provide the additional budgetary support it needs to operate.

ERS provides its members with three types of service: (1) *preparation of reports* (approximately 15–20 per year); (2) *on-call information service,* available to individual institutional members seeking specific information; and (3) *summaries of research* completed by other organizations.

ERS is in Arlington, Virginia.

References: Educational Research Service, *ERS,* Arlington, VA: The Service, Undated Brochure; Educational Research Service, *How to Get the Most from Your ERS Subscription: A Guide for Subscribing School Systems,* Arlington, VA: The Service, 1980; *The School Administrator,* April 1980.

EDUCATIONAL RESOURCES INFORMATION CENTER—See ERIC

(THE) EDUCATIONAL SOFTWARE SELECTOR (TESS)—See EDUCATIONAL PRODUCTS INFORMATION EXCHANGE INSTITUTE

EDUCATIONAL SPECIALIST, an individual who is considered to have a high degree of skill in a field of education or in an educationally related field. Most education specialists have spent many years in training and have achieved high levels of formal education (i.e. advanced degrees). In addition, they tend to have had varied and in-depth experiences, either applied or abstract. Recognition by peers and others helps to establish one's reputation as an educational specialist.

The *Education Specialist Degree* (Ed.S.), sometimes referred to as a Professional Diploma (PD), is a graduate degree earned at an institution of higher education that offers advanced programs in teacher education. Although there is no set number of graduate credit hours one must complete beyond the master's degree level to earn an Ed.S., the range is generally 30–40 semester hours beyond the master's degree. Admission to Ed.S. programs varies from institution to institution, but the entrance requirements are usually more restrictive than those at the master's level. Admission is limited to superior graduate students. Once admitted, the student is expected to follow a planned program. Although there is no dissertation required, a research project must be completed and required examinations passed. In many institutions, the Ed.S. is the highest degree awarded.

References: University of Louisville Graduate School 1978–79 Bulletin; Asa S. Knowles (Editor), *The International Encyclopedia of Higher Education,* San Francisco: Jossey-Bass Publishers, 1977.

EDUCATIONAL TELEVISION—See INSTRUCTIONAL TELEVISION

EDUCATIONAL TELEVISION FACILITIES ACT (Public Law 87-447), federal legislation that authorized grants (on a 50-50 matching basis) for constructing and improving physical facilities for educational telecommunications. Enacted in 1962, the act provided: (1) grants not to exceed $1,000,000 per state for construction of ETV facilities; (2) that university, school, state agency, and community corporation ETV stations would each be eligible for such grants; (3) criteria for distribution of grants; and (4) that there shall be no federal interference or control. Subsequent legislation increased the annual dollar allocations for ETV and revised the matching provisions such that the federal government (through 1981) provided three dollars for every one dollar raised locally.

In 1962, the year in which the act was passed, 74 ETV stations were on the air. By 1975, the number increased to 261. Contributing to that increase was an amendment to the Communications Act of 1934, also passed in 1962, that required manufacturers of television receivers to provide for reception of all VHF and UHF channels. (Significantly, 163 of the 261 ETV stations operating in 1975 were UHF stations.)

References: Robert J. Blakely, *To Serve the Public Interest: Educational Broadcasting in the United States*, Syracuse, NY: Syracuse University Press, 1979; Public Law 87-447, *United States Statutes at Large, 1962* (Volume 76), Washington, DC: U.S. Government Printing Office, 1963; Donald N. Wood and Donald G. Wylie, *Educational Telecommunications*, Belmont, CA: Wadsworth Publishing Company, Inc., 1977.

EDUCATIONAL TESTING SERVICE (ETS), a private, nonprofit organization devoted to measurement and research. The organization grew out of a 1946 study funded by the Carnegie Foundation for the Advancement of Teaching and carried out under the direction of James Bryant Conant, President of Harvard University. Dr. Conant examined national testing operations that were administered by nonprofit agencies. These agencies were the College Entrance Examinations Board, The Educational Record Bureau, the Cooperative Test Service, National Committee on Teacher Examinations of the American Council on Education, and the Graduate Record Office of the Carnegie Foundation. From this study came the recommendation that a new organization be formed that would provide research, test development, test construction, publications, and administrative coordination of the tests listed. It was to be part of the American Council on Education. This suggestion was later changed to provide independent status for ETS.

The Carnegie Foundation made a grant of $750,000 to fund the new organization. The Col-

lege Board (CEEB) tests became the core of ETS. ETS presently develops and publishes many specific tests, the best known of which are the Scholastic Aptitude Test (SAT), Preliminary Scholastic Aptitude Test (PSAT), Graduate Record Examination (GRE), National Teachers Examination (NTE), and the College Level Examination Program (CLEP).

ETS's main office is in Princeton, New Jersey. (See COLLEGE-LEVEL EXAMINATION PROGRAM; GRADUATE RECORD EXAMINATION; and SCHOLASTIC APTITUDE TEST.)

References: Educational Testing Service, *About ETS*, Princeton, NJ: The Service, Undated Brochure; Educational Testing Service, *ETS Annual Report, 1987*, Princeton, NJ: The Service, 1987.

EDUCATIONAL VOUCHERS—See VOUCHERS

EDUCATION COMMISSION OF THE STATES (ECS), an organization formed by interstate compact. Its principal function is to assist governors, state legislators, and educators with the improvement of education. Its governing body is drawn from each of these three groups. ECS was formed in 1966. Almost all states, Puerto Rico, and the Virgin Islands are members. Headquartered in Denver, Colorado, the commission employs a full-time staff that renders a variety of services to member states and possessions. It administers projects, drafts model legislation, provides technical assistance, sponsors forums, publishes materials and research findings, and maintains a communication link with the federal government. The National Assessment of Educational Progress (NAEP) was a major project with which the commission was involved; it no longer has the NAEP contract. (See NATIONAL ASSESSMENT OF EDUCATIONAL PROGRESS.)

Reference: Education Commission of the States, *Annual Report: 1977 New Directions*, Denver, CO: The Commission, 1977.

EDUCATION CONSOLIDATION IMPROVEMENT ACT, an education act that was part of the omnibus Budget Reconciliation Act passed in the first session of the 97th United States Congress (Public Law 97–35, August 13, 1981). The omnibus Budget Reconciliation Act had 27 titles, ranging from agriculture to the health professions. Most education programs were included in Title V of the act. The initial authorization covered fiscal years 1982–1984. The act itself superseded the Elementary and Secondary Education Act of 1965 and other various federal education acts.

Chapter 1 (Subchapter)—Financial Assistance to Meet Special Educational Needs of Disadvantaged Children and Chapter 2 (Subchapter)—Consolidation of Federal Programs for Elementary and Secondary Education are the two major chapters of the act; Chapter 3, the other section of the act, is a "general provisions" section of the law. Chapter 1 was formally Title 1 of the Elementary and Secondary Education Act.

The authorization of funds for Chapter 1 was not to exceed $3,480,000,000 for fiscal years 1983–1984. The amount authorized for Chapter 2 was $589,368,000 for each of the fiscal years 1982, 1983, and 1984. Authorization of the act has been amended and extended several times by the United States Congress. (See ELEMENTARY AND SECONDARY EDUCATION ACT.)

References: United States Code Annotated, Title 20 Education 1681 to End, St. Paul, MN: West Publishing Co., 1986; *United States Code Congressional and Administrative News, 97th Congress—First Session 1981*, (Volume 1, 95 STAT), St. Paul, MN: West Publishing Co., 1982; *United States Congressional and Administrative News, 98th Congress—First Session 1983* (Volume 1, 97 STAT), St. Paul, MN: West Publishing Co., 1984.

EDUCATION FOR ALL HANDICAPPED CHILDREN ACT—See PUBLIC LAW 94–142

EDUCATION FOR ECONOMIC SECURITY ACT (Public Law 98–377), passed by the United States Congress on August 11, 1984, provided assistance to mathematics and science programs in elementary, secondary, and postsecondary schools (and colleges). The act's prime purpose was to improve the quality of mathematics and science instruction in the United States. Under the act: teacher institutes were authorized through the National Science Foundation (Title I) for the training, retraining, and inservicing of elementary and secondary school teachers in the fields of mathematics and science. Congressional Merit Scholarships (for those taking mathematics, science, and engineering in college) were established and state and local agencies were helped to improve the skills of teachers and improve instruction in mathematics and science (Title II). NSF Programs for Partnerships (business, colleges, schools) in Education for Mathematics, Science, and Engineering (Title III) were initiated. In addition, Presidential Awards for Teaching Excellence in Mathematics and Science (Title IV) were established. Recognition of local

programs in mathematics and science (Title VI) were started. Assistance in the development of magnet schools (Title VII) was included, and a provision not related to mathematics and science, Title VIII—the Equal Access Act, was attached to Public Law 98–377.

Under the Equal Access Act, public secondary schools, which receive federal monies and which have a limited open forum, cannot deny equal access or a fair opportunity to students who wish to conduct a meeting within the limited open forum basis because of the religious, political, philosophical, or other content nature of the speech to be presented. There are restrictions on such meetings, such as: it is to be voluntary, student-initiated, not sponsored by the school, and does not interfere with the orderly conduct of the school. (See NATIONAL SCIENCE, ENGINEERING, AND MATHEMATICS AUTHORIZATION ACT OF 1986.)

Reference: United States Code Congressional and Administrative News, 98th Congress—Second Session, 1984 (Volume 1), St. Paul, MN: West Publishing Co., 1985.

EDUCATION INDEX, a serial publication listing current references to education that are written in the English language. The *Education Index*, first published in 1929, is a cumulative author and subject index. Twenty-nine cumulative volumes of the *Index* were produced from 1929-32 to 1978-79. Principal listings are taken from educational periodicals; selected yearbooks, book reviews, and monographs are also included. Selection of periodicals to be indexed is determined by a vote of subscribers. A committee of the American Library Association advises the publisher, H. W. Wilson Company, on indexing and general publication policy.

References: Carter Alexander and Arvid J. Burke, *How to Locate Educational Information and Data: An Aid to Quick Utilization of the Literature of Education* (Fourth Edition), New York: Bureau of Publications, Teachers College, Columbia University, 1958; Mary Louise Hewitt (Editor), *Education Index: July 1978–June 1979* (Volume 29), New York: The H. W. Wilson Company, 1979; Marda Woodbury, *A Guide to Sources of Educational Information*, Washington, DC: Information Resources Press, 1976.

EDUCATION PROFESSIONS DEVELOPMENT ACT (EPDA), federal legislation enacted in 1967 for the purpose of meeting the shortage of qualified educational personnel in the nation's elementary and secondary schools. Provisions for a variety of training programs were made to help realize this objective. One group of programs was designed to improve the education of children from low-income families. It included the Career Opportunities Program, Teacher Corps, and the Urban/Rural School Development Program. A second group consisted of programs designed to reinforce the preparation of all educational personnel. These were the Teacher Trainers Program (Triple-T) and one that authorized creation of teacher centers, the Training Complexes Program. A third cluster of programs was comprised of programs intended to meet shortages of educational personnel in areas such as bilingual education, early childhood education, vocational education, special education, school leadership, and pupil personnel services. The fourth and final group included programs to meet special needs for educational personnel. It included the School Personnel Utilization Program, which sought to bring about institutional change, and the Teacher Development for Desegregating Schools Program.

Each of the foregoing programs was administered by the Bureau of Educational Personnel Development, U.S. Office of Education. A Media Specialists Program, also authorized by EPDA, was administered by the Office's Bureau of Libraries and Educational Technology. EPDA expired in 1976, although continuation of several of its component programs was later authorized in separate legislation. (See CAREER OPPORTUNITIES PROGRAM; TEACHER CENTER; TEACHER CORPS; and TRIPLE-T PROGRAM.)

References: Bureau of Educational Personnel Development, *Education Professions Development Act: Facts About Programs for 1971-72*, Washington, DC: U.S. Office of Education, July 1970; Don Davies, "Education Professions Development Act: An Inside Perspective" in Alan Gartner, et al. (Editors) *Paraprofessionals in Education Today*, New York: Human Services Press, 1977; Public Law 90-35, *United States Statutes at Large, 1967* (Volume 81), Washington, DC: U.S. Government Printing Office, 1968.

EDUCATION RESEARCH INFORMATION CENTER—See ERIC

EFFORT, FINANCIAL—See FINANCIAL EFFORT

EGALITARIANISM—See ELITISM

EIGHT-FOUR PLAN—See ORGANIZATIONAL PLANS

EIGHT-YEAR STUDY, a field demonstration of selected secondary school graduates, carried out between 1933 and 1941. The Progressive Education Association, concerned over the extent to which college entrance requirements were then dominating the high school curriculum, sponsored the study.

Between 1936 and 1939, 1,475 graduates from the 30 secondary schools who participated in the study entered 300 cooperating colleges and universities. The graduates were paired with an equal number of graduates from other high schools. Matching variables included sex, race, aptitude, age, interest, family background, and type of home community. Careful matching was imperative since the alumni from the 30 schools ranked higher than the average college entrant in intelligence.

Analysis of the students' success in college indicated that those from the more experimental or progressive of the 30 schools were not handicapped in their college work. It was also found that those who came from participating schools that engaged in the greatest amount of innovation achieved better in college than did their counterparts from the control (or more traditional) school population. (See PROGRESSIVE EDUCATION ASSOCIATION.)

References: Wilford M. Aikin, *The Story of the Eight-Year Study* (Volume I of the Adventure in American Education Series), New York: Harper and Brothers, 1942; Wilford M. Aikin, "The Story of the Eight-Year Study" in Carl H. Gross and Charles C. Chandler (Editors), *The History of American Education Through Readings*, Boston: D. C. Heath and Company, 1964; John W. Best, *Research in Education* (Third Edition), Englewood Cliffs, NJ: Prentice-Hall, Inc., 1977; William Van Til, *Education: A Beginning*, Boston: Houghton Mifflin Company, 1971.

ELECTIVE COURSES, those optional courses or programs not generally prescribed for students in a given curriculum or program. Elective courses often are used to expand the "general education" of a student. They can be used to "humanize" or broaden a highly specialized curriculum, or they can be used by students for a variety of personal reasons (e.g. personal interest).

Typical programs in high schools and colleges have specific curriculum distributions that include: (1) *required courses* (e.g. Algebra I, II, Mathematics 101, 102, English Literature 200, 201); (2) *restricted electives* (a student must take a course in mathematics, English Literature, physical science, and so on but is free to select any course as long as it meets the stated restrictions or comes from a bank of acceptable courses); and (3) *free electives* (a student may take any course he/she selects). In all cases, the elective approach is used to broaden and give more personal flexibility to the student.

References: Morton Alpren (Editor), *The Subject Curriculum: Grades K-12,* Columbus, OH: Charles E. Merrill Books, Inc., 1967; John I. Goodlad, et al., *The Changing School Curriculum,* New York: The Fund for the Advancement of Education, 1966; Frederick Rudolph, *Curriculum: A History of the American Undergraduate Course of Study Since 1636,* San Francisco: Jossey-Bass Publishers, 1978; Daniel Tanner and Laurel N. Tanner, *Curriculum Development: Theory Into Practice* (Second Edition), New York: Macmillan Publishing Company, Inc., 1980.

ELECTRONIC AMPLIFICATION, a system that amplifies sound to improve the hearing of the partially deaf. Although such systems do provide significant assistance to some, they generally do not raise hearing levels to the normal range.

Two types of amplification equipment are the *hearing aid,* a battery-powered device with adjustable volume control, and *auditory trainers.* The latter are more sophisticated than the former and are often used in classrooms. They are essentially miniature broadcasting stations. Teachers wear microphones (transmitters); hearing impaired children wear headphones (receivers). A wire loop, replacing outmoded wires that connected transmitters and receivers, is placed around the perimeter of the classroom and, like a radio transmitter, serves to disperse sounds to receivers.

References: R. E. Hartbauer, *Aural Habilitation: A Total Approach,* Springfield, IL: Charles C. Thomas, Publisher, 1975; Alice H. Streng, et al., *Language, Learning, and Deafness: Theory, Application, and Classroom Management,* New York: Grune and Stratton, 1978.

ELEMENTARY AND SECONDARY EDUCATION ACT (ESEA), omnibus federal legislation (enacted in 1965) designed to improve the quality of education at the elementary and secondary school levels.

Title I, the best known of the act's six titles, was included for the purpose of meeting the special educational needs of children of low-income families. Disbursements to local educational agencies (LEA's) were authorized on the basis of the number of low-income children residing in an LEA. In 1973, the benefits of Title I were estimated to be reaching 5,000,000 to 6,000,000 low-income children. Services provided included, but were not limited to, programs such as remedial reading, compensatory mathematics, and special summer programs. Between 1977 and 1979, the annual ap-

propriation for Title I averaged $2,300,000,000 a year.

In the 1965 legislation, Title II of ESEA allocated funds for school library resources and textbooks in public and private schools. Title III made grants available to stimulate needs and services and to encourage development of exemplary programs. Educational research and training was encouraged under Title IV. Title V made funds available to assist states in strengthening leadership resources of their educational agencies and to help them meet the educational needs of their constituencies. Title VI contained miscellaneous provisions of an administrative nature.

The Elementary and Secondary Education Act of 1965 was superseded by the 1981 Education Consolidation Improvement Act. The functions of Title I, ESEA, are now funded under Chapter 1 of Title V of the new consolidation law; all of Titles II–V are found in Chapter 2. (See EDUCATION CONSOLIDATION IMPROVEMENT ACT.)

References: Stephen K. Bailey and Edith K. Mosher, *ESEA: The Office of Education Administers a Law,* Syracuse, NY: Syracuse University Press, 1968; Milbrey W. McLaughlin, "Implementation of ESEA Title I: A Problem of Compliance" in Dale Mann (Editor), *Making Change Happen?* New York: Teachers College Press, 1978; Office of Evaluation and Dissemination, U.S. Office of Education, *Annual Evaluation Report on Programs Administered by the U.S. Office of Education, FY 1978,* Washington, DC: The Office, 1978; Public Law 89–10, *United States Statutes at Large, 1965* (Volume 79), Washington, DC: U.S. Government Printing Office, 1966; *United States Congressional and Administrative News, 97th Congress—First Session 1981* (Volume 95 STAT. 441–482), St. Paul, MN: West Publishing Co., 1982; *United States Statutes at Large,* Volume 99, Part I, Washington, DC: U.S. Government Printing Office, 1987.

ELEMENTARY SCHOOL, the basic institution of education that, in the United States, provides education for all young children of all of the people. In public schools, that education is free. Although numerous functions have been assigned to it during its almost two-century existence, the primary one continues to be the teaching of reading. Citizenship and computational skills are other traditional components of the elementary school's curriculum. Numerous other functions have been added over the years in response to the changing needs and demands of society.

Elementary schools are usually divided into grade levels (e.g. K-6, K-4), a structure introduced in the Quincy Grammar School (1848). In recent years, the emergence of the middle school has resulted in a reduction of the number of grade levels since these intermediate schools frequently include one or more of the so-called intermediate grades (i.e. grades 4–6).

Varying organizational templates are employed in the elementary school, the most widely used being the self-contained classroom. In the 20th century, other templates have been introduced in some schools including departmentalization, nongraded classes, team teaching, and, in recent years, open classrooms. In contrast to the typical high school teacher, who is a subject specialist, the typical elementary school teacher is a subject generalist responsible for teaching most subjects comprising the elementary school curriculum.

Since the 1970s, declines in the country's total number of elementary school children have been reported. Nevertheless, the total population remains high. (In 1980, the National Center for Education Statistics reported almost 31,000,000 students enrolled in grades K–8, of whom 3,600,000 attended nonpublic schools. Corresponding figures for 1970 were almost 37,000,000 total and 4,100,000 nonpublic.) Enrollment is expected to begin increasing again during the mid-1980s. (See COMMON SCHOOLS.)

References: Nancy B. Dearman and Valena W. Plisko, National Center for Education Statistics, *The Condition of Education, 1980 Edition*, Washington, DC: U.S. Government Printing Office, 1980; John I. Goodlad and Harold G. Shane (Editors), *The Elementary School in the United States* (NSSE 72nd Yearbook, Part II), Chicago: University of Chicago Press, 1973; John Jarolimek and Clifford D. Foster, *Teaching and Learning in the Elementary School* (Third Edition), New York: Macmillan Publishing Company, Inc., 1985.

ELEMENTARY SCHOOL COUNSELING, the provision of specialized counseling services to elementary school students by persons trained in the field of guidance and counseling. Until recently, school counseling services were typically limited to the senior high school level. Since the early 1960s, the number of elementary school counselors has increased dramatically, actually tripling between 1968 and 1971.

The two broad functions of the elementary counselor are development of human potential and prevention of maladjustment. Donald Keat identified a list of seven more specific functions that grow out of these broader ones and that, collectively, define the role of the elementary school counselor. They are: (1) *counseling* with children and adults; (2) *collaborating* with others, especially classroom teachers; (3) *coordination* of counseling with other supportive services available in the school; (4) *communication,* especially with students; (5) *curriculum development,* in cooperation with others; (6) *fostering* child growth and development; and (7) *teaching coping behaviors.*

Literature on elementary school counseling stresses that counselors, to be effective, must work closely with administrators, teachers, students, parents, community residents, and other of the district's support personnel.

References: Kenneth M. Dimick and Vaughn E. Huff, *Child Counseling,* Dubuque, IA: Wm. C. Brown Company, Publishers, 1970; Donald B. Keat, *Fundamentals of Child Counseling,* Boston: Houghton Mifflin Company, 1974; Richard C. Nelson, *Guidance and Counseling in the Elementary School,* New York: Holt, Rinehart and Winston, Inc., 1972; William H. Van Hoose, et al. (Editors), *Elementary-School Guidance: A Composite View,* Boston: Houghton Mifflin Company, 1973.

ELEMENTARY SCHOOL PRINCIPAL, professional administrator responsible for the management of an elementary school. In the middle of the 19th century, with the advent of graded schools and the rapid growth of cities, the need for persons to serve as controlling heads of elementary schools was recognized. One of the first cities to appoint such leaders (initially called principal-teachers because they were expected to teach as well as to administer) was Cincinnati. By 1920, the number of principals had grown considerably and the first national organization of elementary school principals was formed (as an affiliate of the NEA). Currently, approximately 25,000 elementary school principals belong to the independent National Association of Elementary School Principals.

Elementary principals qualify for their positions by earning state certificates. Requirements normally include successful completion of a graduate training program and relevant teaching experience. A national survey of elementary principals (1978) revealed that the average principal: (1) was a white male, married, 46 years of age; (2) held a masters degree; (3) earned $21,500 for 11 months of work; (4) administered a K–6 building, located in a suburban or rural area, with an enrollment of 430 pupils; and (5) supervised 18 full-time teachers (90 percent of whom were women).

In his/her daily work, the elementary school principal performs numbers of functions. Among the more important are serving as a member of an administrative team, as a community leader, as an advocate for students, as an instructional leader and supervisor, as monitor of a communication system, as a business administrator, as an authority on child development and curriculum, and as builder of a wholesome school climate.

References: Larry W. Hughes and Gerald C. Ubben, *The Elementary Principal's Handbook: A Guide to Effective Action* (Third Edition), Boston: Allyn and Bacon, 1989; William L. Pharis, "U.S. Principals: The Inside Story," *National Elementary Principal*, March 1979; William L. Pharis and Sally B. Zakariya, *The Elementary School Principalship in 1978: A Research Study*, Arlington, VA: National Association of Elementary School Principals, 1979.

ELEMENTARY SCIENCE STUDY (ESS), a collection of science units developed by the Education Development Center, Newton, Massachusetts, and distributed by the Webster Division of McGraw-Hill. Lacking sequence and continuity, ESS cannot correctly be characterized as a program; rather, it is a collection of materials, packaged as kits, that the individual teacher or school district can use independently or incorporate into the local curriculum as need and conditions warrant. Emphasis is not placed on teaching or concepts; instead, children, working individually or in small groups, are provided with materials that they are encouraged to use for the purpose of making observations and reaching conclusions. Materials have been developed for grades K–8.

Several scientists, teachers, and psychologists, in the early 1960s, participated in writing conferences at which some of the early ESS materials were prepared. Included were some of the leading educators who, previously, had worked on PSSC (Physical Science Study Committee), the high school physics program.

ESS kits are shipped as complete packages. They include all materials needed to study a particular unit together with teacher guides, student work sheets, and, in some instances, booklets for student use. (See PHYSICAL SCIENCE STUDY COMMITTEE.)

References: Glenn O. Blough and Julius Schwartz, *Elementary School Science and How to Teach It* (Fifth Edition), New York: Holt, Rinehart and Winston, Inc., 1974; Arthur A. Carin and Robert B. Sund, *Teaching Science Through Discovery* (Third Edition), Columbus, OH: Charles E. Merrill Publishing Company, 1975; William K. Esler, *Teaching Elementary Science*, Belmont, CA: Wadsworth Publishing Company, Inc., 1973; Howard J. Hausman, *Choosing a Science Program for the Elementary School* (Occasional Paper No. 24), Washington, DC: Council for Basic Education, October 1976; J. David Lockard (Editor), *Science and Mathematics Cur-*

ricular Developments Internationally, 1956–1974, College Park, MD: Science Teaching Center, University of Maryland (Joint Project with the Commission on Science Education, American Association for the Advancement of Science), 1974.

ELITISM, the identification/selection of individuals on the basis of one or more relatively superior characteristics, traits, or abilities. Education elitism has tended to be defined in terms of intellectual ability. Socioeconomic status (home/social background) has considerable influence on what children learn. For that reason, the separation of children based on scholastic attainment has also tended to separate children along socioeconomic lines.

Until the 20th century, school curriculum was based on an elitist (i.e. survival of the fittest) model of education. This was particularly true at the high school and college levels. During the 1800s, most high school graduates attended college, and therefore much of the high school curriculum was college oriented. However, relatively few children enrolled in or graduated from high school; even fewer of those who attended elementary school ever attended college. Thus, the programs at the high school and college levels were designed for academically oriented students who, in most instances, came from economically privileged families. Until compulsory school attendance laws were extended to include 16-year-olds, and until tax supported high schools were deemed legal, high schools were academically and socially elitist.

Numerous factors and forces have served to make American education less elitist. They include the move toward mass public education, compulsory school attendance laws, the drive for educational equality and equality of opportunity, social and economic changes, alternative school programs, open admissions to public colleges, and mainstreaming.

The opposite of elitism is egalitarianism (i.e. education open to all, regardless of background).

References: Don Adams and Gerald M. Reagan, *School and Social Change in Modern America*, New York: David McKay Company, Inc., 1972; Vernon F. H. Haubrich and Michael W. Apple (Editors), *Schooling and the Rights of Children*, Berkeley, CA: McCutchan Publishing Corporation, 1975; Jacob Klein, *American Values and American Education*, New York: Exposition Press, 1973; Andrew Kopan and Herbert Walberg (Editors), *Rethinking Educational Equality*, Berkeley, CA: McCutchan Publishing Corporation, 1974; Lawrence Kotin and William F. Aikman, *Legal Foundations of Compulsory School Atten-*

dance, Port Washington, NY: Kennikat Press, Inc., 1980; Edward P. Morgan, *Inequality in Classroom Learning*, New York: Praeger Publishers, 1977.

EMANCIPATED MINOR, a minor entitled to treatment as an adult after demonstrating that he/she is essentially in control over his/her life. In addition, the emancipated minor must show that he/she has no intention of returning to the residence of his/her parents.

In education, the matter of emancipated minors is generally raised in connection with legal residence. Emancipated minors may, by law, establish legal residence as do adults. By doing so, they are often entitled to free tuition or reduced tuition benefits available only to local (i.e. state) residents. (See RESIDENT STUDENT.)

References: Shervert H. Frazier, et al., *A Psychiatric Glossary: The Meaning of Terms Frequently Used in Psychiatry*, New York: Basic Books, Inc., Publishers, 1975; Leroy J. Peterson, et al., *The Law and Public School Operation* (Second Edition), New York: Harper and Row, Publishers, 1978.

EMILE—See ROUSSEAU, JEAN J.

EMINENT DOMAIN, a legal term relating to condemnation of private property. The power to acquire property via eminent domain is vested in the state and federal governments. Most states, in turn, have granted the power of eminent domain to local governmental units including boards of education.

A school board may condemn private property for educational purposes subject to specific restrictions included in its state's statutes. They commonly require the board to: (1) ensure that "due process" has been granted to the property owner; (2) pay a fair market price for the property being acquired; and (3) limit its condemnation activity to property located within the local school district.

References: Richard D. Gatti and Daniel J. Gatti, *Encyclopedic Dictionary of School Law*, West Nyack, NY: Parker Publishing Company, Inc., 1975; E. Edmund Reutter, Jr. and Robert R. Hamilton, *The Law of Public Education* (Second Edition), Mineola, NY: The Foundation Press, Inc., 1976.

EMOTIONAL DISTURBANCE, a broad classification of behaviors that signify psychological abnormalities. Children classified as emotionally disturbed are included in the broad group of exceptional children. For numerous reasons, there does not appear to be a set definition for emotional disturbance. For example, different cultures and socioeconomic levels may have different definitions. Professional people may also disagree as to its meaning (i.e. teachers may have a different basis than psychologists for determining who is emotionally disturbed). Finally, in children, problem behavior caused by emotional disturbance may be more transitory than in adults, or children not emotionally disturbed may only manifest such disturbances at one time or another. Before children are classified as being emotionally disturbed, considerable testing and observation by competent personnel is usually performed.

Many children who are classified as emotionally disturbed are far from being mentally deficient. There are many causes for such disturbance (e.g. mental, physical, environmental-home, social). Individualized education and the assistance of qualified professionals are needed to help such children. (See AUTISM.)

References: Harvey F. Clarizo and George F. McCoy, *Behavioral Disorders in Children* (Second Edition), New York: Thomas Y. Crowell, 1976; Martin Herbert, *Emotional Problems of Development in Children*, New York: Academic Press, 1974; James M. Kaufman, *Characteristics of Children's Behavior Disorders*, Columbus, OH: Charles E. Merrill Publishing Company, 1977; Denis H. Stott, et al., *Taxonomy of Behavioral Disturbances*, London, England: University of London Press Ltd., 1975.

EMPATHY, the capacity to understand and to share the feelings of another person or group of people. It is a form of behavior characterized by warmth, understanding, and emotional identification. When empathizing with an individual, one sees the other person's world as if it were his/her own. Group empathy involves putting oneself into the place of a whole class of people (e.g. the aged, the poor, or the Native Americans).

When a teacher accepts students for who they are and can understand their concerns, abilities, aspirations, needs, cultural, social, and ethnic backgrounds, the teacher is said to have empathy for them. Empathy is considered a very important trait for teachers to have both in and out of the classroom. It has long been considered a learned social response; recently, however, several psychologists have advanced the position that selected simple empathic responses are present at birth.

References: Ronald T. Hyman (Editor), *Teaching: Vantage Points for Study* (Second Edition), Philadelphia: J. B. Lippincott Company, 1974; Steven R. Yussen and John W. Santrock, *Child Development: An Introduction* (Second Edition), Dubuque, IA: Wm. C. Brown Company, Publishers, 1978.

EMPIRICAL VALIDITY—See VALIDITY

EMPIRICISM, a philosophical theory concerned with the experiential nature of knowledge and meaning. Perceptions (what one believes or sense-impressions) and communication (discourse or discussion between or among the parties involved) are important elements in empiricism.

Empiricism has its roots in the works of John Locke and David Hume and, more recently, Bertrand Russell and John Anderson. John Anderson, in 1927, took the position that, in discussion or inquiry, any proposition can be treated as (a) a conclusion to be proved from premises accepted; (b) a premise accepted to be used in proving some conclusion; (c) a hypothesis to be tested by the observation of the truth or falsity of the conclusions drawn from it; or (d) an observation to be used in determining the truth or falsity of conclusions drawn from a hypothesis.

Empiricism is also a method that tests theories through observations and experimentation.

References: John Anderson, *Studies in Empirical Philosophy,* Sydney, Australia: Angus and Robertson, Ltd., 1962; Charles E. Jarrett, et al., (Editors), *New Essays on Rationalism and Empiricism,* Guelph, Canada: Canadian Association for Publishers in Philosophy, 1978; Mark Levensky, *Human Factual Knowledge,* Englewood Cliffs, NJ: Prentice-Hall, Inc., 1971; Godfrey Vesey (Editor), *Impressions of Empiricism,* New York: St. Martin's Press, 1976.

EMPLOYMENT ANTI-DISCRIMINATION LAWS—See ANTI-DISCRIMINATION LAWS, EMPLOYMENT

ENDOMORPHY—See CONSTITUTIONAL TYPES

ENGINEERED CLASSROOM, first developed in California by Frank Hewitt (1967) as an educational program for emotionally disturbed children. It is a highly structured behavioral approach employing a number of behavior modification techniques. The teacher is the behavioral engineer. He/she assigns tasks, provides contingency management (rewards learning and other behaviors), and structures a well-defined classroom with specific limits of behavior. The classroom is divided into three major areas: (1) mastery center (reading, writing, arithmetic); (2) exploratory center (science, communication, art); and (3) order center (activities dealing with attention, active responses, and direction following). The pedagogical basis for

the engineered classroom is behavioral psychology, with reinforcement, task stimulation, and intervention techniques constituting a major part of the activities used by the teacher. The 240-minute day is broken down into 15-minute periods. A new task is given to a child by the teacher at the start of each period.

References: Don Bushell, Jr., *Classroom Behavior,* Englewood Cliffs, NJ: Prentice-Hall, Inc., 1973; Norris G. Haring and E. Lakin Phillips, *Analysis and Modification of Classroom Behavior,* Englewood Cliffs, NJ: Prentice-Hall, Inc., 1972; E. Philip Trapp and Philip Himelstein (Editors), *Readings on the Exceptional Child* (Second Edition), New York: Appleton-Century-Crofts, Inc., 1972.

ENGINEERING CONCEPTS CURRICULUM PROJECT (ECCP), a problem-oriented, experimental, and interdisciplinary course designed for high school students. ECCP was initiated (1963) by the Commission on Engineering Education for the purpose of helping students to understand and to appreciate how tools, invented by man, have improved mankind. Following some preliminary field testing, a conference was called (1965) to develop a final draft of a course titled *The Man-Made World.* Secondary school science teachers, engineers, professors, and scientists were involved in this course writing activity.

The Man-Made World was designed to satisfy several specific objectives, including the following: (1) to develop technical literacy of students; (2) to help students to understand the way in which technology has affected society; (3) to study the ways in which man copes with nature; (4) to appreciate the precise role mathematics plays in communicating ideas; and (5) to develop an awareness of engineering and its contributions to society. The course consists of three parts: *Logic and Computers, Models and Measurement,* and *Energy and Control.* Special print and nonprint materials developed for the course include texts, teachers' manuals, tests, filmstrips, transparencies, audiotapes, games, and laboratory equipment.

ECCP offices are at the State University of New York at Stony Brook. Funding support for the project was provided by the National Science Foundation as well as Exxon, U.S. Steel, and McGraw-Hill.

References: Richard E. Haney, *The Changing Curriculum: Science,* Washington, DC: Association for Supervision and Curriculum Development, NEA, 1966; Paul D. Hurd, *New Curriculum Perspectives for Junior High School Science,* Belmont, CA: Wadsworth Publishing Company, Inc., 1970; J. David Lockard (Editor), *Science and Mathematics Curricular Developments Internationally, 1956–1974,*

College Park, MD: Science Teaching Center, University of Maryland (Joint Project with the Commission on Science Education, American Association for the Advancement of Science), 1974.

ENGLISH AS A SECOND LANGUAGE (ESL), the teaching of English to non-English speaking students. With the increasing number of children born in the United States whose primary language is not English, and because English is not the dominant language spoken in many homes, ESL programs have been developed to meet the English language needs of linguistic minority students. Many such programs exist in urban schools throughout the United States and in many areas of the southwestern section of the United States.

English as a second language not only includes the teaching of the English language, but also includes cultural adjustment elements. ESL materials are a vital part of many bilingual education programs used in the schools. (See BILINGUAL-BICULTURAL EDUCATION; BILINGUAL INSTRUCTION; and TEACHING ENGLISH TO SPEAKERS OF OTHER LANGUAGES.)
References: Donna M. Johnson and Duane H. Roen, *Richness in Writing: Empowering ESL Students*, New York: Longman, Inc., 1989; Judith Wells Lindfors, *Children's Language and Learning* (Second Edition), Englewood Cliffs, NJ: Prentice-Hall, Inc., 1987.

ENRICHMENT PROGRAMS, curricular activities that increase the quality/quantity of new learning opportunities consistent with the learner's achievement level. Often discussed (and debated) in the literature as an alternative to acceleration of gifted pupils, enrichment programs require a high degree of individualized planning on the part of the teacher. John Gowan and George Demos suggested that enrichment programs will be successful to the extent that the student: (1) is encouraged to search for new and additional information; (2) is provided with leadership opportunities; (3) is able to pursue personal interests; (4) is able to engage in creative as well as routine work assignments; (5) can develop and use his/her own initiative; and (6) engages in in-depth activities that are in fact broadening.

Some school systems, James Gallagher pointed out, believing that a meaningful enrichment environment for gifted elementary school pupils cannot be provided in the regular heterogeneously grouped classroom, have created a variety of special organizational arrangements for them. Included are: (1) *special schools* for the gifted; (2) *special classes;* (3) *modified special classes* that provide special grouping/programs for part of the school day; and (4) *itinerant teachers* who provide regular classroom teachers with specialized help and who do some teaching of intellectually superior students.
References: James J. Gallagher, "The Gifted Child in Elementary School" in Wayne Dennis and Margaret W. Dennis (Editors), *The Intellectually Gifted: An Overview,* New York: Grune and Stratton, 1976; John C. Gowan and George D. Demos, *The Education and Guidance of the Ablest,* Springfield, IL: Charles C. Thomas, Publisher, 1964; Daniel P. Keating, "Secondary School Programs" in A. Harry Passow (Editor), *The Gifted and the Talented: Their Education and Development* (NSSE 78th Yearbook, Part I), Chicago: University of Chicago Press, 1979.

ENTRANCE AGE—See SCHOOL ENTRANCE AGE

ENTROPY, a concept that describes a tendency toward disorder, or even chaos in an established system. As order is defined in a system, the entropy of the system decreases.

In communication theory, entropy is proportional to the number of messages (information) that can be produced by a message source. Informational entropy is concerned with information gained by the receiver. As information is transmitted, entropy decreases; this is called negative entropy (or negentropy).
References: Rudolf Carnap, *Two Essays on Entropy,* Berkeley, CA: University of California Press, 1977; Y. S. Touloukian, *The Concept of Entropy in Communication, Living Organisms, and Thermodynamics,* Lafayette, IN: Purdue University, 1956; John F. Young, *Information Theory,* New York: John Wiley and Sons, 1971.

ENTRY BEHAVIOR, or entering behavior, a term used in educational psychology to describe the skills and knowledges, specifically related to the instructional objectives of a course or instructional unit, that the student brings with him/her to the course/unit. Pre-tests are frequently administered to determine what students actually know or to ascertain what remediation may be necessary to ensure instructional success. Entry behavior information is also used to help the teacher to adapt instruction to the student's entry level, to group children for instructional purposes, and to provide a data base against which future (post-test) results can be compared.

Exit, or terminal behaviors, are also assessed before and after a training program is implemented, this to determine specific instructional outcomes.

References: Richard C. Anderson and Gerald W. Faust, *Educational Psychology: The Science of Instruction and Learning,* New York: Dodd, Mead and Company, 1973; Saul Axelrod, *Behavior Modification for the Classroom Teacher,* New York: McGraw-Hill Book Company, 1977; Anthony R. Ciminero, et al. (Editors), *Handbook of Behavioral Assessment,* New York: John Wiley and Sons, 1977; David W. Johnson, *Educational Psychology,* Englewood Cliffs, NJ: Prentice-Hall, Inc., 1979.

ENUMERATION—See RATIONAL COUNTING

ENURESIS, or bedwetting, the involuntary expulsion of urine, often during sleep. The condition, most frequently found among young children, has been attributed to more than one source, many of them psychological. Emotional disturbance, delayed maturation, aggressive behavior, dependent behavior, and low level of adjustment to new situations are some of the factors that authorities have found to be related to enuresis. The incidence of bedwetting attributable to organic problems is low, usually less than 10 percent of the total cases. Researchers have noted that bedwetting may be hereditary, with incidence of family-related bedwetting ranging from a reported 17 percent in one study to as high as 60 percent found in others.

The incidence of bedwetting is highest between ages zero and three and decreases with chronological age. Most cases are corrected by the time the child approaches puberty. The condition is slightly more prevalent among boys than girls.

References: Warren R. Baller, *Bed-Wetting: Origins and Treatment,* New York: Pergamon Press, Inc., 1975; Mordecai Kaffman and Esther Elizur, *Infants Who Become Enuretics: A Longitudinal Study of 161 Kibbutz Children,* Chicago: Society for Research in Child Development, 1977.

ENVIRONMENTAL EDUCATION, defined in federal legislation as "the educational process dealing with man's relationship with his natural and manmade surroundings, and includes the relation of population, pollution, resource allocation and depletion, conservation, transportation, technology, and urban and rural planning to the total human environment" (Public Law 91-516, p. 1312).

In schools, the environmental education curriculum, an interdisciplinary one, is frequently problem centered with prevailing environmental issues serving as catalysts for study and instruction. All parts of a problem (e.g. air pollution) are examined; solutions are then proffered. The process of analyzing and formulating solutions may be carried out in any number of contexts (e.g. ecology, geography, conservation, economics, resource management). S. Audean Allman and associates pointed out that environmental education may be taught at all grade levels, is frequently offered as a content area in science, and, to be effective, requires the teacher to serve as facilitator rather than dispenser of knowledge. Increasing numbers of environmental programs are being offered by the country's colleges and universities.

References: S. Audean Allman, et al., *Environmental Education: Guidelines and Activities for Teachers,* Columbus, OH: Charles E. Merrill Publishing Company, 1976; Roger Bybee, et al., *Teaching about Science and Society,* Columbus, OH: Merrill Publishing, 1984; Phyllis M. Ford, *Principles and Practices of Outdoor/Environmental Education,* New York: John Wiley and Sons, Inc., 1981; Public Law 91–516, *United States Statutes at Large, 1970–71* (Volume 84, Part I), Washington, DC: U.S. Government Printing Office, 1971.

ENVIRONMENTAL EDUCATION ACT (Public Law 91-516), federal legislation enacted in 1970 that seeks to overcome the deterioration of the country's environment and ecological balance through improved understanding and related education. The act authorized establishment of an environmental education office within the Office of Education. Expenditures were authorized to: (1) encourage development of new and improved curricula that would enhance environmental quality; (2) establish model programs through which these curricula may be demonstrated and evaluated; (3) distribute curricular materials for use in educational programs; (4) provide training programs for teachers, public service personnel, community-business-labor leaders, and government employees at all levels of government; (5) support the creation of outdoor ecological study centers; (6) support community education programs; and (7) prepare and distribute environmental/ecological materials by mass media.

References: Public Law 91-516, *United States Statutes at Large, 1970–1971* (Volume 84, Part I), Washington, DC: U.S. Government Printing Office, 1971; Public Law 91-665, *United States Statutes at Large, 1970–1971* (Volume 84, Part II), Washington, DC: U.S. Government Printing Office, 1971.

EPILEPSY, a condition characterized by abnormal electrical discharges in the brain followed by a wide variety of involuntary activities (seizures). Some types of epilepsy are caused by brain injury; in many other cases, however, epilepsy can not be attributed to such injury. The actual seizure is a product of a group of disrupted neurons, in the brain, that develop an abnormal, rhythmic, synchronous discharge. Rather than operating individually, as would be expected, the neurons tend to group together, thus releasing a large electrical force in the brain.

The old classification of seizures included *Petit Mal* (entire brain, lasts about 5 to 30 seconds), *Grand Mal* (entire brain, a major seizure), and *Psychomotor* (disturbance in the temporal lobe). The new International Classification of Seizures describes seizures in terms of the area of the brain affected. They are (1) *partial seizures with elementary symptomatology* (motor, sensory, autonomic, compound); (2) *partial seizures with complex symptomatology* (with impairment of consciousness, cognitive, affective, psychosensory, psychomotor, compound); (3) *partial seizure secondarily generalized;* (4) *generalized seizures* (involving both sides of the brain); (5) *unilateral;* and (6) *unclassified.*

Use of drugs is the most common treatment, with surgery being limited to a few patients. Other treatments are being developed. Epilepsy can be caused by injury to the brain before, during, or after birth; therefore, it is not restricted to any one group of people.

References: Howard Gardner, *The Shattered Mind,* New York: Alfred A. Knopf, 1975; Robert B. Johnston and Phyllis R. Magrab (Editors), *Developmental Disorders,* Baltimore, MD: University Park Press, 1976; Dominick P. Purpura, et al. (Editors), *Experimental Models of Epilepsy,* New York: Raven Press, 1972; Harry Sands and Frances C. Minters, *The Epilepsy Fact Book,* New York: Scribner's, 1977; Owsei Temkin, *The Falling Sickness* (Second Edition), Baltimore, MD: The Johns Hopkins Press, 1971.

EPISTEMOLOGY, a field of philosophy concerned with knowledge and truth. According to one educational philosopher (Charles Marler), it involves "the study of the possibility, the limits, the development and the validation of knowledge-claims" (p. 103). Another philosopher (Milton Hunnex) described it as a field of philosophy that "comprises the systematic study of the nature, sources, and validity of knowledge" (p. 3).

Epistemology is one of several basic realms of philosophy. The others are *ontology,* the study of reality; *axiology,* which deals with values; and *logic,* which deals with valid reasoning. Axiology is comprised of two divisions: aesthetics and ethics. (See AXIOLOGY; ONTOLOGY; and LOGIC.)

References: Milton D. Hunnex, *Philosophies and Philo-*

sophers (Revised Edition), San Francisco: Chandler Publishing Company, 1971; Charles D. Marler, *Philosophy and Schooling,* Boston: Allyn and Bacon, Inc., 1975.

EQUAL ACCESS ACT—See EDUCATION FOR ECONOMIC SECURITY ACT

EQUALIZATION, FINANCIAL, a principle of educational financing whose implementation serves to remove the wealth disparities that exist among different school districts. Such disparity, it is held, provides educational advantages to students residing in relatively wealthy districts and, conversely, places students in poor districts at a decided disadvantage.

The actual carrying out of financial equalization is done at the state level. State funds, supplementing local funds available in poorer districts, are used to bring the minimal per-pupil support level (expressed in dollars) to the point where the student will be assured of receiving an adequate education. State programs designed to achieve financial equalization are known as foundation programs. (See FINANCIAL ABILITY; FINANCIAL EFFORT; FOUNDATION PROGRAMS; and STATE AID.)

References: Percy E. Burrup, *Financing Education in a Climate of Change* (Second Edition), Boston: Allyn and Bacon, Inc., 1977; John E. Corbally, Jr., *School Finance,* Boston: Allyn and Bacon, Inc., 1962; Ralph B. Kimbrough and Michael Y. Nunnery, *Educational Administration: An Introduction,* New York: Macmillan Publishing Company, Inc., 1976; Paul R. Mort and Walter C. Reusser, *Public School Finance: Its Background, Structure, and Operation* (Second Edition), New York: McGraw-Hill Book Company, 1951.

EQUILIBRIUM, ORGANIZATIONAL, a management concept describing the "needs-inducements" relationship in organizations. Equilibrium exists when institutional needs (goals) and the personal needs of individuals serving in organizations are both being satisfied. Administrators work to realize equilibrium, because it is presumed to be productive and satisfactory. Profit, growth, customer satisfaction, and service illustrate organizational needs. Individual needs can be physical or psychological: working conditions, esprit, salary, hours, and so on. The concept of equilibrium may be applied to a total organization or to any unit within the total organization.

Students of organization point out that change frequently occurs during periods of disequilibrium.

References: Chester I. Barnard, *The Functions of the Executive,* Cambridge, MA: Harvard University Press, 1938; Richard C. Lonsdale, "Maintaining the Organization in Dynamic Equilibrium" in Daniel E. Griffiths (Editor), *Behavioral Science and Educational Administration* (NSSE 63rd Yearbook, Part II), Chicago: University of Chicago Press, 1964; Robert G. Owens, *Organizational Behavior in Schools,* Englewood Cliffs, NJ: Prentice-Hall, Inc., 1970.

EQUIPMENT, a financial accounting term for generally nonconsumable items such as furniture, machines, books, and instruments. These items may be instructional or noninstructional, fixed or movable. For budget purposes, an item of equipment is charged against capital outlay.

The U.S. Office of Education has defined *equipment* as an item possessing *each* of the following characteristics: (1) it retains its original shape and size with use; (2) it is nonexpendable; (3) its cost is such that capitalization is justified; and (4) it retains its identity even when incorporated into a more complex unit or substance. (See CAPITAL OUTLAY and SUPPLY.)

References: Percy E. Burrup, *Financing Education in a Climate of Change* (Second Edition), Boston: Allyn and Bacon, Inc., 1977; John Greenhalgh, *Practitioner's Guide to School Business Management,* Boston: Allyn and Bacon, Inc., 1978; Charles T. Roberts and Allan R. Lichtenberger, *Financial Accounting Classifications and Standard Terminology for Local and State School Systems,* Washington, DC: U.S. Department of Health, Education, and Welfare, 1973.

ERGONOMICS, the study of people and their adjustment to the environment. Ergonomics is a science that tries most specifically to adapt the working conditions to the worker. The study includes not only the work area, but the design of machines and other tools that would be compatible with human physiological and psychological characteristics as well. It has been termed *human interface engineering.* Ergonomics plays a major role in the design of educational software as well as the microcomputer screen, where efforts to increase the contrast between characters and background, to reduce screen reflection and to arrange text to maximize learning are a few examples of the important contributions the science of ergonomics is making to education.

Reference: Robert M. Mason, "Ergonomics: The Human and the Machine," *Library Journal,* February 15, 1984.

ERIC, popular acronym for the Educational Resources Information Center, a network of decentralized information centers. Funding, monitoring, and policymaking related to ERIC are under the auspices of the U.S. Department of Education's Office of Educational Research and Improvement (OERI).

ERIC acts as an archive of educational publications. It collects, screens, and disseminates reports; prepares interpretive summaries, reviews, and bibliographies on important educational topics; provides copies of educational documents at nominal cost; and services its several information centers located throughout the country. Presently, 16 clearinghouses are located throughout the United States. Each is responsible for searching out and processing material in the educational area (discipline) assigned to it (e.g. Educational Management: University of Oregon; Handicapped and Gifted Children: Council for Exceptional Children). Material selection and processing for inclusion in ERIC's computer base is carried out in accordance with ERIC guidelines.

In addition to the clearinghouses, three new system components have been added: *Access ERIC* that provides systemwide coordination, training, materials development to make ERIC more accessible and useful; *Adjunct clearinghouses* that provide services beyond the sixteen clearinghouses; *ERIC Partners* who will distribute and advertise ERIC materials or services.

Reference tools published by ERIC include: (1) *Thesaurus of ERIC Descriptors,* a listing of vocabulary terms used in the system; (2) *Resources in Education,* a monthly abstract journal announcing recent research reports; (3) *Current Index to Journals in Education,* including almost 800 education publications; (4) *Director of ERIC Microfiche Collections;* and (5) *Survey of ERIC Data Base Search Services.* (See APPENDIX V: ERIC CLEARING HOUSES.)

References: Educational Resources Information Center, *How to Use ERIC,* Washington, DC: U.S. Government Printing Office, Undated; Office of Educational Research and Improvement; Educational Networks Division, *Directory of Institutional Projects Funded by OERI,* Washington, DC: The Office, January 1986; Dorothy A. Slawsky and Ted Brandhorst, *A Bibliography of Publications About the Educational Resources Information Center,* Washington, DC: ERIC, December 1978; Marda Woodbury, *Selecting Materials for Instruction: Media and the Curriculum,* Littleton, CO: Libraries Unlimited, Inc., 1980.

ERROR PATTERN ANALYSIS, a procedure that can be used by the classroom teacher to identify word recognition miscues on the part of an individual student. By listing all the errors (word recognition miscues) next to the word found in the text read, the teacher can determine not only if the meaning has been changed but also the type of error made (e.g., whole word substitution, omission, reversal, etc.). Any major pattern of error can thus be identified; comprehension weakness can be identified as well. Error pattern analysis is a qualitative analysis approach in informal reading inventories used by teachers in the schools.

References: Joan P. Gipe, *Corrective Reading Techniques for the Classroom Teacher*, Scottsdale, AZ: Gorsuch Scarisbrick, Publishers, 1987; J. Johns, *Basic Reading Inventory*, Dubuque, IA: Kendall/Hunt Publishing Co., 1981; M. L. Woods and A. J. Moe, *Analytical Reading Inventory* (Second Edition), Columbus, OH: Charles E. Merrill, 1981.

ESSAY TEST, an examination in which the respondent answers a question with an original, narrative (one or more sentences) statement. Given the response latitude inherent in this type of test, no single answer can be considered as the only correct one. The evaluator's assessment of an essay test answer is largely subjective; furthermore, it is one of the most difficult of tests for an examiner to evaluate. Supporters of the test indicate that the essay test: (1) requires relatively little time to construct; (2) makes it possible to gauge a student's breadth (command) of knowledge; (3) tends to reduce guessing on the part of the respondent; and (4) requires ample time for completion by the student.

The task of scoring an essay test can be facilitated if four procedures are followed: (1) the respondents cannot be identified by name; (2) the examination is scored on a question-by-question rather than pupil-by-pupil basis; (3) grading of spelling, English usage, penmanship, and so on is completed separately from evaluation of content; and (4) several readers evaluate each test.

The use of essay tests has been traced back approximately 4,000 years.

References: Robert L. Ebel, *Essentials of Educational Measurement* (Third Edition), Englewood Cliffs, NJ: Prentice-Hall, Inc., 1979; Tom Kubiszyn and Gary Borich, *Educational Testing and Measurement: Classroom Application and Practice* (Second Edition), Glenview, IL: Scott Foresman and Company, 1987; Dale P. Scannell and D. B. Tracy, *Testing and Measurement in the Classroom*, Boston: Houghton Mifflin Company, 1975.

ESSENTIALISM, a philosophically eclectic and relatively recent educational theory identified with names such as William C. Bagley, Thomas Briggs, Isaac L. Kandel, and, most recently, William Brickman. The essentialist movement in education began in 1938 and spread during the Great Depression and most World War II years. It sees essential subject matter as the core of the educative process with responsibility for content vested in the teacher, not the child. Emphasis is placed on mastery of the basics of education, discipline, and rigorous standards. Although essentialists, in some instances, hold views similar to those of perennialists, they are far less inclined to support almost exclusive reliance on the classics. Their tolerance for selected contributions made by progressive education constitutes yet another distinction.

There is no single essentialist philosophy per se. Although this movement's supporters are grounded in different philosophical schools, including idealism and realism, collectively they constitute a 3 R's basic subject matter emphasis. (See BAGLEY, WILLIAM; KANDEL, ISAAC L.; PERENNIALISM; and PROGRESSIVE EDUCATION.)

References: George Kneller, *Introduction to the Philosophy of Education* (Second Edition), New York: John Wiley and Sons, 1971; Van Cleve Morris, *Philosophy and the American School: An Introduction to the Philosophy of Education,* Boston: Houghton Mifflin Company, 1961.

ESTABLISHMENT CLAUSE, that part of the First Amendment of the U.S. Constitution that reads: "Congress shall make no law respecting an establishment of religion or prohibiting the free exercise thereof." This clause has served as the basis for the church and state separation concept that has existed in the United States for over two centuries. It is also the basis upon which numerous U.S. Supreme Court decisions involving religion and education have been made (e.g., *Aguilar v. Felton, Everson v. Board of Education, McCollum v. Board of Education*). In addition to precluding the establishment of a religion, the clause provides that Congress may not prohibit the free exercise of religion. This provision is frequently referred to as the "free-exercise" clause. (See *AGUILAR v. FELTON, EVERSON v. BOARD OF EDUCATION* and *Mc-COLLUM CASE.*)

References: William R. Hazard, *Education and the Law: Cases and Materials on Public Schools* (Second Edition), New York: The Free Press, 1978; Frank R. Kemerer and Kenneth L. Deutsch, *Constitutional Rights and Student Life: Value Conflict in Law and Education*, St. Paul, MN: West Publishing Company, 1979; Eugene T. Conners, *Religion and the Schools: Significant Court Decisions in the 1980s*, Bloomington, IN: Phi Delta Kappa, 1988; Charles R. Kniker, *Teaching about Religion in the Public Schools*, Bloomington, IN: Phi Delta Kappa, 1985.

ESTEEM—See SELF-ESTEEM

ETCHING, the art of preparing etched metal plates and using them to print designs or pictures. These plates are usually made of copper or zinc. The design or picture is carved into the plate by means of an acid that follows the lines of the graphic template previously drawn by an etching needle. Ink is rolled on the plate after the etching has been completed. The plate is then pressed (by machine) on the material to receive the picture, usually paper or fabric. The etching technique is not only a graphic art form, but it is used in printing as well.

Etching can be inscribed directly with a pointed steel needle or jewel point. Although most etching is done on metal, it can be done on glass too.

Multicrayon engraving is a form of etching. Students use crayon over crayon on colored paper. They then etch, engrave, or scrape with a short-blade a design or picture, with the various crayon colors becoming the lines, background, and so on.

The process of etching has been traced to the medieval practice of decorating metal armor through the use of acid.

References: Fitz Roy Carrington (Editor), *Prints and Their Makers,* Boston: Houghton Mifflin Company, 1916; Ruari McLean, *Victorian Book Design and Colour Printing,* Berkeley, CA: University of California Press, 1972; Charles S. Papp and Robert A. Brown, *The Magic of Color Printing: For Art Classes, Printers and Laymen Who Deal in Printing,* Riverside, CA: American Visual Aid Books, 1970; Frank Wachowiak and David Hodge, *Art in Depth: A Qualitative Program for the Young Adolescent,* Scranton, PA: International Textbook Company, 1970; Gabriel P. Weisberg and Ronnie L. Fakon, *Between Past and Present: French, English, and American Etching, 1850–1950,* Cleveland, OH: Cleveland Museum of Art, 1977.

ETHICS, a branch of philosophy concerned with the practice and conduct of individuals and groups. Ethics includes various areas of study; choice between or among alternatives that lead to right or wrong decisions (deontology, or theory of obligation); philosophical values of "good" or "bad" (axiology); and the combination of deontology and axiology that forms the major portion of ethics called normative ethics. The emphasis of ethics is on the conduct of man and the understanding of that conduct. "Good," "bad," obligation, freedom, social relations, morals, mores, reality, nature of man, and analytic analysis are all a part of the study of ethics. (See AXIOLOGY; DEONTOLOGY; and VALUES.)

References: John Dewey, *Outlines of a Critical Theory of Ethics,* New York: Hillary House, 1891 (Reissued, 1957); T. D. Mabbott, *An Introduction to Ethics,* London, England: Hutchinson University Library, 1966; Henry B. Veatch, *For an Ontology of Morals,* Evanston, IL: Northwestern University Press, 1971; Carl Wellman, *Morals and Ethics,* Glenview, IL: Scott, Foresman and Company, 1975.

ETHNIC HERITAGE PROGRAM, a federal program approved by Congress in 1972 "in recognition of the principle that all persons in the educational institutions of the Nation should have an opportunity to learn about the differing and unique contributions to the national heritage made by each ethnic group" (p. 346). The enabling legislation, Section 504 of Public Law 92-318, makes grants available to help educational organizations with the planning, establishing, and operation of ethnic heritage studies programs. Development and dissemination of curriculum materials in elementary and secondary schools as well as colleges and universities, public or private, is encouraged.

Reference: Public Law 92-318, *United States Statutes at Large, 1972* (Volume 86), Washington, DC: U.S. Government Printing Office, 1973.

ETHNIC STUDIES—See MULTICULTURAL EDUCATION

ETHNOGRAPHIC RESEARCH, a qualitative research approach originally developed by anthropologists to help with the study of cultures. The method is now being used in many other fields as well. The school or classroom is one area where ethnographic research can be used to study groups of people and even animals.

Ethnographic research is descriptive. Observational data such as reports of people's written or spoken words, their actions/reactions, and the manner in which they act in given situations are made in case-study fashion. This observational information is frequently suggested by other sources of information. Included in the approach is: (1) the participant observer; (2) the utilizing of informants; (3) the positing of descriptive, structural, and contrast questions; (4) the analysis of interviews; and (5) the keeping of ethnographic records. Findings and conclusions are based on the various data collected.

References: Walter R. Borg and Meredith D. Gall, *Educational Research: An Introduction* (Fifth Edition), New York: Longman, Inc., 1989; L. R. Gay, *Educational Research: Competencies for Analysis and Application* (Third Edition), Columbus, OH: Merrill Publishing Company, 1987; Judith P. Goetz and Margaret D. LeCompte, *Ethnography and Qualitative Design in Educational Research*, Orlando, FL: Academic Press, Inc., 1984.

ETHOLOGY—See ANIMAL PSYCHOLOGY

ETIOLOGY, the study of factors that cause disease. The term may be applied to both physical and mental disorders.

References: Bernard Dixon, *Beyond the Magic Bullet*, New York: Harper and Row, Publishers, 1978; John P. Friel (Editor), *Dorland's Illustrated Medical Dictionary* (Twenty-fifth Edition), Philadelphia: W. B. Saunders Company, 1974; D. G. Garan, *Against Ourselves: Disorders from Improvements Under the Organic Limitedness of Man*, New York: Philosophical Library, 1979; Robert M. Goldenson, *The Encyclopedia of Human Behavior: Psychology, Psychiatry, and Mental Health* (Volume I), Garden City, NY: Doubleday and Company, Inc., 1970.

EUCLID, a disciple of Plato and author of a 13-volume treatment of Greek geometry and number theory written around 300 B.C. Euclid's *Elements of Geometry* was based on the works of mathematicians and philosophers who were his predecessors. Books I–IV, VII, and IX were based on the works of the Pythagorean mathematicians, and the work of Archytes provided the basis for Volume VIII. Eudoxus's works are found in Books V, VI, and XII; Theaetetus's contributions appear in Books X and XIII.

Euclid's works, which did not include any practical applications (they do today), were handed down from ancient Greece to ancient Rome and then survived the Middle Ages in Arabic translations before appearing in their present form. For many centuries, the axioms, postulates, and definitions of Euclidean Geometry had been the accepted base for all geometry. In the 1700s and 1800s, however, mathematicians began to question Euclid's geometry. Bolyai (1802–60), Gauss (1777–1855), Lobachevsky (1792–1856), and Riemann (1826–1866) were all mathematicians who contributed to the field of non-Euclidean Geometry by challenging various elements of Euclid's work. Until the advent of "modern mathematics" in the schools in the late 1950s, Euclidean Geometry was the basic geometry found in American schools and in American textbooks.

References: Jacques Derrida, *Edmund Husserl's Origin of Geometry: An Introduction*, Stony Brook, NY: Nicolas Hays, Ltd., 1978; Marvin Jay Greenberg, *Euclidean and Non-Euclidean Geometries*, San Francisco: W. H. Freeman and Company, 1974; Don Pedoe, *Geometry and the Liberal Arts*, New York: St. Martin's Press, 1976.

EURHYTHMICS—See DALCROZE METHOD

EVALUATION, the process of making judgments about the worth or appraised value of whatever is being considered. An object, an event, a person, a program, a policy, or a complex organization can be evaluated. The process by which a judgment is made may be systematic and complex, or it can be quite simplistic. It can range from a few (even one) observations, results of a single test, or a discussion to highly involved and complex evaluation research designs that involve large-scale data gathering, computers, statistical analysis, and the efforts of many highly trained professionals.

The basic function of evaluation is to provide information for decision making. At one time, formal program evaluation occured at the end of a program (summative evaluation). Today, formal program evaluation procedures can be designed that enable decision makers to receive information during the development and implementation of a program (formative evaluation), thus enabling appropriate program changes to be made before it is too late to make such adjustments. (See FORMATIVE EVALUATION and SUMMATIVE EVALUATION.)

References: Jack L. Franklin and Jean H. Thrasher, *An Introduction to Program Evaluation*, New York: John Wiley and Sons, 1976; W. James Popham, *Educational Evaluation* (Second Edition), Englewood Cliffs, NJ: Prentice-Hall, 1988; Emil J. Posavac and Raymond J. Carey, *Program Evaluation: Methods and Case Studies* (Third Edition), Englewood Cliffs, NJ: Prentice-Hall, 1989; Robert M. Rippey (Editor), *Studies in Transactional Evaluation*, Berkeley, CA: McCutchan Publishing Corporation, 1973; Herbert C. Schulberg and Jeanette M. Jerrell (Editors), *The Evaluator and Management*, Beverly Hills, CA: Sage Publications, Inc., 1979.

EVALUATION, PROGRAM, the assessment of the value, worth, or merit of a particular educational program. Such assessment provides the information necessary to determine if program goals are being met.

There are many approaches to program evaluation including procedures commonly used in research. Pre-tests, post-tests, random sampling, and Latin Square designs are illustrative.

The two general types of program evaluation are formative and summative evaluations. *Formative evaluation* occurs during the life of the program and provides feedback for improvement. *Summative evaluation* is completed at the end of the program at which time evaluators can determine if final program goals have been met. (See DISCREPANCY EVALUATION MODEL; FORMATIVE EVALUATION; and SUMMATIVE EVALUATION.)

References: Joint Committee on Standards for Educational Evaluation, *Standards for Evaluations of Educational Programs, Projects, and Materials*, New York: McGraw-Hill Book Company, 1981; W. James Popham, *Educational Evaluation* (Second Edition), Englewood Cliffs, NJ: Prentice-Hall, 1988; Emil J. Posavac and Raymond J. Carey, *Program Evaluation: Methods and Case Studies* (Third Edition), Englewood Cliffs, NJ: Prentice-Hall, 1989; Bruce W. Tuckerman, *Evaluating Instructional Programs*, Boston: Allyn and Bacon, Inc., 1979.

EVALUATION, TEACHER, program for the appraisal of teacher performance. Guidelines for carrying out such programs are normally detailed in local board of education policy statements. Teacher evaluation involves the collection of information about the teacher and assessment of this information in the context of the total school setting. The assessment serves two purposes: (1) identifying the ways in which the teacher can be helped to grow professionally, and (2) helping school administrators to make proper management decisions.

A survey of teacher evaluation research, completed and reported by Benjy Levin, indicated that educational organizations/institutions employ combinations of six approaches (modes) when evaluating teachers: (1) use of *student ratings,* a particularly widespread practice in institutions of higher education; (2) *classroom observations* by principals or supervisors; (3) use of *observation instruments* (e.g. Flanders Interaction Analysis System); (4) *self-evaluation* by teachers; (5) *product evaluation,* which uses student growth measures (as shown on tests); and (6) use of special "*teaching tests.*"

Programs for evaluating teachers are not uniform from one school agency to another. Nevertheless, several common elements are found in most of them. They include printed *criteria* that indicate desirable competencies and that consist of person, product, and process measures. *Forms* for classroom observation and evaluation are also used. In addition, the program normally includes a number of *classroom observations,* preparation of at least one *written evaluation* each year, a procedure for the teacher to read and, if desired, provide

rebuttal to the evaluation, and a *grievance procedure* for appealing questionable evaluations. Special procedures usually exist for the evaluation of probationary teachers. (See FLANDERS INTERACTION ANALYSIS.)

References: John A. Centra, *Determining Faculty Effectiveness*, San Francisco: Jossey-Bass Publishers, 1979; Joan P. S. Kowalski, *Evaluating Teacher Performance*, Arlington, VA: Educational Research Service, Inc., 1978; Benjy Levin, "Teacher Evaluation—A Review of Research," *Educational Leadership*, December 1979; Renfro C. Manning, *The Teacher Evaluation Handbook*, Englewood Cliffs, NJ: Prentice-Hall, 1988; M. Donald Thomas, *Performance Evaluation of Educational Personnel* (PDK Fastback 135), Bloomington, IN: The Phi Delta Kappa Educational Foundation, 1979.

EVERSON v. BOARD OF EDUCATION, the first case brought before the U.S. Supreme Court (1946) in which the Establishment Clause, First Amendment of the U.S. Constitution, was applied to education. At issue was a disagreement involving a program of reimbursement to parents of both public and parochial school children for school bus fares, a program authorized by a New Jersey statute. The Ewing Township Board of Education was challenged for providing such reimbursement, the appellant (a taxpayer) arguing that reimbursement to parents whose children were enrolled in a parochial (Catholic) school violated the provisions of the First Amendment. In a five to four decision, the Supreme Court sustained the program, reasoning that the action was constitutional since no monies or support were contributed to the school. The decision permits, but does not require, public transportation for parochial school children. (See CHILD BENEFIT THEORY.)

References: Committee for Public Education and Religious Liberty v. Nyquist, 413 U.S. 756, 93 S.Ct. 2955 (1973); *Everson v. Board of Education*, Supreme Court of the United States, 1947, 330 U.S. 1, 67 S.Ct. 504, 91 L.Ed. 711; Earl Hoffman, "Milestones on the Road to Parochiad," *NASSP Bulletin*, December 1974; Frank R. Kemerer and Kenneth L. Deutsch, *Constitutional Rights and Student Life: Value Conflict in Law and Education*, St. Paul, MN: West Publishing Company, 1979; *Sloan v. Lemon*, 413 U.S. 812, 93 S.Ct. 2982 (1973); Dale E. Twomley, *Parochiad and the Courts*, Berrien Springs, MI: Andrews University Press, 1979.

EXCELLENCE IN EDUCATION PROGRAMS— See OFFICE OF EDUCATIONAL RESEARCH AND IMPROVEMENT and SCHOOL RECOGNITION PROGRAMS

EXCEPTIONAL CHILDREN, students in need of some form of special education. Categories of exceptionality include children with: (1) *sensory handicaps* (including hearing and vision disorders); (2) *mental deviations,* including the gifted as well as the mentally retarded; (3) *communication disorders;* (4) *learning disabilities;* (5) *behavior disorders;* and (6) *health impairments,* including orthopedic conditions, birth defects, and neurological defects. Exceptional children, other than the gifted, are considered handicapped. (See HANDICAPPED INDIVIDUALS and PUBLIC LAW 94-142.)

References: William H. Berdine and A. Edward Blackhurst (Editors), *An Introduction to Special Education* (Second Edition), Boston: Little, Brown and Company, 1985; Daniel P. Hallahan and James M. Kauffman, *Exceptional Children: Introduction to Special Education* (Fourth Edition), Englewood Cliffs, NJ: Prentice-Hall, 1988; William L. Heward and Michael D. Orlansky, *Exceptional Children: An Introductory Survey of Special Education,* Columbus, OH: Merrill Publishing Company, 1988; Maynard C. Reynolds and Jack W. Birch, *Teaching Exceptional Children in All America's Schools: A First Course for Teachers and Principals,* Reston, VA: The Council for Exceptional Children, 1977.

EXCHANGE TEACHERS, teachers who teach, study, lecture, engage in research, or pursue similar educational activities for a period in another country. In some cases, a teacher from another country replaces the teacher who left on an "exchange program." The major emphasis for teacher exchanges came from the Fulbright Act (P.L. 584, 79th Congress, 1946), the Smith-Mundt Act (P.L. 402, 80th Congress, 1948), and the Mutual Educational and Cultural Exchange Act (the Fulbright-Hays Act, P.L. 87-256, 87th Congress, 1961). Once the United States and participating countries sign agreements, the program is administered through the Department of State with help from other U.S. agencies such as the Department of Education.

There are other programs that provide teachers an opportunity to become exchange teachers. Some are university sponsored; others are funded by private agencies and/or organizations. Their prime purposes are: (1) to provide experiences for teachers from many countries to visit, live, and teach in a foreign country; (2) to enhance international education and understandings; and (3) to provide empirical resources for countries that might not have such resources.

References: Richard W. Breslin and Paul Pedersen, *Cross-Cultural Orientation Programs,* New York: Gardner Press, Inc., 1976; Steven E. Deutsch, *International Education and Exchange,* Cleveland, OH: The Press of Case

Western Reserve University, 1970; Walter Johnson and Francis J. Colligan, *The Fulbright Program: A History,* Chicago: University of Chicago Press, 1965; Irwin J. Sanders and Jennifer C. Ward, *Bridges to Understanding,* New York: McGraw-Hill Book Company, 1970.

EXECUTIVE PROFESSIONAL LEADERSHIP (EPL), a term coined by Neal Gross and Robert E. Herriott in their 1965 study of selected elementary school principals. That investigation had two main objectives: (1) to test the assumption that effective leadership by the principal would produce important consequences for the school, and (2) to identify (isolate) the determinants of educational leadership exhibited by these principals.

Neal Gross and Robert Herriott's definition of EPL, as used in their study, "is the effort of an executive of a professionally staffed organization *to conform to a definition of his role that stresses his obligation to improve the quality of staff performance*" (underlining ours) (p. 22).

Reference: Neal Gross and Robert E. Herriott, *Staff Leadership in Public Schools: A Sociological Inquiry,* New York: John Wiley and Sons, 1965.

EXECUTIVE SESSIONS, meetings that are closed to the general public. Closed meetings of this sort are conducted by school boards or other governing boards when privileged and/or sensitive information is to be discussed. Personnel matters that relate to a particular employee and preliminary discussions of possible school building sites, knowledge of which could handicap the board financially, are illustrative of the items legitimately discussed in executive session.

In recent years, numbers of states have passed "sunshine laws" that are designed to limit or to preclude executive sessions and thus increase the amount of official business to be transacted during open meetings. (See SUNSHINE ACTS.)

References: Archie R. Dykes, *School Board and Superintendent: Their Effective Working Relationships,* Danville, IL: The Interstate Printers and Publishers, Inc., 1965; Charles E. Reeves, *School Boards: Their Status, Functions, and Activities,* New York: Prentice-Hall, Inc., 1954.

EXEMPTED CHILD, or nonserved child, a child of compulsory school age who is not required to attend school. The reason for excusing the individual is the lack of a program that meets his/her special educational needs. Such waiver is almost always restricted to certain populations of handicapped children.

References: Combined Glossary: Terms and Definitions from the Handbooks of the State Educational Records and Reports

Series, Washington, DC: National Center for Education Statistics, U.S. Department of Health, Education, and Welfare, 1974; Carter V. Good (Editor), *Dictionary of Education* (Third Edition), New York: McGraw-Hill Book Company, 1973.

EXISTENTIAL COUNSELING, an approach to counseling whose therapy is based on several points of view, combining some elements of existentialism with elements of humanism. For this reason, some have criticized it as lacking in methodological rigor. Essentially, the existential counselor works to develop a oneness with his/her client, trying to see the world through the eyes of the client. Considerable emphasis is placed on understanding of the individual. This counseling approach is predicated on the assumption that individuals, having free wills, must ultimately accept responsibility for their own actions. The job of the counselor is to help clients to develop self-awareness and eventually help them to make free choices for which they will be willing to accept responsibility. The heart of the technique is its emphasis on human-to-human relationships.
References: Gerald Corey, *Theory and Practice of Counseling and Psychotherapy,* Monterey, CA: Brooks/Cole Publishing Company, 1977; Charlotte Buhleu and Melanie Allen, *Introduction to Humanistic Psychology,* Monterey, CA: Brooks/Cole Publishing Company, 1972; Bruce Shertzer and Shelley C. Stone, *Fundamentals of Counseling* (Third Edition), Boston: Houghton Mifflin Company, 1980; E. L. Tolbert, *An Introduction to Guidance,* Boston: Little, Brown and Company, 1978.

EXISTENTIALISM, a philosophy that focuses on the nature of human existence and most particularly the existence of a single individual. According to this philosophy, man can discover basic truths about him/herself. The world has neither purpose nor meaning when apart from man. There is no right or wrong standard on which to base decisions in existentialism; rather, individuals are forced to make a choice from among alternatives (including "not to select"). Soren Kierkegaard is considered the founder of the philosophy (he died in 1855). Nietzsche, Husserl, Heidegger, Sartre, Pascal, Buber, and Dostoevsky are among the better known existentialists.
References: Wesley Barnes, *The Philosophy and Literature of Existentialism,* Woodbury, NY: Barron's Educational Series, Inc., 1968; Robert D. Cumming, *Starting Point,* Chicago: University of Chicago Press, 1979; Fernando R. Molina (Editor), *The Sources of Existentialism as Philosophy,* Englewood Cliffs, NJ: Prentice-Hall, Inc., 1969.

EXIT BEHAVIOR—See ENTRY BEHAVIOR

EXPECTANCY LEVEL, the degree of accomplishment, attainment and/or behavior that is anticipated of an individual or a group by another individual or group. It is a term educators use frequently to set anticipated performance goals based on students' test scores. Generally, the expectancies are set in relationship to others. For example, one student might feel that another student is more able; therefore, the first student will wait until the "more able" student reacts before taking action.

Expectancy levels may be set through interactions with individuals; power-prestige relationships; stereotyping; fear; known skills, abilities, or prior performance; age; and maturation. Such levels must be set realistically. If they are too high for an individual or group, frustrations and antagonisms may be produced. If they are too low, abilities and skills of the individuals involved might not develop.
References: Joseph Berger, et al., *Expectation Status Theory: A Theoretical Research Program,* Cambridge, MA: Winthrop Publishers, Inc., 1974; Joseph Berger, et al., *Status Characteristics and Social Interaction.* New York: Elsevier Scientific Publishing Company, Inc., 1977.

EXPERIENCE CHART, the chart on which a teacher writes stories and/or records of experiences that have been dictated by one child or a group of children. Stories may be written on chart paper, the chalkboard, or on regular paper. Experience charts can be used to stimulate writing, as an adjunct to reading, or as a way of helping students to express ideas clearly. In some instances, the experience chart is an effective tool for motivating poor readers to read, the premise being that a child who has dictated a story will encounter success in reading it after it has been written for him/her.

C. M. Lee and R. V. Allen identified four types of charts: (1) *personal language chart* (described above), the chart that permits the student to express himself/herself and subsequently to see his/her own language in print; (2) *work chart,* a functional chart on which daily class or individual activities are recorded; (3) *narrative chart,* the recording of actual or mythical experiences that are frequently reproduced and collated into class reading booklets; and (4) the *reading skills chart,* which develops skills diagnosed as necessary for a number of children to master.
References: Estill Alexander, Jr. et al., *Teaching Reading,*

Boston: Little, Brown and Company, 1979; Victor Froese, "Diagnostic Teaching of Composition" in Carl Braun and Victor Froese (Editors), *An Experience-Based Approach to Language and Reading*, Baltimore: University Park Press, 1977; C. M. Lee and R. V. Allen, *Learning to Read Through Experience*, New York: Appleton-Century-Crofts, Inc., 1963; Walter T. Petty, et al., *Experiences in Language: Tools and Techniques for Language Arts Methods* (Second Edition), Boston: Allyn and Bacon, Inc., 1976.

EXPERIENTIAL LEARNING—See LEARNING, EXPERIENTIAL

EXPERIMENTAL DESIGN, an approach used by researchers to test hypotheses. In a true experimental design, the researcher has control over independent variables (those factors to be tested and/or manipulated), the criterion (dependent) variable, the assignment of subjects to treatment conditions, and the environment. Although most experimental research is performed in the laboratory, true experiments can also be performed in nonlaboratory settings such as classrooms.

There are many experimental designs that can be used by a researcher. Selection of the most appropriate one depends on the treatment, conditions, and the hypotheses to be tested. One of the most common is the pre-post design, where subjects are assigned randomly to a treatment (experimental) group and a control (receives no treatment) group. Each group is given a pre-test. The experimental group receives the treatment while the control does not; then, both groups are post-tested and the results of the testing are analyzed. (See QUASI-EXPERIMENTAL DESIGN.)
References: Donald Campbell and Julian Stanley, *Experimental and Quasi-Experimental Designs for Research*, Chicago: Rand McNally and Company, 1966; William M. Hays, *Statistics* (Fourth Edition), New York: Holt, Rinehart and Winston, Inc., 1988; W. James Popham, *Educational Evaluation* (Second Edition), Englewood Cliffs, NJ: Prentice-Hall, 1988.

EXPERIMENT IN INTERNATIONAL LIVING, a privately financed program, founded in 1931 by Donald Watt, that plans group education travel for students and places them in homes of a host country (be it the United States or other countries). About eight to ten students and an academic director form a group that spends a semester studying in a foreign culture. The program includes language study, living in homes rather than hotels, study of the host culture, and independent study.

The Experiment in International Living established a School for International Training in Brattleboro, Vermont in 1964. The school awards master's degrees. In the 1960s, the Experiment in International Living was involved in the training of Peace Corps members. Headquarters for the Experiment in International Living is in Putney, Vermont.
References: Richard W. Breslin and Paul Pedersen, *Cross-Cultural Orientation Programs*, New York: Gardner Press, Inc., 1976; Steven E. Deutsch, *International Education and Exchange*, Cleveland, OH: The Press of Case Western Reserve University, 1970; William Peters, *Passport to Friendship*, Philadelphia: J. B. Lippincott Company, 1957; Cummins E. Speakman, Jr., *International Exchange in Education*, New York: The Center for Applied Research in Education, Inc., 1966.

EX POST FACTO ANALYSIS—See POST HOC ANALYSIS

EXPRESSIVE APHASIA—See APHASIA

EXPULSION, the indefinite removal (separation) of a student from school. Because of the gravity of this form of action, the decision to expel a student is made by the board of education following recommendation for expulsion by the school administration. Expulsion of a student normally takes place after very detailed due process hearings have been conducted. The school board's decision is subject to review by the courts. (See SUSPENSION.)
References: Edward C. Bolmeier, *Legality of Student Disciplinary Practices*, Charlottesville, VA: The Michie Company, 1976; Eugene T. Connors, *Student Discipline and the Law* (PDK Fastback 121), Bloomington, IN: The Phi Delta Kappa Educational Foundation, 1979.

EXTENDING CONCEPTS THROUGH LANGUAGE ACTIVITIES (ECOLA), an extension of the language experience approach to the teaching of language and reading comprehension. Although developed as an approach for first language readers, the method can be adapted to a variety of groups. ECOLA can be employed with non-native speakers if the students' oral and written responses are in their native tongues.

ECOLA consists of five steps: (1) determining a reason/purpose for reading the selection; (2) silent reading guided by both the purpose question and an established criterion task; (3) writing of personal interpretations of the selection that reflect both the purpose and the assigned task; (4) sharing of interpretations by students and instructor in an open exchange; (5) writing, either individually or in groups, a second interpretation to be compared with the first. This entire approach enables the reader to understand the constructive and altering nature of the comprehension process. (See LANGUAGE EXPERIENCE APPROACH.)

References: John G. Barnitz, *Reading Development of Non-Native Speakers of English*, ERIC Clearinghouse on Language and Linguistics, New York: Harcourt Brace Jovanovich, Inc., 1985; M. T. Smith-Burke, "Extending Concepts through Language Activities" in J. A. Langer and M. T. Smith-Burke (Editors), *Reader Meets Author/Bridging the Gap: A Psycholinguistic and Sociolinguistic Perspective*, Newark, DE: International Reading Association, 1982.

EXTENSION PROGRAMS, originally those educational and service programs that provided information, guidance, and technical assistance to farmers and people living in rural areas. Large-scale extension programs did not start in the United States until 1862 with the passage of land grant legislation (Morrill Act). Establishment of the Department of Agriculture and passage of the Smith-Lever Act (1914), the legislation that established the Cooperative Extension Service, served to increase services of this sort. Agricultural societies, as early as 1785, were providing limited services and education to farmers in the United States. By 1840, traveling teachers of agriculture were available in most European nations.

Today, extension services are available to rural America in every state, and extension service personnel work out of land-grant colleges/universities, in cooperation with the Department of Agriculture, to make this possible. Extension programs include formal college credit classes, advisory information, soil analysis, home economics information, and other similar services.

In nonrural areas, the term *extension programs* is usually used to describe those courses and programs (usually nonagricultural) that are offered off-campus to accommodate students who do not reside near a college campus. Although not always, extension programs usually add flexibility to colleges and universities in their course offerings and requirements for entrance. Extension programs of a continuing education nature may carry continuing education or academic credit. (See CONTINUING-EDUCATION UNIT.)

References: Louis T. Benezet and Frances W. Magnusson, *Building Bridges to the Public: New Directions for Higher Education*, San Francisco: Jossey-Bass Publishers, 1979; Bruce Crouch and Shankarish Chamala, *Extension Education and Rural Development* (Volume 2), New York:

Wiley-Interscience, 1980; Patricia A. Thrash, "Monitoring Educational Change: Evaluating Institutions with Off-Campus Programs," *North Central Association Quarterly*, Winter 1979.

EXTERNAL DEGREE, a degree earned by an individual based on a program of preparation that does not follow a traditional pattern of collegiate or university study and the work for which need not be completed on the campus of the institution granting the degree. The external degree grew out of: the changes in the internal degree (degrees earned on campus that follow a prescribed program); the extension degree (programs offered off campus); the adult degree (programs designed for the mature person and the life-style he/she follows); and the assessment degree (emphasizes assessment and demonstration of competence). Interest in the external degree developed during the 1960s in the United States. As of 1979, external degree programs were still evolving with no set model or standard being followed.

External degrees range from Associate, B.S. and B.A., through the doctorate. Some of the institutions conferring external degrees are SUNY—Empire State (New York); Minnesota Metropolitan State College; Community College of Vermont; Extended University of the University of California; University Without Walls (Union of Experimenting College and Universities), and Nova University (Florida). External degree programs exist in foreign countries as well.

References: Cyril O. Houle, *The External Degree*, San Francisco: Jossey-Bass Publishers, 1973; Stephen H. Spurr, *Academic Degree Structures: Innovative Approaches*, New York: McGraw-Hill Book Company, 1970.

EXTERNAL STORAGE, the device that contains computer programs and data separate from the unit. In personal computers, information is stored as magnetic spots on oxide surfaces. The three most common forms of external storage used with personal computers are cassette tapes, floppy discs, and hard discs. Unless write-protected, these units can be erased and used again. As new information is written, it automatically replaces what was there. Write-protection avoids accidental erasure. This involves marking the tape or floppy disc by either removing a plastic tab from the tape's case or covering up a notch on the disc's jacket. Most hard discs cannot be write-protected. (See FLOPPY DISC and HARD DISC.)

References: Grace Murray Hopper and Steven L. Mandell, *Understanding Computers*, St. Paul, MN: West Publishing Company, 1984; David R. Sullivan, et al., *Computing Today: Microcomputer Concepts and Application,* Boston: Houghton Mifflin Company, 1985.

EXTERNAL VALIDITY—See VALIDITY, INTERNAL-EXTERNAL

EXTRACLASS ACTIVITIES, also known as extracurricular or cocurricular activities, those activities and events planned by a school but not traditionally part of regular classroom course work. There is considerable debate over the use of the term *extracurricular* as a synonym for these activities, since the term *extracurricular* implies activities outside the curriculum. Ralph Tyler and others defined curriculum as being all the learning that is planned by the school; thus, *extraclass* or *cocurriculum* are considered to be more accurate terms to use.

Activities such as band, drama clubs, sports teams, 4-H Clubs, arts and crafts, debate, and student government are examples of extraclass or cocurricular activities commonly found in schools, especially secondary schools. Considerable learning takes place in these activities, and they have considerable meaning for most students who participate in them. At one time, credit was not awarded for such activities, but this has been changing over the years.

References: Dwight W. Allen and Eli Seifman, *The Teacher's Handbook,* Glenview, IL: Scott, Foresman and Company, 1971; John D. McNeil, *Curriculum: A Comprehensive Introduction,* Boston: Little, Brown and Company, 1977; Daniel Tanner and Laurel N. Tanner, *Curriculum Development,* New York: Macmillan Publishing Company, Inc., 1975; J. Lloyd Trump and Delmas F. Miller, *Secondary School Curriculum Improvement: Meeting Challenges of the Times* (Third Edition), Boston: Allyn and Bacon, Inc., 1979; Ralph Tyler, "The Curriculum—Then and Now" in *Proceedings of the 1956 Invitational Conference on Testing Problems,* Princeton, NJ: Educational Testing Service, 1957.

EXTRACURRICULAR ACTIVITIES—See EXTRACLASS ACTIVITIES

EXTROVERSION—See INTROVERSION AND EXTROVERSION

EYE CONTACT, people looking into each others eyes during periods of social interaction. Such contact is considered to be an important part of interpersonal communication. Michael Argyle and Janet Dean summarized eye contact research and found that contact is more evident: (1) during periods of listening rather than speaking; (2) when the personal relationship between communicating individuals is close; (3) when the topic being discussed is less personal; and (4) when there is a developmental history of eye contact. These same investigators report five purposes served by eye contact: (1) to obtain feedback; (2) to indicate that communication is or will be proceeding (e.g. getting the attention of a waiter); (3) to satisfy certain personal needs; (4) to establish a social relationship; and (5) to establish an equilibrium between one's need for recognition and avoidance.

A study reported by Steven Beebe confirmed that a public speaker who manifests high or moderate levels of eye contact during his/her presentations is perceived (by audience members) as being more credible than one exhibiting low levels of eye contact.

Eye contact is a subject of interest to students of nonverbal communication as well as those interested in speech. (See NONVERBAL COMMUNICATIONS.)

References: Michael Argyle and Janet Dean, "Eye Contact, Distance and Affiliation," *Sociometry,* September 1965; Steven A. Beebe, "Eye Contact: A Nonverbal Determinant of Speaker Credibility," *The Speech Teacher,* January 1974.

EYE-VOICE SPAN (EVS), a reading term for the distance between the point on a line of print to which the eyes have moved ahead during oral reading and the point to which the voice has come in verbalizing words. In the case of silent reading, it is the distance between the point to which the eyes have moved ahead and the point at which reader interpretation is taking place. For adult readers, the span consists of several words.

Reading researchers measure EVS by having a subject read aloud from an illuminated passage. Illumination is suddenly turned off or the printed word disappears through use of some mechanical device. The span of words read by the subject after the printed material has disappeared is then recorded and identified as the reader's EVS. Recent studies of EVS suggest that able readers normally end their EVS at some natural or convenient stopping point such as the end of a phrase.

References: Aaron S. Carton, *Orientation to Reading,* Rowley, MA: Newbury House Publishers, Inc., 1976; Dolores Durkin, *Teaching Them to Read* (Third Edition), Boston: Allyn and Bacon, Inc., 1978; Edward B. Fry, *Elementary Reading Instruction,* New York: McGraw-Hill Book Company, 1977.

FACE VALIDITY—See VALIDITY

FACT-FINDING, a collective bargaining term for a particular type of impasse resolution somewhat different from mediation. In fact-finding, the fact-finder(s) hear(s) the arguments offered by both parties involved in collective bargaining and then proffer(s) recommendations. This activity may take place after or in place of mediation. (See COLLECTIVE BARGAINING and MEDIATION.)

References: Alan E. Bent and T. Zane Reeves, *Collective Bargaining in the Public Sector: Labor-Management Relations and Public Policy,* Menlo Park, CA: The Benjamin/ Cummings Publishing Company, Inc., 1978; Harold S. Roberts, *Labor-Management Relations in the Public Service,* Honolulu, HI: University of Hawaii Press, 1970.

FACTOR ANALYSIS, a multivariate (statistical) technique used to reduce a large number of measured variables into constructs (factors) that explain the intercorrelations among the variables. The primary purposes of factor analysis are statistical simplicity, psychological meaningfulness, and provision of a description of the relationships among multiple variables.

For example, a researcher may have 25 variables that were collected from a given group of data sources. To assess the meaningfulness of the interrelationships among the variables, and to reduce the number of variables with which to work, factor analysis is used. From the 25, perhaps only 7 factors (constructs) of appreciable importance (and in order of importance) may be generated. Other nonimportant factors are apt to be generated too, but they are no longer considered in the analysis. Through the use of factor loadings, the contributions of each of the 25 variables to the 7 factors can be evaluated, with the largest loadings indicating the greatest contributions. These loadings not only determine the input of the factors (constructs) but also provide a basis for naming them as well.

Factor analysis is a complex, mathematically-involved procedure. A matrix of correlations among the variables is constructed, unrotated factors are extracted, the remaining factors are rotated (to make each factor independent of the other), and then the rotated factor matrix is analyzed. This technique developed from the works of Charles Spearman, Cyril Burt, Karl Pearson, and Louis Thurstone. There are different factor analytical approaches available to the researcher such as principal-factor, centroid, and oblique multiple factor.

References: Anne Anastasi, *Psychological Testing* (Sixth Edition), New York: Macmillan Publishing Company, 1988; Walter R. Borg and Meredith D. Gall, *Educational Research: An Introduction* (Fifth Edition), New York: Longman, Inc., 1989; Harry H. Harman, *Modern Factor Analysis* (Third Edition), Chicago: University of Chicago Press, 1976.

FACULTY EXCHANGE CENTER (FEC), a nonprofit program to facilitate the exchange of faculty among colleges and universities. The program is administered by faculty, for faculty match themselves with one or more colleagues listed in a directory and make all the arrangements for an exchange (such as agreements between the department chairs and deans of the respective institutions).

The Faculty Exchange Center provides the directory of faculty from institutions where English is the language of instruction. The center also provides a housing supplement for exchanges during the summer, holidays, and sabbatical leaves. Faculty from the United States, Canada, Hong Kong, New Zealand, Australia, New Guinea, Israel, Egypt, Spain, Sweden, France, Greece, India, Holland, Ireland, and the United Kingdom are listed in the directory.

The Faculty Exchange Center was started in 1973 and is presently located in Lancaster, Pennsylvania. Institutional and individual memberships are available.

Reference: Faculty Exchange Center, *Directory, Fall 1987,* Lancaster, PA: FEC, 1987.

FACULTY MEETING, an official gathering of an institution's faculty, carried out in accordance with established rules, policies, and/or traditions of the institution. These may be convened on a *calendar* (i.e. bimonthly) or *as-needed* basis. Ideally, faculty meetings are carried out in a businesslike manner and in accordance with procedures that are known to all concerned. Such procedures normally include items such as the planning and publishing of a meeting agenda, voting rights, parliamentary procedure, and the recording/distribution of minutes.

In the elementary and secondary schools, the building principal generally chairs faculty meetings. In colleges and universities, the chair may be the dean or a faculty member chosen for this role by the faculty.

Research on faculty meetings tends to show that teachers are frequently dissatisfied with them. Contributing to this disenchantment are several factors, including the following: (1) poor planning; (2) little opportunity for meaningful faculty participation; (3) topics discussed hold little interest for the teachers; (4) failure of the leader to strive for consensus; and (5) "climate" variables such as poor place, time, and length of meeting.

The literature on faculty meetings tends to distinguish those that are conducted for *administrative* purposes and those designed to promote the *inservice development* of teachers.

References: Lester W. Anderson and Lauren A. Van Dyke, *Secondary School Administration* (Second Edition), Boston: Houghton Mifflin Company, 1972; F. Don James, "Faculty Organization and Administration" in Asa S. Knowles (Editor), *Handbook of College and University Administration* (Volume 2), New York: McGraw-Hill Book Company, 1970; Donald G. MacKenzie, "Small-Group Process Skills Necessary for Effective Meetings," *NASSP Bulletin,* April 1979; Albert H. Shuster and Don H. Stewart, *The Principal and the Autonomous Elementary School,* Columbus, OH: Charles E. Merrill Publishing Company, 1973.

FACULTY SENATE, a representative body of a college, university, or school faculty that participates in the institution's policymaking and decision-making process. The extent or scope of policymaking or decision making is a function of factors such as: (1) type of school, college or university; (2) enrollment size; (3) status (i.e. public or private); (4) authority delegated, mandated, or prohibited; (5) organizational structure; (6) nature of the institution; (7) administrative style or leadership of the chief school administrator; and (8) legal limitations (i.e. where the ultimate authority rests). Some faculty senates are very powerful, others are not. There is no set scope of their power, authority, or influence other than that faculty senates are an instrument of faculty governance.

Faculty senates are usually elected by the faculty. Although membership in some instances may be restricted to senior faculty, most senates are proportionally representative. Some are not restrictive with respect to either rank or size. Faculty senates are more commonly found at institutions of higher education than at high schools or other educational institutions.

References: Thad L. Hungate, *Management in Higher Education,* New York: Teachers College, Columbia University, 1964; James A. Perkins, *The University as an Organization,* New York: McGraw-Hill Book Company, 1973; A. K. Rice, *The Modern University,* London, England: Tavistock Publishing, 1970.

FAMILY EDUCATIONAL RIGHTS AND PRIVACY ACT—See BUCKLEY AMENDMENT

FAMILY-LIFE EDUCATION—See SEX EDUCATION

FAMILY RESOURCES EDUCATION, a component of the home economics curriculum that focuses on home management (planning, implementation, decision making), consumerism, family life cycle, family system, microenvironment, financial management, family roles, housekeeping, consumer skills, parenthood education, child development and guidance, and other areas related to the occupation of homemaking. A more traditional term used in home economics for this area of study is *Consumer and Homemaking Home Economics.* Family resources education programs are generally offered at the high school level. The Future Homemakers of America (FHA) organization is generally an integral part of the program. (See CONSUMER EDUCATION; FUTURE HOMEMAKERS OF AMERICA; HOME ECONOMICS; and HOMEMAKING.)

References: A. S. Csaky, *99 Ways to a Simple Lifestyle,* Bloomington, IN: Indiana University Press, 1977; Ruth E. Deacon and Francille M. Firebaugh, *Family Resource Management: Principles and Applications,* Boston: Allyn and Bacon, Inc., 1980; Irene Oppenheim, *Management of the Modern Home,* New York: Macmillan Publishing Company, Inc., 1972; Constantino Lluch, et al., *Patterns in Household Demand and Saving,* Oxford, England: Oxford University Press, 1977.

FARSIGHTEDNESS—See HYPEROPIA

FEDERAL CONTROL, in education, the fact or fear that local decision-making latitude is being or will be assumed by the federal government to the extent that federal aid to, and activities in, education increase. The Tenth Amendment of the Constitution prescribes that education in the United States is a state function. Over the years, however, the states have delegated many responsibilities for operating the schools to local communities. Thus, a tradition of local control of education, stronger in the United States than in most other countries of the world, has emerged. As part of that tradition, direct federal control of the public schools has been resisted.

In recent years, federal contributions to education have increased significantly with corresponding increases in educational activities recorded. Students of federal control have identified numbers of factors that, directly or indirectly, have accounted for increased educational decisioning being carried out at the federal level. Some of the principal ones are: (1) more frequent efforts by the federal government to resolve major social problems (e.g. educating the handicapped); (2) court decisions made for the purpose of assuring universal equality of educational opportunity; (3) increasing power of what David Cohen called "private government" (i.e. powers granted to agencies such as testing firms that are neither elected or accountable to the public); and (4) increases in the size and status of the federal bureaucracies impacting on education (e.g. creation of the U.S. Department of Education).

In a recent Gallup poll, a national sample of the public was asked: "In your opinion, who should have the greatest influence in deciding what is taught in the public schools here—the federal government, the state government, or the local school board?" (p. 36). Respondents answered as follows: federal government, 9 percent; state government, 15 percent; local school board, 68 percent; don't know, 8 percent. These data indicate that, notwithstanding heightened educational activity by the federal government, popular sentiment remains strongly in favor of local control.

References: David K. Cohen, "Tendencies in Public School Governance" in Jane Newitt (Editor), *Future Trends in Education Policy,* Lexington, MA: Lexington Books, 1979; William C. French, "Local Control Under Attack" in Mary F. Williams (Editor), *Government in the Classroom: Dollars and Power in Education* (Proceedings of The Academy of Political Science), Montpelier, VT: Capital City Press, 1978; George H. Gallup, "The 12th Annual Gallup Poll of the Public's Attitudes Toward the Public Schools," *Phi Delta Kappan,* September 1980.

FEEDBACK, any information supplied by others, or the environment, to an individual or an organism that initially requested the response such that the information is used to affect a reaction. The crucial aspects of feedback are: (1) information is requested by one organism, but is generated by someone or something else; (2) the information must be received; (3) information must be considered by the individual (or organism); and (4) the

information is used in the development of a reaction. Acceptance of the information, or a decision not to take action and/or to allow the environment to stay static, can be considered a reaction. Feedback need not be verbal. Nonverbal communication supplies a considerable amount of feedback to individuals and organisms. Heat, odors, light, color, and noises are forms of feedback, in addition to language, facial, and body expressions. (See FEEDBACK LEARNING.)

References: James Deese, *General Psychology,* Boston: Allyn and Bacon, Inc., 1967; Richard S. Lazarus, *The Riddle of Man,* Englewood Cliffs, NJ: Prentice-Hall, Inc., 1974.

FEEDBACK LEARNING, a major part of learning in which an organism or person learns from the information supplied by feedback. Learning occurs when a feedback loop is completed. That is, one organism stimulates (causes a reaction in) another, and the second organism sends a message to the first (feedback) as a result of the initial action.

Behavioral and conditioning psychologists, as well as behavior modification specialists, make use of feedback learning. Reward and punishment used in such psychology and techniques are based on positive or negative feedback. (See FEEDBACK.)

References: James Deese, *General Psychology,* Boston: Allyn and Bacon, Inc., 1967; Richard S. Lazarus, *The Riddle of Man,* Englewood Cliffs, NJ: Prentice-Hall, Inc., 1974.

FEINBERG LAW, New York legislation, passed in 1949, that authorized that state's Board of Regents to draft a list of subversive organizations and to disqualify members of such groups from teaching in the state's public schools. The law was challenged but declared to be constitutional (*Adler v. Board of Education, 1952*) by the U.S. Supreme Court. The Supreme Court later reversed itself (*Keyishian v. Board of Regents, 1967*), ruling that such prohibition violated the First Amendment.

References: Adler v. Board of Education, 342 U.S. 485, 72 S.Ct. 380, 96 L.Ed. 517 (1952); Newton Edwards, *The Courts and the Public Schools: The Legal Basis of School Organization and Administration* (Third Edition), Chicago: University of Chicago Press, 1971; David Fellman, *The Supreme Court and Education* (Third Edition), New York: Teachers College, 1976; *Keyishian v. Board of Regents of University of State of New York,* 385 U.S. 589, 87 S.Ct. 675, 17 L.Ed. 2d 629 (1967) (Case No. 61).

FELLOWSHIPS, grants made to students to pursue an education, primarily at the graduate level. The money is usually nontaxable and is generally awarded on the basis of merit as opposed to financial need. The dollar value of the fellowship varies by institution, the graduate program taken, or the sponsor of the fellowship. The purpose of a fellowship is to support an individual's education by providing expenses for his/her education and some living expenses. Thus, recipients are generally restricted from being otherwise employed.

There are three types of fellowships: research, sponsored, and teaching. *Research fellowships* require an individual to participate in some type of formal research. A *sponsored fellowship* is supported by an agency outside the institution (e.g. National Science Foundation Fellowships, Fulbright-Hays Fellowships). A *teaching fellow* is required to devote a percentage of time to teaching as part of his/her educational program. (See GRADUATE ASSISTANTS.)

References: Definitions of Student Personnel Terms in Higher Education, Washington, DC: U.S. Department of Health, Education, and Welfare, 1968; James Harvey, *The Student in Graduate School,* Washington, DC: American Association of Higher Education, 1972; Carl Kaysen, *Content and Context: Essays on College Education,* New York: McGraw-Hill Book Company, 1973.

FELLOW, TEACHING—See FELLOWSHIPS

FERNALD METHOD, a multisensory approach to remedial reading developed at a University of California clinic school in the 1920s. In 1943, Grace Fernald, one of those who did pioneer work with the method, reported on its use with normal individuals who were disabled readers and with retarded children. Basically, the method makes use of language experience techniques and tracing. It consists of four stages: (1) with his/her finger, the learner traces a word that has been copied on a piece of rough paper, says the word aloud before and after tracing it, and then attempts to write the word without using the copy; (2) the student writes a word after looking at it but does not go through tracing procedure; (3) the child learns a word by viewing it in print (not copied for him/her by the teacher); and (4) the reader is able to recognize parts of new words, or new words, on the basis of previous experience. The V-A-K-T method of teaching reading is a contracted version of the Fernald method. (See V-A-K-T.)

References: Grace Fernald, *Remedial Techniques in Basic School Subjects,* New York: McGraw-Hill Book Company,

1943; George Kaluger and Clifford J. Kolson, *Reading and Learning Disabilities* (Second Edition), Columbus, OH: Charles E. Merrill Publishing Company, 1978; Samuel A. Kirk, et al., *Teaching Reading to Slow and Disabled Learners,* Boston: Houghton Mifflin Company, 1978.

FEUERSTEIN'S INSTRUMENTAL ENRICHMENT (FIE), an approach used in the development of cognitive skills. It is based on developing a child's cognitive abilities through mediated learning experiences that include a set of procedures and materials (Learning Potential Assessment Devices and children's interaction (mediation) with adults while using these materials.

The materials were first developed by Reuven Feuerstein and colleagues in 1979 to be used by disadvantaged, low-performing Israeli adolescents. The materials are being used extensively in U.S. schools for cognitive development and the teaching of thinking skills. Feuerstein's materials include classroom instructional procedures and 14 paper-and-pencil booklets—Organizations of Dots, Orientation in Space (two booklets), Comparisons, Categorizations, Analytic Perceptions, Family Relations, Temporal Relations, Numerical Progressions, Instructions, Illustrations, Representational Stencil Design, Transitive Relations, and Syllogisms. There is considerable teacher-student and student-student discussion (mediation), as well as having students induce principles from their work in the booklets and then applying the principles to content areas.

References: Reuven Feuerstein, et al., *The Dynamic Assessment of Retarded Performers: The Learning Potential Assessment Device, Theory, Instruments, and Techniques,* Baltimore, MD: University Park Press, 1979; Reuven Feuerstein, et al., *Instrumental Enrichment: An Intervention Program for Cognitive Modifiability,* Baltimore, MD: University Park Press, 1980; Joel M. Savell, et al., "Empirical Status of Feuerstein's 'Instrumental Enrichment' (FIE) Technique as a Method of Teaching Thinking Skills," *Review of Educational Research,* Volume 56, Number 4; Winter 1986.

FIELD EXPERIENCE EDUCATION, off-campus educational programs carried out under the auspices of an educational institution but not directly supervised by it. Individual faculty members involved in field-experience programs are normally referred to as supervisors and typically receive load credit for overseeing the activities of students working in the field.

John Duley indicated that field experience education consists of at least eight types of programs.

They are: (1) *cross-cultural education,* in which the student studies in a cultural environment different from his own; (2) *preprofessional training,* of which student teaching and medical internship are examples; (3) *career exploration;* (4) *cooperative work experience,* on-the-job training related to the student's program of study; (5) *service-learning internship,* a learning experience that also serves to meet a social need (e.g. nurse's aide, assuming it is a school-sponsored activity); (6) *social-political action,* an experience related to bringing about social reform; (7) *personal growth and development* (e.g. participating in a wilderness survival program); and (8) *field research.*

The Society for Field Experience Education, formed in 1972 and located at Michigan State University, can be contacted for further information concerning field experience education. (See COOPERATIVE VOCATIONAL EDUCATION; INTERNSHIP; and STUDENT TEACHING.)

Reference: John Duley (Editor), *Implementing Field Experience Education,* San Francisco: Jossey-Bass Publishers, 1974.

FIELD HOUSE, a facility that provides an enclosed and unobstructed space that is adaptable to both indoor and outdoor sport activities. It is not intended to be a substitute for a gymnasium, nor should it be the sole facility to accommodate physical education and recreation programs.

Field houses are quite common on college campuses. They serve many purposes, such as: instruction in physical education service courses; practice for intercollegiate sports; intramural and intercollegiate competition; informal activities; spectator sport activities; community use (sports, bands, commencement exercises for local schools, exhibits, etc.); facilities for large group examinations; and cocurricular activities. Functions taking place in field houses are limited by the space and nature of the facilities. The sizes of field houses vary, again depending on functions, costs, demands, and actual physical facilities planned. Depending on the facilities and equipment needed, such buildings can cost millions of dollars to build exclusive of funds required to staff and operate them.

References: Athletic Institute and American Association for Health, Physical Education, and Recreation, *Planning Facilities for Athletics, Physical Education and Recreation* (Revised), Washington, DC: American Association for Health, Physical Education, and Recreation, 1974; Kenneth A. Penman, *Planning Physical Education and Athletic Facilities in Schools,* New York: John Wiley and Sons, 1977.

FIELD TRIP, or school excursion, an organized trip that is primarily educational and that is made by a group of students as part of the regular school program. Such trips are normally organized and directed by classroom teachers. Costs for field trips may be defrayed by the school system, although it is not uncommon for students to be asked to pay trip costs. Written parental permission is almost always required before a student may participate.

Trips related to social studies and science are the most common. Places visited include sites such as museums, farms, parks, hatcheries, nature centers, stores, the post office, factories, zoos, historical sites, and government buildings.

Effective field trips require careful planning and follow-through by the teacher. Significant phases include: (1) planning; (2) arranging; (3) visiting; (4) classroom follow-up; and (5) evaluation.

References: Shirley A. Brehm, *A Teacher's Handbook for Study Outside the Classroom,* Columbus, OH: Charles E. Merrill Publishing Company, 1969; Edgar Dale, *Audiovisual Methods in Teaching* (Third Edition), New York: The Dryden Press, 1969; Walter A. Wittich and Charles F. Schuller, *Instructional Technology: Its Nature and Use* (Sixth Edition), New York: Harper and Row, Publishers, 1979.

FINANCIAL ABILITY, the economic capacity of a school district or state to support public education. One technique commonly employed to determine financial ability at the *local level* is to relate the district's total assessed valuation to its ADM (Average Daily Membership). ADM is divided into total assessed valuation; the quotient thus obtained is known as "assessed valuation per ADM." This approach is imperfect given the fact that property may not be assessed (evaluated) uniformly from one district to another. Adjustments are often made to correct for such assessment inequities.

Other ratios are used to calculate the financial ability of *states* to support education. A measure commonly used for this purpose relates personal income of all state residents to the number of school-aged children in that same state. (See AVERAGE DAILY ATTENDANCE; AVERAGE DAILY MEMBERSHIP; and FOUNDATION PROGRAMS.)

References: John E. Corbally, Jr., *School Finance,* Boston: Allyn and Bacon, Inc., 1962; Russell S. Harrison, *Equality in Public School Finance,* Lexington, MA: Lexington Books, 1976; Allan Odden, *Alternative Measures of School District Wealth* (Report No. F 76-6), Denver, CO: Education Finance Center, Education Commission of the States, December 1976.

FINANCIAL AID—See STUDENT FINANCIAL AID

FINANCIAL EFFORT, the degree to which a jurisdiction (e.g. school district or state) expends money to support the purchase of goods and services.

At the *local* school district level, general comparison of tax rates or expenditures per pupil may be used to determine effort. They are not perfect measures, however, inasmuch as neither takes into account the financial *ability* of a district to support such expenditures. A more precise procedure, one developed under the direction of Paul Mort, is determined by dividing true valuation per student into the number of dollars spent per pupil.

Financial effort at the *state* level may also be computed in different ways. A relatively accurate measure is one arrived at by dividing a state's per capita personal income into its net current expenditures for public education. (See FINANCIAL ABILITY and MORT, PAUL R.)
References: John E. Corbally, Jr., *School Finance*, Boston: Allyn and Bacon, Inc., 1962; Roe L. Johns and Edgar L. Morphet, *The Economics and Financing of Education: A Systems Approach* (Third Edition), Englewood Cliffs, NJ: Prentice-Hall, Inc., 1975.

FINE ARTS, the general term used in the arts to denote works created for aesthetic enjoyment and/or expression. The fine arts generally include painting, sculpture, print making, music, literature, poetry, and dance. Fine art objects are enjoyed primarily for their aesthetics rather than for their practical or utilitarian value.
References: Donald L. Ehresmann, *Fine Arts: A Bibliographic Guide to Basic Reference Works, Histories, and Handbooks* (Second Edition), Littleton, CO: Libraries Unlimited, Inc., 1979; Joshua C. Taylor, *Fine Arts in America*, Chicago: University of Chicago Press, 1979.

FINGER PAINTING, an art activity in which an individual uses his or her fingers to apply paint. Because of the availability of nontoxic finger paints, their ease of application and cleaning up, and the creativity that can be expressed regardless of artistic skill, finger painting is a widespread activity, one especially popular in elementary school art programs.
References: Francis R. Fast, *Finger Painting: An Outline of Its Origins and History*, Ridgewood, NJ: Women's Club of Ridgewood, NJ, 1945; Mariene Linderman, *Art in the Elementary School: Drawing, Painting and Creating for the Classroom*, Dubuque, IA: Wm. C. Brown Company, Publishers, 1979; Ann S. Wiseman, *Finger Paint and Pudding Paints*, Reading, MA: Addison-Wesley Publishing Company, 1980.

FINGER PLAY, a technique used with primary age children as a form of creative drama. Using this technique, children can "act out" plays, poems, songs, or feelings using appropriate finger movements. Finger play can be used to teach number concepts as well as size and position concepts. Finger play can also be a very important part of the language arts program in the primary grades, lending itself readily to development of storytelling and acting skills in young children. It can also be employed to help a child feel comfortable in front of a group of children.
References: Paul S. Anderson and Diane Lapp, *Language Skills in Elementary Education* (Third Edition), New York: Macmillan Publishing Company, Inc., 1979; Paul C. Burns and Betty L. Broman, *The Language Arts in Childhood Education* (Third Edition), Chicago: Rand McNally College Publishing Company, 1975.

FINGER SPELLING, a manual communication system used with and by deaf individuals. As its name suggests, the system consists of specific finger positions on one hand and includes a separate position for each letter of the alphabet. Some letters (e.g. "o," "c," and "l") are readily recognizable because their configurations closely resemble the shapes of the letters themselves. Finger spelling is easier to learn than is a sign language, lends itself better to exact translation from English, but requires more time and concentration. Experienced adult finger spellers can communicate comfortably at the rate of 60 words per minute. (See ROCHESTER METHOD and SIGN LANGUAGE.)
References: Harry Bornstein, "Sign Language in the Education of the Deaf" in I. M. Schlesinger and Lila Namir (Editors), *Sign Language of the Deaf: Psychological, Linguistic, and Sociological Perspectives*, New York: Academic Press, 1978; Daniel P. Hallahan and James M. Kauffman, *Exceptional Children: Introduction to Special Education*, Englewood Cliffs, NJ: Prentice-Hall, Inc., 1978; R. E. Hartbauer, *Aural Habilitation: A Total Approach*, Springfield, IL: Charles C. Thomas, Publisher, 1975.

FIRST INTERNATIONAL MATHEMATICS STUDY—See INTERNATIONAL ASSOCIATION FOR THE EVALUATION OF EDUCATIONAL ACHIEVEMENT

FIRST PROFESSIONAL DEGREE, an advanced academic degree usually required of those seeking to pursue careers in any number of professions. The National Center for Education Statistics defines it as follows: "An academic degree which requires at least 2 academic years of previous college work for entrance and at least 6 academic years of college work for completion. Beginning in 1965–66, NCES classification includes the following degrees: law (LL.B or J.D.); dentistry (D.D.S. or D.M.D.); medicine (M.D.); veterinary medicine (D.V.M.); chiropody or podiatry (D.S.C. or D.P.); optometry (O.D.); osteopathy (D.O.); pharmacy (D. Pharm.); and theology (B.D.)" (p. 258).

Reference: Nancy B. Dearman and Valena W. Plisko, *The Condition of Education* (1979 Edition), Washington, DC: National Center for Education Statistics, U.S. Department of Health, Education, and Welfare, 1979.

FISCAL INDEPENDENCE, a term used to describe school districts that have complete financial authority over their own business affairs. Fiscally independent systems prepare their own budgets and have the power to raise taxes to support them. In contrast, fiscally dependent districts are obligated to seek financial support from other jurisdictions (e.g. city councils, township boards). The large majority of American school districts are fiscally independent.

References: Percy E. Burrup, *Financing Education in a Climate of Change* (Second Edition), Boston: Allyn and Bacon, Inc., 1977; Stephen J. Knezevich and John G. Fowlkes, *Business Management of Local School Systems,* New York: Harper and Brothers, 1960; Charles E. Reeves, *School Boards: Their Status, Functions, and Activities,* New York: Prentice-Hall, Inc., 1954.

FIXATION PAUSE, a term whose several meanings are each concerned with the idea of remaining or being at a particular point. In terms of psychosexual development, fixation occurs when an individual stays at one stage of development because of libidinal impulses (e.g. stays at the oral gratification stage).

Fixation can occur visually such that an image is focused directly on the fovea of the eye, and the eyes converge only on that object. Fixation is also said to occur when an animal cannot distinguish between a correct and incorrect response.

References: William A. Dember and James J. Jenkins, *General Psychology,* Englewood Cliffs, NJ: Prentice-Hall, Inc., 1970; Robert B. Lawson, et al., *Principles and Methods of Psychology,* New York: Oxford University Press, 1975; Kurt Schlesinger, et al., *Psychology: A Dynamic Science,* Dubuque, IA: Wm. C. Brown Company, Publishers, 1976.

FIXED CHARGES, a category of the school budget that includes recurring expenses of a generally stable nature. They include insurance premiums, contributions made by the district to retirement programs (including social security), and rent. (See SCHOOL BUDGET.)

References: John Greenhalgh, *Practitioner's Guide to School Business Management,* Boston: Allyn and Bacon, Inc., 1978; Leon Ovsiew and William B. Castetter, *Budgeting for Better Schools,* Englewood Cliffs, NJ: Prentice-Hall, Inc., 1963; Paul Reason, *Financial Accounting for Local and State School Systems,* Washington, DC: U.S. Government Printing Office, 1957.

FLAG SALUTE REQUIREMENT, a controversial issue revolving around the right of a school district or a state to require every child to salute the flag. In 1940, in a lawsuit involving a group of Jehovah's Witnesses and the Minersville School District (Pennsylvania), the U.S. Supreme Court ruled that the school district was not violating First Amendment rights of children by requiring them to salute the flag. The ruling was strongly criticized throughout the country. In 1943, the issue was reconsidered by the high court. This time, the flag salute requirement of a state (West Virginia) was challenged, again by a group of Jehovah's Witnesses. The court reversed its earlier ruling on the grounds that the flag salute and pledge requirement infringed on an individual's "sphere of intellect and spirit" that the First Amendment protects.

References: Board of Education of Minersville School District v. Gobitis, 310 U.S. 586, 60 S.Ct. 1010, 84 L.Ed. 998, 1375 (Pa. 1940); Edward C. Bolmeier, *Landmark Supreme Court Decisions on Public School Issues,* Charlottesville, VA: The Michie Company, 1973; E. Edmund Reutter, Jr. and Robert R. Hamilton, *The Law of Public Education* (Second Edition), Mineola, NY: The Foundation Press, Inc., 1976; *West Virginia State Board of Education v. Barnette,* 319 U.S. 624, 63 S.Ct. 1178 (1943).

FLANAGAN, EDWARD J. (July 13, 1886–May 15, 1948), Catholic priest who earned international attention as the founder of Boys Town. Father Flanagan was born in Ireland and moved to the United States at the age of 18. In 1906, he earned the A.B. degree at Mt. St. Mary's College, Maryland. He later studied in Europe, qualifying for ordination at Innsbruck, Austria, in 1912.

From 1912 to 1917, Flanagan worked in Omaha, Nebraska, where he established the Workingman's Hotel. He then decided to establish an orphanage for young boys, one based on his conviction that environmental factors did more to influence the behavior of youth than did heredity. His famous statement, "There is no such thing as a bad boy" reflected that conviction.

In 1922, after occupying two temporary homes, Flanagan purchased a large farm on the outskirts of Omaha that ultimately became the present Boys Town. By 1939, Boys Town became an incorporated city serving 500 youths. During his lifetime, the founder of that city worked with 5,000 young men.

Flanagan died in Berlin, Germany, while inspecting youth facilities being operated there by army personnel. (See BOYS TOWN.)

References: Boys Town: Memories and Dreams, Boys Town, NE: Father Flanagan's Boys Home, Undated Booklet; H. W. Casper, "Flanagan, Edward Joseph" in *New Catholic Encyclopedia* (Volume V), New York: McGraw-Hill Book Company, 1967; "Flanagan, Edward Joseph" in Edward J. Delaney and James E. Tobin, *Dictionary of Catholic Biography*, Garden City, NY: Doubleday and Company, Inc., 1961; Fulton Oursler and Will Oursler, *Father Flanagan of Boys Town*, Garden City, NY: Doubleday and Company, Inc., 1949.

FLANDERS INTERACTION ANALYSIS, a system for recording and analyzing classroom processes. Numerous systems like this have been created of which the Flanders system, developed in the late 1950s by Ned A. Flanders and others at the University of Minnesota, is perhaps best known. Teaching behavior is analyzed by recording selected classroom events at three-second intervals. Trained recorders use a ten-category form to note classroom interactions. Seven of the categories are used when the teacher is speaking (e.g. "praises or encourages," "asks questions"); two are used when children speak (e.g. "pupil talk-response"); and one indicates periods of silence. Results of such analyses are frequently used to help teachers to understand their respective teaching styles.

References: Ned A. Flanders, *Analyzing Teacher Behavior*, Reading, MA: Addison-Wesley Publishing Company, 1970; E. C. Wragg, *Teaching Teaching*, London, England: David and Charles, Inc., 1974.

FLANNELBOARD, also known as cloth board or feltboard, a displaying device used by teachers. The flannelboard can be purchased or made easily by the teacher. It consists of a plywood or masonite panel to which a stretched piece of flannel is fastened. Hooks screwed into one edge of the panel permit the device to be suspended. Physical flexibility is increased by placing the flannelboard on an easel.

Letters, geometric shapes, animal figures, numbers, and other symbols cut from scraps of flannel or felt (of different, contrasting colors) are easily displayed because they adhere readily to the flannelboard. Other coarse-surfaced materials such as sandpaper or styrofoam may also be used to make symbols.

The flannelboard is particularly useful when new information/concepts need to be presented sequentially and/or visually.

References: James W. Brown, et al., *AV Instruction: Technology, Media, and Methods* (Fifth Edition), New York: McGraw-Hill Book Company, 1977; Carlton W. H. Erickson and David H. Curl, *Fundamentals of Teaching with Audiovisual Technology* (Second Edition), New York: The Macmillan Company, 1972; Walter A. Wittich and Charles F. Schuller, *Instructional Technology: Its Nature and Use* (Sixth Edition), New York: Harper and Row, Publishers, 1979.

FLAT GRANTS, state school funds distributed to local school districts on a per-unit basis. Numbers of teachers employed or numbers of students enrolled are the units commonly considered when apportionments are made. A modification of the uniform flat grant, the variable flat grant, utilizes a weighting system that recognizes that educational costs vary by grade level or type of program (e.g. special education). Unit allocations are adjusted (weighted) accordingly. A limitation of the flat grant system is its failure to recognize that the needs, costs, and wealth of school districts vary from one school system to another. (See FOUNDATION PROGRAMS.)

References: Walter I. Garms, et al., *School Finance: The Economics and Politics of Public Education*, Englewood Cliffs, NJ: Prentice-Hall, Inc., 1978; Roe L. Johns and Edgar L. Morphet, *The Economics and Financing of Education: A Systems Approach*, Englewood Cliffs, NJ: Prentice-Hall, Inc., 1975.

FLES, widely used acronym for *Foreign Language* in the *Elementary Schools*, a foreign language program for presecondary school children. Started in the United States after World War II, and reaching its height in the 1950s, FLES has remained an important part of the elementary curriculum in many schools. Although relatively new to the United States, such programs have existed for numerous years in many parts of the world. FLES is based on the assumption that the early years in a child's development are the best time for starting foreign language instruction. Although there is general agreement with respect to this assumption, there appears to be no agreement among specialists about the best age for language learning.

FLES programs normally emphasize the audio-lingual approach to language instruction. Reading, writing, and grammar are not usually made a part of the program in the primary grades. Such skills are introduced in the upper elementary grades, if at all.

There are many problems and value questions that arise in connection with the establishment of a FLES program. Some are: (1) What language should be introduced? (2) At what grade should the program begin? (3) Who should participate in the program? (4) How should it be taught? (5) How much time should be devoted to FLES instruction (e.g. 15 minutes twice or three times a week; 20 minutes twice or three times a week?) and (6) How can articulation with secondary schools best be achieved? (See FOREIGN-LANGUAGE INSTRUCTION.)

References: Theodore Andersson, *Foreign Language in the Elementary School,* Austin, TX: University of Texas Press, 1969; Theodore Andersson and Mildred Boyer, *Bilingual Schooling in the United States,* Austin, TX: National Educational Laboratory Publishers, Inc., 1978; Marguerite Erikson, et al., *Foreign Languages in the Elementary School,* Englewood Cliffs, NJ: Prentice-Hall, Inc., 1964; Wilga M. Rivers, *Teaching Foreign Language Skills,* Chicago: University of Chicago Press, 1968; Wilga M. Rivers, *Speaking in Many Tongues* (Expanded Second Edition), Rowley, MA: Newbury House Publishers, Inc., 1976; Albert Valdman (Editor), *Trends in Language Teaching,* New York: McGraw-Hill Book Company, 1966.

FLEXIBLE SCHEDULE, a schedule consisting of variable time periods based on the educational needs and demands of a program, teacher(s) or student(s). Flexible scheduling allows the school to consider and/or to take advantage of variables such as team teaching, cooperative and individualized planning, class size, individualized instruction, group work, and other innovative instructional methods, techniques, or organizational structures.

Rather than following a set time schedule (e.g. six periods a day), a class (or individual) may be scheduled for a 50-minute chemistry period one day and a 120-minute period the next, depending on the need. Or a class might not repeat the same schedule twice. Modular schedules are a form of flexible scheduling. With the advent of the computer, such scheduling can be accomplished quite efficiently. Flexible schedules can be used for the year-round school, permitting students to start

their studies at different times of the year and begin vacations at different times. (See MODULAR SCHEDULING and YEAR-ROUND SCHOOL.)

References: Carl Braun and Ted Giles, *Strategies for Instruction and Organization,* Calgary, Alberta, Canada: Detselig Enterprises Limited, 1976; Willard Elsbree, et al., *Elementary School Administration and Supervision* (Third Edition), New York: American Book Company, 1967; Richard A. Gorton, *School Administration,* Dubuque, IA: Wm. C. Brown Company, Publishers, 1976; John D. McLain, *Year-Round Education,* Berkeley, CA: McCutchan Publishing Corporation, 1973.

FLEXNER, ABRAHAM (November 13, 1866–September 21, 1959), prominent teacher credited with reforming medical education in America. In 1910, after being commissioned by the Carnegie Foundation for the Advancement of Teaching to study medical training practices, Flexner published the results of his investigation under the title *Medical Education in the United States and Canada.* In the report, he proposed numbers of major reforms including the suggestion that the number of medical schools be reduced, from 155 to 31. The majority of his recommendations were adopted, resulting in significant upgrading of medical training institutions and the introduction of rigorous training standards.

Flexner's educational achievements were extensive. They included: (1) operation of a secondary school; (2) Director of the Institute for Advanced Study at Princeton, New Jersey; and (3) Secretary of the General Education Board. He wrote numerous books and articles dealing with education.

References: Abraham Flexner, *Abraham Flexner: An Autobiography,* New York: Simon and Shuster, 1960; Abraham Flexner, *Medical Education in the United States and Canada: A Report to the Carnegie Foundation for the Advancement of Teaching,* New York: D. B. Updike, The Merrymount Press, 1910 (Reprinted in 1960 by Science and Health Publications, Inc.).

FLOPPY DISC or **DISKETTE,** an external secondary storage unit for the microcomputer. Since the microcomputer has a relatively limited built-in memory capacity, it is nearly always used with an additional storage device. The floppy disc generally comes in two sizes: 8-inch or 5¼-inch. The larger disc has more storage capacity. A smaller disc (sub–4-inch) is also available; however, although easier to use, it stores less data.

Data are stored on the discs as magnetized spots. These are arranged in concentric tracks. Storage capacity of a floppy disc is dependent on how the disc is formatted (i.e., data on one side or data on both sides, which is double density—double the data recorded in the same space). The type of disc drive within the personal computer system determines which formats can be utilized. Data can be accessed randomly on a floppy disc rather than being read or written sequentially, as is the case with magnetic tape. Random access increases the speed of data transfer (reading from or writing to) with the floppy disc. (See EXTERNAL STORAGE.)

References: Grace Murray Hopper and Steven L. Mandell, *Understanding Computers,* St. Paul, MN: West Publishing Company, 1984; David R. Sullivan, et al., *Computing Today: Microcomputer Concepts and Applications,* Boston: Houghton Mifflin Company, 1985.

FLOW CHART, a graphic that portrays a set of specified operations performed, or to be performed, on data. It is used to show both the flow of the problem-solving process as well as the individual (specific) operations to be completed. Different symbols (e.g. rectangles, parallelograms) are used to indicate the nature of each specific operation; direction arrows, or flowlines, connect the successive operations. Use of relatively complex flow charts has increased considerably with the advent of data processing.

Not all flow charts are as complex as those described above. Relatively simple ones may be used to describe an instructional process or to illustrate some sequence of events. An example of a simple flow chart is the graphic "How a Bill Becomes a Law," which civics teachers have used for years to describe the several steps intervening between the introduction of a bill by a congressman and its eventual enactment into law. (See PERT.)

References: Ned Chapin, *Flowcharts,* Princeton, NJ: Auerbach Publishers, 1971; James W. Estes and B. Robert Ellis, *Elements of Computer Science,* San Francisco: Canfield Press, 1973; Peter Stark, *Computer Programming Handbook,* Blue Ridge Summit, PA: Tab Books, 1975.

FOLLOW-THROUGH PROGRAM, a federal program developed to ensure that educational gains made by children who had been in pre-school programs (especially Headstart Programs) are continued. The original Follow-Through Program made federal funds available to schools for programs that provided instructional support for Kindergarten through grade 3 classes. It had previously been found that many of the Headstart gains had been lost once economically and socially disadvantaged children entered regular school programs.

Follow-Through Programs are comprehensive. They include special instruction, free medical and dental care, psychological counseling, social services, free lunches and breakfasts, and parent training through paraprofessional skill development. There is no set Follow-Through model. Instead, the local educational agency adopts the one that best fits its needs.

Follow-Through Programs were established through the 1967 Amendments to the Economic Opportunity Act of 1964. In 1974, Follow-Through was authorized by Title V of the Community Services Act. In 1986 Follow-Through was authorized under Title II of the Human Services Reauthorization Act. (See HUMAN SERVICES REAUTHORIZATION ACT OF 1986.)

References: Rita C. Bobowski, "Federal Funds Follow Through," *American Education,* March, 1977; Public Law 90-222, *United States Statutes at Large, 1967* (Volume 81), Washington, DC: U.S. Government Printing Office, 1968; Public Law 93-644, *United States Statutes at Large, 1974* (Volume 88, Part 2), Washington, DC: U.S. Government Printing Office, 1976.

FOODS AND NUTRITION, that part of the home economics curriculum that focuses on the use, planning, preparation, function, and values of food that humans consume. The broad areas of psychology, sociology, anthropology, economics, agriculture, education, and geography, as well as the physical sciences (e.g. chemistry) are included as part of the study of foods and nutrition.

Foods and nutrition is one of the major areas of home economics. Within the area, numerous specific topics and related problems are studied. They include, but are not limited to, food availability, calories, carbohydrates, fats, vitamins, basal metabolism, diet, dieticians, restaurant and restaurant management, kitchen design and use, meal preparation, meal service, meal planning, food chemistry, and food sanitation. Although some of these topics related to foods and nutrition are to be found in many other curricula, elementary and secondary, major study of the area usually takes place in high schools, vocational and trade schools, and colleges and universities offering instruction in home economics. (See HOME ECONOMICS.)

References: Arnold E. Bender, *Food Processing and Nutrition,* London, England: Academic Press, 1978; *Handbook of Food Preparation* (Seventh Edition), Washington, DC: American Home Economics Association, 1975; Daniel

Melnick, *A Teaching Manual on Food and Nutrition for Non-Science Majors* (Revised Edition), Washington, DC: Nutrition Foundation, Inc., 1979; H. M. Sinclair and G. R. Howat (Editors), *World Nutrition and Nutrition Education*, Oxford, England: Oxford University Press, 1980.

FORCED-CHOICE ITEM, an item in a forced-choice instrument. A forced-choice instrument, or rating form, is made up of items in each of which a respondent *must* select the one description that best or least describes the individual person or subject being rated. In some cases, all possible answers (descriptions) from which the respondent must select will adequately describe the person/subject being rated. Regardless, the rater must select the most appropriate descriptor in accordance with the directions of the instrument. Two or more such descriptors may accompany each item.

Some rating forms have lists of descriptors that discriminate between superior and inferior individuals/subjects; others do not. If the rater selects words from the list that discriminates, the person/subject being rated receives a score. If words from the nondiscriminating list are selected, the individual/subject being rated is not scored.

References: Henry C. Lindgren and Donn Byrne, *Psychology: An Introduction to a Behavioral Science* (Third Edition), New York: John Wiley and Sons, 1971; Aaron Q. Sartaom, et al., *Psychology: Understanding Human Behavior* (Fourth Edition), New York: McGraw-Hill Book Company, 1973; Ross Stagner and Charles M. Solley, *Basic Psychology*, New York: McGraw-Hill Book Company, 1970.

FORCE-FIELD ANALYSIS, a method of separating factors in the psychological field (environment). It may be used with an individual or groups of individuals. The analysis is based on the works of Kurt Lewin, a social psychologist. Lewin felt that behavior was a function of a person in a particular psychological environment at a given time, and that dynamic interaction of the environment and the person at that particular time would determine the behavior of the person. Lewin termed this psychological field *life space*.

For example, if given a reversible figure test, a field-dependent person is distracted by the perceptual background cues and has trouble separating perceptual elements. A field-independent person has less of a problem.

References: Jonathan L. Freedman, et al., *Social Psychology*, Englewood Cliffs, NJ: Prentice-Hall, Inc., 1970; Elliott McGinnies, *Social Behavior: A Functional Analysis*, Boston: Houghton Mifflin Company, 1980; Harold Mey, *Field-theory: A Study of its Applications in the Social Sciences*, New York: St. Martin's Press, 1965; Edward E. Sampson, *Social Psychology and Contemporary Society* (Second Edition), New York: John Wiley and Sons, 1976.

FORD FOUNDATION, a private philanthropic institution established in 1936 by the Ford Family. Since its inception, it has expended $5,000,000,000 including grants to almost 7,500 American and foreign institutions and awards to over 100,000 individuals. It has been active in each of the 50 states and in 96 foreign countries.

The foundation's many approaches (strategies) have been grouped as follows: (1) building and improving institutions; (2) generating and disseminating knowledge; (3) developing individual talents; (4) stimulating support from diverse sources; and (5) contributing to public policy. These activities are carried out by three divisions: National Affairs; Education and Research; and International. The Education and Research Division has supported work in areas such as equity in public school financing, equal educational opportunity for minorities and women, higher education policies, and the needs of adolescents.

Headquartered in New York City, the foundation also maintains overseas field offices in Latin America, the Middle East, Africa, Asia, and the Pacific. Its 1978–79 biennial budget was $221,100,000, smaller than the $365,500,000 and $294,700,000 allocated, respectively, in 1974–75 and 1976–77. Assets reported for 1978 were $2,291,480,000.

References: Ford Foundation, *Current Interests of the Ford Foundation: 1978 and 1979*, New York: The Foundation, 1979; Ford Foundation, *Ford Foundation Annual Report: 1978*, New York: The Foundation, 1978; Richard Magat, *The Ford Foundation at Work: Philanthropic Choices, Methods, and Styles*, New York: Plenum Press, 1979.

FOREIGN LANGUAGE INSTRUCTION, techniques and practices used in the teaching of a foreign language. Foreign language instruction can be broken down into two periods: pre-reading and reading. During the *pre-reading period*, students practice the sound skills of language (oral or conversational prose is stressed). Teaching strategies may include choral mimicry, chain drill, questions and answers, and pattern drill (repetition, substitution, transformation). The *reading period* is more formal. Emphasis here is on learning the technical, written, and reading aspects of the language, the literature of the language, and the culture of the country(ies) of the language.

Language instruction may include visual materials (e.g. labels, maps, clock dials, chalkboards), dramatics, flash cards, slides, movies, motion pictures, records, audio tapes, television, video tapes, language laboratories, programmed instruction, dictation, directed writing, copying, reading modern texts in the language, and reading of the classical literature. Foreign language instruction in the 1970s stressed individualization as opposed to the traditional, large group (or class) instruction.

References: Jermaine D. Arendt, et al. (Editors), *Foreign Language Learning, Today and Tomorrow,* New York: Pergamon Press, Inc., 1979; Dale Lange and Charles J. James (Editors), *Foreign Language Education: A Reappraisal,* Skokie, IL: National Textbook Company, 1972; Gerald E. Logan, *Individualized Foreign Language Learning: An Organic Approach,* Rowley, MA: Newbury House Publishers, Inc., 1973; Raymond R. Renard and Jacques Van Vlasselear, *Foreign Language Teaching with an Integrated Methodology: The S.G.A.V. Methodology,* Paris, France: Didier Publishing Company, 1976.

FOREIGN LANGUAGES IN THE ELEMENTARY SCHOOL—See FLES

FORENSICS, in a general sense, is public speaking or debating. Defined more restrictively, it is the study of argumentation and formal debate. In schools, debating and public speaking clubs and teams are involved in forensic activities. They are often guided by specific rules and guidelines such as those followed during debates. Formal classes in public speaking provide forensics instruction. They are offered in many high schools and colleges.

Forensics also applies to specialized areas such as: forensic medicine, forensic chemistry, forensic psychiatry. In these instances, forensics applies to expert courtroom testimony. (See DEBATE.)

References: Abne M. Eisenberg and Joseph A. Ilardo, *Argument: A Guide to Formal and Informal Debate,* Englewood Cliffs, NJ: Prentice-Hall, Inc., 1980; Donald Klopf and Ronald E. Cambra, *Academic Debate: Practicing Argumentative Theory* (Second Edition), Denver, CO: Morton Publishing Company, 1979; C. G. Tedeschi, et al. (Editors), *Forensic Medicine: A Study in Trauma and Environmental Hazards,* Philadelphia: W. B. Saunders Company, 1977.

FORMAL ORGANIZATION—See ORGANIZATION

FORMATIVE EVALUATION, assessment that takes place during the developmental (formative) stages of a program or a product. Empirical research methodologies are used in formative evaluation. This information may then be used to alter a program, to revise materials, to restructure a program design, or to reconsider goals and objectives. The terms *formative* and *summative* evaluation were first made popular by Michael Scriven in his 1967 AERA monograph. (See EVALUATION, PROGRAM and SUMMATIVE EVALUATION.)

References: W. James Popham, *Educational Evaluation* (Second Edition), Englewood Cliffs, NJ: Prentice-Hall, 1988; Emil J. Posavac and Raymond J. Carey, *Program Evaluation: Methods and Case Studies* (Third Edition), Englewood Cliffs, NJ: Prentice-Hall, 1989; Michael Scriven, "The Methodology of Evaluation" in *Perspectives of Curriculum Evaluation,* AERA Monograph Series on Curriculum Evaluation, No. 1, Chicago: Rand McNally and Company, 1967.

FORTRAN (FORmula TRANslator), a computer language first developed by IBM for computers manufactured by that company. It was designed to instruct the computer to solve algebraic problems. FORTRAN I was developed in 1957 for the IBM 704 machine. FORTRAN II followed (for the same machine). It was later adopted for use with most computers and became the most popular scientific programming language. FORTRAN IV was published in 1962.

The American Standards Association (ASA) later developed USA Standard Basic FORTRAN (similar to FORTRAN II) and the USA Standard FORTRAN (about the same as FORTRAN IV). (See COMPUTER LANGUAGE and COMPUTER PROGRAM.)

References: Charles B. Kreitzberg and Ben Shneiderman, *FORTRAN PROGRAMMING,* New York: Harcourt Brace Jovanovich, Inc., 1975; Donald D. Spencer, *Programming with USA Standard FORTRAN and FORTRAN IV,* Waltham, MA: Blaisdell Publishing Company, 1969.

FOSTER, MARCUS A. (March 31, 1923–November 6, 1973), Oakland, California Superintendent of Schools who was assassinated in a school parking lot following a school board meeting. A black administrator who had previously won national recognition for his work as a reformer in Philadelphia's public schools, Foster was shot by members of the Symbionese Liberation Army. In letters to local newspapers, the group claimed credit for the shooting and attempted to justify it on the grounds that he was an enemy of black people.

As an educator, Foster stressed the importance of having black students develop self-esteem and a

sense of black awareness. He was promoted to the post of Philadelphia's Associate Superintendent (for community relations) before being appointed to the Oakland superintendency.
References: Hugh J. Scott, "Marcus A. Foster: Tribute and Reflection," *Phi Delta Kappan,* February 1974; Harry C. Silcox, "In Memory of Marcus A. Foster, 1923–1973," *Harvard Educational Review,* February 1974.

FOUNDATION PROGRAMS, financial support efforts that are designed to achieve some degree of equality of educational opportunity for all public school children in a given state. A foundation program, John Corbally wrote, is "an educational program which is the minimum, desirable, educational program to be guaranteed for each child in a state" (p. 130). It begins with considerations such as class size, number and kind of resource teachers needed, and administrators needed. Once the minimum, desirable program has been described, it is expressed in dollars-per-pupil terms. State funds are subsequently apportioned to local districts to guarantee the minimal, desirable program for each child enrolled, the exact amount of state support dependent upon local conditions such as number of students, district wealth, and district effort.

George Strayer and Robert Haig, in a report prepared for a New York State Educational Finance Commission, were the first (1923) to propose use of the foundation program concept. (See EQUALIZATION, FINANCIAL; FINANCIAL ABILITY; FINANCIAL EFFORT; and STATE AID.)
References: Percy E. Burrup, *Financing Education in a Climate of Change* (Second Edition), Boston: Allyn and Bacon, Inc., 1977; John E. Corbally, Jr., *School Finance,* Boston: Allyn and Bacon, Inc., 1962; Walter I. Garms, et al., *School Finance: The Economics and Politics of Public Education,* Englewood Cliffs, NJ: Prentice-Hall, Inc., 1978; Paul R. Mort and Walter C. Reusser, *Public School Finance: Its Background, Structure, and Operation* (Second Edition), New York: McGraw-Hill Book Company, 1951; George D. Strayer and Robert M. Haig, *Financing of Education in the State of New York,* New York: The Macmillan Company, 1923.

FOUNDATION SCHOOL, a Jewish day school in which secular and religious programs are offered, from pre-school through sixth grade. Most of these institutions are independent private schools conducted under Conservative or Orthodox jurisdictions. Foundation schools, although they have a strong religious education program, have a better balance between secular and religious programs

than do Yeshiva institutions. (See JEWISH EDUCATION and YESHIVA.)
References: Lloyd P. Gartner (Editor), *Jewish Education in the United States,* New York: Teachers College Press, 1969; Louis Grossmann, *The Aims of Teaching in Jewish Schools: A Handbook for Teachers,* Cincinnati, OH: Teachers Institute of the Hebrew Union College, 1919; Joseph Kaminetsky, "Jewish Education, United States" in Lee C. Deighton (Editor), *The Encyclopedia of Education* (Volume 5), New York: The Macmillan Company and The Free Press, 1971.

FRANKLIN'S ACADEMY, a quasi-public preparatory school whose program was designed by Benjamin Franklin. A description of this program was contained in Franklin's *Proposals Relating to the Education of Youth in Pennsylvania* (1749). The academy program that Franklin proposed had several distinctive features: (1) English was to be taught on an equal footing with Latin and Greek; (2) utilitarian subjects for vocational preparation such as gardening, commerce, mechanics, science, and history were to be included; and (3) the academy was to consist of three departments: English, Latin, and Mathematics. He further suggested that the academy grounds include gardens and an orchard for study and leisure time use by the students. A well-equipped library was also suggested.

Shortly after Franklin's *Proposals* was published, he began to solicit contributions for the creation of his proposed academy. By November of 1749, a 24-member Board of Trustees for the school was created. Unfortunately for Franklin, some of his original ideas were ignored or modified by the board (e.g. English was subordinated to the teaching of Latin and Greek). Nevertheless, much of the program uniqueness he had suggested became a part of the school that came to be called the Philadelphia Academy.

A building was purchased by the trustees in February 1750 with some fiscal support provided by the Philadelphia City Council. Classes were started on January 7, 1751, with approximately 145 boys enrolled. Within five years, and with considerable urging by Franklin, the scope of the academy was broadened to include college level work; the trustees were authorized to confer college degrees. In time, this institution came to be known as the University of Pennsylvania.
References: Carl and Jessica Bridenbaugh, *Rebels and Gentlemen: Philadelphia in the Age of Franklin,* New York: Reynal and Hitchcock, 1942 (Reprinted in 1978 by Greenwood Press); R. Freeman Butts, *A Cultural History of Western Education: Its Social and Intellectual Foundations,*

New York: McGraw-Hill Book Company, 1955; Edward P. Cheyney, *History of the University of Pennsylvania: 1740–1940*. Philadelphia: University of Pennsylvania Press, 1940.

FRATERNITY, a social or honorary society/club usually made up of males. Fraternities in the United States had their origins in debating societies and formal clubs that wanted to control literary societies. In the eastern colleges in the United States, fraternities replaced debating societies starting in 1840. In the midwestern colleges, debating societies and fraternities coexisted.

Phi Beta Kappa, the first Greek-letter society (fraternity) was founded December 5, 1776, at the College of William and Mary. Chi Delta Theta of Yale University, founded in 1821, was similar in nature to Phi Beta Kappa. Although Phi Beta Kappa was founded as a social organization, it evolved into an honorary academic fraternity (the choice of a Greek name appeared to be by chance).

Kappa Alpha Society at Union College (1825) provided the model upon which many modern fraternities are based. Fraternities have evolved over the years with many changing their functions and organizational structure. Individuals wishing to join fraternities must be invited by the organization, go through varying types of initiations, develop close relationships with their "fraternity brothers," and follow determined rules, rituals, and oaths. Many fraternities have "houses" where members live and eat during the school year.

Women's fraternities are called sororities. Because of various laws against certain types of discrimination, many honorary or professional fraternities are changing their charters; some even prefer to be known as *societies*.

Although not as extensive, there do exist high school fraternities. These tend to be social. (See PHI BETA KAPPA and SORORITY.)

References: Thomas A. Leemon, *The Rites of Passage in a Student Culture,* New York: Teachers College Press, 1972; John Robson (Editor), *Baird's Manual of American College Fraternities* (Nineteenth Edition), Menasha, WI: George Banta Company, Inc., 1977; Henry D. Sheldon, *Student Life and Customs,* New York: Arno Press and the New York Times, 1969.

F-RATIO, a statistical procedure by which researchers can estimate the probability that two variances came from the same population by random sampling. It can also be used to determine if the variances came from two populations with the same variance. The test for the homogeneity of variance is computed by using the formula

$$F = \frac{\text{larger variance}}{\text{smaller variance}}$$

There is a distribution of *F*-ratios that can be computed mathematically. When the *F*-ratio is used as a statistical test, it is referred to as the *F* test. (See ANALYSIS OF VARIANCE and VARIANCE.)

References: L. R. Gay, *Educational Research: Competencies for Analysis and Application* (Third Edition), Columbus, OH: Merrill Publishing Company, 1987; William M. Hays, *Statistics* (Fourth Edition), New York: Holt, Rinehart and Winston, Inc., 1988; Bruce W. Tuckman, *Conducting Educational Research* (Second Edition), New York: Harcourt Brace Jovanovich, Inc., 1978.

FREE EXERCISE CLAUSE—See ESTABLISHMENT CLAUSE

FREE SCHOOLS, alternative schools that grew out of the activities of civil rights movements, radical political groups, and counterculture groups that existed during the late 1960s and early 1970s in the United States. The free school movement began in California in 1967. Although the first free schools were designed as alternative institutions for minority children (as opposed to the traditional schools), some free schools were designed for adults. For example, some focused on providing adults with education concerning legal or consumer problems. The one bond that all free schools have in common is the rejection of authority within the free school as well as authority external to it. Thus, the free school is as much an educational institution as it is a model for a new society or relationship for all involved in it. Authority, traditional rewards, punishment, and other traits found in most schools do not exist in these schools.

References: Steve Bhoerman and Joel Denker, *No Particular Place to Go: The Making of a Free High School,* New York: Simon and Schuster, 1972; Jane Lichtman, *Bring your own Bag: A Report on Free Universities,* Washington, DC: American Association for Higher Education, 1973; Ann Swidler, *Organization without Authority: Dilemmas of Social Control in Free Schools,* Cambridge, MA: Harvard University Press, 1979.

FREQUENCY DISTRIBUTION, a set of numbers first arranged from either the highest to the lowest, or the reverse, with the frequency of occurrence counted for each number. A set of numbers such as 1, 2, 2, 2, 3, 3, 3, 3, 4, 5, 5, 6 may be displayed as a frequency distribution, as follows:

Score	f (frequency)
6	1
5	2
4	1
3	4
2	3
1	1

If there are too many scores, numbers may be grouped such that the frequency of numbers within an equally spaced group is summarized:

Scores	f (frequency)
5-6	3
3-4	5
1-2	4

Such number groupings are known as *intervals*.
References: Anne Anastasi, *Psychological Testing* (Sixth Edition), New York: Macmillan Publishing Company, 1988; Frederick J. Gravetter and Larry B. Wallman, *Statistics for the Behavioral Sciences: A First Course for Students of Psychology and Education*, St. Paul, MN: West Publishing Company, 1985.

FREUD, SIGMUND (May 6, 1856–September 23, 1939), founder of psychoanalysis, born in Freiberg, Moravia (now Pribor, Czechoslovakia), and died in London. When he was three years of age, his family moved to Vienna where he lived until Nazi persecution forced him to flee to London in 1938.

Freud was heavily influenced by his mother who was 20 years younger than his father. He was an extremely bright child and student. Freud studied at the University of Vienna where he did physiological research from 1876 to 1881. In 1886, after receiving the M.D. degree, he set up a private practice as a neurologist. From 1886 to 1895, Freud studied neurosis and discovered the relationship of psychology and neurosis. In addition, he developed a simple theory of the sexual causation of neurosis. Between 1895 and 1899, Freud developed self-analysis (which led to psychoanalysis) and published *Studies on Hysteria* (1895) and *The Interpretation of Dreams* (1900). From 1900 until his death, Freud's theories had significant effects on the development of psychoanalysis, especially his expositions of *the id* (instinctual impulses), *the ego* (that part of the psychic that is concerned with reality), and *the superego* (that which restrains the id and the ego). His id psychology, the first system of psychoanalytic psychology, was developed between 1900 and 1914; his ego psychology was worked on from 1914 until his death.
References: Penelope Balogh, *Freud: A Biological Introduction*, New York: Scribner's, 1971; Reuben Fine, *A History of Psychoanalysis*, New York: Columbia University Press, 1979; Sigmund Freud, *An Autobiographical Study*, New York: W. W. Norton and Company, Inc., 1935; Helen W. Puner, *Freud: His Life and His Mind*, New York: Howell, Soskin, Publishers, 1947.

FRIEND OF EDUCATION AWARD, formal honor conferred each year by the national Education Association (NEA) upon "a friend of education who, through his leadership, acts, and support, has contributed to the betterment of education" (Friend of Education Award, p. 1). President Lyndon Johnson, in 1973, was the first individual to be so honored. NEA criteria indicate that the award may be granted for a specific accomplishment or for a long-term contribution. Individual members of the NEA, local associations, or state associations may recommend nominees. Finalists' qualifications are reviewed by an NEA screening committee with the final selection forwarded to the Board of Directors for final approval. (See APPENDIX VI: FRIEND OF EDUCATION AWARD WINNERS.)
References: National Education Association, *Addresses and Proceedings of the One Hundred and Ninth Annual Meeting Held in Detroit, Michigan* (Volume 109), Washington, DC: The Association, 1971; National Education Association, *Friend of Education Award 1980*, Washington, DC: The Association, 1980.

FROEBEL, FRIEDRICH W. A. (April 21, 1782–June 21, 1852), famous 19th-century German educator. Froebel is most noted for founding the "garden of children" (better known as Kindergarten) in 1837. The name itself reflected Froebel's desire to have children developed fully rather than only to be schooled. He formulated a child-centered program where children played and learned through such playing. In his most important work, *The Education of Man* (1877), Froebel stressed the importance of character, purposeful play activities that lead to learning, and the relationship of God, nature, and man. The care and education of young children was perceived to be extremely important and constituted a major part of Froebel's educational design. He had a major impact on education throughout Europe and the United States.

Froebel was heavily influenced by his own childhood. His mother died when he was 9 months old, and his stepmother did not treat him kindly. At 15, he was apprenticed to a forester; later, he became a teacher. These experiences had considerable influence on his thoughts and writing.
References: Robert B. Downs, *Friedrich Froebel,* Boston: Twayne Publishers, 1978; Friedrich Froebel, *Mother's Songs, Games and Stories.,* New York: Arno Press, 1976 (Reprinted from Mutter und Kose-lieder, 1843); Evelyn M. Lawrence (Editor), *Friedrich Froebel and English Education,* London, England: Routledge and Kegan Paul, 1969.

FROSTIG MOVEMENT SKILLS TEST, an experimental evaluation instrument designed to measure strengths and weaknesses in the sensory-motor areas of children, ages 6–12. The test battery was initially developed (in its experimental state) in 1967 and ultimately published in 1972. Six summary scores are produced. They are: (1) hand-eye coordination; (2) strength; (3) balance; (4) visually guided movement; (5) flexibility; and (6) a total score. The test is individually administered, in about 20–25 minutes, although groups of three or four children can take the test together. It is not a group test, thus cannot be administered to an entire class at one time. Each of the areas (e.g. hand-eye coordination, strength) is measured through several subtests. The test was authored by Russell E. Orpet and is published by Consulting Psychologists Press, Inc.
References: Oscar K. Buros (Editor), *The Eighth Mental Measurements Yearbook* (Volume II), Highland Park, NJ: The Gryphon Press, 1978; Marianne Frostig, *Selection and Adaptation of Reading Methods,* San Rafael, CA: Academic Therapy Publications, 1973.

FROSTIG PROGRAM FOR THE DEVELOPMENT OF VISUAL PERCEPTION, generally a paper-and-pencil program that focuses on the remediation of the following visual perception skills: eye-motor coordination, figure-ground relationships, form constancy, position in space, and spatial relationships. The program emphasizes individual instruction and close monitoring of each child. Included in the program are activities and exercises for remediation or skill development as well as development of gross and fine muscle coordination, body image concepts, and total perceptual functions. Although the program does include motor tasks, its major focus is on visual perceptual skill improvement. (See FROSTIG TEST.)
References: Marianne Frostig and D. Horne, *The Frostig Program for the Development of Visual Perception,* Chicago:

Follett Publishing Company, 1964; Arthur S. Reber and Don L. Scarborough (Editors), *Toward a Psychology of Readings: The Proceedings of the CUNY Conferences,* Hillsdale, NJ: Lawrence Erlbaum Associates, Publishers, 1977; Lucille B. Strain, *Accountability in Reading Instruction,* Columbus, OH: Charles E. Merrill Publishing Company, 1976.

FROSTIG TEST, a test of visual perception developed by Marianne Frostig to measure five visual perceptual skills: (1) eye-motor coordination; (2) figure-ground; (3) form constancy; (4) position in space; and (5) spatial relations. Seven scores are generated, one each for the five skills, plus a total score (perceptual age) and a perceptual quotient.

The perceptual quotient (P.Q.) is similar to an I.Q. score. It is suggested that any child with a P.Q. below 90 receive special visual training. The test is designed for children between the ages of three and eight and can be given in a group setting in less than one hour. A specific program has been developed to provide remedial perceptual training in the five skill areas. (See FROSTIG PROGRAM FOR THE DEVELOPMENT OF VISUAL PERCEPTION.)
References: Susanna Pflaum-Connor, *Aspects of Reading Education,* Berkeley, CA: McCutchan Publishing Corporation, 1978; John F. Savage and Jean F. Mooney, *Teaching Reading to Children with Special Needs,* Boston: Allyn and Bacon, Inc., 1979.

FRUSTRATION LEVEL, the point at which a particular item of reading material causes the student to read with difficulty. Different measures are used to ascertain the level at which such frustration (inability to cope) is encountered. Some authorities count the actual number of words a child must be "told" as he/she reads aloud (e.g. 3 or more words missed out of a sequence of 19 indicates that the frustration level has been reached). Other approaches consider percentage of words missed (e.g. more than 10 percent and comprehension less than 50 percent) when ascertaining the frustration level for a particular student.
References: Paul S. Anderson and Diane Lapp, *Language Skills in Elementary Education* (Third Edition), New York: Macmillan Publishing Company, Inc., 1979; Mark W. Aulls, *Developmental and Remedial Reading in the Middle Grades,* Boston: Allyn and Bacon, Inc., 1978; Paul C. Burns and Betty L. Broman, *The Language Arts in Childhood Education* (Fourth Edition), Chicago: Rand McNally College Publishing Company, 1979.

F SCALE, an instrument originally used in the area of personality and attitude measurement as a covert assessment of fascist tendencies. It is now used more commonly as an assessment of authoritarianism.

The F Scale grew out of a series of studies that originally (1944–50) focused on the personality correlates of antisemitism conducted by the Berkeley Public Opinion Study and the Institute of Social Research (U. of California). Four scales, A–S (Antisemitism), E (Ethnocentrism), PEC (Politico-Economic Conservatism), and the F (Fascism), were developed during the studies.

The F Scale underwent several revisions. Form 78 had 38 items, Form 60 had 34 items, and Forms 40 and 45 had 30 items each. Forms 40 and 45 assessed nine cluster areas: conventionalism, authoritarian submission, authoritarian aggression, anti-intraception (opposition to the subjective, the imaginative, the tender-minded), superstition and stereotyping, power and toughness, destructiveness and cynicism, projectivity, and sex (exaggerated concern with sexual mores).

References: Theodor W. Adorno, et al., *The Authoritarian Personality*, New York: W. W. Norton and Company, Inc., 1969; Richard Christie and Joan Havel, "Is the F Scale Irreversible?" *The Journal of Abnormal and Social Psychology*, March 1958; David W. McKinney, Jr., *Authoritarian Personality Studies: An Inquiry Into the Failure of Social Science Research to Reduce Demonstrable Knowledge*, Hawthorne, NY: Moulton Publishers, 1973.

FULBRIGHT-HAYS ACT (P.L. 87-256), federal legislation enacted in 1961 that seeks to promote *foreign language training* and *area studies* in American schools and institutions of higher education. Named for its congressional sponsors, Senator William Fulbright and Representative Wayne Hays, the legislation is officially known as the Mutual Educational and Cultural Exchange Act of 1961.

Section 102(b) (6) of the act provides fellowships for individual scholars to do research and/or strengthen their language skills in different parts of the world. In the 1977 fiscal year, the program supported 118 doctoral dissertation research fellowships, 23 group projects, 20 curriculum consultant grants, and 52 faculty research fellowships. Annual appropriations to support the program have ranged from $830,000 in 1971 to $3,000,000 in 1978.

The Fulbright Act of 1946, forerunner to Fulbright-Hays, authorized proceeds from sale of surplus property abroad to be used for the international exchange of professors and students as a way to promote international understanding. Fulbright-

Hays consolidated the relevant programs of the original Fulbright Act and other cultural exchange legislation that had previously been enacted.

References: Walter Johnson and Francis J. Colligan, *The Fulbright Program: A History*, Chicago: University of Chicago Press, 1969; Office of Planning, Budgeting and Evaluation, Office of Education, U.S. Department of HEW, *Annual Evaluation Report on Programs Administered by the U.S. Office of Education*, Washington, DC: The Office, 1977; Public Law 87-256, *United States Statutes at Large, 1961* (Volume 75), Washington, DC: U.S. Government Printing Office, 1961.

FULL-STATE ASSUMPTION (FSA), or a full-state funding, a policy proposal that would have the individual states assume 100 percent responsibility for the financial support of public schools. The proposal's overriding purpose is to achieve financial equity among school districts. Proponents of FSA offer several arguments in support of this concept, three of which follow: (1) it would reduce the "financial support" disparity that exists among school districts in a given state; (2) reliance on the property tax as a major funding source for education would be lessened; and (3) individual state legislatures would be more inclined to heed seriously the needs of public education.

Perhaps the most compelling argument against such a proposal is the loss of local control that some authorities feel would result. A second objection is the fear that wealthy, "pilot" school districts would have their programs reverted to a level of mediocrity by virtue of having their support levels constrained, perhaps even reduced.

A well-publicized FSA proposal was the 1972 report of the Fleischmann Commission, prepared in New York State. (See FINANCIAL ABILITY and FINANCIAL EFFORT.)

References: Charles Benson, *Equity in School Financing: Full State Funding* (PDK Fastback 56), Bloomington, IN: The Phi Delta Kappa Educational Foundation, 1975; Alan K. Campbell, "State Assumption of Financial Responsibility for Elementary and Secondary Education" in Joel A. Berke, et al., *Financing Equal Educational Opportunity: Alternatives for State Finance*, Berkeley, CA: McCutchan Publishing Corporation, 1972; *The Fleischmann Report: On the Quality, Cost, and Financing of Elementary and Secondary Education in New York State* (Volumes I–III), New York: The Viking Press, 1973.

FULL-TIME EQUIVALENT (FTE), or full-time student equivalent, a calculation used in education, particularly higher education, to convert part-time enrollment to equivalent full-time students. This statistic is now used widely in view of the large number of part-time students enrolled in colleges and universities. The formula for making the conversion is:

$$\text{FTE} = \frac{\text{Total credit hrs. earned by p/t students}}{\text{No. of credit hrs. of average full-time course load}}$$

To illustrate, 9,000 credit hours earned by part-time students at a college where 15 credits is the average course load yields a full-time equivalency of 600 students.

At institutions where part-time faculty members are employed, the term *full-time faculty equivalency is* frequently used, usually for budgetary purposes or to compute faculty-student ratios.

References: William E. Hopke (Editor), *Dictionary of Personnel and Guidance Terms: Including Professional Agencies and Associations,* Chicago: J. G. Ferguson Publishing Company, 1968; Asa S. Knowles (Editor), *The International Encyclopedia of Higher Education* (Volume 1), San Francisco: Jossey-Bass Publishers, 1977.

FUNCTIONAL ILLITERACY, the inability of an individual to respond to practical reading tasks. Such tasks include ordering from a menu, understanding newspaper articles, ordering from a department store catalog, and using want ads correctly.

Precise statistics concerning functional illiteracy in the United States are not available, one reason being that the term *functional illiteracy* is defined operationally and differently from one investigation to another. This lack of precision notwithstanding, the incidence of functional illiteracy is high, especially among unemployed youth. One investigator (David Harmon) estimated that one-half of Americans aged 25 and over may be functionally illiterate.

The U.S. Office of Education defines an illiterate as a learner who has completed fewer than eight years of formal schooling. This measure is considered to be conservative, because it does not consider either the quality of education received or basic skills mastery as measured by standardized tests. Others define a functional illiterate as a person over 16 years of age who cannot read at the 6th grade reading level.

References: D. Harmon, "Illiteracy: An Overview," *Harvard Educational Review* 40, 1970; Walter R. Hill, *Secondary School Reading: Process, Program, Procedure,* Boston: Allyn and Bacon, Inc., 1979; Carman St. John Hunter and David Harmon, *Adult Illiteracy in the United States: A Report to the Ford Foundation,* New York: McGraw-Hill Book Company, 1979.

FUND FOR THE ADVANCEMENT OF EDUCATION, experimental arm of the Ford Foundation's education program. The fund, established in 1951 and terminated in 1967, was, when first constituted, an independent organization with its own Board of Directors. In 1957, to achieve closer working relationships with its parent organization, the fund became the foundation's Education Division.

The fund's several activities, according to Roy E. Larsen (in his foreword to Paul Woodring's *Investment in Innovation*), fell into five categories: (1) improving teacher training; (2) recognizing the importance of citizen interest in education; (3) new technologies (notably classroom television); (4) civil rights in education; and (5) national assessment and accountability of education. Specific fund-sponsored projects, some of which precipitated controversy within the education profession, included: The Arkansas Program, a five-year teacher training program; MAT (Master of Arts in Teaching) programs; educational television grants, including the Hagerstown, Maryland, project and the Midwest Program on Airborne Television Instruction; the Bay City, Michigan, program to provide teacher aides; the Dual Progress Plan (departmentalization in the elementary school); numerous grants to support black colleges; and a project to assess the progress of children in several subject fields (national assessment).

During the 16 years of its existence, the fund spent over $65,000,000, most of it to support innovative education. (See DUAL PROGRESS PLAN; MASTER OF ARTS IN TEACHING; MIDWEST PROGRAM ON AIRBORNE TELEVISION INSTRUCTION; NATIONAL ASSESSMENT OF EDUCATIONAL PROGRESS; and PARAPROFESSIONALS IN EDUCATION.)

References: Decade of Experiment: The Fund for the Advancement of Education, 1951–61, New York: The Fund for the Advancement of Education, April 1961; *The Fund for the Advancement of Education: A Report for 1959–1961,* New York: The Fund for the Advancement of Education, November 1961; *The Fund for the Advancement of Education: A Report for 1961–62,* New York: The Fund for the Advancement of Education, January 1963; Paul Woodring, *Investment in Innovation: An Historical Appraisal of the Fund for the Advancement of Education,* Boston: Little, Brown and Company, 1970.

FUND FOR THE IMPROVEMENT OF POSTSECONDARY EDUCATION (FIPSE), an organizational unit established in the U.S. Office of

Education (later, the Department of Education) to implement provisions of the 1972 Education Amendments Act dealing with improvement of postsecondary education. The fund's Director supervises a professional staff that operates in accordance with policies established by FIPSE's Board of Advisors.

Grants are awarded and programs administered in accordance with purposes set forth in Section 404, Title III, of the 1972 legislation. Eight such purposes, any or all that need to be addressed in grant applications, were listed in the act: "(1) encouraging the reform, innovation, and improvement of postsecondary education, and providing equal educational opportunity for all; (2) the creation of institutions and programs involving new paths to career and professional training, and new combinations of academic and experimental learning; (3) the establishment of institutions and programs based on the technology of communications; (4) the carrying out in postsecondary educational institutions of changes in internal structure and operation designed to clarify institutional priorities and purposes; (5) the design and introduction of cost-effective methods of instruction and operation; (6) the introduction of institutional reforms designed to expand individual opportunities for entering and reentering institutions and pursuing programs of study tailored to individual needs; (7) the introduction of reforms in graduate education, in the structure of academic professions, and in the recruitment and retention of faculties; and (8) the creation of new institutions and programs for examining and awarding credentials to individuals, and the introduction of reforms in current institutional practices related thereto" (p. 328).

References: Fund for the Improvement of Postsecondary Education, *The Comprehensive Program: Information and Application Procedures, Fiscal Year 1980,* Washington, DC: The Fund, 1979; Public Law 92-318, *United States Statutes at Large, 1972* (Volume 86), Washington, DC: U.S. Government Printing Office, 1973; Public Law 94-482, *United States Statutes at Large, 1976* (Volume 90, Part 2), Washington, DC: U.S. Government Printing Office, 1978.

FURTHER EDUCATION, an administrative term frequently (although not exclusively) used in European countries. It is used in England and Wales to describe education that: (1) is offered to students who are beyond compulsory school age; (2) includes adult education and work of a technical and vocational nature offered by institutions such as polytechnics, agricultural colleges and institutions, teacher training institutions, and special colleges of further education; (3) excludes, and is distinguished from, traditional higher education programs offered by universities (although some polytechnics do offer master's degree courses); and (4) is available to students on either a part-time or full-time basis. Franklin Parker reported that, in 1975, approximately 4,000,000 further education students were enrolled in British further education classes with most attending part-time or in the evening. The coexistence of universities and further education institutions has created what is known as Britain's dual system of higher education, a system applauded by many because of the greater educational opportunities it provides to a larger number of students than did the previous unitary, elitist (ladder) system of higher education.

At Charles University, Prague, Czechoslovakia, the European Information Centre for Further Education of Teachers, established in 1973, another type of further education takes place. There, international programs and research efforts are conducted, primarily for the benefit of teacher educators in eastern European nations.

References: European Information Centre of the Charles University for Further Education of Teachers, *Series: Information Review,* May 1979; W. A. Campbell Stewart, "Further Education" in Asa S. Knowles (Editor), *The International Encyclopedia of Higher Education* (Volume 4), San Francisco: Jossey-Bass Publishers, 1977; Franklin Parker, *British Schools and Ours* (PDK Fastback 122), Bloomington, IN: The Phi Delta Kappa Educational Foundation, 1979; Willem van der Eyken (Editor), *Education, the Child and Society: A Documentary History 1900-1973,* Hammondsworth, Middlesex, England: Penguin Education, 1973.

FUTURE FARMERS OF AMERICA (FFA), national organization of high school students (ages 14-21) who are preparing for careers in agriculture or any number of agriculturally related occupations. Any student enrolled in a vocational agriculture program is eligible for active membership. The many and practical activities conducted by FFA (local, state, and national) are adjuncts to the more formalized classroom instruction that these students receive in school. All are designed to develop the leadership skills of members.

FFA was organized in 1928 and chartered by the U.S. Congress in 1950. It presently consists of over 500,000 members associated with any of 8,200 chapters located in each of the states, Puerto Rico, and the Virgin Islands. Individual state associations help to coordinate chapter activities. The Future Farmers of America Foundation, Inc., supported by business, industry, organizations, and individuals, supports FFA through incentive awards.

FFA has headquarters in Alexandria, Virginia. Its national convention, the largest student convention in the United States, is held annually in Kansas City, Missouri. A magazine, *The National Future Farmer,* is published bimonthly and sent to all members. In 1971, the FFA Alumni Association was formed to make it possible for former FFA members to continue their support of the organization.

References: Future Farmers of America, *The FFA Organization,* Alexandria, VA: Future Farmers of America, Undated Booklet; Future Farmers of America, *1979 Official Manual,* Alexandria, VA: Future Farmers of America, 1979.

FUTURE HOMEMAKERS OF AMERICA (FHA),

nonprofit vocational organization for young men and women enrolled in home economics and related courses. Founded in 1945, FHA has a current membership of 500,000 in 12,500 chapters that are based in middle schools and junior and senior high schools. The organization has chapters in each of the 50 states plus the District of Columbia, Puerto Rico, and the Virgin Islands. FHA is sponsored jointly by the American Home Economics Association and the U.S. Department of Education.

Chapters are of two types: (1) *FHA chapters,* which emphasize projects dealing with consumer education, homemaking, and family life education, and (2) *HERO chapters,* concerned with job preparation and careers. The two groups of chapters work to fulfill FHA's principal objective: "to help youth assume their roles in society through Home Economics Education in areas of personal growth, family life, vocational preparation and community involvement" (Fact Sheet).

FHA's main office is in the American Home Economics Association Building, Washington, DC.

References: Future Homemakers of America, *Of Youth, for Youth, by Youth: Case Statement for Future Homemakers of America,* Washington, DC: Future Homemakers of America, 1979; Future Homemakers of America, *Fact Sheet,* Washington, DC: Future Homemakers of America, Undated Brochure.

FUTURE TEACHERS OF AMERICA (FTA),

an organization that had its genesis in the 1937 report of the National Education Association's Horace Mann Centennial Committee. Of 12 recommendations included in that report was one that suggested that, as a continuation of Horace Mann's work in the selection and preparation of teachers, there be established in each community "Future Teachers of America" groups that would work to interest the most promising young people in teaching as a career. The recommendation was accepted by the NEA Board of Directors on June 28, 1937.

During the years immediately following the organization's creation, FTA groups established in high schools were known as *clubs;* counterpart units in colleges and universities were known as *chapters.* Later, after Student NEA (the college-level student organization) was established, high school units became known as *chapters.* In 1955, responsibility for administration of FTA was vested in NEA's National Commission on Teacher Education and Professional Standards.

The first FTA chapter was granted to the Horace Mann Club in the Laramie High School, Laramie, Wyoming.

By 1974, FTA's name was changed to Student Action for Education (SAE). In 1975, SAE was "disestablished" as a national organization when NEA's Board of Directors adopted a resolution that essentially made SAE units the responsibility of local and state educational associations. (See STUDENT NEA.)

References: National Commission on Teacher Education and Professional Standards, *Twenty-Five Years: The Genesis of Future Teachers of America and the Student National Education Association,* Washington, DC: The National Education Association, 1962; National Education Association, *NEA Handbook for Local, State, and National Associations, 1973-74,* Washington, DC: The Association, 1973; National Education Association, *Official Minutes of the Executive Committee and the Board of Directors, February 14-16, 1975,* Washington, DC: The Association, 1975.

FUTURISM,

a broad field of study that focuses on what the entire society, or its subsets, will look like in the future. Those involved in futurism deal with alternatives, anticipated results, and the interactive effects that technology, available resources, quality of life, changes in culture, and the psychology of humans have on each other as one projects from the present to the future. Futurists are found in virtually every field and discipline, including education, economics, population, weather, psychology, transportation, space, weaponry, energy, and oceanography to list but a few. Futurists tend not to rely solely on data projections; rather, they use a variety of methods from many fields to describe the future and what it might look like to those living during that period.

References: Robert Bundy (Editor), *Images of the Future: The Twenty-First Century and Beyond*, Buffalo, NY: Prometheus Books, 1976; Foreign Policy Association (Editors), *Toward the Year 2018*, New York: Cowles Education Corporation, 1968; John D. Pulliam and Jim R. Bowman, *Educational Futurism*, Norman, OK: University of Oklahoma, 1974; Alvin Toffler, *Future Shock*, New York: Random House, 1970; Alvin Toffler (Editor), *Learning for Tomorrow: The Role of the Future in Education*, New York: Vintage Books, 1974.

GALLAUDET COLLEGE, the world's only liberal arts college for the deaf. Located in Washington, D.C., and subsidized by the federal government, this accredited institution offers a diversity of baccalaureate programs, master's degrees in audiology and education, and a doctorate in special education administration of the hearing impaired. It is governed by a 21-member board that includes members of Congress. The institution was established as Kendall School in 1856, attained college status in 1864, and underwent several name changes until acquiring its present name. Edward M. Gallaudet, for whose father (Thomas) the college is named, served as the institution's Superintendent and later as its first President. (See GALLAUDET, THOMAS H.)

References: W. Todd Furniss (Editor), *American Universities and Colleges* (Eleventh Edition), Washington, DC: American Council on Education, 1973; Gallaudet College, *Gallaudet College Catalogue, 1977–78*, Washington, DC: The College, 1977.

GALLAUDET, THOMAS H. (December 10, 1787–September 10, 1851), American clergyman who helped to establish the country's first free school for the deaf (opened 1817 in Hartford, Connecticut). It was Alice Cogswell, deaf daughter of a family friend, in whose case Gallaudet took an early interest. Her condition so interested him that he ultimately left the ministry to undertake a career as educator of the deaf. Dr. Cogswell, Alice's father, arranged for Gallaudet to visit Europe and study methods of teaching the deaf then being used in England and France. The school operated by French Abbe Roch A. C. Sicard, one in which Gallaudet spent considerable time as student and observer, served as model for his own institution. Gallaudet's school employed signing (manual method) as the vehicle for communication with and among the deaf.

In 1821, he married Sophia Fowler, a former student who had been deaf from birth. Two of their eight children also pursued careers as educators for the deaf. Edward, their youngest son, later became first President of Gallaudet College, a national institution named for his father, Thomas.

Thomas Gallaudet graduated from Yale College in 1805 and Andover Theological Seminary in 1814. Many of his articles and books, written between 1818 and 1841, did much to influence the future direction of education of the deaf in the United States. (See GALLAUDET COLLEGE.)

References: Mildred S. Fenner and Eleanor C. Fishburn, *Pioneer American Educators,* Port Washington, NY: Kennikat Press, Inc., 1968; Raymond Quist, "Gallaudet, Thomas Hopkins" in John F. Ohles (Editor), *Biographical Dictionary of American Educators* (Volume 2), Westport, CT: Greenwood Press, 1978.

GAMES, activities in which players assume simulated roles or play without assuming roles. They include either competition [against other players] or cooperation [with other players]. Games must include rules, decision-making alternatives, and procedures for achieving objectives. The base for games is game theory.

Games can be quite complex and mathematical. They can be classified as two-person-zero sum or two-person-nonzero sum (either of the two can be competitive or cooperative). Nonzero sum games are won, but not at the cost of a loser. Zero sum games are won at the cost of a loser. The sum of the winner and the losses of the loser always equals 0, thus the name *zero sum*. When more than two people play, games are classified as n-person games. Some games simulate an environment (e.g. war games, a large corporation) but others do not (e.g. chess, bridge).

Games are excellent for teaching, training, and operational studies. For these reasons, they are used by schools (all levels), the military, business, social sciences, ecologists, political scientists, economists and many other institutions and disciplines in the society. (See GAME THEORY; MANAGEMENT GAMES; and SIMULATION.)

References: Irene W. Bell and Jeanne E. Wiechert, *Basic Classroom Skills through Games,* Littleton, CO: Libraries Unlimited, Inc., 1980; James H. Case, *Economics and the Competitive Process,* New York: New York University Press, 1979; G. I. Gibbs (Editor), *Handbook of Games and Simulation Exercises,* Beverly Hills, CA: Sage Publications, Inc., 1974; Robert E. Horn and Ann Cleaves (Editors), *The Guide to Simulations/Games for Education and Training* (Fourth Edition), Beverly Hills, CA: Sage Publications, Inc., 1980; Martin Shubik, *The Uses and Methods of Gamery,* New York: Elsevier Scientific Publishing Company, Inc., 1975.

GAME THEORY, a highly complex, mathematical, and analytical base upon which decision-making games are developed. It includes solutions as well as various possible decision-making alternatives. Game theory takes risk and probabilities into account. Inasmuch as two or more players must be involved in playing a particular game, each player has some control over what happens, but no player has complete control. In addition, chance plays a role in the outcomes. Thus, interdependency as well as uncertainty are important aspects of game theory. (See GAMES and MANAGEMENT GAMES.)

References: Michael Bacharach, *Economics and the Theory of Games*, Boulder, CO: Westview Press, 1977; Morton D. Davis, *Game Theory*, New York: Basic Books, Inc., Publishers, 1970; M. T. Fryer, *An Introduction to Linear Programming and Matrix Game Theory*, London, England: Edward Arnold Publishers, Ltd., 1978.

GARY PLAN, well-known example of the educational platoon system introduced in the Gary, Indiana, school system by Superintendent of Schools William Wirt. In 1907, the 33-year-old Wirt (former student of John Dewey) assumed the Gary superintendency, coming from Bluffton, Indiana, where some of his progressive ideas had already been put to work.

Each school in Gary was established as a neighborhood (community) school. Service rooms such as gymnasiums, shops, and auditoriums were put to use as regularly used instructional stations with the result that fewer traditional classrooms were needed. A two-platoon plan was developed with half of the children studying the traditional subjects and the remaining half (platoon) engaged in specialized activities using the school's several service rooms.

Gary's schools were open day and night. At one time, more adults than school-age children were being served by the school system.

Wirt and the Gary Plan received considerable publicity during the World War I era, prompting a fair number of critics as well as supporters to visit Gary and to react to what they had seen. In spite of the criticism, over 200 cities had adopted the plan by 1929. Wirt retained the Gary superintendency until his death in 1938. (See PLATOON SCHOOL.)

References: Ronald D. Cohen and Raymond A. Mohl, *The Paradox of Progressive Education. The Gary Plan and Urban Schooling*, Port Washington, NY: Kennikat Press, Inc., 1979; Lawrence A. Cremin, *The Transformation of the School: Progressivism in American Education, 1876–1957*, New York: Alfred A. Knopf, 1968.

GATES, ARTHUR I. (September 22, 1890– August 24, 1972), a leading educational psychologist who made major contributions to the fields of language arts and reading. In 1928, he developed the "Intrinsic Method" for teaching reading. This method included the identification of basic skills needed in reading, identification of problem areas, reading materials organized to provide systematic and graded practice in skill development, diagnostic testing, and materials of interest to young readers.

Gates recognized the need for diagnostic tests and was responsible for the construction of many such instruments. Among them were: the Gates-Strong Health Knowledge Test; the Gates-MacGinitie Reading Test; and the Gates-MacGinitie Reading Readiness Test. He also wrote several books on psychology and education. Other of his writings included reading and spelling books and numerous articles.

Arthur Gates was born in Red Wing, Minnesota. He attended school in California, and earned a Ph.D. (in 1917) from Columbia University. Gates joined the faculty of Teachers College, Columbia in 1917. (See GATES-MACGINITIE READING TESTS and GATES-MACGINITIE READING READINESS TEST.)

References: John T. Guthrie (Editor), *Aspects of Reading Acquisition*, Baltimore, MD: The Johns Hopkins Press, 1976; Robert L. Thorndike, *Arthur I. Gates*, Washington, DC: National Academy of Education, 1973; Miles V. Zintz, *The Reading Process* (Second Edition), Dubuque, IA: Wm. C. Brown Company, Publishers, 1975.

GATES-MACGINITIE READING READINESS TEST, an examination that measures readiness for beginning readers. The test contains subtests in the areas of listening comprehension, auditory and visual discrimination, ability to follow directions, letter recognition, visual-motor coordination, and word recognition. (See READING PREDICTION and READING READINESS.)

Reference: John F. Savage and Jean F. Mooney, *Teaching Reading to Children with Special Needs*, Boston: Allyn and Bacon, Inc., 1979.

GATES-MACGINITIE READING TESTS, a series of reading examinations developed by Arthur I. Gates and Walter H. MacGinitie and published by Houghton Mifflin. Two scores are available (vocabulary and comprehension) for three levels: A, grade 1; B, grade 2; and C, grade 3. Level CS, for grades 2.5–3, provides a speed and accuracy score.

Levels D (grades 4–6), E (grades 7–9), and F (grades 10–12) all provide vocabulary, comprehension, and speed and accuracy scores. All tests are group administered with answer sheets that can be machine or manually scored.

Reference: Oscar K. Buros (Editor), *The Seventh Mental Measurements Yearbook* (Volume II), Highland Park, NJ: The Gryphon Press, 1972.

GATTEGNO, CALEB—See CUISENAIRE NUMBER-IN-COLOR PLAN and WORDS-IN-COLOR

GEMEINSCHAFT and **GESELLSCHAFT,** terms coined by Sociologist Ferdinand Toennies to distinguish two types of social relationship. *Gemeinschaft,* a German word meaning "community," describes a primary social group in which members are related along personal and/or communal lines (e.g. family, work team, small rural community). Successes and failures are shared by all members. *Gesellschaft* describes a secondary social group that is more utilitarian and in which relationships among individuals (e.g. those working in a school system) tend to be impersonal, even contractual.

According to Toennies, the change from relatively simple and close-knit rural societies to more complex and less personal ones has been accelerated by economic trade. This shift has been accompanied by changes in the size, structure, and purposes of schools.

References: Werner J. Cahnman and Rudolf Heberle (Editors), *Ferdinand Toennies on Sociology: Pure, Applied, and Empirical,* Chicago: University of Chicago Press, 1971; G. Duncan Mitchell (Editor), *A Dictionary of Sociology,* Chicago: Aldine Publishing Company, 1968.

GENERAL BUSINESS EDUCATION—See BUSINESS EDUCATION

GENERAL EDUCATION, those subjects and experiences that curriculum authorities believe should be common to all pupils and students. The purpose of general education (sometimes referred to as the common learnings) is to make an individual culturally literate. Although there is no common agreement concerning what constitutes the elements of a general education, there are some wide areas of agreement (e.g. language-skill development, mathematics, reading, natural sciences, history and social studies, and literature). Given its emphasis on basic skill development, much general education is concentrated in the elementary school.

At the college and high school level, general education comprises those subject areas studied by all students, regardless of major. Within the general education group, there can be great latitude in the selection of specific courses. Some students, for example, may take the course, "American Writers" to satisfy one of their general education requirements and others may enroll in "Eastern European Writers" to fulfill the same requirement. (See CULTURAL LITERACY and LIBERAL EDUCATION.)

References: Kenneth E. Eble, *A Perfect Education,* New York: The Macmillan Company, 1966; Alvin C. Eurich, *High School 1980,* New York: Pitman Publishing Corporation, 1970; Faculties of Andover, Exeter, Lawrenceville, Harvard, Princeton, and Yale, *General Education in School and College,* Cambridge, MA: Harvard University Press, 1952; Alan C. Purves, "General Education and the Search for a Common Culture" in Ian Westbury and Alan C. Purves (Editors), *Cultural Literacy and the Idea of General Education,* Chicago: National Society for the Study of Education, 1988.

GENERAL ELECTRIC STUDIES—See HAWTHORNE EFFECT

GENERAL EQUIVALENCY DIPLOMA (GED)—See TEST OF GENERAL EDUCATIONAL DEVELOPMENT

GENETIC STUDIES OF GENIUS, a set of five volumes describing the results of a longitudinal study of 1,000 high I.Q. boys and girls (12 years old) from California. The study was started by Lewis M. Terman, a famous educational psychologist, in 1922. In 1928, an additional 528 students were added to the study. Terman and his associates identified these intellectually gifted children and then measured them on many physical, intellectual, and social qualities. He compared these children with nonhigh I.Q. children using the same measures. In addition, Terman made arrangements to monitor his population of gifted children during their periods of adolescence, adulthood, and later maturity.

Contacts with the original students, their parents, their teachers, and eventually their spouses were maintained from 1922 (1922, 1927–28, 1936, 1939–40, 1945, 1950, 1955). Dr. Terman died in 1956. His project was continued until 1972, first by Melita Oden (1968) and then by Robert Sears and Lee Cronbach (1972). As a result of Terman's works, many "myths" concerning the gifted and talented were questioned and destroyed. This investigation also provided an excellent study of the life cycle of a particular group of people. (See LONGITUDINAL STUDIES and TERMAN, LEWIS.)

References: A. Harry Passow (Editor), *The Gifted and the Talented: Their Education and Development* (NSSE 78th Yearbook, Part I), Chicago: University of Chicago Press, 1979; Lewis M. Terman, et al., *Genetic Studies of Genius: Mental and Physical Traits of a Thousand Gifted Children* (Volume 1), Stanford, CA: Stanford University Press, 1925.

GEOGRAPHY, a science concerned with the study and the description of the Earth. In years past, geography was taught as a discrete subject. Today, in many school systems, it constitutes one of several fields of study comprising the social studies.

The content of geography was perhaps best described by John Morris when he indicated that this subject serves to answer three questions: "(1) Where is the item or place being discussed located? (2) Why is it there and why is it as it is? (3) What is its relationship to man?"

In teaching about different parts of the world and how, in each case, man interacts with his environment, different kinds of geography are used. John Michaelis identified them as (1) *physical geography,* the study of Earth's physical features (e.g. climate, bodies of water); (2) *regional geography,* in which common characteristics of a particular area are studied; (3) *cultural geography,* the study of peoples' life-styles and their relationships to local resources; (4) *locational geography;* and (5) *historical geography,* the study of geographical changes over extended periods of time.

Current emphasis in the teaching of geography is in the direction of having children learn concepts through in-depth study of selected areas rather than simply memorizing a wide array of facts. (See SOCIAL STUDIES.)

References: Paul R. Hanna, et al., *Geography in the Teaching of Social Studies: Concepts and Skills,* Boston: Houghton Mifflin Company, 1966; John Jarolimek, *Social Studies in Elementary Education* (Fourth Edition), New York: The Macmillan Company, 1971; John U. Michaelis, *Social Studies for Children in a Democracy: Recent Trends and Developments* (Sixth Edition), Englewood Cliffs, NJ: Prentice-Hall, Inc., 1976; John W. Morris, "Geography—Separate Course or Integrated," *Journal of Geography,* May 1965.

GEORGE-BARDEN ACT (Public Law 79-586), federal vocational education legislation enacted in 1946. The act approximately doubled dollar allocations for the support of home economics, agricultural, trade and industry, and distributive education. (Support for these areas had already been included in several of this act's legislative forerunners.) Practical nursing was added as a vocational education area eligible for federal support. (See GEORGE-DEEN ACT.)

References: Calfrey C. Calhoun and Alton V. Finch, *Vocational and Career Education: Concepts and Operations,* Belmont, CA: Wadsworth Publishing Company, Inc., 1976; Public Law 79-586, *United States Statutes at Large, 1946* (Volume 60, Part I), Washington, DC: U.S. Government Printing Office, 1947.

GEORGE-DEEN ACT (Public Law 74-673), federal legislation enacted in 1936. The act, like its forerunner, the George-Ellzey Act, made federal funds available to support these areas of vocational education: home economics education, agricultural education, and trade and industry education. The total annual appropriation was $12,000,000. Two other features made this a historically significant act: (1) an appropriation of $1,200,000 annually was added to support distributive education, and (2) broadened coverage that, for the first time, entitled the territories of the United States to federal vocational education funding. The George-Barden Act of 1946 amended the George-Deen Act in 1946. (See GEORGE-ELLZEY ACT and GEORGE-BARDEN ACT.)

References: Calfrey C. Calhoun and Alton V. Finch, *Vocational and Career Education: Concepts and Operations,* Belmont, CA: Wadsworth Publishing Company, Inc., 1976; Public Law 74-673, *Statutes of the United States of America, 1936* (Part I), Washington, DC: U.S. Government Printing Office, 1936.

GEORGE-ELLZEY ACT (Public Law 73-245), federal legislation that replaced the George-Reed Act. The act extended appropriations for home economics education and agricultural education; funding for trade and industry education was also included. The legislation covered the years 1935 through 1937 and authorized annual appropriations of $3,000,000. The George-Ellzey Act was replaced by the George-Deen Act of 1936. (See GEORGE-DEEN ACT and GEORGE-REED ACT.)

References: Calfrey C. Calhoun and Alton V. Finch, *Vocational and Career Education: Concepts and Operations,* Belmont, CA: Wadsworth Publishing Company, Inc., 1976; Public Law 73-245, *The Statutes of the United States of America, 1934* (Part I), Washington, DC: U.S. Government Printing Office, 1934.

GEORGE-REED ACT (Public Law 70-702), federal legislation enacted in 1929 that made federal monies available to support home economics education and agricultural education. Funds totalling $7,500,000 were allocated for the five-year period, 1930–34. When the law expired in 1934, it was replaced by the George-Ellzey Act. (See GEORGE-ELLZEY ACT.)

References: Calfrey C. Calhoun and Alton V. Finch, *Vocational and Career Education: Concepts and Operations*, Belmont, CA: Wadsworth Publishing Company, Inc., 1976; Public Law 70-702, *The Statutes at Large of the United States of America* (Volume 45, Part I), Washington, DC: U.S. Government Printing Office, 1929.

GERMAN MEASLES—See RUBELLA

GERONTOLOGY, the scientific study of aging. As a field study, it is relatively new. Gerontology consists of two branches: physical and social. The former comprises clinical and biological investigations of aging, and the social branch encompasses those studies of aging undertaken by behavioral scientists.

Several specializations within the field of gerontology have recently emerged. One is *social gerontology,* which Marvin Koller defined as "the study of the impact of aging upon individuals and society and the subsequent reactions of individuals and society to aging" (p. 4). Another is *educational gerontology,* which another authority (David Peterson) defined as "the study and practice of instructional endeavors for and about aged and aging individuals" (p. 7). Its specific components include: (1) education for the middle aged and older; (2) education about aging; and (3) the preparation of persons working with or planning to work with older people. Still other specializations are *industrial gerontology* and *psychogerontology.*

References: Rosamonde R. Boyd and Charles G. Oakes (Editors), *Foundations of Practical Gerontology* (Second Edition-Revised), Columbia, SC: University of South Carolina Press, 1973; Marvin R. Koller, *Social Gerontology*, New York: Random House, 1968; David A. Peterson, "Toward a Definition of Educational Gerontology" in Ronald H. Sherron and D. Barry Lumsden (Editors), *Introduction to Educational Gerontology*, Washington, DC: Hemisphere Publishing Corporation, 1978.

GESELL, ARNOLD L. (June 21, 1880–May 29, 1961), noted medical doctor and child psychologist who observed, studied, and recorded the growth and development of children. He was especially interested in the behavior of children. Dr. Gesell founded The Yale Clinic for Child Development at Yale University in 1911 and served as its director until its closing in 1948. In 1950, Francis Ilg, Louise Bates Ames, and Janet Learned founded The Gesell Institute of Child Development, Inc. in New Haven, Connecticut, with Arnold Gesell as an active consultant. Gesell authored or coauthored several notable books that were outgrowths of work carried out in the clinic and the institute. They were: *The First Five Years of Life* (1940), *Infant and Child in the Culture of Today* (1943), *The Child from Five to Ten* (1946), and *Youth, The Years from Ten to Sixteen* (1956).

References: Arnold Gesell, et al., *Youth, The Years from Ten to Sixteen,* New York: Harper and Row, Publishers, 1956; Francis Ilg and Louise B. Ames, *Child Behavior,* New York: Harper and Row, Publishers, 1955; Catherine Landreth, *The Psychology of Early Childhood,* New York: Alfred A. Knopf, 1959; John R. Silvestro, "Gesell, Arnold Lucius" in John F. Ohles (Editor), *Biographical Dictionary of American Educators* (Volume 2), Westport, CT: Greenwood Press, 1978; Harold C. Stuart and Dane G. Prugh (Editors), *The Healthy Child,* Cambridge, MA: Harvard University Press, 1960.

GESELLSCHAFT—See GEMEINSCHAFT AND GESELLSCHAFT

GESTALT PSYCHOLOGY, a branch of cognitive psychology that holds that human nature is organized into patterns of wholes, or totalities. The psychology grew out of the work on human perceptions by German psychologists Max Wertheimer, Wolfgang Köhler, and Kurt Koffka. Disagreeing with associate behaviorists, they contended that psychological phenomena are organized and synthesized into a whole rather than being a collection of specific parts or elements. The word *gestalt* is a German term for which there is no precise English translation.

Gestalt therapy, or counseling, was developed by Frederick Perls in the 1940s and 1950s. The elements of Gestalt psychology found in the therapy are closure, projection according to need, behavior as a whole, and behavior viewed within the environment.

References: George I. Brown, et al. (Editors), *The Life Classroom,* New York: The Viking Press, 1975; William R. Passons, *Gestalt Approaches in Counseling,* New York: Holt, Rinehart and Winston, Inc., 1975; Fritz Perls, *The Gestalt Approach and Eye Witness to Therapy,* Palo Alto, CA: Science and Behavioral Books, 1973.

GETZELS-GUBA MODEL, a theoretical framework that describes an organization as a social system consisting of a hierarchical role structure. Certain behavioral expectations are associated with each role. Developed by Jacob W. Getzels and Egon G. Guba, the model includes two dimensions widely known to students of educational administration: the nomothetic and the idiographic. The *nomothetic* (organizational) is made up of those institutional goals, roles, and role expectations that give partial direction to an individual's organizational behavior. The *idiographic* is the personal dimension. It recognizes that no two individuals are alike. Each has his/her own personality and needs disposition system that also influence one's organizational behavior.

The model's authors pointed out that observed behavior within the organization results from the interaction of these two dimensions. Affecting this behavior, they indicated, are personal/institutional factors such as individual and institutional conflict, effectiveness, efficiency, satisfaction, specific leadership-followership styles (idiographic, nomothetic, or transactional, the last intermediate between the other two), and morale.

References: Jacob W. Getzels, "Administration as a Social Process" in Andrew W. Halpin (Editor), *Administrative Theory in Education*, Chicago: Midwest Administration Center University of Chicago, 1958; Jacob W. Getzels and Egon G. Guba, "Social Behavior and the Administrative Process," *School Review*, Winter 1957.

GHETTO, an area or locality, usually in urban communities, where people of a particular group live. The first ghettoes can be traced to Europe where, during the Middle Ages, Jews were forced to live and work apart from the rest of the population. Perhaps because of the great restrictions placed on the people who lived in the ghettoes of Europe, a social, religious, and at times a political structure developed. Certain language customs, literature, music, and even a mental set evolved.

Today, the term *ghetto* has assumed a broader meaning, one including economic as well as social factors, although it still is a place where a single group of people tend to live. Ghettoes are found in urban areas of countries, the places where poor people tend to live. Many of their residents stay because they don't have the money to move into other areas. At one time in America, housing restrictions and social attitudes in urban communities also forced people to live in ghettoes, even if they had the financial ability to move elsewhere. Ghettoes are often developed through the migration of people. Today in America there are ghettoes where one racial group (e.g. black), one language group (e.g. Spanish), or a single religious group (e.g. Jewish) predominates. Although ghettoes in America during the early 1900s had a protective function for those who couldn't speak English and/or were socially and culturally different, there were many negative factors associated with them too, such as crime, poor education, depressed housing, social problems, and health. Many educational problems reflect the social, economic, and health problems found in ghettoes.

References: Harold X. Connolly, *A Ghetto Grows in Brooklyn*, New York: New York University Press, 1977; Yisrael Gutman and Livia Rothkirchen (Editors), *The Catastrophe of European Jewry*, New York: Ktav Publishing House, Inc., 1976; Kenneth L. Kusmer, *A Ghetto Takes Shape*, Urbana, IL: University of Illinois Press, 1976.

G.I. BILL OF RIGHTS, or the Serviceman's Readjustment Act of 1944, federal legislation enacted to provide various civilian readjustment benefits to World War II veterans. Benefits included educational allowances for those whose education had either been delayed or interrupted by military service. Educational allowances (tuition, fees, books, and a monthly stipend) were authorized for veterans admitted to approved schools of all kinds, colleges, and universities. The length of time for which one could draw benefits was related to his/her length of military service.

In 1952, the bill was extended to accommodate Korean War veterans. Direct payments to institutions were terminated; instead, the veteran received a larger subsistence allowance out of which he/she paid tuition. By 1960, an estimated 10,000,000 veterans had availed themselves of the bill's benefits. As a consequence of the G.I. Bill, college and university enrollments soared to record levels.

Subsequent legislation (e.g. 1966 and 1967) made educational benefits available to Vietnam War veterans. They, like their Korean War counterparts, had a fixed number of years in which to make use of these benefits. Today (1990) service personnel and the government each contribute to an education fund that can be used by the ex-service person to pay for schooling (tuition).

References: Public Law 346, *United States Statutes at Large, 1944* (Volume 58, Part I), Washington, DC: U.S. Government Printing Office, 1945; Public Law 550, *United States Statutes at Large, 1952* (Volume 66), Washington,

DC: U.S. Government Printing Office, 1953; Public Law 89-358, *United States Statutes at Large, 1966* (Volume 80), Washington, DC: Government Printing Office, 1967; Public Law 90-77, *United States Statutes at Large, 1967* (Volume 81), Washington, DC: U.S. Government Printing Office, 1968; Alice M. Rivlin, *The Role of the Federal Government in Financing Higher Education*, Washington, DC: The Brookings Institution, 1961.

GIFTED CHILD, a classification of children who are endowed with a high intellectual ability or a unique performance ability (e.g. art, music, physical or sports ability, leadership, or mechanical ability). An individual found to be gifted in a performance area is normally classified as being *talented*.

It is not always easy to identify gifted children. Scores on standardized intelligence tests (e.g. Stanford-Binet) are frequently used for this purpose; cutoff scores are not absolute, varying from definition to definition. Identification by teachers is another method employed, often in conjunction with other measures. Other tests (e.g. creativity, child development, logical development, maturity, and discrimination tests) are also used.

Interest in the gifted child has manifested itself almost cyclically in the United States. The work of Lewis Terman in the 1920s, Paul Witty in the 1930s, J. P. Guilford, Jacob Getzels, and Philip Jackson in the 1950s, and E. Paul Torrance in the 1960s helped to revive this interest from time to time. In the late 1970s, interest in the gifted developed out of the national concern for all exceptional children.

There is considerable controversy over whether gifted school children should be separated from other students or mainstreamed into a regular classroom. Supporters of the mainstreaming approach contend that, although a gifted child may be superior to other children intellectually or in terms of talents, he/she develops at a normal rate when other child development factors are considered. (See GENETIC STUDIES OF GENIUS; TALENTED AND GIFTED; and TERMAN, LEWIS.)

References: Marsha M. Correll, *Teaching the Gifted and Talented* (PDK Fastback 119), Bloomington, IN: The Phi Delta Kappa Educational Foundation, 1978; Gary A. Davis and Sylvia B. Rimm, *Education of the Gifted and Talented* (Second Edition), Englewood Cliffs, NJ: Prentice-Hall, Inc., 1989; William L. Heward and Michael D. Orlansky, *Exceptional Children: An Introductory Survey of Special Education*, Columbus, OH: Merrill Publishing Company, 1988; Frances D. Horowitz and Marion O'Brien (Editors), *The Gifted and Talented: Developmental*

Perspectives, Washington, DC: American Psychological Association, 1985; Jean Laubenfels, *The Gifted Student, An Annotated Bibliography*, Westport, CT: Greenwood Press, 1977; A. Harry Passow (Editor), *The Gifted and the Talented: Their Education and Development* (NSSE 78th Yearbook, Part I), Chicago: University of Chicago Press, 1979.

GILLINGHAM METHOD, a multisensory reading method developed by Anna Gillingham in the 1930s and based on the work of Samuel Orton. The method relies heavily on phonics and consists of eight steps, or *linkages*. The initial step involves association of a letter with a symbol and its particular sound. Visual, auditory, and kinesthetic (tracing) exercises are each used successively as individual letter sounds are combined to form words. In the eighth (final) step, the learner is expected to write a phonogram after it has been sounded by the teacher. The method emphasizes drill and repetition. Originally designed for dyslexic children with average or above-average intelligence, the Gillingham approach has been reported to be successful with some learners, less so with others.

References: Anna Gillham and Bessie Stillman, *Remedial Training*, Cambridge, MA: Educators Publishing Service, 1960; Anna Gillingham and Bessie Stillman, *Remedial Teaching for Children with Specific Disability in Reading, Spelling, and Penmanship*, Cambridge, MA: Educators Publishing Service, 1968; George Kaluger and Clifford J. Kolson, *Reading and Learning Disabilities* (Second Edition), Columbus, OH: Charles E. Merrill Publishing Company, 1978; Samuel A. Kirk, et al., *Teaching Reading to Slow and Disabled Learners*, Boston: Houghton Mifflin Company, 1978.

GIRL GUIDES—See GIRL SCOUTS OF THE U.S.A.

GIRL SCOUTS OF THE U.S.A. (GSUSA), an organization for girls founded in 1912 by Juliette Gordon Low. When formed, it was known as Girl Guides, named for the English organization after which it was modelled. Eventually, the name was changed to Girl Scouts of the United States of America.

Membership includes over 2,500,000 girls (including 20,000 handicapped and 30,000 living abroad) and more than 500,000 adult volunteers (men and women). The organization's purpose is "to inspire girls with the highest ideals of character, conduct, patriotism and service that they may become happy and resourceful citizens" (Yakes and Akey, p. 709).

GSUSA sponsors programs directed at specific

age groups: Brownie Girl Scouts (ages 6-8); Junior Girl Scouts (9-11); Cadette Girl Scouts (12-14); and Senior Girl Scouts (14-17). Publications are *American Girl,* a monthly; *Daisy,* published nine times a year; and *Girl Scout Leader,* which appears six times annually. GSUSA headquarters is in New York City.

References: Girl Scouts of the U.S.A., *Girl Scouts of the U.S.A.: Annual Report 1978,* New York: GSUSA, 1979; Peter Romanofsky (Editor), "Girl Scouts of the United States of America" in *Social Service Organizations* (Volume I), Westport, CT: Greenwood Press, 1978; Nancy Yakes and Denise Akey (Editors), *Encyclopedia of Organizations* (Thirteenth Edition), Detroit: Gale Research Company, 1979.

GLOBAL EDUCATION, also known as international education, a program that stresses the complexities of global interdependence. Problems and changes of a worldwide nature are studied in a manner that emphasizes the relatedness rather than the differences among the inhabitants of the world. Examples of problems/changes studied are the world population increase, pollution, communication, economic productivity, and the impact of growing literacy on international affairs.

The concept of global education, although viewed favorably by many educators, has yet to become an integral part of the American school curriculum. Harold Shane offered several reasons for this: (1) the tradition of isolationism in the United States; (2) the tendency of educators to favor traditional programs that are not likely to generate community controversy; (3) traditional methods of teaching about world affairs; (4) limited teaching materials dealing with global education; and (5) the crowded curriculum which precludes introduction of new subjects such as global education.

References: James Becker, *Education for a Global Society* (PDK Fastback 28), Bloomington, IN: The Phi Delta Kappa Educational Foundation, 1973; David C. King, "Global Education," *ASCD Curriculum Update,* October 1980; Harold G. Shane, "International Education in the Elementary and Secondary School" in Harold G. Shane (Editor), *The United States and International Education* (NSSE 68th Yearbook, Part I), Chicago: University of Chicago Press, 1969.

GOAL, a statement describing a broad intent or purpose. Broad statements of this sort, known as *general goals,* need to be broken down into *specific goals* if meaningful evaluation is to take place. Specific goals constitute an important component of the *goals approach,* an evaluation procedure that entails matching of performance outcomes with specific goal statements. Some critics of the movement to use performance objectives point out that, too often, performance objectives have a "buckshot" character, because they are based on *general* rather than *specific* goals. Such practices, they contend, can lead to superficial and/or incomplete evaluation.

Educators are principally concerned with two categories of goals: those that seek to bring about changes in learners and those that relate to intended changes in institutional (e.g. school, district) direction or procedures. (See EVALUATION; GOAL-FREE EVALUATION and INSTITUTIONAL GOALS and OBJECTIVES.)

References: Robert F. Mager, *Goal Analysis,* Belmont, CA: Fearon Publishers, 1972; H. H. McAshan, *The Goals Approach to Performance Objectives,* Philadelphia: W. B. Saunders Company, 1974.

GOAL-FREE EVALUATION (GFE), a program evaluation approach developed by Michael Scriven in 1971. The model assesses the "side effects" and "unanticipated effects" of an educational program rather than focusing on the stated or projected program goals.

Used in a formative evaluation mode, GFE supplies data and information that might increase the success of a program by enabling program personnel to respond to weaknesses and problems.

Rather than using stated goals, the goal-free evaluator can focus on needs of those in the program and/or the agency needs. The evaluation is free of the constraints often required when a program evaluation must assess strictly for goal achievement. In many educational programs, the "unanticipated effects" may be more important than the effects planned for (goals) in the original proposal. GFE may be used in conjunction with the more traditional summative goal based evaluations. (See FORMATIVE EVALUATION and SUMMATIVE EVALUATION.)

References: Michael Scriven, "Evaluation Perspectives and Procedures" in W. James Popham (Editor), *Evaluation in Education,* Berkeley, CA: McCutchan Publishing Corporation, 1974; W. James Popham, *Educational Evaluation* (Second Edition), Englewood Cliffs, NJ: Prentice-Hall, 1988.

GOSLIN, WILLARD (September 24, 1899–March 7, 1969), noted educator and school administrator. In 1948, Goslin was serving as Minneapolis's Superintendent of Schools and concurrently holding office as President of the American Association of School Administrators. That year he accepted the superintendency of the Pasadena (California) Public Schools, a move that was to bring him considerable fame as well as disappointment.

A progressive educator, he soon found himself the center of criticism from a vigorous and reactionary minority of Pasadena's residents who criticized him not only for his advocacy of progressive education but also for his "ideological" leanings toward UNESCO, sex education, and racial integration of the schools. The criticism ultimately forced him to resign his position, an action that stunned professional educators throughout the country.

In September of 1951, Goslin became head of the Division of School Administration and Community Development at George Peabody College for Teachers. The NEA gave him their American Education Award for 1952. In 1961, Seoul University awarded Goslin an honorary doctorate for his work as coordinator of a Korean teacher education project, hailing him as "the father of modern education in Korea."

References: David Hulburd, *This Happened in Pasadena,* New York: The Macmillan Company, 1951; *New York Times,* March 8, 1969, p. 27; *Who's Who in America, 1950–51* (Volume 26), Chicago: A. N. Marquis Company, 1950.

GOSS V. LOPEZ, noted and controversial U.S. Supreme Court decision that set forth minimal constitutional requirements relating to suspension of students for up to ten days. Plaintiffs (Columbus, Ohio, students who had been suspended by their principal during student disturbances) filed a complaint alleging that, although the principal had the authority to suspend students, they were denied due process (a hearing) guaranteed by the Constitution's Fourteenth Amendment.

In 1975, on a five to four vote, the U.S. Supreme Court addressed the matter of short suspensions (those not exceeding ten days) and ruled that due process in such instances requires: (1) that the student be given oral or written notice of the charges against him; (2) that "there need be no delay between the time 'notice' is given and the time of the hearing.... (T)he disciplinarian may informally discuss the alleged misconduct with the student minutes after it has occurred"; (3) that in certain recurring instances, "students whose presence poses a continuing danger to persons or property or an ongoing threat of disrupting the academic process may be immediately removed from school"; and (4) that schools were not obligated to "afford the student the opportunity to secure

counsel, to confront and cross-examine witnesses supporting the charge or to call his own witnesses to verify his version of the incident." The Court emphasized that these requirements applied only to suspensions not exceeding ten days. "Longer suspensions or expulsions for the remainder of the school term, or permanently," it ruled, "may require more formal procedures."

References: Goss v. Lopez, 419 U.S. 565, 95 S.Ct. 729, 42 L.Ed. 2d 725 (1975); Frank R. Kemerer and Kenneth L. Deutsch, *Constitutional Rights and Student Life: Value Conflict in Law and Education,* St. Paul, MN: West Publishing Company, 1979.

GOULDNER MODEL, a framework developed by Alvin Gouldner that identifies and contrasts two distinct role identities. The two, each of which exists in educational organizations, are the *locals* and the *cosmopolitans.* Three factors are used to determine whether a given employee has a local orientation or a cosmopolitan one: (1) loyalty to the school; (2) commitment to area of specialization or professional skills; and (3) reference-group orientations (e.g. closer identification with national counterparts vs. identification with local colleagues).

Gouldner applied his model to a small liberal arts college. On the basis of his analysis (using factor analysis), six rather than the originally anticipated two factors were identified. Four were of the local type and two of the cosmopolitan type. The *local types* were: (1) the *dedicated* professors, highly committed to the college; (2) the *true bureaucrats,* those concerned with the security of the organization; (3) the *home guard,* persons having close personal ties to the organization; and (4) the *elders,* those with many years of service in the organization. The *cosmopolitan types* were: (1) the *outsiders,* individuals highly committed to their specialty, less so to the school; and (2) the *empire builders,* those with high national visibility but yet committed to their local academic department.

References: Alvin W. Gouldner, "Cosmopolitans and Locals: Toward an Analysis of Latent Social Roles," *Administrative Science Quarterly,* December 1957 and March 1958: Daniel E. Griffiths, "The Professorship in Educational Administration: Environment" in Donald J. Willower and Jack A. Culbertson (Editors), *The Professorship in Educational Administration,* Columbus, OH: University Council for Educational Administration, 1964; Thomas J. Sergiovanni and Fred D. Carver, *The New School Executive: A Theory of Administration* (Second Edition), New York: Harper and Row, Publishers, 1980.

GRADED SCHOOL, a school organized on a grade level basis. In graded schools, children are normally grouped according to chronological age. Curriculum is compartmentalized with specific learning activities assigned to each grade level. Students progress through the school program by being promoted from one grade level to another. The usual length of a grade level assignment is one year.

The first American graded school was the Quincy Grammar School (Massachusetts), established in 1848. Five years later, in Oswego, New York, Superintendent Edward A. Sheldon enlarged upon the graded concept by creating a 3-3-3-4 organizational plan, one that divided the 13-year school program into separate primary, junior, senior, and high schools. The contemporary and more familiar 8-4 and 6-3-3 organizational plans came later.

Numerous advantages and disadvantages have been associated with graded schools. Advantages include the ease with which grades and classes can be organized, the narrowing of instructional ranges through division of teacher labor, permitting recitations to be directed to relatively large groups of comparably aged children, and compartmentalization of curriculum. Critics of the graded school argue that its lock-step character deters individuality, the structure lacks flexibility, bright and slower students are hurt because instruction is geared to the average child, time losses are found for many students, and stigma results when students experience nonpromotion. (See ORGANIZATIONAL PLANS; OSWEGO MOVEMENT; and QUINCY GRAMMAR SCHOOL.)

References: Philip A. Cowen, "How the Graded School System Developed" in Marian P. Franklin, *School Organization: Theory and Practice*, Chicago: Rand McNally and Company, 1967; *Elementary School Organization: Purposes, Patterns, Perspective*, Washington, DC: National Education Association, 1961; William J. Shearer, "The Typical Graded School" in Oscar T. Jarvis (Editor), *Elementary School Administration: Readings*, Dubuque, IA: Wm. C. Brown Company, Publishers, 1969.

GRADE-EQUIVALENT SCALES, relative measures similar to age-equivalent scales. Grade-equivalency scores are derived in a similar manner. The mean test score for children at each grade level is calculated for a particular test. Subsequently, each mean test score is assigned a grade designation. For example, the average tenth grader scores a 20 on a particular test; thus, 20 is converted to a grade equivalency of tenth grade. If a sixth grader scores a 20 on the test, he/she has a grade-equivalent score of 10, and if an adult scores a 20 on the same test, his/her grade-equivalent score is also tenth grade.

There are several problems associated with the use of grade-equivalent scales/scores. They include measurement issues of regression, reliability of the tests, and interpretations. Grade-equivalent scores should not be used as a basis for comparison among tests nor should they be used as the sole basis to interpret students' test scores. (See AGE-EQUIVALENT SCALES/SCORES.)

References: William A. Angoff, "Scales, Norms, and Equivalent Scores" in Robert L. Thorndike (Editor), *Educational Measurement*, Washington, DC: American Council on Education, 1971; Lee J. Cronbach, *Essentials of Psychological Testing* (Fourth Edition), New York: Harper and Row, Publishers, 1984; Tom Kubiszyn and Gary Borich, *Educational Testing and Measurement: Classroom Application and Practice* (Second Edition), Glenview, IL: Scott Foresman and Company, 1987; William A. Mehrens and Irvin J. Lehmann, *Using Standardized Tests in Education*, New York: Longman, Inc., 1987.

GRADE INFLATION, a recent trend in which two significant changes have been noted with respect to teachers' grading practices. First, grades awarded to students tend to be higher in many schools and colleges than in years past. A second and concommitant change is a rise in mean grade point averages. Accompanying these changes has been increasing use of grading alternatives such as the pass/fail option.

In a study of high-grading professors at a major eastern university, Kurt Geisinger divided his sample of 165 undergraduate professors into three equal groups: high graders, middle-level graders, and low graders. Factors that he found correlating with high-grading were: (1) relatively small class size, and (2) faculty members' individual criteria used for grading ("the more comparative an instructor's grading orientation is, the more likely he/she is to give low grades"). Personal knowledge of the student also influences grading practice.

References: Kurt F. Geisinger, "Who are Giving All Those A's? An Examination of High-Grading College Faculty," *Journal of Teacher Education*, March–April 1980; Angus H. Paul, "Grade Inflation Halted, But Not Reversed, Study Finds," *The Chronicle of Higher Education*, October 14, 1980; Sidney Suslow, "Grade Inflation: End of a Trend?" *Change*, March 1977.

GRADE-POINT AVERAGE (GPA), a mathematical measure used to describe the level of grades earned by an individual student. Grade-point averages are mathematically calculated means that range from 0 to 4. In most colleges, students receive letter grades to which quality points are assigned: A = 4, B = 3, C = 2, D = 1, and F = 0. The quality points are multiplied by the number of semester (or quarter) hours assigned to each course. These are summed and then divided by the total number of credit hours involved. For example:

Course	Grade	Semester (or Quarter) Hours	Quality Points
English 100	A	3	= 12
Math 426	B	3	= 9
History 360	B	3	= 9
Physical Ed 100	A	4	= 16

Total 13 s.h.   = 46

$$\text{Grade-point average} = \frac{46}{13} = 3.54$$

GPA is calculated for a single semester (or quarter). *Cumulative* GPA for work completed in a single institution is calculated on the basis of *all* courses taken at that particular institution. Pass/fail and noncredit courses are usually not calculated into the GPA. Grade-point and cumulative grade-point averages are used to determine honors, academic probation, admission to graduate school, and eligibility for graduation.
References: Humphrey Doermann, *Crosscurrents in College Admissions* (Revised Edition), New York: Teachers College Press, Columbia University, 1970; Howard Kirshenbaum, et al., *Wad-Ja-Get? The Grading Game in American Education,* New York: Hart Publishing Company, Inc., 1971; Harold S. Wechsler, *The Qualified Student,* New York: John Wiley and Sons, 1977.

GRADING ON THE CURVE, an evaluation system in which student grades are distributed on the basis of the normal distribution curve. This practice assumes that the performance of students is normally distributed. This assumption, not always tenable, constitutes the system's most serious weakness. (A second limitation is the fact that, in a classroom, small numbers of students are involved.)

As the figure below indicates, grades are predetermined and related directly to the normal distribution curve. Most grades (C) fall within the middle range; grades of A and B are equivalent to the number of D's and F's. The percentage distribution of A's, B's, C's, and so on is flexible and can be adjusted by the evaluator with symmetry of grade distribution maintained. (See NORMAL DISTRIBUTION CURVE.)
References: Norman E. Gronlund, *Improving Marking and Reporting in Classroom Instruction,* New York: Macmillan Publishing Company, Inc., 1974; James S. Terwilliger, *Assigning Grades to Students,* Glenview, IL: Scott, Foresman and Company, 1971.

GRADUATE ASSISTANTS, graduate students who are hired and paid for teaching, administration, or research in an institution of higher education. Because of the time commitments of such functions, graduate students are rarely permitted to carry full-time graduate loads (as is the case with fellowships). Graduate assistants either work with professors in a team teaching situation or are given full responsibility for teaching classes (usually at the undergraduate level). Those involved in research are normally involved in work of the institution's or professor's choosing. Not all graduate assistant assignments have a direct relationship to the student's graduate program. Nevertheless, the graduate assistant is required to be enrolled in a graduate degree program. Graduate assistantships are usually contracted for a year at a time and do not accrue credit towards tenure. The salaries of graduate assistants vary as a function of institu-

Grading on the Curve

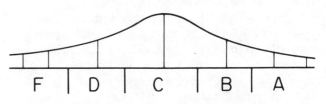

Normal Curve and Sample Distribution of Grades

tional and job expectations. The most common salary ranges between $3,000 and $4,000 a year. (See FELLOWSHIPS.)

References: Robert H. Davis, et al., *Commitment to Excellence,* East Lansing, MI: Michigan State University, 1976; *Definitions of Student Personnel Terms in Higher Education,* Washington, DC: U.S. Department of Health, Education, and Welfare, 1968; G. Kerry Smith, *The Troubled Campus,* San Francisco: Jossey-Bass Publishers, 1970.

GRADUATE COUNCIL, a group of graduate faculty members that either recommends or sets policies dealing with graduate education in a particular institution of higher education. Graduate councils are concerned with issues such as curriculum, standards for student admissions, standards for graduation, and standards for the appointment of graduate faculty members. Council members may be elected by members of the graduate faculty or they may be appointed. In most institutions, graduate council members are elected.

The role, authority, and influence of graduate councils are a function of the institutions' governance structure and/or the members themselves. On many campuses, they are considered the de facto governing group for all graduate-level programs.

References: William H. Cowley, *Presidents, Professors, and Trustees,* San Francisco: Jossey-Bass Publishers, 1980; Paul Jedamus, et al., *Improving Academic Management,* San Francisco: Jossey-Bass Publishers, 1980; John D. Millett, *New Structures of Campus Power,* San Francisco: Jossey-Bass Publishers, 1978; Gary L. Riley and L. Victor Baldridge, *Governing Academic Organizations,* Berkeley, CA: McCutchan Publishing Corporation, 1977.

GRADUATE MANAGEMENT ADMISSION TEST (GMAT), a standardized test developed and administered by Educational Testing Service, Princeton, N.J. It was initially developed in 1954 and titled Admission Test for Graduate Study in Business. The purpose of the test is to provide measures of selected mental abilities found to be necessary in the study of business at the graduate level. Many graduate schools use Graduate Management Admission Test scores for admission purposes—these scores provide one base for predicting success in an institution's graduate business program. (Those with higher scores will most likely be more successful than those with lower scores—however, this is not true for all cases.)

The GMAT includes the following areas to be assessed: *Verbal*—reading comprehension, analysis of situations, sentence corrections, critical thinking;

and *Mathematics* (quantitative)—problem solving, data sufficiency, data evaluation, date application. Three scores are provided, *Verbal* (0–60), *Mathematics* (quantitative) (0–60), and *Composite* (total) (200–800). The composite score is similar to the score provided by the Graduate Record Examination, with a range from 200 to 800, a mean of 500, and a standard deviation of 100. (See GRADUATE RECORD EXAMINATION.)

References: Gino Crocette, et al., *GMAT, Graduate Management Admission Test,* New York: ARCO Publishing, Inc., 1987; James V. Mitchell, Jr., *The Ninth Mental Measurements Yearbook,* Lincoln, NE: The Buros Institute of Mental Measurement, The University of Nebraska Press, 1984.

GRADUATE RECORD EXAMINATION (GRE), an examination developed by Educational Testing Service (ETS) that has become part of the admissions procedure of many graduate schools. The GRE was first administered in 1937 by the Carnegie Foundation for the Advancement of Teaching and the graduate deans of four eastern universities. Two types of tests are presently available. The first, the General Test, measures developed ability. The second, the Subject Test, measures achievement in a specific field of study. Although many graduate schools require scores from both tests, some require a General Test score only. Neither the Graduate Record Examination nor ETS set minimum scores. They are established by the individual graduate school.

The General Test yields three subscores, (verbal, quantitative, and analytic), whose scores generally range from 220 to 800 each. A score of 500 corresponds approximately to the 50 percentile. The Subject Test scores may range from 240 to 980 depending on the particular test used. There are 20 Subject Tests available, including biology, music, computer science, education, and sociology. Nine of the Subject Tests generate subscores. (See EDUCATIONAL TESTING SERVICE and GRADUATE RECORD EXAMINATIONS BOARD.)

Reference: 1978–79 Guide to the Use of the Graduate Record Examinations, Princeton, NJ: Educational Testing Service, 1978.

GRADUATE RECORD EXAMINATIONS BOARD, formed in 1966 to set policies for the GRE program administered by the Educational Testing Service. The GRE program includes the GRE tests, several other standardized tests, research information, publications, and advisory services to graduate schools. The board, although independent, is affiliated with the Association of Graduate Schools as well as the Council of Graduate Schools in the United States. Also falling within its purview are the Graduate School Foreign Language Testing Program, the Test of English as a Foreign Language, other assessment programs, research in graduate education and teaching, and sponsorship of workshops on graduate education. The board sets policies; ETS, functioning as its executive agent, implements them. (See EDUCATIONAL TESTING SERVICE and GRADUATE RECORD EXAMINATION.)

Reference: 1978–79 Guide to the Use of the Graduate Record Examinations, Princeton, NJ: Educational Testing Service, 1978.

GRAMMAR, the study of the rules of a language and the relationship of words to each other in a sentence. It is concerned with the generalization of statements that then become the base or structure of a language. Grammar is interested in the syntax of a language as well as its phonology. The study of the structure of language is called linguistics. It is from linguistics that grammatical texts are developed.

Grammar is made up of grammatical theory, language and word classifications, phonology, change, synchronic universals, and dischronic generalizations. Recent research dealing with *traditional* grammar teaching and its relationship to written composition indicates that the former has little effect on the latter. Teaching of *modern* grammar, however, has been shown to have a positive effect.

Grammatical texts date back to ancient Mesopotamia (about 1600 B.C.). Grammar and grammatical texts were first developed in an attempt to preserve classical literature.

References: Erwin A. Esper, *Analogy and Association in Linguistics and Psychology,* Athens, GA: University of Georgia Press, 1973; Joseph Greenberg, *Anthropological Linguistics: An Introduction,* New York: Random House, 1968; Patrick Groff, "Is Grammar Teaching Worthwhile?" *Practical Applications of Research,* March 1980; Dell Hymes, *Studies in the History of Linguistics,* Bloomington, IN: Indiana University Press, 1974.

GRAMMAR-TRANSLATION METHOD, a foreign language instructional method that stresses the written word. Emphasis is placed on translation, bilingual vocabulary lists, accurate writing of the language, considerable drill and practice, literary significance, and knowing rules and excep-

tions. Actual oral use (communication) is not stressed.

The grammar-translation method had its origins in the teaching of Latin and Greek. Modern language teachers initially used the approach to gain acceptance for nonclassical languages in the schools. The opposite of grammar translation is the direct method. (See CLASSICAL LANGUAGES and DIRECT METHODS.)

References: Wilga M. Rivers, *Teaching Foreign-Language Skills,* Chicago: University of Chicago Press, 1968; David Webb, *Teaching Modern Language,* London, England: David and Charles, Inc., 1974.

GRAND MAL SEIZURE, severe form of epileptic seizure involving convulsions. The individual experiencing a grand mal seizure will usually have a sudden loss of consciousness with a spasm or tightening of all the muscles. Not all muscles tighten simultaneously. At times the individual is apt to bite his/her tongue; loss of control of natural functions may also occur. Contraction of the chest may cause a gurgling, groaning, or even a loud cry. The duration of such a seizure can range from less than 1 minute to more than 30 minutes. Seizures usually come singularly, although it is not totally uncommon for a person to go into a deep sleep or coma. Weakness, nausea, severe headaches, and other problems may manifest themselves after a person comes out of the deep sleep or coma. (See EPILEPSY and PETIT MAL SEIZURE.)

References: John Guerrant, et al., *Personality in Epilepsy,* Springfield, IL: Charles C. Thomas, Publisher, 1962; Daniel P. Hallahan and James M. Kauffman, *Exceptional Children: Introduction to Special Education,* Englewood Cliffs, NJ: Prentice-Hall, Inc., 1978; William G. Lennox, *Science and Seizures,* College Park, MD: McGrath Publishing Company, 1970; Samuel Livingston, *Living with Epileptic Seizures,* Springfield, IL: Charles C. Thomas, Publisher, 1963.

GRANTS-IN-AID, financial grants made available to individuals or to agencies. Several forms of such assistance exist. Some better known examples include: (1) periodic allocations that the federal government makes to states for the support of a specific program; (2) regular allocations of money made available to students in need of financial assistance (regardless of academic distinction); (3) allocations made to support a research project; and (4) gifts of money made to talented students regardless of financial need (e.g. athletic grant-in-aid, music grant-in-aid).

References: Carter V. Good (Editor), *Dictionary of Educa-*

tion (Third Edition), New York: McGraw-Hill Book Company, 1973; William E. Hopke (Editor), *Dictionary of Personnel and Guidance Terms: Including Professional Agencies and Associations,* Chicago: J. G. Ferguson Publishing Company, 1968; Asa S. Knowles (Editor), *The International Encyclopedia of Higher Education* (Volume 1), San Francisco: Jossey-Bass Publishers, 1977.

GRAPHEME, a letter or group of letters symbolizing the smallest unit of writing. The grapheme is to the written word what the phoneme is to the spoken word. Examples of a grapheme are *sh* in shoe, *p* in nap, and *ph* in telephone. Some symbols, such as *b,* can be graphemes or phonemes, depending on use. To make the distinction clear, linguists write the grapheme as *b,* the phoneme as /b/. (See PHONEME and PHONICS.)
References: Dolores Durkin, *Teaching Them to Read* (Third Edition), Boston: Allyn and Bacon, Inc., 1978; Edward Fry, *Reading Instruction for Classroom and Clinic,* New York: McGraw-Hill Book Company, 1972.

GRATIFICATION, DELAY OF, reinforcement (gratification) that does not immediately follow the behavior with which it is connected. For example, a particular behavior may occur and the individual is not rewarded until two hours later. This delay of gratification from the reward may weaken the effect the reward is supposed to have on the particular behavior. In fact, the delayed reward may be mistakenly associated with another behavior that is actually closer in time to the delayed reward itself. Gratification may be induced internally as well as externally.

In behavioral psychology, delayed gratification weakens the Law of Effect (immediacy of reinforcement). If a child performs well in a situation, and circumstances permit, he/she should be told (rewarded) immediately. If the child is told two or three days later about how well he/she has done, the reward will not have the same strong effect. In some instances, the child may even think that he/she is being rewarded for another performance that might have occurred closer to the time the child was complimented.
References: Clifford T. Morgan and Richard King, *Introduction to Psychology* (Fifth Edition), New York: McGraw-Hill Book Company, 1975; Roger Ulrich, et al., *Control of Human Behavior* (Volume 2), Glenview, IL: Scott, Foresman and Company, 1970; Robert S. Woodworth and Harold Schlosberg, *Experimental Psychology* (Revised Edition), New York: Henry Holt and Company, 1953.

GRAY, WILLIAM S. (June 5, 1885–September 8, 1960), noted professor of reading and "father" of the Dick and Jane books. Gray served on the University of Chicago faculty (1914–50), a tenure that included 14 years as dean of that institution's education faculty. Before joining the University of Chicago faculty, he saw service as a teacher, as a principal, and as director of the laboratory school, Illinois State Normal University. His research and writings did much to influence the teaching of reading in the United States as did his service as coeditor of Scott-Foresman's widely used basic reading series. Gray helped to found the International Reading Association and, in 1956, served as that organization's president. He also served as president of the American Education Research Association.
Reference: Donavon Lumpkin, "Gray, William Scott" in John F. Ohles (Editor), *Biographical Dictionary of American Educators* (Volume 2), Westport, CT: Greenwood Press, 1978.

GREATER CLEVELAND MATHEMATICS PROGRAM (GCMP), a modern mathematics program for grades K–6 started in 1959 by the Educational Research Council of Greater Cleveland. The program is based on the discovery approach and focuses on logic and mathematical structure. The purpose of focusing on mathematical structure is to enable students to interpret new situations and enhance problem solving by utilizing the patterns and mathematical structures of a given problem or situation. (See NEW MATHEMATICS.)
References: Calhoun C. Collier and Harold H. Lerch, *Teaching Mathematics in the Modern Elementary School,* New York: The Macmillan Company, 1969; Educational Research Council of Greater Cleveland, *Key Topics in Mathematics for the Intermediate Teacher,* Chicago: Science Research Associates, 1962; Michael L. Mahaffey and Alex F. Perrodin, *Teaching Elementary School Mathematics,* Itasca, IL: F. E. Peacock Publishers, Inc., 1973.

GREGG, JOHN R. (June 17, 1867–February 23, 1948), developer of the well-known shorthand method that carries his name. Gregg was born in Ireland. He moved to the United States in 1893 where many of his books, most relating to the Gregg method, were published. He founded the Gregg Publishing Company, which subsequently became a division of the McGraw-Hill Publishing Company and was later turned over to Northwestern University. The Gregg shorthand system has been adapted for use in French, Spanish, German, Italian, Portuguese, Polish, and Esperanto. (See SHORTHAND.)
References: Louis A. Leslie, *The Story of Gregg Shorthand,* New York: McGraw-Hill Publishing Company, 1964; F.

Addington Symonds, *John Robert Gregg: The Man and His Work*, New York: McGraw-Hill Publishing Company, 1963.

GRIEVANCE PROCEDURES, systems that permit employees and employers to settle labor disputes. Formal grievances may be filed by one employee or a group of employees; representatives of management may also initiate them. They may involve purported violations of the labor agreement (contract) or violations of law, or the filing party may seek to clarify working conditions about which the labor agreement is silent or vague.

Grievance procedures normally detail the appeal steps to be followed when disputes arise and the time period within which formal grievances are to be filed. When appeal steps (i.e. reporting and seeking resolution of grievances through normal administrative channels) fail to resolve the grievance, the matter is generally referred to arbitration. (See ARBITRATION.)

References: William B. Castetter, *The Personnel Function in Educational Administration* (Third Edition), New York: Macmillan Publishing Company, Inc., 1981; W. D. Heisel, *New Questions and Answers on Public Employee Negotiation*, Chicago: International Personnel Management Association, 1973; C. Wilson Randle and Max S. Wortman, Jr., *Collective Bargaining: Principles and Practices* (Second Edition), Boston: Houghton Mifflin Company, 1966; Arthur A. Sloane and Fred Witney, *Labor Relations*, Englewood Cliffs, NJ: Prentice-Hall, Inc., 1967.

GROUP COHESIVENESS, the "togetherness" of a group. Contributing to the process of group cohesiveness are factors such as: (1) the degree of attractiveness group members have for each other; (2) the extent to which members wish to remain together; (3) commonality of purpose or perspective; and (4) the morale of the group. Football teams, fraternities, families, and clubs are examples of groups that are often highly cohesive. Students of group cohesiveness commonly study variables such as interaction (attraction) between/among group members, satisfaction, group productivity, and the behavior (often conforming behavior) of group members.

References: Ronald L. Applbaum, et al., *The Process of Group Communication*, Chicago: Science Research Associates, Inc., 1974; Marvin E. Shaw, *Group Dynamics: The Psychology of Small Group Behavior*, New York: McGraw-Hill Book Company, 1971.

GROUP COUNSELING, a process in which an interpersonal relationship is established between a counselor and a group of clients (usually ten or fewer) for the purpose of discussing and helping to resolve the clients' personal problems. Three-way interaction takes place in group counseling sessions: (1) group-to-member; (2) member-to-member; and (3) counselor-to-client(s). Although occasional decision making takes place, most attention is given to satisfaction of prevailing emotional needs.

Group counseling offers several advantages not found in the one-to-one (counselor and client) approach. They include: (1) the opportunity to communicate with others and thereby develop effective interpersonal relationships; (2) group support and encouragement; (3) the opportunity to be accepted by a group; and (4) the sense of "safety" that comes from belonging to a group. Group counselors, to be effective, need to be self-aware, open, flexible, tolerant, warm, mature, and good listeners. (See GROUP GUIDANCE.)

References: Don C. Dinkmeyer and James J. Muro, *Group Counseling* (Second Edition), Itasca, IL: F. E. Peacock Publishers, Inc., 1979; Merle Ohlsen, *Group Counseling* (Second Edition), New York: Holt, Rinehart and Winston, Inc., 1977; E. L. Tolbert, *An Introduction to Guidance: The Professional Counselor*, Boston: Little, Brown and Company, 1982; James P. Trotzer, *The Counselor and the Group: Integrating Theory, Training, and Practice*, Monterey, CA: Brooks/Cole Publishing Company, 1977.

GROUP DYNAMICS, a field of study that focuses on the action and interaction of a group and the members of the group. The early research of Kurt Lewin, Ronald Lippitt, Dorwin Cartwright and other psychologists, carried out between 1920 and 1950, was concerned with factors such as types of leadership (e.g. authoritarian, democratic), group atmosphere, group goals, and group structure. In recent years, the focus of group dynamics has been on social process (e.g. social comparison, cognitive dissonance, and group decision making) as well as the development of strategies to be used within groups. Although there are many definitions for a group (e.g. two or more people interacting with each other and affecting each other; or a collection of people who develop a relationship, such that individual needs are satisfied), the interactions of individuals and the meeting of needs of these individuals within a group are central to most definitions.

References: Hermann Brandstaller, et al. (Editors), *Dynamics of Group Decisions*, Beverly Hills, CA: Sage Publications, Inc., 1978; Dorwin Cartwright and Alvin Zander (Editors), *Group Dynamics: Research and Theory*, Evanston, IL: Row, Peterson and Company, 1953; P.

Paul Hare, *Handbook of Small Group Research* (Second Edition), New York: The Free Press, 1976; Marvin E. Shaw, *Group Dynamics: The Psychology of Small Group Behavior*, New York: McGraw-Hill Book Company, 1971.

GROUP GUIDANCE, a teaching approach in which the guidance counselor or teacher devotes major time to the imparting of information to a group of students. Topics are normally chosen by the instructor and presentations tend to focus on content. Groups are usually of class size but can be larger when resource or time constraints require.

Topics are diverse as the range of these illustrative subjects illustrates: "choosing your college," "improving study skills," and "how to interview for a job." These topics may be taught in the homeroom, during a regularly scheduled class period, as part of an assembly program or career-day program or even on a field trip. (See GROUP COUNSELING.)

References: Harold W. Bernard and Daniel W. Fullmer, *Principles of Guidance* (Second Edition), New York: Harper and Row, Publishers, 1977; Edward C. Glanz, *Guidance: Foundations, Principles, and Techniques* (Second Edition), Boston: Allyn and Bacon, Inc., 1974; E. L. Tolbert, *An Introduction to Guidance: The Professional Counselor*, Boston: Little, Brown and Company, 1982.

GROUP INVESTIGATION, an approach to Cooperative Learning developed by S. Sharon and Y. Sharon in the 1970s. (See COOPERATIVE LEARNING.)

Reference: S. Sharon and Y. Sharon, *Small-Group teaching*, Englewood Cliffs, NJ: Education Technology Publications, 1976.

GROUP TESTS, examinations administered concurrently to more than one individual. Group tests are usually designed to permit quick scoring and commonly consist of printed test items, often of the multiple-choice type. Such tests are easy to administer; the individual administering them need not be highly trained (as opposed to persons administering individual tests). As a result of the development of group tests, large-scale norms are now available that enhance the conduct of large-scale educational research. Many intelligence and achievement tests have been designed as group tests (e.g. Otis-Lennon Mental Ability Test, SAT, ACT, Stanford Achievement Test). Notwithstanding the many advantages associated with such tests, there are several disadvantages as well. They include possible statistical errors, bias, and problems with reading levels. (See INDIVIDUAL TESTS and MULTIPLE-CHOICE ITEM.)

References: Arthur R. Jensen, *Bias in Mental Testing*, New York: The Free Press, 1979; Orval G. Johnson, *Tests and Measurements in Child Development*, San Francisco: Jossey-Bass Publishers, 1976; Paul Kline, *Psychometrics and Psychology*, New York: Academic Press, 1979.

GROUP THEORY, in the field of group dynamics, those theories used to explain the interactions and workings of groups as well as individuals within such groups. Topics such as T-groups, tasks, roles, structure, work, functions, norms, leadership, and process are covered by various theories of group dynamics.

Group theory in mathematics refers to theories used in the manipulation of particular "sets." A set is considered a group if it has certain mathematical properties, elements, and relationships (e.g. closure, identity, inverse, associativity). (See SETS.)

References: P. B. Bhattscharya and S. K. Jain, *First Course in Group Theory*, New Delhi, India: Wiley Eastern Private, Ltd., 1972; John S. Rose, *A Course on Group Theory*, Cambridge, England: Cambridge University Press, 1978; Harleigh B. Trecker, *Social Group Work: Principles and Practices*, New York: Association Press, 1972.

GROWTH-CURVE METHOD OF PREDICTING POPULATIONS—See PREDICTING PUPIL POPULATION

GRUBE METHOD, a method of teaching mathematics to young children that was introduced in Germany (1842) by A. W. Grube. The method required the teacher to concentrate on small groups of whole numbers (e.g. 1–10) and to teach all four processes in connection with each number rather than teaching each process separately. Once this group of numbers was mastered, the next group of higher numbers (e.g. 11–20) was studied.

H. G. Good illustrated the method as follows: "For example," he wrote, "the exercises on the number 2 were as follows: $2 = 1 + 1; 2 - 1 = 1; 2 - 2 = 0; 2 = 2 \times 1; 2 = 1 \times 2; 2 \div 1 = 2; 2 \div 2 = 1$. On the number 3, there were ten such combinations, and on the number 4, thirteen" (p. 431).

The Grube method enjoyed some popularity in the United States during the 1800s but soon lost favor, as it did in Germany, for being tedious and relatively ineffective.

References: Florian Cajori, *A History of Elementary Mathematics with Hints on Methods of Teaching* (Revised and Enlarged Edition), New York: The Macmillan Company, 1917; H. G. Good, *A History of American Education* (Second Edition), New York: The Macmillan Company, 1968; *A History of Mathematics Education in the United*

States and Canada (32nd Yearbook), Washington, DC: National Council of Teachers of Mathematics, 1970.

GUARANTEED STUDENT LOAN PROGRAM

(GSLP), or Guarantee Agency Program, refers to programs administered by guarantee agencies and to the Federally Insured Student Loan Program (FISLP). Loans are made to individual undergraduate or graduate students who are enrolled in a college program on at least a half-time basis. Banks, credit unions, and other lending institutions make these long-term loans available at a relatively low interest rate but are under no legal obligation to do so. In 1980–81, qualified undergraduate students were able to borrow up to $12,500 and graduate students up to $25,000 (including undergraduate loans). Repayment begins six months after graduation or after the student has ceased being at least a half-time (six semester hour) enrollee. Loan interest is paid by the federal or state government during enrollment regardless of family income. Borrowers have up to ten years in which to repay their loans. (See STUDENT FINANCIAL AID.)

References: Chester E. Finn, Jr., *Scholars, Dollars, and Bureaucrats,* Washington, DC: The Brookings Institution, 1978; Elinor Lenz and Marjorie H. Shaevitz, *So You Want to Go Back to School: Facing the Realities of Reentry,* New York: McGraw-Hill Book Company, 1977.

GUIDANCE AND COUNSELING, two forms of

service rendered by a counselor.

Although used together frequently, the terms guidance and counseling have different meanings. *Counseling* is an interaction process often involving a client (student) and a counselor. When the relationship is one-to-one, the counselor helps the client to understand himself/herself and his/her problems. Successful counseling results in the client being better able to adjust to his/her environment. *Guidance* includes counseling plus other types of activities (e.g. correspondence with a social agency, conferring with a student's classroom teacher, collecting and making college catalogs available to students, lecturing to health class about dating). It is generally regarded as a series of diverse services designed to help the individual solve problems associated with development; to acquire information relevant to career planning, placement; and so on. It may include appraisal procedures, teacher-parent consultation, and follow-up studies.

References: Preston K. Munter, et al., *Counseling Students,* Dover, MA: Auburn House Publishing Company, 1988; John J. Pietrofesa, *Guidance: An Introduction,* Chicago:

Rand McNally College Publishing Company, 1980; E. L. Tolbert, *An Introduction to Guidance: The Professional Counselor,* Boston: Little, Brown and Company, 1982.

GUIDANCE COUNSELOR, trained guidance

specialist who, in a school or school system, works: (1) directly with students; (2) consultatively with parents and teachers; and (3) in team fashion with pupil personnel colleagues, the faculty, and/or the administration. The major duties performed by guidance counselors include but are not limited to activities such as directing the student services personnel program, assisting with pupil placement, maintaining student cumulative records, coordinating standardized-testing programs, career counseling, and developing close working relationships with various community agencies.

Although increasing numbers of elementary schools are employing full-time guidance counselors, their number is small. Considerably more are used at the secondary school level. In 1975–76, almost 50,000 (FTE) counselors were working in American secondary schools with a reported ratio of 1 counselor for every 522 students.

Most guidance counselors receive their training at the graduate level and are state certified. Counselor education, provided by over 400 colleges and universities, requires a minimum of one to two years of graduate study including a supervised practicum and field (internship) experiences. (See GUIDANCE AND COUNSELING and GUIDANCE SERVICES.)

References: Edward F. DeRoche and Jeffrey S. Kaiser, *Complete Guide to Administering School Services,* West Nyack, NY: Parker Publishing Company, Inc., 1980; Donald G. Mortensen and Alan M. Schmuller, *Guidance in Today's Schools* (Third Edition), New York: John Wiley and Sons, 1976; Bruce Shertzer and Shelley C. Stone, *Fundamentals of Guidance* (Third Edition), Boston: Houghton Mifflin Company, 1976; E. L. Tolbert, *An Introduction to Guidance: The Professional Counselor,* Boston: Little, Brown and Company, 1982.

GUIDANCE SERVICES, activities performed by

professional counselors that help to further a student's normal development and to improve adjustment during his/her career as a student. Writers in the field identify at least five basic guidance services: (1) individual inventory, or detailed record keeping about individual students; (2) information services (e.g. college information, career information); (3) counseling services, or help with educational and personal-social problems; (4) placement and followup; and (5) consultation services, including contacts with teachers, community, and the home.

Almost 50,000 counselors perform guidance services in American schools. An estimated 90 percent of them work on the secondary school level. *References:* Claire C. Cole, *Guidance in the Middle School: Everyone's Responsibility*, Fairburn, OH: National Middle School Association, 1981; Edward F. DeRoche and Jeffrey S. Kaiser, *Complete Guide to Administering School Services*, West Nyack, NY: Parker Publishing Company, Inc., 1980; Allan A. Glatthorn, *Curriculum Leadership*, Glenview, IL: Scott, Foresman and Company, 1987; E. L. Tolbert, *An Introduction to Guidance: The Professional Counselor*, Boston: Little, Brown and Company, 1978.

GUIDE WORDS, the first and last words of a dictionary page that appear at the top of each page. Guide words are used to assist dictionary users to locate words rapidly. Effective use of guide words requires that the learner have a thorough understanding of alphabetical order. In the elementary school, children are taught to use guide words as part of the language arts curriculum (dictionary skill). *References:* Harry A. Greene and Walter T. Petty, *Developing Language Skills in the Elementary Schools* (Fourth Edition), Boston: Allyn and Bacon, Inc., 1971; Paul S. Anderson and Diane Lapp, *Language Skills in Elementary Education* (Third Edition), New York: Macmillan Publishing Company, Inc., 1979.

GYMNASIUM, an indoor structure containing special gymnastic and/or other sports equipment where people participate in physical activities (e.g. indoor sports and games) as well as systematic physical exercise.

The history of the gymnasium dates back to ancient Greece (about 500 B.C.). When first developed, the gymnasium was a place where free men were required to provide their sons with instruction in gymnastics as well as literary training. Thus, the early gymnasiums were centers for social and intellectual as well as physical activities. The Academy, Lyceum, and Kynosarges were major intellectual centers (gymnasiums) in ancient Greece. From these origins, the modern gymnasiums of Germany emerged, secondary schools that prepared students for college.

Today, most American high schools and middle schools have full gymnasiums; many elementary schools, being smaller in size, do not. In their place, elementary school buildings often include "all-purpose" rooms that are equipped as gymnasiums but serve as cafeterias and/or auditoriums as well. *References:* Charles A. Bucher, *Foundations of Physical Education* (Eighth Edition), St. Louis, MO: The C. V. Mosby Company, 1979; Elsie C. Burton, *The New Physical Education for Elementary School Children*, Boston: Houghton Mifflin Company, 1977; Earle F. Zeigler (Editor), *A History of Sport and Physical Education to 1900*, Champaign, IL: Stipes Publishing Company, 1973.

GYMNASTICS, exercises, calisthenics, and/or apparatus activities designed to improve or develop one's physical condition. Gymnastics includes strength, flexibility, endurance, movement, control, and coordination exercises. Activities such as tumbling and floor exercises, as well as exercises performed on the balance beam, parallel bars, side horse, or flat mats are part of gymnastics. Selected dance and body movement are also included. The use of space, speed, movement, working with a partner, and body flight are skills that one must normally master in gymnastics.

Gymnastics dates back to the time of the ancient Greeks and Romans. Although popular in Europe during the late 1700s, it was not introduced into the United States until 1885 (by German refugees). Gymnastics is found in many school physical education curricula. (See GYMNASIUM; MOVEMENT EDUCATION; and SOKOLS.) *References:* Reuben B. Frost, *Physical Education*, Reading, MA: Addison-Wesley Publishing Company, 1975; E. Mauldon, et al., *Teaching Gymnastics and Body Control*, Boston: Plays, Inc., 1975; Mary L. Schreiber, *Women's Gymnastics,*, Pacific Palisades, CA: Goodyear Publishing Company, Inc., 1969.

HALFWAY HOUSE, a transitional living facility, public or private, that accommodates and provides support services to individuals who have been released from an institution and are returning to independent living in the community. Included among the institutions from which they have been released are state facilities for the handicapped, prisons, and hospitals. The halfway house, Harold Raush and Charlotte Raush reported, is commonly referred to as a "bridge" in the literature, one that expedites one-way, or single-direction, movement *from* the institution *to* the community. Halfway houses may also serve the handicapped population that has never been institutionalized but, due to circumstances (e.g. health of parents), has nowhere else to reside.

In ideal cases, halfway houses are located in communities similar to those to which the individual will be returning. Programs available, according to W. H. Pearce, should provide numerous services including: (1) a home; (2) vocational counseling and help in finding employment; (3) financial support; (4) educational/recreational opportunities; (5) personal counseling; and (6) a supportive environment.

Various kinds of structures have been used for halfway houses: older homes, former motels, hospitals or apartment houses; and rural farm buildings. The number and ages of halfway house residents vary, with some preferring a mixed-age group. Specially trained staff is available to work with residents, individually and in groups.

The first American halfway houses were organized in the 19th century, with Massachusetts, New York, and Pennsylvania credited with having the earliest of them.

References: Harry E. Allen, et al., *Halfway Houses,* Washington, DC: Law Enforcement Assistance Administration, U.S. Department of Justice, November 1978; Oliver J. Keller, Jr. and Benedict S. Alper, *Halfway Houses: Community-Centered Correction and Treatment,* Lexington, MA: D. C. Heath and Company, 1970; W. H. Pearce, "Reintegration of the Offender into the Community—New Resources and Perspectives," *Canadian Journal of Corrections,* Volume 12, No. 4, 1970; Harold L. Raush and Charlotte L. Raush, *The Halfway House Movement: A Search for Sanity,* New York: Appleton-Century-Crofts, Inc., 1968.

HALL, G. STANLEY (February 1, 1844–April 24, 1924), child psychologist who introduced the child study movement and formulated the modern concept of adolescence. He was an early psychologist in America and helped to establish psychology as an academic discipline. Hall felt that psychology could reform education; furthermore, that the development and education of children was the most important function of society. The center of scientific psychology for G. Stanley Hall comprised childhood, sex, and psychopathology.

He taught at Johns Hopkins University and, in 1889, founded and became President of Clark University. He was responsible for bringing Sigmund Freud and Carl G. Jung to Clark to lecture in 1909. Some of his most notable students were John Dewey, Arnold Gesell, and Lewis M. Terman.

References: G. Stanley Hall, *Aspects of Child Life and Education,* Boston: Ginn and Company, 1907 (Reprinted by Arno Press in 1975); G. Stanley Hall, *Life and Confessions of a Psychologist.,* New York: D. Appleton and Company, 1923; Dorothy Ross, *G. Stanley Hall,* Chicago: University of Chicago Press, 1972.

HALO EFFECT, a type of rating error or observer bias that reduces or makes questionable the reliability of an observation. Halo effect is said to be present when the observer forms an early, general, overall opinion of the individual being observed and allows the opinion to influence subsequent observations. In some cases, the halo effect may help the individual being observed, because the general overall opinion is positive and, therefore, the individual may be overrated. In the opposite situation, where the overall opinion is negative, underrating may occur. In either case, the ratings are questionable. Halo effect may influence ratings in studies and in decision-making situations and may even influence relationships between teachers and students.

References: Anne Anastasi, *Psychological Testing* (Sixth Edition), New York: Macmillan Publishing Company, Inc., 1988; Walter R. Borg and Meredith D. Gall, *Educational Research,* (Fifth Edition) New York: Longman, Inc., 1989; Norman E. Gronlund, *Measurement and Evaluation in Teaching* (Fifth Edition), New York: Macmillan Publishing Company, 1985.

HANDEDNESS, preference for the use of either the right or left hand. There are many theories that have been developed to explain handedness.

Attributions range from inherited trait, environmental factors, eye preference, asymmetry of the brain, relationship to learning, blood supply to the brain, brain weight, arm length, how infants are carried, to brain injury. Many authorities believe that handedness is a function of neurological factors (e.g. the functions of one cerebral hemisphere as opposed to another) or the pattern of functional asymmetry of the brain.

Left-handed children continue to encounter problems in school, primarily because some of the instructional equipment tends to be designed for right-handed children. Years ago, a left-handed child was forced to learn to write with the right hand. This is no longer required; to the contrary, such practice is discouraged by child development specialists. (See AMBIDEXTERITY; LATERALITY; and SINISTRAL.)

References: Minnie Gieseck, *The Genesis of Hand Preference,* Washington, DC: National Research Council, 1936; Jeannine Herron (Editor), *Neuropsychology of Left-handedness,* New York: Academic Press, 1980; Gerd Sommerhoff, *Logic of the Living Brain,* London, England: John Wiley and Sons, 1974.

HANDICAPPED INDIVIDUALS, as defined by Public Law 94-142, are persons who are aged 3–21 and, in varying degrees, are mentally retarded, hard of hearing, deaf, speech impaired, visually handicapped, seriously emotionally disturbed, orthopedically impaired, deaf-blind, or multi-handicapped or those with specific learning disabilities that require special education and related services. Authors of this legislation estimated that, in 1975, there were more than 8,000,000 handicapped children in the United States.

Other definitions do not limit this condition to any particular age group. (See EXCEPTIONAL CHILDREN and PUBLIC LAW 94-142.)

References: National School Public Relations Association, *Educating All the Handicapped: What the Laws Say and What the Schools are Doing,* Arlington, VA: The Association, 1977; Public Law 94-142, Education for All Handicapped Children Act of 1975, in *United States Code: Congressional and Administrative News,* 94th Congress-First Session, 1975, St. Paul, MN: West Publishing Company, 1975.

HANDWRITING, an encoding process that permits a writer to put his ideas to paper.

Frank Freeman, in 1915, identified six characteristics of handwriting that continue to be recognized today. Presented in order of their importance to legibility, they are: (1) *letter form;* (2) *spacing,* between and within words; (3) *slant,* notably its consistency; (4) *letter size* (tall, middle size, small); (5) *alignment,* or the resting of letters on the base line; and (6) *line quality,* or the consistency of the writing pressure, whether light or heavy.

Two styles of writing taught in the schools are *manuscript,* taught first, and *cursive,* introduced later.

Among the factors contributing to poor handwriting are: (1) improper positioning (of the hand, paper, and/or body); (2) poor control of the arm, hand, and finger muscles; and (3) problems relating to any or all of the characteristics listed by Freeman. (See CURSIVE WRITING; MANUSCRIPT WRITING; and PALMER METHOD.)

References: Frank N. Freeman, "An Analytical Scale for Judging Handwriting," *Elementary School Journal,* Volume 15, 1915; John M. Kean and Carl Personke, *The Language Arts: Teaching and Learning in the Elementary School,* New York: St. Martin's Press, 1976; Marie Marcus, *Diagnostic Teaching of the Language Arts,* New York: John Wiley and Sons, 1977.

HARD DISC, an external data storage unit. It is useful if a great deal of storage space is necessary since the hard discs can store more data than floppy discs. They are made of rigid aluminum platters which support a highly polished oxide recording surface. Invented before floppy discs, hard discs have been the primary external storage system for large computers. Like floppy discs, they are random access storage devices.

Hard discs transfer data more quickly than floppy discs because they spin faster. However, hard discs are noisier and more sensitive than floppy discs. It is their sensitivity that has slowed their use in portable computers. A practical application of the hard disc is word processing. An entire book can be stored on a single hard disc, making storage and alterations of text much simpler. (See FLOPPY DISC and RANDOM ACCESS MEMORY.)

References: Grace Murray Hopper and Steven L. Mandell, *Understanding Computers,* St. Paul, MN: West Publishing Company, 1984; David R. Sullivan, et al., *Computing Today: Microcomputer Concepts and Applications,* Boston: Houghton Mifflin Company, 1985.

HARDWARE, COMPUTER, that part of the computer system made up of electronic and electromechanical equipment (e.g. transistors, resistors, chips, circuits, diodes, gates, and disks). Computer hardware includes: operator console, central processing unit (CPU), input-output terminals, printers, displays, and special-purpose devices. Computer hardware cannot function without computer software (computer programs). Computer software is written either to solve problems for the user or to operate the computer. Hardware and software are integrated into what is commonly called a computer system. (See COMPUTER LANGUAGE and COMPUTER PROGRAM.)

References: Marshall D. Abrams and Philip G. Stein, *Computer Hardware and Software: An Interdisciplinary Introduction,* Reading, MA: Addison-Wesley Publishing Company, 1973; Boris Beizer, *The Architecture and Engineering of Digital Computer Complexes* (Volume 1), New York: Plenum Press, 1971.

HARVARD PROJECT PHYSICS—See PROJECT PHYSICS

HASKELL INDIAN JUNIOR COLLEGE, a postsecondary school for Indians located in Lawrence, Kansas. The college, established in 1884, is one of the oldest educational institutions to be supported by the federal government. It is operated by the Bureau of Indian Affairs to fulfill, in part, the government's treaty obligations to the Indian people. Enrollment at the college is limited to students who are at least one-fourth Indian. Tuition, room, and board are free. Haskell Indian Junior College won Kansas state accreditation as a junior college in 1970. It confers Associate of Arts and Associate of Applied Science degrees as well as work-skill diplomas and certificates. Haskell's faculty is divided into five instructional divisions and a Learning Resource Center. It enrolls approximately 1,100 students who come from over 100 Indian tribes and 31 states.

Reference: Haskell Indian Junior College, *Haskell Indian Junior College Bulletin, 1977-79,* Lawrence, KS: The College, 1976.

HATCH ACT, federal legislation enacted in 1887 that sought to strengthen agricultural research at already established land-grant agricultural institutions. Congress originally provided $15,000 to each state annually for research and experimentation to be carried out in agricultural experiment stations under the direction of land-grant colleges.

Section 2 of the act required the experiment stations to conduct "original researches or verify experiments on the physiology of plants and animals; the diseases to which they are severely subject, with the remedies for the same; the chemical composition of useful plants at their different stages of growth; the comparative advantages of rotative cropping as pursued under a varying series of crops; the capacity of new plants or trees for acclimation; the analysis of soils and water; the chemical composition of manures, natural or artificial, with experiments designed to test their comparative effects on crops of different kinds; the adaptation and value of grasses and forage plants; the composition and digestibility of the different kinds of food for domestic animals; the scientific and economic questions involved in the production of butter and cheese; and such other researches or experiments bearing directly on the agricultural industry of the United States" (pp. 440-41). Section 4 prescribed that bulletins and progress reports be published at each station at least once in three months.

This legislation is not to be confused with Chapter 410 (also known as the Hatch Act, but a different one) that, when originally passed by the 76th Congress, specifically precluded any officer or employee of the federal government from taking part in political management or in political campaigns.

References: Lloyd E. Blauch, *Federal Cooperation in Agricultural Extension Work, Vocational Education, and Vocational Rehabilitation,* New York: Arno Press and the New York Times, 1969; Chapter 314, *United States Statutes at Large, December 1885 to March 1887,* Washington, DC: U.S. Government Printing Office, 1887; Chapter 410, *United States Statutes at Large, 1939* (Volume 53, Part 2), Washington, DC: U.S. Government Printing Office, 1939.

HAWLEY, GIDEON (September 26, 1785–July 17, 1870), educational administrator who was the first state Superintendent of Common Schools (New York) in the United States (1813–21) until his office was abolished. Because of his success in organizing the schools of his state, he came to be known as the Father of the Common Schools in New York. Hawley served as Secretary of the Board of Regents, University of the State of New York, from 1814 to 1841, and helped to establish New York's first normal school (Albany, 1843).

A lawyer by profession, Hawley was also a pioneer in the development of railroading in New York. He served on the Board of Regents of the Smithsonian Institution, Washington, DC (1846–61). His book *Essays on Truth and Knowledge* was published in 1856.

References: Norman J. Bauer, "Hawley, Gideon" in John F. Ohles (Editor), *Biographical Dictionary of American Educators* (Volume 2), Westport, CT: Greenwood Press,

1978; *Who Was Who: Historical Volume 1607-1896*, Chicago: Marquis Who's Who, 1963.

HAWTHORNE EFFECT, a condition in which the very fact that a person knows that he or she is involved in an experiment leads to performance improvement by that person. For example, if teachers and students know that they are involved in a research study, the chances are great that improvement will be generated by virtue of their having such knowledge. Thus, the Hawthorne Effect and not the experimental technique itself may account for whatever improvement may be noted. In such cases, individuals are motivated to do better by virtue of being selected.

The name Hawthorne comes from a series of experiments performed at the Hawthorne Plant of the Western Electric Company, Chicago, from 1927 to 1932. Studies on illumination in three departments found that the attention given workers generated increases in production.

References: Walter R. Borg and Meredith D. Gall, *Educational Research* (Fifth Edition), New York: Longman, Inc., 1989; W. James Popham, *Educational Evaluation* (Second Edition), Englewood Cliffs, NJ: Prentice-Hall, 1988; Rodney W. Skager and Carl Weinberg, *Fundamentals of Educational Research*, Glenview, IL: Scott, Foresman and Company, 1971.

HAZELWOOD SCHOOL DISTRICT v. KUHL-MEIER (case #86–836), a United States Supreme Court case (January 13, 1988), where the Court ruled 5–3 that a Missouri high school principal had the right to delete articles on divorce and teenage pregnancy from a school newspaper. It was a censorship and First Amendment case.

Justice Bryon R. White wrote the majority opinion for the Court. In the decision, he made the distinction between tolerating particular student speech (as in *Tinker v. Des Moines* Independent School District) and whether the First Amendment requires a school to affirmatively promote particular student speech. Educators do not violate free speech by having editorial control over style and content in school-sponsored expressive activities (in this case, the articles were written and edited as part of a journalism class) if such action is related to legitimate pedagogical concerns. (See *TINKER v. DES MOINES INDEPENDENT SCHOOL DISTRICT.*)

Reference: Cheryl M. Fields, "Supreme Court Backs Official Who Censored School Newspaper, Skirts Issue at Colleges," *The Chronicle of Higher Education*, Volume 34, November 19, January 20, 1988.

HEADMASTER, in the United States, the title usually bestowed upon the academic and executive leader of a nonsectarian private school.

This title has a different meaning in England and some other English-speaking countries where it is used as a synonym for the American "school principal." George Baron pointed out that, in England, the headmaster customarily enjoys considerable decision-making latitude with respect to the local school's program and personnel.

Reference: George Baron, *Society, Schools and Progress in England*, Oxford, England: Pergamon Press, 1965; G. Terry Page and J. B. Thomas, *International Dictionary of Education*, London, England: Kogan Page Ltd., 1977.

HEADSTART—See OPERATION HEADSTART

HEAD TEACHER, an administrative title that, according to Henry Otto and David Sanders, identifies "those who *teach full time* (emphasis ours) throughout the official school day and attend to selected administrative duties during afterschool, evening, and weekend hours" (p. 293). Head teachers, who work almost exclusively at the elementary school level, may or may not be certified as school principals. Surveys conducted by the NEA Department of Elementary School Principals (later renamed the National Association of Elementary School Principals) indicate a marked decrease in educators holding this title. In 1968, 3.8 percent of all elementary school building administrators surveyed were referred to as Head Teachers. By 1978, the percentage dropped to 0.5 percent. (See SUPERVISING PRINCIPAL and TEACHING PRINCIPAL.)

References: Henry J. Otto and David C. Sanders, *Elementary School Organization and Administration* (Fourth Edition), New York: Appleton-Century-Crofts, Inc., 1964; William L. Pharis and Sally B. Zakariya, *The Elementary School Principalship in 1978: A Research Study*, Arlington, VA: National Association of Elementary School Principals, 1979.

HEALTH EDUCATION, one of the largest fields of study allied to physical education. Unlike physical education, which relates to vigorous muscular activity, health education seeks to develop sound health habits, adequate health knowledge, and proper attitudes toward health. It consists of three components: (1) health instruction; (2) health services; and (3) health environment. *Health Instruction* is most often taught as a separate subject field at all levels, Kindergarten through college. Its content may include, but is not limited to, care of the body, disease prevention, sex education, and the problems of smoking, alcohol, and drug abuse. *Health services* refers to the specialized medical services rendered by physicians and nurses. The third component, *health environment*, is concerned with the total setting within which schooling takes place and is normally the responsibility of the school principal and his/her custodial staff. (See HEALTH SERVICES.)

References: Charles A. Bucher, *Administration of School Health and Physical Education Programs* (Seventh Edition), St. Louis, MO: The C. V. Mosby Company, 1979; Reuben B. Frost, *Physical Education; Foundations, Practices, Principles*, Reading, MA: Addison-Wesley Publishing Company, 1975; Jesse H. Haag, *School Health Program* (Third Edition), Philadelphia: Lea and Febiger, 1972; Charles C. Wilson and Elizabeth A. Wilson (Editors), *Healthful School Environment*, Washington, DC and Chicago: National Education Association of the United States and the American Medical Association, 1969.

HEALTH INSURANCE—See HOSPITAL INSURANCE

HEALTH-OCCUPATIONS EDUCATION, a general term used to describe the formal education (curriculum) and training, preservice and inservice, relating to the health professions. Such education may include on-the-job training, short training programs, or intensive as well as extensive programs leading to a degree and/or credentials. Included among the health professions are the dental occupations (e.g. dentists, dental assistants, hygienists), medical practitioners (e.g. chiropractors, optometrists, physicians), medical technologists, medical assistants, nurses, therapists, rehabilitation personnel, health service administrators, and pharmacists.

Many vocational high schools, trade schools, hospitals, private schools, community colleges, colleges and universities, and professional and graduate schools are involved in different facets of health-occupations education. Earning of state certificates/licenses or the passing of examinations are frequently required before one can engage in the practice of a particular health occupation.

Numerous teacher training institutions prepare health-occupations educators to work in vocational high schools, trade schools, and community colleges. (See HEALTH PROFESSIONS.)

References: E. Joy Hill and Julie Cave, *Catalog of Performance Objectives: Criterion-Referenced Measures and Performance Guides for Dental Assistants*, Frankfort, KY: Bureau of Vocational Education, 1975; George E. Miller and Thomás Fülöp (Editors), *Educational Strategies for the*

Health Professions, Geneva, Switzerland: World Health Organizations, 1974; *Occupational Outlook Handbook, 1980-81 Edition*, Washington, DC: U.S. Department of Labor, 1980.

HEALTH, PHYSICAL EDUCATION, AND RECREATION (HPER), a curriculum category that combines the fields of *health education, physical education,* and *recreation.* Because all three fields are closely interrelated, it is not uncommon for universities and colleges to offer courses through one department/school that include all three fields and frequently carry HPER as its title. All three areas include study in subject fields such as physiology, movement, kinesiology, clinical medicine, physics, biomechanics, athletics, sports medicine, psychology, sociology, and environmental studies. Higher education students can specialize in any of the three areas and pursue programs reflecting their individual interests (e.g. recreation for the physically handicapped, physical education for the elderly).

In recent years, *dance* has been added to many programs as a fourth field within this curriculum category. In some institutions of higher education, departments/schools of HPER have had their titles broadened to include this fourth category and are known as departments/schools of HPERD. (See DANCE; HEALTH EDUCATION; PHYSICAL EDUCATION; and RECREATION.)

References: Charles A. Bucher, *Foundations of Physical Education* (Eighth Edition), St. Louis, MO: The C. V. Mosby Company, 1979; Richard G. Kraus and Barbara L. Bates, *Recreation Leadership and Supervision: Guidelines for Professional Development*, Philadelphia: W. B. Saunders Company, 1975; Michael L. Pollock, et al., *Health and Fitness Through Physical Activity*, New York: John Wiley and Sons, 1978; Roy J. Shephard and Hugues Lavalle (Editors), *Physical Fitness Assessment: Principles, Practices, and Application*, Springfield, IL: Charles C. Thomas, Publisher, 1978.

HEALTH PROFESSIONS, or health occupations, a general term that includes all of the health-delivery and health-related professions (e.g. school nurses, physicians, dentists, pharmacists, dental assistants, medical technologists, medical technicians and medical assistant occupations, nurses, therapists, dietitians, dispensing opticians, and others who render health services).

In 1978, approximately 4,400,000 people worked in the various health professions. Of them, the physician is the highest paid. Generally, his/her education is the longest, most expensive, and most intensive. In contrast, various health aides are the lowest paid; their work requires the least amount of training, sometimes consisting of on-the-job training only. (See HEALTH-OCCUPATIONS EDUCATION.)

References: Ruth F. Odgers and Burness G. Wenberg (Editors), *Introduction to Health Professions*, St. Louis, MO: C. V. Mosby Company, 1972; *Occupational Outlook Handbook* (1980–81 Edition), Washington, DC: U.S. Department of Labor, 1980; John Rafferty (Editor), *Health Manpower and Productivity*, Lexington, VA; Lexington Books, 1974.

HEALTH SERVICES, programs that provide health care. They can range from services offered to the general population in large urban hospitals to those available in small county offices. In many poor areas, clinics are the prime source of the delivery of health care.

School health services (K–12) are administered by health professionals working with and/or employed by the school district. Nurses or nurse-teachers provide first aid, encourage good health practices, and, when certified, many also teach health subjects. Schools are usually restricted by state laws and regulations that limit the level and extent of treatment and drugs they can provide to students. Physicians and psychiatrists are sometimes engaged to provide consultant services or to provide treatment authorized by state law.

Colleges usually have a health service facility for students and, sometimes, staff/faculty. Here, short-term services of an emergency nature are provided, with limitations frequently imposed concerning the type of medicine available. They sometimes sponsor physical examinations for those students who may need them; innoculations may also be provided. (See HEALTH EDUCATION and SCHOOL NURSE.)

References: Annette Lynch, *Redesigning School Health Services*, New York: Human Services Press, Inc., 1983; Kerry J. Redican, Larry K. Olsen, and Charles R. Baffi, *Organization of School Health Programs*, New York: Macmillan Publishing Company, 1986.

HEARING CLINICIAN —See AUDIOLOGIST

HEARING LOSS, a decrease (deficiency) in the ability of a person to hear sounds. Hearing loss is an auditory defect such that certain responses made by hearing persons will not be made by individuals who suffer from a hearing loss. All individuals whose auditory skills fall below normal are said to suffer a hearing loss. The degree of loss may be mild, moderate, severe, or profound.

All people with a hearing loss are classified as "hearing impaired." "Deafness" and "hard of hearing" are subgroups of the *hearing impaired* category. The hard of hearing limits are: 150 db at the low end and 95 db at the high end of the decibel scale. A deaf person has auditory channels that cannot or do not serve normally as a hearing organ. A true deaf person can hear no sounds. (See DEAFNESS.)

References: Julia Davis, *Our Forgotten Children: Hard-of-Hearing Pupils in the Schools*, Minneapolis, MN: University of Minnesota, Audio Visual Library Service, 1977; John J. O'Neill, *The Hard of Hearing*, Englewood Cliffs, NJ: Prentice-Hall, Inc., 1964; Donald F. Moores, *Educating the Deaf: Psychology, Principles, and Practices*, Boston: Houghton Mifflin Company, 1978.

HEGGE-KIRK-KIRK METHOD, a remedial reading method developed for use with children who are mentally retarded or those who are reading disabled and functioning at first-, second-, or third-grade reading levels. It is a highly structured phonic method, especially in its early stages, with much emphasis placed on drill. Considerable time is devoted to practice in blending sounds, starting with relatively simple letter combinations (e.g. oo, sh) and proceeding to more complex combinations such as those italicized in these sample words: *pre*vent, solu*tion*, or fan*cy*.

The method is multisensory, making use of the V-A-K-T approach. Certain teaching techniques are stressed as aids to learning, including emphasis on left-to-right progression and the use of concrete associative aids (clues). Several principles of learning such as repetition, one response for one symbol, and social reinforcement are used. (See LEFT-TO-RIGHT ORIENTATION and V-A-K-T.)

References: George Kaluger and Clifford J. Kolson, *Reading and Learning Disabilities* (Second Edition), Columbus, OH: Charles E. Merrill Publishing Company, 1978; Samuel A. Kirk, et al., *Teaching Reading to Slow and Disabled Learners*, Boston: Houghton Mifflin Company, 1978.

HERBART, JOHANN E. (May 4, 1776–August 14, 1841), considered the "father of the scientific study of education." Herbart was born in Germany and taught at the University of Göttingen and Königsberg where he wrote books on philosophy and pedagogy. His educational contributions included: (1) establishing one of the earliest pedagogical seminaries attached to a university, at Königsberg; (2) formulation of a multistep teaching-learning theory composed of preparation, presentation, association, and application; and (3) suggesting that academic subjects be correlated around a concentrated core.

Herbart approached education using complex concepts of metaphysics and psychology. He saw education related directly to other bodies of knowledge and built these relationships into a very involved system that included elements of ethics, metaphysics, psychology, and pedagogy. Primarily, Herbart sought to make children moral rather than learned or technologically competent.

Herbart did not gain international fame during his lifetime. It was not until 1865 that Herbartianism became a major force in education. His fame reached American shores at the end of the 19th century. In 1895, the Herbart Club became the National Herbart Society for the Scientific Study of Teaching that, in 1902, became the National Society for the Study of Education. By 1906, the Herbart movement began to wane. (See NATIONAL SOCIETY FOR THE STUDY OF EDUCATION.)

References: Harold B. Dunkel, *Herbart and Herbartianism,* Chicago: University of Chicago Press, 1970; Johann E. Herbart, *The Science of Education,* Boston: D. C. Heath and Company, 1896; Daniel N. Robinson (Editor), *Significant Contributions to the History of Psychology, 1750–1920,* Washington, DC: University Publications of America, 1977.

HEREDITY, the process by which an organism produces other similar organisms, with qualities transmitted from parents to children. Because there is considerable interrelationship between heredity and environment, it is often difficult to isolate a purely inherited trait. For example, heredity may play a role in the *probability* that an individual may come down with a particular disease (e.g. cancer, heart disease). It also plays a role in determining some physical characteristics. Yet, studies examining the relationships between heredity and environment have cast doubt on earlier definitions of inherited traits or characteristics. Prenatal care is one example, demonstrating that environment can affect child development.

The effects of heredity on human behavior may be more indirect than direct; such effects have not been confirmed, however. This is particularly true with respect to its effects on intelligence.

Some scientists feel that the effects of heredity can be controlled through genetic engineering.

The subject of genetic engineering has precipitated heated debates among geneticists and social scientists alike.

References: Anne Anastasi, *Common Fallacies about Heredity, Environment, and Human Behavior,* Iowa City, IA: American College Testing Program, 1973; Charles R. Darwin, *The Descent of Man and Selection in Relation to Sex* (Second Edition), New York: D. Appleton and Company, 1902; Laurence E. Karp, *Genetic Engineering,* Chicago: Nelson-Hall, Inc., 1976; Alberto Oliverio (Editor), *Genetics, Environment and Intelligence,* Amsterdam, Holland: Elsevier North-Holland, Inc., 1977.

HERZBERG, FREDERICK—See MOTIVATION-HYGIENE THEORY

HETEROGENEOUS GROUPING—See HOMOGENEOUS AND HETEROGENEOUS GROUPING

HEURISTIC, refers to methods of instruction and learning that focus on discovery and on the solving of problems. In keeping with this form of instruction, students are encouraged to discover solutions, principles, theories, and laws by themselves rather than just being passive receivers of knowledge. The teacher facilitates heuristic learning by providing opportunities for the learner to question, to challenge, to draw inferences, and to reach conclusions. The heuristic approach is not new to teaching; it was used by Socrates in ancient Athens. Other terms sometimes used for the heuristic approach to learning are inquiry method, discovery method, deductive and inductive methods, reflective thinking, and problem solving. (See DEDUCTIVE APPROACH; DISCOVERY METHOD; INQUIRY METHOD; and SOCRATIC METHOD.)

References: Leonard H. Clark and Irving S. Starr, *Secondary School Teaching Methods* (Third Edition), New York: Macmillan Publishing Company, Inc., 1976; Bruce R. Joyce, *New Strategies for Social Education,* Chicago: Science Research Associates, Inc., 1972; Daniel Tanner and Laurel N. Tanner, *Curriculum Development: Theory into Practice* (Second Edition), New York: Macmillan Publishing Company, Inc., 1980.

HIDDEN CURRICULUM, that part of the school curriculum that is not explicit and public. The cultures of both the school and the classroom impact student development. For example, the number of square feet per student in a classroom, the relation of teachers to students, the reward system, and even the physical environment of the school are elements of the curriculum. Patience, competitiveness, and compliant behaviors are a few of the skills learned as a result of different dimensions of the hidden curriculum. Time is a part of the unwritten curriculum as well—both its use and location. The arts are rarely taught to elementary children in the morning; when students are "fresh," they are exposed to the rigors of the "basic" skills, thus prioritizing those subjects intellectually. It has been suggested that the placement of subjects into time periods has an effect on student commitment to the subject; switching subjects each 50 minutes may not encourage extended involvement. In general, the hidden curriculum of a school is dependent on the kind of place it is, the organizational structure it employs, and the approach to teaching it espouses.

References: Michael W. Apple, *Ideology and Curriculum,* London: Routledge and Kegan Paul, 1979; Elliot W. Eisner, *The Educational Imagination* (Second Edition), New York: MacMillan Publishing Company, 1985; Philip Jackson, *Life in the Classroom,* New York: Holt, Rinehart and Winston Inc., 1968; Mark Lepper and Paul Greene (Editors), *The Hidden Cost of Reward,* New York: Holsted Press, 1978.

HIERARCHY OF NEEDS—See MASLOW'S HIERARCHY OF NEEDS

HIGHER HORIZONS, a New York City public schools program that sought to raise the achievement and aspiration levels of disadvantaged students by providing them with extra (compensatory) services. Higher Horizons had its origins in a demonstration project, begun in 1956, that involved Harlem's Junior High School No. 43 and George Washington High School. In that pilot program, half of the junior high school's seventh, eighth, and ninth graders (N = 1,400) were provided with: (1) small-class remedial reading instruction; (2) expanded guidance services (1 counselor: 200 students) that included work with parents; and (3) enrichment experiences such as field trips and special counseling services provided by outside career and college counselors. Special appropriations averaging $100 per pupil at the junior high school and $250 at the senior high school levels supported these extra services.

The pilot program's results, as reported by school officials, were successful. For example, of the 114 pupils entering George Washington High School in 1959, approximately 75 percent went on to complete high school. Of 85 students graduating in 1962, 51 went on to some form of higher education.

The program was expanded in 1959 under the name Higher Horizons. It involved 52 elementary schools and 13 junior high schools, grades 3–9; in 1962, 10 high schools were added. At the high school level, much program responsibility was vested in the language arts department. Research reports indicated that, at the high school levels, the program succeeded in reducing the absence rate, improved classroom behavior, and improved teacher morale.

Higher Horizons, when extended to schools throughout the city, did not prove to be as effective as was the pilot program. Numerous reasons, including poor financial support, have been offered to explain this fact.

References: Regina Barnes, "Higher Horizons: A Promising Program for Secondary Schools," *Clearinghouse,* October 1965; Mary E. Meade, "A View at Higher Horizons," *High Points,* February 1965; Diane Ravitch, *The Great School Wars: New York City, 1805–1973: A History of the Public Schools as Battlefield of Social Change,* New York: Basic Books, Inc., Publishers, 1974; Frederick Shaw, "Educating Culturally Deprived Youth in Urban Centers," *Phi Delta Kappan,* November 1963.

HIGH SCHOOL—See SECONDARY SCHOOL

HIGH SCHOOL: A REPORT ON SECONDARY EDUCATION IN AMERICA—See NATIONAL REFORM REPORTS (1980–86)

HIGH SCHOOL AND BEYOND, the second of two longitudinal studies being carried out by the National Center for Education Statistics (NCES). It was designed to complement the center's initial longitudinal study, "The High School Class of 1972." The 1980 high school sophomores and seniors (36,000 from each class) included in the "High School and Beyond" study were enrolled in approximately 1,100 public and private secondary schools. By design, black and Hispanic students were more heavily represented than in the total population at large.

Much of the original data collected about each of the study's participants was identical to data collected in behalf of students who are part of the "High School Class of 1972" study. This comparability of information will permit the surveyors to identify between-group similarities and differences in the years ahead. Additional information about students included in the 1980 study was also collected (e.g. data about parents of the seniors).

NCES plans to survey subsamples of the "High School and Beyond" participants every three years, with particular attention to be given to "the educational, vocational, and personal development of young people as they move from high school into adult life" (p. 23). (See HIGH SCHOOL CLASS OF 1972; LONGITUDINAL STUDIES; and NATIONAL CENTER FOR EDUCATION STATISTICS.)

Reference: Iris Garfield, *The Condition of Education (Part 2): NCES Programs and Plans,* Washington, DC: National Center for Education Statistics, U.S. Department of Education, 1980.

HIGH SCHOOL CLASS OF 1972, the first of two longitudinal studies being carried out by the National Center for Education Statistics (NCES). A total of 21,000 seniors who were attending 1,200 public and private schools in 1972 are the study's subjects. The sample was deliberately skewed to include a disproportionately larger sample of schools located in low-income areas. Original data collected about each subject included information such as test scores, career-plan information, type of high school curriculum completed, and grade-point average. Follow-up surveys of the 1972 seniors, carried out in 1973, 1974, 1976, and 1979, elicited information about their post-high school educational experiences, marriage and family, attitudes, and aspirations.

Preliminary findings, reported in 1980 by NCES, indicated that: (1) subjects were inclined to be unrealistic about their career aspirations (more than half indicated a preference for professional-technical careers); (2) high school curricula appear to have had little relation to graduates' success in the labor market; and (3) factors such as socioeconomic status, family income, and ability correlated positively with student success.

NCES plans to continue surveying this population of subjects in the years ahead. (See HIGH SCHOOL AND BEYOND; LONGITUDINAL STUDIES; and NATIONAL CENTER FOR EDUCATION STATISTICS.)

Reference: Iris Garfield, *The Condition of Education (Part 2): NCES Programs and Plans,* Washington, DC: National Center for Education Statistics, U.S. Department of Education, 1980.

HIGH SCHOOL EQUIVALENCY DIPLOMA —See TEST OF GENERAL EDUCATIONAL DEVELOPMENT

HINDU-ARABIC NUMERATION SYSTEM, official name for our base-ten number system, which was conceived by the Hindus and introduced to Europe by the Arabs. The first country reported to have used the system widely was India. Historians believe that when first introduced (300–600 A. D.), the system consisted of nine numerals; the zero was added two or three centuries later. The Hindu-Arabic numeration system was not used widely in Europe until the 17th century, although some Europeans had known of its existence 500 years earlier.

The advantage of this particular numeration system is that all mathematical processes can be carried out without the aid of mechanical devices such as the abacus. (See ABACUS.)

References: Rosalie Jensen, *Exploring Mathematical Concepts and Skills in the Elementary School,* Columbus, OH: Charles E. Merrill Publishing Company, 1973; D. E. Smith and W. J. Le Veque, "Numerals and Numeral Systems" in *Encyclopaedia Britannica* (Volume 16), Chicago: Encyclopaedia Britannica, Inc., 1968.

HISTOGRAM, also known as a bar graph. A histogram is a graphic method of displaying a basic set of data such that a number of frequencies (observations) fall or are grouped within a set cell, boundary, or class interval. The cell boundaries have a determined set width (e.g. 28.5–31.5, 31.5–34.5). The height of each bar is determined by the number of observations included in the cell boundary. If there were 205 observations with scores ranging from 29.39 to 41.00, frequencies might be grouped and displayed as shown on page 249. Since observations fall within a cell, there is no way a single observation can be isolated through the use of a histogram.

Histograms can also be used to display nominal data graphically. For example, percentages of student participants, grouped by grade, could be displayed as shown on page 264.

References: Harold O. Kiess, *Statistical Concepts for the Behavioral Sciences,* Boston: Allyn and Bacon, 1989; David S. Moore and George P. McCabe, *Introduction to the Practice of Statistics,* New York: W. H. Freeman and Company, 1989; Gilbert Sax, *Principles of Educational and Psychological Measurement and Evaluation* (Third Edition), Belmont, CA: Wadsworth Publishing Company, 1989.

HISTORICAL RESEARCH, a research procedure that, according to Robert Daniels, involves: (1) finding evidence of past events; (2) sifting, sorting, and interpreting the evidence; and (3) showing what really happened, and how and why. In some cases, generalizations can be made to allow for analogies and predictions.

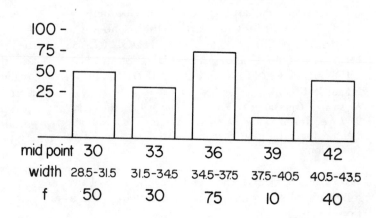

Histogram

mid point	30	33	36	39	42
width	28.5-31.5	31.5-34.5	34.5-37.5	37.5-40.5	40.5-43.5
f	50	30	75	10	40

Historical research has methodological rigor that includes considerations/factors such as definitions, assumptions, stating the problem, hypothesis(es), criteria of proof, analysis of sources, establishment of authenticity and credibility, and internal and external synthesis. Historical research can be interdisciplinary (with anthropology, sociology, economics, etc. included). Sources may be found in different parts of the world, although many primary and secondary sources are discovered in American libraries, archives, private documents, and collections. Historical research, although primarily based on literature, can also be quantitative (e.g. the analysis of school board elections from 1850 to 1900). In some research, information used for analysis is collected through interviews (spoken memories) of those involved in an event. This is called oral history. (See ORAL HISTORY.)

References: Walter R. Borg and Meredith D. Gall, *Educational Research: An Introduction* (Fifth Edition), New York: Longman, Inc., 1989; Philip C. Brooks, *Research in Archives*, Chicago: University of Chicago Press, 1969; James Hooper, *Oral History*, Chapel Hill, NC: University of North Carolina Press, 1979; Fred N. Kerlinger, *Foundations of Behavioral Research* (Third Edition), New York: Holt, Rinehart and Winston, Inc., 1986; Carla J. Stoffle and Simon Karter, *Materials and Methods for History Research*, New York: Libraryworks, 1979.

HIV (HUMAN IMMUNODEFICIENCY VIRUS)—See ACQUIRED IMMUNE DEFICIENCY SYNDROME

HOLMES GROUP, initially a consortium of education deans, from research universities in the United States who were concerned with the quality of teacher preparation. In 1983, the Johnson Foundation sponsored a meeting of 17 education deans to investigate ways to improve the quality of teacher education. The original deans' group was ex-

Histogram Showing Percentages by Grade

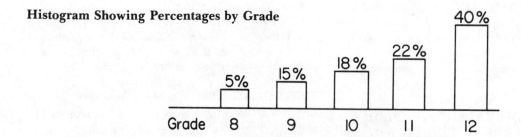

panded to 23 several months later. They met at the Johnson Foundation's Wingspread Conference Center to discuss reform in teacher education. Meetings continued for 18 months, culminating with a report entitled *Tomorrow's Teachers* (1986). The group was partially funded through the United States Secretary of Education Discretionary Fund (Secretary Terrell Bell), the Ford Foundation, the Carnegie Corporation of New York, and the *New York Times* Foundation. The group was named after Henry W. Holmes, Dean of the Harvard Graduate School of Education in the 1920s. Invitations for charter membership in the Holmes Group were issued to 123 institutions in the summer of 1986. At least 1 public university in each state was invited to join. (See *TOMORROW'S TEACHERS, A REPORT OF THE HOLMES GROUP.*)

References: Frank B. Murray, "Goals for the Reform of Teacher Education: An Executive Summary of the Holmes Group Report," *Phi Delta Kappan*, Volume 68, Number 1, 1986; Holmes Group, *Tomorrow's Teachers, A Report of the Holmes Group*, East Lansing, MI: The Holmes Group Inc., 1986.

HOME ADVISOR—See HOME DEMONSTRATION AGENT

HOMEBOUND TEACHER, the teacher who instructs students who, for physical or mental reasons, are unable to attend school and will likely be absent for a significant time. Such teachers tend to be generalists. They teach basic courses such as reading, mathematics, and social studies. Although the homebound teacher develops his/her own program, it is usually similar to the program being taught in the regular classroom. The amount of work, expectations, and scope of program offered through homebound instruction are, in part, determined by the student's disability. Homebound teachers also work with children who are hospitalized for an extended time.

Rules and regulations governing homebound instruction are variable. Most homebound teachers are fully qualified and certified as regular and/or special education teachers. With the advent of mainstreaming and implementation of laws governing the education of exceptional children, the need for homebound instruction for certain children is expected to decline because many of these children will be attending school.

References: Leslie W. Kindred, et al., *The Intermediate Schools*, Englewood Cliffs, NJ: Prentice-Hall, Inc., 1968; Charles W. Telford and James M. Sawrey, *The Excep-*

tional Individual (Second Edition), Englewood Cliffs, NJ: Prentice-Hall, Inc., 1972; William R. Van Osdol and Don G. Shane, *An Introduction to Exceptional Children* (Second Edition), Dubuque, IA: Wm. C. Brown Company, Publishers, 1974.

HOME DEMONSTRATION AGENT, professional home economist who gives instruction in the areas of home economics, family living, child care, social and cultural adjustment, and consumer needs. Such instruction is offered on site and, usually, in rural areas. The position of home demonstration agent was established in 1914 with the passage of the Smith-Lever Act as part of the newly created Cooperative Agricultural Extension Service. Many home demonstration agents, although employed by land-grant colleges, work out of county offices.

Home demonstration agents are usually individuals who hold home economics degrees or who have had extensive course work in a variety of home economic subjects. They work with children and youth (e.g. 4-H Clubs), adults, and the elderly. (See HOME ECONOMICS; LAND GRANT COLLEGES; and SMITH-LEVER ACT.)

References: Marjorie East, *Home Economics: Past, Present, and Future*, Boston: Allyn and Bacon, Inc., 1980; Jeanne Paris, *Your Future as a Home Economist*, New York: Richards Rosen Press, Inc., 1970; Mildred Thurow Tate, *Home Economics as a Profession* (Second Edition), New York: McGraw-Hill Book Company, 1973.

HOME ECONOMICS, a field of study usually divided into at least five parts: (1) housing; (2) foods and nutrition; (3) clothing and textiles; (4) human development and the family; and (5) home management and family economics. Elements of philosophy, the arts, literature, chemistry, biology, psychology, sociology, economics, mathematics, usually in applied form, are to be found in each of these five components.

Although some form of home economics teaching is offered at all levels of the school curriculum, formal and structured instruction begins at the secondary school level. Home economics is typically offered in a comprehensive junior, middle, and senior high school as part of the general educational program of the school. It may also be offered with a career focus, either in a comprehensive high school or in a vocational or regional vocational school. At the college level, home economics courses are available for personal development of students. Often, however, students majoring in home economics do so for career and/or inservice preparation purposes. College graduates who have majored in home economics are usually eligible to pursue such careers as home economics teacher, fashion designer, dietitian, nutritionist, or specialist in child development. Programs and careers in home economics are open to both males and females. (See AREA VOCATIONAL EDUCATION SCHOOL and VOCATIONAL HOME ECONOMICS.)

References: Marjorie East, *Home Economics: Past, Present, and Future,* Boston: Allyn and Bacon, Inc., 1980; Donna Goldfein, *Everywoman's Guide to Time Management,* Millbrae, CA: Les Femmes Publishers, 1977; Eileen E. Quigley, *Introduction to Home Economics* (Second Edition), New York: Macmillan Publishing Company, Inc., 1974; Kathryn E. Walker and Margaret E. Woods, *Time Use: A Measure of Household Production of Family Goods and Services,* Washington, DC: Center for the Family of the Home Economics Association, 1976.

HOME ECONOMICS-RELATED OCCUPATIONS (HERO), those occupations that fall within the broad field of home economics. Examples are home economics teacher (high school, college), dietitian, interior decorator, stylist, dressmaker, cook, chef, hostess, nursery school or early childhood teacher, textile researcher, household equipment consultant, home economist in business, and apparel designer. Each includes some homemaking activities as part of its occupational preparation. HERO covers all occupational strata, including the semiskilled and even unskilled labor categories. Often, Future Homemakers of America chapters are organized along special interest lines and according to home economics-related occupations. (See FUTURE HOMEMAKERS OF AMERICA.)

References: Home Economics Teacher Educators, *Competencies for Home Economics Teachers,* Ames, IA: Iowa State University Press, 1978; Frances T. Parker, *Home Economics: An Introduction to a Dynamic Profession,* New York: Macmillan Publishing Company, Inc., 1980; Mildred Thurow Tate, *Home Economics as a Profession* (Second Edition), New York: McGraw-Hill Book Company, 1973.

HOMEMAKING, those courses in the school curriculum (usually, but not exclusively, in home economics) that focus on skills and activities needed (1) to establish a good home, and (2) to satisfy the needs of family members living in the home. Homemaking covers a variety of skills and topics including home management, nutrition, child care, cooking equipment selection and use, finances, psychology, interior design, values, clothing selection, and clothing repair. (See FAMILY RE-

SOURCES EDUCATION and HOME ECONOMICS.)

References: Marjorie East, *Home Economics: Past, Present, and Future,* Boston: Allyn and Bacon, Inc., 1980; Eleanore L. Kohlmann, *Home Economics for Young Men: A Teaching Guide,* Ames, IA: The Iowa University Press, 1975; Bess Myerson, *The Complete Consumer Book: How to Buy Everything Wisely and Well,* New York: Simon and Schuster, 1979.

HOME ROOM, originally a period in a middle school or senior high school student's schedule included to permit teachers to perform administrative tasks such as taking of attendance, reading announcements, and collecting of milk money. Its function has since been expanded to include group guidance, career exploration, and club programs as well as assemblies and comparable types of activities.

In large schools, the home room provides students the opportunity to identify with one peer group for at least part of the school day and to develop school or class spirit. Assignment to a home room is frequently done alphabetically rather than by grouping students according to curriculum and/or ability.

The home room may be scheduled at almost any time although the most popular times are either at the beginning of or near the middle of the school day.

References: Mary E. Detjen and Erwin W. Detjen, *Home Room Guidance Program for the Junior High School Years,* New York: Houghton Mifflin Company, 1940; Leslie W. Kindred, et al., *The Intermediate Schools,* Englewood Cliffs, NJ: Prentice-Hall, Inc., 1968; Harry C. McKown, *Home Room Guidance,* New York: McGraw-Hill Book Company, 1934.

HOMEWORK, school assignments that the student is normally expected to complete at home and during nonschool hours. The literature of education reveals two general facts: (1) the teaching profession is not of a common mind with respect to the educational value of homework, and (2) limited research of substance has been undertaken regarding the effects of homework. Arguments used in support of homework assignments, frequently subjective, include: (1) it teaches self-reliance; (2) it improves home-school ties; and (3) it supplements (reinforces) work done in the classroom. Those opposing homework argue that: (1) it has yet to be shown to impact positively on achievement; (2) children need free time after school for play and family activities; and (3) homework assignments are not always carefully thought out by the teacher.

Some general findings indicate that: (1) length of homework assignments tend to increase with educational level; (2) the type of assignment sometimes influences its value; and (3) many school systems require homework, with type of assignment determined by the teacher. The popularity of homework has increased in recent years with some authorities attributing this resurgence to the back-to-the-basics movement.

A National Assessment of Educational Progress (NAEP) survey of 17-year-olds, reported in 1976, indicated that: (1) students who did most homework and least television viewing did best on the NAEP mathematics test; (2) availability of reading materials in the home correlated with high scores; and (3) the absence of a specific space in which to study at home did not have a bearing on test scores.

Elizabeth Yeary offered some suggestions for meaningful home-study assignments: (1) be sure students understand the assignment; (2) limit assignments to concepts/ideas explained in class or understood by the learner; (3) avoid "overassigning" in terms of time; and (4) make assignments interesting.

References: William D. Hedges, "Homework" in Lee C. Deighton (Editor), *The Encyclopedia of Education* (Volume 4), New York: The Macmillan Company and The Free Press, 1971; Wayne H. Holtzman, "Study" in Robert L. Ebel (Editor), *Encyclopedia of Educational Research* (Fourth Edition), New York: The Macmillan Company, 1969; Elizabeth E. Yeary, "What About Homework?" *Today's Education*, September–October 1978.

HOMOGENEOUS AND HETEROGENEOUS GROUPING,

contrasting approaches to the classification and assignment of students to classes or groups. *Homogeneously* grouped students are assigned on the basis of intelligence, ability, or achievement. In schools employing this approach, students are generally rank-ordered and then separated into smaller units such as classes/groups for the "slow," "average," or "bright learners." *Heterogeneously* grouped students are generally assigned without regard to ability or achievement levels. When such random assignments are made, they normally do not cut across grade level lines except when nongrading or other organizational templates stressing individualization of instruction are employed.

One writer (Herbert Thelen), after surveying the literature on grouping, reported no convincing support for the hypothesis that ability grouping fosters academic achievement. The homogeneous vs. heterogeneous controversy in education remains, however, in spite of such conclusions. Special education programs, bilingual programs, and renewed interest in special classes for talented and gifted children have served to rekindle the sparks of this controversy. (See ABILITY GROUPING.)

References: Warren Findley and Miriam Bryan, *The Pros and Cons of Ability Grouping* (PDK Fastback 66), Bloomington, IN: The Phi Delta Kappa Educational Foundation, 1975; James E. Rosenbaum, *Making Inequality: The Hidden Curriculum of High School Tracking,* New York: John Wiley and Sons, 1976; Herbert A. Thelen, *Classroom Grouping for Teachability,* New York: John Wiley and Sons, 1967.

HONORARY DEGREE, an academic degree conferred by an institution of higher education in recognition of an individual's *distinguished public service* or *outstanding creative attainment*. It is less frequently awarded for commercial, vanity, or even publicity reasons.

The first honorary degrees in the United States were awarded by Harvard University in 1692. One of the recipients was Increase Mather, Harvard's President, who received the Doctor of Sacred Theology degree. The indiscriminate and widespread practice of conferring honorary degrees during the latter half of the 19th century precipitated justifiable criticism from numbers of educators. For example, in the 1870s, the number of honorary Ph.D.'s awarded was actually greater than the number of earned ones. The abuses that contributed to this imbalance have long since been corrected.

In recent years, honorary degrees have tended to be doctorates. The most popular, presented in frequency order, are: doctor of laws, doctor of humane letters, doctor of divinity, doctor of science, and doctor of letters.

Common recipients of honorary degrees are college and university presidents, university trustees, educators, scientists, military leaders, authors and artists, and political leaders. The actual number of such degrees was reported annually by the U.S. Office of Education from 1874 to 1944. Presently, the American Council on Education publishes these statistics every four years.

References: Walter C. Eells and Harold A. Haswell, *Academic Degrees: Earned and Honorary Degrees conferred by Institutions of Higher Education in the United States* (OE-5400 8A, Bulletin 1960, No. 28), Washington, DC: Office of Education, U.S. Department of H.E.W., 1960 (Republished by Gale Research Company, Detroit,

1970); Stephen E. Epler, *Honorary Degrees: A Survey of their Use and Abuse*, Washington, DC: American Council on Public Affairs, 1943; Asa S. Knowles (Editor), *The International Encyclopedia of Higher Education* (Volume 1), San Francisco: Jossey-Bass Publishers, 1977.

HONOR ROLL, a periodic listing and announcement of students who have distinguished themselves academically. The roll is published at given times (e.g. term, year) and identifies those pupils who meet or exceed some predetermined standard (e.g. 3.7 grade-point average). In institutions of higher education, the roll is commonly referred to as the "dean's list."

Reference: Combined Glossary: Terms and Definitions from the Handbooks of the State Educational Records and Reports Series, Washington, DC: National Center for Education Statistics, U.S. Department of Health, Education, and Welfare, 1974.

HONORS PROGRAMS, programs or courses, offered in colleges and high schools, that have been designed for high achievers. Because these courses or programs are intended to challenge the intellectually able learner, they present, and have more in-depth subject matter than do regular courses or programs. Candidates for honors work are carefully screened with attention given to factors such as: (1) scores earned on standardized achievement, aptitude, and intelligence tests; (2) recommendations; (3) interviews; (4) past grades; (5) mental and emotional stability; and (6) interest. In the case of high school students, parental approval is usually required as a condition for enrollment.

Generally, acceptance into honors programs is restricted to a limited number of students. Participating faculty members are also selected with care. Honors students are traditionally given more freedom in course selection and the way in which they fulfill course requirements. In some colleges and universities, honors programs or courses are restricted to certain academic departments. In others, the honors programs are administered by larger academic units such as colleges of Arts and Science, Business Administration, or Education.

References: William M. Alexander, *The Changing Secondary Curriculum*, New York: Holt, Rinehart and Winston, Inc., 1967; Arthur M. Cohen, et al., *A Constant Variable*, San Francisco: Jossey-Bass Publishers, 1971; Russell M. Cooper (Editor), *The Two Ends of the Log: Learning and Teaching in Today's College*, Minneapolis, MN: University of Minnesota Press, 1958, Asa S. Knowles (Editor), *The International Encyclopedia of Higher Education* (Volume 1), San Francisco: Jossey-Bass Publishers, 1977.

HOPKINS, MARK (February 4, 1802–June 17, 1887), noted teacher of philosophy and President at Williams College. Hopkins graduated from Williams College in 1824, earned his medical degree at the Berkshire Medical School (1829), and thereupon returned to Williams as Professor of Moral Philosophy and Rhetoric. He was elected to the presidency in 1836 and occupied that office for 36 years. The D.D. degree was conferred upon him by Dartmouth (1837) and Harvard (1841) Universities; the LL.D. was awarded to him by the New York State Board of Regents (1857) and Harvard University (1886).

Hopkins was best remembered for his skill as a teacher. U.S. President James A. Garfield, one of his former students, immortalized him with these words: "The ideal college is Mark Hopkins on one end of a log and a student on the other."

In its 1888 report, the National Education's Committee on Necrology recognized Hopkins as follows: "Teaching was his great work. He could, indeed, do all things well. His quickness of perception, his excellent judgment, his conscientious fidelity, enabled him to succeed in all the work of college administration; but he felt that his place was in the class-room. He was truly a prince among teachers. Probably no college president, no college teacher, has ever impressed young men more strongly" (p. 662).

Hopkins is also remembered for his sermons, speeches, and his writings (e.g. *Lectures on the Moral Science*, 1862; and *An Outline Study of Man*, 1873).

References: I. W. Andrews, "President Mark Hopkins" (Report of Committee on Necrology), Chicago: *The Journal of Proceedings and Addresses of the National Education Association, Session of the Year 1887*, 1888; Frederick Rudolph, *Mark Hopkins and the Log: Williams College, 1836–1872*, New Haven, CT: Yale University Press, 1956.

HORACE'S COMPROMISE: THE DILEMMA OF THE AMERICAN HIGH SCHOOL—See NATIONAL REFORM REPORTS (1980–86)

HORNBOOK, the earliest form of textbook whose use in Europe has been traced as far back as 1450. The hornbook consisted of a printed page over which was placed a transparent horn (a plastic-like sheet) that served to protect the page from the fingers of its many readers. The page was glued to a thin, wooden paddle. Some hornbooks had two pages, one fastened to either side of the paddle.

Hornbooks were used rather widely in England and in America. The earliest ones contained the letters of the alphabet; variations which came later also included prayers and/or religious quotations.

References: Elwood P. Cubberly, *Readings in Public Education in the United States: A Collection of Sources and Readings to Illustrate the History of Educational Practice and Progress in the United States,* Boston: Houghton Mifflin Company, 1934 (Reprinted in 1970 by Greenwood Press); Carter V. Good (Editor), *Dictionary of Education* (Second Edition), New York: McGraw-Hill Book Company, 1959; Andrew W. Tuer, *History of the Horn-Book* (Volume 1), Amsterdam, The Netherlands: S. Emmering, 1971.

HOSPITAL INSURANCE, or health insurance, a form of personal welfare insurance that school boards and other educational agencies often make available to their employees. Such insurance, normally sponsored on a group basis, is a fringe benefit that defrays, partially or totally, surgical and hospital costs that may be incurred should the employee become ill. In some instances, the cost of such insurance is assumed solely by the employer; in others, employer and employee each contribute to the cost.

Hospital insurance programs, Frederick Hill and James Colmey pointed out, "may include: (1) room and board benefits . . . ; (2) allowance for other hospital charges; (3) in-hospital doctor's calls; (4) X-ray and laboratory benefits; (5) radiation therapy; (6) maternity benefits; and (7) surgical benefits based on a standard schedule of operation costs" (p. 211).

References: Frederick W. Hill and James W. Colmey, *School Business Administration in the Smaller Community,* Minneapolis, MN: T. S. Denison and Company, Inc., 1964; Oscar T. Jarvis, et al., *Public School Business Administration and Finance: Effective Policies and Practices,* West Nyack, NY: Parker Publishing Company, Inc., 1967; Francis P. King and Thomas J. Cook, *Benefit Plans in Higher Education,* New York: Columbia University Press, 1980.

HOWARD UNIVERSITY, a private institution of higher education that was organized shortly after the Civil War and chartered by Congress in 1867. Early financial support came from the Freedmen's Bureau. (General Otis H. Howard, whose name the university carries, was a founder of the bureau.) Howard University has been receiving special federal support since its inception, with regular annual appropriations made since 1924. The institution maintains a special relationship with the U.S. government through the U.S. Department of Education.

Although Howard University's enrollment is open to students of all races, its student body is made up largely of black Americans, reflecting the institution's special responsibility for selection and training of black students. Howard University has trained approximately 40,000 black professionals in fields such as law, medicine, theology, education, nursing, pharmacy, dentistry, engineering, architecture, and business. It currently consists of 17 schools and colleges with a combined enrollment of approximately 10,000. The institution attracts students from all states and some 90 foreign countries.

References: *Howard University Bulletin, '80–'81,* Washington, DC: The University, 1980; Office of the Federal Register, National Archives and Records Service, *United States Government Manual, 1980–81,* Washington, DC: U.S. Government Printing Office, 1980.

HUMAN ENGINEERING, the use of human factors in the design and application of equipment, products, and environments to ensure that the latter are of optimal service to human beings. In human engineering, there is an interaction between task analysis, information, and equipment design. The equipment configurations provide information such that there is appropriate man-machine interfacing, operation, and maintenance procedures.

Human engineering includes human sensory processes, information input, visual displays, auditory and tactual displays, speech communications, and various mediation activities. Physical activities such as human motor activities and tool and contact devices are considered. Work space and other environmental (e.g. noise, light) concerns are also part of human engineering. Other names for human engineering are: human factors engineering; biomechanics; engineering psychology; ergonomics (in many European countries); and applied experimental psychology. The field of study is interdisciplinary. Engineers, anthropologists, physicians, physiologists, and psychologists are carrying out research in the area.

References: Ernest T. McCormick, *Human Factors Engineering* (Third Edition), New York: McGraw-Hill Book Company, 1970; David Meister, *Human Factors: Theory and Practice,* New York: Wiley-Interscience, 1971; E. R. Tichouer, *The Biomechanical Basis of Ergonomics,* New York: Wiley-Interscience, 1978.

HUMANISTIC EDUCATION, as used currently, is education that places stress on the social and psychological development of the individual. Intellectual development is also an important part of humanistic education; however, major emphasis is given to self-actualization, feelings, acceptance, concern and respect for others, valuing, social action, interpersonal and human relations, and similar aspects of the human experience. Although there is no universally accepted definition of a humanistic education program, the elements cited above are common to most such programs.

Humanistic education is not new. Educators such as Aristotle, S. Thomas Aquinas, Desiderius, Erasmus, Locke, Rousseau, and Pestalozzi were humanistic in their approaches to education and hence can be considered to have been humanistic educators.

References: Cecil H. Patterson, *Humanistic Education,* Englewood Cliffs, NJ: Prentice-Hall, Inc., 1973; Carl Weinberg (Editor), *Humanistic Foundations of Education,* Englewood Cliffs, NJ: Prentice-Hall, Inc., 1972; Richard H. Weller (Editor), *Humanistic Education: Visions and Realities,* Berkeley, CA: McCutchan Publishing Corporation, 1976.

HUMANISTIC PSYCHOLOGY, a school of psychology that focuses on the whole person rather than any particular personality component. Humanistic psychology is concerned with love, creativity, self-worth, self-actualization, values, affection, and other similar areas of the human experience. It is a "third" force in psychology in relationship to the psychoanalytic and behavioristic schools.

Humanistic psychology has its origins in the works and theories of Abraham Maslow. Humanistic psychologists banded together in the 1960s to form an organization known today as the Association for Humanistic Psychology. (See ASSOCIATION FOR HUMANISTIC PSYCHOLOGY.)

References: Janice T. Gibson and Louis A. Chandler, *Educational Psychology: Mastering Principles and Applications,* Boston: Allyn and Bacon, 1988; James O. Lugo and Gerald I. Hershey, *Living Psychology* (Second Edition), New York: Macmillan Publishing Company, Inc., 1976; Aaron Q. Sartain, et al., *Psychology: Understanding Human Behavior* (Fourth Edition), New York: McGraw-Hill Book Company, 1973.

HUMANITIES, the very broad classification of studies concerned with the experiences and self-expression of man as he searched for the meaning of life. The study of language, the arts, philosophy, and history comprise the core of the humanities. Humanities are distinct from the physical, applied, and social sciences. They are often called "the liberal studies."

Humanities courses are integrative and lend themselves to interdisciplinary teaching. Modern humanities courses tend to focus on the broad experiences of man as opposed to being limited to studies of history or literature that focus on a given theme or historical time period. For example, values and value systems may be studied in some humanities courses; the great social documents (e.g. the Bible, American and French Constitutions, or Magna Carta) may be studied in others.

Humanities courses can be found in both high school and college curricula.

References: Otto Bird, *Cultures in Conflict: An Essay in the Philosophy of the Humanities,* Notre Dame, IN: University of Notre Dame Press, 1976; John Ferguson and Arthur Marwick, *Humanities and the Study of Civilization,* Bletchley, England: Open University Press, 1970; Walter A. Kaufmann, *The Future of the Humanities,* New York: Reader's Digest Press, 1977.

HUMAN RELATIONS, a field of study concerned with the individual and his/her relationships with others in all types of environments and organizations and under varying conditions. Although the individual is an important part of human relations, it is his/her interactions and reactions with others that are the major foci.

The study of human relations includes elements of psychology, sociology, and anthropology. Theories and concepts of human relations grow out of these disciplines. The development of appropriate human relations skills is important in school, industry, business, the home, recreation, and anywhere else where people interact (actively or passively) with each other. Motivation, personality, prior experiences, knowledge, attitudes, facility to communicate, and physical attributes are among the factors that affect human relations. In recent years, human relations has been stressed as a vehicle for improving race relations in the United States.

References: Morton Bard and Joseph Zacker, *The Police and Interpersonal Conflict: The Third-Party Intervention Approaches,* Washington, DC: Police Foundations, 1976; Robert A. Georges and Michael O. Jones, *People Studying People: The Human Element in Fieldwork,* Berkeley, CA: University of California Press, 1980; Robert L. Selman, *The Growth of Interpersonal Understanding and Clinical Analysis,* New York: Academic Press, 1980.

HUMAN SERVICES, a relatively new (and interdisciplinary) service field that embraces formerly separate systems such as health, mental health, corrections, family services, and public aid. Human services lacks a commonly accepted definition for several reasons: (1) it is still an emerging profession; (2) traditionalists in the field's component areas (e.g. health, corrections) tend to see their respective areas as the core of human services; and (3) commitment to the interdisciplinary character of human services has frequently been nominal. Mark Yessian noted that the lack of common definition notwithstanding, human services programs have some basic characteristics: (1) more than one categorical service may be provided; (2) client education as well as client care are provided; (3) the purpose of human services is to help individuals to become self-sufficient; and (4) services are furnished in some areas not yet served by other professionals.

Human services usually provide delivery services (e.g. health, geriatric) and include a strong counseling component.

In recent years, numbers of colleges of education have broadened their offerings to include human services training programs, undergraduate and/or graduate. Some have been motivated by the fact that several components of human services involve teaching roles, others by a desire to offset retrenching enrollments. Other colleges and schools within the university community have also begun to sponsor their own training programs.

References: Robert Agranoff, "Achieving Relevance between Human Services Practice and Human Services Education" in Joann Chenault and Fran Burnford, *Human Services Professional Education: Future Directions,* New York: McGraw-Hill Book Company, 1978; Barbara Brittingham and William F. Kelly, "Teacher Education and Human Services: Pointing the Way Toward Change," *Journal of Teacher Education,* September–October 1980; Joann Chenault and Fran Burnford, *Human Services Professional Education: Future Directions,* New York: McGraw-Hill Book Company, 1978; Ann Di Stefano, "Pragmatic Approach to Human Services Program Design," *Journal of Teacher Education,* September–October 1980; Mark R. Yessian, "Commentary: Major Issues and Recommendations for Change" in Joann Chenault and Fran Burnford, *Human Services Professional Education: Future Directions,* New York: McGraw-Hill Book Company, 1978.

HUMAN SERVICES REAUTHORIZATION ACT OF 1986 (Public Law #99–425), passed by the United States Congress on September 30, 1986, authorized appropriations for the years 1987–90 for Headstart Programs (Title I), Follow-Through Programs (Title II), Dependent Care State Grants (Title III), Community Services Block Grants (Title IV), Low-Income Home Energy Assistance Programs (Title V), Child Development Associate Scholarship Assistance (Title VI), Excellence in Education Program (Title VII), Hours of Employ-

ment of Batboys and Batgirls (Title VIII), and funds to conduct a study to compile a complete list of beginning reading instruction programs and methods. (See FOLLOW-THROUGH PROGRAM; OPERATION HEADSTART; and SCHOOL RECOGNITION PROGRAMS.)

Reference: United States Code Congressional and Administrative News, 99th Congress—Second Session, 1986 (Volume 1), St. Paul, MN: West Publishing Co., 1987.

HUNT LECTURES—See CHARLES W. HUNT LECTURES

HUTCHINS, ROBERT MAYNARD (January 17, 1899–May 15, 1977), President of the University of Chicago from 1929 to 1945, its Chancellor from 1945 to 1951, and an outspoken supporter of the perennialist movement in education. He believed that education should focus on intellectual development and develop intellectual powers. Educational institutions, according to Hutchins, are designed to do just that. Education, he believed, should not be an ad hoc experience, nor should it be directed toward immediate needs. It should not change constantly, nor be vocational in design. It should not be preprofessional, nor should it be utilitarian. Rather, education should develop the mind. Dr. Hutchins also believed that human nature is rational and that knowledge is based on universal truths. Consequently, Dr. Hutchins believed that the school curriculum should consist of permanent studies. These studies are perennial. Study of the classics, the great books, rhetoric, logic, mathematics, philosophy, and grammar, in his view, should comprise the school curriculum.

Hutchins's educational activities included: (1) chairmanship of the Board of Educators, Encyclopaedia Britannica; (2) associate directorship of the Ford Foundation; (3) presidency of the Fund for the Republic; and (4) editorship of *Great Books of the Western World.* His principal writings included *The Higher Learning in America* (1936), *Education for Freedom* (1943), and *The Learning Society* (1968). (See PERENNIALISM.)

References: Allan C. Ornstein, *An Introduction to the Foundations of Education,* Chicago: Rand McNally College Publishing Company, 1977; Del Weber, *Hutchins and Conant: A Contrast in Educational Views,* Tempe, AZ: Bureau of Educational Research and Services, 1965.

HYGIENE THEORY—See MOTIVATION-HYGIENE THEORY

HYPERACTIVE CHILD, a child who is excessively active and has a short attention span. The hyperactive child is socially immature, is easily distracted, is uninhibited, and is impulsive. As a result, he/she suffers from many learning deficits. Hyperactivity is usually identified early in a child's life.

Before 1941, hyperactivity was considered to be either a form of schizophrenia or mental retardation. Today, hyperactive children are classified as having either a maturational lag, hyperkinetic reaction, immaturity of the nervous system, perceptual-motor problems, minimal cerebral dysfunction, or minimal brain dysfunction. Minimal brain dysfunction is the most common classification.

Hyperactive children are often assigned to regular classrooms. Multidimensional approaches and teacher strategies are required to work effectively with them. The classroom teacher normally works closely with the child's parents, his/her special education teacher, a psychologist, and a medical doctor in planning and carrying out these strategies. (See HYPERKINESIS.)

References: Frank P. Alabiso and James C. Hansen, *The Hyperactive Child in the Classroom,* Springfield, IL: Charles C. Thomas Publisher, 1977; James S. Cangelosi, *Classroom Management Strategies: Gaining and Maintaining Students' Cooperation,* New York: Longman, Inc., 1988; Ben F. Feingold, *Why Your Child is Hyperactive,* New York: Random House, 1975; William L. Heward and Michael D. Orlansky, *Exceptional Children: An Introductory Survey of Special Education,* Columbus, OH: Merrill Publishing Company, 1988.

HYPERACTIVE CHILD SYNDROME—See ATTENTION DEFICIT DISORDER

HYPERKINESIS, a multifaceted syndrome of a hyperkinetic impulse disorder, manifested by excessive motor activity on the part of a child. The syndrome is characterized by motor restlessness, impulsiveness, learning difficulty, and a low frustration level (tolerance). Students and children who are hyperkinetic are classified as having minimal brain dysfunction (MBD).

Although controversial, stimulant drug treatment can help some MBD-hyperkinesis; a multiple teaching and treatment approach must be used. Any of several factors contribute to hyperkinesis (e.g. genetic, developmental lag, specific learning disability, environment, emotional problems, and family problems). (See ATTENTION DEFICIT DISORDER and HYPERACTIVE CHILD.)

References: Frank P. Alabiso and James C. Hansen, *The Hyperactive Child in the Classroom,* Springfield, IL: Charles

C. Thomas, Publisher, 1977; Eric Denkoff and Leon Stern (Editors), *Minimal Brain Dysfunction: A Developmental Approach,* New York: Masson Publication, USA, Inc., 1979; Herbert E. Rie and Ellen D. Rie (Editors), *Handbook of Minimal Brain Dysfunctions: A Critical View,* New York: John Wiley and Sons, 1980.

HYPERKINETIC, excessive motor activity. Children who suffer from hyperkinesia are classified as hyperactive. There are many terms used to characterize a hyperactive child, e.g. hyperactivity, hyperkinetic impulse disorder, MBD (minimal brain dysfunction), hypermobility neurosis, and organic driveness.

Hyperactive children may have physical and/or learning problems. Among them are short attention span, extremely high motor activity, low frustration level, problems of poor perception, and conceptualization problems. Since there are many problems associated with the condition, no single or simple procedure can be used to manage hyperactive children. Intervention approaches may center around changes in the actual educational environment, direct modification (via behavior management techniques), placement outside the home, and/or medication programs. (See ATTENTION DEFICIT DISORDER.)

References: Marvin J. Fine, *Principles and Techniques of Intervention with Hyperactive Children,* Springfield, IL: Charles C. Thomas, Publisher, 1977; Dorothy O. Lewis, et al., *Delinquency and Psychopathology,* New York: Grune and Stratton, 1976.

HYPERKINETIC SYNDROME—See ATTENTION DEFICIT DISORDER, HYPERKINETIC

HYPEROPIA, or farsightedness, an eye condition characterized by poor vision at close range. The condition is brought about because of a shortened eyeball from front to back. This causes images to appear behind the retina. Hyperopia is usually corrected with use of convex lenses that cause light rays to focus on the retina rather than behind it.

One survey of partially seeing school children in special education programs reported that hyperopia was the second ranking visual impairment found. Hyperopic children commonly suffer from fatigue, a condition the teacher can alleviate by providing rest periods and by alternating close work with distant vision activities (e.g. chalkboard).

References: Randall K. Harley and G. Allen Lawrence, *Visual Impairment in the Schools,* Springfield, IL: Charles C. Thomas, Publisher, 1977; Leo J. Kelly and Glenn A. Vergason, *Dictionary of Special Education and Rehabilitation,* Denver, CO: Love Publishing Company, 1978;

Harold G. Scheie and Daniel M. Albert, *Textbook of Oph-thalmology* (Ninth Edition), Philadelphia: W. B. Saunders Company, 1977.

HYPOTHESES, attempts on the part of the researcher to explain, tentatively, what has happened or what might happen in a given situation. Hypotheses are quite specific and are usually based on prior research (experiences); hence, they may be considered to be "educated guesses" or reasonable explanations. In quantitative research, hypotheses are tested. Because of the nature of educational research, most hypotheses are never proven. In some qualitative projects, hypotheses are actually generated by the research.

Research hypotheses are stated as declarative statements, e. g. "There is a relationship between learning and lighting" (nondirectional); "There is a positive relationship between the amount learned and the amount of lighting" (directional). Null (statistical) hypotheses are used many times in research, because they are appropriate to particular statistical procedures. They indicate that there will be *no* significant (statistical) differences (or relationships) between or among variables. If a null hypothesis is *not* rejected, then any relationship that does exist would be a chance one. If it is rejected, then any relationship that does exist exists beyond a chance factor. (See TESTS OF SIGNIFICANCE and TYPE I (ALPHA) AND TYPE II (BETA) ERRORS.)

References: Walter R. Borg and Meredith D. Gall, *Educational Research: An Introduction* (Fifth Edition), New York: Longman, Inc., 1989; L. R. Gay, *Educational Research: Competencies for Analysis and Application* (Third Edition), Columbus, OH: Charles E. Merrill Publishing Company, 1987; Melvin R. Novick and Paul H. Jackson, *Statistical Methods for Educational and Psychological Research*, New York: McGraw-Hill Book Company, 1974.

I/D/E/A (INSTITUTE FOR THE DEVELOPMENT OF EDUCATIONAL ACTIVITIES), an educational affiliate of the Charles F. Kettering Foundation, created in 1965. The prime function of I/D/E/A is to encourage and speed the implementation of positive changes in elementary and secondary schools. I/D/E/A also serves as the primary outlet for all of the Kettering Foundation's programs and activities in education.

I/D/E/A is regularly involved in, or sponsors projects that are consonant with, its objectives. Recently, for example, I/D/E/A's Research Division, under the direction of Dean John I. Goodlad, UCLA, was involved in a five-year study of the human and organizational influences that operate during periods of educational change and improvement. Eighteen schools from 18 southern California school districts were involved in the study. From the five-year study grew various models and mechanisms not only to study but to facilitate and promote change.

The Change Program for Individually Guided Education (IGE), an earlier effort, was developed by I/D/E/A. IGE was used in 1,700 schools in 38 states and 70 American-sponsored overseas schools in 1977. *Principals' Inservice Program,* a third project, is a new administrators' development program created by I/D/E/A. (See INDIVIDUALLY GUIDED EDUCATION.)

References: Carmen M. Culver and Gary J. Hobin (Editors), *The Power to Change: Issue of the Innovative Educator* (A Charles F. Kettering Foundation Program), New York: McGraw-Hill Book Company, 1973; Danforth Foundation and I/D/E/A, *Education for Responsible Citizenship: The Report of the National Task Force on Citizenship Education,* New York: McGraw-Hill Book Company, 1977; I/D/E/A, *Principals' Inservice Program, An Overview,* Dayton, OH: Charles F. Kettering Foundation, 1980; Jon S. Paden, *Reflections for the Future,* Dayton, OH: Institute for Development of Educational Activities, Inc., 1978.

IDEALISM, one of the oldest branches of philosophy that holds "that ultimate reality is spiritual in nature rather than physical, mental rather than material" (George Kneller, p. 8). Idealists propose that self is the reality of experience, ultimate reality is based on the nature of thought. Idealism holds that reality is a unified system of things (conceptions, perceptions), each related to the other. It is a system of thinking in which ideas or ideals are the basic element of the universe. They are considered to be more important than physical matter. Idealism has its roots in the works of philosophers such as Socrates, Plato, Descartes, Spinoza, Kant, and Hegel.

Idealism, in a general sense, refers to behaviors that are based on deeply held principles and/or philosophies (e.g. a commitment to a particular political party). In such cases, those who believe strongly in the principles and/or philosophies will continue to do so even under extremely difficult conditions or in the face of difficult consequences.

References: James D. Butler, *Four Philosophies and their Practice in Education and Religion* (Third Edition), New York: Harper and Row, Publishers, 1968; George Kneller, *Introduction to the Philosophy of Education* (Second Edition), New York: John Wiley and Sons, 1971; Ben Lazare Mijuskovic, *The Achilles of Rationalist Arguments: The Simplicity, Unity, and Identity of Thought and Soul From the Cambridge Platonists to Kant,* The Hague, Holland: Martinus Nijhoff, 1974; Friedrich W. J. Schelling, *System of Transcendental Idealism (1800),* Charlottesville, VA: University Press of Virginia, 1978.

IDIOGRAPHIC-NOMOTHETIC DIMENSIONS —See GETZELS-GUBA MODEL

ILLUMINATION LEVELS, specific degrees of light intensity recommended for instructional areas in a school building. Light intensity is expressed in footcandle units as measured by a light meter. (One footcandle is the intensity of light from a candle striking a surface at a distance of one foot.)

Minimum standards for different school areas were originally recommended by the Illuminating Engineering Society but have been increased since then. Basil Castoldi, a school plant authority, reported current recommended levels to be as follows: (1) 30–50 footcandles for classrooms, libraries, study halls, offices, and shops; (2) 60–80 footcandles for special education, drafting, typing, and sewing rooms; (3) 20–30 footcandles for physical education and reception rooms; (4) 15–25 footcandles for auditoriums, cafeterias, and similar general service rooms; and (5) 10–20 footcandles for open corridors and storerooms.

References: American Institute of Architects, et al., *American Standard Guide for School Lighting,* New York:

Illuminating Engineering Society, 1962; Basil Castoldi, *Educational Facilities: Planning, Remodeling, and Management,* Boston: Allyn and Bacon, Inc., 1977.

IMMERSION PRINCIPLE, a technique used in foreign language instruction in which students are completely surrounded by the targeted language to be learned. The emphasis in such an approach is audio-lingual. The student develops language skills from initial listening, from active speaking (conversation), and from reading and writing. There is little interference from distracting stimuli (nontargeted language). In addition, a long and intense time is spent in the foreign language environment.

The success of early immersion programs such as the U.S. Navy's Japanese Language School (1941), the Army Air Force Spanish and Portuguese program under the Works Projects Administration (1941), the Inter-American Training Center (1942), and the Army Specialized Training Program (started in 1942) led to the further development of the immersion technique. Many immersion programs are called "intensive" or "total immersion" programs. Their specific characteristics are: (1) direct language is spoken; (2) a large block of time is scheduled (usually in terms of full days and many weeks); and (3) initial emphasis is on oral communication.

References: J. Wesley Childers, *Foreign Language Teaching,* New York: The Center for Applied Research in Education, Inc., 1964; Ralph M. Hester, et al., *Teaching a Living Language,* New York: Harper and Row, Publishers, 1970; C. V. Russell, *Post-O-Level Studies in Modern Foreign Language,* Oxford, England: Pergamon Press, Inc., 1970.

IMPACT AID, or impacted areas program, financial assistance that the federal government provides to those school districts in which federal activities (e.g. military installations, certain defense industries) have created a financial burden. The Lanham Act (1941) originally provided assistance of this type, making possible the construction and operation of community facilities such as schools. Nine years later, Public Laws 815 and 874 continued this form of aid to school systems and made it ongoing.

The legislation is popular in numbers of school systems. Accordingly, attempts by various administrations to repeal these laws in the interest of achieving federal economies have not been successful. (See PUBLIC LAWS 815 AND 874.)

References: Lawrence L. Brown III, et al., "A Proposal to Rationalize the Federal Program of Impact Aid Assistance to School Districts," *Journal of Education Finance,* Winter 1979; Roe L. Johns and Edgar L. Morphet, *The Economics and Financing of Education: A Systems Approach* (Third Edition), Englewood Cliffs, NJ: Prentice-Hall, Inc., 1975; Mike M. Milstein, *Impact and Response: Federal Aid and State Education Agencies,* New York: Teachers College Press, Columbia University, 1976; Public Laws 815 and 874, *United States Statutes at Large, 1950-51* (Volume 64, Part I), Washington, DC: U.S. Government Printing Office, 1952.

IMPASSE, a collective bargaining term for a situation where parties to negotiation find themselves deadlocked (i.e. unable to resolve their differences). In the public sector, these situations normally lead to mediation, fact-finding, or compulsory binding arbitration. (See ARBITRATION; FACT-FINDING; and MEDIATION.)

References: William B. Castetter, *The Personnel Function in Educational Administration* (Third Edition), New York: Macmillan Publishing Company, Inc., 1981; J. Joseph Loewenberg and Michael H. Moskow (Editors), *Collective Bargaining in Government: Readings and Cases,* Englewood Cliffs, NJ: Prentice-Hall, Inc., 1972; Harold S. Roberts, *Labor Management Relations in the Public Service,* Honolulu, HI: University of Hawaii Press, 1970.

IMPEDANCE—See ACOUSTICS

IMPLICIT CURRICULUM—See HIDDEN CURRICULUM

IMPRESS READING METHOD—See NEUROLOGICAL IMPRESS METHOD

IMPREST FUND—See PETTY CASH

IMPROVISATION—See DALCROZE METHOD

INBASKET—See SIMULATION

INCLUSION PROCESS, a direct instruction model of teaching thinking skills. The approach begins with an analysis of the curriculum being taught, and is designed to complement that knowledge base with a process that leads to increased reasoning ability. Originally developed by A. M. Worsham (1982) as part of her doctoral dissertation, the process includes eight steps:

1. Analysis of the current curriculum objectives to ascertain the thinking strategies requisite to mastery;

2. Assessment of the learners' intellectual needs that are related to the curriculum objectives;

3. Development of a list of thinking skills commensurate with curriculum requirements and student needs;

4. Development of a long-range plan to sequence thinking skills;

5. Definition of each thinking skill;

6. Delineation of the steps required to apply each skill;

7. Application of the skills within the content curriculum;

8. Evaluation of effectiveness.

References: A. Whimbey and L. S. Whimbey, *Intelligence Can Be Taught*, New York: Bantam Books, 1976; Antoinette M. Worsham, *The Effects of Think—A Language Arts Thinking Skills Program on Scholastic Aptitude Tests (SAT) Verbal Scores at a Baltimore City Senior High School*, doctoral dissertation, University of Maryland, 1982; Antoinette R. Worsham and C. R. Austin, "Effects of Teaching Thinking Skills on SAT Scores," *Educational Leadership*, November 1983; Antoinette M. Worsham and Anita J. Stockton, *A Model for Teaching Thinking Skills: The Inclusion Process*, Bloomington, IN: Phi Delta Kappa Educational Foundation, 1986.

INCREMENTAL BUDGETING, an approach to budgeting that uses the previous year's appropriation as a starting point. To this base, an incremental increase or decrease is made.

Critics of this budgeting method contend that it is weak, because: (1) the total budget is not subjected to scrutiny; (2) it promotes increased spending, especially in those instances where new programs are likely to be added; and (3) the decision maker is not compelled to make hard choices. This method's principal advantage is its relative ease of preparation. Zero-based budgeting and PPBS are two of several alternative budget approaches that, according to some authorities, can overcome the weaknesses attributed to the traditional incremental approach. (See PLANNING, PROGRAMMING, BUDGETING, EVALUATION SYSTEM; and ZERO-BASE BUDGETING.)

References: Jerry J. Herman, *Administrator's Practical Guide to School Finance*, West Nyack, NY: Parker Publishing Company, Inc., 1977; Aaron Wildavsky, *Budgeting: A Comparative Theory of Budgetary Processes*, Boston: Little, Brown and Company, 1975; Aaron Wildavsky, *The Politics of Budgetary Process* (Second Edition), Boston: Little, Brown and Company, 1974.

INDEPENDENT STUDY, a self-directed approach to the acquisition of knowledge and/or competence. In an independent study program or course, a student plans and carries out learning activities on his/her own. In most cases, independent study is carried out under the guidance of an instructor or teacher. The role of the instructor, however, is usually limited to the giving of direction.

Independent study can be found at any level of education, elementary through graduate school. A good deal of postschool or postcollege education is acquired through independent study, much of it informal. At the college level, degree students may register for a limited number of courses designated as independent studies. At the elementary and secondary levels, independent study is normally carried out as part of a study unit.

A principal goal of education is to develop in all students the skills necessary to conduct meaningful independent study.

References: William M. Alexander and Vynce A. Hines, *Independent Study in Secondary Schools* (Cooperative Research Project No. 2969), Gainesville, FL: University of Florida, 1966; David W. Beggs III and Edward G. Buffie (Editors), *Independent Study: Bold New Venture*, Bloomington, IN: Indiana University Press, 1965; Paul L. Dressel and Mary M. Thompson, *Independent Study*, San Francisco: Jossey-Bass Publishers, 1973; Robert B. Kozma, et al., *Instructional Techniques in Higher Education*, Englewood Cliffs, NJ: Educational Technology Publications, 1978.

INDEX SALARY SCHEDULE, or ratio schedule, a technique used by some school systems for determining salaries to be paid to school administrators and other nonteaching employees. The index schedule uses the system's single salary schedule for teachers as a base. An index (weighting) is then established for each nonteaching or leadership post. To determine a given administrator's (or other nonteaching employee's) salary, his/her salary as a teacher is then multiplied by the appropriate index.

The following table illustrates indexes used in a hypothetical school district:

Position	Index (Weighting)
Teacher Aide	0.50
Teacher	1.00
Chairperson	1.35
Elementary Principal	1.65
Middle School Principal	1.85
High School Principal	2.00

The index schedule has at least two major advantages. First, it simplifies the salary negotiation process, and, second, it attempts to establish structural interrelationships that take varying job responsibilities into account. (See SINGLE SALARY SCHEDULE.)

References: William B. Castetter, *The Personnel Function in Educational Administration* (Third Edition), New York: Macmillan Publishing Company, Inc., 1981; William B. Castetter and Richard S. Heisler, *Planning the Financial Compensation of School Administrative Personnel*, Philadelphia: Center for Field Studies, Graduate School of Education, University of Pennsylvania, 1974; Jay E. Greene, *School Personnel Administration*, Philadelphia: Chilton Book Company, 1971; Gertrude N. Stieber, *Methods of Scheduling Salaries for Principals*, Arlington, VA: Educational Research Service, Inc., 1975.

INDIAN, also known as native American, a racial classification of people whose definition has not been clearly and uniformly established. In Title IV, PL 92-318 (Indian Education Act), Congress defined *Indian* as follows: "For the purpose of this title (IV), the term 'Indian' means any individual who (1) is a member of a tribe, band, or other organized group of Indians, including those tribes, bands, or groups terminated since 1940 and those recognized now or in the future by the State in which they reside, or who is a descendant, in the first or second degree, of any such member, or (2) is considered by the Secretary of the Interior to be an Indian for any purpose, or (3) is an Eskimo or Aleut or other Alaska Native, or (4) is determined to be an Indian under regulations promulgated by the Commissioner, after consultation with the National Advisory Council on Indian Education, which regulations shall further define the term 'Indian'" (p. 345). An earlier functional definition, provided by the United States Census Bureau, is contained in this statement: "In addition to fullblooded American Indians, persons of mixed white and Indian blood are included in this category if they are enrolled on an Indian tribal or agency roll or if they are regarded as Indians in the community" (p. xi).

In some anthropological classifications of race, Indians are listed as Mongoloids. In Latin America, Brewton Berry pointed out, the definition is exclusively cultural rather than biological.

References: Brewton Berry, *Race and Ethnic Relations* (Third Edition), Boston: Houghton Mifflin Company, 1965; Richard M. Burkey, *Ethnic and Racial Groups: The Dynamics of Dominance*, Menlo Park, CA: Benjamin/Cummings, 1978; Public Law 92-318, *United States Statutes at Large, 1972* (Volume 86), Washington, DC: U.S. Government Printing Office, 1973; *U.S. Census of Populations 1960: United States Summary, General Population Characteristics*, Washington, DC: U.S. Government Printing Office, 1961.

INDIAN BOARDING SCHOOL, a school for Native American students that provides its charges with full-time care during a school term. The boarding school is a residential institution offering meals, health services, and dormitory facilities in addition to instructional service.

The earliest such boarding school was established in Pennsylvania (1879) as an off-reservation institution. Years later, as the number of Indian boarding schools increased, more and more were located on Indian reservations and administered by the federal government (Bureau of Indian Affairs).

The 1978 edition of the *Reference Encyclopedia of the American Indian* lists 75 boarding schools being operated by the Bureau of Indian Affairs. (See BUREAU OF INDIAN AFFAIRS.)

References: Barry T. Klein, *Reference Encyclopedia of the American Indian* (Third Edition, Volume I), Rye, NY: Todd Publications, 1978; S. Lyman Tyler, Bureau of Indian Affairs, *A History of Indian Policy*, Washington, DC: U.S. Government Printing Office, 1973.

INDIAN EDUCATION, a general term used to describe educational programs (all levels) available to native Americans. In 1975, according to the U.S. Comptroller General, approximately 190,000 Indian children between the ages of 5 and 18 were enrolled in public, federal, private, and mission schools. The Bureau of Indian Affairs (BIA), the federal agency responsible for operating BIA reservation schools and dormitories, estimates that 72 percent of these students were enrolled in public schools (including several located on Indian reservations), 23 percent in federal schools, and about 5 percent in mission and other schools.

Over the years, Indian education has been fraught with problems. William Demmert listed several points attesting to the existence of such problems, including: (1) low educational level (8.4 years for all Indians); (2) low levels of academic achievement, with Indian students lagging their nonIndian counterparts significantly; and (3) high dropout rates. Several reasons for these data have been suggested over the past 50 years. In his 1928 study of Indian education, for example, Lewis Meriam cited three: (1) the fact that Indians have had little control over their own affairs, including education; (2) poor quality of service received from public officials; and (3) cultural difference problems resulting from the imposition of the white man's value system on Indian cultures. Many of these same conditions continue to thwart educational progress today. Exacerbating the problem, Demmert pointed out, is the fact that only a small minority of Indian children are taught by Indian teachers. Commenting on this, Demmert stated "An obstacle here is the lack of Indian adult examples present in the formal educational process, a situation that must be corrected if the first years in school are to be happy or acceptable ones for the youngsters" (p. 8).

Recent studies of Indian education have been completed by the U.S. Comptroller General (1972 and 1977), the U.S. Senate Committee on Indian Education, and Professor Robert J. Havighurst. All identify the problems noted by Demmert. (See BUREAU OF INDIAN AFFAIRS; INDIAN BOARDING SCHOOL; INDIAN EDUCATION ACT; INDIAN SELF-DETERMINATION; and JOHNSON-O'MALLEY ACT.)

References: William G. Demmert, Jr., "Indian Education: Where and Whither?" *American Education,* August–September 1976; *Information About: Facts on American Indians and Alaskan Natives,* Washington, DC: Bureau of Indian Affairs, U.S. Department of the Interior, November 1977; Walter F. Mondale and George D. Fisher, "Indian Education: A National Disgrace" (Dialogue between the Senator from Minnesota and the President of the NEA) in Alfred Lightfoot (Editor), *Inquiries into the Social Foundations of Education,* Chicago: Rand McNally and Company, 1972; *Report of the Comptroller General of the United States: Concerted Effort Needed to Improve Indian Education,* Washington, DC: U.S. General Accounting Office, January 1977; S. Lyman Tyler, *A History of Indian Policy,* Washington, DC: U.S. Department of the Interior, 1973.

INDIAN EDUCATION ACT (P.L. 92-318, Title IV), federal legislation enacted in 1972 that has as its purpose the improvement of educational opportunities for Indian children and adults.

Part B of the act authorizes distribution of funds to state and local educational agencies engaged in any or all of the following activites: (1) projects of a planning, pilot, or demonstration nature that test or demonstrate effective instructional programs (e.g. bilingual/bicultural); (2) provision of special services (e.g. testing, counseling) not regularly or widely available to Indian children; (3) preservice/inservice training programs for teachers, aides, and others serving Indian children; and (4) dissemination of information regarding successful programs or activities. *Part C* has reduction of illiteracy among Indian adults as its principal goal.

In recent years, federal appropriations for Part B have exceeded those for Part C by approximately a 3.5:1 ratio.

References: Office of Planning, Budgeting and Evaluation, *Annual Evaluation Report on Programs Administered by the U.S. Office of Education, Fiscal Year 1977,* Washington, DC: The Office, 1977; Public Law 92-318, *United States Statutes at Large, 1972* (Volume 86), Washington, DC: U.S. Government Printing Office, 1973.

INDIAN SELF-DETERMINATION, governmental policy designed to increase the involvement of Indians and Native Alaskans in the management of their own affairs. Such involvement includes policymaking as well as decision-making activities. The self-determination movement began to receive serious national attention toward the end of the 1960s with increased Indian leadership being sought out for areas affecting Indians, education included. More Indian adults than ever before are presently serving on special committees, school boards, and commissions and are otherwise involved in giving direction to the nature and content of curriculum for Indian youth. Special efforts are also being made to elevate larger numbers of Indian teachers to school leadership positions. The Indian Education Act (1972) was the first piece of legislation of its kind to mandate active participation by Indians and Native Alaskans in activities falling within the act's purview. (See INDIAN EDUCATION ACT.)

References: Title IV, Public Law 92-318, *United States Statutes at Large, 1972* (Volume 86), Washington, DC: U.S. Government Printing Office, 1973; S. Lyman Tyler, Bureau of Indian Affairs, *A History of Indian Policy,* Washington, DC: U.S. Government Printing Office, 1973.

INDIVIDUAL EDUCATION PLAN (IEP), a requirement included in Public Law 94-142 (Education for All Handicapped Children Act of 1975). Sections 121a.222–224 of the law require the local educational agency to develop, annually, an individualized education program for each handicapped child. Those planning the student's program must include a representative of the local agency other than the child's teacher(s), the child's teacher(s), one or both of the child's parents, the child (where appropriate), and others chosen by the parent or agency.

IEPs normally include: (1) information on the child; (2) evaluation deficiencies (academic, social, vocational); (3) long- and short-term goals; (4) remedial procedures/techniques; (5) evaluation procedures; and (6) signed consent of parent(s) or guardian(s).

References: Edward D. Fiscus and Colleen J. Mandell, *Developing Individualized Education Programs*, St. Paul, MN: West Publishing Company, 1983; Daniel P. Hallahan and James M. Kauffman, *Exceptional Children: Introduction to Special Education* (Fourth Edition), Englewood Cliffs, NJ: Prentice-Hall, 1988; National School Public Relations Association, *Educating All the Handicapped: What the Laws Say and What Schools are Doing*, Arlington, VA: The Association, 1977; Public Law 94–142, *Education for all Handicapped Children Act of 1975, in United States Code: Congressional and Administrative News*, 94th Congress-First Session, 1975, St. Paul, MN: West Publishing Company, 1975; Judy W. Wood, *Mainstreaming: A Practical Approach for Teachers*, Columbus, OH: Merrill Publishing Company, 1989.

INDIVIDUALIZED INSTRUCTION, a teaching approach that permits a child to progress at his/her own pace with the guidance of a teacher. Instruction and instructional modes are geared to the individual child. Instruction is nongraded. This enables a child to move as quickly and as far as he/she is capable. Individualization does not mean that a child always works alone, or that a teacher is no longer responsible for the child. To the contrary, careful records must be kept in order for a teacher to diagnose, to record progress, and to maximize the potential of the approach.

There are many advantages in individualized instruction accruing to students and teachers. Among student advantages are: self-pacing; immediate feedback (depending on the mode of instruction); and greater depth. For the teacher, individualization provides: freedom from teaching many of the routine basic skills; better assessment of individual student needs; more time spent with individual children; better guidance by the teacher rather than just lecturing; and greater variety of techniques from which to select.

There are many forms of individualized instruction. Individually Prescribed Instruction, Project "PLAN," Individualized Guided Education, and learning packets are but a few. (See INDIVIDUALLY GUIDED EDUCATION; INDIVIDUALLY PRESCRIBED INSTRUCTION; LEARNING PACKETS; and PROJECT "PLAN.")

References: James E. Duane, *Individualized Instruction: Programs and Materials*, Englewood Cliffs, NJ: Educational Technology Publications, 1973; Glen Heathers, "Individualized Instruction" in Richard I. Miller (Editor), *Catalyst for Change: A National Study of ESEA Title III (PACE)*, Washington, DC: U.S. Government Printing Office, 1967; G. Ray Musgrave, *Individualized Instruction: Teaching Strategies Focusing on the Learner*, Boston: Allyn and Bacon, Inc., 1975.

INDIVIDUALIZED READING, an instructional approach that features relatively little group instruction; instead, students read from books that are of interest to them and that they have chosen. Children read at their own rate using literature books rather than textbooks. They confer individually with their teacher concerning material read. Skill teaching is usually offered on an individualized basis, although provision can be made for small group instruction when difficulties common to two or more students are noted. Records of each pupil's reading progress are maintained. The program requires a generous inventory of books (one author recommends ten per student) appealing to various interest and ability levels.

Individualized reading began in Europe and was used widely in the United States during the 1950s. Since then, several variations have emerged, many of which combine individualized reading with more traditional (group) approaches.

References: Dolores Durkin, *Teaching Them To Read* (Third Edition), Boston: Allyn and Bacon, Inc., 1978; Lyman C. Hunt, "Philosophy of Individualized Reading" in Althea Berry, et al. (Editors), *Elementary Reading Instruction: Selected Materials* (Second Edition), Boston: Allyn and Bacon, Inc., 1974; Eddie C. Kennedy, *Methods in Teaching Developmental Reading*, Itasca, IL: F. E. Peacock Publishers, Inc., 1974; Eddie C. Kennedy, *Classroom Approaches to Remedial Reading* (Second Edition), Itasca, IL: F. E. Peacock Publishers, Inc., 1977.

INDIVIDUALLY GUIDED EDUCATION (IGE), an alternative approach to education at the elementary and middle school levels. IGE has accommodation of individual differences among children as its principal feature. It attends to different rates of learning, levels of achievement, learning styles, motivation, as well as variations in other psychological and personal factors.

The IGE originated in the Wisconsin Research and Development Center for Cognitive Learning in 1964 under the leadership of Herbert J. Klausmeier. The system is made up of seven components, many of which function simultaneously. The seven components are: (1) the multiunit school organization; (2) instructional programming for the individual student; (3) evaluation for decision making; (4) curriculum materials compatible with IGE; (5) home-school-community relations; (6) facilitative environment for IGE; and (7) continuing research and development.

Instruction and Research (I & R) units replace the "traditional" classroom in IGE's multiunit organization. IGE is nongraded and requires the services of a unit leader, three or four staff teachers, an instructional aide, student teachers, and 100 to 150 students. An IIC (Instructional Improvement Committee), made up of the principal and unit leaders, parents, the IIC director, and special teachers, oversees the program at the local building level. There is also provision for a Systemwide Program Committee (SPC). There are differential roles in IGE, and the traditional roles of school personnel change under the system. The Instructional Programming Model (IPM) that focuses on programming for individual students is the base of IGE. (See INDIVIDUALIZED INSTRUCTION.)
References: Journal of Teacher Education, Fall 1976; Edward J. Nussel, et al., The Teacher and Individually Guided Education, Reading, MA: Addison-Wesley Publishing Company, 1976; Juanita S. Sorenson, et al., The Unit Leader and Individually Guided Education, Reading, MA: Addison-Wesley Publishing Company, 1976.

INDIVIDUALLY PRESCRIBED INSTRUCTION (IPI), an approach to education based on placement tests and teacher-developed prescriptions. The student involved in IPI takes a placement or diagnostic test. The results are analyzed and a specific instructional plan is developed for him/her by the teacher. Students move from level to level depending on their individual rates of achievement. IPI uses a great deal of programmed instruction, self-paced learning, and computer-assisted instruction materials. IPI programs also include a variety of instructional materials and modes. Under the IPI approach, the teacher's role changes dramatically with greater emphasis placed on management of the learning environment as well as diagnosis and counseling.

A system of Individually Prescribed Instruction was developed in 1963 by the Learning Research and Development Center, University of Pittsburgh, at the Oakleaf Elementary School, in suburban Pittsburgh under the direction of Drs. Glaser, Bolvin, and Lindvall of the Univeristy. Research for Better Schools, in Philadelphia, field tested and disseminated IPI. (See INDIVIDUALIZED INSTRUCTION and RESEARCH FOR BETTER SCHOOLS.)
References: Harriet Talmage, Systems of Individualized Education, Berkeley, CA: McCutchan Publishing Corporation, 1975; Robert A. Weisgerber (Editor), Developmental Efforts in Individualized Learning, Itasca, IL: F. E. Peacock Publishers, Inc., 1971; Robert A. Weisgerber, Perspectives in Individualized Learning, Itasca, IL: F. E. Peacock Publishers, Inc., 1971.

INDIVIDUAL TESTS, usually sophisticated tests that are administered on a one-to-one basis. Examiners present one problem at a time, either orally or by showing a picture or toy. The examinee responds to each problem thus posed. Administering and scoring of individual tests requires considerable skill on the part of the examiner, a skill usually acquired through special training and extensive experience. In many cases, individual tests are administered in a clinic where the examiner can establish rapport with, and maintain the interest of, the examinee. The examiner looks for signs of test anxiety, fatigue, or other factors that could interfere with test administration. They are less of a problem with group tests.

Many intelligence tests are administered on an individual basis. The most notable are the Stanford-Binet Scales and the Wechsler Scales. (See GROUP TESTS.)
References: Lewis Aiken, Psychological and Educational Testing, Boston: Allyn and Bacon, Inc., 1971; Norman E. Gronlund, Measurement and Evaluation in Teaching (Fifth Edition), New York: Macmillan Company, Inc., 1985; Vito Perrone, The Abuses of Standardized Testing (PDK Fastback 92), Bloomington, IN: The Phi Delta Kappa Educational Foundation, 1977.

INDO-EUROPEAN LANGUAGES, a family of languages that includes languages from Europe, America, and some countries of Asia. Included are the following subgroups: (1) Germanic (English, German, Dutch, Swedish, Danish, Norwegian, Icelandic, Yiddish, Afrikaans); (2) Romance languages (Italian, French, Spanish, Portuguese, Rumanian); (3) Celtic (Irish, Scottish, Welsh); (4) Slavic (Russian, Polish, Czech, Slovak, Ukrainian, Bulgarian, Serbo-Croatian); (5) Baltic (Lithuanian, Latvian); (6) Iranian (Pashto, Persian, Kurdish); and (7) Indic or Indo-Aryan (Sanskrit, Hindi, and other languages spoken in India, Pakistan, Bangladesh, Sri Lanka, and Nepal).
References: Kenneth Katzner, The Languages of the World, New York: Funk and Wagnalls, 1975; C. F. Voegelin and F. M. Voegelin, Classification and Index of the World's Languages, New York: Elsevier North-Holland, Inc., 1977.

INDUCTION PERIOD (INTO TEACHING), typically the first few years of employment as a teacher. It is one of the most crucial stages in a teacher's career—most often following the completion of a preservice teacher education program, and it is the period where the greatest socialization into the profession, the classroom, and the school district occurs. Concerns about the role of the teacher; acceptance by students, parents, and administrators; and discipline and classroom management are just a few of the problems facing the newly employed teacher.

Several states have recognized the importance of the first year of the newly certified teacher, and as such have passed legislation to aid in the induction of the new teacher into the classroom. Often this is in the form of extending the initial certification process by including an "internship" of one year before full certification is issued. The internship is structured to be supportive (as opposed to being solely evaluative), and usually includes a support team made up of teachers, administrators, and often college personnel. Georgia, Florida, Kentucky, Louisiana, and New Jersey are now a few of the states that have mandated an internship for all newly certified teachers as an aid in the induction process.

Many school distrcts recognize the special needs of teachers during the induction stage and provide specialized in-service assistance. Also, many teacher preparation institutions are providing similar help as well. The revised NCATE (National Council for the Accreditation of Teacher Education) Standards require that teacher preparation institutions provide support, during the first year of employment, for their graduates. (See INTERNSHIP and TEACHER WARRANTY PROGRAM.)

References: Peter J. Burke, Judith C. Christensen, and Ralph Fessler, *Teacher Career Stages: Implications for Staff Development,* Bloomington, IN: Phi Delta Kappa, 1984; Gary A. Griffin (Editor), *Staff Development,* 82nd yearbook of the National Society for the Study of Education, Chicago: The University of Chicago Press, 1983; Kevin Ryan, *The Induction of New Teachers,* Bloomington, IN: Phi Delta Kappa, 1986.

INDUCTIVE APPROACH, an avenue in logic or reasoning that goes from the specific to the general. Started by Francis Bacon (1561–1626), inductive reasoning gives man more flexibility in reasoning and places increased emphasis on observation. Numerous authorities believe that children can and should be encouraged to use the inductive reasoning approach in the classroom. For example, they can study (observe) the habits of ants in an ant farm and then draw general conclusions about all ants. Inductive reasoning is only as strong as the number of observations made and as strong as the observer's ability to draw conclusions from them.

References: Bruce W. Tuckman, *Conducting Educational Research* (Second Edition), New York: Harcourt Brace Jovanovich, Inc., 1978; Debolt B. Van Dalen and William J. Meyers, *Understanding Educational Research,* New York: McGraw-Hill Book Company, 1966.

INDUSTRIAL ARTS CURRICULUM PROJECT (IACP), an innovative instructional system in which students (grades 7 and 8, or 8 and 9) learn how to work efficiently with men, materials, tools, and techniques. The curriculum was developed in 1965 by educators from Ohio State University, the University of Illinois, and the Cincinnati Public Schools.

IACP consists of two year-long courses. In the first, *The World of Construction,* students study on-site construction projects. In the second course, *The World of Manufacturing,* they learn about industrial technology, observing how human, mechanical, and material resources are integrated to achieve effective production. Both courses involve regular classroom as well as laboratory experiences.

References: John R. Lindbeck, *Practical Guide to Industrial Arts Education,* New York: The Center for Applied Research in Education, Inc., 1972; Donald G. Lux and Willis E. Ray, *The World of Construction,* Bloomington, IL: McKnight and McKnight Publishing Company, 1971; Donald G. Lux and Willis E. Ray, *The World of Manufacturing,* Bloomington, IL: McKnight and McKnight Publishing Company, 1971; Donald A. Maley, *The Industrial Arts Teacher's Handbook: Techniques, Principles, and Methods,* Boston: Allyn and Bacon, Inc., 1978.

INDUSTRIAL ARTS EDUCATION, a broad program of studies, pursued for general educational purposes, that deals with technology. Students learn about technological tools, materials, equipment, occupations, processes, and products as well as the problems/benefits associated with industrial societies. Elementary, middle school, and senior high school curricula are integrated to form a total K–12 program.

In 1975, the American Vocational Association published *Industrial Arts in Education,* a succinct overview of industrial arts education. In that document, industrial arts programs were described as meeting seven specific learning goals for students: (1) developing an understanding of industry and its place in society; (2) discovering personal talents, aptitudes, interests, and potential for careers in technology; (3) developing an understanding of industrial processes; (4) developing basic skills in the use of tools and machines; (5)

developing problem-solving and creative abilities related to industrial materials, processes, and products; (6) discovering career opportunities and industrial job requirements; and (7) developing traits that will facilitate procurement and maintaining of employment.

Industrial arts education has been broadened considerably since the time such programs were still known as manual training classes. Mary-Margaret Scobey pointed out that many current industrial arts education practices, especially those in the elementary school, can be traced back to the writings of two groups of individuals: (1) John Comenius, John Locke, Jean Jacques Rousseau, Johann Pestalozzi, and Friedrich Froebel, men who urged sensory learning through the handling of materials and tools; and (2) Frederick Bonser and Lois Mossman who, in 1923, recommended that industrial arts emphasize the study of manufacturing processes. (See MANUAL TRAINING and PRACTICAL ARTS.)

References: American Vocational Association, *Industrial Arts in Education* (Fourth Edition), Washington, DC: The Association, May 1975; Robert D. Brown, *Industrial Education Facilities: A Handbook for Organization and Management*, Boston: Allyn and Bacon, Inc., 1979; John R. Lindbeck, *Practical Guide to Industrial Arts Education*, New York: The Center for Applied Research in Education Inc., 1972; Donald A. Maley, *The Industrial Arts Teacher's Handbook: Techniques, Principles, and Methods*, Boston: Allyn and Bacon, Inc., 1978; Mary-Margaret Scobey, *Teaching Children About Technology*, Bloomington, IL: McKnight and McKnight Publishing Company, 1968.

INDUSTRIAL PSYCHOLOGY, a branch of psychology devoted to the study of business, governmental, and industrial work problems and the means by which those problems may be resolved (and organizational efficiency enhanced) through application of psychological principles. Typical areas investigated by the industrial psychologist are hiring and firing practices, employee training, morale, human engineering, sales, and vocational guidance.

References: Frank J. Landy and Don A. Trumbo, *Psychology of Work Behavior*, Homewood, IL: The Dorsey Press, 1976; Harold J. Leavitt and Louis R. Pondy, *Readings in Managerial Psychology* (Second Edition), Chicago: University of Chicago Press, 1973; Duane P. Schultz, *Psychology and Industry Today* (Second Edition), New York: Macmillan Publishing Company, Inc., 1978; G. D. Wilson, "Industrial Psychology" in H. J. Eysenck, et al. (Editors), *Encyclopedia of Psychology*, New York: The Seabury Press, 1979.

INDUSTRIAL TECHNOLOGY—See TECHNICAL EDUCATION

INFANT EDUCATION, educational and enrichment experiences provided infants and toddlers who range in age from birth to about age 3. One of the main functions of infant education is to furnish stimulation for maximum growth and development. Authorities consider that the years before age 3 are important for sound physical, social, and intellectual skill development and that, for this reason, attention to such development should be a significant part of early childhood (preschool) education. The concept of infant education differs from infant care in that it is predicated on the kinds of programs that foster such development.

Infant education can be enhanced in the home by instructing parents on ways to provide their offspring with a sound intellectual, social, and physical environment. Teachers who provide such instruction are called "parent educators." Some infant education programs can be found in day care centers. (See DAY CARE; EARLY CHILDHOOD EDUCATION; and PARENT EDUCATION.)

References: Marjorie L. Hipple, *Early Childhood Education: Problems and Methods*, Pacific Palisades, CA: Goodyear Publishing Company, Inc., 1975; Jane Findley, et al. (Editors), *A Planning Guide to the Preschool Curriculum: The Child, The Process*, Winston-Salem, NC: Kaplan Press, 1976; Dale G. Range, et al. (Editors), *Aspects of Early Childhood Education: Theory to Research to Practice*, New York: Academic Press, 1980.

INFANT SCHOOL—See BRITISH INFANT SCHOOL

INFERENTIAL STATISTICS, statistical procedures that allow researchers to draw conclusions (or make statements) about a larger group from data drawn from only part of the group. In inferential statistics, the larger group is the *population* for which a conclusion or statement is made. The smaller group is called the *sample*. A population may consist of all those living in a country, in a town, or in a classroom. Although the size and nature of the population may vary, the sample taken from the population must be descriptive or representative of it. There are many approaches to sampling: cluster, interval, random, stratified, and with or without replacement.

Probability is used in inferential statistics. Through the use of probability, researchers can make inferences from a sample to a population about an event or an observed characteristic based on a certain level of chance. Analysis of Variance, F-ratio, t-tests, and z-tests are but a few inferential statistical procedures available. (See ANALYSIS OF VARIANCE; F-RATIO; HYPOTHESES; t-TEST; TYPE I (ALPHA) AND TYPE II (BETA) ERRORS; and z-SCORE.)

References: Frederick J. Gravetter and Larry B. Wallman, *Statistics for the Behavioral Sciences: A First Course for Students of Psychology and Education*, St. Paul, MN: West Publishing Company, 1985; James H. McMillan and Sally Schumacher, *Research in Education: A Conceptual Introduction* (Second Edition), Glenview, IL: Scott, Foresman and Company, 1989.

INFLUENCING, an element of administrative process used to produce behavior consonant with organizational goals. One means available for influencing organizational behavior is the exercise of authority that a superior has over his/her subordinates. When authority is invoked, the superior commands and the subordinate obeys. Authority, however, is not the only approach to influencing, nor is it always the most viable one. As some authorities point out, terms such as *persuade* or *suggest* imply other forms of influence, these latter not necessarily authority related. For example, when suggestion is used to influence, the individual to whom the suggestion is directed is not obligated to carry it out perfunctorily. Instead, he/she enjoys the element of choice, the freedom to act or not to act on the basis of the merits of the suggestion.

Russell Gregg pointed out that the administrator, in addition to exercising authority, can influence through the use of group action or by creating the kind of climate that will bring about influence sans threat or the suggestion of reprisal. Examples of the techniques he suggested for producing such a climate include developing organizational loyalties, making information available to all who can use it, and providing inservice growth opportunities.

References: Allan R. Cohen, et al., *Effective Behavior in Organizations* (Revised Edition), Homewood, IL: Richard D. Irwin, Inc., 1980; Russell T. Gregg, "The Administrative Process" in Roald F. Campbell and Russell T. Gregg (Editors), *Administrative Behavior in Education,* New York: Harper and Brothers, 1957; Herbert A. Simon, *Administrative Behavior: A Study of Decision-Making Processes in Administrative Organization* (Second Edition), New York: The Macmillan Company, 1961.

INFORMAL ORGANIZATION, an organizational term used to identify the extralegal structures found within a complex organization. Where formal organization addresses the official roles and duties normally found in line and staff charts, informal organization is involved with the unofficial group (or clique) relationships that exist in organizations. Informal groups have no official basis for their existence. Because of the latent power inherent in such structures, however, they are frequently able to influence official decision making. In schools, informal organizations include primary groups such as the "old guard," "the bowling group," or "the young Turks."

References: Peter M. Blau, *The Dynamics of Bureaucracy,* Chicago: University of Chicago Press, 1955; Richard A. Gorton, *School Administration and Supervision: Important Issues, Concepts, and Case Studies* (Second Edition), Dubuque, IA: Wm. C. Brown Company, Publishers, 1980; Lawrence Iannaccone, "An Approach to Informal Organization of the School" in Daniel E. Griffiths (Editor), *Behavioral Science and Educational Administration* (NSSE 63rd Yearbook, Part II), Chicago: University of Chicago Press, 1964.

INFORMAL READING INVENTORY (IRI), an informal measure of a child's ability to read and comprehend text. The goal is to determine the reader's *instructional* reading level (reading level of the material the individual can understand with instructor assistance) and *independent* reading level (level of material she/he can read unassisted). Although commercial inventories are available from different publishers, the IRI is usually constructed from the basal reading series used within the school. In increasing levels of difficulty, individuals are requested to read previously selected passages and to answer between 5 and 10 comprehension questions. Different types of reading material are sampled in both oral and silent reading experience. Errors are recorded as the person reads, for later analysis. An IRI provides valuable information about a person's sight vocabulary, types of word recognition skills implemented, and general reading levels. (See ERROR PATTERN ANALYSIS.)

References: Paul C. Burns, Betty D. Roe, and Elinor P. Ross, *Teaching Reading in Today's Elementary School* (Third Edition), Boston: Houghton-Mifflin Company, 1984; Patrick J. Finn, *Helping Children Learn To Read*, New York: Random House, 1984; Joan P. Gipe, *Correction Reading Techniques for the Classroom Teacher*, Scottsdale, AZ: Gorsuch Scarisbrick Publishers, 1987; Betty D. Roe, et al., *Secondary School Reading Instruction: The Content Areas*, Boston: Houghton Mifflin Company, 1983.

INFORMATION PROCESSING, in humans, a process that involves: (1) the receiving of information (input); (2) internalizing of the information received (decision making); and (3) acting on the results of decision making (output). Information is received through various sensory means (visual, auditory, somatic, taste, smell, etc.) and then encoded. Cognition (mentally reacting to the information) and mediation (decision making) subsequently take place followed by the sending of messages (e.g. intended, or overt action; nonovert action such as rapid heart beat or galvanic skin responses) that may be considered output. Information processing is an important part of the cognitive process in humans.

Information processing is also used in computer systems. Information is put into the computer (input) in some usable form for later retrieval, either to provide information or to assist with the making of decisions. The return of this information to the user is referred to as output. Examples of the forms in which output is provided include actual listing of data, abstracts, full texts, and data analyses. Outputs are usually provided in symbolic form (i.e. either printed on paper or in an optic display). (See COGNITION; COGNITIVE DOMAIN; COMPUTER LANGUAGE; COMPUTER PROGRAM; and INFORMATION SCIENCE.)

References: Paul D. Eggen, et al., *Strategies for Teachers: Information Processing Models in the Classroom,* Englewood Cliffs, NJ: Prentice-Hall, Inc., 1979; W. K. Estes (Editor), *Human Information Processing,* Hillsdale, NJ: Lawrence Erlbaum Associates, Publishers, 1978; Roy Lachman, et al., *Cognitive Psychology and Information Processing: An Introduction,* Hillsdale, NJ: Lawrence Erlbaum Associates, Publishers, 1979; Helen M. Townley, *Systems Analysis for Information Retrieval,* London, England: A. Deutsch in Association with the Institute of Information Scientists, 1978.

INFORMATION SCIENCE, the study of information, including: (1) its nature and properties; (2) the manner in which it is generated and governed; and (3) how it is processed. Computers, telecommunication equipment, and machine systems are used in conjunction with such study.

Behavioral scientists, system theorists, engineers, designers of information systems, computer scientists, and specialists in cybernetics all contribute to the basic body of knowledge making up information science. The science has developed its own set of theorems and definitions and is quite logical and mathematical.

References: Forest W. Horton, Jr., *How to Harness Information Resources: A Systems Approach,* Cleveland, OH: Association for Systems Management, 1974; Frederick W. Lancaster, *Toward Paperless Information Systems,* New York: Academic Press, 1978; K. Samuelson, et al., *Information Systems and Networks,* Amsterdam, Holland: Elsevier North-Holland, Inc., 1977.

INFORMATION THEORY, the mathematical base of communication models. It has been stated that information theory is predicated on one theorem, namely, that information is transmitted through a noisy channel at any rate less than channel capacity with an arbitrarily small probability of error. This theorem is called the *fundamental theorem of information theory.* Information theory treats terms and concepts such as information, channel, capacity, source, entropy, encoder, decoder, destination, receiver, distortion, memory, and connecting codes.

References: Silviu Guiasu, *Information Theory with Applications,* New York: McGraw-Hill Book Company, 1977; Douglas S. Jones, *Elementary Information Theory,* Oxford, England: Clarendon Press Ltd., 1979; A. M. Mathai and P. N. Rathie, *Basic Concepts in Information Theory and Statistics,* New York: John Wiley and Sons, 1975.

INITIAL TEACHING ALPHABET (i.t.a.), an augmented alphabet designed to simplify the teaching of reading to beginners, developed in 1959 by Sir James Pitman. When first introduced, it was known as the Augmented Roman Alphabet. Sir James Pitman boasted a famous grandfather, Sir Isaac Pitman, inventor of the shorthand system that carries his name.

In i.t.a., the beginning student is required to learn but one fixed form (letter) for each of the English language's 45 sounds. Different letter configurations, to distinguish capital from lowercase letters, do not exist. Instead, the single forms are printed with larger type to denote the capital. Digraphs (forms made up of two characters) are fused together to give the appearance of a single letter. The initial teaching alphabet's 45 letters include 27 consonants. Its 17 vowels plus "y," which might be classified as either a vowel or a consonant, make up the rest of the alphabet.

Having mastered i.t.a., the student is then expected to transfer to the traditional orthography (t.o.). (See PITMAN, SIR ISAAC.)

References: John A. Downing, *The ITA Symposium,* New York: New York University Press, 1968 (Printed Originally by the Foundation for Educational Research in England and Wales, 1967); John A. Downing and William Latham, *Evaluating the Initial Teaching Alphabet: A Study of the Influence of English Orthography on Learning to Read and Write,* London, England: Cassell, 1967; Maurice Harrison, *The Story of the Initial Teaching Alphabet,* New York: Pitman Publishing Company, 1964.

INITIATING STRUCTURE—See LEADER BEHAVIOR DESCRIPTION QUESTIONNAIRE

INK BLOT TEST—See RORSCHACH TEST

IN LOCO PARENTIS, a legal doctrine that affirms that teachers stand "in the place of the parent" while pupils are in school. This status grants authority to the teacher that is essentially similar to that of the parent. Under the "in loco parentis" doctrine, teachers are granted authority to establish rules for pupils and to enforce those rules within the jurisdictional limits provided by law.

References: Edward C. Bolmeier, *Legality of Student Disciplinary Practices,* Charlottesville, VA: The Michie Company, 1976; E. Edmund Reutter, Jr., *Legal Aspects of Control of Student Activities by Public School Authorities,* Topeka, KS: National Organization on Legal Problems of Education, 1970.

INNER SPEECH—See SUBVOCALIZATION

INQUIRY METHOD, an instructional approach in which students use systematized problem-solving procedures to find answers to questions. Questions are usually those that are of interest to learners and/or based on their needs.

A major purpose of the inquiry method is to generate innovative/resourceful thinking on the part of students. To achieve this aim, the role of the teacher becomes less directive, differing markedly from traditional teaching in which the instructor, a central figure in the teaching-learning process, is expected to be the imparter of information. Inquiry requires a permissive learning climate, one in which students cooperatively investigate different aspects of a problem. Concurrently, the teacher functions as resource person and guide, refraining from imposing his/her authority or desires upon the students. The method lends itself to several subject fields, particularly science and social studies.

References: Leonard H. Clark and Irving S. Starr, *Secondary School Teaching Methods* (Third Edition), New York: Macmillan Publishing Company, Inc., 1976; Kenneth H. Hoover, *The Professional Teacher's Handbook: A Guide for Improving Instruction in Today's Middle and Secondary Schools* (Abridged Second Edition), Boston: Allyn and Bacon, Inc., 1976; John A. McCollum, *Ah Hah! The Inquiry Process of Generating and Testing Knowledge,* Santa Monica, CA: Goodyear Publishing Company, Inc., 1978.

INSERVICE EDUCATION, or continuing education, a program of planned activities designed to improve the quality of services rendered by employees. In education, its overriding purpose is improvement of instructional practices. Unlike preservice education, which has to do with the training of practitioners-to-be, inservice education serves those already trained and employed.

Inservice education of teachers takes many forms. A large number of teachers continue their professional growth by enrolling in university courses. Some participate in workshops, courses, or institutes sponsored by local schools or school systems. Others learn through travel and visitation. Of late, increasing numbers of teachers have been enrolling in local teacher center programs. (See CONTINUING EDUCATION and TEACHER CENTER.)

References: Ben M. Harris, et al., *Inservice Education: A Guide to Better Practice,* Englewood Cliffs, NJ: Prentice-Hall, Inc., 1969; Louis J. Rubin (Editor), *Improving Inservice Education: Proposals and Procedures for Change,* Boston: Allyn and Bacon, Inc., 1971.

INSTITUTE, a higher education term that has several meanings. When used in the context of *organization,* institute refers to either a unit within an organization that carries out research and/or instruction in a particular field or to an independent unit such as a technical or vocational institute that offers nondegree type of course work. When used as an *instructional* term, institute is a type of short course that is more intensive than a conference and similar to a workshop.

References: William E. Hopke (Editor), *Dictionary of Personnel and Guidance Terms: Including Professional Agencies and Associations,* Chicago: J. G. Ferguson Publishing Company, 1968; Asa S. Knowles (Editor), *The International Encyclopedia of Higher Education* (Volume 1), San Francisco: Jossey-Bass Publishers, 1977; G. Terry Page and J. B. Thomas, *International Dictionary of Education,* London, England: Kogan Page Ltd., 1977.

INSTITUTIONAL GOALS, aims/purposes established by an organization or institution. They give direction to the activities of individuals working in organizations. Institutional goals are usually set by coalitions of decision-making units, or groups of people, all working within an organizational structure. These groups or units define the overall roles, functions, and commitments of the organization. There are times, however, when certain broad institutional goals are set by people outside the organization. For example, college and school goals may be set by laws that established the educational institution. This could be true of hospitals, too. More specific goals, and policies as well, are more likely to be established by individuals who work for the organization. (See GOAL.)

References: Marcus Alexis and Charles F. Wilson, *Organization Decision-Making*, Englewood Cliffs, NJ: Prentice-Hall, Inc., 1967; Melvin J. Stanford, *Management Policy*, Englewood Cliffs, NJ: Prentice-Hall, Inc., 1979; Paul E. Torgersen and Irwin T. Weinstock, *Management: An Integrated Approach*, Englewood Cliffs, NJ: Prentice-Hall, Inc., 1972; Geoffrey Vickers, *Towards a Sociology of Management*, New York: Basic Books, Inc., Publishers, 1967.

INSTRUCTIONAL MEDIA—See MEDIA

INSTRUCTIONAL RESOURCE CENTER—See LEARNING RESOURCE CENTER

INSTRUCTIONAL TELEVISION (ITV), an audio-visual procedure that makes it possible to bring an array of multimedia learning experiences to a large number of students. Although ITV is used here as a generic term, some writers distinguish *instructional television* (ITV) from *educational television* (ETV). Where such distinctions are made, ITV refers to limited programming (e.g. closed-circuit or the playing of a videotape in one classroom); ETV, on the other hand, is applied to programs of a cultural and general education nature that are broadcast by public television stations.

The typical classroom equipped for television learning provides for both open- and closed-circuit viewing. Equipment is also available for playback of programs that have been recorded earlier, for recording of live programs and for off-the-air recording. Videotapes or video discs can be used for recording and playback.

The advent of ITV has provided numerous instructional opportunities for both teachers and learners alike. Student television productions, for example, an increasingly popular school activity, provide "active" experience opportunities for both populations. Television teaching has also provided new career opportunities for the limited number of teachers who devote all or part of their time to this type of work. Finally, and especially at the postsecondary level, ITV has made it possible for large numbers of viewers to study (and even to earn college credit) while viewing television in their homes. (See VIDEO DISCS and VIDEOTAPE.)

References: Jerrold Ackerman and Lawrence Lipsitz (Editors), *Instructional Television: Status and Directions*, Englewood Cliffs, NJ: Educational Technology Publications, 1977; James W. Brown, et al., *AV Instruction: Technology, Media, and Methods* (Fifth Edition), New York: McGraw-Hill Book Company, 1977; Mary L. Crow, *Teaching on Television*, Arlington, TX: Faculty Development Resource Center, University of Texas at Arlington, 1977; Robert Heinich, Michael Molenda, and James D. Russell, *Instructional Media and the New Technologies of Instruction* (Second Edition), New York: John Wiley and Sons, 1985; Robert L. Hilliard and Hyman H. Field, *Television and the Teacher: A Handbook for Classroom Use*, New York: Hastings House, Publishers, 1976; Wilbur Schramm (Editor), *Quality in Instructional Television*, Honolulu, HI: University Press of Hawaii, 1972.

INSTRUMENTAL CONDITIONING, a school of psychology within the general field of behavioristic psychology that is an extension of classical conditioning. In instrumental conditioning, the conditioning takes place when a response causes a stimulus to occur and the response-stimulus pairing causes that response to either increase or decrease in number or rate. For example, in instrumental conditioning, a dog could be taught to produce food (stimulus) by hitting a particular bar (response). The stimulus (food in the example) rewards or reinforces the behavior (response-hitting the bar). The reinforcement or reinforcing stimulus is similar to the unconditioned stimulus in classical conditioning. E. L. Thorndike, in 1898, introduced his "law of effect" and thus set the stage for instrumental conditioning. B. F. Skinner experimented with schedules of reinforcement in the 1930s and provided the base for programmed learning and instruction as well as many forms of behavior modification techniques that are now found in schools. William Glasser has developed *Control Theory*, which is the opposite of response-stimulus conditioning. (See CLASSICAL CONDITIONING and CONTROL THEORY.)

References: Donald L. King, *Conditioning: An Image Approach*, New York: Gardner Press, Inc., 1979; Howard Rachlin, *Introduction to Modern Behaviorism* (Second Edition), San Francisco: W. H. Freeman and Company, 1976.

INSTRUMENTAL MUSIC, a part of the school music curriculum in which children are taught to perform musically, alone or in groups, using standard musical instruments. Instrumental instruction normally begins in the elementary school (intermediate grades), with small groups of children being taught together, and continues as part of the participating student's secondary school program. In some schools, children are taught to use recorders and other preband instruments before being introduced to standard musical instruments. Although instrumental music instruction normally begins in the elementary school, it is usually possible for a student to start such instruction while in secondary school.

Traditional instrumental instruction includes the teaching of notation, good habit patterns, care of the instrument, and skills. Instruments chosen generally include those that are part of the string, percussion, woodwind, and brass families, with choices influenced by such personal factors as the student's interest and physical size as well as such practical considerations as availability or cost (purchase vs. rental vs. loan from the school district). A major advantage of school instrumental music programs is that they afford opportunity for ensemble (band or orchestra) experience.

In recent years, instrumental music has been broadened in some schools to become "comprehensive musicianship" or "aesthetic education" that involves teaching musicianship, music history and literature, and music theory along with instrumental music education. The purpose of this more encompassing approach is to develop a well-rounded musician. (See AESTHETIC EDUCATION.)

References: Neal E. Glenn, et al., *Secondary School Music: Philosophy, Theory, and Practice,* Englewood Cliffs, NJ: Prentice-Hall, Inc., 1970; Charles R. Hoffer, *Teaching Music in the Secondary Schools* (Second Edition), Belmont, CA: Wadsworth Publishing Company, Inc., 1973, Harry E. Moses, *Developing and Administering a Comprehensive High School Music Program,* West Nyack, NY: Parker Publishing Company, Inc., 1970; Bennett Reimer, *Philosophy of Music Education,* Englewood Cliffs, NJ: Prentice-Hall, Inc., 1970.

INSURANCE, cooperative sharing of risk of financial or other types of loss. In the majority of states, legal obligation for maintaining a sound insurance program for school systems rests with the local school board. Such a program normally includes the following types of coverage: (1) fire; (2) liability; (3) workmen's compensation; (4) crime; (5) vehicle; (6) boiler and machinery; (7) student accident; and (8) employee insurance (i.e. medical). A few states (e.g. North Carolina) have state-operated programs with varying types of coverage provided.

Self-insurance is sometimes practiced by large school districts. In such cases, the decision to self-insure is based on the belief that it is less expensive to self-insure than it is to buy insurance protection from commercial companies. Self-insurance usually involves the establishment of a reserve fund that is phased in as its size grows (owing to regular contributions made and proceeds from investment).

Another approach to insurance is the collaborative trust. Risks are shared through the pooling of school districts and the development of safety programs. One example of this arrangement is the New England Safety Insurance Collaborative; another is the New York State Safety Group.

References: Association of School Business Officials of the U.S. and Canada, *School Business Affairs,* April 1979; Percy E. Burrup, *Financing Education in a Climate of Change* (Second Edition), Boston: Allyn and Bacon, Inc., 1977; I. Carl Candoli, et al., *School Business Administration: A Planning Approach* (Second Edition), Boston: Allyn and Bacon, Inc., 1978; John Greenhalgh, *Practitioner's Guide to School Business Management,* Boston: Allyn and Bacon, Inc., 1978.

INTANGIBLE PROPERTY—See PROPERTY TAX

INTEGRATED INSTRUCTIONAL INFORMATION RESOURCE (IIIR)—See EDUCATIONAL PRODUCTS INFORMATION EXCHANGE INSTITUTE

INTEGRATED STUDIES, or correlated studies, programs designed such that: (1) the materials are arranged in a related order, with content building on the preceding content; (2) material in one subject area is related to or uses content in another area (e.g. integrating history, mathematics, and English into a unit or lesson); and (3) school subject material is related to the out-of-school environment. The term *integrated* or *correlated studies* was used and advocated by John Dewey and other educators at the turn of the 20th century. This concept has been incorporated into organizational structures such as the Core Curriculum, Dual Progress Plan, and the Dalton Plan. (See CORE PROGRAM; DALTON PLAN; and DUAL PROGRESS PLAN.)

Reference: National Council of Teachers of English, *A Correlated Curriculum,* New York: D. Appleton-Century Company, 1936.

INTEGRATION, RACIAL, a term originally used interchangeably with "desegregation" but that, in recent years, has come to have a meaning of its own, namely, social assimilation of minority students in a culturally diverse school. Racial *desegregation* brings together students of different races for educational purposes. *Integration* follows desegregation and is said to have been realized when minority group students are accepted as social equals and accorded true equality of educational opportunity. Over the last quarter-century, carefully planned strategies by school personnel have been shown to expedite realization of school integration.

Harvard Professor Thomas F. Pettigrew, student of race relations and the schools, was one of the first to distinguish *integration* from *segregation*. (See DESEGREGATION and RACIAL BALANCE.)

References: James H. Bash, *Effective Teaching in the Desegregated School* (PDK Fastback 32), Bloomington, IN: The Phi Delta Kappa Educational Foundation, 1973; National School Public Relations Association, *Desegregation: How Schools Are Meeting Historic Challenge*, Arlington, VA: The Association, 1973; Thomas F. Pettigrew, *Racially Separate or Together?* New York: McGraw-Hill Book Company, 1971; Nancy H. St. John, *School Desegregation Outcomes for Children*, New York: John Wiley and Sons, 1975.

INTEGRATION, SUBJECT MATTER, the combining of subject matter into broad fields of study, into a core curriculum, or into a combined field such that subject matter is highly synthesized.

For example, a course titled "Modern Man" may integrate various subject areas: philosophy, political science, psychology, literature, history, fine arts, economics, medicine, and many other areas as they relate to the nature of modern man. Although these are discrete subjects, they are not taught separately. Rather, they are taught as a cluster with attention given to their contributions to, or effects upon mankind.

References: Ronald C. Doll, *Curriculum Improvement* (Second Edition), Boston: Allyn and Bacon, Inc., 1970; John I. Goodlad, et al., *Curriculum Inquiry*, New York: McGraw-Hill Book Company, 1979; Daniel Tanner and Laurel N. Tanner, *Curriculum Development: Theory into Practice* (Second Edition), New York: Macmillan Publishing Company, Inc., 1980.

INTELLIGENCE, the ability or capacity to perform mental tasks of reasoning and comprehension. The abstract term itself is a complex psychological construct.

Intelligence is made up of a multiplicity of abilities and factors, and there are several definitions, or models, of intelligence. For example, Joy P. Guilford's model of intelligence includes the interaction of various *operations* (cognition, memory, divergent thinking, convergent thinking, evaluation); *products* (units, classes, relations, systems, transformations, implications); and *contents* (figural, symbolic, semantic, behavioral). Raymond

B. Cattell classified intelligence into two broad groups: *biological endowment* (fluid intelligence) and *experimental educative-acculturative influences* (crystallized intelligence). There are other models and definitions too.

Intelligence can be influenced by many factors. Examples of these are: socioeconomics; opportunities for intellectual development; range of experiences; childrearing practices; parental attitudes; degree and level of education; cultural influences; and age. Often, intelligence is measured by an intelligence test with a "general ability" score (I.Q. Score) provided. (See INTELLIGENCE QUOTIENT.)

References: Lee J. Cronbach, *Educational Psychology* (Third Edition), New York: Harcourt Brace Jovanovich, Inc., 1977; Joy P. Guilford, *Nature of Human Intelligence*, New York: McGraw-Hill Book Company, 1968; John L. Horn and Raymond B. Cattell, "Refinement and Test of the Theory of Fluid and Crystallized General Intelligence," *Journal of Educational Psychology*, Volume 57, 1966; William A. Mehrens and Irvin J. Lehmann, *Using Standardized Tests in Education*, New York: Longman Inc., 1987; Philip E. Vernon, *Intelligence: Heredity and Environment*, San Francisco: W. H. Freeman and Company, 1979; W. Bruce Walsh and Nancy E. Betz, *Tests and Measurement*, Englewood Cliffs, NJ: Prentice-Hall, Inc., 1985.

INTELLIGENCE QUOTIENT (I. Q.), a standard score that provides an interpretation of construct intelligence, regardless of the age of the individual. The I.Q. score was first used with the 1916 version of the Stanford-Binet tests. (The Stanford-Binet tests were American translations and revisions by Lewis Terman of Stanford University of the Binet-Simon tests.) The I.Q. score had its origins in 1908 when Alfred Binet introduced the concept of mental age.

The I.Q. score is a ratio of mental age (MA) to chronological age (CA) multiplied by 100.

$$IQ = \frac{MA}{CA} \times 100$$

If a child has a mental age of 12 and a chronological age of 10, then his/her I.Q. = 120. If another child has a mental age of 10 and a chronological age of 12, then his/her I.Q. = 83. Since the I.Q. is a standard score, its means and standard deviations for a particular set of tests must be the same. In most tests, the mean for the I.Q. scores is 100 with a standard deviation of 15 or 16.

There are many problems associated with the use of I.Q. scores. Among them are: misinterpretations and abuses of the score; problems with the definition of the concept of intelligence; nonlinearity of intellectual development; socioeconomic influences on educational development; and problems with the comparisons of "general ability" to specific abilities. (See CHRONOLOGICAL AGE; INTELLIGENCE; MENTAL AGE; STANDARD DEVIATION; and TERMAN, LEWIS.)

References: Lee J. Cronbach, *Educational Psychology* (Third Edition), New York: Harcourt Brace Jovanovich, Inc., 1977; Lee J. Cronbach, *Essentials of Psychological Testing* (Fourth Edition), New York: Harper and Row, Publishers, 1984; W. Bruce Walsh and Nancy E. Betz, *Tests and Measurement*, Englewood Cliffs, NJ: Prentice-Hall, Inc., 1985.

INTELLIGENCE TESTS, instruments designed to measure mental tasks of reasoning and comprehension. These tests measure either general ability or specific abilities. Some are administered individually, others as group tests.

Examples of *individual tests* are: Bayley Scales of Infant Development (ages 2–30 months); Cooperative Preschool Inventory (ages 3–6); Haptic Intelligence Scale for Adult Blind; Pictorial Test of Intelligence (ages 3–8); the Quick Test (ages 2 and over); Slosson Intelligence Test (ages 2 weeks and over); Stanford-Binet Intelligence Scale (ages 2 and over); Wechsler Adult Intelligence Scale, or WAIS (ages 16 and over); Wechsler Intelligence Scale for Children, or WISC (ages 5–15); and the Wechsler Preschool and Primary Scale of Intelligence, or WPPSI (ages 4–6.5).

Group tests include: Academic Alertness "AA" (adult); Analysis of Learning Potential (grades 1–12); Boehm Test of Basic Concepts (grades K–2); California Short-Form Test of Mental Maturity (K–12, adults); Cognitive Abilities Test (K–3); Cooperative School and College Ability Tests (grades 4–14); Doppelt Mathematical Reasoning Tests (grades 16–17 and employees); Goodenough-Harris Drawing Tests (ages 3–15); Lorge-Thorndike Intelligence Tests (grades 12–13, also grades 3–13); Miller Analogies Tests (candidates for graduate school); Otis-Lennon Mental Ability (grades K–12); Quick Word Tests (grades 4–12, average adults, college and professional adults); SRA Short Test of Educational Ability (grades K–12); and the Thurstone Test of Mental Alertness (grades 9–12 and adults).

In addition, there are many *specific intelligence tests.* A few examples are: Closure Flexibility (Concealed Figures) (industrial employees); Concept Assessment Kit-Conservation (ages 4–7); Hidden Figures Test (grades 6–16); Illinois Test of Psycholinguistic Ability (ages 2–10); Perceptual Speed (grades 9–16); Remote Associates Test (college and adults); and the Torrance Test of Creative Thinking (K–graduate school).

Tests in Print II lists 67 individual, 159 group, and 53 specific intelligence tests. (See INTELLIGENCE and INTELLIGENCE QUOTIENT.)

References: Oscar K. Buros (Editor), *Tests in Print II,* Highland Park, NJ: The Gryphon Press, 1974; Oscar K. Buros (Editor), *The Eighth Mental Measurements Yearbook* (Volume I), Highland Park, NJ: The Gryphon Press, 1978; Lee J. Cronbach, *Essentials of Psychological Testing* (Fourth Edition), New York: Harper and Row, Publishers, 1984; William A. Mehrens and Irvin J. Lehmann, *Using Standardized Tests in Education*, New York: Longman, Inc., 1987; W. Bruce Walsh and Nancy E. Betz, *Tests and Measurement*, Englewood Cliffs, NJ: Prentice-Hall, Inc., 1985.

INTELLIGENT COMPUTER-ASSISTED INSTRUCTION (ICAI), computer-assisted instructional programs that diagnose learners' errors and provide instruction appropriate to their strengths and/or weaknesses (e.g., error patterns). ICAI is an adaptive program that permits instruction to fit the knowledge base of the learner at each stage or level of instruction. ICAI utilizes artificial intelligence to adapt to a learner's level and to provide instruction with regard to what is to be learned. There are three major components of ICAI: (1) command of knowledge or subject matter domain, including the "ability" to solve problems within the context of the domain; (2) a comprehensive model of the learner(s)—to understand and represent each learner at a given level; and (3) ability to provide instruction that is appropriate to both the subject matter and the learner at a given point in time. ICAI programs are being used in the military and by physicians. (See ARTIFICIAL INTELLIGENCE.)

References: Lyn Corno and Richard E. Snow, "Adapting Teaching to Individual Differences Among Learners" in Merlin C. Wittrock (Editor), *Handbook of Research on Teaching* (Third Edition), New York: Macmillan Publishing Co., 1986; Neill Graham, *The Mind Tool, Computers and Their Impact on Society* (Fourth Edition), St. Paul, MN: West Publishing Co., 1986; Harold F. O'Neil, Jr., et al., "Research in Teaching in the Armed Forces" in Merlin C. Wittrock (Editor), *Handbook of Research on Teaching* (Third Edition), New York: Macmillan Publishing Co., 1986.

INTERACTION ANALYSIS—See FLANDERS INTERACTION ANALYSIS

INTERACTIVE MODEL OF READING, a theory of reading that accepts both a meaning-based approach (top-down model of reading) and a sound-symbol approach (bottom-up model of reading) as impacting the reading process. A reader uses both processes in the reading act. She/he may substitute a synonym consistent with text (top-down) and later in the same passage use phonics to decode a word which then leads to meaning (bottom-up). Different reading purposes can trigger different processes: i.e., in reading a novel for enjoyment, the reader uses the fewest cues to predict meaning; however, when studying for a test, she/he will read a selection word-for-word. Developed by Rumelhart (1976), the model suggests that all information sources (i.e., letter, sound, syntax, semantics, and experience) available to the reader operate together and in any order. Since reading is neither a pure top-down or bottom-up process, some experts believe that the interactive model has the most value when transferred to the practical teaching of reading. (See BOTTOM-UP MODEL OF READING and TOP-DOWN MODEL OF READING.)

References: Patrick J. Finn, *Helping Children Learn to Read,* New York: Random House, 1985; Lenore H. Ringer and Carol K. Weber, *A Language-Thinking Approach to Reading Diagnosis and Teaching,* New York: Harcourt Brace Jovanovich, Publishers, 1984; David E. Rumelhart, *Toward an Interactive Model for Reading* (Technical Report No. 56), Center for Human Information Processing, San Diego, CA: University of California, 1976.

INTERDISCIPLINARY STUDIES, interrelated sets of courses and activities from a variety of fields or disciplines. They are more often found in colleges and universities than in elementary or secondary schools. Interdisciplinary courses are usually issue or problem oriented, thus a lowing for various disciplines to have input on an issue or problem being studied. Structure and identifiable disciplines are found within such courses. Interdisciplinary courses can be quite substantive and variable with respect to difficulty. There are occasional problems associated with the implementation of interdisciplinary courses, primarily because some institutions have designed them along the lines of the core curriculum or else have made the courses too general. In most cases, interdisciplinary courses require a considerable depth of knowledge of the disciplines involved. (See CORE PROGRAM.)

References: Anthony Blasi, et al., *Toward an Interpretive Sociology,* Washington, DC: University Press of America, 1978; Harry Finestone and Michael F. Shugrue (Editors), *Prospects for the 70's,* New York: Modern Language Association, 1973; Joseph J. Kockelmans (Editor), *Interdis-*

ciplinarity and Higher Education, University Park, PA: Pennsylvania State University Press, 1979.

INTEREST INVENTORIES, instruments developed to assess the interests an individual has in a particular activity, usually a vocation or occupation. It has been found that people in a particular occupation tend to have similar interests. Although several inventories that measured a person's interests existed in the early 1900s, it wasn't until 1919–20, during a graduate seminar at Carnegie Institute of Technology in Pittsburgh, that the modern interest inventories were developed. The Strong Vocational Interest Blank (SVIB) was one of the major tests developed during the seminar.

When completing the inventory, individuals are asked to circle whether they "like," "dislike," or are "indifferent" to selected occupations, school subjects, amusements, activities, and types of people. Another part of the SVIB requires a ranking of activities, comparison of interests, and personal rating of abilities. The Strong-Campbell Interest Inventory (1974) is a revised version of SVIB.

Other types of inventories include the Kuder-Preference Record; the Minnesota Vocational Interest Inventory; Kuder General Interest Survey; Holland Vocational Preference Inventory; Interest Self-Rating Inventory; and the Project TALENT Interest Inventory.

References: Anne Anastasi, *Psychological Testing* (Sixth Edition), New York: Macmillan Publishing Company, Inc., 1988; Robert L. Ebel, *Essentials of Educational Measurement* (Third Edition), Englewood Cliffs, NJ: Prentice-Hall, Inc., 1979; Bert A. Goldman and John L. Saunders, *Directory of Unpublished Experimental Mental Measures* (Volume I), New York: Behavioral Publications, 1974.

INTERGOVERNMENTAL ADVISORY COUNCIL ON EDUCATION (IACE), a council that provides assistance and advises the president, the Congress, and the secretary of education on education as related to intergovernmental policies and relations. It brings together federal, state and local governmental representatives with those from the private sector to discuss educational issues and federal educational programs. In addition to these activities, the council may review proposed, as well as existing, rules and regulations to assess their impact on education at the federal, state, local, and private levels.

The U.S. Congress passed Public Law 96–88 which established the council in 1979. The president appoints the 20 members. Membership is composed of elected state and local officials, individuals from business, students, parents, and representatives from public and private education (elementary, secondary, and post-secondary). In 1985 the council was composed of a certified public accountant, several state senators/representatives, a private school teacher, a vice principal of a public high school, a local PTA president, a former mayor, a former school administrator, college instructors, a college administrator, a college trustee/regent, local elected officials, a state commissioner of labor, and a director of a department at the state level. The under secretary of education serves as an ex-officio member of the council. (See *(A) REPORT TO THE PRESIDENT OF THE UNITED STATES, NATIONAL NETWORKING CONFERENCE.*)

Reference: Intergovernmental Advisory Council on Education, *A Report to the President of the United States, National Networking Conference, Topic: Teacher Preparation and Retention*, Washington, DC: The Council, 1985.

INTERIOR DESIGN, a component of the home economics curriculum that focuses on the use of space within a building with principal attention given to aesthetic, functional and psychological use. The interrelationships of people, manmade items, use and function, and the total environment are major concerns of interior designers. Interior design is also considered a specialized field within architecture.

Programs for those pursuing careers as interior designers may be found in vocational and trade schools, architecture schools and colleges, art schools and colleges, and in certain other colleges and universities. Art, architecture, mechanical drawing, storage, living space, free drawing, watercolors, two/three-dimensional design, home furnishings, textiles, color design, psychology, economics, and management make up the typical interior design curriculum. (See HOME ECONOMICS.)

References: Phyllis S. Allen, *Beginnings of Interior Environment* (Revised Edition), Provo, UT: Brigham Young University Press, 1977; Erica Brown, *Interior Views: Design At Its Best*, New York: The Viking Press, 1977; Jose Wilson and Arthur Leaman, *Decorating American Style*, Boston: New York Graphic Society, 1975.

INTERMEDIATE SCHOOL, an organizational term that has two meanings. When used generically, intermediate school refers to any school that is positioned organizationally between the elementary school and senior high school levels and that

serves middle-years children. Junior high schools and middle schools, collectively, are sometimes referred to as intermediate schools. When used more narrowly, the term refers to the school, in a 6-2-4 or 4-4-4 school system, which houses the middle grades. (See JUNIOR HIGH SCHOOL and MIDDLE SCHOOL.)

References: Frederick S. Calhoun, *Organization of the Middle Grades: A Summary of Research*, Arlington, VA: Educational Research Service, Inc., 1983; Harl R. Douglass, "What Type of Organization of Schools?" in George C. Stoumbis and Alvin W. Howard (Editors), *Schools for the Middle Years: Readings*, Scranton, PA: International Textbook Company, 1969; Sylvester Kohut, Jr., *The Middle School: A Bridge between Elementary and High Schools* (Second Edition), Washington, DC: National Education Association, 1988; Maurice McGlasson, *The Middle School: Whence? What? Whither?* (PDK Fastback 22), Bloomington, IN: The Phi Delta Kappa Educational Foundation, 1973.

INTERMEDIATE UNIT, an administrative organization that has its own board and/or officer and that, historically, has been positioned between the local school district and the state education agency. Intermediate school units are not uniform with respect to form or function.

One type of intermediate unit, and one of the earliest to be formed in the United States, is organized along county lines. A county superintendent, functioning as liaison between local districts and the state, is responsible for maintenance of standards in areas such as certification, pupil attendance, and finance. Another type of intermediate unit, the intermediate school district (ISD), involves the voluntary union of two or more (usually small) school districts for the purpose of providing specialized services that the districts, individually, are unable to provide. Some are organized along county lines, others regionally; ISDs permit small districts to avail themselves of relatively specialized instructional services (e.g. teachers of the blind), effective inservice programs, research services, and instructional material, even while maintaining their autonomy. Examples of the latter type are the Board of Cooperative Educational Services, found in New York State, and Nebraska's Educational Service Units.

References: Louis Bruno, *The Intermediate School District*, Olympia, WA: Association of Intermediate School District Superintendents, 1972; Roald F. Campbell, et al., *The Organization and Control of American Schools* (Fourth Edition), Columbus, OH: Charles E. Merrill Publishing Company, 1980; Stephen J. Knezevich, *Administration of Public Education* (Second Edition), New York: Harper and Row, Publishers, 1969; Emery Stoops, et al., *Handbook of Educational Administration: A Guide for the Practitioner,* Boston: Allyn and Bacon, Inc., 1975.

INTERNAL CONSISTENCY—See RELIABILITY

INTERNAL MEMORY, the primary storage unit for data and programs within the computer. It is part of the actual internal hardware. The internal memory is composed of integrated circuits printed on small chips made from larger silicon crystals.

A large number of electronic cells are found on the surface of each chip. Each cell is either full or empty; thus all its possible states can be represented by two digits within the binary system—zero and one. Each of the binary digits is called a *bit* (short for binary digit). Eight or nine bits grouped together is a byte. A byte is a unit sufficiently large to represent any character. The symbol K is used to measure memory; it represents 2^{10} or 1,024. Thus, a 16K bit chip is a memory chip with 16,384 binary storage cells. Similarly, the terms *kilobit* and *kilobyte* mean 2^{10} bits or bytes of memory. If a computer has less than 16KB of memory, it is limited to very small programs. At least 64KB of memory is needed to make a personal computer useful to school or business applications. The two major types of internal memory are READ ONLY MEMORY (ROM) AND RANDOM ACCESS MEMORY (RAM). (See RANDOM ACCESS MEMORY and READ ONLY MEMORY.)
References: Grace Murray Hopper and Steven L. Mandell, *Understanding Computers,* St. Paul, MN: West Publishing Company, 1984; David R. Sullivan, et al., *Computing Today: Microcomputer Concepts and Applications,* Boston: Houghton Mifflin Company, 1985.

INTERNAL VALIDITY—See VALIDITY, INTERNAL-EXTERNAL

INTERNATIONAL ASSOCIATION FOR THE EVALUATION OF EDUCATIONAL ACHIEVEMENT (IEA), an organization headquartered in Ghent, Belgium, which is responsible for ongoing IEA Studies which were initiated in 1959. IEA has three major functions: (1) educational research on an international scale (cross-cultural comparative studies); (2) research that provides facts that will help in solving significant educational problems and issues; and (3) allowing member countries of IEA to participate in cooperative projects.

In 1976 IEA published a nine-volume, cross-cultural comparative assessment in science, mathematics, reading comprehension, foreign languages, literature, and civic education. Students (250,000) from 22 nations and teachers (50,000) were involved. A major finding of the study was that schools do make a difference in a child's education and development, and this was true across various cultures.

Two IEA major studies that had an impact on education in the United States were the First International Mathematics Study (1964) and the Second International Mathematics Study (1985). Both studies were comprehensive surveys of teaching and learning of mathematics in the schools; 12 countries were in the first study and 20 countries were in the second. Student achievement and attiudes were assessed through internationally developed tests and questionnaires. Targeted populations were 8th- and 12th-graders (the 12th-graders were enrolled in advanced college-preparatory courses). The following countries were involved in the second study: Belgium (Flemish), Belgium (French), Canada, England and Wales, Finland, Japan, France, Hong Kong, Hungary, Israel, Luxembourg, the Netherlands, New Zealand, Nigeria, Scotland, Swaziland, Sweden, Thailand, and the United States. U.S. students were at best, near or below the international average in achievement at both the 8th- and 12th-grade levels in both studies. Criticism of the mathematics curriculum in the United States followed the publication of both studies.
References: International Association for the Evaluation of Educational Achievement, *International Studies in Evaluation* (nine volumes), New York: John Wiley, 1976; Curtis C. McKnight, et al., *The Underachieving Curriculum: Assessing U.S. School Mathematics from the International Perspective,* Champaign, IL: Stipes Publishing Co., 1987; William H. Shubert, *Curriculum, Perspective, Paradigm, and Possibility,* New York: Macmillan Publishing Co., 1986; Daniel Tanner and Laurel N. Tanner, *Curriculum Development, Theory into Practice* (Second Edition), New York: Macmillan Publishing Co., Inc., 1980.

INTERNATIONAL COUNCIL ON EDUCATION FOR TEACHING (ICET), an organization founded in 1953 to provide services and programs on a worldwide basis. ICET is a nongovernmental association of educational organizations, institutions, and individuals, and a nongovernmental member of UNESCO.

The organization has four major thrusts. They are: (1) improve the quality of the preparation of teachers, administrators, and other educational personnel; (2) facilitate cooperation between higher education, government and the private sector in developing a network of resources; (3) develop an international forum for the exchange of information and ideas; (4) help institutions develop curriculum and alternative (nontraditional) educational approaches.

A board of directors and a board of trustees govern ICET. Directors are nominated from among leaders in higher education; the directors establish policy for the organization. The trustees come from corporate and government representatives, and promote cooperative programs. A permanent secretariat is located in the National Center for Higher Education in Washington, DC.

The council sponsors an annual ICET World Assembly (the 35th World Assembly was held July 18–22, 1988, in Sydney, Australia), as well as publishing the ICET *International Yearbook in Teacher Education*, a biannual newsletter, and other documents. Low-cost educational travel programs and special conferences, programs, and activities in international education are sponsored by ICET.

ICET is a founding member of the consortium for International Cooperation in Higher Education (CICHE). The consortium, established in 1980, provides a major contact for those outside the United States who wish access to higher education in this country. (See UNITED NATIONS EDUCATIONAL, SCIENTIFIC AND CULTURAL ORGANIZATION.)

Reference: International Council on Education for Teaching, *An International Association of Decision-Makers in Education, Government, and Business Dedicated to Development through Education*, Washington, DC: The Council, undated.

INTERNATIONAL EDUCATION—See GLOBAL EDUCATION

INTERNATIONAL FEDERATION OF SECONDARY TEACHERS—See WORLD CONFEDERATION OF ORGANIZATIONS OF THE TEACHING PROFESSION

INTERNATIONAL FEDERATION OF TEACHERS' ASSOCIATIONS—See WORLD CONFEDERATION OF ORGANIZATIONS OF THE TEACHING PROFESSION

INTERNATIONAL INTER-VISITATION PROGRAM IN EDUCATIONAL ADMINISTRATION (IIP), a program that is sponsored by the University Council for Educational Administration and implemented every four years. It was estab-

lished in 1966 with the financial support of the W. K. Kellogg Foundation. The purpose of the program is to bring together senior practitioners and scholars in educational administration from many countries for an intensive three-week program of conferences and visitations. During these sessions, participants exchange information and examine the educational systems in the host country. Programs have been conducted in North America (1966); Australia (1970); Great Britain (1974); Canada (1978); Nigeria (1982); Hawaii, Fiji, and New Zealand (1986); and the United Kingdom of the Netherlands (1990). (See UNIVERSITY COUNCIL FOR EDUCATIONAL ADMINISTRATION.)

Reference: The University Council for Educational Administration, "Sixth IIP Takes Participants to Hawaii, Fiji and New Zealand." *UCEA Review*, Volume 28, Number 1, 1986.

INTERNATIONAL READING ASSOCIATION (IRA), an organization consisting of teachers, reading specialists, administrators, researchers, and others who have reading instruction as an interest in common. The association is made up of 70,000 members in 60 countries. IRA was formed in 1956 when the International Council for the Improvement of Reading Instruction and the National Association for Remedial Teaching merged. Its main headquarters is in Newark, Delaware, with branch offices in Paris and Buenos Aires.

IRA includes over 1,000 councils and national affiliates in 25 countries. It publishes 10–15 books a year and three journals: (1) *The Reading Teacher,* monthly, October–May; (2) *Journal of Reading,* monthly, October–May; and (3) *Reading Research Quarterly.*

IRA has three general goals: (1) the improvement of reading instruction; (2) promoting the lifetime reading habit; and (3) promoting individual reader proficiency.

References: International Reading Association, *Fact Sheet,* Newark, DE: The Association, Undated Sheet; International Reading Association, *Read, You'll Never Be the Same Again,* Newark, DE: The Association, Undated Brochure.

INTERNATIONAL YEARBOOK OF EDUCATION, an annual reference book that was published by the International Bureau of Education and UNESCO. Of particular interest to comparative educators, the *Yearbook* reported on the conditions of education in selected UNESCO countries. Published in English and French, it first appeared

in 1948 and ceased publication in 1969.
References: John W. Best, *Research in Education* (Third Edition), Englewood Cliffs, NJ: Prentice-Hall, Inc., 1977; Eugene P. Sheehy, *Guide to Reference Books* (Ninth Edition), Chicago: American Library Association, 1976.

INTERNATIONAL YEARBOOK ON TEACHER EDUCATION—See INTERNATIONAL COUNCIL ON EDUCATION FOR TEACHING (ICET)

INTERNATIONAL YEAR OF THE CHILD (IYC),

a one-year observance (proclaimed by a United Nations General Assembly Resolution) that had as one of its objectives "to provide a *framework for advocacy* (emphasis ours) on behalf of children and for enhancing the awareness of the special needs of children on the part of decision-makers and the public." The resolution was passed in 1976, one that designated 1979 as the official IYC. The idea for an IYC was suggested by Canon Joseph Moerman, President of the International Catholic Child Bureau, and endorsed by numbers of interested nongovernmental agencies throughout the world.

Most reviewers agree that the 1979 observance was successful, with much responsibility for its success attributed to the decentralized and diversified manner in which it was carried out. Different countries each established their own program foci, thus assuring relevancy. Brazil's program, for example, focused on the needs of urban children, Liberia's on the rural child. Other examples of program foci included Kenya, school milk; United Kingdom, the establishment of children's legal centers; and, in Sri Lanka, the creation of children's nutrition centers. Priority areas established by the United States "were: child nurturing, health, education, juvenile justice, development of the individual through recreation, play and the arts, equal opportunity and cultural diversity, impact of media on children, and children around the world" (Interim Report, p. 95).

Each country's program was carried out under the direction of a national commission. Responsibility for coordination of post-1979 activities related to IYC has been assigned to UNICEF. (See UNITED NATIONS INTERNATIONAL CHILDREN'S EMERGENCY FUND.)
References: Maggie Black, "International Year of the Child: A Year that Worked," *Development Forum,* January-February 1980; Marian W. Edelman, "Justice for Children Everywhere," *Today's Education,* February–March 1979; International Year of the Child Secretariat, *International Year of the Child 1979: Interim Report,* June 30, 1980.

INTERNSHIP, an extended field experience normally carried out under the direction of a training institution and scheduled as the culminating part of a professional training program. The purpose of the internship is to provide the trainee with on-the-job training under the tutelage of an experienced practitioner and/or a university supervisor. Internships have long been required of students engaged in the study of such fields as medicine and dentistry.

In education, administrative internships have been completed by thousands of students aspiring to various educational leadership positions (e.g. principalship). Some are completed under the auspices of a university; others, sometimes referred to as cadet programs, are sponsored by school systems seeking to prepare their own professional employees for leadership posts. The first university-sponsored internship program in educational administration was introduced by New York University's Professor Frithiof (Fritz) Borgeson in 1931).

An increasing number of states and teacher training institutions are introducing and/or requiring teacher internships. They normally require extended (e.g. one-year) field experience in the classroom and chronologically follow the traditional student teaching experience.

Interns frequently receive some nominal compensation for their service. (See COOPERATING ADMINISTRATOR.)
References: Roald F. Campbell, et al., *Introduction to Educational Administration* (Fifth Edition), Boston: Allyn and Bacon, Inc., 1977; Don R. Davies, *The Internship in Educational Administration,* Washington, DC: Center for Applied Research in Education, 1962; Horton C. Southworth, et al., *Internship in Teacher Education* (47th Yearbook), Washington, DC: The Association for Student Teaching, 1968.

INTERPERSONAL BEHAVIOR, behavior manifested by an individual in the context of other individuals. Such elements as self-direction, experiencing feelings, empathy, responsiveness, inadequacy, loneliness, isolation, hostility, alienation, apathy, frustration, understanding, loyalty, cooperation, assertiveness, and permissiveness influence interpersonal behavior with the nature and magnitude of behavior depending on the situation and the individuals involved.
References: Irwin Altman and Dalmas A. Taylor, *Social*

Penetration: The Development of Interpersonal Relationships, New York: Holt, Rinehart and Winston, Inc., 1973; Lee J. Cronbach, *Educational Psychology* (Third Edition), New York: Harcourt Brace Jovanovich, Inc., 1977; George M. Gazda, et al., *Human Relations Development: A Handbook for Educators* (Second Edition), Boston: Allyn and Bacon, Inc., 1977; Richard T. Ofshe (Editor), *Interpersonal Behavior in Small Groups*, Englewood Cliffs, NJ: Prentice-Hall, Inc., 1973.

INTERPERSONAL INTELLIGENCE, an ability that enables humans to make distinctions among themselves. This intelligence is one of the seven biologically based intelligences that make up the Theory of Multiple Intelligences (MI Theory). The biological origins of interpersonal intelligences are derived from three factors: (1) the prolonged childhood of humans, which includes a close bonding with the mother; (2) humans as "social animals" do things that require the cooperative efforts of many people; and (3) the frontal lobes of the brain effect personality behaviors and traits that influence interpersonal actions. Individuals who successfully interact with the public and/or with large numbers of individuals (for examples, teachers, or police) must have a highly developed interpersonal intelligence in order to be successful. As with the other intelligences found in the MI Theory, an individual uses several intelligences along with interpersonal intelligence to focus on solving interpersonal problems. (See BODILY-KINESTHETIC INTELLIGENCE; INTELLIGENCE; INTRAPERSONAL INTELLIGENCE; LINGUISTIC INTELLIGENCE; MULTIPLE INTELLIGENCE THEORY; MUSICAL INTELLIGENCE; SPATIAL INTELLIGENCE.)
References: Howard Gardner, *Frames of Mind*, New York: Basic Books, 1976; Michael P. Grady and Emily E. Lueke, *Education and the Brain*, Bloomington, IN: Phi Delta Kappa, 1978; Joseph Walter and Howard Gardner, "The Development of Educational Intelligence" in F. R. Link (Editor), *Essays on the Intellect*, Alexandria, VA: Association for Supervision and Curriculum Development, 1986.

INTRAPERSONAL INTELLIGENCE, the ability to know one's self as a means of guiding one's behavior according to Multiple Intelligence Theory (MI Theory). A person's own feelings and emotions are the center of intrapersonal intelligence. The frontal lobes of the brain effect major personality changes. Intrapersonal intelligence is difficult to identify; frequently, other intelligences that comprise the Multiple Intelligence Theory are used to symbolically manifest, or illustrate, the intraper-

sonal aspects of one's intelligence. Intrapersonal and Interpersonal intelligences often influence each other. The biological basis of intrapersonal intelligence, aside from the frontal lobe factor, is more inductive than it is with the other six intelligences of the MI Theory. (See BODILY-KINESTHETIC INTELLIGENCE; INTELLIGENCE; INTERPERSONAL INTELLIGENCE; LINGUISTIC INTELLIGENCE; LOGICAL-MATHEMATICAL INTELLIGENCE; MULTIPLE INTELLIGENCE; MUSICAL INTELLIGENCE; and SPATIAL INTELLIGENCE.)
References: Howard Gardner, *Frames of Mind*, New York: Basic Books, 1976; Michael P. Grady and Emily A. Lueke, *Education and the Brain*, Bloomington, IN: Phi Delta Kappa, 1978; Joseph Walter and Howard Gardner, "The Development and Education of Intelligence" in F. R. Link (Editor), *Essays on the Intellect*, Alexandria, VA: Association for Supervision and Curriculum Development, 1986.

INTERVAL—See FREQUENCY DISTRIBUTION

INTERVAL SCALE—See DATA and SCALE OF MEASUREMENT

INTERVIEW, a form of communication in which two individuals consult on a face-to-face basis. Its unique characteristics, identified by one group of authorities (Richard Huseman, et al.), include: (1) *purpose,* which distinguishes the interview from social conversation; (2) *dyadic* (two-person) *interaction;* (3) *structure,* including three stages: opening, body, and closing; (4) *context,* the environment in which the interview takes place (e.g. principal's office); and (5) *exchange of information.*

Huseman and his colleagues identified four major types of interview: (1) the *employment* interview; (2) the *performance appraisal* interview, a part of the employee evaluation process; (3) the *correction* interview, which seeks to bring about a change in behavior; and (4) the *grievance* interview, for hearing and acting on employee complaints. Other types are the *exit, counseling, induction,* and *sales* interviews.

In education, interviews are used as management tools by administrators and as vehicles for helping students by school counselors.

To increase the likelihood of satisfactory interviews, interviewers are expected to place interviewees at ease, to demonstrate interest in the interviewee and his/her problem, to be good listeners, and to plan conferences in which no more than two or three topics are to be discussed.

References: Richard C. Huseman, et al., *Interpersonal Communication in Organizations,* Boston: Holbrook Press, Inc., 1976; Sir James Robert Marks, et al., *Handbook of Educational Supervision: A Guide for the Practitioner* (Second Edition), Boston: Allyn and Bacon, Inc., 1978; H. Lee Rust, *Jobsearch: The Complete Manual for Jobseekers,* New York: American Management Association, 1979.

INTRAMURALS, also known as intramural sports or intramural athletics, a term that literally means "within the walls." Unlike extramural athletics, a program of sports competition involving participants from two or more schools, intramurals refers to all sports activities conducted within, and involving the students of a single school. The term *intramurals* was coined by a University of Michigan Latin instructor, A. S. Whitley.

Before recognition of intramural activities as a legitimate component of a school's physical education and athletics program, intramural activities in the United States were carried out (for two centuries) informally by high school and university students themselves. Such recognition finally was achieved in the 20th century.

Intramurals are currently carried out in many elementary schools (intermediate grades), secondary schools, colleges, and universities. Ideally, authorities suggest, all students should be encouraged to participate regardless of skill levels. Games and activities should generate pleasure for all who take part.

These same authorities suggest: (1) that responsibility for intramural programs should be vested in the physical education department; (2) that necessary facilities and equipment should be provided within the school budget; and (3) that one individual be designated to direct them.

References: Charles A. Forsythe and Irvin A. Keller, *Administration of High School Athletics* (Sixth Edition), Englewood Cliffs, NJ: Prentice-Hall, Inc., 1977; Ronald W. Hyatt, *Intramural Sports: Organization and Administration,* St. Louis, MO: The C. V. Mosby Company, 1977; James A. Peterson (Editor), *Intramural Administration: Theory and Practice,* Englewood Cliffs, NJ: Prentice-Hall, Inc., 1976.

INTRODUCTORY PHYSICAL SCIENCE (IPS), a physical science course designed for the purpose of improving science teaching at the junior high school (usually grades 8–9) level. Work on IPS was initiated in 1963 by Educational Services Incorporated. The course, which was field tested before final versions of the textual materials were pre-

pared, has study of matter as its principal focus. It is designed to serve as a comprehensive terminal course for students not interested in pursuing further science study as well as a basic course for students intending to enroll in biology, chemistry, and/or physics courses. Classroom lectures and laboratory work are an integral part of IPS.

Course materials include a text, a teacher's guide, tests, and special laboratory material.

References: Gerald Abegg, "Interaction: Key to IPS Philosophy," *The Science Teacher,* April 1970; Alfred T. Collette, *Science Teaching in the Secondary School: A Guide for Modernizing Instruction,* Boston: Allyn and Bacon, Inc., 1973; Richard E. Haney, *The Changing Curriculum: Science,* Washington, DC: Association for Supervision and Curriculum Development, NEA, 1966; J. David Lockard (Editor), *Science and Mathematics Curricular Developments Internationally, 1956–1974,* College Park, MD: Science Teaching Center, University of Maryland (Joint Project with the Commission on Science Education, American Association for the Advancement of Science), 1974.

INTROVERSION AND EXTROVERSION, a construct in personality that was first popularized by the psychologist C. G. Jung (1923). Jung postulated that individuals deal with four components of mental activity: (1) sense perception vs. (2) intuition; and (3) thinking vs. (4) feeling in a particular manner or way to produce eight psychological types. He produced theoretical definitions of introversion/extroversion (I/E) that grew out of his 1923 work.

Generally, an *introvert* is one who will deal with, or is preoccupied with his/her own ideas, feelings, perceptions as opposed to dealing with other people and things. An *extrovert* is a relatively outgoing individual who reacts more to his/her social and physical environment and is more inclined to deal with people and things. Most individuals tend to have a balance between one extreme and the other, although an orientation toward one or the other does not appear to be harmful.

References: Richard Lynn, *An Introduction to the Study of Personality,* London, England: The Macmillan Book Company, 1971; Kenneth J. Shapiro and Irving E. Alexander, *The Experience of Introversion: An Integration of Phenomenological, Empirical and Jungian Approaches,* Durham, NC: Duke University Press, 1975; Marie-Louise von Franz, *C. G. Jung: His Myth in Our Time,* New York: G. P. Putnam's Sons, 1975.

INVESTING IN OUR CHILDREN: BUSINESS AND THE PUBLIC SCHOOLS—See NATIONAL REFORM REPORTS (1980–86)

IOWA TESTS OF BASIC SKILLS (ITBS), general achievement test batteries published by Houghton Mifflin. The grade range for the *Iowa Tests of Basic Skills* is grades 1–8 for skills such as reading, arithmetic, spelling, and language usage. The *Modern Mathematics Supplement* to the ITBS covers grades 3–9 and can be considered an update of the ITBS Arithmetic Concepts Test. There are two forms, short and long. The long form includes study skills. The *Iowa Tests of Educational Development* for grades 9–12 include tests on interpreting reading materials in literature, social studies, and the natural sciences.

References: Anne Anastasi, *Psychological Testing* (Fourth Edition), New York: Macmillan Publishing Company, Inc., 1976; Oscar K. Buros (Editor), *The Seventh Mental Measurements Yearbook* (Volume I), Highland Park, NJ: The Gryphon Press, 1972; J. Raymond Gerberich, *Specimen Objective Test Items,* New York: Longmans, Green and Company, 1956.

I.Q. TESTS—See INTELLIGENCE TESTS

ISOLATION, SOCIAL, the removing of group contacts and interactions from an individual. This can be done involuntarily, such as solitary confinement in prison, or voluntarily (e.g. going on a trip and intentionally becoming isolated from individuals for a period of time). A form of social isolation can also occur when an individual is no longer accepted by a group or social organization, yet is not physically removed from it.

Since social interactions are extremely important to most individuals, involuntary social isolation can have a significant effect on the individual involved. Psychological problems, or deviant behavior, could be an outcome of such isolation. Social isolation of individuals can occur in almost any group or environment, schools included. (See SOCIOGRAM and SOCIOMETRICS.)

References: Arthur Brittain, *The Prevatised World,* London, England: Routledge and Kegan Paul, 1977; Suzanne Gordon, *Lonely in America,* New York: Simon and Schuster, 1976; Paul Halmos, *Solitude and Privacy,* New York: Philosophical Library, 1953.

ITINERANT TEACHER, a teacher specially trained to work with individual students during part(s) of the school day. The teaching service rendered by itinerant teachers, essentially tutorial in nature, supplements the instruction provided by the individual student's regular classroom teacher. It most often involves working with mainstreamed students (visually impaired, gifted, and other exceptional children). Although teaching is the major responsibility of the itinerant teacher, he/she is also likely to be involved in related activities such as procuring special instructional materials, conferring with parents, assessing students, or participating in case conferences.

References: Maynard C. Reynolds and Jack W. Birch, *Teaching Exceptional Children in All America's Schools: A First Course for Teacher and Principals,* Reston, VA: The Council for Exceptional Children, 1977; Bernard G. Suran and Joseph V. Rizzo, *Special Children: An Integrative Approach.* Glenview, IL: Scott, Foresman and Company, 1979.

JACQUES-DALCROZE, EMILE (July 6, 1865–July 1, 1950), frequently referred to as Dalcroze, Viennese-born composer and music educator whose method of music teaching (the Dalcroze method) did much to influence music education in Europe and the United States. The method, which involves music learning through rhythmic body movement, had an influence on modern ballet as well.

Dalcroze's basic theories about music education were set forth in two of the several publications that he authored: *Rhythm, Music and Education* (1921) and *Eurhythmics, Art and Education* (1930). An earlier book, *Methode Jacques-Dalcroze* (1907–14), contained various exercises and suggested musical accompaniments. Dalcroze also composed over 1,000 songs, most for children and intended for use in his classes. He also is credited with creating 39 musical pageants, 85 chamber works, 125 piano pieces, 175 chorus numbers (with piano accompaniment), 200 chorus numbers (with orchestral accompaniment), 3 concertos for violin and orchestra, and several miscellaneous musical works, most for school use.

In 1915, Dalcroze formed the Institut Jacques-Dalcroze in Geneva. Branches of this school were later formed in Europe and North America. One of these, the Dalcroze School of Music (New York), specializes in teaching his methods and is authorized to issue a Dalcroze Teachers Certificate. (See DALCROZE METHOD and DALCROZE SCHOOL OF MUSIC.)

References: Bruce Bohle (Editor), *The International Cyclopedia of Music and Musicians* (Tenth Edition), New York: Dodd, Mead and Company, 1975; Beth Landis and Polly Carder, *The Eclectric Curriculum in American Music Education: Contributions of Dalcroze, Kodaly, and Orff*, Washington, DC: Music Educators National Conference, 1972.

JEWISH COMMUNITY CENTERS—See YOUNG MEN'S/YOUNG WOMEN'S HEBREW ASSOCIATION

JEWISH EDUCATION, educational programs found in Jewish supplementary schools, Jewish day schools, Hebrew colleges, and summer camping programs. Jewish *supplementary* schools augment the public, or non-Jewish elementary and secondary schools, with Judaic, religious, and Hebrew language studies with classes taking place either in the late afternoon, on Saturday, or on Sunday. Jewish *day* schools usually have a dual program consisting of Jewish and general studies. Students attend them as they would public schools, every day, morning and afternoon. Many day schools have grades ranging from Kindergarten to 12.

There is no set Jewish Education curriculum, nor is it restricted to only religious study. Curricula vary according to the school, congregation, or sponsoring organization; the purposes of the school (i.e. supplementary, day school, college); and, in the case of day schools, the requirements of a particular state. In most cases, the Jewish day school offers secular programs similar to those found in public schools. Courses are often integrated with nonsecular content such as Hebrew, Judaic studies, and Jewish culture. In the United States, day schools integrate the secular and religious worlds of the student.

Jewish day and supplementary schools exist in countries other than the United States and Israel. For example, in 1975 there were six Jewish high schools in Mexico City. There are many such schools offering Jewish Education in Canada. In the United States, in 1978, there were 1,715 Jewish congregational, day, communal, and Yiddish schools. Most of these schools were supplementary; however, 523 were day schools.

References: Bennett Ira Solomon, "A Critical Review of the Term 'Integration' in the Literature on the Jewish Day School in America," *Jewish Education*, Winter 1978; Shimon Samuels, "A Research Note on Jewish Education in Mexico," *The Jewish Journal of Sociology*, December 1978.

JOB ANALYSIS—See JOB DESCRIPTION

JOB CORPS, an antipoverty training program authorized by the Economic Opportunity Act of 1964. The thrust of the program is to help poor youth to become trained and upwardly mobile citizens. Job Corps Centers are located throughout the United States. They were designed so that Job Corps participants would have to live in the center rather than at home. Members of Job Corps receive basic education as well as skill training.

Initially, the Job Corps plan was designed for men; women's centers were added later as part of the enacting legislation. In the 1970s, coeducational facilities were provided. There are three types of centers: (1) rural; (2) urban; and (3) women's. All provide residential facilities, health care, educational and vocational programs, and counseling. Many Job Corps Centers are operated, under contract, by large corporations as well as by social service organizations.

The Job Corps program came under attack from its very beginning and, in the judgment of some, never reached its potential in terms of numbers to be served. It has succeeded in training 750,000 youth to date.

References: Sai A. Levitan and Benjamin H. Johnson, *The Job Corps: A Social Experiment That Works,* Baltimore, MD: Johns Hopkins Press, 1975; Public Law 88-452, *United States Statutes at Large, 1964* (Volume 78), Washington, DC: U.S. Government Printing Office, 1965; Christopher Weeks, *Job Corps: Dollars and Dropouts,* Boston: Little, Brown and Company, 1967.

JOB DESCRIPTION, a written document which is prepared to describe a particular organizational position or role. Job descriptions are normally written in operational (functional) terms and provide three kinds of information in addition to the job title: (1) the duties and rights associated with the position; (2) standards of performance (including qualifications) expected by the employer; and (3) relationships with other positions in the organization. The typical school system has three categories of positions: (1) *administrative;* (2) *instructional service* (e.g. reading consultant, chemistry teacher); and (3) *supporting service,* a category that includes disparate, noninstructional positions such as secretary, bus driver, and cook.

References: R. Oliver Gibson and Herold C. Hunt, *The School Personnel Administrator,* Boston: Houghton Mifflin Company, 1965; Jay E. Greene, *School Personnel Administration,* Philadelphia: Chilton Book Company, 1971.

JOHN DEWEY SOCIETY FOR THE STUDY OF EDUCATION AND CULTURE, an organization founded in 1935 that encourages the study of educational and cultural problems that are of special concern to the teaching profession. Two vehicles have been used to implement these objectives: sponsorship of meetings and publication of research.

From 1937 to 1963, the society published annual yearbooks that were edited by prestigious people such as William Kilpatrick, Theodore Brameld, and Harold Rugg. Between 1963 and 1970, annual *Studies in Educational Theory* were produced, these replacing the yearbooks. Currently, the society sponsors and publishes the annual John Dewey Lecture, an event that dates back to 1958. Lectures are delivered in conjunction with the annual meetings of the American Association of Colleges for Teacher Education.

References: Henry Harap, "The Beginnings of the John Dewey Society," *Educational Theory,* Spring 1970; John Dewey Society, *The John Dewey Society for the Study of Education and Culture,* Gainesville, FL: The Society, Undated Brochure; Henry C. Johnson, Jr., "Reflective Thought and Practical Action: The Origins of the John Dewey Society," *Educational Theory,* Winter 1977.

JOHNSON-O'MALLEY ACT, federal legislation enacted in 1934 that authorized the Secretary of the Interior "to enter into a contract or contracts with any State or Territory having legal authority so to do, for the education, medical attention, agriculture assistance, and social welfare . . . of Indians in such State or Territory, through the qualified agencies of such State or Territory, and to expend under such contract . . . moneys appropriated by Congress for the education, medical attention, agricultural assistance, and social welfare . . . of Indians in such State" (p. 596). Insofar as education was concerned, the act provided subsidies to public school districts that enrolled Indian children.

During the two or three decades immediately following its enactment, the Johnson-O'Malley measure failed to bring about any significant educational reform, primarily because of "control" differences between the Bureau of Indian Affairs, the agency responsible for its implementation, and the states. In the 1970s, similar "control" differences developed, this time between public school districts and Indian organizations that were arguing for increased Indian involvement in the awarding of contracts. This resulted in a policy change that gave Indian groups authority to negotiate Johnson-O'Malley contracts. Today, the Johnson-O'Malley Act is but one of several pieces of legislation making federal funds available for the support of Indian education.

References: Chapter 147, *Statutes of the United States of America* (Part I), Washington, DC: U.S. Government Printing Office, 1934; N.A.A.C.P. Legal Defense and Educational Fund, Inc., *An Even Chance,* New York: The Fund, 1971; Margaret C. Szasz, *Education and the American Indian: The Road to Self-Determination Since 1928* (Second Edition), Albuquerque, NM: University of New Mexico Press, 1977.

JOHNSTON TEST—See SWEEP-CHECK TEST

JOINT COUNCIL ON ECONOMIC EDUCATION (JCEE), sometimes referred to as the Joint Council, an independent, nonprofit, nonpartisan organization (incorporated in 1949) dedicated to improving the quality and quantity of economic education throughout the United States. The association maintains over 200 centers on college campuses and about 600 cooperating school systems on a dollar-matching basis, providing them with instructional materials, consultant services, and staff development workshops. The association is based in New York City and is officially affiliated with numerous educational leadership associations at all levels.

In pointing up the need for effective economic education, JCEE documents the depth and breadth of economic illiteracy in the United States. Facts such as the following are offered: (1) only about a quarter of American secondary schools offer a course in economics; (2) in schools where economics is offered, approximately 7 percent of the students take the course; (3) only about 3 percent of all high school students ever take an economics course; and (4) only half of all social studies teachers have taken one or more economics courses.

References: Joint Council on Economic Education, *Checklist,* New York: The Council, Spring 1980; Joint Council on Economic Education, *Economic Illiteracy: Can We Afford It Any Longer?* New York: The Council, Undated Brochure.

JOPLIN PLAN, an intergrade method of grouping students for the teaching of reading. Named for Joplin, Missouri, the city in which it originated, the plan requires that teachers follow a relatively common daily schedule. During the reading period, children are assigned to different rooms on the basis of their achievement levels. Under this plan, a sixth grade student, for example, may be assigned to any reading level, grades 3 through 7 or 8. Variations of the Joplin Plan, some involving small groups of teachers, are used in other school districts. Critics of this grouping arrangement fault it on the grounds that intraclass grouping, needed to individualize instruction even further, frequently does not take place.

References: Donald C. Cushenbery, *Reading Improvement in the Elementary School,* West Nyack, NY: Parker Publishing Company, Inc., 1969; Albert J. Harris and Edward R. Sipay, *How to Teach Reading,* New York: Longman, Inc., 1979; Harry W. Sartain, "Organizational Patterns of Schools and Classrooms for Reading Instruction" in

Helen M. Robinson (Editor), *Innovation and Change in Reading Instruction,* Chicago: University of Chicago Press, 1968.

JOURNAL WRITING, an ongoing narrative log of real events that have been observed, experienced, or learned. It is a means of putting personal experiences into language. Unlike a diary, where the intent is to maintain privacy, a journal is read by others.

The technique is applicable to all age groups. In a school setting, time is generally allotted on a scheduled basis for journal entries. The initial focus might be on a specific event, subject, or relationship. Students are directed to record observations and thoughts as they relate to the topic; this is referred to as a specialized journal. Students summarize and share entries weekly in an effort to improve communication skills. A miscellaneous journal might be introduced after experience with specialized journal—such journal entries are not limited to specified topics. Again, summary statements are encouraged at logical junctures. Journal writing provides intensive practice in written communication.

References: James Moffett and Betty Jane Wagner, *Student-Centered Language Arts and Reading K–8: A Handbook for Teachers,* Boston: Houghton Mifflin Company, 1983; Lyndon W. Searfoss and John E. Readance, *Helping Children Learn to Read,* Englewood Cliffs, NJ: Prentice-Hall Inc., 1985; Charles Temple and Jean Wallace Gilbert, *Language Arts: Learning Processes and Teaching Practices,* Boston: Little, Brown and Company, 1984.

JUNIOR ACHIEVEMENT (JA), a program of youth economic education that stresses learning by doing. Participants, working in groups of approximately 20 students and under the direction of adult (volunteer) advisers, form, operate, and eventually liquidate their own businesses. Most JA companies are manufacturing companies. Students hold weekly two-hour meetings at which time they elect officers and prepare their own products (e.g. T-shirts, art reproductions) for sale by the membership. At the close of the school year, the businesses are liquidated with profits used to pay dividends to stockholders and, in some cases, distributed among company members as profit-sharing. The principal purpose of Junior Achievement is to teach students the workings of the free enterprise system.

JA was conceived in 1919 by a corporation president, Horace A. Moses, with the assistance of Theodore N. Vail, former president of the American Telephone and Telegraph Co. Moses was impressed with the 4-H Club movement and created JA as its urban counterpart for business. Early programs were aimed at 8-12-year-olds; later experience indicated that it is better suited for older (high school) students. The JA movement expanded rapidly after World War II. By 1977, it involved over 250,000 students and approximately 30,000 volunteer advisers.

In addition to the company program described above, JA sponsors a group of "Economic Awareness" programs. One, *Project Business,* involves eighth- and ninth-grade students who learn about business from a local member of the business community who visits their classroom once a week for a semester. Other such programs are *Applied Management* (for college students of business) and *Job Education,* a summer work program that seeks to provide disadvantaged youth with job skills.

JA is subsidized exclusively by the business community, with some supplementary funding provided by businesses and individuals. The organization's national offices are in Stamford, Connecticut.

References: Annual Report 1978-79, Stamford, CT: Junior Achievement, Inc., 1979; *Employee Relations Bulletin: Junior Achievement,* Waterford, CT: Bureau of Business Practice, Undated Special Report; "History of Junior Achievement" (Mimeographed Fact Sheet). Stamford, CT: Junior Achievement, Inc., March 1978; *Junior Achievement: What's It All About?* Stamford, CT: Junior Achievement, Inc., A Brochure, 1976.

JUNIOR COLLEGE,

a two-year, postsecondary institution of higher education. Although the terms *junior college* and *community college* are sometimes treated as synonyms, there are several characteristics that usually (not always) give the junior college a uniqueness of its own: (1) it is liberal arts oriented; (2) it is a private institution, sometimes church related; and (3) it does not limit enrollment to local students. The term *junior college* is sometimes used generically to describe all two-year institutions of higher education including technical schools and community colleges.

The first junior college was created by President William Harper, University of Chicago, in 1896 when he used the term to designate that institution's lower division (freshman and sophomore years).

Privately supported two-year institutions in the United States numbered 283 in 1978-79 with a combined enrollment of slightly more than 150,000 students. (See COMMUNITY COLLEGE.)

References: Maurice R. Duperre, "Short-Cycle Education" in Asa S. Knowles (Editor), *The International Encyclopedia of Higher Education* (Volume 8), San Francisco: Jossey-Bass Publishers, 1977; Tyrus Hillway, *The American Two-Year College,* New York: Harper and Brothers, 1958; Andrew J. Pepin, *Fall Enrollment in Higher Education, 1977: Final Report,* Washington, DC: National Center for Education Statistics, U.S. Department of HEW, 1979; Arthur Podolsky and Carolyn R. Smith, *Education Directory, Colleges and Universities: 1977-78,* Washington, DC: National Center for Education Statistics, U.S. Department of HEW, 1979.

JUNIOR GREAT BOOKS DISCUSSION PROGRAM,

a program of interpretive reading and discussion geared to students in Grades 2 through 12. The program operates under the aegis of the Great Books Foundation which was established in 1947. The foundation selects and publishes its own paperback books for use in discussion groups. It also trains discussion leaders who conduct the programs.

The primary goals of the Junior Great Books Discussion Program are to improve students' comprehension and to have them think independently about the selection and develop a love of literature. These goals are achieved via discussions that focus on story interpretation. The method of interpretation is called *shared inquiry* since leader and participants anticipate new learning as a result of the discussion. Although used as part of the curriculum in many programs for gifted students, the Great Books Foundation emphasizes the value of the Junior Great Books Discussion Program for all students.

References: Richard P. Dennes and Edwin P. Moldof, *A Handbook on Interpretive Reading and Discussion,* Chicago: The Great Books Foundation, 1984; Robert M. Hutchins, *Great Books,* New York: Simon and Schuster, 1954; Lyndon W. Searfoss and John E. Readance, *Helping Children Learn to Read,* Englewood Cliffs, NJ: Prentice-Hall Inc., 1985.

JUNIOR HIGH SCHOOL,

an educational institution designed to meet the unique educational needs and abilities of students during early adolescence. Introduced after World War I, the junior high school provided what many believed to be a necessary alternative to the 8-4 educational plan, the then dominant school organization template in America. The junior high school program, carried out in a separate and often specially designed building, normally accommodated students in departmentalized grades 7, 8, and 9. By 1940, the 6–3–3 organizational plan had virtually replaced the 8–4 template.

Different writers ascribed varying purposes to the junior high school. Among the most common were: (1) to meet the individual and unique needs of early adolescents; (2) to provide prevocational training and opportunities for exploration; (3) to make counseling and guidance services available; and (4) to develop good citizenship through active participation in the school community.

In recent years, the middle school has begun to replace the junior high school as the school district's intermediate institution, a change at least partly attributable to growing disenchantment with the actual achievements of the junior high school. (See INTERMEDIATE SCHOOL; MIDDLE SCHOOL; and ORGANIZATIONAL PLANS.)

References: Joseph S. Butterweck, "Junior High School" in Harry N. Rivlin and Herbert Schueler (Editors), *Encyclopedia of Modern Education*, New York: The Philosophical Library of New York City, 1943; Frederick S. Calhoun, *Organization of the Middle Grades: A Summary of Research*, Arlington, VA: Educational Research Service, Inc., 1983; William T. Gruhn and Harl R. Douglass, *The Modern Junior High School* (Second Edition), New York: Ronald Press Company, 1956; Leonard V. Koos, *Junior High School Trends*, Westport, CT: Greenwood Press, 1969.

JUVENILE DELINQUENCY, offenses by children that, in most states, would be crimes if committed by adults. Over the years, laws and court practices have not been uniform with respect to either the definition of delinquency or procedures for coping with it.

In the United States, crimes by youth increased more than 144.0 percent between 1960 and 1975. Department of Justice data report the percentage of all crimes that were committed by juveniles in 1976: 52.6 percent, motor vehicle thefts; 51.5 percent, burglary; 43.0 percent, larceny; 35.5 percent, robbery; 17.0 percent, aggravated assault; 17.3 percent, forcible rape; and 9.2 percent, murder.

Clemens Bartollas and Stuart Miller indicated that four approaches (philosophies) for treating children in trouble have been used in this century. They are: (1) *parens patriae,* in which the courts become guardians of the offender and seek to have him/her treated not as a criminal but as a ward of the state; (2) *due process,* in which no position is taken with respect to the offender's guilt or innocence but every effort is made to ensure fair legal treatment; (3) *reintegration,* programs designed to help all but hard-core offenders to reenter community life; and (4) *punishment.*

References: Clemens Bartollas and Stuart J. Miller, *The Juvenile Offender: Control, Correction, and Treatment,* Boston: Holbrook Press, Inc., 1978; Delbert S. Elliott, *Explaining Delinquency and Drug Abuse,* Beverly Hills, CA: Sage Publications, 1984; LeMar T. Empey, *American Delinquency: Its Meaning and Construction,* Homewood, IL: The Dorsey Press, 1978; Howard B. Kaplan, *Patterns of Juvenile Delinquency,* Beverly Hills, CA: Sage Publications, 1984; U.S. Department of Justice, *Federal Bureau of Investigation: Uniform Crime Reports, 1976,* Washington, DC: U.S. Government Printing Office, 1977.

KALAMAZOO CASE, a landmark legal decision relating to public support of secondary schools. In 1874, a group of Kalamazoo parents contested the school board's right to include secondary education as part of the common school system and to collect taxes therefor. The Michigan State Supreme Court declared the board's action to be legal, thereby establishing a precedent that facilitated the establishment of free public secondary schools in Michigan and other states as well.
References: Stuart v. School Dist. No. 1 of Village of Kalamazoo, 30 Mich. 69 (1874); E. Edmund Reutter, Jr. and Robert R. Hamilton, *The Law of Public Education* (Second Edition), Mineola, NY: The Foundation Press, Inc., 1976.

KANAWHA COUNTY, West Virginia, site of a 1974 school boycott brought on to protest adoption of certain textbooks deemed to be "dirty, anti-Christian, anti-American" (p. 8). Numerous fundamentalist church members and leaders were involved. Coal miners and other local workers staged wildcat strikes to support the textbook protesters. Instances of physical violence also took place. School attendance dropped significantly; later, schools were closed temporarily to protect the students. The boycott, which attracted national attention, involved several issues: intellectual freedom; the right of parents to be involved in textbook selection; charges of "secular humanism" being taught; and exposing students to values alien to those held by some in the local culture.
Reference: Franklin Parker, *The Battle of the Books: Kanawha County* (PDK Fastback 63), Bloomington, IN: The Phi Delta Kappa Educational Foundation, 1975.

KANDEL, ISAAC L. (January 22, 1881–June 14, 1965), noted educational historian, professor of comparative education, and critic of the progressive education movement. He taught at Teachers College, Columbia University (1913–47). Before 1913 he was a faculty member at the Royal Academical Institute of Belfast, Ireland (1906–8). Kandel authored numerous books, perhaps the best known being *Comparative Education* (1933). Following his retirement from Teachers College, he inaugurated the professorship of American Studies at the University of Manchester, England (1948–50). Kandel was born in Rumania and received much of his education in England before earning the doctorate at Teachers College.
References: William W. Brickman, "I. L. Kandel," *School and Society,* October 30, 1965; William W. Brickman, "Kandel, Isaac Leon" in John F. Ohles (Editor), *Biographical Dictionary of American Educators* (Volume 2), Westport, CT: Greenwood Press, 1978.

KANT, IMMANUEL (April 22, 1724–February 12, 1804), well-known and influential philosopher who was born in Konigsberg, East Prussia. His best known work is *Critique of Pure Reason* (1781).

About 1770, Kant began to theorize about the workings of the mind, the concept of causality, perceptions, and reality. His teachings and writings led people to look at the mind in a different way. The mind, according to Kant, was far more important and complex than was then thought. His approach, however, was based on reason and philosophy, not psychology. His works included *Critique of Pure Reason* (1781); *Critique of Practical Reason* (1788); and *Critique of Judgement* (1789–90). He also wrote on the philosophy of law and the philosophy of religion.
References: Raymond E. Fancher, *Pioneers of Psychology,* New York: W. W. Norton and Company, 1979; C. Lewy (Editor), *Kant: An Introduction,* Cambridge, England: Cambridge University Press, 1978; Allen W. Wood, *Kant's Rational Theology,* Ithaca, NY: Cornell University Press, 1978.

KAPPA DELTA PI (KDP), an honor society open to men and women in the field of education. The organization was founded in 1911 at the University of Illinois. Membership is open to upper division and graduate students whose academic work places them in the upper 20 percent of their respective institutions. The society publishes two quarterlies, *The Educational Forum* and the *Kappa Delta Pi Record.* In 1977, Kappa Delta Pi's 400,000 members belonged to 321 active chapters. The organization's headquarters is in West Lafayette, Indiana.
Reference: John Robson (Editor), *Baird's Manual of American College Fraternities* (Nineteenth Edition), Menasha, WI: Baird's Manual Foundation, 1977.

KELLOGG FOUNDATION, more accurately the W. K. Kellogg Foundation, a philanthropic organization named for its founder, Will Keith Kellogg. Kellogg established the foundation in 1930 after his ready-to-eat breakfast cereal company had achieved national prominence and was prospering. The resources of the foundation, he decreed, were to be used "for the application of knowledge to the problems of people" (Brochure, p. 1).

In 1979, the foundation's assets approached $800,000,000. By that year, its cumulative expenditures exceeded $480,000,000. In 1978-79, 660 projects in the United States, Canada, Latin America, Europe, and Australia were receiving W. K. Kellogg Foundation assistance.

The foundation's current efforts are confined to three broad program areas: agriculture, education, and health. The educational area has four foci: (1) improving learning processes; (2) strengthening the family; (3) helping youth develop educational, career, and leadership potential; and (4) enhancing lifelong learning in the adult years.

The foundation's main office is in Battle Creek, Michigan, where officers and staff, guided by a ten-member Board of Trustees, transact the business of the organization.

References: W. K. Kellogg Foundation, *W. K. Kellogg Foundation* (a Brochure), Battle Creek, MI: The Foundation, June 1979; W. K. Kellogg Foundation, *W. K. Kellogg Annual Report/1979*, Battle Creek, MI: The Foundation, 1979; W. K. Kellogg Foundation, *W. K. Kellogg Foundation: The First Half Century, 1930-1980*, Battle Creek, MI: The Foundation, 1979.

KERNER COMMISSION REPORT, official report tendered by the U.S. National Advisory Commission on Civil Disorders following the July 1967 civil unrest in Newark, N.J., and Detroit. President Lyndon Johnson appointed this advisory commission, headed by Otto Kerner, to investigate the causes of the civil disorders that had spread through many of the large urban centers of the United States. The report attempted to answer three questions: (1) What happened? (2) Why did it happen? and (3) What can be done to prevent it from happening again?

The commission investigated unrest in several large urban areas; the disorders and their causes were then described. The commission made many recommendations designed to prevent such disorders from reoccurring, these dealing with topics such as employment, education, justice, and the role of news media.

References: James W. Button, *Black Violence*, Princeton, NJ: Princeton University Press, 1978; David T. Farmer, *Civil Disorder Control*, Chicago: Public Administration Service, 1968; *U.S. National Advisory Commission on Civil Disorders*, Washington, DC: U.S. Government Printing Office, 1968.

KETTERING FOUNDATION, officially the Charles F. Kettering Foundation, a nonprofit or-

ganization whose overriding purpose is "to advance knowledge and to find creative solutions to human problems" (Key Facts). The foundation was incorporated in 1927 by the inventor and researcher Charles F. Kettering (1876-1958), whose name it carries. When first organized, its primary emphasis was scientific research. In recent years, the programs it supports have been broadened to include: (1) *science and technology,* a group of activities that seek to increase world food supplies and to decrease crop losses due to weather; (2) *international affairs,* a broad effort designed to strengthen people-to-people communications at the international level and to find ways in which individual U.S. citizens can be involved in shaping U.S. foreign policy; (3) *education,* with principal support given to the I/D/E/A Change Program for Individually Guided Education, studies of schooling in the United States, and analyses of educational policy issues; and (4) *urban affairs,* consisting of several projects that seek to strengthen urban communities and development of a coordinated national urban policy.

In 1978, the foundation's assets totalled over $72,000,000. Appropriations for the same year exceeded $7,000,000 including $2,078,746 for science and technology projects; $1,896,423 for education; $697,127 for urban affairs; $563,922 for international affairs; and $211,573 for exploratory research. A 13-member Board of Trustees guides the foundation. Kettering Foundation's main office is in Dayton, Ohio. (See I/D/E/A and INDIVIDUALLY GUIDED EDUCATION.)

References: Charles F. Kettering Foundation, *Annual Report 1978*, Dayton, OH: The Foundation, 1978; Charles F. Kettering Foundation, *Key Facts About the Charles F. Kettering Foundation*, Dayton, OH: The Foundation, Undated Brochure.

KEYES V. SCHOOL DIST. NO. 1, a lawsuit in which the public schools of Denver, Colorado, were charged with operating administratively segregated schools. The plaintiffs, a group of black, white, and Hispanic parents, brought the case before the U.S. Supreme Court in 1973. Lower courts had found Denver guilty of de jure segregation, a finding supported by the U.S. Supreme Court. As part of its ruling, the Court instructed school officials to desegregate the entire school system with black and Hispanic students to be considered together when defining a segregated school.

This case is considered to be significant, historically, because it marked the first time that the U.S.

Supreme Court ordered the desegregation of a northern school district. (See DE JURE SEGREGATION.)

References: Frank R. Kemerer and Kenneth L. Deutsch, Constitutional Rights and Student Life: Value Conflict in Law and Education, St. Paul, MN: West Publishing Company, 1979; Keyes v. School Dist. No. 1 (Denver, Colorado), 413 U.S. 189 (1973); E. Edmund Reutter, Jr. and Robert R. Hamilton, The Law of Public Education (Second Edition), Mineola, NY: The Foundation Press, Inc., 1976.

KIBBUTZ, a voluntary communal settlement started in 1909 by Jewish pioneers in what was called Palestine (now Israel). Most Kibbutzim are agricultural. Some are paramilitary and others are engaged in light industry, such as fabrication of plastics. Kibbutz federations, a development of networks of Kibbutzim, with central planning, coordinating, and governing organizations have developed. These federations have prevented the individual Kibbutzim from being isolated and have made them a political as well as a social force in Israel.

Kibbutzim have developed their own ideologies, life-styles, and procedures. Child-rearing, the educational system, and family structure in the Kibbutzim have become the focus of interest on the part of many Western educators, psychologists, and researchers. Kibbutzim have certain characteristics in common: noncompetition, socialistic design, egalitarian, highly democratic (direct democracy), unique family structure, high peer orientation, and pioneering. The word Kibbutz means "meeting or gathering."

References: Dan Leon, The Kibbutz: A New Way of Life, Oxford, England: Pergamon Press, 1969; A. I. Rabin, Kibbutz Studies, Lansing, MI: Michigan State University Press, 1971.

KILPATRICK, WILLIAM HEARD (November 20, 1871–February 13, 1965), noted teacher educator and disciple of progressive education. A friend of John Dewey and an exponent of Dewey's educational philosophy, Kilpatrick did much to influence curricular change in American schools. He was a critic of programs made up of traditional and disparate subjects; as an alternative, he developed and promoted the project method of education. He was also an outspoken critic of the Montessori system of education.

Kilpatrick earned his doctorate at Columbia University and taught at Teachers College, Columbia University, from 1909 to 1938. Before that he taught and served as a school principal in Geor-

gia, taught mathematics at Mercer University, and for a time (1903–5) served as that institution's Acting President. (Kilpatrick earned the A.B. and A.M. degrees at Mercer.)

A prolific writer, Kilpatrick authored numerous books in which his philosophical and curricular beliefs were articulated. They included Foundations of Method (1925), Education and the Social Crisis (1932), and Philosophy of Education (1951). He was a fellow of the American Association for the Advancement of Science.

References: Joseph C. Bronars, Jr., "Kilpatrick, William Heard" in John F. Ohles (Editor), Biographical Dictionary of American Educators (Volume 2), Westport, CT: Greenwood Press, 1978; Educational Theory, January 1966 (Memorial Issue of W. H. Kilpatrick); Samuel Tenenbaum, William Heard Kilpatrick, New York: Harper and Row Publishers, Inc., 1951.

KINESICS, the study of body motion, or "body language," a form of communication. Kinesics is one manifestation of nonverbal communication. Students of kinesics point out that: (1) decodable information about an individual and his/her feelings can be gleaned from study of gestures; (2) different parts of the body may be used to communicate information or feelings; (3) different cultural groups may employ their own systems of body language; (4) the alert teacher can learn much about students by consciously observing their body motions; and (5) students are sensitive to teachers' gestures and body movements.

Facial gestures, eye movements, use of hands, and body stance are each capable of communicating information nonverbally. For example, according to Gerard Nierenberg and Henry Calero, hands on hips connotes readiness; tapping of fingers on table may signify boredom or impatience; rubbing hands together indicates a positive expectation; and placing one's foot on a desk communicates dominance. One example of between-culture differences is eye contact. In the Navajo Indian culture, avoidance of eye contact is used to suggest recognition of authority; in the white culture, such avoidance is perceived to be a sign of disrespect.

References: H. Thomas Hurt, et al., Communication in the Classroom, Reading, MA: Addison-Wesley Publishing Company, 1978; Marie Marcus, Diagnostic Teaching of the Language Arts, New York: John Wiley and Sons, 1977; Gerard I. Nierenberg and Henry H. Calero, How to Read a Person Like a Book, New York: Pocket Books, 1973.

KINESIOLOGY, the science of human motion. The father of kinesiology is considered to be Aristotle (384–322 B.C.). He studied human and animal movement and wrote about his studies in *Parts of Animals, Movement of Animals, and Progression of Animals.* Teachers and therapists use some of his concepts today.

Human motion is affected by the skeleton, nervous and muscular systems, physics, and biochemistry. These parts of the human body, as well as their chemical elements and physics, interact with each other during movement. Thus, all must be considered in movement studies. The study of movement is not only important in athletics, dance, and other overt physical activities, but it is also important in speech. As related to speech, kinesiology is concerned with muscle movement and its effect upon the development of sound.

Research in kinesiology requires a great deal of equipment; hence, the development of special laboratories. Many of these are called biomechanic laboratories where physicians, psychologists, engineers, anatomists, physical therapists, and physical education specialists participate in joint studies on the movement of the human body.

References: John M. Cooper and Ruth B. Glassow, *Kinesiology,* St. Louis, MO: The C. V. Mosby Company, 1976; Marilyn M. Hinson, *Kinesiology,* Dubuque, IA: Wm. C. Brown Company, Publishers, 1977; J. R. Poortmans (Editor), *Medicine and Sport Biochemistry of Exercise* (Volume 3), Basel, Switzerland: S. Karger, 1969.

KINESTHESIA, the awareness, through sensations, of the movement of speech muscles. When an individual speaks, not only are auditory sense data (sounds) being produced, but kinesthetic sensitivity data (physical feelings) are also being supplied the individual by muscles and tendons. Kinesthetic awareness helps to develop correct patterns in speech and consequently aids in the production of correct speech sounds. The loss or reduction of such kinesthetic sensitivities, such as in the tongue, may contribute to functional articulatory defects. (See KINESIOLOGY.)

References: John Dickinson, *Proprioceptive Control of Human Movement,* London, England: Lepus Books, 1974; Lucilla Nicolosi, et al., *Terminology of Communication Disorders,* Baltimore, MD: The Williams and Wilkins Company, 1978.

KNOWLEDGE, the facts, information, principles, and truths to which the mind has access. Knowledge is used as a resource for inquiry and deliberation. Because knowledge is based on numbers of factors (e.g. experiences, observations, beliefs, cultural influences, semantics, philosophical bases), it appears to be relative and subject to change. Knowledge can be analyzed and made to meet certain conditions such as truth, belief, and justification. The question, "What is knowledge?" has generated considerable debate among philosophers over the years.

In a classroom, knowledge may be demonstrated through activities such as athletics (having a skill knowledge), having someone give the "correct" or desired answer (conceived as having knowledge of the subject), or helping someone become acquainted with someone else (becoming familiar). Often, knowledge is understood to mean only the acquisition of facts or information per se; however, as these illustrations indicate, it has many meanings.

References: Nicholas Abercrombie, *Class, Structure, and Knowledge: Problems of the Sociology of Knowledge,* New York: New York University Press, 1980; Jerome S. Bruner, *On Knowing: Essays for the Left Hand* (Expanded Edition), Cambridge, MA: Belknap Press of Harvard University, 1979; Burkart Holzner and John H. Marx, *Knowledge Application,* Boston: Allyn and Bacon, Inc., 1979; Isaac Levi, *The Enterprise of Knowledge,* Cambridge, MA: The MIT Press, 1980.

KODÁLY METHOD, an approach to music education developed by the Hungarian, Zoltán Kodály. Geared primarily toward young children, variations of the Kodály method have been used widely in American elementary schools. The method's overriding goal is to help all children to become musically literate.

The Kodály method is vocal (as opposed to instrumental); it is also child-developmental (i.e. new learnings are introduced with consideration given to different stages in the development of children). Children's chants, nursery rhymes, and other simple music familiar to the young learner are used to start the program, followed by folk music. Other features of the method include: (1) the movable-*do* system in which *do* is the home tone in major modes, regardless of key, and *la* the minor mode; (2) a syllable system used to teach rhythm; and (3) the use of hand signs (developed by John Carwen in 1870), a kinetic activity that provides one sign for each note of the scale and that is used to help with teaching melody. As students progress, they come to study composed music and eventually learn to sight-read with little difficulty. (See KODÁLY, ZOLTÁN.)

References: Lois Choksy, *The Kodály Method: Comprehensive Music Education from Infant to Adult,* Englewood Cliffs, NJ: Prentice-Hall, Inc., 1974; Michael L. Mark,

Contemporary Music Education, New York: Schirmer Books (Macmillan), 1978.

KODÁLY, ZOLTÁN (December 16, 1882–March 6, 1967), Hungarian composer and music educator who originated the Kodály method of music instruction. Born in Kecskemet, Hungary, to parents who were amateur musicians, he studied piano as a child and taught himself to play the violin and cello. After attending a Catholic gymnasium for eight years, he was admitted to the Franz Liszt Academy of Music in Budapest where he studied composition.

After graduating from the academy, Kodály and Béla Bartók undertook to collect Hungarian folk music, eventually accumulating hundreds of songs. This effort helped Kodály with the writing of his doctoral dissertation, "The Strophic Structure of the Hungarian Folk Song."

Kodály began writing music for children in the 1920s, much of it based on Hungarian folk music, and later began teaching music courses to teachers in training. His teaching career spanned over three decades during which time he produced numerous instructional materials. They led to formulation of a method of teaching music to children that presently carries his name and is used in many countries of the world. (See KODÁLY METHOD.)

References: Michael L. Mark, *Contemporary Music Education,* New York: Schirmer Books, 1978; Oscar Thompson and Bruce Bohle (Editors), *The International Cyclopedia of Music and Musicians* (Tenth Edition), New York: Dodd, Mead and Company, 1975.

KOMENSKY, JAN AMOS—See COMENIUS, JAN AMOS

KUDER-RICHARDSON FORMULAS, measures of test reliability developed by M. W. Richardson and G. F. Kuder in 1937. They were designed to measure the internal consistency of a test. Unlike the correlational approach to assessing internal consistency, the Kuder-Richardson Formulas are calculated using the results of individual test items. Although there are several K-R formulas, the most common ones used are Numbers 20 and 21. Because the formulas are quite easy to calculate, they are recommended for use with teacher-made tests.

References: Walter B. Borg and Meredith D. Gall, *Educational Research: An Introduction* (Fifth Edition), New York: Longman, Inc., 1989; George K. Cunningham, *Educational and Psychological Measurement,* New York: Macmillan Publishing Company, 1986; Robert L. Ebel, *Essentials of Educational Measurement* (Third Edition), Englewood Cliffs, NJ: Prentice-Hall, Inc., 1979.

KUHLMANN-ANDERSON TESTS: A MEASURE OF ACADEMIC POTENTIAL, a multilevel battery of tests for grades K, 1, 2, 3–4, 4–5, 5–7, 7–9, and 9–13. The term *academic potential* is used because the test scores can be used to predict academic performance. The test is relatively focused and specific as opposed to measuring the general construct of intelligence. The Kuhlmann-Anderson Test is a group test, published by Personnel Press. It was first published in 1927 as the Kuhlmann-Anderson Intelligence Tests by Educational Test Bureau of Minneapolis.

Reference: Anne Anastasi, *Psychological Testing* (Fourth Edition), New York: Macmillan Publishing Company, Inc., 1976; Milton G. Holmen and Richard Doctor, *Educational and Psychological Testing,* New York: Russell Sage Foundation, 1972.

LABIALS, refers to the lips. In speech articulation, labials are those sounds that are produced with the aid of the lips. The letters "P" and "M" are produced by the lips only; other sounds, such as "F", are produced by the contact of the lips and the teeth. The latter are called labio-dentals.

There are many spoken words that rely on the proper use of the lips. Consequently, speech problems may develop as the result of lip disorders. One problem source that produces profound speech disturbances is the congenital cleft lip and cleft palate. Such malformations create a disconfiguration of many speech structures that, in turn, cause significant alterations in articulation and resonation. Even though surgery may correct many cleft lips and cleft palates, speech clinicians have to work with the individuals to correct/reduce many of the speech problems. (See CLEFT PALATE.)

References: William H. Perkins, *Speech Pathology: An Applied Behavioral Science*, St. Louis, MO: The C. V. Mosby Company, 1971; Charles V. Riper, *Speech Correction* (Fourth Edition), Englewood Cliffs, NJ: Prentice-Hall, Inc., 1963; W. Dean Wolfe and Daniel J. Goulding, *Articulation and Learning*, Springfield, IL: Charles C Thomas, Publisher, 1973.

LABORATORY INSTRUCTION, a form of teaching that stresses experiential learning and that provides learners with hands-on experiences. This form of instruction is commonly employed to teach science, engineering, foreign languages, and certain vocational subjects. Working in specially equipped rooms or areas (laboratories), students study independently or in small groups, observing, experimenting, and/or researching concepts presented earlier via lecture or reading. Some laboratory experiences (e.g. foreign language) provide practice opportunities that are not normally available in classrooms where the lecture is the prevailing instructional method.

Yet another form of laboratory experience is the one employed by social and behavioral scientists who, through the use of small-group laboratories, hope to produce changes in individuals.

Research carried out to ascertain the value of laboratory instruction has yielded mixed results. Different investigators have found that such instruction is better suited for some students than others, that the laboratory tends to be effective in specific areas of instruction, and that the value of the laboratory approach used (e.g. inductive vs. deductive) varies with student ability.

References: Kenneth D. Benne, et al. (Editors), *The Laboratory Method of Changing and Learning: Theory and Application*, Palo Alto, CA: Science and Behavior Books, Inc., 1975; Brian Farrington, "Language Laboratory" in Derick Unwin and Ray McAleese (Editors), *The Encyclopedia of Educational Media Communications and Technology*, Westport, CT: Greenwood Press, 1978; Robert B. Kozma, et al., *Instructional Techniques in Higher Education*, Englewood Cliffs, NJ: Educational Technology Publications, 1978; John W. Thornton, *The Laboratory: A Place to Investigate*, Washington, DC: American Institute of Biological Sciences, 1972.

LABORATORY SCHOOLS, campus-based and university-affiliated schools that enroll elementary and/or secondary school-aged children and that are used as training arms for schools/colleges of education. Professionals employed in laboratory schools are normally master teachers. They are expected to serve as role models for teachers-to-be (usually student teachers) and to work closely with education professors in either a research or demonstration capacity.

One laboratory school investigator (Evan Kelley) surveyed almost 200 laboratory schools to determine their function(s). Seven specific functions were reported (these listed in rank order): (1) observation; (2) demonstration; (3) student teaching; (4) participation; (5) experimentation; (6) research; and (7) inservice training.

In recent years, the number of laboratory schools has been declining. Reasons for this include cost and the fact that laboratory school children are not always representative of the community's total population. Clifford Rotton's study of discontinued laboratory schools (1967) revealed that schools that were closed had *student teaching* as their primary function; those still operating listed *observation* as their number one activity.

References: Charles F. Cardinell, "New Paths for America's Laboratory Schools," Bethesda, MD: ERIC Document Reproduction Service (ED 153-997), 1978; Evan H. Kelley, *College-Controlled Laboratory Schools in the United States, 1964*, Washington, DC: American Association of Colleges for Teacher Education, 1964; Clifford C. Rotton, "Study to Determine the Factors Contributing to the Discontinuance of College Controlled Laboratory Schools," Unpublished Doctoral Dissertation, 1967; William Van Til, *The Laboratory School: Its Rise and Fall?* Terre Haute, IN: Indiana State University, 1969.

LAISSEZ-FAIRE LEADERSHIP—See DEMOCRATIC-AUTOCRATIC LEADERSHIP STYLES

LAMINATION—See MATERIALS PRESERVATION

LANCASTRIAN SYSTEM, an early attempt to provide basic and inexpensive education to large numbers of students. The system was developed in England (1798) by Joseph Lancaster and introduced shortly thereafter in the United States. Because of its relatively low cost, it won favor with the American school societies (forerunners of free public schools) that were then attempting to make education available to the masses.

The Lancastrian System called upon a teacher to train his brightest students and to use them as monitors; monitors, in turn, were responsible for teaching approximately ten students each. Once organized, the system permitted one teacher to "teach" up to 600 children. The system, though crude, also aided teacher training.
Reference: Carl E. Kaestle, *Joseph Lancaster and the Monitorial School Movement: A Documentary History,* New York: Teachers College Press, Columbia University, 1973.

LAND GRANT COLLEGES, those institutions of higher education that were initially supported by the Morrill Act of 1862 (federal funds). These institutions were to have low tuition and were to offer agricultural, mechanical, and other kinds of practical courses. Over the years, many of the states established land grant institutions (e.g. Iowa State University, Michigan State University) as a result of the Morrill Act; others have contracted these functions to private or semiprivate institutions. For example, New York State's land grant supported programs are found in Cornell University, a private university. These universities have become major research centers, especially in the applied areas of agriculture and industry. Today, land grant colleges and universities offer agricultural programs plus almost any other program commonly offered by other universities and colleges. (See MORRILL ACT and SECOND MORRILL ACT. Also see APPENDIX VII: LAND GRANT COLLEGES AND UNIVERSITIES.)
References: G. Lester Anderson (Editor), *Land-Grant Universities and Their Continuing Challenge,* East Lansing, MI: Michigan State University Press, 1976; Allen Herman, *Open Door to Learning,* Urbana, IL: University of Illinois Press, 1963; Allan Nevins, *The State Universities and Democracy,* Urbana, IL: University of Illinois Press, 1962; Earle D. Ross, *Democracy's College,* New York: Arno Press, 1969.

LANGUAGE, a method of communication among individuals that contains a system of words and a set of rules governing the use of those words. Lois Bloom and Margaret Lahey defined language as "knowledge of a code for representing ideas about the world through a conventional system of arbitrary signals for communication" (p. 23). They go on to point out that there are three basic dimensions to language: (1) *content,* what people talk about or understand; (2) *form,* the acoustic, phonetic, or configurational form of utterances; and (3) *use,* reasons for communication and ways in which individuals communicate.

The four processes, or skills of language are: (1) *listening;* (2) *speaking;* (3) *writing;* and (4) *reading.*

Most children have mastered pronunciation and syntax by the time they enter school. That knowledge is expanded and developed in school through the spectrum of activities making up the language arts. Walter Petty and associates have identified three broad sets of language competencies necessary for successful functioning in society, hence those to be taught in school. They are the competencies: (1) *necessary for receiving communication* (understandings and attitudes, comprehension abilities, aural decoding, and visual decoding); (2) *necessary for expression to others* (understandings and attitudes, organization and composition, oral communication skills, and written communication skills); and (3) *necessary for locating information* (understandings and attitudes as well as locational abilities).
References: Lois Bloom and Margaret Lahey, *Language Development and Language Disorders,* New York: John Wiley and Sons, 1978; Dorothy Grant Hennings, *Communication in Action: Teaching the Language Arts* (Third Edition), Boston: Houghton Mifflin Company, 1986; Walter T. Petty and Julie M. Jensen, *Developing Children's Language,* Boston: Allyn and Bacon, Inc., 1980; Charles Temple and Jean Wallace Gillet, *Language Arts: Learning Processes and Teaching Practices* (Second Edition), Glenview, IL: Scott, Foresman and Company, 1989.

LANGUAGE ACQUISITION DEVICE—See NATIVISTIC THEORY

LANGUAGE ARTS, a component of the school curriculum that includes reading, writing, speech, and listening. These elements of the language arts are taught as tools, or skills, of communication with particular attention given to usage of language symbols (words, letters, sounds, etc.). In recent years, it has been recommended that visual communication, including nonprint media and nonverbal communication, be taught as part of the language arts.

References: Dorothy Grant Hennings, *Communication in Action: Teaching the Language Arts* (Third Edition), Boston: Houghton Mifflin Company, 1986; Charles Temple and Jean Wallace Gillet, *Language Arts: Learning Processes and Teaching Practices* (Second Edition), Glenview, IL: Scott, Foresman and Company, 1989.

LANGUAGE DISORDERS, or language impairment, a broad descriptive term applied to individuals who manifest abnormal language skills and behaviors. Disorders in terms of reception, vocabulary, form, structure, or content and its use may be considered language disorders. They may range from mild to extreme.

Children who suffer from cerebral palsy, autism, or aphasia have varying degrees of language disorders, as do some children with brain dysfunctions. There are many factors that contribute to language disorders, including intellectual, sensory, physical, maturational, and emotional factors; neurological problems; and, social-cultural differences. Some causes are unknown. (See APHASIA; AUTISM; BRAIN DAMAGE; and CEREBRAL PALSY.)

References: William H. Berdine and A. Edward Blackhurst (Editors), *An Introduction to Special Education* (Second Edition), Boston: Little, Brown and Company, 1985; Lois Bloom and Margaret Lahey, *Language Development and Language Disorders*, New York: John Wiley and Sons, 1978; Alfonso Caramazza and Edgar B. Zurif (Editors), *Language Acquisition and Language Breakdown: Parallels and Divergencies*, Baltimore, MD: Johns Hopkins University Press, 1978; Herbert E. Rie and Ellen D. Rie, *Handbook of Minimal Brain Dysfunctions: A Critical View*, New York: John Wiley and Sons, 1980; R. W. Rieber (Editor), *Language Development and Aphasia in Children, New Essays and a Translation of Kindersprache and Aphasia by Emil Fröschels*, New York: Academic Press, 1980.

LANGUAGE EXPERIENCE APPROACH, an instructional method that builds on the experiences of the learner. This method was formulated to facilitate students' language development. When following the language experience approach, students' experiences (rather than printed materials) provide the content for language study.

Events such as field trips, holiday celebrations, and athletic events, in which one or more learners participated, are recorded (written down), often on large chart paper (experience chart). The language and thinking of the children themselves are used, a step that ultimately helps the learner to become aware of: (1) the similarity between his/her spoken and written language, and (2) eventually, the similarity between his/her printed language and the printed language of others. Students read each experience chart, the last step in integrating the development of four language skills (listening, speaking, writing, and reading).

References: Carole Cox, *Teaching Language Arts*, Boston: Allyn and Bacon, Inc., 1988; R. Van Allen, *Language Experiences in Communication*, Boston: Houghton Mifflin Company, 1976; R. Van Allen and Gladys C. Halvorsen, "The Language-Experience Approach to Reading Instruction," *Contributions in Reading*, No. 27, Boston: Ginn and Company, 1960; Robert M. Wilson and Craig J. Cleland, *Diagnostic and Remedial Reading for Classroom and Clinic* (Sixth Edition), Columbus, OH: Merrill Publishing Company, 1989.

LANGUAGE LABORATORY, a study area especially equipped to facilitate the teaching and learning of languages. The typical laboratory consists of a teacher's console and individual study areas in which students, using headsets and microphones, can listen to spoken language via specially prepared lessons (e.g. tapes) and then hear themselves as they attempt, orally, to replicate the language passages just heard. The teacher, using the console, can: (1) listen to individual student recitations; (2) communicate separately with each student; or (3) communicate with the entire class. Less complex laboratories do not have consoles. In such cases, students select and use tapes as they would a library book. Language laboratories were first introduced in the 1950s.

References: Julian Dakin, *The Language Laboratory and Language Learning*, London, England: Longman Group Ltd., 1973; Walter F. Davison, *The Language Laboratory: A Bibliography, 1950–1972* (Mimeographed), Pittsburgh, PA: University Center for International Studies, 1973; Derick Unwin and Ray McAleese (Editors), *The Encyclopedia of Educational Media Communications and Technology*, Westport, CT: Greenwood Press, 1978.

LANGUAGE USAGE—See USAGE

LANTERN SLIDES, one of the oldest audio-visual devices used to project an enlarged image onto a screen. The slides were standardized in the United States at 3¼ by 4 inches, consisting of photographic positive images on glass. Slides of smaller dimensions are more widely used today. Some slides are prepared commercially. Teachers and students may prepare lantern slides by using special pens to write/draw on glass, by typing or drawing on cellophane, and so on. Lantern slide projectors are used to recreate these images.

References: Fred J. Pula, *Application and Operation of Audiovisual Equipment in Education*, New York: John Wiley and Sons, 1968; Raymond Wyman, *Mediaware: Selection, Operation, and Maintenance* (Second Edition), Dubuque, IA: Wm. C. Brown Company, Publishers, 1976.

L'ASSOCIATION CANADIENNE d'EDUCATION—See CANADIAN EDUCATION ASSOCIATION

LATERAL DOMINANCE, the specific and unique functions of each of the two human cerebral hemispheres. The right and left hemispheres exist in a symbiotic relationship in which the functions are complementary. Each side of the brain performs particular tasks that the other side doesn't like to do (e.g. the right over space, the left over time). Visual similarities are dominant in the right hemisphere and concepts are dominant in the left. There is a great deal of lateral dominance research being completed, some of it suggesting that the retrieval processes and cerebral laterality are related to coding strategies, thus influencing learning and educational strategies.

References: Stuart T. Dimond (Editor), *Hemisphere Function in the Human Brain*, New York: John Wiley and Sons, 1974; Walter T. Friedlander (Editor), *Current Reviews of Higher Nervous Systems Dysfunction*, New York: Raven Press, 1975; B. R. Hergenhahn, *An Introduction to Theories of Learning* (Third Edition), Englewood Cliffs, NJ: Prentice-Hall, Inc., 1988; Marcel Kinsbourne (Editor), *Asymmetrical Function of the Brain*, New York: Cambridge University Press, 1978.

LATERALITY, the general use of one part of the body as opposed to its counterpart. Right (dextrality) or left (sinistrality) handedness are examples of laterality because of a preference for the use of a particular hand in completing a task, especially when only one hand might be needed. Studies have led to the conclusion that the dominance of one side (right or left) of the cerebral hemisphere over the other causes laterality with respect to motor activities. Research on the functions of the brain and the effects of laterality on various learning and perceptual disorders is continuing. Laterality relates to the eyes, hands, feet, and even hearing. (See AMBIDEXTERITY; CEREBRAL DOMINANCE; MIXED DOMINANCE; and SINISTRAL.)

References: Edward C. Carterette and Morton P. Friedman (Editors), *Handbook of Perception*, New York: Academic Press, 1978; Carl W. Cotman and James L. McGaugh, *Behavioral Neuroscience: An Introduction*, New York: Academic Press, 1980; J. Z. Young, *Programs of the Brain*, Oxford, England: Oxford University Press, 1978.

LATIN GRAMMAR SCHOOL, a type of secondary school, most often a college preparatory school, developed in England and brought to America during the colonial period. The Boston Latin School, founded in 1635, was the first and one of the better known such schools to operate in the colonies. Most Latin grammar schools, also known as grammar schools, were located in New England. They admitted young boys (usually seven- and eight-year-olds) who had already learned to read and prepared them for college.

Programs took approximately seven years to complete; Latin grammar was studied almost exclusively, although some also taught Greek. In a sense, they proved to be class (private) schools, attended by boys whose parents could afford to pay the tuition that most required. The cost factor, coupled with the impracticality of curricula, prompted many young men to enter academies when such schools became available after 1750.

References: R. Freeman Butts, *A Cultural History of Western Education: Its Social and Intellectual Foundations*, New York: McGraw-Hill Book Company, 1955; Pauline Holmes, *A Tercentenary History of the Boston Public Latin School, 1635–1935*, Cambridge, MA: Harvard University Press, 1935; Robert W. Richey, *Planning for Teaching: An Introduction to Education* (Fourth Edition), New York: McGraw-Hill Book Company, 1968.

LAUBACH LITERACY PROGRAM, a tutorial program for adult illiterates. The program was originally designed by Presbyterian missionary Frank Laubach (1943) to instruct the Moros of the Philippine Islands. Employing a pictorial method, Laubach employed newly literate individuals as peer tutors. Since its inception, the program has been in continuous operation in different parts of the world. Volunteer tutoring remains a major thrust of the approach.

The program is divided into four levels designed to take nonreaders from zero to sixth-grade level. Material is intended for adolescents and adults. The material is available through New Readers Press publishers, a branch of the Laubach Literacy Foundation. Most cities have local representatives of the Laubach program who cooperate with groups interested in adopting the system.

References: Arthur Heilmen, *Principles and Practices of Teaching Reading* (Third Edition), Columbus, OH: Charles E. Merrill Publishing Company, 1972; Frank Laubach, *Learn English the New Way*, Syracuse, NY: New Readers Press, 1962.

LAU v. NICHOLS, a United States Supreme Court decision rendered in 1974. It held that schools, by not providing English language instruction for non-English speaking children, were denying these children their civil rights by failing to provide a meaningful opportunity to participate in public education. In ruling on this case, the Supreme Court found the San Francisco School District had violated Section 601 of the Civil Rights Act of 1964 for approximately 1,800 students of Chinese ancestry by not providing appropriate educational experiences.

From this decision came the Office of Civil Rights (of the U.S. Department of Health, Education and Welfare, Summer of 1975) *Task Force Findings Specifying Remedies Available for Eliminating Past Educational Practices Ruled Unlawful under Lau v. Nichols.* This report became the base for school district compliance, identification of linguistically different students, and the provision of instructional programs to meet the needs of such students. In addition, in 1974, federal bilingual legislation (P.L. 93-380) was extended greatly from its limited focus under Title VII of the Elementary and Secondary Education Act.

References: Bernard Spolsky and Robert L. Cooper (Editors), *Case Studies in Bilingual Education*, Rowley, MA: Newbury House Publishers, Inc., 1978; Perry A. Zirkel (Editor), *A Digest of Supreme Court Decisions Affecting Education*, Bloomington, IN: Phi Delta Kappa, 1978.

LAW OF EFFECT—See GRATIFICATION, DELAY OF

LAW-RELATED EDUCATION (LRE), as defined by the U.S. Office of Education Study Group on Law-Related Education, "means education to give people an adequate base of knowledge, understanding, and training about the law, the legal process, and the legal system that, as part of their general education, enables them to be more informed and effective citizens" (p. 1). Law-related education goes beyond the traditional, rote learning of civics, instead challenging students to raise questions about the law and to suggest what it should be rather than what it is.

LRE proponents suggest that this is a subject that, in the past, has been taught incidentally as part of civics, history, citizenship education, and social studies. They argue that it should be made a key part of a revitalized curriculum at all school levels. The study group, cited above, suggests that LRE include components such as fundamental legal principles, the Bill of Rights and Constitutional law, the role and limits of law in a democracy, the use of law in avoiding conflicts/controversies, and an assessment of our judicial system's strengths and weaknesses.

Interest in LRE has increased considerably in recent years, heightened by: (1) passage of the national Law-Related Education Act of 1978; (2) the study group's final report on LRE; and (3) the encouragement of foundations and such organizations as the American Bar Association. (See LAW-RELATED EDUCATION ACT.)

References: Application for Grants Under the Law-Related Education Program, Washington, DC: U.S. Department of Health, Education, and Welfare, 1980; Mary S. Furlong and Lee Arbetman, "Learning About Law: Law-Related Education is Creating a Renaissance in Civic Education," *Education Leadership*, October 1980; Steven Y. Winnick (Chairperson), *Final Report of the U.S. Office of Education Study Group on Law-Related Education*, Washington, DC: U.S. Department of Health, Education, and Welfare, September 1, 1978.

LAW-RELATED EDUCATION ACT (Public Law 95-561), federal legislation enacted in 1978 that authorized the Commissioner of Education to make grants and contracts available for the purpose of encouraging law-related education programs. The act cited seven types of activities that such funding could support: (1) awareness activities (e.g. helping the public to understand what law-related education is); (2) program support at all educational levels, elementary through university, for pilot programs; (3) providing clearinghouse assistance; (4) training of educators and law-related personnel; (5) research and evaluation; (6) involvement of law-related organizations in the provision of law-related education activities; and (7) youth internships for non-classroom law experiences. (See LAW-RELATED EDUCATION.)

References: Federal Register, Volume 45, No. 185, September 22, 1980; Public Law 95-561, Law-Related Education Act, *Application for Grants Under the Law-Related Education Program*, Washington, DC: Department of Health, Education, and Welfare, 1980.

LEADER BEHAVIOR, the observed behavior of leaders as they carry out their duties in a formal organization. In education, some of the earliest studies of leader behavior were conducted by Andrew Halpin (1955 and 1957) using the Leader Behavior Description Questionnaire, a two-dimensional instrument developed at Ohio State University. One dimension was *initiating structure* (establishing organization and procedures), the other *consideration* (establishing rapport with members of the organization). Effective leaders were found to score high on both dimensions. A paradigm for the study of administrator behavior was later (1966) proposed by Halpin. It consisted of four "panels" (components): (1) the organization task; (2) administrator behavior; (3) variables associated with administrative behavior; and (4) criteria of administrator "effectiveness."

Ralph Stogdill, in 1974, summarized research in which specific leadership characteristics (factors) had been identified and studied by three or more investigators. The most frequently occurring factors, he found, were: (1) social and interpersonal skills; (2) technical skills; (3) administrative skills; (4) intellectual skills; (5) leadership effectiveness and achievement; (6) social nearness, friendliness; (7) group task supportiveness; and (8) task motivation and application.

In recent years, new theoretical frameworks have been developed to help study leader behavior. They include *organizational contingency theory* (which considers the differing degrees of environmental turbulence and its relationship to organizational structure), *path-goal theory* (which holds that the behavior of subordinates is motivated by the behavior of the leader), and *situational leadership theory* (a theory that suggests that leader behavior should be determined primarily by the situation in which he/she works).

References: Daniel E. Griffiths, "Another Look at Research on the Behavior of Administrators" in Glenn L. Immegart and William L. Boyd (Editors), *Problem-Finding in Educational Administration*, Lexington, MA: Lexington Books, 1979; E. Mark Hanson, *Educational Administration and Organizational Behavior*, Boston: Allyn and Bacon, Inc., 1979; Paul Hersey and Kenneth Blanchard, *Management of Organizational Behavior: Utilizing Human Resources* (Third Edition), Englewood Cliffs, NJ: Prentice-Hall, Inc., 1977; Andrew W. Halpin, "The Leader Behavior and Leadership Ideology of Educational Administrators and Aircraft Commanders," *Harvard Educational Review* 25, 1955; Andrew W. Halpin, *The Leadership Behavior of School Superintendents*, Chicago: Midwest Administration Center, University of Chicago, 1959; Andrew W. Halpin, *Theory and Research in Administration*, New York: The Macmillan Company, 1966; Thomas J. Sergiovanni and Fred D. Carver, *The New School Executive: A Theory of Administration* (Second Edi-

tion), New York: Harper and Row, Publishers, 1980; Ralph M. Stogdill, *Handbook of Leadership: A Survey of Theory and Research*, New York: The Free Press, 1974.

LEADER BEHAVIOR DESCRIPTION QUESTIONNAIRE, frequently referred to as the LBDQ. Developed by John K. Hemphill and Alvin E. Coons, this instrument examines two dimensions of a leader's behavior: consideration and structure. Leaders scoring high in *consideration* demonstrate concern, warmth, and trust for subordinates. Those scoring high on the *initiation of structure* dimension tend to be task oriented, concerned with goals, organization, and realization of high organizational productivity. Several forms of the LBDQ have been developed and used in numerous leadership studies.

References: Andrew W. Halpin, *The Leadership Behavior of School Superintendents* (Second Edition), Chicago: Midwest Administration Center, University of Chicago, 1959; John K. Hemphill and Alvin E. Coons, "Development of the Leader Behavior Description Questionnaire" in Ralph M. Stogdill and Alvin E. Coons (Editors), *Leader Behavior: Its Description and Measurement*, Columbus, OH: Ohio State University Press, 1957.

LEADERS IN EDUCATION, a directory of biographical sketches published by the R. R. Bowker Company. The 1974 (fifth) edition of *Leaders in Education* contains approximately 17,000 biographies. Persons listed include university officers, professors of education, educational researchers, educational authors, and leaders of educational foundations. The directory was first published in 1932. Recent editions have been edited by Jacques Cattell Press.

Reference: Jacques Cattell Press (Editors), *Leaders in Education* (Fifth Edition), New York: R. R. Bowker Company, 1974.

LEARNING, a change in behavior or attitude that is a result of an experience. The change in behavior or attitude need not necessarily be observed (i.e. learning may occur without an overt change in behavior evident). Learning is an active process; the learner must interact with a stimulus or condition. The external stimulus or condition may be a classroom, a teacher, other learners, the physical environment, sound, a book, a movie, television, an incident, and so on. An example of an internal stimulus or condition may be one's desire to reanalyze or reconceptualize previously learned materials. Much, although not all, learning occurs in schools in a classroom. Because learning itself is highly individualistic, an activity that facilitates learning for one learner may not do so for another.

References: Benjamin S. Bloom, *Human Characteristics and School Learning*, New York: McGraw-Hill Book Company, 1976; W. K. Estes (Editor), *Handbook of Learning and Cognitive Processes* (Volume I), Hillsdale, NJ: Lawrence Erlbaum Associates, Publishers, 1975; B. R. Hergenhahn, *An Introduction to Theories of Learning* (Third Edition), Englewood Cliffs, NJ: Prentice-Hall, Inc., 1988.

LEARNING BLOCK, that which prevents or interferes with learning. There are three basic types of learning blocks: physical, psychological, educational.

The *physical block* may be caused by damage to a particular section of the brain. It may also be caused by changes in electrical excitation to the brain for a period of time. Inability to see, hear, or perform a physical task may also constitute a physical block.

Psychological blocks may be caused by factors such as past experiences, emotional problems on the part of the learner, low self-concept, poor perceptions of what is being learned, disinterest in the learning activity, failure, level of difficulty causing frustration and/or anxieties, value conflicts, or attitudes.

The learner's lack of skills and abilities in a particular area may cause *educational learning blocks*. One's inability to read or perform a specific task at a particular skill level (such as in physical education, shop) or poor cognitive base can cause blocks of this type.

Many of the blocks are interrelated and tend to manifest themselves in individualized ways.

References: Don E. Hamachek, *Behavior Dynamics in Teaching, Learning, and Growth*, Boston: Allyn and Bacon, Inc., 1975; O. Hobart Mowrer, *Learning Theory and the Symbolic Process*, New York: John Wiley and Sons, 1960; William L. Mikulas, *Concepts in Learning*, Philadelphia: W. B. Saunders Company, 1974.

LEARNING CENTERS—See LEARNING LABORATORY

LEARNING CLIMATE, the type of atmosphere or conditions in which learning takes place. In the classroom, the teacher generally establishes the learning climate. It can range from being accepting and free to being punitive and threatening. The learning climate can directly affect how children and students learn. For example, learning authorities have demonstrated that classes in which the learning climate is accepting and constructive tend to enhance learning.

Although physical factors such as heat, light, noise, and other distractions are also capable of influencing learning climate, interpersonal relationships developed in the classroom are considered to be the major determiners. Consequently, the teacher is viewed as a major element in the classroom atmosphere.

References: Lilian G. Katz, et al. (Editors), *Current Topics in Early Childhood Education* (Volume II), Norwood, NJ: Ablex Publishing Corporation, 1979; Albert H. Shuster and Milton E. Ploghoft, *The Emerging Elementary Curriculum* (Second Edition), Columbus, OH: Charles E. Merrill Publishing Company, 1970.

LEARNING, CONCEPTUAL, the grouping together of different items, things, events, or words according to a common characteristic or trait. The items may be real, but the concept is abstract. For example, a student may study the structures of governments of several countries and then group the governments according to whether or not they are democratic. In this example, the term *democratic* is the concept.

Concept learning is extremely important for children and students, for it enables them to bring together and manipulate complex subject matter into a systematic form and facilitates communication. As one gets older, the concepts learned are more complex and abstract.

References: Muriel Beadle, *A Child's Mind*, Garden City, NY: Doubleday and Company, Inc., 1971; Robert M. Gagné, *The Conditions of Learning* (Third Edition), New York: Holt, Rinehart and Winston, Inc., 1977; Jean Piaget, *Science of Education and the Psychology of the Child*, New York: Orion Press, 1970; Wayne A. Wickilgren, *Learning and Memory*, Englewood Cliffs, NJ: Prentice-Hall, Inc., 1977.

LEARNING CONTRACT, an agreement between a student and an instructor that specifies the amount/type of student work to be completed. It is at the same time a commitment and a plan for an individual student project. The contract indicates the skills or new learnings to be acquired by the student, time to be spent on the project, learning approaches to be used, criteria for evaluation, and the amount of credit to be awarded once the project has been successfully completed. Learning contracts are normally employed with adult learners. This particular instructional strategy has been used with varying degrees of success, notably by non-traditional institutions of higher education.

References: Neal R. Berte (Editor), *Individualizing Education by Learning Contracts*, San Francisco: Jossey-Bass Publishers, 1975; Wayne Blaze and John Nero, *College De-*

grees for Adults, Boston: Beacon Press, 1979.

LEARNING DISABILITIES, a special education term for children who exhibit a discrepancy between their ability to achieve and their demonstrated achievement. The discrepancy generally refers to the skill areas of reading, mathematics, and writing and the broader areas of perception and language.

Learning disabled children are not mentally retarded; most fall within the normal range of intelligence. For this reason, many of the definitions used for learning disabilities are exclusionary in nature (i.e. they indicate what learning disabilities is not). Common to most definitions are four elements: (1) academic retardation; (2) uneven developmental pattern; (3) learning difficulties not attributable to mental retardation, emotional disturbance, or environmental disadvantage; and (4) the child may or may not show demonstrable deviation in central nervous functioning.

The term *learning disabilities* was first used in the early 1960s and became widespread as the result of parent activism generated through the Association for Children with Learning Disabilities. (See SPECIFIC LEARNING DISABILITIES.)
References: Daniel P. Hallahan and James M. Kauffman, *Exceptional Children: Introduction to Special Education* (Fourth Edition), Englewood Cliffs, NJ: Prentice-Hall, Inc., 1988; Norris G. Haring and Barbara Bateman, *Teaching the Learning Disabled Child,* Englewood Cliffs, NJ: Prentice-Hall, Inc., 1977; Thomas C. Lovitt, *Introduction to Learning Disabilities,* Boston: Allyn and Bacon, 1989; Gerald Wallace and James A. McLoughlin, *Learning Disabilities: Concepts and Characteristics* (Third Edition), Columbus, OH: Charles E. Merrill Publishing Company, 1988.

LEARNING, DISCRIMINATION, the ability to make different responses to very similar stimuli. For example, a learner may respond by tapping his/her foot to a red light, but not to a green light. When a child learns to read, the child must learn to make discriminations among letters that look almost alike.

There are many types of discriminations an individual must learn. Shapes, colors, and sounds are but a few. Discrimination learning occurs in infants and becomes fully developed in the elementary grades. Discrimination learning is the base upon which much learning occurs. Although the school is one place where one learns to discriminate between and among various stimuli, a good deal of such learning also occurs outside the school. Play-

ing games at an early age helps young children to develop such skills.
References: Jack A. Adams, *Learning and Memory: An Introduction,* Homewood, IL: The Dorsey Press, 1976; Ralph Garry and Howard L. Kingsley, *The Nature and Conditions of Learning* (Third Edition), Englewood Cliffs, NJ: Prentice-Hall, Inc., 1970; Merlin C. Wittrock (Editor), *Learning and Instruction,* Berkeley, CA: McCutchan Publishing Corporation, 1977.

LEARNING, EXPERIENTIAL, sometimes referred to as real-life learning or experience-based learning, the learning that results from having lived through an event. Warren Willingham pointed out that experiential learning is of two types. The first consists of those *nonsponsored* real-life experiences that typically are learned in other than institutional settings. Examples include learning that results from travel, volunteer work, and job experience. The second type is made up of *institutionally sponsored* activities that have been designed to help students relate (apply) formal learning to practical situations. Student teaching and various forms of internship are illustrations of this latter category.

The term *experiential learning* is also used to describe a methodology that: (1) provides students with experiences that are relevant to them; (2) involves other than a passive student role; and (3) provides students with coping skills necessary to evaluate the world about them and to make good decisions. Careful preplanning and effective questioning by the teacher, as well as a climate in which students are free to explore and to express their ideas, serve to maximize the amount of learning likely to take place. This method may be used to teach virtually all subjects making up the school curriculum.
References: Muriel S. Karlin and Regina Berger, *Experiential Learning: An Effective Teaching Program for Elementary Schools,* West Nyack, NY: Parker Publishing Company, Inc., 1971; Byron G. Massialas and Joseph B. Hurst, *Social Studies in a New Era: The Elementary School as a Laboratory,* New York: Longman, Inc., 1978; Warren W. Willingham, "Critical Issues and Basic Requirements for Assessment" in Morris T. Keeton and Associates, *Experiential Learning,* San Francisco: Jossey-Bass Publishers, 1976.

LEARNING LABORATORY, a facility in which a learner is taught the basic cognitive skills as well as the learning and study habits necessary to succeed academically. Learning laboratories are usually designed to meet individual needs, primarily to help students overcome learning problems. They contain instructional equipment and devices as well as a considerable amount of self-instructional material (e.g. programmed instruction and multimedia kits). To the extent that budgets permit, learning laboratories are staffed by trained professionals. Some are well equipped, containing specially designed facilities; others consist of a section of a classroom devoted to helping children or students improve their learning skills. At the elementary and secondary levels, such facilities are called laboratories. At the posthigh school level, they are sometimes called learning centers. Learning centers are usually larger and better equipped than their counterparts at the lower levels. They also have broader functions, including tutoring and preparation for professional examinations. (See LABORATORY INSTRUCTION.)

References: Mario D. Fantini and Gerald Weinstein, *The Disadvantaged: Challenge to Education,* New York: Harper and Row, Publishers, 1968; Gerald R. Firth and Richard D. Kimpston, *The Curricular Continuum in Perspective,* Itasca, IL: F. E. Peacock Publishers, Inc., 1973; Martha Maxwell, *Improving Student Learning Skills,* San Francisco: Jossey-Bass Publishers, 1979.

LEARNING MODULE, another term for a learning unit. A learning module tends to be a self-standing or self-contained learning experience, but it is also a part of a broader instructional design. A series of learning modules is organized to achieve general and/or specific objectives. Sequentially, modules proceed from the simple to the complex or from the restrictive to the general.

The design of the module depends on its purpose and function. In the classroom, learning activity packets (LAPS) are examples of a complex learning module, and even they range in levels of complexities and difficulties. Modules may be designed for specific learners who have particular learning problems, or they may be designed for all learners. (See LEARNING PACKETS.)

References: Ronald C. Doll, *Curriculum Improvement,* Boston: Allyn and Bacon, Inc., 1970; George J. Mouly, *Psychology for Effective Teaching* (Third Edition), New York: Holt, Rinehart and Winston, Inc., 1973.

LEARNING PACKETS, or learning-activity packages, protocol materials designed to foster individualization of instruction. Generally, learning packets include: a pre-test to determine prior knowledge; a self-test (determines whether a student is ready for the mastery test); a mastery test, to assess what a student knows after completing a packet; information on what a student is to learn or study (a list of specific skills to be achieved); suggestions for using variable approaches and varieties of learning resources (multimedia) to learn or acquire the specific skills; and enrichment activities. Usually, learning packets are consumable because each student interacts actively with the materials contained in the packets, particularly the tests.

Several benefits accrue from use of learning packets: (1) students proceed at their own rate of learning; (2) they select the best media through which to learn; (3) they are encouraged to master information retrieval skills; (4) a great deal of student decision making is involved; and (5) they produce more individual interactions with the teacher. A major advantage of learning packets is that they can be teacher developed and made, thus meeting individual school and community needs. (See INDIVIDUALIZED INSTRUCTION.)

Reference: Patricia S. Ward and E. Craig Williams, *Learning Packets: New Approach to Individualizing Instruction,* West Nyack, NY: Parker Publishing Company, Inc., 1976.

LEARNING, PERCEPTUAL, learning that is based on how an individual interprets a given learning situation. Perceptual learning is concerned with how an individual internalizes (processes or interprets) the new learning. Needs, wants, anxieties, values, attitudes, and interests are just a few of the forces that condition the internalizing process. It is these forces that greatly affect what is learned or not learned by a student. (See COMPREHENSION; LEARNING; and PERCEPTIONS.)

References: D. W. Hamlyn, *Experience and the Growth of Understanding,* London, England: Routledge and Kegan Paul, Ltd., 1978; David Klahr (Editor), *Cognition and Instruction,* Hillsdale, NJ: Lawrence Erlbaum Associates, Publishers, 1976; H. Ronald Pulliam and Christopher Dunford, *Programmed to Learn: An Essay on the Evolution of Culture,* New York: Columbia University Press, 1980.

LEARNING POTENTIAL ASSESSMENT DEVICE—See FEUERSTEIN'S INSTRUMENTAL ENRICHMENT

LEARNING RESOURCE CENTER, a school facility that integrates and provides four types of service to support the institution's instructional program. The services are: (1) *library;* (2) *audiovisual;* (3) *instructional development;* and (4) *alternate* (nontraditional) instructional modes. The center has learning as its focus, a factor that accounts for its status as a service (rather than storage) unit.

Service that teachers and students alike receive from the learning resource center is intended to facilitate individual learning, inquiry, change, and experimentation. That service takes the form of consultation as well as exposure to various instructional materials.

References: Lowell Horton and Phyllis Horton, *The Learning Center: Heart of the School,* Minneapolis, MN: T. S. Denison and Company, Inc., 1973; Gary T. Peterson, *The Learning Center: A Sphere for Nontraditional Approaches to Education,* Hamden, CT: The Shoe String Press, Inc., 1975.

LEARNING, SEQUENTIAL, in psychology, the learning of a series of responses in which the first response facilitates the second response, the second the third, and so on. This sequencing helps to shape the behavior of the learner.

In the classroom, sequential learning is achieved through a series of ordered experiences, each building on the other and each forming the base for the learning that is to take place in the subsequent learning experience. It is quite important for the teacher to design learning experiences in a sequence, thus permitting the learner to bring prior experiences to the new learning situation. Mathematics is an example of an academic discipline that is based on sequential learning. Subjects such as English and science also lend themselves to sequential learning.

References: Richard C. Anderson, et al., *Schooling and the Acquisition of Knowledge,* Hillsdale, NJ: Lawrence Erlbaum Associates, Publishers, 1977; E. A. Bilodeau and Ina McD. Bilodeau (Editors), *Principles of Skill Acquisition,* New York: Academic Press, 1969; Robert M. Gagne, *The Conditions of Learning* (Third Edition), New York: Holt, Rinehart and Winston, Inc., 1977; Clifford T. Morgan and Richard King, *Introduction to Psychology* (Fourth Edition), New York: McGraw-Hill Book Company, 1971.

LEARNING SETS, a large number of related or similar problems that help an organism "learn how to learn." Learning of similar tasks results in improved speed of learning. Harry Harlow, in 1949, showed that through the use of learning sets (discrimination-learning problems), monkeys became more proficient at learning new problems. They learned to identify (disseminate) relevant and irrelevant stimuli used in the new problem through the learning sets. A learning set can either facilitate learning of similar materials or hinder learning of material that does not fit the set. There

is considerable division of opinion about the use or success of learning sets. Some primates have shown good learning set performance, others have not. More research into learning sets needs to be completed to understand how and why they are effective in some cases and not in others.

References: W. K. Estes (Editor), *Handbook of Learning and Cognitive Processes* (Volume I), Hillsdale, NJ: Lawrence Erlbaum Associates, Publishers, 1975; Wayne A. Wickelgren, *Learning and Memory,* Englewood Cliffs, NJ: Prentice-Hall, Inc., 1977.

LEARNING, SOCIAL, those learning activities that help a human to become integrated into a particular society. The acquisition of such learning is called socialization. Socialization begins to occur at birth and continues throughout an individual's life.

There are many ways a person becomes involved in social learning. Individuals can learn through observation. Parents, brothers, sisters, and relatives influence the social learning of an individual. Peers are another important source of social learning. Teachers and other adults also help children to acquire social learning. Social learning occurs in all societies and in all environments with the school a major provider of such learning. (See ACCULTURATION).

References: Nicholas T. Anastasiow, et al. (Contributing Consultants), *Educational Psychology,* Del Mar, CA: CRM Books, 1973; Robert L. Morasky, *Learning Experiences in Educational Psychology,* Dubuque, IA: Wm. C. Brown Company, Publishers, 1973.

LEARNING STYLE, sometimes called cognitive style, the actual way in which an individual accepts and processes information while learning. Prior experiences often help to shape the learning style used by the learner. There are many learning styles. According to Marshall Rosenberg, they fall into any of four general categories: (1) rigid-inhibited; (2) undisciplined; (3) acceptance-anxious; and (4) creative. The creative learner is an independent thinker, one who maximizes his/her abilities, can work by him/herself, enjoys learning, and is self-critical. This last category constitutes the ideal, incorporating the learning styles preferred by most students of learning.

Since prior experience contributes to the way a person learns, the teacher must establish a learning climate that is supportive and helps the learner to develop the desired creative learning style. (See COGNITIVE STYLE and LEARNING CLIMATE.)

References: Joseph S. Renzulli and Linda H. Smith, *Learning Styles Inventory: A Measure of Student Preference for Instructional Technique*, Mansfield, CT: Creative Learning Press, 1978; Marshall Rosenberg, *Diagnostic Teaching*, Seattle, WA: Special Child Publications, 1968; Laurel N. Tanner and Henry Clay Lindgren, *Classroom Teaching and Learning*, New York: Holt, Rinehart and Winston, Inc., 1971; Herman A. Witkin and Donald R. Goodenough, *Cognitive Styles: Essence and Origins-Field Dependence and Field Independence*, New York: International Universities Press, 1980.

LEARNING TEAM—CONTROL THEORY

LEARNING THEORY, the psychological principles (system) that attempt to explain the learning process. Although learning is studied by physiologists, biochemists, and others in the physical sciences, it is the psychologist who has developed, studied, and tested learning theories. These studies began in the laboratory of the psychologist.

There are many learning theories. Among the best known are: connectionism (E. L. Thorndike); classical conditioning (Ivan Pavlov); operant conditioning (B. F. Skinner); gestalt (Max Wertheimer, Wolfgang Koehler, Kurt Lewin); functionalism; stimulus-sampling model (William Estes); developmental; information processing; and Jean Piaget's theory. Each has its supporters, as well as critics who reject a theory on the grounds that it fails, for one reason or another, to explain how an individual learns.

References: Robert M. Gagne and Leslie Briggs, *Principles of Instructional Design* (Second Edition), New York: Holt, Rinehart and Winston, Inc., 1979; B. R. Hergenhahn, *An Introduction to Theories of Learning* (Third Edition), Englewood Cliffs, NJ: Prentice-Hall, Inc., 1988; Ernest R. Hilgard and Gordon H. Bower, *Theories of Learning* (Third Edition), New York: Appleton-Century-Crofts, Inc., 1966.

LEARNING TOGETHER, an approach to Cooperative Learning developed by D. Johnson and R. Johnson in the 1970s. (See COOPERATIVE LEARNING.)

Reference: D. Johnson and R. Johnson, *Learning Together and Alone*, Englewood Cliffs, NJ: Prentice-Hall, Inc., 1975.

LEARNING, VERBAL AND NONVERBAL, learning that deals with oral or written language communication (verbal) or with nonlanguage communication such as body language (gestures, pointing, body movements) or geometric shapes.

Both types of learning change behavior. Often it is the nonverbal learning that is the more effective.

Both verbal and nonverbal learning is a function of the particular culture a person is in; both contribute to the development of perceptions. It is apparent that there are significant language differences among nations, and even within a country there can be major language differences. Nonverbal learning can also be quite different from culture to culture.

Teachers should be aware that both verbal and nonverbal learning occurs in a classroom and should be able to capitalize on such learnings. At times, what is communicated through nonverbal learning is different from what is being taught verbally.

Psychologists, aware of the nonverbal learning phenomenon, have developed nonverbal tests. These instruments are usually used with children or adults manifesting verbal skill problems. (See LEARNING and NONVERBAL COMMUNICATIONS.)

References: Jack A. Adams, *Learning and Memory: An Introduction*, Homewood, IL: The Dorsey Press, 1976; Merlin C. Wittrock (Editor), *Learning and Instruction*, Berkeley, CA: McCutchan Publishing Corporation, 1977; Miles V. Zintz, *The Reading Process* (Second Edition), Dubuque, IA: Wm. C. Brown Company, Publishers, 1975.

LEAST RESTRICTIVE ENVIRONMENT (LRE), statutory language relating to the education of handicapped children. The term appears as a regulatory requirement in Public Law 94-142, the Education for All Handicapped Children Act. The regulation requires states and local education agencies to see that each handicapped child's educational placement in a regular class, special class, special school, home instruction program, hospital instruction program, or institution is consistent with his/her individualized educational program and provides an educational setting appropriate to his/her educational needs. The intent of the regulation is deinstitutionalization to the greatest extent possible with maximum mainstreaming opportunities made available to the handicapped child. (See MAINSTREAMING and SPECIAL EDUCATION PLACEMENT CASCADE.)

References: Daniel P. Hallahan and James M. Kauffman, *Exceptional Children: Introduction to Special Education* (Fourth Edition), Englewood Cliffs, NJ: Prentice-Hall, 1988; National School Public Relations Association, *Educating All the Handicapped: What the Laws Say and What Schools are Doing*, Arlington, VA: The Association, 1977; Public Law 94–142, "Education for All Handicapped Children Act of 1975" in *United States Code: Congressional and Administrative News*, 94th Congress—First Session, 1975, St. Paul, MN: West Publishing Company, 1975; Judy W. Wood, *Mainstreaming: A Practical Approach for Teachers*, Columbus, OH: Merrill Publishing Company, 1989.

LEAVE OF ABSENCE, authorized absence from employment that is normally granted for a fixed period and that does not sever (or even jeopardize) an individual's employment status. Leaves serve two general purposes: (1) meeting the needs of the individual employee, and/or (2) improving the employee's productivity.

School board policies determine the *types* and *conditions* of leaves granted to teachers and other school employees. Leaves are commonly granted for illness, maternity, travel or study, observance of religious holidays, and military service. Leave conditions vary from district to district and may include constraints such as limiting the number of days allowed for each leave, requiring verification of illness (for sick leave), or restricting study leaves to tenured personnel. (See MATERNITY LEAVE; PERSONAL LEAVE; and SABBATICAL LEAVE.)

References: William B. Castetter, *The Personnel Function in Educational Administration* (Third Edition), New York: Macmillan Publishing Company, Inc., 1981; R. Oliver Gibson and Herold C. Hunt, *The School Personnel Administrator*, Boston: Houghton Mifflin Company, 1965.

LECTURE METHOD, a mode of instruction involving communication of information by one individual (e.g. teacher, master, reader) to a group of listeners (learners). This instructional method has been traced to ancient times, was used by Socrates and other early scholars, and is reported to have been the popular vehicle for instruction in medieval universities. Today, the lecture method is used widely at all levels of education.

Proponents of the lecture method cite at least four principal advantages associated with it: (1) it is relatively economical; (2) whole fields of knowledge can be communicated by a living teacher; (3) learners can be aroused intellectually and thus encouraged to pursue additional knowledge independently; and (4) the teacher "grows" in an inservice sense by virtue of having to prepare a lecture. Critics of the method cite numerous shortcomings, including the following: (1) the relatively passive role of the learner; (2) students come to view knowledge as a closed system; and (3) information is not always presented objectively.

Some research indicates that students tend to respond positively to the lecture method when there is evidence that the lecturer: (1) knows his subject; (2) organizes it well; and (3) demonstrates personal commitment to the subject under study.

References: N. L. Gage and David C. Berliner, *Educational Psychology* (Second Edition), Chicago: Rand McNally College Publishing Company, 1979; Robert B. Kozma, et al., *Instructional Techniques in Higher Education*, Englewood Cliffs, NJ: Educational Technology Publications, 1978; John McLeish, "The Lecture Method" in N. L. Gage (Editor), *The Psychology of Teaching Methods* (NSSE 75th Yearbook, Part I), Chicago: University of Chicago Press, 1976.

LEE-CLARK READING READINESS TEST, a standardized test used to determine the readiness of a child for beginning formal reading instruction. The test produces four scores: *letter symbols, concepts, word symbols,* and *total.*

The test is one of the oldest reading readiness tests available, having first been published in 1931. Its latest revision was prepared in 1962. It is most valuable as a supplement to teacher judgment since the readiness factors that are evaluated are rather limited when considering all the influences affecting reading readiness. The test is used in grades K–1. The California Test Bureau of McGraw-Hill publishes the Lee-Clark Reading Readiness Test.

References: Clifford L. Bush and Mildred H. Huebner, *Strategies of Reading in the Elementary Schools* (Second Edition), New York: Macmillan Publishing Company, Inc., 1979; George D. Spache and Evelyn B. Spache, *Reading in the Elementary School*, Boston: Allyn and Bacon Inc., 1973.

LEFT-TO-RIGHT ORIENTATION, a reading objective considered to be learned once a reader demonstrates automatic left-to-right motion of the eyes when reading a printed passage. Such eye movement is not natural; it must be learned. Reading readiness programs consist of various exercises designed to teach left-to-right sequence. They include: (1) games that teach the difference between left and right; (2) observing the teacher as he/she writes from left to right; (3) arranging/viewing pictures from left to right; and (4) mechanical aids that have left-to-right exposure controls.

References: Mary A. Hall, et al., *Reading and the Elementary School* (Second Edition), New York: D. Van Nostrand Company, Inc., 1979; Robert M. Wilson, *Diagnostic and Remedial Reading for Classrooms and Clinic* (Second Edition), Columbus, OH: Charles E. Merrill Publishing Company, 1972.

LEGASTHENIA, a reading disability. Afflicted individuals cannot encode and/or decode a word or letter and are unable to recognize that words are written forms of verbal communication. The cause of legasthenia is unknown. (See APHASIA.)

References: William E. Davis, *Educator's Resource Guide to Special Education,* Boston: Allyn and Bacon, Inc., 1980; Constance M. McCullough (Editor), *Inchworm, Inchworm: Persistent Problems in Reading Education,* Newark, DE: International Reading Association, 1980; Harold A. Solan (Editor), *The Psychology of Learning and Reading Difficulties,* New York: Simon and Schuster, 1973.

LEMON v. KURTZMAN, an educationally significant legal case in which the U.S. Supreme Court (1971) ruled unconstitutional a 1968 Pennsylvania statute that permitted direct financial support (state aid) to parochial schools. The statute authorized reimbursement to be paid directly for certain educational services provided by these schools. Eligible for reimbursement were teachers' salaries, textbooks, and instructional materials that were used specifically for secular purposes. Approximately 1,100 nonpublic (principally Roman Catholic) schools were receiving as much as $5,000,000 annually for such reimbursements.

The Pennsylvania statute, along with a similar Rhode Island statute, The Rhode Island Salary Supplement Act, was not supported on the grounds that the granting of direct aid to parochial schools constitutes entanglement of governmental affairs and religious affairs, a violation of the First Amendment's Establishment Clause.

When does aid to nonpublic schools not violate the Establishment Clause? In rendering its decision on *Lemon v. Kurtzman,* the Supreme Court offered three guidelines: (1) the statute must be secular in purpose; (2) its primary effect should be to neither advance nor inhibit religion; and (3) the statute should not foster excessive entanglement of governmental and religious affairs. (See ESTABLISHMENT CLAUSE.)

References: *Committee for Public Education and Religious Liberty v. Nyquist,* 413 U.S. 756, 93 S.Ct. 2955 (1973); Frank R. Kemerer and Kenneth L. Deutsch, *Constitutional Rights and Student Life: Value Conflict in Law and Education,* St. Paul, MN: West Publishing Company, 1979; *Lemon v. Kurtzman,* Supreme Court of the United States, 1971, 403 U.S. 602, 612; *Sloan v. Lemon,* 413 U.S. 812, 93 S.Ct. 2982 (1973).

LESSON PLANS, written statements indicating content to be covered and methods to be employed in the teaching of a lesson or a unit. Normally completed by the individual who will be doing the teaching, lesson plans are prepared for at least three principal reasons: (1) to maximize the likelihood of effective learning taking place; (2) to expedite teaching; and (3) to provide directions for possible substitute teachers. They typically are written after the teacher has: (1) decided what goals he/she intends to realize; (2) ascertained where the students are in terms of readiness and ability; and (3) determined the teaching approaches to be employed and a strategy for assessing their effectiveness.

Lesson plans, ideally, provide for a motivational activity designed to stimulate student interest. The teaching approaches (methods) may include any number of activities in addition to the lecture: demonstrations, use of audio-visual devices, guest speakers, field trips, reading activities, written work, and so on. Homework assignments, if any, are planned as extensions of classroom activities and are normally incorporated into the lesson plan.

References: James M. Cooper (Editor), *Classroom Teaching Skills: A Handbook,* Lexington, MA: D. C. Heath and Company, 1977; Ellen H. Furman, *The New Teacher's Complete Reference Guide or the First Years Are the Hardest,* Minneapolis, MN: T. S. Denison and Company, Inc., 1973; Richard M. Henak, *Lesson Planning for Meaningful Variety in Teaching,* Washington, DC: National Education Association, 1980; Abraham Shumsky, *In Search of Teaching Style,* New York: Appleton-Century-Crofts, Inc., 1968.

LEWIN, KURT (September 9, 1890–February 12, 1947), German-born psychologist who won fame for his contributions to group dynamics research and for originating field theory. Lewin received his doctorate at the University of Berlin and taught there from 1921 to 1933. The rise of Nazism caused him to move to the United States where, over the years, he was associated with several universities.

While at the State University of Iowa (1935–44), he participated in research that focused on democratic, autocratic, and laissez-faire leadership styles. In 1945, he moved to the Massachusetts Institute of Technology where he organized the Research Center for Group Dynamics.

Lewin worked to apply experimental methodology to the study of social phenomena. His works focused on how people worked in groups, what motivated them, and what inhibited them in group situations. His complex models of the factors and forces affecting behavior did much to influence modern social psychology. (See AUTOCRATIC LEADERSHIP and DEMOCRATIC LEADERSHIP.)

References: Richard C. Clark, "Lewin" in *The McGraw-Hill Encyclopedia of World Biography*, New York: McGraw-Hill Book Company, 1973; Alfred J. Marrow, *The Practical Theorist: The Life and Work of Kurt Lewin*, New York: Teachers College Press, 1977.

LIBEL, a legal term relating to written and published statements that expose living persons to ridicule, hatred, or contempt. "Publication" is any communication directed to a person or persons other than the individual libelled. The law has treated libel more seriously than slander because of the permanency inherent in written communications. Teachers, other school officials, and school board members enjoy "qualified privilege" (immunity from suit) when it can be demonstrated that information they have written about someone was done so in line of duty and not intended to defame that individual. (See SLANDER and TORT LIABILITY.)

References: Leroy J. Peterson, et al., *The Law and Public School Operation* (Second Edition), New York: Harper and Row, Publishers, 1978; Max Radin, *Law Dictionary* (Second Edition), Dobbs Ferry, NY: Oceana Publications, Inc., 1970; Rennard Strickland, et al., *Avoiding Teacher Malpractice: A Practical Legal Handbook for the Teaching Professional*, New York: Hawthorn Books, Inc., 1976.

LIBERAL EDUCATION, currently defined as a form of education that is broad and general as opposed to being specialized or preparing one for a vocation/profession. Since the time of Aristotle, the term liberal education has had several meanings. He saw it as an end in itself, a vehicle for *knowing* and one to be pursued by members of the leisure class. During the Middle Ages, it was understood to mean an education consisting of the then seven liberal arts: grammar, rhetoric, logic, arithmetic, geometry, astronomy, and music. With the advent of the social and physical sciences, the content approach to defining liberal education proved to be impractical; *purpose* gave way to *content*. John Dewey, in 1913, concluded that "liberal education becomes a name for the sort of education that every member of the community should have: the education that will liberate his capacities and thereby contribute both to his own happiness and his social usefulness" (p. 6). Liberal education goes beyond general education and cultural literacy in its functions, purposes, and goals. Liberal education focuses on freeing the imagination and intelligence, while general education and cultural literacy, often coming from the liberal arts, have a more focused and restrictive purpose.

In high schools, colleges, and universities, the liberal arts, sometimes referred to as the general education component of the curriculum, include the arts and sciences. At the college level, Mark Van Doren noted, the curriculum is devoted to two kinds of concurrent activities: "learning the arts of investigation, discovery, criticism, and communication, and achieving at first hand an acquaintance with the original books, the unkillable classics, in which these miracles have happened" (pp. 144–45).

Teacher-education programs usually include a liberal (general) education block of courses. At the undergraduate level, this block may comprise one-third to one-half of the total program. (See CULTURAL LITERACY and GENERAL EDUCATION.)

References: Peter F. Carbone, Jr., "Liberal Education and Teacher Preparation," *Journal of Teacher Education*, May-June 1980; John Dewey, "Liberal Education" in Paul Monroe (Editor), *A Cyclopedia of Education* (Volume 4), New York: The Macmillan Company, 1913 (Republished by Gale Research Company, Detroit, 1968); Edward Ducharme, "Liberal Arts in Teacher Education: The Perennial Challenge," *Journal of Teacher Education*, May-June 1980; Sheldon Rothblatt, "General Education on the American Campus: A Historical Introduction in Brief" in Ian Westbury and Alan C. Purves (Editors), *Cultural Literacy and the Idea of General Education*, Chicago: National Society for the Study of Education, 1988; Mark Van Doren, *Liberal Education*, Boston: Beacon Press, 1959; Charles Wegener, *Liberal Education and the Modern University*, Chicago: University of Chicago Press, 1978.

LIBERTY AND LEARNING IN THE SCHOOLS, HIGHER EDUCATION'S CONCERNS (A REPORT BY THE COMMISSION ON ACADEMIC FREEDOM AND PRE-COLLEGE EDUCATION)—See COMMISSION ON ACADEMIC FREEDOM AND PRE-COLLEGE EDUCATION

LIBRARY—See SCHOOL LIBRARY

LIBRARY OF CONGRESS (LC), national research library established in 1800 and located in Washington, D.C. A service arm of Congress, LC was initially charged with procurement of books necessary for the use of Congress. Although its function and activities have been broadened considerably since its establishment, 10 of LC's 52 divisions (Congressional Research Service) continue to provide Congress, its committees, and employees with answers to official inquiries that may number 2,000 a day when Congress is in session. Over the years, LC has either been assigned or assumed a broad spectrum of other activities. They include, but are not limited to, library service for the blind and physically handicapped; maintaining valuable manuscripts, including musical scores; operating the U.S. Copyright Office; preparation of bibliographies; distribution of cataloging information; and operation of an interlibrary loan system. Financial support comes from Congressional appropriations and gifts from foundations.

The Librarian of Congress, the organization's director, is appointed by the President with the advice and consent of the Senate.

References: John Y. Cole (Editor), *The Library of Congress in Perspective,* New York: R. R. Bowker Company, 1978; Office of the Federal Register, National Archives and Records Service, *United States Government Manual, 1978/ 79,* Washington, DC: U.S. Government Printing Office, May 1, 1978; Richard L. Williams, "The Library of Congress Can't Hold All Man's Knowledge—But it Tries," *Smithsonian,* April 1980.

LIBRARY OF CONGRESS CLASSIFICATION, an enumerative system for classifying and shelving of books. First outlined in 1897 by Dr. Herbert Putnam, Library of Congress Librarian, the system has been undergoing revision on a fairly regular basis. The system's principal categories, each of which has its own special subdivisions (classes) and corresponding indexes, follows:

A   General Works; Polygraphy
B   Philosophy; Religion
C   Auxiliary-Sciences of History
D   Universal and Old World History
E-F American History
G   Geography; Anthropology; Folk-lore; Manners and Customs; Sports and Games
H   Social Sciences; Economics; Sociology
J   Political Science
K   Law
L   Education
M   Music
N   Fine Arts
P   Language and Literature
Q   Science
R   Medicine
S   Agriculture
T   Technology
U   Military Science
V   Naval Science
Z   Bibliography and Library Science

Because of its complexity, the system is generally used in large (e.g. university) libraries. A single, comprehensive index does not exist for the entire system. A list of headings, however, published as *Subject Headings,* comes reasonably close to fulfilling this need.

References: Leonard M. Harrod, *The Librarians' Glossary of Terms Used in Librarianship and the Book Crafts,* New York: Seminar Press, 1971; John P. Immroth, "Library of Congress Classification" in Allen Kent, et al. (Editors), *Encyclopedia of Library and Information Science* (Volume 15), New York: Marcel Dekker, Inc., 1975; *Library of Congress Subject Headings* (Eighth Edition), Washington, DC: Library of Congress, 1975.

LIDS—See TAX AND EXPENDITURE LIMITATIONS

LIFE ADJUSTMENT EDUCATION, a broad general curriculum approach that focused on preparing all children and youth to: (1) be good citizens (present, future); (2) be better adjusted to home life; (3) be prepared to work in the society; and (4) be more accepting of themselves. The program was designed for all children. Those who were not in a specific vocational program or college preparatory program, it was assumed, would benefit most from such a program.

Although the program was to cover all grades (K–12), it had a more identifiable curriculum structure in grades 7 through 12. One approach to the life adjustment education program was to utilize community resources and facilities, to use life experiences in the school, and to attempt to transfer school learning to life situations.

The life adjustment education movement began in the middle 1940s and was at its highest point of popularity in the late 1940s and early to middle 1950s.

References: James A. Fitzgerald and Patricia G. Fitzgerald, *Methods and Curricula in Elementary Schools,* Milwaukee, WI: The Bruce Publishing Company, 1955; George J. Mouly, *Psychology for Effective Teaching* (Third Edition), New York: Holt, Rinehart and Winston, Inc., 1973; Franklin R. Zeran (Editor), *Life Adjustment Education in Action,* New York: Chartwell House, 1953.

LIFELONG EDUCATION, sometimes referred to as lifelong learning, a concept that seeks to extend educational opportunity beyond the traditional attendance periods of elementary and secondary school. Several features give lifelong education its uniqueness: (1) education is seen as a lifelong (birth-to-death) activity; (2) all community agencies work as educational partners with the school; (3) the educational program is sufficiently flexible to meet the needs of diverse, yet motivated, learners who possess a range of abilities and interests; and (4) education is provided at the time it is needed.

References: Arthur J. Cropley and Ravindra H. Dave, *Lifelong Education and the Training of Teachers*, New York: UNESCO Institute for Education, Hamburg, and Pergamon Press, 1978; Paul Lengrand, *An Introduction to Lifelong Education*, London, England: Croom Helm, 1975; Donald W. Mocker and George E. Spear, *Lifelong Learning: Formal, Nonformal, Informal, and Self-Directed*, Columbus, OH: The ERIC Clearinghouse on Adult, Career and Vocational Education, 1982; Tom Schuller and Jacquette Megarry (Editors), *Recurrent Education and Lifelong Learning* (World Yearbook of Education, 1979), London, England: Kogan Page Ltd., 1979.

LIGHTHOUSE DISTRICT, a term used in educational finance for school systems that are "pilot" in nature (i.e. they offer exemplary programs). It is usually a district that: (1) expends relatively more than most school systems to support public education; (2) is affluent with respect to financial ability; (3) is often located in suburbia; and (4) has a reputation for offering quality programs. The lighthouse district is frequently a pioneer district, one that "leads the way" and serves as a figurative "beacon of light" for all other districts. (See FINANCIAL ABILITY.)

References: Michael W. Kirst, "Research Directions for the Impact of School Finance Return on High Wealth, High Expenditure Suburban School Districts," Paper prepared for the National Institute of Education, May 1978; Jane Sjogren, "Assessing the Impact of School Finance Reforms Upon Lighthouse School Districts," *Journal of Education Finance*, Summer 1980.

LIKERT SCALE, a five-point scale used to quantify the responses of subjects or students to a set of statements reflecting attitudes, beliefs, or judgments. This scale was developed by Rensis Likert in 1932 and has been used extensively in attitude research ever since.

Individuals are asked to respond to a series of statements that are either favorable or unfavorable, e.g. "Latin should be included in the comprehensive high school," or "Students who take Latin in high school are better prepared for college," or "Women are not as academically talented as men." Each subject (or student) responds to each item using a five-point scale.

The five points on the scale are: *strongly agree, agree, undecided, disagree,* and *strongly disagree* (or some similar and balanced expressions of agreement or disagreement). Intervals between each point on the scale are assumed to be equal; hence, each point on the scale is assigned a number value, usually *strongly agree* = 5, to *strongly disagree* = 1. The assignment of numbers and the direction of agreement are arbitrary. Scores are derived by either the summation of the responses or by averaging them. An example of a modified Likert-type scale is the Minnesota Teacher Attitude Inventory.

References: Anne Anastasi, *Psychological Testing* (Sixth Edition), New York: Macmillan Publishing Company, Inc., 1988; Fred N. Kerlinger, *Behavioral Research: A Conceptual Approach*, New York: Holt, Rinehart and Winston, Inc., 1979; Gilbert Sax, *Principles of Educational and Psychological Measurement and Evaluation* (Third Edition), Belmont, CA: Wadsworth Publishing Company, 1989; Bruce W. Tuckman, *Conducting Educational Research* (Second Edition), New York: Harcourt Brace Jovanovich, Inc., 1978.

LINE AND STAFF CHART, a graphic indicating the coordinative relationships between (1) superiors and subordinates, and (2) administrators and support staff. These relationships are depicted on "line and staff" charts. The higher a job title is placed on the chart, the greater is its status. Solid and dotted lines connect the several positions shown. *Solid lines* indicate authority channels, or the chain of command; *dotted lines* are used to identify staff positions, those that provide supportive services. In recent years, line and staff charts have been criticized for ignoring the functional yet sometimes informal units and relationships that exist in organizations and that regularly cut across line-staff roles.

References: William B. Castetter, *The Personnel Function in Educational Administration* (Third Edition), New York: Macmillan Publishing Company, Inc., 1981; Thomas J. Landers and Judith G. Myers, *Essentials of School Management*, Philadelphia: W. B. Saunders Company, 1977.

LINEAR PROGRAMMING, a format used in many early programmed instruction materials. In linear programmed materials, each frame is followed, in a specific sequence and development, by either: (1) a more difficult frame; (2) an informational frame; (3) a review frame; (4) a reinforcer frame; or (5) a test frame. Every student who uses a specific linear program follows the program, frame by frame, in a specific and predetermined order and sequence.

Students may proceed through a linear program at different speeds, or they may use a different linear program (based on a specific intellectual level), but their behaviors are shaped and controlled in a predetermined and specifically described manner. Classical experimental psychology is the foundation on which linear programming is built. B. F. Skinner was one of the first developers of this approach. (See BRANCHING PROGRAMMING and PROGRAMMED INSTRUCTION.)

References: Donald H. Bullock, *Programmed Instruction: The Instructional Design Library* (Volume 14), Englewood Cliffs, NJ: Educational Technology Publications, 1978; Allen D. Calvin, *Programmed Instruction: Bold New Venture*, Bloomington, IN: Indiana University Press, 1969; Susan M. Markle, *Good Frames and Bad: A Grammar of Frame Writing* (Second Edition), New York: John Wiley and Sons, 1969.

LINGUISTIC INTELLIGENCE, one of the seven biologically based intelligences that comprise the theory of multiple intelligence (MI Theory). Linguistic intelligence has its biological origin in a specific area of the brain (left hemisphere), where sentences are produced. Although humans speak different languages, the production and use of language is universal—all people possess language ability; hence, they possess linguistic intelligence according to the MI Theory. Linguistic intelligence makes possible an individual's ability to acquire language and to understand linguistic rules and principles. Although linguistic ability may exist in all humans, language has a social/cultural base. It follows a fairly consistent development that includes meanings that are set from outside the individual (although in young children this is not always true), initial comprehension, and expression or production. (See BODILY-KINESTHETIC INTELLIGENCE; INTELLIGENCE; INTERPERSONAL INTELLIGENCE; INTRAPERSONAL INTELLIGENCE; LANGUAGE; LINGUISTICS; LOGICAL-MATHEMATICAL INTELLIGENCE; MULTIPLE INTELLIGENCE THEORY; MUSICAL INTELLIGENCE; and SPATIAL INTELLIGENCE.)

References: Hans Furth, *Piaget and Knowledge*, Englewood Cliffs, NJ: Prentice-Hall, Inc., 1969; Howard Gardner, *Frames of Mind*, New York: Basic Books, 1976; Joseph Walter and Howard Gardner, "The Development and Education of Intelligence" in F. R. Link (Editor), *Essay on the Intellect*, Alexandria, VA: Association for Supervision and Curriculum Development, 1986.

LINGUISTICS, the study of sounds that humans make when speaking to each other. Linguists study these sounds to understand their nature and their function (i.e. regularities, order, patterns). From these studies come generalizations, theories, and conclusions.

The study of linguistics is not new. It dates back to 1818 and the work of Erasmus Rask, a pioneer in this field. The study of linguistics went through many periods, starting with comparative (philology), then to structural, and now transformational-generative grammar stages. Although there is a great deal of controversy over linguistics in the classroom, there are general areas of agreement. For example, there is agreement that children know their language by age six; that language acquisition does not take place by chance; that each dialect is complex; that there is no inferior language or dialect; that oral talk and written language are different; and that languages change overtime. (See PHILOLOGY.)

References: Paul S. Anderson, *Linguistics in the Elementary Classroom*, New York: The Macmillan Company, 1971; Sara W. Lundsteen, *Children Learn to Communicate*, Englewood Cliffs, NJ: Prentice-Hall, Inc., 1976.

LINKING, a change process in which individuals or institutions interested in adopting innovations are brought together (linked) with sources that originated the innovation. A communication network is normally established that makes it possible for individuals or organizations (e.g. school districts) to avail themselves of the various forms of assistance (human, conceptual, technical, etc.) that the resource agencies or agents can provide. Such assistance can come from within an organization or from the outside. One example of a linking agent is the agricultural extension agent. By keeping himself abreast of new developments in agricultural research, usually at universities, he is in a position to advise and assist farmers (those desiring innovation) on the best ways to produce and market their products.

References: Ronald G. Havelock, et al., *Planning for Innovation through the Dissemination and Utilization of Knowledge,* Ann Arbor, MI: Institute for Research, Center for Research on Utilization of Scientific Knowledge, 1969; Nicholas Nash and Jack Culbertson (Editors), *Linking Processes in Educational Improvement*, Columbus, OH: University Council for Educational Administration, 1977.

LIPREADING, also known as speech reading or visual communication, a communication skill used by some deaf and hard of hearing persons. The skill involves reading of a speaker's lips and grasping the ideas being transmitted. This approach, when used in combination with physical clues such as gestures or facial expressions, has come to be called the *total communication* system of communication.

The first lipreading text was written in 1620 by Juan P. Bonet, a Spaniard. Since then, lipreading has been used and researched widely throughout Europe and in the United States. (See TOTAL COMMUNICATION.)

References: R. E. Hartbauer, *Aural Habilitation: A Total Approach,* Springfield, IL: Charles C. Thomas, Publisher, 1975; John J. O'Neill and Herbert J. Oyer, *Visual Communication for the Hard of Hearing: History, Research, Methods,* Englewood Cliffs, NJ: Prentice-Hall, Inc., 1961.

LISP, a computer language that was developed by John McCarthy in the 1960s to be used in artificial intelligence, studies. It is exact and unambiguous, and is considered a process-description language. Because functions precede their arguments, LISP is considered a prefix language.

LISP manipulates abstract symbols (ATOMS) and combinations of symbols (called lists). LISP is the language used in computational linguistics, robotics, pattern recognition, game playing, and other areas that utilize artificial intelligence languages. (See ARTIFICIAL INTELLIGENCE.)

References: Daniel P. Friedman, *The Little LISPer,* Chicago, IL: Science Research Associates, 1974; Ken Tracton, *Programmer's Guide to LISP,* Blue Ridge Summit, PA: TAB Books, Inc., 1980.

LISPING, or parasigmatism, an articulation defect. Lisping can be identified when a child has problems articulating /s/, /z/, /f/, /ʒ/, /tf/, and /dʒ/ sounds. He or she generally has problems with /s/ and /z/ and usually substitutes with the "th" sound. Improper tongue placement or disorder in the articulatory mechanism causes a lisp. There are several different types of lisps: interdental, lateral, lingual, nasal, occluded, protrusion, and substitutional.

There are also various levels of lisping. Many children do not always substitute the "th" sounds when articulating words and, therefore, the misarticulation may not be noticed by the classroom teacher. Teachers and speech clinicians working with parents can help children with this type of articulation problem. (See ARTICULATION, SPEECH.)

References: Stephen E. Blache, *The Acquisition of Distinctive Features,* Baltimore, MD: University Park Press, 1978; Jill G. DeVilliers and Peter A. DeVilliers, *Language Acquisition,* Cambridge, MA: Harvard University Press, 1978; Leija V. McReynolds and Deedia L. Engmann, *Distinctive Feature Analysis of Misarticulation,* Baltimore, MD: University Park Press, 1975.

LISTENING, more than hearing, involves both *hearing* and *using* the message (information) of the acoustical event. Listening is the first language skill to appear in humans. Children learn to listen even before they learn to speak. Oral language is the base for all language-art skills, and even at the college level, listening in class is extremely important.

Many influences and factors affect listening. Type of presentation, length, mind set, relevance, social concerns, motivation, distractors, body language, noise pollution, and psychological and physical problems are all factors that influence listening for many individuals. Noise pollution is now becoming a major factor, particularly in urban societies. Noise levels above 85 decibels can eventually cause a loss of hearing for sounds in the range crucial for understanding of human speech. Hence, language-arts programs in the school should not only concentrate on improving listening skills, but they should also call attention to those factors that influence listening.

Research conducted in the area of listening indicates that the average student devotes more time in a day to listening than to speaking. Language arts, of which listening is a part, stresses the development of good listening skills because of the close relationship that exists between it and reading.

References: Lillian M. Logan, et al., *Creative Communication,* Toronto, Canada: McGraw-Hill Ryerson Limited, 1972; Sara W. Lundsteen, *Children Learn to Communicate,* Englewood Cliffs, NJ: Prentice-Hall, Inc., 1976.

LISTENING, MUSICAL, an instructional element of a school's total music curriculum. Although some consider musical listening to be a passive activity, music educators see it as an active perceptual process that helps the student learn to enjoy music. Its ultimate goal is to have the student want to listen to music and to derive aesthetic satisfaction from it.

In the lower elementary grades, listening instruction calls students' attention to simple musical elements such as tempo and dynamics (loudness and softness); listening for particular orchestral instruments is another. Older children are taught to listen for mood, particular dance forms, recurring themes, and so on. At the high school level, regularly scheduled classes are offered that seek to refine sensitivity and increase enjoyment of music through listening. Different course titles are used, including Music Appreciation, Understanding Music, Music Listening, and Survey of Music.

References: Malcolm E. Bessom, et al., *Teaching Music in Today's Secondary Schools: A Creative Approach to Contemporary Music Education,* New York: Holt, Rinehart and Winston, Inc., 1974; Charles Leonard and Robert W. House, *Foundations and Principles of Music Education* (Second Edition), New York: McGraw-Hill Book Company, 1972; Aleta Runkle and Mary L. Eriksen, *Music for Today: Elementary School Methods* (Third Edition), Boston: Allyn and Bacon, Inc., 1976.

LITERACY—See FUNCTIONAL ILLITERACY

LITERATURE, those books, poems, essays, letters, documents, and other printed materials considered to have social, cultural, or intellectual value and interest. In school programs, literature is read and studied at all levels for its inherent value. Most literary works are not written for the classroom per se, although some may occasionally appear in textbooks. Most literature appears in separate volumes. Examples are children's books (e.g. *Many Moons* by James Thurber; *The Biggest Bear* by Lynd Ward), written for children but not intended for use as language arts textbooks.

The literature of a society reflects that society; thus, in school programs, literature has a major role to play in teaching the student about his/her and other cultures. It frequently provides experiences that are not otherwise available to the reader. Some literature provides a look back into history, while some is essentially projective in nature. Finally, literature exists in all disciplines and areas of the society; thus, it can not be considered to be the sole domain of English/language arts programs.

References: Nora L. Goddard, *Literacy: Language-Experience Approaches,* London, England: The Macmillan Book Company, 1974; Mary J. Lickteig, *An Introduction to Children's Literature,* Columbus, OH: Charles E. Merrill Publishing Company, 1975; Glenna Sloan, *The Child as Critic: Teaching Literature in the Elementary School,* New York: Teachers College Press, 1975; Sylvia Spann and Mary B. Culp (Editors), *Thematic Units in Teaching English and the Humanities: First Supplement,* Urbana, IL: National Council of Teachers of English, 1977.

LOCAL BOARD OF EDUCATION—See BOARD OF EDUCATION, LOCAL

LOCAL EDUCATIONAL AGENCY (LEA), a legal term included in several pieces of educational legislation passed by Congress. It refers to the administrative unit responsible for carrying out a public education program at the local level. The specific definition included in Title VI of the Elementary and Secondary Education Act reads as follows: "The term 'local educational agency' means a public board of education or other public authority legally constituted within a State for either administrative control or direction of, or to perform a service function for, public elementary or secondary schools in a city, county, township, school district, or other political subdivision of a State, or such combination of school districts or counties as are recognized in a State as an administrative agency for its public elementary or secondary schools. Such term also includes any other public institution or agency having administrative control and direction of a public elementary or secondary school" (Title VI, p. 56).

Reference: Public Law 89-10, *United States Statutes at Large, 1965* (Volume 79), Washington, DC: U.S. Government Printing Office, 1966.

LOCALS—See GOULDNER MODEL

LOCAL SCHOOL ADMINISTRATIVE UNIT—See SCHOOL DISTRICT ORGANIZATION

LOCATIONAL SKILLS, or locating skills, a reading term that encompasses numerous specific skills a reader must master for the purpose of seeking information in printed sources. They include the ability to: (1) find words appearing in an alphabetized list; (2) find a specific page using a table of contents; (3) know how to determine the meaning or pronunciation of a word with the help of a glossary; (4) make use of reference books such as dictionaries and encyclopedias; and (5) locate materials in a library.

One author (Edward Dolch) proposed that successful teaching of locational skills should lead to the development of certain habits: (1) covering the field; (2) evaluating sources; (3) employing rapid reading methods; (4) using reference aids; and (5) organizing information collected to make a good report.

References: Martha Dallman, *Teaching the Language Arts in the Elementary School* (Third Edition), Dubuque, IA: Wm. C. Brown Company, Publishers, 1976; Edward M. Dolch, *Psychology and Teaching of Reading,* Westport, CT: Greenwood Press, 1970 (Reprint of a book originally published by Garrard Press, 1951); Lucille B. Strain, *Accountability in Reading Instruction,* Columbus, OH: Charles E. Merrill Publishing Company, 1976.

LOCKE, JOHN (August 29, 1632–October 28, 1704), an English philosopher who, in his earlier years, was a supporter of the monarchy at the time of Charles II of England. In later years, John Locke became politically liberal. Although primarily a philosopher, he had collateral interests in economics, medicine, diplomacy, religion, and education.

In 1693, he wrote *Thoughts Concerning Education*. For his day, his views on education were quite progressive. For example, he felt that the poor and girls should be educated. He included health, good character, economics, and the arts in education. Locke also believed that reward and punishment in education were not appropriate; that learning rules per se had little value; and that education should serve the nation through the action of happy, prepared, and useful individuals. Other of his writings included *Essay Concerning Human Understanding* (1687), *Two Treatises of Government* (1690), and *A Letter Concerning Toleration* (1690).

References: John Locke, *The Correspondence of John Locke*, Oxford, England: Clarendon Press, 1976; John L. Mackie, *Problems from Locke*, Oxford, England: Clarendon Press, 1976; Peter Schouls, *The Imposition of Method: A Study of Descartes and Locke*, Oxford, England: Clarendon Press, 1980.

LOGIC, a broad field of study that is utilized by many disciplines including philosophy, mathematics, language, communications, reasoning, and physical science; the scientific study of inference.

Terms such as *propositions, arguments, conclusions, premises, inductive, valid, fallacy, syllogism, hypothesis,* and *symbolic* are used in the teaching of logic.

The two major approaches to a logical argument, deductive and inductive, are different in the way one determines the validity of a conclusion. In the *deductive* approach, the premises provide evidence that the conclusion is valid. In the *inductive*, premises are used to establish the probability of the validity of the conclusion. Another approach, *symbolic logic*, appeared in many "modern mathematics" texts in the late 1950s. It is used to teach the basic understandings of mathematics.

Logic can be taught in schools at almost any level providing it is appropriate to the level of the children.

References: Patrick Bastable, *Logic: Depth Grammar of Rationality*, Dublin, Ireland: Gill and Macmillan, 1975; Raymond Bradley and Norman Swartz, *Possible Worlds: An Introduction to Logic and Its Philosophy*, Indianapolis, IN: Hackett Publishing Company, 1979; Jonas Langer, *The Origins of Logic: Six to Twelve Months*, New York: Academic Press, 1980.

LOGICAL-MATHEMATICAL INTELLIGENCE, one of the seven biologically based intelligences found in the Multiple Intelligence Theory (MI Theory). All humans possess this intelligence, although the verbal nature of the intellect is influenced heavily by culture.

Often an individual may arrive at a solution to a problem before being able to verbalize the solution or proof. Piaget called this logical-mathematical experience: experience that is acquired through one's own inner actions, rather than through physical experiences. An example is the learning of the concept of mathematical sets through the observation of a group of similar objects, such as a group of round objects made of glass. Because certain areas of the brain are primarily involved in mathematical calculations, support for the biological base of this intelligence can be put forward; mathematically gifted children and idiot savants provide additional support for this intellect. Logical-mathematical intelligence rarely operates without other intellectual supports, such as linguistic intelligence. (See BODILY-KINESTHETIC INTELLIGENCE; INTELLIGENCE; INTERPERSONAL INTELLIGENCE; INTRAPERSONAL INTELLIGENCE; LINGUISTIC INTELLIGENCE; MULTIPLE INTELLIGENCE THEORY; MUSICAL INTELLIGENCE, and SPATIAL INTELLIGENCE.)

References: Howard Gardner, *Frames of Mind*, New York: Basic Books, 1976; Herbert Ginsberg, and Sylvia Opper, *Piaget's Theory of Intellectual Development, An Introduction*, Englewood Cliffs, NJ: Prentice-Hall, Inc., 1969; Michael P. Grady and Emily A. Luecker, *Education and the Brain*, Bloomington, IN: Phi Delta Kappa, 1978; Joseph Walter and Howard Gardner, "The Development and Education of Intelligences" in F. R. Lind (Editor), *Essays on the Intellect*, Alexandria: VA: Association for Supervision and Curriculum Development, 1986.

LOGICAL POSITIVISM, a school or movement of philosophy that developed from the logical contributions of Auguste Comte, John Stuart Mill, and Wilhelm Ostwald. The base for logical positivism is the belief that knowledge should be restricted to the "positive" facts of experience. These three philosophers stressed methods and science. They were interested in the prediction of data, and used hypotheses and theories as their tools.

In the 1920s and 1930s, the logical positivists felt that language was misused, and that much of the language used had no meaning to people. They argued that many academic logical arguments had no meaning because they could neither be verified nor falsified.

References: Barry Gross, *Analytic Philosophy: An Historical Introduction,* New York: Pegasus Press, 1970; Christopher Peacocke, *Holistic Explanation: Action, Space, Interpretation,* Oxford University Press, 1979; Richard Von Mises, et al., *Positivism: A Study in Human Understanding,* Cambridge, MA: Harvard University Press, 1951.

LOGO, a computer language developed for use with children to encourage learning. The language is "user friendly": It is easily learned. Logo's success with children has resulted in the misconception that it is not suitable for use as a serious language. Although easy to use, Logo has serious applications similar to those of other computer languages. Logo was developed at MIT and grew out of research on artificial intelligence. It was developed to facilitate thinking and problem solving.

Turtle graphics is a graphics package provided with Logo. It was designed to teach logic and reasoning. Central to the package is the turtle—an imaginary creature that can be moved across the screen. The turtle can be moved backward and forward a given number of steps, and also to the right and left a specified number of degrees. Given a few procedures, an individual can create any shape. Children's interest is maintained in this interactive exchange with the graphics. Children can learn to program in Logo as soon as they can read. (See ARTIFICIAL INTELLIGENCE and LISP.)

References: Alfred Glossbrenner, *How to Buy Software,* New York: St. Martin's Press, 1984; Seymour Papert, *Mindstorms: Children, Computers, and Powerful Ideas,* Brighton, MA: Harvester Press, 1980; Charles F. Taylor, *The Master Handbook of High-Level Microcomputer Language,* Blue Ridge Summit, PA: Tab Books Inc., 1984.

LONGITUDINAL STUDIES, those research studies that measure and record progress made by one group of individuals over an extended period. Successive numbers of measurements are taken on the subjects under study. The Eight-Year Study (1930 to 1938), a famous longitudinal study carried out under the direction of Wilford Aikin, was nationwide and included 1,475 students from 30 selected high schools that used the progressive education approach. Another 1,475 students not involved in such programs were matched with them. Students were assessed in terms of academic achievement, artisticability, and cocurricular activity.

Lewis M. Terman and associates, in another well-known longitudinal study, examined 1,000 gifted children from 1922 until Terman's death in 1956. Melita Oden completed the 1960 follow-up, and the final study of these children was completed in 1962 by Robert Sears and Lee Cronbach. Occupation, family income, marital status, health, general adjustment, and feelings of accomplishment were among the variables investigated.

Project TALENT, a third such study, is a nationwide 20-year study that started in 1960 with the assessment of 440,000 students in grades 9–12 from over 1,300 high schools (5 percent of the high schools in the United States). Their talents, aptitudes, abilities, and interests were measured. Follow-up studies of these students are being conducted at regular intervals (1, 5, 10, and 20 years following high school graduation). (See EIGHT-YEAR STUDY; GENETIC STUDIES OF GENIUS; PROJECT TALENT; and TERMAN, LEWIS.)

References: John C. Flanagan, et al., *Design for a Study of American Youth,* Boston: Houghton Mifflin Company, 1962; A. Harry Passow (Editor), *The Gifted and the Talented: Their Education Development* (NSSE 78th Yearbook, Part I), Chicago: University of Chicago Press, 1979.

LORGE-THORNDIKE INTELLIGENCE TESTS, a group intelligence test series available for grades K–1, 2–3, 4–6, 7–9, and 9–13 and for adults. Separate verbal and nonverbal tests are available for grades 4 and above. Figure analogies, figure classifications, and number series are included as tasks in the nonverbal tests. No language is required for the nonverbal tests; however, the directions are given orally. The tests are published by Houghton Mifflin Company and were constructed by Irving Lorge, Robert L. Thorndike, and Elizabeth Hagen. The verbal test takes 35 minutes to complete, and the nonverbal requires 27 minutes to administer.

References: The Lorge-Thorndike Intelligence Tests, Boston: Houghton Mifflin Company, 1964; Robert L. Thorndike and Elizabeth Hagen, *Measurement and Evaluation in Psychology and Education* (Fourth Edition), New York: John Wiley and Sons, 1977.

LOYALTY OATHS, statements sometimes required of applicants seeking teacher certification and/or public school employment. Usually, such oaths seek assurance of the applicant's allegiance to country and to state. The courts have generally supported the right of school districts and universities to require such affirmations but have imposed numerous constraints designed to deter use of negative oaths (assurances that one has not or will not belong to a subversive organization).

References: Knight v. Regents of the University of the State of New York, 269 F. Supp. 339 (S.D.N.Y. 1967); E. Edmund Reutter, Jr. and Robert R. Hamilton, *The Law of Public Education* (Second Edition), Mineola, NY: The Foundation Press, Inc., 1976.

MADISON PROJECT, a supplementary modern mathematics program developed as part of an experimental teaching program at Syracuse University and Webster College. The Madison Project was designed to be used along with the regular mathematics program.

The program stresses intuitive algebraic and geometric concepts. Discovery and explanation by students are encouraged. It is designed to be an enrichment supplement with some materials used as low as grade 2 and others in senior high school. Abstract axiomatic algebra, coordinate geometry, and the study of functions are its principal mathematical contents.

Robert B. Davis started the first experimental work at Madison Junior High School in Syracuse, N.Y.; hence the name, Madison Project. A second experimental center was later established at Webster College, Missouri.

References: Robert B. Davis, *Discovery in Mathematics,* Menlow Park, CA: Addison-Wesley Publishing Company, 1964; Robert B. Davis, *Discovery in Mathematics: A Test for Teachers,* Menlo Park, CA: Addison-Wesley Publishing Company, 1964; C. W. Schminke, et al., *Teaching the Child Mathematics,* Hinsdale, IL: The Dryden Press, 1973.

MAGIC SQUARES, numbers in a square arranged in such a way that the sum of each row, column, and diagonal is the same. Magic squares have been traced back 3,000 years and are said to have been used first in China. They are used by teachers to help children understand number patterns and relationships. Completed magic squares (Example A) and those to be completed by children (Example B)

each have instructional value. (Example A appears in Albrecht Dürer's painting, Melancolia, completed in 1514. In Example B, the answer must equal 1³/₈.)

References: Jeanne Bendick and Marcia Levin, *Mathematics Illustrated Dictionary: Facts, Figures and People Including the New Math,* New York: McGraw-Hill Book Company, 1965; Joseph Crescimbeni, *Treasury of Classroom Arithmetic Activities,* West Nyack, NY: Parker Publishing Company, Inc., 1969; Alvin M. Westcott, *Creative Teaching of Mathematics in the Elementary School* (Second Edition), Boston: Allyn and Bacon, Inc., 1978.

MAGNET SCHOOL, a public elementary or secondary school whose program possesses sufficient uniqueness to attract students of all races. Magnet schools exist in almost all states; most are found in urban areas where racial integration of schools has been established as a goal by school districts and/or the courts. Part of their popularity can be attributed to the fact that, enrollment being voluntary, such schools are more readily received by white citizens than is "forced busing."

A study of magnet schools, completed for the U.S. Office of Education by Abt Associates, identified the factors that made them appealing to students. Listed in rank order, the five most appealing features identified for magnet *elementary* schools were: (1) program; (2) faculty; (3) voluntary nature of magnet; (4) alternative nature of magnet; and (5) parent involvement. Factors making *secondary* magnet schools attractive, also rank ordered, were reported to be: (1) program; (2) voluntary nature of magnet; (3) alternative nature of magnet; (4) school location; and (5) principal.

Magic Squares

Example A

16	3	2	13
5	10	11	8
9	6	7	12
4	15	14	1

Example B

$\frac{1}{8}$		$\frac{1}{4}$	$\frac{3}{8}$
	$\frac{3}{8}$	$\frac{1}{8}$	
	0	$\frac{7}{8}$	$\frac{1}{2}$
$\frac{7}{8}$			0

Magnet schools are usually identified as offering quality education and programs that stress one or a few curricular specialties. Examples of such specialties are science, vocational education, and honors at the secondary level. Frequently found elementary school specialties include the "open" concept, "fundamental" schools, and a program for the gifted.

Charles McMillan pointed out that the various definitions of magnet schools appearing in law and professional literature each include four criteria: (1) they must offer unique programs; (2) curricula should appeal to students of all races; (3) schools must be racially mixed and unsegregated; and (4) the schools must be open to students of all races on a voluntary basis.

References: Abt Associates, *Study of the Emergency School Aid Act Magnet Program*, A Report to the U.S. Office of Education: Contract No. OE–300–77–393; Nolan Estes and Donald Waldrip (Editors), *Magnet Schools: Legal and Practical Realities*, Piscataway, NJ: New Century Education Corporation, 1978; Charles B. McMillan, "Magnet Education in Boston," *Phi Delta Kappan*, November 1977; Charles B. McMillan, *Magnet Schools: An Approach to Voluntary Desegregation* (PDK Fastback 141), Bloomington, IN: The Phi Delta Kappa Educational Foundation, 1980; Mary Haywood Metz, *Different by Design: The Context and Character of Three Magnet Schools*, New York: Routledge and Kegan Paul Inc., 1986.

MAINFRAMES, large-scale, centrally located, general-purpose computer systems. They are multi-task, with tasks occurring simultaneously, and have a variety of uses. These are used in large corporations, governmental agencies, and other organizations where large volumes of data (batch) must be processed, complex analysis is required, and speed is a factor. Much of the capabilities of the mainframe, such as overlapping operations, large memory with dynamic allocation, and time-sharing, can now be accomplished via minicomputers and by some microcomputers.

The first mainframe electromechanical computer (Mark I) was developed at Harvard University in 1944; it used punched paper tapes and punched cards. The first electronic computer (using vacuum tubes) was developed at the University of Pennsylvania by T. Presper Eckert, John W. Mauchly, and others in 1946 (called ENIAC—Electronic Numerical Integrator and Computer). The first mass-produced mainframe was the Remington Rand Corporation UNIVAC I (Universal Automatic Computer) in 1951. International Business Machines (IBM) built its first mainframe in 1953 (Model 701); as the field developed, these corporations went into the computer field. First-generation computers used vacuum tubes, second-generation computers were composed of transistors, third-generation computers were composed of integrated circuits, and the fourth generation are made up of microminiature circuits. (See MINICOMPUTERS and PERSONAL COMPUTER.)

References: Nikitas A. Alexandridis, *Microprocessor System Design Concepts*, Rockville, MD: Computer Science Press, Inc., 1984; Charles K. Kinzer, et al., *Computer Strategies for Education*, Columbus, OH: Merrill Publishing Co., 1986; Roger S. Walker, *Understanding Computer Science*, Dallas, TX: Texas Instruments, Inc., 1981.

MAINSTREAMING, a grouping practice that involves assigning exceptional students to classes largely made up of nonhandicapped students. Prompted by Public Law 94-142 and reinforced by the Education of the Handicapped Acts enacted by individual state legislatures, mainstreaming calls for education of children in the least restrictive educational environment. The mainstreaming concept calls for flexible programs such that an individual education plan (IEP) is developed for each handicapped child.

Mainstreaming requires schools to: (1) work closely with the mainstreamed child's parents; (2) screen and assess handicapped children accurately and continuously; (3) provide a multidisciplinary team of support personnel (e.g. psychologist) to work with the student, his/her parents, and regular teachers; (4) make appropriate placement; and, as indicated above, (5) provide the individualized instruction needed, including the services of supplementary personnel such as itinerant teachers and consultants. (See EXCEPTIONAL CHILDREN; INDIVIDUAL EDUCTION PLAN; ITINERANT TEACHER; LEAST RESTRICTIVE ENVIRONMENT; and PUBLIC LAW 94-142.)

References: Daniel P. Hallahan and James M. Kauffman, *Exceptional Children: Introduction to Special Education* (Fourth Edition), Englewood Cliffs, NJ: Prentice-Hall, 1988; Maynard C. Reynolds and Jack W. Birch, *Teaching Exceptional Children in All America's Schools*, Reston, VA: The Council for Exceptional Children, 1977; Judy W. Wood, *Mainstreaming: A Practical Approach for Teachers*, Columbus, OH: Merrill Publishing Company, 1989.

MAINTENANCE OF PLANT, a school budget category that includes costs for maintaining, replacing, or repairing property. Such upkeep costs sustain the value of the asset. Representative of the expenditures assigned to the "maintenance of plant" category are replacement of furnaces, painting, and salaries for such maintenance personnel as carpenters, masons, plumbers, and so on. (See SCHOOL BUDGET.)

References: Leon Ovsiew and William B. Castetter, *Budgeting for Better Schools,* Englewood Cliffs, NJ: Prentice-Hall, Inc., 1963; Paul Reason, *Financial Accounting for Local and State School Systems,* Washington, DC: U.S. Government Printing Office, 1957; Charles T. Roberts and Allan R. Lichtenberger (Editors), *Financial Accounting* (State Educational Records and Report Series: Handbook II, Revised), Washington, DC: National Center for Educational Statistics, U.S. Department of Health, Education, and Welfare, 1973.

MAJORS AND MINORS, terms used in most institutions of higher education to describe a student's main subject specialization (major) and a second subject concentration (minor) that normally involves completion of fewer courses. A liberal arts student, for example, may major in English and minor in Geography while an Education undergraduate may major in Elementary Education and minor in Library Science. Each college or university prescribes the number of courses or credit hours required to complete a particular major or minor field of specialization, requirements that normally need to be completed in order to qualify for graduation.

References: Asa S. Knowles (Editor), *The International Encyclopedia of Higher Education* (Volume 1), San Francisco: Jossey-Bass Publishers, 1977; G. Terry Page and J. B. Thomas, *International Dictionary of Education,* London, England: Kogan Page Ltd., 1977.

MAKING THE GRADE—See NATIONAL REFORM REPORTS (1980–86)

MALOCCLUSION, a condition that results when the natural closure and fitting together of the upper and lower teeth is improper. The position of the maxillary and mandibular first permanent molars is the major point of fit.

A classification of malocclusion, consisting of three distinct categories, was first developed in 1907 by Edward H. Angle. Other classifications are used today.

Aside from the health problems caused by malocclusion, significant speech and psychological problems can result as well. Teachers, working cooperatively with dentists, speech clinicians, and school psychologists can help to minimize adjustment problems that students may exhibit as the result of this deformity.

References: Peggy Dalton and W. J. Hardcastle, *Disorders of Fluency and Their Effects on Communication,* London,

England: E. Arnold, Ltd., 1977; John V. Irwin, *Disorders of Articulation,* Indianapolis, IN: The Bobbs-Merrill Company, Inc., 1972; William H. Perkins, *Speech Pathology: An Applied Behavioral Science* (Second Edition), St. Louis, MO: C. V. Mosby Company, 1977; Lee E. Travis (Editor), *Handbook of Speech Pathology and Audiology,* New York: Appleton-Century-Crofts, Inc., 1971.

MALPRACTICE—See *PETER DOE v. SAN FRANCISCO UNIFIED SCHOOL DISTRICT*

MAN: A COURSE OF STUDY (MACOS), controversial program of cultural study developed for middle school children by the Education Development Center, Newton, Massachusetts. The program, consisting principally of booklets and audio-visual materials, was distributed commercially in 1969. It presented man as a unique species: capable of language, able to function in a complex organization, possessing the capacity to modify his environment, and able to explain the world in which he lives. Used by approximately 500 school districts, MACOS was initially supported by a $4,800,000 grant from the National Science Foundation (NSF).

Critics of the program leveled two principal charges against MACOS: (1) it purportedly exposed children to questionable topics such as "adultery, bestiality, cannibalism, infanticide, and senilicide" (Peter Dow, p. 80), and (2) it provided a way for the federal government to become involved in school curriculum matters. One critic, George Weber of the Council for Basic Education, added yet another criticism, contending that MACOS contained an air of indoctrination by implying that "cultural relativism and environmental determinism are the only 'scientific' answers to the place of man in society" (p. 82). Objections such as these prompted Congress to legislate that NSF may no longer promote or market instructional materials for schools.

References: Peter B. Dow, "MACOS: The Study of Human Behavior as One Road to Survival," *Phi Delta Kappan,* October 1975; *Man: A Course of Study,* Newton, MA: Education Development Center, 1969; George Weber, "The Case Against Man: A Course of Study," *Phi Delta Kappan,* October 1975; Jeannette Wilson and Bob L. Taylor, "The Effects of MACOS on Intermediate-Grade Children's Attitudes," *Education,* March–April 1978.

MANAGEMENT BY OBJECTIVES (MBO), a planning technique developed by Peter Drucker. Major goals and objectives, to which all members of the institution are ostensibly committed, constitute the heart of MBO. Once they have been identified and agreed to, they are refined into lower orders of objectives and assigned to various levels of the administrative hierarchy for implementation. Ongoing evaluation of the latter takes place with major goal evaluation occurring once a predetermined time segment (e.g. 12 months) has passed. Provision is made for recycling of activities and/or adjustment of goals on the basis of the formal evaluation.

References: American Association of School Administrators, *Management by Objectives and Results,* Arlington, VA: The Association, 1973; Peter F. Drucker, *The Practice of Management,* New York: Harper and Row, Publishers, 1954; Jong S. Jun, *Management by Objectives in Government: Theory and Practice,* Beverly Hills, CA: Sage Publications, Inc., 1976.

MANAGEMENT GAMES, simulation exercises introduced in the 1950s as a management-training technique. Since then, many undergraduate and graduate courses, especially in the field of business administration (some in educational administration), have come to make use of management games, usually as a culmination activity. Sometimes called gaming, or decision gaming, the technique requires the participant to assume a role and to make real-life decisions, using information previously learned, in the hope of resolving one or more problems posed by the game (e.g. a marketing problem faced by a small corporation). Some games are played by individual participants, others by teams.

Janet Schriesheim and Chester Schriesheim undertook a content analysis of 100 books and articles dealing with game effectiveness and found that claims that business games teach or foster decision-making skills, planning and forecasting skills, and recognition of the interrelationships in business have a large degree of support. Other claims relating to factors such as communication skills and organizing ability did not have much support in the literature. They concluded their report with the observation that the number of empirical studies in these areas is small; more research dealing with management game effectiveness is needed. (See GAME THEORY and SIMULATION.)

References: John G. H. Carlson and Michael J. Misshank, *Introduction to Gaming: Management Decision Simulations,* New York: John Wiley and Sons, 1972; Bill R. Darden and William H. Lucas, *The Decision Making Game: An Integrated Operations Management Simulation,* New York: Appleton-Century-Crofts, Inc., 1969; Janet F. Schriesheim and Chester A. Schriesheim, "The Effectiveness of Business Games in Management Training," *Training and Development Journal,* May 1974.

MANN, HORACE (May 4, 1796–August 2, 1859), Secretary of Massachusetts' first State Board of Education. A lawyer who became Secretary after first serving in the Massachusetts legislature, Mann won fame as an educational pioneer and leader. He espoused free and universal education for girls as well as boys. He founded the country's first state normal schools, supported the teaching of moral character, and encouraged the construction of well-planned school buildings. He also called for other reforms such as improved teacher training, practical curricula, and better supervision of schools.

Mann served as board Secretary for 12 years. He published annual reports in which his sometimes controversial ideas were set forth and that ultimately served to popularize American public education. He resigned the secretaryship to enter Congress and later became President of Antioch College.

Mann authored numerous articles. Books that he wrote were *Lectures on Education* (1845), *A Few Thoughts for a Young Man* (1850), and *Powers and Duties of Woman* (1853).

References: Lawrence A. Cremin (Editor), *The Republic and the School: Horace Mann on the Education of Free Men,* New York: Teachers College, Columbia University, 1957; Frank P. Graves, *Great Educators of Three Centuries: Their Work and Its Influence on Modern Education,* New York: AMS Press, Reprinted 1971.

MANPOWER DEVELOPMENT AND TRAINING ACT (MDTA), federal legislation enacted in 1962 that established occupational training and retraining programs for the country's labor force. One of the War on Poverty programs, MDTA required the federal government "to appraise the manpower requirements and resources of the Nation, and to develop and apply the information and methods needed to deal with the problem of unemployment resulting from automation and technological changes and other types of persistent unemployment" (p. 24).

Responsibility for implementing MDTA was assigned jointly to the Departments of Labor and Health, Education, and Welfare.

In 1963, MDTA was amended with emphasis redirected to stress training for disadvantaged persons and youth.

References: Garth L. Mangum, *MDTA: Foundation of Federal Manpower Policy,* Baltimore, MD: The Johns Hopkins Press, 1968; Public Law 87-415, *United States Statutes at Large, 1962* (Volume 76), Washington, DC: U.S. Government Printing Office, 1963.

MANUALISM, a system of communication for the deaf. Sign language and/or finger spelling are used as substitutes for speech. (See FINGER SPELLING; SIGN LANGUAGE; and TOTAL COMMUNICATION.)

References: R. E. Hartbauer, *Aural Habilitation: A Total Approach,* Springfield, IL: Charles C. Thomas, Publisher, 1975; Leo J. Kelly and Glenn A. Vergason, *Dictionary of Special Education and Rehabilitation,* Denver, CO: Love Publishing Company, 1978; Donald F. Moores, *Educating the Deaf: Psychology, Principles, and Practices,* Boston: Houghton Mifflin Company, 1978.

MANUAL TRAINING, a general term applied to that part of the school curriculum that focuses on the development of handwork skills. The term was used by educators and the public during the late 1800s and up to the 1930s. In elementary schools, manual training included instruction in the use of tools, apparatus, and various homemaking equipment as well as the use of various arts and crafts. At the secondary level, it tended to consist of shopwork (woodwork, mechanical drawing, metalwork) and homemaking (sewing, cooking, utilization of home appliances) courses.

Initial justification for the introduction of manual training in the school curriculum was based on the principle that general education would be enhanced through the use of hands-on experiences. For example, it was held that the study of fractions would be more meaningful if students utilized them when working with building materials. Manual training led to the development of industrial arts and the more occupationally and industrially oriented curriculum, later titled vocational and/or industrial education.

Manual training in schools was started in Europe (about 1858). It wasn't until 1878 that manual training was begun in the United States. In 1880, manual training was introduced into a St. Louis high school. High schools devoted exclusively to the teaching of manual training were started in 1884. (See INDUSTRIAL ARTS EDUCATION and VOCATIONAL EDUCATION.)

References: Charles A. Bennett, *History of Manual and Industrial Training Up to 1870,* Peoria, IL: The Manual Arts Press, 1926; *Industrial Education,* Washington, DC: American Federation of Labor, 1910; Albert T. Paulter, *Teaching Shop and Laboratory Subjects,* Columbus, OH: Charles E. Merrill Publishing Company, 1971.

MANUSCRIPT WRITING, or printing, a simple form of handwriting used in most primary grades. Manuscript lettering is very similar to the type of print used in primary reading books. This makes it possible to teach both writing and reading using the same alphabet. Another reason accounting for its popularity among primary grade teachers is the simplicity with which letters are made. Manuscript letters consist of straight lines and circles; the pencil is lifted from the paper after each stroke has been made. These factors reduce fatigue for the young learner whose muscles have yet to mature.

In most school systems, a dual system of handwriting is used. Manuscript writing is taught in the first grade with transfer to cursive handwriting generally taking place in the second or third grades. (See CURSIVE WRITING.)

References: Martha Dallman, *Teaching the Language Arts in the Elementary School* (Third Edition), Dubuque, IA: Wm. C. Brown Company, Publishers, 1976; Mildred R. Donoghue, *The Child and the English Language Arts* (Third Edition), Dubuque, IA: Wm. C. Brown Company, Publishers, 1979.

MARKING SYSTEMS, formal policies and procedures for evaluating and reporting student progress. An authority on the subject (Norman Gronlund) indicated that such systems serve four functions: (1) *instruction* (providing feedback to students, a vehicle for motivating students, etc.); (2) *information,* primarily to keep parents informed of students' progress; (3) *guidance;* and (4) *administrative* (determining eligibility for promotion, placement, etc.). A national survey of reporting methods used by teachers, completed in 1970 by the NEA Research Division, found that report cards employing *letter grades* were most widely used (72 percent by elementary teachers, 83 percent by secondary teachers). Other relatively common methods were: *parent-teacher conferences* (60 percent, 20 percent); *written descriptions* of a student's performance (24 percent, 10 percent); and *number grades* (e.g. 1, 2, 3) (10 percent, 9 percent).

Report cards commonly report on work habits, attitudes, and student effort as well as academic progress. Criteria for academic grading vary from one school system to the next. Some systems grade a student's progress relative to progress of other students; some determine grades in terms of each student's potential; and, finally, some employ the criterion-referenced approach that measures every student against some predetermined and common standard. Attempts to modify evaluation systems frequently meet with resistance and often result in a substitution of one symbol system for another. (See PARENT-TEACHER CONFERENCES and REPORT CARD.)

References: Norman E. Gronlund, *Improving Marking and Reporting in Classroom Instruction,* New York: Macmillan Publishing Company, Inc., 1974; Woodrow Mousley, "Report Cards Across the Nation," *Phi Delta Kappan,* March 1972; Research Division, NEA, "Marking and Reporting Pupil Progress," *Research Summary 1970 S-1,* Washington, DC: National Education Association, 1970.

MASLOW'S HIERARCHY OF NEEDS, a theory of human motivation conceived by psychologist Abraham H. Maslow. Published in 1954, the theory has been studied widely by both behaviorists and educators. The theory holds that five sets of basic needs motivate an individual; furthermore, that they tend to be related to each other hierarchically. The lower order needs include the *physiological* (e.g. need for food, water, sleep) and the *safety* needs. As these needs are satisfied, the individual is motivated to satisfy higher order needs. The latter include those relating to *belongingness and love;* the *esteem needs* (e.g. need for achievement, adequacy, prestige, status); and the need for *self-actualization,* a term that Maslow explained as man being true to his own nature (or, "What a man *can* be he *must* be"). As needs are satisfied, they cease to function as motivators. Maslow contended that the needs do not operate as single determiners of behavior. Rather, most behavior is multimotivated (i.e. produced by several needs operating simultaneously).

References: Janice T. Gibson and Louis A. Chandler, *Educational Psychology: Mastering Principles and Applications,* Boston: Allyn and Bacon, 1988; Abraham H. Maslow, *Motivation and Personality* (Second Edition), New York: Harper and Row, Publishers, 1970.

MASON, LOWELL (January 8, 1792–August 11, 1872), referred to by some musicologists as the father of American music education. He is remembered as the first teacher of music in Boston; many believe he was the first in the country.

Born in Massachusetts, Mason demonstrated musical ability at an early age and mastered several musical instruments before his 20th birthday. As a young man, he moved to Georgia where, on a part-time basis, he gave several solo performances, vocal and instrumental, and directed musical groups. He also wrote original church music that was published in Boston by the Handel and Haydn Society. The society succeeded in bringing him

back to Boston where, from 1827 to 1831, he held office as that organization's President.

In 1833, Mason helped establish the Boston Academy of Music that, in addition to being an academy for vocal and musical instruction, sought to introduce music in the public schools. In 1838, he taught music gratuitously in the public schools of Boston. Later that year, he became that system's Superintendent of Music. He later taught music to blind students and turned his attention to popularizing music education to the public through lectures and writing.

References: Samuel L. Flueckiger, *Lowell Mason's Contribution to the History of Music Education in the United States,* Unpublished Doctoral Dissertation: Ohio State University, 1936; Lloyd F. Sunderman, *Historical Foundations of Music Education in the United States,* Metuchen, NJ: The Scarecrow Press, Inc., 1971.

MASSACHUSETTS LAWS OF 1642 AND 1647, early school laws passed at the urging of Puritan church leaders. Both pieces of legislation are historically significant, because they constituted the bases upon which the American public school was built. The Massachusetts Law of 1642 required officials of each town to inspect schools and homes to ensure that children were being taught "to read and understand the principles of religion and the capital laws of the country." Fines were to be levied against those failing to comply. The 1642 legislation was the first in America prescribing compulsory education for children.

The Massachusetts Law of 1647, also known as the Old Deluder Satan Act, was the first in America to provide for compulsory elementary and secondary schools. Every town with at least 50 householders was required to appoint and pay the salary of a teacher of reading and writing. Towns with 100 householders or more were required to provide a "grammar" (i.e. secondary or university preparatory) school.

References: Elwood P. Cubberly, *Public Education in the United States: A Study and Interpretation of American Educational History,* Cambridge, MA: Riverside Press, 1962 (Published in 1919 by Houghton Mifflin Company); Adam M. Drayer, *The Teacher in a Democratic Society: An Introduction to the Field of Education,* Columbus, OH: Charles E. Merrill Publishing Company, 1970.

MASSACHUSETTS TEST—See SWEEP-CHECK TEST

MASTER OF ARTS IN TEACHING (MAT), a master's level degree designed to meet the professional training needs of college graduates who, as undergraduates, did not prepare themselves for careers as teachers. Popular during the post-World War II era of teacher shortages, the MAT normally required students to complete at least one academic year of study including required courses in education and, for prospective secondary schoolteachers, a major field concentration (e.g. chemistry, mathematics). An internship or equivalent field experience was an integral part of the program. Fellowships, federal grants, foundation-supported grants, and scholarships were frequently offered to those matriculating in an MAT program.

References: Southern Regional Educational Board, *Master of Arts in Teaching Programs in the South*, Atlanta, GA: Southern Regional Education Board, March 1965; Stephen H. Spurr, *Academic Degree Structures: Innovative Approaches*, New York: McGraw-Hill Book Company, 1970.

MASTER'S DEGREE, a graduate degree that normally requires one year of postbaccalaureate study in either a subject field or education. Three of the most commonly conferred degrees are the Master of Arts (M.A.), the Master of Science (M.S.), and the Master of Education (M.Ed.). Degree requirements vary from one institution to another and from one program to another. For example, some require the writing of a thesis and others do not. The master's degree is especially popular among teachers inasmuch as most faculty salary schedules include increments for completion of this degree.

In 1977–78, an estimated 356,000 master's degrees were conferred in the United States. Of this number, approximately 145,000 were in the field of education.

References: Asa S. Knowles (Editor), *Handbook of College and University Administration*, New York: McGraw-Hill Book Company, 1970; Janet A. Mitchell, *Higher Education Exchange: 78/79*, Princeton, NJ: J. B. Lippincott Company, 1978.

MASTER TEACHER, a formal title and usually the highest designation earned by teachers as a result of their meritorious contributions as excellent teachers in the classroom and their contributions to education. Most often master teachers earn more than regular teachers as a result of a differentiated or merit salary scale that recognizes them. Master teacher plans that have been implemented usually include a career ladder that leads to the designation of master teacher, a difference in salary paid to them on the master teacher salary scale, and a defined system to identify master teachers. Master teacher plans may be restricted to one school district, such as the one that exists in the Charlotte-Mecklenburg, North Carolina, school district, or it may be statewide, such as in the state of Tennessee (although Tennessee did drop the designation "master teacher" from its legislation).

Although the identification and differential rewarding of master teachers is not new, (such as master teachers found in the differentiated staffing plans of the 1950s and 1960s) and the need to attract highly talented individuals to teaching through a reward system that recognizes excellence in the classroom is generally recognized, there is still considerable concern about master teacher plans. The criterion used in the selection of the master teacher is but one of the issues. Other issues include length of designation, periodic reevaluations, and the nature of the career ladder steps leading to the master teacher designation (or salary scale). (See CAREER LADDERS FOR TEACHERS, DIFFERENTIATED STAFFING, MENTOR TEACHER, and MERIT PAY.)

References: Susan M. Johnson, *Pros and Cons of Merit Pay*, Bloomington, IN: Phi Delta Kappa, 1984; David E. Kapel, et al., "Linking Career Ladders with Demonstration Schools: A Proposed Cooperative Model," *Journal of Teacher Education*, Volume 36, Number 3, 1985; David Lipsky and Samuel B. Bacharach, "The Single Salary Schedule vs. Merit Pay: An Examination of the Debate," *NEA Research Memo*, June 1983; Richard W. Moore, *Master Teachers*, Bloomington, IN: Phi Delta Kappa, 1984.

MASTERY LEARNING, learning that occurs when an individual has reached a minimum level of performance that has been established as an objective for a particular skill or concept. Such performance is necessary to establish a level of competence.

The mastery model is based on the assumption that almost all can learn basic skills and knowledges when the curriculum is structured to be appropriate for past learning, the mode of instruction is good, and time is adequate. The main parts of the mastery model are: *objectives* (expressed in behavioral terms); *preassessment; instruction* (adapted to the nature and level of the objectives and the history of the learner); *diagnostic assessment; prescription;* and *postassessment*.

Mastery learning has been the base for programmed instruction; it has its modern origins in the writings of J. Franklin Bobbitt, Ralph Tyler,

Robert Glaser, John Carroll, and, more recently, Benjamin Bloom.

References: James H. Block (Editor), *Mastery Learning: Theory and Practice,* New York: Holt, Rinehart and Winston, Inc., 1971; James H. Block and Lorin W. Anderson, *Mastery Learning in Classroom Instruction,* New York: Macmillan Publishing Company, Inc., 1975; Benjamin S. Bloom, *Human Characteristics and School Learning,* New York: McGraw-Hill Book Company, 1976; *Educational Leadership* (Theme Issue), November 1979; Peter H. Martorella, et al., *Concept Learning: Designs for Instruction,* Scranton, PA: Intext Educational Publishers, 1972; Kay P. Torshen, *The Mastery Approach to Competency-based Education,* New York: Academic Press, 1977.

MATCHING GRANT, also known as a challenge grant or matching-fund grant, monies awarded to an institution by a funding agency for the support of a project. The monies are awarded with the understanding that the recipient institution will "match" the funding agency's contribution using local (often nongovernmental) resources. The amount of "match" is variable, depending on the funding agency's policies and guidelines. Some accept a "match" as low as 1 percent; others require a 50 percent "match." The recipient institution's contributions may be in the form of cash (hard match) or, in lieu of cash, soft match services such as office space, equipment, and/or personnel may be substituted.

The fact that local matching resources are available does not guarantee grant support.

References: Annual Register of Grant Support, 1979–80 (Thirteenth Edition), Chicago: Marquis Who's Who, 1979; Stephen E. Nowlan, et al. (Editors), *User's Guide to Funding Resources,* Radnor, PA: Chilton Book Company, 1975; Virginia P. White, *Grants: How to Find Out About Them and What to Do Next,* New York: Plenum Press, 1975.

MATCHING TEST, a specialized form of the multiple-choice test. Examinees are presented with two columns of listings, one containing *premises* (Column A), the other *responses* (Column B). The examinee is expected to pair (or match) individual premises with individual responses on the basis of some specific association or for the purpose of completing a correct statement.

Several suggestions for construction of matching tests have been made by testing specialists: (1) lists should be homogeneous; (2) response lists should contain single words, numbers, or short phrases; (3) lists should be kept relatively short, each containing 5–12 premises and responses; (4) the number of premises and responses should not be equal; (5) directions should be clear; and (6) grammatical consistency should be maintained.

The matching test's strengths include ease of scoring, objectivity, and the fact that a variety of areas in the lower levels of the cognitive domain can be tested. One principal weakness is that the test measures only recognition; another is that it is difficult to use when measurement at the higher cognitive domain levels is desired.

References: Tom Kubiszyn and Gary Borich, *Educational Testing and Measurement: Classroom Application and Practice* (Second Edition), Glenview, IL: Scott Foresman and Company, 1987; Jon C. Marshall and Loyde W. Hales, *Classroom Test Construction,* Reading, MA: Addison-Wesley Publishing Company, 1971.

MATERIALS PRESERVATION, various procedures used to keep instructional materials in usable condition over a long period. *Lamination* of materials is one procedure (placing paper material between two plastic sheets and permanently bonding the two together, using a laminating machine). *Dry-mount* (using a dry-mount press) is another, one in which paper material is affixed to dry-mount paper and pressed for five seconds at about 225°F. *Slides* or *photographs* are still another way to preserve paper as well as three dimensional materials without saving the original. By preserving materials, teachers can develop a collection of various successful teaching aids for classroom instruction.

References: John R. Bullard and Calvin E. Mether, *Audiovisual Fundamentals: Basic Equipment and Simple Materials Production* (Second Edition), Dubuque, IA: Wm. C. Brown Company, Publishers, 1979; Kendrick Coy, *Multi-Sensory Educational Aids from Scrap,* Springfield, IL: Charles C. Thomas, Publisher, 1979; Kit Laybourne and Pauline Cianciolo (Editors), *Doing the Media,* New York: McGraw-Hill Book Company, 1978.

MATERNITY LEAVE, an absence from employment granted to pregnant employees. Before 1974, it was common for boards of education to mandate that pregnant teachers begin their maternity leaves "x" months before, and not return to work for "y" months following, childbirth. Such mandatory leaves were ruled unconstitutional by the U.S. Supreme Court in that year. Before 1974, mandatory maternity leaves were based on the then prevailing view that they assured continuity of instruction by making the employment of relatively long-term substitute teachers possible. (See *CLEVELAND BOARD OF EDUCATION v. LAFLEUR.*)

References: Broward County Board of Education, *Policy Handbook,* Ft. Lauderdale, FL: The Board, 1977; William

B. Castetter, *The Personnel Function in Educational Administration* (Second Edition), New York: Macmillan Publishing Company, Inc., 1976.

MATHEMATICAL MODEL, a systematic, logico-mathematical means of quantitative and qualitative analysis of factors in an educational system. Such models provide maximum approximations of the interactions of the factors being studied. They may also be used for the optimal planning of educational systems. A mathematical model is an algebraic, geometric, or statistical description, or representation, of a system and/or subsystems, an event, or a theory. All elements in the factors under study are converted to numerical values and inserted into the mathematical model for use with a computer.

Such models help to explain the present dynamics of a system or subsystem, future trends, and consequences of decisions made at a particular time under particular conditions. Manpower predictions, theory building, financial needs (present and future), and the development of training plans can be products of such analyses. The results are only approximations of "what might be" and are the products of calculations from the interrelations of factors as determined by the constraints of the logical and mathematical design of the model itself.

Models in education can be divided into at least two major subclassifications. *Micromodels* include the elements of psychology, physiology, didactics, attitudes, goals, and teacher-student interactions. *Macromodels* include factors such as number of teachers, number of students, cubic footage, tax ratables, and financial resources.

References: Paul A. Ballonoff (Editor), *Mathematical Models of Social and Cognitive Structures*, Urbana, IL: University of Illinois Press, 1974; M. A. Bermant, et al., *Mathematical Models and Educational Planning*, Washington, DC: Joint Publications Research Service, Department of Commerce, 1973; John G. Kemeny and H. Laurie Snell, *Mathematical Models in the Social Sciences*, Boston: Ginn and Company, 1962.

MATTHEW EFFECT, an educational sequence in which early achievement results in an increased rate of subsequent learning in addition to a more efficient utilization of new educational experiences. The phenomena was named after the gospel according to Matthew: "For unto every one that hath shall be given, and he shall have abundance: but from him that hath not shall be taken away even that which he hath" (25–29). This effect is apparent when reviewing findings that indicate that early positive learning experiences result in a more ef-

ficient use of new learning. The Matthew effect may arise for a variety of reasons: early and frequent reward; greater exposure to a broader environment; and self-selection of peers. Often termed the "rich get richer" syndrome, the Matthew effect is a major source of achievement variance in various areas of schooling.

References: R. Merton, "The Matthew Effect in Science," *Science*, Volume 159, January, 1968; K. E. Stanovich, "Matthew Effect in Reading: Some Consequences of Individual Difference in the Acquisition of Literacy," *Reading Research Quarterly*, Vol. 21, Number 4, 1986; H. J. Walberg and S. Tsai, "Matthew Effect in Education," *Educational Research Quarterly*, Volume 20, Number 3, 1983.

MATURITY, SOCIAL, the level of social skills/activities attained by an individual. Social maturity is measured relative to the norms of a particular age group. For example, at age four a child should be able to perform certain self-help activities such as washing one's hands and playing competition games; at age ten, he/she should be able to perform more complex activities and have highly developed social interactions with his/her peers. There is usually a relationship between chronological age and social maturity, but it is not uncommon for a child to be functioning at a lower level of social maturity than would be expected for his/her age.

Social maturity is very important in classrooms, for children or youth who are socially immature are likely to have social adjustment problems and, often, learning difficulties as well. Factors contributing to social maturity include diverse variables such as the family, social and educational experiences, physical development, neighborhood environment, and peer pressures.

References: David P. Barash, *Sociobiology and Behavior*, New York: Elsevier North-Holland, Inc., 1977; Wilbur Doise, *Groups and Individuals: Explanations in Social Psychology*, Cambridge, England: Cambridge University Press, 1978; Bernard Seidenberg, et al., *Social Psychology: An Introduction*, New York: The Free Press, 1976.

McCOLLUM CASE, a lawsuit that challenged the right of public schools to release students from classes so that they might receive religious instruction from sectarian teachers in the students' regular school building. This case involved the public schools of Champaign, Illinois. In 1948, the United States Supreme Court ordered discontinuance of this practice on the grounds that it involved "too great" a cooperation between religion and government and thus violated the Establishment of

Religion Clause of the First Amendment of the United States Constitution. (See ESTABLISHMENT CLAUSE.)

References: People of State of Illinois ex. rel. McCollum v. Board of Education, 333 U.S. 203, 68 S.Ct. 461, 92 L.Ed. 649 (1948), (Case No. 2); E. Edmund Reutter, Jr. and Robert R. Hamilton, *The Law of Public Education* (Second Edition), Mineola, NY: The Foundation Press, Inc., 1976.

McGUFFEY READERS, a reading series used extensively in the United States during the middle half of the 19th century (1840–80). The Rev. Dr. William Holmes McGuffey, whose name the series carries, issued his First and Second Readers in 1836. They were later enlarged to a series of seven books titled *The McGuffey Eclectic Readers* (Primer, First-Sixth Eclectic Reader). The series made use of the "phonic," "word," and "alphabet" methods. Black and white illustrations accompanied selections that were frequently concerned with morals, science, history, art, philosophy, economics, and politics. Virtue and good work were themes regularly stressed in the readers.

Over 125,000,000 copies of the readers were sold; yet Rev. McGuffey received only $1,000 in royalties inasmuch as he had sold his rights outright to the first publisher of the texts. (See McGUFFEY, WILLIAM H.)

References: William H. McGuffey, *The McGuffey Eclectic Readers* (Revised Edition), New York: American Book Company, Undated; Adolphe E. Meyer, *An Educational History of the American People* (Second Edition), New York: McGraw-Hill Book Company, 1967; Nila Banton Smith, *American Reading Instruction,* Newark, DE: International Reading Association, 1974.

McGUFFEY, WILLIAM H. (September 23, 1800–May 4, 1873), educator and compiler of the best-known textbooks ever written in America, the McGuffey Readers. McGuffey taught in the schools of Ohio and Kentucky and later served as instructor of ancient languages and philosophy at Miami University, Ohio, before accepting the presidency of Cincinnati College. In 1839, he became President of Ohio University, Athens, Ohio. McGuffey served for four years as Pastor of a Presbyterian church before entering university administration.

It was at Miami University that McGuffey began to compile his readers. The first was published in 1836. Others, totalling seven in the series, appeared between 1836 and 1857 and were valued by generations of Americans for their frank patriotism and literary selections. (See McGUFFEY READERS.)

References: Benjamin F. Crawford, *William Holmes McGuffey: The Schoolmaster to our Nation,* Delaware, OH: Carnegie Church Press, 1963; Robert H. Hoexter, "McGuffey, William Holmes" in John F. Ohles (Editor), *Biographical Dictionary of American Educators* (Volume 2), Westport, CT: Greenwood Press, 1978; John A. Nietz, *Old Textbooks,* Pittsburgh, PA: University of Pittsburgh Press, 1961; John H. Westerhoff III, *McGuffey and his Readers: Piety, Morality, and Education in Nineteenth-Century America,* Nashville, TN: Abingdon, 1978.

MEAD, MARGARET (December 16, 1901–November 15, 1978), internationally acclaimed anthropologist. A writer and social critic, she was the most influential anthropologist in her time. Dr. Mead studied psychology at Barnard College and then went on to earn her doctorate in anthropology at Columbia University. One of her earliest works, *Coming of Age in Samoa* (1928), was written while she was still in her twenties and subsequently became a classic in its field. In it she reported how young people in Samoa coped with adolescence.

Dr. Mead became a prolific writer, interspersing her writings with numbers of field trips to Oceania and other parts of the world. A bibliography of her extensive publications alone covers approximately 100 pages. The entries reflect the diversity of her professional interests, ranging from Samoa to women's liberation.

Dr. Mead was curator of ethnology at the American Museum of Natural History. She worked there in varying capacities for over two decades. One of her major interests was the interrelationship between personality and culture, with particular emphasis on young people and the childrearing process.

References: Joan Gordan (Editor), *Margaret Mead: The Complete Bibliography, 1925–1975,* The Hague, Netherlands: Mouton, 1976; Margaret Mead, *Coming of Age in Samoa,* New York: Modern Library, 1953; Margaret Mead, *Letters from the Field: 1925–1975,* New York: Harper and Row, Publishers, 1977.

MEAN, or arithmetic mean ($\overline{X}$), synonym for mathematical average. The mean is calculated by adding all numbers (or scores) in a set and dividing the sum by the number of numbers (or scores). It is one of three commonly used measures used to determine central tendency (the others being *median* and *mode*).

Statisticians point to the mean as the most reliable measure of central tendency. This measure is not without weakness, however, since it can be influenced by skewness. Stated differently, relatively large or small scores will increase or decrease the mean. Given this weakness, the median is recommended whenever skewness is likely to affect central tendency. (See CENTRAL TENDENCY MEASURES; MEDIAN; and MODE.)

References: George K. Cunningham, *Educational and Psychological Measurement*, New York: Macmillan Publishing Company, 1986; L. R. Gay, *Educational Research: Competencies for Analysis and Application* (Third Edition), Columbus, OH: Merrill Publishing Company, 1987.

MECHANICAL DRAWING—See DRAFTING

MEDIA, or instructional media, commonly understood to mean instructional machines. Some authorities are inclined to define the term more broadly, describing it as any type of communication employed to transmit knowledge.

Phillip Sleeman and his colleagues divided media into four categories: (1) *printed media* such as books, magazines, brochures; (2) *graphic media,* a grouping that includes items such as charts, maps, bulletin board displays, and overhead transparencies; (3) *photographic media* (e.g. photographs, slides, and motion pictures); and (4) *electronic media.* This last category includes both audio and video recordings.

Media fulfill any of several functions, these usually dictated by the instructor's goals and strategies. Several of these functions have been identified by Robert Kozma, Lawrence Belle, and George Williams. Some media, they indicated, are designed to stimulate recall, others simply to gain attention. Still others may offer guidance, present stimuli, appraise performance, inform, or provide feedback.

Erhard Heidt observed that research has yet to show that a particular medium is superior to others when used with a particular teaching method. He reported: "not only may most media be used effectively for the attainment of a great number of different objectives, but also most objectives may be achieved through any of a variety of media" (p. 500). (See MULTIMEDIA INSTRUCTION.)

References: Erhard U. Heidt, "Media Classification," in Derick Unwin and Ray McAleese (Editors), *The Encyclopedia of Educational Media Communications and Technology,* Westport, CT: Greenwood Press, 1978; Robert Heinich, Michael Molenda, and James D. Russell, *Instructional Media and the New Technologies of Instruction* (Second Edition), New York: John Wiley and Sons, 1985; Jerrold E. Kemp and Don C. Smellie, *Planning, Producing and Using Instructional Media* (Sixth Edition), New York: Harper and Row Publishers, 1989; Robert B. Kozma, et al., *Instructional Techniques in Higher Education,* Englewood Cliffs, NJ: Educational Technology Publications, 1978; Phillip

J. Sleeman, et al., *Instructional Media and Technology: A Guide to Accountable Learning Systems,* New York: Longman, Inc., 1979.

MEDIAN, a measure of central tendency that represents the 50th percentile, or that point in a group of scores (numbers) above which and below which 50 percent of the numbers (or scores) lay. To calculate the median for ungrouped scores, the individual numbers must first be arranged in order of magnitude (e.g. 90, 85, 80, 70, 60). The formula $\frac{N+1}{2}$, where N represents the number of scores, is then employed. Using the five scores given in the illustration, substitutions in the formula are made as follows: $\frac{5+1}{2} = 3$. The answer means that the third score (80) is the median for this particular group of numbers. The formula does not always yield actual scores as the following example illustrates. (Scores, 92, 85, 83, 80, 75, 70; $\frac{6+1}{2} = 3.5$.) In this second illustration, the 3.5 figure means that the median, which falls halfway between the third and fourth scores, is 81.5.

The median for scores that have been grouped in a frequency distribution (e.g. 96–100: 4; 91–95: 7; 86–90: 11; 81–85: 9) can also be calculated. (See CENTRAL TENDENCY MEASURES.)

References: George K. Cunningham, *Educational and Psychological Measurement,* New York: Macmillan Publishing Company, 1986; L. R. Gay, *Educational Research: Competencies for Analysis and Application* (Third Edition), Columbus, OH: Merrill Publishing Company, 1987.

MEDIA SPECIALIST—See SCHOOL LIBRARY MEDIA SPECIALIST

MEDIATED READING, a stage in the process of learning to read. The term specifically designates the stage between reading readiness and fluent reading; the length of time spent in this stage of reading development varies from child to child. This is the stage usually involved with phonic instruction. The learner becomes aware of the visual letter and word equivalents of the spoken language. It is predicated on the understanding that an average 6-year-old understands and speaks his/her language clearly; the challenge of reading is to decode the visual marks on the page to sound. Even a precocious reader goes through a mediated reading stage; however, such a learner may require less overt instruction in sound-letter equivalents to break the code. Short-term memory plays a major role in mediated reading since it keeps the letter elements in mind to form a word, and keeps several words in memory to form a sentence. The mediated reading process is a brief transitional stage when the learner acquires the ability to extract the spoken equivalents of written symbols. Gradually, the learner masters the application of phonic generalizations. These generalizations must be internalized and then applied automatically to reading material.

References: Jeanne Chall, *Stages of Reading Development,* New York: McGraw-Hill, 1983; Seymour W. Itzhoff, *How We Learn to Read,* Ashfield, MA: Paideia Publishers, 1986.

MEDIATION, the use of a neutral third party to help settle disputes that representatives of employees and management are unable to resolve through direct negotiation. Unlike arbitrators, whose recommendations are binding on both parties, mediators work to overcome stalemates through fact-finding, talking, and similar (nonbinding) techniques designed to keep communication channels open.

Mediators may be called upon for help by either or both of the negotiating parties. The federal government and some states have mediation services available to assist public agencies. (See ARBITRATION and COLLECTIVE BARGAINING.)

References: William B. Castetter, *The Personnel Function in Educational Administration* (Third Edition), New York: Macmillan Publishing Company, Inc., 1981; W. D. Heisel, *New Questions and Answers on Public Employee Negotiation,* Chicago: International Personnel Management Association, 1973; Max S. Wortmann, Jr. and C. Wilson Randle, *Collective Bargaining: Principles and Practices* (Second Edition), Boston: Houghton Mifflin Company, 1966.

MEDICAL COLLEGE ADMISSIONS TEST (MCAT), a test used extensively since the 1950s by medical schools as one part of their admission process. Initially the MCAT had four subtests—science, general information, quantitative ability, and verbal. As a result of criticism that the test stressed recall information, MCAT was redesigned in the early 1970s. There are now six subtests: reading, quantitative, biology, chemistry, physics, and science problems (New MCAT, 1977). The test is still highly scientific and quantitatively oriented. The test is published by the Association of American Medical Colleges.

The Medical College Admissions Test is one of several specialized tests used by the health professions. Others are the Allied Health Professions Admissions Test (AHPAT, subtests—verbal ability, reading comprehension, quantitative ability, biology, and chemistry), Dental Aptitude Test (DAT, subtests—academic verbal reasoning, reading comprehension, quantitative reasoning, biology, chemistry, and perceptual ability), and the Pharmacy College Admissions Tests (PCAT, subtests—verbal ability, reading, quantitative ability, biology, and chemistry). These tests were developed to provide better predictability of performance in their respective programs than was provided by either the American College Tests (ACT) or Scholastic Aptitude Test (SAT). (See AMERICAN COLLEGE TESTS and SCHOLASTIC APTITUDE TEST.)

References: Christine H. McGuire, et al., *Handbook of Health Professions Education,* San Francisco, CA: Jossey-Bass Publishers, 1983; National Commission on Allied Health Education, *The Future of Allied Health Education,* San Francisco, CA: Jossey-Bass Publishers, 1980; James R. Schofield, *New and Expanded Medical Schools, Mid-Century to the 1980s,* San Francisco, CA: Jossey-Bass Publishers, 1984.

MEIKLEJOHN, ALEXANDER (February 3, 1872–December 16, 1964), philosopher, educator, and higher education administrator noted for his educational innovations. Upon earning the Ph.D. in philosophy (1897) at Cornell University, he began teaching philosophy at Brown University, his undergraduate alma mater. Four years later, he was appointed to that institution's deanship.

In 1912, Meiklejohn became President of Amherst College (Massachusetts) and almost immediately introduced curricular reforms that stressed academic excellence and the fostering of intelligence. He was discharged from the presidency in 1924. In 1926, he was employed by the University of Wisconsin where he introduced a controversial experimental college that was dissolved in 1933.

Meiklejohn authored seven books including *The Liberal College* (1920), *The Experimental College* (1932), and *Education Between Two Worlds* (1942). He helped to found the American Civil Liberties Union (1920) and served as President of the American Philosophical Association (1923) as well as the American Association of Adult Education (1942). In 1962, he was awarded the presidential Medal of Freedom.

References: James M. Green, "Meiklejohn, Alexander B." in John F. Ohles (Editor), *Biographical Dictionary of American Educators* (Volume 2), Westport, CT: Greenwood Press, 1978; "Meiklejohn, Alexander" in *Who Was Who in*

America (Volume 4), Chicago: Marquis Who's Who, 1968.

MEMORY, recall ability that consists of two processes: *storing information* and *retrieving information.* Psychologists have divided information storage, the first of the processes, into three stages: (1) the act of taking information and absorbing it into the sensory register (e.g. seeing, hearing); (2) short-term storage, as when one is introduced to a stranger at a party and remembers the stranger's name for just the party's duration; and (3) long-term storage consisting of information that is stored forever. The inability to retrieve information is called forgetting.

Researchers point out that some factors enhance retention and others contribute to forgetting. Among the enhancing factors are: (1) *level of learning* (e.g. continued practice, repetition); (2) the *similarity of learning and recall conditions;* (3) *uniqueness of materials learned;* (4) the *meaningfulness* of information learned; and (5) *organization* of material. Contributing to forgetting are so-called interference factors including *limited training, "interfering" material, retention level* (the time between learning and need for recall), and *similarity* of materials being learned. (See MNEMONIC DEVICE.)
References: Lee C. Cronbach, *Educational Psychology* (Third Edition), New York: Harcourt Brace Jovanovich, Inc., 1977; Janice T. Gibson and Louis A. Chandler, *Educational Psychology: Mastering Principles and Applications,* Boston: Allyn and Bacon, 1988; B. R. Hergenhahn, *An Introduction to Theories of Learning* (Third Edition), Englewood Cliffs, NJ: Prentice-Hall, Inc., 1988.

MENTAL AGE (MA), the age level at which an individual is functioning as measured using a standardized test. It is a form of intellectual age used to describe present performance as well as an indirect measure of potential performance.

The MA was first introduced by Alfred Binet in 1908 when the Binet-Simon test of intelligence (1905 version) was revised and increased in size. Binet grouped tests by age levels (e.g. three-year level, four-year level). The level reached by a child that equaled the performance of normal children at a particular age level was considered to be the mental age of that child. For example, if an eight-year-old performed satisfactorily on ten-year-level tests, the mental age of the child was ten. Stated differently, he/she was determined to be ahead of his/her age group (mental age) by two years.

There are interpretation and measurement problems associated with the concept of mental age.

MA tends to shrink with age. Also, intellectual development is accelerated at the earlier ages and decreases as one matures. Past experiences, too, play a role in determining mental age.

To allow for a reliable measure of intelligence that could be interpreted regardless of age, the Intelligence Quotient (I.Q.) was developed for use in the 1916 version of the Stanford-Binet. Mental age is one of two measures used to determine I.Q. The other is chronological age. (See INTELLIGENCE QUOTIENT.)
References: Anne Anastasi, *Psychological Testing* (Sixth Edition), New York: Macmillan Publishing Company, Inc., 1988; Lee J. Cronbach, *Essentials of Psychological Testing* (Fourth Edition), New York: Harper and Row, Publishers, 1984; W. Bruce Walsh and Nancy E. Betz, *Tests and Measurement,* Englewood Cliffs, NJ: Prentice-Hall, Inc., 1985.

MENTAL HEALTH—See MENTAL HYGIENE

MENTAL HYGIENE, a general term that includes all aspects of mental health. It is concerned with the development and maintenance of good mental health and the prevention of mental and personality disorders.

Motivation, frustration, conflicts, compensation, identification, projection, regression, repression, love, hate, need to achieve, need to avoid failure, traits, and environmental conditions may affect or influence the development of good mental health. Consequently, they receive careful consideration as mental hygiene programs are developed.

Mental hygiene programs must be wide in scope, flexible enough to meet individual needs, and designed to help the individual to function effectively as a worker, citizen, and family member. The fostering of good mental health and an active mental hygiene program, authorities indicate, should be a part of all school programs. (See SELF-ACTUALIZATION.)
References: Nicholas S. DiCaprio, *The Good Life: Models for a Healthy Personality,* Englewood Cliffs, NJ: Prentice-Hall, Inc., 1976; Stephen N. Elliott and Joseph C. Witt, *The Delivery of Psychological Services in Schools,* Hillsdale, NJ: Lawrence Erlbaum Associates, Publishers, 1986; Joel Meyers, et al., *Mental Health Consultation in the Schools,* San Francisco: Jossey-Bass Publishers, 1979; Milton G. Thackeray, et al., *Introduction to Mental Health: Field Practice,* Englewood Cliffs, NJ: Prentice-Hall, Inc., 1979.

MENTAL RETARDATION (MR), commonly believed to mean below-average capacity of a student to perform in regular school situations. Mental retardates have (1) significantly subaverage general intellectual functioning, with (2) deficits in adaptive behavior that (3) manifest themselves during the developmental period. All three conditions must be present before the label is assigned to the individual. Special educators use the terms *mild, moderate, severe,* and *profound* to indicate degrees of retardation. A large majority of the retarded population falls within the mild category.

MR can be caused by environmental influences, heredity, infection, genetic influences, or a combination of these. The majority of MR individuals are capable of independent living and are assimilated into their respective communities.

References: William L. Heward and Michael D. Orlansky, *Exceptional Children: An Introductory Survey of Special Education,* Columbus, OH: Merrill Publishing Company, 1988; Judy W. Wood, *Mainstreaming: A Practical Approach for Teachers,* Columbus, OH: Merrill Publishing Company, 1989.

MENTOR TEACHER, a teacher who has the responsibility to assist, guide, and function as a role model in the induction of new teachers into the profession. The mentor teacher also assists in the in-service training of experienced teachers, in addition to serving as a role model. This is done through direct observation of the mentor teacher in his/her classroom, individual and small-group interaction, staff development programs, curriculum development, instructional leadership at the school building as well as district level, and instructional problem solving at the classroom level.

Mentor teacher programs, like master teacher programs, are intended to provide recognition and salary differentials to teachers who have demonstrated mentorious teaching ability and expertise. Mentor teachers, unlike master teachers, have a definite charge to work with other teachers, either at the school building or district-wide level.

In 1983 the California legislature passed the California Educational Reform Act. The Mentor Teacher Program was part of that act and is California's career ladder program. Mentor teachers are appointed for one, two, or three years; are selected by a district selection committee made up of mostly teachers; and must spend 60 percent of their time in the direct instruction of students. (See CAREER LADDERS FOR TEACHERS; MASTER TEACHER; and MERIT PAY.)

References: David E. Kapel, et al., "Linking Career Ladders with Demonstration Schools: A Proposed Cooperative Model," *Journal of Teacher Education,* Volume 36, Number 3, 1985; Roger G. Lowne, *Mentor Teachers: The California Model,* Bloomington, IN: Phi Delta Kappa,

1986; Richard W. Moore, *Master Teachers,* Bloomington, IN: Phi Delta Kappa, 1984.

MERIT PAY, a salary adjustment paid to employees on the basis of qualitative differences in performance. In education, the term has come to mean extra pay for outstanding or meritorious performance (usually teaching). The concept of merit pay is not universally supported among educators. Proponents argue that it stimulates individual improvement, rewards the deserving employee, and is consistent with employment practices in industry. Critics charge that merit pay leads to favoritism, precipitates anxiety and distrust among employees, and cannot be administered objectively until such time as the teaching profession develops instruments that accurately measure teaching performance.

There are different types of merit pay plans found in public schools. One approach is to have two or three salary schedules; only meritorious teachers are put on the list and the highest schedule. Another approach is to grant different salary adjustments based on the assessment of performance. Another approach is to allow teachers to move up a salary scale at an accelerated rate—depending on teacher assessment. Yet another approach allows teachers to go beyond the range of the schedules if deemed meritorious. Another one would give teachers a one-time-only bonus for meritorious service; unlike other plans, the bonus does not remain a part of the teacher's permanent salary. Although merit pay plans are becoming more prevalent in the public schools as a result of the educational reform movements of the 1980s, merit pay is used more frequently in colleges and universities than in public schools. (See CAREER LADDERS FOR TEACHERS; MASTER TEACHER; and NATIONAL REFORM REPORTS (1980–86).)

References: Stayner Brighton and Cecil Hannon, *Merit Pay Programs for Teachers,* Belmont, CA: Fearon Publishers, Inc., 1962; William B. Castetter, *The Personnel Function in Educational Administration* (Third Edition), New York: Macmillan Publishing Company, Inc., 1981; Elwood B. Ehrle and John B. Bennett, *Managing the Academic Enterprise,* New York: American Council on Education, 1988; Susan Moore Johnson, *Pros and Cons of Merit Pay,* Bloomington, IN: Phi Delta Kappa, 1984.

MESOMORPHY—See CONSTITUTIONAL TYPES

META-ANALYSIS, a review technique or ap-

proach used to synthesize, integrate, or summarize the results from a set (all) of research studies in a particular area of investigation. Inductive statistics, or quantitative synthesis, is used in assessing the findings from a body of studies that have investigated the same problem—usually to combine results across these studies. Early meta-analysis focused on the overall relationship between two variables, variations in the size of the correlation of the two variables, or on providing aggregated data to study selected hypotheses. Dr. Gene Glass in 1976 introduced a more systematic, rigorous, and quantitative methodology to integrate or synthesize findings found in a large set of research studies completed in a specific area. There are many problems associated with meta-analysis, such as common definition and use of terms and concepts; sampling procedures used in the individual studies; studies that are flawed but are included in the set of studies used in the analysis; missing data; and publication bias. These concerns notwithstanding, meta-analysis has made a major contribution to the review of bodies of studies. It focuses attention on methodological rigor and standards in such reviews. (See BEST-EVIDENCE SYNTHESIS.)
References: Bruce J. Biddle and Donald S. Anderson, "Theory, Methods, Knowledge, and Research on Teaching" in Merlin C. Wittrock (Editor), *Handbook on Research on Teaching* (Third Edition), New York: Macmillan Publishing Company, 1986; Gene V. Glass, "Integrating Findings: The Meta-Analysis of Research," in Lee S. Shulman (Editor), *Review of Research in Education*, Washington, DC: American Educational Research Association, 1977; Gene V. Glass, "Primary, Secondary, and Meta-Analysis of Research," *Educational Research*, Volume 5, Number 10, 1986; Gene V. Glass, et al., *Meta-Analysis in Social Research*, Beverly Hills, CA: Sage Publications, Incorporated, 1981; Larry V. Hedges, "Issues in Meta-analysis" in Ernst Z. Rothkopf (Editor), *Review of Research in Education*, Washington, DC: American Educational Research Association, 1986.

METACOGNITION, the deliberate control of one's own cognition. Research supports the fact that the greater the individual's awareness and control of his or her thought processes, the better his or her understanding of the thing about which he or she is thinking.

According to Baker and Brown (1984) it is imperative to distinguish between two types of metacognition knowledge: knowledge of cognition and regulation of the cognition. The focus of the first is on the knowledge readers possess relative to their own cognitive resources and the interrelatedness of that knowledge with the demands of reading.

There are important implications derived from this awareness of one's own cognitive processing relative to one's active participation in one's own education. Regulation of cognition, the second type of metacognition, consists of the mechanisms employed by the active learner in ongoing problem solving. Competent readers monitor their comprehension as related to the purposes for reading. (See FEUERSTEIN'S INSTRUMENTAL ENRICHMENT.)
References: L. Baker and Ann L. Brown, "Metacognition Skills of Reading" in P. D. Pearson (Editor), *Handbook of Reading Research*, New York: Longman, 1984; Ann L. Brown, "Metacognition: The Development of Selective Attention Strategies for Learning from Texts" in Harry Singer and Robert B. Ruddell (Editors), *Theoretical Models and Processes of Reading*, Newark, DE: International Reading Association, 1985; Ann L. Brown, "Metacognitive Development and Reading" in Rand J. Spiro, Bertram C. Bruce, and William F. Brewer (Editors), *Theoretical Issues in Reading Comprehension*, Hillsdale, NJ: Lawrence Erlbaum, 1980; Thomas N. Turner, "Comprehension: Reading for Meaning" in J. Estell Alexander (Editor), *Teaching Reading*, Boston: Little, Brown and Company, 1983.

METRIC CONVERSION ACT OF 1975 (PL 94-168), Congressional legislation that: (1) set forth the policy of the United States with respect to the metric system, and (2) authorized creation of a United States Metric Board. Specifically, it stated that "the policy of the United States shall be to coordinate and plan the increasing use of the metric system in the United States and to establish a United States Metric Board to coordinate the *voluntary conversion* (italics ours) to the metric system" (p. 1007).

The board, consisting of 17 members, is appointed by the President with the advice and consent of the Senate. Section 6 of the act calls for the board to plan and carry out programs that will help to implement the act's policy. Eleven specific activities/responsibilities were assigned to the board, including public education, research, and consultation with foreign governments.
Reference: Public Law 94-168, *United States Statutes at Large, 1975* (Volume 89), Washington, DC: U.S. Government Printing Office, 1977.

METRIC SYSTEM, a basic system of weights and measures used in virtually all countries of the world. It was first officially adopted by France in 1795.

The system was changed somewhat in 1960 at the General Conference of Weights and Measures, an international meeting, at which time the Systeme International d'Unites (SI), or the International System of Units, was adopted. SI utilizes seven basic units of measure. Two of the more widely known measures are the *meter*, a linear measure (equal to 39.37 inches) and the *kilogram*, a unit of weight (equal to 2.2 pounds). (Although the cubic meter is SI's official volume measure, the liter, equal to 0.26 U.S. gallons, is more commonly used.) Four other units are the *second*, for time; the *ampere*, for electric current; the *candelo*, for luminous intensity; and the *mole*, for amount of substance. The seventh unit, the *kelvin*, is the basic temperature measure. More commonly used than the scientist's kelvin is the Celsius (C) Scale, with degrees of temperature (0 = freezing point of water; 100 = water's boiling point) expressed in degrees centigrade.

The metric system uses the base-ten number system. Prefixes added to metric units express multiples or parts of each unit in "powers of ten" terms. These are *kilo* (1,000 or 10^3); *hecto* (100 or 10^2); *deka* (10 or 10^1); *deci* (0.1 or 10^{-1}); *centi* (0.01 or 10^{-2}); and *milli* (0.001 or 10^{-3}). Thus, a *kilo*gram equals 1,000 grams and the *centi*meter is equivalent to one 100th of a meter.

The metric system is legal in the United States. Its use has been increasing, although the traditional English system of weights and measures continues to be used widely. Since passage of the Metric Conversion Act of 1975 by the U.S. Congress, American schools have been stressing the teaching of metrics. (See METRIC CONVERSION ACT OF 1975.)

References: Gary G. Bitter, et al., *Activities Handbook for Teaching the Metric System*, Boston: Allyn and Bacon, Inc., 1976; Jon L. Higgins (Editor), *A Metric Handbook for Teachers*, Reston, VA: National Council of Teachers of Mathematics, 1974; Klaas Kramer, *Teaching Elementary School Mathematics* (Fourth Edition), Boston: Allyn and Bacon, Inc., 1978.

METROPOLITAN ACHIEVEMENT TESTS, a battery of group tests that measures achievement in specific areas. The *Primer* is used in grades K.7–1.4; *Primary I*, 1.5–2.4; *Primary II*, 2.5–3.4; *Elementary*, 3.5–4.9; *Intermediate*, 5.0–6.9; *Advanced*, 7.0–9.5; and *High School*, 9–13.

Listening for Sounds and Reading and Numbers are subtests of the Primer. Word Knowledge, Word Analysis, Reading, Mathematics Computation, and Mathematics Concepts make up Primary I. The other levels have several additional subtests such as Mathematics Problem Solving, Science and Social Science, and Spelling. The High School battery includes language arts, social studies, mathematics, and science subtests. Depending on the level, the time required to administer the test ranges from 1 hour and 10 minutes to 4 hours and 30 minutes. The tests are published by Harcourt Brace Jovanovich.

References: William A. Mehrens and Irvin J. Lehmann, *Using Standardized Tests in Education*, New York: Longman, Inc., 1987; Robert L. Thorndike and Elizabeth P. Hagen, *Measurement and Evaluation in Psychology and Education* (Fourth Edition), New York: John Wiley and Sons, 1977; W. Bruce Walsh and Nancy E. Betz, *Tests and Measurement*, Englewood Cliffs, NJ: Prentice-Hall, Inc., 1985.

METROPOLITANISM, the action of metropolitan areas working as wholes rather than as disparate urban vs. suburban organizations and/or governmental units. Robert Havighurst referred to metropolitanism as "a process of action and planning . . . in which an increasing number of organizations take the metropolitan area as their natural area of action" (p. 5). Supporters of metropolitanism see it as a more viable approach to planning than the traditional, often protectionist one in which individual governmental units function independently of each other. Metropolitan planning activities address issues such as transportation, higher education, energy, vocational-technical education, and recreation.

In education, metropolitanism is concerned with the educational opportunities available to all students residing in a given metropolitan area. Recent interest in this subject has been prompted by at least four phenomena: (1) changes in, and the extent of migration between, urban and outlying areas; (2) the realization that individual organizations are becoming increasingly interdependent; (3) court rulings that have mandated merger of some urban and neighboring school districts (e.g. Detroit and Wilmington, Delaware) to achieve racial balance; and (4) as Theodore Reller pointed out, growing recognition that "among society's most difficult problems in education are those of the metropolitan area" (p. 8). (See *MILLIKEN v. BRADLEY* and STANDARD METROPOLITAN STATISTICAL AREA.)

References: Robert J. Havighurst (Editor), *Metropolitanism: Its Challenge to Education* (NSSE 67th Yearbook, Part I), Chicago: University of Chicago Press, 1968; Theodore L. Reller, *Educational Administration in Metropolitan Areas*, Bloomington, IN: The Phi Delta Kappa Educational Foundation, 1974.

METROPOLITAN READINESS TESTS (1976 EDITION), two group-level tests for grades K–1. Level I is for students considered to be low in skill development; Level II is for those considered to be at a normal level of progress in skill development.

Level I has six subtests: Auditory Memory, Rhyming, Letter Recognition, Visual Matching, School Language and Listening, Quantitative Language, and Copying (an optional test).

Beginning Consonants, Sound-Letter Correspondence, Visual Matching, Finding Patterns, School Language, Listening, two quantitative tests that are optional (Quantitative Concepts, Quantitative Operations), and Copying (optional) are subtests that make up Level II. Each level takes from 80 to 90 minutes to administer. The Psychological Corporation of Harcourt Brace Jovanovich publishes both tests.

Reference: Robert L. Thorndike and Elizabeth P. Hagen, *Measurement and Evaluation in Psychology and Education* (Fourth Edition), New York: John Wiley and Sons, 1977.

METROPOLITAN SCHOOL STUDY COUNCIL (MSSC), a cooperative research organization of selected school districts located in New York, New Jersey, and Connecticut. Organized in 1941 by Professor Paul Mort, Teachers College, Columbia University, MSSC works to improve educational quality through mutual exchange and cooperative research. The activities of the council are supported by contributions from member districts and Teachers College.

MSSC pioneered the school study council concept and, since its inception, has produced a large number of significant educational studies.

Reference: Gary A. Griffin and Ann Lieberman (Principal Investigators), "Interactive Research and Development on Schooling" (Proposal Submitted to the National Institute of Education), New York: Teachers College, December 1979.

MICROCOMPUTER—See PERSONAL COMPUTER

MICROFICHE, a French term that means miniature index card. The card, measuring 4 by 6 inches, is a transparency that contains rows of frames. Frames are copies of records, pages in a book, and so on that have been photographed and greatly reduced in size. Because microfiche images are considerably smaller than those appearing on microfilm, the photo-reduced pages of several books can be made to fit on one card. Microfiched material is read by using a microfiche reader, a device that enlarges and projects images onto a screen or a special viewer.

Microfiche is one of several innovations that simplifies information retrieval and greatly reduces storage requirements. (See MICROFILM.)

References: Alice H. Bahr, *Microforms: The Librarians' View, 1978–79,* White Plains, NY: Knowledge Industry Publications, 1978; James W. Brown, et al., *AV Instruction: Technology, Media, and Methods* (Fifth Edition), New York: McGraw-Hill Book Company, 1977; Walter A. Wittich and Charles F. Schuller, *Instructional Technology: Its Nature and Use* (Sixth Edition), New York: Harper and Row, Publishers, 1979.

MICROFILM, one of two principal microforms used in schools and libraries. (The other is microfiche.) Microfilming makes it possible to store large amounts of printed matter in relatively compact storage spaces using the process of photographic miniaturization. Pages of a book, for example, are photographed, reduced in size photographically, and then preserved on 35 mm. microfilm. A roll of microfilm, which resembles a filmstrip, contains a series of such photographs (frames). Microfilms are generally read using a "reader," a device that enlarges and projects each frame onto a reader screen. Print copies may also be made from microfilm. (See MICROFICHE.)

References: Alice H. Bahr, *Microforms: The Librarians' View, 1978–79,* White Plains, NY: Knowledge Industry Publications, 1978; James W. Brown, et al., *AV Instruction: Technology, Media, and Methods* (Fifth Edition), New York: McGraw-Hill Book Company, 1977; Walter A. Wittich and Charles F. Schuller, *Instructional Technology: Its Nature and Use* (Sixth Edition), New York: Harper and Row, Publishers, 1979.

MICROPROCESSOR, the brain within the personal computer, also known as the central processing unit (CPU). Microprocessors can perform a limited number of primary operations called an instruction set. Unless translated from one instruction set to another, programs are not transferable from one microprocessor to another.

A microprocessor's power is dependent on four factors:

1. The number of bits of data that can be processed in a single operation;

2. The number and usefulness of operations in the instruction set;

3. The time it takes to complete an instruction; and

4. The quantity of internal memory that the processor can manage.

The CPU is composed of three units: the *control* unit, which tells all the other parts what to do; the *arithmetic-logic* unit, which executes all arithmetic and logic statements; and the *primary storage* unit, which stores all data and programs within the computer's internal memory. (See INTERNAL MEMORY and PERSONAL COMPUTER.)

References: Grace Murray Hopper and Steven L. Mandell, *Understanding Computers*, St. Paul, MN: West Publishing Company, 1984; David R. Sullivan, et al., *Computing Today: Microcomputer Concepts and Applications*, Boston: Houghton Mifflin Company, 1985.

MICROTEACHING, a scaled-down version of real teaching. The microteaching method is used with individual teacher trainees. It requires the trainee to prepare a teaching lesson that is limited to a short period, involves a small group of learners, and focuses on one specific teaching skill (e.g. "questioning"). The lesson is video-taped and subsequently critiqued by the trainee and his instructor. The tape (feedback) is studied and used as a basis for correcting errors and/or modifying teaching approach(es). The microteaching method was developed at Stanford University in the early 1960s.

References: Dwight Allen and Kevin Ryan, *Microteaching*, Reading, MA: Addison-Wesley Publishing Company, 1969; Robin Barrow and Geoffrey Milburn, *A Critical Dictionary of Educational Concepts*, New York: St. Martin's Press, 1986; Earl J. Montague, *Fundamentals of Secondary Classroom Instruction*, Columbus, OH: Merrill Publishing Company, 1987.

MIDDLE SCHOOL, a school organized to meet the needs of preadolescents and early adolescents in the middle range of grades. The "middle" grades housed in a middle school vary in accordance with local conditions such as availability of school housing and enrollment configurations. In school systems organized on a 4-4-4 basis, the "middle 4" (grades 5 through 8) constitute the middle school. In others, such schools include grades 5-7 or 6-8.

Numerous reasons have been offered to justify the creation of middle schools. They include: (1) growing disenchantment with the junior high school; (2) a desire to have the senior high school again become a four-year institution; (3) the need for more flexible and experimental curricula that, in eclectic fashion, employ the best elements of elementary and secondary schools; and (4) the fact that in some school districts, the existence of a middle school makes racial integration possible at lower grade levels.

Middle school student-grouping patterns are variable. They may include nongrading, self-contained classrooms, and/or departmentalization. The existence of departmentalization in many middle schools has caused relatively more teachers to serve as subject specialists than subject generalists. (See CURRICULUM and INTERMEDIATE SCHOOL.)

References: Joseph Bondi, *Developing Middle Schools: A Guidebook*, Wheeling, IL: Whitehall Company, Publishers, 1978; Frederick S. Calhoun, *Organization of the Middle Grades: A Summary of Research*, Arlington, VA: Educational Research Service, Inc., 1983; Heather S. Doob, *Summary of Research on Middle Schools*, Arlington, VA: Educational Research Service, Inc., 1977; Allan A. Glattorn and Norman K. Spencer, *Middle School/Junior High Principal's Handbook*, Englewood Cliffs, NJ: Prentice-Hall, Inc., 1986; Sylvester Kohut, Jr., *The Middle School: A Bridge Between Elementary and High Schools* (Second Edition), Washington, DC: National Education Association, 1988.

MIDWEST PROGRAM ON AIRBORNE TELEVISION INSTRUCTION (MPATI), an educational experiment, carried out in the 1960s, in which an airborne telecasting studio beamed television programs to schools located in Kentucky, Indiana, Michigan, Ohio, Wisconsin, and Illinois. Initially, MPATI was almost exclusively funded by the Ford Foundation; subsequently, a nonprofit corporation of public and private schools (1,800 in 1964) undertook to manage and pay for much of the program.

MPATI set out to ascertain whether beaming TV programs from a moving airplane could: (1) provide a consistently good signal to all schools, including those in rural areas, and (2) prove more economical than other modes of transmission. Programs were telecast four days each week, approximately five hours a day, and operated on two UHF channels. Courses were developed for students at all academic levels, with course guides made available for use by teachers in the participating schools. Courses for university students were also beamed but they were dropped after one year. Those directed at elementary and secondary schools included programming in fields such as science, mathematics, foreign languages, and social studies.

During its lifetime, MPATI experienced successes and concurrently generated opposition, including resistance from organizations such as AASA, ASCD, and the National Association of Educational Broadcasters. Much of the opposition revolved around the desire for more local autonomy and the belief that increased use should be made of land-based TV stations. MPATI's periodic technical difficulties (usually at the receiver end) were also cited by those in opposition.

Some efforts to evaluate the efficiency of TV instruction over conventional instructional methods were undertaken with several universities participating in some of these evaluations. Universities also played various roles in the preparation of courses.

References: Urban H. Fleege, "Airborne Television, Promising Experiment," *School Science and Mathematics,* May 1962; Kenneth F. Jerkins and Joseph D. Novak, "The Study of Concept Improvement of Junior High School Students Viewing MPATI Telecasts with and without Supplementary Aids," *Science Education,* January–March 1971; Blanche E. Owens, "ETV Airborne TV: Five Year Appraisal," *Nation's Schools,* October 1965; Jerome M. Sachs, "Airborne TV-Teaching and Evaluation," *School Science and Mathematics,* October 1963; Mendel Sherman, "MPATI at the Crossroads," *Phi Delta Kappan,* November 1964; Richard J. Stonesifer, "The Separation Needed Between ETV and ITV," *AV Communication Review,* Winter 1966.

MIGRANT EDUCATION, educational programs usually supported by the federal and state governments for the children of migratory agricultural workers. Since migratory agricultural workers follow the growing seasons, the children who accompany them rarely remain in one location for a full school year. Adding to their learning difficulty is the fact that their living and home support systems are usually poor. Consequently, many of the children have psychological and health as well as educational problems.

Some migrant education programs for children are designed for summer schools or special periods during the rest of the academic year. Programs tend to emphasize language development and other compensatory basic skills. In many areas of the country, the schools are established within migrant agricultural camps during the crop season (or when the migrants arrive in the area). California, Michigan, Florida, Texas, and Washington have the largest number of agricultural migrants. Other states such as New York, New Jersey, and Ohio also have a large number of migrant children. Special migrant education programs for parents have also been developed. Federal funding now requires active parent participation in migrant education programs through Parent Advisory Committees (PACs).

References: Myron Friedman, et al., *Evaluation Design 1978–79: ESAA Title I Migrant Program,* Austin, TX: Aus-

tin Independent School District, 1978; Samir N. Maamary, *Attitudes toward Migration Among Rural Residents,* San Francisco: R & E Research Associates, 1976; Lloyd Morain, *The Human Cougar,* Buffalo, NY: Prometheus Books, 1976; *Rural Education: A Forward Look,* Washington, DC: Department of Rural Education, NEA, 1955.

MILD LEARNING AND BEHAVIOR DISORDERS—See MILD/MODERATE DISORDERS

MILD/MODERATE DISORDERS (MILD LEARNING AND BEHAVIOR DISORDERS), a generic classification of disorders of individuals who have mild learning, behavioral disorders, or social/interpersonal deficits. These deficits fall one to two standard deviations below the average on assessment (criterion and/or norm-referenced) instruments.

Students classified as having a mild/moderate disorder generally remain in a regular classroom for most of the school day. Additional services to moderate the effects of the disorder should be made available. Approximately 6 percent of school-age children will fall under Public Law 94–142 definition of mild learning and behavior disorders; another 7 percent are considered to have such disorders, but will not qualify under the law.

So many factors contribute to mild/moderate disorders that the cause for such problems remains unknown. Often the identification of these disorders does not occur until a child enters school. Poor motivation, poor memory and retention skills, the influences of socioeconomic class, and poor teaching are but a few factors that may contribute to the disorder. (See LEARNING DISABILITIES; MENTAL RETARDATION; PUBLIC LAW 94–142; and SEVERE AND PROFOUND DISORDERS.)

References: Donald Hammill, et al., "A New Definition of Learning Disabilities," *Learning Disability Quarterly,* Volume 4, Number 4, 1981; Michael L. Hardman, et al., *Human Exceptionality, Society, School, and Family* (Second Edition), Boston: Allyn and Bacon, Inc., 1987.

MILLER ANALOGIES TEST (MAT), an examination required by many graduate schools as part of their admissions procedures. It is also used in industry for the filling of certain high-level positions. The test requires 50 minutes to complete and is made up of analogies of increasing complexity. The items come from many academic disciplines. Five parallel forms of the test are available, one of which is reserved for reexaminations. Percentile norms for graduate and professional school students are available in various areas. In addition, norms for several groups of industrial employees are reported. As might be expected, there are wide differences among the norm groups in terms of percentile norms.

The test was first developed at the University of Minnesota (1926) by W. S. Miller. It is now published by the Psychological Corporation. Braille and large-type editions are available. The distribution of the test is restricted, and tests are administered at specific, licensed university centers. Scoring and reporting are done at these centers.

References: Anne Anastasi, *Psychological Testing* (Fourth Edition), New York: Macmillan Publishing Company, Inc., 1976; Oscar K. Buros (Editor), *The Eighth Mental Measurements Yearbook* (Volume I), Highland Park, NJ: The Gryphon Press, 1978.

MILLIKEN v. BRADLEY, sometimes referred to as the *Detroit* case, landmark lawsuit that challenged the right of a district court to mandate the joining of districts in a metropolitan area for the purpose of desegregating an almost all-black city district. Such a consolidation was ordered in 1971 for the purpose of remedying Detroit's desegregation problem. Since Detroit's student body was almost totally black, a district court ruled (on advice of a court-appointed panel) that the Detroit system and 53 neighboring districts be joined to form 15 clusters, each of which would include at least two suburban districts and part of the Detroit system.

The district court's ruling was later supported by the Court of Appeals for the Sixth Circuit. When appealed to the U.S. Supreme Court, however, the decisions of the lower courts were reversed on a five-to-four vote. Those voting to reverse noted that the suburban districts were not de jure contributors to Detroit's desegregation problem. One Justice concluded that "(by) approving a remedy that would reach beyond the limits of the city of Detroit to correct a constitutional violation found to have occurred solely within that city the Court of Appeals thus went beyond the governing equitable principles established in this Court's decisions" (Browning, p.193).

References: R. Stephen Browning (Editor), *From Brown to Bradley: School Desegregation 1954-1974,* Cincinnati, OH: Jefferson Law Book Company, 1975; Frank R. Kemerer and Kenneth L. Deutsch, *Constitutional Rights and Student Life: Value Conflict in Law and Education,* St. Paul, MN: West Publishing Company, 1979; *Milliken v. Bradley,* 418 U.S. 717, 94 S.Ct. 3112, 41 L.Ed. 2d 1069 (1974).

MILLS v. DISTRICT OF COLUMBIA BOARD OF EDUCATION, a 1972 class action suit, on behalf of seven school-aged disabled children, that established civil rights for non–mentally retarded but disabled children. The court ordered the Board of Education for the District of Columbia to provide free and appropriate public education for school-aged children regardless of mental, physical, or emotional disabilities. The court also ordered the District Board of Education to advertise the availability of free educational programs for disabled children and to provide such education to them. The Board of Education had to file educational plans for such children with the court as well.

Along with the PARC Decision, the Mills decision went a long way in establishing the concept of zero rejection in the enrolling of children in public schools. Mills and PARC helped to form the base for Public law 94–142. (See PARC DECISION and PUBLIC LAW 94–142.)

References: Mills v. District of Columbia Board of Education, 348 F. Supp. 866 (D.D.C. 1972); H. Rutherford Turnbull III, *Free Appropriate Public Education, The Law and Children with Disabilities,* Denver, CO: Love Publishing Co., 1986.

MINICOMPUTER, a computer with all the components of a full-size mainframe computer but with a smaller memory. These computers were developed in the late 1960s for specialized applications. A number of minicomputers can be interconnected to share common resources. Costing between $15,000 and $200,000, they are used in engineering, aviation, industrial automation, and word processing. As with the larger computers, time-sharing is possible; however, only 40 to 50 individuals can use the computer simultaneously. (Up to several hundred can use the large mainframe computer at one time.) (See MAINFRAME.)

References: Grace Murray Hopper and Steven L. Mandell, *Understanding Computers,* St. Paul, MN: West Publishing Company, 1984; David R. Sullivan, et al., *Computing Today: Microcomputer Concepts and Applications,* Boston: Houghton Mifflin Company, 1985.

MINICOURSE, a course that is not as long, chronologically, as a traditional educational or training course. A regular course is usually scheduled for a set length of time (e.g. 15 weeks, 1 semester, 1 year) and designed to cover a set amount of material. Being shorter, a minicourse doesn't cover as much material and is often designed as a limited, self-contained training experience.

Minicourses permit the breaking down of a

longer traditional course into segments, thus granting individuals the option to enroll in only one, two, or all of the segments. Each segment carries reduced credit with the total of all segments' credits usually equal to the longer course. For example, a traditional mathematics class may be 15 weeks long and carry 3 semester hours of credit. This same course may be broken down into three segments of 5 weeks with each carrying 1 semester hour of credit (each segment based on a particular area of mathematics).

Other minicourses are specifically designed to be short courses, with reduced credit hours, without being the subset of any longer traditional course.

The minicourse is designed to give the learner more flexibility in registering for a variety of courses. It is also designed to allow experimentation on the part of the learner in terms of subject matter and/or type of instruction received. Minicourses are found in most colleges and high schools. In education, they had their origins in the microteaching studies at Stanford University where self-contained and self-instructional modules were developed to improve teaching techniques. From this model developed the concept of the minicourse now being used in many colleges and schools.
References: Kieran Egan, *Educational Development*, Oxford, England: Oxford University Press, 1979; Harold G. Shane (Editor), *Curriculum Change Toward the 21st Century*, Washington, DC: National Education Association, 1977; Michael D. Stephens and Gordon W. Roderick (Editors), *Higher Education Alternatives*, London, England: Longman Group Ltd., 1978.

MINIMAL BRAIN DYSFUNCTION (MBD), a term often used to describe an organic cause for specific learning disabilities. *Minimal cerebral dysfunction* is another term used for MBD. The elements of minimal brain dysfunction are not clear, for it may include anatomical or physiological lesions in the brain, or it may include deficits in the way information is processed in the brain. Sometimes there is a relationship between MBD and learning disabilities, especially MBD caused by anoxia during birth, but children who may have learning disabilities do not always suffer from MBD or have the disabilities caused by an organic dysfunction.

Attention deficit disorder is a term that has replaced minimal brain dysfunction to describe children who have significant attention problems. MBD has a more restrictive meaning with reference to an organically caused disability. (See ATTENTION DEFICIT DISORDER.)

References: J. L. Matson and J. A. Mulick (Editors), *Handbook for Mental Retardation*, New York: Pergamon Press, 1983; Steven Schwartz and James H. Johnson, *Psychopathology of Childhood*, New York: Pergamon Press, 1985; P. H. Wender, *Minimal Brain Dysfunction in Children*, New York: John Wiley, 1971.

MINIMAL CEREBRAL DYSFUNCTION—See MINIMAL BRAIN DYSFUNCTION

MINIMUM COMPETENCY TESTS, examinations administered to students for the purpose of determining remediation needed, eligibility for grade level promotion, and/or eligibility for graduation from high school. In 1980, over one-half of the states had mandated minimal competency testing programs, some to be administered by state authorities and others by local school districts. Most of these programs were developed after 1976. Some authorities expect large numbers of other states to require minimum competency tests in the years immediately ahead; others anticipate an eventual waning of interest.

A survey supported by the National Institute of Education revealed that: (1) in 1980, 31 states had such programs with 14 of them related to graduation from high school; (2) all tests included reading and computational skills assessments; (3) skills in the areas of language arts and writing were also commonly tested; and (4) considerable provision has been made for learning disabled children.

Sparked by the back-to-the-basics movement, minimum competency testing has produced both supporters and critics. Supporters of the movement argue that it will help to reduce the country's high rate of functional illiteracy. Critics disagree, fearing that it may cause teachers to teach only for the test.
References: Joseph Beckham, *Legal Implications of Minimum Competency Testing* (PDK Fastback 138), Bloomington, IN: The Phi Delta Kappa Educational Foundation, 1980; Dan Kaercher, "A Report to Parents on Minimum Competency Tests," *Better Homes and Gardens*, May 1980; William A. Mehrens and Irvin J. Lehmann, *Using Standardized Tests in Education*, New York: Longman Inc., 1987; Rodney P. Riegle and Ned B. Lovell, *Minimum Competency Testing* (PDK Fastback 137), Bloomington, IN: The Phi Delta Kappa Educational Foundation, 1980; W. Bruce Walsh and Nancy E. Betz, *Tests and Measurement*, Englewood Cliffs, NJ: Prentice-Hall, Inc., 1985.

MINNESOTA MULTIPHASIC PERSONALITY INVENTORY (MMPI), a clinical personality instrument originally designed to differentiate between normal and abnormal personality groups, ages 16 and over, on scales generated by the test. These scales have been used to measure personality on a continuum, as opposed to differentiation of types. MMPI supplies 14 scores: four validity scales (lie, question, validity, test taking attitude) and 10 clinical scales: (1) hypochondriases (Hs); (2) depression (D); (3) hysteria (Hy); (4) psychopathic deviate (Pd); (5) masculinity and femininity (Mf); (6) paranoia (Pa); (7) psychasthenia (Pt); (8) schizophrenia (Sc); (9) hypomania (Ha); and (10) social introversion (Si).

MMPI comes in two forms. They are individual tests that include 550 cards plus sorting guides and a group form that includes 399 items plus 167 research items. In individual testing, examinees respond to statements printed on separate cards with "true," "false," or "cannot say." Statements are printed in a test booklet and responses are recorded on an answer sheet under the group testing condition. Statements cover many areas including health; various symptoms and disorders; attitudes towards sex, religion, social condition; and politics, marital questions, neurotic or psychotic behaviors. A Spanish edition is available.

Since its publication in 1943, the MMPI has generated a great deal of interest and research. (There were 6,000 citations by 1978.) The research has generated over 300 new scales, with several developed for normal populations. The test is published by the Psychological Corporation.

References: Anne Anastasi, *Psychological Testing* (Fourth Edition), New York: Macmillan Publishing Company, Inc., 1976; Oscar K. Buros (Editor), *The Eighth Mental Measurements Yearbook* (Volume I), Highland Park, NJ: The Gryphon Press, 1978.

MINNESOTA SCHOOL MATHEMATICS AND SCIENCE TEACHING PROJECT (MINNEMAST),

a coordinated curriculum for grades K-3 that stresses the interrelationships between mathematics and science. Originally sponsored by the University of Minnesota and supported financially by the National Science Foundation, MINNEMAST consists of sequential units. Printed materials include teachers' manuals, student manuals, and materials kits. The MINNEMAST project also produced a few special texts for teachers and teachers-to-be in an effort to improve the professional preparation of teachers.

References: E. C. Bray, "MINNEMAST, An Elementary Math-Science Program," *School Science and Mathematics,* June 1969; J. David Lockard (Editor), *Science and Mathematics Curricular Developments Internationally, 1956-1974,* College Park, MD: Science Teaching Center, University of Maryland (Joint Project with the Commission on Science Education, American Association for the Advancement of Science), 1974; G. R. Rising, "Research and Development in Mathematics and Science Education at the Minnesota School Mathematics and Science Center and the Minnesota National Laboratory," *School Science and Mathematics,* December 1965.

MINNESOTA TEACHER ATTITUDE INVENTORY,

an instrument designed to assess teacher attitudes toward pupil-teacher relationships. Prospective as well as practicing teachers may take the 150-item inventory. The examinee is asked to respond to each item by indicating whether he/she "Strongly Agrees," "Agrees," "Undecided," "Disagrees," or "Strongly Disagrees" with a particular statement. An example of the type of item is: "Most pupils are resourceful when left on their own." This test has been widely used in research, but, due to the lack of data on test reliability and predictive validity, caution should be used when teacher selection or counseling is involved. The test is published by the Psychological Corporation.

References: Anne Anastasi, *Psychological Testing* (Fourth Edition), New York: Macmillan Publishing Company, Inc., 1976; Oscar K. Buros (Editor), *The Eighth Mental Measurements Yearbook* (Volume I), Highland Park, NJ: The Gryphon Press, 1978.

MINOR—See MAJORS AND MINORS

MIRROR READING,

a reading image problem in which the student reverses letter, word, or sentence order. These symbols are frequently viewed in incorrect order, with left-and-right or even up-and-down confusions evident. Illustrating this disability is the misreading of *b* as *d*, *tab* as *bat*, or *m* for *w*. Psychiatrist Samuel T. Orton, who coined the term *strephosymbolia*, was one of the first to study and report on mirror readers. (See DYSLEXIA and STREPHOSYMBOLIA.)

References: Katrina De Hirsch, "Specific Dyslexia or Strephosymbolia" in Gladys Natchez (Editor), *Children With Reading Problems: Classic and Contemporary Issues in Reading Disability,* New York: Basic Books, Inc., Publishers, 1968; Philip B. Gough, "One Second of Reading" in James F. Kavanagh and Ignatius G. Mattingly (Editors), *Language by Ear and by Eye: The Relationships Between Speech and Reading,* Cambridge, MA: The MIT Press, 1972; Diane Lapp and James Flood, *Teaching Reading to Every Child,* New York: Macmillan Publishing Company, Inc., 1978; Margaret Newton and Michael Thomson, *Dyslexia: A Guide for Teachers and Parents,* London, England: University of London Press Ltd., 1975.

MISCUE,

a reading research term used to describe deviations from what appears on the printed page.

The counting of miscues is used by some teachers to approximate a student's level of reading achievement. Children are asked to read preselected passages, individually and orally. Deviations are recorded (sometimes using a tape recorder), counted, and then analyzed. Major miscue categories include: (1) substituting one word for another; (2) inserting a word that does not appear on the page; (3) omitting a word; and (4) inability to identify a word. Recent miscue research indicates that the counting of such errors is of limited value; more important than such counting, it is suggested, is qualitative assessment of the reader's word identification errors.

References: Dolores Durkin, *Teaching Them to Read* (Third Edition), Boston: Allyn and Bacon, Inc., 1978; Kenneth S. Goodman (Editor), *Miscue Analysis: Applications to Reading Analysis*, Urbana, IL: National Council of Teachers of English, 1973; Daniel R. Hittleman, *Developmental Reading, K–8* (Third Edition), Columbus, OH: Merrill Publishing Company, 1988; Robert M. Wilson and Craig J. Cleland, *Diagnostic and Remedial Reading for Classroom and Clinic* (Sixth Edition), Columbus, OH: Merrill Publishing Company, 1989.

MIXED DOMINANCE, or mixed laterality, a characterization applied to an individual who performs some activities with the right side of the body and others with the left side. For example, an individual may kick a ball with the left foot (left dominant) yet bat a ball with the right hand (right dominant).

Although most people are consistently right or left dominated, virtually everyone can do some things with the opposite (nondominant) side of his/her body. However, there is usually a preference for one side, the dominant one. Laterality is a function of cerebral dominance. (See AMBIDEXTERITY; CEREBRAL DOMINANCE; LATERAL DOMINANCE; and LATERALITY.)

References: Edward C. Carterette and Morton P. Friedman (Editors), *Handbook of Perception,* New York: Academic Press, 1978; Marcel Kinsbourne (Editor), *Asymmetrical Functions of the Brain,* New York: Cambridge University Press, 1978; James L. McGaugh, *Behavioral Neuroscience: An Introduction,* New York: Academic Press, 1980.

MLA COOPERATIVE FOREIGN LANGUAGE TESTS, five tests that measure achievement in separate foreign languages: French, German, Italian, Russian, and Spanish. There are two levels of each test, one for those who have completed one to two years of high school or two semesters of college, and one for students who have completed

three to four years of high school or four semesters of college. Each test consists of four subtests: listening, speaking, reading, and writing. The MLA Cooperative Foreign Language Test is published by Educational Testing Service (Cooperative Tests and Services) in consultation with the Modern Language Association.

References: Oscar Buros (Editor), *The Seventh Mental Measurements Yearbook* (Volume I), Highland Park, NJ: The Gryphon Press, 1972; Rebecca M. Valette, *Modern Language Testing: A Handbook,* New York: Harcourt, Brace and World, Inc., 1967.

MNEMONIC DEVICE, an aid to memory. Complex data are simplified and made easier to remember through the use of such devices. Acronyms and memory crutches such as "thirty days hath September" or "place *i* before *e,* except after *c*" are examples of mnemonic devices. (See MEMORY.)

References: Walter Kintsch, *Memory and Cognition,* New York: John Wiley and Sons, 1977; Herbert Pollan and Gerald Greenberg, *Help Your Child to Remember,* New York: Citadel Press, 1965.

MOBILE, a sculpture in space that, when properly balanced, moves constantly if suspended in an area of circulating air. The mobile, in recent years, has become a respected art form. Oriental wood chimes are an example of mobiles.

The construction of mobiles has become a popular art experience in the schools, one that can be particularly successful at the upper elementary and secondary school levels. Mobiles can be constructed of natural materials exclusively (e.g. pine cones) or handcrafted items such as birds, fish, or butterflies that are made from materials such as paper, pipe cleaners, linoleum, and Christmas tree balls. Normally, thin wire is used as the mobile's skeletal structure. Working up from the bottom (to achieve balance), the natural or handcrafted materials are added. Once completed, mobiles may be suspended from wires that have been strung across the classroom or they may be hung directly from the ceiling.

References: John Harrell, *Basic Media in Education,* Winona, MN: St. Mary's College Press, 1974; Edward L. Mattil, *Meaning in Crafts* (Third Edition), Englewood Cliffs, NJ: Prentice-Hall, Inc., 1971; Ruth Perlmutter, *Construction Projects for Elementary Art,* West Nyack, NY: Parker Publishing Company, Inc., 1975.

MOBILITY AIDS, devices used by handicapped people to assist them in moving from place to place. Mobility aids may range from a simple wooden cane to a complex bus system designed to transport handicapped individuals. For example, there are mobility aids for amputees (e.g. molded propylene braces, direct skeletal attachment prostheses, artificial limbs, electronic wheelchairs) and for blind people (e.g. electronic canes, dog guides, obstacle detectors). With the development of computers and electronics, many more aids are being developed, offering more handicapped people greater mobility. Mobility aids have been devised for almost everyone who has a problem with movement. Many of the mobility aids are used by senior citizens who find that they are not as mobile as they would like to be.

With mainstreaming, more and more classes have children who use mobility aids. With these aids, individuals are able to lead highly productive and rewarding lives and can compete successfully both in school and in the greater society. (See MAINSTREAMING.)

References: Frank Boone, *Rehabilitating America*, New York: Harper and Row, Publishers, 1980; Joseph M. LaRocca and Jerry S. Turem, *The Application of Technological Developments to Physically Disabled People*, Washington, DC: Urban Institute, 1978; Orrin Marx, *Physical Activities for Handicapped Children in the Home*, Iowa City, IA: University Hospital School, 1972; Shirley Perlmutter (Editor), *Neuroanatomy and Neurophysiology Underlying Current Treatment Techniques for Sensorimotor Dysfunction*, Chicago: Center for Handicapped, 1975.

MODE, a statistical term used to denote the score that occurs most frequently in a distribution of scores. No formula is used to determine the mode; this is done by inspection. In this sample list of scores (99, 99, 96, 95, 95, 95, 92, 88, 84, 83, 83), the score "95" appears most frequently; hence it is the mode for this particular distribution. In some distributions, ties may exist (i.e. there may be two scores, each with the same frequency). Such distributions are referred to as being bimodal. (See CENTRAL TENDENCY MEASURES.)

References: George K. Cunningham, *Educational and Psychological Measurement*, New York: Macmillan Publishing Company, 1986; L. R. Gay, *Educational Research: Competencies for Analysis and Application* (Third Edition), Columbus, OH: Merrill Publishing Company, 1987.

MODELS, ANALYTIC, standards or representations used to explain, predict, and, at times, control a given phenomenon or situation. An analytic model is a mathematically and logically constructed system. There are definite principles, theorems, and axioms that are followed to develop analytic models. Data are usually used to verify an analytic model.

Models exist in many fields. Mathematics, biology, engineering, physics, economics, language, communications, sociology, and education are but a few of the areas. A teaching method may be based on a specific model of learning. The model of learning is, in turn, based on a theory of learning.

References: Jane Bridge, *Beginning Model Theory*, Oxford, England: Clarendon Press, 1977; Chen Chung Chang and H. J. Keisler, *Model Theory* (Second Edition), Amsterdam, Holland: North-Holland Publishing, 1977; Ralph D. Kopperman, *Model Theory and Its Application*, Boston: Allyn and Bacon, Inc., 1972.

MODERN FOREIGN LANGUAGES, those languages that are in use today and are taught as foreign languages. Spanish, French, German, Russian, and Chinese are examples of modern foreign languages taught in American schools.

Modern foreign languages were first offered in 18th- and 19th-century American schools, but their acceptance was slow. They were not considered to be as acceptable as the classical languages, notably Latin and Greek. Today, most students prefer to study the modern foreign languages. When first introduced in the schools, modern foreign languages were taught in the traditional manner of the classical languages. A variety of methods and approaches, including individualization, are used today. (See AURAL-ORAL APPROACH; DIRECT METHODS; and GRAMMAR-TRANSLATION METHOD.)

References: Jermaine D. Arendt, et al. (Editors), *Foreign Language Learning, Today and Tomorrow*, Elmsford, NY: Pergamon Press, Inc., 1979; Dale L. Lange, *Foreign Language Education: A Reappraisal*, Skokie, IL: National Textbook Company, 1972.

MODERN LANGUAGE APTITUDE TEST (MLAT), an aptitude test developed in 1958 by John B. Carroll and Stanley Sapon. It is used for placement and selection of modern language students, as well as for research. The test consists of several subtests: Phonetic Script, Words and Sentences, Paired Associates, Number Learning, and Spelling Clues. A score for each as well as a total score can be obtained. The MLAT is appropriate for students in grade 9 and above.

Another test, for grades 3 to 6, is titled the Modern Language Aptitude Test-Elementary (EMLAT). It is made up of four subtests: Hidden Words, Matching Words, Finding Rhymes, and Number Learning. Both the MLAT and the

EMLAT are published by the Psychological Corporation.

References: Oscar Buros (Editor), *Tests in Print II,* Highland Park, NJ: The Gryphon Press, 1974; Joseph Michel, *Foreign Language Teaching: An Anthology,* New York: The Macmillan Company, 1967.

MODERN LANGUAGE ASSOCIATION OF AMERICA (MLA), international organization of 30,000 teachers and others interested in English and the modern languages. MLA was founded in 1883. Its early activities focused on scholarship but have been broadened since to include the enrichment of teaching at all levels of instruction.

MLA's publications include: (1) *PMLA,* a quarterly journal; (2) *MLA International Bibliography,* a three-volume annual listing of books and articles published throughout the world on American and English literature, linguistics, and foreign literatures; (3) *MLA Directory of Periodicals,* published biennially; (4) the *MLA Newsletter;* and (5) numerous books and pamphlets dealing with research and/or teaching in languages and literatures.

Other service activities sponsored by MLA include: (1) an annual convention; (2) a Job Information Service; and (3) awards made to authors of outstanding books and articles in the language field. In addition, members benefit from departmental membership in MLA's Association of Departments of Foreign Languages (ADFL) and the Association of Departments of English (ADE).

MLA's headquarters is in New York City.

References: Modern Language Association, *MLA,* New York: The Association, Undated Brochure; Modern Language Association, *MLA Job Information Service,* New York: The Association, Undated Brochure.

MODERN MATHEMATICS—See NEW MATHEMATICS

MODULAR SCHEDULING, or variable class scheduling, an approach to flexible school program scheduling. Modular scheduling employs "modules" that are small units of time. These scheduling units can be of any length (e.g. 15 or 20 minutes each). Two and three modules may be used for scheduling regular, lecture-type classes with larger numbers of consecutive modules set aside for laboratory work or project-type activities. Modular scheduling was developed as an alternative to the traditional schedule that, in many secondary schools, consists of six to eight uniform, 40-, 45-, or 50-minute periods. Computer usage in

the schools has facilitated the use of modular scheduling.

References: Alexander M. Swaab, *School Administrator's Guide to Flexible Master Scheduling,* West Nyack, NY: Parker Publishing Company, Inc., 1974; W. Deane Wiley and Lloyd K. Bishop, *The Flexibly Scheduled High School,* West Nyack, NY: Parker Publishing Company, Inc., 1968.

MODULE, LEARNING—See LEARNING MODULE

MOEHLMAN, ARTHUR B. (August 10, 1889–May 2, 1952), prominent educational administrator. Before joining the University of Michigan as a Professor of Administration and Supervision (1925–51), he served as teacher, principal, and as Director of Statistics, Publications, and Administrative Research in Detroit. Moehlman authored numerous widely used books in his field, one of the better known being *School Administration* (first published in 1940). Others were: *Public Education in Detroit* (1925); *Public School Relations* (1927); and *Social Interpretations* (1938). In addition, he served as Editor of *Nation's Schools* (1932–48) and was President of The American Educational Research Association in 1929.

Reference: John F. Ohles, "Moehlman, Arthur Bernard" in John F. Ohles (Editor), *Biographical Dictionary of American Educators* (Volume 2), Westport, CT: Greenwood Press, 1978.

MONGOLISM—See DOWN'S SYNDROME

MONTESSORI, MARIA (August 31, 1870–May 6, 1952), first Italian woman to earn an M.D. degree and a pioneer in the study of intellectual development of young children. As a practicing doctor, she worked with "mental defectives." This experience and resulting interest prompted her to pursue pedagogy courses to serve them better. After serving as director of a medical-pedagogical school (which prepared teachers of the mentally retarded and emotionally disturbed), and while teaching at the University of Rome's Pedagogic School, Dr. Montessori was invited to establish Children's House in an impoverished section of Rome. This permitted her to test her ideas, methods, and instructional materials (didactic apparatus) with normal children. The school proved successful and other such schools later opened in Rome and other cities.

Montessori ideas were disseminated internationally via her writings and lectures. Educators from many countries came to observe her programs and to train with her. Before the United States entered World War I, almost 100 Montessori schools were operating in the United States.

Montessori's programs were criticized severely by numerous American educators concerned with her experimentation with discipline and in a book by Professor William Kilpatrick of Teachers College, Columbia University. These criticisms contributed to the post-World War I waning of American interest in Montessori schools. (It has been revived since 1960.)

The Association Montessori Internationale (AMI) was formed in 1929. It served as the worldwide parent organization for schools and societies bearing the Montessori name.

Montessori's significant publications were *The Montessori Method* (1912), *Pedagogical Anthropology* (1913), *The Secret of Childhood* (1936), *The Discovery of the Child* (1948), and *The Absorbent Mind* (1949). (See MONTESSORI METHOD.)

References: William Heard Kilpatrick, *The Montessori System Examined*, Boston: Houghton Mifflin Company, 1914; Rita Kramer, *Maria Montessori: A Biography*, New York: G. P. Putnam's Sons, 1976.

MONTESSORI METHOD, named after its originator, Dr. Maria Montessori. Originally developed to accommodate the learning needs of young mentally handicapped children, the method has been used with normal children as well. Features of the method include training of the senses using materials and exercises developed by Montessori. Instruction is highly individualized with students' activity choices limited to Montessori materials and exercises. Montessori teachers, required to complete special training in the Montessori method, are frequently called upon to observe learners rather than to interact with them.

Popularity of Montessori Schools and method has recently been renewed in the United States. (See MONTESSORI, MARIA.)

Reference: Maria Montessori, *The Montessori Method*, New York: Shocken Books, 1964 (Translated from Italian by Anne E. George; First Published in English in 1912).

MOONEY PROBLEM CHECK LIST, an instrument published by The Psychological Corporation that is designed to identify a student's (counselee's) expressed problems or areas of concern. Since items are not designed to elicit "right" or "wrong" answers, the check list is not a test in the traditional sense. Rather, it is a vehicle that permits an individual to communicate his/her perceived problems to a counselor.

The Mooney Problem Check List has four levels, with different forms available for each. The levels are: (1) junior high school; (2) senior high school; (3) college; and (4) adult. By underlining items included in the check list, respondents identify problems that trouble them in broad categories such as Home and Family, School or Occupation, Morals and Religion, and Sex. The check list, which takes approximately 30 minutes to complete, is easily scored. Its interpretation, however, should be undertaken by a trained counselor or psychologist.

References: Ross L. Mooney and Leonard V. Gordon, *The Mooney Problem Check Lists*, New York: The Psychological Corporation, 1950; Victor H. Noll and Dale P. Scannell, *Introduction to Educational Measurement* (Third Edition), Boston: Houghton Mifflin Company, 1972.

MORAL AND SPIRITUAL VALUES, the moral and value system that forms, or has been proposed as one broad basis for, American public schools. In the United States, moral and spiritual values of an educational nature are *not* identified with any particular religious group or dogma; rather, they are general and often defined operationally.

In 1951, the Educational Policies Commission of the National Education Association published a report titled *Moral and Spiritual Values in the Public Schools.* Ten major moral and spiritual values were identified and suggested as the aims or goals of education. Paraphrased, they were: (1) importance of the individual personality; (2) the individual is responsible for the consequences of his/her own conduct; (3) institutional organizations exist to serve people; (4) mutual consent rather than violence is required; (5) information and opinions liberate the human mind; (6) the highest level of mind, character, and creative ability development should be encouraged; (7) moral standards should be used uniformly when judging individuals; (8) brotherhood rather than self-interest should take precedence; (9) pursuit of individual happiness should be fostered as long as such pursuits do not interfere with the pursuit of happiness by others; and (10) emotional and spiritual experiences should be recognized as being more important than materialism. These recommended values were not universally accepted; in some quarters they generated considerable discussion and controversy.

In the 1970s, morals, values, and valuing were still controversial issues in the public schools. Value clarification, too, produced considerable disagreement. In some instances, they were challenged on philosophical grounds; in others, for legal reasons (i.e. separation of church and state). Given the controversy they generated, specific moral and spiritual values, goals, and aims for education have proven to be difficult, in some cases impossible to set forth explicitly. (See MORAL DEVELOPMENT; VALUES; and VALUES CLARIFICATION.)

References: J. Doyle Casteel and Robert J. Stahl, *Value Clarification in the Classroom*, Pacific Palisades, CA: Goodyear Publishing Company, Inc., 1975; Educational Policies Commission, *Moral and Spiritual Values in the Public Schools*, Washington, DC: National Education Association, 1951; Herbert H. Hyman and Charles R. Wright, *Education's Lasting Influences on Values*, Chicago: University of Chicago Press, 1979; Hugh Rosen, *The Development of Sociomoral Knowledge*, New York: Columbia University Press, 1980.

MORAL DEVELOPMENT, in psychology, stages through which one passes in the process of developing moral reasoning ability. There are two major developmental theories, one produced by Jean Piaget and the other by Lawrence Kohlberg.

Piaget's moral development theory parallels his cognitive states of development. Kohlberg suggested levels and stages of development such as: *preconventional* (Stages 1, 2); *conventional* (Stages 3, 4); and *postconventional,* or principled (Stages 5, 6).

Moral development is an area of concern for philosophers as well. Significant contributions have been made by Plato, Aristotle, Hobbes, Kant, Dewey, and Ross. (See PIAGET, JEAN.)

References: Ronald E. Galbraith and Thomas M. Jones, *Moral Reasoning: A Teaching Handbook for Adapting Kohlberg to the Classroom*, Minneapolis, MN: Greenhaven Press, 1976; Harry C. Jensen and Karen M. Hughston, *Responsibility and Morality: Helping Children Become Responsible and Morally Mature*, Provo, UT: Brigham Young University Press, 1979; Lawrence Kohlberg, "Moral States and Moralization," in Gilbert Geis, et al. (Editors), *Moral Development and Behavior: Theory, Research, and Social Issues*, New York: Holt, Rinehart and Winston, Inc., 1976; Nathaniel Lande and Afton Slade, *Stages: Understanding How You Make Your Moral Decisions*, San Francisco: Harper and Row, Publishers, 1979; Jean Piaget, *The Moral Judgment of the Child*, New York: The Free Press, 1965; Betty A. Sichel, *Moral Education: Character, Community, and Ideals*, Philadelphia: Temple University Press, 1988.

MORALE—See TEACHER MORALE

MORAL EDUCATION, incidental or formal instruction dealing with the rules of conduct or actions of a good-bad, right-wrong nature. In the United States, where religious instruction is not a part of the public school program, moral education is often taught as part of curriculum elements such as citizenship education, social studies, and character development. In countries where religious instruction is an integral component of the school curriculum (e.g. England), moral education is normally made a part thereof.

The literature on this subject contains no uniform, generally accepted definition of *morality.* Equally widespread are the suggestions relating to content, methodology, and goals of moral education instruction. Peter Scharf noted that there are essentially three prevailing (and contrasting) philosophies that illustrate the various approaches to moral education. The first, the *mechanistic* approach, stresses conformity to social expectations with rewards accruing from such conformity. The second philosophy, which he labels as the *romantic,* is consonant with the tenets held by individuals such as Jean Jacques Rousseau, Ivan Illich, and Rudolf Steiner. It essentially strives to protect the individual from a corrupt society, stressing free choice and natural expression. Values clarification, Scharf noted, falls within this approach. The final philosophy, the *dialectical,* has its roots in the writings of Socrates, Plato, Piaget, Kohlberg, and others. It urges rigorous scrutiny of premises as part of the search for truth, with dialectical inquiry the means used to arrive at such truth.

References: Muriel Downey and A. V. Kelly, *Moral Education: Theory and Practice*, London, England: Harper and Row, Publishers, 1978; Janice T. Gibson and Louis A. Chandler, *Educational Psychology: Mastering Principles and Applications*, Boston: Allyn and Bacon, 1988; Peter Scharf, *Moral Education*, Davis, CA: Responsible Action, 1978; Betty A. Sichel, *Moral Education: Character, Community, and Ideals*, Philadelphia: Temple University Press, 1988.

MORE EFFECTIVE SCHOOLS (MES), a New York City Public Schools plan, introduced in 1964, for providing ghetto schools with compensatory services. Sponsored collaboratively with the district's teachers' union and strongly supported by it, MES involved 21 heterogeneously grouped elementary schools whose class sizes were reduced and that received added dollar support for each child enrolled. Extra paraprofessional, counseling, and psychological services were provided. The overall impact of the MES effort was evaluated by the Center for Urban Education in 1967 with the conclusion that it had "made no significant difference in the functioning of children" (Owens and Steinhoff, p. 259). The MES model became an issue in the city's 1967 teacher strike. Numerous claims about the program's successes and failures were made during that period of emotional and political strife.

References: Gloria Channon, "The More Effective Schools," *The Urban Review,* February 1967; Robert G. Owens and Carl R. Steinhoff, "Strategies for Improving Inner-City Schools," *Phi Delta Kappan,* January 1969; David Rogers, *110 Livingston Street: Politics and Bureaucracy in the New York City Schools,* New York: Random House, 1968; Miriam Wasserman, *The School Fix, NYC, USA,* New York: Outerbridge and Dienstfrey, 1970.

MORPHEME, a reading term that refers to the smallest structural unit of meaning in any language. A word may consist of one morpheme (e.g. "taste," "play") or it may be made up of several morphemes (e.g. "distasteful," "player," "players").

The basic word, or morpheme, to which other morphemes are affixed is called a *free morpheme,* or root word. *Bound morphemes* are the affixes (including prefixes and suffixes) that, when connected to free morphemes, create new words having distinct meanings. In the following list of words, free morphemes have been italicized: dis*credit,* dis*credit*ed, *credit*or, pre*view,* pre*view*ers.

The specific meaning of morphemes that are homophones may be inferred when the morpheme is presented in a specific context (e.g. He *bit* the meat. The drill *bit* broke.). (See MORPHOLOGY.)

References: Jean Berko Gleason (Editor), *The Development of Language,* Columbus, OH: Charles E. Merrill Publishing Company, 1985; Daniel R. Hittleman, *Developmental Reading, K–8,* (Third Edition), Columbus, OH: Merrill Publishing Company, 1988.

MORPHOLOGY, the study of form and structure. In language, morphology is the study of word formation that includes inflection, derivations, and compounding. In its more restricted sense, morphology is the study of morphemes and their arrangements in forming words. Morphemes that form words or parts of words are included in the field of morphology. Examples of morphemes are *re, de, un, ish,* and *girl* in words such as *repeat, demand, until,* and *girlish.* A morpheme is the minimal meaningful unit that is part of the word or the word itself.

There is a branch of morphology in science that is concerned with the comparative nature of an organism in terms of form as opposed to function. Two such divergent areas of science that are included in morphology are: palynology (spores, pollen) and topographic features of the earth. (See MORPHEME.)

References: Jean Berko Gleason (Editor), *The Development of Language,* Columbus, OH: Charles E. Merrill Publishing Company, 1985; Daniel R. Hittleman, *Developmental Reading, K–8* (Third Edition), Columbus, OH: Merrill Publishing Company, 1988.

MORRILL ACT, federal legislation passed in 1862, sometimes referred to as the Land Grant College Act. Endowments of land (30,000 acres for each senator and representative) were granted to the states by the federal government. Proceeds from the sale of these lands were to be applied to the maintenance of at least one college offering "practical education." The act prescribed that the study of agriculture, mechanic arts, and military tactics was to supplement traditional "scientific and classical studies." A second Morrill Act, passed in 1890, made federal funds available to each land grant college on an annual basis. (See SECOND MORRILL ACT.)

References: Harry G. Good and James D. Teller, *A History of American Education* (Third Edition), New York: The Macmillan Company, 1973; Arthur B. Moehlman, *School Administration: Its Development, Principles, and Function in the United States* (Second Edition), Boston: Houghton Mifflin Company, 1951.

MORT, PAUL R. (February 21, 1894–May 12, 1962), national authority on the financing of public education. He, together with many of his graduate students at Teachers College, Columbia University (where he taught from 1922 to 1959), played a leadership role in studying and establishing cost-quality relationships in education. Many state legislatures sought his advice on the development of state equalization formulas for financing of education. Much of Mort's fieldwork was carried out in conjunction with the Metropolitan School Study Council, a university-school system study consortium that he helped to found.

Mort's books, including *Public School Finance* (1960), were frequently coauthored with his colleagues at Teachers College. In 1951, he served as President of the American Educational Research Association. (See METROPOLITAN SCHOOL STUDY COUNCIL.)

References: Kenneth J. Frasure, "Mort, Paul R." in John F. Ohles (Editor), *Biographical Dictionary of American Educators* (Volume 2), Westport, CT: Greenwood Press, 1978; Paul R. Mort and Walter C. Reusser, *Public School Finance: Its Background, Structure, and Operation* (Second Edition), New York: McGraw-Hill Book Company, 1951.

MOTIVATION, a psychological concept in human behavior that describes a predisposition toward a particular behavior to satisfy a specific need. Motivation is highly individualized. What drives one person to do something or to react in a particular way may not cause a comparable (or any) reaction in another person even though both may be exposed to identical stimuli or environmental conditions.

There are physiological (e.g. food, water, sleep, sex) and psychological (e.g. achievement, independence, acceptance, love, recognition) needs, as well as drives and goals, that contribute to motivation. Although there are several theories of motivation (e.g. satisfaction of needs, drive-reduction, stimulation, achievement, sensory deprivation), none is universally accepted. Motivation is a major contributor to learning. Consequently, authorities point out, teachers need to identify strategies that encourage motivation to learn within each child.

References: Samuel Bell (Editor), *Motivation in Education,* New York: Academic Press, 1977; Janice T. Gibson and Louis A. Chandler, *Educational Psychology: Mastering Principles and Applications,* Boston: Allyn and Bacon, 1988; Norman A. Sprinthall and Richard C. Sprinthall, *Educational Psychology: A Developmental Approach* (Fourth Edition), New York: Random House, 1987; Gene Stanford, *Activating the Passive Student,* Urbana, IL: National Council of Teachers of English, 1978; Raymond J. Wlodkowski, *Motivation and Teaching,* Washington, DC: National Education Association, 1978.

MOTIVATION-HYGIENE THEORY, a theory developed by Frederick Herzberg and his associates that deals with peoples' job attitudes and motivation. According to the theory, two separate sets of factors operate to influence one's job satisfaction-dissatisfaction. One set, the *dissatisfiers,* relates broadly to conditions of work. Included are variables such as salary, possibility of growth, interpersonal relations, status, supervision, working conditions, and job security. Dissatisfiers serve to meet the lower motivational (hygiene) needs of workers. When absent, job dissatisfaction results. Additionally, they are related to productivity, stability, and general adjustment of the workers. Significantly, the theorists go on to say, the presence of dissatisfiers does not necessarily contribute to worker motivation.

Satisfiers, the second set of factors, satisfy the individual's need for self-actualization and influence worker motivation. They consist of variables such as achievement, recognition, work itself, responsibility, and advancement. When present, satisfiers lead to increased worker performance.

The applicability of the Motivation-Hygiene Theory to education has been established by Thomas Sergiovanni.

References: Frederick Herzberg, et al., *Job Attitudes: Review of Research and Opinion,* Pittsburgh, PA: Psychological Service of Pittsburgh, 1957 (Reprinted in 1978 by University Microfilms International, Ann Arbor, MI); Frederick Herzberg, et al., *The Motivation to Work* (Second Edition), New York: John Wiley and Sons, 1959; Thomas J. Sergiovanni, "Factors Which Affect Satisfaction and Dissatisfaction in Teaching," *Journal of Educational Administration,* May 1967; Thomas J. Sergiovanni and Fred D. Carver, *The New School Executive: A Theory of Administration* (Second Edition), New York: Harper and Row, Publishers, 1980.

MOTIVATION THEORY—See MASLOW'S HIERARCHY OF NEEDS

MOTT FOUNDATION, a philanthropic organization founded in 1926. The foundation was established in Flint, Michigan, by Charles Stewart Mott, an automobile industry executive. Community self-improvement constitutes its principal area of interest. The rapid growth and wide acceptance of the community school concept has been attributed to early and continued support by the Mott Foundation. (See COMMUNITY EDUCATION.)

References: Charles Stewart Mott Foundation, *Foundation for Living,* Flint, MI: The Foundation, Undated; Clarence Young and William Quinn, *Foundation for Living: The Story of Charles Stewart Mott and Flint,* New York: McGraw-Hill Book Company, 1963.

MOVEMENT EDUCATION, or movement exploration, a physical education concept that attempts to help individuals understand the movements of which their bodies are capable. Faced with a physical problem, the learner perceives, ponders, and resolves it intellectually, then proceeds to overcome it physically. Increasingly difficult problems are presented as the student gains self-confidence and acquires new skills. Emphasis is placed on study of basic skills (e.g. running, crawling) in the context of phenomena such as body action, position, and hurling. With the advent of movement education, student self-motivation has begun to replace the traditional and highly structured physical education environment.

Movement education was established in England by Rudolf Laban, a German refugee. It was accepted widely in that country following World War II. In recent years, its popularity has increased in the United States.

References: Donald D. Arnheim and Robert A. Pestolesi, *Elementary Physical Education: A Developmental Approach*

(Second Edition), St. Louis, MO: The C. V. Mosby Company, 1978; Charles A. Bucher, *Foundations of Physical Education* (Fifth Edition), St. Louis, MO: C. V. Mosby Company, 1968; Reuben B. Frost, *Physical Education: Foundations, Practices, Principles,* Reading, MA: Addison-Wesley Publishing Company, 1975; Robert E. Gensemer, *Movement Education,* Washington, DC: National Education Association, 1979.

MULTIBASAL READING PROGRAM, a reading program that makes use of more than one (usually several) basal readers at each grade level, K–6 or K–8. Corresponding workbooks are frequently used as supplements, along with other instructional materials such as games and word cards.
Reference: Grayce A. Ransom, *Preparing to Teach Reading,* Boston: Little, Brown and Company, 1978.

MULTICULTURAL EDUCATION, curricula designed to recognize the integrity, contributions, strengths, and viability of different cultural, language, and social groups in a society. Such programs help students, from all groups, to understand and accept others as equals. They also help students, particularly those from different cultural, social, or language groups, to adjust to the demands of a modern pluralistic society.

Multicultural education should not be confused with Ethnic Studies. Ethnic Studies focus on the history, social structure, differences, contributions, and so forth of a particular group (e.g. the Polish-Americans, blacks, Africans, Mexican-Americans, Cubans, Chinese, Japanese, American Indians, and Jews). Multicultural education, on the other hand, deals with the understandings, acceptances, knowledges, contributions (historical/present), problems, concerns, values, and barriers (language, prejudices, social, economic) of the many subcultures found in a country. These programs also help students to develop skills and coping mechanisms to become self-sufficient in the present as well as meeting the requirements of the future. In the opinion of some, multicultural education should be made a part of the entire educational program rather than consisting of just a few limited experiences and/or courses (such as Ethnic Studies or bilingual courses). This broad perception prompts many to speak of "education that is multicultural" rather than multicultural education.

Although multicultural education received financial support and encouragement from the United States Government through the Elementary and Secondary Education Act, Civil Rights Act, and other laws of the 1960s, multicultural education is not new. Nor is it unique to American systems. England and Israel have had such programs for many years. (See ACCULTURATION.)
References: Dolores E. Cross, et al., *Teaching in a Multicultural Society,* New York: The Free Press, 1977; Hilda Hernandez, *Multicultural Education: A Teacher's Guide to Content and Process,* Columbus, OH: Merrill Publishing Company, 1989; Manuel Ramirex III and Alfredo Castaneda, *Cultural Democracy: Bicognitive Development and Education,* New York: Academic Press, 1974; Pamela L. Tiedt and Iris M. Tiedt, *Multicultural Teaching: A Handbook of Activities, Information, and Resources* (Second Edition), Boston: Allyn and Bacon, Inc., 1986.

MULTIHANDICAPPED, or multiple handicapped, an individual who has two or more conditions that are classified as being handicapping and that thwart learning and/or participation in the regular classroom. Because of better medical care, the incidence of multiple-handicapped children surviving birth has increased. The incidence of the multiple handicapped in the general population has increased as a consequence. Handicaps may be congenital or acquired from diseases or accidents.

Some examples of multihandicapped conditions are: cerebral palsy (CP)-mental retardation, CP-hearing impaired, CP-speech defects, mentally retarded-deaf, deaf-blind, and blind-speech. Multiple handicapped students pose a complex problem for regular and special education teachers not only in terms of learning and movement, but also in terms of management. Educational programs providing special services are available in many school districts, these designed to meet the special physical, educational, and psychological needs of such children.
References: William L. Heward and Michael D. Orlansky, *Exceptional Children: An Introductory Survey of Special Education,* Columbus, OH: Merrill Publishing Company, 1988; Frank J. Menolascino, et al., *Beyond the Limits,* Seattle, WA: Special Child Publications, 1974; David A. Sabatino and Ted L. Miller (Editors), *Describing Learner Characteristics of Handicapped Children and Youth,* New York: Grune and Stratton, 1979; James M. Wolf and Robert M. Anderson, *The Multiple Handicapped Child,* Springfield, IL: Charles C. Thomas, Publisher, 1969.

MULTIMEDIA INSTRUCTION, the combining of two or more types of media to form a new learning package. John Haney and Eldon Ullmer indicate that the term *multimedia* may apply to any or all of three presentational forms. The first involves the concurrent use of two audio-visual devices (e.g. tape recorder and slide projector.) The second entails the use of separate devices that the teacher and/or students use sequentially as a particular topic is studied (e.g. displaying a plaster of paris model, followed by use of a filmstrip, followed by the showing of a 16 mm. sound film). The final form, most difficult of the three to prepare, requires the projection of several simultaneous images using numerous screens and different types of projection media (usually slides and motion pictures) to fill all areas of a viewer's peripheral vision.

Commercially prepared multimedia kits, designed for self-instruction, are available in numerous subject fields. They typically include items such as instruction booklets, self-tests, slides, recordings, and filmstrips that students, working at their own rates, utilize under the general supervision of the teacher.

References: John B. Haney and Eldon J. Ullmer, *Educational Media and Teacher*, Dubuque, IA: Wm. C. Brown Company, Publishers, 1970; Robert Heinich, Michael Molenda, and James D. Russell, *Instructional Media and the New Technologies of Instruction* (Second Edition), New York: John Wiley and Sons, 1985; Jerrold E. Kemp and Don C. Smellie, *Planning, Producing and Using Instructional Media* (Sixth Edition), New York: Harper and Row Publishers, 1989.

MULTIPLE-CHOICE ITEM, a test question that consists of a stem and three or more possible answers from which the student chooses the best answer to complete a statement or to solve a problem. Many authorities consider this type of question to be effective; for this reason, it is popular among those who construct standardized tests.

The multiple-choice test enjoys several advantages: (1) it can be used to test virtually all kinds of subject matter; (2) scoring is easy, readily adapted to machine scoring by use of a separate answer sheet; (3) it can be used to measure instructional objectives at all levels of the cognitive domain; and (4) numerous questions can be answered in a relatively short period. Like all tests, the multiple-choice type also has some weaknesses, the principal one being the difficulty of preparing good test items.

References: Tom Kubiszyn and Gary Borich, *Educational Testing and Measurement: Classroom Application and Practice* (Second Edition), Glenview, IL: Scott Foresman and Company, 1987; Jon C. Marshall and Loyde W. Hales, *Classroom Test Construction*, Reading, MA: Addison-Wesley Publishing Company, 1971; Fred M. Smith and Sam Adams, *Educational Measurement for the Classroom Teacher* (Second Edition), New York: Harper and Row, Publishers, 1972.

MULTIPLE INTELLIGENCE THEORY (MI THEORY), a theory of intelligence that has its base in the biological regions of individual problem-solving skills. The theory deals with skills that are found universally in humans, although MI theory recognizes that individual culture effects the manifestation of problem solving skills in a given society. Since it is neurally based, each intelligence comes into play as a result of internally and externally presented information. Figures/shapes/pictures, language (oral and written), and mathematics, although culturally derived or manifested for most humans, exist as capacities within all humans; therefore, they are included in the theory. An adult will use and amalgamate several of the intelligences; these intelligences rarely operate in isolation or singularly. The seven intelligences that make up the multiple intelligences theory are: musical, bodily kinesthetic, logical-mathematical, linguistic, spatial, interpersonal and intrapersonal. (See BODILY-KINESTHETIC INTELLIGENCE; INTELLIGENCE; INTERPERSONAL INTELLIGENCE; INTRAPERSONAL INTELLIGENCE; LINGUISTIC INTELLIGENCE; LOGICAL-MATHEMATICAL INTELLIGENCE; MUSICAL INTELLIGENCE; and SPATIAL INTELLIGENCE.)

References: Howard Gardner, *Frames of Mind*, New York: Basic Books, 1976; Michael P. Grady and Emily Luecke, *Education and the Brain*, Bloomington, IN: Phi Delta Kappa, 1978; Joseph Walters and Howard Gardner, "Crystallizing Experiences: Discovering an Intellectual Gift" in R. Sternbery and J. Davidson (Editors), *Studies in Giftedness*, Cambridge: Cambridge University Press, 1984; Joseph Walters, and Howard Gardner, "The Development and Education of the Intelligences" in F. R. Link (Editor), *Essays on the Intellect*, Alexandria, VA: Association for Supervision and Curriculum Development, 1986.

MULTIPLE SCLEROSIS (MS), a disease with no known cure that attacks the nerves of the central nervous system by destroying a fatty protective tissue (myelin) in the spinal cord and leaving scar tissue (sclerotic). Sensory impairment is the most common symptom. However, as the disease progresses, other symptoms appear including vision problems, uncontrollable jerking, staggering, and speech impairment. The disease is a crippler but it is not classified as terminal per se.

Multiple sclerosis symptoms may go into remission for a period of years. The disease will not have disappeared, however, and the symptoms will return. Emotions play a major role in MS, particularly as the disease goes in and out of remission. MS attacks all groups and social classes, normally striking those between the ages of 20 and 40.

References: June L. Bigge, *Teaching Individuals with Physical and Multiple Disabilities,* Columbus, OH: Charles E. Merrill Publishing Company, 1976; E. E. Bleck and Donald A. Nagel (Editors), *Physically Handicapped Children: A Medical Atlas for Teachers,* New York: Grune and Stratton, 1975; Julian S. Myers (Editor), *Orientation to Chronic Disease and Disability,* New York: Macmillan Book Company, 1965; Jules Saltman, *Multiple Sclerosis: New Hope in an Old Mystery,* New York: Public Affairs Committee, 1962.

MULTIVERSITY, a term used to describe an organizationally large university with numerous identifiable component units such as schools, colleges, campuses, and/or centers. It is most commonly used when referring to: (1) a large university made up of relatively autonomous institutions (e.g. City University of New York, University of California), or (2) a university that has a main campus and several satellite (branch) campuses. Coining of the term *multiversity* has been attributed to Clark Kerr, one-time President of the University of California.

References: Clark Kerr, *The Uses of the University,* Cambridge, MA: Harvard University Press, 1963; Asa S. Knowles (Editor), *The International Encyclopedia of Higher Education* (Volume 1), San Francisco: Jossey-Bass Publishers, 1977; G. Terry Page and J. B. Thomas, *International Dictionary of Education,* London, England: Kogan Page Ltd., 1977; Nicholas von Hoffman, *The Multiversity: A Personal Report on What Happens to Today's Students at American Universities,* New York: Holt, Rinehart and Winston, Inc., 1966.

MUSCULAR DYSTROPHY (MD), a disease that attacks and deteriorates the voluntary muscles of the body. There are three main types of MD: (1) that which usually attacks a child between the ages of 2 and 5; (2) that which attacks adolescents; and (3) that which affects adults (usually between ages 30 and 50). The first type attacks the calf muscles and the wasting muscles swell with fatty deposits (35 percent of the cases are hereditary). The adolescent MD first attacks the face muscles, shoulders, and upper arms (heredity is a factor here as well). MD that affects adults begins in the shoulders and/or pelvic girdle. Muscle wasting also results in the latter two types of cases.

Although the patient suffers no pain from MD, he or she becomes helpless from the disease. It is usually the complications caused by MD that cause death. It is rare for an early-affected MD victim to survive his/her adolescence.

References: June L. Bigge, *Teaching Individuals with Physical and Multiple Disabilities,* Columbus, OH: Charles E. Merrill Publishing Company, 1976; E. E. Bleck and Donald A. Nagel (Editors), *Physically Handicapped Children: A Medical Atlas for Teachers,* New York: Grune and Stratton, 1975; Frank R. Ford, *Diseases of the Nervous System* (Sixth Edition), Springfield, IL: Charles C. Thomas, Publisher, 1973; Joan K. McMichael, *Handicap,* Pittsburgh, PA: University of Pittsburgh Press, 1971; William L. Nyhan and Edward Edelson, *The Heredity Factor,* New York: Grosset and Dunlap, Publishers, 1976.

MUSICAL APTITUDE, or musicality, the abilities and capacities needed for musical achievement. The term *musical aptitude* is frequently used interchangeably with *musical talent.* In the literature of music education, various definitions are used to describe musical potential. Some authors are inclined to distinguish *ability* from *aptitude,* suggesting that the term *ability* includes *achievement* but *aptitude* does not. Most appear willing to settle for an operational definition that normally reflects scores on one or more tests of musical aptitude (sometimes coupled with teacher judgment).

Carl E. Seashore was a pioneer in the area of musical aptitude testing. Current editions of the Seashore Measures of Musical Talents (first published in 1919) comprise six testing components: pitch, rhythm, time, timbre, loudness, and tonal memory. Among the other standardized tests of musical aptitude available to the music teacher are The Wing Standardized Test of Musical Intelligence, The (Gaston) Test of Musicality, and The (Gordon) Musical Aptitude Profile. (See WING STANDARDIZED TESTS OF MUSICAL INTELLIGENCE.)

References: Richard Colwell, *The Evaluation of Music Teaching and Learning,* Englewood Cliffs, NJ: Prentice-Hall, Inc., 1970; Charles R. Hoffer, *Teaching Music in the Secondary Schools* (Second Edition), Belmont, CA: Wadsworth Publishing Company, Inc., 1973; Paul R. Lehman, *Tests and Measurements in Music,* Englewood Cliffs, NJ: Prentice-Hall, Inc., 1968; Herbert Wing, *Tests of Musical Ability and Appreciation* (Second Edition), Cambridge, England: Cambridge University Press, 1968.

MUSICAL INTELLIGENCE, one of the seven biologically based intelligences found in the Multiple Intelligence Theory (MI Theory). This intelligence is found in all humans, since music is found in all cultures—although it may be produced and/or manifested differently. The presence of high levels of musical abilities or talents in some very young children would indicate that such abilities or talents have a biological, rather than a totally learned, base. Musical intelligence often works in consort with one or more of the other intelligences included in the Multiple Intelligence Theory. The playing of an instrument requires not only the perception of sound but its production through bodily movement and the reading of symbols. (See BODILY-KINESTHETIC INTELLIGENCE; INTELLIGENCE; INTERPERSONAL INTELLIGENCE; INTRAPERSONAL INTELLIGENCE; LINGUISTIC INTELLIGENCE; MULTIPLE INTELLIGENCE THEORY; and SPATIAL INTELLIGENCE.)

References: Howard Gardner, *Frames of Mind*, New York: Basic Books, 1976; Joseph Walter and Howard Gardner, "The Development and Education of Intelligences" in F. R. Link (Editor), *Essays on the Intellect*, Alexandria, VA: Association for Supervision and Curriculum Development, 1986.

MUSIC CAMP—See SUMMER MUSIC CAMP

MUSIC EDUCATION, comprehensive school curriculum/process offering a broad variety of music instruction. Frequently taught by specialist teachers of music, particularly in larger schools, music education includes listening and performance activities; composing is also encouraged in many cases.

Music education was first instituted in Boston schools by Lowell Mason (1838). It was subsequently adopted by virtually all other school systems. Early programs emphasized singing and the reading of music. Currently, music is accepted as an academic discipline that seeks to develop the talents of the musically gifted as well as understanding and aesthetic responsiveness of all students.

General goals for music programs include helping the student to: (1) develop skill in music (including listening and performance); (2) become an intelligent critic of major types of serious music; (3) acquire knowledge of music (i.e. history of music, form and design); and (4) recognize music as an international language and vehicle of international goodwill. (See MASON, LOWELL and MUSIC EDUCATORS NATIONAL CONFERENCE.)

References: Malcolm E. Bessom, et al., *Teaching Music in Today's Secondary Schools: A Creative Approach to Contemporary Music Education*, New York: Holt, Rinehart and Winston, Inc., 1974; William J. Ellena, *Curriculum Handbook for School Executives*, Arlington, VA: American Association of School Administrators, 1973; Music Educators National Conference, "Goals and Objectives for Music Education," *Music Educators Journal*, December 1970; Robert E. Nye and Vernice T. Nye, *Music in the Elementary School* (Fourth Edition), Englewood Cliffs, NJ: Prentice-Hall, Inc., 1977.

MUSIC EDUCATORS NATIONAL CONFERENCE (MENC), a national organization of music educators. An estimated 65,000 music educators working in schools, colleges, and universities belong to the organization. Headquartered in Reston, Virginia, MENC provides its members with numerous services. Books, brochures, and audiovisuals are prepared and made available on a low-cost basis.

MENC's national conventions are conducted in even-numbered years. In odd-numbered years, division conventions are held. Fifty affiliate state units help to carry out the business of the organization. MENC's official publication is the *Music Educators Journal*, published nine times annually (September–May). Other periodicals are a quarterly, the *Journal of Research in Music Education* and a newsletter, *Music Power*.

References: Music Educators National Conference, *Information Sheet*, Reston, VA: The Conference, April 1979; Music Educators National Conference, *MENC: Dedicated to the Advancement of Music Education*, Reston, VA: The Conference, Undated Brochure.

MUSIC, INSTRUMENTAL—See INSTRUMENTAL MUSIC

MUSICOLOGY, the scholarly study of musical composition and its history. Paul Pisk stated: "(T)he appropriate definition of musicology would be the investigation of music, its structure, tradition, and style" (p. 1467). Vincent Duckles and his colleagues noted that there are two principal viewpoints regarding the definition of "musicology," one that sees it as a *scholarly method*, the other perceiving it as an *area of knowledge*.

References: Gilbert Chase, "Musicology, History, and Anthropology: Current Thoughts" in John W. Grubbs (Editor), *Current Thought in Musicology*, Austin, TX: University of Texas Press, 1976; Vincent Duckles, et al., "Musicology" in Stanley Sadie (Editor), *The New Grove Dictionary of Music and Musicians* (Volume 12), London, England: Macmillan Publishers Limited, 1980; Paul A. Pisk, "Musicology" in Bruce Bohle (Editor), *The Interna-*

tional Cyclopedia of Music and Musicians (Tenth Edition), New York: Dodd, Mead and Company, 1975.

MYOPIA, or near-sightedness, a visual impairment caused by failure of the eye to focus normally. Distant objects appear blurred; near objects are seen clearly. Myopic children constitute the largest group of partially seeing school pupils. In classrooms, they frequently have difficulty seeing the board or reading other than large print materials. Eyeglasses with concave lenses are used to correct this impairment.

Reference: Randall K. Harley and G. Allen Lawrence, *Visual Impairment in the Schools,* Springfield, IL: Charles C. Thomas, Publisher, 1977.

NARCOTICS, a family of drugs that includes opium, morphine, heroin, codeine, as well as non-opiate synthetic drugs (e.g. methadone, meperidine). Narcotics act primarily on the central nervous system and are effective and powerful.

Narcotics are used in medicine and have been used to relieve pain, as a tranquilizer, and in cough medicine. However, narcotics are addictive and therefore dangerous. Excessive use of narcotics can lead to death, comas, respiratory problems, and many other physical and emotional complications. For this reason, most schools have drug-abuse programs in their curricula to educate children and teenagers about the dangers of narcotics.

Although narcotics abuse became a major problem in the schools during the 1960s, their appearance is not recent. They were sold openly in drugstores and in grocery and general stores and were prescribed freely by physicians during the 1800s in the United States. Many patent medicines contained narcotics during the 1800s. (See DRUG; DRUG ABUSE; and DRUG-ABUSE EDUCATION.)

References: Barry Brown, *Addicts and Aftercare,* Beverly Hills, CA: Sage Publications, Inc., 1979; Sidney Cohen, *The Drug Dilemma* (Second Edition), New York: McGraw-Hill Book Company, 1976; The Drug Abuse Council, *The Facts about "Drug Abuse,"* New York: The Free Press, 1980; Vincent P. Zarcone, *Drug Addicts in a Therapeutic Community,* Baltimore, MD: York Press, 1975.

NASAL, a voice quality involving unusual resonance such as, but not limited to, that found in cleft-palate speech. The nasal passage, used for intake of air, also contributes to sound production. Although the size and shape of the nasal passage cannot easily be altered or modified, they do influence the vocal tract system by either the soft palate hanging in a down position or being retracted (raised). The nature of the soft palate movement contributes to the characteristics of the voice through nasal resonance. Some voice disorders can be caused by malfunctioning of the soft palate or by an obstruction to the nasal cavities. Such disorders are called denasality (i.e. problems producing the nasal consonants).

References: William A. Ainsworth, *Mechanisms of Speech Recognition,* New York: Pergamon Press, Inc., 1976; Peggy Dalton and W. J. Hardcastle, *Disorders of Fluency and Their Effects on Communication,* London, England: E. Arnold, Ltd., 1977; Wendell Johnson and Dorothy

Moeller, *Speech Handicapped School Children* (Third Edition), New York: Harper and Row, Publishers, 1967; Leija McReynolds and Deedra L. Engmann, *Distinctive Feature Analysis of Misarticulation,* Baltimore, MD: University Park Press, 1975.

NATIONAL ACADEMY FOR SCHOOL EXECUTIVES (NASE), a unit within the American Association of School Administrators that sponsors various inservice programs of interest to educational administrators (e.g. collective bargaining). They are available to AASA members at reduced rates and are offered in different parts of the country. First introduced in 1969, NASE programs consist of seminars and institutes as well as Contract Programs (programs designed to meet the special needs of a single school system or agency). In recent years, NASE programs, collectively, have been atracting over 3,000 participants annually. (See AMERICAN ASSOCIATION OF SCHOOL ADMINISTRATORS.)

References: American Association of School Administrators, *Annual Report,* Arlington, VA: The Association, 1980; *The School Administrator,* April 1980.

NATIONAL ACADEMY OF EDUCATION, an independent group of schools and distinguished educators. All members of the Academy are elected in recognition of their contributions to the field of education (not all members of the academy are university professors). The academy has from time to time been asked by the United States government to comment on significant educational issues and to provide in-depth reports and reviews. One of the most recent reports was written by Lamar Alexander and H. Thomas James. This report focused on the National Assessment of Educational Progress (NAEP). The National Academy of Education is presently located at the Harvard Graduate School of Education in Cambridge, Massachusetts. (See NATIONAL ASSESSMENT OF EDUCATIONAL PROGRESS.)

Reference: National Academy of Education, *The Nation's Report Card, Improving the Assessment of Student Achievement,* Cambridge, MA: The Academy, 1987.

NATIONAL ADVISORY COUNCIL ON INDIAN EDUCATION (NACIE), a 15-member committee charged with the responsibility of advising Congress and the Commissioner (now Secretary)

of Education on programs in which Indian children and adults participate. NACIE is appointed by the President of the United States: its members are Indians and Alaskan natives. The committee was formed on June 23, 1972, in compliance with Public Law 92–318.

References: National Advisory Council on Indian Education, *Indian Education is "Sui Generis": Of Its Own Kind* (Sixth Annual Report to the Congress of the United States), Washington, DC: The Association, June 1979; Public Law 92–318, *United States Statutes at Large, 1972* (Volume 86), Washington, DC: U.S. Government Printing office, 1973.

NATIONAL ALLIANCE OF BLACK SCHOOL EDUCATORS, INC. (NABSE), an organization of black teachers and administrators. When founded in 1970, the organization was known as the National Alliance of Black School Superintendents (NABSS), and its membership was limited to black school superintendents. In 1973, membership qualifications were broadened to include all individuals directly or indirectly involved in education. As a consequence of this move, the alliance, in 1980, was organized into seven commissions: (1) Policy Development in Public Education Commission; (2) District Administration Commission, for central administration personnel; (3) Local School Administration Commission, for school building leaders (e.g. principals); (4) Instruction and Instructional Support Commission; (5) Higher Education Commission; (6) Special Project Administration Commission; and (7) Program Development, Research and Evaluation Commission.

NABSE members may avail themselves of several services offered by the organization. They include: (1) receiving *NABSE Quarterly*, the alliance's official journal; (2) participation in annual conferences; (3) participation in NABSE's national "Black Educator's Data Bank"; (4) participation in programs to eliminate racism in education; and (5) receiving notices of various job opportunities.

NABSE's headquarters is in Washington, D.C.

References: The National Alliance of Black School Educators, *NABSE* (A Brochure), Washington, DC: The Alliance, 1980; *NABSE Quarterly*, Fall 1980.

NATIONAL ART EDUCATION ASSOCIATION (NAEA), "an organization devoted to the advancement of the professional interests and competence of those teaching art at all educational levels" (unpaginated brochure). NAEA was founded in 1947 when four regional associations agreed to consolidate to form the larger national association.

Publications produced by NAEA include four periodicals: *Art Education*, published eight times each year; *Studies in Art Education*, a report on significant research, published three times annually; *Art Teacher*, a journal for elementary and secondary teachers of art; and a newsletter, *NAEA Newsletter*. Additionally, the association publishes books, pamphlets, and related materials of interest to its membership.

NAEA's main office is in Reston, Virginia. The national office works closely with affiliated associations located in each of the 50 states. The NAEA States Assembly, with representatives from each state, establishes policies and plans.

Reference: National Art Education Association, *Publications*, Reston, VA: The Association (Brochure), 1979.

NATIONAL ASSESSMENT OF EDUCATIONAL PROGRESS (NAEP), an information-gathering project that tests a nationally representative sample of children, ages 9, 13, and 17 (grades 3, 7, and 11) every two years. Some young adults are surveyed, too. NAEP has been refunded under Public Law 98–511, Section 405(e), 1984; it received 4 million dollars from the U.S. government for 1986.

Achievement is assessed, and national trends identified in the following areas of learning: reading, writing, literacy, mathematics, science, technology (computer competence), history, geography, civics, music, art, literature, and occupational attitudes. Not all learning areas are tested in each year of the assessment. NAEP was started in 1969–70 and originally was contracted to the Education Commission of the States by the National Center for Education Statistics. Presently, the Educational Testing Service of Princeton, N.J., has the NAEP contract.

A review of the structure, design, and directions of NAEP was undertaken by a study group of the National Academy of Education as requested by U.S. Secretary of Education William J. Bennett in 1986. A report, titled *The Nation's Report Card*, suggested changes and expansion of NAEP. It was suggested that the transition grades, 3, 4, 8, and 12 be assessed rather than those presently assessed, and that more assessment information at the state and local levels be provided. The creation of an Educational Assessment Council, add-on assessments at the state and local levels, and the assessment of private school students were also among the suggestions made by the study group. The study group was chaired by Lamar Alexander, governor of Tennessee, and H. Thomas James, president emeritus of the Spencer Foundation. (See EDUCATION COMMISSION OF THE STATES and NATIONAL CENTER FOR EDUCATION STATISTICS.)

References: Lamar Alexander and H. Thomas James, *The Nation's Report Card,* Cambridge, MA: National Academy of Education, 1987; Department of Elementary School Principals, National Education Association, *National Assessment of Educational Progress: Some Questions and Comments* (Revised), Washington, DC: The Association, 1968.

NATIONAL ASSOCIATION FOR PUBLIC CONTINUING AND ADULT EDUCATION (NAPCAE),

a national organization of approximately 6,000 adult educators. Its principal purpose is to give leadership to, and to support implementation of, public continuing and adult education programs. Organized in 1952, NAPCAE has 7 national, 1 regional, and 33 state affiliates.

The association provides numerous services to its members. Information is imparted through three regular publications: *Pulse,* published six times annually; *Techniques,* also published six times a year; and *NAPCAE Exchange,* appearing three times annually; and through numerous special publications that suggest practical ideas to members. As part of its legislative program, NAPCAE works closely with state and federal legislators concerning adult education legislation. The services of program consultants are made available through a special consultant network. An annual conference, held each fall, and more frequent workshops are also sponsored each year.

NAPCAE's main office is in Washington, D.C.

References: National Association for Public Continuing and Adult Education, *Membership Information: Current Publications,* Washington, DC: The Association, Undated Brochure; Nancy Yakes and Denise Akey (Coeditors), *Encyclopedia of Associations* (Fourteenth Edition), Detroit: Gale Research Company, 1980.

NATIONAL ASSOCIATION FOR THE ADVANCEMENT OF COLORED PEOPLE (NAACP),

an organization formed by black and white citizens (1909) to obtain racial justice for all Americans. Currently, the work of the association is being carried out by approximately 1,700 branches located throughout the United States, West Germany, and other parts of the world. Total individual memberships exceed 400,000.

NAACP has sought to eliminate racial discrimination through the ballot box, the courts, and by influencing public opinion. Among its several ef-

forts to correct injustices have been: (1) efforts to have civil rights laws enacted (e.g. Civil Rights Acts of 1957, 1960, 1964, 1965, and 1968); (2) helping to pass the 1968 Open Housing Act; (3) prison reform programs; (4) school desegregation efforts (e.g. *Brown v. Board of Education of Topeka*); (5) achieving military justice for black servicemen; and (6) elimination of job discrimination based on racist personnel practices. NAACP activities directly related to education have included efforts to eliminate racial stereotypes in textbooks, challenging the validity of certain standardized tests, and encouraging young black people to remain in school.

Crisis, the oldest black magazine in the United States, is published by NAACP and boasts a readership of 250,000.

References: National Association for the Advancement of Colored People, *National Association for the Advancement of Colored People: Its Story, Its Program and Objectives,* New York: The Association, Undated Brochure; National Association for the Advancement of Colored People, *Update,* New York: The Association, Winter 1978; Mary White Ovington, *How the National Association for the Advancement of Colored People Began,* New York: The Association, 1914, Undated Reprint; Harry A. Ploski and Warren Marr II (Editors), *The Negro Almanac: A Reference Work on the Afro-American* (Third Edition), New York: The Bellwether Company, 1976; Lubomyr R. Wynar, *Encyclopedic Directory of Ethnic Organizations in the United States,* Littleton, CO: Libraries Unlimited, Inc., 1975.

NATIONAL ASSOCIATION FOR THE EDUCATION OF YOUNG CHILDREN (NAEYC),

a professional organization whose principal objectives are "to serve and act on behalf of the needs and rights of young children, with focus on the provision of educational services and resources to adults who work with and for children" (*Books, etc.,* p. 2). NAEYC was founded in 1926, growing out of a small group of nursery school advocates calling themselves the Committee on Nursery Schools. For several years it was known as the National Association for Nursery Education. Current membership includes 31,000 individuals interested in various facets of early childhood education.

NAEYC's journal, available to all members, is *Young Children* (known earlier as the *NANE Bulletin,* later as the *Journal of Nursery Education*). Other services available to members include books of interest to early childhood educators, an annual conference, and information services covering a broad range of subjects. NAEYC also remains in close contact with federal officials and legislators on matters of interest to its membership.

Over 200 affiliate groups operating at local and state levels are a part of the national association. NAEYC's headquarters staff is in Washington, D.C.

References: "NAEYC's First Half Century, 1926-1976," *Young Children,* September 1976; National Association for the Education of Young Children, *Books, etc.,* Washington, DC: The Association, 1979-80; National Association for the Education of Young Children, *NAEYC Annual Conference,* Washington, DC: The Association, 1980.

NATIONAL ASSOCIATION FOR WOMEN DEANS, ADMINISTRATORS, AND COUNSELORS (NAWDAC), professional organization seeking to improve educational opportunities and services for women and girls at all educational levels. Formed in 1916, NAWDAC's present membership roll exceeds 2,200. Its annual conference brings together professional women educators who work together to implement the goals of the association. These purposes are also carried out through regional workshops and the efforts of the organization's 30 state associations.

NAWDAC publishes the *Journal of NAWDAC,* a quarterly, plus numerous monographs of interest to its members. The organization sponsors a limited number of internships. The Ruth Strang Research Award, an annual award, is used to encourage research excellence, especially among new professionals. NAWDAC supports federal legislation intended to bring about the fair treatment of women. Members are entitled to join one of NAWDAC's six sections: (1) Elementary, Middle and Junior High School Section; (2) High School Section; (3) Community and Junior College Section; (4) College Section; (5) University Section; and, (6) Continuing Education Section. The organization's main offices are in Washington, D.C. (See STRANG, RUTH M.)

Reference: National Association for Women Deans, Administrators, and Counselors, *The Power of a Professional Experience . . . NAWDAC,* Washington, DC: The Association, Undated Brochure.

NATIONAL ASSOCIATION OF BIOLOGY TEACHERS (NABT), formed in 1938, the sole organization in the United States specifically devoted to helping teachers with the improvement of biology teaching. NABT works to encourage regional activities for teachers of biology, to address issues that involve biology, and to serve as the membership's official voice at the national level.

The association's service activities for members include: (1) sponsorship of an annual national con-

vention; (2) publication of two periodicals, *The American Biology Teacher,* appearing nine times each year, and *News and Views,* the association's bimonthly newsletter; (3) conducting specific topic seminars designed to increase and update teachers' knowledge base; and (4) sponsorship (since 1962) of the Outstanding Biology Teacher Award, which recognizes outstanding biology teachers in every state and Puerto Rico.

NABT's headquarters is in Reston, Virginia.

References: National Association of Biology Teachers, *Profile of the National Association of Biology Teachers,* Reston, VA: The Association. Undated Flier; National Association of Biology Teachers, *Outstanding Biology Teacher Award* (Brochure), Reston, VA: The Association, 1980.

NATIONAL ASSOCIATION OF COLLEGES AND TEACHERS OF AGRICULTURE (NACTA), a national professional organization dedicated to improvement of college teaching of agriculture. Formed in 1955, NACTA works: "(1) to provide all institutions a forum for discussion of questions and problems related to the improvement of college level instruction in agriculture; (2) to improve higher education in agriculture through examination and discussion of curricula, course organization, teaching techniques, facilities and materials; and (3) to encourage and promote the general availability of instruction in agriculture and research supporting this instruction" (unpaginated brochure).

NACTA provides its members (employed classroom teachers and administrators of agricultural subjects working at the postsecondary school level) with several services. The organization's official publication, the *NACTA Journal,* is distributed quarterly. Two major and several regional awards are made annually. The major awards are: (1) the Ensminger-Interstate-NACTA Distinguished Teacher Award to the most outstanding college teacher of agriculture, and (2) the E. B. Knight NACTA Journal award for the outstanding agricultural publication of the year. An annual conference is sponsored by NACTA. The association, with business offices at Sam Houston State University, Texas, also helps institutions to sponsor local workshops.

References: National Association of Colleges and Teachers of Agriculture, *NACTA,* Huntsville, TX (Sam Houston University): The Association, Undated Brochure; *NACTA Journal,* June 1980.

NATIONAL ASSOCIATION OF EDUCATIONAL BROADCASTERS (NAEB), an organization of individuals interested in public and educational telecommunications. Membership consists of two major groups: (1) those employed in public and educational telecommunications, and (2) those aspiring to such positions. NAEB's principal goals are: (1) to foster a high level of professionalism, and (2) to promote effective communication among working professionals.

Members are invited to affiliate with an NAEB professional council of their choosing. Councils, essentially subgroups of the association, are: Broadcast Education, Development, Engineers, Financial Officers, Graphics and Design, Instruction, Personnel, Production Managers, Production, Public Information, Radio, Research, State Administrators, TV Programming, TV Station Managers, and Volunteer Coordinators.

Opportunities available to members include participation in the organization's annual meeting and receipt of several publications. The latter are *PTR-Public Telecommunications Review* (published bimonthly), *Current*, a biweekly newspaper, and the NAEB *Annual Directory*. A job-matching résumé service (PACT) is available to experienced professionals. Various awards are made to individuals whose work in telecommunications has been judged to be distinctive. Seminars and workshops are sponsored for the benefit of members working for public radio and TV stations, governmental agencies, industry, and academic institutions. Leadership training programs are also sponsored.

NAEB's main offices are in Washington, D.C.
Reference: National Association of Education Broadcasters, *Come Join Us: NAEB,* Washington, DC: The Association, Undated Brochure.

NATIONAL ASSOCIATION OF EDUCATIONAL OFFICE PERSONNEL (NAEOP), formerly the National Association of Educational Secretaries, the only national organization in the United States for educational office personnel. Founded in 1934, NAEOP is committed to the professional growth of its members and works to have them recognized as members of the educational team.

The association makes numerous services available to its members: (1) conferences and institutes, the latter including college-level courses and inservice activities that carry continuing education units; (2) the Professional Standards Program through which a certificate is issued that is based on experience, education, and professional activities; and (3) numerous publications covering topics of interest to members and including *The National*

Educational Secretary, NAEOP's official (quarterly) publication.

The association's main office is in Arlington, Virginia.
Reference: National Association of Educational Office Personnel, *Your Future Is Now,* Arlington, VA: The Association, 1979.

NATIONAL ASSOCIATION OF EDUCATIONAL SECRETARIES—See NATIONAL ASSOCIATION OF EDUCATIONAL OFFICE PERSONNEL

NATIONAL ASSOCIATION OF ELEMENTARY SCHOOL PRINCIPALS (NAESP), a professional organization founded in 1921 by 51 elementary school principals. It was accepted as a department within the National Education Association in that same year. From 1921 to 1970, the organization was known as the Department of Elementary School Principals, NEA. In 1972, it became an independent organization and assumed its present name.

NAESP is headquartered in Alexandria, Virginia. The association publishes *Principal* (a quarterly journal), *Communicator* (a biweekly newsletter), and numerous books, handbooks, and pamphlets related to the elementary principalship. The 26,000 members have opportunities to become involved in various committees such as Black Concerns, Concerns of Nonpublic Schools, Large City Concerns, and Middle School Principals.
References: Encyclopedia of Associations (19th Edition), Detroit: Gale Research Company, 1985; National Association of Elementary School Principals, "What Does NAESP Mean for You?" Alexandria, VA: The Association, Undated Booklet.

NATIONAL ASSOCIATION OF INDEPENDENT COLLEGES AND UNIVERSITIES (NAICU), an organization of independent institutions of higher education whose general purpose, as stated in the association's by-laws, is "to plan, conduct, coordinate, supervise and finance activities which promote the well-being of the independent sector of higher education within the nation's historic dual system of public education" (p. 17). Formed in 1976 to replace the National Council of Independent Colleges and Universities, NAICU has a potential membership of 1,200 private (denominational and nondenominational) institutions. It serves as the national voice for independent colleges and universities in the United States.

In 1977, a companion organization to NAICU, the National Institute of Independent Colleges and Universities, was formed. The institute is responsible for carrying out research and legal services activities. It studies proposed and present public policies as they impact on independent institutions of higher education and/or their students.

NAICU and the institute have headquarters in Washington, DC.

Reference: National Association of Independent Colleges and Universities, *NAICU: General Information Brochure,* Washington, DC: The Association, 1979.

NATIONAL ASSOCIATION OF INDEPENDENT SCHOOLS (NAIS),

an organization that works to assist and strengthen independent schools. NAIS was formed in 1962 by merger of two organizations, the Independent Schools Education Board and the National Council of Independent Schools. In 1965, the Council for Independent School Aid was annexed.

Institutional memberships, which presently number approximately 1,000, are open to nonprofit nondiscriminatory schools that: (1) hold membership in an NAIS-affiliated regional unit; (2) are recognized by a regional accrediting association; and (3) have been in continuous operation for at least five years. Active membership is open to schools in the United States that meet these criteria; schools outside of the United States may qualify for affiliate membership.

NAIS publishes *Independent School,* a quarterly. Its national headquarters is in Boston, Massachusetts.

References: National Association of Independent Schools, *National Association of Independent Schools* (Unpublished Mimeographed Brochure), Boston: The Association, 1979; National Association of Independent Schools, *NAIS: Catalogue 1978–79,* Boston: The Association, 1978.

NATIONAL ASSOCIATION OF INTERCOLLEGIATE ATHLETICS (NAIA),

an association that organizes and administers collegiate athletics. Although it is a national organization, much of NAIA's work is carried out by its 31 districts, each operating with its own chair and district executive committee. It is an autonomous organization, established in 1940 as the National Association of Intercollegiate Basketball. Its current name, which reflects NAIA's involvement in sports other than basketball, was adopted in 1952.

In 1980, 515 accredited four-year colleges and universities were members of NAIA. As members,

they are obligated to abide by NAIA standards (e.g. player eligibility rules). Almost half of the member institutions have enrollments under 1,000; approximately two-thirds are private (mostly church related). An estimated 100,000 student athletes enrolled in these institutions participate in NAIA programs.

The association sponsors national championships in: basketball, golf, outdoor track and field, tennis, football (two divisions), cross country, swimming, baseball, soccer, gymnastics, indoor track and field, ice hockey, and volleyball. The NAIA Basketball Championship Tournament, inaugurated in 1937 and conducted annually in Kansas City, Missouri, is the largest and oldest such championship in the world. In August 1980, a women's division was established that sponsors championships for women. At the time the division was created, plans were made to provide ten women's championships.

NAIA has its headquarters in Kansas City, Missouri.

References: "Addendum A," Kansas City, MO: National Association of Intercollegiate Athletics, Mimeographed and Undated Flier; *National Association of Intercollegiate Athletics,* Kansas City, MO: The Association, Undated Flier.

NATIONAL ASSOCIATION OF SECONDARY SCHOOL PRINCIPALS (NASSP),

the nation's largest organization of secondary school administrators. Founded in 1916, NASSP has its headquarters in Reston, Virginia. In 1978, it reported a membership of 35,000.

The association provides its members with numerous benefits: the services of a full-time staff attorney; liability insurance; curriculum and research publications prepared under NASSP's direction; and numerous leadership development programs. The association works closely with state organizations of secondary school administrators and cooperates with other national organizations to promote programs or legislation of interest to its members. The National Honor Society and the Junior Honor Society, organizations that recognize outstanding student achievement, are sponsored by NASSP. The *NASSP Bulletin,* a journal, is published monthly, September through May. (See NATIONAL HONOR SOCIETY.)

References: National Association of Secondary School Principals, *NASSP and You,* Reston, VA: The Association, Undated Booklet; Mary Wilson Pair (Editor), *Encyclopedia of Associations* (Twelfth Edition), Detroit: Gale Research Company, 1978.

NATIONAL ASSOCIATION OF STATE BOARDS OF EDUCATION (NASBE), an organization of state boards of education that was formed in 1959. NASBE provides a variety of services to the more than 550 individuals serving on state and territorial boards of education. (In 1980, 55 of the 57 states and territories had such boards.)

The services provided by NASBE include: (1) *training,* with emphasis given to improvement of boardmanship skills; (2) *national conventions,* which focus on critical educational issues and at which organizational policy is established; (3) *two newsletters, Focus* (published ten times a year) and *Potomac Review* (published monthly while Congress is in session); (4) *other publications,* including books, monographs, and reports; (5) *consultation,* including site visits; (6) *special meetings and conferences,* many carried out regionally; and (7) *special projects* initiated in response to members' requests.

NASBE's main office is in Washington, D.C. (See BOARD OF EDUCATION, STATE.)

References: National Association of State Boards of Education, *NASBE: Services to State Education Policy Makers,* Washington, DC: The Association, Undated Brochure; National Association of State Boards of Education, *National Association of State Boards of Education,* Washington, DC: The Association, 1980.

NATIONAL ASSOCIATION OF STATE DIRECTORS OF TEACHER EDUCATION AND CERTIFICATION (NASDTEC), an organization of directors and other officers who work in a state education department and who have responsibility for implementing state laws relative to teacher education and/or teacher certification. The association's principal purpose, as set forth in its Constitution, is "to exercise leadership in matters related to the preparation and certification of professional school personnel" (p. 1).

NASDTEC was organized in 1922. Its 1979 membership consisted of representatives from each of the 50 state departments of education plus the District of Columbia and Puerto Rico.

A major project of NASDTEC is the publication of its *Standards for State Approval of Teacher Education,* a document used by numbers of states and teacher training institutions as guides for the development/evaluation of teacher education programs. NASDTEC does not operate a certification reciprocity system; nevertheless, use of the Standards does serve to facilitate certification. Some states give special consideration to out-of-state applicants who have completed preparation programs based on NASDTEC Standards.

References: Constitution of The National Association of State Directors of Teacher Education and Certification (Mimeographed; Revised August 16, 1979), Salt Lake City, UT: The Association, 1979; National Association of State Directors of Teacher Education and Certification, *Standards for State Approval of Teacher Education* (Revised), Salt Lake City, UT: The Association, 1979.

NATIONAL ASSOCIATION OF STATE UNIVERSITIES AND LAND GRANT COLLEGES (NASULGC), oldest higher education association in the United States. NASULGC traces its beginnings to 1887 when land-grant leaders formed the Association of American Agricultural Colleges and Experiment Stations. Another organization, the National Association of State Universities, was organized in 1895 to serve the needs of state universities. In 1963, these two associations merged to form NASULGC.

Approximately 150 member institutions belong to NASULGC, about half of which are land-grant colleges and universities. The association, with headquarters in Washington, D.C., keeps Congress informed of member institutions' needs and contributions in areas such as research, teaching, and extension. Five offices carry out much of the work of the association: (1) Governmental Relations for Higher Education; (2) Governmental Relations for Agriculture and Natural Resources; (3) Communication Services (serving the media and responsible for publications, films, and recordings); (4) Special Programs (clearinghouse for information on subjects such as collective bargaining, urban affairs, and affirmative action); and (5) Advancement of Public Negro Colleges. NASULGC's Senate, which is made up of the chief executives of member institutions, is its legislative and policymaking body. In addition to specific reports and publications, the association publishes four newsletters: *The Circular Letter, For Your Information, The International Letter,* and *Advancement Newsletter.* (See APPENDIX VII: LAND GRANT COLLEGES AND UNIVERSITIES.)

Reference: National Association of State Universities and Land-Grant Colleges, *Facts '79,* Washington, DC: The Association, 1979.

NATIONAL ASSOCIATION OF STUDENT COUNCILS (NASC), an organization made up of approximately 10,000 local secondary school student councils. Created in 1932 through the efforts of its first President, Warren Shull, NASC was first affiliated with the National Education Association.

Since 1943, its organizational sponsor has been the National Association of Secondary School Principals. First organized as the National Association of Student Government Officers, it became the National Association of Student Officers in 1936 and in 1940 acquired its present name.

NASC works to strengthen local student councils and to bring about increased student involvement in all phases of the school program. Numerous strategies are used to help with the implementation of these goals. The creation of new student councils is encouraged; state associations of student councils are organized; and assistance is provided, as needed, to local and state groups. Additionally, NASC sponsors summer workshops, conducts surveys, holds annual conventions, publishes yearbooks, promotes international understanding through international leadership programs, and publishes *Student Advocate*, a magazine published nine times each year.

A 14-member advisory committee (7 regional student members and 7 regional principal and adviser representatives) channels organizational recommendations to the NASSP Board of Directors through the National Association of Secondary School Principals' Office of Student Activities. (See NATIONAL ASSOCIATION OF SECONDARY SCHOOL PRINCIPALS.)

Reference: Office of Student Activities, *Student Council Handbook,* Reston, VA: National Association of Secondary School Principals, 1978.

NATIONAL ASSOCIATION OF TEACHERS' AGENCIES (NATA),

an organization that accredits commercial teacher (placement) agencies. The association's purpose, as described in its literature, "is to promote ethical and professional services for schools and candidates" (unpaginated brochure). In 1979, NATA's list of accredited members consisted of 14 agencies located in 11 states.

The first American teacher agency was formed in Philadelphia in 1835. NATA was organized in 1914. Today, the majority of accredited agencies are managed by former teachers or school administrators.

Reference: National Association of Teachers' Agencies, *Accredited Members: National Association of Teachers' Agencies,* Washington, DC: The Association, 1979.

NATIONAL ASSOCIATION OF TRADE AND TECHNICAL SCHOOLS (NATTS),

an organization made up of American private schools that offer training (job-oriented) in trade and technical fields. Membership is limited to schools that have been accredited by NATTS. The NATTS Accrediting Commission sends field examiners to institutions seeking accreditation, limiting its investigations to schools that are private and that have been in existence for at least two years.

The association's *Handbook of Trade and Technical Careers and Training* lists 95 careers for which students can prepare in two years or less. Representative of the entire list are: diesel mechanic, surveyor, PBX switchboard operator, barber/hairstylist, and medical laboratory technician.

NATTS' main offices, including the association's Accrediting Commission, are in Washington, D.C.

References: National Association of Trade and Technical Schools, *NATTS: An Introduction,* Washington, DC: The Association, Undated Brochure; National Association of Trade and Technical Schools, *Handbook of Trade and Technical Careers and Training* (1979–80 Edition), Washington, D.C.: The Association, 1979.

NATIONAL BOARD FOR CERTIFIED COUNSELORS (NBCC),

an independent, nonprofit organization that promotes national certification for counselors. The board was started in 1982 by the American Association for Counseling and Development.

A board of professionals grants certification to counselors who meet the standards set by the National Board for Certified Counselors. Those who are certified may use "NCC" after their name to indicate that they have met the board standards and follow the NBCC Code of Ethics. Those who are certified have either a master or doctorate in counseling (or a related field) and two years professional counseling, including a supervised counseling experience, and have passed a counselor certification examination. NBCC certification holds for five years and may be renewed by meeting specific requirements set by NBCC. (See AMERICAN ASSOCIATION FOR COUNSELING AND DEVELOPMENT.)

References: American Association for Counseling and Development, *Keep Pace with Your Profession! Join AACD,* Alexandria, VA: The Association, undated; National Board for Certified Counselors, *What Is a National Certified Counselor?* Alexandria, VA: The Board, undated.

NATIONAL CATHOLIC EDUCATIONAL ASSOCIATION (NCEA),

largest private, professional educational organization in the world whose principal purpose is to help with the professional growth of Catholic educators. Its membership is drawn from three segments of the Catholic community in the United States: individual Catholic educators, Catholic educational institutions (all levels), and other interested groups such as parents and board members.

NCEA was founded in 1904. In that year, three organizations (Educational Conference of Seminary Faculties, founded in 1898; Association of Catholic Colleges, 1899; and the Parish School Conference, 1902) agreed to unite. Early pioneers in the organization were Thomas J. Conaty, Rector, Catholic University of America, who laid the groundwork for NCEA, and Francis W. Howard, the association's first Secretary General, who served in that capacity for 25 years.

NCEA's service activities include sponsorship of a national convention, maintaining statistics for member institutions through the NCEA Data Bank, and publication of books, pamphlets, and multimedia materials. Several periodicals are sent to all members including *Momentum,* a quarterly journal, and *Alive,* a general newsletter. NCEA's main office is in Washington, D.C.

References: Donald C. Horrigan, *The Shaping of NCEA,* Washington, D.C.: National Catholic Educational Association, 1978; National Catholic Educational Association, *Membership Information: Celebrating 75 Years of Professionalism,* Washington, D.C.: The Association, 1980; National Catholic Educational Association, *NCEA Publications,* Washington, DC: The Association, Undated Brochure.

NATIONAL CENTER FOR EDUCATION STATISTICS (NCES), was the principal federal agency responsible for collecting and reporting statistics on American education. Section 406 (b) of the General Education Provisions Act, later amended, charged the center with collection and dissemination of "statistics and other data related to education in the United States and in other nations. The Center shall . . . collect, collate, and from time to time, report full and complete statistics on the condition of education in the United States; conduct and publish reports on specialized analyses of . . . such statistics; . . . and . . . report on education activities in foreign countries" (p. ii).

NCES maintained a core of statistics on institutions and students. Its reports provided information on important issues such as declining enrollments, supply and demand of professionals in specific teaching fields, financing of education, minority students in postsecondary institutions, and academic achievement of students.

NCES was originally an organizational component of the Education Division, U.S. Department of Health, Education, and Welfare. In early 1980, NCES became one of the three units in the Office of Educational Research and Improvement (OERI) of the U.S. Department of Education, and in 1985 the responsibilities of NCES were assumed by the Center for Statistics under a reorganization of OERI. (See OFFICE OF EDUCATIONAL RESEARCH AND IMPROVEMENT.)

References: Office of Management, *Department of Education's Mission and Organizational Manual,* Washington, DC: U.S. Department of Education, Revised June 1, 1987; Shirley Radcliffe (Editor), *The Condition of Education: 1978 Edition,* Washington, DC: National Center for Education Statistics, 1978.

NATIONAL CENTER ON CHILD ABUSE AND NEGLECT—See CHILD ABUSE PREVENTION AND TREATMENT ACT

NATIONAL CENTER ON EDUCATION AND THE ECONOMY, an organization for policy analysis and assistance. The center grew out of the work of the Carnegie Forum on Education and the Economy. The first president of the center was Marc Tucker, who was also the executive director of the Carnegie Forum.

The National Center on Education and the Economy was started in January 1988 with a grant from the Carnegie Corporation and financial support from the state of New York. The center's thrust is to produce new ideas for restructuring education (for higher levels of performance) and to help those interested in implementing the ideas. The National Center on Education and Economy was initially based in Washington, D.C., but moved late in 1988 to Rochester, New York, to help the Rochester Public School system implement its educational program and structure. That was based, in part, on recommendations found in *A Nation Prepared: Teachers for the 21st Century.* (See CARNEGIE FORUM ON EDUCATION AND THE ECONOMY and *A NATION PREPARED: TEACHERS FOR THE 21ST CENTURY.*)

References: Carnegie Corporation of New York, press release, New York: Carnegie Corporation, January 4, 1988; National Center on Education and the Economy, *Press Release: New York's Governor Cuomo Announces Major Commitment toward Launching National Center on Education and the Economy,* Washington, DC: The Center, January 4, 1988.

NATIONAL CHILDREN'S BOOK WEEK, an annual event held during the third week of November in American schools, libraries, and bookstores. The purpose of the celebration is to encourage the reading and enjoyment of children's books.

The idea for National Children's Book Week originated with Franklin K. Mathiews, librarian for the Boy Scouts of America. He suggested such a celebration in a speech delivered to the 1915 Booksellers Convention. In 1916, the American Booksellers Association and the Boy Scouts sponsored a Good Book Week. In1919, the American Library Association agreed with Mathiews that the country needed a Children's Book Week, an idea that soon became reality and was eventually supported by librarians, publishers, booksellers, and scout leaders.

The growth of the celebration led to creation of the Children's Book Council (CBC) in 1945. Since then, CBC has helped to support Children's Book Week. The council serves as headquarters for National Children's Book Week. (See CHILDREN'S BOOK COUNCIL.)

References: Children's Book Council, Inc., *National Children's Book Week: A Brief History,* New York: The Council, Undated Brochure; Allen Kent and Harold Lancour (Editors), *Encyclopedia of Library and Information Science* (Volume IV), New York: Marcel Dekker, Inc., 1970.

NATIONAL CITIZENS COMMISSION FOR THE PUBLIC SCHOOLS (NCCPS),

an organization of citizens (noneducators) devoted to school improvement work. The commission was incorporated in 1949 with financial support from the Carnegie Corporation and the General Education Board. Harvard University President James B. Conant had suggested, some six years earlier, that a national commission of laymen be formed to improve the public relations of the public schools. NCCPS was created in response to that suggestion. Its primary purpose was described by its chairman, Roy E. Larsen, as being "a promoter of local citizen activity—a catalytic agent, a clearinghouse, an encourager of independent, democratic action—with no pronouncements or pattern of our own to impose but with the single message that citizens everywhere must take responsibility for making the schools as good as they want them to be" (Dreiman, p. xi). NCCPS records indicate that, to the organization's knowledge, only 17 school communities had citizens' committees operating when the organization was formed; by 1957, that number had increased to 15,000. The story of NCCPS (which was replaced by the National Citizens Council for Better Schools in 1956) is reported by David Dreiman in his book *How to Get Better Schools.* The National Citizens Council for Better Schools ceased to exist in 1959.

References: Roald F. Campbell, et. al., *The Organization and Control of American Schools* (Fourth Edition), Columbus, OH: Charles E. Merrill Publishing Company, 1980; David B. Dreiman, *How to Get Better Schools: A Tested Program,* New York: Harper and Brothers, 1956.

NATIONAL COLLEGIATE ATHLETIC AS- SOCIATION (NCAA),

a voluntary organization of almost 900 colleges, universities, conferences, and organizations concerned with intercollegiate athletics. Formed in 1906, NCAA fulfills numerous purposes and services. They include: (1) establishment and enforcement of standards for competitive athletics; (2) supervision of regional and national collegiate athletic contests; (3) compilation and distribution of collegiate athletic records/statistics; and (4) service as a national discussion, legislative, and administrative body in matters of intercollegiate athletics.

NCAA's annual convention is its final authority and governing body. Numerous subunits carry out the routine work of the association: an 18-member elected council; an executive committee; 30 general committees; and 12 sports committees (for rule making and tournament supervision), including 7 to administer women's championships. NCAA, for competition purposes, has been divided into three divisions. Finally, the organization consists of eight geographical districts that facilitate largely administrative kinds of work.

Effective 1981–82, NCAA created 53 national championships in 20 sports. Included are 10 championships for women.

The largest share of the association's budget is supported out of proceeds from meets/tournaments and television income. NCAA's national office is in Shawnee Mission, Kansas.

References: National Collegiate Athletic Association: General Information (with Addendum), Shawnee Mission, KS: The National Collegiate Athletic Association, September 1978; *USA: 1776, 1976; NCAA: 1906, 1976,* Shawnee Mission, KS: The National Collegiate Athletic Association, February 1976.

NATIONAL COMMISSION ON TEACHER EDUCATION AND PROFESSIONAL STAN- DARDS (NCTEPS),

a body established by the National Education Association in 1946 for the purpose of strengthening teacher education, recruiting and selecting teachers, and upgrading requirements for teacher certification. Commonly referred to as the TEPS Commission, NCTEPS consisted of nine members who constituted a cross-section of the teaching profession. All were appointed by the NEA.

The commission's activities were numerous and, on the whole, successful. It advocated that all prospective teachers should hold a baccalaureate degree, including study in professional education. Creation of professional standards boards at the state level was recommended. The need for stronger accreditation practices was identified. These needs were stressed during conferences sponsored by NCTEPS, in position papers, and by the commission's consultants to school systems, state and federal agencies, universities, and professional organizations. TEPS groups established at the state level worked to implement the commission's recommendations.

Several of NCTEPS's functions were later (through 1973–74) assumed by the NEA's Council on Instruction and Professional Development.

References: Linda E. Morris, "National Commission on Teacher Education and Professional Standards" in Lee C. Deighton (Editor), *The Encyclopedia of Education* (Volume 6), New York: The Macmillan Company and The Free Press, 1971; *NEA Handbook, 1973–74,* Washington, DC: National Education Association, 1973.

NATIONAL COMMISSION ON THE REFORM OF SECONDARY EDUCATION,

a group of citizens and educators whose report, tendered in 1973, included numerous recommendations for improvement of American secondary education. The study was sponsored by the Kettering Foundation. The commission's Chairman was B. Frank Brown.

The commission's deliberations resulted in the positing of 32 specific recommendations. They called for changes such as: (1) formulation of goals by each secondary school; (2) revitalization of curriculum and support services; (3) expansion of career education opportunities; (4) providing students with a global (total human environment) education; (5) making alternatives to the comprehensive high school available at the local district level; (6) increased use of instructional television; (7) developing school security plans and keeping records of violence; (8) elimination of corporal punishment; (9) reducing the school-learning age to 14; and (10) elimination of racism and sexism in schools.

Reference: National Commission on the Reform of Secondary Education, *The Reform of Secondary Education: A Report to the Public and the Profession,* New York: McGraw-Hill Book Company, 1973.

NATIONAL COMMUNITY EDUCATION ASSOCIATION (NCEA),

organized in 1966 to promote the concept of community education. The organization is divided into eight geographical regions. Within them, approximately 100 centers, housed in colleges/universities, school districts, or state departments of education conduct activities designed to encourage growth of community schools at the school district level: (1) conducting workshops and training programs; (2) providing resource help to school districts; (3) developing graduate degree programs; (4) conducting research and evaluation projects; and (5) helping to develop state associations.

In its early years, NCEA received major financial support from the Charles Stewart Mott Foundation. Membership presently exceeds 4,000. Publications distributed regularly to members are *Community Education Journal,* a quarterly, and a monthly newsletter, *Community Education Today.* In 1978, NCEA's main offices were moved from Flint, Michigan, to Washington, D.C. (See COMMUNITY EDUCATION and MOTT FOUNDATION.)

References: Thomas L. Fish, "Building a New NCEA," *Community Education Journal,* October 1978; Everett E. Nance, "The Center Scene—A Lively Network," *Community Education Journal,* October 1978; National Community Education Association, *Official By-Laws for the National Community Education Association,* Washington, DC: The Association, 1978.

NATIONAL CONFERENCE OF PROFESSORS OF EDUCATIONAL ADMINISTRATION (NCPEA),

a flexibly structured and operated association of professors interested in the field of educational administration. The organization has no official list of members, no dues, and no permanent headquarters. Conferences are conducted once each year on different university campuses. They are planned by NCPEA's Chairman, an individual chosen by the organization's governing body (a nine-member Planning Committee).

NCPEA was organized in 1947 after Walter Cocking, then Editor of *The School Executive,* and a few of his contemporaries discussed the need for such a group. The first NCPEA conference was held in Endicott, N.Y., in that same year. Since then, work conferences have been attended by approximately 150 professionals, about half of whom participate on a regular basis. These meetings serve as an inservice vehicle for participating professors. Members of professors' families also attend the annual conferences and participate in programs designed especially for them.

Reference: J. Donald Herring, et al., *National Conference of Professors of Educational Administration: 1947–1977,* National Conference of Professors of Educational Administration, 1977.

NATIONAL CONGRESS OF PARENTS AND TEACHERS, or National PTA,

a volunteer organization primarily concerned with the welfare of children. It was founded in 1897 by Alice M. Birney and Phoebe A. Hearst. Since then the organization's membership has grown to approximately 6,400,000. National PTA, headquartered in Chicago, is made up of 31,000 local school associations (PTAs). State branches serve as liaison units between National PTA and its local associations.

National PTA serves children's needs via three broad programs: (1) child advocacy; (2) parent education; and (3) service to children, families, and schools. The recent opening of a Washington Office of Governmental Relations reflects the organization's increasing involvement as a lobbying group for children and education.

National PTA publishes *PTA Today,* a periodical; *PTA Communique,* a newsletter; and *What's Happening in Washington,* a legislative newsletter.

References: The National PTA, *The National PTA: What It Is, What It Does,* Chicago: The Association, 1978; The National PTA, *PTA Directions: 1978, 1979,* Chicago: The Association, 1978.

NATIONAL COUNCIL FOR THE ACCREDITATION OF TEACHER EDUCATION (NCATE),

the only nationally recognized accrediting agency in the field of teacher education. NCATE accredits undergraduate and graduate teacher education programs (elementary and secondary) as well as programs that prepare school service personnel (e.g., principals, counselors). In 1979, 550 (approximately 40 percent of all) teacher training institutions enjoyed NCATE accreditation.

Standards for the Accreditation of Teacher Education, a criteria manual published and periodically revised by NCATE, lists standards for Basic Programs and Advanced Programs. They are made available as a guide to both the institution seeking accreditation and to the site visitation team that is responsible for confirming the accuracy of the institution's Institutional Report (self-study).

NCATE was organized in 1952 and chartered in 1954. Numerous national professional organizations are represented on the council. Currently, the National Education Association and the American Association of Colleges for Teacher Education each have eight representatives seated. Eleven other professional organizations are each represented by one voting representative. (See

ACCREDITING AGENCIES AND ASSOCIATIONS.)

References: A. L. Fritschel, "The 1979 NCATE Standards: Implications for Teacher Education Programs," *Journal of Teacher Education,* January–February 1978; Lyn Gubser, "NCATE's Director Comments on the Tom Critique," *Phi Delta Kappan,* October 1980; National Council for the Accreditation of Teacher Education, *Standards for the Accreditation of Teacher Education,* Washington, DC: The Council, 1979; Alan R. Tom, "NCATE Standards and Program Quality: You Can't Get There From Here," *Phi Delta Kappan,* October 1980.

NATIONAL COUNCIL FOR THE SOCIAL STUDIES (NCSS),

founded in 1921 for the purpose of unifying numerous local, state, and regional organizations then working in various social studies education fields. They included groups of historians, geographers, political scientists, economists, and sociologists. Currently an independent organization, NCSS was, until 1973, an affiliate of the National Education Association.

NCSS publishes books, guides, research reports, and curriculum materials of interest to its 23,000 members from 50 states and 69 foreign countries. Its official journal, *Social Education,* is published seven times per year, from September through May. In addition, NCSS publishes *The Social Studies Professional* five times per year. The council's affiliates include 44 state and 43 local groups.

NCSS's annual meetings are conducted at Thanksgiving time. Some of them are held jointly with other professional associations. The council's main office is in Washington, D.C.

References: National Council for the Social Studies, *Highlights of National Council History* (Mimeographed), Washington, DC: The Council, October 1979; National Council for the Social Studies, *NCSS Membership Benefits,* Washington, DC: The Council, 1987; National Council for the Social Studies, *NCSS Publications for Social Studies Educators,* Washington, DC: The Council, Undated Brochure; Nancy Yakes and Denise Akey (Editors), *Encyclopedia of Associations* (Fourteenth Edition), Detroit: Gale Research Company, 1980.

NATIONAL COUNCIL OF TEACHERS OF ENGLISH (NCTE),

the world's largest subject-matter organization. Headquartered in Urbana, Illinois, NCTE has improvement of English and language arts instruction (Kindergarten through university) as its major goal. More than 100,000 elementary, secondary, and college-level teachers, librarians, and others interested in the council's goals and programs belong to NCTE. Over 130 local, state, and regional councils are also affiliated with the parent council.

NCTE consists of three divisions: the Elementary, Secondary, and College sections, which publish their own journals. Respectively, they are *Language Arts* (formerly *English Education*), *English Journal*, and *College English*. The council sponsors numerous conventions, institutes, and workshops each year. It also supports an extensive publishing program.

Since 1957, NCTE has given achievement awards for writing to graduating high school seniors. Names of award winners are published annually. Almost 900 were made in 1980.

References: National Council of Teachers of English, *NCTE*, Urbana, IL: The Council, Undated Brochure; National Council of Teachers of English, *NCTE Achievement Awards in Writing, 1979*, Urbana, IL: The Council, 1979.

NATIONAL COUNCIL OF TEACHERS OF MATHEMATICS (NCTM), a professional organization concerned with improvement of mathematics education. NCTM is headquartered in Reston, Virginia. Its levels of interest extend from elementary schools through junior colleges and teacher training institutions. Individual and institutional memberships currently exceed 75,000. *The Mathematics Teacher,* published nine times annually, has secondary and postsecondary instruction as its principal foci. *Arithmetic Teacher,* published eight times annually, deals with mathematics instruction at the elementary school level. NCTM also publishes the *Journal for Research in Mathematics Education,* the *NCTM Newsletter,* and a magazine for secondary school students, *The Mathematics Student.*

Reference: Mary Wilson Pair (Editor), *Encyclopedia of Associations* (Twelfth Edition), Detroit: Gale Research Company, 1978.

NATIONAL COUNCIL ON VOCATIONAL EDUCATION—See PERKINS (CARL D.) VOCATIONAL EDUCATION ACT

NATIONAL DEFENSE EDUCATION ACT (Public Law 85-864), federal legislation passed in 1958. The act, frequently referred to as NDEA, contained three major thrusts: (1) loans and fellowships to college and university students; (2) aid to the states for strengthening instruction in mathematics, science, and foreign languages as well as counseling services and area vocational programs; and (3) aid to researchers seeking ways to improve teaching. NDEA was passed in response to the Soviet Union's launching of Sputnik. The legislation reflected Congress's desire to strengthen the quality level of American schools, notably in the fields of mathematics and science. Several of NDEA's titles were later amended. Approximately $3,000,000,000 were appropriated for NDEA in the decade following its passage. Currently, the program emphasizes foreign language instruction and international studies.

References: Mike M. Milstein, *Impact and Response: Federal Aid and State Education Agencies,* New York: Teachers College Press, 1976; Public Law 85-864, *United States Statutes at Large, 1958* (Volume 72, Part 1), Washington, DC: U.S. Government Printing Office, 1959; Sidney C. Suffrin, *Administering the National Defense Education Act,* Syracuse, NY: Syracuse University Press, 1963.

NATIONAL DIFFUSION NETWORK (NDN), a system for nationwide dissemination of exemplary educational programs. The network, established in 1974 as part of the U.S. Office of Education, is currently a component unit in the U.S. Department of Education.

The network's total operation involves three steps. First, programs deemed to be exemplary are evaluated by a group called the *Joint Dissemination Review Panel.* These jurors assess the program using six criteria: (1) Did a change occur? (2) Was the effect consistent enough and observed often enough to be statistically significant? (3) Was the effect educationally significant? (4) Can the intervention be implemented in another location with the likelihood of comparable impact? (5) How likely is it that the observed effects resulted from the intervention? and (6) Is the presented evidence believable and interpretable? Second, each program chosen for dissemination is identified as a *Developer/Demonstrator* (DD) and becomes part of the NDN. Finally, *State Facilitators* work to promote the DDs in their respective geographical areas. State Facilitators may be associated with state departments of education, local school districts, intermediate school districts, or an institution of higher education.

School districts interested in adopting a particular program receive training (16–24 hours) from the DD with adoption costs shared three ways: by the adopting school, the State Facilitator, and the DD. Further information about NDN may be obtained from NDN, Division of Educational Replication, U.S. Department of Education.

References: Ellen Czeh and Mary McMurrer, "NDN: Pacesetter for Educational Improvement," *Momentum,* February 1980; Far West Laboratory for Educational Research and Development, *NDN: A Success Story,*

Washington, DC: U.S. Office of Education, June 1978; G. Kasten Tallmadge, *The Joint Dissemination Review Panel Ideabook*, Washington, DC: U.S. Office of Education, October 1977.

NATIONAL DIRECT STUDENT LOANS (NDSL), low interest loans extended to needy students enrolled in institutions of higher education. Interest payments begin after the student completes his/her studies. The NDSL loan program makes loan capital available to the colleges and universities. The federal share of the program is 90 percent, with the remaining 10 percent provided by the institution. Loans are processed by the college/university. Loan limits, as of 1980-81, were $3,000 for the first two years of college, $6,000 for a B.A. or B.S. program, and $12,000 for graduate study (including monies borrowed under NDSL for undergraduate work). Maximum repayment period is ten years with a minimum of $30 monthly repayment required. (See STUDENT FINANCIAL AID.)

References: Charles E. Finn, Jr., *Scholars, Dollars, and Bureaucrats*, Washington, DC: The Brookings Institution, 1978; Elinor Lenz and Marjorie H. Shaevitz, *So You Want to Go Back to School: Facing the Realities of Reentry*, New York: McGraw-Hill Book Company, 1977.

NATIONAL EDUCATION ASSOCIATION (NEA), largest professional organization in the United States. Its basic purposes include working for improved education (schools and colleges) and enhancing the status of teachers. The NEA's parent organization was the National Teachers Association (NTA) formed in 1857.

NEA was formed in 1870 when three formerly separate organizations (National Teachers Association, National Association of School Superintendents, and the Normal School Association) agreed to merge. By 1920, the association had grown so large that a representative assembly system was introduced for the purpose of transacting business. In 1966, NEA and the American Teachers Association, a black educators organization, merged. More recently, several organizations of administrators (e.g. elementary school principals) that had previously operated as separate NEA departments withdrew from the parent organization and became autonomous. However, all educational employees (e.g., support personnel) can now become members of the NEA.

NEA members receive a variety of publications, including *NEA Today*. The association produces numerous other publications including research reports concerning teachers' salaries, school finance, and retirement systems. Other benefits include legal services, an attorney referral program, employment liability insurance, accidental death insurance, life insurance, and a variety of other personal services.

NEA is made up of several affiliates including 52 state-level associations and approximately 13, 250 local units. NEA represents faculty in 370 institutions of higher education. Total membership was 1,919,773 in 1989. The association's main offices are in Washington, D.C. (See NATIONAL TEACHERS ASSOCIATION; also see APPENDIX VI: FRIEND OF EDUCATION AWARD WINNERS; APPENDIX XI: PAST PRESIDENTS OF THE AMERICAN TEACHERS ASSOCIATION; APPENDIX XVII: PAST PRESIDENTS OF THE NATIONAL EDUCATION ASSOCIATION; and APPENDIX XXI: SECRETARIES AND EXECUTIVE DIRECTORS OF THE NATIONAL EDUCATION ASSOCIATION OF THE UNITED STATES.)

References: National Education Association, *National Education Association: A Brief Description*, Washington, DC: The Association, June 1976; National Education Association, *NEA Handbook: 1988–89*, Washington, DC: The Association, 1988; Edgar B. Wesley, *NEA, The First Hundred Years: The Building of the Teaching Profession*, New York: Harper and Brothers, 1957.

NATIONAL EDUCATION ASSOCIATION CODE OF ETHICS—See CODE OF ETHICS OF THE EDUCATION PROFESSION

NATIONAL ENDOWMENT FOR THE ARTS—See NATIONAL FOUNDATION ON THE ARTS AND HUMANITIES

NATIONAL ENDOWMENT FOR THE HUMANITIES—See NATIONAL FOUNDATION ON THE ARTS AND HUMANITIES

NATIONAL FACULTY DIRECTORY, a regularly published directory that lists almost 500,000 teaching faculty members working in over 3,000 American institutions of higher education. Also listed are teaching faculty members on the staffs of over 100 Canadian institutions. Individuals listed are those who have classroom teaching as their primary responsibility. Most junior college, college, and university faculty members are included.

National Faculty Directory is published annually by the Gale Research Company, Detroit, Michigan. The first edition appeared in 1970.

Reference: The National Faculty Directory, 1980 (Volumes 1

and 2) (Tenth Edition), Detroit: Gale Research Company, 1979.

NATIONAL FOUNDATION FOR THE IMPROVEMENT OF EDUCATION,

a nonprofit foundation established in 1969 by the National Education Association. Its principal aim is the improvement of educational quality, with particular attention given to teaching-learning problems. Governing the foundation is a Board of Directors consisting of 9-15 members. The foundation's offices are in the National Education Association's headquarters, Washington, D.C. (See NATIONAL EDUCATION ASSOCIATION.)

Reference: National Education Association, *NEA Handbook: 1977-78,* Washington, DC: The Association, 1977.

NATIONAL FOUNDATION ON THE ARTS AND HUMANITIES,

a federal agency that works to support national advancement in the arts and the humanities. The foundation, created in 1965, consists of three subunits. The first of these, the *National Endowment for the Arts,* promotes development of the arts in the United States by encouraging dissemination of high-quality arts, helping cultural institutions, encouraging artistically gifted individuals, and preserving our cultural heritage through the arts. A second subunit, the *National Endowment for the Humanities,* supports creation and distribution of knowledge in fields such as language, linguistics, history, philosophy, archaeology, history of the arts, and philosophy. The third subunit, the *Federal Council on the Arts and Humanities,* coordinates the work of the two endowments.

Each of the two endowments and the federal council receives policy direction from its own council.

Grant information inquiries should be addressed to the appropriate endowment. Annual reports prepared by each endowment may be obtained from the U.S. Government Printing Office, Washington, D.C.

References: National Endowment for the Arts, *Annual Report, 1979,* Washington, DC: The Endowment, 1979; National Endowment for the Humanities, *Fourteenth Annual Report, 1979,* Washington, DC: U.S. Government Printing Office, 1979; Office of the Federal Register, National Archives and Records Service, General Services Administration, *United States Government Manual, 1978/79,* Washington, DC: U.S. Government Printing Office, 1978.

NATIONAL HONOR SOCIETY (NHS),

an organization of local high school students who are high academic achievers. Membership in the local chapter is limited to tenth, eleventh and twelfth grade students who have a minimum grade-point average of 85 percent, a "B" average, or its equivalent. Members are elected to NHS by a faculty council that consists of the principal and at least four faculty members. A faculty adviser, normally designated by the principal, works closely with the local chapter. Each chapter's constitution is subject to approval by the organization's National Council.

NHS is sponsored by the National Association of Secondary School Principals (NASSP). Operational activities of the society are carried out by the National Council but responsibility for its governance is vested in the Board of Directors of NASSP.

The original proposal to form a national honor society was made in 1919 by J. G. Masters, then Principal of Omaha's Central High School. NHS was formed in 1921, with this statement a part of the founding resolution: "The organization . . . would have a strong tendency to improve scholarship and to place the regular and faithful performance of academic work in its proper place in the estimation of the school body. . . . (It) would counteract a prevailing tendency among secondary schools to place undue emphasis upon individual performance in the various athletic events" (p. 3).

NASSP reports that NHS chapters exist in over 20,000 public and private high schools, with 350 to 400 new chapters added each year.

Reference: National Honor Society Handbook (Revised), Reston, VA: National Association of Secondary School Principals, 1978.

NATIONAL INSTITUTE OF EDUCATION (NIE),

was a unit of the U.S. Department of Education. NIE was created by Congress in 1972. It served as the federal government's agency for educational research and development.

Grants underwritten by NIE fulfilled either or both of the institute's principal missions: to promote equality of educational opportunity and to improve educational practice. The grants fell within three broad areas of study: (1) educational policy and organization; (2) teaching and learning; and (3) dissemination and the improvement of practice. The majority of NIE's funds were used to support long-term research and development programs. Although NIE followed the practice of inviting proposals through official Requests for Proposals (RFPs), some funds were allocated to sponsor worthy unsolicited proposals. In early 1980, NIE became one of the three units in the Office of Educational Research and Improvement

(OERI) of the U.S. Department of Education, and in 1985 the responsibilities of NIE were assumed by the Office of Research under a reorganization of OERI. (See OFFICE OF EDUCATIONAL RESEARCH AND IMPROVEMENT.)

References: National Institute of Education, *Funding Opportunities at NIE: FY 1979* (Revised), Washington, DC: The Institute, 1979; National Institute of Education, *National Institute of Education: Summary of the Reorganization Plan*, Washington, DC: The Institute, June 1978; Office of Management, *Department of Education's Mission and Organizational Manual*, Washington, DC: U.S. Department of Education, Revised June 1, 1987.

NATIONAL JUNIOR COLLEGE ATHLETIC ASSOCIATION (NJCAA), an organization that promotes and supervises a national program of junior college sports activities. NJCAA was formed in 1936 and, since then, has become a large association, divided into 22 regions with separate men and women directors heading each. The organization's purposes, as set forth in its constitution, are "to promote and foster junior college athletics on intersectional and national levels so that results will be consistent with the total educational program of its members" (Handbook, p. 21). Membership is open to junior colleges and comparable institutions accredited at either the state or regional levels.

NJCAA sponsors championship tournaments, meets, and games in the following sports: baseball (men), basketball (men and women), cross country (men and women), football (men), spring golf (men), gymnastics (women), ice hockey (men), marathon (men), soccer (men), fast-pitch softball (women), swimming/diving (men and women), tennis (men and women), indoor track and field (men and women), outdoor track and field (men and women), volleyball (women), and wrestling (men). Invitational tournaments, meets, and games are available in bowling (men and women), fall golf (men), field hockey (women), golf (women), gymnastics (men), judo (men), lacrosse (men), and snow skiing (men and women).

NJCAA's national office is in Hutchinson, Kansas.

References: George E. Killian (Editor), *Official Handbook and Casebook of the National Junior College Athletic Association* (Revised), Hutchinson, KS: The Association, August 1, 1980; *National Junior College Athletic Association*, Hutchinson, KS: The Association, 1980–81.

NATIONAL MERIT SCHOLARSHIPS, financial awards given to academically talented high school graduates by the National Merit Scholarship Program. The program is operated by a private non-profit organization located in Evanston, Illinois, called the National Merit Scholarship Corporation.

The corporation was founded in 1955 and made possible by a $20,000,000 grant from the Ford Foundation and a $500,000 grant from The Carnegie Corporation. Business corporations, colleges, and other groups and organizations also support the program.

About one million high school students take the Preliminary Scholastic Aptitude Test–National Merit Scholarship Qualifying Test (PSAT-NMSQT) to qualify for the scholarships. Nearly 6,000 scholarships are awarded annually, valued at over $21 million. The actual dollar amounts of each scholarship awarded are based on financial need. Students who qualify as semifinalists, the top half of 1 percent of the students in each state, are widely recruited by colleges throughout the nation.

References: Oreon P. Keeslar, *Financial Aids for Higher Education*, Dubuque, IA: Wm. C. Brown Company, Publishers, 1974; Nancy McCormack, "Financial Aid" in Lee C. Deighton (Editor), *The Encyclopedia of Education* (Volume 4), New York: The Macmillan Company and The Free Press, 1971; Chester E. Finn, Jr., *Scholars, Dollars, and Bureaucrats*, Washington, DC: The Brookings Institution, 1978; Oreon P. Keeslar, *Financial Aids for Higher Education*, Dubuque, IA: Wm. C. Brown Company, Publishers, 1974; Hubert S. Sacks, et al., *Hurdles*, New York: Atheneum, 1978.

NATIONAL REFORM REPORTS (1980–86), a group of reports or books published by a variety of national groups or organizations, scholars in the field, or various agencies of the United States government. The reports were generated by a concern for the level of education in the United States, low standardized test scores of students in the schools, and the change within the American economy to service and technology. These reports called for reform of public education at the elementary, secondary, and higher levels of education, and/or called for reform of teacher education and training. Although *A Nation at Risk: The Imperative for Educational Reform* (1986), *Tomorrow's Teachers, A Report of the Holmes Group* (1986), and the *Paideia Proposal* (1983) had a significant impact on the American public and helped to shape public opinion with regard to the need for educational reform, there were other reports or books that added to the reform movement during that period as well. These included: Ernest L. Boyer's *High School: A Report on Secondary Education in America* (1983); Business–Higher Education Forum's *America's Competitive Challenge: The Need for a National Re-*

sponse (1983); College Board Educational Equality Project's *Academic Preparation for College: What Students Need to Know and Be Able to Do; Bryer's College: The Undergraduate Experiences in America* (1987); Education Commission of the States Task Force on Education for Economic Growth's *Action for Excellence* (1983); John I. Goodland's *A Place Called School: Prospects for the Future* (1983); National Science Board Commission on Precollege Education in Mathematics, Science and Technology's *Educating Americans for the 21st Century: A Report to the American People and the National Science Board* (1983); Vita Pearone's *Portraits of High School, A Supplement to High School: A Report on Secondary Education* (1985); Research and Policy Committee of the Committee for Economic Development's *Investing in Our Children: Business and the Public Schools* (1986); Theodore R. Sizer's *Horace's Compromise: The Dilemma of the American High School* (1984); Tommy M. Tomlinson and Herbert J. Walberg's *Academic Work and Educational Excellence* (1986); and the Twentieth Century Fund Task Force on Federal Elementary and Secondary Education Policy's *Making the Grade* (1983). (See *(A) NATION AT RISK: THE IMPERATIVE FOR EDUCATIONAL REFORM; (A) NATION PREPARED: TEACHERS FOR THE 21ST CENTURY; PAIDEIA PROPOSAL;* and *TOMORROW'S TEACHERS: A REPORT OF THE HOLMES GROUP.*)

References: Dean Corrigan, *Agenda for Educational Reform*, College Station, TX: Texas A&M University, 1986; A. Harry Passow, *Reforming Schools in the 1980's, A Critical Review of the National Reports*, New York: Clearinghouse on Urban Education, Teachers College, Columbia University, 1984.

NATIONAL RETIRED TEACHERS ASSOCIATION (NRTA), organized in 1947 by the California Retired Teachers Association. Dr. Ethel Percy Andrus was elected organizing President in that year. Four other state organizations of retired teachers joined the national unit in that same year. By 1977, NRTA grew to 1,451 local and state chapters with a combined membership of 534,401.

NRTA's membership is not limited to retired teachers. Anyone who ever worked or is working in some field of education may join. The organization publishes the *NRTA Journal*, a bimonthly magazine, and a monthly newspaper, the *NRTA News Bulletin*. Numerous services are available to members: a consumer program, the Tax Aide program, a pharmacy service, travel assistance, a driver-improvement program, and an Institute of Lifetime Learning that sponsors regional speakers

and workshops. NRTA lobbies for legislation of interest to its members.

References: National Retired Teachers Association, *31 Years of Achievement: 1947–1978*, Washington, DC: The Association, 1978; Mary Wilson Pair (Editor), *Encyclopedia of Associations* (Twelfth Edition), Detroit: Gale Research Company, 1978.

NATIONAL SCHOOL BOARDS ASSOCIATION (NSBA), organized in 1940 as the National Council of State School Boards Association. In 1948, it became the NSBA. Institutional memberships include 52 state and territorial school board associations and approximately 2,000 local school boards.

Several component groups operate within the NSBA structure. They are: (1) the Council of Urban Boards of Education; (2) the Council of School Attorneys; (3) the Council of School Board Negotiators; (4) the Federal Policy Coordinators; (5) the Large District Forum; (6) the Rural School District Forum; (7) the Council of School Board Association Communicators; and (8) the NSBA Technology Network.

Headquartered in Alexandria, Virginia, NSBA works to strengthen state school boards ssociations, to keep local boards informed on educational matters, and, in cooperation with educators and the laity, to advance the quality level of American public education. Additionally, it sponsors a national convention for school board members. The *American School Board Journal* is published by NSBA. A monthly publication, *The Executive Educator*, was introduced in January 1979. NSBA publishes *School Board News* every two weeks during the year.

References: National School Boards Association, *Officers and Directors, 1980–81*, Washington, DC: The Association, 1980, Brochure; Mary W. Pair (Editor), *Encyclopedia of Associations*, Detroit: Gale Research Company, 1978; Edward M. Tuttle, *School Board Leadership in America*, Danville, IL: The Interstate Printers and Publishers, Inc., 1958.

NATIONAL SCHOOL DEVELOPMENT COUNCIL (NSDC), a chartered, nonprofit corporation that is a confederation of school study or development councils (such as the Capital Area School Development Association, Albany, NY; East Texas School Study Council, Commerce, TX: and Arkansas School Study Council, Fayetteville, AR), which are found throughout the United States. It is governed by a board of directors and officers elected by the board. Representatives from the northeast, northwest, southwest, and southeast are members of the board of directors as stipulated by the NSDC bylaws.

The council's functions are as follows: assist directors of local and regional development councils; help local/regional groups to form councils; help to disseminate information among councils; provide training sessions; establish a resource pool for workshops, in-service education, and conferences; participate in cooperative research; share information and publications among councils; sponsor *Catalyst for Change*, a journal published by East Texas State University; and provide two awards—Executive Secretary Exchange and Cooperative Leadership Awards. The executive director and the headquarters of NSDC are located in Sudbury, Mass.

References: National School Development Council, *National School Development Council,* Undated Brochure; National School Development Council, *NSDC Information Packet,* Sudbury, MA: The Council, 1988.

NATIONAL SCHOOL LUNCH PROGRAM, a nationwide effort that makes relatively inexpensive (in some cases free) lunches available to school children. Although state aid and monies collected from students and teachers help to defray the cost of the program, federal subsidies constitute a significant share of total receipts. Federal aid for school lunches includes contributions of surplus agricultural commodities as well as reimbursement for milk and free meals served to children. Recent estimates indicate that the program costs the federal government over $2,500,000,000 annually.

Schools desirous of receiving federal support for their lunch programs are required to offer a Type A lunch. Intended to ensure a nutritious meal, the Type A lunch, as of 1981, was required to contain five components: (1) one-half pint of milk; (2) two ounces lean meat, poultry, fish, or alternate; (3) vegetables and fruit; (4) one teaspoon of butter or fortified margarine; and (5) bread.

One of the earliest evidences of feeding school children dates back to 1853. During and since the 1940s, several pieces of federal legislation were passed that either introduced or expanded the school lunch program. In 1946, the National School Lunch Act (to be administered by the Department of Agriculture) was enacted by Congress. Significant amendments included the 1966 Child Nutrition Act (which authorized breakfast programs) and Public Law 94-105, enacted in 1975.

References: Mary de Garmo Bryan, "The Sixty Years' Growth of School Feeding," *Nation's Schools,* June 1955; John Greenhalgh, *Practitioner's Guide to School Business*

Management; Boston: Allyn and Bacon, Inc., 1978; Lewis Lyman, "The National School Lunch Program: Boon or Boondoggle?" *Phi Delta Kappan,* February 1979; Public Law 79-396, *United States Statutes at Large, 1946* (Volume 60), Washington, DC: U.S. Government Printing Office, 1947; Public Law 89-642, *United States Statutes at Large, 1966* (Volume 80), Washington, DC: U.S. Government Printing Office, 1967; Public Law 94-105, *United States Statutes at Large, 1975* (Volume 89), Washington, DC: U.S. Government Printing Office, 1977.

NATIONAL SCHOOL PUBLIC RELATIONS ASSOCIATION (NSPRA), an organization that attempts to meet two purposes: (1) the specific needs of a relatively small group of professional communicators (its membership), and (2) the informational needs of American and Canadian educators, board members, and parents. NSPRA was organized in 1935 during a National Education Association convention. Early activities (1930s and 1940s) were limited almost exclusively to members' needs and interests. In 1950, NSPRA became a Department of NEA; approximately two decades later, it became an independent organization. In 1975, membership was opened to eligible Canadians and the Canadian provinces were added as NSPRA regions.

By 1970, over 5,000,000 printed and audiovisual materials prepared by NSPRA had been sold throughout the United States. Well known to school administrators are two NSPRA weeklies: *Education USA* and *Federal Funding Alert.* Services to members include a resource center containing ideas for school communication, research assistance, a national conference (seminar), workshops, a personal clearinghouse for individuals seeking public relations positions, and awards made to chapters and individuals.

NSPRA's main office is in Arlington, Virginia.

References: "An Inside Look at the National School Public Relations Association," *Journal of Educational Communication,* November–December 1975; National School Public Relations Association, *It's Time to Get Serious About School Public Relations,* Arlington, VA: Undated Brochure.

NATIONAL SCIENCE EDUCATIONAL FACILITIES LABORATORIES, part of the National Science Foundation's "Institutional Science Programs." NSF initiated this construction program in fiscal year 1960, providing matching funds for the erection of new, or the renovation of existing, research laboratories for graduate science education. These laboratories were designed to facilitate graduate science training and high-level scientific research. Included in them were extensive equipment for training and research in biological science, oceanography, physical science, engineering, social science, and computer science.

As part of the laboratory thrust, NSF also funded equipment grants, institutional base grants, and science development grants (to develop scientific centers of excellence). All of these grants were part of the United States effort to encourage science education as a part of the post-Sputnik era. The program was in effect until 1968.

Reference: The National Science Foundation, Its Present and Future, Washington, DC: Committee on Science and Astronautics, U.S. House of Representatives, Eighty-Ninth Congress, 1966.

NATIONAL SCIENCE, ENGINEERING, AND MATHEMATICS AUTHORIZATION ACT OF 1986

(P.L. 99–159), approved by the United States Congress on November 22, 1985, a broad-based law that authorized appropriations for: Title I—National Science Foundation, special commissions; Title II—Education for Economic Security Reauthorization; Title III—Library Services Program; Title IV—Minority Institutions Science Improvement Programs and Migrating Children Records System; Title V—Harry S. Truman Memorial Scholarship Program; Title VI—Amended Education of the Handicapped Act; Title VII—amended the Carl D. Perkins Vocational Education Act (technical amendments); and Title VIII—Higher Education Programs, National Direct Student Loans, and the National Graduate Fellows Program. Over $1,521,156,000 was authorized under this act for 1986 alone. (See EDUCATION FOR ECONOMIC SECURITY ACT; NATIONAL SCIENCE FOUNDATION; PERKINS (CARL D.) VOCATIONAL EDUCATION ACT; and PUBLIC LAW 94–142.)

Reference: United States Code Congressional and Administrative News, 99th Congress—First Session, 1985 (Volume 1), St. Paul, MN: West Publishing Co., 1986.

NATIONAL SCIENCE FOUNDATION (NSF),

the leading federal supporter of science in the United States. NSF was formed in 1950 by the National Science Foundation Act (later amended). This legislation provided for a policymaking body, a 24-member National Science Board, and a Director, each to be appointed to six-year terms by the President of the United States with the advice and consent of the Senate.

The foundation's basic purpose is to promote and advance scientific progress in the United States. It does this by supporting research and education projects in the behavioral, biological, engineering, environmental, mathematical, physical, and social sciences. In the area of science education, NSF activities include identification and encouragement of scientific talent, projects to improve science teaching, and incentives for bringing about more participation in the sciences by women, minorities, and the handicapped. NSF was reauthorized to receive funds under the National Science, Engineering, and Mathematics Act of 1986. (See NATIONAL SCIENCE, ENGINEERING, AND MATHEMATICS ACT AUTHORIZATION OF 1986.)

References: Chapter 171, "National Science Foundation Act of 1950," *United States Statutes at Large, 1950–51* (Volume 64, Part I), Washington, DC: U.S. Government Printing Office, 1952; Milton Lomask, *A Minor Miracle: An Informal History of the National Science Foundation,* Washington, DC: National Science Foundation, 1975; National Science Foundation, *Guide to Programs: Fiscal Year 1979,* Washington, DC: The Foundation, 1979; Office of the Federal Register, National Archives and Records Service, General Services Administration, *United States Government Manual, 1978/79,* Washington, DC: U.S. Government Printing Office, 1978.

NATIONAL SCIENCE TEACHERS ASSOCIATION (NSTA),

an organization of elementary, secondary, and college science teachers. NSTA was formed in 1944 through merger of two science teachers' organizations: the American Science Teachers Association and the American Council of Science Teachers. Over 40,000 members presently belong to the association.

NSTA publishes three journals, each directed to a specific level of interest. These are *Science and Children,* for elementary school science teachers; *The Science Teacher,* for secondary school teachers and administrators; and *Journal of College Science Teaching,* devoted to science teaching at the college level. The association produces special publications of interest to members, sponsors a national convention as well as regional conferences, and makes other benefits (e.g. insurance) available to members. NSTA's headquarters is in Washington, D.C.

Reference: Robert H. Carleton, *The NSTA Story: 1944–1974,* Washington, DC: National Science Teachers Association, 1976.

NATIONAL SOCIETY FOR THE STUDY OF EDUCATION (NSSE),

an organization that seeks to promote discussion of significant educational issues through research and publication. NSSE's yearbooks have come to be viewed as among the most authoritative volumes published in education. The organization's Board of Directors selects yearbook topics that are subsequently prepared by experts working under the direction of a yearbook editor. Two-part yearbooks are published each year. Other works are also published as part of NSSE's Contemporary Educational Issues Series.

The first NSSE Yearbook appeared in 1902. Part I, edited by Lucy M. Salmon, was titled *Some Principles in the Teaching of History*. Part II (W. M. Davis and H. M. Wilson, editors) carried the title, *The Progress of Geography in the Schools*.

NSSE offices are in Chicago. Yearbooks are distributed by the University of Chicago Press. (See HERBART, JOHANN E.)

References: National Society for the Study of Education, *The Gifted and Talented: Their Education and Development* (NSSE 78th Yearbook, Part I), Chicago: University of Chicago Press, 1979; Nancy Yakes and Denise Akey (Editors), *Encyclopedia of Associations* (Volume 1, Thirteenth Edition), Detroit: Gale Research Company, 1979.

NATIONAL STUDENT ASSOCIATION—See UNITED STATES STUDENT ASSOCIATION

NATIONAL STUDENT LOBBY—See UNITED STATES STUDENT ASSOCIATION

NATIONAL STUDY OF SCHOOL EVALUATION (NSSE), a professional organization devoted to the support of school evaluation and self-evaluation. When formed in 1933, NSSE was known as the Cooperative Study of Secondary School Standards. Its best-known publication, a pioneering work in the field of school evaluation, is *Evaluative Criteria* (revised several times). Other publications produced by NSSE are: (1) *Secondary School Evaluative Criteria;* (2) *Middle School/Junior High School Evaluative Criteria;* (3) *Elementary School Evaluative Criteria;* (4) *Evaluation Guidelines for Multicultural/Multiracial Education;* (5) *Student Opinion Inventory;* (6) *Teacher Opinion Inventory;* and *Parent Opinion Inventory.* The organization also supports original research in the area of school evaluation.

NSSE is composed of 25 representatives from the six regional accrediting associations in the United States who constitute the general committee. This body oversees the work of NSSE. An Executive Committee (one member elected from each region) is elected by the Board of Directors, as is the board Chairman. NSSE's main office is in Arlington, Virginia. (See ACCREDITATION and ACCREDITING AGENCIES AND ASSOCIATIONS.)

Reference: National Study of School Evaluation, *Introducing National Study of School Evaluation,* Arlington, VA: NSSE, Undated Brochure.

NATIONAL TEACHER CORPS—See TEACHER CORPS

NATIONAL TEACHER EXAMINATIONS (NTE), or NTE programs standardized and objective examinations for persons completing undergraduate teacher education programs or advanced students training in specific educational fields. A 12-member NTE policy council, made up of representatives from state departments of education, teacher training institutions, and school districts, establishes testing policies; the Educational Testing Service conducts the testing program for the council.

The tests consist of: (1) the Core Battery, made up of three individual tests titled: "Communication Skills," "General Knowledge," "Professional Knowledge," and (2) *Specialty Area Tests* in over 25 fields such as audiology, early childhood education, educational administration/supervision, and Spanish. Collectively, the tests cover three domains: (1) general education; (2) professional education; and (3) subject-field specialization.

Since 1970, the right of districts and state departments to use NTE for different purposes has been challenged in the courts. In *United States v. South Carolina* (1977), for example, a Federal District Court ruled that South Carolina's use of the tests for teacher certification was constitutional. In other suits, some districts have been enjoined from using NTE as the sole criterion for making personnel retention decisions or for evaluating teaching performance. In yet other cases, some districts have been supported in their use of NTE as a basis for teacher selection.

References: Educational Testing Service, *National Teacher Examinations: 79/80 Bulletin of Information,* Princeton, NJ: The Service, 1979; National Teacher Examinations Policy Council, *Guidelines for Using the National Teacher Examinations,* Princeton, NJ: Educational Testing Service, 1979; *NTE News,* writer, 1982; David R. Turner, *How to Score High on the National Teacher Examination,* New York: Arco Publishing Company, 1976.

NATIONAL TEACHER OF THE YEAR, annual award conferred upon the American teacher deemed to be the best in teaching. The National Teacher of the Year Program, instituted in 1952, is sponsored by three organizations: Encyclopedia Britannica Companies; the Council of Chief State School Officers; and Good Housekeeping Magazine.

Each year, chief state school officers are asked to nominate a candidate from their state or territory. (Procedures for selecting each State Teacher of the Year vary from one state to the next.) An anonymous selection committee is then appointed by the council, which reviews data on each candidate, selects the finalists, and eventually identifies the National Teacher of the Year. Committee members serve without pay and represent a cross-section of professional educational organizations. In the spring of each year, the National Teacher of the Year, in a White House ceremony, receives a special trophy from the President of the United States. (See COUNCIL OF CHIEF STATE SCHOOL OFFICERS; also see APPENDIX XXIV: THE TEACHER OF THE YEAR.)

References: Mary S. Miller, "1980 Teacher of the Year," *Good Housekeeping,* May 1980; *National Teacher of the Year,* Undated Press Release, Anna M. Rosenberg Associates, New York.

NATIONAL TEACHERS ASSOCIATION (NTA), forerunner to the National Education Association. The NTA was formed in 1857 "to elevate the character and advance the interests of the profession of teaching, and to promote the cause of popular education in the United States" (Cubberly, p. 709). Its membership was limited to public schoolteachers. In 1870, two professional organizations, The American Normal School Association and the National Association of School Superintendents, merged with NTA to form the National Education Association. (See NATIONAL EDUCATION ASSOCIATION.)

References: Elwood P. Cubberly, *Public Education in the United States: A Study and Interpretation of American Educational History,* Cambridge, MA: The Riverside Press, 1962 (Published originally by Houghton Mifflin Company, 1914); William M. French, *America's Educational Tradition: An Interpretative History,* Boston: D. C. Heath and Company, 1964.

NATIONAL UNION OF TEACHERS (NUT), largest teachers' organization in England and Wales. Membership in the union is open to all qualified teachers. Founded in 1870, and originally known as The National Union of Elementary Teachers, NUT's current membership exceeds 450,000.

Local associations of NUT are located throughout England and Wales. County/metropolitan divisions serve a coordinating function, as do the or-

ganization's 12 regional councils, the next larger of NUT's units. The organization's principal governing body is its Executive Committee, a 48-member body that is made up of NUT officers and representatives as well as representatives of two organizational partnerships affiliated with the union. An annual conference, which is held at Easter, is the union's supreme authority. Local associations are represented at the conference with the number of such representatives based on the local association's membership size.

Services to members are numerous. Two journals are published (each twice a year): the *Secondary Education Journal* and the *Primary Education Review.* Other services include, but are not limited to: (1) a legal aid service; (2) full-time officials in each region available to assist members with professional problems; (3) personal accident and other types of insurance; (4) savings and investment opportunities available through the union's Building Society; (5) a personal loan program; and (6) participation in Countdown, a service in the United Kingdom that makes it possible for cardholders to receive discounts on numerous cash purchases.

NUT's headquarters is in London.

References: National Union of Teachers, *An Invitation to Join the Effective Teachers' Organization,* London, England: The Union, 1980; National Union of Teachers, *Financial Services and Benefits for Members,* London, England: The Union, 1980; National Union of Teachers, *NUT Rules,* London, England: The Union, 1979; National Union of Teachers, *NUT School Representatives' Handbook: Extracts,* London, England: The Union, 1979; National Union of Teachers, *The Report of the Executive* (Annual Conference), London, England: The Union, 1980.

A NATION AT RISK: THE IMPERATIVE FOR EDUCATIONAL REFORM, a report on the quality of education in the United States as presented by the National Commission on Excellence in Education. The report was delivered to Terrell H. Bell, United States Secretary of Education, in April 1983.

Findings focused on curriculum content, knowledge expectations, time spent in task-oriented learning, and quality of teaching. Based on the reported findings, recommendations for improvement were put forth in each area: increased high school graduation requirements to improve curriculum content; more rigorous and measurable standards in all schools, with colleges raising admission requirements; more time allocated to basic instruction; and improvement in the quality of and respect for people in the teaching profession. In addition, recommendations were included in the areas of leadership and fiscal support.

The report had a major impact on the educational community and was one of the prime factors in the reformation of schools in the middle 1980s. As a result, many schools and teacher training institutions reassessed and changed requirements.
References: National Commission on Excellence in Education, *A Nation at Risk: The Imperative for Educational Reform*, Washington, DC: United States Government Printing Office, April 1983; Tommy M. Tomlinson and Herbert J. Walberg, *Academic Work and Educational Excellence, Raising Student Productivity*, Berkeley, CA: McCutchan Publishing Corp., 1986.

A NATION PREPARED: TEACHERS FOR THE 21st CENTURY, the report of the Task Force on Teaching as a Profession, an outgrowth of the Carnegie Forum on Education and the Economy (May 1986). In pursuit of excellence in the schools, the task force proposed the following reforms:

1. Establish a national credentialing board to ensure high standards for teachers;
2. Restructure schools to allow teachers more decision-making powers in attaining state and local goals while holding the teachers accountable for student progress;
3. Restructure teaching to include Lead Teachers as mentors;
4. Require an undergraduate degree in the arts and sciences as prerequisite to pedagogical study;
5. Develop a Master in Teaching degree to include internship and residency in schools;
6. Attract minority students to teaching;
7. Relate teacher incentives to student performance and provide adequate support services; and
8. Make teacher salaries and opportunities competitive with those of other professionals.

References: Carnegie Forum on Education and the Economy, *A Nation Prepared: Teachers for the 21st Century*, New York: Carnegie Corporation of New York, 1986; Marc Tucker and David Madel, "The Carnegie Report—A Call for Redesigning the Schools," *Phi Delta Kappa*, Volume 62, Number 1, 1986.

(THE) NATION'S REPORT CARD—See NATIONAL ASSESSMENT OF EDUCATIONAL PROGRESS (NAEP)

NATIVE AMERICAN—See INDIAN

NATIVE LANGUAGE, when used in referring to a person possessing limited English-speaking ability, means the language normally used by that person. In the case of children, federal legislation defines native language as the language normally used by the parents of the child.
Reference: Public Law 93-380, "Amendments to the Elementary and Secondary Education Act of 1965," *United States Statutes at Large* (Volume 88, Part I), Washington, DC: U.S. Government Printing Office, 1976.

NATIVE SPEAKER, an individual who was born in a culture and knows the language of that culture. There are times when an individual learns a foreign language so thoroughly that he or she can speak it fluently, knows and understands the culture, and, consequently, can pass as a native speaker.

Native speakers can be used as teachers of their language. They are sometimes used as resource persons for teachers of modern foreign languages.
References: Mary Finocchiaro, *Teaching Children Foreign Languages,* New York: McGraw-Hill Book Company, 1964; Mary Finocchiaro and Michael Bonomo, *Foreign Language Learner: A Guide for Teachers,* New York: Regents Publishing Company, Inc., 1973; Wilga M. Rivers, *Teaching Foreign-Language Skills,* Chicago: University of Chicago Press, 1968.

NATIVISTIC THEORY, a theory that holds that all people are born with a *predisposition* to learn a native (their first) language. Since the predisposition is considered to be innate, learning a language is natural. It is an activity found in all cultures and linguistic patterns. The ease of basic language acquisition is the same for all people because of this innate phenomenon known as a language-acquisition device (LAD). (See COGNITIVE THEORY IN FOREIGN LANGUAGE ACQUISITION.)
References: Edward D. Allen and Rebecca M. Valette, *Classroom Techniques: Foreign Languages and English as a Second Language,* New York: Harcourt Brace Jovanovich, Inc., 1977; Kenneth Chastain, *Developing Second-Language Skills: Theory to Practice* (Second Edition), Chicago: Rand McNally College Publishing Company, 1976.

NATURALISM, a school of philosophy that holds that the physical universe (nature) is reality. Exponents of this philosophy believe that education should: (1) follow the ways of nature (be naturalistic); (2) conform to the natural growth and development of children; (3) focus on the natural activities and interests of children; and (4) change as society changes. John Dewey was one of the major naturalistic philosophers of the 20th century.

Naturalism is also used in literature and arts when the methods of science and its logic are applied to literary and fine arts works.

References: John Dewey, *Experience and Education,* New York: Macmillan and Company, 1938; Samuel Morris Eames, *Pragmatic Naturalism,* Carbondale, IL: Southern Illinois University Press, 1977; Lilian R. Furst and Peter N. Skrine, *Naturalism,* London, England: Methuen and Company, Ltd., 1971; Ram A. Mall, *Naturalism and Criticism,* The Hague, Holland: Nijoff, 1975.

NATURAL METHOD—See DIRECT METHODS

NAVAL RESERVE OFFICERS TRAINING CORPS (NROTC), a college program that leads to graduation with a bachelor's degree and a commission as either a Naval Reserve Ensign or a Marine Corps Reserve Second Lieutenant. The program is open to male and female students, although some university NROTC programs do not accept women students.

While at college, the NROTC student completes a regular academic program. Concurrently, he/she registers for naval science courses. Beginning with the junior year, the student receives a monthly, tax-free subsistence allowance for up to 20 months. He/she participates in a summer training cruise lasting four to six weeks. NROTC graduates are required to fulfill a three-year active duty obligation in either the U.S. Navy or the Marine Corps.

General requirements for admission to an NROTC program include: (1) age (17.0, not to exceed 27.5 by June 30 the year of graduation); (2) U.S. citizenship; (3) sound physical health; (4) a good record (academic, moral, extracurricular); (5) willingness to bear arms and to support the U.S. Constitution; and (6) acceptance into a college or university offering an NROTC program.

Reference: Navy Recruiting Command, *NROTC: Navy-Marine Corps College Programs,* Arlington, VA: Department of the Navy, Undated Brochure.

NEARSIGHTEDNESS—See MYOPIA

NEEDS ASSESSMENT, a procedure for determining the discrepancy, or difference, between what an organization *is* achieving and what it *wants* to achieve. N. L. McCaslin and Janice Lave defined it as "a process for determining the difference between 'what is' and 'what should be' occurring." After the needs (discrepancies) have been identified, they are ranked in order of priority. Various approaches are used to arrive at consensus regarding priority rankings.

In school systems, the procedure is used to identify instructional as well as noninstructional goals and objectives. Its popularity as an assessment tool within the total evaluation process is increasing, in and out of education.

References: Fenwick W. English and Roger A. Kaufman, *Needs Assessment: A Focus for Curriculum Development,* Washington, DC: Association for Supervision and Curriculum Development, 1975; N. L. McCaslin and Janice Lave, *Needs Assessment and Career Education: An Approach for States,* Columbus, OH: The Center for Vocational Education, The Ohio State University, 1976; Keith A. Neuber, et al., *Needs Assessment: A Model for Community Planning,* Beverly Hills, CA: Sage Publications, Inc., 1980; W. James Popham, *Educational Evaluation* (Second Edition), Englewood Cliffs, NJ: Prentice-Hall, 1988.

NEEDS THEORY, a collective term used to describe several different theories that relate human needs (physical and/or psychological) to drive, motivation, achievement, or reactions-actions. Among the major constructs permeating these theories are the following: (1) need may motivate or drive an activity, affecting both the type and magnitude of the behavior; (2) motivation for change in behavior occurs when there is disequilibrium within the organism because the organism has the need for equilibrium; (3) the need for reduction of tension may cause the motivation to act to reduce that tension in an organism; and (4) unmet needs (physical, psychological) may cause many different types of reactions (e.g. aggression, withdrawal).

Needs theory has been applied to many theories of psychological behavior (e.g. Clark Hull, Kurt Lewin, Henry Murray, Abraham Maslow). Several theories of achievement and/or motivation are based, in part, on a particular needs theory.

References: Charles N. Cofer, *Motivation and Emotion,* Glenview, IL: Scott, Foresman and Company, 1972; David C. McClelland, et al., *The Achievement Motive,* New York: Appleton-Century-Crofts, Inc., 1953; Edward T. Murray, *Motivation and Emotion,* Englewood Cliffs, NJ: Prentice-Hall, Inc., 1964; Wallace A. Russell (Editor), *Milestone in Motivation,* New York: Appleton-Century-Crofts, Inc., 1970; Bernard Weiner, *Theories of Motivation,* Chicago: Markham Publishing Company, 1972.

NEGLIGENCE, a legal term referring to the liability of one party to an injured party for an injury attributable to the unintentional action of the first party. The Supreme Court of Oregon defined negligence as "the doing of that thing which a reasonably prudent person would not have done, or the failure to do that thing which a reasonably prudent person would have done in like or similar circumstances" (Peterson, p. 252). Teachers and other school officials may be liable for negligent conduct.

Injured parties must establish three facts to prove that the party charged was negligent: (1) the defendant had a duty to protect the injured party against unreasonable risk; (2) the defendant failed to exercise that duty; and (3) the defendant's breach of duty was the proximate cause of the complainant's injury. (See TORT LIABILITY and PROXIMATE CAUSE.)

References: Biddle v. Mazzocco, 284 P.2d 364 (Oregon 1955); Leroy J. Peterson, et al., *The Law and Public School Operation* (Second Edition), New York: Harper and Row, Publishers, 1978.

NEGRO EDUCATION—See BLACK EDUCATION

NEGRO HISTORY WEEK—See BLACK HISTORY MONTH

NEIGHBORHOOD SCHOOLS—See ATTENDANCE AREA

NEIGHBORHOOD YOUTH CORPS (NYC), developed in 1965 by the Office of Economic Opportunity as a work-training, in-school, and summer program for disadvantaged youth to discourage school dropouts. Unlike Job Corps participants, trainees did not have to leave home to participate in the Youth Corps. NYC was designed to provide part-time employment to students in grades 9–12 and thus permit them to remain in school. The out-of-school component (for those equivalent in age to students in grades 9–12) was designed to improve participants' employment potential.

There was considerable questioning about whether NYC met its objectives; nevertheless, in 1973 the program was continued as part of the Comprehensive Employment and Training Act.

References: Comptroller General of the United States, *Review of Economic Programs,* Washington, DC: U.S. Government Printing Office, 1969; Robert H. Haveman, *A Decade of Federal Antipoverty Programs,* New York: Academic Press, 1977; U.S. Office of Economic Opportunity, *Catalog of Federal Domestic Assistance,* Washington, DC: Executive Office of the President, 1969.

NEILL, A.S.—See SUMMERHILL

NEO-SCHOLASTICS—See THOMISM

NEO-THOMISTS—See THOMISM

NEUROLOGICAL IMPRESS METHOD, a read-along approach that involves both learner and instructor. Developed by Heckelman in 1966, the method is effective with disabled readers. Its success is credited to the establishment of a neurological memory trace when the learner sees words in print while simultaneously hearing his own and the instructor's voice saying the words. Students hear accurate, fluid, oral reading through this process.

Material selected for the approach begins at the student's independent reading level. Students are directed to read fluently, not to be concerned with accuracy, and to disregard illustrations. At the outset, the instructor reads slightly louder and faster; as the student gains confidence, the instructor reads softer and a bit slower than the student. Gradually, the material increases in difficulty until it approaches the actual age/grade level of the learner.

References: Robert G. Heckelman, "Using the Neurological Impress Remedial Technique," *Academic Therapy Quarterly,* 1966, Volume 1, Number 4; Robert G. Heckelman, "The Neurological Impress Method of Remedial Reading Instruction," *Academic Therapy Quarterly,* Volume 4, Number 4, Summer, 1969; Margaret Ann Richek, Lynne K. List, and Janet W. Learner, *Reading Problems: Diagnosis and Remediation,* Englewood Cliffs, NJ: Prentice-Hall Inc., 1983; William H. Rupley and Timothy R. Blair, *Reading Diagnosis and Remediation: Classroom and Clinic* (Second Edition), Boston: Houghton Mifflin Company, 1983.

NEWBERY MEDAL, an award presented annually for the outstanding American children's book of the year, and originally proposed by Frederic G. Melcher. Melcher decided to name the medal in honor of John Newbery, an 18th-century London bookseller who was among the first of his trade to give special attention to juvenile books. The first Newbery medal was awarded in 1922 to Hendrik Willem van Loon, author of *The Story of Mankind.* (See APPENDIX VIII: JOHN NEWBERY MEDAL AWARD WINNERS.)

References: Mary Hill Arbuthnot, *Children and Books* (Third Edition), Chicago: Scott, Foresman and Company, 1964; Charlotte S. Huck and Doris A. Young, *Children's Literature in the Elementary School* (Third Edition), New York: Holt, Rinehart and Winston, Inc., 1976.

NEW MATHEMATICS, also referred to as modern mathematics, a term used to describe the mathematics programs introduced in the late 1950s and early 1960s to "reform" school mathematics instruction. Although the mathematical concepts reintroduced into the school programs were neither new nor modern, at least two elements were added that made the new mathematics distinctive. These were *logic* and *abstraction*. Symbols, concepts, and notations were introduced to: (1) help students understand the basic concepts of mathematics; (2) aid in improving abilities; (3) develop a precise language; (4) help students discover ideas, relationships, and generalizations; and (5) develop an enjoyment of the subject. Logic, set theory, number systems, axiomatics, probability, and Boolean Algebra were all reintroduced into most of these new mathematics curricula.

The School Mathematics Study Group (SMSG) had a major impact on the content and study of mathematics at the secondary school level, as did the Greater Cleveland Mathematics Program, developed for grades K–6. Numerous other modern mathematics programs were developed for all academic levels.

In recent years, increasing disenchantment with the new mathematics has taken place among laymen and professionals alike. (See GREATER CLEVELAND MATHEMATICS PROGRAM and SCHOOL MATHEMATICS STUDY GROUP.)
References: Leslie A. Dwight, *Modern Mathematics for the Elementary Teacher,* New York: Holt, Rinehart and Winston, Inc., 1966; Howard Fehr and Jo McKeeby Phillips, *Teaching Modern Mathematics in the Elementary School,* Reading, MA: Addison-Wesley Publishing Company, 1967; Nathan J. Fine, *An Introduction to Modern Mathematics,* Chicago: Rand McNally and Company, 1965.

NEWSPRINT, an inexpensive paper, found in many classrooms, that is used for many purposes: art, reading, arithmetic, science, and so on. The paper comes in pads or rolls, is extremely easy to handle, and will take soft pencil, crayon, felt pen, charcoal, or soft writing devices. Because it is made from wood pulp, newsprint is not very durable. Given its relatively low cost, teachers tend to use newsprint once and then immediately discard it.
References: James W. Brown, et al., *AV Instruction: Technology Media and Methods* (Fourth Edition), New York: McGraw-Hill Book Company, 1973; Ralph Mayer, *A Dictionary of Art Terms and Techniques,* New York: Thomas Y. Crowell, 1969; Adelaide Sproul, *With a Free Hand: Painting, Drawing, Graphics, Ceramics, and Sculpture for Children,* New York: Reinhold Book Company, 1968.

NEW ZEALAND EDUCATIONAL INSTITUTE (NZEI), largest and oldest organization of teachers in New Zealand. Formed in 1883, NZEI has a current membership exceeding 21,000. Its *Policy Document* cites two of the organization's major pur-

poses: (1) serving as "the voice of teachers on professional questions and working conditions alike" (p. 7), and (2) "to advance the cause of education generally whilst upholding and maintaining the just claims of members individually and collectively" (p. 7).

As a service to its members, NZEI maintains a unique counseling service; publishes a journal, *National Education;* publishes yearbooks and other materials for teachers through two organizationally owned subsidiaries, Education House Ltd. and Deslandes; and carries out research of interest to New Zealand educators.

NZEI is a member of the World Confederation of Organizations of the Teaching Profession. Its main offices are in Wellington. (See WORLD CONFEDERATION OF ORGANIZATIONS OF THE TEACHING PROFESSION.)
References: New Zealand Educational Institute, *Manual for Counselors,* Wellington, New Zealand: The Institute, January 1978; "New Zealand Educational Institute" (Mimeographed Fact Sheet), Wellington, New Zealand: The Institute, Undated; New Zealand Educational Institute, *Policy Document,* Wellington, New Zealand: The Institute, 1980.

NOMINAL SCALE—See DATA and SCALE OF MEASUREMENT

NOMOTHETIC DIMENSION—See GETZELS-GUBA MODEL

NONBASAL READING PROGRAMS, reading approaches that do not follow or employ the systematic and sequential elements common to basal reading programs. Nonbasal programs include individualized reading, the language-experience approach, and the eclectic method of teaching reading. (See ECLECTIC READING METHOD; INDIVIDUALIZED READING; and LANGUAGE EXPERIENCE APPROACH.)
References: Eddie C. Kennedy, *Methods in Teaching Developmental Reading,* Itasca, IL: F. E. Peacock Publishers, Inc., 1974; Wilma H. Miller, *The First R: Elementary Reading Today* (Second Edition), New York: Holt, Rinehart and Winston, Inc., 1977.

NONCERTIFIED PERSONNEL—See AUXILIARY PERSONNEL and CLASSIFIED PERSONNEL

NONDIRECTIVE TECHNIQUE, an approach sometimes used in counseling, group therapy, and psychotherapy that seeks to have the individual reorganize, reorder, or alter attitudes and behaviors through his/her own introspection, actions, and/or reactions. The nondirective technique is affective in nature and based on the principle that the individual is restricted by his/her emotions; furthermore, that by developing free expression, opening up new emotional and affective avenues and alternatives, developing accepting behaviors, and reducing internal emotional conflicts, the individual will better understand him/herself. He/she will also understand what may be causing a problem(s). Ultimately, he/she will be helped to adjust emotionally.

Nondirective therapy in psychotherapy was developed in the 1940s by Carl Rogers and called client-centered therapy. In nondirective therapy, the therapist helps the client work out his/her problem, but the therapist doesn't prejudge him/her. Thus, the client has the potential to solve his/her own problems and need not "lean heavily" on experts.

References: Howard Kirschenbaum, *On Becoming Carl Rogers,* New York: Delacorte Press, 1979; David G. Martin, *Learning-based Client-centered Therapy,* Monterey, CA: Brooks/Cole Publishing Company, 1972; Irving H. Paul, *The Form and Technique of Psychotherapy,* Chicago: University of Chicago Press, 1978; Carl R. Rogers, *Counseling and Psychotherapy: Newer Concepts in Practice,* Boston: Houghton Mifflin Company, 1942; Carl R. Rogers, et al., *Client-centered Therapy, Its Current Practice, Implications, and Theory,* Boston: Houghton Mifflin Company, 1951.

NONGRADED SCHOOL, an organizational (continuous progress) plan adopted by many elementary schools for use at the primary level such that children can theoretically advance at their own rates in all subjects. Some middle and high schools have adopted the plan as well. Curriculum content, reading in particular, is divided into sequential steps. Children move through the sequence at their own speed. Grade-level designations are eliminated. For slower students, this reduces the traumatic experience of failure. The plan also allows gifted children to move faster than they would under a traditional structure. With the nongraded or continuous progress plan, no formal promotion or advancement takes place at the end of each grade level.

In years past, many one-room schools had elements of the nongraded concept incorporated into their structure.

Research concerning the continuous progress plan has neither supported nor rejected the claims of those advocating it. Problems relating to the plan include curriculum articulation and the establishment of structured achievement levels.

References: Ruth C. Cook and Ronald C. Doll, *The Elementary School Curriculum,* Boston: Allyn and Bacon, Inc., 1973; Frank R. Dufay, *Ungrading the Elementary School,* West Nyack, NY: Parker Publishing Company, Inc., 1966; John Goodlad and Robert Anderson, *The Nongraded Elementary School* (Second Edition), New York: Harcourt, Brace and World, Inc., 1963; J. Murray Lee, *Elementary Education: Today and Tomorrow,* Boston: Allyn and Bacon, Inc., 1966; Daniel Tanner and Laurel N. Tanner, *Curriculum Development,* New York: Macmillan Publishing Company, Inc., 1975.

NONOPERATING DISTRICTS, school districts that do not operate schools of their own. Such districts are legal administrative units managed by an elected school board. The large majority of nonoperating districts have small numbers of children of school age who are enrolled in neighboring school districts and whose tuition is paid for by the nonoperating district. A much smaller number have no children of school age. The number of nonoperating districts has been decreasing steadily.

A 1958 AASA commission on school district organization was critical of such districts, charging that they "serve more as protectors of low property tax rates than as providers for children's educational needs. They are administrative units whose true purposes have withered and lost real meaning" (p. 87).

The National Center for Education Statistics, in 1979, reported a total of 278 nonoperating districts in the United States.

References: Commission on School District Organization, *School District Organization,* Washington, DC: American Association of School Administrators, 1958; Nancy B. Dearman and Valena W. Plisko, *The Condition of Education, 1979 Edition,* Washington, DC: National Center for Education Statistics, U.S. Department of HEW, 1979.

NONPARAMETRIC STATISTICS, those statistical procedures that are used with distribution-free data or when the sample size is very small. Distribution-free tests make no assumptions about the parent population from which the samples are drawn.

Nonparametric procedures are used with data whose scales are nominal (e.g. male or female; black, white, or green; American, English, or Russian) or ordinal (1st, 2nd, 3rd; poor, fair, best, etc.); where the distribution of the data is unknown or highly questionable; or when the sizes of the groups being studied are small. Several common nonparametric tests are: Wilcoxon matched pairs signed-ranks test; chi-square; Kruskal-Wallis one-way analysis of variance; and Kendall's Tau. Although there are times when nonparametric procedures are easier to use than parametric procedures, many researchers prefer to use parametric procedures, if possible. (See PARAMETRIC STATISTICS.)

References: Wayne W. Daniel, *Applied Nonparametric Statistics,* Boston: Houghton Mifflin Company, 1978; Jean D. Gibbons, *Nonparametric Methods for Quantitative Analysis,* New York: Holt, Rinehart and Winston, Inc., 1976; Erich L. Lehmann, *Nonparametrics: Statistical Methods Based on Ranks,* San Francisco: Holden-Day, 1975; James H. McMillan and Sally Schumacher, *Research in Education: A Conceptual Introduction* (Second Edition), Glenview, IL: Scott, Foresman and Company, 1989; Sidney Siegel, *Nonparametric Statistics for the Behavioral Sciences,* McGraw-Hill Book Company, 1956.

NONPUBLIC SCHOOLS, also classified as private schools. Such institutions are not operated by a governmental agency. They can be divided into two general classifications: (1) church-owned or church-related, and (2) nonchurch-owned or nonchurch-related schools. These schools, most of which are not profit-making institutions, range from preschool to trade schools to universities.

The major parochial school groups are those schools related to and/or operated by various Catholic religious orders. In some sections of the United States (e.g. Philadelphia, Boston, Chicago), the Catholic parochial school system is almost as large as the public school system. Although Catholic schools existed in the 1700s in the United States, their major rise and development started in the 1800s with the increased migration of Catholics to the United States. Protestant schools can be traced back to American Colonial times, with many different groups establishing such institutions. There are Jewish and Black Moslem religious schools, too.

Many private schools, mostly in the eastern states, were founded some time ago. Phillips Andover Academy (1778) is an example. Many of the early private schools in America, particularly the boarding schools, were established by religious groups. These had classical educational programs and were organized to develop and train gentlemen or as finishing schools for girls.

Numerous controversies surround nonpublic education in the United States. They include or relate to: (1) the role of private schools in American education; (2) tax support for selected programs; (3) the elite nature of some of the schools and their programs; and (4) public school integration. Nonpublic schools are found in every section and state in the United States; consequently, they affect American education at all levels and in every area. (See PAROCHIAL SCHOOLS.)

References: Leonard Baird, *The Elite Schools,* Lexington, MA: Lexington Books, 1977; Otto Kraushaar, *Private Schools: From the Puritans to the Present,* Bloomington, IN: The Phi Delta Kappa Foundation, 1976; Daniel Sullivan, *Public Aid to Nonpublic Schools,* Lexington, MA: Lexington Books, 1974.

NONSERVED CHILD—See EXEMPTED CHILD

NONSTANDARD ENGLISH, the English spoken and written by individuals who come from environments where other languages and dialects are spoken and who do not speak or write the standard English normally taught in the schools and accepted by the culture. There are many nonstandard Englishes spoken and written throughout the English-speaking world (e.g. black English, calypso English). Often, they are used by native born citizens who live in social-economic environments different from those of the dominant society. The nonstandard Englishes have phonological and grammatical variations that distinguish them from standard English. As a result, children and adults who speak a nonstandard English frequently have problems with listening, speaking, writing, spelling, reading, and using standard English.

The standard English taught in one English-speaking country (e.g. United States) may be different, to some degree, from the English spoken in another English-speaking country (e.g. England).

Since all languages have value, purposes, and functions, and no one language can be considered superior to another, some authorities point out that individuals who use nonstandard English are not inferior to those who use standard English. For this reason, it is stressed that they should not be made to feel inferior. (See BLACK ENGLISH.)

References: Bonnie Lass and Beth Davis, *The Remedial Reading Handbook,* Englewood Cliffs, NJ: Prentice-Hall, Inc., 1985; Donna E. Norton, *The Effective Teaching of Language Arts,* Columbus, OH: Charles E. Merrill Publishing Company, 1980; Catherine Wallace, *Learning to Read in a Multicultural Society,* New York: Prentice Hall, 1988.

NONVERBAL COMMUNICATIONS, those messages communicated by individuals through the use of a part of the body. Gestures, head movements, hand movements, facial expressions, gazes, spatial position, postures, bodily contact, tones of voice, and clothing are but a few examples of nonverbal communications.

All animals use body communication; humans use it extensively. Human nonverbal communication is learned; meanings and types are a function of factors such as the area of the world, the culture of the individuals involved, sex, age, and education.

Nonverbal communications can be used in support of verbal communication or to replace it. At times, the nonverbal may actually be opposite to what is being said. Nonverbal communications express emotions and attitudes very effectively, either consciously or unconsciously.

Considerable nonverbal communication takes place in the school. Accordingly, authorities advise teachers and counselors to be sensitive to their own and students' messages being sent and received through nonverbal actions and movements. (See PROXEMICS.)

References: Michael Argyle, *Bodily Communication,* New York: International Universities Press, 1975; Robert G. Harper, et al., *Nonverbal Communication: The State of the Art,* New York: John Wiley and Sons, 1978; Walburga von Raffler-Engel and Bates Hoffer (Editors), *Aspects of Nonverbal Communication: A Handbook,* San Antonio, TX: Trinity University, 1977.

NORMAL CAPACITY, or student capacity of a school building, the number of students that a school plant can accommodate: (1) for instructional purposes; (2) on a given school day; and (3) on a single session basis. Capacities are normally calculated in accordance with state school building standards.

References: Combined Glossary: Terms and Definitions from the Handbooks of the State Educational Records and Reports Series, Washington, DC: National Center for Education Statistics, U.S. Department of Health, Education, and Welfare, 1974.

NORMAL DISTRIBUTION CURVE, known at times as the Gaussian Curve or the DeMoiovre's Curve, a distribution of scores that forms a bell-shaped curve in which the distribution of scores is symmetrical from the mean. In such a distribution, there is the same number of cases below the mean as there is above the mean. The mean (average), the mode (the score that occurs most often), and the median (point in the distribution below which 50 percent of the cases lie) are one and the same point.

In nature, there are many normal distributions. Often the normal distribution is theoretical. *Standard scores* are based on a normal distribution curve. Through the use of a normal distribution curve and the conversion of a raw score to a standard score, researchers can determine the theoretical expected frequency of a particular score. (See CENTRAL TENDENCY MEASURES and STANDARD DEVIATION.)

References: Lou M. Carey, *Measuring and Evaluating School Learning,* Boston: Allyn and Bacon, Inc., 1988; David S. Moore and George P. McCabe, *Introduction to the Practice of Statistics,* New York: W. H. Freeman and Company, 1989.

NORMAL SCHOOLS, the nation's earliest professional schools for the training of teachers, first established (1839–40) in Massachusetts. Similar schools were already operating in France, Germany, England, and Italy.

The minimal training program, a one-year curriculum, consisted of reading, writing, grammar, arithmetic, orthography (spelling), and geography. Students selected for a second year of training took

Normal Distribution Curve

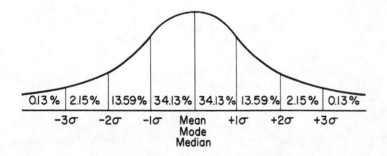

additional work in fields such as drawing, music, bookkeeping, navigation, physiology, history, and the natural sciences. Methodologies of teaching, as related to each of these study areas, were also studied. Model schools, forerunners of today's university laboratory schools, were attached to each normal school.

Most early normal schools were private institutions. As time passed, and the popularity of normal schools increased, the majority became public, two-year, posthigh school institutions whose programs led to the granting of a teaching license. A graduate could, if he/she so desired, take additional work and qualify for the bachelor's degree. Some normal schools sponsored three- and four-year programs, a few offering the Bachelor of Pedogogics degree upon completion of a four-year course of study.

References: Nicholas Murray Butler, *Education in the United States*, American Book Company, 1910; Harry G. Good and James D. Teller, *A History of American Education* (Third Edition), New York: The Macmillan Company, 1973.

NORM GROUP, a representative group of individuals whose test scores are used to establish a set of norms for standardized tests. A norm group can be representative of an extremely large population (all 15-year-old girls in the United States), or the group may be more restricted in its representation (15-year-old girls in Omaha, 15-year-old girls in a particular school, etc.).

Since norms are established from a norm group, it is extremely important that the norm group be representative of whatever population is to be used as the comparative or base-line group against which an individual's test scores will be compared or from which interpretations are to be made. A major problem attendant to interpreting individual test scores is the fact that the norm group is either unknown or perhaps inappropriate to the individual being tested. (See NORM-REFERENCED TESTS and NORMS.)

References: Lou M. Carey, *Measuring and Evaluating School Learning*, Boston: Allyn and Bacon, Inc., 1988; Arthur Jensen, *Bias in Mental Testing*, New York: The Free Press, 1979; David S. Moore and George P. McCabe, *Introduction to the Practice of Statistics*, New York: W. H. Freeman and Company, 1989.

NORM-REFERENCED TESTS, standardized examinations in which an individual's performance is compared (evaluated) in relation to the performance of others (i.e. a norm group). Most standardized tests administered in the schools are norm-referenced instruments (e.g. intelligence, achievement, aptitude, and interest).

There are many problems and concerns associated with the use of norm-referenced tests. One major problem is the definition (description) or appropriateness of the norm group used to establish the comparative base. Another is the nature and type of tests written. A third relates to breadth of examination. A large number of test items is not needed to establish variability within a very large norm group; yet, if the norm-referenced test is used to assess the level of a student's knowledge in a field, it is possible that decisions will be made on the basis of only a small number of test items.

Norm-referenced tests deal with relative relationships, and criterion tests deal with a set standard or level (e.g. 90 out of 100, 85 percent correct) of performance below which a person is not considered to have met the standard. (See CRITERION-REFERENCED TEST.)

References: Frederick B. David (Chair), *Standards for Educational Psychological Tests*, Washington, DC: American Psychological Association, 1974; Victor R. Martuza, *Applying Norm-Referenced and Criterion-Referenced Measurement in Education*, Boston: Allyn and Bacon, Inc., 1977; William A. Mehrens and Irvin J. Lehmann, *Using Standardized Tests in Education*, New York: Longman, Inc., 1987; Vito Perrone, *The Abuses of Standardized Testing* (PDK Fastback 92), Bloomington, IN: The Phi Delta Kappa Educational Foundation, 1977.

NORMS, in educational and psychological measurement, those performance standards that are established by a reference group. Norms are usually determined empirically by testing a representative group and then calculating that group's test performance. For example, a representative sample of 16-year-old boys may be given a particular test and their average test scores then calculated. This average, or norm, can be used as a reference score to interpret scores on the test when administered to other individuals. Raw scores on a test have little meaning unless compared with other interpretive data, such as a norm. Norms can be calculated from national samples and/or those established locally.

There are many types of norms: mental age, grade equivalents, percentiles, standard scores, and deviation IQ. Norms are extremely important for use with non-referenced and standardized tests.

In terms of social behavior, norms are those behaviors that are accepted and practiced by a particular group. These norms are established over a long period of time (e.g. the norms of a community).

References: Anne Anastasi, *Psychological Testing* (Sixth Edition), New York: Macmillan Publishing Company, Inc., 1988; D. L. Bayless, et al., *Considerations and Procedures in National Norming*, Iowa City, IA: American College and Testing Programs, 1974; Arnold Birenbaum and Edward Sagarin, *Norms and Human Behavior*, New York: Praeger Publishers, 1976; David S. Moore and George P. McCabe, *Introduction to the Practice of Statistics*, New York: W. H. Freeman and Company, 1989; Joseph Raz, *Practical Reason and Norms*, London, England: Hutchinson, Ltd., 1975.

NORTHWEST ORDINANCE—See
ORDINANCE OF 1785

NOTATION, MUSICAL, printed symbols that make possible the reading and writing of music. Some music educators hold that individuals unable to understand the graphic language of music are musically illiterate. Others disagree, contending that mastery of notation is not a requisite to understanding and appreciation of music. When notation is taught as part of a school's music education program, it is done on an "as needed" basis, with this visual experience normally preceded by the aural.

Notation provides the reader with two kinds of information. First, it indicates how a melody rises and falls (pitch). Second, it tells how long each sound lasts (rhythm). Mastery of notation involves knowledge of rhythm, pitch, clefs, time signatures, rests, and key signatures. (See PITCH and RHYTHM.)

References: Willi Apel, *Harvard Dictionary of Music* (Second Edition), Cambridge, MA: The Belknap Press of Harvard University Press, 1970; Ian D. Bent, et al., "Notation" in Stanley Sadie (Editor), *The New Grove Dictionary of Music and Musicians* (Volume 13), London, England: Macmillan Publishers Limited, 1980; Malcolm E. Bessom, et al., *Teaching Music in Today's Secondary Schools: A Creative Approach to Contemporary Music Education*, New York: Holt, Rinehart and Winston, Inc., 1974; Bernarr Rainbow, *Music in the Classroom* (Second Edition), London, England: Heinemann Educational Books, Ltd., 1971.

NUFFIELD PROJECT, or the Nuffield Foundation Mathematics Teaching Project, an innovative program of mathematics teaching carried out in England and Wales. Inaugurated in 1964 and directed by Dr. Geoffrey Matthews, the project employed a discovery-type approach to learning for 5–13-year-olds. According to Matthews, the project was to "be designed to help (the children) connect together many aspects of the world around them, to introduce them gradually to the process of abstract thinking, and to foster in them a critical, logical, but also creative, turn of mind" (Vosper, p. 370).

The project was initially funded by the Nuffield Foundation to last from 1964 to 1970 but later had its funding extended. It included diverse activities such as: (1) preparation of teachers' guides that stressed student understanding, individualized pacing, activity-based methods, and small group instruction; (2) inservice teacher education, much of it carried out through teachers' centers; (3) special instructional apparatus; (4) films; (5) use of activity cards that posed open-ended kinds of problems; and (6) experimental resequencing of curriculum (e.g. postponing teaching of division until fractions had been taught).

In the Nuffield program, the teacher performed two basic roles: (1) providing children with challenging learning (discovery) materials, and (2) helping children to infer patterns and to see number relationships. Providing children with answers to problems was discouraged.

References: Edith E. Biggs and James R. MacLean, *Freedom to Learn: An Active Learning Approach to Mathematics*, Don Mills, Ontario, Canada: Addison-Wesley Publishing Company, 1969; Norbert Maertens, "What Lies Ahead: Exercising Options with Emerging Programs" in C. W. Schminke and William R. Arnold (Editors), *Mathematics Is a Verb: Options for Teaching*, Hinsdale, IL: The Dryden Press, 1971; A. G. Vosper, "Nuffield Foundation Mathematics Teaching Project" in L. R. Chapman (Editor), *The Process of Learning Mathematics*, Oxford, England: Pergamon Press, Inc., 1972.

NULL HYPOTHESIS—See HYPOTHESES

NUMBER LINE, technically a geometric ray, a multipurpose device used in the teaching of mathematics. The number line is made by following three simple steps (see illustration): (1) drawing a line, with arrows placed at each end to designate infinity; (2) labeling one point on the line "0"; and (3) using a unit of measure (e.g. inch, centimeter), labeling other points on the line at equal intervals. Numbers to the right of "0" are positive, those to the left negative.

Number lines may be used to teach any of several mathematical concepts or processes. Examples include: (1) "less than" vs. "greater than"; (2) addition, subtraction, multiplication, and division; (3) fractions; and (4) negative numbers. Superimposed over the number line in the illustration are numbers grouped together by arrows that show

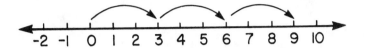

Number Distribution Line

how the concept of division-with-remainder can be explained graphically. (The problem: 10 ÷ 3 = 3 R1.

References: Rosalie Jensen, *Exploring Mathematical Concepts and Skills in the Elementary School,* Columbus, OH: Charles E. Merrill Publishing Company, 1973; William D. McKillip, et al., *Mathematics Instruction in the Elementary Grades,* Morristown, NJ: Silver Burdett Company, 1978; William Zlot, *Elementary School Mathematics: Teaching the Basic Skills,* New York: Thomas Y. Crowell, 1976.

NUMERICAL STAFFING ADEQUACY, a useful measure used to report the ratio of total students in a school or school district to the total number of professional employees employed in that same unit. In most instances, "professional employees" are considered to be certified personnel. Numerical staffing adequacy is generally reported as the number of professional employees per 1,000 students. The formula used to determine this measure is:

$$NSA = \frac{\text{Total professional employees}}{\text{Total students}} \times 1,000$$

The National Education Association reports that, nationally, numerical staffing adequacy among school districts ranges from 40 to almost 100 professionals per 1,000 students.

This measure has proven successful in research dealing with quality of education. Several of the *adaptability studies* conducted at Teachers College, Columbia University, in the 1940s and 1950s also made use of this measure. (See ADAPTABILITY, ORGANIZATIONAL; CLASS SIZE; and PUPIL-TEACHER RATIO.)

References: Class Size (Reference and Resource Series), Washington, DC: National Education Association, 1977; Charles E. Danowski and James N. Finch, "Teacher Preparation and Numerical Adequacy," *IAR Research Bulletin,* 6: 7–10, No. 3; 1966; Donald H. Ross (Editor), *Administration for Adaptability* (Volumes I and III), New York: Metropolitan School Study Council, Columbia University, 1951.

NURSE-TEACHER—See SCHOOL NURSE

NURSERY SCHOOL—See PRE-SCHOOL

NURSING EDUCATION, those training programs designed to prepare individuals for the different nursing occupations (i.e., registered nurse, RN; licensed practical nurse, LPN; nursing aide, orderly, and attendant).

There are several classifications within each nursing occupation. For example, within the RN category, there are hospital nurses, private duty nurses, community health nurses, office nurses, occupational health or industrial nurses, school nurses, nurse administrators, and nurse educators. Although there is considerable commonality in their training programs, some variations are made to accommodate this occupational diversity.

RN nursing programs include classroom instruction and a supervised clinical experience in various health facilities. Anatomy, psychology, sociology, other behavioral sciences, microbiology, family medicine, nutrition, and nursing are all a part of the RN training curriculum. Students completing RN programs may be awarded a diploma from a hospital or private school (in the case of two- or three-year programs), an associate degree from a community college (after completing a two-year program), a bachelor's degree (usually a four-year program in a college or university), and advanced degrees (masters or doctoral degrees) for those who wish to pursue advanced study in nursing or nursing education.

LPNs usually have a year of training, but nursing aides, orderlies, and attendants may receive lesser amounts of formal instruction. In some cases, aides, orderlies, and attendants receive on-the-job training only.

A few vocational high schools offer selected nursing occupation programs.

References: Bernice E. Anderson, *Nursing Education in Community and Junior College,* Philadelphia: J. B. Lippincott, Company, 1968; Madeline M. Leninger, *Transcultural Nursing,* New York: John Wiley and Sons, 1978; *Occupational Outlook Handbook, 1980–81 Edition,* Washington, DC: Bureau of Labor Statistics, U.S. Department of Labor, 1980; Callista Roy (Editor), *Introduction to Nursing: An Adaptation Model,* Englewood Cliffs, NJ: Prentice-Hall, Inc., 1976; Lily M. Turnbull and Helena Pizurki (Editors), *Family Planning in the Education of Nurses and Midwives,* Geneva, Switzerland: World Health Organization, 1973.

OBJECTIVES, those learning or behavioral outcomes that are planned and that a program or experience is designed to accomplish. Objectives may be very broad and difficult to measure, or they may be specific and stated in behavioral terms to facilitate their measurement and observation.

There are several types of objectives. *Educational objectives* are those that give direction to an educational curriculum. They are sometimes called educational goals or aims. Ralph Tyler, in 1950, suggested that key sources for the development of statements of ends (educational objectives) are suggested by studying: (1) the learner; (2) contemporary life outside the school; and (3) the ideas of subject matter specialists. Such objectives, when set forth in writing, should be precise, significant, and attainable. Educational objectives tend to be broad (e.g. "to develop a love for learning"; "to develop good citizens").

Instructional objectives are those outcomes dealing with the aims of specific instructional areas (e.g. "to develop competent writers"; "to develop competent readers"; "to develop an appreciation for fine arts"). These objectives, also broad, have sometimes been classified as goals or aims by many educators.

Finally, there are *behavioral objectives.* They are specific and precise, focus on a particular skill or outcome, and are written with a limited specific expectation for the individual. Behavioral objects should have the following elements: (1) time limit; (2) statement of what the learner is expected to do; and (3) the criteria with which to measure the attainment of the objective. An example of a behavioral objective is: "after completing a chapter on addition, a student will be able to solve correctly 50 out of 60 randomly selected simple addition problems." A series of behavioral objectives can lead to formulation of broader educational or instructional objectives. (See BEHAVIORAL OBJECTIVES and GOAL.)

References: Robert F. Mager, *Preparing Instructional Objectives*, Palo Alto, CA: Fearon Publishers, Inc., 1962; Earl J. Montague, *Fundamentals of Secondary Classroom Instruction*, Columbus, OH: Merrill Publishing Company, 1987; Daniel Tanner, *Using Behavioral Objectives in the Classroom*, New York: Macmillan Publishing Company, Inc., 1972; Ralph W. Tyler, *Basic Principles of Curriculum and Instruction*, Chicago: University of Chicago Press, 1950.

OBJECTIVE TEST, an examination containing items that are of two types: (1) the *constructed-response* type, which requires the examinee to provide a short answer from recall, and (2) the *select* type (e.g. matching, true-false, multiple choice) in which a correct or best answer is chosen (recognized) from among those furnished by the test's creator.

If constructed properly, objective tests can be extremely valid and reliable. Scoring is relatively simple; hence corrected tests can be returned quickly to students. These tests also overcome many of the weaknesses inherent in the essay test. Critics of objective tests argue that they are not readily adapted for testing higher cognitive levels. (See ANALOGIES TEST ITEM; COMPLETION TEST; ESSAY TEST; MATCHING TEST; MULTIPLE CHOICE ITEM; and TRUE-FALSE TEST.)

References: Anne Anastasi, *Psychological Testing* (Sixth Edition), New York: Macmillan Publishing Company, 1988; George K. Cunningham, *Educational and Psychological Measurement*, New York: Macmillan Publishing Company, 1986.

OBSERVATIONAL TECHNIQUES, various procedures used to analyze behavior by watching what individuals or groups of individuals actually do. Observation techniques range from informal or incidental observing to the use of sociograms, one-way screens, and visual or tape recordings. Among the most complex systematic observational techniques, such as Flanders's interaction analysis, are those requiring extended observations by trained observers. The purpose of observation, regardless of technique, is to collect valid and reliable information as efficiently as possible. Such information is then used to assess a situation (usually interactions among individuals in that given situation over a period of time) and to develop alternatives and/or changes needed to enhance or maximize the situation.

Various observational schemes are available for classroom use. The teacher can be the observer, but most often an outside observer is utilized. When interaction analyses are to be made, students' and teachers' behaviors (verbal, nonverbal) are usually coded and placed into appropriate categories that fit into a particular scheme. From them, information concerning classroom interactions, including student-to-student and teacher-to-student, can be culled and strategies formulated. (See FLANDERS INTERACTION ANALYSIS and SOCIOGRAM.)

References: Millie C. Almy and Celia Geniski, *Ways of Studying Children: An Observational Manual for Early Childhood Teachers* (Revised Edition), New York: Teachers College Press, 1979; Edmond J. Amidon and John B. Hough (Editors), *Interaction Analyses: Theory, Research, and Application*, Reading, MA: Addison-Wesley Publishing Company, 1967; Robin Barrow and Geoffrey Milburn, *A Critical Dictionary of Educational Concepts*, New York: St. Martin's Press, 1986; Ned A. Flanders, *Analyzing Teaching Behaviors*, Reading, MA: Addison-Wesley Publishing Company, 1970; Donald D. Hammill (Editor), *Assessing the Abilities and Instructional Needs of Students*, Austin, TX: Pro-Ed, Inc., 1987.

OBSESSIVE-COMPULSIVE, a neurosis that occurs in combination, with either the obsessive condition or the compulsive condition dominating. In the *obsessive* state, the individual has continued disagreeable or disturbing thoughts. Where obsessions predominate, the individual is preoccupied with ideas, a condition that interferes with his/her daily life.

Those in the *compulsive* state are involved with acts or action. If a person doesn't act, there may also be a great deal of anxiety generated. Often the actions reflect overconcern with phenomenal phobias such as cleanliness, safety, or superstitions.

Although all people have had short-lived compulsions, the obsessive-compulsive person has the problem for an extended period and is both depressed and anxious as a result.

References: Frederick H. Allen, *Psychotherapy with Children*, Lincoln, NE: University of Nebraska Press, 1979; Melvin Gray, *Neurosis: A Comprehensive and Critical View*, New York: Van Nostrand Reinhold Company, 1978; Jane W. Kessler, *Psychopathology of Childhood*, Englewood Cliffs, NJ: Prentice-Hall, Inc., 1966.

OCCUPATIONAL EDUCATION—See TECHNICAL EDUCATION and VOCATIONAL EDUCATION

OCCUPATIONAL THERAPY (OT), a planned program of purposeful activities designed to enable physically or mentally handicapped individuals to function effectively in the world of work. Occupational therapy is often a major part of the total treatment of handicapped individuals. Particular attention is given to their need for physical and emotional adjustment. Because OT involves some form of work, it (the work) by its very nature becomes a form of therapy. In some cases, occupational therapy stresses only simple activities that prepare the individual for daily living (e.g. how to grasp a fork). More complex forms of OT are used that aim for a higher level of attainment, these adjusted to the individual's potential for mastering them successfully. Occupational therapy is a planned program designed to maximize an individual's potential and adjustment. Its goals reflect, and are a function of, the individual's handicap.

Occupational therapy is part of a larger rehabilitation program that involves the services of doctors, nurses, physical therapists, speech therapists, and other required rehabilitation specialists. Highly trained occupational therapists provide the professional services for OT.

Formal training and certification prepare one for a career as an occupational therapist. Programs range from four-year bachelor degree curricula (offered by colleges/universities) to one-year certification programs (sponsored by vocational schools or community colleges). Occupational therapist assistants are required to complete the less extensive training programs. Curricula usually include course work in the physical, biological, and behavioral sciences, application of occupational therapy theory, and internships in agencies or hospitals.

Special examinations developed by the American Occupational Therapy Association must be passed in order for one to become a registered occupational therapist (OTR) or certified occupational therapy assistant (COTA).

References: Lloyd V. Briggs, *Occupation as a Substitute for Restraint in the Treatment of the Mentally Ill*, New York: Arno Press, 1973; Joan M. Erikson, et al., *Activity, Recovery, Growth: The Communal Role of Planned Activities*, New York: W. W. Norton and Company, Inc., 1976; Joel A. Levitch, *Occupational Therapy: A New Life for the Disabled*, New York: Public Affairs Committee, 1968.

OCTAVE, a musical term for notes that, on a diatonic scale, are seven notes apart. Stated differently, an octave is the interval between the first and eighth notes of the diatonic scale. In acoustical terms, an octave is achieved when the frequency of a given tone (e.g. á = 440) is doubled (á = 880). When such doubling of vibrations occurs, the new tone appears to be a duplicate of the original one, at a higher sound.

References: Willi Apel, *Harvard Dictionary of Music* (Second Edition, Revised and Enlarged), Cambridge, MA: The Belknap Press of Harvard University Press, 1970; William Drabkin, "Octave" in Stanley Sadie (Editor), *The New Grove Dictionary of Music and Musicians* (Volume 13), London, England: Macmillan Publishers Limited, 1980; J. A. Westrup and F. L. Harrison (Revised by Conrad Wilson), *The New College Encyclopedia of Music*, New York: W. W. Norton and Company, Inc., 1976.

ODYSSEY: A CURRICULUM FOR THINKING,

a program intended to increase students ability to perform intellectual tasks. Developed at Harvard University, the curriculum combines research on cognition with that on direct instruction. The program was developed for use by heterogeneously grouped classes in both elementary and middle schools. The approach is eclectic in nature; materials reflect a variety of theories of cognitive development—i.e., Socratic inquiry, Piagetian analysis, and Brunnerian discovery and exploration. The focus is on long-term development that will transfer to other subjects and to continued growth after formal schooling. There are approximately 100 separate lessons. Materials include six teacher manuals and six student texts. Materials are intended to follow predetermined order beginning as early as Grade Four.

References: M. J. Adams, "Project Intelligence," *Human Intelligence International Newsletter*, Winter 1984; Elena Wright, "Odyssey: A Curriculum for Thinking" in Arthur L. Costa (Editor), Alexandria, VA: Association for Supervision and Curriculum Development, 1985.

ODYSSEY OF THE MIND PROGRAM (formerly OLYMPICS OF THE MIND),

an extracurricular activity targeted for gifted students. Participants work in groups to solve assigned problems. Organization of the program reflects much of the organization found in the athletic olympics. Teams of volunteers are coached in training sessions by coaches who help the group members extend and improve their divergent creative problem-solving abilities. The teams are then presented problems to solve within a time frame; these problems are assigned dependent on the age level of the team. The competitions range from intramural events to worldwide involvements. Judges are selected by the coordinators of the specific event to represent many areas of expertise.

References: James L. Gallagher, *Teaching the Gifted Child* (Third Edition), Boston: Allyn and Bacon Inc., 1985; C. Samuel Micklus and T. Gourley, "Olympics of the Mind," *Coaches Manual*, Glassboro, NJ: Creative Competition, 1982; C. Samuel Micklus and Carole Micklus, "Odyssey of the Mind" *Program Handbook: Instructional Manual for Teams and Coaches*, Glassboro, NJ: Creative Competition, 1989.

OEDIPUS COMPLEX,

a Freudian concept relating to an offspring's sexual interest in a parent of the opposite sex. Girls will at first identify with the mother and boys with the father; the girls then mentally replace their mother in the mother-father relationship, and the boys mentally replace their fathers. Thus, the mother becomes the love object for boys, while the father becomes the love object for girls. At the same time, resentment and anger mounts toward the parent being replaced.

This complex is strongest between the ages of three and five. Considerable anxiety, aggression, fear, guilt, and hostility are manifested during this period toward both parents, each for different reasons.

The term was named by Freud after Oedipus, of Greek legend, who unknowingly killed his father and married his mother. Later, having discovered what he had done, Oedipus blinded himself as self-punishment.

References: Raymond J. Corsini, *Current Psychotherapies* (Second Edition), Itasca, IL: F. E. Peacock Publishers, Inc., 1979; Otto Fenichel, *The Psychoanalytic Theory of Neurosis*, New York: W. W. Norton and Company, Inc., 1945; Jane W. Kessler, *Psychopathology of Childhood*, Englewood Cliffs, NJ: Prentice-Hall, Inc., 1966.

OFFICE OF CIVIL RIGHTS,

a generic term for the several offices in the federal government responsible for enforcing various civil rights laws pertaining to their respective departments. Within the Department of Education (DE), the Office of Civil Rights is responsible for the administration and enforcement of departmental policies that prohibit discrimination with regard to race, sex, religion, color, or national origin in programs and activities receiving federal financial assistance from the DE. Other such offices are: the Office of Civil Rights in the Department of Health and Human Services; the Civil Rights Division in the Department of Justice; Equal Opportunity Office, Department of Housing and Urban Development; Departmental Office of Civil Rights, Department of Transportation; and six other similar offices within various departments and units of the federal government. Similar offices exist at state and local levels.

References: Joan M. Burke, *Civil Rights*, New York: R. R. Bowker Company, 1974; Bernard Schwartz (Editor), *Civil Rights*, New York: Chelsea House Publishers, 1980.

OFFICE OF ECONOMIC OPPORTUNITY (OEO), a federal agency within the Executive Office of the President, created by the Economic Opportunity Act of 1964. It was responsible for planning and coordinating advocacy programs for the poor, specifically those programs established by the act. Many of them served specific target populations (e.g., preschoolers, migrants). Responsibility for the administration or oversight of some was delegated to other federal agencies. According to the 1964 legislation, the Director of OEO was responsible for coordinating the overall War on Poverty.

Numerous educational or educationally related programs were either a part of OEO's operation or delegated to other agencies by OEO. Job Corps, Headstart, Upward Bound, and Vista were some of the programs administered by OEO itself. Examples of delegated educational programs were the Neighborhood Youth Corps (Department of Labor) and Adult Basic Education (Department of HEW).

In 1967, Congress provided for the establishment of a 21-member National Advisory Council on Economic Opportunity. It performed two functions: (1) advising the Director of the OEO, and (2) reviewing and reporting on the effectiveness of OEO operations.

In 1973, all but three of OEO's programs were or had been transferred to other executive departments. By the middle 1970s, OEO had ceased to function as an independent federal agency. (See COMMUNITY ACTION PROGRAM and ECONOMIC OPPORTUNITY ACT.)

References: "Death of the OEO," *Newsweek,* March 5, 1973; National Advisory Council on Economic Opportunity, *Seventh Annual Report,* Washington, DC: The Council, June 1974; Office of Economic Opportunity, *The Quiet Revolution,* Washington, DC: The Office, Undated; Office of the Federal Register, National Archives and Records Service, *United States Government Manual, 1974–75* (Revised), Washington, DC: U.S. Government Printing Office, September 1, 1974; "The Wasting of OEO," *Newsweek,* July 9, 1973.

OFFICE OF EDUCATIONAL RESEARCH AND IMPROVEMENT (OERI), a branch of the U.S. Department of Education that initially included the National Institute of Education (NIE), the National Center for Education Statistics (NCES), and the Center for Libraries and Education Improvement (CLEI). (Under the 1980 Department of Education Organization Act, NIE, NCES, and CLEI became the three units that made up OERI.) In 1985, using the 1980 authorization, OERI was reorganized by the U.S. Secretary of Education into five programs under an assistant secretary of education, appointed by the president and approved by the U.S. Senate. The programs are: *Information Services*—includes Educational Resources Information Center (ERIC); *Library Programs*—includes Library Development and Public Library Support; *Programs for the Improvement of Practice*—includes Regional Educational Laboratories, School Recognition Programs (Excellence in Education), the National Diffusion Network, Chapter 2 Secretary's Discretionary Fund, and the Secretary's Discretionary Funds (from the Education for Economic Security Act) for Sciences, Mathematics, Computer Learning and Critical Foreign Languages; *Office of Research*—includes most of the responsibilities of the National Institute of Education, 14 research centers, basic and applied research in four divisions (Learning and Instruction, Schools and School Professionals, Higher Education and Adult Learning, Education and Society Division); *Center for Statistics*—includes most of the responsibilities of the National Center for Education Statistics and five divisions (Condition of Education, Elementary and Secondary Education Statistics, General Surveys and Analysis Branch, Special Surveys and Analysis Branch, and Postsecondary Education Statistics). A National Council on Education Research has a major advisory role in OERI. (See APPENDIX XX: RESEARCH AND DEVELOPMENT CENTERS; ERIC; NATIONAL CENTER FOR EDUCATION STATISTICS; NATIONAL INSTITUTE OF EDUCATION; REGIONAL LABORATORIES; and SCHOOL RECOGNITION PROGRAMS.)

References: William Bennett, U.S. Secretary of Education, personal communication (report to) to U.S. Representative Augustus F. Hawkins, chair: House Committee on Education and Labor, July 2, 1985; Office of Management, *Department of Education's Mission and Organizational Manual,* Washington, DC: U.S. Department of Education, Revised June 1, 1987; United States Department of Education News (news release), *Bennett Proposes Major Restructuring of Department of Education Research, Statistical, and Education Improvement Activities,* Washington, DC: U.S. Department of Education, July 2, 1985.

OFFSET, a procedure in printing. An impression (words, letters, pictures, design) is transferred from a plate, block, stone, and so on to paper or some other surface. In lithographic printing, a rubber roller or blanket is passed over an inked plate. The roller is then run over a surface, depositing the impression. By following this two-step process, the artist or printer need not reverse the design, for the roller picks up a reverse image from the plate and then reverses it again on the surface.

Offset can be done by photographing a "copy" and then preparing a plate to be used in an offset duplicator. This provides considerable flexibility and use by schools that have offset duplicators in their vocational education print shops. Offset duplicators range in size from tabletop models to complete multicolor, sheet-fed offset printing presses. *References: Monsen Type Manual,* Chicago: Thormod Monsen and Son, 1922; Jean Peters (Editor), *The Bookman's Glossary,* New York: R. R. Bowker and Company, 1975; George Stevenson, *Graphic Arts Encyclopedia* (Second Edition), New York: McGraw-Hill Book Company, 1979; James Sutton and Alan Bartram, *An Atlas of Typeforms,* New York: Hastings House, 1968.

OGIVE, a distribution curve of cumulative percentages or proportions derived from normally distributed data. Another name for an ogive distribution is S-shaped (sometimes percentage) curve distribution. The figure below is an ogive that was derived from the quantitative data appearing immediately above it.

Score	Frequencies	Cumulative Frequencies	Cumulative Percentage
56–60	2	78	100.0
51–55	3	76	97.4
46–50	8	73	93.4
41–45	11	65	83.3
36–40	14	54	69.2
31–35	15	40	51.3
26–30	10	25	32.1
21–25	8	15	19.2
16–20	4	7	9.0
11–15	3	3	3.8
6–10	0	0	0.0

References: Joy P. Guilford and Benjamin Fruchter, *Fundamental Statistics in Psychology and Education* (Sixth Edition), New York: McGraw-Hill Book Company, 1978; Richard P. Runyon and Audrey Haber, *Fundamentals of Behavioral Statistics* (Third Edition), Reading, MA: Addison-Wesley Publishing Company, 1976.

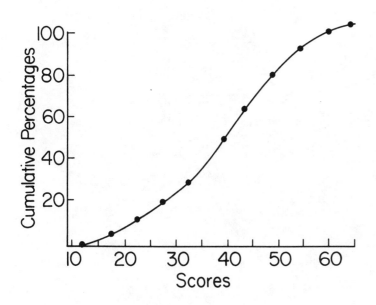

Sample Ogive

OLD DELUDER SATAN ACT—See MAS-SACHUSETTS LAWS OF 1642 AND 1647

OLYMPICS OF THE MIND—See ODYSSEY OF THE MIND PROGRAM

OMBUDSMAN, an office created by the Swedish Constitution of 1809 and subsequently adopted in countries such as Finland, Denmark, Norway, and New Zealand. A watchdog for Parliament as well as the people, the Ombudsman is empowered to prosecute officials who are guilty of breach of duty. He/she has access to public records and may interrogate officials at all levels while investigating purported breaches.

The office and title have been adopted by many agencies and organizations in the United States, including schools and universities. Expected to be both available and impartial, the typical American Ombudsman may only recommend and publicize. He/she is expected to resolve grievances, to improve administration, and to suggest needed legislation.

References: Stanley V. Anderson, *Ombudsman Papers: American Experience and Proposals,* Berkeley, CA: Institute of Governmental Studies, University of California, Ber-

keley, 1969; Walter Gellhorn, *Ombudsman and Others: Citizens' Protectors in Nine Countries,* Cambridge, MA: Harvard University Press, 1966.

ONE-TAILED AND TWO-TAILED TESTS, tests that designate the "region of rejection" of hypotheses in educational research. The "region of rejection," or "critical region," in a sampling distribution is the area (level) of statistical significance used in hypothesis testing. A sampling distribution is formed by the calculations of a statistic from samples, of a set size, taken from a population. One-tailed and two-tailed tests, rather than being particular formulae (tests), are really the regions of the distribution used to reject a hypothesis. A researcher uses a specific test (e.g. *F*-ratio, t-test) and then determines whether to reject a hypothesis by using either one or two regions of a distribution to determine the level of significance. (See below.)

The "region of rejection" utilizing the one-tailed tests may be at one or the other end of a sampling distribution. Two-tailed test regions are found at both ends of the distribution.

If a directional hypothesis is tested, a one-tailed test is used. When a nondirectional or null hypothesis is tested, a two-tailed test is used. The

One-Tailed Tests

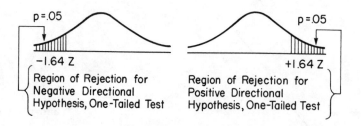

Two-Tailed Tests

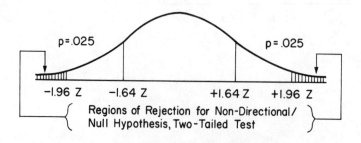

significance level of a two-tailed test is more difficult to reach than that of a one-tailed test. (See HYPOTHESES and TESTS OF SIGNIFICANCE.)
References: Walter R. Borg and Meredith D. Gall, *Educational Research: An Introduction* (Fifth Edition), New York: Longman, Inc., 1989; Harold O. Kiess, *Statistical Concepts for the Behavioral Sciences*, Boston: Allyn and Bacon, 1989.

ONE-TO-ONE CORRESPONDENCE, a mathematical term, involves the matching of one member in a set to a member in another set. This concept of pairing, taught to young children, is basic to counting. By involving learners in numbers of concrete experiences, the teacher helps children to understand one-to-one correspondence. Examples of such experiences follow: (1) having a child pass out one crayon to each student in class; (2) finding partners, one boy and one girl; and (3) pairing one chair with one desk. Children are taught that two sets that have the same number are *equivalent*. Once one-to-one correspondence is used for understanding more sophisticated number concepts such as *greater than* or *less than* are then taught.
References: Hunter Ballew, *Teaching Children Mathematics*, Columbus, OH: Charles E. Merrill Publishing Company, 1973; Donald D. Paige, et al., *Elementary Mathematical Methods*, New York: John Wiley and Sons, 1978; Louise B. Scott and Jewell Garner, *Mathematical Experiences for Young Children*, St. Louis, MO: Webster Division, McGraw-Hill Book Company, 1978.

ONTOLOGY, in philosophy the study of what is real. It is the central part of metaphysics, which asks what is real about the universe, material objects, persons, being, mind, and so on. Ontology addresses questions such as "What do we mean when we say that something *is*?" Paul Tillich defined it as the study of "the character of everything that is insofar as it is."
References: J. Donald Butler, *Four Philosophies and Their Practice in Education and Religion* (Third Edition), New York: Harper and Row, Publishers, 1968; William H. Halverson, *A Concise Introduction to Philosophy* (Second Edition), New York: Random House, 1972; Paul Tillich, *Systematic Theology* (Volume I), Chicago: University of Chicago Press, 1951.

OPAQUE PROJECTOR, an audio-visual device used to project natural color images of graphic materials (books, photos, etc.) onto a screen. Early models used oil or gas lamps for illumination. Later, the use of mirrors and incandescent lamps in the projector served to improve its usefulness in classrooms. Notwithstanding these improvements, the opaque projector's principal limitation continues to be its relatively inefficient light output. Room darkening and the use of a 1,000 watt lamp help to improve images; even with these changes, however, they remain approximately 20 percent as bright as those projected by a slide projector. This difference is caused by diffusion that takes place after light strikes the graphic being projected.

Early opaque projectors were sometimes referred to as Balopticans or Delineascopes. In England, they are known as episcopes.
References: John R. Bullard and Calvin E. Mather, *Audio-Visual Fundamentals: Basic Equipment Operation and Sample Materials Production*, Dubuque, IA: Wm. C. Brown Company, Publishers, 1974; Raymond Wyman, *Mediaware: Selection, Operation, and Maintenance* (Second Edition), Dubuque, IA: Wm. C. Brown Company, Publishers, 1969.

OPEN ADMISSIONS, or open enrollment admissions, a policy for admitting students to colleges and universities regardless of their academic record. In recent years, such policies have been promulgated by a desire to bring about social change through attraction of students from low socioeconomic populations. These free-access policies have generated spirited debates over their educational efficacy with considerable resistance coming from the university community. Critics argue that incoming students who lack basic skills are incapable of completing their studies at a satisfactory level of performance; that open admissions dilutes academic standards; and, finally, that the compensatory (remedial) programs required for many open admissions students are costly and hence drain resources that should be available to better qualified students. Many community colleges and other state-supported institutions of higher education have regularly (sometimes provisionally) admitted all graduates of their states' high schools, a more traditional approach to open admissions.
References: Anne F. Decker, et al., *A Handbook on Open Admissions: Success, Failure, Potential*, Boulder, CO: Westview Press, 1976; Herbert S. Sacks (Editor), *Hurdles: The Admissions Dilemma in American Higher Education*, New York: Atheneum, 1978.

OPEN EDUCATION, an approach to schooling that possesses many of the characteristics found in the "progressive" schools of the 1930s and 1940s. The open education concept was popularized in the United States in the 1960s and often modeled after the British infant schools. Features of the open classroom include small group (frequently individualized) instruction, flexible scheduling, an abundance of instructional materials, numerous learning activities taking place concurrently in open space classrooms, considerable self-directed learning, experimentation, and an open relationship between teacher and learner. Students are encouraged to learn at their own pace and do so in a nonthreatening environment.

References: Heather S. Doob, *Summary of Research on Open Education,* Arlington, VA: Educational Research Service, Inc., 1974; Ewald B. Nyquist and Gene R. Hawes (Editors), *Open Education: A Sourcebook for Parents and Teachers,* New York: Bantam Books, 1972; Lillian S. Stephens, *The Teacher's Guide to Open Education,* New York: Holt, Rinehart and Winston, Inc., 1974.

OPEN ENROLLMENT—See OPEN ADMISSIONS

OPEN SCHOOL—See OPEN EDUCATION

OPEN SYSTEM THEORY—See ORGANIZATIONAL BEHAVIOR

OPEN UNIVERSITY, nontraditional British institution of higher education whose program is designed to meet the needs of the adult learner unable to fit into the traditional system of higher education. Sir Walter Perry, the first chief administrative officer of Open University of the United Kingdom, attributed the Open University concept to three postwar educational trends: (1) new developments in the field of adult education; (2) educational broadcasting; and (3) promotion of egalitarianism in education.

Open University of the United Kingdom, first opened to students in January 1971, accepts part-time students of varied abilities and backgrounds. These students study for their degrees while at home using diverse instructional media/strategies such as radio, television, correspondence courses, prescribed reading, summer schools, and self-assessment materials. Close cooperation is maintained with national television and the British Broadcasting Company, linkages vital to the program.

The Open University concept, heavily subsidized by the British government, has proven popular. Recent estimates indicate that over 80,000 applicants file for admission each year, of whom about 25 percent are accepted. The idea is popular abroad also, with an estimated 30 countries having introduced variations of the Open University concept.

References: Naomi E. McIntosh, et al., *A Degree of Difference: The Open University of the United Kingdom,* New York: Praeger Publishers, 1977; Walter Perry, *The Open University,* San Francisco: Jossey-Bass Publishers, 1977; Brian Silcock, "Britain's Stay-at-Home Scholars," *Phi Delta Kappan,* December 1979; Jeremy Tunstall (Editor), *The Open University Opens,* London, England: Routledge and Kegan Paul, 1974.

OPERANT BEHAVIOR, behavior shaped by reinforcements after a response rather than the reinforcement (or stimulus) itself eliciting the response. Operant behavior is a subset of a psychology of learning developed by B. F. Skinner.

Operant behavior experimentation's historical base can be traced to classical conditioning psychology. B. F. Skinner, the major developer of operant behavior, stipulated that in operant behavior, the reinforcement is contingent upon a response (S_1RS_2). In the classical conditioning approach, the reinforcer is paired with the stimulus (S_1S_2R).

Operant conditioning serves to strengthen operant behavior by controlling and continuously shaping the behavior of an organism (man, animal) through schedules of reinforcements. In such conditioning, the behavior is made more probable or, in fact, more frequent. Operant conditioning and operant behavior form the psychological learning theory behind programmed instruction and modern teaching machines.

Operant conditioning is controversial, with some educators charging that it is a form of mind control. (See BEHAVIORAL MODIFICATION; PROGRAMMED INSTRUCTION; and SKINNER BOX.)

References: J. Mark Ackerman, *Operant Conditioning Techniques for the Classroom Teacher,* Glenview, IL: Scott, Foresman and Company, 1972; Janice T. Gibson and Louis A. Chandler, *Educational Psychology: Mastering Principles and Applications,* Boston: Allyn and Bacon, 1988; James G. Holland and B. F. Skinner, *The Analysis of Behavior,* New York: McGraw-Hill Book Company, 1961; B. F. Skinner, *Science and Human Behavior,* New York: The Macmillan Company, 1953; Norman A. Sprinthall and Richard C. Sprinthall, *Educational Psychology: A Developmental Approach* (Fourth Edition), New York: Random House, 1987.

OPERANT CONDITIONING—See OPERANT BEHAVIOR

OPERATION HEADSTART, also known as Head

Start or Project Head Start, a nationwide program conceived to provide education and achievement opportunities for young children from poverty environments. Headstart was established by the Office of Economic Opportunity during the summer of 1965 as part of the government's broader anti-poverty effort. The program was designed for preschool children. It not only teaches selected readiness skills, but provides social, medical, nutritional, and psychological support services as well. Professional teachers and teacher aides are involved in Headstart programs. Parents and volunteers are part of the program as well. Many urban and rural communities operate Headstart programs. Research has shown that children have benefited from the program. (See FOLLOW-THROUGH PROGRAM and HUMAN SERVICES REAUTHORIZATION ACT OF 1986).

References: Sarah T. Curwood, *Project Head Start,* Boston: Massachusetts Committee on Children and Youth, 1966; Clara M. Riley, *Head Start in Action,* West Nyack, NY: Parker Publishing Company, Inc., 1967; Alice M. Rivlin and P. Michael Timpane (Editors), *Planned Variation in Education,* Washington, DC: The Brookings Institution, 1975; Julian C. Stanley (Editor), *Preschool Programs for the Disadvantaged,* Baltimore, MD: John Hopkins University Press, 1972; Edward Zigler and Jeanette Valentine (Editors), *Project Head Start: A Legacy of the War on Poverty,* New York: The Free Press, 1979.

OPERATION OF PLANT, a category of the school budget that includes the housekeeping expenses of a school system. These are costs incurred to keep buildings usable on a daily basis. Custodial supplies, heating costs, utilities, and salaries for custodians are normally charged against this budget category. (See SCHOOL BUDGET.)

References: Leon Ovsiew and William B. Castetter, *Budgeting for Better Schools,* Englewood Cliffs, NJ: Prentice-Hall, Inc., 1963; Emery Stoops, et al., *Handbook of Educational Administration: A Guide for the Practitioner* (Second Edition), Boston: Allyn and Bacon, Inc., 1981.

OPERATION PUSH, *P*eople *U*nited to *S*ave *H*umanity, an organization working to build a strong economic base within America's black communities. Operation PUSH was founded in 1971 by the Rev. Jesse Jackson, former associate of the Rev. Martin Luther King. The organization views increased economic power for black Americans as a logical sequel to the civil rights and civil power movements of the 1950s and 1960s. One of its principal goals is greater black participation in the ownership and production of U.S. goods and services.

Urban schools, in which large numbers of black students are enrolled, are seen as an important vehicle for realization of PUSH's goals. Black students are urged to accept more responsibility for their own education. Exhortations such as "I am somebody" and "Nobody will save us, from us, for us, but us" are used to dramatize this plea. The organization's EXCEL program, begun in 1977, is devoted to the mission of educational improvement.

Operation PUSH has its national headquarters in Chicago.

References: Thomas S. Gunnings and Barbara B. Gunnings, "In Defense of EXCEL," *Phi Delta Kappan,* January 1979; Jesse L. Jackson, "Give the People a Vision," *New York Times Magazine,* April 18, 1976; Operation Push Inc., Untitled and Undated Public Relations Memorandum.

ORAL HISTORY, historical information that is obtained through preplanned interviews with prominent people and tape recorded. The individual collecting such information is referred to as an oral historian. Those being interviewed speak from first-hand knowledge and are generally free to impose restrictions (e.g. date when the interview may be made public) that the oral historian and his/her associates are obligated to honor.

The oral history movement originated in 1948, with some initial interviews arranged by Allan Nevins. Creation of the Oral History Association at Columbia University gave the movement considerable impetus.

The oral history interview involves several steps: (1) careful researching of the topic by the oral historian; (2) planning the interview (which includes making of arrangements with the person to be interviewed and arriving at a prerecording understanding; (3) conducting the interview; (4) outlining the completed tape; (5) preparing written transcripts, when feasible; and (6) arranging for storage and distribution.

Numerous oral history collections are presently in existence around the world. A guide to help with location of specific oral history interviews, *Oral History Collections,* has been published by the R. R. Bowker Company.

References: Willa Baum, *Oral History for the Local Historical Society* (Second Edition, Revised), Nashville, TN: American Association for State and Local History, 1977; Elizabeth B. Mason and Louis M. Starr (Editors), *The Oral History Collection of Columbia University,* New York: Oral History Research Office, 1979; Jane McCracken (Editor), *Oral History: Basic Techniques,* Manitoba,

Canada: Manitoba Museum of Man and Nature, 1974; Alan M. Meckler and Ruth McMullin, *Oral History Collections*, New York: R. R. Bowker Company, 1975; Karen J. Winkler, "Oral History: Coming of Age in the 1980's," *The Chronicle of Higher Education*, October 14, 1980.

ORALISM—See AURAL-ORAL APPROACH

ORAL READING, a method of reading instruction that requires a student to read aloud to the teacher and/or fellow students. Both oral and silent reading experiences are included in developmental reading programs, each serving separate sets of purposes. Oral reading permits the teacher to gauge a student's general reading progress, particularly word identification skill and fluency. Additionally, this method: (1) provides practice in oral presentation; (2) helps to develop acceptable speech patterns; and (3) helps to develop listening skills.

One author (Eldon Ekwall) calls attention to several specific reading errors that can be identified from oral reading. They include: (1) omissions; (2) insertions; (3) substitutions; (4) mispronunciations; (5) inversions and reversals (e.g. "was" for "saw," "p" for "b"); and (6) disregard of punctuation. (See READING REVERSALS.)

References: Eldon E. Ekwall, *Locating and Correcting Reading Difficulties* (Third Edition), Columbus, OH; Eldon E. Ekwall, *Diagnosis and Remediation of the Disabled Reader*, Boston: Allyn and Bacon, Inc., 1976; Margaret A. Richek, Lynne K. List, and Janet W. Lerner, *Reading Problems: Assessment and Teaching Strategies* (Second Edition), Englewood Cliffs, NJ: Prentice-Hall, Inc., 1989; Harry Singer and Dan Donlan, *Reading and Learning from Text* (Second Edition), Hillsdale, NJ: Lawrence Erlbaum Associates, Publishers, 1989.

ORDINAL SCALE—See DATA and SCALE OF MEASUREMENT

ORDINANCE OF 1785, the earliest federal land-grant act. It provided that, in the Northwest Territory (areas lying north of the Ohio River and east of the Mississippi River), the 16th section of each township was to be set aside for the maintenance and operation of public schools. Townships were set up to consist of 36 square miles, these divided into 36 sections that measured 1 square mile each. The 13 original states were excluded from the ordinance's provisions as were a few others. Ohio, admitted to the Union in 1802, was the first state to benefit educationally from this act. In the Northwest Ordinance of 1787, another act regulating settlement of new territories, Congress prescribed:

"Religion, morality, and knowledge being necessary to good government and the happiness of mankind, schools and the means of education shall be forever encouraged."

References: Adam M. Drayer, *The Teacher in a Democratic Society: An Introduction to the Field of Education*, Columbus, OH: Charles E. Merrill Publishing Company, 1970; Francis N. Thorpe (Editor), *The Federal and State Constitutions, Colonial Charters, and Other Organic Laws* (Volume 2), Washington, DC: U.S. Government Printing Office, 1909.

OREGON CASE, a suit that challenged the right of a state to require children to attend public schools. In 1922, an Oregon initiative action required normal children of school age to enroll in that state's public schools. Three years later, the United States Supreme Court supported an injunction against implementation of this action on the grounds that it interfered with the rights of individuals operating private schools as a business. The ruling also affirmed the right of parents to make educational decisions in behalf of their children. Finally, the court decreed that although the state could establish regulations for the operation of nonpublic schools, it could not eliminate these institutions.

References: Pierce v. Society of Sisters, 268 U.S. 510, 45 S.Ct. 571, 69 L.Ed. 1070 (1925); E. Edmund Reutter, Jr. and Robert Hamilton, *The Law of Public Education* (Second Edition), Mineola, NY: The Foundation Press, Inc., 1976.

ORFF METHOD, also known as Orff Schulwerk, a child-centered approach to the teaching of music developed by the German composer and music educator Carl Orff. His approach to music instruction has been adopted by numerous music educators around the world.

Orff based his approach on the belief that the musical development of children should essentially parallel the evolution of music history (e.g. rhythm comes before melody, and melody precedes harmony). The method begins with what Orff has called *elemental* music. Chanting, clapping, echo clapping, and so on are used to provide rhythmic experiences. Body movements such as patschen (patting the knees with one's hands), foot tapping, and finger snapping are also used as aids to the teaching of rhythm. Students are then introduced to musical instruments designed by Orff and are encouraged to experiment with rhythm patterns, simple melodies, and ostinato figures. The teaching of melody and harmony follows.

In the United States, the American Orff-

Schulwerk Association, formed at Ball State University in 1963, helps to promote information about the Orff approach.

References: Beth Landis and Polly Carder, *The Eclectic Curriculum in American Music Education: Contributions of Dalcroze, Kodaly, and Orff,* Washington, DC: Music Educators National Conference, 1972; Michael L. Mark, *Contemporary Music Education,* New York: Schirmer Books (Macmillan), 1978; Robert W. Winslow and Leon Dallin, *Music Skills for Classroom Teachers* (Fifth Edition), Dubuque, IA: Wm. C. Brown Company, Publishers, 1979.

ORGANIZATION, or formal organization, a group of individuals who help to implement the goals of an institution by performing separate but interrelated and coordinated functions within it. Methods exist to replenish members as well as the materials they require.

One writer (Robert Weiss) cited four characteristics of an organization. They are: (1) a set of individuals in *offices* (jobs); (2) sets of specific *functional activities* (duties) associated with each office; (3) *organizational goals* to which the staff contribute; and (4) a system of *coordinative relationships* (structure) connecting the various office-holders.

Tables of organization, also known as line and staff charts, are graphics that depict the way in which authority and responsibility are assigned within formal organizations. (See INFORMAL ORGANIZATION and LINE AND STAFF CHART.)

References: Amitai Etzioni (Editor), *Complex Organizations: A Sociological Reader,* New York: Holt, Rinehart and Winston, Inc., 1964; E. Mark Hanson, *Educational Administration and Organizational Behavior,* Boston: Allyn and Bacon, Inc., 1979; Thomas J. Sergiovanni and Fred D. Carver, *The New School Executive: A Theory of Administration* (Second Edition), New York: Harper and Row, Publishers, 1980; Robert S. Weiss, *Processes of Organization,* Ann Arbor, MI: Survey Research Center, Institute for Social Research, University of Michigan, 1956.

ORGANIZATIONAL BEHAVIOR, a systematic and largely interdisciplinary attempt to understand how an individual behaves as a member of an organization. An organizational psychologist (Joe Kelly) defined organizational behavior as "the study of the behaviours and attitudes of man in an organizational setting; the organization's effect on his perceptions, feelings, and actions; and his effect on the organization, particularly how his behaviour affects the achievement of the organization's purposes" (p. 1).

Organizational behavior in schools, as in other complex organizations, has been and continues to be studied using three broad, conceptual (theoretical) frameworks. They are: (1) *classical organization theory,* an attempt to assess organizational behavior in terms of productivity and organizational efficiency; (2) *social systems theory,* a framework reflecting the belief that individual needs and organizational needs are interdependent, hence need to be studied jointly; and (3) *open system theory,* an approach that holds that an organization (and its components) has an interdependent relationship with its environment; changes in one produce changes in the other.

References: Andrew J. DuBrin, *Fundamentals of Organizational Behavior: An Applied Perspective,* New York: Pergamon Press, Inc., 1974; E. Mark Hanson, *Educational Administration and Organizational Behavior,* Boston: Allyn and Bacon, Inc., 1979; Joe Kelly, *Organizational Behaviour,* Homewood, IL: Richard D. Irwin and Dorsey Press, 1969.

ORGANIZATIONAL CLIMATE, the psychological structure of organization. Terms such as *atmosphere, tone,* or *character* are sometimes used when an attempt is made to characterize a unit's climate. In schools, as in other formal organizations, organizational climate is studied by examining the behavior of employees. This behavior, in turn, is produced by numbers of interrelated variables. They include the unit's economic conditions, leadership style, organizational structure, policy, values, and personnel characteristics.

One instrument used to measure the organizational climate of schools is the Organizational Climate Description Questionnaire (OCDQ), pioneered by Andrew Halpin and Don Croft. Another is the Organizational Climate Index, developed by George Stern and Carl Steinhoff. (See ORGANIZATIONAL CLIMATE DESCRIPTION QUESTIONNAIRE.)

References: Andrew J. DuBrin, *Fundamentals of Organizational Behavior: An Applied Perspective,* New York: Pergamon Press, Inc., 1974; Allan A. Glatthorn and Norman K. Spencer, *Middle School/Junior High Principal's Handbook,* Englewood Cliffs, NJ: Prentice-Hall, Inc., 1986; Robert G. Owens, *Organizational Behavior in Schools,* Englewood Cliffs, NJ: Prentice-Hall, Inc., 1970.

ORGANIZATIONAL CLIMATE DESCRIPTION QUESTIONNAIRE (OCDQ), an instrument for measuring the "organizational climate" of a school. The OCDQ, developed by Andrew W. Halpin and Don B. Croft, has been used extensively by school administrators as well as educational researchers. The questionnaire is based on the perceived behaviors of principals and teachers.

OCDQ consists of eight parts, or subsets. Four of them focus on the behavior of the principal as perceived by teachers; another four deal with teacher behavior, also as perceived by teachers.

Halpin and Croft administered the OCDQ to a national sample of elementary schools. On the basis of data collected, they identified six discernible patterns (or school profiles) that they called "climate types." They were: (1) open climate; (2) autonomous climate; (3) controlled climate; (4) familiar climate; (5) paternal climate; and (6) closed climate. Specific patterns of perceived teacher and principal behavior differentiate one climate type from each of the others. (See ORGANIZATIONAL CLIMATE.)

References: Andrew W. Halpin and Don B. Croft, *The Organizational Climate of Schools,* Chicago: Midwest Administration Center, University of Chicago, 1963; Robert G. Owens, *Organizational Behavior in Schools,* Englewood Cliffs, NJ: Prentice-Hall, Inc., 1970.

ORGANIZATIONAL CONTINGENCY THEORY—See LEADER BEHAVIOR

ORGANIZATIONAL DISTANCE, the number of authority levels separating members of a formal organization. Large and organizationally complex organizations such as city or county school districts are frequently characterized as having vertically "tall," or hierarchical, organizational structures. In such cases, the organizational distance between (or number of authority levels separating) a teacher and the school superintendent is greater than is the case in rural and other smaller school systems. (See ORGANIZATIONAL SPACE.)

References: Amitai Etzioni (Editor), *Complex Organizations: A Sociological Reader,* New York: Holt, Rinehart and Winston, Inc., 1964; Daniel E. Griffiths, et al., *Organizing Schools for Effective Education,* Danville, IL: The Interstate Printers and Publishers, Inc., 1962.

ORGANIZATIONAL PLANS, vertical grade patterns used within school districts. Various combinations of grade levels are assigned to a school, usually for a relatively long period. Four of the most common organizational plans are the Eight-Four (8-4) Plan, the Six-Three-Three (6-3-3) Plan, the Six-Two-Four (6-2-4) Plan, and the Six-Six (6-6) Plan. Kindergarten (K), although not represented in the titles of these plans, is nevertheless found in virtually every one of them. Nursery (N) Programs are also to be found, although on a much smaller scale and not universally.

The 8-4 plan involves eight years of elementary and four years of high school study. It was the traditional plan used through the early decades of this century and continues to be used today, particularly in rural areas. The 6-3-3 and 6-2-4 plans gained popularity across the country as junior high schools and middle schools were formed to accommodate the unique developmental and instructional needs of early adolescents. (See GRADED SCHOOL; JUNIOR HIGH SCHOOL; and MIDDLE SCHOOL.)

References: Edgar L. Morphet, et al., *Educational Administration: Concepts, Practices, and Issues,* Englewood Cliffs, NJ: Prentice-Hall, Inc., 1959; Robert W. Richey, *Planning for Teaching: An Introduction to Education* (Sixth Edition), New York: McGraw-Hill Book Company, 1979.

ORGANIZATIONAL SPACE, the behavioral distances separating members of an organization. The nature and extent of organizational space can be inferred by observing organizational members' behavior.

Social psychologists Daniel Katz and Robert Kahn described four types of separation relating to organizational space. The first, *geographical separation,* describes the physical distances between organizational subsystems, a separation that can impede effective communication. In a college, for example, two academic departments are geographically separated as a result of being housed in different buildings. *Functional separation,* the second type, is evident when groups of employees with like interests voluntarily segregate themselves from other employees. This type of separation is illustrated when school secretaries choose to eat together in a dining room open to all employees. A third type, one reflecting *status* or *prestige* differences among workers, is operating when one observes that school custodians are not likely to be found socializing regularly with school principals. The final type of separation is based on *power differences.* In this case, chain-of-command relationships serve to determine formal communication channels even while discouraging informal patterns between persons possessing markedly different degrees of power.

Reference: Daniel Katz and Robert L. Kahn, *The Social Psychology of Organizations* (Second Edition), New York: John Wiley and Sons, 1978.

ORGANIZATIONAL SUBSYSTEM, a secondary or subordinate system into which organizations are divided. Two students of organizational behavior (Paul Lawrence and Jay Lorsch) have identified four factors that differentiate one subsystem from another: (1) *formality of structure,* or the varying rules and processes unique to each subsystem; (2) *interpersonal orientation,* with variations depending on degree of emphasis on people as opposed to task; (3) *time orientation,* concern with short-term vs. long-term matters; and (4) *goal orientation.* These categories were developed following their study of ten corporations.

Organizational subsystems exist in schools and school systems as they do in industrial or governmental organizations. Although they may sometimes operate as quasi-independent units, organizational integration is required to bring about meaningful collaboration among them. Major responsibility for achieving such integration is, of course, vested in the organization's leadership. (See ORGANIZATIONAL SPACE.)

References: E. Mark Hanson, *Educational Administration and Organizational Behavior,* Boston: Allyn and Bacon, Inc., 1979; Daniel Katz and Robert L. Kahn, *The Social Psychology of Organizations* (Second Edition), New York: John Wiley and Sons, 1978; Paul R. Lawrence and Jay Lorsch, *Organization and Environment: Management Differentiation and Integration,* Cambridge, MA: Harvard University Graduate School of Business Administration, 1967.

ORGANIZATION CHART—See LINE AND STAFF CHART

ORGANIZING, an element of the administrative process that deals with the assignment of specific tasks to individuals in an organization for the purpose of meeting predetermined objectives. One student of organization (Robert Weiss) identified three broad problem categories relating to organizing, problems with which executives (school administrators included) cope on a fairly regular basis. *Allocation,* the first of them, involves the matching of people to prescribed job responsibilities. It includes the act of creating new positions as well as the hiring of personnel to fill vacancies. *Adaptation,* the second broad problem area, has to do with resolution of personnel difficulties stemming from the unwillingness or inability of individual employees to fulfill their job responsibilities. The final area, *coordination,* is concerned with directing the energies of all employees toward realization of the organization's goals. (See INFORMAL ORGANIZATION and ORGANIZATION.)

References: Russell T. Gregg, "The Administrative Process" in Roald F. Campbell and Russell T. Gregg (Editors), *Administrative Behavior in Education,* New York: Harper and Brothers, 1957; Robert S. Weiss, *Processes of Organization,* Ann Arbor, MI: Survey Research Center,

Institute for Social Research, University of Michigan, 1956.

ORIENTATION OF STAFF, a personnel administration effort designed to welcome and to help first-time or reassigned employees adjust to their new jobs. R. Oliver Gibson and Herold Hunt defined it as "a form of induction into a social system, with its formal and informal organization, its purposes and procedures, its rights and duties already attached to other positions, and the various expectations that help define the newcomer's role" (p. 184).

The format of orientation programs conducted by school systems is variable. A common practice is to invite new teachers to a special one-day or two-day orientation meeting before the start of the academic year. At such meetings, newcomers are welcomed by school officials and receive general information concerning the school district, the local school community, their respective school buildings, and the profession. Handbooks, policy statements, rules and regulations, and so on are normally distributed at this time. In some school systems, the orientation effort extends throughout the newcomer's initial year of employment with new teachers, especially, receiving assistance from such resource persons as the principal, an assigned "buddy" teacher, or a department chairperson.

References: R. Oliver Gibson and Herold C. Hunt, *The School Personnel Administrator,* Boston: Houghton Mifflin Company, 1965; Joan P. S. Kowalski, *Orientation Programs for New Teachers,* Arlington, VA: Educational Research Service, Inc., 1977.

ORTHOGRAPHY, the proper or standard spelling of words in a language. Proper spelling is important at all levels of language since the meaning of a word can change greatly with the juxtaposing of even a single letter.

The English language is one of the more complicated languages in which to master appropriate spelling. Although there are only 26 letters to represent the 44 different sounds found in English, there are many variations. A single symbol may represent more than one sound, depending on the context. In toto, there exist at least 2,000 different letter combinations to represent the 44 sounds.

Efforts to reform English language spelling can be traced to the work of John Hart (1554). Sir James Pitman's Initial Teaching Alphabet (i.t.a.), another such reform effort, became popular in some American and English schools during the 1960s. (See INITIAL TEACHING ALPHABET;

SPELLING; and SPELLING DEMONS.)

References: Ruel A. Alhed, *Spelling: The Application of Research Findings,* Washington, DC: National Education Association, 1977; Uta Frith (Editor), *Cognitive Processes in Spelling,* London, England: Academic Press, 1980; Charles Read, *Children's Categorization of Speech Sounds in English,* Urbana, IL: National Council of Teachers of English, 1975.

ORTHOPEDICALLY HANDICAPPED CHILDREN, children with disorders of the musculoskeletal system (bones, joints, and muscles) such that movement is made difficult, if not impossible, causing a handicap. Many times the orthopedically handicapped child has undergone extensive surgery, hospitalization, and physical therapy. Not only may learning difficulties be brought on by the orthopedic problem, but there may be accompanying significant emotional problems as well. Special educational programs that include physical therapy can be designed to facilitate the emotional, educational, and physical development of such children.

There is a wide variety of orthopedic handicaps. Some may not affect movement too adversely, and others can be quite extreme. Examples include: clubfoot; congenital vertical talus; leg-length discrepancy; Osgood-Schlatter disease; congenital dislocated hip; Legg-Perthes disease; scoliosis; arthritis; rheumatoid arthritis; various muscle, brain, and spinal cord diseases; and bone tumors. Many orthopedic problems can be corrected through surgery or medical/physical therapy if identified and acted upon early enough.

References: Eugene E. Bleck and Donald A. Nagel (Editors), *Physically Handicapped Children,* New York: Grune and Stratton, 1975; Nancy E. Hilt and William Schmitt, Jr., *Pediatric Orthopedic Nursing,* St. Louis, MO: C. V. Mosby, 1975; Ruth Velleman, *Serving Physically Disabled People,* New York: R. R. Bowker Company, 1979.

OSWEGO MOVEMENT, an effort begun by Oswego, N.Y., Superintendent Edwin A. Sheldon when he undertook to incorporate the ideas of Johann Pestalozzi into his school system. Sheldon established the school district in 1853 and later created a normal school in Oswego in which Pestalozzian ideas and methods were taught. The movement stressed object teaching, a method designed to stimulate: (1) acquisition of knowledge through observation and inquiry, physically using the five senses; (2) reasoning; and (3) individual judgment. Special instructors were brought to Oswego from England to assist with training of teachers in the Pestalozzian method. The schools and the training institution attracted large numbers of visitors. The thousands of highly regarded Oswego Normal School alumni did much to spread the ideas of the Oswego movement all over the United States where they were employed. (See PESTALOZZI, JOHANN HEINRICH.)

References: Elwood P. Cubberly, *Public Education in the United States: A Study and Interpretation of American Educational History,* Cambridge, MA: The Riverside Press, 1962 (Originally Published in 1919 by Houghton Mifflin Company); Harry G. Good and James D. Teller, *A History of American Education* (Third Edition), New York: The Macmillan Company, 1973.

OTIS QUICK-SCORING MENTAL ABILITY TEST, a group intelligence test that had as its base the Simon-Binet Scale and the Otis Self-Administering test (one of the first group intelligence tests developed). This genesis is not surprising given the fact that Arthur Otis (1886–1964), author of the tests, was a student of Terman, the psychologist who developed the Stanford-Binet tests. The Quick-Scoring Test was first published in 1936, with three levels: *Alpha* (for grades 1–4); *Beta* (4–9); and *Gamma* (9–13).

The Otis Quick-Scoring Test was designed to measure a broadly based general mental ability, although there has been some question concerning this assertion. The Otis Quick-Scoring Test, used until 1954, has been revised and incorporated into the Otis-Lennon Mental Ability Test. (See TERMAN, LEWIS.)

References: Joy P. Guilford and Ralph Hoepfner, *The Analysis of Intelligence,* New York: McGraw-Hill Book Company, 1971; Kathryn W. Linden and James D. Linden, *Modern Mental Measurement: A Historical Perspective,* Boston: Houghton Mifflin Company, 1968; Jerome M. Sattler, *Assessment of Children's Intelligence,* Philadelphia: Saunders Publishing Company, 1974.

OTOLOGIST, the physician who specializes in the biological functions of hearing. The otologist diagnoses diseases of the ear, identifies the causes of hearing loss, and treats pathologies of the auditory system. He/she treats many of the problems of the mechanics of the auditory system that cause hearing impairment such as congenital malformations, blockages, external otitis, allergies, infections, and mastoidectomy.

The otologist and the audiologist complement each other. The otologist treats diseases and malformations and the audiologist is concerned with diagnostic testing of hearing and assisting an individual to overcome hearing impairment through nonmedical means. The otologist is a physician; the audiologist is not. (See AUDIOLOGIST.)

References: Lawrence R. Boies, et al., *Fundamentals of Otolaryngology,* Philadelphia: W. B. Saunders Company, 1964; Hallowell Davis and S. Richard Silverman, *Hearing and Deafness* (Fourth Edition), New York: Holt, Rinehart and Winston, Inc., 1978; Hayes A. Newby, *Audiology* (Fourth Edition), Englewood Cliffs, NJ: Prentice-Hall, Inc., 1979.

OUTDOOR EDUCATION, school activities that seek to develop ecological awareness by having learners study in the out-of-doors. Field trips of a camping nature are sponsored to achieve numerous specific educational objectives, including: (1) appreciation of the out-of-doors as an enrichment for living; (2) appreciation of the physical environment and natural resources; (3) love of adventure; (4) democratic living with other children and adults; (5) mastery of recreation skills; and (6) learning safety. Some school districts operate their own camps to which classes are sent for short periods. Others make use of local, state, and/or federal preserves/parks.

References: Wynlee Crisp, *Development and Use of the Outdoor Classroom: An Annotated Bibliography,* Metuchen, NJ: The Scarecrow Press, Inc., 1975; Phyllis M. Ford, *Principles and Practices of Outdoor/Environmental Education,* New York: John Wiley and Sons, Inc., 1981; Charles A. Lewis, Jr., *The Administration of Outdoor Education Programs,* Dubuque, IA: Kendall/Hunt Publishing Company, 1975; T. M. Parker and K. I. Meldrum, *Outdoor Educators,* London, England: J. M. Dent and Sons Limited, 1973; Julian W. Smith, et al., *Outdoor Education* (Second Edition), Englewood Cliffs, NJ: Prentice-Hall, Inc., 1972.

OVERHEAD PROJECTION, the projecting onto a screen of a large, bright image using a transparency and an overhead projector. The overhead projector, sometimes called "the electronic chalkboard," has come to be one of the most widely used audio-visual devices in the classroom.

Transparencies can be purchased commercially or prepared readily using any of these commonly used processes: (1) the *thermal process,* a method that involves placing a special transparency film over material (e.g. page from a book) to be projected and running these through a thermal copier; (2) the *diazo process,* a more complex method; and (3) the *photographic method.* A simpler but more limited procedure, one requiring no special equipment, involves drawing or tracing images directly on to a sheet of acetate. Transparencies can be prepared using different colors. Presentations in which step-by-step information is to be imparted can be facilitated by using overlays. They are a set of transparencies that are superimposed over each other as the teacher discusses each step. (Illustrating the use of overlays is a presentation on the human body. The first transparency may present the skeletal structure, followed by separate and successive transparencies which add the organs, the muscles, the nervous system, etc.).

One author (Morton Schultz) cited several advantages in using the overhead projector: (1) teacher faces the class when presenting material; (2) the overhead projector can be used in a lighted room; (3) the transparency is permanent; (4) the projector is light in weight; and (5) using a grease pencil or felt pen, the teacher can write directly on the transparent material.

References: Robert V. Bullough, *Creating Instructional Materials* (Second Edition), Columbus, OH: Charles E. Merrill Publishing Company, 1978; Robert Heinich, Michael Molenda, and James D. Russell, *Instructional Media and the New Technologies of Instruction* (Second Edition), New York: John Wiley and Sons, 1985; Jerrold E. Kemp and Don C. Smellie, *Planning, Producing and Using Instructional Media* (Sixth Edition), New York: Harper and Row Publishers, 1989; Morton J. Schultz, *The Teacher and Overhead Projection: A Treasury of Ideas, Uses and Techniques,* Englewood Cliffs, NJ: Prentice-Hall, Inc., 1965.

OVERHEAD TRANSPARENCY—See TRANSPARENCIES

PACING—See CONTROLLED READING

PAIDEIA PROPOSAL, a curriculum reform for all elementary and secondary pupils offered by the Paideia Group (Mortimer J. Adler, the noted philosopher was chair of the group). The proposal presents a single-track academic core curriculum to include the native language, a foreign language, literature, fine arts, mathematics, natural science, history, geography, and social studies. In addition, students would take 12 years of physical education, and be involved with drama, industrial arts, music, and the visual arts. This required curriculum is to be presented through three modes of teaching: *didactic* instruction for acquiring basic knowledge; *coaching* and supervised practice to develop intellectual skills; and *Socratic* or *maieutic* teaching (the questioning approach) in seminars to allow for further development and understanding. The proposal is built on the theory that basic schooling is only one phase in the total process of education. Schooling must give the learner the tools and incentive to continue the education process throughout a lifetime.
References: Mortimer J. Adler (Chair), *Paideia Problems and Possibilities*, New York: MacMillan Publishing Company, 1983; Mortimer J. Adler (Chair), *The Paideia Proposal*; New York: MacMillan Publishing Company, 1980; John D. McNeil, *Curriculum: A Comprehensive Introduction* (Third Edition), Boston: Little, Brown and Company, 1985.

PALATALS, a category of sounds made by the tongue (tip or blade) approaching the palate. There are two types of palatals in the English language. They are *frontal* and *central*.

Palatalization, which occurs when the broad surface of the blade of the tongue comes into contact with the hard palate, is found in most languages. It is an important phenomenon to understand and master when teaching or learning a second language.
References: Jean D. Bowen, *Patterns of English Pronunciation*, Rowley, MA: Newbury House Publishers, Inc., 1975; Willard Espy, *Say It My Way*, Garden City, NY: Doubleday Publishing Company, 1980; Abraham H. Lass and Betty Lass, *Dictionary of Pronunciation*, New York: The New York Times Press, 1976.

PALMER, AUSTIN N. (December 22, 1857–November 16, 1927), handwriting teacher and developer of the Palmer Method of handwriting. Although born in New York State, Palmer moved to Cedar Rapids, Iowa, as a young man and thereafter considered it to be his home. He was, from boyhood, interested in penmanship, practical handwriting, as well as ornamental penmanship.

In 1877, the Cedar Rapids Business College was established (an institution Palmer purchased in 1885). Palmer was invited to teach there and, in 1844, founded a magazine, *Western Penman* (later *American Penman*), which was devoted to the subject of penmanship. He used this publication to promote pen art, later known as the Palmer Method, and also to attack the use of copy books that were then being used widely in elementary schools. Notwithstanding considerable resistance from their publishers, Palmer was able to bring about the demise of copy books by the turn of the century. He published Palmer Method lessons (to replace copy books) in *Western Penman* that led to adoptions of his approach in New York City, certain other American districts, and by Canadian Catholic parochial schools.

Palmer worked closely with teachers, stressing the view that only trained teachers could teach penmanship effectively. Before he died, Palmer had trained over 50,000 teachers (directly or via correspondence) to employ materials that were being used by an estimated 12–15,000,000 public and private school children. Millions of copies of his lesson manual were sold in connection with this effort. (See PALMER METHOD.)
Reference: W. C. Henning, "A. N. Palmer," Paper Prepared in 1965 and Delivered for Him at the 18th Annual Convention of the International Association of Master Penmen and Teachers of Handwriting.

PALMER METHOD, a commercial program for the teaching of handwriting. The method's overriding objective is to teach good legible handwriting done with ease and speed. Both manuscript and cursive writing are taught. Materials include a series of student manuals with accompanying teachers' editions as well as numbers of supplementary teaching aids such as charts, overhead transparencies, and paper (slant line instruction sheets, wall cards, and desk cards). The method was developed in the latter part of the 19th century by Austin N. Palmer and is currently published by the A. N. Palmer Company. (See PALMER, AUSTIN N.)

References: Committee Guide for Use by Elementary Handwriting Committees Preparing to Select a Handwriting Program, Schaumburg, IL: The A. N. Palmer Company, 1980; *Palmer Method Handwriting: 1980 Catalog,* Schaumburg, IL: The A. N. Palmer Company, 1980.

PAPIER-MÂCHÉ, an art material used to create three-dimensional forms. Shredded paper or paper strips, mixed with glue, wheat paste, or wallpaper paste, constitute the basic materials needed to do papier-mâché work. Paper that has been mixed with the glue is applied to an armature (i.e. the base used to support the limp paper until it dries). Empty containers, strips of wood, cans, rolled newspaper, foil, and plastecine are examples of base materials that can be used as armatures. Another method involves using an easel brush to apply glue over each strip of paper.

Paper is applied a piece at a time after the desired basic shape has been formed with the armature, and criss-crossed for added strength. Once the object (e.g. puppet, mask, sculpture) has been formed and allowed to dry, it is painted. Sealers such as varnish or shellac are then added for luster and to increase longevity.

References: Leslie A. Baker, The Art Teacher's Resource Book, Reston, VA: Reston Publishing Company, Inc., 1979; Robert V. Bullough, Sr., *Creating Instructional Materials* (Second Edition), Columbus, OH: Charles E. Merrill Publishing Company, 1978.

PARADIGM, a descriptive representation of a model, system, or pattern that can be used to describe a theory or concept. A paradigm can be depicted graphically, usually with blocks and lines, as indicated below. Such illustrations do not consti-

tute the theory or concept; rather, they are used to reinforce the more extensive narrative description.

Paradigms are used in many fields and disciplines. They can be used to describe and illustrate an economic system, social concepts, learning, a theory of psychology, logic, thinking, and so on. Paradigms help to identify and illustrate how the components of a particular system, theory, or concept are interrelated.

References: Beryl L. Bellman and Benetta Jules-Rosette, *A Paradigm for Looking,* Norwood, NJ: Ablex Publishing Corporation, 1977; Robert G. Colodney (Editor), *Paradigms and Paradoxes,* Pittsburgh, PA: University of Pittsburgh Press, 1972; John G. Grumm, *A Paradigm for the Comparative Analysis of Legislative Systems,* Beverly Hills, CA: Sage Publications, Inc., 1973.

PARAMETER—See POPULATION

PARAMETRIC STATISTICS, those statistical procedures used to assess data usually taken from samples of a population. Since it is rare to know the parameters (quantity characteristics) of a population, sample data are used. A quantity computed from sample data is known as a "statistic." The following assumptions should be met when using parametric statistical procedures: (1) the population(s) is (are) normally distributed around the mean; (2) population variances are approximately equal when two or more populations are being compared; (3) the measures have equal intervals (interval scaling, ratio scaling); and (4) the scores are independent.

Sampling, inferences, probability, normal distributions, randomization, and measurement error are all important in parametric statistics. Student "t," analysis of variance, and F distributions are common parametric statistical procedures. (See NONPARAMETRIC STATISTICS.)

References: George E. P. Box, et al., *Statistics for Experimenters,* New York: John Wiley and Sons, 1978; L. R.

Sample Paradigm

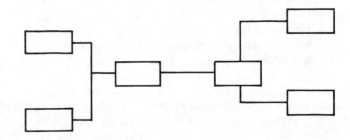

Gay, *Educational Research: Competencies for Analysis and Application* (Third Edition), Columbus, OH: Merrill Publishing Company, 1987; James H. McMillan and Sally Schumacher, *Research in Education: A Conceptual Introduction* (Second Edition), Glenview, IL: Scott, Foresman and Company, 1989.

PARAPLEGIA, a neuromuscular problem that results in dysfunction or paralysis of the lower half of the body, including both legs. Disease or accidents involving the spinal cord usually cause the dysfunction or paralysis. For example, cerebral palsy may lead to dysfunction in both legs. An injury or wound can also bring about paraplegia.

Although there may be major emotional problems associated with the condition, it does not affect the intellectual ability or functioning of the individual involved. Many paraplegia students can participate easily in most regular classroom programs.

References: Eugene E. Bleck and Donald A. Nagel (Editors), *Physically Handicapped Children: A Medical Atlas for Teachers,* New York: Grune and Stratton, 1975; Harold D. Love, *Teaching Physically Handicapped Children,* Springfield, IL: Charles C Thomas, Publisher, 1978; Philip Safford and Dena C. Arbitman, *Developmental Intervention with Young Physically Handicapped Children,* Springfield, IL: Charles C Thomas, Publisher, 1975.

PARAPROFESSIONALS IN EDUCATION, noncertified school aides. The term *paraprofessionals* is often used interchangeably with other job titles such as *aide, auxiliary school personnel, teacher aide,* and *educational assistant.*

In 1953, Bay City, Michigan, as part of an experiment, employed and paired paraprofessionals with regular teachers. They performed noninstructional (usually clerical) duties, thus freeing the teacher to devote more time to teaching. After two years, the experiment failed to show any significant change in pupil achievement. Nevertheless, the movement to use paraprofessionals increased in popularity throughout the United States. Different districts hired them for different reasons: to ease budget; to improve curriculum; or simply to provide needed help (instructional or service-oriented) as enrollments grew.

The movement received considerable impetus from federal antipoverty programs introduced in the 1960s. Some higher education institutions developed training programs, of up to two years, that were geared to meet the needs of aides and schools. The paraprofessional movement began to decline in the 1970s, however, for economic and other reasons. Today, aides continue to be used, some to meet unique needs (e.g. using bilingual aides to bolster bilingual programs).

References: Nan Coppock and Ian Templeton, *Paraprofessionals: School Leadership Digest,* Arlington, VA: National Association of Elementary School Principals, 1974; Arthur Pearl, "An Analysis and Perspective" in Alan Gartner, et al. (Editors), *Paraprofessionals in Education Today,* New York: Human Sciences Press, 1977; Paul C. Shank and Wayne McElroy, *The Paraprofessionals or Teacher Aides: Selection, Preparation and Assignment,* Midland, MI: Pendell Publishing Company, 1970.

PARAPSYCHOLOGY, the study (field) of psychic phenomena. It deals with exchanges between individuals or between individuals and objects that are extrasensorimotor. That is, the exchanges are not dependent on the senses and/or muscles. Psi is the Greek letter used to identify an individual's extrasensorimotor ability.

Parapsychology is almost 100 years old, but the Duke University studies of ESP (Estrasensory Perception), which began in 1933, played a major role in the development of the field. Dr. Joseph B. Rhine of Duke University invented the word *para* (beyond) *psychology,* meaning "beyond that which can be explained by psychology." Phenomena such as clairvoyance, ESP, telepathy, out-of-body experience, poltergeist, precognition, psychokinesis (PK), and retrocognition are among the areas studied in parapsychology.

References: John L. Randall, *Parapsychology and the Nature of Life,* New York: Harper and Row, Publishers, 1975; Gertrude R. Schmeidler (Editor), *Parapsychology: Its Relation to Physics, Biology, Psychology and Psychiatry,* Metuchen, NJ: The Scarecrow Press, Inc., 1976; Betty Shapin and Lisette Coly (Editors), *The Philosophy of Parapsychology,* New York: Parapsychology Foundation, 1977.

PARC DECISION, a 1971 court case that resulted in a consent decree that extended equal educational opportunities to handicapped children. The Pennsylvania Association for Retarded Children took the Commonwealth of Pennsylvania to court to ensure that *all* children would have an opportunity to a free public education. It was held that (1) all mentally retarded children can benefit from an educational program, (2) the state of Pennsylvania must provide a free public education to all children between the ages of 6 and 21, including mentally retarded children, (3) the state cannot deny mentally retarded children access to that education, and (4) the state must place mentally retarded children in free public programs that are appropriate for the children.

PARC was one of the major court decisions that granted rights to the handicapped and led to the passing of Public Law 94–142. Public schools could not reject or exclude a child because that child was mentally retarded; it established the principle of zero rejection in the state of Pennsylvania. (See *MILLS v. DISTRICT OF COLUMBIA BOARD OF EDUCATION and PUBLIC LAW 94–142.*)

References: Pennsylvania Association for Retarded Children v. Commonwealth of Pennsylvania, 334 F. Supp. 1257, 343 F. Supp. 279 (E.D. Pa. 1971, 1972); H. Rutherford Turnbull III, *Free Appropriate Public Education, The Law and Children with Disabilities*, Denver, CO: Love Publishing Co., 1986.

PARENT EDUCATION, generally defined as programs/efforts that seek to inform parents about various aspects of childrearing and thereby make better parents of them. Parent education is also referred to as "parenting," "parenting education," or "education for parenthood." Parent education programs may be carried out with groups of parents or by working with individuals. Although most parent education is carried out with parents of preschool children, it has also proved successful with other parent populations (e.g. parents of the handicapped).

Shari Nedler and Oralie McAfee pointed out that recent surveys of prospective parent education participants indicated greatest interest in gaining information about: (1) child growth and development; (2) treating a child like a person; and (3) caring for health problems. Evelyn Pickarts and Jean Fargo suggested that parent education programs should include: (1) a "teachable" content; (2) a content general enough to be used with various class and cultural groups; (3) instructors who are educators; (4) sufficient flexibility to meet participants' needs and interests; and (5) topics that offer new information rather than those that attempt to remediate or focus on parent failures.

References: Doreen Croft, *Parents and Teachers: A Resource Book for Home, School, and Community Relations*, Belmont, CA: Wadsworth Publishing Company, Inc., 1979; Shari E. Nedler and Oralie D. McAfee, *Working with Parents: Guidelines for Early Childhood and Elementary Teachers*, Belmont, CA: Wadsworth Publishing Company, Inc., 1979; Evelyn Pickarts and Jean Fargo, *Parent Education: Toward Parental Competence*, New York: Appleton-Century-Crofts, Inc., 1971; Kevin J. Swick and R. Eleanor Duff, *What Research Says to the Teacher: Parenting*, Washington, DC: National Education Association, 1979.

PARENTS ANONYMOUS (PA), a voluntary, nonreligious, self-help, crisis-intervention organization for parents who abuse their children. PA was founded in 1970 by a child abuser and her therapist, Leonard Lieber.

Members belonging to local chapters meet once a week as a group and discuss (voluntarily) their respective difficulties with an eye to supporting each other and finding satisfactory alternatives to abusive behavior. Before PA's founding, society sought to resolve problems attendant to child abuse by: (1) separating the child from his/her parent(s), an action that often created new problems for the child, or (2) punishing the parent. PA believes it provides a viable alternative to these earlier courses of action.

PA members do not pay dues. They may choose to remain anonymous by electing to use only their first names. Local chapters choose their own leader who, in turn, receives resource help from a *sponsor*, a professional in the field of mental health.

PA publishes a newsletter, *P.A. Frontiers*, and relatively inexpensive literature dealing with child abuse. Its national office is in Torrance, California. (See CHILD ABUSE.)

References: Losing Your Kool With Your Kids? Torrance, CA: Parents Anonymous, Undated Brochure; Patte Wheat and Leonard L. Lieber, *Hope for the Children: A Personal History of Parents Anonymous*, Minneapolis, MN: Winston Press, 1979.

PARENT-TEACHER CONFERENCES, face-to-face meetings between a child's teacher and the child's parent(s). The individual parent-teacher conference, an extension of the individualized instruction movement, provides teachers with an opportunity to learn about students directly from their parents and also permits them to report on students' progress/problems as well.

A survey conducted by the NEA Research Division revealed that 60 percent of the elementary teachers and 20 percent of the secondary teachers sampled used the parent-teacher conference as a method of reporting. Many school systems have formalized such conferences, either substituting them for, or alternating them with, written report cards.

Parent-teacher conferences take other forms as well. Some are unscheduled, taking place when parent or teacher feels there is a need for one. Another type involves a teacher and parent(s) of a preschool child slated for enrollment. Still others are of the group variety, bringing a teacher and several (or all) parents together for a meeting. (See INDIVIDUAL EDUCATION PLAN.)

References: Robert L. Canady and John T. Seyfarth, *How Parent-Teacher Conferences Build Partnerships* (PDK

Fastback 132), Bloomington, IN: The Phi Delta Kappa Educational Foundation, 1979; James N. Casavis, *Principal's Guidelines for Action in Parent Conferences,* West Nyack, NY: Parker Publishing Company, Inc., 1970; Norman E. Gronlund, *Improving Marking and Reporting in Classroom Instruction,* New York: Macmillan Publishing Company, Inc., 1974; Stuart M. Losen and Bert Diament, *Parent Conferences in the Schools: Procedures for Developing Effective Partnership,* Boston: Allyn and Bacon, Inc., 1978.

PARKER, FRANCIS W. (October 9, 1837–March 2, 1902), educational reformer and founder of the progressive education movement. John Dewey, associated with Parker in Chicago, referred to him as the father of progressive education. Parker's educational career, interrupted by service in the Union Army during the Civil War, included administrative headship of the Dayton, Ohio, and Quincy, Massachusetts, school systems. He later served as Principal of the Cook County Normal School in Chicago and as President of the Chicago Institute, an organization that subsequently became the University of Chicago's Department of Education. A study trip to Berlin, in 1871, exposed him to the philosophies of Comenius, Pestalozzi, Herbart, and Froebel.

In Dayton and Quincy, Parker implemented numerous curricular changes that presaged several educational reforms in American schools. They included adapting curriculum to the needs of individual learners; placing instructional emphasis on discovery; use of field trips; adding science and drawing to the curriculum; placing more reliance on active approaches to learning with a corresponding decline in dependence on textbooks; and correlating subject matter.

Parker's writings related directly to the reforms he espoused. *Talks on Teaching* (1896) was one of several books he authored.

References: Lawrence A. Cremin, *The Transformation of the School: Progressivism in American Education, 1876–1957,* New York: Alfred A. Knopf, 1961; Elinor Kline and David W. Moore, "Colonel Francis Parker and Beginning Reading Instruction," *Reading Research and Instruction,* Volume 26, Number 3, 1987; Adolphe E. Meyer, *Grandmasters of Educational Thought,* New York: McGraw-Hill Book Company, 1975; Frederick C. Neff and Joseph Engle, "Parker, Francis W." in John F. Ohles (Editor), *Biographical Dictionary of American Educators* (Volume 2), Westport, CT: Greenwood Press, 1978; William Van Til, *Secondary Education: School and Community,* Boston: Houghton Mifflin Company, 1978.

PAROCHIAD, the use of state and/or federal funds to support parochial schools, directly or indirectly. For years, numerous state constitutions have provided for the fiscal support of schools and specifically preclude the use of public funds for the support of private/parochial education. These constitutional provisions are based on one category of the Establishment Clause, First Amendment of the U.S. Constitution, which has often been used as a basis for disallowing public aid to sectarian institutions.

Over the last half-century, however, several events and court decisions have given legal sanction to some forms of parochiad, while others, deemed to go beyond the "verge" of impermissable state aid, have continued to be resisted by the courts. Examples of events/decisions that have won court endorsement include *Everson v. Board of Education* (permitting reimbursement of bus fares to parents of public and parochial school children), *Cochran v. Louisiana State Board of Education* (permitting use of public monies to furnish textbooks to private school children, and the decision that created the "child-benefit theory"), and federal programs providing varying forms of assistance to both public and private school children (e.g. National Defense Education Act).

Some decisions in which parochiad has been denied include *Sloan v. Lemon* (which concluded that a Pennsylvania law providing partial tuition reimbursement to parents of parochial school children was unconstitutional), *Lemon v. Kurtzman* (which resulted in a similar ruling concerning another Pennsylvania law, one that attempted to reimburse parochial schools for teachers' salaries, textbooks, and materials provided in conjunction with the teaching of secular subjects). See CHILD BENEFIT THEORY; *COCHRAN v. LOUISIANA BOARD OF EDUCATION; EVERSON v. BOARD OF EDUCATION;* and *LEMON v. KURTZMAN.*)

References: Gaston D. Cogdell, *What Price Parochiad?* Silver Springs, MD: Americans United, 1970; Earl Hoffman, "Milestones on the Road to Parochiad," *NASSP Bulletin,* December 1974; Frank R. Kemerer and Kenneth L. Deutsch, *Constitutional Rights and Student Life: Value Conflict in Law and Education,* St. Paul, MN: West Publishing Company, 1979; Stephen J. Pollak, "Parochiad: End of the Line?" *Today's Education,* November–December 1973; Dale E. Twomley, *Parochiad and the Courts,* Berrien Springs, MI: Andrews University Press, 1979.

PAROCHIAL SCHOOLS, educational institutions that are church related. In the United States, schools associated with the Roman Catholic church constitute the largest group of parochial schools. In 1978–79, they enrolled 3,274,000 elementary and secondary school students, or approximately 7 percent of the nation's total K–12 population. Among the first Protestant groups to sponsor parochial schools were the Calvinists, Lutherans, Episcopalians, Quakers, and Dutch Reformed. Since the mid-1800s, schools have also been operated by various Methodist and Baptist groups as well as Seventh Day Adventists, Assemblies of God, Churches of Christ, and other sects. Most Hebrew schools in the United States were established after 1940. In 1976–77, enrollments reported for the larger, other than Catholic parochial schools were as follows: Lutheran, 214,000; Baptist, 99,700; Episcopal, 83,700; Jewish, 67,900; Presbyterian, 53,500; and Seventh Day Adventist, 53,300. An additional 418,900 students were enrolled in other sectarian schools.

Enrollment trends indicate that Catholic school enrollment, although still the largest among all parochial schools, decreased from 1965–66 to 1978–79 (5,481,300 to 3,274,000), and the combined enrollments of all other parochial schools increased during the same period (482,200 to 1,053,000). (See CATHOLIC SCHOOLS; CHRISTIAN SCHOOLS; NONPUBLIC SCHOOLS; and YESHIVA.)

References: A Statistical Report on U.S. Catholic Schools, 1979–80 (Excerpt from *Catholic Schools in America, 1980*), Washington, DC: National Catholic Educational Association, 1980; Otto F. Kraushaar, *Private Schools: From the Puritans to the Present* (PDK Fastback 78), Bloomington, IN: The Phi Delta Kappa Educational Foundation, 1976; Lewis J. Sherrill, *Presbyterian Parochial Schools, 1846–1870,* New York: Arno Press and the New York Times, 1969 (Originally Published by Yale University Press, 1932).

PART SINGING, or singing in harmony, a musical activity carried out by two or more singers without benefit of accompaniment. It is frequently taught as an approach to the study of harmony.

In schools, any of several preliminary song types may be taught before the teaching of actual harmony. They include *dialogue* songs, or songs that are divided into two or more parts with groups of singers taking turns singing their assigned sections; *rounds* (e.g. "Row Your Boat"), in which the same melody is sung by two or more groups, but not at the same time; *descants* (e.g. "Silent Night"), two independent melodies sung together; or *songs with harmonic endings.* These song-types are generally taught progressively with learners, in each case, instructed to listen and to discern the relationships between the different parts being sung. To facilitate mastery of part singing, students at

first learn their sections by rote. Actual singing in harmony (two and three parts) can be taught successfully in the intermediate grades of elementary school. Special interest groups such as choirs or choruses make it possible for elementary and high school children to perform for audiences and demonstrate their ability to do part singing.

References: Willi Apel, *Harvard Dictionary of Music* (Second Edition), Cambridge, MA: The Belknap Press of Harvard University Press, 1970; Marvin Greenberg and Beatrix MacGregor, *Music Handbook for the Elementary School,* West Nyack, NY: Parker Publishing Company, Inc., 1972; Robert E. Nye and Vernice T. Nye, *Music in the Elementary School* (Fourth Edition), Englewood Cliffs, NJ: Prentice-Hall, Inc., 1977; Aleta Runkle and Mary L. Eriksen, *Music for Today: Elementary School Methods* (Third Edition), Boston: Allyn and Bacon, Inc., 1976.

PARTS OF SPEECH, in traditional grammar, the classification of words according to their function or the ideas they express. Depending on which classification system is used, there are seven to ten different parts of speech. Among the most common, presented here with their respective meanings, are: (1) *noun,* the name of a person, place, or thing; (2) *pronoun,* a word that can be used in place of a noun (e.g. he, it); (3) *adjective,* a word that modifies a noun (e.g. *big* house); (4) *verb,* a word that shows action or indicates a state of being (e.g. run, is); (5) *adverb,* a word that modifies a verb, an adjective, or another adverb; (6) *preposition,* a word that introduces a phrase; (7) *conjunction,* a word that connects words, phrases, or clauses (e.g. or); and (8) *article,* the words "a," "an," and "the." (See GRAMMAR.)

References: Gertrude A. Boyd and Daisy M. Jones, *Teaching Communication Skills in the Elementary School* (Second Edition), New York: D. Van Nostrand Company, Inc., 1977; Paul C. Burns and Betty L. Broman, *The Language Arts in Childhood Education* (Third Edition), Chicago: Rand McNally College Publishing Company, 1975.

PASCAL, a computer language developed in 1971 by Kiklaus Wirth, a Swiss computer scientist. He named the language after Blaise Pascal, who is credited with developing the first mechanical calculating machine in 1642 (the machine was called the Pascaline). PASCAL was designed to be a teaching language, is based on structured programming, and develops strong programming habits in students, thus facilitating the learning of other languages. PASCAL is a language with a source code that must be translated into machine executable object code by a compiler (complied language);

thus, it is more complex than other languages. It is used most often in college and university computer science courses. Because the Educational Testing Service's Advanced Placement Examination in Computer Science is based on PASCAL, schools below the college level are utilizing it in some of their computer science courses. (See BASIC and LOGO.)

References: James Lockard, et al., *Microcomputers for Educators,* Boston, MA: Little, Brown and Co., 1987; Paul F. Merrill, et al., *Computers in Education,* Englewood Cliffs, NJ: Prentice-Hall, Inc., 1986.

PATH ANALYSIS, an approach comprised of several different statistical procedures used to analyze the causal interrelationships of a set of variables. Before path analysis can be used appropriately, a theory concerning the structure of the causal model underlying the variables to be assessed must be developed by the researcher. The researcher must be able to identify which variables influence others. The researcher must also make the measurements and data collection fit the model.

For example, a researcher may wish to analyze the relationship of five variables. One of the variables might be highly influenced by two variables, one might be influenced by three variables, and one might be influenced by four. The resultant path analysis, illustrated below, shows the direct and indirect, as well as the feedback or reciprocal relationships among the five variables.

Path analysis was first developed by Sewall Wright, a biologist and geneticist, between 1910 and 1930. The procedure has been adapted to the social sciences with the advent of high-speed and high-capacity computers.

References: Daniel J. Amick and Herbert J. Walberg (Editors), *Introductory Multivariate Analysis for Educational, Psychological, and Social Research,* Berkeley, CA: McCutchan Publishing Corporation, 1975; Jacob Cohen and Patricia Cohen, *Applied Multiple Regression/Correlation Analysis for the Behavioral Sciences,* Hillsdale, NJ: Lawrence Erlbaum Associates, Publishers, 1975; David R. Heise, *Causal Analysis,* New York: John Wiley and Sons, 1975.

PATH-GOAL THEORY—See LEADER BEHAVIOR

PATTERNING, in psychology, the process by which external signals are transposed into a meaningful perceptual experience. In language learning, it refers to the combining of basic elements in a language to build messages. It can also be used in verbalization to develop conversational patterns (e.g. expanding conversation beyond simple questions and answers). In perceptual development, patterning refers to the recognition of relationships between similar and dissimilar objects. Illustrating this type of patterning is the child who can place similar objects together.

Patterning, as used by Glen Doman and Carl Delacato (Institutes for the Achievement of Human Potential), is a technique of reprogramming the brains of brain-injured children. It involves the manipulation of arms, legs, and head movements (by five individuals each working on a separate appendage) such that the brain will receive sensory messages. This is intended to activate the live cells within the injured brain and increase/improve the level of neurological development.

References: Christopher Alexander, *The Timeless Way of Building,* New York: Oxford University Press, 1979; Patricia I. Myers and Donald D. Hammell, *Methods for Learning Disorders* (Second Edition), New York: John Wiley and Sons, 1976; Stephen K. Reed, *Psychological Process in Pattern Recognition,* New York: Academic Press, 1973.

Example of Path Analysis

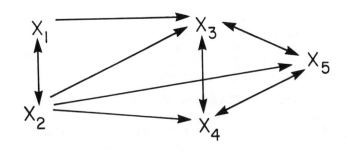

PAUPER SCHOOLS, early American schools set aside for the children of the poor. The pauper school concept, common to the southern and middle colonies, originated in England. It was particularly popular in New Jersey, Pennsylvania, Delaware, Maryland, Virginia, and Georgia. Those enrolled in pauper schools were either orphans or offspring of the poor. Children of the upper and middle classes, on the other hand, either attended private (including denominational) schools or received instruction from tutors.

Provision for pauper schools was included in numbers of state constitutions. The pauper school concept began to be challenged during the late 18th and early 19th centuries, principally on the grounds that the idea of special schools for special classes was antiethical to the "man is created equal" doctrine. Eventually, free state schools, open to children of all social classes, replaced the increasingly unpopular pauper schools.
References: Elwood P. Cubberly, *Public Education in the United States: A Study and Interpretation of American Educational History,* Cambridge, MA: Houghton Mifflin Company (Riverside Press), 1962; Edgar W. Knight (Editor), *A Documentary History of Education in the South Before 1860* (Volume I), Chapel Hill, NC: University of North Carolina Press, 1949.

PAVLOV, IVAN P. (September 14, 1849–February 22, 1936), Russian physiologist known internationally for his research in the areas of blood circulation, the digestive glands, and conditioned reflexes. His work in conditioning established that the nervous activity of the dog is based on reflex action. Such activity, he concluded, was a response to stimuli found inside or outside the animal. Pavlov identified two types of reflexes: *unconditioned,* or innate reactions to given stimuli, and the *conditioned* (or acquired) responses. His research did much to influence the psychology of learning. In 1904, Pavlov was awarded the Nobel Prize for his work on the physiology of digestive glands. He is also known as an early leader in the behaviorist group of psychologists.
References: Ezras A. Asratyan, *I. P. Pavlov: His Life and Work,* Moscow, USSR: Foreign Language Publishing House, 1953; B. P. Babkin, *Pavlov: A Biography,* Chicago: University of Chicago Press, 1949.

PEABODY, ELIZABETH P. (May 16, 1804–January 3, 1894), first American educator to establish an English-speaking Kindergarten in the United States (Boston). Peabody was a student in a private school operated by her mother and later, at the age of 16, opened her own private school. She

was later introduced to the Kindergarten idea and to the writings of Froebel by Mrs. Carl Schurz, a woman who earlier had established a German-speaking Kindergarten in Wisconsin.

Peabody's Kindergarten was opened in 1860, in her own home, and quickly grew in popularity. She later traveled to Germany to study Kindergarten programs there. In 1870, she persuaded Boston to open the first public Kindergarten in the United States.

Her writings included several books dealing with Kindergarten (e.g. *Kindergarten in Italy,* 1872, and *Letters to Kindergarteners,* 1886). From 1873 to 1877, she edited the *Kindergarten Messenger.* Her two sisters (Mrs. Horace Mann and Mrs. Nathaniel Hawthorne, educator and illustrator, respectively) were equally successful in their career endeavors.
References: Mildred S. Fenner and Eleanor C. Fishburn, *Pioneer American Educators,* Port Washington, NY: Kennikat Press, Inc., 1968; Ann Stankiewicz, "Peabody, Elizabeth Palmer" in John F. Ohles (Editor), *Biographical Dictionary of American Educators* (Volume 2), Westport, CT: Greenwood Press, 1978; Louise Hall Tharp, *The Peabody Sisters of Salem,* Boston: Little, Brown and Company, 1950.

PEABODY, GEORGE (February 18, 1795–November 4, 1869), successful merchant and international financier. A bachelor throughout his lifetime, Peabody amassed a fortune that he shared philanthropically with others. Numerous foundations, institutes, museums, and libraries were formed or supported by Peabody money. Many, including George Peabody College for Teachers (now a part of Vanderbilt University) in Nashville, Tennessee, bear his name. Peabody was born in Massachusetts, spent his early adult years in Georgetown and Baltimore, and moved permanently to England in 1837. The Peabody Education Fund (1867) was particularly influential on all later education trusts, funds, and foundations.
Reference: Franklin Parker, *George Peabody: A Biography,* Nashville, TN: Vanderbilt University Press, 1971.

PEABODY PICTURE VOCABULARY TEST (PPVT), a simple test of intelligence for use with subjects aged 2.5 to 18.0 years. The test consists of 150 items, or plates, each containing four pictures. The examiner calls out the name of one object depicted on a plate after which the child is expected to point to the correct (corresponding) picture. Although the PPVT correlates reasonably well with more sophisticated intelligence instruments, reading authorities value it more as an indicator of vocabulary development than as a measure of intelligence.

Reference: Lloyd M. Dunn, *Expanded Manual Peabody Picture Vocabulary Test,* Circle Pines, MN: American Guidance Services, 1965; George D. Spache, *Investigating the Issues of Reading Disabilities,* Boston: Allyn and Bacon, Inc., 1976.

PEACE CORPS, an agency of the U.S. government that makes American volunteers with specialized skills available to work with people of developing nations. The Peace Corps Act (1961) established the corps and set forth its basic purposes: "to promote world peace and friendship through a Peace Corps, which shall make available to interested countries and areas men and women of the United States qualified for service abroad and willing to serve, under conditions of hardship if necessary, to help the peoples of such countries in meeting their needs for trained manpower, and to promote a better understanding of the American people on the part of the peoples served and a better understanding of other peoples on the part of the American people" (p. 612).

Volunteers (presently working in over 60 countries) render two years of service following 10–14 weeks of training. They work in vocational areas such as agriculture, health education, economic and community development, and home economics. Each receives a nominal living allowance and a readjustment allowance following completion of service. Volunteers receive basic instruction in the language of the host country and normally reside in native housing.

In 1971, Peace Corps and Vista (another service agency) were consolidated to form the omnibus service organization, ACTION. (See ACTION and VISTA.)

References: Robert G. Carey, *The Peace Corps,* New York: Praeger Publishers, 1970; *Peace Corps* (Action Pamphlet No. 4200.3), Washington, DC: ACTION, April 1979; *Public Law 87-293, United States Statutes at Large, 1961* (Volume 75), Washington, DC: U.S. Government Printing Office, 1961.

PEDIATRICS, or pediatry, a field of medicine devoted to disease treatment and health care of children. It evolved as a medical specialization in the middle 1900s and did much, in cooperation with other medical specialties, to reduce infant mortality in the United States.

During the first half of the 20th century, pediatricians (physicians specializing in health care of children) tended to concentrate on children's infectious diseases. The field was later broadened to include areas such as the behavioral and social aspects of children's health, nutrition, and the problems of the handicapped. Very recently, subspecialties within pediatrics have emerged. Some concentrate on specific age groups; others reflect physician interest in medical areas such as pediatric cardiology, pediatric hematology, neonatal prenatal medicine, and nephrology.

In the United States, the American Board of Pediatrics, Inc., establishes criteria for certification of pediatricians and administers both the written and oral examinations requisite to certification.

References: Directory of Medical Specialists (Nineteenth Edition, Volume 2), Chicago: Marquis Who's Who, 1979–80 (Published for the American Board of Medical Specialties); Victor C. Vaughan, III, et al., *Nelson Textbook of Pediatrics* (Eleventh Edition), Philadelphia: W. B. Saunders Company, 1979.

PEER GROUP, or peer culture, a group of associates who tend to be of the same age and developmental level. Relationships among peer group members are transitory, yet often intensive. The influence of the peer group on the individual is greatest during adolescence, the period when the youth is approaching adulthood physically but is still dependent on others for his/her basic needs. It is during this developmental stage that the influence of parents and home is often overshadowed, even displaced by that of peers.

Peer group influence may be positive or negative. As a reference group, the peer group, although informal, serves several functions. David Ausubel, in 1954, identified several that a later writer, Don Hamachek, modified in view of more recent research data. Among the functions listed are these: (1) in varying degrees, to replace the family; (2) to provide group members with stability and to serve as a source of self-esteem; (3) to insulate and protect members from adult coercions; and (4) to provide standards of behavior (a function about which all authorities are not in agreement). (See SELF-ESTEEM.)

References: David P. Ausubel, *Theory and Problems of Adolescent Development,* New York: Grune and Stratton, 1954; Don E. Hamachek, *Psychology in Teaching, Learning and Growth* (Second Edition), Boston: Allyn and Bacon, Inc., 1979; Robert J. Havighurst and Daniel U. Levine, *Society and Education* (Fifth Edition), Boston: Allyn and Bacon, Inc., 1979; Harry H. Vorrath and Larry K. Brendtro, *Positive Peer Culture,* Chicago: Aldine Publishing Company, 1974.

PEER TUTORING, or peer teaching, a procedure in which students tutor or teach other students.

There are generally two types of peer tutoring. In the first type, tutors and tutees are from the same grade. In the second type, older children tutor or teach younger children. The latter type is sometimes referred to as cross-age tutoring. Considerable learning and social growth has been attributed to both the tutor and tutee as a result of peer tutoring. Peer tutoring as teaching can be used to supplement regular classroom instruction, but authorities recommend that it not be used as a substitute for teacher instruction.

Peer teaching has another, but similar, meaning when used in teacher education. Here, teacher education students present a demonstration lesson or an instructional strategy to their peers and have them critique it. The advantage of this method is that it provides "learners" (peers) with immediate feedback.

References: David W. Johnson and Roger T. Johnson, *Learning Together and Alone,* Englewood Cliffs, NJ: Prentice-Hall, Inc., 1975; Peggy Lippitt, *Students Teach Students* (PDK Fastback 65), Bloomington, IN: The Phi Delta Kappa Educational Foundation, 1975; Barry Nelson, *An Experiment in Cross-Age Peer Interaction,* Clarks Summit, PA: Abington Heights Middle School, 1979; Keith J. Topping, *The Peer Tutoring Handbook: Promoting Cooperative Learning,* Cambridge, MA: Brookline Books, 1988; James C. Tyson and Mary Ann Carroll, *Conceptual Tools for Teaching in Secondary Schools,* New York: Houghton Mifflin Company, 1970.

PELL GRANT—See BASIC EDUCATIONAL OPPORTUNITY GRANT

PENMANSHIP—See HANDWRITING

PENTATONIC SCALE—See SCALE, MUSICAL

PERCENTILE, a point or score below which a given percentage of scores is found. The total number of scores (cases) is divided into 100 equal parts. The points that separate the 1 percent parts are called centiles. Thus, the 50th centile, or 50th percentile, is the point below which 50 percent of the scores lie. The 14th centile (percentile) is that point below which 14 percent of the scores are found, and 90 percent of the cases are below the 90th percentile. By definition, it is impossible to be in the 100th percentile, since a score must be part of the distribution and no score can be outside its own set of scores.

The percentile may be used to describe the shape of a frequency. It is used frequently to interpret individual test scores. Many standardized tests report scores in terms of percentile rankings. Per-

centile rank is another method of expressing a distribution of scores such that if 27 percent of the students in a standardized test made scores below 240, the student making a score of 240 would have a percentile rank of 27. Percentiles may be used in the computation of other statistics as well.

References: Lou M. Carey, *Measuring and Evaluating School Learning,* Boston: Allyn and Bacon, Inc., 1988; Gilbert Sax, *Principles of Educational and Psychological Measurement and Evaluation* (Third Edition), Belmont, CA: Wadsworth Publishing Company, 1989.

PERCEPTIONS, the ways in which an individual "sees" things. The study of perceptions concerns the appearance of things. Perceptions may reflect accurately the object (veridical) being viewed, or they may not (illusion).

Each of the human senses plays a role in the development of perceptions (e.g., hearing, vision, taste, smell, feel). Factors such as past experiences, the unknown, attitudes, values, and misinformation may also help to develop and to influence perceptions. Thus, perceptions are of interest not only to psychology but to philosophy as well. One's perceptions of another person may dictate how that other person reacts to him/her. Knowing this, teachers are urged to be alert to inaccurate perceptions of their students toward others or themselves.

Perception, as related to the senses, may include size, dimension, direction, movements, shape, orientation, or color. These perceptions help the individual to differentiate between and among similar but different sensory stimuli. Children with such perceptual problems may develop highly inaccurate perceptions and thus can be significantly handicapped. (See PERCEPTUAL DISORDERS.)

References: Floyd H. Allport, *Theories of Perception and the Concept of Structure,* New York: John Wiley and Sons, 1955; Irvin Rock, *An Introduction to Perception,* New York: Macmillan Publishing Company, Inc., 1975; George A. Miller and Philip N. Johnson-Laird, *Language and Perception,* Cambridge, MA: Harvard University Press, 1976; Richard D. Walk and Herbert L. Pick, Jr. (Editors), *Perceptions and Experience,* New York: Plenum Press, 1978.

PERCEPTUAL DISORDERS, those disorders that impact on the ability of a person, regardless of age or intellectual ability, to see, hear, taste, touch, or smell an object, person, or event. An individual who has a perceptual problem may not be able to: recognize discriminatory features in speech, form or shape, or symbols (e.g. reading, mathematics); use these features in sensory and motor acts; recall discriminatory features; integrate intersensory information; or relate information to motor functions.

There may be physical and/or neurological causes for perceptual disorders. The most common perceptual disorders are caused by hearing or visual handicaps. Regardless of the causes, and because an individual cannot differentiate or interpret between and among sensory stimuli, perceptual disorders have a significant (adverse) impact on learning, frequently creating learning disabilities. Language disorders are not included in the perceptual disorder category. (See PERCEPTIONS.)

References: William M. Cruickshank and Daniel R. Hallahan, *Perceptual and Learning Disabilities*, Syracuse, NY: Syracuse University Press, 1975; Bill R. Gearheart, *Special Education for the 80's*, St. Louis, MO: The C. V. Mosby Company, 1980; Daniel P. Hallahan and James M. Kauffman, *Exceptional Children: Introduction to Special Education* (Fourth Edition), Englewood Cliffs, NJ: Prentice-Hall, 1988.

PERCEPTUAL LEARNING—See LEARNING, PERCEPTUAL

PERENNIALISM, an educational theory that is grounded in the philosophy of classical realism and that stresses the teaching of knowledge as eternal truth. It holds that the school should develop the intellectual faculties of the child by exposing him/her to prominent works (e.g. great books) in basic subjects, notably literature, fine arts, languages, history, philosophy, mathematics, and science. Exercising of the mind is achieved through the use of memory and reasoning exercises. Completion of assignments that may be distasteful to the learner but that exercise his/her will is seen as an important instructional method because, it is held, it leads to character building and realization of true self-discipline. The names of Robert Maynard Hutchins, Mortimer J. Adler, Sir Richard Livingstone, and Jacques Maritain are closely identified with the principles of perennialism.

References: George Kneller, *Introduction to the Philosophy of Education* (Second Edition), New York: John Wiley and Sons, 1971; Van Cleve Morris, *Philosophy and the American School: An Introduction to the Philosophy of Education,* Boston: Houghton Mifflin Company, 1961.

PERFORMANCE-BASED TEACHER EDUCATION—See COMPETENCY-BASED TEACHER EDUCATION

PERFORMANCE BOND, a school business administration term referring to written assurance, made by a contractor, that all parts of his/her contract will be performed faithfully. Should the contractor default, the bonding company can be required to pay for another contractor engaged to complete unfinished work. The premium charged for the bond may be paid to a surety company by either the contractor or the owner (e.g. school district). Performance bonds, in addition to assuring satisfactory performance, also discourage the incompetent, dishonest, or financially overcommitted from bidding.

References: Basil Castoldi, *Educational Facilities: Planning, Remodeling, and Management,* Boston: Allyn and Bacon, Inc., 1977; Roe L. Johns and Edgar L. Morphet, *The Economics and Financing of Education: A Systems Approach* (Third Edition), Englewood Cliffs, NJ: Prentice-Hall, Inc., 1975.

PERFORMANCE CONTRACTING, a services-for-pay arrangement in which a school system engages one or more outside agencies (usually private) to carry out specified academic activities with predetermined populations of students. Expected achievement gains are established as goals; they give activities their direction. The actual amount paid is determined on the basis of performance, or the actual academic growth realized.

Numerous school districts introduced performance contracting experimentally during the early 1970s. Considerable attention was given to specialized reading and mathematics instruction for disadvantaged learners. Funding, in most instances, was provided by the Office of Economic Opportunity (OEO). The Texarkana Public Schools were among the first to experiment with performance contracting.

Evaluations of the federally funded projects were carried out by the OEO and the Rand Corporation. Findings were qualified and the results mixed. (See OFFICE OF ECONOMIC OPPORTUNITY.)

References: American Association of School Administrators, *The School Executive's Guide to Performance Contracting,* Washington, DC: The Association, 1972; Roald F. Campbell and James E. Lorion, *Performance Contracting in School Systems,* Columbus, OH: Charles E. Merrill Publishing Company, 1972.

PERFORMANCE TESTS, nonverbal or nonlanguage tests designed for individuals who have a language (e.g. reading, learning, or sight) problem. Children who cannot read, are very young (preschool), who come from homes where the language of the printed test is not used (cross-cultural), who are not "word" oriented or have other verbal problems, or who have a particular handicap often are given performance tests as a substitute for verbally oriented tests. These examinations are designed to measure intellectual ability. The Merrill-Palmer Scale of Mental Tests, the Minnesota Preschool Scale, the California Preschool Social Competency Scale, Cultural Fair Intelligence Test, the Arthur Point Scale of Performance Tests, Non-Verbal Intelligence Tests for Deaf and Hearing Students, and the Pictorial Test of Intelligence are examples of performance tests.

References: Anne Anastasi, *Psychological Testing* (Fourth Edition), New York: Macmillan Publishing Company, Inc., 1976; Oscar K. Buros (Editor), *The Eighth Mental Measurements Yearbook* (Volumes I and II), Highland Park, NJ: The Gryphon Press, 1978; Sidney L. Pressey, et al., *Psychology in Education*, New York: Harper and Brothers, 1959.

PERKINS (CARL D.) VOCATIONAL EDUCATION ACT (Public Law 98–524), which was passed by the United States Congress on October 19, 1984, amended the Vocational Education Act of 1963 to expand and improve vocational-technical education. Its purpose is to develop human resources and reduce unemployment by: (1) assisting states to expand and improve quality vocational education; (2) providing people who are disadvantaged, handicapped, adults, single parents, those with limited English proficiency, and incarcerated (in correctional institutions) with program support; and (3) providing support in other vocationally oriented areas. Funds for 1985 were authorized to the amount of $835,300,000. Titles of the Act are: I—Vocational Education Assistance to the States, II—Basic State Grants for Vocational Education, III—Special Programs, IV—National Programs, and V—General Provisions. The act not only includes support for direct vocational training, but also includes support in career guidance and counseling, industry-education partnerships, research, demonstration programs, and the establishment of a national Council on Vocational Education (17 members) to advise the president, Congress, and the secretary of education on the effectiveness of P.L. 98–524. The act was renewed in 1989. (See NATIONAL SCIENCE, ENGINEERING, AND MATHEMATICS AUTHORIZATION ACT OF 1986, VOCATIONAL EDUCATION and VOCATIONAL EDUCATION ACT OF 1963.)

Reference: United States Code Congressional and Administrative News, 98th Congress—Second Session, 1984 (Volume 2), St. Paul, MN: West Publishing Co., 1985.

PERIODICALS, publications (except newspapers) that are issued on a regular basis. Periodicals consist chiefly of magazines and journals. In recent years, the terms *periodical, magazine,* and *journal* have come to be used interchangeably. Before the 19th century, *periodical* was used as an adjective (e.g. periodical literature).

The first magazine to be published in the United States (1741) was *American Magazine or a Monthly View of the British Colonies.* According to the Standard Periodical Directory, over 50,000 periodicals are currently produced in the United States and Canada.

Periodicals constitute an important component of school, college, and university library collections. Accrediting organizations frequently require a minimum number of periodicals to be included in such collections with the type of periodicals determined by the institution's curriculum.

Education Index, a serial publication, lists articles, by subject and author, that appear in the major professional journals in the field of education. (See EDUCATION INDEX and PROFESSIONAL JOURNALS.)

References: Education Index, New York: The H. W. Wilson Company, 1980; S. E. Wimberly Library, Florida Atlantic University, *Library News* (Mimeographed), Fall 1979, Boca Raton, FL: The Library, 1979; Frank L. Mott, *A History of American Magazines, 1741–1850,* Cambridge, MA: The Belknap Press of Harvard University Press, 1957.

PERSONAL COMPUTER (PC), a small (desktop) computer. First introduced in mid–1970, the personal computer has gone through many changes. Today, the average person can learn to use a personal computer within a short time.

The microprocessor is the heart of the personal computer. It is a circuit built on a single silicon chip to execute a program: a programmable processing circuit. Although many smaller companies entered the field at its early stage (1977–81), the larger computer manufacturers did not enter the market until the 1980s. By the mid–1980s, companies were working on integrated systems to integrate the hardware of one company with that of others. Computer networks were formed to tie computers together. For example, a personal computer can be tied to a large mainframe via telephone. In addition, companies developed integrated software which permitted more ease and versatility.

References: Grace Murray Hopper and Steven L. Mandell, *Understanding Computers,* New York: West Publishing Company, 1984; David R. Sullivan, et al., *Computing*

Today: Microcomputer Concepts and Applications, Boston: Houghton Mifflin Company, 1985.

PERSONALITY, a psychological construct that has many definitions. However, it can generally be defined in terms of behavior that is: predictable; unique to the individual; multidimensional; measurable; indicative of the way an individual adjusts to his/her environment; hierarchical; most often learned; and consistent.

Personality traits do not usually include cognitive or intellectual variates; yet intelligence may be a basic factor. Rather, the traits are classified in terms of affective dimensions such as emotions, value orientations, and temperament. Personality is influenced by heredity; yet it is continually being developed and altered throughout life. It has a psycho-neural-bio-chemical base. There are several theories of personality, each tending to stress a particular view or focus (e.g. instinct, social, free will, determinism, simple and mechanistic, complex and dynamic). (See PERSONALITY TESTS.)
References: Dennis B. Bromley, *Personality Description in Ordinary Language*, New York: John Wiley and Sons, 1977; Raymond B. Cattell and Ralph M. Dreger (Editors), *Handbook of Modern Personality Theory*, Washington, DC: Hemisphere Publishing Corporation, 1977; Kenneth H. Craik and George E. McKechnie (Editors), *Personality and the Environment,* Beverly Hills, CA: Sage Publications, Inc., 1978.

PERSONALITY TESTS, instruments and procedures used to assess or evaluate personality. They range from individual projective tests to observations, including tests and approaches such as the Rorschach Ink Blots, Murray's Thematic Apperception Test (TAT), Doll Play, Minnesota Multiphasic Personality Inventory (MMPI), Semantic Differential, Cattell 16 Personality Factor Inventory, Conditioned Eyeblink Response, self-report questionnaires, observations, sociometry, interviews, rating scales, and locus of control tests. Since there is no universally accepted definition of personality, no universally accepted list of personality traits, and several theories of personality, there is no universally accepted personality test. Most personality assessment procedures, at one time or another, have been challenged on the grounds of questionable reliability and validity.
References: Orval G. Johnson and James W. Bommarito, *Tests and Measurements in Child Development*, San Francisco: Jossey-Bass Publishers, 1971; Tom Kubiszyn and Gary Borich, *Educational Testing and Measurement: Classroom Application and Practice* (Second Edition), Glenview, IL: Scott Foresman and Company, 1987; William A.

Mehrens and Irvin J. Lehmann, *Using Standardized Tests in Education*, New York: Longman, Inc., 1987.

PERSONALITY TRAIT, a description of a generalized reaction disposition of an individual. It represents the way an individual reacts consistently over time as opposed to a single reaction. A personality trait is an enduring attribute. Such traits are used in describing the personality of an individual or a group. Often, traits are assumed from overt behavior; thus, there is a question concerning the identification and measurement of such traits.

Illustrative of personality tests that measure traits are: Guilford Zimmerman Temperament Survey (general activity, ascendance, sociability, etc.); Thurstone Temperament Schedule (active, vigorous, impulsive, dominant, etc.); and the Cattell Sixteen Personality Factor Questionnaire (cyclothymia, liking for people, surgency, cheerful, optimistic, etc.).
References: Lee J. Cronbach, *Educational Psychology* (Third Edition), New York: Harcourt Brace Jovanovich, Inc., 1977; Richard I. Lanyon and Leonard D. Goodstein, *Personality Assessment*, New York: John Wiley and Sons, 1971; Merle J. Moskowitz and Arthur R. Orgel, *General Psychology: A Core Text in Human Behavior*, Boston: Houghton Mifflin Company, 1969.

PERSONAL LEAVE, a leave of absence that grants an employee a limited number of days off each year for the purpose of attending to "personal business." School boards granting such leaves typically limit the number of personal leave days (e.g. 2-3 a year), specify that they are not accruable from one year to the next, and differentiate personal leave from professional or sick leave. Personal leaves may be used for such purposes as attending a family member's funeral, taking title to a house, or getting married.
References: William B. Castetter, *The Personnel Function in Educational Administration* (Third Edition), New York: Macmillan Publishing Company, Inc., 1981; Donald E. Davis and Neal C. Nickerson, *Critical Issues in School Personnel Administration*, Chicago: Rand McNally and Company, 1968.

PERSONAL SPACE—See PROXEMICS

PERSONNEL ADMINISTRATOR, in education, the individual responsible for overseeing the employment program of professional employees as well as employees who perform support services (e.g. secretaries, custodians). The personnel administrator carries out two broad functions, these consistent with local school board policies: (1) allocating human resources in such a way that the objectives of the school system can best be realized, and (2) providing rewards to the district's employees. The more specific duties and activities subsuming these functions include personnel recruitment, selection, orientation, and evaluation; designing and/or monitoring the organization's welfare program (salaries, fringe benefits, retirement, etc.); working to maintain a wholesome organizational climate; and collective bargaining, including appropriate provision for grievance procedures.

In large school districts, full-time personnel directors facilitate the system's personnel program under the direction of the superintendent and in collaboration with school building administrators and other central office administrators. They are normally seen as staff (as opposed to line) responsibilities. In smaller systems, these responsibilities are carried out directly by the superintendent in collaboration with building principals. (See LINE AND STAFF CHART.)

References: William B. Castetter, *The Personnel Function in Educational Administration* (Third Edition), New York: Macmillan Publishing Company, Inc., 1981; R. Oliver Gibson and Herold C. Hunt, *The School Personnel Administrator,* Boston: Houghton Mifflin Company, 1965.

PERT, a widely used acronym that stands for *P*rogram *E*valuation and *R*eview *T*echnique. PERT was conceived in 1958 by the United States Navy Special Projects Office as an aid to planning. It has since been adopted and used widely by educational planners. PERT calls for a graphic depiction, or flow-chart, showing the relationship between the various steps (or tasks) that lead to completion of a complex project. A network of *events* and *activities* constitutes the heart of the PERT system. (See FLOW CHART.)

References: Paul Barnetson, *Critical Path Planning: Present and Future Techniques,* London, England: Newnes Books, Hamlyn Publishing Group, 1968; Harry F. Evarts, *Introduction to PERT,* Boston: Allyn and Bacon, Inc., 1964.

PESTALOZZI, JOHANN HENRICH (January 12, 1746–February 17, 1827), noted Swiss educator whose educational ideas accorded generally with those of Comenius and Rousseau. Influenced himself by reading Rousseau's *Emile,* Pestalozzi's views on learning and teaching methodology, in turn, influenced pedagogues such as Friedrich Froebel, Johann Herbart, Horace Mann, and Oswego's Edwin Sheldon. They included the belief that

teaching should: (1) proceed from the concrete to the abstract; (2) involve learner observations obtained through use of all senses; and (3) permit the child to learn and to develop at his/her own ability level. Pestalozzi believed that three basic drives (impulses) were present in all men: the primitive, the social, and the ethical. Education, he argued, results in the subordination of the first two to the ethical impulse.

Pestalozzi developed many of his ideas by observing needy children whom he took into his own home, through operation of an orphanage, and, finally, through observation and experimentation in his own institute at Yverdon, Switzerland, which attracted visitors from around the world. He stressed education for citizenship and education as a government responsibility rather than a church function.

References: Thomas A. Barlow, *Pestalozzi and American Education,* Boulder, CO: University of Colorado Libraries, 1977; Elwood P. Cubberly, *Public Education in the United States: A Study and Interpretation of American Educational History,* Cambridge, MA: The Riverside Press, 1962 (Originally Published in 1919 by Houghton Mifflin Company); Frank P. Graves, *Great Educators of Three Centuries: Their Work and Its Influence on Modern Education,* New York: AMS Press, 1971; Heinrich Pestalozzi, *The Education of Man: Aphorisms,* New York: Greenwood Press, 1969 (Copyright 1951 by Philosophical Library, Inc.).

PETER DOE v. SAN FRANCISCO UNIFIED SCHOOL DISTRICT, a lawsuit in which a high school graduate sought recovery in tort on the grounds of educational malpractice. Peter Doe (an alias) charged that the school district was responsible for the fact that he was functionally illiterate even after attending the San Francisco schools for 13 years. The district, he argued further, owed him a "duty of care" and was obligated to educate him to at least the eighth-grade level. The case received national attention because of the fundamental question it posed: Can a school district be found guilty of educational malpractice (negligence) for the academic shortcomings of its students?

A California trial court dismissed the case whereupon Doe appealed to a California court of appeals. That court heard the case and then ruled against the plaintiff. Several reasons were offered in support of the decision, including these: (1) lack of standards by which to determine the district's duties; (2) fear that an affirmative decision would establish a precedent, one that would invite and produce numerous similar suits against school systems; and (3) testimony indicating that factors not controllable by school officials influence educational achievement.

Doe subsequently appealed to the California Supreme Court. That court, in 1976, refused to hear the case, in effect leaving the question of malpractice unresolved.

References: David A. Abel and Lindsay A. Conner, "Educational Malpractice: One Jurisdiction's Response" in Clifford P. Hooker (Editor), *The Courts and Education* (NSSE 77th Yearbook, Part I), Chicago: University of Chicago Press, 1978; *Peter Doe v. San Francisco Unified School District*, 60 C.A. 3d 819; Arlene H. Patterson, "Professional Malpractice: Small Cloud, but Growing Bigger," *Phi Delta Kappa*, November 1980.

PETIT MAL SEIZURE, the most frequent seizures of epilepsy. Because the symptoms are so slight, their presence is often overlooked. Loss or impairment of consciousness is short and abrupt (5–30 seconds, rarely longer) with such a seizure. Rhythmic twitching of eyelids or eyebrows may be present at the rate of about three per second.

Petit mal seizures are more prominent during adolescence, and they occur more frequently than do grand mal seizures. The dysrhythmia, measured by the electroencephalogram (E.E.G.), of the petit mal alternate from fast to slow at a rate of three per second. Because the petit mal seizures are so slight as compared with the grand mal, they have also been called "minor seizures" or "absences." (See EPILEPSY and GRAND MAL SEIZURE.)

References: Michael Myslobodsky, *Petit Mal Epilepsy*, New York: Academic Press, 1976; Dominick P. Purpura, et al. (Editors), *Experimental Models of Epilepsy*, New York: Raven Press, 1972; Donald B. Tower, *Neurochemistry of Epilepsy*, Springfield, IL: Charles C. Thomas, Publisher, 1960.

PETTY CASH, or imprest fund, a designated sum of monies set aside for the purpose of paying for relatively inexpensive items. Such funds are normally used when it is inconvenient or relatively expensive to process a formal voucher. In school districts, responsibility for maintaining petty cash funds and related records is usually assigned to specific individuals (e.g. building principals, program directors).

Receipts for cash purchases made are submitted periodically to: (1) replenish the fund, and (2) allow for necessary accounting (processing) of all monies spent.

References: Combined Glossary: Terms and Definitions from the Handbooks of the State Educational Records and Reports

Series, Washington, DC: National Center for Education Statistics, U.S. Department of Health, Education, and Welfare, 1974; John Greenhalgh, *Practitioner's Guide to School Business Management*, Boston: Allyn and Bacon, Inc., 1978; Jerry M. Rosenberg, *Dictionary of Business and Management*, New York: John Wiley and Sons, 1978.

PHARMACY COLLEGE ADMISSIONS TEST—
See MEDICAL COLLEGE ADMISSIONS TEST

PHI BETA KAPPA (PBK), a national honorary society established in 1776 on the College of William and Mary campus. The second and third PBK chapters were established in 1780 and 1781, respectively, at Yale and Harvard universities. The term *chapter* came into being in 1845 when two additional Connecticut universities (Trinity and Wesleyan) received charters. Women were first inducted, in 1875, by the University of Vermont chapter.

Election to Phi Beta Kappa has long symbolized a high level of intellectual achievement in the liberal arts and sciences. In 1977, the society consisted of 225 active chapters with a total living membership of 325,000.

PBK is governed by a council made up of three delegates elected from each chapter. The organization's senate, made up of 24 members elected by the council, serves as the society's executive body.

Reference: John Robson (Editor), *Baird's Manual of American College Fraternities* (Nineteenth Edition), Menasha, WI: Baird's Manual Foundation, Inc., 1977.

PHI DELTA KAPPA (PDK), professional fraternity in education. Its 116,000 members are men and women who are recognized educational leaders or graduate students with leadership potential. PDK's overriding purpose is the promotion of quality education. The fraternity consists of over 500 chapters scattered through the United States, its possessions, Canada, western Europe, and the Philippines, PDK's headquarters is in Bloomington, Indiana.

PDK makes three of its publications available to all members. *Phi Delta Kappan*, considered by many to be the outstanding journal in education, is published ten times annually. *News, Notes, and Quotes*, a newsletter, appears five times a year. *Application of Research*, a relatively new publication, is distributed quarterly.

PDK's *Fastbacks*, brief yet authoritative booklets dealing with timely educational issues, were introduced in 1972. Books, monographs, and research reports published by the fraternity are also disseminated widely.

Reference: Phi Delta Kappa, *Introduction to Phi Delta Kappa,* Bloomington, IN: The Fraternity, 1979.

PHI EPSILON KAPPA (PEK), national professional fraternity for persons working in health, physical education, recreation, or safety. The organization's purposes include continuing service to the field of HPER and the promotion of related research. PEK was founded in 1913 at the Normal College of American Gymnastics Union in Indianapolis. Seven years later, when a chapter was established on the campus of De Paul University, it became a national fraternity. PEK currently consists of over 100 chapters with a combined individual membership of approximately 25,000. Its official publication, *The Physical Educator,* is published four times annually. The fraternity's headquarters is located in Indianapolis, Indiana.

References: P. Nicholas Kellum, "Phi Epsilon Kappa: Serving the Profession," *The Physical Educator,* October 1975; Phi Epsilon Kappa, *The Articles of Incorporation and By-Laws of Phi Epsilon Kappa Fraternity* (Adopted March 30, 1974), Indianapolis, IN: The Fraternity, Undated Booklet.

PHI KAPPA PHI (PKP), an honor society organized in 1897 by students at the University of Maine, Orono. The organization, when formed, was known as the Lambda Sigma Eta Society. A year later, in honor of the Congressional act that subsidized land-grant colleges, it was renamed the Morrill Society. Phi Kappa Phi became a national society in 1900 and assumed its present name at that time.

The society consists of 225 chapters located in 49 states, the District of Columbia, Puerto Rico, and the Philippines. Undergraduate as well as graduate students are members. To be eligible for membership, undergraduates must be seniors who, scholastically, rank in the top 10 percent of their respective classes. A limited number of faculty members and alumni may also be elected to membership.

Phi Kappa Phi's main office is on the Louisiana State University Campus, Baton Rouge, Louisiana.

References: Phi Kappa Phi, *The Honor Society of Phi Kappa Phi,* Baton Rouge, LA: Undated Brochure; Edward Schriver, *In Pursuit of Excellence: The Honor Society of Phi Kappa Phi, 1897–1971,* Orono, ME: University of Maine Press, 1971.

PHILOLOGY, the study of language. Philologists are interested in examining languages scientifically (e.g. linguistics); additionally, they study their history, evolution, and relationships with other languages.

Reference: Carter V. Good (Editor), *Dictionary of Education* (Third Edition), New York: McGraw-Hill Book Company, 1973.

PHILOSOPHY, a field of study that searches for an understanding of values, reality, and theory through reasoning, logic, and discourse. It is chiefly speculative rather than observational. Through philosophy, the general beliefs, concepts, and attitudes that groups and/or individuals hold can be identified, assessed, and evaluated.

Philosophy of education, a subset of this field of study, can be divided into two general areas. The *normative* or speculative area involves a line of reasoning derived from a metaphysical position and is concerned with qualitative judgments regarding the aims and purposes of education. The *analytical* approach is concerned with the explication and clarification of basic terminology and concepts used in education.

The general elements in philosophy include: epistemology, metaphysics, ethics and value theory, aesthetics, logic, semantics, language, philosophies of science, man and society, and religion. At its simplest, philosophy probes the reasons behind ideas, events, and things.

References: Harry Broudy, et al., *Philosophy of Education,* Urbana, IL: University of Illinois Press, 1967; Frederick C. Gruber, *Historical and Contemporary Philosophies of Education,* New York: Thomas Y. Crowell, 1973; Ralph B. Winn (Editor), *John Dewey: Dictionary of Education,* New York: Philosophical Library, 1959 (Reprinted in 1972 by Greenwood Press).

PHOBIA, a generic term used by psychiatrists and psychologists to describe an individual's obsessive and persistent fear of an object or situation. An individual with a phobia avoids that which threatens loss of control over his/her activities and does so ritualistically.

Some commonly known phobias are *acrophobia,* the fear of heights; *xenophobia,* the fear of strangers; *claustrophobia,* the fear of being in an enclosed space; *algophobia,* the fear of pain; and *mysophobia,* the fear of dirt and contamination from germs. Psychiatrists have identified over 200 different phobias. (See SCHOOL PHOBIA.)

References: Shervert H. Frazier, et al., *A Psychiatric Glossary: The Meaning of Terms Frequently Used in Psychiatry,* New York: Basic Books, Inc., Publishers, 1975; Isaac M. Marks, *Fears and Phobias,* New York: Academic Press, 1969; S. Rachman, *Phobias: Their Nature and Control,* Springfield, IL: Charles C Thomas, Publisher, 1968; Leon Salzman, *The Obsessive Personality: Origins, Dynamics and Therapy* (Revised Edition), New York: Jason Aronson, Inc., 1973.

PHONEME, a symbol that represents a particular sound element. The symbol "s," for example, is the phoneme used to describe the "s" sound appearing in words such as *lust, muss, place, answer,* and *cite.* Although the sound elements used in the foregoing illustrations are not exactly alike, they are sufficiently similar to warrant identification using the common phoneme "s." The English language has 45 phonemes. (See GRAPHEME and PHONICS.)

References: Alan Garnham, *Psycholinguistics: Central Topics,* London: Methuen and Co., 1985; Jean Berko Gleason (Editor), *The Development of Language,* Columbus, OH: Charles E. Merrill Publishing Company, 1985; Albert J. Harris and Edward R. Sipay, *How to Increase Reading Ability* (Eighth Edition), New York: Longman, Inc., 1985.

PHONETICS, the study of speech sounds. Linguists, in whose domain the study of phonetics falls, point out that there are three ways to approach the study of phonetics. The first method, and the oldest, is known as *articulatory* (or *physiological*) *phonetics.* It involves study of the various speech organs (e.g. tongue, vocal cords, teeth) and the manner in which they combine to produce speech sounds. A second approach, *acoustic phonetics,* examines the effects that moving parts (e.g. vocal cords) have on the air that surrounds them. Vowels and consonant changes are studied. These variations result from corresponding energy changes produced by different tongue, lip, cord, and so on positions. The final approach, *auditory phonetics,* deals with the perception of sounds by the listener.

Phonetics is frequently (and incorrectly) confused with phonics. (See PHONICS.)

References: Jean Berko Gleason (Editor), *The Development of Language,* Columbus, OH: Charles E. Merrill Publishing Company, 1985; Sadanah Singh and Kala S. Singh, *Phonetics Principles and Practices,* Baltimore: University Park Press, 1982; Michael Stubbs, *Educational Linguistics,* New York: Basil Blackwell Inc., 1986.

PHONICS, an approach to reading instruction in which the student is taught to recognize the relationships between graphic symbols (letters or letter combinations) and the speech sounds they represent. Stated more technically, it is the teaching of grapheme-phoneme correspondence. Phonics normally refers to one direction of correspondence: looking at the grapheme, or printed symbol, and then saying the phoneme, or speech sound. (Correspondence in the opposite direction is called spelling.) Although teachers sometimes (and incorrectly) use *phonics* and *phonetics* interchangeably, the terms are not synonymous. (*Phonetics* refers to the specific study of the sounds of a language.)

Reading authorities speak of two approaches to the teaching of phonics: synthetic phonics and analytic phonics. In *synthetic phonics,* the child is taught the names of phonic elements (letters and blends) in isolation as well as the sounds they each represent. These are then blended together to form words (e.g. *b-at*). *Analytic phonics,* the system employed in many basal readers, makes use of known elements to determine the pronunciation of unknown elements or words. (see GRAPHEME; PHONEME; and PHONETICS.)

References: Dolores Durkin, *Teaching Them to Read* (Fifth Edition), Boston: Allyn and Bacon, 1989; Eldon E. Ekwall, *Diagnosis and Remediation of the Disabled Reader,* Boston: Allyn and Bacon, Inc., 1976; Pose Lamb and Richard Arnold, *Reading: Foundations and Instructional Strategies,* Belmont, CA: Wadsworth Publishing Company, Inc., 1976; Robert M. Wilson and Craig J. Cleland, *Diagnostic and Remedial Reading for Classroom and Clinic* (Sixth Edition), Columbus, OH: Merrill Publishing Company, 1989.

PHONOGRAMS, or word families used by reading teachers to help improve students' reading skills. They are clusters of letters that tend to have the same sound in whatever words they appear. Examples of phonograms are *ink, all,* and *ale.* As a skill exercise, students are asked to place different consonants or blends before each phonogram for the purpose of creating different words. In the instance of the phonogram *ink,* several words can thus be created: *pink, rink, blink, sink,* and so on. It has been reported that as many as 170 ending phonograms appear in elementary reading vocabularies.

References: Eldon E. Ekwall, *Diagnosis and Remediation of the Disabled Reader,* Boston: Allyn and Bacon, Inc., 1976; Eddie C. Kennedy, *Methods in Teaching Developmental Reading,* Itasca, IL: F. E. Peacock Publishers, Inc., 1974.

PHONOLOGY, the study of distinctive sounds (phonemes) that make up a language. Phonemes are the smallest unit of sound in a language. The English language, authorities report, consists of approximately 45 phonemes.

Phonology is one of four components that linguists study as they examine a language's expression system. The remaining three are phonetics, morphology, and syntax. (See MORPHOLOGY; PHONEME; PHONETICS; and SYNTAX.)

References: Paul S. Anderson and Diane Lapp, *Language*

Skills in Elementary Education (Third Edition), New York: Macmillan Publishing Company, Inc., 1979; Mildred R. Donoghue, *The Child and the English Language Arts* (Third Edition), Dubuque, IA: Wm. C. Brown Company, Publishers, 1979; John M. Kean and Carl Personke, *The Language Arts: Teaching and Learning in the Elementary School,* New York: St. Martin's Press, 1976.

PHYSICAL BLOCK—See LEARNING BLOCK

PHYSICAL EDUCATION (P.E.), a field of study that embraces numerous interests that have general body development through gross physical activity in common. Most writers in the field point out that physical education serves to produce cognitive and affective changes in students as well as the better known ones that fall within the psychomotor domain.

Several movement skills are taught in physical education classes at all grade levels. They include, but are not limited to, running, climbing, jumping, crawling, swinging, twisting, and stretching. Games, gymnastics, sports, and dance are activities in which these and similar skills are learned and applied.

Physical education is also a profession, one whose members have received extended (minimally college-level) training and whose career is devoted to the overall development of individuals through the use of physical activities.
References: Charles A. Bucher, *Foundations of Physical Education* (Fifth Edition), St. Louis, MO: C. V. Mosby Company, 1968; William H. Freeman, *Physical Education in a Changing Society,* Boston: Houghton Mifflin Company, 1977; Reuben B. Frost, *Physical Education: Foundations, Practices, Principles,* Reading, MA: Addison-Wesley Publishing Company, 1975.

PHYSICAL HEALTH DISORDER, a physical health problem that, according to two authorities (Bernard Suran and Joseph Rizzo): (1) requires medical attention or hospitalization; (2) cannot be cured or corrected readily; and (3) serves to prevent an individual from leading a normal life.

I. B. Pless and J. W. B. Douglas prepared a system for classifying physical disorders. Three principal categories are used: type, duration, and severity. *Type* includes motor (e.g. orthopedia), sensory (e.g. hearing), and cosmetic (e.g. eczema) disabilities. The second category, *duration,* is broken down into three subclassifications: permanent, indefinite, and temporary disabilities. The final category, *severity,* consists of mild, moderate, and severe disabilities. This classification system lends itself to use by both medical and nonmedical professionals.

References: I. B. Pless and J. W. B. Douglas, "Chronic Illnesses in Childhood: Part I, Epidemiological and Clinical Characteristics," *Pediatrics,* 1971; Bernard G. Suran and Joseph V. Rizzo, *Special Children: An Integrative Approach,* Glenview, IL: Scott, Foresman and Company, 1979.

PHYSICALLY HANDICAPPED STUDENTS, those students who have a physical impairment (defect) such that they could be significantly limited with respect to development, adjustment, or education. Physical handicaps can be caused by disease, accidents, inheritance, prenatal development, or by accidents occurring during birth. Such impairment may result from any number of causes including defects of nerves, muscles, bones; absence of a limb(s); curvature of the spine; wry neck complications; infantile paralysis; hemophilia; arthritis; muscular dystrophy; results of rheumatic fever; diabetes; nephrosis; asthma; heart disease; sickle cell anemia; cerebral palsy; or cystic fibrosis. The list of causes of physical handicaps is quite long.

Today, as a result of medical advances, new prosthetics and technologies, changes in architecture, new educational programs due to mainstreaming, advances in physical therapy, and changes in attitudes, the physically handicapped student is more likely to lead an active and rewarding life and participate in most, if not all, school programs.
References: Eugene E. Bleck and Donald S. Nagel (Editors), *Physically Handicapped Children,* New York: Grune and Stratton, 1975; Harold D. Love, *Teaching Physically Handicapped Children,* Springfield, IL: Charles C. Thomas, Publisher, 1978; Shirley Perlmutter, *Neuroanatomy and Neurophysiology Underlying Current Treatment Techniques for Sensorimotor Dysfunction,* Chicago: Center for Handicapped Children, 1975.

PHYSICAL SCIENCE STUDY COMMITTEE (PSSC), a group of university and high school teachers who, in 1956, undertook to develop an innovative beginning physics course. Principal support for the effort came from a National Science Foundation grant. Hundreds of individuals were involved in the development of the new course, an effort that took four years to complete. Two of the group's leaders (whose names have been closely associated with PSSC) were Professors Jerrold R. Zacharias and Francis L. Friedman, both of the Massachusetts Institute of Technology.

The PSSC course reflected a new approach to the teaching of physics. Rather than having physics taught as a series of relatively disjointed topics, with stress on technology and recall, the PSSC course presented physics as a unified science with emphasis placed on basic principles. Laboratory exercises were designed to lead students to make discoveries for themselves, in research method fashion, with the help of leading questions that replaced the prescriptive laboratory approach common to traditional courses. Tests and other instructional materials all supported the idea of concept mastery. *Physics*, a textbook developed by the PSSC, constituted the heart of the course. It was published in 1960 and revised in 1965. The text's four parts (The Universe; Optics and Waves; Mechanics; and Electricity and Atomic Structure) were divided into a total of 34 chapters. Considerable field testing of the PSSC material preceded its publication.

References: David Kutliroff, *Physics Teacher's Guide: Effective Classroom Demonstrations and Activities,* West Nyack, NY: Parker Publishing Company, Inc., 1970; J. David Lockard (Editor), *Science and Mathematics Curricular Developments Internationally, 1956–1974,* College Park, MD: The Science Teaching Center, University of Maryland (Joint Project with the Commission on Science Education, American Association for the Advancement of Science), 1974; Physical Science Study Committee, *Physics* (Second Edition), Boston: D. C. Heath and Company, 1965.

PHYSICAL THERAPY, procedures used to relieve pain and restore movement through the rehabilitation of individuals who have suffered a physical injury or disease. Physical therapists make use of a variety of physical agents in their treatment. They include heat, cold, water, ultrasonic energy, ultraviolet light, weights and pullies, and muscular manipulation as well as many electrical/mechanical instruments and devices. The therapist works closely with other professionals (e.g. physicians, occupational therapists, psychologists) as part of a medical team in the treatment of pain and loss of movement. Physical therapy is practiced in most hospitals and in many schools where children with rehabilitative physical handicaps are enrolled. Physical therapy as practiced by the therapist is considered to be both an art and a science.

To be licensed as a physical therapist, a state test must be passed. To qualify for the examination, an individual must hold a four-year bachelor's degree in physical therapy or a degree in a related area (e.g. biology, physical education) and have a certificate in physical therapy. Physical therapy curriculum usually includes: anatomy, physiology, neuro-anatomy, biomechanics, human growth and development, and other related subjects.

References: James E. Griffin and Terence K. Karselis, *Physical Agents for Physical Therapists,* Springfield, IL: Charles C. Thomas, ' Publisher, 1978; Bernice Krumhansl, *Opportunities in Physical Therapy* (Revised Edition), Louisville, KY: Vocational Guidance Manuals, Inc., 1974; Paul H. Pearson and Carol E. Williams (Editors), *Physical Therapy Services in the Developmental Disabilities,* Springfield, IL: Charles C Thomas, Publisher, 1972.

PIAGET, JEAN (August 9, 1896–September 16, 1980), a Swiss scientist who studied the developmental psychology of children. He was also a recognized zoologist and genetic epistemologist. Piaget made major contributions to the field of philosophy, religion, sociology, logic, and mathematics as well as psychology.

His major contributions to education were in the area of conceptual development of children (i.e. all children pass through distinct stages of intellectual development: sensory motor, preoperational, concrete operational, and formal operational, from birth to about age 16). His formulizations were based on extensive and systematic observations of children. His research and theories have had a strong impact on all levels of education, educational programs, and instruction. Their greatest impact has been on early childhood and elementary education programs and instruction. Instruction based on Piagetian theories and principles has, to some extent, been used in some institutions of higher education as well.

Piaget published his first paper at the age of ten, one dealing with the albino sparrow. He earned the doctorate (Natural Science) at the University of Neuchâtel, Switzerland in 1918. He later taught at numbers of Swiss and French universities. His record of service included codirectorship of the Institute of J. J. Rousseau in Geneva (1933–80) and, in 1955, founding of the International Center of Genetic Epistemology.

Included among his numerous literary contributions (more than 50 books) were *The Language and Thought of the Child* (1925), *The Psychology of Intelligence* (1947), *An Introduction to Genetic Epistemology* (three volumes, 1950), *The Development of Thought* (1977), and *Behavior and Education* (1978).

References: Jean Claude Brinquier, *Conversation with Jean Piaget,* Chicago: University of Chicago Press, 1980; Barbel Inhelder and Jean Piaget, *The Growth of Logical Thinking from Childhood to Adolescence,* New York: Basic Books, Inc., Publishers, 1958; Jean Piaget, *Behavior and Evaluation,* New York: Pantheon Press, 1978; Jean Piaget, *The Development of Thought: Equilibration of Cognitive Structures,* New York: The Viking Press, 1977.

PICTURE BOOK, a book of illustrations (images) that contains little or no printed matter. Content is varied. A type of picture book commonly found in schools and children's libraries is the one designed for preschool children. More sophisticated kinds of picture books, with varying subjects, styles, and themes, are published for adults.

References: Stephen F. Gordon, *Making Picture Books: A Method of Learning Graphic Sequence,* New York: Van Nostrand Reinhold Company, 1970; Zena Sutherland and May Hill Arbuthnot, *Children and Books* (Fifth Edition), Glenview, IL: Scott, Foresman and Company, 1977; Jerry J. Watson, "Picture Books for Young Adults," *The Clearing House,* January 1978.

PICTURE DICTIONARY, a dictionary designed to serve very young children and that is used as a forerunner to the nonpicture dictionary. In the picture dictionary, individual pictures accompany each word. In this way, the learner is helped to remember new words and, to a lesser extent, to learn new ones.

Numerous publishers have produced picture dictionaries. A list of them appears in Dallman's *Teaching the Language Arts in the Elementary School.*

Picture dictionaries may also be created by classes of children.

References: Paul S. Anderson and Diane Lapp, *Language Skills in Elementary Education* (Third Edition), New York: Macmillan Publishing Company, Inc., 1974; Martha Dallman, *Teaching the Language Arts in the Elementary School* (Third Edition), Dubuque, IA: Wm. C. Brown Company, Publishers, 1976.

PICTURE FILE, a collection of pictures usually assembled by the individual teacher. Picture files consist of mounted pictures that have been taken from magazines, posters, and so on and that have been classified into specific groupings such as teaching units (e.g. transportation, science).

One writer (Betty Chaney) identified several uses for such files, including: (1) to stimulate discussion; (2) to stimulate imagination; (3) to motivate creative writing; (4) to provide information; and (5) to develop size-shape discriminations.

Key questions about each picture can serve to stimulate discussion. Examples of such questions are: What time of the year is it? How does this person feel? and What do you think of it?

References: Paul C. Burns and Betty L. Broman, *The Language Arts in Childhood Education* (Fourth Edition), Chicago: Rand McNally College Publishing Company, 1977; Betty B. Chaney, *Stimulating Language Development in Early Childhood: Communication Skills, Speaking, Reading, and Writing,* Millburn, NJ: R. F. Publishing, Inc., 1976.

PICTURE LIFT—See COLOR LIFT

PIERCE v. SOCIETY OF THE SISTERS—See *OREGON* CASE

PILOT STUDY, sometimes referred to as pilot testing, a preliminary or "trial run" investigation that precedes the carrying out of any investigation or project. Its basic purpose is to determine how the design of the subsequent study can be improved and/or to identify flaws in the instruments (e.g. questionnaires) or textual materials to be used. The number of participants in the pilot group is normally smaller than the number scheduled to take part in the subsequent study.

Pilot studies are also used to refine new courses, especially those for which special materials (including textbooks) are being developed.

References: Ralph H. Jones, *Methods and Techniques of Educational Research,* Danville, IL: The Interstate Printers and Publishers, Inc., 1973; Bruce W. Tuckman, *Conducting Educational Research,* New York: Harcourt Brace Jovanovich, Inc., 1972; William Wiersma, *Research Methods in Education: An Introduction* (Second Edition), Itasca, IL: F. E. Peacock Publishers, Inc., 1975.

PIMSLEUR LANGUAGE APTITUDE BATTERY, an instrument used to assess language aptitude. It is made up of six parts: (1) *Grade-Point Average,* grades received in English, social studies, mathematics, and science; (2) *Interest;* (3) *Vocabulary,* synonyms for 24 English words; (4) *Language Analysis,* selection of foreign language equivalents of English sentences; (5) *Sound Discrimination;* and (6) *Sound-Symbol Association.* Five scores are available: Grade-Point Average; Interest; Verbal (Vocabulary and Language Analysis); Auditory (Sound Discrimination and Sound-Symbol Association); and Total.

References: Oscar Buros (Editor), *The Seventh Mental Measurements Yearbook* (Volume I), Highland Park, NJ: The Gryphon Press, 1972; Rebecca M. Valette, *Modern Language Testing: A Handbook,* New York: Harcourt, Brace and World, Inc., 1967.

PIMSLEUR MODERN FOREIGN LANGUAGE PROFICIENCY TESTS, three separate examinations that measure proficiency in one of the following languages: French, German, or Spanish. These tests can be used for first or second level courses in grades 7–12 or first- or second-semester college-level courses. Each consists of four subtests. They measure listening, speaking, reading, and writing. The Pimsleur Modern Foreign Language

Proficiency Tests are published by Harcourt, Brace and World.

References: Oscar Buros (Editor), *The Seventh Mental Measurements Yearbook* (Volume I), Highland Park, NJ: The Gryphon Press, 1972; Rebecca M. Valette, *Modern Language Testing: A Handbook,* New York: Harcourt, Brace and World, Inc., 1967.

PINTNER-CUNNINGHAM PRIMARY TEST, a standardized examination used in the primary grades to measure academic aptitudes. First published in 1923 by Rudolf Pitner, Bess V. Cunningham, and Walter N. Durost, it provides an index of a primary grade student's ability to understand abstract symbols. The Pintner-Cunningham Primary Test is part of the Pintner General Ability Tests battery that consists of the Pintner-Cunningham Primary Test (for grades K-2), the Pintner-Durost Elementary Test (grades 2-4), the Pintner Intermediate Test (grades 5-8), and the Pintner Advanced Test (grades 9-12).

References: Oscar K. Buros (Editor), *The Fifth Mental Measurements Yearbook,* Highland Park, NJ: The Gryphon Press, 1959; Oscar K. Buros (Editor), *Tests in Print II,* Highland Park, NJ: The Gryphon Press, 1974.

PITCH, the highness or lowness of a musical note. The pitch of a tone is determined by the number of vibrations produced per second by a string, air column, or other sound-producing agent. The higher the number of vibrations, the higher is the pitch.

To establish a uniform musical system, a pitch standard has been established that is recognized internationally. Known as *concert pitch,* the standard is 440 cycles (vibrations) per second for the A above middle C. This standard, agreed to at a 1939 conference sponsored by the International Standards Association, replaced the standard of 435 that had been established in 1859. (Some European orchestras continue to use 435 as a standard pitch.)

Music teachers employ various approaches to help students understand pitch. They range from the use of high and low hand exercises (to indicate high and low pitch) done to music to the teaching of pitch symbols (e.g. letters, notes).

References: Willi Apel, *Harvard Dictionary of Music* (Second Edition), Cambridge, MA: The Belknap Press of Harvard University Press, 1970; Bruce Boehle (Editor), *The International Cyclopedia of Music and Musicians* (Tenth Edition), New York: Dodd, Mead and Company, 1975; Marvin Greenberg and Beatrix MacGregor, *Music Handbook for the Elementary School,* West Nyack, NY: Parker Publishing Company, Inc., 1972.

PITCH PIPE, a device used by music teachers and choir leaders to set the pitch for a group of singers. It is a small pipe with a movable stopper that enables the user to produce any of the pitches of an octave. Its use has been traced at least as far back as the 18th century. Present-day pitch pipes, although still widely used, are not as accurate as tuning forks.

References: Willi Apel, *Harvard Dictionary of Music* (Second Edition), Cambridge, MA: The Belknap Press of Harvard University Press, 1970; Bruce Boehle (Editor), *The International Cyclopedia of Music and Musicians* (Tenth Edition), New York: Dodd, Mead and Company, 1975.

PITMAN, SIR ISAAC (January 4, 1813–January 12, 1897), English phonographer who developed the phonetic shorthand system that bears his name. The Pitman shorthand system was the first to experience commercial success. Pitman was also a champion of phonetic spelling.

Pitman enrolled in a normal school at the age of 18. Upon completion of his teacher training, he was appointed a master in 1832. Five years later, he opened a private school at Bath, called the Phonetic Institute, whose curriculum included shorthand.

His *Stenographic Shorthand,* published in 1837, explained his shorthand system. *Phonography,* another of his books, appeared in 1840. Pitman was knighted by Queen Victoria in 1894. The Pitman shorthand system was introduced in the United States by his brother, Benjamin. (See SHORTHAND.)

References: Isaac Pitman's Shorthand Instructor: An Exposition of Isaac Pitman's System of Phonography, New York: Isaac Pitman and Sons, 1905; "Pitman, Sir Isaac" in Louis Shores (Editor), *Collier's Encyclopedia* (Volume 19), New York: Macmillan Educational Corporation, 1975.

PLACEBO, in drug experiments, the inert (produces no chemical or medical reaction) substance given the control group, as opposed to the drug being tested that is given to the experimental group. When this is done, neither the experimental nor the control group knows which is actually receiving the "experimental" drug. Any differences found between the two otherwise similar groups can thus be attributed to the experimental drug.

Some people feel better just by believing that they have received a drug. Thus, if control group participants report improvement, and only the experimental group received the drug, such reported differences could be attributed to psychological reactions.

References: Christopher F. Monte, *Psychology's Scientific Endeavor,* New York: Praeger Publishers, 1975; Philip T. Runkel and Joseph E. McGrath, *Research on Human Behavior,* New York: Holt, Rinehart and Winston, Inc., 1972; Georges Thines, *Phenomenology and the Science of Behavior,* Boston: G. Allen and Unwin, 1977.

PLACE-BOUND AND CAREER-BOUND SUPERINTENDENTS, a motivational distinction between chief school administrators who rise to the top in a school district through promotion as opposed to those who enter the superintendency from outside the system. According to Richard Carlson, who studied career patterns of these administrators, "the place-bound superintendent is more interested in place than career and ... the opposite is true for the career-bound superintendent" (pp. 41–42). He reported further that, among superintendents, there is an imbalance with career-bound administrators outnumbering their place-bound counterparts. Finally, he noted a tendency for larger school systems to choose their superintendents from within the system.

Reference: Richard O. Carlson, *School Superintendents: Careers and Performance,* Columbus, OH: Charles E. Merrill Publishing Company, 1972.

A PLACE CALLED SCHOOL: PROSPECTS FOR THE FUTURE—See NATIONAL REFORM REPORTS (1980–86)

PLACEMENT, an element of career planning. The placement process, when defined narrowly, involves helping individuals to secure employment. In education, these individuals are normally senior-level students or alumni. In recent years, the concept of placement has been defined more broadly, reflecting the several career-development activities with which placement officers are now involved (e.g. career counseling, career planning). As a consequence of this change, the names of institutional offices have likewise been broadened, from "Placement Office" to names such as "Career Counseling and Placement Office," "Career Services," and "Career Planning and Placement Office."

Most institutions of higher education currently include such offices as part of their organizational structure. These are also found, although far less frequently, in high schools. Placement offices, in addition to their counseling and planning function, play a liaison role, calling qualified applicants to the attention of prospective employers.

References: André G. Beaumont, et al., *A Model Career Counseling and Placement Program,* Bethlehem, PA: College Placement Services, Inc., 1978; C. Randall Powell and Donald K. Kirts, *Career Services Today: A Dynamic College Profession,* Bethlehem, PA: The College Placement Council, Inc., 1980.

PLACE VALUE, a mathematical term used in our numeration system. The value that a particular digit represents depends on: (1) the symbol used for that digit, and (2) its position (or placement) in relation to the units' place. For example, the digit *3* appears in each of the following numbers: 301.6, 123.9, and 14.3. Its specific value is different in each case, however, owing to placement differences. In the first number, 3 represents *three hundreds;* in the second, it represents *three ones,* or 3 *units;* and in the final number, it represents *three-tenths of a unit.* In our number system, called the Hindu-Arabic numeration system, the zero is used as a space-holder when "not any" is to be shown for a particular column. (See HINDU-ARABIC NUMERATION SYSTEM.)

References: Hunter Ballew, *Teaching Children Mathematics,* Columbus, OH: Charles E. Merrill Publishing Company, 1973; Donald F. Devine and Jerome E. Kaufmann, *Mathematics for Elementary Education,* New York: John Wiley and Sons, 1974; Rosalie Jensen, *Exploring Mathematical Concepts in the Elementary School,* Columbus, OH: Charles E. Merrill Publishing Company, 1973; William Zlot, *Elementary School Mathematics: Teaching the Basic Skills,* New York: Thomas Y. Crowell, 1976.

PLACE VALUE CHART, an instructional device used to help children understand the place value of numbers. Sometimes referred to as a pocket chart, it consists of objects that can be bundled readily (e.g. ice cream sticks, strips of cardboard) into sets of ten and a chart containing "pockets."

A simple place value chart, with inserts representing the number 124, appears on page 437.

Children's understanding of place values is facilitated through use of place value charts. For example, they are helped to see that a "bundle" representing *10 ones* is the same as a single insert appearing in the *tens* column or that *12 ones* has the same value as *1 ten and 2 ones.*

References: Hunter Ballew, *Teaching Children Mathematics,* Columbus, OH: Charles E. Merrill Publishing Company, 1973; William D. McKillip, *Mathematics Instruction in the Elementary Grades,* Morristown, NJ: Silver Burdett Company, 1978; William Zlot, *Elementary School Mathematics: Teaching the Basic Skills,* New York: Thomas Y. Crowell, 1976.

Place Value Chart

PLANNING, a conscious preparation for action. In administration, the planning process is a means to some organizational end. One or more goals are established; related data (including resources and restraints) are collected and studied; alternative approaches to realization of the goal(s) are identified and weighed; and, finally, the alternative chosen (frequently a compromise) is implemented. Thereafter, plans are monitored and modifications made as needed.

Educational planning may involve individuals (e.g. teachers, principals, maintenance personnel) or groups such as administrative teams, committees of teachers, or specially appointed task forces. Normally, plans of a relatively complex nature are developed by more than one individual.

In recent years, specific strategies for planning of change have been developed for use in both educational and business organizations. Examples include PPBES, PERT, and Management by Objectives. (See MANAGEMENT BY OBJECTIVES; PERT; and PLANNING, PROGRAMMING, BUDGETING, EVALUATION SYSTEM.)

References: Stephen P. Gibert, *Planning for the Future: Long-Range Planning for Associations,* Washington, DC: Foundation of the American Society of Association Executives, 1973; Russell T. Gregg, "The Administrative Process" in Roald F. Campbell and Russell T. Gregg (Editors), *Administrative Behavior in Education,* New York: Harper and Brothers, 1957; Dan E. Schendel and Charles W. Hofer (Editors), *Strategic Management: A New View of Business Policy and Planning,* Boston: Little, Brown and Company, 1979; Jesse B. Sears, *The Nature of the Administrative Process: With Special Reference to Public School Administration,* New York: McGraw-Hill Book Company, 1950.

PLANNING, PROGRAMMING, BUDGETING, EVALUATION SYSTEM (PPBES), also known as PPBS, a systems approach to budgeting. PPBES is a comprehensive and long-range process that em-

ploys a program-by-program budget rather than the traditional line-item budget. Goals and activities are developed for each program and subsequently evaluated with consideration given to their cost-effectiveness. Considerable research on PPBES was developed and reported by the RAND Corporation during the 1950s and 1960s. The approach was popularized after being introduced into the Department of Defense by Secretary Robert McNamara.

References: I. Carl Candoli, et al., *School Business Administration: A Planning Approach* (Second Edition), Boston: Allyn and Bacon, Inc., 1978; Harry J. Hartley, *Educational Planning-Programming-Budgeting: A Systems Approach,* Englewood Cliffs, NJ: Prentice-Hall, Inc., 1968; Larry W. Hughes and Gerald C. Ubben, *The Elementary Principal's Handbook: A Guide to Effective Action* (Third Edition), Boston: Allyn and Bacon, 1989; NEA Committee on Educational Finance, *Planning for Educational Development in a Planning, Programming, Budgeting System,* Washington, DC: National Education Association, 1968; Research Corporation of the Association of Schoool Business Officials, *Program Planning-Budgeting-Evaluation System Design,* Chicago: The Corporation, December 1968.

PLASTER OF PARIS, a material used in studios and classrooms for casting and modeling. Plaster of paris, which can also be used in molds, is easy to handle because it can be mixed with water and sets quickly. It is made out of calcinated or dehydrated gypsum.

When set, plaster of paris becomes hard and can subsequently be carved without difficulty. It can be colored, waxed, shellacked, or varnished. Plaster of paris dates back to ancient times when it was used to create life or death masks.

References: Charles Chaney and Stanley Skee, *Plaster Mold and Mold Making,* New York: Van Nostrand Reinhold Company, 1978; Mariene Linderman, *Art in the Elementary School: Drawing, Painting and Creating for the*

Classroom, Dubuque, IA: Wm. C. Brown Company, Publishers, 1979; Adelaide Sproul, *With a Free Hand: Painting, Drawing, Graphics, Ceramics, and Sculpture for Children,* New York: Reinhold Book Company, 1968.

PLASTIC PAINTS, used by painters and in many art classes, are paints made from acrylic resin that has a polymethylmethacrylate acid base as opposed to a polymer base as found in other types of acrylic-based paints. Acrylic paints dry quickly and do not yellow as do other types of paints. (See POLYMER PAINTS.)

References: Ralph Mayer, *A Dictionary of Art Terms and Techniques,* New York: Thomas Y. Crowell, 1969; Margaret Walch, *The Color Source Book,* New York: Scribner's, 1979.

PLATO, computer-assisted instruction (CAI) in elementary reading (grades 1 and 2) and mathematics (grades 4–6). One hundred terminals were installed within more than 40 classrooms for the initial study. Piloting of the program occurred in the mid–1970s. Volunteer teachers were trained to use the strategy. Uniform daily time allocations of 30 minutes for math instruction for the older students and 15 minutes of reading lessons for primary grades were devised, although great time variability was reported by the pilot groups. The goal of PLATO was to integrate CAI with the ongoing classroom curriculum; it was an alternate delivery system for the traditional curriculum content. Evaluation of the pilot program noted the effect teachers had on the program. Contributions of computerized instruction to student achievement were masked by teacher effects. The myth that CAI was impervious to outside impact was destroyed. (See Computer-Assisted Instruction.)

References: Marianne Amarel, "The Classroom: An Instructional Setting for Teachers, Students, and the Computer" in Alex Cherry Wilkinson (Editor), *Classroom Computers and Cognitive Science,* New York: Academic Press, 1983; CERL (Construction Enginnering Research Laboratory), *Demonstration of the PLATO IV Computer-Based Education System, Final Report* (NSF Contract C–723), Urbana, IL: University of Illinois, 1977; Charles K. Kinzer, et al. (Editor), *Computer Strategies for Education,* Columbus, OH: Merrill Publishing Company, 1986; S. Swinton, M. Amarel, and J. Morgan, *The PLATO Elementary Demonstration: Educational Outcome Evaluation, Final Report* (ESSPR 78–11) Princeton, NJ: Educational Testing Service, 1978.

PLATOON SCHOOL, or platoon plan, a form of school organization used by numerous American school districts during the early part of the 20th century. The platoon plan typically divided the school population into two groups. While one group (Platoon A) was receiving instruction in basic "homeroom" subjects such as reading, writing, and arithmetic, another (Platoon B) was studying subjects taught in specially equipped facilities (e.g. art room, shop, gymnasium). At a predetermined time, both groups changed places. This arrangement served to achieve a balance between academic work and social-creative activities. It also increased pupil capacity by about 40 percent without requiring extra staff.

The first platoon school was organized (1900) in Bluffton, Indiana, by Superintendent of Schools William Wirt. Wirt later became superintendent in Gary, Indiana, where he introduced the better known and somewhat similar Gary Plan. (See GARY PLAN.)

References: Elementary School Organization: Purposes, Patterns, Perspective, Washington, DC: National Education Association, 1961; W. Virgil Nestrick, "Platoon School—Platoon Plan" in Harry N. Rivlin and Herbert Schueler (Editors), *Encyclopedia of Modern Education,* New York: Philosophical Library, 1943.

PLAY THERAPY, a nondirective activity through which individuals (whether children or adults) can express themselves and develop without the pressure of evaluation or the pressure of change. Play is usually defined in terms of age: children "play," adults participate in "recreation," and the retired are involved in "leisure activities."

Play therapy is a technique that affords opportunity for self-expression, for gaining faith in one's self, and for achieving emotional relaxation. It also provides challenge, exploration, fulfillment, and independence for the person involved. For the observer (e.g. therapist, teacher), play therapy makes it possible to see what the individual can do or how he/she feels. It also provides a basis for designing appropriate educational, psychological, or therapeutic programs.

Although play therapy has been used for individuals with emotional, mental, or physical handicaps, the basic principles of play are used in education and the classroom, particularly at the preschool and elementary levels. It is important to note that play is a function of evolution, anthropology, psychology, and sociology. Thus, the manifestation of play therapy in one society or social class may be quite different from that in another.

References: Virginia M. Axline, *Play Therapy,* Boston: Houghton Mifflin Company, 1947; Clark E. Moustakas, *Children in Play Therapy,* New York: McGraw-Hill Book Company, 1953; Mary Reilly (Editor), *Play as Exploratory*

Learning, Beverly Hills, CA: Sage Publishing Company, Inc., 1974; Otto Weininger, *Play and Education*, Springfield, IL: Charles C Thomas, Publisher, 1979.

PLESSY v. FERGUSON, an early court case dealing with the "separate-but-equal" concept and racial segregation. In 1890, a Louisiana statute was enacted that provided for equal-but-separate railroad passenger car accommodations for the white and colored races. Two years later, Homer A. Plessy, a Negro, was arrested for refusing to leave a passenger car set aside for whites. Plessy took his case to court on the grounds that such segregation violated his rights as provided by the Fourteenth Amendment of the U.S. Constitution, and he lost.

In 1896, the U.S. Supreme Court supported the lower court decision. It agreed that the Fourteenth Amendment's object was "to enforce the absolute equality of the two races before the law." However, it found nothing in the Louisiana statute that denied equal protection. Thus, the "separate but equal concept" was given legal sanction by the highest court in the land.

Although *Plessy v. Ferguson* did not deal specifically with schools, the Plessy doctrine was used to justify separate but equal schools until the U.S. Supreme Court (*Brown v. Board of Education of Topeka*), in 1954, reversed itself and found it to be unconstitutional. (See *BROWN v. BOARD OF EDUCATION OF TOPEKA*.)

References: Edward C. Bolmeier, *Landmark Supreme Court Decisions on Public School Issues*, Charlottesville, VA: The Michie Company, 1973; Richard Kluger, *Simple Justice: The History of Brown v. Board of Education and Black America's Struggle for Equality*, New York: Alfred A. Knopf, 1976; *Plessy v. Ferguson*, 163 U.S. 537 (1896).

PLOWDEN REPORT, a study of English primary schools conducted in 1967 by the Central Advisory Council for Education. It was titled *Children and Their Primary Schools*. Lady Plowden was chairperson of the council.

The report, containing 197 recommendations, was one of the major educational reform documents published in England during the 1960s. In it, the council encouraged the growth of middle schools and called for a closer relationship between home and school. The report also called for educational experiences that would benefit all children, regardless of social circumstances. (The document's authors were highly influenced by research in child development, especially by the works of Piaget.) Identification of educational priority areas was called for and the government was urged to provide corresponding funding priorities. Nursery schools, community schools, and better education for immigrants were among the other topics discussed in the report.

References: John Lawson and Harold Silver, *A Social History of Education in England*, London, England: Methuen and Company, Ltd., 1973; David Wardle, *The Rise of the Schooled Society*, London, England: Routledge and Kegan Paul, 1974.

PLURALISM, a term used to denote the existence of more than one social, cultural, ethnic, religious, or racial group in an area. Cultural, ethnic, religious or racial pluralism exists in the United States as a result of history. From the very start, the population of the United States has comprised more than one group (e.g. native Americans and various colonists lived next to, or near, each other). The establishment of slavery added another racial dimension to the population. Immigration in the 1800–1900s introduced many different ethnic, religious, racial, and cultural groups to the United States. All of these historical factors contributed to the pluralism that exists in the country today.

Pluralism is not only a cause, but is also considered by some to be a justification for education that is multicultural. Prompted by the sizable number of American, Mexican-American, Native-American, Asian-American, Puerto Rican, and Indo-Chinese children attending public schools in the United States, various multicultural education programs (including bilingual-bicultural education) have been started throughout the country. (See *BILINGUAL-BICULTURAL EDUCATION* and *MULTICULTURAL EDUCATION*.)

References: Robert A. Dahl, *Democracy in the United States: Promise and Performance*, Chicago: Rand McNally Book Company, 1972; Edgar G. Epps (Editor), *Cultural Pluralism*, Berkeley, CA: McCutchan Publishing Corporation, 1974; George L. Hicks and Philip E. Leis (Editors), *Ethnic Encounters: Identities and Contexts*, North Scituate, MA: Duxbury Press, 1977; Thomas R. Lopez and Albert W. Vogel (Editors), *No One Model American*, Toledo, OH: University of Toledo, College of Education, 1979.

POLICY, defined by Roald Campbell and associates as "an authoritative decision which guides other decisions" (p. 166). At the school district level, policies are adopted by the board of education. They are written guidelines that give direction to the administrator(s) and other employees responsible for carrying them out and also establish decision-making parameters. Unlike rules and regulations, which are specific and prescriptive, policies establish the board's motive and allow the administrator to exercise his/her own judgment when implementing them.

Policies may cover general areas such as pupil transportation, use of school property, field trips, purchasing, and relations with the press. Personnel policies normally address topics such as personnel evaluation, grievance procedures, salary schedules, and assignment of responsibility.

Policies, authorities stress, need to be written, prepared objectively, and modified as needed. In addition to charting directions for decision makers, policies serve other purposes: (1) they avoid misunderstandings; (2) provide organizational continuity even as board composition changes; and (3) help to orient new board members.

Policies affecting education are also established or called for by actions taken at the federal level (e.g. affirmative action), at the state level, and by the courts.

References: Administration Committee, *Boardmanship: A Guide for the School Board Member,* Sacramento, CA: California School Boards Association, 1967; Ben Brodinsky, *How a School Board Operates* (PDK Fastback 88), Bloomington, IN: The Phi Delta Kappa Educational Foundation, 1977; Roald F. Campbell, et al., *The Organization and Control of American Schools* (Fourth Edition), Columbus, OH: Charles E. Merrill Publishing Company, 1980; Edward M. Tuttle, *School Board Leadership in America: Policy Making in Public Education* (Revised Edition), Danville, IL: The Interstate Printers and Publishers, Inc., 1965.

POLICY-RECORDING SYSTEMS, or policy manuals, systems for classifying and maintaining policies established by policymaking bodies such as boards of education. Written policies are coded and, to facilitate changes (revisions, additions, deletions), are usually maintained in a loose-leaf binder.

Classification systems for recording school board policies are not identical, although, in 1970, the National School Boards Association introduced a system, subsequently adopted by numbers of boards, that arranges policies into 13 broad groups or classes. They are:

A School District Organization
B School Board Operations
C General School Administration
D Fiscal Management
E Business Management
F Facility Expansion Program
G Personnel
H Negotiations
I Instructional Program
J Students

K General Public Relations
L Interorganizational Relations
M Relations with Other Education Agencies

References: Rodney L. Bartels, *A Handbook of Model School Board Policies for Effective Community Education Programs,* Omaha, NE: Educational Policy Development Associates, 1973; William B. Castetter, *The Personnel Function in Educational Administration* (Third Edition), New York: Macmillan Publishing Company, Inc., 1981; National School Boards Association, *School Board Policy Development for the '70s,* Evanston, IL: The Association, 1970; Prentice-Hall Editorial Staff, *School Executives Guide,* Englewood Cliffs, NJ, 1964.

POLYMER PAINTS, paints with a particular acrylic base. There are two types of acrylics in this group of paints: water-emulsion acrylics and solvent-based acrylics. Both have acrylic polymer as the primary ingredient. The colors produced by acrylic polymer-based paints are extremely durable and have degrees of brilliance. These are called polymer colors.

References: A. Maerz and M. Rea Paul, *A Dictionary of Color* (Second Edition), New York: McGraw-Hill Book Company, 1950; Margaret Walch, *The Color Source Book,* New York: Scribner's, 1979.

POPULATION, a term used in educational research for an entire group having unique characteristics or properties. The group is well defined and may be large. A population may be: all people in a country, state, city, or school building; all girls in the seventh grade in a particular school; and so on. A population may also consist of objects, animals, reactions, or people.

Frequently, populations are so large that researchers are not always able to test, assess, or evaluate all of their members. When this happens, a sample from the population is studied.

The numbers that describe the characteristics of a population are called parameters. They are designed using Greek symbols (e.g. μ stands for mean, or average, and σ for standard deviation).

References: Joy P. Guilford and Benjamin Fruchter, *Fundamental Statistics in Psychology and Education* (Sixth Edition), New York: McGraw-Hill Book Company, 1978; Vicki F. Sharp, *Statistics for the Social Sciences,* Boston: Little, Brown and Company, 1979.

PORTAL SCHOOL, a school in which a university and a group of schools work closely together in the preparation of teachers. The portal school concept was originally carried out as part of the Temple University-Philadelphia Plan with competency-based teacher education and field work included as key elements. The Temple University-Philadelphia model brought the resources of the Philadelphia public school system and Temple University together to train teachers for, and to educate the children in, the inner city. University resources were focused on a few inner-city schools. Methods classes, for example, were taught in the inner-city classroom utilizing children already enrolled. Methodological examples used were consistent with the ongoing curriculum of the inner-city school.

Funded and developed by the National Teacher Corps, the portal school concept was subsequently implemented by several local Teacher Corps projects in Ohio, Georgia, Pennsylvania, New York, and Colorado.

References: Linda Lutonsky (Editor), *Portal Schools* (Final Report), Washington, DC: The Council of the Great City Schools, 1973; Gilbert F. Shearron and Charles E. Johnson, *Portal Schools for the Georgia Educational Model,* Athens, GA: College of Education, University of Georgia, 1971.

PORTLAND PROJECT, a high school science teaching project, initiated in 1962, that sought to integrate the disciplines of biology, chemistry, physics, behavioral science, environmental science, and mathematics. Originally funded by the National Science Foundation, The Portland Public Schools (Oregon), Portland State College, Reed College, and Oregon State University, the project eventually resulted in the development of a three-year curriculum that integrated the ideas and materials of several innovative courses including the Chemical Bond Approach, Physical Science Study Committee physics, the Chemical Educational Materials Study course, and Project Physics. The integrated program was predicated on the assumption that the teaching of discrete courses for chemistry, biology, and physics is an obsolete approach; furthermore, that these discrete courses frequently contain overlapping ideas. Thus, both time and effort could be saved by integrating these subjects.

Portland Project offices were located at Portland State University. (See CHEMICAL BOND APPROACH; CHEMICAL EDUCATION MATERIAL STUDY; PHYSICAL SCIENCE STUDY COMMITTEE; and PROJECT PHYSICS.)

References: Alfred T. Collette, *Science Teaching in the Secondary School: A Guide for Modernizing Instruction,* Boston: Allyn and Bacon, Inc., 1973; Michael A. Fiasca, "Integration of the Sciences," *The American Biology Teacher,* April 1970; J. David Lockard (Editor), *Science and Mathematics Curricular Developments Internationally, 1956–1974,* College Park, MD: Science Teaching Center, University of Maryland (Joint Project with the Commission on Sci-

ence Education, American Association for the Advancement of Science), 1974.

PORTRAITS OF HIGH SCHOOL, A SUPPLEMENT TO HIGH SCHOOL: A REPORT ON SECONDARY EDUCATION—See NATIONAL REFORM REPORTS (1980–86)

POSDCORB, an acronym introduced by Luther Gulick to help management officials and students of administration to remember what he believed to be the essentials of administrative process. POSDCORB, considered outdated by current writers in the management field, stands for the following process elements: *p*lanning, *o*rganizing, *s*taffing, *d*irecting, *co-o*rdinating, *r*eporting, and *b*udgeting.

Reference: Luther Gulick, "Notes on the Theory of Organization" in Luther Gulick and L. Urwick (Editors), *Papers on the Science of Administration,* New York: Institute of Public Administration, Columbia University, 1937.

POST-HOC ANALYSIS, a broad term referring to any analysis undertaken after the fact or event. In educational research, one such analysis is known as *ex post facto analysis* in which causes are inferred from the effects. That is, the effects already exist and the researcher attempts to determine what factors, conditions, and/or circumstances caused them. For example, a researcher may want to determine past personal and educational factors that lead to success in a particular field. He may identify a group of individuals from the field and then analyze their educational backgrounds and past personal traits to isolate possible causal factors that lead to success. There are many problems with this approach, because there are no, or limited, research controls over the study. Ex post facto research is not considered experimental.

In a more restricted sense, post hoc tests are those multiple-comparison procedures that are used in experimental research, after an analysis of variance test has been calculated, to compare group means (either pair-wise or in combination). Scheffé, Duncan, Newman-Keuls, and Tukey are all examples of post hoc tests. (See EXPERIMENTAL DESIGN.)

References: L. R. Gay, *Educational Evaluation of Measurement: Competencies for Analysis and Application* (Third Edition), Columbus, OH: Charles E. Merrill Publishing Company, 1987; Frederick J. Gravetter and Larry B. Wallman, *Statistics for the Behavioral Sciences: A First Course for Students of Psychology and Education,* St. Paul, MN: West Publishing Company, 1985; Harold O. Kiess, *Statistical*

Concepts for the Behavioral Sciences, Boston: Allyn and Bacon, 1989.

POSTSECONDARY EDUCATION, education offered beyond high school. Initially, the term was used to describe instruction offered in grades 13 and 14, usually for youth from ages 16–20. Such instruction was available in community colleges, area vocational schools, technical institutes, adult education schools, vocational schools, junior colleges, or special educational units attached, organizationally, to four-year colleges or universities.

The definition of postsecondary education has been expanded and is now commonly used to describe all education offered beyond high school. With the advent of lifelong education, better access to educational opportunities, greater demand for knowledge, changes in the philosophy of education, and changing careers/patterns, the original (and restricted) definition for postsecondary education has little value or meaning.

Postsecondary educational opportunities are found in most communities in the United States; they may or may not be publicly funded. Most industrialized nations provide postsecondary education programs and facilities.

References: Mortimer J. Adler, *Reforming Education*, Boulder, CO: Westview Press, 1977; Edmund J. King, et al., *Post-Compulsory Education II*, London, England: Sage Publications, Inc., 1975; Harland E. Samson, *Post-Secondary Distributive Education*, Washington, DC: U.S. Office of Education, Bureau of Adult, Vocational, and Library Programs, 1969.

POTTER'S WHEEL, a device with a rotating horizontal disk that is used by potters to mold clay. Molding is done by hand with the help of water and special potter's tools. Through the use of inward pressure (to make a taller form) or downward pressure (to make a flatter form) as the lump of clay is rotated at varying speeds, the potter can mold a desired shape.

Potter's wheels can be foot driven, such as a kickwheel, or they can be power driven. They are found in many ceramic art classrooms. Potter's wheels were used in ancient Egypt and China.

References: Dora M. Billington (Revised by John Colbeck), *The Technique of Pottery*, London, England: B. T. Batsford, Ltd., 1974; Willis G. Lawrence, *Ceramic Science for the Potter*, Philadelphia: Chilton Book Company, 1972; Bernard H. Leach, *A Potter's Book*, New York: Transatlantic Arts, 1976; Elsbeth S. Woody, *Pottery on the Wheel*, New York: Farrar, Straus and Giroux, Inc., 1975.

POWER, an organizational term used to describe the ability of one individual, or an entity, to influence another individual or group to behave in a certain way. Formal authority granted to individuals in an organization is known as legitimate power. The democratic use of power is supported in the literature of educational administration; the use of force or manipulation as a means for influencing others is not recognized as a desirable way to implement organizational goals.

Two authorities on this subject (J. R. P. French and Bertram Raven) have identified five "bases of power." They are: (1) *reward power,* based on the belief that one individual can provide rewards for another; (2) *coercive power,* predicated on the belief that one individual possesses the ability to punish another; (3) *referent power,* power that stems from the desire of one individual to identify with another; (4) *expert power,* based on the assumption that someone has specialized knowledge; and (5) *legitimate power,* defined above.

References: H. Randolph Bobbitt, Jr., et al. (Editors), *Organizational Behavior: Understanding and Prediction* (Second Edition), Englewood Cliffs, NJ: Prentice-Hall, Inc., 1978; Allan R. Cohen, et al., *Effective Behavior in Organizations* (Revised Edition), Homewood, IL: Richard D. Irwin, Inc., 1980; J. R. P. French and B. Raven, "The Bases of Social Power" in Dorwin Cartwright (Editor), *Studies in Social Power*, Ann Arbor, MI: Institute for Social Research, University of Michigan, 1959; Daniel E. Griffiths, *Human Relations in School Administration*, New York: Appleton-Century-Crofts, Inc., 1956.

POWER MECHANICS, a vocational education field of study that deals with the control and conversion of energy into power. It makes considerable use of applied physics. Within the field there are three general subspecialties: (1) mechanical; (2) electrical; and (3) fluid. *Mechanics* includes the study of gears, pulleys, clutches, and other mechanical devices. The *electrical* subspecialty deals with topics such as generators and circuits. *Fluid* mechanics has to do with hydraulic and pneumatic pumps, filters, controls, motors, pressure, and so on. Power mechanics can include nuclear and solar energy as well as traditional and mechanical sources. Power mechanics is taught in specialized vocational courses in high schools and trade schools and as a part of some industrial arts programs in junior high school.

References: Richard R. Bailie, *Energy Conversion Engineering*, Reading, MA: Addison-Wesley Publishing Company, 1978; Archie W. Culp, Jr., *Principles of Energy Conversion*, New York: McGraw-Hill Book Company, 1979; G. Harold Silvius and Ralph C. Bohn, *Planning and Organizing Instruction* (Second Edition), Bloomington, IL: McKnight and McKnight Publishing Company, 1976.

POWER STRUCTURE, the system of authority or influence that permits some individuals to influence or affect others.

John R. P. French and Bertram Raven identified five types of power within organizations: coercive, reward, legitimate, experts, and referent. Some power is based on a superior-subordinate relationship in an organization hierarchy (coercive, reward, legitimate), and other power is based on the perception people have of individuals (expert, referent). A management structure is designed to include formal superior-subordinate relationships. However, the real power structure does not always accord with these structured organizational relationships. Stated differently, real power within an organization is not always held by persons holding designated authority positions.

In the larger society, the power structure consists of those individuals who make the major decisions that influence the community. Often they are individuals who have money or family/social prestige. More often than not, they are not the elected officials of the community, and they tend to be few. (See AUTHORITY and POWER.)

References: Henry L. Bretton, *The Power of Money: A Political-Economic Analysis with Special Emphasis on the American Political System,* Albany, NY: State University of New York Press, 1980; John R. P. French and Bertram Raven, "The Bases of Social Power" in Dorwin Cartwright and A. F. Zander (Editors), *Group Dynamics* (Second Edition), Evanston, IL: Row, Peterson, and Company, 1960; Hubert G. Hicks, et al., *Organizations: Theory and Behavior,* New York: McGraw-Hill Book Company, 1975; Walter R. Nord (Editor), *Concepts and Controversy in Organizational Behavior* (Second Edition), Pacific Palisades, CA: Goodyear Publishing Company, Inc., 1976.

POWER TESTS, examinations constructed to include items of varying degrees of difficulty. Included are items that are so difficult that no one taking the test is expected to solve them. Power tests are designed to prevent anyone from obtaining a perfect score.

A perfect score would prevent knowing how high a person could score. Thus, a power test, with enough difficult items, provides a high enough ceiling to assess an individual's capabilities.

In actual practice, many standardized tests, to varying degrees, are a combination of power and speed tests. That is, the tests have differing levels of difficulty and time limits. Knowledge of the proportion of a test that is power, and the proportion that is speed, will help in the interpretation of the scores. (See SPEED TESTS.)

Reference: Anne Anastasi, *Psychological Testing* (Sixth Edition), New York: Macmillan Publishing Company, Inc., 1988; Gilbert Sax, *Principles of Educational and Psychological Measurement and Evaluation* (Third Edition), Belmont, CA: Wadsworth Publishing Company, 1989.

PPBES—See PLANNING, PROGRAMMING, BUDGETING, EVALUATION SYSTEM

PRACTICAL ARTS, that part of the school curriculum that teaches practical skills and related knowledge in subjects such as industrial arts, home economics, general business (including typing), and general agriculture. Most of them are offered at the junior and senior high school levels. Unlike vocational education courses (which are designed to prepare students for the world of work), the practical arts are made available as exploratory offerings and for the purpose of helping students to live fuller lives as adults.

The practical arts movement in the United States, begun between 1800 and 1900, was heavily influenced by Pestalozzian philosophy. Discrete courses such as drawing, manual training, and agriculture were commonplace at that time. Except for some title and content changes, most remain in the curriculum today.

References: Roy W. Roberts, *Vocational and Practical Arts Education: History, Development, and Principles* (Second Edition), New York: Harper and Row, Publishers, 1965; F. Theodore Struck, "Practical Arts Education" in Harry N. Rivlin and Herbert Schueler (Editors), *Encyclopedia of Modern Education,* New York: Philosophical Library, 1943.

PRAGMATISM, a uniquely American contribution to Western philosophy whose name was coined by Charles Sanders Peirce (1839–1914), a chemist and scientist. It has its modern origins in Peirce's article: "How to Make Our Ideas Clear" in the *Popular Science Monthly* (1878). Pragmatism has a practical empiricism as its base, is action oriented, and tests truth in terms of consequences. Pragmatism has attempted to assimilate modern science into philosophy without being dominated by science per se. To date, the four major pragmatists have been Charles Sanders Peirce, William James, George Herbert Mead, and John Dewey. Each stressed different approaches to pragmatism: Peirce, *logical methods;* James, *experience;* Mead, *symbolism;* and Dewey, *intelligence.* Although pragmatism developed since the late 19th century, it has had significant influence on education through the progressive education era. (See DEWEY, JOHN B. and PROGRESSIVE EDUCATION.)

References: Samuel M. Eames, *Pragmatic Naturalism,* Carbondale, IL: Southern Illinois University Press, 1977; William James, *Essays in Radical Empiricism,* Cambridge, MA: Harvard University Press, 1976; John E. Smith, *Purpose and Thought: The Meaning of Pragmatism,* New Haven, CT: Yale University Press, 1978.

PREDICTING PUPIL POPULATION, a statistical procedure undertaken for the purpose of projecting future school enrollments. Data resulting from such procedures help to forecast school district needs in areas such as school housing, personnel, and budget.

Roscoe Brown pointed out that three of the better known methods for predicting pupil population are: (1) the *growth-curve method,* which relies on past school enrollments to project future populations; (2) the *birth-survival method,* a method based on a ratio arrived at by determining the percentage of children born "x" years ago who subsequently enter/remain in school; and (3) the *corrected promotion method* that, grade by grade, determines the percentage of students promoted at the end of one year who actually reenroll the following year. The last method is considered to be the most accurate of the three.

Each method makes use of basic population data that school officials need to collect and maintain. Included are the results of the federal decennial census, results gleaned from the local school district (usually annual) census, information concerning land availability and utilization practices (zoning), in- and out-migration patterns, new housing starts, and birthrates. (See SCHOOL CENSUS.)
References: Roscoe C. Brown, Jr., *Predicting School Enrollments,* New York: The Center for School Services, School of Education, New York University, 1961; School Buildings Committee, Metropolitan School Study Council, *Some Things to Consider in Forecasting School Enrollments: A Guide for School Administrators and Laymen,* New York: The Council, November 1953.

PREDICTION, STATISTICAL, the attempt to forecast attributes or measurements from other attributes or measurements through the use of statistical procedures. For example, predicting incidence of poverty from racial classifications demonstrates the use of one attribute to predict another. Illustrating the prediction of an attribute based on a measurement is the forecasting of poverty on the basis of intelligence scores. Predicting intelligence scores from socioeconomic level is an example of forecasting a measurement from an attribute. Predicting reading scores from intelligence scores illustrates measurement prediction from measurement.

There are many statistical procedures that can be used. The one selected depends, to a great extent, on which of the above-described predictions is involved. Least squares, standard error of estimate, correlation, regression, and multiple correlations are but a few of the statistical procedures that might be employed.
References: Donald Ary, et al., *Introduction to Research in Education* (Second Edition), New York: Holt, Rinehart and Winston, Inc., 1979; Joy P. Guilford and Benjamin Fruchter, *Fundamental Statistics in Psychology and Education* (Sixth Edition), New York: McGraw-Hill Book Company, 1978.

PREENGINEERED SCHOOLS, school buildings, or parts thereof, that are prefabricated and mass produced. Some are assembled using stock plans; others can be built using locally designed plans.

Preeingineered schools generally cost less than conventionally constructed schools, with cost savings increasing in proportion to the size of the building. Other advantages associated with preengineered schools include speed of construction (approximately $33\frac{1}{3}$–50 percent reduction in construction time), less need for on-site labor, flexibility, and predictable cost. Disadvantages include increased time and dollar costs that result when architectural modifications are made and, in the judgment of some, a less pleasing aesthetic appearance.
References: Basil Castaldi, *Educational Factilities: Planning Remodeling, and Management,* Boston: Allyn and Bacon, Inc., 1977; Douglas M. Jurney, "Pre-Engineered Buildings and School Construction," *School Business Affairs,* June 1979.

PREJUDICE, a stereotyped attitude, positive or negative, that individuals feel toward a group or division of people or toward members of such groups or divisions. Nationalistic pride is an example of positive prejudice; untruthful and derogating statements about a group illustrates negative prejudice. Evidences of prejudice are to be found in all societies.

Prejudice, David Dressler pointed out, is an emotional attitude that predisposes an individual to react toward a group in a certain way. It is not synonymous with *discrimination* although the two terms are frequently related. Prejudice is an internal phenomenon, one not always discernible, and discrimination is an observable behavior. George Simpson and J. Milton Yinger indicated that one can be prejudiced but, by controlling that prejudice, discrimination does not take place. Conversely, some discrimination is not causally related to prejudice. "The net effect of prejudice," Gordon

Allport wrote, "is to place the object of prejudice at some disadvantage not merited by his own misconduct" (p. 9). (See DISCRIMINATION.)

References: Gordon W. Allport, *The Nature of Prejudice,* Cambridge, MA: Addison-Wesley Publishing Company, 1954; David Dressler, *Sociology: The Study of Human Interaction,* New York: Alfred A. Knopf, 1969; George E. Simpson and J. Milton Yinger, *Racial and Cultural Minorities* (Third Edition), New York: Harper and Row, Publishers, 1965.

PREP, a structured, pre-reading group discussion method to elicit knowledge related to the subject of the reading (Langer, 1982). The teacher selects, from the text, a concept or picture that will encourage discussion and focusing on the main idea. For example, in a chapter entitled *The Birth of Democracy,* the word *democracy* could be selected. Putting the word *democracy* before the group, the teacher requests students to contribute anything that comes to mind on hearing the word. All contributions are recorded without judgment in a place clearly visible (board, overhead, or chart). Next, the teacher asks respondents to tell what made them think of each idea. Students begin to focus on personal thinking strategies and to see the interrelatedness of ideas. Any erroneous ideas are eliminated at this point. Finally, students are asked what new ideas relative to the concept *democracy* they have learned as a result of the discussion. In addition to relating prior knowledge to the new concept, the teacher is able to assess the students' level of understanding of the new concept from the number and types of responses elicited.

References: John G. Barnitz, *Reading Development of Non-Native Speakers of English* (ERIC Clearinghouse on Languages and Linguistics), New York: Harcourt Brace Jovanovich Inc., 1985; J. A. Langer, "Facilitating Text Processing: The Elaboration of Prior Knowledge" in J. Langer and M. Trika Smith-Burke (Editors), *Reader Meets Author/Bridging the Gap: A Psycholinguistic and Sociolinguistic Perspective,* Newark, DE: International Reading Association, 1982; Lenore H. Ringler and Carol K. Weber, *A Language-Thinking Approach to Reading Diagnosis and Teaching,* New York: Harcourt Brace Jovanovich, Publishers, 1984.

PRE-POST-TESTING, an evaluation procedure in which parallel (or equal forms) tests are administered to a group of individuals before and after a treatment. The test given *before* treatment (e.g. experiment, administration of drugs, instruction) is called the pre-test; the test given *after* the treatment is referred to as the post-test.

There may be several purposes for a pre-test. For example, an experimenter may wish to determine if groups of individuals participating in a program or experiment are initially equal with respect to skills, attitudes, or knowledges in a particular area. Or the experimenter may wish to determine the initial ability or skill level(s) of a particular group.

The amount learned (difference between pre- and post-test scores) can be determined only when pre-test and post-test scores are available. Relationships and predictions can be determined using pre-test scores together with other relevant data. Post-test scores can be used for comparative purposes between or among groups.

There may be a problem of testing effect when using a pre-test in an experiment, because subjects may be influenced (e.g. practice, shaping attitudes) by the pre-test. In spite of this possibility, pre-test–post-test designs continue to be used in educational and psychological research studies. (See HAWTHORNE EFFECT.)

References: Donald Campbell and Julian C. Stanley, *Experimental and Quasi-Experimental Designs for Research,* Chicago: Rand-McNally and Company, 1966; Lou M. Carey, *Measuring and Evaluating School Learning,* Boston: Allyn and Bacon, Inc., 1988; Emil J. Posavac and Raymond J. Carey, *Program Evaluation: Methods and Case Studies* (Third Edition), Englewood Cliffs, NJ: Prentice-Hall, 1989.

PREPRIMERS, soft-covered books that are an integral part of a basal (basic) reading series and designed for use with very young (beginning) reading students. Sequentially, preprimers are introduced *after* students have satisfactorily mastered the first volume in the reading series (frequently referred to as a readiness book) and *before* the primer (the first hard-covered book in the series).

Basal reading series typically include three or four preprimers. They are designed to introduce students to the printed word using a controlled vocabulary. Each of the preprimers introduces 20–30 new words, usually in association with a picture. At first, single words are introduced, one page at a time. In the last preprimer, complete sentences appear on a given page.

In recent years, the terms *preprimer* and *primer* have been replaced by the term *level,* ostensibly to discourage the practice of limiting use of a particular book to a particular school year. In response to growing criticism of basal readers, publishers have been working to modify their purportedly simplistic vocabulary (e.g. look, look; oh, oh) and to heighten interest in their content. (See PRIMERS.)

References: Albert J. Harris and Edward R. Sipay, *How to Increase Reading Ability: A Guide to Developmental and Remedial Methods* (Sixth Edition), New York: Longman, Inc., 1975; Arthur W. Heilman, *Principles and Practices of Teaching Reading* (Third Edition), Columbus, OH: Charles E.Merrill Publishing Company, 1972.

PRESCHOOL, or nursery school, a school designed for children whose ages generally fall between three and five years. There are many types of preschools. They include: custodial schools; Montessori schools; industrial models that favor the academic child; child-development or maturational schools; and "open classroom" schools similar to the British Infant Schools.

Preschools are not viewed today as "play centers" in the narrow sense since the value of play as a highly cognitive as well as socializing experience has been well documented. A child can enjoy and learn in such an environment where a wide variety of materials, music, books, art, blocks, free time, organized play, and problem solving and socializing experiences can be planned and implemented under professional guidance. Many health needs are identified and taken care of in nursery schools.

Nursery schools were first organized in the United States (1920s) at Teachers College, Columbia University, and at the Merrill Palmer School of Motherhood and Home Training, Detroit, as experimental centers. Since 1933, there has been significant federal support for such schools as a result of the Great Depression, World War II, and the advent of compensatory education programs. Today, nursery school education is an important field in teacher preparation (Early Childhood Education). (See COMPENSATORY EDUCATION.)

References: William Blatz, et al., *Nursery Education: Theory and Practice*, New York: William Morrow and Company, Inc., 1935; Sarah H. Leeper, et al., *Good Schools for Young Children*, New York: Macmillan Publishing Company, Inc., 1974; Evelyn G. Pitcher and L. B. Ames, *The Guidance Nursery School*, New York: Harper and Row, Publishers, 1975.

PRESIDENT, COLLEGE AND UNIVERSITY, the chief executive officer of an institution of higher education. (These institutions include two-year community colleges, four-year colleges, and universities.) Before the Civil War, college presidents headed relatively small institutions. Many of them were members of the clergy who spent some part of their time teaching, preaching, and writing.

In recent years, as colleges and universities became considerably larger and more complex, the role of the president increased in complexity. Today, governing boards (trustees, regents, etc.) expect their presidents to provide general superintendence over all aspects of the institutions they head. In the exercise of their duties, they are expected: (1) to be both academic as well as financial managers; (2) to play a development role (finding new sources of income); (3) to recommend and implement policy; and (4) to mediate differences that may arise between groups of faculty or between the public (including legislatures) and the institution.

Frederick Bolman pointed out that, in recent years, college and university presidents have been facing four critical problems: (1) demands by students to have a greater voice in institutional governance; (2) similar demands by faculties; (3) state, regional, and national planning activities (including the problem of finding a place for both private and public institutions) that impinge on institutional sovereignty and test the conceptual/political skills of the presidents; and (4) financial accountability, a problem that grows larger as more and more institutions and agencies of government compete for money with higher educational institutions.

The National Center for Education Statistics reported that, in 1978, there were 3,130 institutions of higher education and branches in the United States. Of this number, 1,174 were two-year colleges; 1,644 (a slight majority) were privately controlled institutions. (See BOARD OF TRUSTEES, COLLEGE AND UNIVERSITY and COMMUNITY COLLEGE.)

References: Frederick deW. Bolman, "The Administrator as Leader and Statesman" in G. Kerry Smith (Editor), *Stress and Campus Response*, San Francisco: Jossey-Bass Publishers, 1968; Michael D. Cohen and James G. March, *Leadership and Ambiguity: The American College President* (General Report Prepared for the Carnegie Commission on Higher Education), New York: McGraw-Hill Book Company, 1974; W. H. Cowley, *Presidents, Professors, and Trustees*, San Francisco: Jossey-Bass Publishers, 1980; Nancy B. Dearman and Valena W. Plisko, *The Condition of Education: Statistical Report*, Washington, DC: National Center for Education Statistics, U.S. Department of Health, Education, and Welfare, 1979; Joseph F. Kauffman, *At the Pleasure of the Board*, Washington, DC: American Council on Education, 1980; Barry M. Richman and Richard N. Farmer, *Leadership, Goals, and Power in Higher Education*, San Francisco: Jossey-Bass Publishers, 1974.

PRIMARY SCHOOL, a school enrolling young children, normally of Kindergarten through grade 3 age. Primary education had its origins in colonial

America when primary schools enrolled 30 to 40 young students and stressed the development of reading skills for religious purposes. The primary grades were later viewed as a vehicle for teaching the basic skills of reading, writing, and computation. During the 1800s, arts and crafts, science, geography, social studies, music, and physical education were added to the curriculum. The modern elementary school evolved from the primary school. Today's elementary school, in contrast to the primary school of the 1800s, can be divided into three levels: preprimary (grades or levels below grade 1); primary grades (1–3); and upper elementary grades (4–6).

References: Calhoun C. Collier, et al., *Modern Elementary Education: Teaching and Learning,* New York: Macmillan Publishing Company, Inc., 1976; William B. Rogan and Gene D. Shepherd, *Modern Elementary Curriculum* (Fourth Edition), New York: Holt, Rinehart and Winston, Inc., 1971; Bernard Spodek, *Teaching in the Early Years,* Englewood Cliffs, NJ: Prentice-Hall, Inc., 1972.

PRIMERS, reading books designed for use with young students. Primers are an integral part of basal-reading series, each a program that typically employs the developmental approach to reading instruction. The primer is usually the first hard-covered reader given to the child; sequentially, it is used *after* the student has successfully completed the program's three or four preprimers. Primers repeat and build on vocabulary as well as content found in the series' preprimers. A given primer may introduce 100–150 new words.

Recent criticism of basal reading programs has prompted changes in vocabulary and content as well as increased use of enrichment devices such as games, records, tapes, and filmstrips. Another noted change has been the inclination of several textbook publishers to substitute "levels" for terms such as *primer* and *preprimer,* a move intended to encourage greater individualization of reading instruction. (See PREPRIMERS.)

References: Albert J. Harris and Edward R. Sipay, *How to Increase Reading Ability: A Guide to Developmental and Remedial Methods* (Sixth Edition), New York: Longman, Inc., 1975; Arthur W. Heilman, *Principles and Practices of Teaching Reading* (Third Edition), Columbus, OH: Charles E. Merrill Publishing Company, 1972.

PRIME SPONSOR, a term used in connection with certain federal legislation. Specifically, it is the organization, public or private, authorized to contract with a federal agency for the purpose of carrying out one or more programs. The agency may actually carry out the program itself or subcontract to have it implemented.

In 1973, Public Law 93-203 (the Comprehensive Employment Training Act), an example of such federal legislation, provided that prime sponsors shall be: (1) a state; (2) a unit of general local government that has a population of 100,000 or more persons; or (3) any combination of units of local government. "A limited number of existing concentrated employment program grantees serving rural areas having a high level of unemployment" (p. 841) could also qualify as prime sponsors.

References: Garth Magnum and David Snedeker, *Manpower Planning for Local Labor Markets,* Salt Lake City, UT: Olympus Publishing Company, 1974; Public Law 93-203, *United States Statutes at Large, 1973* (Volume 87), Washington, DC: U.S. Government Printing Office, 1974.

PRINCETON PLAN, a school desegregation scheme in which schools in close proximity to each other are paired. One predominantly white and one predominantly minority school serving the same grades are matched. Although there are many variations of the pairing that originated in Princeton, New Jersey (in 1948), the most common approach followed is one in which two grade K–6 schools are divided in such a way that one school will enroll all students in grades K–3 and the other will have all grade 4–6 students. By doing this, both schools share the merged school populations; furthermore, the school populations are desegregated. The original plan merged two Princeton elementary schools' attendance areas, with students being assigned to grades K–5 in one school and grades 6–8 in the other.

References: Bentley Edwards and Frederick M. Wirt, *School Desegregation in the North,* San Francisco: Chandler Publishing Company, 1967; Frank W. Lutz, *Toward Improved Urban Education,* Worthington, OH: Charles A. Jones Publishing Company, 1970; National School Public Relations Association, *Desegregation: How Schools Are Meeting Historic Challenge,* Arlington, VA: The Association, 1973.

PRINCETON PROJECT—See SECONDARY SCHOOL SCIENCE PROJECT

PRINCIPAL, the executive officer of an individual elementary or secondary school building. In years past, when school sizes were still relatively small, one teacher was frequently designated the head or "principal-teacher." As school enrollments grew, the principalship evolved into a full-time management position and the word *teacher* was dropped from the title. Functions of the principalship at the building level include budgeting, supervision of faculty and staff, instructional leadership, student personnel administration, record management, and other tasks prescribed by law and school board policy.

The principal is administratively responsible to the superintendent of schools or one of his assistants. There are over 100,000 principals and assistant principals currently working in American public schools. (See ELEMENTARY SCHOOL PRINCIPAL and SENIOR HIGH SCHOOL PRINCIPAL.)

References: Lester W. Anderson and Lauren A. Van Dyke, *Secondary School Administration* (Second Edition), Boston: Houghton Mifflin Company, 1972; Donald A. Erikson and Theodore L. Reller (Editors), *The Principal in Metropolitan Schools*, Berkeley, CA: McCutchan Publishing Corporation, 1978; James M. Lipham and James A. Hoeh, Jr., *The Principalship: Foundations and Functions*, New York: Harper and Row, Publishers, 1974; William H. Roe and Thelbert L. Drake, *The Principalship* (Second Edition), New York: Macmillan Publishing Company, Inc., 1980.

PRINTING INKS, inks that are used in printing. There are different types of printing ink, depending on the type of printing to be done (i.e. *letterpress,* relief printing used in the printing of most books and newspapers; *lithographic,* or *plane graphic,* printing from a flat surface; *flexographic,* printing with rubber plates and a liquid ink, used in printing paper bags, food wrappers; and *gravure,* intaglio printing in which steel and copperplate engraving plates are used). Letterpress and lithographic printing use paste inks, and flexographic and gravure printing use a liquid ink.

There are many types of ink made from a variety of natural and man-made compounds. Printing inks can be used in highly specialized areas of printing, such as inks for wallpaper and magnetic inks for checks used in banking. They are used extensively in classroom art projects as well.

Printing inks date back to ancient China and Egypt.

References: D. E. Bisset, et al., *Printing Ink Manual* (Third Edition), Philadelphia: International Ideas, Inc., 1979; J. I. Duffy, *Printing Inks: Developments Since Nineteen Seventy-Five,* Park Ridge, NJ: Noyes Data Corporation, 1980; James Moran, *Printing Presses,* Berkeley, CA: University of California Press, 1973.

PRINT MATERIALS, those communication media that make use of the printed word. Significant among such materials are textbooks, reference books, periodicals, trade books, pamphlets, and newspapers. It has been estimated that almost two-thirds of school instructional time is spent using print materials; nevertheless, these materials, on average, account for only one-quarter of 1 percent of a school's total operating budget. (See PERIODICALS; TEXTBOOKS; and TRADE BOOK.)

References: James W. Brown, et al., *AV Instruction: Technology, Media, and Methods* (Fifth Edition), New York: McGraw-Hill Book Company, 1977; Marda Woodbury, *Selecting Instructional Materials* (PDK Fastback 110), Bloomington, IN: The Phi Delta Kappa Educational Foundation, 1978; Marda Woodbury, *Selecting Materials for Instruction: Media and the Curriculum,* Littleton, CO: Libraries Unlimited, Inc., 1980.

PRISON SCHOOLS, or prison education, instructional programs operating in various prisons for the benefit of the incarcerated. In the United States, prison education was first started by the Pennsylvania Quakers in the 1700s for salvation, moral development, and penitence reasons. Illiterate prisoners were taught to read and write so that Bible studies could be completed. In the late 1800s, more formal and extensive prison schools were introduced with basic educational and vocational programs available. By the 1940s, high school education was made available in many prisons. In 1957, the first college-level program (Southern Illinois University) was introduced.

Prison education has a basic personal rehabilitation thrust concerned with increasing opportunities and job accesses for prisoners. The prison schools are quite extensive, since many of the prisoners are undereducated, with many illiterate. Today, many types and levels of education are available in prisons. They range from elementary programs to vocational education to higher education. In 1975, there were 920 full-time educators of inmates in the United States, most working in state or federal prisons.

References: Michael V. Reagen and Donald M. Stoughtov (Editors), *School Behind Bars: A Descriptive Overview of Correctional Education in the American Prison System,* Metuchen, NJ: The Scarecrow Press, Inc., 1976; Robert Roberts, *Imprisoned Tongues,* Manchester, England: Manchester University Press, 1968; Marjorie Seashore, et al., *Prisoner Education,* New York: Praeger Publishers, 1976.

PRIVATE SCHOOLS—See NONPUBLIC SCHOOLS

PROBABILITY, a mathematical system used to

infer the likelihood of an event or outcome. The theory of probability was originally developed to be used with games of chance. Currently, probability theory has many other applications, most particularly to science and research. When an experimenter is uncertain about his/her findings, he/she must guess or infer the stability of the results. Probability theory allows the investigator to evaluate the "risk" of a particular decision. It can also be used to determine the "odds" that an event will/will not occur.

Through the use of probability, a statistician can determine significance levels that then enable the researcher to make informed decisions. For example, researchers know that chance may play a part in determining the results of a study. The lower the chance level (1 out of a 100, $p = 0.01$, is a better risk than 5 out of a 100, $p = 0.05$), the more confidence the researcher can place in his/her decision.

Probability theory is used extensively in inferential statistics and hypothesis testing in educational research. (See HYPOTHESES and INFERENTIAL STATISTICS.)

References: Henry L. Alder and Edward B. Roessler, *Introduction to Probability and Statistics* (Sixth Edition), San Francisco: W. H. Freeman, 1977; William M. Hays, *Statistics* (Fourth Edition), New York: Holt, Rinehart and Winston, Inc., 1988; David S. Moore and George P. McCabe, *Introduction to the Practice of Statistics*, New York: W. H. Freeman and Company, 1989.

PROBLEM-RAISING METHOD, or problem-method approach, an instructional technique that uses (or creates) various problems as media for learning. The solving of problems, or the searching for solutions to specific problems is used as a basis for facilitating learning. Problem raising often uses as problems the current and relevant issues facing students. Such personalized strategies are in keeping with the belief, held by many authorities, that often the more effective approach to learning social issues is to become involved in such issues. Consequently, games and simulations are often used. In other cases, students are placed in a limited situation and are faced with developing a solution to remove themselves from that situation. The problem-raising approach helps to develop thinking, problem-solving skills and strategies, and decision-making ability. Problem-raising methods can be used in most school disciplines and curriculum areas. (See PROBLEM SOLVING and SIMULATION.)

References: Carole E. Greenes, et al., *Successful Problem Solving Technique*, Palo Alto, CA: Creative Publications, 1977; Philip A. Heath and Thomas Weible, *Developing*

Social Responsibility in the Middle School, Washington, DC: National Education Association, 1979.

PROBLEM SOLVING, defined by the National Council of Supervisors of Mathematics as "the process of applying previously acquired knowledge to new and unfamiliar situations" (p. 2). Nicholas Branca pointed out that the term is all-encompassing. While agreeing that it is, in some instances, a *process,* he pointed out that it may also be a *goal* (e.g. problem solving is a goal of mathematics) or a *skill* (e.g. minimum-competency tests frequently treat problem solving as a mathematical skill).

Educational institutions, elementary through the university level, are devoting increasing amounts of time to the formal teaching of problem solving, this to correct deficiencies noted in National Assessment of Education Progress reports and similar research findings. These studies indicate that students experiencing problem-solving difficulties are frequently unable to analyze the problem with which they are coping. One approach to problem-solving instruction, first introduced by Benjamin Bloom and Lois Broder, requires individual students to "think aloud" as they solve problems, thus permitting the teacher to "observe" the thought processes employed. (See NATIONAL ASSESSMENT OF EDUCATIONAL PROGRESS.)

References: Benjamin S. Bloom and Lois Broder, *Problem-Solving Processes of College Students,* Chicago: University of Chicago Press, 1950; Nicholas A. Branca, "Problem Solving as a Goal, Process, and Basic Skill" in Stephen Krulik and Robert E. Reys (Editors), *Problem Solving in School Mathematics* (1980 Yearbook), Reston, VA: The National Council of Teachers of Mathematics, Inc., 1980; Thomas P. Carpenter, et al., "Problem Solving in Mathematics: National Assessment Results," *Educational Leadership,* April 1980; National Council of Supervisors of Mathematics, *Position Paper on Basic Mathematical Skills,* Washington, DC: National Institute of Education, 1977; Arthur Whimbey, "Students Can Learn to Be Better Problem Solvers," *Educational Leadership,* April 1980.

PROCESS/PRODUCT EVALUATION, program evaluation concerned with the performance characteristics of a program and its output or outcomes. The *process* aspects of the evaluation include program monitoring, client tracking, cost accounting, compliance with external regulations, indicators of adequacy (standards, accessibility), the degree to which goals are being pursued, as well as the interactions of the program itself. In a school, factors such as teacher style, teacher techniques, school climate, administrator style, and the school curriculum can be considered as elements of process.

Product evaluation focuses on how students have changed as a result of a program. It is concerned with goal attainment. Testing, observations, data collection, follow-up surveys, and so on are methods that can be used in product evaluation. Positive changes in student achievement, attitudes, or behavioral manifestations illustrate the types of product, or output, that may be recorded in a school program.

References: W. James Popham, *Educational Evaluation* (Second Edition), Englewood Cliffs, NJ: Prentice-Hall, 1988; Emil J. Posavac and Raymond J. Carey, *Program Evaluation: Methods and Case Studies* (Third Edition), Englewood Cliffs, NJ: Prentice-Hall, 1989; Bruce W. Tuckman, *Evaluating Educational Programs*, Boston: Allyn and Bacon, Inc., 1979.

PROFESSION, the occupational classification that, when included in a hierarchical ordering of occupational groups, ranks in the top position (above the semiprofessional, skilled, and unskilled job categories). Sociologists are in general agreement that numerous criteria must be considered when attempting to ascertain if a particular occupation is in fact professional. The professional, one investigator (Edgar Schein) reported after reviewing the literature on this subject, is an individual who: (1) works in a full-time occupation; (2) has made a lifetime commitment to his/her job; (3) possesses specialized knowledges and skills through extensive study; (4) is committed to serving the needs of clients objectively and does so by using standardized approaches; and (5) makes judgments for clients on the basis of superior knowledge. Other criteria used in the definition relate to autonomy matters such as occupational self-governance, peer review, and standards for admission into the occupation.

Is the teacher a professional? That question was studied by a special commission of the American Association of Colleges for Teacher Education. Its members reported that teaching meets some, but not all, of the criteria noted above; accordingly, it was concluded that teaching is more correctly a *semiprofession*. Specific recommendations for helping teaching to become a profession were included in the commission's report.

References: Robert B. Howsam, et al., *Educating a Profession*, Washington, DC: American Association of Colleges for Teacher Education, 1976; Edgar H. Schein, *Professional Education*, New York: McGraw-Hill Publishing Company, 1972.

PROFESSIONAL JOURNALS, periodicals published exclusively for the purpose of advancing a particular field or profession. Professional journals contain information and news of interest to its readership: (1) activities of colleagues; (2) current and future organizational activities/meetings; and (3) information on research, inventions, discoveries, new procedures, and new movements.

Professional journals in the United States are not new. The *American Journal of Science* was founded in 1818; the *Journal of the Franklin Institute at Philadelphia* was first published in 1825; *Scientific American* appeared in 1845; and the *American Journal of the Medical Sciences* was established in 1820.

Virtually every identifiable profession has one or more professional journals. Many are published by, and often reflect views of, professional organizations. Others, although sponsored by a professional organization, do not necessarily reflect their sponsors' opinions. Still others are independent of any professional organization. Although many people outside a profession may read such journals, the target audience is largely made up of practicing and prospective professionals.

The Directory of Publishing Opportunities in Journals and Periodicals (1979) lists over 3,400 specialized and professional journals; *Ulrich's International Periodicals Directory* (1979) lists 62,000. As a result of the large number of journals, several journal indexes are published. One of them, the *Current Index to Journals in Education* (CIJE), is published monthly and covers approximately 780 major education and education-related journals. (See EDUCATION INDEX and PERIODICALS.)

References: Current Index to Journals in Education, Phoenix, AZ: Oryx Press, 1980; *Directory of Publishing Opportunities in Journals and Periodicals* (Fourth Edition), Chicago: Marquis Academic Media, 1979; John E. Drewry, *Some Magazines and Magazine Makers,* Boston: The Stratford Company, 1924; *Ulrich's International Periodicals Directory* (Eighteenth Edition), New York: R. R. Bowker Company, 1979.

PROFESSORSHIP IN EDUCATION, a collective term used to describe faculty members employed in schools, colleges, and departments of education. The U.S. Office of Education recently reported that education faculty (including physical and health education instructors) accounted for almost 15 percent of all faculty members, who, in 1972–73, taught or did research in America's two-year colleges, four-year colleges, and universities. These faculty members are presently working in approximately 1,100 four-year American colleges and universities.

The education professorship is approximately a century old. Erwin Johanningmeier and Henry Johnson wrote that one of the first such positions was established at the University of Michigan in 1879, a chair created to promote the study of educational science and to help with the preparation of secondary schoolteachers. The number of such positions increased throughout the country during the late 1800s, accelerated by the opening of larger and larger numbers of high schools. By 1890, these same investigators reported, education professorships were established "in thirty-one institutions, chairs of pedagogy attached to another subject (usually philosophy and sometimes psychology) in forty-five more, and seven universities reported lectureships" (pp. 7–8). The addition of graduate programs, and sponsorships of the doctorate in education, further accelerated the number of education professorships.

During its evolution, the education professorship has been primarily concerned with the preparation of educational professionals. The status accorded teacher educators is relatively low on most campuses. Some authorities aver that this group's preoccupation with preparation at the expense of educational inquiry (research) is one factor contributing to this low status. Other status deterrents that have been suggested include: (1) the positioning of most teacher education programs at the undergraduate rather than graduate level, and (2) the fact that large numbers of teachers had to be prepared, virtually on a crash basis, between 1860 and 1930 and following World War II.

References: Merle L. Borrowman, "About Professors of Education" in Ayers Bagley (Editor), *The Professor of Education: An Assessment of Conditions*, Minneapolis, MN: College of Education, University of Minnesota, 1975 (for the Society of Professors of Education); David L. Clark and Gerald Marker, "The Institutionalization of Teacher Education" in Kevin Ryan (Editor), *Teacher Education* (NSSE 74th Yearbook, Part II), Chicago: University of Chicago Press, 1975; Erwin V. Johanningmeier (Editor), *Science of Education and the Education Professoriate* (Society of Professors of Education Occasional Papers Series—Set #10), DeKalb, IL: College of Education, Northern Illinois University, 1978 (for the Society of Professors of Education); Erwin V. Johanningmeier and Henry C. Johnston, Jr., "The Education Professoriate: A Historical Consideration of Its Work and Growth" in Ayers Bagley (Editor), *The Professor of Education: An Assessment of Conditions*, Minneapolis, MN: College of Education, University of Minnesota, 1975 (for the Society of Professors of Education); National Center for Education Statistics, *Digest of Education Statistics 1979*, Washington, DC: U.S. Government Printing Office, 1979.

PROFILE, a graphic representation used to describe an individual, a group, a region, or even an industry in terms of relative positions, strengths, or dynamics on several different measures or characteristics. There are many types of profiles. They range from line graphs on a single grid to full written descriptions appearing in book form. The basic purpose of a profile is to illustrate or describe the characteristics of the individual, group, and so on concerned. A profile can be used to illustrate individual or group vocational interests, aptitudes, test scores, strengths and weaknesses in a given area (e.g. reading or physical growth), or it can be employed for diagnostic, counseling, or planning purposes.

References: *Barron's Profiles of American Colleges* (Volume 1, Eleventh Edition), Woodbury, NY: Barron's Educational Series, Inc., 1978; *Profile of Medical Practice*, Chicago: Center for Health Services Research and Development, AMA, 1979; Sadanand Singh and John Lynch (Editors), *Diagnostic Procedures in Hearing, Language, and Speech*, Baltimore, MD: University Park Press, 1978; John Stellern, et al., *Introduction to Diagnostic-Prescriptive Teaching and Programming*, Glen Ridge, NJ: Exceptional Press, 1976.

PROGNOSIS, prediction or forecast of a future outcome based on existing information or data. Teachers, psychologists, reading specialists, medical doctors, counselors, and others engage extensively in prognosis. For example, a counselor may look at the results of a set of standardized psychological test scores, a set of achievement test scores, and the past educational record of a student and conclude that the student may or may not be successful if he/she takes a particular course or program, attempts a particular activity, or makes a specific career choice. Prognosis can be used when developing individualized educational programs, for placement purposes, or to predict the outcome of a diagnosis or treatment. Since the accuracy of prognosis is based on many factors (e.g. validity of data, attitudes, intelligence, ability of the person making the prognosis, skills, chance), one must be careful when using the procedure. Ideally, as many factors as possible should be considered.

References: John F. Darne and Albert R. Brinkman, *Guidance in Business Education* (Third Edition), Cincinnati, OH: South-Western Publishing Company, 1961; Nate L. Gage and David C. Berliner, *Educational Psychology*, Chicago: Rand McNally College Publishing Company, 1975; George D. Spache, *Diagnosing and Correcting Reading Disabilities*, Boston: Allyn and Bacon, Inc., 1976; William M. Walsh (Editor), *Counseling Children and Ado-*

lescents, Berkeley, CA: McCutchan Publishing Corporation, 1975.

PROGRAM ARTICULATION—See ARTICULATION, PROGRAM

PROGRAM, EDUCATIONAL, a general term used to classify a group of educational activities or courses that (1) have common goals or objectives, or (2) can be used to achieve common goals or objectives. Some programs may be large (with many subprograms), and others are relatively small and simple. Educational programs are usually a subset of a larger curriculum. For example, special education in one university may be the larger curriculum classification, and a set of courses in learning disabilities, leading to certification, may be one of the many educational programs offered within special education. In another institution, special education may be considered the program and learning disabilities a subprogram.

There are several common elements found in all programs: (1) they are made up of a series of activities or courses; (2) the activities or courses are sequential in design; (3) the activities or courses are well organized; (4) the programs are educationally goal oriented; (5) activities are identifiable as a program; and (6) usually, educational programs are more stable in terms of time than are projects, institutes, or other ad hoc training programs. Although complex, programs can be evaluated in terms of outcomes and costs.
References: Harry J. Hartley, *Educational Planning-Programming-Budgeting: A Systems Approach,* Englewood Cliffs, NJ: Prentice-Hall, Inc., 1968; Lynn L. Morris and Carol T. Fitz-Gibbon, *How to Deal with Goals and Objectives,* Beverly Hills, CA: Sage Publications, Inc., 1978; Satish Parekh, *Long Range Planning,* New York: Change Magazine Press, 1977; B. W. Vaughan, *Planning in Education,* Cambridge, England: Cambridge University Press, 1978.

PROGRAM EVALUATION—See EVALUATION, PROGRAM

PROGRAM EVALUATION AND REVIEW TECHNIQUE—See PERT

PROGRAMMED INSTRUCTION, a highly structured and individualized system of teaching. Introduced in the 1950s, largely as the result of B. F. Skinner's work in the area of learning reinforcement, programmed instruction is sequential and developmental. Information is presented to the learner using a *text, teaching machine,* or a *computer*

with questions interspersed throughout the program. The information is broken down into small units called frames that may consist of brief explanations, inductive stimuli, or materials requiring learner response. The student learns promptly whether or not his/her answer is correct, thereby receiving immediate reinforcement. Questions may be of the multiple-choice or open-ended type. Programs are designed to ensure relatively high learner success. (See COMPUTER-ASSISTED INSTRUCTION and TEACHING MACHINES.)
References: Edward B. Fry, *Teaching Machines and Programmed Instruction: An Introduction,* New York: McGraw-Hill Book Company, 1963; J. L. Hughes, *Programmed Instruction for Schools and Industry,* Chicago: Science Research Associates, Inc., 1962; Phil C. Lange (Editor), *Programmed Instruction* (NSSE 66th Yearbook, Part II), Chicago: University of Chicago Press, 1967; Jerome P. Lysaught and Clarence M. Williams, *A Guide to Programmed Instruction,* New York: John Wiley and Sons, 1963.

PROGRESSIVE EDUCATION, an educational movement that began during the latter part of the 19th century and whose influence on American and European schools was preeminent throughout much of the first half of the 20th century. The movement in America had its roots in numbers of concurrent events: (1) the national call for social reform (including curtailment of child-labor practices); (2) demographic changes (notably industrialization, urbanization, and school population growth); (3) growing dissatisfaction with the schools' traditional curriculum; and (4) the writings of educational reformers such as Francis W. Parker (whom John Dewey called "the father of progressive education") and John Dewey himself.

John L. Childs characterized progressive education as the work of educators "who have combined the psychological principles of child growth with the moral principles of democracy and have developed the conception that the supreme aim of education should be the nurture of an individual who can take responsibility for his own continued growth" (ASCD Yearbook, p. 1). The movement's key elements, which this quotation captures, were: (1) attention to child growth and development; (2) teaching the ideals of democracy; (3) learner self-direction; and (4) rational problem solving. Phrases such as "purposeful learning," "learning through doing," the "whole child," and "the power of choice" were often used to explain (or condemn) the movement.

Two major events served to strengthen and expand progressive education: (1) creation of the

Progressive Education Association in 1919, and (2) the Eight-Year Study, a research study, sponsored by the association, that indicated successes of progressive-educated youths. (See DEWEY, JOHN B.; EIGHT-YEAR STUDY; PARKER, FRANCIS W.; and PROGRESSIVE EDUCATION ASSOCIATION.)

References: Lawrence A. Cremin, *The Transformation of the School: Progressivism in American Education, 1876-1957,* New York: Alfred A. Knopf, 1961; George F. Kneller, *Introduction to the Philosophy of Education* (Second Edition), New York: John Wiley and Sons, 1971; James B. MacDonald, "Introduction" in James R. Squire (Editor), *A New Look at Progressive Education* (1972 Yearbook), Washington, DC: Association for Supervision and Curriculum Development, 1972.

PROGRESSIVE EDUCATION ASSOCIATION (PEA), an organization formed to foster innovative education and to evaluate the effectiveness of the progressive education movement. The association was organized in 1919 and eventually disbanded in 1955. During its 36-year existence, PEA proved to be a significant force for promoting educational reforms, particularly those consistent with the teachings of John Dewey and William Kilpatrick. The Eight-Year Study was carried out under its auspices. (See EIGHT-YEAR STUDY and PROGRESSIVE EDUCATION.)

References: Lawrence A. Cremin, *The Transformation of the School: Progressivism in American Education, 1876-1957,* New York: Alfred A. Knopf, 1961; Patricia A. Graham, *Progressive Education, From Arcady to Academe: A History of the Progressive Education Association, 1919-1955,* New York: Teachers College Press, 1967.

PROGRESSIVE vs. REGRESSIVE TAXES, terms used by economists to distinguish taxes that are based on ability to pay from those that, relatively, impose more heavily on persons less able to pay. *Progressive* taxes are taxes whose rates increase as the tax base increases. The progressive income tax is one example. *Regressive* taxes, in contrast, are those whose rates decrease as the tax base increases. Few such taxes exist. More common is the *proportional* tax (frequently confused with the regressive tax), one whose rate does not vary as the tax base varies. Most sales and excise taxes fall within this last classification.

Many school finance authorities contend that the property tax, a tax not always indicative of ability to pay, is too often used to support education at the local level. This imposes unduly on those least able to support schools. For that reason, the authorities have urged increased reliance on state support of

education, partly because many states use the personal income tax (a progressive tax) as a revenue source.

References: James M. Buchanan, *The Public Finances: An Introductory Textbook* (Third Edition), Homewood, IL: Richard D. Irwin, Inc., 1970; John E. Corbally, *School Finance,* Boston: Allyn and Bacon, Inc., 1962.

PROJECT ENGLISH, a 1960s program designed to improve the teaching of English in American secondary schools. The project was organized in 1961 and soon after became known as the English Program of the Office of Education. Several concurrent activities, Michael Shugrue reported, were carried out during the course of the project, these falling into any of four principal categories; (1) *curriculum study centers,* in which new instructional materials were developed; (2) *study centers for teacher preparation,* centers that sought improved ways to train English teachers; (3) *demonstration centers,* where research and experimentation were carried out in curriculum areas such as reading and literature; and (4) *individual research projects,* which dealt with an array of topics related to English instruction.

Numerous documents produced in Project English centers have been processed for inclusion in the ERIC system. (See ERIC.)

References: Robert F. Hogan, "As Others See Us: An Interview after the Fact," *English Journal,* May 1966; Bernard O'Donnell, "NCTE/ERIC and Project English," *English Journal,* September 1968; Michael F. Shugrue, "National English Projects and Curriculum Change," *NASSP Bulletin,* April 1967.

PROJECT FOLLOW-THROUGH—See FOLLOW-THROUGH PROGRAM

PROJECT HEADSTART—See OPERATION HEADSTART

PROJECTION, a defense (or ego) mechanism in which an individual unknowingly attributes his/her own characteristics to others or foists onto others motives that cause him/her anxiety. For example, a mother may ascribe to her daughter a strong desire to become a successful dancer, when, in fact, it is the mother herself who possesses this desire. Similarly, an individual may condemn members of a particular minority group for being hostile when all the time the individual is actually projecting his/her own hostility on the group. By condemning others through projection one shields himself/herself from reality (self-awareness).

References: Jerome Kagan and Ernest Havemann, *Psy-*

chology: An Introduction (Second Edition), New York: Harcourt Brace Jovanovich, Inc., 1972; Merle J. Moskowitz and Arthur R. Orgel, *General Psychology: A Core Text in Human Behavior*, Boston: Houghton Mifflin Company, 1969; Norman D. Sundberg, *Assessment of Persons*, Englewood Cliffs, NJ: Prentice-Hall, Inc., 1977; W. Edgar Vinacke, *Foundations of Psychology*, New York: Van Nostrand Reinhold Company, 1968.

PROJECTIVE TECHNIQUES, clinical tools used by psychologists to elicit personality data that are not voluntarily reported by a person being tested. Projective testing instruments are so constructed that a wide range of complex responses can be elicited. These responses are then used to identify and evaluate the underlying (or real) dynamics and personality characteristics of the person being tested. This type of testing has been criticized from time to time with critics questioning whether responses correctly reflect subjects' perceptions.

Several of the projective techniques commonly used are: Bender-Gestalt; Blacky Pictures; Children's Apperception Test; Draw-A-Person; House-Tree-Person; Make-A-Picture Test; Michigan Picture Test; Rorschach Inkblot Test; and the Word Association Test.

References: Edna A. Lerner, *Projective Use of the Bender-Gestalt*, Springfield, IL: Charles C Thomas, Publisher, 1972; Bernard I. Murstein (Editor), *Handbook of Projective Techniques*, New York: Basic Books, Inc., Publishers, 1965; Norman D. Sundberg, *Assessment of Persons*, Englewood Cliffs, NJ: Prentice-Hall, Inc., 1977; Constance Tarczan, *An Educator's Guide to Psychological Tests*, Springfield, IL: Charles C Thomas, Publisher, 1975.

PROJECT ON INSTRUCTION, or the Project on the Instructional Program of the Public Schools, a National Education Association undertaking authorized in 1959. Sometimes compared with such other well-known NEA efforts as the 1918 statement of the "Seven Cardinal Principles" or the 1938 and 1961 Educational Policies Commission statements, the Project on Instruction undertook to identify critical concerns relating to American Education and to offer recommendations relating to each. A 14-member National Committee and a headquarters staff, directed by Dr. Ole Sand, carried out the project.

Schools for the Sixties, an early project publication, addressed 12 questions (e.g. Who should make what decisions about education? What is the school's role in dealing with serious national problems such as youth unemployment and juvenile delinquency? How should the content of the curriculum be organized?). These 12 questions

produced 33 recommendations. *Schools for the Seventies*, another of the project's several publications, appeared later.

References: John I. Goodlad, Project on the Instructional Program of the Public Schools, *Planning and Organizing for Teaching*, Washington, DC: The Association, 1963; Warren T. Greenleaf and Gary A. Griffin, *Schools for the Seventies and Beyond: A Call to Action*, Washington, DC: National Education Association, 1971; Richard I. Miller, Project on the Instructional Program of the Public Schools, *Education in a Changing Society*, Washington, DC: The Association, 1964; National Committee of the NEA Project on Instruction, *Schools for the Sixties*, New York: McGraw-Hill Book Company, 1963.

PROJECT PHYSICS, formerly known as Harvard Project Physics, an effort to design a new physics course that would attract average high school students who normally would not choose to study this subject. The project, headquartered at Harvard University, began in 1964 with financial support contributed by the federal government, Harvard University, and several foundations. A new course was developed that accommodated a wide range of student abilities, emphasized the humanistic background of physics, and required but a minimal mathematics background. It made a variety of instructional approaches available to the teacher including lectures, demonstrations, laboratory experiences, independent study, and use of the several multimedia materials (including texts, filmloops, and transparencies) expressly designed for this course. The course was field tested in 1967 and, by 1969–70, was adopted by 400 secondary schools. It was subsequently used in several foreign countries as well. A 1975 edition of the course sought to gear its reading level to the average grade 9–10 reader.

References: Alfred T. Collette, *Science Teaching in the Secondary School: A Guide for Modernizing Instruction*, Boston: Allyn and Bacon, Inc., 1973; J. David Lockard (Editor), *Science and Mathematics Curricular Developments Internationally, 1956–1974*, College Park, MD: Science Teaching Center, University of Maryland (Joint Project with the Commission on Science Education, American Association for the Advancement of Science), 1974.

PROJECT "PLAN", or *Program for Learning in Accordance with Needs*, a highly individualized educational system (preschool–grade 12) that utilizes a computer to collect information concerning the progress and performance of students. Information about the student is fed into a terminal at each school for processing. Feedback is then made available to students and teachers. Each student's individualized program of study (POS) is stored in the computer.

Project "PLAN" is a system made up of: instructional objectives; teaching-learning units (TLUs); criterion tests; and a computer management and information program. The teaching-learning unit centers on a particular instructional objective found in the PLAN system. It serves as a guide to sundry learning activities, these designed to help the student meet a particular objective. Many different materials, instructional modes, and approaches may be suggested by a TLU. The objectives, tests, POS, and management system are stored in the computer.

Project "PLAN" is marketed by the Westinghouse Learning Corporation. "PLAN" was conceptualized in 1961 at the American Institutes for Research in the Behavioral Sciences under the direction of John C. Flanagan. From 1967 to 1971, "PLAN" was operated experimentally by AIR and Westinghouse (the year Westinghouse joined "PLAN"). Numerous schools throughout the United States use "PLAN." (See INDIVIDUALIZED INSTRUCTION.)

References: James E. Duane, Individualized Instruction—Programs and Materials, Englewood Cliffs, NJ: Educational Technology Publications, 1973; Harriet Talmage, Systems of Individualized Education, Berkeley, CA: McCutchan Publishing Corporation, 1975.

PROJECT TALENT, a 20-year longitudinal study undertaken to study the relationship between young people's career choices and their interests, aptitudes, and education. The study, supported by the U.S. Office of Education, was conducted by the American Institutes for Research under the direction of John C. Flanagan.

In 1960, an extensive battery of aptitude tests, achievement tests, and interest inventories was administered to 440,000 secondary school pupils in over 1,300 public and private schools. Literally hundreds of findings resulted. Early reports provided several significant and disparate findings. Included were the observations that: (1) the best predictor of high school success was the amount of learning acquired before grade 9; (2) teachers' salaries and student learning were highly correlative variables; and (3) seniors in large high schools tended to perform better in mathematics and science than did their small high school counterparts. Results of a five-year follow-up study, published in 1973, provided separate profiles characterizing 1960 students who entered 12 occupational groups

(e.g. construction trades, business administration). References: John C. Flanagan, et al., Design for a Study of American Youth (Volume I), Boston: Houghton Mifflin Company, 1962; John C. Flanagan, "Project Talent," NEA Journal, January 1964; John C. Flanagan, et al., The Career Data Book: Results from Project Talent's Five-Year Follow-up Study, Palo Alto, CA: American Institutes for Research, 1973.

PROJECT UPWARD BOUND—See UPWARD BOUND

PROMOTION OF STUDENTS, the vertical advancement of learners from one grade level to the next. The majority of students are promoted at the close of each academic year. Those few who, for academic or other reasons, are required to repeat a grade are said to have been retained. In even a smaller number of cases, able learners are accelerated, often by "skipping a grade."

Retention rates have decreased significantly since the turn of the century. At the elementary school level, they were reported to be 16 percent in 1909, 10 percent in 1933, and 8.3 percent in 1957.

Research indicates that retention appears to do little to improve students' subsequent academic performance. (See ACCELERATION and SOCIAL PROMOTION.)

References: Bertha B. Friedman and William A. Kelly, "Promotion" in Harry N. Rivlin and Herbert Schueler (Editors), Encyclopedia of Modern Education (Volume 2), New York: The Philosophical Library of New York City, 1943 (Reissued in 1969 by Kennikat Press); Virgil E. Herrick, "Elementary Education Programs" in Chester W. Harris (Editor), Encyclopedia of Educational Research (Third Edition), New York: The Macmillan Company, 1960.

PROPERTY TAX, the principal source of public school revenue raised at the local school level. Recent estimates indicate that approximately 98 cents of every tax dollar raised locally for school purposes come from the property tax.

Property is of three types: (1) real property, or land and permanent improvements thereon; (2) tangible property, such as equipment, livestock, and business inventories; and (3) intangible property, a category including stocks, bonds, and so on. For tax purposes, the definition of property varies from one state to another; most jurisdictions, however, tend to tax real property only.

Property is assessed (evaluated) for tax purposes. The assessed valuation may be its actual market value or a percentage thereof. A taxpayer's property tax is determined by multiplying the assessed valuation of the owner's property times the jurisdiction's uniform tax rate. Although the property tax has several advantages as a vehicle for raising money, it has been criticized for its failure to tax equitably (i.e. in accordance with a taxpayer's real wealth). (See PROGRESSIVE vs. REGRESSIVE TAXES.)

References: Robert J. Garvue, *Modern Public School Finance*, New York: The Macmillan Company, 1969; Oscar T. Jarvis, et al., *Public School Business Administration and Finance: Effective Policies and Practices*, West Nyack, NY: Parker Publishing Company, Inc., 1967; Richard W. Lindholm (Editor), *Property Taxation and the Finance of Education*, Madison, WI: University of Wisconsin Press, 1974.

PROPRIETARY SCHOOL, a type of nonpublic educational institution, independent of any church, that is privately owned and operated for the purpose of making a profit for its owners. Many proprietary schools offer curricula in vocational and business areas. Students normally enroll in such schools to learn a skill and thus facilitate their entry into the job market.

Reference: Frances C. Thomson (Editor), *The New York Times Guide to Continuing Education in America*, New York: Quadrangle Books, 1972.

PROVOST, traditionally the chief academic officer in an institution of higher education. Some institutions use the title Vice-President for Academic Affairs, others Provost to designate the individual responsible for all educational programs. The Provost reports directly to the college or university President, is second in command, and typically has deans, library directors, and research directors under his/her jurisdiction. Faculty appointments and academic budgets are included among the Provost's responsibilities.

In recent years, the title has often been given to the administrator charged with managing a particular campus that is part of a multicampus institution. In these cases, the Provost may or may not be the second in command.

References: Elwood B. Ehrle and John B. Bennett, *Managing the Academic Enterprise*, New York: American Council on Education, 1988; Asa S. Knowles (Editor), *Handbook of College and University Administration*, New York: McGraw-Hill Book Company, 1970; Stanley Salmen, *Duties of Administrators in Higher Education*, New York: The Macmillan Company, 1971.

PROXEMICS, the study of space as related to communication. Researchers include it within the broad classification of nonverbal communication.

Territoriality and personal space are space terms closely associated with proxemics. *Territoriality* has to do with space that is fixed in a geographical sense. In classrooms, for example, students may choose seats during the first day of class and continue to occupy them thereafter. In a sense, they have "carved out" territories for themselves and may even defend them aggressively should others dare to trespass. *Personal space* is similar to territoriality except that space claimed is not fixed geographically. To illustrate, a student may enter a cafeteria, find a vacant table, and set his/her books atop it as though staking a claim. Here, too, intruders may provoke a negative reaction.

Within classrooms, seating arrangements (e.g. by rows, horseshoe arrangement, or group seating at tables) have been studied. These studies demonstrate that the degree of interaction between teacher and individual pupils is related to seating arrangements. In a seating-by-rows arrangement, for example, pupils seated in the front-central area of the classroom (nearest the teacher) have greatest interaction; conversely, those seated in the rear and along the far sides interact least.

References: Edward T. Hall, *The Silent Language*, New York: Fawcett World Library, 1967; M. Thomas Hurt, et al., *Communication in the Classroom*, Reading, MA: Addison-Wesley Publishing Company, 1978; Marie Marcus, *Diagnostic Teaching of the Language Arts*, New York: John Wiley and Sons, 1977.

PROXIMATE CAUSE, a legal term (derived from the Latin *causa proxima*) that is used in the context of tort liability. The definition of *proximate cause* appearing in *Ballentine's Law Dictionary* has become the standard one: "That cause, which, in natural and continuous sequence, unbroken by any efficient intervening cause, produces the injury, and without which the result would not have occurred" (p. 1017). In education, the term is frequently used in negligence cases where the action (or failure to act) by teachers or other school officials is alleged to be the cause for an injury.

References: William S. Anderson (Editor), *Ballentine's Law Dictionary* (Third Edition), Rochester, NY: The Lawyer's Co-operative Publishing Company, 1969; David Mellinkoff, *The Language of the Law*, Boston: Little, Brown and Company, 1963; Harold H. Punke, *The Teacher and the Courts*, Danville, IL: The Interstate Printers and Publishers, Inc., 1971.

PSYCHOANALYTIC THERAPY, a long-lasting therapy normally used with clients suffering from severe emotional problems with treatment carried out by a trained psychoanalyst. Based largely on the work of Freud and his followers, the therapy seeks to help clients gain control over their emotions through techniques such as dream analysis and exploration of the unconscious. The ultimate aim is to reconstruct the personality and to have the client's unconscious become his/her conscious. Much of the unconscious-to-conscious change comes about through talking with the therapist.

Psychoanalytic theory holds that personality is heavily influenced by early experiences. For this reason, possible failure to cope with psychosexual stages of development is examined and held to be a root cause of personality problems. The stages are: (1) *oral;* (2) *anal;* (3) *genital;* (4) *latency;* (5) *puberty;* and (6) *adult genital.* The theory also holds that personality structure is based on: (1) the *id,* that part that seeks immediate gratification; (2) the *ego,* a reality component that intelligently regulates (reconciles) basic instincts and the individual's outside environment; and (3) the *superego,* the moral element concerned with issues of rightness and wrongness that were instilled by early (usually parental/family) experiences.

References: Norman Abeles, "Psychodynamic Theory" in Herbert M. Burks, Jr. and Buford Stefflre, *Theories of Counseling* (Third Edition), New York: McGraw-Hill Book Company, 1979; Gerald Corey, *Theory and Practice of Counseling and Psychotherapy,* Monterey, CA: Brooks/Cole Publishing Company, 1977; E. L. Tolbert, *An Introduction to Guidance,* Boston: Little, Brown and Company, 1978.

PSYCHODRAMA, a technique used in psychotherapy that provides an individual the opportunity to enact his/her problem rather than just talking about it. Dr. Jacob Levy Moreno, M.D., created and introduced psychodrama (1921) in Austria. The technique includes verbal, nonverbal, and physical movement actions. Sociodrama and role playing are techniques based on psychodrama models.

Psychodrama, a very powerful tool, is intended for use by those trained in the technique. Emotional problem solving, development of helping relationships, acceptance, honesty, self-observations, group observations, and understanding of one's problems are all part of the approach.

Psychodrama is a structured experience in which the therapist participates actively in what is discussed. It is a technique used with groups, generally; others in the group take part in the psychodrama. (See ROLE PLAYING and SOCIODRAMA.)

References: Howard A. Blatner, *Acting-In,* New York: Springer Publishing Company, Inc., 1973; Ira A. Greenberg (Editor), *Group Hypnotherapy and Hypnodrama,* Chicago: Nelson-Hall, Inc., 1977; Jacob Moreno, et al., *The First Psychodramatic Family,* Beacon, NY: Beacon House, 1964; Adaline Starr, *Rehearsal for Living,* Chicago: Nelson-Hall, Inc., 1977.

PSYCHOLINGUISTICS, an interdisciplinary science (psychology and linguistics) that focuses on the mental processes that form the base of language and its use (i.e. human ability to speak and understand language). This field of study covers a broad range of topics. The nature of human languages versus animal language, structure of language, linguistic units and speech behavior, the psychological base for the meaning of words, grammar and speech, language acquisition, symbolism, and language and speech disorders are the generally accepted areas of study for psycholinguists. Within these groupings are found subtopics such as cognition, transformational generative grammar (initially developed by Noam Chomsky, 1957), word association, semantic meaning of words, syntax, phonological features and performances, speech perceptions, theory of language acquisition, and language and cognitive development. Psycholinguistic studies have had a major impact on reading and the teaching of reading in the schools. (See TRANSFORMATIONAL GENERATIVE GRAMMAR.)

References: Helen S. Cairns and Charles E. Cairns, *Psycholinguistics: A Cognitive View of Language,* New York: Holt, Rinehart and Winston, Inc., 1976; Alan Garnham, *Psycholinguistics: Central Topics,* London: Methuen and Co., 1985; Jean Berko Gleason (Editor), *The Development of Language,* Columbus, OH: Charles E. Merrill Publishing Company, 1985; Daniel R. Hittleman, *Developmental Reading: A Psycholinguistic Perspective,* Chicago: Rand McNally College Publishing Company, 1978.

PSYCHOLOGICAL BLOCK—See LEARNING BLOCK

PSYCHOLOGICAL-TESTING-IN-THE-SCHOOL CONTROVERSY, an issue that has been raised since the 1960s concerning the validity and reliability of many standardized tests administered to urban and/or rural school children. Criticisms made have been both educational and social in nature. Many of the concerns focus on the standardized intelligence tests administered to children with minority (i.e., different social, cultural, ethnic, non-English speaking, or racial) or rural backgrounds. They were not appropriate, it has been charged by some professionals and laymen alike, because many such tests were normed utilizing middle-class nonurban children whose background and life experiences were different from those of children who were not from traditional middle-class backgrounds. In addition, it has been charged, many minority and rural children are inappropriately placed in special school programs because their placements are/were based on such psychological test results. Many of the psychological tests have since been renormed or use urban based norms only. Nevertheless, there is still a concern that such psychological instruments are unfair when used with minority students.

Some psychological tests assess personalities and values. It has been charged by some that schools do not have a right to make such assessments, and that this is an invasion of the home and the rights of parents. Others have charged that a middle-class bias exists in such tests. (See NORMS and NORM GROUP.)

References: Frederick G. Brown, Guidelines for Test Use: A Commentary on the Standards for Educational and Psychological Tests, Washington, DC: National Council on Measurement in Education, 1980; Francesco Cordasco (Editor), The Bilingual-Bicultural Child and the Question of Intelligence, New York: Arno Press, 1978; Arthur R. Jensen, Bias in Mental Testing, New York: The Free Press, 1979; Mark N. Ozer, A Cybernetic Approach to the Assessment of Children: Toward a More Humane Use of Human Beings, Boulder, CO: Westview Press, 1979.

PSYCHOLOGIST, SCHOOL—See SCHOOL PSYCHOLOGIST

PSYCHOLOGY, a discipline that studies human behavior to explain the actions of people (how they feel, think, and react). The roots of psychology can be traced to Democritus (370 B.C.) who believed that human nature can be understood as a system. Plato, Aristotle, and Galen contributed to psychology through their attempts to understand, systematically, the structure and workings of man. Modern psychology can be traced to René Descartes (1596–1650). John Locke, George Berkeley, and David Hume all made significant contributions to the discipline's development. But it wasn't until the 19th century that psychology moved from being philosophical and theoretical to a discipline of testing and experimentation.

Although some psychologists may study behavior of other animals (rats, birds, dogs, etc.), the discipline's prime purpose is to focus on, and explain, human behaviors. There are many subdivisions of psychology. Three principal ones are: comparative psychology (comparison of behavior between various living organisms); clinical psychology (diagnosis and therapy for the correction of disorders); and developmental psychology (effects of growth on human behavior). Other specialized forms of psychology include child psychology, social psychology, industrial psychology, and adolescent psychology. (See AMERICAN PSYCHOLOGICAL ASSOCIATION; ANIMAL PSYCHOLOGY; CHILD PSYCHOLOGY; COLOR PSYCHOLOGY; COMPARATIVE PSYCHOLOGY; EDUCATIONAL PSYCHOLOGY; INDUSTRIAL PSYCHOLOGY; and SOCIAL PSYCHOLOGY.)

References: Richard S. Lazarus, The Riddle of Man, Englewood Cliffs, NJ: Prentice-Hall, Inc., 1974; Aaron Q. Sartain, et al., Psychology: Understanding Human Behavior (Fourth Edition), New York: McGraw-Hill Book Company, 1973; W. Porter Swift, General Psychology, New York: McGraw-Hill Book Company, 1969; Walter M. Vernon, Introductory Psychology (Second Edition, Revised), Chicago: Rand McNally College Publishing Company, 1976.

PSYCHOMOTOR DOMAIN, the third of three broad general classifications of behaviors found in the taxonomies of Benjamin Bloom and associates. (The other two domains are the cognitive and affective.) It covers those behaviors and objectives that emphasize or deal with motor skills. In 1956, when Bloom and his colleagues formulated their taxonomies, they did not develop specific psychomotor taxonomies; rather, they simply "recognized the existence of this domain."

Robert Kibler, Larry Baker, and David Miles (1970) developed a classification of the psychomotor domain made up of gross bodily movements, finely coordinated bodily movements, nonverbal communication behaviors, and speech behaviors. (They were not necessarily placed in a hierarchical order of skills, as would be the case in a taxonomy.) Gross Bodily Movements (1.00) were divided into movements involving the Upper Limbs (1.10), Lower Limbs (1.20), and Two or More Bodily Limbs (1.30). Finely Coordinated Movements (2.00) include Hand-Finger Movements (2.10), Hand-Eye Coordination (2.20), Hand-Ear Coordination (2.30), Hand-Eye-Foot Coordination (2.40), and Other Combinations of Hand-Foot-Eye-Ear Movements (2.50). Nonverbal Communications (3.00) includes Facial Expression (3.10), Gestures (3.20), and Bodily Movements (3.30). Finally, Speech Behaviors (4.00) are made up of Sound Production (4.10), Sound-Word Formation (4.20), Sound Projection (4.30), and Sound-Gesture Coordination (4.40).

Although the behaviors in the psychomotor domain are considered by many as concerns of physical education, home economics, industrial education, and other similar disciplines, there is a general recognition on the part of educators that the psychomotor domain is an important part of total human behavior. Psychomotor behaviors are found in all learning environments. This domain, authorities stress, must be considered a part of most, if not all, classroom activities. (See AFFECTIVE DOMAIN and COGNITIVE DOMAIN.)

References: Benjamin S. Bloom, et al., *Taxonomy of Educational Objectives: Handbook I, Cognitive Domain*, New York: David McKay Company, Inc., 1956; Robert J. Kibler, et al., *Behavioral Objectives and Instruction*, Boston: Allyn and Bacon, Inc., 1970; Robert N. Singer (Editor), *The Psychomotor Domain: Movement Behaviors*, Philadelphia: Lea and Febiger, 1972.

PSYCHOMOTOR SKILLS, those skills that include the action or coordination of the mind and the muscle (i.e. muscular movements are the direct result of a mental process). Psychomotor skills are extremely important in the development of children. For example, handwriting would be impossible without fine motor coordination and control. Speaking requires psychomotor skills in the movement of the tongue and jaw muscles. Running and sitting require movements of various muscles. Playing any game or sport requires various psychomotor skills.

From the time a child is born, his/her psychomotor skills are developing. Schools are responsible for seeing that students' psychomotor skills are developed along with their cognitive and affective skills. Many learning problems, authorities indicate, may be a direct result of poor psychomotor skill development. (See AFFECTIVE DOMAIN; COGNITIVE DOMAIN; and PSYCHOMOTOR DOMAIN.)

References: Daniel D. Arnheim and William A. Sinclair, *The Clumsy Child*, St. Louis, MO: C. V. Mosby Company, 1975; Ray H. Barsch, *Perceptual-Motor Curriculum*, Seattle, WA: Special Child Publications, 1967; Louise Skinner, *Motor Development in the Preschool Years*, Springfield, IL: Charles C. Thomas, Publisher, 1979.

PSYCHOSIS, a severe mental state (mental illness) characterized by ignoring of reality and seriously disordered behavior. This disorder has several classifications. The most common is schizophrenic. *Schizophrenic reactions*, in turn, can be broken down into: paranoid, catatonic, hebephrenic, simple, schizo-affective, and other subclassifications. Another group of psychoses are *affective reactions:*

pooled-depressed and manic. *Psychoneurotic* and *personality* are two other classifications of psychosis. All of them are considered acute psychotic types.

Psychosis can be associated with any of several factors. They include heterosexual rejection, drugs, adolescent psychosexual development, childbirth, and marital stress. Psychotic development is influenced by character structure, human (physical) development itself, interpersonal interactions, and the alteration of consciousness. Because psychosis is a complex mental illness, it requires treatment by competent medical and psychological personnel.

References: Malcolm B. Bowers, *Retreat from Sanity*, New York: Human Sciences Press, 1974; Hans J. Eysenck and Sybil B. G. Eysenck, *Psychoticism as a Dimension of Personality*, London, England: Hodder and Stoughton, 1976; Maurice Lorr, *Exploration in Typing Psychotics*, Oxford, England: Pergamon Press, Inc., 1966; M. Schou and E. Stromgren (Editors). *Origin, Prevention and Treatment of Affective Disorders*, London, England: Academic Press, 1979.

PUBERTY, the period in the development of boys and girls when secondary sexual characteristics develop and the organs of reproduction become functional. During this period, a significant growth spurt (increased height and weight, muscular development, physical changes in the body, and changes in the circulation of hormones) normally takes place. (*Pubescere*, in Latin, means "to grow hair").

Puberty can last for several years. It generally marks the beginning of adolescence. However, there is no consensus among psychologists concerning the exact relationship of puberty to adolescence. During puberty, boys and girls usually experience psychological and physiological adjustment difficulties, many brought on by the fact that they are frequently perceived to be neither children nor adults. Relationships with friends, teachers, and parents can change drastically during this period. Although boys normally reach puberty between the ages of 13½ and 14 years, and girls between 12 and 13 years, there is considerable variability among individuals. Some girls have reached puberty at age 10 but others have not done so until age 15. Similar variability exists for boys. Many cultures throughout the world observe puberty as a significant event and have special rituals or services to mark it. (See ADOLESCENCE.)

References: Sylvia Brody and Sidney Axelrod, *Mothers, Fathers, and Children*, New York: International Universities Press, Inc., 1978; Yehudi A. Cohen, *The Transaction from Childhood to Adolescence,* Chicago: Aldine Publishing Company, 1964; Boyd R. McCandless, *Adolescents: Behavior and Development,* Hinsdale, IL: The Dryden Press, 1970; Barbara Baker Sommer, *Puberty and Adolescence,* Oxford, England: Oxford University Press, 1978.

PUBLIC LAW 94–142, the Education for All Handicapped Children Act of 1975, a revision of previously enacted legislation (Public Law 93–380) that also dealt with education of the handicapped. Public Law 98–199 (enacted in 1983) and Public Law 99–457 (passed in 1986) amended the Education for All Handicapped Children Act of 1975. The laws cover children and students who are enrolled in preschool, elementary, secondary, and adult education programs. PL 94–142 was enacted to improve educational opportunities for the estimated 8,000,000 handicapped children in the United States (of whom 1,000,000 were then excluded from the public schools). The act was designated to achieve four objectives: (1) assuring that all handicapped children have free public and appropriate education available to them; (2) assuring that the rights of handicapped children and their parents are protected; (3) helping states and local communities to provide adequate education for the handicapped; and (4) assessing, in a quality control sense, the education of such children. These laws provide federal funds to state and local educational agencies. States applying for funds must submit a State Annual Program Plan to the U.S. Secretary of Education. This plan must show how the laws, and their subsequent regulations, are complied with throughout the state. (See HANDICAPPED INDIVIDUALS; INDIVIDUAL EDUCATION PLAN; LEAST RESTRICTIVE ENVIRONMENT; MAINSTREAMING; *MILLS v. DISTRICT OF COLUMBIA BOARD OF EDUCATION;* and *PARC DECISION.)*

References: Bureau of Education for the Handicapped, *Progress Toward a Free Appropriate Public Education: A Report to Congress on the Implementation of Public Law 94–142, The Education for All Handicapped Children Act,* Washington, DC: U.S. Office of Education, January 1979; Council for Exceptional Children, *Public Law 99–457, the Education of the Handicapped Act, Amendments of 1986,* Reston, VA: The Council, 1987; National School Public Relations Association, *Educating All the Handicapped: What the Laws Say and What Schools Are Doing,* Arlington, VA: The Association, 1977; Public Law 94–142, *Education for All Handicapped Children Act of 1975,* in *United States Code: Congressional and Administrative News,* 94th Congress-First Session, 1975, St. Paul, MN: West Publishing Company, 1975; Marilyn Rauth, *The Education for All Handicapped Children Act (PL 94–142): Preserving Both Children's and*

Teacher's Rights, Washington, DC: American Federation of Teachers, AFL-CIO, Undated Booklet, No. 436; H. Rutherford Turnbull, III, *Free Appropriate Public Education, the Law and Children with Disabilities,* Denver, CO: Love Publishing Co., 1986.

PUBLIC LAW 98–199—See PUBLIC LAW 94–142

PUBLIC LAW 98–377—See EDUCATION FOR ECONOMIC SECURITY ACT

PUBLIC LAW 98–524—See PERKINS (CARL D.) VOCATIONAL EDUCATION ACT

PUBLIC LAW 99–457—See PUBLIC LAW 94–142

PUBLIC LAWS 815 and **874,** special-purpose grants enacted in 1950 by the U.S. Congress. Sometimes referred to as impacted-areas legislation, these laws provide special funding to school districts enrolling relatively large numbers of children whose parents work or live on federal property or whose parents are engaged in other federally connected activities. Public Law 815 makes school building construction aid available to eligible school systems. Public Law 874 provides funds for current operations. (See IMPACT AID.)

References: Oscar T. Jarvis, et al., *Public School Business Administration and Finance: Effective Policies and Practices,* West Nyack, NY: Parker Publishing Company, Inc., 1967; Public Laws 815 and 874, *United States Statutes at Large* (Volume 64, Part I), Washington, DC: U.S. Government Printing Office, 1952.

PUBLIC RELATIONS, or external relations, the relationship that an organization establishes with its public. Its overriding purpose, one author (Robert Ross) averred, is to assist the organization to obtain and maintain a positive and prosperous social climate. Another authority (Philip Lesly) saw public relations as being more than publicity. Rather, he wrote, it "can be defined as helping an organization and its publics accommodate to each other" (p. 632). Although larger organizations, including school systems, employ specialists to manage their public relations programs, every member of the unit, regardless of its size, has some responsibility for contributing to effective relationships with the public.

Numerous purposes have been associated with school public relations programs. Some of the major ones are: (1) to keep the public informed; (2)

to establish confidence in the schools; (3) to strengthen the parent-school partnership to the advantage of students; and (4) to develop an appreciation of education's potential.

Most school systems utilize a variety of public relations approaches including: (1) provision of opportunities for citizen participation; (2) preparation of special school publications; (3) use of newspapers, radio, and television; and (4) sponsorship of information meetings.

References: James J. Jones and Irving W. Stout, *School Public Relations: Issues and Cases*, New York: G. P. Putnam's Sons, 1960; Philip Lesly (Editor), *Lesly's Public Relations Handbook* (Second Edition), Englewood Cliffs, NJ: Prentice-Hall, Inc., 1978; Robert D. Ross, *The Management of Public Relations: Analysis and Planning External Relations*, New York: John Wiley and Sons, 1977.

PUBLIC SCHOOL, an elementary or secondary school in the United States that is: (1) tax supported; (2) universal; and (3) available free of charge to the children of a community's legal residents. The term is sometimes used when referring to a public school building. In Great Britain, "public schools" are endowed (actually private) secondary schools.

Various forms of public schools existed in the American colonies during the 17th and 18th centuries. By the 1820s, common schools were operating in numerous communities. Enrollments grew steadily throughout the 19th and 20th centuries, reaching a total (K–12) enrollment of almost 48,000,000 in 1978.

In his 1893 book, *The Public School System of the United States,* J. M. Rice identified four elements that, at the time, were exerting influence on the public schools: (1) the public at large; (2) the boards of education; (3) the superintendent and his staff; and (4) the teachers. In recent years, the courts and the U.S. Congress have begun to exert such influence as well. In spite of interventions by the courts and Congress, the American public schools remain virtually unique in that they are decentralized and controlled largely by the communities in which they are located.

Educational historians have attributed numerous successes and shortcomings to the American public school movement. One such historian, Lawrence Cremin, noted that the public school has never functioned independently or in isolation. He attributed its successes, when they have occurred, to "a configuration of education that has usually included families, churches, and Sunday schools, all committed to similar or complementary values"

(p. 58). Others, usually students of educational administration, have long fought for a suitable finance base to support the public school on the grounds that cost and quality tend to be correlative.

References: Lawrence A. Cremin, *Public Education*, New York: Basic Books, Inc., Publishers, 1976; Nancy B. Dearman and Valena W. Plisko, *The Condition of Education, 1980 Edition*, Washington, DC: National Center for Education Statistics, U.S. Department of Education, 1980; Brian Gardner, *The Public School: A Historical Survey*, London, England: Hamish Hamilton, 1973; Richard Pratte, *The Public School Movement: A Critical Study*, New York: David McKay Company, Inc., 1973; J. M. Rice, *The Public School System of the United States*, New York: The Century Company, 1893 (Reprinted in 1969 by Arno Press and the New York Times).

PUPIL ACCOUNTING, also known as child accounting, a record-keeping system for maintaining significant information about students. Comprising pupil accounting are activities such as admission and registration of students, attendance, school census, discipline, and work permits. In school districts, pupil accounting is usually carried out at both the building and central office levels.

References: Carter V. Good (Editor), *Dictionary of Education* (Third Edition), New York: McGraw-Hill Book Company, 1973; William E. Hopke (Editor), *Dictionary of Personnel and Guidance Terms: Including Professional Agencies and Associations*, Chicago: J. G. Ferguson Publishing Company, 1968.

PUPIL-ACTIVITY FUND, a financial record (fund) of student-activity transactions (expenditures and receipts) that are school sponsored. Such activities (e.g. athletic events, plays) are supported, from pupils, tickets of admission, and gate receipts.

Reference: Combined Glossary: Terms and Definitions from the Handbooks of the State Educational Records and Reports Series, Washington, DC: National Center for Education Statistics, U.S. Department of Health, Education, and Welfare, 1974.

PUPIL PERSONNEL SERVICES, the supportive services that assist children in educational, career, and personal/social development. They include the areas of guidance, placement, counseling services, appraisal and assessment services, attendance, school social work, information services, follow-up services, and health. The term *pupil personnel services* is being replaced by the newer *student personnel services.* (See DIRECTOR OF PUPIL PERSONNEL SERVICES.)

References: Donald G. Mortensen and Allen M. Schmuller, *Guidance in Today's Schools* (Third Edition), New

York: John Wiley and Sons, 1976; Merle Ohlsen, *Guidance Services in the Modern School* (Second Edition), New York: Harcourt Brace Jovanovich, Inc., 1974; John J. Pietrofesa, et al., *Counseling: Theory, Practice and Research*, Chicago: Rand McNally College Publishing Company, 1978.

PUPIL-TEACHER RATIO, a statistic sometimes used to report class size. This measure is generally employed to compare one local school building against others. Pupil-teacher ratio is determined by dividing the total number of students in a building by the total number of teachers assigned to that building (PTR = Total students/Total teachers). Much of this measure's lack of reliability reflects the fact that the term *teacher* is not uniformly defined from one school or one school district to another. In some instances, for example, supervisors are considered to be teachers; in other cases, they are not. (See CLASS SIZE and NUMERICAL STAFFING ADEQUACY.)

References: Class Size (Reference and Resource Series), Washington, DC: National Education Association, 1977; Paul J. Porwoll, *Class Size: A Summary of Research*, Arlington, VA: Educational Research Service, Inc., 1978.

PURCHASE ORDER, written instrument issued by an authorized official (e.g. school district purchasing agent) for the purchase of supplies, materials, or services. Purchase orders are directed to specific vendors once all required bidding procedures, if any, have been completed. The order form normally includes: (1) complete description of materials requested; (2) the quantity desired; (3) delivery instructions; (4) unit price; and (5) a purchase order number.

References: John Greenhalgh, *Practitioner's Guide to School Business Management*, Boston: Allyn and Bacon, Inc., 1978; Sam B. Tidwell, *Financial and Managerial Accounting for Elementary and Secondary School Systems*, Chicago: The Research Corporation Association of School Business Officials, 1974.

PURCHASE REQUISITION—See REQUISITION

PURCHASING, in education the ordering and procurement of school materials, instructional and noninstructional. Percy Burrup pointed out several tasks and problems attendant to the purchasing process, including the following: (1) determining the materials needed; (2) ascertaining quantity and quality of materials to be purchased; (3) synchronizing need and delivery times; (4) procuring the quality of material needed while not exceeding budgetary constraints; (5) keeping unsuccessful bidders happy; and (6) explaining to school personnel why the quality or manufacture of a requested item may not accord exactly with the item purchased.

School board policies normally specify how and by whom purchasing may be implemented. Such policies standardize procedures, an important safeguard for both the school district and the designated purchasing official. Authorities recommend that purchasing policies specify factors such as the need for specifications, bidding procedures, and standardization of items purchased in large quantity.

Large school districts maintain full-time purchasing personnel who, in addition to the aforementioned duties, are also responsible for maintaining current vendor lists, overseeing supply storage and distribution, and maintaining inventory systems. (See BIDDING CYCLE and COMPETITIVE BIDS.)

References: Percy E. Burrup, *Financing Education in a Climate of Change* (Second Edition), Boston: Allyn and Bacon, Inc., 1977; John Greenhalgh, *Practitioner's Guide to School Business Management*, Boston: Allyn and Bacon, Inc., 1978.

PUSH, OPERATION—See OPERATION PUSH

Q

QUADRIVIUM—See TRIVIUM AND QUAD-RIVIUM

QUARTER, ACADEMIC, one of four terms making up the academic calendar for colleges and universities. Collectively, the first three quarters are about the same length as a two semester academic calendar (about 38 weeks) and constitute the work of one academic year. The fourth quarter is usually a summer school term.

Students attending a college/university employing the quarter system do not take as many courses during a quarter as do their counterparts taking courses during a regular semester. There are advantages to the quarter system. They are: More frequent advising and counseling; more frequent articulation with high schools and other colleges; and more flexibility in offering modular courses. There are disadvantages, too: costs involved in starting and stopping a new term; possible time pressures on students; and more frequent registration.

Most colleges follow the regular two-semesters-per-academic-year plan. (See SEMESTER.)
References: Asa S. Knowles (Editor), *Handbook of College and University Administration,* New York: McGraw-Hill Book Company, 1970; Lloyd C. Oleson, "Calendars, Academic" in Asa S. Knowles (Editor), *The International Encyclopedia of Higher Education* (Volume 3), San Francisco: Jossey-Bass Publishers, 1977; Richard J. Petersen and Geneva C. Davis, *Education Directory, Colleges and Universities, 1979–80,* Washington, DC: National Center for Education Statistics, U.S. Department of Education, May 1980.

QUARTILE, one of three points that separate a distribution of scores into four equal parts: (1) the highest quarter; (2) the high middle quarter; (3) the low middle quarter; and (4) the lowest quarter. The lowest 25 percent of the scores are included in the lowest quarter, and the highest 25 percent in the highest quarter. Through mathematical interpolation, the two middle quarters can be determined. The two middle quarters are called the interquartile range.
References: Frederick T. Gravetter and Larry B. Wallman, *Statistics for the Behavioral Sciences: A First Course for Students of Psychology and Education,* St. Paul, MN: West Publishing Company, 1985; Norman E. Gronlund, *Measurement and Evaluation in Teaching* (Fifth Edition), New York: Macmillan Publishing Company, 1985.

QUASI-EXPERIMENTAL DESIGN, a broad term used to describe research designs in which full experimental conditions (control) are not present. Lack of randomization, for example, may be one of the missing conditions. Another illustration involves the use of intact groups (classes) such as those found in many schools that may have to be involved in an experiment. The researcher has no option but to use them if he/she wants to proceed with the experiment. By using such nonrandomized groups, the internal and external validity of the design and results may be subject to question.

There are different quasi-experimental designs that, if followed, can enhance the validity of a study and its results. They include time series; counterbalanced designs; separate-sample pre-post-test, separate-sample pre-post-test control group design; and multiple-time series. (See VALIDITY.)
References: Donald T. Campbell and Julian C. Stanley, *Experimental and Quasi-Experimental Designs for Research,* Chicago: Rand McNally and Company, 1963; L. R. Gay, *Educational Research: Competencies for Analysis and Application* (Third Edition), Columbus, OH: Merrill Publishing Company, 1987; William Wiersma, *Research Methods in Education* (Third Edition), Itasca, IL: F. E. Peacock Publishers, Inc., 1980.

QUESTIONING, instructional interrogation employed by a teacher to make students think, to call attention to a particular subject, or to seek answers. Research on teacher questioning indicates that: (1) next to lecturing, teachers spend more time posing questions than expressing any other verbal utterance; (2) pupils' thought patterns, as expressed through recitation, relate closely to teachers' questions; and (3) pupil behavior is influenced by teachers' questions.

Several systems for classifying questions have been proposed. One authority (Ronald Hyman) suggested that there are four cognitive process kinds of questions, the first three of which are manifest in classrooms on a fairly regular basis. They are: (1) *definitional* questions, those that require a student to define a word or phrase (e.g. What is Agriculture?); (2) *empirical* questions, questions that require the student not only to recall the facts but to see relationships among them using his/her sense perceptions (e.g. Would the United States have been involved in World War II if we had a Republican president in 1940?); (3) *evaluative* questions, queries seeking opinions and/or justifications for those opinions (e.g. Why do you like that painting?); and (4) *metaphysical* questions, those that seek theological beliefs (e.g. Is God dead?).

Two reading authorities (Larry Harris and Carl Smith) proposed another four-category classification system, this one related directly to their own field of specialization. The categories are: (1) *identification*, requiring the reader to recall or locate information; (2) *analysis*, requiring reasoning based on reading; (3) *evaluation*, judging information against a standard; and (4) *application*, requiring one to do something with information read.

References: Larry A. Harris and Carl B. Smith, *Reading Instruction: Diagnostic Teaching in the Classroom* (Second Edition), New York: Holt, Rinehart and Winston, Inc., 1976; Ronald T. Hyman, *Strategic Questioning*, Englewood Cliffs, NJ: Prentice-Hall, Inc., 1979; Robert W. Richey, *Planning for Teaching: An Introduction to Education* (Sixth Edition), New York: McGraw-Hill Book Company, 1979.

QUESTIONNAIRE, instrument (form) distributed to prospective respondents for the purpose of gathering facts, opinions, interests, or attitudes. The validity of the questionnaire method for gathering such information depends on the representativeness of the sample to whom instruments are directed and on the truthfulness (accuracy) of the respondents. Many authorities have come to question the scientific value of this method because representativeness and truthfulness are difficult to establish.

Items included in a questionnaire may be open-ended questions. Steps that are believed to encourage relatively high return rates include: (1) inclusion of a brief cover letter in which the purpose of the survey is explained; (2) sponsor is identified; (3) instructions for completion are clear; (4) items are objective; (5) format is attractive; (6) instrument length is kept to a minimum; and (7) where possible, the respondent remains anonymous.

References: John W. Best, *Research in Education* (Third Edition), Englewood Cliffs, NJ: Prentice-Hall, Inc., 1977; Earl J. McCallon and Emajean McCray, *Designing and Using Questionnaires*, Austin, TX: Learning Concepts, 1975.

QUINCY GRAMMAR SCHOOL, a landmark elementary school made innovative in 1848 by John D. Philbrick (1818–86). Located in Boston, the school was organized on a grade-level basis with one teacher assigned to each grade. Single desks were used instead of two-pupil ones. Drawing and music were added to the curriculum of the time. This new organizational structure grew in popularity and became the forerunner of the self-contained classroom, an organizational arrangement still used widely in American elementary schools. (See SELF-CONTAINED CLASSROOM.)

References: Virgil E. Herrick, et al., *The Elementary School*, Englewood Cliffs, NJ: Prentice-Hall, Inc., 1956; National Elementary Principal, *Elementary School Organization: Purposes, Patterns, Perspective*, Washington, DC: National Educational Association, 1961.

QUINMESTER PLAN, a year-round school plan that divides the school year into five nine-week sessions. In the Dade County Public Schools, Florida, where the plan was pioneered at the secondary school level (1971) and used up to 1978, quinmester students were required to attend school during any four of the 45-day quinmesters, thus satisfying the state's attendance requirement of 180 school days. Advantages cited by supporters of the quinmester plan included the following: (1) curriculum innovation, a claim based on the fact that a variety of minicourses were developed in each subject field to fit the 45-day schedule; (2) its year-round character that, theoretically at least, permits acceleration for the student willing to enroll in five quinmesters a year; and (3) a variety of vacation options for both teachers and students. (See MINICOURSE.)

References: Debra D. Nygaard, *Evaluations of Year-Round School Programs*, Arlington, VA: Educational Research Service, Inc., 1974; National School Public Relations Association, *Year-Round School; Districts Develop Successful Programs*, Washington, DC: The Association, 1971; Glenys G. Unruh and William M. Alexander, *Innovations in Secondary Education* (Second Edition), New York: Holt, Rinehart and Winston, Inc., 1974.

RACE, a biological term used to designate related populations possessing identifiable and hereditary (transmittable) characteristics. It refers to a breeding population that, for reasons of geography or culture, tends to breed within itself. Scientists often use the term broadly to distinguish groups of fish, birds, and so on, as well as man.

Among humans, races evolved as man began to migrate and to settle in different parts of the globe. Variations in skin color, physical characteristics, and blood chemistry developed as adaptations to climate or because of isolating barriers. UNESCO, which has issued several formal statements on race (with the help of prominent scientists), in its *First Statement* concurred with most anthropologists that present-day mankind can be classified into three major racial divisions: (1) Mongoloid; (2) Negroid; and (3) Caucasoid.

Race is a collective (group) term; however, not all individuals within a race possess all the characteristics used to identify a given population. This fact notwithstanding, as sociologists are aware, unsupportable efforts have been made throughout history to label individuals (usually along inferiority-superiority lines) solely on the basis of racial affiliation. Well-known examples of such efforts (racism) have included Nazi Germany's anti-Semitic Nürnberg laws that forbade marriage between Jews and Germans and miscegination statutes that existed in several American states until being ruled unconstitutional in 1966.

References: Richard A. Goldsby, *Race and Races*, New York: The Macmillan Company, 1971; Ashley Montagu, *Statement on Race* (Third Edition), New York: Oxford University Press, 1972.

RACIAL BALANCE, a goal achieved when the racial makeup of a school is approximately equal to the racial composition of the total community. For example, in a school district with an 80 percent white-20 percent black racial makeup, the system is considered to be balanced racially if that 80–20 percent ratio is reflected, approximately, in the enrollments of the individual schools.

References: Carter V. Good (Editor), *Dictionary of Education* (Third Edition), New York: McGraw-Hill Book Company, 1973; National School Public Realtions Association, *Desegregation: How Schools Are Meeting Historic Challenge*, Arlington, VA: The Association, 1973; Nancy H. St. John, *School Desegregation Outcomes for Children*, New York: John Wiley and Sons, 1975.

RACIAL INTEGRATION—See INTEGRATION, RACIAL

RACIAL SEGREGATION—See SEGREGATION, RACIAL

RACISM, defined (1970) by the United States Commission on Civil Rights as any attitude, action, or institutional structure that subordinates a person or group because of his/her race or color. Racism may be unintentional, with one individual not consciously aware that he/she is relegating another individual to some inferior position for reasons of race or color, or it may be carried out overtly. In the United States, racism normally takes the form of white supremacy and black (also Native American, Hispanic) inferiority, a phenomenon some historians have traced to early Europe and one reinforced by the period of slavery in America.

The psychological effect of racism on certain American minority groups has been telling. Commenting on this from the perspective of black children, Psychologist Kenneth Clark has written: "By the age of seven, most Negro children have accepted the reality that they are, after all, dark skinned. But the stigma remains; they have been forced to recognize themselves as inferior. Few if any Negroes ever fully lose that sense of shame and self-hatred" (p. 78).

Studies of school systems and school practices have identified several manifestations of institutional racism. They include: (1) failure to provide minority students with worthy role models, a failure attributed to institutional hiring practices; (2) failure to recognize the achievements of minority people in the schools' curricula or instructional materials; (3) low expectations of minority students; and (4) until recently, limited postsecondary educational opportunities for minority students.

References: Kenneth B. Clark, "The Psychology of the Ghetto" in David M. Reimers (Editor), *Racism in the United States: An American Dilemma?* New York: Holt, Rinehart and Winston, Inc., 1972; Institute for the Study of Educational Policy, *Equal Educational Opportunity: More Promise Than Progress*, Washington, DC: Howard University Press, 1978; Phi Delta Kappa Teacher Education Project on Human Rights, *A Guide for Improving Public School Practices in Human Rights*, Bloomington, IN: Phi Delta Kappa, 1975.

RANDOM ACCESS MEMORY (RAM), one of two major types of internal memory used in a computer. RAM can be written to or read from. Information stored in RAM can be changed; thus, it is called a destructive write; permanent (nondestructive read) information is stored in Read Only Memory (ROM). When the power is turned off, everything in RAM is automatically erased. Even a short interruption in the power supplied to the computer will erase RAM. In most personal computers, RAM holds the application program being used, the data used by that application program, and anything else that changes frequently. (See INTERNAL MEMORY and READ ONLY MEMORY.)

References: Grace Murray Hopper and Steven L. Mandell, *Understanding Computers*, St. Paul, MN: West Publishing Company, 1984; David R. Sullivan, et al., *Computing Today: Microcomputer Concepts and Application*, Boston: Houghton Mifflin Company, 1985.

RANDOM NUMBERS—See TABLE OF RANDOM NUMBERS

RANDOM SAMPLING, a technique used to select participants or objects from a larger group of objects or population such that every person or object in the larger group or population has an equal and independent chance of being selected. The purpose of a random sample approach is to develop a small group that will be representative of the larger group of objects or population from which it came. The results obtained from the random sample can then be assumed to be true of the larger group or population. If carried out correctly, random sampling is both effective and cost/time efficient. It is used extensively in educational survey and industrial research projects.

Random sampling can be done without replication (once a person or object is selected, the person or object is removed from further consideration) or with replication (the person or object, even though selected, can be selected again). In a lottery, a winner would rather have random sampling with replication for obvious reasons.

There are times when a simple random sample approach is not appropriate. For example, if 30 percent of a given population is made up of individuals with incomes over $70,000, 40 percent with incomes from $40,000 to 70,000, and 30 percent with incomes below $40,000, and the researcher wants to be sure that the sample reflects these income proportions, a stratified random sample should be used. The *stratified random sample* approach would require that 30 percent of the sample would randomly be selected from the upper income group, 40 percent from the middle income group, and 30 percent from the lowest income group of the given population.

References: L. R. Gay, *Educational Research: Competencies for Analysis and Application* (Third Edition), Columbus, OH: Merrill Publishing Company, 1987; W. James Popham, *Educational Evaluation* (Second Edition), Englewood Cliffs, NJ: Prentice-Hall, 1988; Bill Williams, *A Sampler on Sampling*, New York: John Wiley and Sons, 1978.

RANGE, a very general measure of statistical variability. In any group of numbers (including scores), the distance between the highest and lowest of these constitutes the range. Range indicates "spread" or "scatter" and is of some use when between-group comparisons are made. To illustrate, one might speak of the temperature highs and lows for Monday as being 47–81 degrees and 61–78 degrees for Tuesday. Tuesday's range was relatively smaller than Monday's. In schools, ranges are of some use in comparing test scores for different groups of students. The problem with using the range is that it depends upon only two scores.

References: Joy P. Guilford and Benjamin Fruchter, *Fundamental Statistics in Psychology and Education* (Sixth Edition), New York: McGraw-Hill Book Company, 1978; Celeste McCollough and Loche Van Atta, *Introduction to Descriptive Statistics and Correlation: A Program for Self-Instruction*, New York: McGraw-Hill Book Company, 1965.

RAPPORT, the quality of the relationship between two or more people. Good rapport exists when individuals have mutual respect for each other in a warm and accepting environment. In the classroom, good rapport, whether teacher-pupil or pupil-pupil, is an important educational consideration, because it can facilitate learning and the development of positive interpersonal relationships.

The technique for establishing rapport between two or more individuals is a function of factors such as the physical and social environment, the personalities of the individuals involved, the reasons for being in the environment, age and/or age differences, past histories or experiences, and the congruency of goals on the part of the individuals. Although the techniques used to establish and maintain it are different for preschool, elementary, middle, high school, and college teachers, the basic factors are the same for all levels.

References: Leonard J. Clark and Irving S. Starr, *Secondary School Teaching Methods* (Third Edition), New York: Macmillan Publishing Company, Inc., 1976; Kenneth H.

Hoover, *Secondary/Middle School Teaching,* Boston: Allyn and Bacon, Inc., 1977; Melodie A. McCarthy and John P. Houston, *Fundamentals of Early Childhood Education,* Cambridge, MA: Winthrop Publishers, Inc., 1980.

RATING SCALES, instruments used to assess the quality of a particular trait, characteristic, or attribute with assessment usually based on predetermined criteria (scale). There are many types of rating scales. Some are numerical, such as those used by judges in sports (e.g. records, speed). Others are more descriptive (e.g. excellent, fair, very poor), and still others force the rater to decide whether the individual displays/demonstrates more of one trait than another (forced-choice). Other forms include graphics, check lists, and multiple-choice items.

Rating scales are frequently used as part of the psychological evaluation process. They can be used in personality assessment, in guidance, in the selection of careers, in evaluating teachers, and for ascertaining instructional effectiveness. Rating scales have limitations, because their use frequently reflects the limitations of the rater applying them. Subjectively, prior experience, bias, perceptions, memory, inaccurate observations, expectations, and pressures may also play a part in influencing rating. This is true even when a self-rating scale is used.

References: Lewis R. Aiken, Jr., *Psychological and Educational Testing,* Boston: Allyn and Bacon, Inc., 1971; Lou M. Carey, *Measuring and Evaluating School Learning,* Boston: Allyn and Bacon, Inc., 1988; Gilbert Sax, *Principles of Educational and Psychological Measurement and Evaluation* (Third Edition), Belmont, CA: Wadsworth Publishing Company, 1989.

RATIONAL COUNTING, or enumeration, the ability to count for the purpose of determining the number of objects in a group. Unlike rote counting, which has no mathematical meaning for the child, rational counting involves establishment of a one-to-one relationship (or correspondence) between a number name and an object. A teacher of young children who has them count the number of students present each day, or count books, is teaching rational counting. Authorities indicate that the physical touching of objects being counted facilitates mastery of rational counting. (See ONE-TO-ONE CORRESPONDENCE and ROTE COUNTING.)

References: Herbert Ginsburg, *Children's Arithmetic: The Learning Process,* New York: D. Van Nostrand Company, Inc., 1977; Donald D. Paige, et al., *Elementary Mathematical Methods,* New York: John Wiley and Sons, 1978.

RATIONAL-EMOTIVE THERAPY (RET), a counseling approach formulated by Albert Ellis. It is predicated on the belief that human beings are born with the capacity to do rational thinking as well as irrational thinking. Ellis identified several "irrational ideas" held by individuals that, in turn, produce (are causally related to) emotions that lead to various forms of self-criticism, even self-destruction. Examples of irrational ideas included: (1) "the idea that it is a dire necessity for an adult human being to be loved or approved by virtually every significant other person in his community" and, (2) "the idea that one should be thoroughly competent, adequate, and achieving in all possible respects if one is to consider oneself worthwhile" (Ellis, 1967, p. 84).

RET works to change the individual's personality by attacking his/her irrational self-destructing beliefs. The role of the RET counselor is to help the client formulate effective and rational goals and to substitute them for those predicated on irrational thinking. The approach may be used at the elementary, secondary, college, and adult levels.

References: Gerald Corey, *Theory and Practice of Counseling and Psychotherapy,* Monterey, CA: Brooks/Cole Publishing Company, 1977; Albert Ellis, *Reason and Emotion in Psychotherapy,* New York: Lyle Stuart, 1967; Albert Ellis, "The Rational-Emotive Approach to Counseling" in Herbert M. Burks, Jr. and Buford Stefflre, *Theories of Counseling* (Third Edition), New York: McGraw-Hill Book Company, 1979; John J. Pietrofesa, et al., *Guidance: An Introduction,* Chicago: Rand McNally College Publishing Company, 1980.

RATIONALISM, a philosophy based on the principle that reason is the base for reality. Faith, sense experiences, and fact, per se, are not seen as being the test of the truth of reality. Rather, logical relationships are viewed as the basis for establishing reality. Descartes, Spinoza, Leibniz, and Hegel are considered to have been rationalists, although each was different from the other in approach when addressing these questions: What is reality? and What is truth?

References: S. I. Benn and G. W. Mortimore (Editors), *Rationality and the Social Sciences,* London, England: Routledge and Kegan Paul, 1976; Charles E. Jarrett, et al. (Editors), *New Essays on Rationalism and Empiricism,* Guelph, Canada: Canadian Association for Publishing in Philosophy, 1978; Genevieve Rodis-Lewis, *Descartes et le Rationalisme,* Paris, France: Presses Universitaires de France, 1966.

RATIONAL NUMBERS, a mathematical term for that set of all integers that can be expressed in the form a/b or $a \div b$ where b is not zero. Rational numbers, essentially ratios between two integers, can be expressed as fractional numbers or as decimals.

References: Hunter Ballew, *Teaching Children Mathematics,* Columbus, OH: Charles E. Merrill Publishing Company, 1973; Donald F. Devine and Jerome E. Kaufmann, *Mathematics for Elementary Education,* New York: John Wiley and Sons, 1974.

RATIO SCALE—See DATA

RAW SCORE, the original score or number of points earned on a given test. If a student answers 85 items correctly on a test, his/her raw score is 85. If, on the other hand, a student were to receive 2 points for every correct answer, and he/she had 85 items correct, the raw score would be 170.

References: Lou M. Carey, *Measuring and Evaluating School Learning,* Boston: Allyn and Bacon, Inc., 1988; Gilbert Sax, *Principles of Educational and Psychological Measurement and Evaluation* (Third Edition), Belmont, CA: Wadsworth Publishing Company, 1989.

REACTION TIME, the time between the stimulation of a particular sensory organ (vision, hearing, feeling) and the organism's response to the stimulus. For example, the time between a child's placing his/her hand on a hot pan and the time the child removes his/her hand is called reaction time. Reaction time can be very short or relatively long. Depending on the desired outcomes, individuals can be trained to reduce reaction time or to increase it. In sports, it is usually the goal of the individual to reduce reaction time.

Reference: Kurt Schlesinger and Philip M. Groves, *Psychology: A Dynamic Science,* Dubuque, IA: Wm. C. Brown Company, Publishing, 1976.

READABILITY, a reading term that refers to the ease or difficulty with which a reader understands a printed passage. Teachers, textbook authors, and publishers each weigh readability carefully, knowing that textbooks that are too difficult for students to read are of little value to either student or teacher.

Various readiability formulas have been developed for the purpose of ascertaining the reading level of a given book. Representative passages are analyzed with attention given to factors such as average sentence length, number of "hard" words, and number of prepositional phrases. Since the early 1920s, several readability formulas have been published. Among the better known ones are those created by Irving Lorge, Edward Dolch, George Spache, Edgar Dale, Jeanne Chall, Rudolf Flesch, and Edward Fry.

References: Dolores Durkin, *Teaching Them to Read* (Fifth Edition), Boston: Allyn and Bacon, 1989; W. B. Gray, Jr., *How to Measure Readability,* Philadelphia: Dorrance and Company, 1975; Diane Lapp, James Flood, and Nancy Farnan, *Content Area Reading and Learning: Instructional Strategies,* Englewood Cliffs, NJ: Prentice-Hall, 1989; Robert S. Laubach and Kay Koschnick, *Using Readability: Formulas for Easy Adult Materials,* Syracuse, NY: New Readers Press, 1977.

READING, a process that involves the oral interpretation of written language. Some years ago, William Gray, noted authority on the subject, defined reading as a four-step process. The four steps, each interrelated with the other three, are: (1) *word perception,* the ability to recognize a printed word and to know its meaning; (2) *comprehension,* the ability to infer ideas from groups of words; (3) *reaction,* a step in which the reader interacts intellectually and emotionally with what has been read; and (4) *integration,* the absorbing of ideas read in the context of one's experience and making them a part of one's personal background. Apropos of the last step (integration), Lawrence Carrillo made this observation: "meaning obtained from a page derives from readers' experiential background and is not likely to be identified with the writer's intent. . . . (W)hen we read we *give* meaning to the print; we do not *take* meaning from it" (p. 2).

Reading may also be defined as the key element of the school curriculum. The teaching of reading, Miles Zintz pointed out, consists of four major tasks: (1) helping the learner to develop a basic sight vocabulary; (2) teaching word attack skills; (3) teaching that reading is a thinking, not a word-calling, process; and (4) providing the learner with considerable easy reading practice.

In recent years, a significant change has taken place with respect to teaching of reading—from meaning emphasis to code emphasis.

References: Lawrence W. Carrillo, *Teaching Reading: A Handbook,* New York: St. Martin's Press, 1976; Jeanne Chall, *Reading 1967–1977: A Decade of Change and Progress* (PDK Fastback 97). Bloomington, IN: The Phi Delta Kappa Educational Foundation, 1977; Dolores Durkin, *Teaching Them to Read* (Fifth Edition), Boston: Allyn and Bacon, 1989; William S. Gray, *On Their Own in Reading,* Chicago: Scott, Foresman and Company, 1948; Albert J. Harris and Edward R. Sipay, *How to Increase Reading Ability* (Eighth Edition), New York: Longman, Inc., 1985.

READING ACCELERATOR, a mechanical device for pacing reading. This reading machine has a moving shutter that exposes one line of printed material at a time. The rate at which the shutter moves down a page can be regulated. The accelerator is designed to increase the rate of reading by progressively shortening the time in which a line of print is exposed.

References: Emerald Dechant, *Diagnosis and Remediation of Reading Disability,* West Nyack, NY: Parker Publishing Company, Inc., 1968; Miles V. Zintz, *Corrective Reading* (Third Edition), Dubuque, IA: Wm. C. Brown Company, Publishers, 1977.

READING AGE, a student's level of reading ability stated in years. For example, a child whose reading level is comparable to that of the average 11-year-old is said to have a reading age of 11.

Reading test norms are used to determine reading age. Chronological age is not considered.

References: Diane Lapp and James Flood, *Teaching Reading to Every Child,* New York: Macmillan Publishing Company, Inc., 1978; Delwyn G. Schubert, *A Dictionary of Terms and Concepts in Reading* (Second Edition), Springfield, IL: Charles C. Thomas, Publisher, 1969.

READING CLUES—See CLUES (READING)

READING COMPREHENSION, the process of discriminating visual features that appear on a printed page and inferring meaning therefrom. The reader relies on his/her experience to gain such understanding, including the application of previously learned reading skills.

Reading authorities have identified three, sometimes four, levels of reading comprehension. They are: (1) *literal comprehension,* the simple understanding of ideas explicitly stated; (2) *interpretive comprehension,* the inference of ideas implied by the author; (3) *critical comprehension,* the ability to assess the accuracy or worth of materials read; and (4) *creative comprehension,* the ability to apply meaning to one's own life.

References: Albert J. Harris and Edward R. Sipay, *How to Increase Reading Ability* (Eighth Edition), New York: Longman, Inc., 1985; Arthur W. Heilman, Timothy R. Blair, and William H. Rupley, *Principles and Practices of Teaching Reading* (Sixth Edition), Columbus, OH: Charles E. Merrill Publishing Company, 1986.

READING GAMES, activities and devices of a fun nature with which children play but that are designed to foster interest in, or to provide practice with, some aspect of reading. Some games may be purchased commercially; others can be constructed by the teacher. The number and types of games are virtually endless. Examples are: matching exercises; crossword puzzles; vowel dominoes; card games; sight-word games; and picture riddles. Miles Zintz conceded the value of certain carefully chosen games but cautioned that their principal emphasis should be on skill acquisition rather than play per se.

References: Martha Langham and Nancy M. Peterson, *Open Your Cupboards to Learning Center Games: Activities for Reinforcing Math and Reading Skills for Teacher and Parent Involvement,* Phoenix, AZ: Skills Reinforcement Systems, 1975; D. F. Nicolson and Glenda M. C. Williams, *Word Games for the Teaching of Reading,* London, England: Pitman Publishing, 1975; Miles V. Zintz, *The Reading Process: The Teacher and the Learner,* Dubuque, IA: Wm. C. Brown Company, Publishers, 1970.

READING IS FUNDAMENTAL (RIF), a national nonprofit organization whose program is designed to motivate children to read. Although RIF is national in scope, most of its work is carried out by over 1,000 local community projects in the 50 states and the Virgin Islands.

Local projects are staffed by volunteers who choose and purchase a wide variety of paperback books for children, pre-Kindergarten through grade 12. Funds to purchase the books are raised locally with the help of civic, fraternal, and business organizations. Under the provisions of Congress's Inexpensive Book Distribution Program, 50 percent of the book costs are borne by the federal government.

Local book distributions take place at least three times annually. Children and their parents are invited to these distributions and are given books of their own choosing. RIF's popularity is based on two key, yet simple, ideas: freedom of choice (children select their own books), and pride of ownership (they get to keep the books).

RIF was conceived and organized by Mrs. Robert S. McNamara, the organization's first national chairperson. (See BASIC SKILLS AND EDUCATIONAL PROFICIENCY PROGRAMS and RIGHT TO READ.)

Reference: Reading Is Fundamental, Inc., *Reading Is Fundamental: 1977,* Washington, DC: RIF, 1977.

READING LEVELS, a rough indicator of the functional levels of reading for the individual. Generally determined by administering an Informal Reading Inventory (IRI), there are four levels of operation based upon familiarity with, and difficulty of the material:

1. The *dependent* level is the level at which there are almost no oral reading errors (< 2 percent) and ex-

cellent comprehension (> 90 percent). No assistance is necessary in reading.

2. The *instructional* level challenges the reader more. Oral reading may be conducted with 95 percent accuracy and comprehension can fall to 75 to 80 percent. It is assumed that teacher assistance is provided at this level.

3. The *frustration* level involves numerous difficulties with oral reading (error > 10 percent) and very poor comprehension of less than 50 percent. Material cannot, and should not, be read at this level.

4. The *capacity* level is the highest level of material understood when the passage is read to the individual. Comprehension is at the 75 percent level of accuracy.

Although these levels apply to all instructional material, the terms are usually used in referring to an individual's performance within a basal reading series.

References: Paul C. Burns, et al., *Teaching Reading in Today's Elementary Schools* (Third Edition), Boston: Houghton Mifflin Company, 1984; Patrick J. Finn, *Helping Children Learn to Read*, New York: Random House, 1984.

READING PREDICTION, the practice of predetermining success in reading. During the 1930s, 1940s, and 1950s, numerous reading readiness tests were developed for use with preprimary and primary grade students.

Early identification of successful readers involves the assessment of specific prereading skills. They include: (1) alphabet recognition, or letter knowledge; (2) whole-word recognition; (3) vocabulary; and (4) visual discrimination, or the ability to distinguish specific shapes and forms (e.g. b-d, saw-was). (See READING READINESS and VISUAL DISCRIMINATION.)

References: Dolores Durkin, *Teaching Them to Read* (Third Edition), Boston: Allyn and Bacon, Inc., 1978; Diane Lapp and James Flood, *Teaching Reading to Every Child*, New York: Macmillan Publishing Company, Inc., 1978.

READING RATE, the speed with which a student is able to read a passage containing a known number of words. Rates for oral and silent reading are different, particularly among intermediate grade and secondary school students. Researchers report that oral reading rate increases to 130–40 words a minute by the end of the third grade and generally levels off thereafter. Silent reading is also reported to average 130–40 words a minute at that grade level but continues to increase by approximately 10 words a year. The average American high school graduate reads 250 words a minute.

Several factors cause reading rates to fluctuate: (1) the reason, or purpose, for doing the reading; (2) the reader's general familiarity with the material being read; (3) the setting (e.g. lighting conditions); and (4) the reader's physical and/or psychological condition.

References: Dolores Durkin, *Teaching Them to Read* (Fifth Edition), Boston: Allyn and Bacon, 1989; Edward Fry, *Elementary Reading Instruction*, New York: McGraw-Hill Book Company, 1977; Edward Fry, *Reading Instruction for Classroom and Clinic*, New York: McGraw-Hill Book Company, 1972; Arthur W. Heilman, Timothy R. Blair, and William H. Rupley, *Principles and Practices of Teaching Reading* (Sixth Edition), Columbus, OH: Charles E. Merrill Publishing Company, 1986.

READING READINESS, a state of maturity and development that will permit a child to begin to learn to read. Several factors influence reading readiness: (1) social-emotional maturity; (2) intelligence; (3) physical factors (e.g. eye-hand coordination and visual-auditory discrimination); (4) understanding of oral language; (5) work habits; and (6) interest in reading. Classroom exercises and experiences designed to develop each of these factors need to be introduced by the teacher to facilitate readiness. They range from specific practice exercises such as matching of geometric forms to the displaying of attractive books in the classroom.

Numerous commercially prepared reading readiness tests are available to the teacher. Valid tests of this type serve two useful purposes: (1) predicting a child's readiness to read, and (2) diagnosis of specific reading skills. (See READING PREDICTION.)

References: Roger Farr and Nicholas Anastasiow, *Tests of Reading Readiness and Achievement: A Review and Evaluation*, Newark, DE: International Reading Association, 1971; Albert J. Harris and Edward R. Sipay, *How to Increase Reading Ability* (Eighth Edition), New York: Longman, Inc., 1985; Arthur W. Heilman, Timothy R. Blair, and William H. Rupley, *Principles and Practices of Teaching Reading* (Sixth Edition), Columbus, OH: Charles E. Merrill Publishing Company, 1986.

READING REVERSALS, a term referring to different types of perceptual errors. In some instances, individual letters are confused by the reader (e.g. *b* for *d*). In others, total words are reversed (e.g. *was* for *saw*). In still others, partial juxtaposition or confusion of letters is involved as when the student reads *ever* for *even* or *arm* for *ram*. In a fourth type of reversal, the reader juxtaposes words, thereby distorting sentence meaning (e.g. *The man chased the dog* is read as *The dog chased the man*).

Reading authorities note that occasional reversals are common among young (beginning) readers. Reversal patterns are considered serious, and symptomatic of visual perception problems, if: (1) the reversal is repeated regularly; (2) reversal patterns are apparent in different perception situations (words, letters, numbers, etc.); and (3) the reversal pattern persists over an extended period.

Numerous methods may be used by the teacher to correct remediable reversal problems. They include placing emphasis on left-to-right sequence in reading, kinesthetic exercises (e.g. tracing), and use of a pointer (pencil or finger) to guide reading. *References:* Albert J. Harris and Edward R. Sipay, *How to Increase Reading Ability: A Guide to Developmental and Remedial Methods* (Sixth Edition), New York: David McKay Company, Inc., 1975; Philip L. Safford, *Teaching Young Children with Special Needs,* St. Louis, MO: The C. V. Mosby Company, 1978.

READING SUPERVISOR, the individual in a school or school system responsible for designing, implementing, and evaluating the educational unit's total reading program. He/she may carry the title Reading Supervisor; another title commonly used is Director of Reading. Principal duties associated with this leadership post include: (1) helping individual classroom teachers; (2) material selection and distribution; (3) evaluating teachers; (4) assessing program via testing and/or personal observation; (5) diagnosis of student needs; and (6) sponsorship of inservice activities for teachers. *Reference:* Leslie A. Burg, et al., *The Complete Reading Supervisor: Tasks and Roles,* Columbus, OH: Charles E. Merrill Publishing Company, 1978.

READING TEXTBOOKS—See BASAL READERS

READ ONLY MEMORY (ROM), one of two major types of computer internal memory. ROM can be compared to a book because information can be read but not changed. ROM is used to build often-used programs into computers, whereas RAM (Random Access Memory) stores information that can be changed. In many personal computers, ROM stores operating instructions, a simple version of the BASIC programming language, and frequently used application programs. For example, the microprocessors in microwave ovens, cars, and video games are instructed in their functions by a program stored in Read Only Memory (ROM). Read Only Memory instructions are hard-wired;

thus, the only way to change the contents is to rewire the circuits in the computer. (See INTERNAL MEMORY; MICROPROCESSOR; PERSONAL COMPUTER; and RANDOM ACCESS MEMORY.)
References: Grace Murray Hopper and Steven L. Mandell, *Understanding Computers,* St. Paul, MN: West Publishing Company, 1984; David R. Sullivan, et al., *Computing Today: Microcomputer Concepts and Applications,* Boston: Houghton Mifflin Company, 1985.

REALITY THERAPY, an approach to counseling in which the client is taught productive and appropriate behavior. Although used often on young, incarcerated individuals, reality therapy can also be employed effectively in the classroom.

This form of therapy, promoted by William Glasser, reflects its author's distrust of psychoanalysis. Reality therapy requires the client (delinquent) to be realistic, recognizing that his/her behavior is irresponsible. The counselor then describes responsible (acceptable) behavior that, if substituted for irresponsible behavior, can lead to acceptance and success identity. Reality therapy possesses other characteristics: it rejects the idea of mental illness; it focuses on present behavior; and it stresses success while eliminating punishment. *References:* Gerald Corey, *Theory and Practice of Counseling and Psychotherapy,* Monterey, CA: Brooks/Cole Publishing Company, 1977; William Glasser, *Schools Without Failure,* New York: Harper and Row, Publishers, 1969; Robert E. Wubbolding, *Using Reality Therapy,* New York: Harper and Row Publishers, Inc., 1988.

REAL LEADER—See STATUS LEADER

REAL PROPERTY—See PROPERTY TAX

REBUS APPROACH, a reading method that uses symbols or pictures in place of certain printed words. For example, the symbol *3* may be used in place of *three* or a *picture of a bird* may be used in lieu of the word *bird.* These symbols, or pictographs, permit the child who is unfamiliar with a word (or words) to read a complete sentence by "reading" words and/or pictographs as needed. The Rebus approach is sometimes used with beginning readers, at other times with disabled learners. The *Peabody Rebus Reading Program* is a commercially prepared program that employs this approach.
References: Samuel A. Kirk, et al., *Teaching Reading to Slow and Disabled Learners,* Boston: Houghton Mifflin Company, 1978; Richard W. Woodcock and Charlotte R. Clark, *Peabody Rebus Reading Program,* Circle Pines, MN:

American Guidance Service, 1969; Miles V. Zintz, *The Reading Process: The Teacher and the Learner*, Dubuque, IA: Wm. C. Brown Company, Publishers, 1970.

RECALL ELECTIONS, special elections initiated by citizens of a jurisdiction, including school districts in some states, to remove elected officials from office. Recall elections are conducted in accordance with state law. They are normally preceded by the preparation of a recall petition that a prescribed percentage of qualified voters are required to sign.

Judges, legislators, and school board members, in different states, are subject to recall. This action on the part of the citizenry reflects lack of trust in the particular elected official.

Reference: Philip K. Piele (Editor), *The Yearbook of School Law: 1978*, Topeka, KS: National Organization on Legal Problems of Education, 1978.

RECIPROCITY IN TEACHER CERTIFICATION—See NATIONAL ASSOCIATION OF STATE DIRECTORS OF TEACHER EDUCATION AND CERTIFICATION

RECITAL, a public musical performance (vocal or instrumental) involving one, sometimes two, performers. When more than two performers are involved, the performance is referred to as a "concert." Historians report that the term *recital* was first used in 1840 in connection with London performances given by Franz Lizst. Recital programs are planned carefully to achieve any of several objectives, including: (1) providing students of music with an opportunity to demonstrate their musical abilities in public; (2) fulfilling a performance requirement frequently expected of college, university, and conservatory students majoring in music; (3) providing professional musicians with an opportunity to perform in public; and (4) providing the audience with an enjoyable musical experience.

References: Shirlee Emmons and Stanley Sonntag, *The Art of the Song Recital*, New York: Schirmer Books (Macmillan), 1979; J. A. Westrup and F. L. Harrison (Revised by Conrad Wilson), *The New College Encyclopedia of Music*, New York: W. W. Norton and Company, Inc., 1976.

RECOGNITION, in psychology, the discrimination between a new stimulus and one that has already been observed. It is a measure of retention since the subject must remember the stimulus that has already been seen.

It has been found that recall of unpleasant stimuli (particularly words) takes longer than does recognition of neutral or pleasant stimuli. Recognition of another person implies acceptance and/or status, for the observer remembers the individual. The time for actual recognition to take place after a stimulus is presented is called the *threshold of recognition.*

In testing, a recognition item is one that requires the respondent to identify the correct response (item) from a list of possible responses (items) presented.

References: Kurt Schlesinger and Philip M. Groves, *Psychology: A Dynamic Science*, Dubuque, IA: Wm. C. Brown Company, Publishers, 1976; Marvin Schroth and Derald W. Sue, *Introductory Psychology*, Homewood, IL: The Dorsey Press, 1975; James O. Whittaker, *Introduction to Psychology*, Philadelphia: W. B. Saunders Company, 1970.

RECONSTRUCTIONISM, a philosophy of education (some have called it a "movement") that holds that a major purpose of schooling is to bring about social reform (reconstruction). Claiming that many of its tenets are consistent with findings of the biosocial sciences, reconstructionism argues for education to work for accommodation of social and cultural needs. It champions the practice and preservation of democracy. Reconstructionists want the teacher to show the need for social reform, but to do so democratically by having students examine all sides of an issue. A method of teaching recommended by reconstructionists involves group activity.

The reconstructionist movement began in the early 1930s, led by prominent teacher educators such as George S. Counts and Harold O. Rugg. It was more recently expounded by Theodore Brameld and is sometimes called social reconstructionism.

References: Theodore Brameld, *Toward A Reconstructed Philosophy of Education*, New York: The Dryden Press, 1956; George Kneller, *Introduction to the Philosophy of Education* (Second Edition), New York: John Wiley and Sons, 1971; Van Cleve Morris, *Philosophy and the American School: An Introduction to the Philosophy of Education*, Boston: Houghton Mifflin Company, 1961.

RECORDER, a musical instrument frequently used with young children. Some music instructors use it for the purpose of teaching students to read music. Others employ it to provide learners with preband or preorchestra experience. The instrument enjoys popularity with adults as well.

The recorder, developed centuries ago, produces sounds having a flutelike quality. The sounds are produced by using one of two fingering systems (Baroque or German) on the instrument's eight holes. Fingers on both hands are used. Although there are four kinds of recorders that can be used to produce four-part harmony (C-Soprano, F-Alto, C-Tenor, and F-Bass), the C-Soprano is the one most commonly used in the schools.

The recorder is known by different names in different parts of the world: *flûte-à-bec* in French; *blockflöte* in German; and *flauto dolce* in Italian.

References: Patricia Hackett, et al., *The Musical Classroom: Models, Skills, and Backgrounds for Elementary Teaching,* Englewood Cliffs, NJ: Prentice-Hall, Inc., 1979; Edgar Hunt, "Recorder" in Stanley Sadie (Editor), *The New Grove Dictionary of Music and Musicians* (Volume 15), London, England: Macmillan Publishers Limited, 1980; Robert W. Winslow and Leon Dallin, *Music Skills for Classroom Teachers* (Fifth Edition), Dubuque, IA: Wm. C. Brown Company, Publishers, 1979.

RECREATION, a leisure-time activity that one pursues voluntarily and from which one derives personal satisfaction or pleasure. Additionally, it provides a release for one's physical, mental, and/or creative resources. Frequently associated with the term *play,* recreation is pursued with a minimum of goals or compulsions. One recreation authority (Maryhelen Vannier) wrote that recreation possesses four characteristics: (1) it is both a creative and re-creative activity; (2) it can be either passive or active; (3) it generally takes place during one's free time; and (4) through it, one can learn how to live the full life.

Organized recreation programs are sponsored by communities, schools, camps, and industry to meet the leisure-time needs of people of all ages and all abilities. They include both indoor and outdoor activities such as arts and crafts, dancing, drama, sports, camping, music, and all types of games.

References: Richard G. Kraus, *Recreation and the Schools: Guides to Effective Practices in Leisure Education and Community Recreation Sponsorship,* New York: The Macmillan Company, 1964; Maryhelen Vannier, *Recreation Leadership* (Third Edition), Philadelphia: Lea and Febiger, 1977; Donald C. Weiskopf, *A Guide to Recreation and Leisure,* Boston: Allyn and Bacon, Inc., 1975; Thomas S. Yukic, Fundamentals of Recreation (Second Edition), New York: Harper and Row, Publishers, 1970.

REDUCTION IN FORCE (RIF), a set of organizational strategies designed to reduce the number of school (or higher education) employees as a direct consequence of declining enrollments. Various approaches to RIFing have been used since the late 1960s, the period when public school enrollments in the United States began to decline, particularly at the elementary school level. The American Association of School Administrators has identified four policies, or bases for determining layoffs, developed by local boards of education: (1) seniority; (2) merit; (3) a "mixed" system that takes factors such as academic training, experience, length of service, and performance into account; and (4) board-administration prerogative.

References: William B. Castetter, *The Personnel Function in Educational Administration* (Third Edition), New York: Macmillan Publishing Company, Inc., 1981; Shirley B. Neill and Jerry Custis, *Staff Dismissal: Problems and Solutions* (AASA Critical Issues Report), Sacramento, CA: Education News Service (for the American Association of School Administrators), 1978.

REFERENCE GROUP, that group of people or objects used as a base for comparing and assessing an individual's responses, perceptions, attitudes, or values. For example, a teacher may use, as a reference, the test results of a group of middle-class children when evaluating the actual test results of a group of nonmiddle-class children. Having done this, the teacher may then determine that the nonmiddle-class children did or did not do very well.

Many times the use of a reference group may be more subconscious than conscious on the part of one individual. That is, the person doesn't realize that he or she is comparing a person with individuals from another group. Generally, the use of a reference group as a comparison base is a product of past experiences with that reference group. It is important to choose carefully the reference group (if any) used by individuals when attempting to evaluate the judgments or responses of individuals. Congruency between the nature of the reference group used and the group being evaluated is very important, otherwise the judgments, perceptions, attitudes, and so on developed may not be justified.

Reference groups are often used by individuals to make judgments about themselves. (See NORM GROUP.)

References: Arthur R. Jensen, *Bias in Mental Testing,* New York: The Free Press, 1980; David E. Lavin, *The Prediction of Academic Performance,* New York: John Wiley and Sons, 1965; Kurt Schlesinger and Philip M. Groves, *Psychology: A Dynamic Science,* Dubuque, IA: Wm. C. Brown Company, Publishers, 1976.

REFLECTION-IN-ACTION—See REFLECTIVE TEACHING

REFLECTIVE TEACHING LESSONS (RTL)— See REFLECTIVE TEACHING

REFLECTIVE TEACHING or PRACTICE, an approach used in teaching in which a problem (in teaching or learning) is first set or interpreted in theory, experiences, and understandings, and then a solution to the problem is developed through testing, self-evaluations, and a series of revisions. It is inquiry-oriented, and, as the title states, it is reflective. The origins of reflection teaching are found in the works of John Dewey.

Donald Schon (1974) has developed a theory of reflection-in-action that requires problem setting (or diagnosis), testing, and belief in personal causation (personal or professional values used in setting the problem, and responsibility for actions taken). Another approach to reflective teaching includes action or reflection through recollections, representation, analysis, and a conceptual base for future reference (N. B. Garman, 1986). Donald Cruickshank (1987) has developed a series of reflective teaching lessons (RTL) to be used by preservice teacher education majors—in these lessons, the teacher and learner reflect upon the teaching and learning. Reflective teaching is used in clinical supervision and as a part of preservice education in some universities. (See CLINICAL SUPERVISION and DEWEY, JOHN B.)

References: C. Argyris and D. Schon, *Theory in Practice: Increasing Professional Effectiveness*, San Francisco: Jossey-Bass, Inc., 1974; Donald R. Cruickshank, et al., "Evaluation of Reflective Teaching Outcomes," *Journal of Educational Research*, Volume 75, Number 1, 1981; Donald R. Cruickshank, *Reflective Teaching, the Preparation of Student Teaching*, Reston, VA: Association of Teachers Educators, 1987; John Dewey, *How We Think*, Chicago: Henry Regnery, 1933; John Dewey, "The Relationships of Theory to Practice in Education," in C. A. McMurray (Editor), *The Third Yearbook of the National Society for the Study of Education* (Part I), Chicago: University of Chicago Press, 1904; N. B. Garman, "Reflection, the Heart of Clinical Supervision: A Modern Rationale for Professional Practice," *Journal of Curriculum and Instruction*, Volume 2, Number 1, 1986; Peggy Kirby, *Reflective Practice as a Predictor of Teacher Effectiveness*, unpublished doctoral dissertation, University of New Orleans, 1987; Donald A. Schon, *The Reflective Practitioner: How Professionals Think in Action*, New York: Basic Books, 1983.

REFLEX, an automatic response by an organism to a stimulus. The reflex, or reflex reaction, is in some instances innate and carried out without conscious effort. Examples of such reflex reactions include the quick removing of the hand after it touches a hot stove, dilation or contraction of the pupil of the eye in response to sudden changes in light intensity, and sneezing. Some reflex reactions involve but one muscle; others, such as the reaction produced in response to a sudden loud noise, may involve many parts of the central nervous system.

Conditioned responses, also referred to as classical conditioning, are *learned* (not innate) responses. Pavlov's well-known experiment, in which a dog salivated once learning to associate food with a particular stimulus (e.g. light, a particular sound, touch) was one of the first to be carried out in the field of classical conditioning. The conditioned reflex continues as long as the conditional stimulus is present. Once the conditional stimulus is removed, the response wanes and eventually ceases to occur. (See OPERANT BEHAVIOR and PAVLOV, IVAN P.)

References: Jerome Kagan and Ernest Havemann, *Psychology: An Introduction* (Second Edition), New York: Harcourt Brace Jovanovich, Inc., 1972; Merle J. Moskowitz and Arthur R. Orgel, *General Psychology: A Core Text in Human Behavior*, Boston: Houghton Mifflin Company, 1969; *Psychology Today: An Introduction* (Second Edition), DelMar, CA: CRM Books, 1972.

REGENTS, trustees of a board that governs (sets policies for) a state institution of higher education or a statewide system of higher education. The actual span of control of this corporate body depends on state statutes. For example, in California the Regents of California are the governing board for the major state-supported universities (e.g. UCLA, Berkeley); in New York, the Board of Regents governs all state-supported universities and colleges in the State University of New York System; and in Nebraska, the Board of Regents governs the University of Nebraska System but not the state colleges (which are governed by a separate board). Boards of regents for state systems of higher education may be appointed by the governor, elected by the people of a state, or chosen using a combination of these two selection procedures. (See BOARD OF TRUSTEES, COLLEGE AND UNIVERSITY.)

References: Frederick E. Baldeston, *Managing Today's University*, San Francisco: Jossey-Bass Publishers, 1974; Eugene C. Lee and Frank M. Bowen, *The Multicampus University*, New York: McGraw-Hill Book Company, 1971; *Regents of the University of California v. Bakke*, Washington, DC: University Publications of America, 1978.

REGENTS PRAYER, developed by the New York State Board of Regents and suggested for use in the state's public schools. The prayer reads: "Almighty God, we acknowledge our dependence upon Thee, and we beg Thy blessings upon us, our parents, our teachers and our country." Purported to be nonsectarian and simply intended to teach moral and spiritual values, its legality was challenged. In 1962, the United States Supreme Court declared the prayer's recitation in school to be unconstitutional on the grounds that it constituted a religious activity sponsored by the state in violation of the Establishment of Religion Clause of the First Amendment. This ruling was significant because it involved the first prayers-in-school case to be brought before the U.S. Supreme Court. (See ESTABLISHMENT CLAUSE.)

References: Engel v. Vitale, 370 U.S. 421, 82 S.Ct. 1261, 8 L.Ed. 2d 601, 1962; William E. Griffiths, Religion, the Courts, and the Public Schools: A Century of Litigation, Cincinnati, OH: The W. H. Anderson Company, 1966; E. Edmund Reutter, Jr. and Robert R. Hamilton, The Law of Public Education (Second Edition), Mineola, NY: The Foundation Press, Inc., 1976.

REGIONAL ACCREDITING ASSOCIATIONS— See ACCREDITING AGENCIES AND ASSOCIATIONS

REGIONAL LABORATORIES, independent, nonprofit research and development organizations funded by the U.S. federal government to meet regional educational needs. They were first supported under Title IV of the U.S. Elementary and Secondary Education Act of 1965. Twenty laboratories were first funded, these located in most sections of the United States (e.g. New York City, Center for Urban Education; Charleston, W. Va., Appalachia Educational Laboratory; Berkeley, Calif., Far West Laboratory). By 1986, only 9 regional laboratories were still in existence.

The original functions of the regional laboratories included model building, sponsorship of demonstration projects, dissemination of new ideas and technologies, and the carrying out of applied basic research. Questions concerning the validity of their regional thrusts and concern over the administrative control of the laboratories were issues that were debated among educators, with some of these issues creating problems for the laboratories. In recent years, the laboratories have been funded by the National Institute of Education and then by the Programs for the Improvement of Practice of the Office of Educational Research and Improvement (OERI). Their principal mission is still educational improvement through research and development and technical assistance.

The nine regional laboratories should not be confused with the 14 Research and Development Centers funded by the Office of Research of the Office of Educational Research and Improvement (OERI). The latter were established in 1963 primarily for research in particular educational areas (e.g. Learning Research and Development Center, University of Pittsburgh). Both the laboratories and centers can be viewed as augmenting each other's functions. (See APPENDIX XIX: REGIONAL EDUCATIONAL LABORATORIES and OFFICE OF EDUCATIONAL RESEARCH AND IMPROVEMENT.)

References: Robert A. Dentler, "Regional Laboratories and Development Centers" in Lee C. Deighton (Editor), The Encyclopedia of Education (Volume 7), New York: The Macmillan Company and The Free Press, 1971; Office of Management, Department of Education's Mission and Organizational Manual, Washington, DC: Department of Education, Revised June 1, 1987; Office of Educational Research and Improvement; Educational Networks Division, Directory of Institutional Projects Funded by OERI, Washington, DC: OERI, January 1986; Panel for the Review of Laboratory and Center Operations, Research and Development Centers and Regional Educational Laboratories: Strengthening and Stabilizing a National Resource, Washington, DC: U.S. Department of Health, Education, and Welfare, 1979; Marda Woodbury, Selecting Materials for Instruction: Media and the Curriculum, Littleton, CO: Libraries Unlimited, Inc., 1980.

REGISTERED SCHOOL BUSINESS ADMINISTRATOR, a certificate issued by the Association of School Business Officials of the United States and Canada (ASBO) to school business officials who meet criteria that ASBO developed and that became effective on December 31, 1972. To qualify for the certificate, applicants must: (1) be active ASBO members; (2) have, as a school or college staff employee, major responsibility for many of the business categories comprising school business administration (e.g. financial affairs, transportation, school lunch); (3) hold a master's degree in school business administration or educational administration; and (4) have completed five years of satisfactory service in some area of school business administration, including three years as a school business administrator.

Another certificate issued by ASBO, Registered School Business Official, is available to eligible ASBO members who "have overall administrative responsibility for a specific (specialized) phase or phases of school business administration in a school system" (p. 107). Separate criteria, including a bachelor's degree, have been established for this latter credential. (See ASSOCIATION OF SCHOOL BUSINESS OFFICIALS OF THE UNITED STATES AND CANADA.)

Reference: Frederick W. Hill, et al., *The School Business Administrator* (Bulletin No. 21, Revised), Chicago: Research Corporation of the Association of School Business Officials, 1970.

REGISTER OF ATTENDANCE—See ATTENDANCE REGISTER

REGISTRATION, in higher education the act of enrolling in a college, university, or in a particular program or course. In most colleges and universities, registration usually occurs just before a term begins. In higher education, the individual responsible for the registration process is called the registrar.

Under compulsory school attendance, a child of legal school age (unless excused) must be enrolled in school. A parent registers (enrolls) him/her but once, a process permitting the child to remain continuously enrolled until graduation, transfer, or legal termination of his/her studies. Registration is required each time a child of legal school age moves to a new community or, in some communities, graduates to a higher level school (e.g. elementary to middle school, or middle school to high school). (See COMPULSORY EDUCATION.)

References: Asa S. Knowles, *Handbook of College and University Administration,* New York: McGraw-Hill Book Company, 1970; Michael S. Katz, *A History of Compulsory Education Laws* (PDK Fastback 75), Bloomington, IN: The Phi Delta Kappa Foundation, 1976; Edmund J. Mullen, "Registrar" in Asa S. Knowles (Editor), *The International Encyclopedia of Higher Education* (Volume 8), San Francisco: Jossey-Bass Publishers, 1977.

REGRESSION, a pyschological term that has two meanings. In the context of child development, regression refers to temporary lapses that occur in the otherwise normal growth (physical or intellectual) of learners. Smooth development is interrupted; the child reverts to an earlier level of behavior but later resumes normal development. Such lapses are likely to recur until the newly learned level of performance is mastered completely. Illustrating this form of regression is the child who barely learns to ride a bicycle one week, frequently falls from it the next, and then goes on to master bicycling.

The second form of regression is a type of withdrawal. It involves a reverting to infantile or immature behavior by those who face difficult problem-solving situations. The severity of this form of regression, which in extreme instances may become a kind of schizophrenia, is often measured in terms of its duration.

References: Gary S. Belkin and Jerry L. Gray, *Educational Psychology: An Introduction,* Dubuque, IA: Wm. C. Brown Company, Publishers, 1977; Morris E. Eson, *Psychological Foundations of Education* (Second Edition), New York: Holt, Rinehart and Winston, Inc., 1972; M. Ray Loree, *Psychology of Education,* New York: Ronald Press Company, 1965.

REGRESSIVE TAXES—See PROGRESSIVE vs. REGRESSIVE TAXES

REHABILITATION, the process by which an individual is restored to fullest capacity through retraining or education. The goal is to make him/her independent and able to live a full, meaningful life in the larger society. Rehabilitation programs are carried out by many social and medical agencies. There are rehabilitation programs for: those on drugs, alcoholics, ex-prisoners, the physically handicapped, the hearing impaired, the emotionally disturbed, older citizens, and so on. Some programs are found in large hospitals, others in group homes or small transition workshops, and still others in schools. Rehabilitation programs are frequently involved and complex, entailing medical and psychological treatment, extensive counseling, social work activities, specialized education, and economic skill development.

References: John G. Cull and Richard E. Hardy (Editors), *Rehabilitation Facility Approaches in Severe Disabilities,* Springfield, IL: Charles C. Thomas, Publisher, 1975; Patricia T. Flaherty and Corrine W. Larson, *Key to Joint Mobility,* Minneapolis, MN: Sister Kenny Institute, 1977; Robert Martinson, et al., *Rehabilitation, Recidivism, and Research,* Hackensack, NJ: National Council on Crime and Delinquency, 1976; John E. Muthard, *Personnel and Research Utilization in Rehabilitation,* Gainesville, FL: University of Florida, 1975.

REHABILITATION ACT, or Public Law 93–112, federal legislation enacted in 1973 that provided that handicapped persons may not be discriminated against on the basis of their handicap. Section 504 is the base of this antidiscrimination act; it prohibits state and local governments or any private organization (that receives federal funds) from discriminating against qualified handicapped individuals because of their handicap. Section 504 also bars discrimination in preschool, through adult education, and in social service organizations. In addition, the act: (1) mandated the elimination of architectural barriers that make buildings inaccessible to the handicapped; (2) created an Architectural and Transportation Barriers Compliance Board to ensure compliance with the act; (3) required certain federal contractors to "take affirmative action to employ and advance in employment qualified handicapped individuals" (p. 393); and (4) made grants available to states for the purpose of rehabilitating the handicapped.

The Rehabilitation Act of 1973 replaced the Vocational Rehabilitation Act. (See ARCHITECTURAL BARRIERS.)

References: Public Law 93–112, *United States Statutes at Large, 1973* (Volume 87), Washington, DC: U.S. Government Printing Office, 1974; H. Rutherford Turnbull III, *Free Appropriate Public Education: The Law and Children with Disabilities*, Denver, CO: Love Publishing Co., 1986.

REINFORCEMENT, the impact that a reinforcer has on an organism such that behavior is affected. If a behavior is likely to continue, or start, as a result of a positive reinforcer, *positive reinforcement* is said to have occurred. On the other hand, if a behavior is likely to stop, or decrease, as a result of a negative reinforcer, then *negative reinforcement* has taken place.

Reinforcement is used widely in the field of operant behavior psychology. B. F. Skinner did extensive research work in this field, particularly with schedules of reinforcement (timing of the presentation of reinforcing stimuli).

Elements of reinforcement are found in programmed instruction and behavior modification. In the case of behavior modification, for example, food can be used as a positive reinforcer (electric shock would be a negative reinforcer). Its effect on the behavior of a person would then be the reinforcement.

In the classroom, praise can have a positive reinforcement effect on the motivation and achievement of students. (See MOTIVATION and OPERANT BEHAVIOR.)

References: Robert F. Biehler, *Psychology Applied to Teaching*, Atlanta, GA: Houghton Mifflin Company, 1974; Janice T. Gibson and Louis A. Chandler, *Educational Psychology: Mastering Principles and Applications*, Boston: Allyn and Bacon, 1988; R. M. Gilbert and J. R. Millenson (Editors), *Reinforcement*, New York: Academic Press, 1972; Werner K. Honig and J.E.R. Staddon (Editors), *Handbook of Operant Behavior*, Englewood Cliffs, NJ: Prentice-Hall, Inc., 1977; Burrhus F. Skinner, *Contingencies of Reinforcement*, New York: Appleton-Century-Crofts, Inc., 1969.

RELEASED TIME, cooperative arrangements that permit public school children to leave school, usually toward the end of the school day, for the purpose of receiving church-sponsored religious instruction. Such release is permitted upon written request of the child's parent. Nonparticipating students remain in school until the time for regular dismissal.

In 1952, the U.S. Supreme Court ruled that such release is legal and that it does not serve to establish a religion. Criteria used in arriving at this decision were: (1) the state must be neutral, not favoring any particular religion, and (2) public funds may not be spent, in any way, to aid sectarian instruction.

Earlier (1948), the U.S. Supreme Court had ruled (*McCollum v. Board of Education*) that religious leaders could not come into the public schools to offer such instruction. (See *McCOLLUM* CASE and SHARED TIME.)

References: David Fellman, *The Supreme Court and Education* (Third Edition), New York: Teachers College Press, 1976; William R. Hazard, *Education and the Law: Cases and Materials on Public Schools* (Second Edition), New York: The Free Press (Macmillan), 1978; Leroy J. Peterson, et al., *The Law and the Public School Operation* (Second Edition), New York: Harper and Row, Publishers, 1978; David Tavel, *Church-State Issues in Education* (PDK Fastback 123), Bloomington, IN: The Phi Delta Kappa Educational Foundation, 1979; *Zorach v. Clauson*, 343 U.S. 306, 72 S.Ct. 679, 96 L.Ed., 954 (N.Y. 1952).

RELIABILITY, in testing, a term that refers to the fact that a test is consistent in what it measures. The more consistent a test, the higher is its reliability. High reliability is desirable (ideally approaching +1.00). Technically, reliability is the proportion of true variance generated by a test. The ideal test is both highly *reliable* and *valid*.

Coefficients of reliability can be determined (estimated) through various techniques. *Internal consistency* (e.g. Spearman-Brown, Kuder-Richardson procedures, odd-even, parallel-forms, split-half) among the items in the test and *test-retest* (the test is administered twice to the same people and the association between the two sets of scores is calculated) are the two basic approaches to measurement of reliability. Correlational (association) relationships are used to determine the coefficients of reliability.

There are many factors that influence test reliability. Some are: (1) the nature of the group tested (homogeneity, heterogeneity); (2) ability level; (3) conditions of testing; (4) time; (5) the nature of the tests; and (6) whether a test is a speed or power test.

References: Anne Anastasi, *Psychological Testing* (Sixth Edition), New York: Macmillan Publishing Company, Inc., 1988; Walter R. Borg and Meredith D. Gall, *Educational Research: An Introduction* (Fifth Edition), New York: Longman, Inc., 1989; George K. Cunningham, *Educational and Psychological Measurement*, New York: Macmillan Publishing Company, 1986.

RELIGION IN THE SCHOOLS, an issue that permeates the pages of textbooks in fields of study such as school law and the history of American education. Unlike many national systems of education throughout the world that incorporate religion and/or religious instruction into their curricula, the tradition of American public education has been to operate programs in basically a secular environment. This tradition, in large measure, is based on the Establishment Clause of the U.S. Constitution's First Amendment.

Over the years, numerous court cases have been initiated by individuals intent on infusing religion into the public school curriculum or by others equally intent on resisting such infusion attempts. Bible reading and prayer recitation in the schools constitute one type of effort to infuse religion. Several Supreme Court decisions (e.g. *McCollum v. Board of Education, Engel v. Vitale,* and *Abington School District v. Schempp*) have served to ban such activities. In response to such bans, released-time policies have emerged as alternatives and have won court approval. These policies, carried out in cooperation with local religious officials, permit students to leave school at certain times during the week for the purpose of receiving religious instruction.

Another broad category of cases involves protests by individuals who challenge certain school practices on religious grounds. Sex education, moral education, teaching about evolution, and even flag saluting are instructional activities that have precipitated litigation. Many have been adjudicated on the basis of whether they promoted religion or simply involved the teaching about religiously related subjects.

A third category of cases relates to the use of public monies to support educational programs being carried out by nonpublic schools, including auxiliary services such as transportation. In these cases, several court decisions have tended to support use of public monies for those segments of the curriculum that are nonreligious or those that are designed to aid the student rather than the sectarian institution. (See ABINGTON SCHOOL DISTRICT v. SCHEMPP; CHILD BENEFIT THEORY; McCOLLUM CASE; and RELEASED TIME.)

References: Frank R. Kemerer and Kenneth L. Deutsch, *Constitutional Rights and Student Life: Value Conflict in Law and Education*, St. Paul, MN: West Publishing Company, 1979; David L. Kirp and Mark G. Yudof, *Educational Policy and the Law: Cases and Materials*, Berkeley, CA: McCutchan Publishing Corporation, 1974; David Tavel, *Church-State Issues in Education* (PDK Fastback 123), Bloomington, IN: The Phi Delta Kappa Educational Foundation, 1979.

REMEDIAL READING, a corrective approach to reading that involves helping students to develop particular reading skills not acquired in the developmental reading program. Word-recognition difficulties are identified (e.g. visual-discrimination or sound-discrimination problems); corrective steps are then taken to overcome the student's specific recognition problem(s).

One authority (Eddie Kennedy) identified seven competencies needed before a student can read independently: (1) visual discrimination; (2) sound discrimination; (3) letter recognition; (4) sound recognition; (5) sound blending; (6) recognition of word meanings; and (7) ability to use word-attack skills. He also called attention to the need for direct instruction and practice when teaching specific word-attack skills.

Another authority (Miles Zintz) provided an operational definition for *remedial reading*. It is corrective instruction, he said, "provided outside the framework of the total group teaching situation." In contrast, *corrective reading* is "remedial reading . . . applied by the regular classroom teacher within the framework of the daily instruction" (p. 34). (See WORD-ATTACK SKILLS.)

References: Albert J. Harris and Edward R. Sipay, *How to Increase Reading Ability* (Eighth Edition), New York: Longman, Inc., 1985; Robert M. Wilson and Craig J. Cleland, *Diagnostic and Remedial Reading for Classroom and Clinic* (Sixth Edition), Columbus, OH: Merrill Publishing Company, 1989.

REMEDIATION, a process that corrects a deficit. In education, remediation programs are designed to correct student behaviors and/or skills and are used in all subject areas (e.g. mathematics, reading, handwriting, spelling, language arts, science). They have been found to be effective with children who have learning problems.

At one time, remediation focused only on one

deficit, but presently remedial programs focus on the whole learner. Remedial programs include any or all of the following: (1) modified course content; (2) alterations, modifications, and changes in the mode of instruction; (3) possible behavioral modification techniques; (4) possible changes in the learning environment (including a physical change); (5) extensive evaluations; and (6) individualization.

In postsecondary education, programs that focus on the whole learner, rather than being remedial only, are termed *developmental*. (See STUDENT DEVELOPMENT PROGRAMS.)

References: James N. Blake, *Speech, Language and Learning Disorders*, Springfield, IL: Charles C. Thomas, Publisher, 1971; K. Patricia Cross, *Accent on Learning*, San Francisco: Jossey-Bass Publishers, 1976; Marianne Frostig and Phyllis Maslow, *Learning Problems in the Classroom*, New York: Grune and Stratton, 1973; Philip H. Mann, et al., *Handbook in Diagnostic Prescriptive Teaching* (Second Edition), Boston: Allyn and Bacon, Inc., 1979.

REPORT CARD, a written report that informs parents of their child's progress in school. In many school systems, parent-teacher conferences and/or letters from the teacher supplement (or replace) such written reports. The report card is the single most commonly used reporting vehicle in American schools.

Report card format varies within and among school systems. Different formats for Kindergarten, primary, intermediate, middle, and senior high schools are not uncommon. Each may contain numerous separate sections including those that report: (1) achievement in specific subject or skill areas; (2) achievement in the context of the student's ability; (3) record of attendance and punctuality; and (4) social adjustment. Written comments by the teacher and provision for comments by parents are also commonly included. Where a child's achievement or social adjustment is reported relatively, letter, number, or general measures (e.g., "satisfactory" vs. "unsatisfactory") are used. Report cards are issued periodically, usually on a quarterly basis. Most educators agree that the card is most useful when used in conjunction with parent-teacher conferences. (See MARKING SYSTEMS.)

References: Lester W. Anderson and Lauren A. Van Dyke, *Secondary School Administration* (Second Edition), Boston: Houghton Mifflin Company, 1972; Norman M. Chansky, "A Critical Examination of School Report Cards From K Through 12," *Reading Improvement*, Fall 1975.

A REPORT TO THE PRESIDENT OF THE UNITED STATES, NATIONAL NETWORKING CONFERENCE, TOPIC: TEACHER PREPARATION AND RETENTION, a report issued by the Intergovernmental Advisory Council on Education in 1985. The report was a product of a two-day conference attended by a variety of educational groups from the local, state, and national levels. Also included were groups that represented the private sector, professional organizations, business, civil rights groups, and labor. Elected officials from all three levels of government participated in the meeting.

Ten recommendations were made which focused on teacher supply and demand; teacher certification; multiple routes into teaching; preservice education design; induction supervision; retraining of teachers for critical shortage areas; teacher evaluation; incentives to attract and retain talented teachers; and private-sector (industry) participation and development of resource networks. (See INTERGOVERNMENTAL ADVISORY COUNCIL ON EDUCATION.)

Reference: Intergovernmental Advisory Council on Education, *A Report to the President of the United States, National Networking Conference, Topic: Teacher Preparation and Retention*, Washington, DC: The Council, 1985.

REPRESSION, a psychological term that refers to the unconscious exclusions (rejection) of impulses, thoughts, or experiences that would prove painful and/or disagreeable to consciousness. Repression is a defense mechanism that serves, temporarily at least, to reduce tension. It is practiced in varying degrees by all individuals. Some psychologists urge that children be permitted to work in a relatively open learning environment, one that will permit them to express their feelings, reduce pent up emotions, and thus keep repression to a minimum.

References: Glenn M. Blair, et al., *Educational Psychology* (Third Edition), New York: The Macmillan Company, 1968; Leland E. Hinsie and Robert J. Campbell, *Psychiatric Dictionary* (Fourth Edition), New York: Oxford University Press, 1970.

REQUEST, an acronym for reciprocal questioning, ReQuest is a reading technique that involves both learner and instructor in a process of silent reading followed by alternate questioning and answering. Utilization of the technique promotes instructor modeling of both good questioning skills and answers to questions posed by the learner. The ReQuest technique was originally developed by

A. V. Manzo in 1969 as an intermediary step between teacher-directed comprehension lessons and lessons that allow for more active interaction with the material. As the learner becomes more comfortable with the procedure, she/he will take over more responsibility for the questioning. In 1977, L. W. Searfoss and E. K. Dishner developed an expanded ReQuest format which included directions for the instructor on text selection. One of the goals of the strategy is to encourage an inquiring attitude toward reading.

References: Anthony V. Manzo, "The ReQuest Procedures," *Journal of Reading*, Volume 13, Number 2, 1969; David W. Moor, John E. Readance, and Robert J. Rickelman, *ReQuest in Prereading Activities for Content Area Reading and Learning*, Newark, DE: International Reading Association, 1982; Lyndon W. Searfoss and Ernest K. Dishner, "Improving Comprehension through the ReQuest Procedure," *Reading Education: A Journal for Australian Teachers*, Volume 2, Autumn 1977; Lyndon W. Searfoss and John E. Readance, *Helping Children Learn to Read*, Englewood Cliffs, NJ: Prentice-Hall Inc., 1985.

REQUISITION, or purchase requisition, a written request for specified goods or services. In school districts or institutions of higher education, requisitions are normally directed to the official who has been authorized to make purchases. A requisition is not a purchase order.

Purchasing officials utilize the requisition as the basic instrument for seeking quotations/bids from prospective vendors.

References: Combined Glossary: Terms and Definitions from the Handbooks of the State Educational Records and Reports Series, Washington, DC: National Center for Education Statistics, U.S. Department of Health, Education, and Welfare, 1974; Jerry M. Rosenberg, *Dictionary of Business and Management*, New York: John Wiley and Sons, 1978.

RESEARCH FOR BETTER SCHOOLS (RBS), a regional educational laboratory originally established in Philadelphia under Title IV of the Elementary and Secondary Education Act. The region served by RBS includes the states of Delaware and New Jersey and the eastern section of Pennsylvania. RBS was established, as were all regional laboratories, as an independent, nonprofit corporation with a governing board charged with determining the laboratory's objectives and policies and responsible for administering its personnel and budget.

RBS has been involved in a variety of research and developmental projects, many carried out in close collaboration with local school districts. Its programs have addressed topics such as citizen education, career education, community education, child development, school improvement projects, reading, urban education, and school management. The laboratory has prepared numerous texts dealing with educational concerns, research reports, monographs, and educational design proposals. RBS initiated a newsletter, *Classroom Interaction Newsletter,* on classroom interaction in 1962. (See REGIONAL LABORATORIES.)

References: Walter R. Borg and Meredith D. Gall, *Educational Research* (Second Edition), New York: Longman, Inc., 1971; *Classroom Interaction Newsletter,* Philadelphia: Research for Better Schools (1962 to 1974); Louis Rubin (Editor), *Educational Reform for a Changing Society: Anticipating Tomorrow's Schools,* Philadelphia: Research for Better Schools (Published by Allyn and Bacon, Inc.), 1978.

RESEARCH METHODS IN EDUCATION, those rigorous, systematic, and scientific techniques and approaches used to assess an educational program, evaluate a new/old technique, evaluate educational technologies, answer a specific educational question, test hypotheses, or develop new knowledges and/or extend present knowledges.

There are many research methods and designs available to the educational researcher. Experimental and quasi-experimental designs, ex post facto, survey, historical (written, oral), ethnographic, literary, and summative and formative evaluations of programs are most commonly used. Many of the methods include specific statistical procedures and/or complex designs. By comparison, others are quite simplistic. The particular research method used must be appropriate to the problem at hand, the data available, the nature of the environment, and the skill of the researcher. (See ETHNOGRAPHIC RESEARCH; EXPERIMENTAL DESIGN; FORMATIVE EVALUATION; QUASI-EXPERIMENTAL DESIGN; SUMMATIVE EVALUATION; and SURVEY METHOD.)

References: Walter R. Borg and Meredith D. Gall, *Educational Research: An Introduction* (Fifth Edition), New York: Longman, Inc., 1989; L. R. Gay, *Educational Research: Competencies for Analysis and Application* (Third Edition), Columbus, OH: Merrill Publishing Company, 1987.

RESIDENTIAL SCHOOL, an educational institution, public or private, that boards and provides designated care to individuals assigned to it by virtue of having extensive health or severe behavior problems. Such care includes specialized instruction offered on a relatively small group basis. In the United States, the handicapped populations most commonly found in residential schools are the mentally retarded, the mentally ill, the blind, and the deaf.

One of the earliest such institutions to be established was a school for mental defectives, located in Paris (1837) and the creation of Edward Seguin. In the United States, the first public facility for defectives was opened in Massachusetts (1846). Many of the later public residential schools to be opened were originally established as private institutions.

The philosophy undergirding American residential schools has changed over the years. Many of these institutions were originally created for the purpose of aiding the residents. Segregation from the society at large was, and in some cases continues to be, seen as a way of helping the handicapped learner to acquire coping skills and to do so in a nonhostile environment. During the first half of the 20th century, however, the philosophical emphasis began to change with considerable attention given to protecting society from the handicapped, especially the mentally handicapped, and purportedly keeping them happy by keeping them together. More recently, the philosophical pendulum has again changed direction with increased attention being given to "deinstitutionalization," a concept designed to have the handicapped individual assigned to his/her least restrictive environment and one in which some degree of interaction with the total society is included.

Alfred Baumeister predicted that, in the years ahead, residential schools are likely to be smaller and more closely integrated with the community and will increasingly emphasize short-term care. (See DEINSTITUTIONALIZATION; LEAST RESTRICTIVE ENVIRONMENT; and SPECIAL EDUCATION PLACEMENT CASCADE.)

References: Alfred A. Baumeister, "The American Residential Institution: Its History and Character" in Alfred A. Baumeister and Earl Butterfield (Editors), *Residential Facilities for the Mentally Retarded*, Chicago: Aldine Publishing Company, 1970; Pat Bickersteth, "There Is a Positive Side to Sheltering," *Education and Training of the Mentally Retarded*, April 1978; Donovan Jones, "Residential Versus Local School Programs: A Response," *Education of the Visually Handicapped*, Summer 1978; Philip Roos, "Evolutionary Changes of the Residential Facility" in Alfred A. Baumeister and Earl Butterfield (Editors), *Residential Facilities for the Mentally Retarded*, Chicago: Aldine Publishing Company, 1970.

RESIDENTIAL STUDENT, a college or univer-

sity student who, during part or all of his/her college years, resides in college residence halls (dormitories) or in fraternity/sorority housing. In years past, students typically occupied such housing units during their four years of college study. In recent years, however, because numerous new colleges have been opened in close physical proximity to students' homes, and for economic reasons, increasing numbers of students have elected to commute to institutions of higher education.

Some research has been undertaken to compare the characteristics of *residential* and *commuter* students. These studies report numerous findings, including the fact that *residential* students: (1) are more often supported financially by parents or loans; (2) have more frequent interchanges with the faculty; (3) are more active in fraternity/sorority and other extracurricular activities; (4) are more satisfied with their college; and (5) are less likely to fail courses or to be placed on academic probation.

In the 1970's, residential housing programs witnessed a decline in the *in loco parentis* doctrine and an increase in coeducational student housing. (See IN LOCO PARENTIS.)

References: Arthur W. Chickering, *Commuting Versus Resident Students*, San Francisco: Jossey-Bass Publishers, 1975; Carolyn Cridler-Smith, *Survey of Academic Support Programs in Residence Halls, 1978-79*, Westfield, MA: Association of College and University Housing Officers, 1979; David Decoster and Phyllis Mable, *Student Development and Education in College Residence Halls*, Washington, DC: American College Personnel Association, 1974; Michael Korff and Larry N. Horton, "Student Housing" in Asa S. Knowles (Editor), *The International Encyclopedia of Higher Education* (Volume 3), San Francisco: Jossey-Bass Publishers, 1977.

RESIDENT STUDENT, as distinct from nonresident student, in education, the student who is considered to be a legal resident of a particular state or school district. Since many institutions of higher education charge higher tuition for nonresident than resident students, the status of a student's residency (and even his/her admissability as a student) has serious economic implications for both student and institution. Criteria employed to determine residency include factors such as year-round home address, place of filing tax returns, state in which licensed to drive, and address for voter registration purposes. The courts have generally supported the right of colleges and universities to make the resident-nonresident distinction and have also held that a requirement calling for one academic year's durational residency to establish legal residency is reasonable.

School districts are obligated to enroll residents of legal school age without payment of tuition. The residency status of the child's parents is used to determine his/her residency status. Boards of education may establish tuition requirements/policies for nonresidents enrolled in their respective school systems.

The terms *resident student* and *residential student* are not synonymous, the latter referring to students who reside in an institution that has boarding facilities (e.g. residential school). (See ATTENDANCE AREA and RESIDENTIAL STUDENT.)
References: M. M. Chambers, *The Colleges and the Courts: The Developing Law of the Student and the College,* Danville, IL: The Interstate Printers and Publishers, Inc., 1972; *Combined Glossary: Terms and Definitions from the Handbooks of the State Educational Records and Reports Series,* Washington, DC: National Center for Education Statistics, U.S. Department of Health, Education, and Welfare, 1974; Leroy J. Peterson, et al., *The Law and the Public School Operation* (Second Edition), New York: Harper and Row, Publishers, 1978; D. Parker Young and Donald D. Gehring, *The College Student and the Courts* (Revised Edition), Asheville, NC: College Administration Publications, Inc., August 1977.

RESOURCE ROOM, a special class equipped to meet the educational needs of students with specific learning disabilities, mild mental retardation, or mild emotional-behavioral problems. The resource room is the one to which the mainstreamed child is sent for part of the school day. Here he/she receives specialized instruction from a special (resource) teacher. Such instruction supplements the instruction provided by the child's regular teacher in the regular classroom.

Bill Gearheart, a special educator, developed several guidelines for, and characteristics of, the resource room. They call for: (1) resource rooms in every school building; (2) time each week for resource teachers and regular teachers to meet; (3) a resource room load not to exceed 15–20 students; (4) no more than 3–4 children in the resource room at any given time; (5) 90–120 minutes of daily resource-room assistance for each child; (6) involving resource teacher in decisions affecting student placement; (7) involving resource and regular teachers in parent conferences; (8) close operating relationships between resource teacher and all other professional personnel in the school; and (9) provision of full-size classroom(s) for use as resource room(s). (See MAINSTREAMING.)
References: Bill R. Gearheart, *Learning Disabilities: Educa-*

tional Strategies (Second Edition), St. Louis, MO: The C. V. Mosby Company, 1977; Bernard G. Suran and Joseph V. Rizzo, *Special Children: An Integrative Approach,* Glenview, IL: Scott, Foresman and Company, 1979; Gerald Wallace and James A. McLoughlin, *Learning Disabilities: Concepts and Characteristics* (Second Edition), Columbus, OH: Charles E. Merrill Publishing Company, 1979; J. Lee Wiederholt, et al., *The Resource Teacher: A Guide to Effective Practices,* Boston: Allyn and Bacon, Inc., 1978.

RESOURCE TEACHER, a specialist teacher who works individually with children who have learning and/or behavior problems. The resource teacher supports the regular classroom teacher. Services such as analytic, remedial, developmental, or tutorial teaching are normally provided by the resource teacher. The resource teacher may have to work on the behaviors of children too. These services are generally provided in a separate (resource) room. There are times, however, when a resource teacher may actually prefer to be in the regular classroom working along with the regular teacher.

Resource teachers and resource rooms had their historical origins in special rooms for handicapped children or in the early remedial reading rooms where teachers and students generally worked alone. Today, resource teachers work cooperatively with regular classroom teachers to develop individualized educational programs for those who need them. It is not uncommon for a child to spend most of his/her time in the regular classroom and part of the time away from the class, working in a resource room on an individualized remedial program. (See REMEDIATION and RESOURCE ROOM.)
References: Marianne Frostig and Phyllis Maslow, *Learning Problems in the Classroom,* New York: Grune and Stratton, 1973; J. Lee Wiederholt, et al., *The Resource Teacher: A Guide to Effective Practices,* Boston: Allyn and Bacon, Inc., 1978.

RÉSUMÉ, a written summary of one's experience that is submitted as a supplement to, sometimes in lieu of, a job application. Prospective employers find numerous uses for résumés. Primarily, however, they use these documents to gain an overall impression of the job applicant or to determine whether or not an applicant's record of experience warrants an interview invitation.

Résumés are not uniform in terms of format. Traditionally, however, they contain the following categories of information about the job candidate:

(1) *personal information* such as age, address, health, height-weight, marital status, number and ages of children, and telephone numbers; (2) *education*, including degrees earned, program majors, institutions attended, and dates of attendance; (3) *record of employment*, a listing of previous positions held, inclusive dates of employment, and duties; and (4) *other information* such as organizational affiliations, hobbies, awards received, and names/addresses of references. A fifth category, *research and publications*, is normally expected of individuals seeking appointment to academic positions.
References: Fred D. Newell, *How to Get That Job*, Flagstaff, AZ: Northland Press, 1974; H. Lee Rust, *Job Search: The Complete Manual for Jobseekers*, New York: American Management Associations, 1979.

RETIREMENT FOR TEACHERS, programs whose primary purpose is to provide income to teachers (i.e. professional educators) who have retired. Membership in retirement systems for public school teachers, whether state or local, is mandatory. *Statewide* retirement systems are of three types: (1) those organized for teachers only; (2) education employees' systems with membership open to nonprofessional as well as professional employees; and (3) those to which all state/local employees (including teachers) belong. Major *local* systems are those operating for the benefit of teachers in a given city (e.g. New York City, Omaha). One of the earliest retirement systems, a local one, was established in Chicago in 1895.

Contribution patterns vary among the systems. Some (e.g. Florida) are supported exclusively by the state; in other systems (e.g. Arizona), employer and employee each make contributions.

The 1954 amendment to the Social Security Act made it possible for a majority of teachers to participate in the Social Security program as well as their regular retirement programs. In some systems, Social Security supplements the teacher retirement system; in others, the two are integrated.

As of 1977, 68 percent of the systems surveyed by the NEA had provisions for normal retirement at age 60 or earlier. Retirement systems frequently offer more than retirement benefits. Among them are disability benefits, death benefits before retirement, and survivor benefits. Depending on the system, service credit may be granted for military service or out-of-state service. Among the weaknesses associated with several systems is the penalty paid by the mobile teacher who, because he/she may have taught in more than one state, frequently finds himself/herself denied recognition for out-of-state service. (See VESTING.)
References: Franklin Parker, "Educators Facing Retirement: A Bibliographical Essay," *Phi Delta Kappan*, June 1976; W. William Schmid, *Retirement Systems of the American Teacher*, New York: Fleet Academic Editions, Inc. (in cooperation with the American Federation of Teachers, AFL-CIO), 1971; Theodor Schuchat, *Planning the Rest of Your Life* (PDK Fastback 61), Bloomington, IN: The Phi Delta Kappa Educational Foundation, 1975; Sharon M. Vernier, *Teacher Retirement Systems: Summary of the 1977 Survey* (NEA Research Memo), Washington, DC: The National Education Association, 1979.

RETREAT, the practice of group isolation, originally used by religious orders for individual and/or group meditation and prayer, often in a secluded environment. In such cases, retreat participants were/are isolated from day-to-day activities to permit them to concentrate on spiritual renewal.

Today, retreats are used by many nonreligious organizations for generally the same purposes: (1) to achieve isolation from the usual day-to-day routines, concerns, and problems; (2) to permit participants to concentrate on a particular subject area or topic; and (3) to develop "organizational" or individual renewal. Many educational organizations use the retreat as a means of bringing professional staff together, in a relaxed environment, for inservice or staff development purposes.
References: J. Victor Baldridge and Terrence E. Deal, *Managing Change in Educational Organizations*, Berkeley, CA: McCutchan Publishing Corporation, 1975; Mike M. Milstein (Editor), *Schools, Conflicts, and Change*, New York: Teachers College Press, 1980; Charles Moeller, *L'Homme Modern Devant le Salut*, Paris, France: Editions Ouvrières, 1965.

RETURN SWEEP, a reading term that describes the ability of a reader to shift his/her eyes from the end of one printed line to the beginning of the next. As a result of inaccurate return sweep, some lines may be skipped, others repeated; "losing place" frequently results. Eye movement photographs are sometimes used to help with detection and analysis of eye coordination problems such as return sweep.
Reference: Albert J. Harris and Edward R. Sipay, *How to Increase Reading Ability: A Guide to Developmental and Remedial Methods* (Sixth Edition), New York: David McKay Company, Inc., 1975.

REVENUE SHARING, a federal financing program that provides states and local communities with blocks of money for the purpose of meeting local needs. This program, inaugurated in 1972, permits states and communities to determine needs and to make allocations, features that distinguish revenue sharing from most other federal support programs. Grants are made subject to broad guidelines set forth by the federal government.

References: Paul R. Dommel, *The Politics of Revenue Sharing*, Bloomington, IN: Indiana University Press, 1974; Walter F. Scheffer (Editor), *General Revenue Sharing and Decentralization*, Norman, OK: University of Oklahoma Press, 1976.

REVERSAL ERRORS—See READING REVERSALS

RHEUMATIC FEVER, a disease stemming from a Group A streptococcal (upper respiratory tract) infection. It can affect one or more of the following areas of the body: joints (migratory arthritis); the brain (chorea); the heart (carditis); tissues (subcutaneous nodules); and the skin (esythema marginatum). Children between the ages of 4 and 18 are most likely to contract the disease, especially those living in overcrowded conditions or suffering from malnutrition.

The consequences of rheumatic fever can be quite severe. For example, carditis may leave a patient with a heart murmur, cardiac failure, or valvular deformity; arthritis, mild or severe, can affect the joints; chorea, which may also be mild or severe, can result in total incapacity as the result of severe chorea. Rheumatic fever can recur if a patient with a previous history of the disease fails to have a streptococcal infection treated. Children who have the residual effects of rheumatic fever (especially carditis) are sometimes classified as physically handicapped. Such classification depends on the severity of the effects.

References: Paul B. Beeson and Walsh McDermott (Editors), *Textbook of Medicine* (Fourteenth Edition), Philadelphia: W. B. Saunders Company, 1975; David N. Holvey (Editor), *The Merck Manual*, Rahway, NJ: Merck Sharp and Dohme Research Laboratories, 1972; Clarence Wilbur Taber, *Taber's Cyclopedic Medical Dictionary* (Eleventh Edition), Philadelphia: F. A. Davis Company, 1970.

RHYTHM, a musical term describing the grouping of sounds and silences that have varying duration. The concept of rhythm is taught using methods adapted to the age or musical sophistication of the learner. They include body movement, dance, use of rhythm instruments, notation, and the playing of traditional musical instruments.

References: Grosvenor Cooper and Leonard B. Meyer, *The Rhythmic Structure of Music*, Chicago: University of Chicago Press, 1960; Walter Dürr, et al., "Rhythm" in Stanley Sadie (Editor), *The New Grove Dictionary of Music and Musicians* (Volume 15), London, England: Macmillan Publishers Limited, 1980; Robert E. Nye and Vernice T. Nye, *Music in the Elementary School* (Fourth Edition), Englewood Cliffs, NJ: Prentice-Hall, Inc., 1977.

RHYTHM BAND, a group activity used to facilitate the rhythmic development of young children. Band members play simple percussion instruments such as drums, sticks, cymbols, blocks of wood, and tambourines. They may be purchased or made by the children themselves. Rhythm bands are used to help children keep time to music, to distinguish loud from soft sounds, and to develop a feeling for strong and weak beats.

References: Parks Grant, *Music for Elementary Teachers* (Second Edition), New York: Appleton-Century-Crofts, Inc., 1960; John Hawkinson and Martha Faulhaber, *Rhythms, Music and Instruments to Make*, Chicago: Albert Whitman and Company, 1975.

RICKOVER, HYMAN GEORGE, known as the "father of the atomic submarine," was born in the village of Makow, Poland on January 27, 1900; he died on July 8, 1986. Admiral Rickover's father was a tailor in Poland who settled in New York City in 1899 and sent for his family in 1903 (dates not verifiable). The family moved later to Chicago. Hyman Rickover attended John Marshall High School in Chicago and then the Naval Academy (class of 1922). Richover's only ship command was that of a minesweeper (USS Finch) in China in 1937. Rickover received a MS in Electrical Engineering from Columbia University in 1929. In 1946 he was assigned to the Manhattan Project in Oak Ridge, Tennessee thus starting his major career of merging atomic energy with ships.

In addition to Rickover's contributions to the U.S. Navy, he was a critic of American education during the 1950s and 1960s. He was a strong supporter of the "back-to-the-basics" movement. He wanted education to stress the traditional three Rs. He thought highly of the European education, and most particularly of the Soviet system of education. Two of his most popular books on education are: *Education and Freedom* (1959) and *American Education, A National Failure* (1963). (See BACK-TO-THE-BASICS.)

References: Norman Polmar and Thomas B. Allen, *Rickover*, New York: Simon and Schuster, 1982; Hyman Rickover, *American Education, A National Failure*, New York: Dutton Publishers, 1963; Hyman Rickover, *Education and Freedom*, New York: Dutton Publishers, 1959.

RIF—See READING IS FUNDAMENTAL

RIGHT TO READ, a federal program introduced to improve the reading skills of all citizens. Created by Public Law 93-380, amended in 1975 (Public Law 94-194), and with the National Reading Improvement Program as its major activity, Right to Read: (1) encouraged education agencies within each state to work to eliminate illiteracy; (2) recommended a process for assessing literacy needs; (3) supported instructional programs, carried out at the local level, to meet those needs; (4) served as a clearinghouse for collecting and disseminating information about reading techniques, strategies, and so on; (5) provided help with instructional and staff development programs; and (6) attempted to involve private and other governmental agencies in activities which addressed literacy needs.

Right to Read comprised six programs: (1) state level leadership and training programs; (2) reading improvement programs for low-performing preschool and elementary children; (3) reading academies aimed at illiterate (inschool and out-of-school) youth and adults; (4) special projects that made use of reading specialists at the classroom level; (5) dissemination efforts; and (6) distribution of inexpensive books (under contract with Reading is Fundamental, Inc.).

Public Law 95-561 broadened the program to focus on "basic skills" (which the legislation defined as mathematics, reading, and oral and written communication). The modified program, which in effect replaced Right to Read, became known as the Basic Skills and Educational Proficiency Programs. (See BASIC SKILLS AND EDUCATIONAL PROFICIENCY PROGRAMS and READING IS FUNDAMENTAL.)

References: Federal Register, Volume 41, No. 103, May 26, 1976; Shirley A. Jackson, *Annual Report: The Right to Read, Fiscal Year 1978,* Washington, DC: Office of Education, U.S. Department of Health, Education, and Welfare, 1978; Public Law 93-380, *United States Statutes at Large, 1974* (Volume 88, Part I), Washington, DC: U.S. Government Printing Office, 1976; Public Law 94-194, *United States Statutes at Large, 1975* (Volume 89), Washington, DC: U.S. Government Printing Office, 1977.

ROCHESTER METHOD, a system of instruction used with hearing impaired learners. Developed in the Rochester School for the Deaf by Dr. Zenas F. Westervelt (in 1878), the method combines the use, simultaneously, of fingerspelling (a system that uses the fingers of one hand) with speech. (See FINGER SPELLING.)

References: William J. McClure, "The Revival of the Rochester Method" in Irving S. Fusfeld (Editor), *A Handbook of Readings in Education of the Deaf and Postschool Implications,* Springfield, IL: Charles C. Thomas, Publisher, 1967; James A. Pahz, et al., *Total Communication: The Meaning Behind the Movement to Expand Educational Opportunities for Deaf Children,* Springfield, IL: Charles C. Thomas, Publisher, 1978.

ROCKEFELLER FOUNDATION, a philanthropic organization chartered in 1913 and endowed by John D. Rockefeller, Sr. The foundation's general mission is to promote the well-being of mankind throughout the world. In recent years, programs supported or carried out by the foundation have been narrowed to five areas: Arts, Humanities and Contemporary Values; Conquest of Hunger; Equal Opportunity; International Relations; and Population and Health.

The foundation is administered by a President and his executive staff. An independent Board of Trustees controls the organization's policies and budget. The foundation has appropriated approximately $1,500,000,000 since its inception.

References: The Rockefeller Foundation, *The President's Review and Annual Report,* New York: The Foundation, 1977; The Rockefeller Foundation, *The Rockefeller Foundation: Purpose and Program,* New York: The Foundation, Undated Brochure.

RODRIGUEZ v. SAN ANTONIO SCHOOL DISTRICT, a landmark law decision rendered by the U.S. Supreme Court that addressed the matter of disparity in per-pupil expenditures among different Texas school districts. A group of Mexican-American parents whose children were enrolled in a school district with a low property tax base argued that uneven per-pupil expenditures among school districts created a situation that denied children enrolled in low-support districts an equal right to quality education. The plaintiffs argued that the state's financing system violated the equal-protection clause of the U.S. Constitution's Fourteenth Amendment.

Although a federal district court in Texas had previously ruled in favor of the plaintiffs, that ruling was overturned by the U.S. Supreme Court (1973) on the grounds that the U.S. Constitution does not explicitly or implicitly guarantee a right to education. Thus, the unequal expenditures were not held to be discriminatory. The Court went on to support the state's school financing system as a rational one. (See *SERRANO v. PRIEST*.)

References: E. Gordon Gee and David J. Sperry, *Education Law and the Public Schools: A Compendium*, Boston: Allyn and Bacon, Inc., 1978; David L. Kirp and Mark G. Yudof, *Educational Policy and the Law: Cases and Materials*, Berkeley, CA: McCutchan Publishing Corporation, 1974; E. Edmund Reutter, Jr. and Robert R. Hamilton, *The Law of Public Education* (Second Edition), Mineola, NY: The Foundation Press, Inc., 1976; *Rodriguez v. San Antonio Independent School District*, 337 F. Supp. 280 (W.D. Tex. 1971), rev'd 411 U.S. 1, 93 S.Ct. 1278, 36 L.Ed. 2d 16 (1973).

ROKEACH SCALE, or Dogmatism Scale, an instrument developed under the direction of Milton Rokeach for measuring individual differences in openness or closedness of belief systems.

Form D of the scale consists of 66 items. The items are statements to which the respondent is asked to react by indicating a specific degree of agreement or disagreement. For example, as answer to the item: "To compromise with our political opponents is dangerous because it usually leads to the betrayal of our own side," the respondent registers very much agreement, agreement on the whole, little agreement, little disagreement, disagreement on the whole, or very much disagreement. High test scores reflect relatively high levels of dogmatism; low scores indicate relatively low levels of dogmatism.

A shorter version of the scale, Form E, contains the best 40 items selected from Form D.

The Rokeach Scale is used by educational researchers to measure between-group dogmatism differences or, on a pre-post-test basis, to measure changes in an individual's (or group's) belief system. (See DOGMATISM.)

Reference: Milton Rokeach, *The Open and Closed Mind*, New York: Basic Books, Inc., Publishers, 1960.

ROLE, a set of expectations (desired behaviors) associated with a particular job title. These expectations constitute evaluative standards that can be used to assess an incumbent jobholder's effectiveness.

References: William B. Castetter, *The Personnel Function in Educational Administration* (Third Edition), New York: Macmillan Publishing Company, Inc., 1981; Richard A. Gorton, *School Administration and Supervision: Important Issues, Concepts, and Case Studies* (Second Edition), Dubuque, IA: Wm. C. Brown Company, Publishers, 1980; Neil Gross, et al., *Explorations in Role Analysis: Studies of the School Superintendency Role*, New York: John Wiley and Sons, 1966.

ROLE CONFLICT, an organizational problem resulting from incompatible job expectations. Role conflicts are of two types: intrarole and interrole. *Intrarole conflicts* exist when an incumbent jobholder works with different groups whose expectations of him/her are not congruent. For example, faculty members may expect their department chairperson to serve as their advocate, but the chairperson's supervisor may expect him/her to behave as the department's monitor. *Interrole conflicts* arise when an individual fulfills two roles (e.g. teacher and mother) and the expectations of one conflict with the expectations of the other.

The Getzels-Guba model is a model sometimes used for understanding role conflict. (See GETZELS-GUBA MODEL.)

References: Richard A. Gorton, *School Administration and Supervision: Important Issues, Concepts, and Case Studies* (Second Edition), Dubuque, IA: Wm. C. Brown Company, Publishers, 1980; Neal Gross, et al., *Explorations in Role Analysis: Studies of the School Superintendency Role*, New York: John Wiley and Sons, 1966; Donald E. Tope, et al., *The Social Sciences View School Administration*, Englewood Cliffs, NJ: Prentice-Hall, Inc., 1965.

ROLE NORM, a rule of behavior or specific observable behavior associated with a particular status or position. For the elementary principal, examples of role norms include: (1) "review with teachers written evaluations of their work," or (2) "take an active part in community affairs." (See ROLE and ROLE CONFLICT.)

References: John M. Foskett, *The Normative World of the Elementary School Principal*, Eugene, OR: The Center for the Study of Educational Administration, 1967; Donald E. Tope, et al., *The Social Sciences View School Administration*, Englewood Cliffs, NJ: Prentice-Hall, Inc., 1965.

ROLE-PERSON THEORY—See GETZELS-GUBA MODEL

ROLE PLAYING, a form of simulation used for training purposes. Participants are assigned a role (e.g. parent, principal, pupil) and asked to act out that role, realistically, as they interact with other role-playing participants. Role playing may be used to demonstrate desirable or undesirable behaviors, for rehearsing, to produce attitude change, to act out problems, or for reporting purposes. (See PSYCHODRAMA and SIMULATION.)

References: Robert C. Hawley, *Value Exploration through Role Playing*, Amherst, MA: ERA Press, Education Research Associates, 1974; Robert B. Kozma, et al., *Instructional Techniques in Higher Education*, Englewood Cliffs, NJ: Educational Technology Publications, 1978; Merle

M. Ohlsen, *Group Counseling* (Second Edition), New York: Holt, Rinehart and Winston, Inc., 1977; John F. Thompson, *Using Role Playing in the Classroom* (PDK Fastback 114), Bloomington, IN: The Phi Delta Kappa Educational Foundation, 1978; E. C. Wragg, *Teaching Teaching*, London, England: David and Charles, Inc., 1974.

ROLLING ADMISSIONS, an admission procedure used in many colleges and universities where admission decisions and notifications are made throughout the year. An applicant applies to a particular institution at any time; the institution receives the application, and, rather than waiting for a particular time (e.g. spring) to inform the applicant, the institution notifies the individual immediately of its decision. Thus, the institution makes admissions decisions continuously. Usually, in return for this expedited procedure, the applicant is required to inform the institution within a prescribed period of his/her intention to accept the admission offer.

Early admissions, somewhat different from rolling admissions, is a process in which students apply early and state that, if accepted, they will attend the institution. As a consequence of students' commitments to attend, the institution then makes admissions decisions early, usually in the fall. Students should not assume that an early admissions program will enable unqualified applicants to be admitted to an institution of higher education. Not all colleges and universities have early admissions programs.

Reference: Herbert S. Sacks, et al., *Hurdles,* New York: Atheneum, 1978.

RORSCHACH TEST, commonly called the "ink-blot" test, a ten ink-blot-figures instrument used as a projective test to reveal an individual's personality structure. Each ink-blot is reproduced on a card that measures 7 by 9½ inches. Five of the ink-blots have colored as well as black ink. They are presented to the subject one at a time. The subject is asked to indicate what each blot suggests or reminds him/her of. Inferences about the individual's personality are made on the basis of these responses.

The Rorschach Test is difficult to score and takes considerable training and education to master. The nature of what is a scorable response, categories for location of responses, categories for determinants (movement, shading, color, or form), and categories for content (human, animal, geography, art, etc.) are all part of the complex scoring procedure.

Justinus Kerner first reported on the use of ink-blots in 1857, but it was Herman Rorschach of Zurich, Switzerland, who, in 1921, developed a standardized ink-blot test. His work was extended by many psychologists following his death in 1922. (See PROJECTIVE TECHNIQUES.)

References: Samuel J. Beck, et al., *Rorschach's Test* (Third Edition), New York: Grune and Stratton, 1961; Paul Lemkau and Bernard Kronenberg (Translators and Editors), *Herman Rorschach's Psychodiagnostics (1924–1942),* New York: Grune and Stratton, 1964; Eugene E. Levitt and Aàre Truumaa, *The Rorschach Technique with Children and Adolescents,* New York: Grune and Stratton, 1972.

ROTC—See AIR FORCE RESERVE OFFICERS TRAINING CORPS; ARMY JUNIOR ROTC; ARMY RESERVE OFFICERS TRAINING CORPS; and NAVAL RESERVE OFFICERS TRAINING CORPS

ROTE COUNTING, the simple recitation (from memory) of number names. Very young children use rote counting in nursery rhymes (e.g. One, two, buckle my shoe...) or rote count (e.g. counting from 1 to 10) without necessarily knowing the mathematical meaning of the numbers being recited. (See RATIONAL COUNTING.)

References: Herbert Ginsburg, *Children's Arithmetic: The Learning Process,* New York: D. Van Nostrand Company, Inc., 1977; Donald D. Paige, et al., *Elementary Mathematical Methods,* New York: John Wiley and Sons, 1978.

ROTE LEARNING, the acquiring of content material through memorization. There is no development of the powers of reasoning involved in rote learning. Facts and information are learned in isolation. The learning of the multiplication tables, for example, is often achieved through rote learning. There are times when rote learning may be the most viable way to acquire content material. Constant (repeated) use of material learned enhances the retention of what was learned through the rote approach.

References: Jack A. Adams, *Learning and Memory: An Introduction,* Homewood, IL: The Dorsey Press, 1976; G. Douglas Mayo (Editor), *Learning and Instructional Improvement Digest,* Englewood Cliffs, NJ: Prentice-Hall, Inc., 1973; Merlin C. Wittrock (Editor), *Learning and Instruction,* Berkeley, CA: McCutchan Publishing Corporation, 1977.

ROUGH ROCK DEMONSTRATION SCHOOL, a school located in Lukachukai, Arizona, on the Navajo Indian Reservation. In 1964, Rough Rock was one of several Bureau of Indian Affairs (BIA) schools serving Indian children. In that year, with

BIA approval and supplementary funding provided by the Office of Economic Opportunity (OEO), it was transformed into a demonstration school that attempted to improve educational opportunity by stressing Indian self-determination. Its multifaceted program included areas of demonstration such as: (1) involving Navajos in policy formulation and program development; (2) featuring Navajo culture, including study of the Navajo language, in the curriculum; (3) inservice training for the school's many staff members; (4) making adult education available to community residents; (5) encouraging close home-school ties; and (6) making the school's facilities and services (e.g. showers, laundry) available to community residents.

A 1968 evaluation of the school, completed at OEO's request, criticized its limited attention to the academic program. A year later, four Navajo leaders conducted another evaluation that praised the school for bringing school and community closer together and for instilling cultural pride in the Navajo people. (See INDIAN SELF-DETERMINATION.)

References: Thomas R. Reno, "A Demonstration in Navajo Education" in R. Merwin Deever, et al. (Editors), *American Indian Education,* Tempe, AZ: Arizona State University, June 1974; Robert A. Roessel, Jr., "An Overview of the Rough Rock Demonstration School" in R. Merwin Deever, et al. (Editors), *American Indian Education,* Tempe, AZ: Arizona State University, June 1974; Margaret C. Szasz, *Education and the American Indian: The Road to Self-Determination Since 1928* (Second Edition), Albuquerque, NM: University of New Mexico Press, 1977.

ROUSSEAU, JEAN J. (June 28, 1712–July 2, 1778), Swiss-born critic of the formal approaches to religion, education, and manners being practiced in Europe during the early 18th century. In contrast, he espoused his doctrine of Naturalism, one that advocated the natural development of the individual learner with considerable attention given to learner needs, learner interests, reason, experimentation, and training of the senses. A romanticist, Rousseau argued against authoritative and formal teaching.

Rousseau's ideas were set forth in his best-known book, *Emile* (1762). This five-part work ("infancy," "childhood," "boyhood," "youth," and "the education of woman") proved to be one of the most significant books published in the 18th century. The educational philosophy presented in *Emile* did much to influence education in western Europe and, later, the United States.

References: Frank P. Graves, *Great Educators of Three Centuries: Their Work and Its Influence on Modern Education,* New York: AMS Press, 1971 (Originally printed in 1912); Jean J. Rousseau, *Emile* (Translated by Barbara Foxley), London, England: Everyman's Library, 1966; Mabel L. Sahakian and William S. Sahakian, *Rousseau as Educator,* New York: Twayne Publishers, 1974.

RUBELLA, or German Measles, a viral disease that can cause deformity in the human fetus when contracted by a mother during her first trimester of pregnancy. It has been estimated that 20,000 to 30,000 children born in the United States after the Rubella epidemic of 1963–64 sustained handicaps, many involving multiple impairments. Deformities attributable to Rubella include deafness, visual impairment, retardation, and cardiac disorders. A vaccine now in use has effectively lessened Rubella-induced impairments by reducing the incidence of German Measles.

References: Lloyd M. Dunn (Editor), *Exceptional Children in the Schools: Special Education in Transition,* New York: Holt, Rinehart and Winston, Inc., 1973; Janet B. Hardy, "Rubella and Its Aftermath," *Children,* May–June 1969; E. Norrby, *Rubella Virus,* New York: Springer-Verlag, 1969.

RURAL EDUCATION, education that takes place in rural communities or small towns. In the United States, by 1975, over 80 percent of the rural population was not living or working on farms. Consequently, the curricula of rural schools have become diverse in structure and design. As a result of consolidation, many one-room school houses, small schools, and small school districts no longer exist.

It is not uncommon to find college preparatory and developed vocational programs being offered in many of the larger rural consolidated schools. The vocational programs may include: agricultural education; business education; trade and industry; home economics; and other such programs normally found in urban and/or suburban schools.

In spite of the consolidation movement, numerous problems continue to affect rural education. Although not found in every rural school district, they include problems normally associated with small populations: weak tax base; higher teacher turnover; limited educational programs; and relatively lower test scores.

References: Barbara B. Israel (Editor), *Attacking Rural Poverty,* Baltimore, MD: Johns Hopkins University Press, 1974; Gertrude H. McPherson, *Small Town Teacher,*

Cambridge, MA: Harvard University Press, 1972; Jonathan P. Sher, *Education in Rural America,* Boulder, CO: Westview Press, 1977; Southern Regional Committee for Family Life, *Educational and Vocational Goals for Rural Youth in the South,* Raleigh, NC: North Carolina Agricultural Experiment Station, 1965.

RURAL/REGIONAL EDUCATION ASSOCIATION (R/REA), a national organization that works to expand educational opportunities in, and to promote research about, education in smaller and rural American communities. The present association grew out of a National Education Association department, the Department of Rural and Agricultural Education. Its name was changed three times thereafter (in 1919 to the Department of Rural Education and in 1969 to the Rural Education Association; in 1975, it assumed its present name).

In carrying out its work as an advocate group for rural education, R/REA makes both individual and institutional memberships available to all interested professionals; publishes a bimonthly newsletter, *Rural/Regional Education News;* sponsors annual conferences; prepares occasional papers and research reports; and works closely with other organizations having an interest in rural education.

The office of the association's field secretaries and editors is in Fredonia, New York.

References: Rural/Regional Education Association, *Rural/Regional Education Association,* Fredonia, NY: The Association, Undated Brochure; *Rural/Regional Education News,* Spring 1980.

SABBATICAL LEAVE, a fringe benefit for teachers commonplace in institutions of higher education and available in some school districts. The leave is granted to strengthen the sponsoring institution and to enhance the professional development of individual faculty members. Sabbaticals are most frequently offered to individuals planning to pursue advanced study, to conduct research, or to improve their overall performance as teachers. Applicants seeking sabbatical leave are generally required to have completed at least six years of satisfactory local service and to submit a leave plan, the latter subject to review by administrators or a committee of peers. Successful applicants may be obligated to remain in the service of the sponsoring institution for at least two years following the sabbatical leave. Personnel policies normally limit the number of faculty members eligible for leave at any one time. Additionally, they guarantee no interruption of other benefits such as retirement eligibility. Although such policies sometimes provide full salary for those on half-year leave or half-salary for teachers on leave for a full year, numerous institutions provide no (or very limited) compensation during periods of leave.

References: William B. Castetter, *The Personnel Function in Educational Administration* (Second Edition), New York: Macmillan Publishing Company, Inc., 1976; Mark H. Ingraham, *The Outer Fringe,* Madison, WI: University of Wisconsin Press, 1965.

SABER-TOOTH CURRICULUM, a parody on education written by Harold Benjamin. (Benjamin used the nom de plume J. Abner Peddiwell, Ph.D.) In this entertaining book, Benjamin tells of a primitive people whose survival depended on their ability to catch fish with bare hands, to club horses, and to frighten away saber-tooth tigers with fire. The teaching of these skills eventually became the curriculum of the primitive people's school. In time, a glacier moved across this primitive land, requiring its occupants to develop new survival skills. Many in the community did, but those controlling the school's curriculum resisted pressures to include the new skills in the school's program. Benjamin's parody points up two facts: (1) that the educational needs of communities change, and (2) that school curriculum is not always responsive to these changing needs. (See BENJAMIN, HAROLD.)

Reference: Harold Benjamin, *The Saber-Tooth Curriculum,* New York: McGraw-Hill Book Company, 1939.

SAFETY EDUCATION, a specific curriculum that focuses on accident prevention and accident loss reduction. Its purpose is to improve the quality of life through the development of appropriate safety habits, skills, attitudes, and knowledges.

Safety education had its origins in 1867 when the State of Massachusetts passed a law providing for factory inspectors. In 1877, Massachusetts required employers to protect workers from hazardous machinery, but it wasn't until the 1920s that safety education became a part of education at the urging of E. George Payne and Albert W. Whitney.

The categories of accidents constituting the major concerns of safety education are: traffic/motor-vehicle/pedestrians; work/occupational; home; and public (accidents that occur in public places or places that are used in a public manner, such as recreational areas). Typical topics covered in safety education include philosophy, theory, trends, costs, and legislation in safety education; school safety programs; recreational hunting, boating, sports; traffic, pedestrian, bicycle, motorcycle safety; and agricultural safety. (See DRIVER EDUCATION.)

References: A. E. Florio, et al., *Safety Education* (Fourth Edition), New York: McGraw-Hill Book Company, 1979; Joseph H. Mroz, *Safety in Everyday Living,* Dubuque, IA: Wm. C. Brown Company, Publishers, 1978; Alton L. Thygerson, *Safety: Concepts and Instruction* (Second Edition), Englewood Cliffs, NJ: Prentice-Hall, Inc., 1976; W. Wayne Worick, *Safety Education: Man, His Machines, and His Environment,* Englewood Cliffs, NJ: Prentice-Hall, Inc., 1975.

SAFETY PATROLS, school-sponsored organizations of older students whose duty it is "to instruct, direct, and control the members of the student body in crossing the streets and highways at or near schools; and, to assist teachers and parents in the instruction of school children in safe pedestrian practices at all times and places" (p. 2). This statement comes from *Policies and Practices for School Safety Patrols,* a publication of the American Automobile Association.

Patrols of this sort began to be used in American schools in the 1920s. Rules for their operation were formulated in 1930 by the American Automobile

Association, the National Congress of Parents and Teachers, and the National Safety Council. Changes in these rules were later made by these and other organizations including the National Education Association and the U.S. Office of Education.

In school districts, safety patrols are organized with the approval of local school boards. Their membership includes older (over grade 5) and reliable students who have parent approval to participate. Insignia such as white or fluourescent Sam Browne belts are used for visibility and identification, especially when members serve as school crossing guards. Student officers and a faculty supervisor oversee the work of safety patrols.

School districts, until recently, invoked the doctrine of governmental immunity to protect themselves against damage suits growing out of injuries to pupils or patrols. Today, however, approximately half of the states permit liability suits against districts.

References: American Automobile Association, *Policies and Practices for School Safety Patrols*, Falls Church, VA: The Association, Undated Brochure; Marion A. McGhehey, *Is Liability a Factor Affecting School Safety Patrol Programs Today?* Falls Church, VA: The American Automobile Association, 1971.

SALARY SCHEDULE, a plan for paying employees. Salary schedules for teachers typically include annual increments that reward experience and advanced (postbaccalaureate) training. Some schedules (approximately 10 percent) also include supplements payable to teachers judged to be meritorious. Granting of extra pay for extra duties such as coaching or yearbook sponsorship is common. The single salary schedule, which entitles teachers to equal pay regardless of sex, marital status, or grade level taught, operates in most American school districts. Salary schedules for administrators and supervisors are sometimes based on the teachers' salary schedule with graduated factors added (e.g. 1.85 × base for elementary school principals, 2.5 × base for the superintendent, etc.) for increased responsibility. Usually, the salary schedule has no contractual status. Rather, it is a policy statement that may be modified at the discretion of the board of education. (See INDEX SALARY SCHEDULE and SINGLE SALARY SCHEDULE.)

References: Leroy J. Peterson, et al., *The Law and Public School Operation* (Second Edition), New York: Harper and Row, Publishers, 1978; Research Division, National Education Association, *Salary Schedules and Fringe Benefits for Teachers, 1972–73* (Research Report 1973-R2), Washington, DC: The Association, 1973; Jean L. Proetsch, *Salary Schedules, 1978–79,* Washington, DC: National Education Association, 1979; E. Edmund Reutter, Jr. and Robert R. Hamilton, *The Law of Public Education* (Second Edition), Mineola, NY: The Foundation Press, Inc., 1976; Gertrude N. Stieber, et al., *Methods of Scheduling Salaries for Teachers,* Arlington, VA: Educational Research Service, Inc., 1978.

SAMPLE, a part of a defined population that is representative of that population. For example, if adolescent girls (population) in a particular city were to be studied, a researcher might select 10 percent of the girls in all the junior and senior high schools of that city. The 10 percent, if selected appropriately, would constitute the *sample* of the population. Gallup, Harris, and Nielsen polls use samples rather than the entire population when they survey the American public.

The use of samples is important because time, adequate funding, and accessibility to an entire population are not always possible. Through appropriate sampling and statistical procedures, inferences from a sample to a population can be made. (See POPULATION and SAMPLING.)

References: Walter R. Borg and Meredith D. Gall, *Educational Research: An Introduction* (Fifth Edition), New York: Longman, Inc., 1989; William M. Hays, *Statistics* (Fourth Edition), New York: Holt, Rinehart and Winston, Inc., 1988.

SAMPLING, a technique used to select a microcosm from a given population. There are several different approaches to selecting a sample. In *random sampling,* everyone has an equal chance to be selected. The selection of one individual does not rest on the selection of another particular individual; that is, the selection is independent. A table of random numbers, a lottery, a bingo cage with numbers, and so on are techniques that illustrate random selection.

Stratified sampling requires breaking the population into segments and then selecting randomly a predetermined number from each segment (or stratum). The entire stratified sample must represent (mirror) the original population. For example, if the population is made up of 60 percent girls, the final sample must also be made up of 60 percent girls.

Cluster sampling is another sampling approach. It is usually used when the population is extremely large. The population is broken down into units or clusters. All individuals within a unit or cluster are then included in the sample once their particular cluster has been selected randomly. Clusters may be broken down into subclusters. Such subdivisions depend on the size of the population, the size of the clusters, and the design of the study. States, counties, cities, or voting wards may be clusters, each a subcluster of the previous cluster and all being subclusters of the United States.

Size of sample is dependent on many factors: the size of the population, costs, and so on. The larger the sample, the more representative it is, if selected appropriately and without bias. The numbers that describe the characteristics of a sample are called statistics. They are designated using Roman symbols; for example, $\bar{X}$ stands for mean (average), N for number of subjects/cases, and s for standard deviation. (See POPULATION; RANDOM SAMPLING; SAMPLE; and TABLE OF RANDOM NUMBERS.)

References: Walter R. Borg and Meredith D. Gall, *Educational Research: An Introduction* (Fifth Edition), New York: Longman, Inc., 1989; L. R. Gay, *Educational Research: Competencies for Analysis and Application* (Third Edition), Columbus, OH: Merrill Publishing Company, 1987; Bill Williams, *A Sampler on Sampling*, New York: John Wiley and Sons, 1978.

SANCTIONS, pressures that labor organizations exert in an effort to have an employer correct what the organization considers to be an injustice or poor working conditions. Of all teacher organizations, the National Education Association (NEA) has been in the forefront with respect to development and use of sanctions. An early form of sanctions was authorized in 1929 when the NEA Code of Ethics was adopted. It provided that teachers must "refuse to accept a position when the vacancy has been created through unprofessional activity or pending controversy over professional policy or the application of unjust personnel practices and procedures."

In 1962, a more concerted form of sanctions was endorsed by the NEA, motivated primarily by a desire to attract new members and to curb the growth of a competing unit, the American Federation of Teachers. This later form of sanctions included several levels of pressure: (1) notifying members of unsatisfactory working conditions in a school system (district or state); (2) requesting members not to seek employment in the system; (3) urging incumbent employees to leave the service of the offending system; and (4) threatening to expel members accepting or continuing employment in the system.

References: Robert C. O'Reilly, *Understanding Collective Bargaining in Education: Negotiations, Contracts and Disputes Between Teachers and Boards,* Metuchen, NJ: The Scarecrow Press, Inc., 1978; Phi Delta Kappan Editorial, "Collective Bargaining and Strikes? Or Professional Negotiations and Sanctions?" *Phi Delta Kappan,* October 1962.

SAVE HARMLESS, a legal term referring to statutes that protect teachers in cases of litigation stemming from their alleged negligence. Some states require local school districts to defend employees when such charges are made against them and to pay any judgments that may result from such litigation. The statutes limit indemnification to actions carried out during the employee's normal performance of his/her duties.

References: Richard D. Gatti and Daniel J. Gatti, *Encyclopedic Dictionary of School Law,* West Nyack, NY: Parker Publishing Company, Inc., 1975; E. Edmund Reutter, Jr. and Robert R. Hamilton, *The Law of Public Education* (Second Edition), Mineola, NY: The Foundation Press, Inc., 1976.

SAVE THE CHILDREN FEDERATION (SCF), a nonprofit agency devoted to assisting needy children through the process of community development. The organization was formed in 1932, during the depression period, to meet the needs of coal miners' children in Appalachia. It has since developed into an agency with a worldwide focus. In 1979, for example, approximately half of SCF's funds were used to support programs in the United States; the remaining monies were spent in 18 foreign countries located in Africa, Asia, Europe, Latin America, and the Middle East. A staff of almost 500 full- and part-time professionals, located throughout the world, carries out SCF's programs.

During its history, SCF has supported programs in different parts of the United States (e.g. Ozarks, Imperial Valley of California, the Navajo Indian Reservation). These early programs frequently involved distribution of clothing contributed by American school children. Inclusion of overseas programs began in the 1940s.

In recent years, SCF has supported self-help programs, the philosophy being that needy children can best be served by addressing the needs of their families and communities. Special attention has been given to need areas such as health and nutrition, women and family development, technology development, and economic development.

SCF's main offices are in Westport, Connecticut.

References: "Save the Children Federation" in Peter Romanofsky (Editor), *Social Service Organizations* (Volume 2), Westport, CT: Greenwood Press, 1978; Save the Children Federation, *Save the Children: 1979 Annual Report*, Westport, CT: The Federation, 1979.

SCALE, a psychological measurement used to represent differences among individuals in performance, abilities, attitudes, and so on. Scales enable different test scores to be compared with each other. The need to convert raw scores to particular scale scores becomes apparent as one realizes that, in most psychological measurements, there is no absolute zero and most scores are not of equal increments. For example, an I.Q. of 100 is not twice the magnitude of an I.Q. of 50. Zero I.Q. has no real meaning, and, in the physical world, 100 pounds is twice that of 50 pounds (theoretically it is possible to have no weight).

The conversion of a raw score to a scale structure is called *scaling.* Usually, scales have a set mean and standard deviation. Consequently, scaled scores can be used for comparative purposes. There are many types of scales. *Percentages correct* is a poor form of a scale, because percentages do not have equal increments; nevertheless, they are used extensively in schools. The *standard score* (Z) has a mean of 0 and a standard deviation of 1.00; the Z Score's mean equals 50 with a standard deviation of 10. *C-scale* is an 11-point scaled score (0–10) with a mean of 5.0 and the standard deviation ranging between a C of 3 and a C of 7. *Stanine scale* has a mean of 5 and a standard deviation of 1.96. Stanine is a 9-unit scale (1–9). Regular classroom test scores can be converted into any of these scaled scores.

Standardized test scores that are scaled should include not only the actual scaling but norm group and equivalent scores in order to interpret the scaled scores as well. Scholastic Aptitude Tests, with a mean of 500 and a standard deviation of 100, are scaled and provide normative and equivalent scores for meaningful interpretation. (See STANDARD SCORES.)

References: William H. Angoff, "Scales, Norms, and Equivalent Score" in Robert L. Thorndike (Editor), *Educational Measurement*, Washington, DC: American Council on Education, 1971; Joy P. Guilford and Benjamin Fruchter, *Fundamental Statistics in Psychology and Education* (Sixth Edition), New York: McGraw-Hill Book Company, 1978.

SCALE, MUSICAL, notes that make up an octave and are presented in order of rising pitches. These notes are arranged in different ways to form different musical compositions.

There are several musical scales, each of which divides the octave differently. The scale used for traditional music is the *diatonic scale,* with two modes (major and minor) and consisting of 7 tones. The *chromatic scale* consists of 12 semitones (a *semitone* is the smallest interval in traditional Western music). The *pentatonic scale* is made up of 5 tones to the octave, and the *whole-tone scale* consists of 6 whole tones to the octave.

References: Robert Fink and Robert Ricci, *The Language of Twentieth Century Music: A Dictionary of Terms,* New York: Schirmer Books (Macmillan), 1975: J. A. Westrup and F. Harrison (Revised by Conrad Wilson), *The New College Encyclopedia of Music,* New York: W. W. Norton and Company, Inc., 1976.

SCALE OF MEASUREMENT, classification of measurement according to specific properties that distinguish one classification from other classifications. There are four basic classifications of measurement (or data): nominal, ordinal, interval, and ratio.

Nominal data are those that fall into separate categories (e.g. American, Russian, English, citizen, noncitizen). *Ordinal* measurements are ordered on some continuum (e.g. first, second, third, hardest, hard, soft). There need not be equal distances between each unit in ordinal data; distance between categories in nominal data also has no meaning.

Interval measures are based on an actual continuum, with equal units starting from an arbitrary origin. Fahrenheit scale is an example of an interval scale. Fifty degrees (50°F) are 25° greater than 25°F; yet 50°F is not twice as hot as 25°F. This is due to the fact that the Fahrenheit scale does not have a true or absolute zero. *Ratio* scales have a true zero and also have equal intervals. Measurements in feet are examples of ratio data. There is a true zero (no measurement at all) and 10 feet is twice that of 5 feet.

References: L. R. Gay, *Educational Research: Competencies for Analysis and Application* (Third Edition), Columbus, OH: Merrill Publishing Company, 1987; Harold O. Kiess, *Statistical Concepts for the Behavioral Sciences,* Boston: Allyn and Bacon, 1989.

SCANNING, a method of rapid reading. Using this method, the student hurriedly looks over one or more pages in search of specific information such as a date, a time, a name, or a price. This searching type of reading is exemplified whenever one uses a telephone directory, a dictionary, a catalogue, or even a menu. Scanning is unique in that it can not be used with spoken language. (See SKIMMING.)

References: Dolores Durkin, *Teaching Them to Read* (Third Edition), Boston: Allyn and Bacon, Inc., 1978; Edward Fry, *Reading Instruction for Classroom and Clinic,* New York: McGraw-Hill Book Company, 1972.

SCAT (COOPERATIVE SCHOOL AND COLLEGE ABILITY TESTS) (Series II), a battery of standardized tests used to evaluate the intellectual ability of a student to complete studies successfully at the next higher level. Separate tests are available for grades 4–6, 7–9, 10–12, and 13–14. Three scores are provided. They are the verbal, quantitative, and total. The test can be administered in a relatively short time (approximately one class period). The SCAT is published by Educational Testing Service.

Reference: Oscar K. Buros (Editor), *The Eighth Mental Measurements Yearbook* (Volume I), Highland Park, NJ: The Gryphon Press, 1978.

SCHEDULES OF REINFORCEMENT, rules that determine when, and in what sequence, reinforcing stimuli are presented to an organism. Schedules of reinforcement involve time, changes in the environment, and the nature of the response (behavioral change) exhibited by the organism affected.

Schedules of reinforcement are used extensively in operant behavior and conditioning. Both C. B. Feister and B. F. Skinner used schedules of reinforcement in their research in the 1940s and 1950s. There are several different general categories of schedules: (1) *fixed time,* reinforcement that occurs after a specific time lapse regardless of response being made; (2) *variable time,* time lapse changes from one reinforcement to another regardless of response being made; (3) *fixed ratio,* reinforcement that occurs after a specific number of responses are made; and (4) *variable ratio,* a schedule that does not require a specific number of responses to occur before a reinforcement stimulus is presented. Interval schedules include time and a fixed ratio schedule. With fixed interval, the time is constant; with variable interval, it is not.

References: G. M. Gilbert and J. R. Millenson (Editors), *Reinforcement: Behavior Analysis,* New York: Academic Press, 1972; Werner K. Honig and J. E. R. Staddon, *Handbook of Operant Behavior,* Englewood Cliffs, NJ: Prentice-Hall, Inc., 1977; K. Daniel O'Leary and Susan G. O'Leary (Editors), *Classroom Management: The Success-*

ful Use of Behavior Modification (Second Edition), New York: Pergamon Press, Inc., 1977; William N. Schoenfeld (Editor), *The Theory of Reinforcement Schedules,* New York: Appleton-Century-Crofts, Inc., 1970.

SCHEMA THEORY, a concept that focuses on the relationship between prior knowledge and comprehension. The theory explains the way in which experiences and related concepts are stored in memory. Schema (schemata, pl.) is the individual's internal explanation of the nature of situations, objects, etc., that are encountered; it is the way knowledge is organized within the brain. These schemata are constantly being altered and/or changed as new knowledge is absorbed.

In reading comprehension, the schemata form the ties between reader and text. With no relatable experience or concepts, a reader would find the understanding of a selection to be most difficult. The importance of a purposeful building of background knowledge through pre-reading activity, structured comprehension follow-through, and experience-based vocabulary development is apparent in order to create the cognitive structures.

References: Marilyn Jager Adams and Allan Collin, "A Schema-Theoretic View of Reading" in Harry Singer and Robert B. Ruddell (Editors); *Theoretical Models and Processes of Reading,* Newark, DE: International Reading Association, 1985; David E. Rumelhart, "Schemata: The Building Blocks of Cognition" in Rand J. Spiro, Bertram C. Bruce, and William F. Brewer (Editors), *Theoretical Issues in Reading Comprehension,* Hillsdale, NJ: Lawrence Erlbaum, 1980; Thomas N. Turner, "Comprehension: Reading for Meaning" in J. Estill Alexander (Editor), *Teaching Reading,* Boston: Little, Brown and Company, 1980.

SCHOLARSHIP, a term that has several meanings: (1) a level of academic achievement attained by an individual; (2) a high-level academic contribution made to an area or a discipline; and (3) an award (usually a stipend) given to an individual to encourage continued education.

When an individual has reached a high level of academic accomplishment in a discipline, he/she is usually recognized for his/her "scholarship" in that area of study. For example, the author of a history text may be recognized by other historians for the scholarship that went into the research and writing of it.

A student receiving honors is being recognized for his/her high academic accomplishments/scholarship. Such honors may be given for scholarship in one field (e.g. mathematics, science,

English) or for an overall record of high academic attainment.

A scholarship may be awarded to an individual for his/her high academic accomplishments or for accomplishments on a test, such as a merit scholarship examination. The purpose of the scholarship is to encourage the individual to improve and expand his/her knowledge, usually through further education and study. Often a stipend is awarded with the scholarship. For example, a four-year scholarship to a college may cover all tuition costs. Scholarships not only benefit the individual but are also a means to attract to an institution a group of high academic achievers. Some scholarships are awarded for other than academic reasons. The most common is the athletic scholarship. However, the general purposes for such scholarships are the same as the academic scholarship (i.e. to encourage the individual to improve himself/herself and/or to attract individuals with unique skills to an institution).

Numerous reference books that list the availability of scholarships to institutions of higher education are available in most libraries.

References: Herbert H. Hyman, et al., *The Enduring Effects of Education,* Chicago: University of Chicago Press, 1975; M. Lorraine Mathies and Elizabeth I. Dixon, *The College Blue Book: Scholarships, Fellowships, Grants and Loans* (Seventeenth Edition), New York: Macmillan Publishing Company, Inc., 1979; Alexander Oleson and John Vosh (Editors), *The Organization of Knowledge in Modern America, 1860–1920,* Baltimore, MD: Johns Hopkins University Press, 1979; Rudolf Pfeiffer, *History of Classical Scholarship from 1300–1850,* Oxford, England: Clarendon Press, 1976; Nicholas C. Proia and Vincent M. Digaspari, *Barron's Handbook of American College Financial Aid* (Third Edition), Woodbury, NY: Barron's Educational Series, Inc., 1978.

SCHOLASTIC APTITUDE TEST (SAT), a test developed by the Educational Testing Service for the College Entrance Examination Board, to be used for college admission decisions, scholarship decisions, and college counseling. These tests are taken by over a million students each year. The Preliminary Scholastic Aptitude Test (PSAT) is taken by high school sophomores and juniors as practice for this test and as a qualifying test for National Merit Scholarships. The SAT consists of two sections: mathematics and verbal (which is subdivided into reading comprehension and vocabulary). The Test of Standard Written English, a multiple-choice test designed to evaluate students' ability to recognize standard written English, is administered in conjunction with the SAT.

Although the word *aptitude* appears in the test's title, SAT scores should not be considered strictly as indicators of general intelligence. Thus caution should be exercised because the test is made up of a combination of items similar to those often found in both intelligence tests and high school achievement tests. SAT scores, when used together with high school grades or class rank, are better predictors of college grade point average than are SAT scores alone. (See COLLEGE BOARD.)

References: Anne Anastasi, *Psychological Testing* (Sixth Edition), New York: Macmillan Publishing Co., 1988; College Entrance Examination Board, *The College Board Annual Report, 1987–88,* New York: The Board, 1988; College Entrance Examination Board, *National Report— 1987 Profile of SAT and Achievement Test Takers,* New York: The Board, 1987.

SCHOOL ACCOUNTING, a system for recording, classifying, reporting, and maintaining a school or school district's financial transactions. School accounting systems include special forms that usually employ standardized terms, definitions, classifications, and procedures and account for all income and disbursements. A well-maintained accounting system fulfills several purposes: (1) provides accurate records for informing and protecting the public; (2) yields information necessary for evaluating programs/personnel; (3) facilitates long- and short-term planning; and (4) provides basic data needed to determine tax levies, for reporting to state agencies, for formulation of school budgets, and for carrying out audits.

The U.S. Office of Education has contributed to the standardization of school accounting procedures by publishing handbooks on a periodic basis (1940, 1948, 1957, 1973) that recommend school accounting procedures.

References: Percy E. Burrup, *Financing Education in a Climate of Change* (Second Edition), Boston: Allyn and Bacon, Inc., 1977; I. Carl Candoli, et al., *School Business Administration: A Planning Approach* (Second Edition), Boston: Allyn and Bacon, Inc., 1978; John Greenhalgh, *Practitioner's Guide to School Business Management,* Boston: Allyn and Bacon, Inc., 1978; U.S. Department of Health, Education, and Welfare, *Financial Accounting Classifications and Standard Terminology for Local and State School Systems* (Publication No. 73-11800), Washington, DC: The Department, 1973.

SCHOOL ADMINISTRATION CENTER, or administration building, the facility or facilities used to house all or some members of a school district's central administrative staff. Such centers may be separate buildings, these normally found in relatively large school systems, or parts (wings) of schools, a not uncommon arrangement in small districts. The school administration center includes any or all of the following kinds of facilities: (1) a meeting room for the board of education; (2) offices for the superintendent and central staff (e.g. business manager, assistant superintendent, personnel director); and (3) service areas (e.g. conference rooms, library, data processing, audiovisual services, printing).

School administration centers may be: (1) specially designed facilities that are owned by the school district; (2) offices or suites that are leased; or (3) buildings such as former schools, stores, and office buildings that have been remodelled and converted for administrative use.

Reference: Commission on School Administration Buildings, *Planning the School Administration Center,* Washington, DC: American Association of School Administrators, 1969.

SCHOOL ARCHITECT, the trained and licensed designer of school facilities. Architects normally work closely with educational planners, the designated representatives of school boards or boards of trustees, to design new school facilities or to remodel existing ones. The architectural planning process consists of six phases: (1) preliminary design planning; (2) schematic design; (3) design development; (4) construction documents preparation; (5) bidding; and (6) construction.

The Council of Educational Facility Planners indicates that there are three principal methods of selecting an architect: (1) design competition, used infrequently in education; (2) direct appointment; and (3) comparative selection, with final choice based on information provided by all competing architects.

Reference: Guide for Planning Educational Facilities, Columbus, OH: Council of Educational Facility Planners, International, 1976.

SCHOOL ATTENDANCE AREA—See ATTENDANCE AREA

SCHOOL-BASED MANAGEMENT, a strategy for improving public education through decentralization of the school system. In districts committed to school-based management, as much decision-making authority as possible is delegated downward, from central office to the local school. Considerable decision-making latitude is given to the local unit in the areas of budget, personnel administration, and curriculum, with principals,

teachers, and parents each involved in such decision making.

In a recent study of Florida's public schools, a group of consultants cited several reasons supporting the concept of school-based management: "decisions made at the school level would be more responsive to the needs of children, would be more consistent with the skills and teaching styles of teachers, would more accurately reflect parent and citizen preferences, and would be better coordinated" (p. 5).

References: Larry W. Hughes and Gerald C. Ubben, *The Elementary Principal's Handbook: A Guide to Effective Action* (Third Edition), Boston: Allyn and Bacon, 1989; Lawrence C. Pierce, *School Site Management,* Palo Alto, CA: Aspen Institute, 1977; Select Joint Committee on Public Schools of the Florida Legislature, *Improving Education in Florida: A Reassessment,* February 1978; David E. Weischadle, "School Based Management and the Principal," *The Clearing House,* October 1980.

SCHOOL BOARD—See BOARD OF EDUCATION, LOCAL

SCHOOL BOND, an instrument of indebtedness or fixed obligation assumed by a school district for the purpose of financing a school building program or for capital outlay. Proceeds are derived from sales of bonds to lenders. Bonds are amortized over extended periods, usually 10, 20, or 30 years. Interest is paid to the bond purchaser with rates determined by numerous factors including the state of the economy or the financial record of the borrowing district. Bonds are of two general types. The first, *term bonds,* are issued for a specific period during which only interest is paid. *Serial bonds,* the second type, are numbered and the repayment schedule is staggered; low numbered bonds mature earlier. The latter type serves to reduce the amount of interest owed. School bonds are generally unsecured obligations backed by the good faith of the state and the promise of the district's taxpayers to repay in accordance with the terms of the bond.

References: Percy E. Burrup, Vern Brimsley, Jr., and Rulon R. Garfield, *Financing Education in a Climate of Change* (Fourth Edition), Boston: Allyn and Bacon, Inc., 1988; National Center for Education Statistics, *Combined Glossary: Terms and Definitions from the Handbooks of the State Educational Records and Reports Series,* Washington, DC: U.S. Department of Health, Education, and Welfare, 1974; Dewey H. Stollar, *Managing School Indebtedness,* Danville, IL: The Interstate Printers and Publishers, Inc., 1967.

SCHOOL BOND RATING, a system employed by bond-rating firms to rank the relative safety and attractiveness of bonds to be sold by a school district. Such ratings influence the bond's appeal in the open market.

Three well-known bond rating firms each use different rating systems. Dun and Bradstreet employs a three-point scale: prime, better good, and medium good. Moody's scale consists of nine categories (Aaa, Aa, A, Baa, Ba, B, Caa, Ca, C) that range from high safety to hopelessly in default. The third rating firm, Standard and Poor's, employs the following symbols: AAA, prime; AA, high grade; A, upper medium grade; BBB, medium grade; BB, lower medium grade; B, slight degree of speculative risk; CCC and CC, increasing degree of speculative risk; and C, DDD, DD, different degrees of default. Several factors influence rating. They include the unit's debt history, nature of the enterprise, financial conditions, management, and general academic conditions. (See SCHOOL BOND.)

Reference: David M. Darst, *The Complete Bond Book: A Guide to All Types of Fixed-Income Securities,* New York: McGraw-Hill Book Company, 1975.

SCHOOL BUDGET, a financial instrument for planning and controlling educational activities. Anticipated expenses and receipts are included, these based on an educational plan. Most school budgets cover a period of one fiscal year. Budgets are prepared by the superintendent of schools for consideration by the local board of education. In some states, boards are empowered to adopt budgets; in others, the instrument requires approval by taxpayers or another governmental agency.

Budget formats have historically differed from one state to another. In recent years, categories and nomenclature recommended by the U.S. Office of Education have helped to standardize budgets. Budget categories recommended are: Administrator, Instructor, Attendance and Health Services, Public Transportation Services, Operation of Plant, Maintenance of Plant, Fixed Charges, Food Services and Student Body Activities, Community Services, Capital Outlay, Debt Service from Current Funds, and Outgoing Transfer Accounts.

References: Judith Bentley, *Busing: The Continuing Controversy,* New York: Franklin Watts, 1982; Walter I. Garms, et al., *School Finance: The Economics and Politics of Public Education,* Englewood Cliffs, NJ: Prentice-Hall, Inc., 1978; William Goldstein, *Selling School Budgets in Hardtimes,* Bloomington, IN: Phi Delta Kappa, 1984; Robert D. Lee, Jr. and Ronald W. Johnson, *Public Budg-*

eting Systems (Second Edition), Baltimore, MD: University Park Press, 1977; Paul L. Reason and Alpheus L. White, *Financial Accounting for Local and State School Systems,* Washington, DC: U.S. Office of Education, 1957; Frederick M. Wirt and Michael W. Kirst, *The Politics of Education, Schools in Conflict* (Second Edition), Berkeley, CA: McCutchan Publishing Corp., 1989.

SCHOOL BUSINESS ADMINISTRATOR, or school business official, a member of the central office staff responsible for managing the school system's business and financial affairs under the direction of the superintendent of schools. Specific duties associated with this position include, but are not limited to: financial planning; accounting; special fund management; purchasing; auditing, planning, operation, and maintenance of plant; transportation; food service operations; insurance; data processing; and school elections. The titles assigned to administrators who perform these duties vary from district to district. Those most commonly used are deputy, associate, or assistant superintendent; business manager; director of business affairs; school business administrator; financial secretary; and clerk-treasurer of the board of education. (See REGISTERED SCHOOL BUSINESS ADMINISTRATOR.)

References: I. Carl Candoli, et al., *School Business Administration: A Planning Approach* (Second Edition), Boston: Allyn and Bacon, Inc., 1978; K. Forbis Jordan, et al., *School Business Administration,* Beverly Hills, CA: Sage Publications, 1985.

SCHOOL/BUSINESS PARTNERSHIPS, a formal relationship between one or more schools and one or more businesses in which the businesses work cooperatively with the schools to improve education. Often individual schools are "adopted" by a business, which may supply equipment or funds for special projects. The business may also supply corporate volunteers who may be matched on a one-to-one partnership with students in a school. These volunteers may function as tutors or mentors. Other approaches to the school/business partnership may include a district-wide multi-school partnership program, executives assigned for a period of time to the school district, corporate membership on school task forces or advisory committees, participation in curriculum development (especially mathematics, science, and computer technology), funded support of in-service education programs for teachers, coparticipation with the school district in grant development for specific projects, development of recognition awards and programs for students and/or teachers, provision of training for nonteacher personnel in the schools, and development district-wide special projects. Often local universities or colleges will join a school/business partnership by supplying staff support of facilities.

Although school/business partnerships are not new (several of the street academies of the 1960s were corporate-sponsored), the concept was encouraged by President Reagan in 1983 when he issued a challenge to improve education through such partnerships. Several of the more notable partnerships are: Young Astronauts Council, Co-operative Federation for Education Experience (Oxford, MA), Rick's Academy (Atlanta), Stanford Mid-Peninsula Urban Coalition (California), and Metropolitan Area Council (New Orleans). (See STREET ACADEMIES.)

References: Carol O'Connell, How to Start a School/Business Partnership, Bloomington, IN: Phi Delta Kappa Educational Foundation, 1985; Manuel J. Justiz and Marilyn C. Kameen, "Business Offers a Hand to Education," Phi Delta Kappa, Volume 68, Number 5, January 1987; Dorothy J. Reller, The Peninsula Academies: Final Technical Evaluation Report, Palo Alto, CA: American Institutes for Research in the Behavioral Sciences, 1984.

SCHOOL CALENDAR, a device for projecting and scheduling major institutional events, usually for a full academic year. Such events normally include items such as: (1) the opening and closing dates of school; (2) holidays; (3) teacher meetings/conventions; (4) major school activities (e.g. plays, athletic events); (5) examinations; and (6) community events, including PTA meetings.

The length of the school year has been increasing steadily over the past 100 years. The National Education Association reports that the school year, in 1975-76, had a median of 180 school days. Data compiled by the National Center for Education Statistics indicate that the school year consisted of an average of 132.2 school days in 1870; 144.3 in 1900; and 172.7 in 1930.

References: Lester W. Anderson and Lauren A. Van Dyke, Secondary School Administration (Second Edition), Boston: Houghton Mifflin Company, 1972; Mary A. Golladay, National Center for Education Statistics, The Condition of Education (1976 Edition), Washington, DC: U.S. Government Printing Office, 1976; National Education Association, Status of the American Public School Teacher, 1975-76, Washington, DC: The Association, 1977.

SCHOOL CENSUS, a community canvass carried out as part of a school district's pupil accounting program. Its basic purpose is to ascertain the number of resident children who are in school, should be in school, or are of preschool age. States normally require districts to conduct a periodic (e.g. annual) school census. Census enumerators, volunteers or paid personnel, are engaged to carry out the canvass, usually during the summer months of the year.

Census data are used in several ways: (1) to identify increases/decreases in the preschool and school-aged populations; (2) to note population shifts within a school district or a particular attendance area; (3) to project budgetary and staffing needs; (4) to establish appropriate bus transportation routes; (5) to enforce state compulsory education laws; and (6) as a basis for periodic updating of a school system's pupil projections.

In elementary schools, the spring roundup (registration) of children provides detailed information about children who will be entering school for the first time.

References: Roald F. Campbell, et al., Introduction to Educational Administration (Third Edition), Boston: Allyn and Bacon, Inc., 1966; Willard S. Elsbree, et al., Elementary School Administration and Supervision (Third Edition), New York: American Book Company, 1967; Edgar L. Morphet, et al., Educational Administration: Concepts, Practices, and Issues, Englewood Cliffs, NJ: Prentice-Hall, Inc., 1959; John F. Putnam, National Center for Education Statistics, Student/Pupil Accounting (State Educational Records and Reports Series: Handbook V, Revised), Washington, DC: U.S. Department of Health, Education, and Welfare, 1974.

SCHOOL-COMMUNITY RELATIONS, a process that permits schools to communicate information of importance to members of their respective communities and vice-versa. Unlike public relations, which is essentially a one-way process (school-to-community), the effective school-community relations program seeks to establish effective two-way communication channels between school and community and strives to achieve consensus with respect to the role of the school.

In some school districts, full-time school-community relations directors are employed. Their work includes, but is not limited to: (1) determining the composition of the community; (2) ascertaining citizens' perceptions and expectations of the schools; (3) regularly informing the community about the work of the school; (4) developing and maintaining effective relations with the media; and (5) sharing community feedback with school-board members and the school system's professional staff.

The overriding purpose of the school-community relations program is to develop understanding and commitment on the part of the community.

References: Roald F. Campbell, et al., *Introduction to Educational Administration* (Fifth Edition), Boston: Allyn and Bacon, Inc., 1977; Richard A. Gorton, *School Administration: Challenge and Opportunity for Leadership,* Dubuque, IA: Wm. C. Brown Company, Publishers, 1976.

SCHOOL DISTRICT ORGANIZATION, or local school administrative unit, a basic unit of school administration that, according to the National Commission on School District Reorganization, has the following characteristics: (1) all schools within the unit are governed by a single board; (2) a chief school officer is responsible to the board for administration of the unit; and (3) for school purposes, is a fiscal unit that, subject to state laws, maintains a district budget and may have tax-levying authority.

In recent years, efforts have been made to reduce the number of public school districts in the United States (through consolidation), primarily to reduce the large number of small and educationally inefficient units. National Center for Education Statistics data attest to the success of that effort. In 1931-32, there were 127,531 school districts in the United States; 94,926 in 1947-48; 31,705 in 1963-64; and 16,112 in 1977-78. The states with the largest number of school districts (fall 1977) are Nebraska (1,138), Texas (1,113), California (1,044), and Illinois (1,030). Those with the fewest school districts are Hawaii (1), Nevada (17), and Maryland (24).

References: American Association of School Administrators, *School District Organization,* Washington, DC: The Association, 1958; Roald F. Campbell, et al., *The Organization and Control of American Schools* (Fourth Edition), Columbus, OH: Charles E. Merrill Publishing Company, 1980; National Center for Education Statistics, *Digest of Education Statistics, 1979,* Washington, DC: U.S. Department of Health, Education, and Welfare, 1979; National Commission on School District Reorganization, *Your School District,* Washington, DC: Department of Rural Education, National Education Association, 1948.

SCHOOL ENTRANCE AGE, the chronological age of a child at the time of entering Kindergarten or grade 1. The problem of trying to determine the best time for a child to enter school is not new; it has existed for centuries. In U.S. school districts, the Kindergarten age requirement tends to range between 5 years 7 months (by February 1) and 5 years 11 months (by September 1).

Some school systems permit admission at earlier ages with predetermined criteria used to establish eligibility. These criteria normally consider any or all of the following: (1) mental age; (2) emotional maturity; (3) social development; (4) physical maturity; (5) academic considerations; (6) preschool experience(s); and (7) I.Q. Research data suggest that any single criterion (e.g. I.Q.) tends not to be reliable. For this reason, clusters of criteria are suggested when considering early admission. Screening for school readiness is sometimes used for the purpose of identifying children likely to become high-risk learners.

Raymond Moore and Dorothy Moore, on the basis of their examination of early schooling, concluded that research has yet to demonstrate lasting benefits from early schooling. They also noted that scientific evidence impressively favors later school admission. These findings notwithstanding, schools continue to be pressured into providing early schooling opportunities and reducing their entrance age requirements.

References: William D. Hedges, *At What Age Should Children Enter First Grade: A Comprehensive Review of the Research,* Ann Arbor, MI: University Microfilms International, 1977; Francis L. Ilg and Louise B. Ames, *School Readiness: Behavior Tests Used at the Gesell Institute,* New York: Harper and Row, Publishers, 1972; Raymond S. Moore and Dorothy N. Moore, *Better Late Than Early,* New York: Reader's Digest Press, 1975; Shirley Zeitlin, *Kindergarten Screening: Early Identification of Potential High Risk Learners,* Springfield, IL: Charles C. Thomas, Publisher, 1976.

SCHOOL EXCURSION—See FIELD TRIP

SCHOOL LIBRARY, an outdated term for what is currently (and widely) referred to as *school library media center.* The traditional school library was a room or suite of rooms in which book collections appropriate to the age groups being served were housed. It was here that books and periodicals were selected, processed, and distributed, often by trained librarians. Librarians were responsible for managing these collections and for helping students, individually or in groups, to make effective use of this resource area.

In the 1960s, both the American Association of School Librarians and the National Education Association's Department of Audio-Visual Instruction encouraged transformation of school libraries into media centers. Media centers continue to include books but are also stocked with various types of media. Personnel assigned to these centers, referred to as school library media specialists, are conversant with both the print and nonprint aspects of media center operation.

In 1975, the American Association of School Librarians and the Association for Educational Communications and Technology (formerly the NEA Department of A-V Instruction) published their revised *Media Programs: District and School,* a set of widely recognized standards for school media centers.

In their book, Betty Martin and Ben Carson enumerated the principal differences between traditional libraries and media centers. (See SCHOOL LIBRARY MEDIA SPECIALIST.)

References: American Association of School Librarians and Association for Educational Communications and Technology, *Media Programs: District and School,* Chicago: American Library Association, 1975; Ruth A. Davis, *The School Library Media Program: Instructional Force for Excellence* (Third Edition), New York: R. R. Bowker Company, 1979; Betty Martin and Ben Carson, *The Principal's Handbook on the School Library Media Center,* Syracuse, NY: Gaylord Professional Publications, 1978.

SCHOOL LIBRARY MEDIA SPECIALIST, the professional who is a school's authority on instructional media. Print and nonprint materials as well as instructionally related equipment fall within the purview of this position. The school library media specialist's duties include, but are not limited to: (1) helping with the selection of instructional materials; (2) developing and overseeing the organization and circulation of such materials; (3) providing resource assistance to curriculum study groups; (4) providing assistance to individual students and teachers; and (5) supervising support staff that may include clerks, technicians, and student workers.

A distinction is sometimes made between certified and noncertified specialists. Licensing of media specialists is required by only a few states, although certification for school librarians is common. (See PRINT MATERIALS.)

References: Robert N. Case and Anna M. Lowrey, "Occupational Definitions: School Library Media Specialist" in Pearl L. Ward and Robert Beacon (Editors), *The School Media Center: A Book of Readings,* Metuchen, NJ: The Scarecrow Press, Inc., 1973; James S. Kinder, *Using Instructional Media,* New York: D. Van Nostrand Company, Inc., 1973; Kay E. Vandergrift, *The Teaching Role of the School Media Specialist,* Chicago: American Library Association, 1979.

SCHOOL MATHEMATICS STUDY GROUP, sometimes referred to as SMSG, was organized in 1958 to improve mathematics teaching in American secondary schools. Funded by the National Science Foundation, SMSG, consisting of 45 people (mainly mathematics professors and secondary school mathematics teachers), met at Yale University. Professor E. G. Begle of Yale University, later of Stanford University, directed the project. The group's task was to develop a model curriculum (including units and textbook outlines) for secondary school mathematics. This work was completed during the summer of 1958.

A second and considerably larger NSF grant was awarded for the purpose of writing the textbooks already outlined and testing these in selected schools. This latter work was carried out over the next several years. Reports from schools included in the SMSG sample indicated general preference for the new materials by students and their teachers. Some reports also indicated that SMSG was influencing the curricula of mathematics education programs in teacher-training institutions.

References: E. G. Begle, "Some Lessons Learned by SMSG," *Mathematics Teacher,* March 1973; William Wooton, *SMSG: The Making of a Curriculum,* New Haven, CT: Yale University Press, 1965.

SCHOOL NURSE, the employee responsible for a school's health services and its health environment. The nurse works under the direction of the school administrator and in close cooperation with teachers, parents, students, and community health agencies. He/she attends to the health and safety needs of students, counsels with students on health matters, arranges for testing and screening, makes referrals, maintains individual pupil health records, and, to the extent that law permits, renders emergency assistance. Those certified to do so also teach health and are known as nurse-teachers. The number of school nurses employed by school boards is increasing. Some states have established nurse-pupil ratios as a guide for school districts. They range from a low of 600:1 to as high as 1,500:1. (See HEALTH EDUCATION and HEALTH SERVICES.)

References: American School Health Association, *Guidelines for the School Nurse in the School Health Program,* Kent, OH: The Association, 1974; Doris Bryan, *School Nursing in Transition,* St. Louis, MO: C. V. Mosby Company, 1973; Annette Lynch, *Redesigning School Health Services,* New York: Human Services Press, Inc., 1983.

SCHOOL OF EDUCATION—See COLLEGE OF EDUCATION

SCHOOL PHOBIA, or "school refusal," a specific type of truancy brought about by a wide range of fears. Although the exact causes of school phobia have yet to be determined with certainty, there is general agreement that this condition is associated with the home. Fear of separation from parent(s) is cited as a major root cause.

Children with school phobia are extremely fearful of school and steadfastly refuse either to attend or to stay in it. Their fear frequently takes the form of physical ailments (e.g. nausea, diarrhea, stomach pains, headaches). (See PHOBIA.)

References: A. H. Denney, *Truancy and School Phobias,* London, England: Priory Press Limited, 1974; Norman Stein and Dennis Bogin, "Individual Child Psychotherapy" in Arnold P. Goldstein (Editor), *Prescriptions for Child Mental Health and Education,* New York: Pergamon Press, Inc., 1978.

SCHOOL PLANT PLANNING, those activities associated with the construction of new, or refurbishing of existing, school facilities. These activities normally require ongoing consultation among a trilogy of professionals: school officials, architects, and contractors.

School plant planning involves, but is not limited to, steps such as: (1) long-range planning, including school population forecasts; (2) determining the programs and students a proposed facility is to accommodate; (3) architect selection; (4) site selection; (5) preparation of a schematic design for the facility; (6) design development following approval of schematic designs; (7) preparation of specifications and related documents; (8) state and/or voter approval, if required; (9) financing plans; (10) bidding; (11) construction; and (12) evaluation during the early period of occupancy. In recent years, increased attention has been given to energy saving, maintenance costs, student safety, and law (e.g. architectural barriers) as new facilities are being planned. (See SCHOOL ARCHITECT and SCHOOL SITE.)

References: Wallace B. Cleland (Editor), *New Tactic for Building: Experience/Analysis/Recommendations from the Detroit Public Schools Construction Systems Program,* Detroit: Office of School Housing, Detroit Public Schools, 1975; Jacques Hallak, *Planning the Location of Schools: An Instrument of Educational Policy,* Paris, France: International Institute for Educational Planning, UNESCO, 1977; Harold L. Hawkins, *Appraisal Guide for School Facilities,* Midland, MI: Pendell Publishing Company, 1973; Harvey H. Kaiser (Editor), *New Directions for Higher Education: Managing Facilities More Effectively,* San Francisco: Jossey-Bass Publishers, 1980; National School Boards Association, *School Facilities Planning* (Research Report No. 1974-2), Evanston, IL: The Association, 1974; David K. Wiles, *Energy, Winter, and Schools: Crisis and Decision Theory,* Lexington, MA: Lexington Books, 1979.

SCHOOL PRAYER—See REGENTS PRAYER and RELIGION IN THE SCHOOLS

SCHOOL PSYCHOLOGIST, a professionally certified individual hired by school districts to diagnose and assess the needs of individual children and to recommend strategies to foster good mental health in these children. School psychologists work closely with children, parents, teachers, and school administrators.

John Pietrofesa suggested that school psychologists perform many functions, among them: (1) to accept referrals for diagnosis and prescription for children with learning problems; (2) to prepare individual evaluations of children (administering tests, observations, etc.); (3) to consult with parents and teachers; (4) to provide services for handicapped children; and (5) to provide inservice education for teachers and administrators. In addition, many are involved in research in various areas, including specific areas of the school curriculum, inservice education, and community concerns.

School psychologists work with other professionals, as a team, to help develop individualized educational programs (IEPs) for those children classified as being handicapped. School psychologists may also work with children who are identified as being gifted or talented. Also, they work with children who have emotional or learning difficulties but may not be classified as being "exceptional."

Universities and colleges sponsor special educational programs that train individuals to become school psychologists. The training, offered at the graduate level, includes considerable study of child development, child psychology, developmental psychology, theories of learning, education, testing (intelligence tests, projective instruments, individual test administration, etc.) and usually a practicum.

References: Arthur A. Attwell, *School Psychologist's Handbook* (Revised Edition), Los Angeles, CA: Western Psychological Services, 1976; Stephen N. Elliott and Joseph C. Witt, *The Delivery of Psychological Services in Schools,* Hillsdale, NJ: Lawrence Erlbaum Associates, Publishers, 1986; William G. Herron, et al., *Contemporary School Psychology,* Scranton, PA: Intext Educational Publishers, 1970; John J. Pietrofesa, et al., *Guidance, An Introduction,* Chicago, IL: Rand McNally College Publishing Company, 1980.

SCHOOL RECOGNITION PROGRAMS, a set of programs to recognize schools for excellence in education and administered by the Office of Educational Research and Improvement (Programs for the Improvement of Practice Section) of the United States Department of Education. The School Recognition Program was first initiated by T. H. Bell, then U.S. secretary of education, in 1982. At first the program was only open to public secondary schools; private secondary schools were included in 1983–84 for recognition (the Council for American Private Education administers the Private Schools Recognition Program for the Department of Education), and elementary public and private schools were included for recognition during the 1985–1986 year.

Schools are nominated, their documentation materials are initially reviewed by an external panel, and then they must undergo a two-day site visit to determine if they meet selected "indicators of success" and have "attributes of success." Site visitors and review panelists discuss each school that is visited before sending a school's name forward to the U.S. secretary of education. Public and private schools from the 50 states, Bureau of Indian Affairs, Department of Defense (Dependent Schools), District of Columbia, Puerto Rico, and the Virgin Islands can be nominated for recognition. Although only 152 schools were recognized as outstanding in 1982–83, almost 300 schools have been listed each year since then. (See COUNCIL FOR AMERICAN PRIVATE EDUCATION; HUMAN SERVICES REAUTHORIZATION ACT OF 1986; and OFFICE OF EDUCATIONAL RESEARCH AND IMPROVEMENT.)

References: James Howard, Exemplary Schools, 1986, Report on the Private Elementary School Recognition Program, Washington, DC: Council for American Private Education, 1986; Pat McKee and Kay McKinney, Good Secondary Schools, What Makes Them Tick? Washington, DC: Office of Educational Research and Improvement, 1986; U.S. Department of Education, Excellence in Elementary, Elementary School Recognition Program 1985–86, Washington, DC: The Department, 1986; U.S. Department of Education, Secondary School Recognition Program, Junior High and Middle School, High School (forms to be filled out by schools), Washington, DC: The Department, 1986; Bruce L. Wilson and Thomas B. Corcoran, Places Where Children Succeed: A Profile of Outstanding Elementary Schools, Philadelphia, PA: Research for Better Schools, 1987.

SCHOOL SECRETARY, the secretary who most directly serves the principal of a school. In a small school, this person is likely to be the only secretary in the building. Illustrative (specific) tasks performed by the school secretary include typing and filing, scheduling of appointments, keeping of student records, receptionist services, recording staff attendance, overseeing petty cash, mail processing, and management of supplies. In a study of Arizona school secretaries, Robert Russell divided secretarial tasks into six broad areas of responsibility: (1) giving assistance and/or support to teachers; (2) working and caring for children; (3) maintaining relations with the community; (4) administering the school office; (5) working with the principal; and (6) working with individual parents.

A survey of American elementary school principals, reported in 1979 by the National Association of Elementary School Principals, revealed that secretarial assistance was available to 88 percent of the respondents. (In 1958, the figure was 50 percent.) A higher percentage obtains in secondary schools.

References: John Greenhalgh, Practitioner's Guide to School Business Management, Boston: Allyn and Bacon, Inc., 1978; William L. Pharis and Sally B. Zakariya, The Elementary School Principalship in 1978: A Research Study, Arlington, VA: National Association of Elementary School Principals, 1979; Robert V. Russell, "The Role of the School Secretary as Perceived by Principals, Teachers, and Other School Secretaries," Unpublished doctoral dissertation, Northern Arizona University, 1973.

SCHOOL SECURITY, as defined by Seymour Vestermark and Peter Blauvelt, is "the process of achieving acceptable levels of risk from crimes against persons and property in the school community" (p. 33). The likelihood of a school having to face serious crime problems, these same authors pointed out, increases with size of school, ages of students, and the degree to which the school is located in an urban environment. Crimes are of two types: (1) crimes against persons, including assaults, robberies, trespassing, and narcotics violations, and (2) crimes against property (e.g. vandalism, burglary, arson).

In its 1978 Safe School Study, the National Institute of Education (NIE) reported to Congress on the extent of crime and violence in American schools. Data indicated that: (1) approximately 8 percent of U.S. schools have serious crime problems; (2) approximately 11 percent of secondary school students have something stolen from them each month; (3) over 25 percent of the schools are vandalized each month; and (4) over 5,000 secondary school (especially junior high school) teachers are physically attacked each month, about a fifth of them requiring medical attention.

School security programs vary from district to district. Those considered to be most effective make use of full-time *professional security personnel* and *security devices* such as specially designed locks, safes, and window/door alarms. The NIE study found that the single most important difference between "safe" and "violent" schools was the strength, dedication, fairness, firmness, and consistency of the school principal.

References: David Boesel (Director), *Violent Schools—Safe Schools: The Safe School Study Report to the Congress* (Volume I), Washington, DC: National Institute of Education, 1978; Robert J. Rubel, *Identifying Your School's Crime Problems: Simple Steps That Preceed* (Sic) *Costly Action,* College Park, MD: Institute for Reduction of Crime, Inc., 1978; Seymour D. Vestermark, Jr. and Peter D. Blauvelt, *Controlling Crime in the School: A Complete Security Handbook for Administrators,* West Nyack, NY: Parker Publishing Company, Inc., 1978.

SCHOOL SITE, the land on which a school building is situated or is scheduled to be built. Minimal site sizes, usually expressed in acres, are prescribed by some state departments of education. Several factors govern site size including the number of students to be housed, the instructional level (e.g. senior high school grades) to be accommodated, other buildings to be erected on the site, the nature of the school's athletic program, community requirements, and parking needs. Site selection takes into account the location of the land relative to population centers and other schools, cost, health and safety conditions, soil conditions, topography, and projected costs for site development. (See SCHOOL PLANT PLANNING.)

References: A.A.S.A. School Building Commission, *Planning America's School Buildings,* Washington, DC: American Association of School Administrators, 1960; Basil Castaldi, *Educational Facilities: Planning, Remodeling, and Management,* Boston: Allyn and Bacon, Inc., 1977.

SCHOOL SOCIAL WORKER, a specially trained social work professional who understands those social, community, and family forces that influence children's functioning in the schools. The school social worker works with teachers, parents, and other professionals on social and emotional problems of children. At one time, school social workers were known as "visiting teachers." Most states require training in social work and/or an advanced degree (master's or above) in social work with an emphasis in school social work before certification can be earned. Many also require school experience.

Although a school social worker uses the casework (i.e. has a case load of children) approach, he/she also focuses on the welfare of school children in general. Basic school social work tasks include: casework; group work; collaboration in a team mode with all school personnel (not just the teacher) on behalf of a child; consultation with school personnel; work in the schools as a professional employee; development of an educational program for teachers and parents; helping the child, parent, and school to utilize the social welfare resources and agencies of the community; assisting in interpreting the schools to the community; and, bringing the community into the schools and the school into the community.

References: Peter R. Day, *Methods of Learning Communication Skills,* Maxwell House, NY: Pergamon Press, Inc., 1977; Edward F. DeRoche and Jeffrey S. Kaiser, *Complete Guide to Administering School Services,* West Nyack, NY: Parker Publishing Company, Inc., 1980; Marilyn Gronbeck, *Social Work Careers,* New York: Franklin Watts, Inc., 1977; Margaret Robinson, *Schools and Social Work,* Boston: Routledge and Kegan Paul, 1978.

SCHOOL STAFFING RATIOS, personnel measures that relate numbers of professionals to students or administrators to teachers. One widely used staffing ratio, not to be confused with average class size, is *pupils per teacher.* It is computed by dividing the total number of all teachers (full time or full-time equivalent) into a school's or school system's total enrollment. The same computational approach is used to determine counselor-student, teacher aide-student, and so on ratios. Administrator to teacher ratios, when reported, generally include relationships such as teachers per administrator, teachers per counselor, or teachers per assistant principal. (See CLASS SIZE.)

References: Nancy B. Dearman and Valena W. Plisko, *The Condition of Education, 1979 Edition,* Washington, DC: National Center for Education Statistics, 1979; Anne Gavin, et al., *School Staffing Ratios, 1977-78,* Arlington, VA: Educational Research Service, Inc., 1978.

SCHOOL SURVEY, a generic term used to describe the procedures and instrumentation employed by school planners to collect specific kinds of information about a school or school system. Once gathered, such information is used to identify needs and to formulate objectives. Several types of surveys are used by school planners: (1) *population surveys,* to forecast future school enrollment; (2) *financial surveys,* studies of school business practices; (3) *comprehensive surveys,* which examine the school system's total instructional and support operations; and (4) *school building surveys,* assessments of existing facilities in relation to program requirements. School surveys may be completed by outside experts, local school personnel, local citizens, or combinations of these groups.

References: Basil Castaldi, *Educational Facilities: Planning, Remodeling, and Management,* Boston: Allyn and Bacon, Inc., 1977; Harold C. Hand, *What People Think About Their Schools: Values and Methods of Public-Opinion Polling as Applied to School Systems,* New York: World Book Company, 1948; Gary R. Hanson, *Evaluating Program Effectiveness,* San Francisco: Jossey-Bass Publishers, 1978.

SCHOOLS-WITHIN-A-SCHOOL, a system for dividing large (usually secondary) schools into smaller, near-autonomous administrative units that are all housed in one building. The system is occasionally referred to as a "house plan." Students are divided horizontally or vertically by grade level, with each component unit consisting of up to 500 pupils. Each of the units may occupy a separate wing, or building area, and will normally have its own counselors and faculty members for teaching of basic courses. Special resource rooms and instructors are shared by all "schools" within the school. Proponents of this organizational arrangement support it as a viable way to preserve the advantages found in small schools and still continue to make a wide range of course offerings available to students.

References: Lester W. Anderson and Lauren A. Van Dyke, *Secondary School Administration* (Second Edition), New York: Houghton Mifflin Company, 1972; Harl R. Douglass, *Modern Administration of Secondary Schools* (Second Edition), Boston: Ginn and Company, 1963; Karl R. Plath, *Schools Within Schools: A Study of High School Organization,* New York: Bureau of Publications, Teachers College, Columbia University, 1965; Robert D. Ramsey, et al., *The Schools-Within-A-School Program: A Modern Approach to Secondary Instruction and Guidance,* West Nyack, NY: Parker Publishing Company, Inc., 1967.

SCHOOLS WITHOUT WALLS, or "open-space schools," educational buildings with few or no interior partitions. Schools without walls are designed to eliminate such conventional "barriers" as rows of classrooms with connecting corridors and to replace them with an open space conducive to increased student-teacher and teacher-teacher interaction. One of the first schools to be built in this fashion (late 1950s) was an elementary school in Carson City, Michigan, designed to accommodate a team teaching program.

In schools without walls, several groups of students and their teacher(s) work in different parts of the open room. Floors are carpeted to keep noise to a minimum. Teachers carefully articulate their schedules to avoid problems of a space and traffic nature.

In a survey of California open schools, John Sugden and Ralph Lovik found: (1) many districts chose the open-school design as a way to keep costs down; (2) teachers reported that the goal of flexible student grouping was achieved; and (3) most (not all) teachers and students were able to adjust to the open space environment.

References: John Bremer and Michael von Moschzisker, *The School Without Walls: Philadelphia's Parkway Program,* New York: Holt, Rinehart and Winston, Inc., 1971; *Profiles of Significant Schools: Schools Without Walls,* New York: Educational Facilities Laboratories, 1971; Curtis Samuels, "From the Open School Room to the Open School," *Education,* Winter 1977; John H. Sugden, Jr., "How Effective Are Open Plan Elementary Schools?" *American School and University,* August 1973.

SCHOOL YEAR—See SCHOOL CALENDAR

SCIENCE—A PROCESS APPROACH (SAPA), an elementary school science program developed by writing teams of teachers, psychologists, and scientists working under the direction of the American Association for the Advancement of Science. This K–6 curriculum, developed between 1963 and 1965, stresses skills in using the *processes* of science rather than fragmented *content.* Processes include observing, classifying, using time-space relations, using numbers, communicating, measuring, inferring, predicting (these taught in grades K–3) as well as six more complex processes introduced in grades 4–6: formulating hypotheses, controlling variables, interpreting data, defining operationally, formulating models, and experimenting.

The course uses no student textbook. Instead, a series of structured lessons is used with materials chosen from the life, physical, and environmental sciences. Each lesson lists prescribed activities and behavioral objectives. (SAPA was one of the first projects to use the behavioral objectives approach.) This prescription affords the teacher little instructional flexibility. SAPA materials come in kits, distributed by the Xerox Corporation through Ginn and Company, which include a teacher's guide and class materials for 30 students.

References: Arthur A. Carin and Robert B. Sund, *Teaching Science through Discovery* (Third Edition), Columbus, OH: Charles E. Merrill Publishing Company, 1975; William K. Esler, *Teaching Elementary Science,* Belmont, CA: Wadsworth Publishing Company, Inc., 1973; Howard J. Hausman, *Choosing a Science Program for the*

Elementary School (Occasional Paper No. 24), Washington, DC: Council for Basic Education, October 1976; J. David Lockard (Editor), *Science and Mathematics Curricular Developments Internationally, 1956–1974*, College Park, MD: Science Teaching Center, University of Maryland (Joint Project with the Commission on Science Education, American Association for the Advancement of Science), 1974; John R. Mayor and Arthur H. Livermore, "A Process Approach to Elementary School Science," *School Science and Mathematics*, May 1969.

SCIENCE CURRICULUM IMPROVEMENT STUDY (SCIS), organized at the University of California, Berkeley (1961), for the purpose of preparing a structured K–6 science program. The curriculum, largely a laboratory program, contains two strands, *physical sciences* and *life sciences*, which are taught at all grade levels. Six fundamental concepts (themes) are drawn from each of the two fields. They constitute the cores of the 12 units making up the curriculum. Laboratory experiences are designed to encourage students to make their own observations and to test their own ideas through experimentation.

The idea for SCIS originated with the project's director, physicist Robert Karplus. Materials developed for use with this science curriculum include teacher manuals, tests, student manuals, laboratory equipment, films, filmstrips, and filmloops.
References: Glenn O. Blough and Julius Schwartz, *Elementary School Science and How to Teach It* (Fifth Edition), New York: Holt, Rinehart and Winston, Inc., 1974; William K. Esler, *Teaching Elementary Science*, Belmont, CA: Wadsworth Publishing Company, Inc., 1973; Howard J. Hausman, *Choosing a Science Program for the Elementary School* (Occasional Paper No. 24), Washington, DC: Council for Basic Education, October 1976; J. David Lockard (Editor), *Science and Mathematics Curricular Developments Internationally, 1956–1974*, College Park, MD: Science Teaching Center, University of Maryland (Joint Project with the Commission on Science Education, American Association for the Advancement of Science), 1974; B. S. Thomson and A. M. Voelker, "Programs for Improving Science Instruction in the Elementary School, SCIS," *Science and Children*, May 1970.

SCIENCE FAIR, an exhibit in which students' science projects are displayed. Science fairs may be used as a culmination for study units or as a way to show students, parents, and teachers the nature and extent of one year's science teaching in a given school. Displays include projects completed by individual students or by groups of students.
References: Charles F. Beck, *The Development and Present Status of School Science Fairs* (Microfilm No. 24,733), Ann Arbor, MI: University Microfilms, 1958; Mary B. Harbeck (Editor), *Second Sourcebook for Science Supervisors*, Washington, DC: National Science Supervisors Association, 1976; Janet Y. Stoffer (Editor), *Science Fair Project Index: 1960–1972*, Metuchen, NJ: The Scarecrow Press, Inc., 1975; Harold E. Tannenbaum and Nathan Stillman, *Science Education for Elementary School Teachers*, Boston: Allyn and Bacon, Inc., 1961.

SCIENCE KIT, packaged collection of items used for teaching/demonstrating the physical or biological sciences. Commercially prepared kits are available for all school levels; comparable (and less expensive) packages may be prepared by the teacher. There are two principal types of science kit: the *general purpose kit*, suitable for numbers of different kinds of experiments and particularly useful in elementary schools, and the *special purpose kit*. The latter type, as its name implies, contains materials suitable for demonstration/experimentation in specific fields of study (e.g. heat, weather, and sound).
References: William K. Esler, *Teaching Elementary Science* (Second Edition), Belmont, CA: Wadsworth Publishing Company, Inc., 1977; Albert Piltz and William J. Gruver, *Science Equipment and Materials: Science Kits* (OE-29049, Bulletin 1963, No. 30), Washington, DC: U.S. Government Printing Office, 1963.

SCIENCE RESEARCH ASSOCIATES ACHIEVEMENT SERIES, a multilevel battery of tests used to assess student growth in reading, mathematics, language arts, social studies, work-study skills, and science. There are five levels: primary 1 (grades 1–2); primary 2 (grades 2–4); blue (grades 4–6); green (grades 6–8); and red (grades 8–9). Since the Achievement Series is limited to grades 1–9, it is often used in conjunction with the Iowa Tests of Educational Development (which cover grades 9–12).

The test is a norm referenced, broad-scale, standardized examination that is used extensively throughout the United States. Science Research Associates (SRA), the test's publisher, provides separate norms for large city, Title I, rural/small town, nonpublic, and high socioeconomic schools.
References: Martha Dallman, *Teaching the Language Arts in the Elementary School* (Third Edition), Dubuque, IA: Wm. C. Brown Company, Publishers, 1976; Donna E. Norton, *The Effective Teaching of Language Arts*, Columbus, OH: Charles E. Merrill Publishing Company, 1980; Thomas Oakland (Editor), *Psychological and Educational Assessment of Minority Children*, New York: Brunner/Mazel, Inc., 1977.

SCIENTIFIC MANAGEMENT, a leadership concept advanced by Frederick W. Taylor in 1910. Taylor's approach to management was predicated on two assumptions: (1) that man is machinelike, and (2) that an individual employee's feelings, personality, and peer group are generally unimportant. Taylor's scientific management model, forerunner to Management by Objectives, emphasized productivity and efficiency. It called for defining a worker's job description with scientific precision; selection and training of workers with similar precision; and a cooperative relationship between worker and supervisor that ensures that work is being performed in accordance with carefully predetermined procedures. The scientific management concept, which included studies of time and motion (essentially moves to establish productivity standards) was one of the early management approaches to influence programs for the training of school administrators.

In recent years, the scientific management movement has been replaced by one that emphasizes human relations as an important management component.

References: Raymond E. Callahan, *Education and the Cult of Efficiency,* Chicago: University of Chicago Press, 1962; Frederick W. Taylor, *Scientific Management, Comprising Shop Management, The Principles of Scientific Management, and Testimony Before the Special House Committee,* New York: Harper and Row, Publishers, 1947.

SCIENTIFIC METHOD, or scientific problem solving, step-by-step procedures that researchers in the various sciences follow when reviewing existing knowledge or pursuing new knowledge. The procedures normally entail: (1) the systematic collection and classification of data relating to a problem; (2) hypothesis development; and (3) testing of the hypothesis using the data collected. The method is taught at all levels in education and is applicable to virtually all of the sciences.

References: Clarence W. Brown and Edwin E. Ghiselli, *Scientific Method in Psychology,* New York: McGraw-Hill Book Company, 1955; Charles A. Ford, et al. (Editors), *Compton's Illustrated Science Dictionary,* Indianapolis, IN: David-Stewart Publishing Company, 1963; Daniel N. Lapedes (Editor), *McGraw-Hill Dictionary of Scientific and Technical Terms* (Second Edition), New York: McGraw-Hill Book Company, 1978; John G. Navarra and Joseph Zafforoni, *Science Today for the Elementary School Teacher,* New York: Harper and Row, Publishers, 1960.

SCOPE AND SEQUENCE, curriculum terms that concern the horizontal and vertical placement of content to be taught. *Scope,* or horizontal organiza-tion, has to do with the side-by-side positioning of curriculum components. For example, the correlating of science and mathematics to create a fourth grade weather unit is a scope activity. *Sequence* addresses the vertical positioning of topics, subjects, or skill areas. Illustrating sequence is the mathematics curriculum that assigns the teaching of whole number addition to first grade and the teaching of addition of fractions to a later grade. One curriculum authority (Albert Oliver) referred to scope as the *what* criterion (i.e. What is to be taught?) and to sequence as the *when* criterion (i.e. When should a particular topic be taught?).

Robert Zais, another curriculum expert, indicated that school authorities face several problems associated with scope and sequence. A major scope problem, he indicated, is the integration of subject matter in an effort to minimize instructional fragmentation. A principal sequence problem, he pointed out, is the difficulty of developing and maintaining cumulative and continuous learning as students progress through the grade levels. Illustrating this latter problem is the traditional (sometimes disjointed) sequencing of secondary school biology, followed by chemistry, then by physics.

References: Allan A. Glatthorn, *Curriculum Leadership,* Glenview, IL: Scott, Foresman and Company, 1987; Albert I. Oliver, *Curriculum Improvement: A Guide to Problems, Principles, and Process* (Second Edition), New York: Harper and Row, Publishers, 1977; Robert S. Zais, *Curriculum: Principles and Foundations,* New York: Harper and Row, Publishers, 1976.

SCOPES TRIAL, a famous trial in which a secondary schoolteacher was charged with the teaching of evolution in violation of state law. Held in Dayton, Tennessee, from July 10 to July 20, 1925, it was known as the "Scopes Monkey Trial," because John Thomas Scopes, a science teacher in Rhea County High School, had taught a passage in a biology textbook that violated an antievolution bill that had been passed four months earlier. The trial attracted national and international attention.

John Scopes, Dr. George Rappleyea, and the American Civil Liberties Union determined to test the Tennessee law. Actually, Dr. Rappleyea, a businessman from Dayton, Tennessee, swore out a warrant against John Scopes (his friend) to test it. Two famous lawyers were involved in the trial: *William Jennings Bryan,* who assisted the Attorney General of Tennessee (Thomas Stewart), and *Clarence Darrow,* who, along with others, spoke for the defense. William Jennings Bryan died only five days after the conclusion of the trial.

John Scopes was found guilty of violating the law and fined $100. The Tennessee Supreme Court later reversed John Scopes's conviction on a technicality not related to the evolution issue. It was not until 1968 that the U.S. Supreme Court ruled against such antievolution legislation. The Tennessee law was repealed in 1967.

References: Leslie Allen (Editor), *Bryan and Darrow at Dayton,* New York: A. Lee and Company, 1925; John Thomas Scopes, *Center of the Storm,* New York: Holt, Rinehart and Winston, Inc., 1967; *The World's Most Famous Court Trial, State of Tennessee v. John Thomas Scopes* (c. 1925), New York: Da Capo Press, 1971.

SCSS CONVERSATIONAL SYSTEM—See STATISTICAL PACKAGE FOR THE SOCIAL SCIENCES

SEARCHES OF STUDENTS, a facet of law enforcement that has been receiving increased attention by the courts. Protests against searches of students and/or their property by school authorities have resulted in court decisions from which a few guidelines may be inferred. First, a few courts have ruled that searches of desks and lockers (by school officials and/or the police) are permissible on the grounds that these items of equipment, although used by students, are the property of the school. Even so, administrators in some states have been advised to seek student permission before undertaking such searches and to do so with the student and a witness present. Second, searches of students' persons may violate their Fourth Amendment rights; accordingly, the courts have been inclined to support such searches only in those instances where the gravity of a problem requires immediate action. Finally, off-campus searches of students that lead to disciplinary action by the schools are least likely to enjoy court sanction.

William Hazard pointed out that schools should publish a policy relating to locker searches, especially in cases involving stolen property. "(I)n the absence of a published policy clearly reserving the right to inspect the contents of school lockers for any purpose," he speculated, "the lockers would probably be held constitutionally secure against searches for contraband" (p. 274).

References: Eve Cary, *What Every Teacher Should Know About Student Rights,* Washington, DC: National Education Association, 1975; William R. Hazard, *Education and the Law: Cases and Materials on Public Schools* (Second Edition), New York: The Free Press, 1978.

SECONDARY SCHOOL, an institution of learning that provides education to youth who have completed elementary and/or middle school programs. A generic term, *secondary school* typically includes grades 7–12 and embraces both the junior high school and senior high school programs. Some definitions narrow the range to grades 9–12.

Most secondary schools are departmentalized. At the senior high school level they provide specialization programs (e.g. college preparation, vocational education). Graduation from a secondary school is usually required for admission to a college.

The major educational focus of such schools is the adolescent student. Secondary teachers usually function as subject specialists and earn certification in the teaching of a particular subject (e.g. history, mathematics, biology).

Secondary schools in the United States had their origins in the Boston Latin Grammar School and the academy (proposed by Benjamin Franklin) of colonial America. The first public supported high school (the English Classical School, later called the English High School) was founded in 1821. Central High School in Philadelphia was founded in 1836.

The National Center for Education Statistics estimated that, in the United States in 1980, total grade 9–12 enrollment was 14,807,000 of whom 13,307,000 were attending public secondary schools. (See FRANKLIN'S ACADEMY and LATIN GRAMMAR SCHOOL.)

References: William N. Alexander, et al., *The High School,* New York: Holt, Rinehart and Winston, Inc., 1971; David G. Armstrong and Tom V. Savage, *Secondary Education: An Introduction,* New York: Macmillan Publishing Co., Inc., 1983; Nancy B. Dearman and Valena W. Plisko, *The Condition of Education, 1980 Edition,* Washington, DC: National Center for Educational Statistics, U.S. Department of Education, 1980; J. Lloyd Trump and Delmas Miller, *Secondary School Curriculum Improvement: Meeting Challenges of the Times,* Boston: Allyn and Bacon, Inc., 1979.

SECONDARY SCHOOL SCIENCE PROJECT (SSP), also known as the Princeton project or by its course title, "Time, Space, and Matter (TSM)." SSSP, essentially though not exclusively an earth science course, was developed at Princeton University by a group of geologists working with selected chemists, physicists, and teachers. The course, titled TSM, was field tested in the early 1960s and later (1966) published by the McGraw-Hill Book Company.

TSM has no textbook for students. Instead, and because the course is inquiry oriented, the student conducts sequenced investigations and, in effect, develops his/her own textbook by recording observations in a blank Student Record Book. The course is divided into three parts: (1) *On the Nature of Things;* (2) *Seeking Regularity in Matter;* and (3) *Interpreting a World of Change.*

Materials include nine Student Investigation Booklets, The Student Record Book, a laboratory kit, teachers' manuals for each of the nine student booklets, tests, audio-visual materials, and a basic volume, *SSSP, Time, Space, and Matter.*
References: Alfred T. Collette, *Science Teaching in the Secondary School: A Guide for Modernizing Instruction,* Boston: Allyn and Bacon, Inc., 1973; Paul D. Hurd, *New Directions in Teaching Secondary School Science,* Chicago: Rand McNally and Company, 1969; J. David Lockard (Editor), *Science and Mathematics Curricular Developments Internationally, 1956–1974,* College Park, MD: Science Teaching Center, University of Maryland (Joint Project with the Commission on Science Education, American Association for the Advancement of Science), 1974; George J. Pallrand, "Time, Space and Matter," *The Physics Teacher,* March 1970; *Time, Space, and Matter: Investigating the Physical World,* St. Louis, MO: Webster Division, McGraw-Hill Book Company, 1966.

SECOND INTERNATIONAL MATHEMATICS STUDY—See INTERNATIONAL ASSOCIATION FOR THE EVALUATION OF EDUCATIONAL ACHIEVEMENT

SECOND MORRILL ACT, land-grant college legislation enacted by Congress at the urging of one of its members, Justin S. Morrill. Passed in 1890, this act built on the original Morrill Act of 1862 by providing annual appropriations to each land-grant college, beginning at $15,000 per annum and increasing to $25,000 per year in ten years. A second (and significant) provision barred appropriations to colleges that denied admission to black students. However, it provided that funds could be granted to segregated institutions that were operating separate educational systems. It was this provision that gave rise to the establishment of agricultural and mechanical colleges in the south. Today, the historically black land-grant institutions account for approximately one-quarter of all American black students enrolled in institutions of higher education. (See MORRILL ACT.)
References: Harry G. Good and James D. Teller, *A His-*

tory of American Education (Third Edition), New York: The Macmillan Company, 1973; National Association of State Universities and Land-Grant Colleges, *Facts '79,* Washington, DC: The Association, 1979.

SECTION 504—See REHABILITATION ACT

SECURITY—See SCHOOL SECURITY

SEED MONEY, funds used to establish (or "seed") a program, project, or organization. Such funds are sometimes used to allow time for the new effort being supported to get underway. They may also be used by a donor (agency, foundation, individual, etc.) to show faith in a proposed effort and/or to encourage others to contribute to it as well.
Reference: Stephen E. Nowlan, et al. (Editors), *User's Guide to Funding Resources,* Radnor, PA: Chilton Book Company, 1975.

SEGREGATION, RACIAL, the separation of people by race. The term *racial segregation* is frequently associated with students who, because of housing patterns, law, or for other reasons, are (were) assigned to a school in which all or a large majority of the students are (were) of one race.

The courts have identified two types of segregation: *de jure* and *de facto.* The former type is used to describe racial segregation that results from laws enacted or actions taken by states, cities, or school boards. The latter type includes cases of racial segregation resulting from housing patterns or other factors for which no direct governmental/juridical action is responsible.

The U.S. Supreme Court, 1954, ruled (*Brown v. Board of Education of Topeka*) that segregation of public school children on the basis of race is unconstitutional. Although the majority of school boards around the country have attempted to desegregate their school systems, residential segregation has made numbers of such attempts difficult to implement. Also, as Nancy St. John pointed out, desegregated schools often maintain classes that are largely segregated (intraschool segregation), a practice receiving the attention of several researchers investigating the academic effects of desegregation. (See BROWN v. BOARD OF EDUCATION OF TOPEKA; DE FACTO SEGREGATION; DE JURE SEGREGATION; DESEGREGATION; and INTEGRATION, RACIAL.)
References: Reynolds Farley, "Residential Segregation and Its Implications for School Integration" in Betsy Levin and Willis D. Hawley (Editors), *The Courts, Social*

Science, and School Desegregation, New Brunswick, NJ: Transaction Books, 1977; National School Public Relations Association, *Desegregation: How Schools Are Meeting Historic Challenge*, Arlington, VA: The Association, 1973; Frank T. Read, "Judicial Evolution of the Law of School Integration Since Brown v. Board of Education" in Betsy Levin and Willis D. Hawley (Editors), *The Courts, Social Science, and School Desegregation*, New Brunswick, NJ: Transaction Books, 1977; Nancy H. St. John, *School Desegregation Outcomes for Children*, New York: John Wiley and Sons, 1975.

SELF-ACTUALIZATION, the full use of one's talents, potentialities, skills, and capacities to reach one's full capability. The concept of self-actualization was first developed fully by Abraham Maslow in the 1940s, 1950s, and 1960s as he formulated his motivational hierarchy. There are five higher order need levels in his hierarchy. They are: (1) physiological; (2) safety; (3) belongingness and love; (4) esteem; and (5) self-actualization (with self-actualization the highest level). Gordon Allport and Carl Rogers also developed self-actualization concepts in the 1950s.

Self-actualizing individuals tend to: accept themselves and others, be autonomous, be nonstereotyped, have deep relationships with others, be problem solvers, and be able to enjoy an experience deeply. The need for self-actualization is the highest level of motivation and cannot be reached (according to Maslow) without satisfying the other lower level needs. (See MASLOW'S HIERARCHY OF NEEDS.)
References: Victor Daniels and Lawrence J. Horowitz, *Being and Caring*, San Francisco: San Francisco Book Company, 1976; Herbert Leff, *Experience, Environment, and Human Potentials*, New York: Oxford University Press, 1978; Richard J. Lowry (Editor), *Dominance, Self-Esteem, Self-Actualization: Germinal Papers of A. H. Maslow*, Monterey, CA: Brooks/Cole Publishing Company, 1973; Abraham H. Maslow, *Motivation and Personality*, New York: Harper and Row, Publishers, 1970.

SELF-CONCEPT—See SELF-ESTEEM

SELF-CONTAINED CLASSROOM, a pattern of organization commonly found in American elementary and some middle schools. Children of similar social maturity are grouped together and work under the direction of a single teacher, normally for one academic year. The instructor, a subject generalist, typically teaches most subjects making up the curriculum. Resource teachers in fields such as art, music, and physical education are frequently available to teach these specialized subjects.

Teacher aides are often available, also, to assist the teacher in selected areas of instruction.

Proponents of the self-contained classroom support it on the basis of several purported advantages: (1) teachers get to know their students well; (2) flexibility of planning; (3) opportunity to individualize instruction; and (4) the opportunity to integrate subjects into units of study.
References: Edith R. Snyder (Editor), *The Self-Contained Classroom*, Washington, DC: Association for Supervision and Curriculum Development, 1960; L. O. Obdell and W. J. Van Ness, "The Self-Contained Classrooms in the Elementary School" in Oscar T. Jarvis (Editor), *Elementary School Administration: Readings*, Dubuque, IA: Wm. C. Brown Company, Publishers, 1969.

SELF-ESTEEM, or self-concept, a judgment about one's self-worth. How the student views himself/herself, research has shown, has much to do with his/her success in school. More important to achievement than tangibles such as new school buildings or modern instructional artifacts is the individual student's view of self. High (positive) self-esteem has frequently been shown to correlate with success in school. High self-esteem students tend to have confidence in their own abilities and believe that they can control their own destinies. On the other hand, low (negative) self-esteem students tend to lack such confidence. Many of this latter group come from low socioeconomic households.
References: David W. Johnson, *Educational Psychology*, Englewood Cliffs, NJ: Prentice-Hall, Inc., 1979; Jerome Kagan and Ernest Havemann, *Psychology: An Introduction* (Second Edition), New York: Harcourt Brace Jovanovich, Inc., 1972; W. Edgar Vinacke, *Foundations of Psychology*, New York: Van Nostrand Reinhold Company, 1968; Ruth C. Wylie, et al., *The Self-Concept: Theory and Research on Selected Topics* (Revised Edition, Volume Two), Lincoln, NE: University of Nebraska Press, 1979.

SELF-FULFILLING PROPHECY, a sociological term that, according to Robert K. Merton, its developer, "is, in the beginning, a *false* definition of the situation evoking a new behavior which makes the originally false conception come true" (p. 195). Jackson Toby, another sociologist, described it as "a cultural definition, initially untrue, which affects interaction in such a way as to generate its own confirming evidence" (p. 606). Illustrating self-fulfilling prophecy is the case of the classroom teacher who believes that black children are intellectually inferior to white children. Believing this, he/she treats them in a way that makes them sensitive to his/her belief. Ultimately, they perform in a relatively inferior manner, in effect fulfilling the instructor's initially fallacious and unfounded prophecy.

Robert Merton pointed out that the self-fulfilling prophecy does not stop working automatically. Planned and deliberate institutional controls are needed to thwart its perpetuation.

References: Robert K. Merton, "The Self-Fulfilling Prophecy," *The Antioch Review,* June 1948; Jackson Toby, *Contemporary Society: An Introduction to Sociology* (Second Edition), New York: John Wiley and Sons, 1971.

SELF-INSURANCE—See INSURANCE

SEMANTIC DIFFERENTIAL TECHNIQUE, a psycholinguistic approach used to assess the perceptions or attitudes of an individual, or group of individuals, to a stimulus (e.g. word, concept). Stimuli are presented to the individual with bipolar adjective words listed under each. The respondent is asked to place an "X" next to the word that best describes the degree of his/her feeling about each stimulus.

The following is the most common form of the semantic differential:

Stimulus ⟶ TELEVISION PROGRAMS
Bipolar Adjectives ⟶ GOOD __: __: __: __: __: __: __: BAD
⟶ BEAUTIFUL __: __: __: __: __: __: __: UGLY

Research has indicated that adjectives fall into various dimensions or factors. The most common dimensions are: *evaluation* (good-bad, beautiful-ugly, sweet-sour, clean-dirty); *potency* (large-small, strong-weak, heavy-light); and *activity* (fast-slow, active-passive, hot-cold).

The semantic differential technique was developed by Charles E. Osgood and associates in the 1950s and had its origins in the studies of the meanings of words. It has been used extensively in several types of research including cross-cultural studies; developmental studies; and experimental, social, clinical psychology investigations.

References: Anne Anastasi, *Psychological Testing* (Sixth Edition), New York: Macmillan Publishing Company, 1988; David E. Kapel, "Attitudes toward Selected Stimuli," *Urban Education,* October 1973; Charles E. Osgood, et al., *The Measurement of Meaning,* Urbana, IL: University of Illinois Press, 1957; James G. Snider and Charles E. Osgood (Editors), *Semantic Differential Technique: A Source Book,* Chicago: Aldine Publishing Company, 1969.

SEMANTIC MAPPING, an instructional strategy that involves the structuring of information in graphic form. The method builds on the learner's prior knowledge. Semantic maps enable the learner to see the interrelatedness of words and concepts. The specific procedure varies according to lesson objectives; however, the lesson generally evolves from a brainstorming session. Students are requested to verbalize words/concepts that they would associate with the stimulus. Through reading and discussion, students verify and amplify their understanding of the concepts (see illustration below). New concepts are related to background knowledge; thus, comprehension improves. Semantic mapping can be used for vocabulary development, as a pre- and post-reading

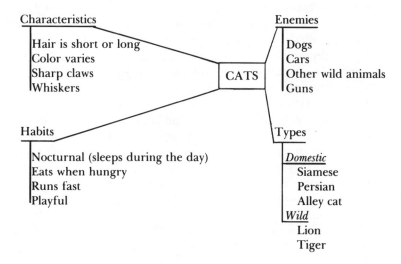

Semantic Map of Cats

Semantic Webbing

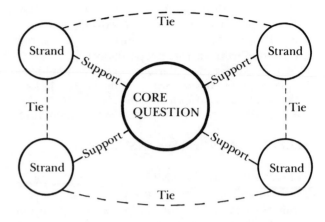

strategy, to help students recall and organize information, read, and as a study skill strategy. As a lesson progresses from pre- to post-reading, the semantic map can be extended. Semantic mapping helps the learner to organize and integrate information, thus facilitating text comprehension. (See SEMANTIC WEBBING and STRUCTURED OVERVIEW.)

References: Joan E. Heimlich and Susan D. Pittelman, *Semantic Mapping: Classroom Application*, Newark, DE: International Reading Association, 1986; D. D. Johnson and P. D. Pearson, *Teaching Reading Vocabulary*, (Second Edition), New York: Holt, Rinehart and Winston, 1984; J. D. McNeil, *Reading Comprehension: New Directions for Classroom Practice*, Glenview, IL: Scott Foresman, 1984.

SEMANTIC WEBBING, a process for visually displaying categories and their interrelatedness (Freedman and Reynolds, 1980). Webbing is used to aid the reader to organize and integrate concepts within a selection. The web consists of a core question which is chosen by the facilitator or teacher. Student answers become the strands of the web. These answers are based on both the story itself and student experiences; the reasons behind the answers are known as the strand supports. The relationship among the strands are known as the strand ties. This process can be employed after completion of a reading or as a predictor in the continued reading of a selection. For example, after reading the portion of *Cinderella* that ends with the stepsisters' departure for the ball, the core question for predictive value could be, "What will Cinderella do next?" (See SEMANTIC MAPPING and STRUCTURED OVERVIEW.)

References: Paul C. Burns, Betty D. Roe, and Elinor P. Ross, *Teaching Reading in Today's Elementary Schools*, Boston: Houghton Mifflin Company, 1984; J. David Cooper, *Improving Reading Comprehension*, Boston: Houghton Mifflin Company, 1986; Glen Freedman and Elizabeth G. Reynolds, "Enriching Basal Reader Lesson with Semantic Webbing," *The Reading Teacher*, March 1980.

SEMESTER, an academic term that usually consists of 15 weeks of classes. The semester system is the calendar system most commonly used by American colleges and universities. (The next most popular is the *quarter* system.) Two semesters make up the traditional academic year, one starting on or about September 1 and the second sometime after the Christmas holiday. (See QUARTER, ACADEMIC.)

Reference: Asa S. Knowles (Editor), *Handbook of College and University Administration*, New York: McGraw-Hill Book Company, 1970.

SEMINAR METHOD, an instructional approach that brings together a group of pupils, usually college-level students, to discuss topics of interest under the direction of a teacher or discussion leader. This instructional technique was used in German universities during the 19th century. During the latter part of that century, the seminar was introduced in American institutions of higher education by a small number of German-trained teachers. Professor Charles Adams was using this method at the University of Michigan as early as 1869. Other American scholars reported to be teaching seminars before 1900 were Henry Adams (Harvard), Herbert Adams (Johns Hopkins), and G. Stanley Hall (Clark).

In recent years, the term *seminar* has come to be used interchangeably with other terms such as *workshop, institute,* and *study group.* The literature on the seminar method of instruction indicates that, to some extent, it is used in junior and senior high schools as well as colleges; furthermore, that it is used in virtually all subject areas.

Operationally, the seminar method requires the teacher to play less of a leadership role than in the lecture method. Much responsibility for discussion and analysis is vested in the students with the teacher functioning as a resource person. (See LECTURE METHOD.)

References: John S. Brubacher and Willis Rudy, *Higher Education in Transition: An American History, 1636–1956,* New York: Harper and Brothers, 1958; Carolyn M. Owen, "The Seminar," *Improving College and University Teaching,* Summer 1970.

SENIOR HIGH SCHOOL—See SECONDARY SCHOOL

SENIOR HIGH SCHOOL PRINCIPAL, the administrator responsible for administering a senior high school. According to a National Association of Secondary School Principals survey, the median size of the public senior high school is 1,000–1,500 students. In 1977, the median salary earned by public high school administrators was $25,600. Effective senior high school principals, the study indicated, devote the major portion of the working day to three primary activities: (1) personnel; (2) program development; and (3) school management. Private and parochial senior high schools make up approximately 13 percent of the country's high schools. Because they are smaller than their public school counterparts, several of their administrators are required to engage in some teaching.

Qualifications for the senior high school principalship vary from state to state. The representative job applicant is required to hold at least a master's degree in educational administration, be certified by his/her state, and have completed three to five years of successful classroom teaching.

References: Lloyd E. McCleary and Scott D. Thomson, *The Senior High School Principalship* (Volume III: The Summary Report), Reston, VA: National Association of Secondary School Principals, 1979; Gilbert R. Weldy, *Principals: What They Do and Who They Are,* Reston, VA: National Association of Secondary School Principals, 1979.

SENSITIVITY TRAINING, a particular kind of group laboratory training designed to help participants better understand and/or improve their ability to relate to themselves, to other individuals, to groups, or to organizations. Sensitivity training does not follow hard and fast rules, nor are procedures (e.g. time period) the same from one sensitivity training laboratory to another. There are some characteristics that they have in common, however: (1) a group of participants who work together for an extended period (e.g. weekend, one week, two weeks); (2) a professional trainer whose principal task it is to establish effective communication links among participants; and (3) intergroup or organizational exercises frequently including use of T-groups.

The overriding purpose of sensitivity training is self-awareness, not therapy. Gerard Egan wrote that it "provides its members a unique opportunity for responsible learning about themselves on intrapsychic and interpersonal levels.... (T)he climate is such as to sustain and even demand examination of personal and interpersonal issues" (p. 10).

References: Arthur Blumberg, "Laboratory Education and Sensitivity Training" in Robert T. Golembiewski and Arthur Blumberg (Editors), *Sensitivity Training and the Laboratory Approach: Readings About Concepts and Applications* (Third Edition), Itasca, IL: F. E. Peacock Publishers, Inc., 1977; Gerard Egan, *Encounter: Group Processes for Interpersonal Growth,* Belmont, CA: Wadsworth Publishing Company, Inc., 1970; Henry C. Smith, *Sensitivity Training: The Scientific Understanding of Individuals,* New York: McGraw-Hill Book Company, 1973.

SEPARATE-BUT-EQUAL DOCTRINE—See *PLESSY v. FERGUSON*

SEQUENCE, CURRICULUM—See SCOPE AND SEQUENCE

SERENDIPITY, an unanticipated beneficial result produced by factors that are unpredictable as well as uncontrollable. Such results, sometimes referred to as "gifts," "bonuses," or "extras," frequently come about through luck rather than plan. The case of a property owner who digs for water and suddenly discovers oil illustrates the meaning of serendipity. In organizations, problem-solving and decision-making activities occasionally produce serendipitous results.

Reference: Andrew J. Du Brin, *Fundamentals of Organizational Behavior: An Applied Perspective,* New York: Pergamon Press, Inc., 1974.

SERIGRAPHY—See SILK SCREEN

SERRANO v. PRIEST, a significant court decision

in which the California State Supreme Court ruled that California's method of financing education, a method based on the wealth of individual school districts, was in violation of the state Constitution. California, like most states, was relying heavily on local property taxes to support its public schools. This method, which the court ruled was in violation of that state's equal protection clause, was found to discriminate against the poor. The court held that the quality of education in school districts populated by large numbers of poor families was inferior to that being provided by districts with wealthier families because dollar support per pupil was lower. The state was instructed to devise a more equitable formula for apportioning monies for education, a mandate that had political and social as well as financial implications not only for California but for all other states using California's method of school support.

In 1973, in a similar case (*Rodriguez v. San Antonio School District*), the U.S. Supreme Court ruled that state systems that use local property taxes to support schools were not in violation of the *federal* Constitution since education is not a fundamental interest provided or protected by the U.S. Constitution. (See *RODRIGUEZ v. SAN ANTONIO SCHOOL DISTRICT.*)

References: David K. Cohen, "Serrano and Its Progeny" in John Pincus (Editor), *School Finance in Transition: The Courts and Educational Reform*, Cambridge, MA: Ballinger Publishing Company, 1974; E. Gordon Gee and David J. Sperry, *Education Law and the Public Schools: A Compendium*, Boston: Allyn and Bacon, Inc., 1978; Arnold J. Meltsner and Robert T. Nakamura, "Political Implications of Serrano" in John Pincus (Editor), *School Finance in Transition: The Courts and Educational Reform*, Cambridge, MA: Ballinger Publishing Company, 1974; *Serrano v. Priest*, 5 Cal. 3d 584, 487 P.2d. 1241, 96 Cal. Rptr. 601 (1971).

SERVICEMEN'S OPPORTUNITY COLLEGES (SOC), a joint civilian-military effort in which over 300 institutions of higher education have been formed into a network that works to meet the educational needs of service personnel and veterans. The SOC program grew out of a 1970 project that was designed to meet the educational needs of returning Vietnam War servicemen. The project was carried out by the American Association of Community and Junior Colleges and funded by the Carnegie Corporation of New York. In 1972, the first SOC program evolved from that project, making lower division courses and programs available to servicemen and women. A year later, the Ameri-

can Association of State Colleges and Universities and ten other higher education associations joined AACJC to make four-year college programs available to servicemen. Since 1974, SOC has been supported by the Department of Defense and a grant from the Carnegie Corporation.

SOC serves more than 250,000 military students each year, doing so in at least three principal ways: (1) offering programs on or near military bases; (2) developing nontraditional modes of instruction for service personnel; and (3) providing "coordinator" services for students who plan, later, to transfer SOC courses to other institutions. (See DEFENSE ACTIVITY FOR NONTRADITIONAL EDUCATION SUPPORT.)

References: Defense Activity for Non-Traditional Education Support, *A Guide to the Acceptance of Non-Traditional Credit in SOC Institutions,* Pensacola, FL: DANTES, May 1979; *SOC Directory, 1979,* Washington, DC: American Association of State Colleges and Universities and American Association of Community and Junior Colleges, 1979.

SET INDUCTION, the actions and/or statements designed to put students in a receptive mind for learning. The first purpose of set induction is to focus student attention. A second reason for set induction is to provide an organizational framework for the lesson. Extension of understanding through example and/or analogy is a third purpose for using set induction strategy. The following are examples of instances when teachers are advised to use set induction: when introducing a long unit of work, a new concept, a period of discussion, a field trip, a guest speaker, or a question-answer session. Set induction provides for a smooth transition from known to unknown material since it employs example, analogy, and student activity. It provides an opportunity to evaluate past learning before moving on to new skills. (See ADVANCE ORGANIZERS.)

References: Nat L. Gage and David C. Berliner, *Educational Psychology,* Chicago: Rand McNally and Co., 1975; Robert M. Gagné and Leslie J. Briggs, *Principles of Instructional Design,* New York: Holt, Rinehart and Winston, 1974; Robert Shostak, "Lesson Presentation Skills" in James M. Cooper (Editor), *Classroom Teaching Skills* (Second Edition), Lexington, MA: D. C. Heath and Co., 1982.

SETS, a mathematical term used to describe a well-defined collection or a class of items, objects, numbers, or individuals. For example, all tenth graders in a particular high school may comprise a set. Other sets may be all books in a library, all automobiles, all Americans, months in a year, numbers, and so forth. The items or objects that make up the set are called *elements*. A set may contain a few elements, many elements, an infinite number of elements, or no elements. When there are no elements in a set it is called a *null set*. Sets have subsets within them. Ford cars, for example, are a subset of all cars, and mathematics books are a subset of all books found in a university library.

There are various relations that could exist among sets; for example:

A *union* of sets *A* and *B*, written as *A U B*.

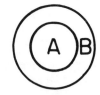

The shaded area is common to both sets *A* and *B*. This is written as *A ∩ B*.

There are many relations that look alike graphically but are not. One must know the various conditions and the many symbols of sets to be able to understand the relations being illustrated.

Sets and set theory are used in the logical development of mathematics.

References: Didier Dubois and Henri Prade, *Fuzzy Sets and Systems: Theory and Applications,* New York: Academic Press, 1979; Helen L. Garstens and Stanley B. Jackson, *Mathematics for Elementary School Teachers,* New York: The Macmillan Company, 1967; William L. Schaaf, *Basic Concepts of Elementary Mathematics,* New York: John Wiley and Sons, 1969; Robert R. Stoll, *Sets, Logic and Axiomatic Theories* (Second Edition), San Francisco: W. H. Freeman, 1974.

SEVERE AND PROFOUND DISORDERS, a generic classification of disorders of individuals who have either one or more deficits in the following areas: intellect, social/interpersonal relations, physical, and sensory. These deficits fall beyond three standard deviations below the average on assessment (criterion and/or norm-referenced) instruments. Most of the individuals who fall into this category have multiple deficits. The deficits these individuals have are manifested in a variety of settings or environments. Mental retardation is the most common disorder found in this classification. However, there are many people who have other severe and profound disorders, such as the deaf-

blind, yet are not mentally retarded. Individuals in this category often need special school environments and services.

The number of individuals classified as severe and profound is quite small. No more than 1 percent of the population could be placed within this category. *Severely* or *profoundly handicapped* or *severely multiply handicapped* are terms that are often used for individuals in this classification. Special equipment, technology, and augmented environments, especially for the deaf or blind, can reduce the "handicap aspects" of the disorder. (See LEARNING DISABILITIES, MENTAL RETARDATION, and MILD/MODERATE DISORDERS.)

References: Michael L. Hardman, et al., *Human Exceptionality, Society, School, and Family* (Second Edition), Boston: Allyn and Bacon, Inc., 1987; A. A. More and L. F. Masters, *Teaching the Severely Mentally Retarded,* Rockville, MD: Aspen Systems Corp., 1980; S. Stainback and W. Stainback, *Integration of Students with Severe Handicaps,* Reston, VA: Council for Exceptional Children, 1985.

SEX EDUCATION, a generalized term that covers the study and teaching of the psychosocial-sexual development of humans. It has no set definition since context is dependent upon the restrictions and mores of the school, locality, and/or country in which this subject is taught.

The major thrust of sex education is to enable an individual to make informed and responsible decisions concerning his/her own sexual conduct. Another area focuses on human sexuality or the comprehensive attributes of a person's maleness or femaleness. Family life and sexual reproduction are also studied as part of sex education, but only one part.

The psychosocial-sexual development of humans is learned or heavily influenced by society, family, religion, and environment. Consequently, most authorities agree that sex education should focus on such psychosocial-sexual development and these influences.

Many schools in the United States offer some form of sex education, usually starting in the upper elementary grades. Others have none, primarily due to the controversial nature of the subject and the still widespread belief in some communities that sex education should be taught at home rather than in school.

John Pietrofesa, who has written widely on sex education, offered the view that effective sex education programs include six elements: (1) the program is developmental rather than remedial; (2) the program recognizes the rights and obligations of parents; (3) the community is involved in developing and carrying out programs; (4) sex education goals are stated objectively; (5) faculty who teach sex education are adequately trained and are volunteers; and (6) the program is subjected to ongoing, systematic evaluation. (See SIECUS.)

References: Sol Gordon and Irving R. Dickman, *Sex Education: The Parent's Role*, New York: Public Affairs Committee, 1977; John J. Pietrofesa, "The School Counselor in Sex Education," *Personnel and Guidance Journal*, March 1976; Norman Rosenzweig and F. Paul Pearsall (Editors), *Sex Education for the Health Professional*, New York: Grune and Stratton, 1978; David R. Stronck (Editor), *Discussing Sex in the Classroom: Readings for Teachers*, Washington, D.C.: National Science Teachers Association, 1982.

SEXISM, originally defined as discrimination on the basis of sex, has more recently come to mean the conscious or unconscious stereotyping of roles on the basis of sex. In recent years, sexism in schools has come under careful scrutiny, because children are especially likely to be influenced by the several manifestations of sexual stereotyping present in the educational environment. Content analyses of textbooks, for example, have shown that these materials are frequently sexist, often portraying women as the weaker sex and associating them with specific vocational roles (e.g. secretaries, maids, nurses). The school organization, especially at the elementary level, is itself likely to reinforce the idea of sexism by depicting teachers as females and the administrators, their superiors, as males. Curriculum, too, has been receiving attention, particularly in those program areas where sexual segregation of students has been traditional (e.g. home economics, physical education, industrial arts).

Two principal sets of reasons account for the recent movement to eliminate sexism in schools: (1) the legal ones, concerned with achieving sexual parity, and (2) those relating to self-concept. The latter reflect research evidence showing that girls often have more negative self-concepts than boys. (See SELF-ESTEEM.)

References: Pauline Gough, *Sexism: New Issue in American Education* (PDK Fastback 81), Bloomington, IN: The Phi Delta Kappa Educational Foundation, 1976; Elizabeth S. Maccia, et al., *Women and Education*, Springfield, IL: Charles C. Thomas, Publisher, 1975.

SHARED TIME, cooperative dual-enrollment programs that permit students to enroll concur-

rently in both public and private (parochial) schools. Such programs usually involve parochial students who, for some part of the school day, enroll in selected public school courses (e.g. laboratories, vocational education offerings) that are not a part of the private school's curriculum. Shared time involves nonreligious offerings, one of the characteristics that distinguishes it from released time programs. (See RELEASED TIME.)

References: William R. Hazard, *Education and the Law: Cases and Materials on Public Schools* (Second Edition), New York: The Free Press (Macmillan), 1978; David Tavel, *Church-State Issues in Education* (PDK Fastback 123), Bloomington, IN: The Phi Delta Kappa Educational Foundation, 1979.

SHELTERED WORKSHOP, defined by the Association of Rehabilitation Facilities as "a work-oriented rehabilitation facility with a controlled working environment and individual vocational goals, which utilizes work experience and related services for assisting the handicapped person to progress toward normal living and a productive vocational status" (p. 88). When first introduced in the early part of the 20th century, sheltered workshops performed a custodial function almost exclusively. In recent years, such workshops have been broadened to help the severely disabled person to secure a job and to become economically self-sufficient.

Workshop participants are normally paid in exchange for the goods and/or services they produce. The kind of work arrangements developed by the agencies sponsoring sheltered workshops include: (1) service contracts (e.g. gardening, janitorial services); (2) industrial subcontract work; (3) repairing and processing of used goods; and (4) manufacturing of new goods.

Sheltered workshops are usually incorporated as nonprofit organizations and are certified (for wage purposes) by the U.S. Department of Labor. Standards for operation have been established by many state governments as well as national organizations such as Goodwill Industries. (See VOCATIONAL REHABILITATION.)

References: Robert M. Goldenson, "The Sheltered Workshop" in Robert M. Goldenson (Editor), *Disability and Rehabilitation Handbook*, New York: McGraw-Hill Book Company, 1978; Nathan Nelson, *Workshops for the Handicapped in the United States: An Historical and Developmental Perspective*, Springfield, IL: Charles C. Thomas, Publisher, 1971; Jay L. Zaetz, *Organization of Sheltered Workshop Programs for the Mentally Retarded Adult*, Springfield, IL: Charles C. Thomas, Publisher, 1971.

SHORTHAND, a general term for systems of

rapid handwriting in which symbols are used to represent letters, words, or phrases. As Hamden Forkner and Ron Deyoung indicated, the word *shorthand* includes three broad, yet distinct, approaches: (1) systems that use symbols for speech sounds or combinations of speech sounds (e.g. Gregg, Pitman systems); (2) machine shorthand, such as Stenotype or Stenograph; and (3) systems such as Speedwriting, Forkner, or Stenospeed that make use of letter and special symbol combinations.

Literally hundreds of shorthand systems have been developed and used over the last 2,000 years. In the United States, where over a hundred systems have been introduced, the Gregg system is the most widely used, although Pitman shorthand continues to be taught in some school systems (and is still rather widely used in Europe).

Research on shorthand has identified different attempts to predict shorthand success using such variables as foreign language aptitude, grade point average, English grades, and so on. None stands out as being a perfect predictor. Accordingly, business educators are urged to consider several measures when attempting to gauge future success of students.

References: Lloyd V. Douglas, et al., *Teaching Business Subjects* (Third Edition), Englewood Cliffs, NJ: Prentice-Hall, Inc., 1973; Hamden L. Forkner and Ron C. Deyoung, "A Historical Development of Shorthand" in Ruth B. Woolschlager and E. Edward Harris (Editors), *Business Education Yesterday, Today, and Tomorrow* (National Business Education Yearbook, No. 14), Reston, VA: National Business Education Association, 1976; Leona Gallion, "The Teaching of Shorthand and Transcription" in Calfrey C. Calhoun and Mildred Hillestad (Editors), *Contributions of Research to Business Education* (National Business Education Yearbook, No. 9), Washington, DC: National Business Education Association, 1971; Louis A. Leslie (Editor), *The Story of Gregg Shorthand: Based on the Writings of John Robert Gregg*, New York: McGraw-Hill Book Company, 1964.

SIBLING RIVALRY, competition between brothers and/or sisters for parental attention and affection. This feeling of conflict often precipitates jealousy, which manifests itself in different ways. For example, a sibling who sees himself/herself as being the unfavored child may become aggressive and engage in fighting or other attention-gaining activities of a negative nature. Another may show signs of despondency and withdraw. Still others may compete openly with the brother or sister perceived to be the favored child. Parents who regularly compare their children or who show decided preference for one over another aggravate such rivalry.

References: Horace B. English and Ava C. English, *A Comprehensive Dictionary of Psychological and Psychoanalytical Terms: A Guide to Usage*, New York: David McKay Company, Inc., 1974; Robert M. Goldenson, *The Encyclopedia of Human Behavior: Psychology, Psychiatry, and Mental Health* (Volume 2), Garden City, NY: Doubleday and Company, Inc., 1970.

SIBLINGS, brothers and/or sisters who are not members of a multiple-birth group (e.g. twins, triplets) and who have one common set of parents. The term appears frequently in the literature of the behavioral and social sciences. (See SIBLING RIVALRY.)

Reference: Carter V. Good (Editor), *Dictionary of Education* (Third Edition), New York: McGraw-Hill Book Company, 1973.

SICKLE CELL ANEMIA, a painful and inherited blood disease that is almost unique to black children. Carried genetically (it is Mendelian-recessive), the disease causes a disorder of hemoglobin, the oxygen-carrying part of the red cells. At times, it causes normally round blood cells to assume a crescent, or sickle-like shape that precludes their free flow through the capillaries. The sickle-shaped cells get lodged in these fine blood vessels, causing extreme pain and damage to the area that has been jammed and thus denied oxygen.

Sickle cell anemia and sickle cell trait are often (and incorrectly) considered to be synonymous terms. *Anemia* refers to the disease, produced when both parents are genetic carriers. *Trait*, on the other hand, refers to those cases where only a single parent is a carrier but is not ill. Anemia affects an estimated 1:400 persons, the trait 1:10.

Anemia pain attacks vary in frequency and length, causing pain in parts of the torso, arms, and legs; joints swell; drowsiness and fever may occur. Life span is shortened with an estimated 50 percent of afflicted children surviving to adulthood.

The disease affects children's school work and social development in several ways and adversely. Those able to attend classes are likely to do so intermittently. When in school, symptoms of fatigue are likely to be noted. Children with serious cases of anemia may require the services of a home teacher.

References: Denis R. Miller and Howard A. Pearson (Editors), *Smith's Blood Diseases of Infancy and Childhood*, St. Louis, MO: The C. V. Mosby Company, 1978; Georgia Travis, *Chronic Illness in Children: Its Impact on Child and Family,* Stanford, CA: Stanford University Press, 1976.

SIECUS, the *Sex Information and Education Council of the U. S.,* a nonprofit organization that provides materials and information for professionals working in the field of human sexuality and sex education. Additionally, it participates in parent education and teacher training programs. Conferences are held and professional publications prepared to help implement the organization's goals. Many of these activities are designed to help teenagers.

SIECUS was founded in 1964 by a Quaker physician, Dr. Mary S. Calderone. Dr. Calderone became SIECUS's first President. SIECUS leaders and the organization itself have been both applauded and attacked for their work with much of the criticism coming from extremist right wing groups.

The *SIECUS Report,* a bimonthly periodical, is published by SIECUS. Guidebooks and resource manuals are distributed through Human Science Press. In 1979, the SIECUS Resource Center and Library became available for outside use (at New York University) as the result of SIECUS's affiliation with NYU's School of Education, Health, Nursing, and Arts Professions.

References: SIECUS, *By 15, All Kids Have Had Sex Education in School . . . in Hallways, Locker Rooms and Washrooms,* New York: The Council, Undated Brochure; SIECUS, *SIECUS Resource Center and Library at NYU,* New York: The Council, Undated Brochure.

SIGHT METHOD OF READING—See SIGHT WORD

SIGHT READING, in music, the ability to sing or play a piece of music at first sight. (Singing a score for practice or study is sometimes referred to as *sight singing.*)

References: Jack Boyd, *Teaching Choral Sight Reading,* West Nyack, NY: Parker Publishing Company, Inc., 1975; Leonhard Deutsch, *Piano: Guided Sight-Reading,* Chicago: Nelson-Hall, Inc., 1977; Anne M. de Zeeuw and Roger E. Foltz, *Sight-Singing and Related Skills* (Revised), Manchaca, TX: Sterling Swift, 1975.

SIGHT VOCABULARY, a reading term referring to the total list of words that a student can recognize. To have a word qualify for inclusion as part of the student's sight vocabulary, he/she must demonstrate ability to read it and to understand its meaning. Teachers help children to expand their sight vocabularies in two principal ways: (1) by helping the child to read (visually discriminate) new words, and (2) by encouraging free or recreational reading.

References: Robert Karlin and Andrea R. Karlin, *Teaching Elementary Reading: Principles and Strategies* (Fourth Edition), San Diego, CA: Harcourt Brace Jovanovich, Publishers, 1987; Barbara E. R. Swaby, *Diagnosis and Correction of Reading Difficulties,* Boston: Allyn and Bacon, 1989; Eldon E. Ekwall, *Diagnosis and Remediation of the Disabled Reader,* Boston: Allyn and Bacon, Inc., 1976; Pose Lamb and Richard Arnold (Editors), *Reading: Foundations and Instructional Strategies,* Belmont, CA: Wadsworth Publishing Company, Inc., 1976.

SIGHT WORD, a reading term used to describe recognition of a word by its configuration (shape) rather than by studying its separate parts and blending them into a whole word. Words may be recognized because of their length (e.g. *cat* vs. *elephant*), unique shape (e.g. grandfather), or some other distinguishing feature of a configurative nature. This visual method of teaching seeks to have learners recognize a word after repeated exposure to it. A limitation of this method is that children with reading disability are inclined to confuse words having similar shapes.

Lists of words are taught for the purpose of developing reading vocabulary. They may consist of basic word lists prepared by reading authorities (the Dolch Word List, for example), high frequency words, key words the student will encounter in a story, or even words having special interest to the learner. (See WORD CONFIGURATION and WORD LISTS.)

References: Eddie C. Kennedy, *Classroom Approaches to Remedial Reading* (Second Edition), Itasca, IL: F. E. Peacock Publishers, Inc., 1977; Florence G. Roswell and Gladys Natchez, *Reading Disability: A Human Approach to Learning* (Third Edition), New York: Basic Books, Inc., Publishers, 1977; S. Jay Samuels, "Modes of Word Recognition" in Harry Singer and Robert B. Ruddell (Editors), *Theoretical Models and Processes of Reading* (Second Edition), Newark, DE: International Reading Association, 1976.

SIGMA SCORES—See z-SCORE

SIGN LANGUAGE, a system of communication, used especially with deaf individuals, that involves the use of hand and finger signs and gestures. Different signs/gestures connote different messages. Often, there is a similarity between the configuration of the gesture and the word or idea being communicated.

American Sign Language (ASL) is a widely used language system deaf persons employ when communicating among themselves. Although ASL is not as complete a communication system as is English (some grammatical features are lacking), it has come to be recognized as a language. Variations of ASL (sometimes referred to as "shortcut" or "pidgin" sign language) are often used in schools for the deaf or other social settings where attempts are made to expedite interlanguage communication (e.g. using English and ASL). Extensive research relating to sign languages and their use has been undertaken in recent years by linguists, anthropologists, sociologists, and psychologists. (See FINGER SPELLING.)

References: Deena K. Bernstein and Ellen Morris Tiegerman, *Language and Communication Disorders in Children* (Second Edition), Columbus, OH: Merrill Publishing Company, 1989; Richard R. Kretschmer, Jr. and Laura W. Kretschmer, *Language Development and Intervention with the Hearing Impaired*, Baltimore, MD: University Park Press, 1978; Alice H. Streng, et al., *Language, Learning, and Deafness: Theory, Application, and Classroom Management*, New York: Grune and Stratton, 1978.

SILENT READING, nonoral reading. Today, school reading programs include the teaching of both silent and oral reading skills. This has not always been the case, however. Until the turn of the century, oral reading skill was being taught almost exclusively. Then, just before World War I, as a result of eye-movement research findings that demonstrated that the average person could read more quickly by doing so silently, the emphasis shifted to silent reading instruction. This change was accompanied by growing interest in reading comprehension, a skill that can best be studied through use of silent reading exercises.

Reading authorities George Spache and Evelyn Spache pointed out that the goals of silent and oral reading instruction are dissimilar. *Silent reading* seeks to improve/increase skills such as reading rate, comprehension, inferring meanings from context, and use of different word analysis approaches. *Oral reading*, on the other hand, is concerned with perfecting such skills as pronunciation, delivery, reaching the listener, and voice control.

References: Dolores Durkin, *Teaching Them to Read* (Fifth Edition), Boston: Allyn and Bacon, 1989; Mary A. Hall, et al.,*Reading and the Elementary School Child* (Second Edition), New York: D. Van Nostrand Company, 1979; Albert J. Harris and Edward R. Sipay, *How to Increase Reading Ability: A Guide to Developmental and Remedial Methods* (Eighth Edition), New York: David McKay Company, Inc. 1989; George D. Spache and Evelyn B. Spache, *Reading in the Elementary School* (Third Edition), Boston: Allyn and Bacon, Inc., 1973.

SILK SCREEN, an art procedure used in stencil printing. A silk open weave cloth is stretched over a frame. Areas not to be printed are blocked out through a variety of techniques. Inks, process oils, tempera colors, dyes, and so on are then forced through the remaining (nonblocked) areas of the cloth by a squeegee to make the print.

Silk screening is used commercially as well as in regular classrooms and with art classes. It can be used on cloth (e.g., T-shirts), dresses, wallpaper, glass, ceramics, paper, and many other materials. Serigraphy is the term applied to silk screen printing done by artists.

References: Clifford T. Chieffo, *Silk-Screen as a Fine Art: A Handbook of Contemporary Silk-Screen Printing*, New York: Van Nostrand Reinhold Company, 1979; James Eisenberg and Francis J. Kafka, *Silk Screen Printing*, Bloomington, IL: McKnight and McKnight Publishing Company, 1957; Mathilda V. Schwalbach and James A. Schwalbach, *Silk-Screen Printing for Artists and Craftsmen*, New York: Dover Publishing Company, Inc., 1980.

SIMULATION, a training method that requires trainees to cope with near-realistic problems or situations. The Link Trainer, used to train World War II pilots, was one of the first sophisticated simulation devices to be developed. Space officials later used simulation as a way of preexperiencing flights and flight problems.

Various forms of simulation are employed in education including the case method of instruction, role playing, and gaming. A more recent simulation development, introduced to education in 1959, is the "in-basket" technique. It requires participants to assume a particular leadership role (e.g. elementary school principal) and to respond to stimulus items that are presented as problems representative of those appearing in a school administrator's in-basket. "In-basket" programs may be used as training devices or to collect data about participants. (See ROLE PLAYING.)

References: Dale L. Bolton, *The Use of Simulation in Educational Administration*, Columbus, OH: Charles E. Merrill Publishing Company, 1971; Jack Culbertson and William Coffield (Editors), *Simulation in Administrative Training*, Columbus, OH: University Council for Educational Administration, 1960.

SINGLE-CONCEPT FILM, short, relatively inexpensive, and simple to use film designed for use by individual learners. Self-threading film cartridges (or loops), commercially prepared or teacher made, are developed for use with lightweight 8 mm projectors. Silent or sound film may be used. The film can be viewed over and over again by the student, a significant feature for students requiring repetition of demonstrations. Single-concept films are not used to teach total units of a curriculum; rather, they present a single point representing but one part of such units. Such films have been in use since the turn of the century.

References: Edgar Dale, *Audiovisual Methods in Teaching* (Third Edition), New York: The Dryden Press, 1969; Walter A. Wittich and Charles F. Schuller, *Instructional Technology: Its Nature and Use* (Sixth Edition), New York: Harper and Row, Publishers, 1979.

SINGLE-PARENT FAMILIES, families in which children are reared by one parent. Census data indicate that, in 1978, there were 6,300,000 single-parent families in the United States. Arthur Norton pointed out that this figure, considerably higher than the 3,000,000 figure reported for 1960 and the almost 4,000,000 recorded in 1970, is in part attributable to the country's high divorce rate. Approximately 90 percent of single-parent families involve a divorced, separated, or single woman and her offspring. About 60 percent of them are working women. In 1978, Norton indicated, single-parent families accounted for 17 percent of all families with children and included a national total of 11,700,000 children under 18 years of age.

A study of children from 1,237 single-parent families, conducted by the National Committee for Citizens in Education, revealed that such children sometimes pose special problems for both the school and the parent, some of which have precipitated the creation of special programs designed to meet the needs of single parents and their children. Problems reported by those surveyed included: (1) some difficulty with scheduling of parent-teacher conferences (because the single parent was employed); (2) the "two-parent" image portrayed in typical school books; (3) communications between school and noncustody parent; and (4) attitudes of some school personnel toward single-parent families.

References: B. Frank Brown, "A Study of the School Needs of Children from One-Parent Families," *Phi Delta Kappan,* April 1980; Phyllis L. C. Falk, "One Out of Five and Largely Ignored," *The National Elementary Principal,* October 1979; National Committee for Citizens in Education, *Single Parent Survey,* Columbia, MD: The Committee, 1980; Arthur J. Norton, "A Portrait of the One-Parent Family," *The National Elementary Principal,* October 1979.

SINGLE SALARY SCHEDULE, a pay scale for automatic determination of a teacher's salary that provides equivalent pay for equivalent training and experiences. No distinction is made for merit or type of position. Thus, a primary grade teacher, a teacher of elementary school music, and a high school physics teacher are each entitled to equal pay presuming their training and experience are equivalent.

Today, the large majority of American school districts utilize the single salary schedule. Before 1920, no system used it.

Indexed (or ratio) salary schedules are gaining popularity throughout the United States. Using the single salary schedule for teachers as a base, various factors are added to yield salary differentials for administrators and even noncertified personnel.

The typical single salary schedule lists years of experience along its vertical axis, preparation level (e.g. B.A., M.A., M.A. plus 30, doctorate) along the horizontal axis. The cell where particular experience and training columns intersect indicates the annual salary to be paid. Although salary ranges vary from one district to another, the ratio of maximum to minimum salaries paid using a given schedule tends to be about 2:1. (See INDEX SALARY SCHEDULE and SALARY SCHEDULE.)

References: William B. Castetter, *The Personnel Function in Educational Administration* (Third Edition), New York: Macmillan Publishing Company, Inc., 1981; Jefferson N. Eastmond, *The Teacher and School Administration,* Boston: Houghton Mifflin Company, 1959; Gertrude N. Stieber, et al., *Methods of Scheduling Salaries for Teachers,* Arlington, VA: Educational Research Service, Inc., 1978.

SINISTRAL, pertaining to the left side of the body or to left-side parts of the body (e.g. left hand, left eye). Persons who are left-handed or left-eyed are sometimes referred to as sinistrals.

Sinistrality refers to left-handedness, dextrality to right-handedness. The derivations of these terms are interesting, dating back to the period of the Romans who associated skill with the right hand and harm with the left. (See HANDEDNESS and LATERALITY.)

References: Horace B. English and Ava C. English, *A Comprehensive Dictionary of Psychological and Psychoanalytical Terms: A Guide to Usage,* New York: David McKay Company, Inc., 1958; Robert M. Goldenson, *The Ency-*

clopedia of Human Behavior: Psychology, Psychiatry, and Mental Health (Volume I), Garden City, NY: Doubleday and Company, Inc., 1970.

SITE SELECTION—See SCHOOL SITE

SITUATIONAL LEADERSHIP THEORY—See LEADER BEHAVIOR

SKEWED DISTRIBUTION, a nonsymmetrical distribution of cases or scores such that a larger number of cases is on one side of the distribution than on the other. Unlike a "normal" distribution where the distribution is symmetrical, with the mean, mode, and median located in the middle, a skewed distribution will not have the three measures of central tendency at the same point.

A positively skewed distribution will have more cases at the lower end of the distribution.

A negatively skewed curve will have more cases at the higher end of the distribution. (See NORMAL DISTRIBUTION CURVE.)

References: Anne Anastasi, *Psychological Testing* (Sixth Edition), New York: Macmillan Publishing Company, 1988; Gilbert Sax, *Principles of Educational and Psychological Measurement and Evaluation* (Third Edition), Belmont, CA: Wadsworth Publishing Company, 1989.

SKILL DEVELOPMENT, activities and programs that enhance quality of performance through training, practice, and experience. Skill development is a product of learning. Included in such learning is stress on efficiency, effectiveness, and capacity.

There are many types of skills, the principle ones being perceptual, motor, and intellectual. None is learned without the utilization of perceptual organs (e.g. ears, eyes), motor coordination, and/or various cognitive processes such as thinking, reasoning, and utilization of previously learned information.

Skill development includes discrimination, perceptual coding, memory, acquisition, motivation, recognition of individual differences, conditions of learning, and the learning process (including learning theory) itself.

In schools, the basics of education are generally considered to be reading, writing, and mathematics. Because they are the basics, skill activities associated with each receive priority attention in the program. This stress notwithstanding, all areas of the curriculum, in varying degrees, require some form of skill development.

References: W. K. Estes (Editor), *Handbook of Learning and Cognitive Processes* (Volume 6), Hillsdale, NJ: Lawrence Erlbaum Associates, Publishers, 1978; Arnold P.

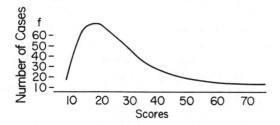

Positively Skewed Curve

Negatively Skewed Curve

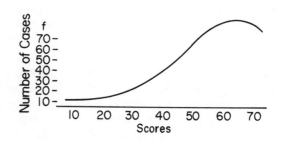

Goldstein, et al., *Skill Training for Community Living*, New York: Pergamon Press, Inc., 1976; Joseph B. Oxendine, *Psychology of Motor Learning*, New York: Appleton-Century-Crofts, Inc., 1968; Alan T. Welford and Lyle E. Bourne (Editors), *Skilled Performance: Perceptual and Motor Skills*, Glenview, IL: Scott, Foresman and Company, 1976.

SKIMMING, the fastest method of speed reading. The reader employing this reading method is only interested in gaining a general idea of the author's message. Comprehension is deliberately sacrificed in favor of speed. One reading authority (Edward Fry) pointed out that a trained reader will achieve 70–80 percent comprehension while reading 500 words a minute. By skimming, that same reader will read 800–1,000 words, but comprehension is reduced to 50–60 percent. (See SCANNING.)
References: Dolores Durkin, *Teaching Them to Read* (Fifth Edition), Boston: Allyn and Bacon, 1989; Edward Fry, *Reading Instruction for Classroom and Clinic*, New York: McGraw-Hill Book Company, 1972; John Langan, *Reading and Study Skills* (Fourth Edition), New York: McGraw-Hill Book Company, 1989; Richard T. Vacca and Jo Anne L. Vacca, *Content Area Reading* (Third Edition), Glenview, IL: Scott, Foresman and Company, 1989.

SKINNER BOX, an enclosed rectangular chamber or box used for experiments of operant conditioning by B. F. Skinner and his associates. For example, a hungry pigeon is placed in the box where the pigeon eventually pecks at a small disk-shaped key placed at one end of the box. A food magazine, which operates automatically, is located directly below the key. When the pigeon pecks at the key, food from the magazine drops. The rate of reinforcement (the dropping of food) can be controlled by the experimenter. Many experimentations on operant behavior were completed using such a box.

At another level, Skinner considered an organism as being an "empty box" and believed that behavior is governed by the direct relationships between stimuli and observable responses. He ignored the internal connections between stimuli and response. Thus, in his view, learning (the changing of behavior) can be shaped through arranging reinforcements (schedules of) contingent upon a response. Operant behavior and operant conditioning formed the base for programmed instruction. (See OPERANT BEHAVIOR; PROGRAMMED INSTRUCTION; and SCHEDULES OF REINFORCEMENT.)
References: James G. Holland and B. F. Skinner, *The Analysis of Behavior*, New York: McGraw-Hill Book Company, 1961; Jean Piaget, *Science of Education and the Psychology of the Child*, New York: The Viking Press, 1971.

SLANDER, a tort that involves false statements made orally about a person and that defame or malign that person. Teachers and other school officials may be liable for proven slanders made about students, other teachers, parents, and so on. However, supportable statements made in line of duty are not actionable as slanders where there was a duty on the part of the teacher to report the matter to the person to whom it was reported. School board members, too, enjoy such immunity or "qualified privilege" while making statements that are a legitimate part of school board meetings and not made with the intention of defaming. (See LIBEL and TORT LIABILITY.)
References: Richard D. Gatti and Daniel J. Gatti, *Encyclopedic Dictionary of School Law*, West Nyack, NY: Parker Publishing Company, Inc., 1975; E. Edmund Reutter, Jr. and Robert R. Hamilton, *The Law of Public Education* (Second Edition), Mineola, NY: The Foundation Press, Inc., 1976; Rennard Strickland, et al., *Avoiding Teacher Malpractice: A Practical Handbook for the Teaching Profession*, New York: Hawthorn Books, Inc., 1976.

SLOYD SYSTEM, an approach to manual arts education developed in Naas, Sweden, in 1868. Conceived by schoolman Otto Salomon and refined with the assistance of Finnish educator Cygnaeus, the system was predicated on the belief that sloyd (Swedish for *manual skill*) teaching should not be limited to preparing students for careers in the trades; rather, it should contribute to one's understanding of the trades as a part of general education.

Goals for educational sloyd were set forth by Otto Salomon in 1896. They were: "(1) to instill a taste for, and a love of, labor in general; (2) to instill respect for rough, honest, bodily labor; (3) to develop independence and self-reliance; (4) to train habits of order, exactness, cleanliness, and neatness; (5) to train the eye and sense of form; to cultivate dexterity of hand and develop touch; (6) to cultivate habits of attention, industry, perseverance, and patience; (7) to promote the development of the physical powers; (8) to directly give dexterity in the use of tools; and (9) to execute exact work" (Lindbeck, p. 25).

The sloyd system also recommended specific methodologies of instruction and formed the basis of a program for training "folk school" teachers. Gustaf Larson introduced the system to the United States (Boston) in 1896.

References: John R. Lindbeck, *Practical Guide to Industrial Arts Education,* New York: The Center for Applied Research in Education, Inc., 1972; Otto Salomon, *The Theory of Educational Sloyd,* Morristown, NJ: Silver Burdett Company, 1896; Mary-Margaret Scobey, *Teaching Children About Technology,* Bloomington, IL: McKnight and McKnight Publishing Company, 1968.

SMITH-HUGHES ACT (Public Law 64-347), federal legislation enacted in 1917 to support vocational education below the college level. The act sought to strengthen the teaching of agriculture, home economics, and industrial subjects by subsidizing salaries of teachers and supervisors in these fields. This was done on a matching (dollar-for-dollar) basis. Provisions were also made for the training of vocational teachers and the creation of a federal Board of Vocational Education. Subsequent amendments to this legislation broadened its scope. (See GEORGE-BARDEN ACT; GEORGE-DEAN ACT; GEORGE-REED ACT; and VOCATIONAL EDUCATION ACT OF 1963.)

References: Calfrey C. Calhoun and Alton V. Finch, *Vocational and Career Education: Concepts and Operations,* Belmont, CA: Wadsworth Publishing Company, Inc., 1976; Public Law 64-347, *The Statutes at Large of the United States of America* (Volume 39, Part I), Washington, DC: U.S. Government Printing Office, 1917; John F. Thompson, *Foundations of Vocational Education: Social and Philosophical Concepts,* Englewood Cliffs, NJ: Prentice-Hall, Inc., 1973.

SMITH-LEVER ACT, federal legislation, passed in 1914, that established cooperative extension programs. The act sought to encourage diffusion (dissemination) of "useful and practical information relating to agriculture and home economics" (p. 372) among the people of the United States. It provided that such dissemination should be done by land grant colleges; furthermore, that such "cooperative extension work shall consist of the giving of instruction and practical demonstrations in agriculture and home economics to persons not attending or resident in said colleges in the several communities, and imparting to such persons information on said subjects through field demonstrations, publications, and otherwise" (p. 373). A total of $480,000 a year was originally appropriated to support these programs.

Reference: Chapter 79, *The Statutes at Large of the United States of America* (Volume 38, Part I), Washington, DC: U.S. Government Printing Office, 1915.

SNELLEN CHART, the most commonly used eye chart for measuring visual acuity. It was named after its developer, a Dutch ophthalmologist. The standard letter chart is often used with literate children. For those unable to read, the "E" symbol chart is substituted. Also, for very young children, a chart with recognizable animals has been developed. Letter or symbol size becomes smaller as one reads downward from the chart's top line. Test results are expressed as a fraction: 20/20, 20/40, 20/200, and so on. In these examples, the numerator represents the testing distance and the denominator the distance at which the normal eye can read a letter or symbol. Thus, a 20/50 score means that the eye being tested reads at 20 feet what the normal eye can read at 50 feet.

References: Clarence H. Graham, et al., *Vision and Visual Perception,* New York: John Wiley and Sons, 1966; Randall K. Harley and G. Allen Lawrence, *Visual Impairment in the Schools,* Springfield, IL: Charles C. Thomas, Publisher, 1977.

SOCIAL ADJUSTMENT—See ADJUSTMENT, SOCIAL

SOCIAL ALIENATION, a sociological term used to describe the estrangement of one or more individuals from the social system. An individual or a group can become separated (alienated) from the social order voluntarily or as the result of renunciation by the social system.

There are many definitions of the term that have been developed from sundry theories of alienation. Some of these early theories were developed by Hegel, Marx, Engels, and Durkheim. Others were originated by Merton, Fromm, Seeman, Sartre, and Weber. In some cases, the alienation theories were more economic or psychological than sociological. The variety of factors that might cause the actual alienation make it difficult to define this term more narrowly.

Individual alienation, as indicated above, can result from withdrawals or as a result of renunciation. Social alienation of a group may occur for these same basic reasons.

References: Frank P. Besag, *Alienation and Education,* Buffalo, NY: Hertillon Press, 1966; Arthur Britton, *The Privatised World,* London, England: Routledge and Kegan Paul, 1978; Carel B. Germain (Editor), *Social Work Practice: People and Environments,* New York: Columbia University Press, 1979; Arnold T. Levine, *Alienation in the Metropolis,* San Francisco: R & E Research Associates, 1977.

SOCIAL DISTANCE—See DISTANCE, SOCIAL

SOCIAL ENGINEERING, a term that became popular during the 1960s when social programs (e.g. Great Society Programs) were conceived, developed, and implemented to effect parts of the social structure and social stratification of the United States.

It is a systematic, planned, and goal-oriented approach with significant social changes that control the intended product. For example, in several Great Society antipoverty programs, not only were the poor to be changed to become economically solvent, but they were also supposed to be changed in terms of their value systems, attitudes, and their place in the social structure.

In many cases, the receivers of social engineering have few participation opportunities available. The results of social engineering are usually more subtle than drastic. Social engineering is not new; many countries have been participating, and continue to participate in varying degrees of social engineering. (See SOCIAL STRATIFICATION.)
References: Tom Honderich (Editor), *Social Ends and Political Means,* London, England: Routledge and Kegan Paul, 1976; Robert R. Mayer, *Social Planning and Social Change,* Englewood Cliffs, NJ: Prentice-Hall, Inc., 1972.

SOCIAL GERONTOLOGY—See GERONTOLOGY

SOCIALLY DISADVANTAGED—See CULTURALLY DEPRIVED

SOCIAL MATURITY—See MATURITY, SOCIAL

SOCIAL MOBILITY, the transition (moving) of an individual from one social position to another. The principal categories reported in the literature dealing with this subject are *horizontal mobility* and *vertical mobility.* Illustrating horizontal mobility are changes of religion, political party affiliation, citizenship, or job status. In none of these examples has the basic social position been changed. Vertical mobility, however, does involve change of social position, from one social level to another. The two kinds of vertical mobility are *ascending* (upward) mobility, frequently associated with educational attainment, and *descending* (downward) mobility. Occupational promotion and demotion serve to illustrate the ascending-descending distinction.

Sociologists also distinguish between *intergenerational* and *intragenerational* social mobility. In the former type, an individual's position (station) is compared with that of his/her parent or grandparent, usually at the same age. In the latter case, the individual is compared against himself/herself at different career points.
References: A. P. M. Coxon and C. L. Jones (Editors), *Social Mobility,* Hammondsworth, Middlesex, England: Penguin Education, 1975; Judah Matras, *Social Inequality, Stratification and Mobility,* Englewood Cliffs, NJ: Prentice-Hall, Inc., 1975; Pitrim A. Sorokin, *Social and Cultural Mobility,* Glencoe, IL: The Free Press, 1959.

SOCIAL PROMOTION, the passing on to the next highest level or grade of a student based on age or social maturity rather than academic accomplishment. Often, social promotion results in 100 percent promotion. Social promotion was used extensively in the United States during the 1930s and 1940s. With the advent of nongraded schools, individualized instruction, and new organizational structures, promotion per se is not as significant an issue in education as it was in that earlier period. The recent concern for quality of education and support of "back to the basics" has made this a relatively unpopular concept among some parents and educators. (See INDIVIDUALLY GUIDED EDUCATION; INDIVIDUALLY PRESCRIBED INSTRUCTION; and NONGRADED SCHOOL.)
References: J. Stanley Ahmann and Marvin D. Glock, *Evaluating Pupil Growth: Principles of Tests and Measurement* (Fifth Edition), Boston: Allyn and Bacon, Inc., 1975; Raymond L. Clemmens, *Obscure Causes of School Failure: A Pediatric Viewpoint,* Pomfret, CT: Orton Society, 1964; Carleton M. Saunders, *Promotion or Failure for the Elementary School Pupil?* New York: Teachers College, Columbia University, 1941.

SOCIAL PSYCHOLOGY, a branch of psychology involving the interdisciplinary study of human behavior. It bridges sociology and psychology. Gordon Allport defined social psychology as "the science which studies the behavior of the individual in so far as his behavior stimulates other individuals, or is itself a reaction to their behavior; and which describes the consciousness of the individual in so far as it is a consciousness of social objects and social reactions" (p. 12). Succinctly, it is the study of human behavior as that behavior is influenced by other persons, groups, and institutions. Illustrative of the topics studied by social psychologists are conformity, attitude development, influence of media on individuals, leadership, group behavior, minorities, and social change.
References: Floyd Henry Allport, *Social Psychology,* Bos-

ton: Houghton Mifflin Company, 1924 (Reprinted in 1967 by Johnson Reprint Corporation); Leigh Marlowe, *Social Psychology: An Interdisciplinary Approach to Human Behavior*, Boston: Holbrook Press, Inc., 1971; Stephen Worchel and Joel Cooper, *Understanding Social Psychology*, Homewood, IL: The Dorsey Press, 1976.

SOCIAL STATUS—See STATUS

SOCIAL STRATIFICATION, the ranking of various social types. A social type is the larger group to which an individual may belong or to which he/she is assigned by others. Within most societies, and most particularly complex or industrial societies, there are many social differentiations (groupings) made among people, either by themselves or by others.

Individuals belonging to the same group make up a social stratum, or social level. Income levels, education levels, inherited social ranks, and/or types of occupations are some of the variables used to differentiate groups of people. Social class differences are also a form of strata.

Although assignment to most stratifications may not be as lasting as a caste (into which one is born and from which he/she can never leave), social stratification can cause great inequities, some having lasting effects. They may last generations, with impact felt at the time an individual is born and lasting through school and into adulthood.

Individuals may, in most societies, move up through the social stratification structure. The attainment of an education has traditionally been one vehicle facilitating upward mobility and consequent social stratification modifications. (See SOCIAL STRUCTURE AND EDUCATION and STATUS.)

References: John E. Bodner, *Immigration and Industrialization's Ethnicity in an American Mill Town*, Pittsburgh, PA: University of Pittsburgh, 1977; Nelson Polsby, *Community Power and Political Theory* (Second Edition), New Haven, CT: Yale University Press, 1980.

SOCIAL STRUCTURE AND EDUCATION, two variables studied by students of social foundations of education and found to be related in numerous respects. Several investigations of social class in America, conducted in the 1930s, 1940s, and 1950s, demonstrated that, although education is generally prized by all Americans, social class differences among students influence the nature and extent of education they receive. Stated differently, different classes do not use education in the same way. Middle class families, for example,

being more future oriented than lower class families, are more likely to make better use of education as a vehicle for upward mobility and to demonstrate a relatively higher level of achievement motivation.

Studies of teachers indicate that most instructional staffs come from middle class backgrounds. Public school boards are heavily populated by business and professional men. Those who serve as university trustees or regents, it has been reported, tend to be higher status people, with personal status closely related to the status of the institution with which they are identified.

Several factors, operating together, have served to make educational opportunity available to the masses of America's young people, social class differences notwithstanding. They include compulsory school attendance laws enacted at the state level, significant federal legislation (e.g. G.I. Bill), court decisions, and the recent rise in the number of public colleges and universities.

Among students enrolled in institutions of higher education, some significant demographic changes have been noted in recent years: (1) more females are pursuing degrees; (2) students tend to be older; and (3) the ratio of racial and ethnic minorities has been increasing.

References: Cole S. Brembeck, *Social Foundations of Education: Environmental Influences in Teaching and Learning* (Second Edition), New York: John Wiley and Sons, 1971; Nancy B. Dearman and Valena W. Plisko, *The Condition of Education (1980 Edition)*, Washington, DC: National Center for Education Statistics, U.S. Department of Education, 1980; Mary A. Golladay, *The Condition of Education (1976 Edition)*, Washington, DC: National Center for Education Statistics, U.S. Department of Health, Education, and Welfare, 1976; Robert J. Havighurst, "Social Class and Education" in James C. Stone and Frederick W. Schneider (Editors), *Readings in the Foundations of Education* (Second Edition), New York: Thomas Y. Crowell, 1971.

SOCIAL STUDIES, an interdisciplinary teaching field that includes elements of history, geography, civics, economics, anthropology, political science, sociology, psychology, and other social-behavioral sciences. "Social studies" as a term first appeared in 1905 and has grown in popularity ever since. The goals of the social studies are essentially two-fold: (1) to provide the learner with knowledge and understanding of society, and (2) to develop attitudes and behaviors that will help him/her to function effectively in it. The subject is frequently taught using units of instruction and may be correlated with the language arts or other curriculum components. The social studies have been criticized on occasion as being too nebulous in content and for their failure to teach adequate social literacy. Critics would prefer that history, geography, etc. be taught as discrete subjects.

References: Arthur W. Foshay (Editor), *The Rand McNally Handbook of Education*, Chicago: Rand McNally and Company, 1963; Howard D. Mehlinger and O. L. Davis (Editors), *The Social Studies* (NSSE 80th Yearbook, Part II), Chicago: University of Chicago Press, 1981; David T. Naylor and Richard A. Diem, *Elementary and Middle School Social Studies*, New York: Random House, 1987; Virginia Richardson-Koehler, et al., *Educators' Handbook: A Research Perspective*, New York: Longman, Inc., 1987.

SOCIAL SYSTEMS THEORY—See ORGANIZATIONAL BEHAVIOR

SOCIAL UTILITY, a theory, principle, or approach used in curriculum development: What is to be taught (activities) in the schools should flow from an objective examination of society. Job analysis was an approach used to determine how people were working and living, and what information, knowledges, and skills were needed to be successful in life. The information that was gathered would then become the objectives of the curriculum.

The Social Utility Theory grew out of the reports of the Committee on Economy of Time that was established in 1911 by the Department of Superintendence of the National Education Association (NEA). The committee was established as a result of public demand in curriculum reform in the public schools. Critics of the day felt that school curriculum was inefficient and ineffective. The committee published four reports in the yearbooks of the National Society for the Study of Education (14th, 16th, 17th, and 18th yearbooks). John Franklin Bobbitt and W. W. Charters were two major proponents of the social utility theory in curriculum development. (See BOBBITT, JOHN FRANKLIN and CHARTERS, WERRETT WALLACE.)

References: Eva L. Baker, "The Technology of Instructional Development" in Robert M. W. Travers (Editor), *Second Handbook of Research in Teaching*, Chicago: Rand McNally and Co., 1973; Daniel Tanner and Laurel N. Tanner, *Curriculum Development Theory into Practice* (Second Edition), New York: Macmillan Publishing Co., 1980.

SOCIODRAMA, a teaching technique in which students act out (dramatize) problems that one or more of them face. The dramatizations are unrehearsed. Unlike role playing, which stresses role behavior, sociodrama has a problem emphasis. Participants and observers alike are expected to learn from sociodrama and thereby develop a better appreciation of the problem(s) under study. (See CREATIVE DRAMATICS and PLAY THERAPY.)

References: Mildred R. Donoghue, *The Child and the English Language Arts* (Third Edition), Dubuque, IA: Wm. C. Brown Company, Publishers, 1979; John M. Kean and Carl Personke, *The Language Arts: Teaching and Learning in the Elementary School*, New York: St. Martin's Press, 1976; Herbert J. Klausmeier and Katharine Dresden, *Teaching in the Elementary School* (Second Edition), New York: Harper and Row, Publishers, 1962.

SOCIOGRAM, a graphic representation showing interpersonal relationships among members of a group. Data are collected from group members and then organized to show individual members' choices, or preferences, for other group members. In a classroom, such data can be collected by having the teacher pose stimulus questions designed to identify preferences for others. For example, students may be asked to assume that they will each be having a party; furthermore, that only two other children from that class may be invited. Students are instructed to name their respective invitees and to list them on a first and second choice basis. Results are then summarized and reported graphically. The resulting chart, or sociogram, identifies group "isolates," "cliques," "stars" (most popular students), and so on.

References: Victor H. Noll and Dale P. Scannell, *Introduction to Educational Measurement* (Third Edition), New York: Houghton Mifflin Company, 1972; Mary L. Northway, *A Primer of Sociometry* (Second Edition), Toronto, Canada: University of Toronto Press, 1967; Merle M. Ohlsen, *Guidance Services in the Modern School* (Second Edition), New York: Harcourt Brace Jovanovich, Inc., 1974.

SOCIOLINGUISTICS, a broad field of study that focuses on the interactions of linguistic and social structure. It developed in the 1960s from the field of anthropology and the introduction of Noam Chomsky's transformational grammar.

Sociolinguistics is concerned with dialects and with rhetoric. Principal emphasis is placed upon the coding of social information through linguistic patterns and approaches and its understanding in a social framework.

Sociolinguistics is often approached at either the microlevel or macrolevel. *Microsociolinguists* study the differences among individuals per se. *Macrosociolinguists* are concerned with differences among individuals as a function of group membership (i.e. sex, race, ethnicity, occupation). Sociolinguists examine variations in language (including indicators, markers, stereotypes), functional models of language (components, rules, dynamics), code switching (bilingualism), and language types (standard, nonstandard, pidginization, national languages, multilanguage societies).

References: Roger T. Bell, *Sociolinguistics: Goals, Approaches, and Problems*, London, England: B. T. Batsford Ltd., 1976; William Labov, *Sociolinguistic Patterns*, Philadelphia: University of Pennsylvania Press, 1973; Pose Lamb and Richard Arnold (Editors), *Teaching Reading: Foundations and Strategies*, New York: Richard C. Owen Publishers, Inc., 1988.

SOCIOLOGY, a behavioral science devoted to the study of human interaction. Such study usually involves disciplined observation on the part of the sociologist. Unlike psychology, which tends to focus on the behavior of individuals, sociology is concerned with group behavior and processes. Subjects such as prejudice, social stratification, group behavior, and culture are included within its purview. Through study of sociology, the learner should be able to: (1) solve personal problems more readily; (2) appreciate the problems of others; and (3) learn how he/she can help to resolve social problems.

References: David Dressler, *Sociology: The Study of Human Interaction*, New York: Alfred A. Knopf, 1969; Edward Shils, *The Calling of Sociology*, Chicago: University of Chicago Press, 1980; Jackson Toby, *Contemporary Society: An Introduction to Sociology* (Second Edition), New York: John Wiley and Sons, 1971.

SOCIOMETRICS, the data, measures, and procedures used in the research and analysis of social groups. Both sociologists and social psychologists use sociometric procedures in their research. A considerable amount of mathematics and statistics can be involved in sociometrics. There are various general approaches used. Observation is one; collecting data from opinionnaires, questionnaires, and sociometric scales or indexes is another.

Examples of sociometric scales/indexes are: Edward's Social-Economic Grouping of Occupations; Chapin's Social Status (Living Room) Scale; Interaction Analysis Procedures; Seashore's Group Cohesiveness Index; Bogardus' Social Distance Scale; Morse Indexes of Employee Satisfaction; Community Attitude Scale; Citizen Political Action Scale; Semantic Differential, Social Insight Scale;

and the Authoritarian Personality (F) Scale. (See SEMANTIC DIFFERENTIAL TECHNIQUE.)

References: Walter R. Borg and Meredith D. Gall, *Educational Research: An Introduction* (Fifth Edition), New York: Longman, Inc., 1989; Fred N. Kerlinger, *Foundations of Behavioral Research* (Third Edition), New York: Holt, Rinehart and Winston, Inc., 1986; Delbert C. Miller, *Handbook of Research Design and Social Measurement* (Third Edition), New York: David McKay Company, Inc., 1977; United Nations Education, Scientific and Cultural Organization, *Main Trends of Research in the Social and Human Sciences*, Paris, France: UNESCO, 1979.

SOCRATES (470 b.c.–399 b.c.), a great ancient Athenian philosopher and teacher who was born in the parish of Alopece (near Athens) and lived during the Age of Pericles. Little is known of Socrates except that which has been recorded by Xenophon, Plato, and Aristophanes. The first two supported Socrates; Aristophanes did not.

Socrates's teaching was done orally. He developed the Socratic method of questioning, one that leads individuals to logical conclusions through the inductive approach. (The goal of his dialectic approach was to reach a true and universal definition; thus, it requires questioning of what is assumed to be true.)

Suspicious of his skepticism and questioning (some of Socrates's disciples had given allegiance to Sparta, Athens's foe), the Athenian government charged Socrates with corrupting the youth of the city. Although he defended himself, he was tried, convicted, and sentenced to death. In 399 b.c., in late May or June, Socrates was put to death by drinking a cup of hemlock. Plato later wrote extensively of Socrates, his trial, and his death. (See DIALECTIC METHOD and SOCRATIC METHOD.)

References: Ronna Burger, *Plato's Phaedrus: A Defense of a Philosophic Art of Writing*, University, AL: University of Alabama Press, 1979; Robert N. Cross, *Socrates, The Man and His Mission*, Freeport, NY: Books for Libraries Press, 1970; Hugh Tredennick (Translator), *Plato: The Last Days of Socrates*, Harmondsworth, NY: Penguin Books, 1969.

SOCRATIC METHOD, a technique of questioning used by the Greek philosopher Socrates. Socrates used the questioning method with his students to help them arrive at definitions and truth.

In the Socratic method, the teacher utilizes questions and discussion to control the information to which students are exposed. In addition, student responses are shaped and directed by the questions. Such questions usually lead students to deeper meanings.

The Socratic method is an approach that is not too dissimilar from the basic approach used in programmed instruction. It is also the base for the "deductive discovery" mode sometimes used by classroom teachers.

References: Francis P. Hunkins, *Involving Students in Questioning*, Boston: Allyn and Bacon, Inc., 1976; Francis P. Hunkins, *Questioning Strategies and Techniques*, Boston: Allyn and Bacon, Inc., 1972.

SOFTWARE, COMPUTER, all the nonhardware (primarily computer and operating programs) used to operate a data processing system. Included are manuals, diagrams, and operating instructions associated with a computer or computer program. Without software, data processing systems could not operate, because they enable the system to translate data from symbols to machine language, to follow directions, to sort data, to manipulate data, and to perform other computer functions. Computer programming is essentially the heart of software.

The field of programming and software engineering, complex and expensive, has grown rapidly in recent years. In 1979, the annual cost of software in the United States alone was estimated to be $20,000,000,000, with relatively similar expansion taking place in American schools and universities. Since then, software has become an ever more significant issue with computers. The purpose and functions of the software, and the compatibility of software and hardware, are extremely important in deciding on the type of computers to use (or purchase) in schools. Some manufacturers design their computers to be compatible with specific computers of a competitor, thus enabling the buyer to use programs (software) interchangeably under certain conditions.

Software now provides a variety of options, such as: word processing, graphics, computer-assisted/computer-managed instruction, sound, statistical packages, spreadsheets, data base "managers," drill, content and heuristic tutorials, problem solving, and higher-order thinking development. (See COMPUTER PROGRAM; FORTRAN; and HARDWARE, COMPUTER.)

References: P. J. Brown (Editor), *Software Portability*, Cambridge, England: Cambridge University Press, 1977; Wayne Cowell (Editor), *Portability of Numerical Software Workshop*, Berlin, West Germany: Springer-Verlag, 1977; Jack A. Culbertson and Luvern L. Cunningham (Editors), *Microcomputers and Education, Eighty-fifth Yearbook of the National Society for the Study of Education (Part 1)*, Chicago: The University of Chicago Press, 1986; Michael Machtey and Paul Young, *An Introduction to the General Theory of Algorithms*, New York: Elsevier North-Holland, Inc., 1978: Peter Wegner, et al. (Editors), *Research Directions in Software Technology*, Cambridge, MA: The MIT Press, 1979.

SOFTWARE EVALUATION OFFICE—See EDUCATIONAL PRODUCTS INFORMATION EXCHANGE INSTITUTE

SOKOLS, Czechoslovak gymnastic society organized when Czechoslovakia was still a part of the Austro-Hungarian Empire. The society was organized as the result of the personal efforts of Miroslav Tyre (1832–84) and Czech patriot Henry Fugner. By 1882, the organization had enough local clubs and a sufficient number of members to sponsor its initial Slet (festival), a meet that included gymnastic exercises with and without apparatus. At one time, up to 400,000 persons were participating in the annual Sokol Slets.

From its inception, the Sokol organization had political as well as athletic interests, a fact that originally annoyed the Austro-Hungarians and later led to its temporary elimination during Czechoslovakia's occupation by Nazi Germany. In recent years, influenced by the Soviet Union's Spartakiada festival, the Czechs have replaced the Slets with a Spartakiada of their own.

Numerous Sokol Societies have been organized in the United States, the first established in St. Louis (1865). They continue to stress gymnastics for persons of all ages.

References: Bruce L. Bennett, et al., *Comparative Physical Education and Sport*, Philadelphia: Lea and Febiger, 1975; C. W. Hackensmith, *History of Physical Education*, New York: Harper and Row, Publishers, 1966; Vera Laska, *The Czechs in America (1633–1977): A Chronology and Fact Book*, Dobbs Ferry, NY: Oceana Publications, Inc., 1978.

SOLFEGE—See DALCROZE METHOD

SOMATOPSYCHOLOGY, the study of bodily deviation (atypical physique) on behavior. (Bodily deviation normally includes both *disability* and *handicap*.) Interest in this field of study has been heightened owing to increased activity in the field of special education and the fact that the world's population of physically disabled persons is larger than ever before.

Lee Meyerson pointed out that somatopsychologists have used different theoretical approaches in studying the relationship between physique and behavior, noting further that each approach has yielded but a limited amount of confirming evidence. Five specific theoretical approaches are identified: (1) there is no relationship between physique and behavior; (2) physique determines behavior; (3) behavior determines physique; (4) behavior and physique may be simultaneously determined by a third variable; and (5) behavior is a function of a person interacting with his environment. (See CONSTITUTIONAL TYPES.)

References: Lee Meyerson, "Somatopsychology of Physical Disability" in William M. Cruikshank (Editor), *Psychology of Exceptional Children and Youth* (Third Edition), Englewood Cliffs, NJ: Prentice-Hall, Inc., 1971; Robert M. Smith and John T. Neisworth, *The Exceptional Child: A Functional Approach,* New York: McGraw-Hill Book Company, 1975.

SORORITY, a group of women friends organized into a college or university social fraternity that has its own individual goals. Many sororities cooperate with their respective institutions of higher education to promote high levels of service and/or scholarship. The earliest sororities to be formed in the United States were Alpha Delta Pi (1851), Phi Beta Phi (1867), and Kappa Apha Theta (1870).

Some sororities have national affiliations; others consist of one group located on a single campus. *Baird's Manual of American College Fraternities* identifies the sororities associated with the National Panhellenic Conference, a women's interfraternity organization. They are: Alpha Chi Omega, Alpha Delta Pi, Alpha Epsilon Phi, Alpha Gamma Delta, Alpha Omicron Pi, Alpha Phi, Alpha Sigma Alpha, Alpha Sigma Tau, Alpha Xi Delta, Chi Omega, Delta Delta Delta, Delta Gamma, Delta Phi Epsilon, Delta Zeta, Gamma Phi Beta, Kappa Alpha Theta, Kappa Delta, Kappa Kappa Gamma, Phi Mu, Phi Sigma Sigma, Phi Beta Phi, Sigma Delta Tau, Sigma Kappa, Sigma Sigma Sigma, Theta Phi Alpha, and Zeta Tau Alpha. In 1977, these NPC sororities claimed a combined membership of approximately 1,500,000.

Selection of members begins with "rushing" of possible prospective members. This is followed by the offering of "bids" to successful rushees, pledging (period in which rushees are examined carefully), and initiation. Often, several sorority members live together in a chapter (or sorority) house while enrolled in college. (See FRATERNITY.)

References: Mark Beach, "Fraternities and Sororities, Social" in Lee C. Deighton (Editor), *The Encyclopedia of Education* (Volume 4), New York: The Macmillan Company and The Free Press, 1971; John Robson (Editor), *Baird's Manual of American College Fraternities* (Nineteenth Edi-

tion), Menashu, WI: Baird's Manual Foundation, Inc., 1977.

SPALDING PLAN—See UNIFIED PHONICS METHOD

SPAN OF CONTROL, a management concept that attempts to limit the number of subordinate positions supervised by a given superior. Lyndall Urwick, exponent of limited spans of control, argued that a given superior should supervise no more than five or six subordinate positions, each having a different job analysis. Critics of the span of control concept argue that it leads to creation of organizations that are pyramidal, frequently too hierarchical, administratively unwieldy, and bureaucratic.

References: Daniel E. Griffiths, et al., *Organizing Schools for Effective Education,* Danville, IL: The Interstate Printers and Publishers, Inc., 1962; Ralph B. Kimbrough and Michael Y. Nunnery, *Educational Administration: An Introduction,* New York: Macmillan Publishing Company, Inc., 1976; Robert G. Owens, *Organizational Behavior in Schools,* Englewood Cliffs, NJ: Prentice-Hall, Inc., 1970; Lyndall Urwick, *The Elements of Administration,* New York: Harper and Brothers, 1943.

SPARTAN EDUCATION, the form of education available in the classical Greek city-state of Sparta. Education was controlled by the state; in most other states, this was an individual family responsibility.

Sparta's educational program reflected the military objectives of the state. Its aims were strength, courage, endurance, patriotism, and obedience. Newborn children were examined; if deemed to be weak, they were either permitted to die or given away. Boys were raised by their mothers to age 7; then between ages 7 and 18, they were assigned to a barracks and taught by older men with military backgrounds. Much emphasis was placed on physical drill. For the next two years, they served as military "cadets," refining their knowledge of the martial arts and receiving instruction of a political nature. This was followed by ten years of full-time military service. Full citizenship status came at the close of this last phase. Girls remained at home, learning the domestic arts from their mothers. Provision was made for them to engage in organized physical development activities.

References: William Boyd and Edmund J. King, *The History of Western Education* (Eleventh Edition), London, England: Adam and Charles Black, 1975; H. I. Marrou (Translated by George Lamb), *A History of Education in Antiquity,* New York: Mentor Books (New American Library of World Literature), 1964.

SPASTIC, a term used to describe poor muscle coordination resulting from muscle spasms. In spasticity, the limb muscles contract strongly or release quickly to resistance (such that they "spring open"). The most common type of cerebral palsy has these characteristics as well. The stretch reflex, the ankle clonus, and the hyperactive knee jerk are all characteristics of spasticity.

Premature babies have a greater tendency for spasticity than do normal term babies. Spasticity may be caused by damage to, or defects in, the brain (the cortical motor area). Some spastic children may also manifest perceptual and visual motor problems. Orthopedic surgery can help some spastic children by relieving the stretch reflex and muscle contracture.

References: Eugene E. Bleck and Donald A. Nagel (Editors), *Physically Handicapped Children: A Medical Atlas for Teachers,* New York: Grune and Stratton, 1975; Harold D. Love and Joe E. Walthall, *A Handbook of Medical, Educational, and Psychological Information for Teachers of Physically Handicapped Children,* Springfield, IL: Charles C. Thomas, Publisher, 1977; Joseph M. LaRocca and Jerry S. Turem, *The Application of Technological Developments to Physically Disabled People,* Washington, DC: Urban Institute, 1978.

SPATIAL IMAGERY, a subset of visual imagery in which form, space, and relationships of the visual imagery are important. It is the reconstitution in the mind of what is seen, what has been seen, or what may never have been seen. The image (in the mind) is not seeing the object itself, nor is it an exact replica per se; rather, it is what the "mind sees."

Students with well-developed spatial imagery ability tend to do well in art, map making, geometry, drafting, shop, mechanical drawing, architecture, and engineering. There are several nonverbal spatial ability tests available. The pencil and paper varieties generally show a cut-out and flattened, three-four dimensional illustration (object) and ask the respondent to select, from one of several choices, the one figure that could be made from the cut-out and flattened illustration.

References: Maurice S. Bartlett, *The Statistical Analysis of Spatial Pattern,* New York: John Wiley and Sons, 1975; Arthur Getis and Barry Boots, *Models of Spatial Processes,* New York: Cambridge University Press, 1978; Robert Sommer, *The Mind's Eye,* New York: Delacorte Press, 1978.

SPATIAL INTELLIGENCE, one of the seven biologically based intelligences found in the Multiple Intelligence Theory (MI Theory). Spatial intelligence derives its biological base, according to the MI Theory, from the fact that the right hemisphere of the brain is the hemisphere that is most responsible for spatial processing. Spatial intelligence provides all humans with the capability to visualize objects from a variety of angles and recognize shapes by an indirect method. It also provides tactile mobility. Visual artists would tend to have a high degree of spatial intelligence. Humans use spatial intelligence to solve a variety of problems, including playing chess, arranging tables and chairs, and making color balances in clothing. Spatial intelligence is used by individuals together with other intelligences in the MI Theory to solve problems. (See BODILY-KINESTHETIC INTELLIGENCE; INTELLIGENCE; INTERPERSONAL INTELLIGENCE; INTRAPERSONAL INTELLIGENCE; LINGUISTIC INTELLIGENCE; LOGICAL-MATHEMATICAL INTELLIGENCE; MULTIPLE INTELLIGENCE THEORY; MUSICAL INTELLIGENCE; and SPATIAL IMAGERY.

References: Hans Furth, *Piaget and Knowledge,* Englewood Cliffs, NJ: Prentice-Hall, Inc., 1969; Howard Gardner, *Frames of Mind,* New York: Basic Books, 1976; M. P. Grady and E. A. Lueke, *Education and the Brain,* Bloomington, IN: Phi Delta Kappa, 1978; Joseph Walter and Howard Gardner, "The Development and Education of Intelligence" in F. R. Link (Editor), *Essays on the Intellect,* Alexandria, VA: Association for Supervision and Curriculum Development, 1986.

SPAULDING, FRANK E. (November 30, 1866– June 6, 1960), prominent school administrator, author, consultant, and university professor. After completing his formal education in the United States and Europe, Spaulding served as superintendent of schools in numerous school districts including Newton (Massachusetts), Minneapolis, and Cleveland. He founded the Department of Education at Yale University and served as its first Chairman (1920–29). A prolific writer, Spaulding authored or coauthored several books in diverse fields such as reading, spelling, and educational administration.

Reference: Lawrence S. Master, "Spaulding, Frank Ellsworth" in John F. Ohles (Editor), *Biographical Dictionary of American Educators* (Volume 3), Westport, CT: Greenwood Press, 1978.

SPEARMAN-BROWN FORMULA, a statistical calculation used to estimate the reliability of a test of N items once the internal consistency (e.g. split-half method) reliability of the original test is known.

The Spearman-Brown formula is also used by test developers to determine the exact extent to which test reliability would be increased if the number of items were increased. (Test reliability increases as its length increases, assuming that like items are added.) (See RELIABILITY and SPLIT-HALF CORRELATION.)

References: Anne Anastasi, *Psychological Testing* (Sixth Edition), New York: Macmillan Publishing Company, 1988; Joy P. Guilford and Benjamin Fruchter, *Fundamental Statistics in Psychology and Education* (Sixth Edition), New York: McGraw-Hill Book Company, 1978.

SPEARMAN RANK DIFFERENCE CORRELATION COEFFICIENT, or Spearman's RHO, a nonparametric correlational technique used to assess the association between two rankings of data for the same individuals. For example, a teacher may rank a group of students from highest to lowest on intelligence and then rank the same group of students from highest to lowest on reading scores. Use of the Spearman rank difference correlation would enable the teacher to assess the relationship of reading to intelligence. In ranking, the values of the scores themselves are not important. More important is their rank order. When rank ordering, the highest score is assigned a rank of 1 and the lowest, the rank equal to the number of students in the class.

The formula is:

$$r_s = 1 - \frac{6\Sigma d^2}{n(n^2 - 1)}$$

Student	Rank on Intelligence Test	Rank on Reading Test	d	d^2
a	2	4	−2	4
b	6	6	0	0
c	1	1	0	0
d	5	3	2	4
e	3	2	1	1
f	4	5	−1	1

$n = 6$ $\hspace{4em}$ $\Sigma d^2 = 10$

$$r_s = 1 - \frac{6\,(10)}{6(36-1)} = 1 - \frac{60}{210} = 1 - 0.285 = 0.714$$

In the above example, there is a relatively strong relationship between rankings on the intelligence test and rankings on the reading test.

The Spearman rank difference correlation can range from −1.00 to +1.00 with 0.00 indicating no association or relationship. (See NONPARAMETRIC STATISTICS.)

References: W. J. Conover, *Practical Nonparametric Statistics,* New York: John Wiley and Sons, 1971; William M. Hays, *Statistics* (Fourth Edition), New York: Holt, Rinehart and Winston, Inc., 1988; Harold O. Kiess, *Statistical Concepts for the Behavioral Sciences,* Boston: Allyn and Bacon, 1989.

SPECIAL EDUCATION, a field of education that provides specially designed instruction to meet the needs of exceptional students. Exceptional students, as defined in Public Law 94-142, are those who, in varying degrees, are mentally retarded, hard of hearing, deaf, speech impaired, visually handicapped, seriously emotionally disturbed, orthopedically impaired, deaf-blind, or multihandicapped or those with specific learning disabilities. Talented and gifted students are frequently considered to be part of the exceptional child population.

Special educators and regular classroom teachers work with exceptional students in a variety of settings and ways. Students assigned to a regular classroom for part or all of the day usually work closely with the regular classroom teacher. In many instances, resource teachers (special educators) are available to provide the regular teacher with consultative assistance. In other cases, the special educator works with the exceptional student for a part of the day, usually in another room. Special (segregated) schools are institutions that typically accommodate students with a particular form of exceptionality. Residential (boarding) schools, often state supported, are also available for students requiring highly specialized services.

The term *special education* may refer to any or all of four services: (1) instruction by specially trained educators; (2) special curricular content; (3) special methodology; and (4) special instructional materials. (See HANDICAPPED INDIVIDUALS; MAINSTREAMING; PUBLIC LAW 94-142; and RESIDENTIAL SCHOOL. Also see articles addressed to separate exceptionalities.)

References: William H. Berdine and A. Edward Blackhurst (Editors), *An Introduction to Special Education* (Second Edition), Boston: Little, Brown and Company, 1985; Lloyd M. Dunn (Editor), *Exceptional Children in the Schools: Special Education in Transition* (Second Edition), New York: Holt, Rinehart and Winston, Inc., 1973.

SPECIAL EDUCATION PLACEMENT CASCADE, a continuum of optional placements for special education students. Often depicted graphically, the eight-level "cascade" was developed by Maynard Reynolds. It lists placement options,

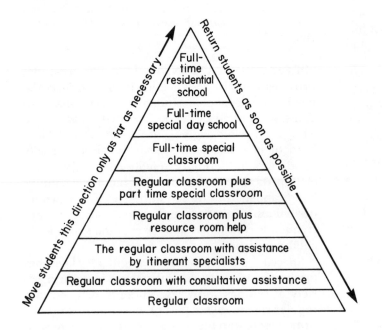

Special Education Placement Cascade

any one of which can apply to a given child at a given point in time. The graphic appearing above was adapted from the one developed by Reynolds. (See ITINERANT TEACHER; LEAST RESTRICTIVE ENVIRONMENT; and MAINSTREAMING.)

References: Evelyn N. Deno, *Instructional Alternatives for Exceptional Children*, Reston, VA: Council for Exceptional Children, 1972; Maynard C. Reynolds, "A Framework for Considering Some Issues in Special Education," *Exceptional Children*, March 1962; Bernard G. Suran and Joseph V. Rizzo, *Special Children: An Integrative Approach*, Glenview, IL: Scott, Foresman and Company, 1979.

SPECIFIC LEARNING DISABILITIES, defined in Public Law 94–142 (Education for All Handicapped Children Act of 1975) as conditions applying to "those children who have a disorder in one or more of the psychological processes involved in understanding or in using language, spoken or written, which disorder may manifest itself in imperfect ability to listen, think, speak, read, write, spell, or do mathematical calculations. These disorders include conditions such as perceptual handicaps, brain injury, minimal brain dysfunction, dyslexia, and developmental aphasia. Such terms do not include children who have learning problems which are primarily the result of visual, hearing, or motor handicaps, of mental retardation, of emotional disturbance, or environmental, cultural, or economic disadvantage" (Section 620, p. 794). Unlike *learning disabilities,* a generic term used to describe a heterogeneous group of disabilities, *specific learning disabilities* refers to a single disability in one area of functioning.

References: Samuel A. Kirk, "Samuel A. Kirk" in James M. Kauffman and Daniel P. Hallahan (Editors), *Teaching Children with Learning Disabilities: Personal Perspectives*, Columbus, OH: Charles E. Merrill Publishing Company, 1976; Thomas C. Lovitt, *Introduction to Learning Disabilities*, Boston: Allyn and Bacon, 1989; Public Law 94–142, *United States Statutes at Large, 1975* (Volume 89), Washington, DC: U.S. Government Printing Office, 1977; B. Marian Swanson and Diane J. Willis, "Children and Youth with Specific Learning Disabilities" in B. Marian Swanson and Diane J. Willis, *Understanding Exceptional Children and Youth*, Chicago: Rand McNally College Publishing Company, 1979.

SPEECH COMMUNICATION ASSOCIATION (SCA), a national organization of communication professionals. Its purposes are "to promote study, criticism, research, teaching and application of the artistic, humanistic, and scientific principles of communication, particularly speech communication" (*Get in Touch,* unpaginated). Founded in

1914, SCA currently enrolls 7,000 members who work in the United States and 20 other countries. The large majority are teachers, administrators, and students working in institutions of higher education.

SCA's nine divisions, each organized around specific areas of communication interest, are: (1) Forensics; (2) Instructional Development; (3) Interpersonal and Small Group Interaction; (4) Interpretation; (5) Mass Communication; (6) Public Address; (7) Rhetorical and Communication Theory; (8) Speech and Language Sciences; and (9) Theatre. Major publications are *Spectra*, a bimonthly newsletter, and three quarterlies: *Quarterly Journal of Speech, Communication Monographs*, and *Communication Education*. Additionally, SCA publishes/produces yearbooks, directories, indexes, special texts, and audio cassettes.

SCA's main office is in Falls Church, Virginia.
References: Speech Communication Association, *Get in Touch, Keep in Touch*, Falls Church, VA: The Association, Undated Brochure; Speech Communication Association, *Publications: Speech Communication Association*, Falls Church, VA: The Association, Undated Brochure; Speech Communication Association, *Spectra*, February 1980; Speech Communication Association, *Speech Communication Association*, Falls Church, VA: The Association, Mimeographed and Undated Fact Sheet.

SPEECH DISCRIMINATION SCORE, the level at which an individual can correctly or incorrectly "hear" words, syllables, or disconnected nonsyllables. The score is found by presenting a list of words or syllables at the acoustical level set by the individual's Speech Reception Threshold (SRT). The speech discrimination score usually falls between 25 and 40 db (decibels) above the SRT. There is disagreement among researchers over the validity of the discrimination score as opposed to the SRT as a measure of hearing ability.

The Speech Reception Threshold is the level of sound pressure at which 50 percent of the test words are repeated correctly. Spondaic words are usually employed to determine SRT, and for the speech-discrimination score, American English speech sounds found in a phonetically balanced (single-syllable) word list are used. (See AUDITORY DISCRIMINATION.)
References: Thomas G. Giolas and Kenneth Randolph, *Basic Audiometry*, Lincoln, NE: Cliffs Notes, Inc., 1977; Aram Glovig (Editor), *Audiometry: Principles and Practices*, Baltimore, MD: The Williams and Wilkins Company, 1965; William Noble, *Assessment of Impaired Hearing*, New York: Academic Press, 1978.

SPEECH PATHOLOGY, a broad field of study concerned with normal communication as well as with disorders in oral communication. Working within this field are speech scientists, speech clinicians, and audiologists as well as those classified as speech pathologists. Speech pathologists are not only concerned with the identification of speech disorders, but with remediation as well.

Delayed speech, aphasia, articulatory disorders, stuttering, voice disorders, and language disorders are all concerns of the speech pathologist. Speech pathologists in the schools work with individual students in a remedial mode and with teachers in developing appropriate educational programs for students with oral communication disorders. (See APHASIA; CLEFT PALATE; DELAYED SPEECH; and STUTTERING.)
References: Stephen B. Blache, *The Acquisition of Distinctive Feature*, Baltimore, MD: University Park Press, 1978; William H. Perkins, *Speech Pathology* (Second Edition), St. Louis, MO: C. V. Mosby Company, 1977; Sadanand Singh and Joan Lynch, *Diagnostic Procedures in Hearing, Language, and Speech*, Baltimore, MD: University Park Press, 1978; Lee Edward Travis, *Handbook of Speech Pathology and Audiology*, New York: Appleton-Century-Crofts, Inc., 1971.

SPEECH PROGRAMS, programs developed to correct articulation and functional articulation disorders (e.g. stuttering, voice problems) through speech and language therapy. These programs are normally supervised by trained speech clinicians.

Programmed materials and equipment have been used in such programs. Their use is called *programmed articulation therapy. Behavior modification* procedures have also been used. *Paired-stimuli techniques* constitute yet another approach. *Psychological treatment*, under certain conditions, can be used as part of an articulation program. Finally, many clinicians employ a *multisensory approach* to therapy that is individually designed. Whatever approach is used, certain common elements are to be found in these programs: auditory discrimination; production of new sounds; learning to use the new sounds; and the carryover and habitual use of the new sounds. (See ARTICULATION, SPEECH.)
References: Lee E. Travis (Editor), *Handbook of Speech Pathology and Audiology*, Englewood Cliffs, NJ: Prentice-Hall, Inc., 1971; W. Dean Wolfe and Daniel J. Goulding, *Articulation and Learning*, Springfield, IL: Charles C. Thomas, Publisher, 1973.

SPEECH READING—See LIPREADING

SPEECH RECEPTION THRESHOLD—See SPEECH DISCRIMINATION SCORE

SPEED READING, rapid reading that Peter B. Smith defined functionally as gaining meaning from the printed page while inspecting more than 1,200 words a minute. (The average reading speed of an adult is approximately 250–300 words a minute.) Research indicates that rapid readers use peripheral vision not only to see words situated to the left or right of a fixation point, but to see those located in lines above and below the fixation point as well. It also indicates that not all people can become speed readers, particularly those with oral-visual barriers (i.e. the individuals who read word-by-word, saying each word to themselves).

Reading authorities are not in agreement with respect to the achievability of speed reading. Several are of the opinion that there are both physiological and psychological limits to speed reading (which some believe to be approximately 800–1,000 words per minute). These disagreements notwithstanding, all agree that selected reading exercises can aid the student to increase his/her reading rate to some degree.

References: John Langan, *Reading and Study Skills* (Fourth Edition), New York: McGraw-Hill Book Company, 1989; G. Harry McLaughlin, "Reading at 'Impossible' Speeds" in Eldon E. Ekwall (Editor), *Psychological Factors in the Teaching of Reading*, Columbus, OH: Charles E. Merrill Publishing Company, 1973; Keith Rayner and Alexander Pollatsek, *The Psychology of Reading*, Englewood Cliffs, NJ: Prentice-Hall, Inc., 1989; Peter B. Smith, "Eye Movements and Rapid Reading Reconsidered," *Fourteenth Yearbook of the National Reading Conference*, 1964.

SPEED TESTS, tests constructed to measure speed of performance. All items in a speed test have a low difficulty level such that all those taking the test can respond correctly to them. Speed tests are designed so that no one can successfully complete them. This is done by including more items in the test than can be completed within the prescribed time limit. Usually, time limits in a speed test are short. Knowledge of whether a test is a speed or a power test is important when interpreting the results. (See POWER TESTS.)

Reference: Anne Anastasi, *Psychological Testing* (Sixth Edition), New York: Macmillan Publishing Company, Inc., 1988.

SPELLING, or orthography, a component of the language arts that teaches students to write words using the proper letters. Standardized spelling began in the United States with the appearance (1828) of Noah Webster's *An American Dictionary of the English Language*. The principal goal of school spelling programs is to teach children to spell the words they are most likely to encounter and use as adults.

Multisensory-multimotor factors condition spelling ability. Accordingly, spelling instruction for normal children will involve having them: (1) hear the word (auditory imagery); (2) say the word (speech imagery); (3) see the word (visual imagery); and (4) feel the word (kinesthetic imagery) using such techniques as imaginary skywriting or tracing letters from sandpaper.

Over the years, several distinct methods of teaching spelling have been developed. They include: (1) the *alphabetical approach*, which stresses mastery of individual letters by being able to name them; (2) the *syllabarium*, or syllable method; (3) the *word method*, which teaches the spelling of a whole word from the beginning rather than by breaking it down into parts; (4) the *phonics method*, whose emphasis is on letter sounds; (5) the *linguistic method*, an approach based on phoneme-grapheme correspondences; and (6) the *"test-study-test"* method. (See CORRECTED-TEST METHOD and SPELLING DEMONS.)

References: Ruel A. Albred, *Spelling Trends, Content, and Methods*, Washington, DC, National Education Association, 1984; Paul R. Hanna, et al., *Spelling: Structure and Strategies*, Boston: Houghton Mifflin Company, 1971; Marie Marcus, *Diagnostic Teaching of the Language Arts*, New York: John Wiley and Sons, 1977.

SPELLING DEMONS, spelling words that are difficult to learn. Contributing to the difficulty are factors such as silent letters, phonetic elements that are irregular, and exceptions to the general rules of spelling. Researchers estimate that 3 percent of the words in the English language are spelling demons. Various lists of spelling demons have been developed by numerous spelling researchers (e.g. James Fitzgerald, Arthur Gates, W. Franklin Jones). Teachers may also prepare such lists by observing and recording the frequency with which individual children (or groups) misspell words on spelling tests or in free writing exercises.

References: Gertrude A. Boyd and E. Gene Talbert, *Spelling in the Elementary School*, Columbus, OH: Charles E. Merrill Publishing Company, 1971; Paul R. Hanna, et al., *Spelling: Structure and Strategies*, Boston: Houghton Mifflin Company, 1971; John F. Savage, *Effective Communication: Language Arts Instruction in the Elementary School*, Chicago: Science Research Associates, Inc., 1977.

SPIRAL CURRICULUM, a term used by Jerome S. Bruner to describe a longitudinal school program in which curriculum "revisit(s) . . . basic ideas repeatedly, building upon them until the student has grasped the full formal apparatus that goes with them" (p. 13). Bruner contended that any subject can be taught to any student, of whatever age, in some honest form. Subjects that are worth knowing at adulthood, he contended, should be introduced as simply as possible to young learners and, in spiral fashion, re-presented as the student progresses through school with each re-presentation building on concepts previously mastered.
Reference: Jerome S. Bruner, *The Process of Education,* Cambridge, MA: Harvard University Press, 1962.

SPIRIT DUPLICATION, a relatively inexpensive and fast process for producing instructional materials in quantity. The word *Ditto,* a brand name, is often (and incorrectly) used when referring to the process.

Spirit duplication involves the use of four items. They are: (1) the *spirit duplicator,* the machine used to prepare copies; (2) the *spirit master,* teacher-made or commercially prepared "original" of the material to be reproduced; (3) *spirit duplicating fluid,* a clear and strong-smelling liquid used to soak the master and activate its dye; and (4) *duplicator paper,* a special paper capable of absorbing and retaining the dye from the master when pressed against it.

Duplicated sheets usually are printed purple, although multiple colors may be used on the master. The spirit duplication process is normally employed when fewer than 100 copies of an item are needed. More than 200 copies may be prepared, however, if quality materials are available and used correctly.
References: John R. Bullard and Calvin E. Mether, *Audiovisual Fundamentals: Basic Equipment Operation, Simple Materials Production* (Second Edition), Dubuque, IA: Wm. C. Brown Company, Publishers, 1979; Michael Goudket, *An Audiovisual Primer,* New York: Teachers College Press, 1973.

SPLIT-HALF CORRELATION, a statistical procedure used to assess the reliability of a test. The procedure involves comparing the odd-numbered items and the even-numbered items that are correct for each individual taking a test. The comparison is made using correlational procedure. The resulting correlation can be used to determine the test's internal consistency, but it is important to remember that the reliability is only for half of a

test. The Spearman-Brown formula can then be used to determine reliability of the full test. (One cannot assume that doubling the split-half correlation will produce an accurate estimate of the full test.) (See RELIABILITY and SPEARMAN-BROWN FORMULA.)
References: Herbert M. Blalock, Jr., *Social Statistics* (Second Edition), New York: McGraw-Hill Book Company, 1979; Joy P. Guilford and Benjamin Fruchter, *Fundamental Statistics in Psychology and Education* (Sixth Edition), New York: McGraw-Hill Book Company, 1978.

SPRING HILL CONFERENCE, a meeting of 37 university/college presidents at the Spring Hill Conference Center near Minneapolis, Minnesota (September 2–4, 1987). The meeting was initiated by Stanford University President Donald Kennedy. Presentations and group meetings focused on the reform of the nation's schools in response to the Carnegie Forum on Education and the Economy's report, *A Nation Prepared: Teachers for the 21st Century.*

As a result of the conference, a letter was written by the presidents to all university/college presidents in the United States encouraging all institutions of higher education to become actively involved in the reform of the nation's schools. The 37 presidents asked the other president to: (1) speak out for education and the importance of teaching at all levels; (2) initiate direct and meaningful affiliations with schools and school districts; (3) enhance the attractiveness of teaching as a career and improve teacher preparation; and (4) bring more minorities into teaching. The education of teachers by all faculties at a university or college is one of the major suggestions made by the presidents. The American Association for Higher Education was asked to coordinate the efforts of the university/college presidents in reforming education in the nation's schools. (See AMERICAN ASSOCIATION FOR HIGHER EDUCATION and *(A) NATION PREPARED: TEACHERS FOR THE 21ST CENTURY.*)
Reference: "The Letter, 37 Presidents Write . . . ," *AAHE Bulletin,* Volume 40, Number 3, November 1987.

SQ3R, a study skill technique that helps students organize, in advance, to make reading purposeful. SQ3R stands for "survey, question, read, recite, and review." When following this technique, a student: (1) *surveys* materials quickly (introductory sentences, headings, etc.); (2) raises *questions* concerning the headings or the topic; (3) *reads* the material to find the answers to questions raised in step 2; (4) *recites* the answers; and, finally, (5) *reviews* and fills in details on what was read. The SQ3R technique facilitates the memorizing process; it can also be used as an "advance organizer." (See ADVANCE ORGANIZERS.)

References: Diane Lapp, James Flood, and Nancy Farnan, *Content Area Reading and Learning: Instructional Strategies,* Englewood Cliffs, NJ: Prentice Hall, 1989; Harry Singer and Dan Donlan, *Reading and Learning from Text* (Second Edition), Hillsdale, NJ: Lawrence Erlbaum Associates, Publishers, 1989.

STAFF BALANCE, a personnel administration effort that, through recruitment and/or inservice activities, seeks to produce a "balanced" school staff. One goal of staff balancing is to eliminate or reduce imbalance in personal characteristics areas such as race, ethnicity, age, and sex. Passage of the Civil Rights Act and other affirmative action legislation has prompted school districts and institutions of higher education to formulate school balance targets. Parity of working conditions (e.g. teaching load) also falls within the purview of staff balance.

Another broad goal involves examination of instructional competencies and the taking of steps designed to overcome or eliminate major weaknesses/inequities. (See AFFIRMATIVE ACTION and CIVIL RIGHTS ACT OF 1964.)

References: Ben M. Harris, et al., *Personnel Administration in Education: Leadership for Instructional Improvement,* Boston: Allyn and Bacon, Inc., 1979; Lewis D. Solomon and Judith S. Hecter, "The Case for Preferential Hiring," *Change,* June 1977.

STAFF DEVELOPMENT, a program of activities that, in education, is most commonly designed to promote the professional growth of teachers. Staff development does not assume a deficiency in the teacher. Rather, it is predicated on the assumption that all employees have a need to grow on the job.

Interest in staff development has been heightened by decreases in student enrollment that, in turn, have reduced the district-to-district mobility of teachers. Given this consequent increase in staff stability, teachers and administrators alike have been promoting staff development programs that one authority (Louis Rubin) believes can be used profitably to improve any or all of four teaching-related factors: (1) teacher's sense of purpose; (2) teacher's perception of students; (3) teacher's knowledge of subject matter; and (4) teacher's mastery of technique.

Creation of teacher centers, granting of sabbatical leaves, use of outside consultants, peer teaching, teacher team planning, and the pairing of teachers ("buddy" system) are examples that illustrate the range of staff development activities available to the professional educator. (See INSERVICE EDUCATION.)

References: Betty Dillon-Peterson, *Staff Development Organizational Development,* Alexandria, VA: Association for Supervision and Curriculum Development, 1981; Stanley M. Elam, Jerome Cramer, and Ben Brodinsky, *Staff Development: Problems and Solutions,* Arlington, VA: American Association of School Administrators, 1986; Allan A. Glatthorn and Norman K. Spencer, *Middle School/Junior High Principal's Handbook,* Englewood Cliffs, NJ: Prentice-Hall, Inc., 1986; Donald C. Orlich, *Staff Development: Enhancing Human Potential,* Boston: Allyn and Bacon, 1989.

STAFF OFFICERS—See LINE AND STAFF CHART

STANDARD DEVIATION, a measure indicating the variability, dispersion, or spread of a set of scores. One of the major measures of variability in statistics, it is used extensively in statistical computations and analyses. The symbols used for standard deviations are *SD*, *s*, and σ. Standard deviation is defined as the square root of the sum of the squared deviations about the mean divided by either the number of cases (for a population, σ) or the number of cases minus one (for a sample, *S*).

When a set of scores is normally distributed (see illustration), standard deviations can be used to interpret frequency distributions. For example, the "T-scores" used in our illustration have a mean ($\bar{x}$) of 50 and a standard deviation of 10. Since the T scores are normally distributed, 68.26 percent of percent range from 60 to 70, with another 13.59 percent ranging from 30 to 40; and 2.14 percent range from 20 to 30, with another 2.14 percent covering the 70 to 80 range. Thus, 99.72 percent of all of the scores range from 20 to 80 (-3σ to $+3\sigma$). If test scores are normally distributed (perfectly symmetrical about their mean and are bell shaped), a standard deviation can be used to describe their dispersion. If, however, the scores are not normally distributed (i.e. skewed), the standard deviation is of limited value.

References: William M. Hays, *Statistics* (Fourth Edition), New York: Holt, Rinehart and Winston, Inc., 1988; David S. Moore and George P. McCabe, *Introduction to*

Standard Deviation Distribution

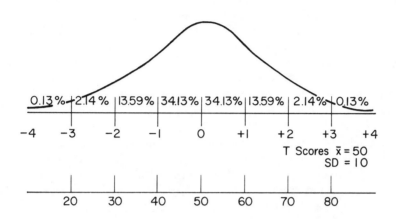

the Practice of Statistics, New York: W. H. Freeman and Company, 1989.

STANDARD ERROR OF ESTIMATES—See STANDARD ERROR OF MEASUREMENT

STANDARD ERROR OF MEASUREMENT, a statistic used to report the accuracy of predicted (or obtained) scores vs. true scores. The smaller the standard error of measurement, the more confidence can be placed in the predicted score of an individual. Standard error of measurement can be used to determine the reliability of a test. Interpretation of real or chance differences of test scores can be made using the standard error of measurement. (See RELIABILITY and STANDARD DEVIATION.)

References: Walter R. Borg and Meredith D. Gall, *Educational Research: An Introduction* (Fifth Edition), New York: Longman, Inc., 1989; David S. Moore and George P. McCabe, *Introduction to the Practice of Statistics*, New York: W. H. Freeman and Company, 1989.

STANDARD ERROR OF THE MEAN, the standard deviation of a set of sample means. If one were to sample equal sets of scores randomly from a given population, and then calculate a mean for each set, a distribution of means would result. If each mean were then to be treated as a single raw score, the standard deviation of these "raw scores" would be the standard error of the mean.

If the equal sets each have an N (number) of 8, the standard error of the mean will be larger than if each set were to have an N of 20. This example illustrates an important point, namely, that the larger the number of cases in each set, the smaller will be the dispersion. In fact, as the N gets larger, the more normal the distribution of mean scores becomes. (See NORMAL DISTRIBUTION CURVE and STANDARD DEVIATION.)

References: L. R. Gay, *Educational Research: Competencies for Analysis and Application* (Third Edition), Columbus, OH: Merrill Publishing Company, 1987; Harold O. Kiess, *Statistical Concepts for the Behavorial Sciences*, Boston: Allyn and Bacon, 1989.

STANDARDIZED TEST, an examination that has been normed against a given population. To achieve standardization, a test is administered to a given population. Means, standard deviations, standardized scores, and percentiles are then calculated. From these data, a table of equivalent scores is produced that allows one to interpret test scores by comparing an individual's score against the performance of the norm group. For example, an individual earns a score of 49 on a standardized test, a score that is equivalent to the 73rd percentile for the norm group. This means that the individual's score was higher than scores earned by 73 percent of the norm group. The 49 in itself has little interpretive value, but the 73rd percentile, a relative bit of information, gives meaning to the score.

Standardized tests must usually be administered in a set way, this to increase the likelihood that the resulting scores are comparable to the norm group.

Standardized tests are not without limitations. Some of the questions that have been raised about them are: (1) What is the nature of the group used as the norm, and how was it formed? (2) How reflective is it of the total population? (3) To what extent may ethnic, racial, and sex bias be present as a result of the nature of the norm group? (4) What assurance is there that individual test items are free of built-in bias? (5) How are the test scores being interpreted? and (6) How are the scores being used by teachers, parents, and school administrators?

Many intelligence and achievement tests used in schools are standardized tests. Given this widespread use, standardized test results have significant impact on both program and students. (See NORM-REFERENCED TESTS and NORMS.)

References: Paul L. Houts (Editor), *The Myth of Measurability*, New York: Hart Publishing Company, 1977; Arthur R. Jensen, *Bias in Mental Testing*, New York: The Free Press, 1980; Tom Kubiszyn and Gary Borich, *Educational Testing and Measurement: Classroom Application and Practice* (Second Edition), Glenview, IL: Scott Foresman and Company, 1987; William A. Mehrens and Irvin J. Lehmann, *Using Standardized Tests in Education*, New York: Longman Inc., 1987; W. Bruce Walsh and Nancy E. Betz, *Tests and Measurement*, Englewood Cliffs, NJ: Prentice-Hall, Inc., 1985.

STANDARD METROPOLITAN STATISTICAL AREA (SMSA), a census measure that conforms to the following Census Bureau criteria: "(1) One city with 50,000 or more inhabitants, or (2) A city with at least 25,000 inhabitants, which, together with those contiguous places (incorporated or unincorporated) having population densities of at least 1,000 persons per square mile, has a combined population of 50,000 and constitutes for general economic and social purposes a single community, provided that the county or counties in which the city and contiguous places are located has a total population of at least 75,000" (p. 1). The SMSA has become an increasingly useful measure given the fact that: (1) larger numbers of people reside in and around cities, and (2) these population concentrations, normally, are socially and economically integrated systems. In 1975, the Census Bureau officially recognized 276 such areas in the United States.

References: Bureau of the Census, *Standard Metropolitan Statistical Areas* (Revised), Washington, DC: U.S. Government Printing Office, 1975; Thomas F. Hoult, *Dictionary of Modern Sociology,* Totowa, NJ: Littlefield, Adams and Company, 1969; George A. Theodorson and Achilles G. Theodorson, *A Modern Dictionary of Sociology,* New York: Thomas Y. Crowell, 1969.

STANDARD SCORES, the scores that result when raw scores are transformed into a standard form with a distribution that has an arbitrary set mean and an arbitrarily set standard deviation. Standard scores are based on the normal distribution curve. Consequently, they can be used to compare the relative position of an individual on two or more tests. Standard scores are used extensively in educational research.

Although z-scores (sigma scores) are a standard score, the most widely used standard score (T or Z score) has a mean of 50 and a standard deviation of 10 and is based on a transformation of the z-score. It can be calculated as follows:

$$\text{T-Score} = 10 \ (z) + 50$$

For example, if a z-score $= 2.1$, the T-score $= 10(2.1) + 50 = 21 + 50 = 71$.

One reason for converting z-scores to another standard score is to eliminate negative values that are found in z-scores. The conversion does not affect the original relationships among the raw scores.

Actually, any standard deviation (s) and mean ($\bar{x}$) can be set in the transformation from z to another standard score (e.g., $s = 50$, $\bar{x} = 100$; $s = 100$, $\bar{x} = 500$, etc.).

PSAT, SAT, Army General Classification Test, the National Teachers Examination, and most test publishers use standard scores in reporting individual and group results. (See SCALE; STANDARD DEVIATION; and z-SCORES.)

References: Lou M. Carey, *Measuring and Evaluating School Learning*, Boston: Allyn and Bacon, Inc., 1988; George K. Cunningham, *Educational and Psychological Measurement*, New York: Macmillan Publishing Company, 1986.

STANDING COMMITTEES—See BOARD OF EDUCATION STANDING COMMITTEES

STANFORD-BINET TEST, an individually administered intelligence test. The test's origin was the Binet-Simon Scale of 1905. The Binet-Simon test was revised in 1908 and again in 1911. It was L. M. Terman of Stanford University whose revision of the Binet-Simon tests, in 1916, gave rise to the intelligence quotient and the Stanford-Binet Test.

The Stanford-Binet Test has been revised several times (1937, 1960, 1972). Although the age range for the test is two to adult (tests are grouped into age levels), the Stanford-Binet is not suitable for use with normal and superior adults. Since the 1960 revision, a deviation I.Q. score is reported. This is a standard score with a mean of 100 and a standard deviation of 16. Any I.Q. between 90 and 110 is considered to be equivalent to an I.Q. of 100. Scores above 110 are considered superior, and scores below 90 are considered inferior. Children classified as "educable," "trainable," and "custodial" have I.Q. ranges of 75–50, 50–25, and below 25, respectively.

The test takes 30–40 minutes to administer. The test procedures are most exact; administration and scoring require the services of a highly trained person. (See INTELLIGENCE QUOTIENT and INTELLIGENCE TESTS.)

References: Anne Anastasi, *Psychological Testing* (Fourth Edition), New York: Macmillan Publishing Company, Inc., 1976; Oscar K. Buros (Editor), *The Eighth Mental Measurements Yearbook* (Volume I), Highland Park, NJ: The Gryphon Press, 1978.

STANINE, a standard score developed during World War II by the Army Air Force Psychology Program. A normal distribution is divided into nine intervals, each called a stanine (*stan*-dard *nine*).

The mean of the stanine scale is 5.00 and the standard deviation is ± 1.96. Because of the grouping, discrimination at the extremes of the distribution is not as fine as in other standard scores. Other limiting characteristics of the stanine make it more difficult to interpret than percentile ranks, another approach to establishing equal intervals. (See PERCENTILE; STANDARD DEVIATION; and STANDARD SCORES.)

References: Lou M. Carey, *Measuring and Evaluating*

School Learning, Boston: Allyn and Bacon, Inc., 1988; Gilbert Sax, *Principles of Educational and Psychological Measurement and Evaluation* (Third Edition), Belmont, CA: Wadsworth Publishing Company, 1989.

STATE AID, or state school financing, financial assistance that states provide to local school districts for the support of public education. In recent years, most states have been assuming increasingly larger shares of the tax burden for education with the nature and extent of support varying from one state to the next. Oscar Jarvis and associates identified several major purposes of state support: (1) social benefit; (2) equalization of educational opportunity; (3) equalization of tax burden; (4) stimulation of local expenditures; (5) distribution of cost among different tax sources; and (6) state control (i.e. ensuring that minimal educational standards are maintained).

In his historical review of school finance in the United States, Percy Burrup identified five periods, or stages of development. They are: (1) the *period of local district responsibility,* when no financial assistance was provided by the state; (2) the *period of emerging state responsibility,* with flat grants and other nonequalizing monies paid to the districts; (3) the *emergence of the foundation program concept,* based on the work of George Strayer and Robert Haig; (4) the *period of refinement of the foundation programs;* and, presently, (5) the *period of emerging power equalization,* with increasing concern being expressed for qualitative improvement of education.

The National Center for Education Statistics reported that, "in 1942, local sources contributed over two-thirds of the total funding (for public education). . . . But by 1978 the proportion of local revenues for elementary and secondary education had dropped to less than half of total revenues. The State share had increased to 44 percent" (p. 138).

There are two basic types of state aid. The first,

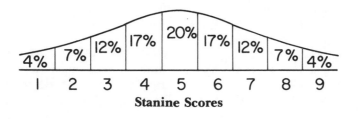

Stanine Scores

flat grant aid, involves distribution of state monies to school districts on the basis of uniform factors such as number of teachers employed or number of pupils in average daily attendance. *Equalization aid,* the second type, attempts to achieve equality of educational opportunity by providing proportionately more aid to poor school districts than to wealthy ones. (See EQUALIZATION, FINANCIAL; FINANCIAL ABILITY; FLAT GRANTS; FOUNDATION PROGRAMS; and STRAYER, GEORGE D.)

References: Percy E. Burrup, *Financing Education in a Climate of Change* (Second Edition), Boston: Allyn and Bacon, Inc., 1977; Nancy B. Dearman and Valena W. Plisko, *The Condition of Education* (1979 Edition), Washington, DC: National Center for Education Statistics, 1979; Oscar T. Jarvis, et al., *Public School Business Administration and Finance: Effective Policies and Practices,* West Nyack, NY: Parker Publishing Company, Inc., 1967; Ralph M. Kimbrough and Michael Y. Nunnery, *Educational Administration: An Introduction,* New York: Macmillan Publishing Company, Inc., 1976.

STATE ANNUAL PROGRAM PLAN—See PUBLIC LAW 94–142

STATE BOARD OF EDUCATION—See BOARD OF EDUCATION, STATE

STATE DEPARTMENT OF EDUCATION, an arm of state government and the agency responsible for monitoring education at the state level. State departments of education are administered by chief state school officers (CSSOs). Some CSSOs are known as *commissioners of education,* others as *state superintendents.* State boards of education oversee state department operations. They establish policies that are implemented by the CSSO and his/her staff.

Principal functions of the state department of education include certification of teachers, school accreditation, recommending educational legislation, distribution of state and federal funds to local school districts, and enforcing education law. In some states, state departments operate special institutions such as state schools for the blind and deaf. (See CHIEF STATE SCHOOL OFFICER.)

References: Burton D. Friedman, *State Government and Education: Management in the State Education Agency,* Chicago: Public Administration Service, 1971; U.S. Department of Health, Education, and Welfare, *State Education Structure and Organization,* Washington, DC: U.S. Government Printing Office, 1964.

STATE EDUCATIONAL AGENCY (SEA), a legal term included in numerous educational laws passed by Congress that, in most instances, is synonymous with *state boards of education.* Public Law 89-10 (ESEA Act of 1965), one such law, defines SEA as meaning "the State board of education or other agency or officer primarily responsible for the State supervision of public elementary and secondary schools, or, if there is no such officer or agency, an officer or agency designated by the Governor or by State law" (p. 47).

Reference: Public Law 89-10, *United States Statutes at Large, 1965* (Volume 79), Washington, DC: U.S. Government Printing Office, 1966.

STATE EDUCATIONAL JOURNAL INDEX, an index of educational articles that have appeared in American state educational journals. Most of the journals indexed (approximately 100) are not included in *Education Index. State Educational Journal Index* is published twice each year.

References: John W. Best, *Research in Education* (Third Edition), Englewood Cliffs, NJ: Prentice-Hall, Inc., 1977; L. Stanley Ratliff (Editor), *State Education Journal Index,* Volume XVII, No. 2, January 1980–June 1980, Westminster, CO: The Editor.

STATE SUPERINTENDENT—See CHIEF STATE SCHOOL OFFICER

STATISTIC, according to colloquial usage, any number describing a group or a classification (e.g. number of boys in a class, mean salary of teachers). (For a more technical definition, see SAMPLING.)

The study of statistics is, however, the analysis of numerical data. This field of study can generally be divided into descriptive or inferential statistics. *Descriptive statistics* describes data, and *inferential statistics* is used to infer or generalize, as well as to describe. (See POPULATION; SAMPLE; and SAMPLING.)

References: Frederick J. Gravetter and Larry B. Wallman, *Statistics for the Behavioral Sciences: A First Course for Students of Psychology and Education,* St. Paul, MN: West Publishing Company, 1985; Shawn L. Weinberg and Kenneth P. Goldberg, *Basic Statistics for Education and the Behavioral Sciences,* Boston: Houghton Mifflin Company, 1979.

STATISTICAL ANALYSIS SYSTEM (SAS), a multipurpose statistical package that provides a variety of analyses for a set of data. SAS was developed in 1972 at the SAS Institute in North Carolina by Anthony J. Barr and colleagues. The SAS package includes a variety of univariate and multivariate statistical procedures (e.g., correlations, chi-square, t-tests, analyses of variance, analyses of covariance, multivariate analysis of variance, factor analysis, etc.). SAS, like other statistical packages such as SPSS, uses a special-purpose language. When it was introduced, SAS was confined to IBM equipment; this is no longer the case.

References: Anthony J. Barr, et al., *A User's Guide to SAS 76,* Raleigh, NC: SAS Institute, Inc., 1976; William J. Kennedy and James E. Gentle, *Statistical Computing,* New York: Marcel Dekker Inc., 1980; John H. Maindonald, *Statistical Computation,* New York: John Wiley and Sons, Inc., 1984; Richard W. Moore, *Introduction to the Use of Computer Packages for Statistical Analysis,* Englewood Cliffs, NJ: Prentice-Hall, Inc., 1978; SAS Institute, *SAS User's Guide, 1979 Edition,* Raleigh, NC: SAS Institute, Inc., 1979.

STATISTICAL PACKAGE FOR THE SOCIAL SCIENCES (SPSS), a comprehensive set of computer programs used in the analysis of social science data. The user of the programs can use natural language in the programs, and is able to transfer data and results between compatible programs with ease.

Dr. Norman H. Nie and others started developing SPSS at Stanford University in 1965. SPSS is a developing system that has undergone many revisions and expansions since its first publication in 1970. It was originally developed for use in large mainframe computers and in a batch process mode (a set of transactions that are processed as a unit). SPSS has developed a conversational mode titled SCSS; this allows the researcher to direct the process by interacting with the computer and SPSS. The SPSS package includes a variety of common statistical procedures, such as: distributions, measures of central tendency, dispersion, correlations, regression, analysis of variance, multivariate analysis of variance, analysis of time series, nonparametric statistics, discriminant analysis, factor analysis, and canonical correlation.

References: C. Hadlai Hull and Norman H. Nie, *SPSS Update 7–9,* New York: McGraw-Hill Book Co., 1980; William R. Klecka, Norman H. Nie, and C. Hadlai Hull, *SPSS Primer,* New York: McGraw-Hill Book Co., 1975; Norman H. Nie, et al., *SCSS, a User's Guide to the SCSS Conversational System,* New York: McGraw-Hill Book Co., 1980; Norman H. Nie, et al. *SPSS* (Second Edition), New York: McGraw-Hill Book Co., 1975.

STATISTICAL SIGNIFICANCE—See TESTS OF SIGNIFICANCE

STATUS, or social status, a specific position in a social organization that can be distinguished from all other positions. One's status determines his/her duties, behaviors, and relationships to persons of other statuses. Sociologists have identified different types of status. Included are: (1) *achieved status,* based on fulfillment of certain requirements that are open to competition (e.g. doctor, professor); (2) *ascribed status,* an inherited position (e.g. sex, age statuses); (3) *nominal status,* a designation that is organizationally ungraded (e.g. brother-in-law); and (4) *ordered status,* positions that are graded, ranked, or hierarchically arranged (e.g. colonel, associate professor).

In bureaucracies, status positions connote a system of superior-subordinate relationships. Prestige, or the esteem ascribed to a particular individual, is related to the position held.

The *role* approach to status was developed by Ralph Linton. He held that status positions are expressed in terms of roles or patterns of behavior that can be associated with each status position (e.g. father, boy scout, librarian).

References: Joseph Berger, et al., *Status Characteristics and Social Interaction: An Expectation-States Approach,* New York: Elsevier Scientific Publishing Company, Inc., 1977; Thomas F. Hoult, *Dictionary of Modern Sociology,* Totowa, NJ: Littlefield, Adams and Company, 1969; Ralph Linton, *The Study of Man,* New York: Appleton-Century-Crofts, Inc., 1936; George A. Theodorson and Achilles G. Theodorson, *A Modern Dictionary of Sociology,* New York: Thomas Y. Crowell, 1969.

STATUS LEADER, the officially designated leader of a group. Status leaders (e.g. principals, supervisors, directors) are formal leaders who carry official titles with which specified duties and responsibilities are associated. The term *status leader* is distinct from *real leader,* the latter term used to identify those individuals whom people (usually in formal groups) follow naturally whether or not they enjoy positions of status. For example, in an elementary school, the principal may be the *status leader* but the school's *real leader* could be a teacher, a secretary, or even a custodian.

Reference: Bernard M. Bass, *Leadership, Psychology, and Organizational Behavior,* New York: Harper and Row, Publishers, 1960.

STEINER, RUDOLF—See WALDORF EDUCATION

STEREOSCOPE, a visual screening instrument. Distances are simulated by optical means, making it possible to reproduce testing conditions identical to those in a 20-foot room. The instrument consists of two lenses that have been placed side by side.

Two nearly identical images (slides) are viewed by the subject being screened, one with each eye. The stereoscope (sometimes referred to as a "tele-binocular," trade name for a well-known stereoscope) is used for testing visual acuity, stereopsis, fusion, and lateral imbalance (phoria); it serves as a basic color testing device as well.

References: Henrik L. Blum, et al., *Vision Screening for Elementary Schools: The Orinda Study,* Berkeley, CA: University of California Press, 1968; Fred W. Jobe, *Screening Vision in Schools,* Newark, DE: International Reading Association, 1976.

STIMULUS-RESPONSE THEORY (S-R Theory), a theory developed from the research of Pavlov, carried out in the early 1900s, that holds that a specific stimulus can elicit a specific response. Pavlov's study of salivary and gastric secretion in dogs when food was presented led to the development of the concepts of conditioned and unconditioned reflexes. *Conditioned reflexes,* according to his theory, are essentially psychological in nature, and *unconditioned reflexes* are more physiological.

Pavlov's conditioning theory evolved from this stimulus-response theory. In turn, the theories of behaviorism, operant control, several learning theories, and schedules of reinforcement grew out of classical conditioning theory. Some of the basic principles of behavior modification procedures can also be traced to S-R theory. Some of the psychologists who extended and applied S-R learning were Clark Hull, E. L. Thorndike, and B. F. Skinner. (See CLASSICAL CONDITIONING; CONDITIONED RESPONSE; PAVLOV, IVAN P.; and REFLEX.)

References: T. Mark Ackerman, *Operant Conditioning Techniques for the Classroom,* Glenview, IL: Scott, Foresman and Company, 1972; F. Robert Brush (Editor), *Aversive Conditioning and Learning,* New York: Academic Press, 1971; W. K. Estes (Editor), *Conditioning of Behavior Theory,* Hillsdale, NJ: Lawrence Erlbaum Associates, Publishers, 1975; Donald L. King, *Conditioning, an Image Approach,* New York: Gardner Press, Inc., 1979.

STIPEND, the amount of money awarded to a student (usually a college student). These awards are made for specific functions or reasons, including assistantships, fellowships, scholarships, and grants-in-aid.

References: William E. Hopke (Editor), *Dictionary of Personnel and Guidance Terms: Including Professional Agencies and Associations,* Chicago: J. G. Ferguson Publishing Company, 1968; Asa S. Knowles (Editor), *The International Encyclopedia of Higher Education* (Volume 1), San Francisco: Jossey-Bass Publishers, 1977.

STORY GRAMMAR, a means of providing rules to define a story's structure to the individual. Knowledge of such structure appears to improve both immediate comprehension and later recall of the story. A simple story grammar can consist of a setting plus a series of events or episodes. Another, more detailed, story grammar could focus on the structures of character, setting, plot, resolution, and theme. Marilyn Sado (1982) offered five general questions to ask in developing an understanding of a story grammar: (1) Where and when did the story occur and who was involved? (setting). (2) What began the chain of events? (initiating event). (3) How did the main character react to this event? (reaction). (4) What did the main character do about it? (action). (5) What occurred as the result of the main character's action? (consequences). It is beneficial to begin the process on an oral level with stories that have easily identified grammars, such as fairy tales.

References: Paul C. Burns, Betty D. Roe, and Elinor P. Ross, *Teaching Reading in Today's Elementary Schools,* Boston: Houghton Mifflin Company, 1984; J. David Cooper, *Improving Reading Comprehension,* Boston: Houghton Mifflin Company, 1986; Marilyn W. Sado, "The Use of Story Grammar in the Design of Questions," *The Reading Teacher,* February 1982.

STORYTELLING, the art or craft of narrating stories. Storytelling is led by one person who performs before a live audience. Narrated stories may be spoken, sung, or even chanted. The storyteller may learn them from printed or mechanically recorded sources as well as from other persons who pass stories along orally. The earliest evidences of storytelling have been traced to ancient Egypt (2000 B.C.).

Principal types of storytelling are: (1) *bardic storytelling,* an age-old form of communication in which the storyteller presents narrations extolling the history of a cultural group, frequently doing so with a musical background; (2) *folk storytelling,* another longstanding type in which stories are told, informally by nonprofessional narrators, at home, at work, or at social gatherings; (3) *religious storytelling,* a vehicle for communicating/promoting religion; and (4) *theatrical storytelling,* a highly developed form of dramatic entertainment performed in theaters.

In schools, storytelling is most frequently led by teachers and librarians. Storytelling by children is encouraged as part of the language arts curriculum. Other storytelling settings include home, hospital, camp, and park.

References: Augusta Baker and Ellin Greene, *Storytelling: Art and Technique* (Second Edition), New York: R. R. Bowker Company, 1987; Nancy E. Briggs and Joseph A. Wagner, *Children's Literature Through Storytelling and Drama* (Second Edition), Dubuque, IA: Wm. C. Brown Company, Publishers, 1979; Jack Maguire, *Creative Storytelling: Choosing, Inventing and Sharing Tales for Children*, New York: McGraw Hill, 1985; Anne Pellowski, *The World of Storytelling*, New York: R. R. Bowker Company, 1977.

STRANG, RUTH M. (April 3, 1895–January 3, 1971), New York-born and trained home economist who emerged as a prominent teacher and author in the field of guidance and counseling. One of the pioneers in this field, she did much to broaden the counseling approach to include teachers as well as those formally trained for guidance positions. In an autobiographical piece, she identified four significant movements in which she was engaged during her career: (1) health education; (2) the guidance movement; (3) improving reading in secondary schools; and (4) the movement away from control-experimental group research approaches "toward a broader, less statistical, more individually oriented type" (p. 390).

Strang received her three academic degrees at Teachers College, Columbia University (Ph.D. in 1926), and, in 1929, joined that faculty as an Assistant Professor of Education. Upon retiring from Teachers College (1960), she accepted employment at the University of Arizona to work in reading.

Her academic and organizational achievements included authorship of several books (student personnel, reading, the gifted; editorship of the *Journal of the National Association of Women Deans and Counselors;* and fellow in the American Association for the Advancement of Science).

References: Diana Scott, "Strang, Ruth May" in John F. Ohles (Editor), *Biographical Dictionary of American Educators* (Volume 3), Westport, CT: Greenwood Press, 1978; Ruth M. Strang, "Ruth M. Strang: An Autobiographical Sketch" in Robert J. Havighurst, *Leaders in American Education* (NSSE 70th Yearbook, Part II), Chicago: University of Chicago Press, 1971.

STRATEMEYER, FLORENCE B. (February 17, 1900–May 10, 1980), noted teacher educator who served on the Teachers College, Columbia University, faculty from 1924 to the year of her retirement, 1965. Her international reputation as a teacher was based on two sets of achievements: (1) her writing, and (2) the large numbers of doctoral students who trained under her and sub-sequently emerged as educational leaders in their own right.

Stratemeyer's major writings included *Working with Student Teachers* (1958) and *Developing a Curriculum for Modern Living* (1947, later revised). Her three degrees (B.A., M.A., and Ph.D.) were earned at Teachers College. Before joining that institution's faculty, she served as teacher and Assistant Principal in the Detroit Public Schools, later as a supervisor of student teachers at Detroit Teachers College.

Reference: "In Memorium: Florence B. Stratemeyer," *AACTE Briefs,* June 1980.

STRATIFIED SAMPLING—See SAMPLING

STRAUSS SYNDROME—See ATTENTION DEFICIT DISORDER

STRAYER, GEORGE D. (November 29, 1876–September 29, 1962), Professor of Education at Teachers College, Columbia University, from 1905 to 1943. Although interested in a spectrum of educational specialties (e.g. mathematics teaching and classroom teaching), he became best known for his work in the field of educational administration. Strayer headed the division of field studies at Teachers College (1921–42) and, for a time, directed that institution's educational administration division (1937–42). Through these positions he became involved in a large number of school surveys. These experiences, in turn, led to his becoming a national authority on school administration generally, cost management specifically.

Strayer published numerous articles and several books in his field. With C. B. Upton as collaborator, he authored an arithmetic textbook series. With another collaborator, Nickolaus Engelhardt, he coauthored three books dealing with administration (e.g. *School Building Problems,* 1927, and another, *The Classroom Teacher,* 1920).

Strayer's reputation led to his election/appointment to several prestigious organizations. He served as President of the National Education Association, as President of the National Society for the Study of Education, as a fellow of the American Association for the Advancement of Science, and as a member of the Educational Policies Commission.

Reference: W. Richard Stephens, "Strayer, George Drayton" in John F. Ohles (Editor), *Biographical Dictionary of American Educators* (Volume 3), Westport, CT: Greenwood Press, 1978.

STREAMING, ability grouping of students. In many countries other than the United States, the term *streaming* is used to denote ability grouping; in the United States, the counterpart term is *tracking*.

Streaming, introduced in Britain during the 1920s, continues to be employed in many British schools, although, in recent years, unstreaming (mixed grouping) has been taking place (especially among infant and primary schools).

There is considerable evidence to show that a relationship frequently exists between curricular streaming and the social strata from which children come.

References: Edward Blishen (Editor), *Encyclopedia of Education*, New York: Philosophical Library, 1970; Fritz Ringer, *Education and Society in Modern Europe*, Bloomington, IN: Indiana University Press, 1979; Nigel Wright, *Progress in Education: A Review of Schooling in England and Wales*, London, England: Croom Helm Ltd., 1977.

STREET ACADEMIES, privately managed, community controlled, and community-based schools that were started in urban inner-city areas in the 1960s. Students who attended such schools were usually from minority groups and were dropouts from the public schools. The principal purpose of these schools was to prepare students to enter college.

Street academies were initially patterned after the southern freedom schools of the 1950s. There was considerable parental control and direction associated with these schools. Street academies have served as models for alternative education plans for urban schooling as well as for programs seeking to bring about greater minority or disadvantaged parent participation in schools.

Although many street academies were funded from private sources (tuition, donations, private grants), others were funded using federal, state, and local public monies. Many have since become part of the public schools. The best-known street academies were: Academies of Transition (Harlem Prep, New York City); Metropolitan Youth Education Center (Denver and Jefferson County, Colorado); New School (Roxbury, Boston); East Harlem Block School (New York City); and the Southeast Free School (Minneapolis, Minnesota). (See ALTERNATIVE EDUCATION.)

References: Gary Coats (Editor), *Alternative Learning Environments*, Stroudsburg, PA: Dowden, Hutchinson and Ross, Inc., 1974; Don Davies (Editor), *Schools Where Parents Make a Difference*, Boston: The Institute for Respon-

sive Education, 1976; Mario Fantini, et al., *Community Control and the Urban School*, New York: Praeger Publishers, 1970; David Rogers, *An Inventory of Educational Improvement Efforts in the New York City Public Schools*, New York: Teachers College Press, 1977; Vernon Smith, et al., *Alternatives in Education: Freedom to Choose*, Bloomington, IN: Phi Delta Kappa, 1976.

STREPHOSYMBOLIA, a perception problem in reading. The reader may have problems distinguishing letters that are physically similar. For example, the individual may not be able to differentiate "b" from "d." Or he/she may perceive words, letters, and numbers in "mirror image" form.

The term *strephosymbolia* was coined by Samuel T. Orton, a University of Iowa psychiatrist, in 1928. Literally, it means "twisted symbols." Orton felt that the reversal of letters, symbols, numbers, and even words was caused by a disturbance in cortical dominance; furthermore, that memory images from the nondominant side of the brain caused the "mirror images."

Strephosymbolia is a primary symptom of dyslexia. (See DYSLEXIA and MIRROR READING.)

References: Arthur L. Benton and David Pearl (Editors), *Dyslexia*, New York: Oxford University Press, 1978; Louis Clarke, *Can't Read, Can't Write, Can't Tak Too Good Either*, New York: Walker and Company, 1973; Herbert E. Rie and Ellen D. Rie, *Handbook of Minimal Brain Dysfunctions*, New York: John Wiley and Sons, 1980.

STRESS, a phenomenon that can be social, psychological, or physiological (or all three) and one precipitated by a threatening, demanding, or physically damaging situation. These situations produce forced changes in the individuals subjected to them. For example, electric shock to the body can cause physical stress, an extremely high sales quota or an uncontrolled classroom can cause psychological stress, and loss of reputation can cause social stress. Stress and reaction to stress includes: (1) stressers, the factors that produce the stress; (2) factors in the environment that may affect the impact of the stressers; (3) the stress itself; and (4) various adaptive behaviors that are the consequence of stress.

Stress can cause or contribute to significant physical, personality, and mental problems. Although most children and adults develop coping behaviors to handle stress, there are times when the force of stress can go beyond the ability of an individual to manage it.

References: Karl G. Albrecht, *Stress and the Manager*, Englewood Cliffs, NJ: Prentice-Hall, Inc., 1979; Aaron Antonovsky, *Health, Stress, and Coping,* San Francisco: Jossey-Bass Publishers, 1979; Daniel A. Girdano and George S. Everly, *Controlling Stress and Tension,* Englewood Cliffs, NJ: Prentice-Hall, Inc., 1979.

STRONG VOCATIONAL INTEREST BLANK (SVIB), a pencil-and-paper interest inventory that consists of 325 items grouped into seven parts: (1) occupations; (2) school subjects; (3) activities; (4) amusements; (5) types of people (day-to-day contact); (6) preference (between paired items); and (7) characteristics (self-description). SVIB is based on the premise that those in similar occupations have similar job preferences and other similar interests. By comparing interests of individuals with those recorded for specific vocational groups, conclusions having occupational implications can be made.

The 1974 revision of the SVIB was retitled the Strong-Campbell Interest Inventory (SCII). This revision involved merger of the SVIB for men and the SVIB for women. The SCII yields information about 124 occupational scales (67 for men and 57 for women). (See INTEREST INVENTORIES.)

References: Anne Anastasi, *Psychological Testing* (Fourth Edition), New York: Macmillan Publishing Company, Inc., 1976; Oscar K. Buros (Editor), *The Eighth Mental Measurements Yearbook* (Volume II), Highland Park, NJ: The Gryphon Press, 1978.

STRUCTURAL ANALYSIS, the breaking up of a word such that its root, prefix, suffix, word family, derivational suffix, inflectional suffix, and/or inflected and derived word are isolated. Through such part-by-part analysis, the word's meaning can be determined. Structural analysis, in addition to dealing with the understanding of meaning, is also concerned with word forms and sound-letter associations.

References: Dolores Durkin, *Teaching Young Children to Read* (Third Edition), Boston: Allyn and Bacon, Inc., 1980; Arthur W. Heilman, Timothy R. Blair, and William H. Rupley, *Principles and Practices of Teaching Reading* (Sixth Edition), Columbus, OH: Charles E. Merrill Publishing Company, 1986; Robert M. Wilson and Craig J. Cleland, *Diagnostic and Remedial Reading for Classroom and Clinic* (Sixth Edition), Columbus, OH: Merrill Publishing Company, 1989; Robert M. Wilson and Mary Anne Hall, *Programmed Word Attack for Teachers* (Second Edition), Columbus, OH: Charles E. Merrill Publishing Company, 1974.

STRUCTURAL GRAMMAR, a form of a descriptive grammar. Structural grammar is a scientific approach to grammar that focuses on sound, on the way language is used, on structural meaning, and on that aspect of grammar that can be observed. Sentences already formed are analyzed. Structural grammar is generally not concerned with the underlying relationship among phonemes and morphemes. (See TRANSFORMATIONAL GENERATIVE GRAMMAR.)

References: Nancy Ainsworth Johnson, *Current Topics in Language,* Cambridge, MA: Winthrop Publishers, Inc., 1976; John P. Kimball, *Formal Theory of Grammar,* Englewood Cliffs, NJ: Prentice-Hall, Inc., 1973; E. Brooks Smith, et al., *Language and Thinking in School* (Second Edition), New York: Holt, Rinehart and Winston, Inc., 1976.

STRUCTURED OVERVIEW, a graphic display of the relationships among the concepts within a course, text, unit, or chapter. The structured overview is founded in David Ausubel's theory of advanced organizers, which indicates that individuals learn new concepts more easily when they are presented in an orderly arrangement. The graphic organization provides students with a structure for assimilating new concepts.

To develop a structured overview, all key words and concepts must be identified. Next, they are organized in such a way as to visually display their interrelatedness. The graphic display can allow for additional concepts as learning proceeds. The structured overview, in addition to its primary value as an advanced organizer, has secondary benefits. It holds the instructor accountable for emphasizing key concepts, and it provides a skeletal guide for note taking and study. (See SEMANTIC MAPPING, SEMANTIC WEBBING.)

References: David Ausubel, *Educational Psychology: A Cognitive View* (Second Edition), New York: Holt, Rinehart and Winston, 1978; Dale D. Johnson and P. David Pearson, *Teaching Vocabulary,* New York: Holt, Rinehart and

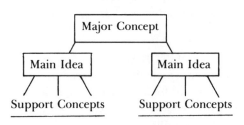

Structured Overview

Winston, 1984; Betty D. Roe, Barbara D. Stoodt, and Paul C. Burns, *Secondary School Reading Instruction: The Content Areas* (Second Edition), Boston: Houghton Mifflin Company, 1983.

STRUCTURE OF INTELLECT (SOI), Joy P. Guilford's theory of intelligence. First used to measure intellect in the early 1960s, it is presently regarded as a problem-solving program for the gifted. However, all individuals have intelligence; the SOI reveals the quality and quantity. SOI assessments analyze 26 intellectual abilities; this information can be used to document various kinds of thinking abilities. SOI is also used as a basis for teaching thinking skills, creativity, and reasoning, since it identifies 90 thinking abilities ranging from the basics to advanced, higher-order thinking. Developmental thinking abilities for a verbally oriented curriculum differ from those required in a quantitative curriculum. SOI separates these two areas to allow for assessment and curriculum development. SOI assessments are group-administered by the classroom teacher.

References: James J. Gallagher, *Teaching the Gifted Child* (Third Edition), Boston: Allyn and Bacon, Inc., 1985; Joy P. Guilford, *Way beyond the I.Q.*, Great Neck, NY: Creative Synergetic Associates, 1977; Mary N. Meeker, "SOI" in Arthur I. Costa (Editor), *Developing Minds*, Alexandria, VA: Association for Supervision and Curriculum Development, 1985; Mary N. Meeker, Robert Meeker, and Gayle Roid, *The Basic SOI Test Manual*, Los Angeles: WPS, 1984.

STUDENT COMMONS AREA, or commons area, that part of a school set aside for unscheduled use by students. Such areas may be used for a number of activities including lounging, reading, smoking (if permitted), and, in some instances, the purchase of refreshments.

Reference: Combined Glossary; Terms and Definitions from the Handbooks of the State Educational Records and Reports Series, Washington, DC: National Center for Education Statistics, U.S. Department of Health, Education, and Welfare, 1974.

STUDENT COUNCILS, student governmental organizations normally found in secondary schools and institutions of higher learning. Their existence serves to fulfill several goals: (1) providing students with an opportunity to learn good citizenship through democratic practice; (2) establishing a wholesome school climate; (3) serving as an advisory body to a school's faculty and administration; and, to the extent that law and local policies permit, (4) participation in the administration of the

school. In some secondary schools, home rooms elect one representative to serve on the council with council officers elected by the total school membership. Other organizational models may also be used (e.g., school officer, club officer, modified government). These variations account for the fact that the size of school councils is not uniform. School councils regularly sponsor/support one or more school projects likely to be of importance to a large segment of the total school population. Examples of such projects include homecoming programs, special assemblies, career day programs, money-making projects, and award programs.

Student council meetings and activities are carried out in accordance with a constitution and bylaws. The council adviser, a faculty member appointed by the administration, works closely with council members and offers guidance as needed.

At the college and university level, the term applied to such organizations is *student government.* (See NATIONAL ASSOCIATION OF STUDENT COUNCILS.)

References: Donald F. Murphy, *Student Structures: Moving Toward Student Government*, Reston, VA: The National Association of Secondary School Principals, 1974; National Association of Secondary School Principals, *The Student Council in the Secondary School*, Washington, DC: The Association, 1962; Office of Student Activities, *Student Council Handbook*, Reston, VA: National Association of Secondary School Principals, 1978; C. Michael Otten, *University Authority and the Student*, Berkeley, CA: University of California Press, 1970.

STUDENT CREDIT HOUR—See CREDIT HOUR

STUDENT DESCRIPTIVE FORM, a standard form used by many teachers in grades 9–12 and made a part of each student's cumulative folder. Using it, teachers rate students on the following: participation in discussion, classroom involvement, independent study, evenness of performance, questioning skills, depth of understanding, responsibility, and consideration of others. The form is published by the National Association of Secondary School Principals.

Reference: Oscar K. Buros, *Personality Tests and Reviews*, Lincoln, NE: University of Nebraska Press, 1970.

STUDENT DESCRIPTIVE QUESTIONNAIRE, a part of the College Board Admissions Testing Program (SAT) designed to provide colleges with background information about their applicants. Completion of this part (a questionnaire) by the applicant is optional.

Information provided by the applicant can assist colleges in making admissions decisions. Information asked for on the student descriptive questionnaire includes ethnic identification, type of high school attended, type of high school program completed, size of high school class, rank in class, educational objectives, housing preference, kinds of assistance needed, and extracurricular interests. The student descriptive questionnaire is similar to the American College Testing Program's (ACT) student questionnaire. (See AMERICAN COLLEGE TESTS and SCHOLASTIC APTITUDE TEST.)

References: Oscar K. Buros (Editor), *The Eighth Mental Measurements Yearbook* (Volume I), Highland Park, NJ: The Gryphon Press, 1978; M. O. Phelps, "Use of the College Board Student Descriptive Questionnaire," *College and University,* Summer 1972.

STUDENT-DEVELOPMENT PROGRAMS, planned student services offered by institutions of higher education to maximize the social, psychological, and educational experiences offered by such institutions. Student development programs seek to integrate various student services (e.g., counseling, housing, health services, student activities, tutoring, student government, social programs) to facilitate the total development of students.

Student development programs utilize concepts, principles, and approaches appropriate to the particular age range of the student population involved.

References: Leonard L. Baird, et al., *Understanding Student and Faculty Life,* San Francisco: Jossey-Bass Publishers, 1980; Arthur Chickering, *Education and Identity,* San Francisco: Jossey-Bass Publishers, 1969; Asa S. Knowles (Editor), *Handbook of College and University Administration,* New York: McGraw-Hill Book Company, 1970; Ted K. Miller and Judith Prince, *The Future of Student Affairs,* San Francisco: Jossey-Bass Publishers, 1976.

STUDENT FINANCIAL AID, a generic term referring to support programs that institutions of higher education sponsor or coordinate for the purpose of assisting their students to meet educational expenses. Most aid programs (state, federal, institutional) are based on a philosophy that holds that the family is primarily responsible for a student's expenses. Aid is used to help finance the difference between the cost of the student's education and what the family can reasonably be expected to pay.

Financial aid includes *grants* (e.g., the Basic Edu-

cational Opportunity Grant), *loans* (e.g. Guaranteed Student Loan), *employment opportunities* (e.g., College Work Study Program), and *scholarships.* In recent years, a large proportion of student financial aid programs has been supported by the federal government.

Surveys of incumbent and prospective students have revealed that: (1) finances are a major factor in determining which, if any, institutions of higher education a student will attend, and (2) educational cost information, reportedly, is not always available to the student. (See BASIC EDUCATIONAL OPPORTUNITY GRANT (BEOG) PROGRAM; COLLEGE WORK-STUDY PROGRAM; GUARANTEED STUDENT LOAN PROGRAM; NATIONAL DIRECT STUDENT LOANS: and SUPPLEMENTAL EDUCATIONAL OPPORTUNITY GRANTS.)

References: College Entrance Examination Board, *Making It Count: A Report on a Project to Provide Better Financial Aid Information to Students,* New York: The Board, Undated Report; Chester E. Finn, Jr., *Scholars, Dollars, and Bureaucrats,* Washington, DC: The Brookings Institution, 1978; *Student Financial Aid, 1980-81,* Boca Raton, FL: Florida Atlantic University, 1980.

STUDENT NEA, National Education Association's affiliate for students preparing to be teachers. Approximately 50,000 students, enrolled in 1,100 institutions of higher education, are members. The organization provides numerous leadership training opportunities in areas such as student rights, political involvement, teacher preparation, and involvement in the organized teaching profession. Student NEA is represented on the NEA Board of Directors and sends voting delegates to the NEA Representative Assembly. Student NEA's official publication is *Impact.* (See NATIONAL EDUCATION ASSOCIATION.)

Reference: National Education Association, *NEA Handbook: 1977-78,* Washington, DC: The Association, 1977.

STUDENT RIGHTS, a broad school law term that relates to the Constitutional rights of students enrolled in schools, colleges, and universities. In general, the courts have respected and supported the right of school officials to govern their own institutions and to establish reasonable codes of conduct for students. In these matters, they have refrained from substituting their own judgments for those of the educators. However, the courts have intervened when, in their judgment, actions by the school or school officials violate the Constitutional rights of students. *Tinker v. Des Moines Independent*

Community School District is a case in point, one in which teenage students were threatened with suspension for wearing black armbands to protest the Vietnam War. Relative to this case, Associate Supreme Court Justice Fortas commented: "Students in school as well as out of school are 'persons' under our Constitution," a statement indicating the Supreme Court's determination to preserve and protect those rights.

Related to student rights are considerations such as suspension and expulsion, dress and hair styles, statutory rights, student newspapers, the right to freely associate, and searches of students and/or their property. To offset misunderstanding and possible litigation, authorities recommend that student handbooks be prepared that describe rules of conduct for students; furthermore, that they be distributed and explained to all students.

References: Joseph Abruscato, *Introduction to Teaching and the Study of Education*, Englewood Cliffs, NJ: Prentice-Hall, Inc., 1985; David G. Armstrong and Tom V. Savage, *Secondary Education: An Introduction*, New York: Macmillan Publishing Co., Inc., 1983; Eve Cary, *What Every Teacher Should Know About Student Rights*, Washington, DC: National Education Association, 1975; Eugene T. Conners, *Student Discipline and the Law* (PDK Fastback 121), Bloomington, IN: The Phi Delta Kappa Educational Foundation, 1979; Thomas J. Flygare, *The Legal Rights of Students* (PDK Fastback 59), Bloomington, IN: The Phi Delta Kappa Educational Foundation, 1975; Patricia A. Hollander, *Legal Handbook for Educators*, Boulder, CO: Westview Press, 1978; D. Parker Young and Donald Gehring, *The College Student and the Courts*, Asheville, NC: College Administration Publications, Inc., 1977.

STUDENT TEACHING, an extended clinical experience for prospective teachers that is usually completed during the final year of the preservice training program. The length of the student teaching experience is variable. Most range from 9 to 18 weeks for full-time student teachers with proportionately longer periods required for those completing the requirement on a part-time basis.

The student teacher is usually assigned to, and understudies, a cooperating (master) teacher in a public or private school. The clinical experience begins with considerable observation on the part of the student teacher followed by increasing opportunities to plan lessons and to teach students.

Student teachers are not paid, are visited regularly by a university supervisor, and receive academic credit for student teaching. Virtually all states require successful completion of student teaching (or its equivalent) for certification.

References: Fillmer Hevener, Jr., *Successful Student Teaching: A Handbook for Elementary and Secondary Student Teachers*, Saratoga, CA: Century Twenty-One Publishing, 1981; James A. Johnson, *A National Survey of Student Teaching Programs*, Baltimore, MD: Multi-State Teacher Education Project (Monograph II), July 1968; Betty D. Roe, Elinor P. Ross, and Paul C. Burns, *Student Teaching and Field Experiences Handbook*, Columbus, OH: Charles E. Merrill Publishing Company, 1984.

STUDENT TEAMS ACHIEVEMENT DIVISIONS (STAD), a cooperative learning approach developed by Robert E. Slavin in the 1970s. STAD can be used in Grades 2 to 12. There are five major components to STAD: class presentations (by the teacher), team study, quizzes, individual improvement scores, and team recognition.

Teaching is usually highly focused on a unit of study and is a function of the teacher. Teams, made up of four or five students that are heterogeneous on ability, sex, and ethnicity, have the primary purpose of preparing its members for the quizzes via worksheets, discussing problems together, comparing solutions, and making corrections. Students take quizzes individually, and their scores are compared to their base scores to determine individual improvement. Certificates or other rewards may be given the teams if their average scores go beyond a criterion point. Teams-Games-Tournaments (TGT) is similar to Student Teams Achievement in every way except that TGT (1) uses academic game tournaments and (2) does not use individual improvement scores. STAD students compete with academically similar students in "divisions" within a tournament. (See COOPERATIVE LEARNING.)

References: Robert E. Slavin, "Student Teams and Achievement Divisions, *Journal of Research and Development in Education*, Volume 12, Number 1, 1978; Robert E. Slavin, *Using Student Team Learning* (Third Edition), Baltimore, MD: The Johns Hopkins University, 1986.

STUDENT YEARBOOK—See YEARBOOK, STUDENT

STUDY ABROAD PROGRAMS, programs that make it possible for students to study in another country, usually for one, two, or more semesters. Many American universities and colleges give credit toward graduation for the experience providing the study program is generally consistent with the individual institution's degree requirements. In many United States colleges, a "junior year abroad" is an acceptable part of the student's undergraduate program.

A student interested in studying abroad may make his/her own arrangements with a foreign university or college, or he/she may do so through either his/her own university, an organization, or foreign country. In most cases, the participating student enrolls for formal courses at the foreign institution of higher education. Some students elect to engage in extensive travel rather than taking formal courses. Generally, where formal course work is the option selected, entrance requirements established by the host institution must be met; in some cases, facility with the language of the host country is also required. Study abroad programs are not to be confused with study tours. (See STUDY TOURS.)

References: John A. Garraty, et al., *The New Guide to Study Abroad* (1978–79 Edition), New York: Harper and Row, Publishers, 1978; *Study Abroad* (Volume XXII, 1979–80, 1980–81), Paris, France: UNESCO, 1978.

STUDY CARREL—See CARREL

STUDY GUIDE, a means of assisting students in reading a text. The study guide focuses student attention on the major concepts within the reading—it may also provide ways to apply new concepts in order to reinforce learning. There are two major approaches to development of a study guide. A *process* guide focuses on the skills necessary to read the specific material (i.e., cause-effect relationships); a *content* guide focuses on the subject matter—it includes purpose setting and comprehension questions. It is possible to synthesize the two types of guides into a single unit.

Study guides allow for grouping within a content area classroom. Differentiated assignments on the study guide could be prepared to accommodate different ability levels. Study guides increase the retention of material read.

References: Paul C. Burns, Betty D. Roe, and Elinor P. Ross, *Teaching Reading in Today's Elementary Schools* (Third Edition), Boston: Houghton Mifflin Company, 1984; Robert Karlin, *Teaching Reading in High School: Improving Reading in Content Areas* (Third Edition), Indianapolis: Bobbs Merrill, 1977; Betty D. Roe, et al., *Secondary School Reading Instruction: The Content Areas*, Boston: Houghton Mifflin Company, 1983.

STUDY HALL, special study area (other than the library) in which students, usually in secondary schools, gather for one or more periods of supervised and independent study. Supervision is provided by one or more members of the faculty.

In years past, it was common for secondary school students to have at least one study hall period included in their respective programs. More recently, the study hall approach has been losing favor with school authorities, for several reasons: (1) it is seen as a "restriction zone," a place for silence; (2) effective supervised study is better achieved in classrooms than in large study hall areas such as cafeterias and auditoriums; (3) study hall assignments are often used to accommodate the needs of schedule rather than student; and (4) supervised study in the study hall often means keeping order rather than providing students with study help.

J. Lloyd Trump and Delmas Miller recommended that other study areas be used (e.g. library, resource centers, special help areas). They suggested that when study halls must be used, they should accommodate no more than 1–3 percent of the school's total enrollment at any one time.

References: Leonard H. Clark and Irving S. Starr, *Secondary School Teaching Methods* (Third Edition), New York: Macmillan Publishing Company, Inc., 1976; J. Lloyd Trump and Delmas F. Miller, *Secondary School Curriculum Improvement* (Second Edition), Boston: Allyn and Bacon, Inc., 1973.

STUDY SKILLS, specific skills taught to students for the purpose of overcoming blocks to learning. Study skills programs are offered at elementary, secondary, and college levels; some are also available to adults who are not attending school. All have one goal in common: teaching the student how to study. Among the skills taught are: (1) note taking; (2) learning how to take a test; (3) improving study conditions (lighting, room temperature, time of day, etc.); (4) using the library; (5) listening; and (6) reading improvement.

References: Jerold W. Apps, *Study Skills for Those Adults Returning to School*, New York: McGraw-Hill Book Company, 1978; John Langan, *Reading and Study Skills* (Fourth Edition), New York: McGraw-Hill Book Company, 1989.

STUDY TOURS, supervised and structured educational trips to a specific area of the world. A study tour is designed to provide groups of students with experiences not available in a traditional classroom setting. Such tours may be sponsored by universities, colleges, and departments as well as professional or other organizations. Study tours are of short duration (e.g. 6 to 12 weeks), are usually scheduled during the summer or during traditional vacation periods, and involve trips to regions within the United States or to foreign countries. The participant pays one price for a study tour that covers costs for meals, hotels, and transportation. If academic credit (graduate or undergraduate) is to be awarded, an additional amount is charged for tuition. The earliest known study tours were organized by the University of Jena in 1892.

Study tours are not to be confused with "study abroad programs." The former involve travel to *different* localities, while study abroad programs are designed for a student to attend (or reside) in *one* institution or place. Also, study abroad programs tend to be of longer duration. Another distinction is that study tours are usually thematic (e.g. focus is on comparative education, art, music, alternative schools) and study abroad programs are structured to resemble a regular formal school program. Finally, study abroad programs entail formal entrance requirements. Study tours, in contrast, have but minimal requirements.

References: John A. Garraty, et al., *The New Guide to Study Abroad* (1978–79 Edition), New York: Harper and Row, Publishers, 1978; *International Programs in Education,* Louisville, KY: University of Louisville and Kentucky State University, Undated; *Study Abroad* (Volume XXII, 1979–80, 1980–81), Paris, France: UNESCO, 1978.

STUTTERING, or dysfluency, a speech defect or disorder that prevents a speaker from moving smoothly from one phoneme to another, even when the speaker has a clear intention to do so. Hesitations, blocking, prolongations, or repetitions of words, syllables, sounds, or mouth positions are characteristics of stuttering and interfere with the speech flow. This, in turn, causes verbal stress.

There are several characteristics of stuttering. They include compressed lips, lingual posturing, mouth held open, holding breath, blinking eyes, dilating nostrils, repetition of syllable strings, interjections, and changes in emotional state. Not all who stutter manifest each of these characteristics. Also, there are varying degrees of the speech defect.

The actual cause of stuttering has not been determined although there is considerable information indicating that emotions (fear, embarrassment, hostility, even excitement that is generated from a positive stimulus) play a role. Various therapies have been used to treat stuttering, such as: relaxation; punishment/reward, servotherapy; psychotherapies; behavior modification; drugs; and rhythmic, timing, and rate control. The ap-

propriate therapy needs to be designed by a well-trained speech clinician.

References: Gerald Jones, *Stuttering: The Disorder of Many Theories,* New York: Farrar, Straus and Giroux, 1977; Martin F. Schwartz, *Stuttering Solved,* Philadelphia: J. B. Lippincott Company, 1976; Charles Van Riper, *The Treatment of Stuttering,* Englewood Cliffs, NJ: Prentice-Hall, Inc., 1973; Marcel E. Wingage, *Stuttering: Theory and Treatment,* New York: Irvington Publishers, Inc., 1976.

SUBJECT-CENTERED CURRICULUM, a school curriculum arranged by subject areas (e.g. algebra, chemistry, social studies, American history). The entire school curriculum (K–12) can be organized in this manner. The subject-centered curriculum has several advantages. It is easy to implement, easy to administer, lends itself to the application of the Carnegie unit, and specialization in a particular field of study can be provided. The subject-centered curriculum has been traced to educational programs existing during medieval times. Although variations in the subject-centered curriculum approach are made from time to time, most schools continue to use a curriculum design structured along subject lines. (See TRIVIUM AND QUADRIVIUM.)

References: Arthur W. Foshay, "How Fare the Disciplines?" *Phi Delta Kappa,* March 1970; Daniel Tanner and Laurel N. Tanner, *Curriculum Development* (Second Edition), New York: Macmillan Publishing Company, Inc., 1980.

SUBSTITUTE TEACHER, a teacher employed as a replacement for an absent, full-time teacher. The substitute teacher is expected, to the greatest degree possible, to continue the normal work routine by implementing lesson plans prepared by the regular teacher. In most instances, boards of education require that substitute teachers be certified.

Substitute teachers may be employed on a day-to-day basis or as annual substitutes called upon to replace regular teachers for up to a full year. A relatively large school system will likely employ a corps of substitutes, some of whom function as permanent substitutes, others as temporary replacements (floaters).

The duties of the substitute are myriad. In addition to teaching, they are expected to: (1) record attendance; (2) implement plans prepared by the regular teacher; (3) report to the principal's office before and after classes are in session; (4) leave a written summary of the day's activities for the regular teacher, including the identification of uncooperative students; (5) contact the principal for assistance with unusual problems; and (6) leave the classroom in order.

References: William B. Castetter, *The Personnel Function in Educational Administration* (Second Edition), New York: Macmillan Publishing Company, Inc., 1976; Donald E. Davis and Neal C. Nickerson, Jr., *Critical Issues in School Personnel Administration,* Chicago: Rand McNally and Company, 1968; Neal Nickerson, Jr., *The Selection and Utilization of Substitute Teachers,* Danville, IL: The Interstate Printers and Publishers, Inc., 1965; Bryce Perkins and Harry A. Becker, *Getting Better Results from Substitutes, Teacher Aides, and Volunteers,* Englewood Cliffs, NJ: Prentice-Hall, Inc., 1966; Herbert E. Robb, "Decline and Fall of the Substitute Teacher," *Journal of Teacher Education,* March–April 1979.

SUBSYSTEM—See ORGANIZATIONAL SUBSYSTEM

SUBVOCALIZATION, reading in which words may be whispered or formed by lips and vocal cords without sound being uttered (often during silent reading). In some cases, the words are formed with almost no noticeable movement of the speech organs (i.e. the words are formed in the mind as inner speech).

Subvocalization may be detected in the following manner: (1) observation of the student while he/she reads silently, to determine if he/she is whispering or moving lips, or (2) placement of the finger tips against the child's vocal cords during silent reading, to detect vibrations.

For the beginning reader, subvocalization is not a major concern since it does not slow down the speed or reading significantly. Subvocalization must be reduced or eliminated for the more mature reader if he/she is to achieve skill as a rapid reader.

References: Guy Bond and Miles Tinker, *Reading Difficulties: Their Diagnosis and Correction* (Fourth Edition), Englewood Cliffs, NJ: Prentice-Hall, Inc., 1979; Lyle L. Lloyd (Editor), *Communication Assessment and Intervention Strategies,* Baltimore, MD: University Park Press, 1976;

George D. Spache, *Diagnosing and Correcting Reading Disabilities,* Boston: Allyn and Bacon, Inc., 1976.

SUICIDE, a growing problem involving American children and youth. Urie Bronfenbrenner pointed out that, among the young, death rate from suicide increased dramatically (almost tripling) between 1951 and 1974, especially for those in their adolescent and postadolescent years. For youth in the 15 to 19 age group it was (in 1970) the fourth ranking cause of death.

Luciano L'Abate and Leonard Curtis reported that, although 90 percent of all adolescents attempting suicide are females, male deaths by suicide outnumber female suicide deaths by a 3:1 ratio. Investigators have noted that death by suicide is highest among Puerto Rican youth, next highest for whites, and lowest for blacks.

William Glasser identified six motivational factors leading to suicide attempts. They are: (1) grief following loss of a love object; (2) self-punishment or blame; (3) cry for help aimed at individuals/agencies outside of the immediate family; (4) revenge aimed at punishing another person; (5) unstable behavior of a psychotic nature; and (6) suicidal games such as Russian roulette and automobile "chicken."

References: Urie Bronfenbrenner, "Who Cares for America's Children?" in Victor C. Vaughan, III and T. Berry Brazelton, *The Family—Can It be Saved?* Chicago: Year Book Medical Publishers, Inc., 1976; William Glasser, *Reality Therapy,* New York: Harper and Row, Publishers, 1965; L. D. Hankoff and Bernice Einsidler, *Suicide: Theory and Clinical Aspects,* Littleton, MA: PSG Publishing Company, 1979; Luciano L'Abate and Leonard T. Curtis, *Teaching the Exceptional Child,* Philadelphia: W. B. Saunders Company, 1975.

SUMMATIVE EVALUATION, the assessment of the overall effectiveness of a program or a product. Unlike formative evaluation, which is carried out during the development of a program, summative evaluation takes place after a program is fully de-

Summative Evaluation

Program Development	Finalized Program Design and Implementation	Completion of a full Cycle of the Program and Output Assessment
FORMATIVE EVALUATION		SUMMATIVE EVALUATION

veloped and implemented. The results of summative evaluations usually are a major concern for policymakers, and the results of formative evaluations are of particular interest to program directors, those working in the program, and program developers. (See graphic on page 551.)

In terms of a program evaluation continuum, summative evaluation starts when formative evaluation ends. (See FORMATIVE EVALUATION.)

References: W. James Popham, *Educational Evaluation* (Second Edition), Englewood Cliffs, NJ: Prentice-Hall, 1988; Emil J. Posavac and Raymond J. Carey, *Program Evaluation: Methods and Case Studies* (Third Edition), Englewood Cliffs, NJ: Prentice-Hall, 1989; Michael Scriven, "The Methodology of Evaluation" in *Perspectives of Curriculum Evaluation,* AERA Monograph Series on Curriculum Evaluation, No. 1, Chicago: Rand McNally and Company, 1967.

SUMMERHILL, a private demonstration school for problem children. Established in England by A. S. Neill shortly after World War I, the school became noted for its nontraditional approaches to learning and teaching. The Summerhill idea is based on several of Neill's convictions concerning childrearing: that every child is born inherently good; that every child should be permitted to live his/her life to the fullest in a climate of love and with a minimum of adult constraints; that learning should be self-motivated, growing out of the child's innate interests; that education should foster self-discipline; that children should grow and study in heterosexual settings; and that a function of education is the development and respect of the student's own dignity.

Summerhill's critics have charged that the program places a premium on affective learning with relatively less concern demonstrated for acquisition of knowledge.

The Summerhill idea received wide attention in the United States following publication of Neill's compendium, *Summerhill: A Radical Approach to Child Rearing.*

References: Harold H. Hart (Editor), *Summerhill: For and Against,* New York: Hart Publishing Company, 1970; Ray Hemmings, *Children's Freedom: A. S. Neill and the Evolution of the Summerhill Idea,* New York: Schocken Books, 1973; William Matthias, "Whatever Happened to Summerhill?" *Childhood Education,* April/May 1979; A. S. Neill, *Summerhill: A Radical Approach to Child Rearing,* New York: Pocket Books, 1977.

SUMMER MUSIC CAMP, a camp whose programs emphasize music instruction in fields such as band, orchestra, chorus, and chamber groups. Such camps usually offer private vocal and instrumental instruction as well. Patrons are normally precollege-age students. A listing of such camps, by state, appears in *The American Music Handbook.*

Reference: Christopher Pavlakis, *The American Music Handbook,* New York: The Free Press, 1974.

SUMMER YOUTH EMPLOYMENT PROGRAM, a federal program designed to provide jobs for economically disadvantaged young people (ages 14–21) during the summer months. Authorization for this program is contained in the Comprehensive Employment Training Act (CETA), passed in 1973. In 1977, almost 1,000,000 jobs for youth were made possible by the program. (See COMPREHENSIVE EMPLOYMENT AND TRAINING ACT.)

References: Office of the Federal Register, National Archives and Records Service, General Services Administration, *United States Government Manual, 1978/79,* Washington, DC: U.S. Government Printing Office, 1978; Public Law 93-203, *United States Statutes at Large, 1973* (Volume 87), Washington, DC: U.S. Government Printing Office, 1974.

SUNSHINE ACTS, federal and state laws that require public institutions (including school districts) to transact governmental business at meetings that are open to the public and that have been announced in advance. Closed meetings are permitted in certain instances (e.g. when certain personnel topics, real estate plans, collective bargaining strategies, etc. are discussed). Florida was the first state to introduce a sunshine act (1905). Since then, all states have passed some form of such legislation.

The federal sunshine act sets forth the purpose of this legislation, as follows: "It is thereby declared to be the policy of the United States that the public is entitled to the fullest practicable information regarding the decision-making processes of the Federal Government. It is the purpose of this Act to provide the public with such information while protecting the rights of individuals and the ability of the Government to carry out its responsibilities" (p. 1241).

References: Craig Gifford, *Boardmanship: A Handbook for School Board Members,* Westerville, OH: Ohio School Boards Association, 1978; Patricia A. Hollander, *Legal Handbook for Educators,* Boulder, CO: Westview Press, 1978; Public Law 94-409, *United States Code: Congressional and Administrative News, 94th Congress, Second Session* (Volume 1), St. Paul, MN: West Publishing Company, 1976.

SUPERINTENDENT, LOCAL, the chief executive officer of a local school district. Louisville and Buffalo established the first such positions in 1837. As school districts consolidated and district enrollments grew, increasing numbers of school boards engaged superintendents to administer the work of the schools. Currently, approximately two-thirds of the country's school districts employ a superintendent of schools.

The superintendent is employed by the local board of education and executes the policies that it develops. As the top school system administrator, he/she regulates the district's decision-making process. Functions of the local superintendency include obtaining and developing personnel, managing the district's funds and facilities, maintaining good community relationships, and general instructional leadership. The number of superintendencies is expected to decrease as the country's school consolidation movement continues.

References: American Association of School Administrators, *The American School Superintendency*, Washington, DC: The Association, 1952; Roald F. Campbell, et al., *The Organization and Control of American Schools* (Fourth Edition), Columbus, OH: Charles E. Merrill Publishing Company, 1980; Marcella R. Dianda, *The Superintendent's Can-Do Guide to School Improvement*, Washington, DC: Council for Educational Development and Research, 1984.

SUPERINTENDENT, STATE—See CHIEF STATE SCHOOL OFFICER

SUPERVISING PRINCIPAL, an administrative title assigned to a school building administrator who does some teaching but spends *the major part* of the work day (e.g. 75 percent) performing administrative and/or supervisory tasks.

According to the National Association of Elementary School Principals' most recent survey of its membership, this formerly familiar job title is currently used in but a relatively few communities. In 1968, NAESP reports, 12.6 percent of the elementary school building administrators surveyed held this title. By 1978, that percentage fell to 1.1 percent.

In New York State, the term has a special meaning, a title held by chief school administrators in certain school districts. (See HEAD TEACHER and TEACHING PRINCIPAL.)

References: Henry J. Otto and David C. Sanders, *Elementary School Organization and Administration* (Fourth Edition), New York: Appleton-Century-Crofts, Inc., 1964; William L. Pharis, *The Elementary School Principalship in 1978: A Research Study*, Arlington, VA: National Association of Elementary School Principals, 1979.

SUPERVISION, a leadership function that has general improvement of the enterprise as its major purpose. In education, the goal of supervision is instructional improvement, including staff development. This objective is realized by helping teachers to perform to the limits of their potential. Supervisors are expected to create organizational climates and decision-making structures that facilitate collaboration and cooperation among faculty members. In recent years, the literature of educational supervision has encouraged effective interpersonal relations and the use of democratic approaches by supervisors.

Supervision in schools is provided by any number of officials. They include building principals, special field supervisors (e.g. supervisors of music), central office personnel, helping teachers, and, in smaller districts, the superintendent of schools.

Key areas of responsibility associated with school supervision include: (1) the selection, orientation, and evaluation of teachers; (2) inservice training; (3) curriculum development; (4) student and program evaluation; (5) instructional supplies and equipment; and (6) group dynamics.

References: Arthur Blumberg, *Supervisors and Teachers: A Private Cold War* (Second Edition), Berkeley, CA: McCutchan Publishing Corporation, 1980; James M. Cooper (Editor), *Developing Skills for Instructional Supervision*, New York: Longman, Inc., 1984; Carl D. Glickman, *Supervision of Instruction: A Developmental Approach*, Boston: Allyn and Bacon, Inc., 1985; Thomas J. Sergiovanni (Editor), *Professional Supervision for Professional Teachers*, Washington, DC: Association for Supervision and Curriculum Development, 1975.

SUPERVISOR, in education, a leader whose principal area of responsibility is instructional improvement. Some authorities have defined supervisor so broadly that the title embraces virtually all educational leadership posts having something to do with instruction (including the principalship). Others, although still employing the term generically, narrow its definition to include only those leaders devoting major time to instructional improvement.

Supervisors (using the narrower definition) serving in the schools of America are known by any number of titles (e.g. Assistant Superintendent for Instruction, Curriculum Consultant, Helping Teacher, Director of Curriculum). Their functions, although not uniform from one school district to another, generally include responsibilities such as: (1) overseeing curriculum development and curriculum change; (2) working with teachers, individually and/or in groups, to increase their instructional effectiveness; and (3) coordinating of programs.

References: Carl D. Glickman, *Supervision of Instruction: A Developmental Approach*, Boston: Allyn and Bacon, Inc., 1985; Gordon MacKenzie, "Role of the Supervisor" in Robert R. Leeper (Editor), *Supervision: Emerging Profession*, Washington, DC: Association for Supervision and Curriculum Development, NEA, 1973; Sir James R. Marks, et al., *Handbook of Educational Supervision: A Guide for the Practitioner* (Second Edition), Boston: Allyn and Bacon, Inc., 1978.

SUPPLEMENTAL EDUCATIONAL OPPORTUNITY GRANTS (SEOG), federally supported grants made directly to needy undergraduate students. Intended to supplement other forms of financial aid, SEOGs are distributed to exceptionally needy students by institutions participating in the program. Awards (as of 1981) range up to $2,000 a year. until a student earns an undergraduate degree. Monies awarded need not be repaid. Allocations are first made on the basis of state high school enrollment figures and are then assigned to individual colleges and universities on the basis of their prior year's utilization of funds.

References: Chester E. Finn, Jr., *Scholars, Dollars, and Bureaucrats*, Washington, DC: The Brookings Institution, 1978; Public Law 89-329, *United States Statutes at Large, 1965* (Volume 79), Washington, DC: U.S. Government Printing Office, 1966; Public Law 90-575, *United States Statutes at Large, 1968* (Volume 82), Washington, DC: U.S. Government Printing Office, 1969.

SUPPLEMENTARY READERS, books and other reading materials used to augment, reinforce, and support the basic reading instructional materials and instructional procedures used in a classroom. Magazines, books, reference books, recreational reading, texts from other fields, and other print materials can be used as supplementary reading materials as long as they are appropriate with respect to reading level, maturation, and interest level of the learner. Under certain conditions, nonprint materials can also be used to supplement the basic reading instructional program.

Supplementary reading materials can be used in all fields of study (e.g. science, social studies, mathematics, art, music).

References: Judith Bechtel, et al., *Reading in the Science Classroom*, Washington, DC: National Education Association, 1980; Richard A. Earle, *Classroom Practice in Reading*, Newark, DE: International Reading Association, 1977; Frank Smith, *Reading Without Nonsense*, New York: Teachers College Press, 1979.

SUPPLY, a financial accounting term for consumable items such as pencils, paper, soap, and electric light bulbs. The U.S. Office of Education has defined *supply* as any item, instructional or noninstructional, possessing *any one* of the following characteristics: (1) the item is consumable; (2) it loses shape or appearance with use; (3) it is expendable (i.e. more likely to be replaced than repaired); (4) it is relatively inexpensive; and (5) it loses its identity when incorporated into a different or more complex substance (See EQUIPMENT.)

References: Percy E. Burrup, *Financing Education in a Climate of Change* (Second Edition), Boston: Allyn and Bacon, Inc., 1977; John Greenhalgh, *Practitioner's Guide to School Business Management*, Boston: Allyn and Bacon, Inc., 1978; Charles T. Roberts and Allan R. Lichtenburger, *Financial Accounting*, Washington, DC: U.S. Department of Health, Education, and Welfare, 1973.

SURVEY METHOD, a research approach used to collect information from a given population (or sample). Survey methods are nonexperimental procedures that focus either on the status quo or seek to ascertain how people feel, think, or perceive (sociological or psychological factors). Interviews, questionnaires/opinionnaires, and field observations are the three techniques used to collect these data. Surveys may be taken of classes, schools, communities, state populations, or national populations. Usually, samples are surveyed when the total population is large.

Survey procedures can be costly and time consuming; accordingly, extensive and careful planning is necessary. This is particularly true when interviews and questionnaires/opinionnaires are to be used. Not only must the items in the survey instrument (questionnaire/opinionnaire) be checked and pretested (piloted), but strategies designed to ensure high rate of response need to be formulated as well.

The nature and number of respondents and nonrespondents must be considered when making inferences from the data collected. (See EXPERIMENTAL DESIGN.)

References: Scarvia B. Anderson, et al., *Encyclopedia of Educational Evaluation*, San Francisco: Jossey-Bass Publishers, 1975; Fred N. Kerlinger, *Foundations of Behavioral Research* (Third Edition), New York: Holt, Rinehart and Winston, Inc., 1986; Emil J. Posavac and Raymond J. Carey, *Program Evaluation: Methods and Case Studies* (Third Edition), Englewood Cliffs, NJ: Prentice-Hall, 1989.

SURVIVAL-SKILLS TESTS, those tests that assess the skills a person should possess to function effectively (survive) in a society. In some cases, the testing materials are not traditional examinations. Rather, they are materials representative of those found and used in adult society. They include maps, newspapers, menus, directions for assembling a toy, application forms, income tax forms, cook books, measuring cups, and so on, any or all of which can be used as assessment instruments. The ability to read, count, follow directions, or complete the instruments are frequently the criterion measures used to confirm attainment of the survival skills.

Many of the various minimum-competency tests required in school districts and states test, to some extent, the skills needed to function successfully in the larger (out-of-school) society. They are constructed to measure the targeted skills, and, in format, tend to be like the traditional pencil-and-paper tests commonly found in the schools. They are criterion-referenced tests; a minimum level (score) is needed to pass. In some states and school districts, a student must pass the minimum competencies tests to qualify for graduation.

Survival skills include more than the basic skills of reading, writing, and arithmetic. Included are social skills, human relations skills, basic skills necessary for employment, citizenship skills, and family living skills. (See CRITERION-REFERENCED TEST and MINIMUM-COMPETENCY TESTS.)

References: David A. Gilman, "Minimum Competency Testing: An Insurance Policy for Survival Skills," *NASSP Bulletin,* March 1977; Alberto Montare, et al., *Basic Skills: What Competencies Shall Be Measured and How?* Paper presented at the American Educational Research Association Annual Meeting in New York, April 1977; Jennifer A. Stevenson, "Survival Reading: An Overview of What, Why, and How," *Wisconsin State Reading Association Journal,* October 1978; William W. Turnbull, *Proficiency in Basic Skills* (Statement Before the Subcommittee on Education, Arts, and Humanities Committee on Human Resources, U.S. Senate), Washington, DC, July 27, 1977.

SUSPENSION, the involuntary absence, by action of the appropriate school authority, of a student from school for a fixed period. Students are normally suspended for disciplinary reasons. This form of control by the school is most frequently exercised at the secondary school level.

Suspensions fall into four general categories: (1) short term; (2) long term; (3) indefinite; and, (4) extracurricular activity. *Short-term suspensions* commonly are for a period not exceeding ten days.

The U.S. Supreme Court, in 1975, ruled (*Goss v. Lopez*) that students have a property interest in education, hence "must be given *some* kind of notice and afforded *some* kind of hearing." The Court ruled further that an informal hearing would be sufficient. *Long-term suspensions* range from more than ten days to a year. They require formal hearing, including the right of the student to be represented by counsel. *Indefinite suspensions* are temporary. They serve to remove the student from a situation or setting deemed to be dangerous to either the student or his peers. *Extracurricular suspensions* deprive the student of what had been considered a privilege: that of participating in extracurricular activities. Court rulings have modified this view by asserting that such activities are an integral part of the student's education; accordingly, they too require informal hearings. (See EXPULSION.)

References: Edward C. Bolmeier, *Legality of Student Disciplinary Practices,* Charlottesville, VA: The Michie Company, 1976; Eugene Connors, *Student Discipline and the Law* (PDK Fastback 121), Bloomington, IN: The Phi Delta Kappa Educational Foundation, 1979; *Goss v. Lopez,* 419 U.S. 565, 95 S.Ct. 729, 42 L.Ed. 2d 725 (1975).

SUSTAINED SILENT READING (SSR), a plan that ensures regularly scheduled time for all personnel within a school to read. Originally presented by Lyman C. Hunt in the 1960s as Uninterrupted Sustained Silent Reading (USSR), the concept is employed in many schools throughout the country.

At a predetermined time and for an established duration (some schools use timers to eliminate clock watching), everyone from the custodial help to the principal relaxes at his/her desk with a leisure reading selection; no "assigned" materials are used. During this silent reading period, no interruptions are permitted. Since the goal of the program emphasizes attitudinal improvement toward reading, reports and records are not encouraged; however, some experts support the use of bulletin boards, information sharing, and inviting others to participate as ways to enhance interest and increase motivation.

References: Lyman C. Hunt, *The Individualized Reading Program: A Guide for Classroom Teaching,* Newark, DE: International Reading Association, 1967; Leonard K. Hong, "Modifying SSR for Beginning Readers," *The Reading Teacher,* May 1981; Robert A. McCracken, "Initiating Sustained Silent Reading," *Journal of Reading,* May 1971.

SUZUKI METHOD, also known as Talent Education, a specific approach to teaching violin to young children. The method is named for its originator, the Japanese music educator Dr. Shinichi Suzuki.

The children with whom the Suzuki method is used may be as young as three years of age. It calls for, but is not limited to: (1) exposing infant children to recorded music, making it an integral part of their environment; (2) technique development that precedes sight reading; (3) memorization of all music by the student; (4) rote teaching (for at least two years); and (5) private lessons, with one of the student's parents always present. Suzuki festivals are held in Japan and some parts of the United States, with participation limited to students taught via the Suzuki method.

In the United States, interest in the method was generated when Suzuki and ten of his Japanese students performed before the 1964 meeting of the Music Educators National Conference. Since then, American adaptations of the method have been made, one being group instruction in place of the individual instruction suggested by Suzuki.

References: John Kendall, *Talent Education and Suzuki*, Washington, DC: Music Educators National Conference, 1966; Michael L. Mark, *Contemporary Music Education*, New York: Schirmer Books (Macmillan), 1978; William Starr, *The Suzuki Violinist*, Knoxville, TN: Kingston Ellis Press, 1976.

SWANN v. CHARLOTTE-MECKLENBURG BOARD OF EDUCATION, 1971 ruling of the U.S. Supreme Court that set forth the obligations of school officials and the authority of district courts in bringing about school desegregation. In 1968–69, the Charlotte-Mecklenburg school system (encompassing the city of Charlotte, North Carolina, and surrounding Mecklenburg County) enrolled 84,000 students. Two-thirds of the 24,000 black students then enrolled were attending schools whose enrollments were 99–100 percent black. A district court determined that the school board was maintaining a segregated system and ordered it to formulate a plan for desegregating its schools. Later, finding the school system's plan to be unacceptable, the court ordered implementation of the recommendations of a court-appointed expert whose recommended plan required busing of some students.

In 1971, after the Court of Appeals had reacted to the district court's plan, the U.S. Supreme Court was asked to rule on it. It did and addressed several points in its decision. It held that: (1) school authorities were obligated "to eliminate invidious racial distinctions"; (2) district courts have the au-

thority to reassign teachers and to oversee future school construction for the purpose of bringing about desegregation; and (3) busing of students may be used to help implement a school system's desegregation plan.

References: Frank R. Kemerer and Kenneth L. Deutsch, *Constitutional Rights and Student Life: Value Conflict in Law and Education*, St. Paul, MN: West Publishing Company, 1979; E. Edmund Reutter, Jr. and Robert R. Hamilton, *The Law of Public Education* (Second Edition), Mineola, NY: The Foundation Press, Inc., 1976; *Swann v. Charlotte-Mecklenburg Board of Education*, Supreme Court of the United States, 1971, 402 U.S. 1, 9 S.Ct. 1267, 28 L.Ed. 2d, 554.

SWEEP-CHECK TEST, an individual examination used to test hearing acuity. An audiometer is set at a predetermined frequency level. If the individual being tested cannot hear the tones at this level, more extensive testing is suggested. The Sweep-Check test is used for purposes of initial screening.

The Massachusetts and Johnston tests are group pure-tone tests that are similar to the Sweep-Check test. They, too, are used for preliminary screening. (See AUDIOMETERS and AUDIOMETRY.)

References: William E. Davis, *Educator's Resource Guide to Special Education*, Boston: Allyn and Bacon, Inc., 1980; Lee Edward Travis, *Handbook of Speech Pathology and Audiology*, New York: Appleton-Century-Crofts, Inc., 1971.

SYLLABICATION, or syllabification, the division of a polysyllabic word into its elements, or syllables. Syllabication is taught as part of language arts or reading for the purpose of helping students to pronounce words correctly and to indicate how words appearing at the end of a line are to be divided.

Numerous syllabication rules exist that relate to either word pronunciation or division. Some authorities believe that they should be taught as part of phonics; others are of the opinion that memorization of these rules is less important than is the inferring of syllabication concepts by the reader/writer.

Paul Anderson and Diane Lapp have listed several of the syllabication rules and have divided them into four major categories. The principal categories follow, with a sample rule or two accompanying each: (1) *determination of a syllable* (the sound of a vowel exists in every syllable); (2) *structural syllabication* (divide between a prefix and a root; divide between two roots); (3) *phonic syllabication* (when two vowel sounds are separated by two consonants, as in "matter," divide between the consonants but consider "ch," "sh," "ph," and "th" as being single consonants); and (4) *accent* (in most words having two syllables, the initial syllable is accented).

References: Paul S. Anderson and Diane Lapp, *Language Skills in Elementary Education* (Third Edition), New York: Macmillan Publishing Company, Inc., 1979; Evelyn B. Spache, *Reading Activities for Child Involvement,* Boston: Allyn and Bacon, Inc., 1972.

SYMPOSIUM, the bringing together of a small group of experts who lecture on a specific topic, each addressing a particular aspect of it. A symposium is generally of short duration (e.g. one session), although some are scheduled to last several days. Moderators are used to introduce the speakers and oversee the question-answer periods following the formal presentations. Symposia are used in almost every field of study. Students, other experts, and interested individuals attend symposia.

References: Asa S. Knowles (Editor), *The International Encyclopedia of Higher Education* (Volume 1), San Francisco: Jossey-Bass Publishers, 1977; Philip R. Lee, et al., *Symposium on Consciousness,* New York: The Viking Press, 1976; James F. Short (Editor), *Symposium on Juvenile Delinquency,* Chicago: University of Chicago Press, 1976.

SYNDROME, repeatedly observed clusters of symptoms. To the trained observer, they indicate a particular clinical condition or disease.

Reference: Leland E. Hinsie and Robert J. Campbell, *Psychiatric Dictionary* (Fourth Edition), London, England: Oxford University Press, 1970.

SYNTAX, that part of grammar concerned with the set of rules of sentence structure such that word order, word relations, and word forms are distributed throughout the sentence to convey a particular meaning. *Hot, a, day, is,* and *it* are words known to most people. The sentence "Hot a day is it" is not a correct sentence, but "It is a hot day" is correct because it follows the appropriate rules of sentence structure (syntax). As a result of syntactical rules, changes in sentence meaning (utilizing the same words) can occur. For example, "Is it a hot day" has a meaning different from "It is a hot day." All languages have syntactical structure. Such structure tends to develop over time through usage and is different from country to country and language to language.

References: Bruce L. Liles, *An Introduction to Linguistics,* Englewood Cliffs, NJ: Prentice-Hall, Inc., 1975; John Lyons, *Semantics* (Volume 2), Cambridge, England: Cambridge University Press, 1977; Dorothy Rubin, *Teaching Elementary Language Arts* (Second Edition), New York: Holt, Rinehart and Winston, Inc., 1980.

SYNTHETIC PHONICS—See PHONICS

TABA, HILDA (December 7, 1902-July 6, 1967), curriculum specialist whose expertise in the areas of curriculum processes, intergroup education, and development of cognitive processes in education won her international recognition. Born in Estonia, where she completed her undergraduate studies, she came to the United States and earned graduate degrees (MA) at Bryn Mawr College and (Ph.D.) Columbia University. Taba served on the faculties of Ohio State University (1936-38), University of Chicago (1939-45 and again between 1948 and 1951), and San Francisco State University (1959-67). Interspersed were assignments as Director of an American Council on Education intergroup project (1945-48) and various research activities and consultancies. At the University of Chicago, she served as Director of Intergroup Education in Cooperating Schools (1948-51).

Taba wrote extensively. Her major book, *Curriculum Development: Theory and Practice*, appeared in 1962. She also edited Studies on Intergroup Education, a series sponsored by the American Council on Education.

References: R. L. Brown, "Taba Rediscovered," *School Teacher*, November 1973; Mary Harshbarger, "Taba, Hilda" in John F. Ohles (Editor), *Biographical Dictionary of American Educators* (Volume 3), Westport, CT: Greenwood Press, 1978; Ruth Larmer, "Developing Work-Study Skills in the Elementary School Social Studies Program through the Taba Teaching Strategies Versus Traditional Approaches," Unpublished Doctoral Dissertation: University of Nebraska (Lincoln), 1973.

TABLE OF ORGANIZATION—See LINE AND STAFF CHART

TABLE OF RANDOM NUMBERS, a statistical table appearing in several research and statistics books whose use makes it possible for the researcher to select a sample of subjects in a random manner. For example, an investigator may wish to survey 35 percent of the faculty members working in a college employing 600 faculty members (600 × 0.35 = 210). To which 210 should queries be directed? The investigator begins by assigning a number to each of the 600 faculty members (001-600). Since 600 is a three-digit number, the investigator then chooses a starting point anywhere in a three-digit table of random numbers. Next, moving in any predetermined direction (e.g. laterally, vertically), he/she writes down the 210 random numbers that appear immediately after the arbitrarily selected starting number. These 210 numbers, each representing a particular faculty member, serve to identify those individuals to be surveyed. (See RANDOM SAMPLING.)

References: Walter R. Borg and Meredith D. Gall, *Educational Research: An Introduction* (Fifth Edition), New York: Longman, Inc., 1989; L. R. Gay, *Educational Research: Competencies for Analysis and Application* (Third Edition), Columbus, OH: Merrill Publishing Company, 1987.

TACHISTOSCOPE, a mechanical device used in the teaching of reading. Tachistoscopes expose letters, words, phrases, or other symbols for limited periods, these generally ranging from fractions of a second to 1.5 seconds. They are used to improve visual perception, or seeing accuracy. Tachistoscopic devices range from simple, teacher-made flash cards to elaborate fixed-time machines that flash images upon a screen. (See CONTROLLED READING.)

References: Emerald Dechant, *Diagnosis and Remediation of Reading Disability*, West Nyack, NY: Parker Publishing Company, Inc., 1968; Miles V. Zintz, *Corrective Reading* (Third Edition), Dubuque, IA: Wm. C. Brown Company, Publishers, 1977.

TACKBROAD—See BULLETIN BOARD

TACTILE LEARNING, learning that takes place through the sense of touch. Tactile learning is the medium used by the blind when learning the Braille system of reading. Tactile learning is also used in teaching beginning lipreading to those with hearing handicaps. Through touch, speech vibrations and word formations can be discerned, thus facilitating mastery of lipreading. Tactile sensitivity involves biophysics, neurophysiology, and psychology.

There is a relationship between vision and touch in form discrimination. Tactile learning facilitates visual perception at certain levels of difficulty. For example, tactile learning is used in the early grades to enhance cognitive learning. Young children may be encouraged to stroke, touch, and handle pets in the classroom to reinforce their study of animals (e.g. their identity, care and feeding, characteristics, shape, size, texture).

Authorities recommend that learning include

many modalities, touching and feeling being one of them.

References: Edward C. Carterette and Morton P. Friedman (Editors), *Handbook of Perception: Feeling and Hurting,* New York: Academic Press, 1978; Tokesuke Kusajima, et al. (Editors), *Visual Reading and Braille Reading,* New York: American Foundation for the Blind, 1974; Ashley Montague, *Touching: The Human Significance of the Skin,* New York: Columbia University Press, 1971; Allan Paivio, *Imagery and Verbal Process,* New York: Holt, Rinehart and Winston, Inc., 1971.

TALENTED AND GIFTED, those individuals who exhibit natural aptitude in a performance or skill area (music, art, dance, sports) or those who demonstrate high cognitive ability/potential. The former (those with the natural aptitude) are classified as being *talented;* the latter are considered to be *gifted.* The two terms are often interchanged in spite of the fact that many talented people do not have high intellectual ability, and, conversely, many gifted people have limited talent in a performance or skill area.

Intelligence test scores are one means used to identify gifted children, but authorities agree that there are weaknesses in a screening procedure that uses I.Q. scores as the sole measure of giftedness. They suggest that more than one criterion be used to identify all such children. The identification of talented children is often just as difficult.

There is considerable disagreement over whether gifted and/or talented children should be separated from other students, have a special curriculum (such as "Talented and Gifted" Programs, Accelerated or Advanced Programs), receive special instruction, or be treated differently.

There are varying degrees of talent and/or giftedness. Some people are extremely talented, others less so. An individual with an I.Q. of 160, for example, is considered to be extremely gifted, and one with an I.Q. of 130, also able intellectually, is not as gifted.

Research indicates that talented and gifted people tend, relatively, to be curious, self-sufficient, alert, more socially oriented, self-confident, nonconforming, innovative, and knowledgeable. (See GIFTED CHILD.)

References: Gary A. Davis and Sylvia B. Rimm, *Education of the Gifted and Talented* (Second Edition), Englewood Cliffs, NJ: Prentice-Hall, 1989; James J. Gallagher, *Teaching the Gifted Child* (Third Edition), Boston: Allyn and Bacon, Inc., 1985; Jean Laubenfels, *The Gifted Student,* Westport, CT: Greenwood Press, 1977; Joanne R. Whitmore, *Giftedness, Conflict, and Underachievement,* Melrose, MA: Allyn and Bacon, Inc., 1980.

TALENT EDUCATION—See SUZUKI METHOD

TALKING-BOOK, a spoken form of a book that has been recorded for use by the blind. Early work (1930s) in perfecting recording machines for this purpose was undertaken by the American Foundation for the Blind. The success of these efforts made it possible to use Congressional appropriations (Pratt-Smoot Act) for the purchase of records.

Currently, two principal sponsors of talking-books are the Library of Congress and Recording for the Blind, Inc. The library lends talking-book machines and recorded books to qualified users. Information about newly available talking-books is included in *Talking Book Topics,* a bimonthly publication distributed free to blind readers. Recording for the Blind, Inc., is a nonprofit, voluntary organization that prepares and distributes talking-books with the assistance of volunteer readers. Books are recorded at the request of blind or physically handicapped patrons. Other organizations (e.g. the John Milton Society, the American Bible Society) make religious talking-books available.

Early talking-books were prepared on discs. Increasing use of cassettes is now being made to prepare these materials. (See LIBRARY OF CONGRESS.)

References: The Encyclopedia Americana (International Edition, Volume 4), New York: Americana Corporation, 1976; Ralph Garretson, "Media Development in Library Services to the Blind and Physically Handicapped" in Frank L. Schick (Editor), *The Bowker Annual of Library and Book Trade Information* (Twentieth Edition), New York: R. R. Bowker Company, 1975; Allen Kent and Harold Lancour (Editors), *Encyclopedia of Library and Information Science* (Volume 2), New York: Marcel Dekker, Inc., 1969.

TANGIBLE PROPERTY—See PROPERTY TAX

TAPE RECORDER, a machine that has the capability of recording, playing, and erasing sound. The audiotape on which sound is recorded, monaurally or stereophonically, consists of a plastic base (glossy side) to which metallic oxide has been affixed (dull side). When recordings are made, magnetic fields are set that, during playback, translate into sound. Tapes may be purchased commercially or prepared by the user.

Tape recorders and playback machines use any of three types of tapes: (1) reel-to-reel; (2) cassette;

and (3) minicassette. Although the cassette recorder has become increasingly popular, a number of schools continue to use the reel-to-reel type. Playing times vary from one type to the next. Reel tapes, played at slow speeds, can play for up to six hours. Cassette tape playing time ranges up to one hour depending on size of cassette. Quality of sound reproduction normally increases with tape speed.

In schools, tape recorders fulfill several instructional purposes. Robert Bullough cited several uses, including the following: (1) to provide individualized instruction; (2) to give directions; (3) to help students who have been absent to catch up on their work; (4) to study voice quality; (5) to record interviews with famous people; (6) to record plays, poetry readings, and so on; and (7) as a vehicle for submission of oral reports by students (in place of traditional written reports).

References: James W. Brown, et al., *AV Instruction: Technology, Media, and Methods* (Fifth Edition), New York: McGraw-Hill Book Company, 1977; Robert V. Bullough, Sr., *Creating Instructional Materials* (Second Edition), Columbus, OH: Charles E. Merrill Publishing Company, 1978; Phillip J. Sleeman, et al., *Instructional Media and Technology: A Guide to Accountable Learning Systems,* New York: Longmans, Inc., 1979.

TAX AND EXPENDITURE LIMITATIONS, various types of ceilings (lids) imposed by states for the purpose of controlling the operational costs and indebtedness of municipalities and school districts. Many such controls were introduced in the 1930s, during the depression period. All had one overriding purpose: limiting tax increases, especially taxes on property.

The approaches used to place a lid on school district expenditures vary from one state to another. Some of the more common include: (1) limiting bonded indebtedness to a certain percentage of a district's total assessed valuation; (2) placing a ceiling on the tax rate; (3) requiring a referendum whenever a proposed operating budget will result in an increased tax rate or one exceeding the legal limit; and (4) requiring certain budgets and/or bond proposals to be approved by an agency of the state or county government. Such constraints are imposed for political as well as legal reasons. In many states, the net (and originally unintended) effect of these constraining efforts has been to increase the ratio of state contributions made for the support of public education and to make more dominant the role of the state.

References: Howard D. Hamilton and Sylvan H. Cohen, *Policy Making by Plebiscite: School of Referenda,* Lexington, MA: Lexington Books, 1974; Seymour Sacks, et al., *City Schools/Suburban Schools: A History of Fiscal Conflict,* Syracuse, NY: Syracuse University Press, 1972; *School District Expenditure and Tax Controls* (Report No. F78-8), Denver, CO: Education Finance Center, Education Commission of the States, August 1978.

TAX-ANTICIPATION NOTES, short-term securities, or promissory notes, issued by state and local governments (including school districts) in anticipation of taxes soon to be collected. Funds derived from these short-term loans make working capital available to governmental units between the time the notes are issued and the time that tax monies are received. In most instances, the notes are retired from tax collections.

References: I. Carl Candoli, et al., *School Business Administration: A Planning Approach* (Second Edition), Boston: Allyn and Bacon, Inc., 1978; David M. Darst, *The Complete Bond Book: A Guide to All Types of Fixed-Income Securities,* New York: McGraw-Hill Book Company, 1975.

TAXONOMY, a systematic approach to the classification of a group of entities. The classifications normally range from simple to complex or from lower to higher order levels. A taxonomy is usually developed according to naturally related groups or groupings based on certain criteria. They are used in many fields or disciplines; biological science and education are but two.

Benjamin S. Bloom and others developed taxonomies for educational objectives in 1956. They divided learning into three domains: cognitive, affective, and psychomotor. Each domain was then refined into subcategories. For example, the cognitive domain was further broken down into: 1.00 knowledge; 2.00 comprehension; 3.00 application; 4.00 analysis; 5.00 synthesis; and 6.00 evaluation. Each classification, in turn, was divided into subclassifications (e.g. for the comprehension classification: 2.10 translation; 2.20 interpretation). Such taxonomies led to the systematic development of behavioral objectives and the designing of specific instructional activities to meet these objectives. (See AFFECTIVE DOMAIN; BEHAVIORAL OBJECTIVES; COGNITIVE DOMAIN; PSYCHOMOTOR DOMAIN; and TAXONOMY.)

References: Benjamin S. Bloom, et al. (Editors), *Taxonomy of Educational Objectives: Handbook I.,* New York: David McKay Company, Inc., 1956; Benjamin S. Bloom, et al.,

Handbook on Formative and Summative Evaluation of Student Learning, New York: McGraw-Hill Book Company, 1971; Richard W. Burns, *New Approaches to Behavioral Objectives* (Second Edition), Dubuque, IA: Wm. C. Brown Company, Publishers, 1977; Daniel Tanner and Laurel N. Tanner, *Curriculum Development* (Second Edition), New York: Macmillan Publishing Company, Inc., 1980.

TEACHER, an instructor. In the public school context (grades K–12), the teacher is an individual who has completed a professional curriculum, is certified to teach, and whose principal duties involve the directing of students' learning experiences. With the exception of some state requirements calling for certification of community college instructors, certification is not required of teachers working at the higher education level.

During America's colonial period, there were wide differences among teachers with respect to training. Frequently, ability to read, write, and compute was the sole criterion for employment. Most teachers were male, although females were occasionally employed in some communities.

Early teacher training was introduced during the first half of the 19th century. Normal schools and teacher institutes were established for this purpose, eventually replaced by college level teacher training programs.

Johanna Lemlech and Merle Marks referred to the 1860–1920 era as the period of professional development. Training programs for teachers were improved; various methodologies were introduced concurrent with the rise of the child-study movement; certification standards, some involving examinations, were imposed by several states; and public awareness and support of education increased. By 1940, four-year training programs were operating in all states, virtually all leading to a baccalaureate degree. Accrediting organizations, many created at the turn of the century, worked to strengthen such programs. Following World War II, teacher organizations, notably the American Federation of Teachers and the National Education Association, helped to escalate teacher militancy and increased both teacher power and political involvement at all levels of government.

Studies of teachers' social composition indicate that few come from the country's upper socioeconomic levels. The relatively low status ascribed to the teaching profession (including low salaries) is no doubt related to this observation.

In 1978, there were 2,460,000 K–12 teachers employed in the United States. Of that number, slightly more than half were working in elementary schools. Included in this figure were an estimated 261,000 nonpublic schoolteachers.

The title "teacher" is also used by noncertified instructors such as private dance, voice, or piano teachers. (See AMERICAN FEDERATION OF TEACHERS; CERTIFICATION; NATIONAL EDUCATION ASSOCIATION; TEACHERS' INSTITUTES; and TEACHER MILITANCY.)

References: Roald F. Campbell, et al., *The Organization and Control of American Schools* (Fourth Edition), Columbus, OH: Charles E. Merrill Publishing Company, 1980; Nancy B. Dearman and Valena W. Plisko, *The Condition of Education, 1980 Edition,* Washington, DC: National Center for Education Statistics, U.S. Department of Education, 1980; Willard S. Elsbree, *The American Teacher: Evolution of a Profession in a Democracy,* Westport, CT: Greenwood Press, 1970 (Originally published in 1939 by the American Book Company); Johanna Lemlech and Merle B. Marks, *The American Teacher: 1776–1976* (PDK Fastback 76), Bloomington, IN: The Phi Delta Kappa Educational Foundation, 1976; Ralph E. Martin, Jr., George H. Wood, and Edward W. Stevens, Jr., *An Introduction to Teaching: A Question of Commitment,* Boston: Allyn and Bacon, Inc., 1988.

TEACHER AIDES—See PARAPROFESSIONALS IN EDUCATION

TEACHER BURNOUT, a feeling experienced by a teacher that he/she has been locked into a professional routine; a stress-related condition that, in extreme cases, may result in physical, emotional, and attitudinal exhaustion. Authorities believe that the "teacher burnout syndrome" (a term relatively new to the literature of education) accounts, in part at least, for the increasing numbers of teachers who are leaving the profession earlier in their careers.

Physical symptoms (e.g. fatigue, weight loss, sleeplessness) as well as psychological symptoms (moodiness, increased irritability, decreased caring for people) accompany the condition. Several causes for teacher burnout have been suggested such as job routines, increased stress, and even fear stemming from pupil violence. Suggested remedies range from simple changes such as acquiring new hobbies to taking extended leaves of absence. Administrators, authorities suggest, can help by changing teachers' assignments on a fairly regular basis.

References: Homer R. Figler, *Overcoming Executive Mid-Life Crisis,* New York: John Wiley and Sons, 1978; Barbara Hendrickson, "Teacher Burnout: How to Recognize It; What to Do About It," *Learning*, January 1979; Sally Reed, "What You Can Do to Prevent Teacher Burnout," *National Elementary Principal*, March 1979.

TEACHER CENTER, a relatively new instructional organization offering education programs. These centers are designed to meet the needs of teachers and the teaching profession through cooperative planning and implementation of inservice programs. Autonomous teacher centers, run by teachers, were developed in England as places where teachers with instructional concerns or problems could go for, and receive help in, informal, nonthreatening, inservice environments.

Unlike the discrete, professional education courses offered by universities or colleges, center offerings tend to be continuous and focus on immediate instructional and/or programmatic needs. Teachers, school administrators, parents, university professors, teacher aides, and even students may be involved in teacher center programs, either as learners or as instructors.

There are many organizational types of teacher centers including consortia, partnerships, autonomous centers, and special focus centers. One of the major hallmarks of teacher centers supported by the United States government (P.L. 94-482) is teacher control. By law, these federally funded centers must have 51 percent of the policy board for each center made up of classroom teachers.

References: Harry H. Bell and John W. Peightel, *Teacher Centers and Inservice Education*, Bloomington, IN: The Phi Delta Kappa Educational Foundation, 1976; Roy A. Edelfelt, *Teacher Centers and Needs Assessment*, Washington, DC: National Foundation for the Improvement of Education, Teacher Center Project, and National Education Association, 1980; Public Law 94-482, *United States Statutes at Large* (Volume 90, Part II), Washington, DC: U.S. Government Printing Office, 1978; *Teacher Centers: Commissioner's Report in the Education Professions*, 1975–76, Washington, DC: U.S. Department of Health, Education, and Welfare, 1977; Robert Thornbury (Editor), *Teachers' Centers*, New York: Agathon Press, 1974.

TEACHER CERTIFICATION—See CERTIFICATION

TEACHER CORPS, a federal program introduced by Congress "to strengthen the educational opportunities available to children in schools having concentrations of low-income families and to encourage colleges and universities to broaden their programs of teacher preparation" (p. 1255). Teacher Corps, a reform program, was authorized in 1965 (Title V, Higher Education Act) and subsequently modified by legislative amendments.

Early Teacher Corps projects were preservice oriented. Junior-level interns completed two-year training cycles that were field based and designed by a participating teacher training institution. In 1974, with the national teacher shortage no longer a serious problem, Teacher Corps projects became demonstration centers for the retraining of experienced teachers. Training cycles were increased to five years and provision made for increased collaboration among participating school districts, their communities, and the training institution. Teacher Corps was phased out of existence in the early 1980s; however, a modified version of Teacher Corps is being proposed in the U.S. Senate (1990).

During the first ten years of the program's operation, Teacher Corps projects involved 11,000 interns and 8,000 teachers. An average annual (national) appropriation of $26,000,000 was made during this period. A significant number of those enrolled in Teacher Corps projects were members of minority groups.

References: National Advisory Council on Education Professions Development, *Teacher Corps: Past or Prologue?* Washington, DC: The Council, 1975; Public Law 89–329, *United States Statutes at Large*, 1965 (Volume 79), Washington, DC: U.S. Government Printing Office, 1966; James P. Steffensen, et al., *Teacher Corps Evaluation*, Omaha, NE: Teacher Corps, University of Nebraska at Omaha, 1978; William Smith, "The American Teacher Corps Programme" in Eric Hoyle and Jacquetta Megarry (Editors), *World Yearbook of Education 1980; Professional Development of Teachers*, London, England: Kogan Page Ltd., 1980; Charles B. Supplee, "An Analysis of Factors in Interunit Management and Governance Influencing Impact of Teacher Corps Programs," Unpublished Doctoral Dissertation: University of Nebraska, 1978.

TEACHER EDUCATION, those formal and informal experiences designed to prepare an individual to become a teacher (preservice) or to improve the professional skills of practicing teachers (inservice). The typical four-year teacher education program consists of basic general education (liberal arts) study, methods courses, field experiences, student teaching, electives, and content courses (e.g. mathematics), the last normally required of prospective middle and high school teachers.

Today, teachers must have a teaching certificate, issued by a state, to be eligible to teach in a public school. (Several states also require licensure of private schoolteachers.) These certificates are issued to an individual who has completed a specific program or course of study. In most cases, a college or university degree (99 percent of 1976 teachers held at least a bachelor's degree) is required for *initial* certification. Teachers may, by completing additional course work, qualify for permanent certification or certification in other fields of education.

Formal programs that focused on the preparation of teachers began in France (1794), where the first normal school was established. The first American normal schools were opened in New England during the early part of the 19th century. Out of the normal schools developed the state teachers colleges (about 1900), most of which, in turn, evolved into multipurpose state colleges (about 1940 and thereafter). Regardless of their nomenclature, these institutions required students to complete specific, planned teacher education programs to graduate with a degree in education and/or qualify for a teaching certificate.

Today, institutions of higher education and other agencies (e.g. teacher centers) are involved in the preservice and inservice education of teachers. Various kinds of continuing education, workshops, seminars, advanced degree programs, and field activities have been designed to meet the preservice or inservice needs of classroom teachers.

At some institutions, teacher education refers only to classroom teaching. At others, the term is used more generically and includes programs preparing administrative and support personnel (e.g. counselors, school psychologists) as well.

Recent studies indicate that approximately 1,600 institutions of higher education sponsor one or more teacher education programs. (See COLLEGE OF EDUCATION; CONTINUING EDUCATION; INSERVICE EDUCATION; NORMAL SCHOOLS; and TEACHER CENTER.)
References: Charles W. Case and William A. Matthes (Editors), *Colleges of Education: Perspectives on Their Future,* Berkeley, CA: McCutchan Publishing Corporation, 1985; Michael J. Dunkin and Bruce J. Biddle, *The Study of Teaching,* New York: Holt, Rinehart and Winston, Inc., 1974; Gene H. Hall and Howard L. Jones, *Competency-based Education: A Process for the Improvement of Education,* Englewood Cliffs, NJ: Prentice-Hall, Inc., 1976; Richard S. Peters, *Education and the Education of Teachers,* London, England: Routledge and Kegan Paul, 1977; Kenneth Ryan (Editor), *Teacher Education* (NSSE 74th Yearbook, Part 2), Chicago: University of Chicago Press, 1975; Susan S. Sherwin, *Teacher Education: A Status Report,* Princeton, NJ: Educational Testing Service, 1974.

TEACHER MILITANCY, group challenges by teachers to administrative and/or community authority. According to one writer (Ronald Corwin), teacher militancy is the expected outcome when increased bureaucratization of organization (the school system) and increased professionalization, forces that are not always compatible, operate concurrently. Teacher militancy takes many forms: (1) strikes; (2) increases in organizational (union) strength; (3) collective bargaining; and (4) political activities.

Although numerous factors have contributed to the rise of teacher militancy in the United States, need for economic gain has been the most compelling. Another is the desire to improve working conditions (e.g. "due process" protection, lighter teaching loads). A third factor is the spirited rivalry between two contending organizations seeking to control the teaching profession, the NEA and the American Federation of Teachers. Another writer on this subject (Marshall Donley) cited the "availability of mechanisms" available to teachers as yet another reason for the rise of teacher militancy, including: (1) state laws that mandate that school boards bargain with teachers, and (2) an ever increasing number of teachers whose working conditions are covered by negotiated contract (1,500,000 in 1973).
References: Ronald G. Corwin, *Militant Professionalism: A Study of Organizational Conflict in High Schools,* New York: Appleton-Century-Crofts, Inc., 1970; Ronald G. Corwin, "The New Teaching Profession" in Kevin Ryan (Editor), *Teacher Education* (NSSE 74th Yearbook, Part II), Chicago: University of Chicago Press; Marshall O. Donley, Jr., *Power to the Teachers: How America's Educators Became Militant,* Bloomington, IN: Indiana University Press, 1976.

TEACHER MORALE, the attitudes and feelings of teachers toward their jobs, peers, and supervisors. In the 1950s and 1960s, a series of teacher morale studies were conducted at New York University under the direction of Professor Frederick L. Redefer. Using a 100-item Morale Tendency Score (MTS) instrument to collect attitudinal data, the study's participants concluded that high-morale teachers, in contrast to low-morale teachers, reported: (1) getting more satisfaction out of teaching; (2) doing more to improve their teaching; (3) engaging in more professional studies; (4) being more active in professional organizations; (5) having more positive attitudes toward fellow teachers; (6) dealing better with authority; and (7) placing teachers higher in community esteem. Also, given such opportunity, they indicated that they would again choose teaching as a career.

In their study of leadership in selected elementary schools, Neal Gross and Robert Herriott concluded that high-morale teachers: (1) are proud of their school; (2) enjoy working in it; (3) exhibit loyalty to the school; (4) cooperate with colleagues; (5) accept the philosophy of the school in which they work; and (6) respect the judgment of their school administrator. Other investigators have found that the principal's leadership style, one encompassing factors such as helpfulness, consideration, and providing for group decision making, correlates positively with high teacher morale. (See TEACHER BURNOUT.)

References: Clyde E. Blocker and Richard C. Richardson, "Twenty-Five Years of Morale Research: A Critical Review," *Journal of Educational Sociology,* January 1963; Richard A. Gorton, *School Administration: Challenge and Opportunity for Leadership,* Dubuque, IA: Wm. C. Brown Company, Publishers, 1976; Neal Gross and Robert E. Herriott, *Staff Leadership in Public Schools: A Sociological Inquiry,* New York: John Wiley and Sons, 1965; National Education Association, *NEA Research Memo* (Research Memo 1963-18), Washington, DC: The Association, August 1963.

TEACHER OF THE YEAR—See NATIONAL TEACHER OF THE YEAR

TEACHERS COLLEGE—See COLLEGE OF EDUCATION

TEACHERS' INSTITUTES, early and relatively inexpensive vehicles for the training of teachers. They normally consisted of lectures on topics such as methods of teaching reading, arithmetic, language, geography, and so on delivered by master teachers and/or invited speakers. Institutes, first introduced by Henry Barnard (1839) in Connecticut, offered programs that were considerably less rigorous than those found in normal schools and that usually lasted from three days to three weeks a year. County superintendents, normal school officials, or state superintendents typically arranged and coordinated institute programs.

Participation in teachers' institutes was generally required of all teachers. Most institutes received financial support from the states, hence were cost-free to the participants.

Teachers' institutes remained popular throughout the early part of the 20th century with 26 of the 48 states reportedly still conducting them as late as 1933. These training programs generally persisted in rural areas of the country that did not yet enjoy the benefits of local normal school programs. Urban communities, in contrast, were inclined to encourage normal school training, especially after the turn of the century.

References: Elwood P. Cubberly, *Public Education in the United States: A Study and Interpretation of American Educational History* (Revised and Enlarged Edition), Cambridge, MA: The Riverside Press, 1962; Willard S. Elsbree, *The American Teacher: Evolution of a Profession in a Democracy,* Westport, CT: Greenwood Press, 1970 (Originally published in 1939 by the American Book Company).

TEACHER STRIKES, work stoppages by teachers designed to cause a school or school system to cease functioning. The strike is usually called to force an employer to grant some concessions in working conditions, including financial remuneration, and normally constitutes the last step in a series of collective bargaining negotiations.

Teacher strikes are illegal in most states. A variety of sanctions against teacher organizations or leaders of teacher organizations have been used throughout the country in reaction to illegal teacher strikes. They include: (1) fines levied against the striking union; (2) fines levied against union leaders; and (3) jailing of union leaders. The imposition of such penalties generally comes about as the result of a failure to honor court injunctions. In spite of these penalties, numerous teacher strikes take place each year. (See ANTISTRIKE LAWS; COLLECTIVE BARGAINING; and TEACHER UNIONS.)

References: Thomas J. Flygare, *Collective Bargaining in the Public Schools* (PDK Fastback 99), Bloomington, IN: The Phi Delta Kappa Educational Foundation, 1977; Robert C. O'Reilly, *Understanding Collective Bargaining in Education: Negotiations, Contracts and Disputes Between Teachers and Boards,* Metuchen, NJ: The Scarecrow Press, Inc., 1978.

TEACHER TURNOVER, a term used to describe the movement of teachers from one position to another (usually outside the school or school district). Teacher turnover can be classified into two broad categories: migration and attrition.

Teachers who leave a teaching position for a similar position in another school or school district are said to have *migrated. Attrition* occurs when a teacher leaves the teaching profession or moves into a nonteaching position (e.g. administration).

When there is considerable demand for teachers, as there was in the late 1950s and 1960s, teachers migrate from one school district to another quite readily. When there is an oversupply of teachers, as was the case in the 1970s, their rate of migration decreases.

Many reasons account for teacher attrition. Some are preventable, such as: teacher stress, lack of success, lack of status. Other attrition factors may not be preventable, such as: mandated retirement age, family moved, personal family considerations, death, entry into other oocupations. (See STRESS and TEACHER BURNOUT.)

References: William S. Graybeal, *Population Trends and Their Implications for Association Planning,* Washington, DC: National Education Association, 1979; William S. Graybeal, *Teacher Supply and Demand in Public Schools, 1978,* Washington, DC: National Education Association, 1979; Dwight E. Mitchell, *Migrant Angels: Why Teachers Quit the Schools,* Palo Alto, CA: (no publisher), 1968; K. George Pedersen, *The Itinerant Schoolmaster,* Chicago: Midwest Administration Center, University of Chicago, 1973.

TEACHER UNIONS, organizations of teachers affiliated with, or operating as independent trade unions. In the United States, the largest such organization is the American Federation of Teachers (AFT), an affiliate of the AFL-CIO. AFT was organized in 1916 and affiliated, shortly thereafter, with what was then the American Federation of Labor. Although its membership level remained relatively low through the World War II period, it has since grown to be one of the major teacher organizations in the country.

In the early 1960s, AFT and the National Education Association (NEA) began to compete aggressively for members. AFT's prestige and influence increased after it won recognition as the official bargaining unit for New York City's public school-teachers, a victory that prompted NEA to become more militant in its relationships with school boards and to maintain what many perceive to be a management-labor relationship with school administrators. Today, many consider NEA to be a union in fact, if not in name.

Teacher unions have traditionally worked to improve working conditions for their members (e.g. salaries, fringe benefits, smaller class sizes) and to support educational changes of benefit to teachers and students. The strike and collective bargaining are among the tools used to help achieve these goals.

In the United States, the number of higher education faculty unions has increased dramatically in recent years. Frank Kemerer and J. Victor Baldridge reported that, in 1966, 11 campuses had faculty bargaining units. By 1975, that figure increased to 430. These investigators also reported that, in 1975, approximately 20 percent of the full-time teaching faculty members in the United States were represented by unions. The major higher education bargaining units are AFT, NEA, and the American Association of University Professors.

Teacher unions have existed for several years in different countries and have attracted varying percentages of teachers as members. The National Union of Teachers (England and Wales), for example, was organized in 1870. In Scotland, approximately 95 percent of all teachers belong to a union. (See AMERICAN FEDERATION OF TEACHERS; AMERICAN ASSOCIATION OF UNIVERSITY PROFESSORS; COLLECTIVE BARGAINING; NATIONAL EDUCATION ASSOCIATION; and TEACHER STRIKES.)

References: Keir Bloomer, "The Teacher as Professional and Trade Unionist" in Eric Hoyle and Jacquetta Megarry, *World Yearbook of Education 1980: Professional Development of Teachers,* London, England: Kogan Page Ltd., 1980; Thomas J. Flygare, *Collective Bargaining in the Public Schools* (PDK Fastback 99), Bloomington, IN: The Phi Delta Kappa Educational Foundation, 1977; William J. Grimshaw, *Union Rule in the Schools: Big-City Politics in Transformation,* Lexington, MA: Lexington Books, 1979; Eugenia Kemble, "Teachers' Unions in the USA: An Aggressive Striving for Professionalism" in Eric Hoyle and Jacquetta Megarry, *World Yearbook of Education 1980: Professional Development of Teachers,* London, England: Kogan Page Ltd., 1980; Frank R. Kemerer and J. Victor Baldridge, *Unions on Campus,* San Francisco: Jossey-Bass Publishers, 1975; Ralph M. Kimbrough and Michael Y. Nunnery, *Educational Administration: An Introduction,* New York: Macmillan Publishing Company, Inc., 1976.

TEACHER WARRANTY PROGRAM, a program designed, usually by a college or a university, to "insure" that beginning teachers graduating from that institution are well prepared and will be successful in the classroom; to that end, the institution develops a procedure to carefully evaluate teachers during their first year on the job and is committed to providing a variety of support services, on a short term basis, as needed, to help those teachers who are having trouble in the classroom. Warranty programs are a form of quality assurance for employing schools.

Telephone consultations, on-site observations, professional development activities, special workshops, and tuition-free in-service courses are some of the support services provided by institutions who have warranty programs. Warranty programs have tended to make teacher education professors and programs more accountable to incoming students and graduates and have forced those programs to reevaluate and design specific skills found in such programs. Teacher warranty programs have enabled institutions of higher education to be more systematically involved in the first year of a teacher's induction period—with both the beginning teacher and the employing school.

Doane College (Nebraska) initiated the first teacher warranty program. Oregon State University–Western Oregon State College, Purdue University, University of Virginia, University of Nebraska-Lincoln, and Grambling State University are but a few of the institutions with teacher warranty programs. (See INDUCTION PERIOD.)

References: John D. Barr, "The Warranty—One Year Later," *Phi Delta Kappan*, Volume 67, Number 2, 1985; *Wingspread Conference on Quality Assurance in Teacher Education*, Sponsored by the OSU–WOSC School of Education and the American Association of Colleges of Teacher Education, (held on May 11, 1986), Washington, DC: American Colleges of Teacher Education, undated.

TEACHING ENGLISH TO SPEAKERS OF OTHER LANGUAGES (TESOL),

a general description of programs that teach English to non-English speaking people. TESOL can be subdivided into two categories: (1) *Teaching English as a Foreign Language* (TEFL), and (2) *Teaching English as a Second Language* (TESL). TEFL stresses literature, culture, and the social aspects of English, and TESL emphasizes communications skill and competence in English. The combination of the two approaches can be found in most TESOL programs. TESOL programs use the aural-oral approach.

TESOL programs are not new. Both the United States and England have had them for many centuries. England made use of TESOL programs in Europe and her colonies, and the United States had programs for American Indians, later for its immigrants. Recently, TESOL programs have been replaced by bilingual programs in many school districts in the United States. Since 1940, both the United States and England have been offering TESOL programs throughout many non-English-speaking countries. (See AURAL-ORAL APPROACH; BILINGUAL-BICULTURAL EDUCATION; and BILINGUAL INSTRUCTION.) TION.)

References: Frank M. Grittner (Editor), *Learning a Second Language* (NSSE 79th Yearbook, Part II), Chicago: University of Chicago Press, 1980; Dorothy Rubin, *Teaching Elementary Language Arts* (Second Edition), New York: Holt, Rinehart and Winston, Inc., 1980.

TEACHING FELLOW—See FELLOWSHIPS

TEACHING LOAD, often defined as the amount of time the teacher spends in the classroom with students (contact hours). Some authorities define teaching load more broadly, including all activities directly related to the duties of a teacher. They include preparation, advising and counseling, marking of papers, and all professional and non-professional duties performed in the school (e.g. lunch or bus duty, committee meetings).

Typically, teaching loads in the high school range from four to six teaching periods a day. At the college or university level, they may range from teaching of one to five courses a semester. In higher education, research work is often reflected in the teaching load.

Several factors enter into the equating of a teaching load. Examples are length of class time, number of students taught, number of sections, number of preparations, size of classes, and types of courses (e.g. lectures, laboratories, seminars). It is frequently difficult to compare teaching loads between or among schools or institutions because of the variations inherent in them.

Most educational institutions establish a standard (minimum) teaching load for administrative purposes.

References: Roald F. Campbell, et al., *Introduction to Educational Administration* (Fifth Edition), Boston: Allyn and Bacon, Inc., 1977; Kenneth E. Eble, *The Craft of Teaching*, San Francisco: Jossey-Bass Publishers, 1978; James R. Marks, et al., *Handbook of Educational Supervision: A Guide for the Practitioner* (Second Edition), Boston: Allyn and Bacon, Inc., 1978.

TEACHING MACHINES, mechanical and electronic devices used for self-instruction. Although teaching machines may be considered to be audiovisual devices, they possess characteristics that make them unique. Some of their distinctive features follow: (1) they require learner responses (overt, covert); (2) they provide various "feedback" information to the learner; (3) they use a systems or logic base and control (e.g. programmed learning, computer programs); (4) they allow, more often than not, for self-pacing of instruction; and (5) they focus on the individual learner as opposed to groups of learners.

In a more technical sense, teaching machines are

the presentation devices, and the programs presented interact with the learner. The programs are based in learning theory, reflect an educational philosophy, do the actual "teaching" or instruction, and are the most important part of any teaching machine.

Teaching machines, as defined above, had their origins in the automatic testing devices developed in the late 1920s by S. L. Pressey. From them and others, research developed to ascertain their instructional effectiveness. The teaching machines and programmed instruction that emerged in the 1950s and 1960s were developed on the basis of this research.

Although there are many different types of teaching machines, the computer and computer programs have replaced programmed textbooks and display devices (teaching machines) as the major type used in many schools. (See COMPUTER-ASSISTED INSTRUCTION; COMPUTER PROGRAM; and PROGRAMMED INSTRUCTION.)

References: Maxwell H. Goldberg, *Cybernation, Systems, and the Teaching of English,* Urbana, IL: National Council of Teachers of English, 1972; Anne Howe and A. J. Romiszowski, *International Yearbook of Educational and Instructional Technology, 1976/77,* New York: Kogan Page Ltd., 1976; Roger E. Levien, *The Emerging Technology,* New York: McGraw-Hill Book Company, 1972; Arthur Lumsdaine and Robert Glaser (Editors), *Teaching Machines and Programmed Learning,* Washington, DC: Department of Audio-Visual Instruction, NEA, 1960; Joseph B. Margolin and Marvin R. Misch, *Computers in the Classroom,* New York: Spartan Books, 1970.

TEACHING METHOD, an instructional process that is recurrent, applicable to more than one subject area, and sufficiently general to be usable by numerous teachers. Teaching methods of relatively long standing include the lecture method, the discussion method, and the tutorial method. More recently developed methods include instructional television and computer-assisted instruction.

Research evidence has yet to emerge to support the notion that, overall, any one method results in greater achievement gains than another. However, when more limited goals/variables are examined, some specific methods and/or strategies do appear to be superior to others. For example, programmed instruction may be an instructional time-saver for individual learners. Also, factors such as classroom management, adaptation to individual differences, class size, teacher decision making, and content can influence the degree to which a given method results in effective learning.

(See DIRECT INSTRUCTION; LECTURE METHOD; PROGRAMMED INSTRUCTION; and TUTORING.)

References: David C. Berliner and N. L. Gage, "The Psychology of Teaching Methods" in N. L. Gage (Editor), *The Psychology of Teaching Methods* (NSSE 75th Yearbook, Part I)., Chicago: University of Chicago Press, 1976; Robert M. W. Travers (Editor), *Second Handbook of Research on Teaching* (A Project of the AERA), Chicago: Rand McNally College Publishing Company, 1973.

TEACHING PRINCIPAL, an administrative title assigned to a school building administrator who spends more than half of his/her work day teaching.

The National Association of Elementary School Principals reported that 14.6 percent of the principals surveyed held this title in 1958. By 1978, that percentage fell to 3.7 percent. (See HEAD TEACHER and SUPERVISING PRINCIPAL.)

References: Department of Elementary School Principals, NEA, *The Elementary School Principalship in 1968,* Washington, DC: The Department, 1968; Gertrude C. Howard, et al., *The Elementary School Principalship: A Research Study,* Washington, DC: Department of Elementary School Principals, NEA, September 1958; William L. Pharis and Sally B. Zakariya, *The Elementary School Principalship in 1978: A Research Study,* Arlington, VA: National Association of Elementary School Principals, 1979.

TEACHING STATIONS, the physical places or locations in a school that require the services of a full-time teacher. In an elementary school with a full complement of classroom and resource teachers, for example, the grade 5 classroom, the art room, the gymnasium, and the Kindergarten classroom are each separate teaching stations.

Reference: Carter V. Good, Editor, *Dictionary of Education* (Third Edition), New York: McGraw-Hill Book Company, 1973.

TEAM-ASSISTED INDIVIDUALIZATION (TAI), an approach to Cooperative Learning developed by Robert E. Slavin, M. Leavey, and Nancy Madden in the early 1980s. The approach combines cooperative learning incentives with an individualized instructional program; motivation, socialization and meeting the diverse needs of each learner are the major thrusts of TAI. Much of the management functions (e.g., record keeping, scoring of tests, etc.) are assumed by the learner. A TAI approach may include: teams—made up of a mix of students; placement tests, curriculum materials; team study methods; team scores (weekly); team recognition (e.g., "superteams," "goodteams," etc.); small group instruction; homework; quick quizzes; and group-paced units. (See COOPERATIVE LEARNING.)

References: Robert E. Slavin, "Team-Assisted Individualization Combining Cooperative Learning and Individualized Instruction in Mathematics" in Robert E. Slavin, et al., (Editors), *Learning to Cooperate, Cooperating to Learn,* New York: Plenum Publishing, 1985; Robert E. Slavin, et al., *Effects of Student Teams and Individualized Instruction on Student Mathematics Achievement, Attitudes, and Behaviors,* Paper presented at the annual convention of the American Educational Research Association, New York, 1982.

TEAMS-GAMES-TOURNAMENTS (TGT)—See STUDENT TEAMS ACHIEVEMENT DIVISIONS

TEAM TEACHING, an umbrella term describing various forms of instructional organization in which two or more teachers work cooperatively with a group of students. Teachers are grouped on the basis of their complementary abilities and skills. To ensure that the most knowledgeable teacher is placed before students, individual instructors are assigned specific roles that reflect these abilities and skills. The team, frequently (not always) led by a team leader, is responsible for instructional planning as well as teaching. Most team teaching models employ flexible scheduling. This allows for individual, small group, and large group instruction on an as-needed basis. Complex versions of team teaching involve use of media, specialized facilities, and nonprofessionals serving as aides.

Team teaching was popularized in the mid-1950s. Distinguished educators such as Francis Keppel, J. Lloyd Trump, and Robert H. Anderson were closely identified with the team teaching movement. (See DIFFERENTIATED STAFFING.)

References: Leslie J. Chamberlain, *Team Teaching: Organization and Administration,* Columbus, OH: Charles E. Merrill Publishing Company, 1969; National Elementary Principal, *Elementary School Organization: Purposes, Patterns, Perspective,* Washington, DC: National Education Association, 1961; Judson T. Shaplin and Henry Y. Olds (Editors), *Team Teaching,* New York: Harper and Row, Publishers, 1964.

TECHNICAL EDUCATION, those educational and training programs that prepare individuals for jobs and occupations requiring technical skills. Technical education is not considered as being equivalent to college-level (baccalaureate) study, although, in recent years, many engineering colleges have introduced technical education curricula (e.g. Industrial Technology). Such programs do not produce engineers or scientists; rather, they prepare individuals for managerial, training, or other such positions allied to engineering.

Technical education is more commonly offered in vocational high schools, trade schools, and many community colleges. At this level, programs can range from relatively short sequences designed to train clerical workers, data processors, craftsmen, and other less technically skilled positions in industry to posthigh school curricula that prepare semiprofessional technicians (e.g. electronics, instrumentation, mechanical technologies). (See VOCATIONAL EDUCATION.)

References: Roy Butler, *Cooperative Vocational Education Program: Staff Development,* Columbus, OH: ERIC Clearinghouse on Vocational and Technical Education, Center for Vocational and Technical Education, Ohio State University, 1973; G. Harold Silvius and Ralph C. Bohn, *Planning and Organizing Instruction* (Second Edition), Bloomington, IL: McKnight and McKnight Publishing Company, 1976; G. Harold Silvius and Estell H. Curry, *Managing Multiple Activities in Industrial Education* (Second Edition), Bloomington, IL: McKnight and McKnight Publishing Company, 1971.

TELEBINOCULAR—See STEREOSCOPE

TELELECTURE, the transmittal of a lecturer's presentation from one location to one or more classrooms that may be located in different (even widely separated) locations. Students in the classroom, using two-way communication capability common to telelecture systems, may question the lecturer. Such questions are heard by all viewers as well as the lecturer. The telelecture technique is used by some universities and for management training. The system consists of amplification equipment located in the lecture room and in each classroom, these connected by standard telephone lines.

References: James W. Brown, et al., *AV Instruction: Technology, Media, and Methods* (Fifth Edition), New York: McGraw-Hill Book Company, 1977; A. J. Romiszowski, *The Selection and Use of Instructional Media,* London England: Kogan Page Ltd., 1974.

TELEVISION—See INSTRUCTIONAL TELEVISION

TEMPERA, a particular type of paint. Pigments, in paste form, are mixed with either egg yolk, milk of figs, gums, varnishes, fatty oil, wax, or other emulsions and then used by the artists on an absorbent fabric. Although different emulsions can be used, the use of egg yolks is most frequently associated with this paint mixture. Consequently, tempera is generally assumed to imply an egg yolk emulsion.

The use of tempera colors dates back to the 1100s and 1200s in Europe, although the ancient Romans and Egyptians used the materials as paint binders.

Tempera colors dry immediately and, over time, harden and become very durable. The colors will last for centuries.

References: Ralph Mayer, *A Dictionary of Art Terms and Techniques,* New York: Thomas Y. Crowell, 1969; Harold Osborne (Editor), *The Oxford Companion to Art,* Oxford, England: Oxford at the Clarendon Press, 1970; Frank Wachowiak and David Hodge, *Art in Depth: A Qualitative Program for the Young Adolescent,* Scranton, PA: International Textbook Company, 1970.

TENURE, permanent job status granted to employees following successful completion of a probationary period. The first law making teacher tenure possible was passed by the Massachusetts legislature in 1886.

Numerous reasons are given in support of teacher tenure laws. Principal arguments are: (1) to protect teachers from unjust dismissal; (2) to keep the schools free from domination by political or other noneducational interests; and (3) to formalize procedures for discharging undesirable teachers. Most states have statutes granting tenure protection for teachers. Most public and private institutions of higher education also grant tenure. The usual probationary period is three years for school district employees and up to seven years for college and university faculty. For tenure purposes, most states have defined "teacher" liberally, granting entitlement to most professional positions except the superintendency.

Tenured personnel may be dismissed for cause (e.g. incompetency, immorality, conduct unbecoming a teacher). School boards are usually required to state specific reasons for dismissal and to grant the teacher a hearing. Tenured teachers may also be dismissed when positions are abolished for bona fide reasons such as a lack of students or staffing reductions following consolidation of school districts.

References: Howard R. Bowen and Jack H. Schuster, *American Professors: A National Resource Imperiled,* New York: Oxford University Press, 1986; Paul H. Morrill and Emil R. Spees, *The Academic Profession: Teaching in Higher Education,* New York: Human Sciences Press, Inc., 1982; Leroy J. Peterson, et al., *The Law and Public School*

Operation (Second Edition), New York: Harper and Row, Publishers, 1978; Robert R. Sherman, *What is Tenure? A Critical Explanation,* Washington, DC: American Federation of Teachers, AFL-CIO, 1973.

TEPS COMMISSION—See NATIONAL COMMISSION ON TEACHER EDUCATION AND PROFESSIONAL STANDARDS

TERMAN, LEWIS (January 15, 1877–December 21, 1956), a professor of education and psychology at Stanford University from 1910 to 1942. In 1916, Terman authored *The Measurement of Intelligence.* His famous Stanford-Binet intelligence test, used widely throughout the country, was introduced in this volume. During World War I, Terman helped to develop the Army Alpha and Beta Tests. He later created the Stanford Achievement Test and several other instruments measuring achievement, personality, and intelligence. He also contributed the term *I.Q.* to the literature of his field.

In 1921, Terman began his well-known longitudinal study of gifted children (those with I.Q.s above 140). His initial group of subjects numbered 1,528, ranged in age from 3 to 18 years, and had a mean I.Q. of 151. The subjects were followed systematically through college, graduate school, and into their respective occupational fields. The study continued after Terman's death.

Included among Terman's writings were: *Mental and Physical Traits of a Thousand Gifted Children* (1925); *Gifted Child Grows Up* (1947); and *The Gifted Group at Midlife* (1959). Some of these were coauthored; the last title appeared posthumously.

In 1923, Terman was recognized for his work by being elected President of the American Psychological Association. (See GENETIC STUDIES OF GENIUS and INTELLIGENCE QUOTIENT.)

References: May V. Seagoe, *Terman and the Gifted,* Los Altos, CA: William Kaufman, Inc., 1975; Lewis M. Terman, *The Measurement of Intelligence,* Boston: Houghton Mifflin Company, 1916.

TERMINAL BEHAVIOR—See ENTRY BEHAVIOR

TERMINAL PROGRAM, an instructional program that normally requires fewer than four years of posthigh school study to complete and that prepares students for employment rather than additional study. In community colleges, where such programs are often found, students may major in terminal programs such as air-conditioning and refrigeration, dental assisting, auto mechanics, auto body repair, and building construction. Terminal programs are also offered in vocational-technical institutes and some four-year colleges. Most community and vocational-technical colleges offer both degree (e.g. A.A.) and nondegree terminal programs.

References: James Cass and Max Birnbaum, *Comparative Guide to Two-Year Colleges and Career Programs,* New York: Harper and Row, Publishers, 1976; Maureen Matheson (Editor), *The College Handbook, 1979–80,* New York: College Entrance Examination Board, 1979.

TERRITORIALITY—See PROXEMICS

TESOL—See TEACHING ENGLISH TO SPEAKERS OF OTHER LANGUAGES

TEST ANXIETY, a state of psychological anxiousness caused, directly or indirectly, by test taking. Some of the many factors that have been known to contribute to test anxiety are poor history of test taking, prior failure, frustration, parental and/or teacher expectations, peer pressure, unrealistic achievement motivation, the physical environment in which a test is administered (e.g. poor lighting, heat in a room), time restrictions, reading level of the test, and test difficulty per se. In some cases, individuals from different socioeconomic levels have different test-taking experiences, with those from lower socioeconomic levels often having less test-taking experience than those from higher levels. Thus, the lower SES group members may have higher test anxiety than do their counterparts from higher SES groups.

References: Anne Anastasi, *Psychological Testing* (Sixth Edition), New York: Macmillan Publishing Company, 1988; Charles D. Hopkins and Richard L. Antes, *Classroom Measurement and Evaluation,* Itasca, IL: F. E. Peacock Publishers, Inc., 1978; Irwin G. Sarason (Editor), *Test Anxiety: Theory, Research and Applications,* Hillsdale, NJ: Lawrence Erlbaum Associates, Publishers, 1980.

TEST BATTERY, examinations composed of several subtests. Each of the subtests measures a different or unique trait, ability, characteristic, or level of knowledge that makes up the larger criterion (measure). Usually, a total score for a test battery is determined by computing a weighted sum of the subtests. There are test batteries, however, where a total score may not be available. In such cases, scores from several individual subtests may be used.

For example, the *Wechsler IQ Test* produces three scores: a verbal I.Q., a performance I.Q., and total I.Q. The verbal and performance I.Q. scores are the sums of six subtests each; the total I.Q. score is derived from the other two I.Q. scores. Illustrating another type of battery is the *General Aptitude Test Battery,* developed by the United States Employment Service (for occupational counseling). It is made up of nine subtests: intelligence; verbal; numerical; spatial; form perception; clerical perception; motor coordination; finger dexterity; and manual dexterity. In counseling, combinations of these subtests may be used selectively, depending on the occupation. (See INTELLIGENCE QUOTIENT.)

References: Anne Anastasi, *Psychological Testing* (Third Edition), New York: Macmillan Publishing Company, Inc., 1968; Robert L. Thorndike, *Educational Measurement* (Second Edition), Washington, DC: American Council on Education, 1971.

TEST OF ENGLISH AS A FOREIGN LANGUAGE (TOEFL), a standardized test used to assess English language skills of those whose native language is not English. The test is frequently required of foreign students applying for admission to colleges and universities in the United States. TOEFL is composed of six subtests: (1) listening; (2) comprehension; (3) English structure; (4) vocabulary; (5) reading comprehension; and (6) writing. The test, which yields scores for each subtest plus a total score, is administered in many non-English-speaking nations throughout the world (about 135). Students take the test before coming to the United States to study. A test kit is available for individuals who wish to know more about TOEFL. Many American colleges and universities set a minimum score for admission of those taking the TOEFL. The test is published by the Educational Testing Service and is administered by the College Entrance Examination Board and the Graduate Record Examination Board.

References: Harriet N. Moreno, et al., *TOEFL,* New York: Arco, 1974; *Understanding TOEFL: Test Kit I,* Princeton, NJ: Test of English as a Foreign Language, 1980.

TEST OF GENERAL EDUCATIONAL DEVELOPMENT (GED), standardized examination that, if passed, qualifies adults who have not completed high school to earn a high school equivalency diploma. Persons who pass the Test of GED are considered to have an academic background equivalent to that of a regular high school graduate. The test may be taken by adults even if they have never attended a high school. A large number of colleges recognize the high school equivalency diploma for admissions purposes.

The Test of General Education Development was developed in 1943 (by the American Council on Education) to accommodate World War II veterans whose high school careers were interrupted by military service. The test, revised in 1973, consists of five subtests: Test I, *Writing Skills* (Spelling 10 percent, English Usage 45 percent, Sentence Correction 30 percent, Logic and Organization 15 percent); Test II, *Social Studies* (Economics 20 percent, Geography 15 percent, Political Science 20 percent, History 25 percent, Behavioral Science 20 percent); Test III, *Science* (Biology 50 percent, Earth Science 20 percent, Chemistry 15 percent, Physics 15 percent); Test IV, *Reading Skills* (General Reading 35 percent, Prose Literature 35 percent, Practical Reading 15 percent, Poetry 10 percent, Drama 5 percent); and Test V, *Mathematics* (Arithmetic 55 percent, Algebra 25 percent, Geometry 20 percent).

Passing scores vary from one state to another. Information about testing centers (locations) and passing scores may be obtained from state departments of education.

Reference: David R. Turner, *The New High School Equivalency Diploma Tests: Secondary Level Test of General Educational Development*, New York: Arco, 1979.

TEST-RETEST—See RELIABILITY

TESTS IN PRINT, an index of tests, test reviews, and literature on specific tests edited by Oscar Krisen Buros, the late Director of the Institute of Mental Measurements. *TESTS IN PRINT* (*I*) was published in 1961 as a guide and index to the first five editions of the *Mental Measurements Yearbook*.

TESTS IN PRINT (*II*) includes: a bibliography of all known tests for English-speaking people; an index for the *Mental Measurements Yearbooks,* up to 1974; "Standards for Educational and Psychological Tests"; bibliographies on the construction, use, and validity of specific tests, through 1971; a list of tests that have gone out of print since 1961; a cumulative name index for each test, with references; publishers' directory and index; an index of names; a scanning index; and several other sections that make the text useful to teachers and school personnel.

Reference: Oscar K. Buros (Editor), *Tests in Print II*, Highland Park, NJ: The Gryphon Press, 1974.

TESTS OF SIGNIFICANCE, statistical procedures used by researchers to determine whether any differences (changes) found in a study occurred by chance or whether the differences are true differences. Such tests are used as bases for rejecting or not rejecting null hypotheses.

Tests of significance are made at a particular probability level. The probability level of $0.05(p = 0.05)$ means that the difference found would be expected to occur 5 out of 100 times by chance. Thus, if a difference did reach the 0.05 level of chance, the researcher would conclude that the difference was significant and would reject the null hypothesis concerning the particular event. The 0.01 level (1 out of 100 times) is more conservative and would result in less null hypothesis rejection; the 0.001 level (1 out of 1,000 times) is even more conservative than either of the others.

There are many statistical tests used to determine levels of significance. *F*-Ratio, t-tests, analysis of variance, and chi square are the ones more commonly used in educational research. (See ANALYSIS OF VARIANCE; CHI SQUARE TEST; *F*-RATIO; HYPOTHESES; t-TEST; and TYPE I (ALPHA) AND TYPE II (BETA) ERRORS.)

References: L. R. Gay, *Educational Research: Competencies for Analysis and Application* (Third Edition), Columbus, OH: Charles E. Merrill Publishing Company, 1987; William M. Hays, *Statistics* (Fourth Edition), New York: Holt, Rinehart and Winston, Inc., 1988; David S. Moore and George P. McCabe, *Introduction to the Practice of Statistics*, New York: W. H. Freeman and Company, 1989.

TESTWISENESS, skill in taking tests demonstrated by individuals who have become accustomed to the tester and/or the process of test taking. Test-naive individuals, Jason Millman and associates pointed out, need to be taught how to take tests if high levels of test validity are to be maintained. (They offered several "principles of testwiseness" to demonstrate the nature and extent of testwiseness.) Lee Cronbach reported that simple improvement in test taking can increase I.Q. test scores by as much as six points. He also cautioned that scores ascribed to very young children are likely to be conditioned by lack of test-taking experience, hence should be interpreted with care.

References: Lee J. Cronbach, *Educational Psychology* (Third Edition), New York: Harcourt Brace Jovanovich, Inc., 1977; Lee J. Cronbach, *Essentials of Psychological Testing* (Fourth Edition), New York: Harper and Row, Publishers, 1984; J. Millman, et al., "An Analysis of Test-Wiseness," *Educational and Psychological Measurement*, Autumn 1965.

TEXTBOOKS, books used by students as a standard work in connection with a particular branch of study. Textbooks, Ernest Hilton reported, are among the oldest of instructional tools used in schools. Their use has increased regularly in recent years, heightened by society's demand for a literate society. Early texts were often value-laden, emphasizing morality. Currently, the type of textbook most commonly used in elementary schools is the basal reader. Textbooks seldom contain new information; rather, they "package" knowledge in some orderly fashion and in keeping with widely used syllabi.

Procedures used to select (adopt) textbooks are of two types, these determined at the state level. States whose laws/regulations require adoption at the state level are known as "state adoption states"; in contrast, "open territory states" leave the matter of selection to the local school district.

Numerous readability formulas have been developed that authors follow and that also provide researchers with a basis for determining a book's difficulty. Research and literature dealing with textbooks generally reflect three areas of interest: (1) aim and function; (2) production and marketing; and (3) selection and evaluation. (See READABILITY.)

References: Lee Burress, et al., *The Students' Right to Know*, Urbana, IL: National Council of Teachers of English, 1982; Raymond English, "The Politics of Textbook Adoption," *Phi Delta Kappan*, December 1980; *El-Hi Textbooks in Print: 1979*, New York: R. R. Bowker Company, 1979; Ernest Hilton, "Textbooks," in Robert L. Ebel (Editor), *Encyclopedia of Educational Research* (Fourth Edition), New York: The Macmillan Company, 1969.

TEXTILES AND CLOTHING, an area of the home economics curriculum concerned with fibers, materials, and the design, care, function, and use of textiles. The use of textiles in clothing and furniture is also studied.

Sociology, psychology, economics, chemistry, art, design, and mathematics are studied as these relate to textiles and clothing. Textiles and clothing includes subjects such as: dress; wardrobe planning; fashion illustration; fabric apparel; textile industry; chemistry; sewing; clothing selection; design elements (color, line, form, shape, texture); merchandising; clothing construction; fiber; clothing care; fashion; and design principles (e.g. balances, proportion, scale). Textiles and clothing, as an area of study, is found in the curricula of numbers of high schools, vocational and trade schools,

and colleges and universities. (See HOME ECONOMICS.)

References: Arline K. Morrison, *Experimental Stitchery and Other Fiber Techniques*, Englewood Cliffs, NJ: Prentice-Hall, Inc., 1977; John M. Woodhouse, *Science for Textile Designers*, London, England: Elek Ltd., 1976; American Home Economics Association, *Textiles Handbook* (Fifth Edition), Washington, DC: The Association, 1974.

T-GROUP, or training group, a technique used in human relations training laboratories that focuses on interpersonal and intrapersonal learnings and relationships. A T-Group is a small, artificially developed primary group of people brought together to learn about themselves, how they affect others, how to interact effectively with others, and group dynamics. By design, it is concerned primarily with process (affectively oriented). The training is nonconventional (i.e. the group decides what it wants to talk about) and involves high levels of intense participation by all individuals. Because it is a training group, it is expected that what is learned by the participants will be "taken home" and used. Each T-Group is led by a trainer or staff member.

The T-Group idea originated in a 1946 workshop held in New Britain, Connecticut. Kurt Lewin, Ronald Lippett, Kenneth Benne, and Leland Bradford were the main professional staff members involved in that historic group session. The next summer the group moved to Gould Academy in Bethel, Maine. The year-round National Training Laboratories (NTL) developed out of these summer workshops. (See SENSITIVITY TRAINING.)

References: Dee G. Appley and Alvin E. Winder, *T-Groups and Therapy Groups in a Changing Society*, San Francisco: Jossey-Bass Publishers, 1973; Leland P. Bradford, et al. (Editors), *T-Group Theory and Laboratory Method*, New York: John Wiley and Sons, 1964; Cary L. Cooper and I. L. Mangham (Editors), *T-Groups*, London, England: Wiley-Interscience, 1971.

THEMATIC TEACHING, the organization of teaching and learning around a specific theme (e.g. love, kinship, morality, family living, war, humor, self-image, decision making). Although themes may be used in a single subject area such as English, sociology, or literature, two or more subject areas may be integrated using a single thematic approach. For example, mathematics, language arts, history, literature, film making, sociology, economics, and psychology may be programmatically integrated around the theme "family living." The thematic approach may be used at all levels of instruction, although it is most often found in grades 7-12 and in higher education. Thematic teaching may be seen as having a relationship to curricular organizations such as Core. Thematic teaching as it is used today was introduced in the 1920s.

References: Dwight L. Burton, et al., *Teaching English Today*, Boston: Houghton Mifflin Company, 1975; Jean L. Flandrin, *Families in Former Times*, Cambridge, England: Cambridge University Press, 1979; Sylvia Spann and Mary Beth Culp, *Thematic Units in Teaching English and the Humanities*, Urbana, IL: National Council of Teachers of English, 1977.

THEORY "X" AND THEORY "Y", a theory relating to motivation of people who work in organizations. Theory "X," appearing at one end of a leadership style continuum, holds that the average person dislikes work, needs to be controlled by higher authority, and prefers being directed. Theory "Y," at the other end, suggests that physical and mental work, like play, are satisfying; that man will exercise self-direction if committed to his organization's goals; that the best rewards are satisfaction of ego and self-actualization; that the average individual can learn to accept and seek responsibility as a matter of course; and, finally, that high levels of creativity and ingenuity are commonly to be found among people. The theory, authored by Douglas M. McGregor, is of interest to administrators, because it calls attention to discrete leadership styles, either of which may be effective or ineffective depending on the situation.

References: Richard A. Gorton, *School Administration and Supervision: Important Issues, Concepts, and Case Studies* (Second Edition), Dubuque, IA: Wm. C. Brown Company, Publishers, 1980; Douglas M. McGregor, *The Human Side of Enterprise*, New York: McGraw-Hill Book Company, 1960.

THERAPY, usually planned activities used in the treatment of a real or imagined problem (medical, psychological, physical). Psychological treatment, drugs, physical therapy, and planned exercises are illustrative of the common therapies used to correct such problems. Other forms of therapy include behavior, client-centered, music, dance, art, nondirective, occupational, play, and supportive.

Therapy may be guided (or administered) by a single therapist or may occur as part of group interaction. Some group therapy is a function of individuals interacting with each other without a therapist; in other groups, a therapist may be leading, directing, or modifying group behavior so that group interactions will have maximal therapeutic value for group members.

References: Billie S. Ables and Jeffrey M. Brandsma, *Therapy for Couples*, San Francisco: Jossey-Bass Publishers, 1977; Paul Nordoff and Clive Robbins, *Therapy in Music for Handicapped Children*, New York: St. Martin's Press, 1972; Charles E. Schaefer, et al., *Therapies for Psychosomatic Disorders in Children*, San Francisco: Jossey-Bass Publishers, 1979.

THIRTY SCHOOLS STUDY—See EIGHT-YEAR STUDY

THOMISM, a body of philosophy based on the medieval scholastic writings of St. Thomas Aquinas (1225-74), the Roman Catholic philosopher and theologian. Reason, faith, and experience are important parts of the Thomistic philosophy. St. Thomas brought together the doctrines of truth and faith through inductive and deductive reasoning. For example, in his *Summa Theologica*, he developed five proofs for the existence of God. The principles of Being, Identity and Noncontradiction, Substance, Sufficient Reasons, Causability (Efficient Causality, Finality), and Absolute Perfection are all part of Thomism. Modern philosophers who have built their philosophies on Thomism are called Neo-Scholastics or Neo-Thomists. (See AQUINAS, ST. THOMAS.)

References: Rudolph G. Bandas, *Contemporary Philosophy and Thomistic Principles*, New York: The Bruce Publishing Company, 1932; Sir Helen John, *Thomist Spectrum*, New York: Fordham University Press, 1966; John S. Morreall, *Analogy and Talking About God: A Critique of the Thomistic Approach*, Washington, DC: University Press of America, 1978.

THORNDIKE, EDWARD L. (August 31, 1874–August 9, 1949), internationally renowned educator, psychologist, and authority on measurement. Thorndike earned his doctorate at Columbia College and later taught at Teachers College, Columbia University (1899-1940). Because of his numerous studies dealing with learning, intelligence, intelligence testing, aptitude testing, and teaching, he came to be called the father of modern educational psychology. His writings, including the three-volume *The Psychology of Learning*, published in 1913-14, did much to influence professional thinking during that period. A vocabulary list containing 10,000 (later 20,000) of the most commonly used words in the English language led to publication of his widely used dictionaries, *Thorndike Century Junior Dictionary* (1935) and the *Thorndike Century Senior Dictionary* (1941).

In the early 1920s, Thorndike was appointed director of Columbia University's Division of Educational Psychology, a unit in the newly created Institute of Educational Research. He held this position until 1940.

During his lifetime, Thorndike authored hundreds of books and articles. He received seven honorary degrees; in 1934, he was honored by being elected to the presidency of the American Association for the Advancement of Science.

References: Geraldine Joncich, *The Sane Positivist: A Biography of Edward L. Thorndike,* Middletown, CT: Wesleyan University Press, 1968; Don C. Locke, "Thorndike, Edward Lee" in John F. Ohles (Editor), *Biographical Dictionary of American Educators* (Volume 3), Westport, CT: Greenwood Press, 1978.

TIAA-CREF, *T*eachers *I*nsurance and *A*nnuity *A*ssociation and *C*ollege *R*etirement *E*quities *F*und, companion nonprofit annuity companies. Their principal purpose is to provide retirement benefits for employees of colleges, universities, independent schools, and a limited number of other educational institutions.

TIAA was founded in 1918 by the Carnegie Foundation for the Advancement of Teaching. Using employee and employer contributions, it invests almost exclusively in fixed-dollar obligations, primarily bonds and mortgages. Proceeds from these investments are used to provide the retiree with a fixed-dollar annual income for life.

CREF, though a separate nonprofit corporation, is closely associated with TIAA. It was established in 1952 as a vehicle through which professors and other TIAA participants could purchase "units" (similar to shares in a mutual fund). Investments in a diversified common stock fund provide the member with a "variable annuity." The market value of these variable annuity units changes with the state of the economy. Theoretically, CREF units, as supplements to TIAA, are designed to provide the retiree with a hedge against inflation, the dollar amount received increasing as common stock market prices move upward.

More than 3,000 institutions participate in the TIAA-CREF program. In 1977, TIAA-CREF assets totalled $6,000,000,000.

References: Best's Insurance Reports, Life-Health (73rd Annual Edition), Oldwick, NJ: A. M. Best Company, 1978; Francis P. King and Thomas J. Cook, *Benefit Plans in Higher Education.,* New York: Columbia University Press, 1980; Teachers Insurance and Annuity Association, *The Role of TIAA-CREF in Higher Education,* New York: The Association, 1977.

TIME, SPACE, AND MATTER—See SECONDARY SCHOOL SCIENCE PROJECT

TINKER v. DES MOINES INDEPENDENT SCHOOL DISTRICT, important law case in which the U.S. Supreme Court ruled (1969) that students had the right to wear antiwar armbands in school. In supporting the right of students to wear armbands in the schools, the Court observed that the "Constitution does not stop at the public school doors like a puppy waiting for his master, but instead it follows the student through the corridors into the classroom, and onto the athletic field" (Eve Cary, p. 28). The First Amendment rights of student expression are to be protected even if the views of some students offend others, the Court ruled, except in those instances where the process of education is "materially and substantially" disrupted by such expressions. Although this case was delimited to the wearing of armbands, it is considered significant because the Court's reasoning affects other forms of student expression as well (e.g. student newspapers).

In keeping with the Tinker decision, subsequent court decisions have held that a school board is within its rights to regulate against insignias (including racial symbols) that are likely to precipitate disruptions. However, in 1988 the U.S. Supreme Court, in *Hazelwood School District v. Kuhlmeier,* ruled that under certain conditions schools can have editorial control over student articles that appear in a school sponsored newspaper. (See *HAZELWOOD SCHOOL DISTRICT v. KUHLMEIER.*)

References: Eve Cary, *What Every Teacher Should Know About Student Rights,* Washington, DC: National Education Association, 1975; Frank R. Kemerer and Kenneth L. Deutsch, *Constitutional Rights and Student Life: Value Conflict in Law and Education,* St. Paul, MN: West Publishing Company, 1979; Leroy J. Peterson, et al., *The Law and the Public School Operation* (Second Edition), New York: Harper and Row, Publishers, Inc., 1978; *Tinker v. Des Moines Independent Community School District,* 393 U.S. 503, 89 S.Ct. 733, 21 L.Ed. 2d 731 (Iowa 1969).

TITLE I—See ELEMENTARY AND SECONDARY EDUCATION ACT

TITLE IX, well-known title of the Education Amendments of 1972 that prohibits discrimination on the basis of sex. It states: "No person in the United States shall, on the basis of sex, be excluded from participation in, be denied the benefits of, or be subjected to discrimination under any education program receiving federal financial assistance" (p.

373). This legislation covers all educational institutions receiving federal financial assistance, preschool through higher education. Excepted are the admissions policies of certain religious schools, sororities and fraternities, and certain youth service organizations (e.g. Girl Scouts, YMCA).

Title IX, contrary to popular opinion, protects males as well as females from discrimination. The regulations for implementing this legislation address several athletic program matters such as having separate teams for each sex in contact sports, equal opportunity for use of athletic facilities, and practice schedule parity. Additionally, they prohibit sex discrimination in pension benefits, employment practices, compensation, financial aid, facilities, and counseling.

References: Robert Cole, "Title IX: A Long Dazed Journey into Rights," *Phi Delta Kappan,* May 1976; Charlotte B. Hallam, "Legal Tools to Fight Sex Discrimination," *Phi Delta Kappan,* October 1973; Public Law 92-318, *United States Statutes at Large, 1972* (Volume 86), Washington, DC: U.S. Government Printing Office, 1973; Norma Raffel, *Title IX: How It Affects Elementary and Secondary Education* (Report No. 80), Denver, CO: Education Commission of the States, 1976.

TOMORROW'S TEACHERS, A REPORT TO THE HOLMES GROUP (1986), focusing on major reforms in teacher education. The report delineated five goals for the reform of teacher education. It then suggested the rationale behind the goals and plans for their attainment. The goals put forth by the Holmes Group are as follows:

1. To make the education of teachers intellectually more solid.
2. To recognize differences in teachers' knowledge, skill, and commitment, in their education, certification, and work.
3. To create standards of entry into the profession—examination and educational requirements—that are professionally relevant and intellectually defensible.
4. To connect our own institutions to schools.
5. To make schools better places for teachers to work, and to learn. (p. 4)

Among the changes suggested in the report are: a three-tiered system of teacher licensing—instructor, professional teacher, and career professional; the abolishment of undergraduate education majors in the university; and the strengthening of education in academic subjects.

References: Holmes Group, *Tomorrow's Teachers, a Report of the Holmes Group,* East Lansing, MI: The Holmes Group Inc., 1986.

TONE, a fixed musical sound that has a certain pitch. More technically, it is the sum of two semitones (e.g. the interval between the notes C and D, F and G, E-flat and F). The term is also used when referring to the musical quality of an instrument or voice.

References: Bruce Bohle (Editor), *The International Cyclopedia of Music and Musicians* (Tenth Edition), New York: Dodd, Mead and Company, 1975; William Drabkin, "Tone" in Stanley Sadie (Editor), *The New Grove Dictionary of Music and Musicians* (Volume 19), London, England: Macmillan Publishers Limited, 1980; J. A. Westrup and F. L. Harrison (Revised by Conrad Wilson), *The New College Encyclopedia of Music,* New York: W. W. Norton and Company, Inc., 1976.

TOP-DOWN MODEL OF READING, a theory of the reading process that views reading as a psycholinguistic guessing game. An efficient reader utilizes the fewest and most productive cues from the text in order to comprehend the author's message; she/he draws on prior experience and learning as well as knowledge of the language in the process. Two early proponents of this meaning-based theory were Kenneth Goodman and Frank Smith. In learning to read, children must be encouraged to use prior knowledge and to predict by making use of everything they know; frequently, their own language and experience form the foundations for the reading program in adhering to this theory (See LANGUAGE EXPERIENCE APPROACH.)

References: Patrick J. Finn, *Helping Children Learn to Read,* New York: Random House, 1985; Kenneth S. Goodman, Reading: A Psycholinguistic Guessing Game, in H. Singer and R. B. Ruddell (Eds.), *Theoretical Models and Processes of Reading,* Newark, DE: International Reading Association, 1970; Lenore H. Ringler and Carl K. Weber, *A Language-Thinking Approach to Reading Diagnosis and Teaching,* New York: Harcourt Brace Jovanovich, Publishers, 1984; Frank Smith, *Understanding Reading: A Psycholinguistic Analysis of Reading and Learning to Read* (2nd Edition), New York: Holt, Rinehart and Winston, 1978.

TORT LIABILITY, a legal term, holds one accountable for wrongdoing, either intentional or through negligence, that causes injury to the person or property of another. Two common torts are *negligence,* which causes personal injury, and *defamation of character.* The law holds that individual citizens, including school children, enjoy certain rights such as freedom from harm and enjoyment of liberty. Tort action is initiated when there is reason to believe that the behavior of one individual violated these rights of another. In tort cases, injured parties seek damages through civil procedure.

In most states, school districts are considered to be immune from tort liability. Teachers employed in these districts are individually liable, however, providing it can be shown that they were negligent and, furthermore, that their negligence was the "proximate cause" of the injury sustained.

Cases of negligence are most often found in a school building's "high danger" areas—gymnasia, playgrounds, shops, and science laboratories. Teachers responsible for supervising these areas have been found to be negligent either for lack of appropriate supervision or for failure to provide and/or insist on use of appropriate safety devices (mats, goggles, etc.). (See NEGLIGENCE and PROXIMATE CAUSE.)

References: Kern Alexander, et al., *Public School Law: Cases and Materials*, St. Paul, MN: West Publishing Company, 1969; Ronald E. Rebore, *Educational Administration: A Management Approach*, Englewood Cliffs, NJ: Prentice-Hall, Inc., 1985; E. Edmund Reutter, Jr. and Robert R. Hamilton, *The Law of Public Education* (Second Edition), Mineola, NY: The Foundation Press, Inc., 1976.

TOTAL COMMUNICATION, a method for teaching language and communication to hearing impaired students. Over the years, either of two distinct methods, the *manual* and the *oral*, have been used to teach deaf pupils. Each method has attracted proponents who, in the main, have been unwilling to see value in any method other than their own. Total communication, a relatively recent approach, is a compromise between the manual and oral philosophies. It makes use of oral speech, speech reading, signing, and finger spelling (manual alphabet) in teaching the deaf. (See AURAL-ORAL APPROACH; FINGER SPELLING; ROCHESTER METHOD; and SIGN LANGUAGE.)

References: Lloyd M. Dunn (Editor), *Exceptional Children in the Schools: Special Education in Transition*, New York: Holt, Rinehart and Winston, Inc., 1973; Maynard C. Reynolds and Jack W. Birch, *Teaching Exceptional Children in All America's Schools: A First Course for Teachers and Principals*, Reston, VA: Council for Exceptional Children, 1977.

TRACKING, an intraschool system for grouping students either on the basis of ability or curriculum. This approach to school organization is employed widely in the high schools of America. In elementary schools, the term *ability grouping* is commonly used.

Research undertaken to test the educational viability of tracking has yielded conflicting findings. Some investigations (e.g. those included in the NEA's 1968 ability grouping survey) have reported some achievement gain associated with tracking; others have found no such relationship. Still other studies have shown that certain segments of the student population (e.g. rapid learners) do profit from tracking based on ability.

Studies of a sociological nature have also been undertaken, primarily to examine the effects of tracking on students from lower socioeconomic families. Some of these have shown that tracking can work to the disadvantage of such pupils by limiting their opportunities and aspirations.

Tracking by curriculum normally separates college-bound from noncollege-bound students. Tracks commonly found are: (1) the *college track;* (2) the *general track,* which includes various academic courses offered at a less demanding level; and (3) the *business* (sometimes called the *vocational*) *track,* which is largely job oriented. (See ABILITY GROUPING and STREAMING.)

References: Glen Heathers, "Grouping" in R. L. Ebel (Editor), *Encyclopedia of Educational Research* (Fourth Edition), New York: The Macmillan Company, 1969; Research Division, National Education Association, *Ability Grouping*, Washington, DC: The Association, 1968; James E. Rosenbaum, *Making Inequality: The Hidden Curriculum in High School Tracking*, New York: John Wiley and Sons, 1976.

TRADE AND INDUSTRIAL EDUCATION (T and I), a curriculum component of vocational education that, as its title suggests, is more vocationally oriented, rather than being oriented toward general education as is the industrial arts curriculum. Trade and industry programs are normally made available to students in the last two years of high school and at the adult level. In recent years, they have received considerable support through federal funding. T and I courses are open to students intent on preparing for a vocational career as well as to those interested in skill acquisition only.

The following programs are representative of the many T and I programs available in many American high schools: air conditioning and refrigeration; arc welding; auto body repairing; carpentry; food trades; landscape gardening; needle trades; plumbing and pipefitting; radio and television repairing; shoe repairing; and upholstering.

References: Rudyard K. Bent and Adolph Unruh, *Secondary School Curriculum*, Lexington, MA: D. C. Heath and Company, 1969; Calfrey C. Calhoun and Alton V. Finch, *Vocational and Career Education: Concepts and Oper-*

ations, Belmont, CA: Wadsworth Publishing Company, Inc., 1976.

TRADE BOOK, a book intended for a general readership (e.g. novel, travel book) and one that the publisher hopes will sell well. Trade books are usually sold in bookstores or are available in libraries for general circulation. Special works such as textbooks, juvenile books, or technical books are not considered to be trade books. Trade paperbacks were first introduced in the United States in 1939.

References: Pyke Johnson, Jr., "The Trade Paperback" in Chandler B. Grannis (Editor), *What Happens in Book Publishing* (Second Edition), New York: Columbia University Press, 1967; Jean Peters (Editor), *The Bookman's Glossary* (Fifth Edition), New York: R. R. Bowker Company, 1975; Marda Woodbury, *Selecting Materials for Instruction: Media and the Curriculum,* Littleton, CO: Libraries Unlimited, Inc., 1980.

TRAINABLE RETARDATES—See MENTAL RETARDATION

TRAINING OF TEACHER TRAINERS—See TRIPLE-T PROGRAM

TRAIT-FACTOR COUNSELING, or trait and factor counseling, a form of counseling used by counselors, rehabilitation personnel, and placement counselors. This counseling approach relies heavily on testing data that describe behavior.

Underlying trait-factor counseling is the belief that behaviors can be measured and grouped to help people see clusters of strengths and weaknesses, thus providing a basis for prognosis. This technique is employed in career guidance/ counseling.

Critics of this approach, while agreeing that trait-factor counseling is used to some extent by numerous counselors, tend to have reservations about it on the grounds that it is mechanistic, not a bona fide theory of counseling, and of limited value, because it fails to take the entire developmental process into account. (See TRAIT THEORY.)

References: E. L. Tolbert, *An Introduction to Guidance,* Boston: Little, Brown and Company, 1978; Stephen G. Weinrach, *Career Counseling,* New York: McGraw-Hill Book Company, 1979; Edmund G. Williamson and Donald A. Biggs, "Trait-Factor Theory and Individual Differences" in Herbert M. Burks, Jr. and Buford Stefflre (Editors), *Theories of Counseling* (Third Edition), New York: McGraw-Hill Book Company, 1979.

TRAIT THEORY, an approach devised by psychologists that seeks to foster understanding of human behavior by describing, comparing, and contrasting the characteristics of individuals. Among the traits holding greatest interest for psychologists and teachers are intelligence, verbal ability, emotional stability, and mechanical aptitude.

Students of leadership have also made use of the trait approach, frequently relating specific personal traits with leadership success. Research results in this area have been inconclusive, sometimes even conflicting. One group of authors (Roald Campbell, et al.) hold that: "It is behavior—the way in which the traits are used—rather than the mere possession of the traits, which becomes crucial" (p. 316).

Alfred Binet, Sir Francis Galton, and James Cattell are testing authorities whose names have long been associated with trait studies. (See TRAIT-FACTOR COUNSELING.)

References: Ralph F. Berdie, et al., *Testing in Guidance and Counseling,* New York: McGraw-Hill Book Company, 1963; Roald F. Campbell, et al., *Introduction to Educational Administration* (Third Edition), Boston: Allyn and Bacon, Inc., 1966; Raymond B. Cattell, *The Scientific Analysis of Personality,* Baltimore, MD: Penguin Books, 1965; Raymond B. Cattell and Ralph M. Dreger (Editors), *Handbook of Modern Personality Theory,* Washington, DC: Hemisphere Publishing Corporation, 1977.

TRANSACTIONAL ANALYSIS (TA), an approach to psychotherapy that employs group interaction. Developed in the late 1950s by American psychiatrist Eric Berne, TA makes extensive use of transactions (communication interactions) between and among clients working in a group.

Participants assume any of three ego states (parent, child, adult), or roles, to help each other understand their needs and behaviors. The *parent* state consists of behaviors, attitudes, and feelings (including the "should's" and "ought's") acquired developmentally from one's parents. The *child* state consists of spontaneous, natural feelings and impulses associated with childhood behavior; it generally reflects dependency and helplessness. The *adult* state is the objective part of personality that sorts through available information to reach a decision. The interaction process relies heavily on the giving of "strokes." They are the positive or negative rewards we seek and receive. They can be communicated verbally or nonverbally.

TA is antideterministic. It assumes that individuals are capable of understanding their need for "strokes"; furthermore, that they are capable of overcoming earlier conditioning and habits such that new goals and behaviors can be brought about. TA's use has increased dramatically for at least three reasons: (1) it is applicable to a variety of client groups; (2) it is relatively inexpensive; and (3) it has been popularized by publications such as Thomas Harris's *I'm O.K.—You're O.K.* and Eric Berne's *Games People Play.*

References: Eric Berne, *Games People Play,* New York: Grove Press, 1964; Eric Berne, *Transactional Analysis in Psychotherapy,* New York: Grove Press, 1961; Gerald Corey, *Theory and Practices of Counseling and Psychotherapy,* Monterey, CA: Brooks/Cole Publishing Company, 1977; Steven E. Elson, "Recent Approaches to Counseling, Gestalt Therapy, Transactional Analysis, and Reality Therapy" in Herbert M. Burks, Jr. and Buford Stefflre (Editors), *Theories of Counseling* (Third Edition), New York: McGraw-Hill Book Company, 1979.

TRANSCRIPT, an official record of a student's academic performance at a particular school or college. Courses undertaken and/or completed by the student are listed together with grades earned. Official transcripts usually carry the institution's official seal and often, when used for such purposes as admissions or employment, must be mailed from one institution to another rather than passing through the hands of the student.

Reference: Combined Glossary: Terms and Definitions from the Handbooks of the State Educational Records and Reports Series, Washington, DC: National Center for Education Statistics, U.S. Department of Health, Education, and Welfare, 1974.

TRANSFORMATIONAL GENERATIVE GRAMMAR, a specific type of generative grammar. The generative grammar of a language establishes the sequence of that language. In a formal and explicitly mathematical manner, it sets the design of the sentence structure (string of elements in a sentence) of the language through linguistic theory, a set of specific statements, or a set of rules. Through generative grammar rules and restrictions, sentences are syntactically well formed. As a result, the grammar of the language is predictive, explicit, has a defined structural description, and is finite.

Generative grammar produces phrase-structure rules for a language. For example, a sentence is made up of a noun phrase (NP) and a verb phrase (VP), S = NP + VP, which in turn can be broken down to its smallest elements by following phrase-structure rules. These phrase-structure rules might be algebraic, depending on the complexities of the sentence. The phrase-structure rules generate a string of symbols that form what is termed the *deep structure* of a sentence. Words are then substituted for the symbols from the lexicon of the language. Transformation rules of a language are followed to produce the *surface structure* of a sentence or sentences. They bring together phrase markers and may delete, substitute, or add to the sentence.

Transformation rules provide the procedures through which the meaning and intent flow from the deep structure (Joe kicked the ball) of a sentence in a manner that is acceptable to speakers of the language; this results in the surface structure of a sentence (Joe, my youngest son, kicked the big yellow ball). Noam Chomsky (1957) has been a major influence in this field. (See PSYCHOLINGUISTICS.)

References: Noam Chomsky, *Syntactic Structures,* The Hague, Holland: Mouton, 1957; Bert Jacobsen, *Transformation-Generative Grammar,* Amsterdam, Holland: North-Holland Publishing, 1977; Owen Thomas and Eugene R. Kantgen, *Transformational Grammar and the Teacher of English* (Second Edition), New York: Holt, Rinehart and Winston, Inc., 1974.

TRANSPARENCIES, "films" used with overhead projectors. Light passes through them, resulting in a picture being projected on a screen, wall, or chalkboard. Transparencies are made of clear X-ray film or acetate sheets. *Handmade transparencies* are readily produced by writing or drawing on an acetate sheet using a grease pencil. This technique is sometimes used by lecturers who use the overhead projector and write/draw as they talk. Such markings can be removed easily from the acetate with the use of a tissue. *Machine-made transparencies* are usually prepared via a thermocopy process (running an original document through a thermocopy machine using special film). They are then individually mounted in a cardboard frame to facilitate handling and to extend transparency life. Transparencies can be made in black and white or in color; also, transparency overlays can be used.

Transparencies are widely used in the schools of the United States and Canada. Teachers have found them to be an excellent aid in the classroom. (See OVERHEAD PROJECTION.)

References: Robert Bullough, Sr., *Creating Instructional Materials* (Second Edition), Columbus, OH: Charles E. Merrill Publishing Company, 1978; Robert Heinich, Michael Molenda, and James D. Russell, *Instructional Media and the New Technologies of Instruction* (Second Edition), New York: John Wiley and Sons, 1985; Jerrold E. Kemp and Don C. Smellie, *Planning, Producing and Using Instructional Media* (Sixth Edition), New York: Harper and Row Publishers, 1989.

TRANSPERSONAL PSYCHOLOGY, a movement in psychology that goes beyond those elements that form an individual's personality. Transpersonal Theory holds that personality is only one part of one's individuality; there is a unity between mind and body; acceptance of all parts of oneself is important; and there should be a willingness to consider a variety of phenomena generated by yoga, biofeedback, meditation, intuition, mysticism, etc.

Although built on psychoanalysis and a behavioral and humanistic theory of psychology, transpersonal psychology does not have a strong research or conceptual base. As a result, it does not, at the present time, have a highly developed definition; several proponents feel that transpersonal psychology would become restricted and limited if a highly developed definition were to be formulated.

References: F. Capra, *The Turning Point: Science, Society, and the Rising Culture*, Toronto, Canada: Bantam Books, 1983; J. Fodiman, "The Transpersonal Stance," in M. Mahoney (Editor), *Psychotherapy Process: Current Issues and Future Directions*, New York: Plenum Press, 1980; J. Vincent Peterson and Bernard Nisenholz, *Orientation to Counseling*, Boston: Allyn and Bacon, Inc., 1987; Charles Tart (Editor), *Altered States of Consciousness*, New York: John Wiley and Sons, 1969.

TRIMESTER, one of three academic terms, each approximately 15 weeks long, that together make up a full academic year. A full range of courses is offered each trimester. Students are expected to attend two out of three trimesters. The trimester calendar is more likely to be used at the college than the secondary school level. (See QUARTER, ACADEMIC and SEMESTER.)

Reference: Asa S. Knowles, *Handbook of College and University Administration*, New York: McGraw-Hill Book Company, 1970.

TRIPLE-T PROGRAM, or Training of Teacher Trainers, a U.S. Office of Education effort to reform teacher education. Supported by National Defense Education Act funds, the program consisted of 58 university projects; it also involved hundreds of schools and some 42,000 people. The project was of short duration (1968–73). The TTT

sought to raise education's quality level by strengthening the trainers of teachers and by making liberal arts faculty members more active partners in teacher education. Some TTT innovations became a regular part of local training programs. Failure of TTT to realize several of its objectives has been attributed to several factors including absence of an underlying program rationale, some hurriedly prepared project proposals, and the dominant role played by professors of education.

References: Malcolm M. Provus, *The Grand Experiment*, Berkeley, CA: McCutchan Publishing Corporation, 1975; Gerald R. Smith, et al., *Stirrings in Teacher Education*, Indiana TTT: School of Education, Indiana University, 1974.

TRIVIUM AND QUADRIVIUM, the two major liberal arts categories taught by university arts faculties during the Middle Ages. The trivium was made up of grammar, logic, and rhetoric, and the quadrivium was composed of astronomy, music, arithmetic, and geometry. The trivium and quadrivium have been traced back to the later Roman period (about 400 A.D.). Some elements of the trivium and quadrivium categories are to be found in the humanities and liberal arts curricula of today's institutions of higher education.

In medieval universities, the trivium was the lower level of the liberal arts curriculum, the quadrivium the upper level. The curriculum was designed to provide a broad education to free men. It was not considered to be either technical or professional education.

References: Joseph C. Kiger, "Disciplines" in Lee C. Deighton (Editor), *The Encyclopedia of Education* (Volume 3), New York: The Macmillan Company and The Free Press, 1971; Asa S. Knowles (Editor), *The International Encyclopedia of Higher Education* (Volume 1), San Francisco: Jossey-Bass Publishers, 1977.

TRUANCY, broadly defined as absence from school without permission (i.e. unexcused absences). Truancy is a continuing problem in most schools. It affects, adversely, the education that the student should be receiving; school district funding is also affected in those states in which state aid is based on average daily attendance. In most cases, parents may be held legally accountable for their child's truant behavior.

There may be many reasons for truancy. Some are: personal problems; learning problems; dislike of school; negative attitudes; inability to get along with peers and/or teachers; employment; family problems; personal convenience; recreation; mental illness; and so on. Often, truancy can be reduced with better understanding of its causes and better communication between school and home. (See ATTENDANCE, SCHOOL.)

References: Larry Bartlett, et al., *Absences, A Model Policy and Rules,* Des Moines, IA: Iowa State Department of Public Instruction, 1978; Carole L. Braden, *Compulsory School Attendance Laws and the Juvenile Justice System* (Criminal Justice Monograph, Volume VIII, No. 3), Huntsville, TX: Sam Houston State University, 1978; Nancy DeLeonibus, "Absenteeism: The Perpetual Problem," *The Practitioner,* October 1978.

TRUE-FALSE TEST, an examination whose test items (questions) are relatively simple declarative statements some of which are true, others false. The respondent answers each item with "True" or "False," sometimes "Right" or "Wrong."

The true-false test's disadvantages, test authorities aver, outweigh its advantages. Among the test's weaknesses are the following: (1) it covers relatively small, sometimes unrelated (even trivial) pieces of information; (2) respondents can guess at the right response; and (3) because of test-writing errors, items may be lengthy or ambiguous, thus confusing to the test taker. Additionally, the inclusion of certain qualifying words unintentionally serves to give the respondent a hint at the correct answer. For example, qualifiers such as *never, always,* or *none* are frequently found in false statements. Conversely, words such as *sometimes, generally,* or *may* are often incorporated into true statements. These qualifiers provide the testwise respondent with an unintended clue.

Advantages of the true-false test include ease of administration and scoring. (See TESTWISENESS.)

References: J. Stanley Ahmann and Marvin D. Glock, *Measuring and Evaluating Educational Achievement,* Boston: Allyn and Bacon, Inc., 1971; Robert L. Ebel, *Essentials of Educational Measurement* (Third Edition), Englewood Cliffs, NJ: Prentice-Hall, Inc., 1979; Tom Kubiszyn and Gary Borich, *Educational Testing and Measurement: Classroom Application and Practice* (Second Edition), Glenview, IL: Scott Foresman and Company, 1987.

TRUTH-IN-TESTING LEGISLATION, state legislation requiring test publishers to make public, to those interested, information concerning each test it publishes, including information about its design, scoring, and use. New York State, in 1979, passed the first Truth-in-Testing Law. The law was concerned with standardized tests administered in New York and used for postsecondary or professional school admissions purposes. (Such tests include the Scholastic Aptitude Test, American College Testing Program, Graduate Record Examination, Miller Analogies Test, Medical College Admission Test, and The Law School Admission Test.

The New York legislation requires that background and statistical information on the tests be made a matter of public record. In addition, the examinee may request to see his/her own answer sheet plus a scoring (answer) key. Thus, the tests become "open tests" rather than secure tests (i.e. where the tests are not a matter of public record). Truth-in-Testing legislation is quite controversial and has generated considerable concern among test publishers because of its technical and legal restrictions, the disclosure requirement, and increased costs directly related to the law.

References: Robert L. Jacobson, "New York's 'Truth-in-Testing' Law called a Threat to Quality of the SAT," *The Chronicle of Higher Education,* November 13, 1979; Winsor A. Lott, *New York's "Truth-in-Testing" Bill: A Cost-Benefit Issue,* Paper presented at the Meeting of the National Consortium on Testing, Arlington, VA, May 1979.

T-SCORES—See STANDARD SCORES

t-TEST, a statistical test used in educational research to determine the level of probability that differences between the means of two groups occurred by chance. The t-test, or t-ratio, was first published by William S. Gosset under the pseudonym of "Student." It is also known as the "Student-t." Gosset was a chemist who worked for a brewery in Ireland when he developed the t-distribution and the t-test.

Since there is a t-distribution, after a "t" is calculated one need only refer to a "t" table to determine probability levels. This enables researchers to test hypotheses. (See TESTS OF SIGNIFICANCE.)

References: Walter R. Borg and Meredith D. Gall, *Educational Research: An Introduction* (Fifth Edition), New York: Longman, Inc., 1989; L. R. Gay, *Educational Research: Competencies for Analysis and Application* (Third Edition), Columbus, OH: Merrill Publishing Company, 1987.

TUITION, financial charges assessed students by an educational institution (e.g. college, university, private elementary or secondary school) to pay for instruction. There is no universally established procedure used by all educational institutions to determine tuition costs. Some institutions charge tuition on the basis of each credit hour or course for which the student is registered. Others impose uniform charges for the semester or year. Tuition for undergraduates is frequently different (lower) than that charged graduate students. Fees charged for a particular purpose (e.g. laboratory fees) supplement rather than being a part of tuition.

Tuition in private institutions is usually higher than in public institutions, primarily because public (tax) monies are used to support part (in some cases, most) of the costs of instruction in public schools and colleges. Tuition costs may change from year to year, depending on such factors as nontuition support received by educational institutions, changes in the cost of living, and so on. In almost all instances, tuition received from students defrays but a part of the total instructional costs of an education.

Reference: Asa S. Knowles, *Handbook of College and University Administration* (Volume I), New York: McGraw-Hill Book Company, 1970.

TUSKEGEE INSTITUTE, a private, nonsectarian institution of higher education enrolling predominantly black students. Located in Tuskegee, Alabama, the institute was founded by Booker T. Washington (in 1881) as a normal school. Its mission was broadened soon thereafter to include agricultural and mechanical programs. In 1896, George Washington Carver assumed directorship of the institution's Department of Agriculture and did much to strengthen agricultural research and education at Tuskegee.

Tuskegee has become a major institution sponsoring many undergraduate and graduate degree programs. Its principal units are the Schools of Applied Sciences, Education, Engineering, Nursing, and Veterinary Medicine. Tuskegee Institute enrolls approximately 3,500 students.

References: Tuskegee Institute, *General Information Catalogue: '76–'78,* Tuskegee Institute, AL: The Institute, 1976; Addie Louise Joyner Butler, *The Distinctive Black College: Talladega, Tuskegee and Morehouse,* Metuchen, NJ: The Scarecrow Press, Inc., 1977; Booker T. Washington (Editor), *Tuskegee: Its People, Their Ideals and Achievements,* D. Appleton and Company, 1905 (Reprinted 1969 by Negro Universities Press).

TUTORING, a one-to-one method of instruction. Differentiating tutoring from individualized instruction is the fact that the former includes individual diagnosis and individual instruction (usually structured) as well. Some research has shown this method to be superior to conventional instruction; other studies have reached the opposite conclusion. Some evidence exists to show that, in certain cases, the educational impact of tutoring may be greater on the tutor than on the tutee.

Nonprofessionals (volunteers, aides, etc.) are sometimes engaged as tutors. They typically receive training from professionals and follow highly structured programs prepared for them.

Tutors have been used for centuries at British institutions of higher education. They normally meet once weekly with their individual tutees and critique essays which the tutee delivers orally. (See PEER TUTORING.)

References: Samuel L. Blumenfeld, *How to Tutor,* New Rochelle, NY: Arlington House, 1973; Douglas G. Ellson, "Tutoring" in N. L. Gage (Editor), *The Psychology of Teaching Methods* (NSSE 75th Yearbook, Part I), Chicago: University of Chicago Press, 1976; Will G. Moore, *The Tutorial System and Its Future,* London: England: Pergamon Press, 1968; Keith J. Topping, *The Peer Tutoring Handbook: Promoting Cooperative Learning,* Cambridge, MA: Brookline Books, 1988.

TWO-TAILED TESTS—See ONE-TAILED AND TWO-TAILED TESTS

TYLER'S MODEL OF CURRICULUM DEVELOPMENT, a linear model developed by Ralph Tyler. The model appeared in a small text that he published (*Basic Principles of Curriculum and Instruction*) for a course he was teaching at the University of Chicago in 1949. Tyler raised four questions in the analysis and development of a curriculum (a course or syllabus): What are the educational purposes or reasons for offering a course? What are the educational objectives (or the students to be helped)? How can the educational experiences be organized effectively? and How are the goals and purposes of the curriculum to be assessed/evaluated?

The primary sources of a curriculum are: (1) the student, (2) the subject matter, and (3) the society/community. From these sources instructional objectives are formulated in the context of both a philosophy of education and a psychology of learning. Content and learning experiences evolve from the instructional objectives. The last element of the model is evaluation—assessing or determining whether the goals, objectives, and purposes of the curriculum have been met. (See OBJECTIVES.)

References: Christopher M. Clark and Penelope L. Peterson, "Teacher's Thought Process," in Merlin C. Wittrock (Editor), *Handbook of Research on Teaching* (Third Edition), New York: Macmillan Publishing Co., 1986; Wanda T. May, "Teaching Students How to Plan: The Dominant Model and Alternatives," *Journal of Teacher Education,* Volume 37, Number 6, 1986; Daniel Tanner and Laurel N. Tanner, *Curriculum Development: Theory into Practice* (Second Edition), New York: Macmillan Publishing Co., Inc., 1980; Ralph Tyler, *Basic Principles of Curriculum and Instruction*, Chicago: University of Chicago Press, 1950; Ralph Tyler, "Desirable Content for a Curriculum Development Syllabus Today" in Alex Molnar and John A. Zahorik (Editors), *Curriculum Theory*, Washington, DC: Association for Supervision and Curriculum Development, 1977.

TYPE I (ALPHA) AND TYPE II (BETA) ERRORS, two of four possible outcomes that may occur when a researcher makes a decision about a null hypothesis. The four possible conclusions to be made by a researcher are: (1) not to reject a true null hypothesis (a correct decision); (2) to reject a false null hypothesis (again a correct decision); (3) to reject a true hypothesis (Type I Error); and (4) not to reject a false hypothesis (Type II Error).

As the probability level used to determine the point of rejection of a null hypothesis becomes smaller (going from $p = 0.05$ to $p = 0.01$), the chance of committing a Type I Error decreases. However, as it becomes harder to reject a hypothesis, it also becomes easier to commit a Type II Error (because a false hypothesis might not be rejected as well). Hence, as researchers decrease the chance of committing one type of error, the chance of making the other increases. (See HYPOTHESES and TESTS OF SIGNIFICANCE.)

References: L. R. Gay, *Educational Research: Competencies for Analysis and Application* (Third Edition), Columbus, OH: Charles E. Merrill Publishing Company, 1987; David S. Moore and George P. McCabe, *Introduction to the Practice of Statistics*, New York: W. H. Freeman and Company, 1989.

TYPOGRAPHY, the process of printing using movable type. It involves design, spacing, copyfitting, layout, type selection, and composition. The individual concerned with the art of printing is called a typographer. There are hundreds of type face designs, sizes, and weights from which the typographer may choose. Selecting the proper type in relation to layout and design of printed text is important in the production of printed material, prompting some to observe that typography is as much an art as it is a technique.

Typography is taught in print shops in some vocational schools.

Johann Gutenberg was the first typographer. He invented movable type in the 15th century.

References: Sandra Ernst, *The ABC's of Typography*, New York: Art Direction, 1977; John Lewis, *Typography: Design and Practice*, New York: Taplinger Publishing Company, 1978; Herbert M. McLuhan, *The Gutenberg Galaxy: The Making of Typography Man*, Toronto, Canada: University of Toronto Press, 1962; *Type Book*, Louisville, KY: Courier-Journal, 1977.

UNDERACHIEVEMENT, a characterization used when an individual's performance or achievement is poorer than it should be, based on his/her ability or potential. The difficulty of determining underachievement is in some part due to how ability and potential are defined, identified, and measured, as well as how performance or achievement are measured.

There are several types (and combinations) of underachievement: (1) *unknown,* a form of underachievement in which one does not know the ability or potential of an individual, consequently the performance or achievement appears to be appropriate. In actuality, the individual may not be achieving or performing up to his/her potential; (2) *high ability* accompanied by low grades and low scores on tests; (3) *high standardized test scores* but low grades; (4) *temporary or situational underachievement* caused by a temporary problem (e.g. illness, divorce in the family, moving); (5) *chronic,* where underachievement is consistent and forms a set pattern of behavior; (6) *one specific area,* underachievement manifested by the individual who has the ability, but doesn't achieve up to expectation in one defined area (e.g. writing, arithmetic, football); (7) *one broad area,* underachievement in a support area (e.g. language arts) that affects achievement in other subject areas; and (8) underachievement in *all general areas.*

There are many reasons accounting for underachievement. They include poor educational background, psychological problems, emotional problems, poor study habits, nonsupport at home, low self-esteem, withdrawal, aggression, social isolation, conflicts at home, overexpectations of parents, underexpectations of parents, physical or medical causes, social/class differences and expectations, and conflicts with teachers.

References: Benjamin Fine, *Underachievers: How They Can Be Helped,* New York: E. P. Dutton and Company, Inc., 1967; Martin Kohn, *Social Competence: Symptoms and Underachievement in Childhood,* Washington, DC: V. H. Winston and Sons, 1977; Learning Library, *Teacher's Strategies,* Springhouse, PA: Springhouse Corporation Book Division, 1987; Joanne R. Whitmore, *Giftedness, Conflict, and Underachievement,* Melrose, MA: Allyn and Bacon, Inc., 1980.

UNESCO—See UNITED NATIONS EDUCATIONAL, SCIENTIFIC AND CULTURAL ORGANIZATION

UNICEF—See UNITED NATIONS INTERNATIONAL CHILDREN'S EMERGENCY FUND

UNIFIED PHONICS METHOD, sometimes referred to as the Spalding Method, a highly structured beginning reading program. The program stresses a spelling-counting approach and the study of some 70 phonograms. Developed by Romalda and Walter Spalding, it consists of six basic elements: (1) pupils say in unison the one or more sounds of each of the phonograms; (2) pupils then write each phonogram, but do not name the letters; (3) all phonograms of two or more letters are called by their sounds; (4) pupils use a word list developed by A. J. Ayres; (5) basic laws of spelling are taught; and (6) actual reading is begun when pupils have learned enough words to be able, instantaneously, to comprehend the meaning of a sentence. The program is highly structured and programmed for both teachers and pupils. (See PHONOGRAMS.)

References: Emerald V. Dechant and Henry P. Smith, *Psychology in Teaching Reading* (Second Edition), Englewood Cliffs, NJ: Prentice-Hall, Inc., 1977; Mildred C. Robeck and John A. R. Wilson, *Psychology of Reading: Foundations of Instruction,* New York: John Wiley and Sons, 1974; Ronalda B. Spalding and Walter T. Spalding, *The Writing Road to Reading,* New York: William Morrow and Company, Inc., 1969.

UNION—See BARGAINING UNIT

UNITED NATIONS EDUCATIONAL, SCIENTIFIC AND CULTURAL ORGANIZATION (UNESCO), an agency of the United Nations whose purpose, as enunciated in its constitution, "is to contribute to peace and security by promoting collaboration among the nations through education, science and culture in order to further universal respect for justice, for the role of law and for the human rights and fundamental freedoms which are affirmed . . . by the Charter of the United Nations" (Ku, p. 88). UNESCO was created on November 4, 1946, with 20 nations joining it as charter members. By 1978, its membership had increased to 144.

In education, UNESCO has been concerned with illiteracy, teacher education, and the general need for education. In 1967, the Experimental World Literacy Programme was established. A

1972 publication, *Learning to Be,* reported on the needs of, and new developments in, the field of education.

UNESCO'S governing organs consist of: (1) *The General Conference,* an assembly to which each member state may appoint five delegates; (2) an *Executive Board,* a 34-member group responsible for executing programs adopted by the Conference; and (3) a *Secretariat* consisting of a Director-General and his/her staff.

UNESCO'S headquarters is in Paris, France.

References: David C. Coyle, *The United Nations and How It Works* (New Edition), New York: Columbia University Press, 1966; *Everyone's United Nations* (Ninth Edition), New York: Department of Public Information, United Nations, December 1979; Min-chuan Ku, *A Comprehensive Handbook of the United Nations* (Volume 2), New York: Monarch Press, 1979.

UNITED NATIONS INTERNATIONAL CHILDREN'S EMERGENCY FUND (UNICEF), a semiautonomous unit within the United Nations that works to help developing nations to improve the conditions of children and youth. Special attention is given to meeting the needs of rural communities and slums. Special projects in fields such as nutrition, education (e.g. textbook preparation), water, community development, food distribution, and agriculture receive UNICEF support. Training programs for teachers and health personnel also fall within UNICEF's purview.

In 1978, over 125 countries contributed to UNICEF's support, providing approximately 75 percent of its budget. The rest of the budget came from individual and group contributions as well as fund-raising projects such as the sale of greeting cards.

Organizationally, UNICEF reports to the Economic and Social Council and the General Assembly. Policies are established by a governing board made up of representatives from 30 countries.

References: Directory of United Nations Information Systems and Services, Geneva, Switzerland: Inter-Organization Board for Information Systems, March 1978; David Dull and Harvey W. Greisman (Editors), *Reference Guide to the United Nations,* New York: United Nations Association of the United States of America, August 1978.

UNITED NEGRO COLLEGE FUND, a fund-raising organization (founded in 1944) that is a federation of 41 independent and fully accredited, predominantly black senior colleges and universities. This organization seeks support for its member institutions on a nationwide level. The 41 institutions are located in 11 southern states and Ohio.

Monies collected are distributed to the institutions according to a formula. A portion of the money is used for scholarships and financial aid. More than 46,000 students benefit each year, with over $5,000,000 in scholarships granted. All scholarships are granted by the member schools rather than the United Negro College Fund.

The Department of Educational Services of the United Negro College Fund provides services to member colleges and universities to help resolve educational and administrative problems. The department also conducts premedical summer courses and "rap sessions" for high school and community college students.

References: Oreon Keeslar, *Financial Aids for Higher Education* (Eighth Edition), Dubuque, IA: Wm. C. Brown Company, Publishers, 1977; Nancy Yakes and Denise Akey (Editors), *Encyclopedia of Associations: Volume I, National Organizations of the U.S.* (Thirteenth Edition), Detroit: Gale Research Company, 1979.

UNITED STATES ARMED FORCES INSTITUTE, USAFI—See DEFENSE ACTIVITY FOR NON-TRADITIONAL EDUCATION SUPPORT

UNITED STATES COMMISSIONER OF EDUCATION, title of the chief executive of the U.S. Office of Education (USOE). Henry Barnard was appointed to the commissionership by President Andrew Johnson in 1867, the year in which the USOE was created. The position became defunct in 1980, 113 years later, as a result of the creation of the cabinet-level U.S. Department of Education, an agency headed by its own Secretary.

While it existed, the post was an appointive one requiring presidential nomination and U.S. Senate endorsement. The Commissioner administered the USOE, subject (in recent years) to the direction and supervision of the Secretary of Health, Education, and Welfare.

The original legislation creating the USOE also prescribed the duties of the Commissioner: "management of the department herein established . . . (and) it shall be the duty of the commissioner of education to present annually to Congress a report embodying the results of his investigations and labors, together with a statement of such facts and recommendations as will, in his judgment, serve the purpose for which this department is established" (p. 434).

Recently, Ernest Boyer, one of the last U.S.

Commissioners, even while conceding that education in the United States is basically the responsibility of the states, argued: "The United States Office of Education must be more than a pipeline for Federal Funding. We have an obligation," he wrote, "to exercise leadership; to bring together colleagues in common endeavor for the good of education; and to remind our constituencies from time to time that while they rightly should take pride in their achievements, they should not allow autonomy to supersede their responsibility to one another... Thus, without intruding on their authority, there is an important function for the Federal Government to perform in supplementing and assisting State and local efforts in education" (p. 2). Implicitly, that supplementary function was a major responsibility of the Commissioner. (See UNITED STATES DEPARTMENT OF EDUCATION and UNITED STATES OFFICE OF EDUCATION. Also see APPENDIX XXVI: UNITED STATES COMMISSIONERS OF EDUCATION.)

References: *Annual Report of the Commissioner of Education: Fiscal Year 1976*, Washington, DC: U.S. Government Printing Office, 1978; Chapter 158 in George P. Sanger (Editor), *The Statutes at Large, Treaties, and Proclamations of the United States of America* (December 1865–March 1867), Boston: Little, Brown, and Company, 1868.

UNITED STATES DEPARTMENT OF EDUCATION (DE), a cabinet-level agency whose creation was passed by Congress and subsequently approved by President Jimmy Carter on October 17, 1979. It became operative on May 5, 1980. The department officially opened its doors in May 1980. (Between 1867 and 1980, federal concerns with education had been attended to by the non-cabinet level U.S. Office of Education.) DE became the nation's 13th cabinet department with Shirley M. Hufstedler, Circuit Judge for the Ninth Circuit, U.S. Court of Appeals, chosen to be the first U.S. Secretary of Education.

Programs formerly the responsibility of the U.S. Office of Education were assigned to DE. In addition, numerous other educational programs (those that had previously been assigned to other federal departments/agencies) were brought together and assigned to the new department. They included: (1) *HEW's* vocational rehabilitation programs plus the education responsibilities of Civil Rights, the National Institute for Education, the National Center for Education Statistics, the Fund for the Improvement of Post Secondary Education, and

the Institute for Museum Services; (2) the *Defense Department's* overseas dependents' schools; and (3) four special institutions (Howard University, Gallaudet College, the National Technical Institute for the Deaf, and the American Printing House for the Blind). The *Justice, Labor, Housing and Urban Development,* and *Agriculture Departments* as well as the National Science Foundation also had educational programs transferred to the new DE. (See UNITED STATES OFFICE OF EDUCATION.)

References: "Secretary Hufstedler Sets Goals for New Department," *American Education*, January–February 1980; Skee Smith, "The U.S. Department of Education," *American Education*, November 1979; "Why a Cabinet Post for Education?" *NEA Reporter,* May/June 1979.

UNITED STATES DEPARTMENT OF HEALTH, EDUCATION, AND WELFARE (HEW), a cabinet agency in the federal government that, until recently, included the U.S. Office of Education. HEW became a department, with its own Secretary reporting directly to the President of the United States, on April 11, 1953. After October 1979, when legislation was passed that authorized the U.S. Office of Education to become the Department of Education, approval was granted for HEW to change its name to the Department of Health and Human Services (HHS). HEW's immediate forerunner was the Federal Security Agency, a lower status unit created in 1939.

While still known as HEW, the department worked to fulfill several goals: (1) to protect and advance the health of American people; (2) to provide every citizen with an opportunity to realize his/her potential through education; and (3) to provide human services. With the exception of educational services, the renamed Department of Health and Human Services continues to see these goals as its principal mission.

The several units remaining in the Department of Health and Human Services include the Office of Civil Rights, the Public Health Service (including the National Institutes of Health), the Health Care Financing Administration, the Social Security Administration, the Office of Consumer Affairs, the Office of Human Development Services, and the Office of the Inspector General.

The Department of HEW's first Secretary, appointed by President Eisenhower, was Mrs. Oveta Culp Hobby. (See UNITED STATES DEPARTMENT OF EDUCATION. Also see APPENDIX XXII: SECRETARIES OF HEALTH, EDUCATION, AND WELFARE.)

References: Department of Health, Education, and Welfare, *This Is HEW*, Washington, DC: The Department, 1978; Rufus E. Miles, *The Department of Health, Education, and Welfare*, New York: Praeger Publishers, 1974; Office of the Federal Register, General Services Administration, *United States Government Manual, 1980–1981*, Washington, DC: U.S. Government Printing Office, May 1980.

UNITED STATES OFFICE OF EDUCATION (USOE), a federal agency created by Congress in 1867. The legislation that created the agency provided that "(t)here shall be established, at the city of Washington, a department of education, for the purpose of collecting such statistics and facts as shall show the condition and progress of education in the several states and territories, and of diffusing such information respecting the organization and management of schools and school systems, and methods of teaching, as shall aid the people of the United States in the establishment and maintenance of efficient school systems, and otherwise promote the cause of education throughout the country." (Sanger, p. 434). The legislation also provided for the appointment of a Commissioner of Education who was to report annually to Congress. President Andrew Johnson chose Henry Barnard to be the first commissioner.

During its history, USOE was at different times assigned to three agencies of the federal government: Department of Interior (1869–1939); Federal Security agency (1939–53); and HEW 1953–80). Over the years, USOE was designated an "Office," a "Department," a "Bureau," and once again an "Office." The principal functions of USOE were: (1) research on education; (2) service to various local, state, national, and international agencies; and (3) administration of federal (educational) grants. Regional offices were established to help carry out the work of the Office.

In 1979, at the urging of President Jimmy Carter, Congress authorized creation of a separate, cabinet-level Department of Education. When the new *department* became operative (on May 5, 1980), the USOE was dissolved and its responsibilities assumed by the new department. (See UNITED STATES DEPARTMENT OF EDUCATION. Also, see APPENDIX XXVI: UNITED STATES COMMISSIONERS OF EDUCATION.)

References: Harry G. Good and James D. Teller, *A History of American Education* (Third Edition), New York: The Macmillan Company, 1973; Harry Kursh, *The United States Office of Education: A Century of Service*, Philadelphia: Chilton Books, 1965; George P. Sanger (Editor), *The Statutes at Large, Treaties, and Proclamations of the United States of America*, Boston: Little, Brown, and Company, 1868.

UNITED STATES STUDENT ASSOCIATION (USSA), an organization created in October 1978 through merger of two student groups: The National Student Association and the National Student Lobby. Its principal mission is lobbying for legislation in which USSA's membership, 275 college and university student bodies, has an interest. USSA is the country's largest officially registered lobbying group for students. Its offices are located in Washington, D.C.

References: Catherine Myers, "Student Group Says Merger Has Given It Greater Clout," *The Chronicle of Higher Education*, September 4, 1979; Nancy Yakes and Denise Akey (Editors), *Encyclopedia of Associations: Volume I, National Organizations of the U.S.* (Fourteenth Edition), Detroit: Gale Research Company, 1980.

UNIT METHOD, sometimes referred to as the "unit of work" method, a teaching approach that cuts across various subject fields and receives much of its direction from pupil interests. (When first introduced, considerable attention was given to pupil planning, doing on the part of students, and appraisal.) Learners and their teacher jointly plan a "unit of work" (e.g. weather, space travel). Learning objectives are identified and specific learning activities are assigned to groups of students.

Once the unit has been studied, a culminating activity is planned that may take the form of an exhibition, a play, a demonstration, or a written report. Teacher-made tests are prepared, these based on the unit's objectives and activities.

Unit method supporters defend it on several grounds: (1) pupils are motivated because units are built around their interests; (2) activities can be adapted to individual learning abilities; (3) cooperative learning is fostered; and (4) learning is interdisciplinary in nature.

References: Fay Adams, *Educating America's Children: Elementary School Curriculum and Methods*, New York: Ronald Press Company, 1946; Bernard G. Kelner, *How to Teach in the Elementary School*, New York: McGraw-Hill Book Company, 1958.

UNITY OF COMMAND, an administrative principle that holds that, to the greatest extent possible, a member of a formal organization (employee) should be subject to orders from but one superior.

This principle, advanced by Luther Gulick, seeks to eliminate the confusion and inefficiency that is likely to develop when a single worker is expected to carry out the wishes of two or more superiors.

Reference: Luther Gulick and L. Urwick (Editors), *Papers on the Science of Administration,* New York: Institute of Public Administration, Columbia University, 1937.

UNIVERSITY COUNCIL FOR EDUCATIONAL ADMINISTRATION (UCEA), a private, nonprofit organization working to improve the preparation of educational administrators. Membership in UCEA is institutional; only universities offering doctoral degrees in educational administration are eligible. Many major American and Canadian institutions belong. UCEA's current efforts include research, student recruitment and placement, strategies for improving leadership practices in the schools, improvement of preparation programs, and development of instructional materials. A Graduate Student Seminar in Educational Administration is offered each year at the American Educational Research Association Annual Meeting, to approximately 40 selected graduate students nominated by UCEA institutions. *UCEA Review* is published three times a year (winter, spring, and fall) by the organization. A full-time staff, governed by the organization's executive committee and the plenary session, is located at Arizona State University in Tempe, Arizona. Prior to being located at Tempe, UCEA was located at Columbia University (1954–59) and the Ohio State University (1959–84).

References: UCEA Review, Volume 30, Spring 1988; University Council for Educational Administration, *An Introduction to UCEA,* Columbus, OH: UCEA, undated.

UNIVERSITY OF CHICAGO SCHOOL MATHEMATICS PROJECT (UCSMP), a mathematics program (K–12) designed to prepare students in the middle-ability (average) range. The project grew out of educational reform reports that made specific recommendations concerning the mathematics curriculum found in the schools (K–12). The project was initially funded by the Amoco Foundation for the years 1983–89. The secondary (7–12) part of the program is designed to help students acquire a mathematical background in order to function in college (regardless of major) and/or in a job. Real-world applications, problem solving, statistics, and use of computers are emphasized throughout the secondary program. Grade 7 includes arithmetic, pre-algebra and pre-geometry; followed by algebra and statistics (Grade 8); ge-

ometry (Grade 9); advanced algebra (Grade 10); and functions, statistics, and computers (Grade 11); in the last year, students are exposed to pre-college mathematics. (See NATIONAL REFORM REPORTS (1980–86).)

References: The College Entrance Examination Board, *Academic Preparation for College,* New York: The College Board, 1985; Conference Board of the Mathematical Sciences, *The Mathematical Sciences Curriculum K–12: What Is Still Fundamental and What Is Not?* Report to the National Science Board Commission on Pre-College Education in Mathematics, Science, and Technology, Washington, DC: The Conference Board, 1983; Zalman Usiskin, "The UCSMP: Translating Grades 7–12 Mathematics Recommendations into Reality," *Educational Leadership,* Volume 44, Number 4, 1986.

UNIVERSITY PRESS, a publishing house, usually nonprofit, owned by a university. These publishing houses are normally interested in producing scholarly work, including paperbacks and reference books. Many, although not all, of the books published are authored by members of the press' own university faculty.

In 1937, the university presses in the United States organized the Association of American University Presses (AAUP) to which Canadian and Mexican presses now also belong. *Scholarly Books in America,* a quarterly bibliography, is prepared by the association and lists all books published by member presses.

The earliest university presses were established in the 15th and 16th centuries in the Sorbonne, at Cambridge, and at Oxford. In the United States, Cornell (1869) and John Hopkins (1878) universities were the first institutions of higher education to establish their own university presses.

References: Charles A. Madison, *Book Publishing in America,* New York: McGraw-Hill Book Company, 1966; Leon E. Seltzer, "University Presses" in Chandler B. Grannis (Editor), *What Happens in Book Publishing* (Second Edition), New York: Columbia University Press, 1967; John Tebbel, *A History of Book Publishing in the United States: The Expansion of an Industry, 1865–1919* (Volume 2), New York: R. R. Bowker Company, 1975.

UNOBTRUSIVE MEASURES, an assessment term for "nonreactive" measures that are administered in such a way that a respondent does not know that he/she is being measured. Often, individuals are required to complete a questionnaire, take a paper-pencil test, or comply with similar requirements that alert them to the fact that they are being assessed. These procedures may cause the individual to "react," sometimes producing changes in behavior and thus raising questions of validity of the measures or the test results. "Nonreactive," or unobtrusive, measures do not produce such results. Observing subjects without their knowledge, reviewing past records of individuals, counting tickets sold to concerts of a particular style of music (to determine musical preferences), counting the number of times particular types of books are selected over other types (to determine reading preferences), and utilizing data banks are a few examples of unobtrusive measuring procedures.

References: Michael Q. Patton, *Qualitative Evaluation Methods,* Beverly Hills, CA: Sage Publications, Inc., 1980; Bernard S. Phillips, *Social Research* (Third Edition), New York: Macmillan Publishing Company, Inc., 1976; Eugene J. Webb, et al., *Unobtrusive Measures: Nonreactive Research in the Social Sciences,* Chicago: Rand McNally and Company, 1966.

UPPER DIVISION COLLEGE, an institution of higher education that confers the baccalaureate degree but that only offers programs at the junior and senior year levels, sometimes at the graduate level as well. Students are admitted to upper division colleges after completing lower division (freshman and sophomore years) at another institution, frequently a junior college. One of the earliest upper division institutions to appear in the United States was the College of the Pacific, in California. Several such colleges were created following World War II, including Flint College (Michigan); Richmond College (New York); and Florida Atlantic University (Florida).

Reference: Robert A. Altman, *The Upper Division College,* San Francisco: Jossey-Bass, Publishers, 1970.

UPWARD BOUND, a federal program designed to assist youth from low-income families who lack a sound high school preparation but who have the potential to pursue postsecondary education. Introduced as part of the Higher Education Act of 1965 (subsequently amended), Upward Bound helps participating students to generate the *skills* and *motivation* necessary to pursue post-high school work successfully. To achieve this, the program works with the student while he/she is still in high school.

Institutions of higher education, the organizations normally receiving Upward Bound grants, typically sponsor programs that have two elements: (1) six- to eight-week summer sessions, often conducted on a college/university campus, during which time skills are taught through use of reme-

dial instruction, tutoring, cultural exposure, and counseling, and (2) continuation of these activities during the regular academic year as supplements to students' basic programs of study.

A federal study, published in 1978, revealed that: (1) more Upward Bound participants enrolled in postsecondary institutions than did their nonparticipating counterparts, and (2) length of participation in the program was related, positively, to rate of enrollment in posthigh school programs.

References: Office of Planning, Budgeting, and Evaluation, U.S. Office of Education, *Annual Evaluation Report on Programs Administered by the U.S. Office of Education: FY1977,* Washington, DC: Department of HEW, 1978; Public Law 89-329, *United States Statutes at Large, 1965* (Volume 79), Washington, DC: U.S. Government Printing Office, 1966.

URBAN AFFAIRS ASSOCIATION (UAA), a professional organization composed of urbanologists from the United States and Canada. Originally formed as the Council of University Institutes for Urban Affairs, the group changed its name in 1981 to reflect the broadening of its membership to include faculty, students, urban program directors, deans, and other urban professionals. The goals of the organization are: (1) disseminate information and research findings about urbanism and urbanization; (2) support development of programs in urban affairs at universities; and (3) foster urban affairs as a profession and field of study. There are institutional programs (over 200), and individual, and student memberships. The Governing Board of 15 members is elected by UAA's institutional members. *The Journal of Urban Affairs, UAA Communication,* and *University Urban Programs* are published by the Association. The headquarters of UAA is located at the University of Delaware, Newark, Delaware.

Reference: Urban Affairs Association, *UAA, Urban Affairs Association,* Undated Brochure.

URBAN EDUCATION, broadly defined as all education (preschool through the university and including postsecondary and technical educational institutions) that occurs in, and is affected by, the various factors generated by an urban environment. Although large city public school districts are typically thought of when considering urban education, religious and nonreligious private schools, located in metropolitan areas, are also influenced by this environment.

Unlike education found in many rural, suburban, and small town schools, urban schools are faced with a variety of concerns. They may include: (1) a large population of poor; (2) a weak tax and funding base; (3) a variety of socially and economically different and unique groups; (4) racially segregated schools and populations; (5) violence; (6) large school populations; (7) old school buildings; (8) low student achievement; (9) middle-class flight from the cities; (10) poor housing and living conditions; (11) changing power/political base and political neglect; and (12) significant teacher turnover. Individually and collectively, these and other similar factors influence education in the urban community, usually adversely. This list of factors serves to indicate that economics, social movements, changing priorities, local, state, and national political concerns, in- and out-migration, culture, energy, inflation, parental demands, and governmental restrictions all influence and lend uniqueness to urban schools.

Not all schooling in the urban community takes place in socially and economically depressed, high-population areas (often called inner-city schools). To the contrary, some urban schools are more like, or superior to, their counterparts in suburban areas. At one time, urban schools were considered to be among the best in the country and were highly regarded.

References: Daniel V. Levine, "The Social Context of Urban Education," in Donald Erickson and Theodore L. Reller (Editors), *The Principal in Metropolitan Schools*, Berkeley, CA: McCutchan Publishing Corporation, 1978; Daniel V. Levine and Robert J. Havighurst (Editors), *The Future of Big-City Schools*, Berkeley, CA: McCutchan Publishing Corporation, 1977; Alfred Lightfoot, *Urban Education in Social Perspective*, Lanham, MD: University Press of America, 1985; Christine E. Sleeter and Carl A. Grant, An Analysis of Multicultural Education in the United States, *Harvard Educational Review*, Volume 57, November 1987; George E. Spear, *Urban Education: A Guide to Information Sources*, Detroit, Gale Research Company, 1978; Herbert J. Walberg and Andrew T. Kopan (Editors), *Rethinking Urban Education*, San Francisco: Jossey-Bass, Publishers, 1972.

USAGE, or language usage, a term used by grammarians to call attention to the variety of language levels used by individuals. Each individual, they report, makes use of several levels of language (informal to formal) and is able to change from one level to another as circumstances or conditions warrant or require.

Helen Lodge and Gerald Trett suggested that there are three basic language levels: (1) nonstandard English; (2) general English; and (3) formal English. Other grammarians use different categorizations. Regardless of the number proposed, authorities are in general agreement that individuals utilize different levels of speech (e.g. casual, formal) and routinely shift from one to another depending on the formality required.

Mildred Donoghue wrote that there are seven "interlocking dimensions" of modern English usage. Different combinations of them result in different language usage variations. The seven are: (1) *socioeconomic-educational*, with type of usage reflecting the speaker's education and/or socioeconomic status; (2) *stylistic*, ranging from formal to casual speech; (3) *sex-based* (e.g. rough masculine); (4) *methodological* (e.g. use of written vs. spoken English); (5) *historical* (e.g. English as it was spoken during the Middle ages vs. modern English); (6) *occupational;* and (7) *geographic.*

References: Mildred R. Donoghue, *The Child and the English Language Arts* (Third Edition), Dubuque, IA: Wm. C. Brown Company, Publishers, 1979; Helen C. Lodge and Gerald L. Trett, *New Ways in English,* Englewood Cliffs, NJ: Prentice-Hall, Inc., 1968; Donna E. Norton, *The Effective Teaching of Language Arts,* Columbus, OH: Charles E. Merrill Publishing Company, 1980.

VACCINATION OF PUPILS, immunization programs for school children instituted to curb the spread of communicable diseases. States frequently require evidence of vaccination as a condition for admission to school. A Michigan statute, enacted in 1970, illustrates the more comprehensive of such legislation. It reads: "All children enrolling in any public, private or parochial or denominational school in Michigan for the first time shall submit either a statement signed by a physician that they have been immunized or protected against smallpox, diptheria, tetanus, pertussis, rubella, measles and poliomyelitis and tuberculin tested . . . ; a statement signed by a parent or guardian to the effect that the child has not been immunized and tuberculin tested because of religious convictions . . . ; or a request . . . that the local health department give the needed injections and . . . test" (Leroy Peterson, p. 292).

The Supreme Court has twice ruled (1920 and 1922) in support of state legislation requiring vaccination for admission to schools. Additionally, school boards and boards of health in several states have been supported by the courts in their attempts to require vaccinations during epidemics. Finally, in response to numerous defenses against vaccination, the courts have held that vaccination does not constitute an invasion of personal rights (especially religious beliefs).

References: Jacobson v. Commonwealth of Massachusetts, 197 U.S. 11, 25 S.Ct. 358, 49 L.Ed. 643 (1905); Leroy J. Peterson, et al., *The Law and Public School Operation* (Second Edition), New York: Harper and Row, Publishers, 1978; E. Edmund Reutter, Jr. and Robert R. Hamilton, *The Law of Public Education* (Second Edition), Mineola, NY: The Foundation Press, Inc., 1976; *Zucht v. King,* 260 U.S. 174, 43 S.Ct. 24, 67 L.Ed. 194 (1922).

V-A-K-T, a multisensory method of teaching reading. The V-A-K-T (*v*isual-*a*uditory-*k*inesthetic-*t*actile) approach has children learn words by seeing, sounding, hearing, tracing, and touching them. It was developed in response to research showing that some children, particularly the psychoneurologically impaired, require multimodal reading instruction. Much of the V-A-K-T method is based on the kinesthetic-sensory method pioneered by Grace Fernald. (See FERNALD METHOD and GILLINGHAM METHOD.)

References: Grace M. Fernald, *Remedial Techniques in Basic School Subjects,* New York: McGraw-Hill Book Company, 1943; Samuel A. Kirk, et al., *Teaching Reading to Slow and Disabled Learners,* Boston: Houghton Mifflin Company, 1978; Russell G. Stauffer, et al., *Diagnosis, Correction, and Prevention of Reading Disabilities,* New York: Harper and Row, Publishers, 1978.

VALIDITY, in testing the extent to which a test measures what it purports to measure. More technically, validity indicates the degree of accuracy of either predictions or inferences that are based upon a test score. There are several types of validity, the principal ones being content, construct, predictive, and face validity.

Content validity, sometimes referred to as curricular validity, indicates the extent to which test items sample the tasks (subject matter) intended to be measured. *Construct validity,* also known as logical validity, reports the extent to which the attribute to be assessed (e.g. musical aptitude) is measured by the test. *Empirical validity,* which includes both predictive and concurrent validity, indicates the extent to which predictions, based on test scores, can be verified when compared with other test scores or an external criterion measure (e.g. grades, success) that measure what is being assessed. Finally, *face validity* refers to the type of validity that reflects acceptance by an examiner or examinee that a test measures what it is supposed to measure (usually a situational test).

The determination of validity can be complex and involved. *Face validity* is the easiest validity to establish, and *construct validity* is usually the most difficult. Authorities stress that it is important that test validity and reliability be established before inferences or predictions based on test results are made. (See RELIABILITY and VALIDITY, INTERNAL-EXTERNAL.)

References: Anne Anastasi, *Psychological Testing* (Sixth Edition), New York: Macmillan Publishing Company, 1988; George K. Cunningham, *Educational and Psychological Measurement,* New York: Macmillan Publishing Company, 1986; William E. Davis, *Educator's Resource Guide to Special Education,* Boston: Allyn and Bacon, Inc., 1980; Lee J. Cronbach, "Test Validation" in Robert L. Thorndike (Editor), *Educational Measurement* (Second Edition), Washington, DC: American Council on Education, 1971.

VALIDITY, INTERNAL-EXTERNAL, procedures used to describe the extent to which research results can be used or interpreted. *Internal validity* refers to the degree to which the results of the study are interpretable within the study itself. *External validity* refers to the degree to which the results can be generalized to other populations, situations, or conditions. Without minimum internal validity, external validity has little meaning.

It is important that both internal and external validity be considered at the time a study is designed. Small changes in how a study is conducted can dramatically affect whether or not the results are hopelessly ambiguous (internal validity) or whether they cannot be generalized (external validity) to other populations or groups.

There are times when an increase in one validity may reduce the other validity. (See EXPERIMENTAL DESIGN.)

References: Walter R. Borg and Meredith D. Gall, *Educational Research: An Introduction* (Fifth Edition), New York: Longman, Inc., 1989; L. R. Gay, *Educational Research: Competencies for Analysis and Application* (Third Edition), Columbus, OH: Merrill Publishing Company, 1987.

VALUES, in sociology the traditions, customs, ideals, mores, and so on of a society that are held in high regard. These may be positive (e.g. honesty) or negative (e.g. cruelty). This makes them bipolar. Values tend to be hierarchical, too. That is, some values are held in higher regard than others.

From values develop morals, or standards of behavior, for individuals, communities, cultural groups, and even nations. Values change over time; consequently, value systems are also in a state of flux.

Children come to school with various values and at different stages of moral development. A student's behavior is often the manifestation of his/her value system. Experiences in the classroom may modify or create a student's positive or negative values vis-á-vis others, him/herself, objects, concepts, education, or whatever may be the focus or product of such experiences.

Philosophers refer to the study of values and value theory as axiology. (See AXIOLOGY and VALUES CLARIFICATION.)

References: Merrill Harmin, et al., *Clarifying Values Through Subject Matter*, Minneapolis, MN: Winston Press, Inc., 1973; David T. Naylor and Richard A. Diem, *Elementary and Middle School Social Studies*, New York: Random House, 1987; Louis E. Raths, et al., *Values and Teaching: Working with Values in the Classroom*, Columbus, OH: Charles E. Merrill Books, Inc., 1966; Evan Simpson, *Reason over Passion: The Social Basis of Evaluation and Appraisal*, Waterloo, Ontario, Canada: Wilfrid Laurier University Press, 1979.

VALUES CLARIFICATION, or value clarification, a process by which an individual is helped to make free value choices after studying a spectrum of options, to prize the choices made, and to behave in a manner that reflects his/her commitment to the value(s) chosen. The process was first described in 1966 by Louis Raths, Merrill Harmin, and Sidney Simon. These authors identified seven specific steps leading to value clarity: (1) choosing from alternatives; (2) making the choice freely; (3) choosing after considering the consequences of each option; (4) prizing, or cherishing the choice made; (5) displaying willingness to affirm the choice(s) publicly; (6) doing something with the choice (acting); and (7) behaving in a consistent manner.

In classrooms, value clarification may be taught using numerous techniques including brainstorming sessions, case studies, value-ranking exercises, and role playing. Lectures by teachers, because of their directive character, are not generally recommended. (See VALUES.)

References: Brian P. Hall, *Value Clarification as Learning Process: A Guidebook*, New York: Paulist Press, 1973; Howard Kirschenbaum, *Advanced Value Clarification*, La Jolla, CA: University Associates, 1977; David T. Naylor and Richard E. Diem, *Elementary and Middle School Social Studies*, New York: Random House, 1987; Louis Raths, et al., *Values and Teaching*, Columbus, OH: Charles E. Merrill Publishing Company, 1966; Sidney Simon, et al., *Values Clarification: A Handbook of Practical Strategies for Teachers and Students*, New York: Hart Publishing Company, 1972.

VANDALISM, the destruction of private or school property. Vandalism of school property ranges from the breaking of a window to serious acts such as the burning of a school building or destruction of school records. Authorities report that most vandals are under the age of 18, with the modal group being the 12–15-year-olds. Schools are targets of the vandal for any number of reasons: (1) they are frequently unoccupied; (2) they are the buildings in which strict discipline is enforced; and (3) as public buildings, they are not seen as being the property of any one individual. Strategies for coping with vandalism include prosecution of vandals, demanding restitution for damages, use of uniformed patrols, installation of alarm systems, and public relations programs that seek to enlist community cooperation in reducing the incidence of school property destruction. (See SCHOOL SECURITY.)

References: Institute for Development of Educational Activities, Inc., *The Problem of School Security*, Dayton,

OH: The Institute, 1974; National School Public Relations Association, *Violence and Vandalism: Current Trends in School Policies and Programs*, Arlington, VA: The Association, 1975; Seymour D. Vestermark, Jr. and Peter D. Blauvelt, *Controlling Crime in the School: A Complete Security Handbook for Administrators*, West Nyack, NY: Parker Publishing Company, Inc., 1978.

VARIABLE, an entity or classification that varies. For example, in a population study there may be several classifications (age, income, height) of subjects. Ages may range from 12 to 50 years, income from 0 to $30,000, and height from 5 to 6-½ feet. Each classification is considered a variable since the units (observations) within each vary. If all the subjects were 6-½ feet tall, height would be a constant.

There are several types of variables found in educational research, the principal ones being independent and dependent. An *independent variable* can be "manipulated" by the researcher and has a consequence on the *dependent variable*. In a research study of the effects of two types of programmed instruction on mathematics skills, for example, the two types of programmed instruction would be the independent variable. The researcher "manipulates" the variable by selecting or determining the modes of instruction. The consequence(s) of the programmed instruction will impact on the dependent variable, the mathematical skills being tested.

In algebra, a variable changes while a constant does not: $X + 3 = Z$; X and Z are variables (each being affected by the value of the other), and 3, having but one value, is a constant.

References: Walter R. Borg and Meredith D. Gall, *Educational Research: An Introduction* (Fifth Edition), New York: Longman, Inc., 1989; L. R. Gay, *Educational Research: Competencies for Analysis and Application* (Third Edition), Columbus, OH: Merrill Publishing Company, 1987; Simon W. Tai, *Social Science Statistics*, Santa Monica, CA: Goodyear Publishing Company, Inc., 1978.

VARIANCE, a measure indicating variability (deviation) of a set of scores from the mean of the set. It is used extensively in many statistical formulae and computations. For example:

Subjects (Observations)	Score	Deviation	Deviation Score Squared
A_1	10	0 (10–10)	0
A_2	8	–2 (8–10)	4
A_3	12	+2 (12–10)	4
A_4	10	0 (10–10)	0
Sum	40	0	8
Mean	10	—	—
Variance	—	—	2.00
Standard Deviation	—	—	1.41

Variance is computed by squaring the deviation (the distance a score is from the mean) of each score, summing the squared deviations, and then dividing the sum by the number of observations. The positive square root of the variance is the standard deviation. (See ANALYSIS OF VARIANCE; *F*-RATIO; and STANDARD DEVIATION.)

References: George K. Cunningham, *Educational and Psychological Measurement*, New York: Macmillan Publishing Company, 1986; L. R. Gay, *Educational Research: Competencies for Analysis and Application* (Third Edition), Columbus, OH: Merrill Publishing Company, 1987.

VERBAL COMMUNICATION, the use of language to convey meaning. In a broad sense, communication may be written, spoken, or both. In a more restrictive sense, verbal communication is oral (speech). In verbal communication, as in nonverbal communication, there is a communicator and a receiver. In verbal communication, both the sender and the receiver communicate through a linguistic system or systems.

Oral communication is complex. Not only is it supported by nonverbal communication (e.g. gestures, frowns), but it includes nuances such as dialect, syntax, semantics, and levels of meaning (intentional, content, interpretative).

As children mature, they progress through various stages of language development. For example, they understand words before they learn to speak. By the time most children enter school, they have learned to communicate using spoken language extensively. (See COMMUNICATION; COMMUNICATION CHANNEL; and NONVERBAL COMMUNICATIONS.)

References: Paul S. Anderson and Diane Lapp, *Language Skills in Elementary Education* (Third Edition), New York: Macmillan Publishing Company, Inc., 1979; Gertrude A. Boyd and Daisy M. Jones, *Teaching Communication Skills in the Elementary School* (Second Edition), New York: D. Van Nostrand Company, Inc., 1977; Clyde W. Jackson, *Verbal Information Systems*, Cleveland, OH: Association for Systems Management, 1974.

VERBATONAL METHOD, a method of instruction used in the field of deafness. Developed by Petar Guberina of Yugoslavia, the method, he reported, "is based on studies of the perception of language by the brain from the sense of hearing of language" (p. 280). Tests using nonsense syllables (logatomes) are used to identify the individual's most sensitive hearing area (i.e. low, medium, or high frequencies). Thereafter, with the help of specially designed hearing aids that filter frequencies, training units are employed that are best suited to the individual. In addition, the speech clinician helps the learner to maximize speech perception through manipulation of any or all of the following variables: (1) frequency; (2) intensity; (3) duration; (4) intonation; (5) rhythm; (6) tension of the articulators; and (7) pause.

References: Carl W. Asp, "Measurement of Aural Speech Perception and Oral Speech Production of the Hearing Impaired" in Sadanand Singh (Editor), *Measurement Procedures in Speech, Hearing, and Language,* Baltimore, MD: University Park Press, 1975; Petar Guberina, "Verbatonal Method and Its Application to the Rehabilitation of the Deaf," *Report of Proceedings of the 41st Meeting of Convention of American Instructors of Deaf,* Washington, DC: U.S. Government Printing Office, 1964; Luciano L'Abate and Leonard T. Curtis, *Teaching the Exceptional Child,* Philadelphia: W. B. Saunders Company, 1975; Michael Rodel, "Visual and Auditory Training for Children" in Jack Katz (Editor), *Handbook of Clinical Audiology* (Second Edition), Baltimore, MD: The Williams and Wilkins Company, 1978.

VERNACULAR LEARNING, learning in a common or nonstandard language rather than in a standard or classical language. For example, standard English is usually used in the classroom as the medium of instruction; yet children frequently "translate" the standard language into common or street language for better understanding. Or, as in the case of Black English, the opposite form of translation may take place. Some educators hold that it might be more appropriate, in some instances, to use the vernacular language as the medium of instruction, especially with children who do not respond to standard language instruction. (See BLACK ENGLISH.)

References: Daphne Brown, *Mother Tongue to English: The Young Child in the Multicultural School,* New York: Cambridge University Press, 1979; Lillian M. Logan, et al., *Creative Communication,* New York: McGraw-Hill Book Company, 1972; *Nonstandard Dialect,* Champaign, IL: National Council of Teachers of English, 1968.

VESTING, a guarantee to a retirement system member of a deferred retirement allowance providing certain conditions are met: (1) completion of a prescribed minimal period of system service (e.g. seven years); (2) nonwithdrawal of retirement contributions; and/or (3) attaining the age at which retirement benefits may begin (e.g. age 60). Specific age and/or service requirements vary from one retirement system to another. Some prescribe only years of service for eligibility; others require that both service and age conditions be met. This guarantee applies even if the member leaves his/her job after meeting the system's service requirements for vesting.

In 1977, according to a National Education Association survey of teacher retirement systems, a total of at least 66 state and local retirement systems to which teachers belonged extended the vesting privilege to their members. (See RETIREMENT FOR TEACHERS.)

References: National Education Association, *NEA Research Memo: Teacher Retirement Systems, Summary of the 1977 Survey,* Washington, DC: The Association, 1979; W. William Schmid, *Retirement Systems of the American Teacher,* New York: Fleet Academic Editions, Inc. (in cooperation with American Federation of Teachers, AFL-CIO), 1971.

VICARIOUS LEARNING, learning that is acquired through sources other than direct contact. Vicarious learning may be a product of listening to the experiences of another individual or individuals. For example, one may learn to fear another person by hearing the experiences a third person had with that particular individual. Or vicarious learning may be the result of a vivid description of an experience in a book where the reader feels as though he or she is experiencing that which is being described (imagination plays a role here). It is also possible to learn vicariously by observing (participating indirectly in) the experiences of another individual. A mother, for example, may vicariously experience the excitement of dancing by watching her child dance on the stage. Vicarious learning and experiences play a part in the educational development of children and adults.

References: Nate L. Gage and David C. Berliner, *Educational Psychology,* Chicago: Rand McNally College Publishing Company, 1975; Karl C. Garrison and Robert A. Magoon, *Educational Psychology,* Columbus, OH: Charles E. Merrill Publishing Company, 1972; Barry Gholson, *The Cognitive-Developmental Basis of Human Learning,* New York: Academic Press, 1980.

VIDEO DISCS, devices that record and store television programs for later playback. Video discs are similar to phonograph records in the sense that they can store programs but do not have a recording capability. Low-power laser beams are used to record (in black and white, or color) and to play back. Programs are recorded on both sides of the disc, with each disc capable of storing up to one hour of programming or over 50,000 still pictures. These still pictures (individual microform frames), authorities suggest, give the video disc considerable potential as a library-reference storage device as well as a system for simply playing back previously recorded television programs.

Robert Gray pointed out that both advantages and disadvantages can be associated with the video disc. Advantages include relatively lower cost (over videotape and player), the possibility of stereo audio being used, ease of operation, greater potential for high-quality color programming, and the possibility of using it to develop low-cost computer-assisted instruction. Disadvantages listed include compatability problems (different manufacturers' discs are not interchangeable), a smaller television screen is used, the fact that it is a playback unit only, and recording with video discs is not possible.

References: James W. Brown, et al., *AV Instruction: Technology, Media, and Methods* (Fifth Edition), New York: McGraw-Hill Book Company, 1977; Robert A. Gray, "Videodiscs: Pros and Cons," *International Journal of Instructional Media*, Volume 5, No. 2, 1977–78; Edward L. Palmer, "New Technologies and New Challenges in Video Education," *National Forum*, Summer 1980.

VIDEO RECORDING, a technique introduced in the 1950s that makes it possible to record both video picture and sound on a single piece of magnetic tape. A special videotape machine is required to play back the tape. Video recording was pioneered for the commercial television industry, with the first black and white videotaped program broadcast on November 30, 1956. Color taping was introduced shortly thereafter.

Video recorders are of two types. The first, the *video tape recorder* (VTR), is reel-to-reel and, much like the reel-to-reel audio tape recorder, requires manual threading. In the second type, the *video cassette recorder* (VCR), tape is contained in a cassette and requires no hand threading. The latter type is used in many classrooms owing to its simplicity and ease of storage. A disadvantage associated with both VTRs and VCRs is that they are frequently incompatible (i.e. the tape prepared on one manufacturer's machine may not be played back on another manufacturer's machine).

Bruce Window identified six ways in which video recordings can be used in education: (1) to record lectures that require repetition; (2) to record demonstrations that are expensive to prepare; (3) to capture special events; (4) to record happenings at which observers are unable to be present; (5) for use in conjunction with independent study; and (6) for exchanges with other institutions. (See VIDEO TAPE.)

References: Charles Bensinger, *The Home Video Handbook* (Second Edition), Santa Barbara, CA: Video-Info Publications, 1979; Robert V. Bullough, Sr., *Creating Instructional Materials* (Second Edition), Columbus, OH: Charles E. Merrill Publishing Company, 1978; Bruce Window, "Video Recording" in Derick Unwin and Ray McAleese, *The Encyclopedia of Educational Media Communications and Technology*, Westport, CT: Greenwood Press, 1978.

VIDEO TAPE, a magnetically sensitive material on which both sound and visual (video) images are recorded. The tape is considerably more sensitive than either a standard 16 mm film or audio tape. Video and audio heads, which are part of the video recorder, produce a magnetic field to which the video tape responds. These impressions are recorded and stored for playback. Black and white or color pictures can be recorded. Tapes can be erased and reused several times.

Care in the handling and storage of videotapes will increase their longevity. Manufacturers suggest that: (1) tapes be kept dust free; (2) temperature and humidity extremes be avoided; (3) tapes be wrapped in plastic bags and stored vertically; (4) reels and cassettes be labeled carefully; and (5) removal of tape from guides or head drum be avoided. (Instead, tape should be wound on to the take-up reel.) (See VIDEO RECORDING.)

References: Charles Bensinger, *The Home Video Handbook* (Second Edition), Santa Barbara, CA: Video-Info Publications, 1979; James W. Brown, et al., *AV Instruction: Technology, Media, and Methods* (Fifth Edition), New York: McGraw-Hill Book Company, 1977.

VISTA, acronym for *V*olunteers in *S*ervice *to* *A*merica, a federal program in which volunteers work to eliminate poverty and poverty-related problems in the United States. VISTA is a sister program to the Peace Corps. Both programs are part of ACTION, an organization created in 1971 when VISTA and Peace Corps were consolidated administratively.

VISTA was formed in 1964 as part of President Lyndon Johnson's War on Poverty. Volunteers work in seven general fields: (1) community services; (2) economic development; (3) knowledge skills (e.g. working with out-of-school bilingual programs); (4) health nutrition; (5) legal rights; (6) housing; and (7) energy conservation.

Special programs involving older volunteers are also a part of ACTION. They are: (1) the Retired Senior Volunteer Program (RSVP); (2) the Foster Grandparent Program (FGP); and (3) the Senior Companion Program (SCP).

VISTA volunteers, numbering in the thousands, render one year of service following a brief training program. To qualify, the volunteer must be at least 18 years of age and possess a needed skill. The volunteer receives limited financial support: (1) nominal monthly and "incidental" allowances, and (2) a modest stipend paid at the close of service. (See ACTION and PEACE CORPS.)
References: ACTION, *Loving, Caring, Sharing, Living: Older American Volunteers in Action* (Pamphlet No. 4500.7), Washington, DC: ACTION, September 1977; ACTION, *VISTA: Put Yourself Where You're Needed* (ACTION Flyer No. 4301.5), Washington, DC: ACTION, August 1978; Public Law 88-452, *United States Statutes at Large, 1964* (Volume 78), Washington, DC: U.S. Government Printing Office, 1964.

VISUAL DISCRIMINATION, the ability of a reader to see similarities and differences among forms such as objects, letters of the alphabet, or words. Essential to successful reading is the ability to distinguish letters and words; for that reason, visual discrimination exercises are included in virtually all reading instruction programs.

An almost limitless number of discrimination exercises may be used by the teacher. Examples include: (1) distinguishing one concrete object (e.g. a dog) from other similar objects; (2) letter discrimination exercises (e.g. underlining the letter that is different: b,b,d,b); (3) word discrimination exercises (e.g. underlining the word that is different: man, man, men, man, man); or (4) matching exercises in which the learner draws lines to connect similar pictures, letters, or words.
References: Albert J. Harris and Edward R. Sipay, *How to Increase Reading Ability* (Eighth Edition), New York: Longman, Inc., 1985; Arthur W. Heilman, Timothy R. Blair, and William H. Rupley, *Principles and Practices of Teaching Reading* (Sixth Edition), Columbus, OH: Charles E. Merrill Publishing Company, 1986; Wayne Otto, et al., *How to Teach Reading*, Reading, MA: Addison-Wesley Publishing Company, 1979.

VISUAL HEARING—See LIPREADING

VISUAL IMPAIRMENT, blindness or partial sightedness. This disability may be defined using legal or educational criteria.

The legal definition of a blind person, accepted by the American Federation for the Blind and incorporated into the Social Security Act of 1935, is one who has visual acuity for distant vision of 20/200 or less in the better eye (with correction) or one whose field of vision is narrowed so that the wider diameter of his/her visual field subtends an angle no greater than 20 degrees. A partially sighted (or partially blind) person is one whose visual acuity falls between 20/70 and 20/200 in the better (corrected) eye.

According to the educational definition of visual impairment, *blind* children are those who need to use braille to read. The *partially blind,* this definition goes on to say, are those who require large print or special conditions to read. (See SNELLEN CHART.)
References: William H. Berdine and A. Edward Blackhurst (Editors), *An Introduction to Special Education* (Second Edition), Boston: Little, Brown and Company, 1985; Donald D. Hammill (Editor), *Assessing the Abilities and Instructional Needs of Students*, Austin, TX: Pro-Ed, Inc., 1987; Daniel P. Hallahan and James M. Kauffman, *Exceptional Children: Introduction to Special Education* (Fourth Edition), Englewood Cliffs, NJ: Prentice-Hall, Inc., 1988; Maynard C. Reynolds and Jack W. Birch, *Teaching Exceptional Children in All America's Schools: A First Course for Teachers and Principals*, Reston, VA: Council for Exceptional Children, 1977.

VISUAL SPEECH RECEPTION—See LIPREADING

VOCABULARY DEVELOPMENT, a facet of reading instruction whose purpose is to increase the number of words known to children. Reading authorities consider this part of the reading curriculum to be important inasmuch as poor reading and limited vocabulary are positively correlated. The vocabulary development program has two objectives: (1) to help students with recognition of sight words, and (2) to expand the student's meaning vocabulary. Sight word recognition is taught using such instructional strategies as phonics, configuration, dictionary skills, and contextual analysis. Expansion of meaning vocabulary is facilitated by using approaches such as: (1) broadening the student's experience (e.g. trips, films); (2) encouraging competent readers to read more widely; and (3) planned (direct) vocabulary instruction. (See SIGHT VOCABULARY.)
References: Albert J. Harris and Edward R. Sipay, *How to Increase Reading Ability* (Eighth Edition), New York: Longman, Inc., 1985; Dale D. Johnson and P. David

Pearson, *Teaching Reading Vocabulary*, New York: Holt, Rinehart and Winston, Inc., 1978; Barbara E. R. Swaby, *Diagnosis and Correction of Reading Differences*, Boston: Allyn and Bacon, 1989; Ellen L. Thomas and H. Alan Robinson, *Improving Reading in Every Class: A Sourcebook for Teachers* (Second Edition), Boston: Allyn and Bacon, Inc., 1977.

VOCAL MUSIC, music that is sung. It may be performed by one voice (solo) or a group of voices (choral). Music historians report that before the 16th century, virtually all music was performed vocally. As time went by, instrumental music began to compete with it as a form of musical presentation.

Today, vocal music is taught in the schools at all educational levels. Activities in which students participate may range from large-group song sessions to carefully rehearsed choral performances by auditioned groups of pupils. In increasing numbers of school districts, vocal music instruction is provided by specially trained and certified teachers who follow carefully planned and sequenced curricula. (See MUSIC EDUCATION.)

References: Willi Apel, *Harvard Dictionary of Music* (Second Edition, Revised and Enlarged), Cambridge, MA: The Belknap Press of Harvard University Press, 1970; Richard L. Dunham and Robert T. Carr, "Music" in Dwight Allen and Eli Seifman (Editors), *The Teacher's Handbook*, Glenview, IL: Scott, Foresman and Company, 1971; Orlando Moss, *Complete Handbook for Teaching Small Vocal Ensembles*, West Nyack, NY: Parker Publishing Company, Inc., 1978; Ray Robinson and Allen Winold, *The Choral Experience: Literature, Materials, and Methods,* New York: Harper's College Press, 1976.

VOCATIONAL BUSINESS EDUCATION—See BUSINESS EDUCATION

VOCATIONAL COUNSELING, or career counseling, the formal process through which an individual makes informed vocational decisions. It is a part of a vocational guidance program. Vocational counseling may be included, formally or informally, in a school curriculum (career education, regular school curriculum, vocational education). A formal program of testing (i.e. personality, psychological, vocational interest, skill, and aptitude tests) are normally made part of the vocational counseling process. In-depth counseling, interviews directed by a trained vocational guidance specialist, or directed exposure to various occupations, trades, or professions are part of the vocational counseling approach.

Vocational counseling as a process not only deals with the knowledges of present and future vocational occupations and economic needs, but it also includes the fields of psychology, sociology, decision making, education, group dynamics, learning theory, developmental theories, model building, phenomenological methodology, formal and informal testing, assessment and evaluation procedures, and counseling research. The focus is on the individual's making an appropriate and realistic assessment of goals, attributes, skills, interests, and so on and consequently making appropriate vocational choices and selections to maximize his/her potential for both the present and the future. Many counseling programs make provisions for organized group counseling.

Vocational counselors are found in schools, in public community and private agencies such as employment services and agencies, and in large businesses. In schools, most vocational counselors have had extensive formal training and education to qualify for certification (most are required to hold advanced degrees in counseling and guidance). Many authorities attribute modern counseling to the development of vocational guidance by Jesse B. Davis, Eli Weaver, and Frank Parsons in the first decade of the 20th century. (See VOCATIONAL GUIDANCE.)

References: Robert F. Glerum and Donna T. Blake, *Vocational Decision Workbook*, Cranston, RI: Carroll Press, 1977; Edwin L. Herr, *Vocational Guidance and Human Development*, Boston: Houghton Mifflin Company, 1974; Robert Hoppock, *Occupational Information* (Fourth Edition), New York: McGraw-Hill Book Company, 1975; Herman T. Peters and James C. Hansen, *Vocational Guidance and Career Development: Selected Readings* (Third Edition), New York: Macmillan Book Company, 1977.

VOCATIONAL EDUCATION, a part of the school curriculum designed to make the student employable in at least one occupation. Federal legislation defines vocational education as including all occupations except those requiring at least a baccalaureate degree or the professions. Vocational education includes the fields of agricultural education, business and office education, distributive education, health occupations education, wage earning, home economics education, trade and industrial education, and technical education.

Various pieces of federal legislation, dating back to 1785, have influenced and expedited the development of vocational education. (See AREA VOCATIONAL EDUCATION SCHOOL; ELEMENTARY AND SECONDARY EDUCATION

ACT; MANPOWER DEVELOPMENT AND TRAINING ACT; MORRILL ACT; NATIONAL DEFENSE EDUCATION ACT; ORDINANCE OF 1785; PERKINS, CARL D., VOCATIONAL EDUCATION ACT; SMITH-HUGHES ACT; VOCATIONAL EDUCATION ACT OF 1963; and VOCATIONAL EDUCATION AMENDMENTS OF 1968.)

References: Calfrey C. Calhoun and Alton V. Finch, *Vocational and Career Education: Concepts and Operations* (Second Edition), Belmont, CA: Wadsworth Publishing Company, Inc., 1982; Rupert N. Evans and Edwin L. Herr, *Foundations of Vocational Education* (Second Edition), Columbus, OH: Charles E. Merrill Publishing Company, 1978; Tim L. Wentling, *Toward Excellence in Secondary Vocational Education*, Columbus, OH: National Center for Research in Vocational Education, 1985.

VOCATIONAL EDUCATION ACT OF 1963 (PL 88–210), federal legislation designed to: (1) extend existing vocational education programs and encourage development of new ones; (2) stimulate research and experimentation; and (3) make work-study programs available to full-time vocational education students. Additionally, the act amended previously enacted vocational education legislation (Smith-Hughes, George-Barden, and National Defense Education Acts). Funds were allocated to the states on a formula basis and were used for specific efforts such as support of programs, strengthening of teacher education, and construction of area vocational educational schools. This act was significantly amended with the passage of the Carl D. Perkins Act of 1984. (See AREA VOCATIONAL EDUCATION SCHOOL; GEORGE-BARDEN ACT; NATIONAL DEFENSE EDUCATION ACT; PERKINS (CARL D.) VOCATIONAL EDUCATION ACT; SMITH HUGHES ACT; and VOCATIONAL EDUCATION AMENDMENTS OF 1968.)

References: Public Law 88–210, *United States Statutes at Large*, 1963 (Volume 77), Washington, DC: U.S. Government Printing Office, 1964; Roy W. Roberts, *Vocational and Practical Arts Education: History, Development, and Principles* (Third Edition), New York: Harper and Row, Publishers, 1971.

VOCATIONAL EDUCATION AMENDMENTS OF 1968 (Public Law 90-576), legislation enacted to amend (virtually rewrite) the Vocational Education Act of 1963. This legislation was omnibus, addressing numerous national vocational education needs. Funds were appropriated to strengthen and/or introduce specific kinds of programs, some requiring state matching. Title I of the amendments provided for: (1) general vocational-education programs; (2) research and training in vocational education; (3) exemplary programs/projects; (4) demonstration residential vocational programs for youths aged 15–21 (including funds to support dormitory construction); (5) consumer and homemaking education; (6) cooperative vocational education programs; (7) work study programs; and (8) curriculum development. Titles II and III contained numerous provisions including the granting of leadership development awards to prospective vocational education leaders. (See VOCATIONAL EDUCATION ACT OF 1963.)

References: Public Law 90-576, *United States Statutes at Large*, 1968 (Volume 82), Washington, DC: U.S. Government Printing Office, 1969; Roy W. Roberts, *Vocational and Practical Arts Education: History, Development, and Principles* (Third Edition), New York: Harper and Row, Publishers, 1971.

VOCATIONAL GUIDANCE, or career guidance, the broad set of services (programs) that help individuals to acquire, assimilate, and use occupational and vocational information that is appropriate to their needs and potential (e.g. vocational abilities, interests, and vocational and personal traits). One of the emphases in vocational guidance is personal/vocational decision making, both group and individual. Another is the area of occupational information. In many vocational guidance programs, placement and follow-up activities are also included.

Both the vocational counselor and the teacher are important participants in the vocational guidance program. Both need to be aware of occupations, occupation literature, current occupational information, techniques of evaluation and assessment, and similar information in order to provide effective vocational guidance. This is especially important for the counselor. Both will use vocational guidance procedures in varying degrees and at various levels as part of the vocational guidance program. (See PLACEMENT and VOCATIONAL COUNSELING.)

References: Calfrey C. Calhoun and Alton V. Finch, *Vocational Education: Concepts and Operations* (Second Edition), Belmont, CA: Wadsworth Publishing Company, 1982; Herman J. Peters and James C. Hansen, *Vocational Guidance and Career Development: Selected Readings* (Third Edition), New York: Macmillan Publishing Company, Inc., 1977.

VOCATIONAL HOME ECONOMICS, a term

used to denote those homemaking and home economics programs that are funded, or partly funded, by the United States government and that are designed to prepare students for wage-earning positions in the home economics field. The origins of such funding date back to 1917 when the Smith-Hughes Act became law. This act allowed federal, state, and local monies to be spent on homemaking programs. As a result of the development of "vocational home economics," home economics expanded from domestic science or domestic arts (cooking, cleaning, needlework) to a much broader field that included subjects such as child development, consumer education, textiles and clothing, food and nutrition, interior design, and family resources. (See CONSUMER EDUCATION; FAMILY RESOURCES EDUCATION; FOODS AND NUTRITION; HOME ECONOMICS; INTERIOR DESIGN; and TEXTILES AND CLOTHING.)

References: Olive A. Hall, *Home Economics: Careers and Homemaking,* New York: John Wiley and Sons, 1958; Marjorie East, *Home Economics: Past, Present, and Future,* Boston: Allyn and Bacon, Inc., 1980; Mildred T. Tate, *Home Economics as a Profession* (Second Edition), New York: McGraw-Hill Book Company, 1973.

VOCATIONAL REHABILITATION, the training for employment of an individual who is physically and/or mentally handicapped. Vocational rehabilitation may include diagnostic service, counseling, occupational and physical therapy, medical therapy, psychological services, training for a specific occupation, books and equipment, job placement, some financial support, tuition for college or technical schools, supervision, transportation, and/or services aimed at specific handicaps (e.g. readers for the blind, sign language specialists).

All states in the United States plus the federal government have agencies concerned exclusively with vocational rehabilitation. Many nonpublic social service agencies are also involved in such rehabilitation.

References: Stephen J. Feldman (Editor), *Readings in Career and Vocational Education for the Handicapped,* Guilford, CT: Special Learning Corporation, 1979; John E. Muthard and Linda M. Crocker, *Knowledge Utilization Resources and Practices of Vocational Rehabilitation Managers,* Gainsville, FL: University of Florida, 1974.

VOLUNTEERS IN SERVICE TO AMERICA— See VISTA

VOUCHERS, or educational vouchers, a plan for changing the traditional system of tax-supported schools. The plan proposes making educational vouchers available to parents of school-aged children, these entitling bearer's children to free education at a public or private school of the parents' choosing. The school would subsequently exchange vouchers received for cash. Several variations of the voucher plan have been put forth. The best known was developed by Christopher Jencks and his associates at Harvard's Center for the Study of Public Policy.

Proponents of the voucher plan support it for different reasons. Some see it as a way to benefit minority children or children of the poor. Others support it as a way to assist parents of children enrolled in nonpublic schools. The voucher idea is opposed by numerous educational organizations and some religious groups. Successful and extensive field testing of the voucher concept, a suggestion included in Jencks' proposal, has yet to take place.

References: Center for the Study of Public Policy, *Education Vouchers: A Report on Financing Education by Payments to Parents,* Cambridge, MA: The Center, December 1970; George R. La Noue (Editor), *Educational Vouchers: Concepts and Controversies,* New York: Teachers College Press, Columbia University, 1972; James A. Mecklenburger and Richard W. Hostrop (Editors), *Education Vouchers: From Theory to Alum Rock,* Homewood, IL: ETC Publications, 1972; Tyll Van Geel, "Parental Preferences and the Politics of Spending Public Educational Funds," *Teachers College Record,* February 1978.

VOWEL CLUSTERS, a general term used in phonics instruction that includes both vowel digraphs and dipthongs. (See DIGRAPH and DIPTHONG.)

Reference: Roger Farr and Nancy Roser, *Teaching A Child to Read,* New York: Harcourt Brace Jovanovich, Inc., 1979.

WALDORF EDUCATION, an independent and nonsectarian school movement based on the writings and teachings of the German educator, Rudolf Steiner. At the invitation of, and with the encouragement of German industrialist Emil Molt, Steiner (in 1919) opened the Freie Waldorf Schule in Stuttgart. The school was coeducational, open to children of all social classes/religions, and independent of political or other forms of interference. Faculty had considerable control over its program.

Since 1919, almost 200 Waldorf schools have been established in many parts of the world. Colleges and special training centers for teachers have been created with curricula devoted to the educational teachings of Steiner. Notwithstanding the common philosophy to which each Waldorf school subscribes, the schools operate as virtually autonomous units.

The Waldorf curriculum is based on the human being's developmental stages as described by Steiner. To accommodate both the cultural and vocational needs of learners, Roy Wilkinson reported, the Waldorf program works to implement four specific goals: (1) training in intellectual and manipulative skills; (2) an awakening of social conscience; (3) cultivating self-expression; and (4) spiritual development.

School organization reflects Steiner's three phases of child development (0 to 6; 7 to 14; and 14 and older). The Infant School, the Middle School, and the Upper School accommodate these age groups, respectively. Middle School teachers are subject generalists; Steiner urged that they remain with and teach the same group of children for the full eight years. Upper School teachers, on the other hand, are subject specialists who are chosen on the basis of their knowledge of subject and their personal convictions.

References: Henry Barnes, "An Introduction to Waldorf Education," *Teachers College Record,* Spring 1980; Rudolf Steiner, *The Education of the Child* (Second Edition), London, England: Rudolf Steiner Press, 1965; E. A. Karl Stockmeyer, *Rudolf Steiner's Curriculum for Waldorf Schools,* London, England: Rudolf Steiner Press, 1969; Roy Wilkinson, *Commonsense Schooling: Based on the Indications of Rudolf Steiner,* Hastings, England: Henry Goulden Limited, 1975.

WASHBURNE, CARLETON (December 2, 1889–November 17, 1968), noted educational innovator and author who gained international recognition while superintendent of the Winnetka, Illinois school district (1919–43). With the help of his faculty, he introduced pre-Kindergarten programs for three- and four-year-olds, an early form of programmed instruction, and elementary guidance programs. The Graduate Teachers College of Winnetka, which he helped to form for the Winnetka schools, trained graduates of liberal arts colleges and prepared them for teaching posts. Instructors were chosen from among the best teachers in the Winnetka system.

Following World War II (1949), Washburne became Director of Teacher Education and Director of the Graduate Division at Brooklyn College, N.Y., a post he held until 1960. From 1961 to 1967, he served as Distinguished Professor, College of Education, Michigan State University.

Washburne earned a doctorate at the University of California and taught science at San Francisco State College for Teachers (1914–19) before assuming the Winnetka superintendency. During his career, he served for four years (1939–43) as President of the Progressive Education Association; chaired yearbook committees for the National Society for the Study of Education; served as Vice-President of the American Educational Research Association; authored over 100 significant books and articles; and served as President of the New Education Fellowship (1947-56). After World War II, working with several federal agencies, he was active in helping to reorganize the public schools of Italy.

References: Larry P. Donahue, "Washburne, Carleton Wolsey" in John F. Ohles (Editor), *Biographical Dictionary of American Educators* (Volume 3), Westport, CT: Greenwood Press, 1978; Carleton W. Washburne, "Carleton Wolsey Washburne" in Robert J. Havighurst (Editor), *Leaders in Education* (NSSE 70th Yearbook, Part II), Chicago: University of Chicago Press, 1971.

WASHINGTON, BOOKER T. (April 5, 1856–November 14, 1915), a prominent black educator in America. Washington was born into slavery. He attended Hampton Institute where he was introduced to ideas and values that gave direction to his future work. In 1880, he founded Tuskegee Institute (Alabama), an institution of higher education for blacks, and directed it until his death. Influencing that institution's curriculum were Washington's belief in the dignity of manual work, his middle-class values, and his commitment to character education. Notwithstanding criticism of his ideas by some young blacks anxious for racial reform (a black militant who opposed Washington's accommodation policy was W. E. B. Dubois), Washington remained America's preeminent black educator throughout his lifetime. (See TUSKEGEE INSTITUTE.)

References: Shirley Graham, *Booker T. Washington: Educator of Hand, Head, and Heart*, New York: Julian Messner, 1955; Louis R. Harlan, *Booker T. Washington: The Making of a Black Leader, 1856–1901*, New York: Oxford University Press, 1972; Booker T. Washington, *Up From Slavery: An Autobiography* (School Edition), Cambridge, MA: The Riverside Press (Reprinted Houghton Mifflin Company, 1928).

WATER COLORS, pigments that use water rather than oil as a vehicle. Color pigments are in a gum arabic binder and are soluble in water. Water colors, when dried, allow light to pass through the colors to reflect off the paper. Also, the grain of the paper on which they have been placed can be seen through water colors. To get lighter color tones, the artist needs only to add water to the color rather than white pigment.

Water colors are easy to handle and use. They are sold in tubes and pans. Water color pans are widely used in elementary school art and general classrooms.

Water colors date back to ancient Egypt and China. They were used extensively in Europe during the Middle Ages in manuscripts.

References: Hale Chatfield, *Water Colors*, Gulfport, FL: Konglomerati Press, 1979; John Holden, *Water Colors: A Complete Teach-Yourself Handbook*, New York: Van Nostrand Reinhold Company, 1980; Mariene Linderman, *Art in the Elementary School: Drawing, Painting, and Creating for the Classroom*, Dubuque, IA: Wm. C. Brown Company, Publishers, 1979.

WEBSTER, NOAH (October 16, 1758–May 28, 1843), lawyer, teacher, author, and lexicographer who is best remembered for authoring a dictionary that has remained a standard reference work since its publication. That work, the two-volume *An American Dictionary of the English Language*, was completed in 1825 and published in 1828. "I finished writing my dictionary in January, 1825.... When I had come to the last word, I was seized with a trembling, which made it somewhat difficult to hold my pen steady for writing. The cause seems to have been the thought that I might

not then live to finish the work . . . (b)ut I summoned strength to finish the last word, and then walking about the room a few minutes, I recovered" (Harvey Warfel, p. 357).

Webster is also remembered for his blue-backed Spelling Book. In 1788, it became the first of his three-part *A Grammatical Institute of the English Language* (1783–85). Other of his books were: *Dissertations on the English Language* (1785); *A Philosophical and Practical Grammar of the English Language* (1807); *Sketches of American Policy* (1785); the four-volume *Elements of Useful Knowledge* (1802–12); and *History of the United States* (1832).

Webster encountered copyright problems in connection with his speller. He worked diligently to protect his interest in it and is reported to have contributed to bringing about reforms in copyright legislation.

References: John F. Ohles, "Webster, Noah" in John F. Ohles (Editor), *Biographical Dictionary of American Educators* (Volume 3), Westport, CT: Greenwood Press, 1978; Harry R. Warfel, *Noah Webster: Schoolmaster to America*, New York: The Macmillan Company, 1936.

WECHSLER ADULT INTELLIGENCE SCALE (WAIS), first published in 1955, an individual test of general intelligence for adults 15 years and older. It had its origins in the Wechsler-Bellevue Intelligence Scale. The scale itself is made up of two component scales, a *Verbal Scale* (consisting of information, comprehension, arithmetic, similarities, digit span, and vocabulary) and a *Performance Scale* (made up of digit symbol, picture completion, block design, picture arrangement, and object assembly).

Mental age is not part of the computation of the I.Q. score in the WAIS; consequently, the score is not expressed as a quotient. The raw scores are converted directly into I.Q. scores (actually a deviation I.Q. score) and are based on the assumption that intelligence is normally distributed. (See DEVIATION I.Q. and WECHSLER-BELLEVUE INTELLIGENCE SCALE.)

References: J. Stanley Ahmann and Marvin D. Glock, *Evaluating Pupil Growth: Principles of Tests and Measurement* (Fifth Edition), Boston: Allyn and Bacon, Inc., 1975; W. Bruce Walsh and Nancy E. Betz, *Tests and Measurement*, Englewood Cliffs, NJ: Prentice-Hall, Inc., 1985; David Wechsler, *Wechsler Adult Intelligence Scale Manual*, New York: Psychological Corporation, 1955.

WECHSLER-BELLEVUE INTELLIGENCE SCALE, an individual intelligence test first published in 1939 (Form I) and designed to assess the intelligence of adults. David Wechsler developed the test for his patients at New York City's Bellevue Hospital. He elected to develop the instrument specifically for adults rather than revise an existing intelligence test designed for children. Items of interest to adults made up the tests; also, speed was not emphasized as much as it is in children's intelligence tests. The Wechsler Adult Intelligence Scale of today is not too dissimilar from the original Wechsler-Bellevue Intelligence Scale. (See WECHSLER ADULT INTELLIGENCE SCALE.)

References: J. Stanley Ahmann and Marvin D. Glock, *Evaluating Pupil Growth: Principles of Tests and Measurement* (Fifth Edition), Boston: Allyn and Bacon, Inc., 1975; Anne Anastasi, *Psychological Testing* (Sixth Edition), New York: Macmillan Publishing Company, Inc., 1988; David Wechsler, *The Measurement of Adult Intelligence* (Third Edition), Baltimore, MD: The Williams and Wilkins Company, 1944.

WECHSLER INTELLIGENCE SCALE FOR CHILDREN (WISC), an individual intelligence test designed for children between the ages of 5 and 15. The test, first designed as a simpler form of the Wechsler-Bellevue Intelligence Scale, was revised in 1974 (WISC-R). There are 12 subtests that make up the WISC (but two digit span and mazes are not used in determining I.Q. They may be used as supplementary tests if time permits.) The WISC's two major scales are *verbal* (consisting of general information, general comprehension, arithmetic, similarities, and vocabulary) and *performance* (made up of picture completion, picture arrangement, block design, object assembly, coding or mazes).

It takes a well-trained examiner to administer the WISC. Although some scoring is objective, certain parts require considerable professional interpretation. A deviation I.Q. score is produced by the WISC. (See DEVIATION I.Q. and WECHSLER-BELLEVUE INTELLIGENCE SCALE.)

References: J. Stanley Ahmann and Marvin D. Glock, *Evaluating Pupil Growth: Principles of Tests and Measurement* (Fifth Edition), Boston: Allyn and Bacon, Inc., 1975; Tom Kubiszyn and Gary Borich, *Educational Testing and Measurement: Classroom Application and Practice* (Second Edition), Glenview, IL: Scott Foresman and Company, 1987; W. Bruce Walsh and Nancy E. Betz, *Tests and Measurement*, Englewood Cliffs, NJ: Prentice-Hall, Inc., 1985; David Wechsler, *Wechsler Intelligence Scale for Children* (Revised), New York: Psychological Corporation, 1974.

WECHSLER PRESCHOOL AND PRIMARY SCALE OF INTELLIGENCE (WPPSI), an indi-

vidual intelligence test designed for children between the ages of four and six, and first developed in 1967. This test is a revision (downward) of the Wechsler Intelligence Scale for Children. Although the instrument consists of 11 subtests, only 10 are used in finding the deviation I.Q. (Sentences, a memory test, is the 11th subtest that can be used as a supplementary test). WPPSI's two major scales are the *verbal* (consisting of information, vocabulary, arithmetic, similarities, and comprehension) and *performance* (made up of animal house, picture completion, mazes, geometric design, and block design).

Like the other Wechsler scales, the WPPSI requires a skilled and highly trained test administrator. The total time required to take the test ranges from 50 to 75 minutes. It can be administered in two sessions. (See WECHSLER INTELLIGENCE SCALE FOR CHILDREN.)

References: Robert P. Ingalls, *Mental Retardation: The Changing Outlook*, New York: John Wiley and Sons, 1978; W. Bruce Walsh and Nancy E. Betz, *Tests and Measurement*, Englewood Cliffs, NJ: Prentice-Hall, Inc., 1985; David Wechsler, *Manual for the Wechsler Preschool and Primary Scale of Intelligence*, New York: Psychological Corporation, 1967.

WEIGHTED ELEMENTARY PUPIL UNIT (WEPU), or weighted classroom unit, an early measure used by school business officials when computing school district per-pupil costs or determining financial need. A base unit of 1.0 was used for all full-time students enrolled in grades 1–6. Adjustments were then made to accommodate: (1) differences in elementary vs. secondary school costs per pupil (e.g. 1.0 for each elementary, 1.3 for each secondary student enrolled); (2) transportation costs and/or adjustments for small classes; and (3) differences in cost of living from one school district to another. After all adjustments were made, weighted pupil costs were determined using the formula:

$$\text{WEPU Costs} = \frac{\text{Total district costs}}{\text{Total district WEPU's}}.$$

In recent years, the *Full-Time Equivalent* (FTE) has replaced the WEPU as a basis for determining adjusted per-pupil costs. (See FULL-TIME EQUIVALENT.)

References: Paul R. Mort, *The Measurement of Educational Need*, Bureau of Publications, Teachers College, Columbia University, 1924; Paul R. Mort and Walter C. Reusser, *Public School Finance: Its Background, Structure, and Operation* (Second Edition), New York: McGraw-Hill Book Company, 1951.

WESTERN INTERSTATE COMMISSION FOR HIGHER EDUCATION (WICHE), a consortium of 13 western states organized for the purpose of creating a regional forum to examine education issues. WICHE was founded in 1953. Member states are Alaska, Arizona, California, Colorado, Hawaii, Idaho, Montana, Nevada, New Mexico, Oregon, Utah, Washington, and Wyoming. Policy decisions are made by the organization's 39 commissioners (three from each member state appointed by their respective governors).

WICHE's major activity is its student exchange program, one that makes it possible for students to enroll in professional programs (e.g. veterinary medicine, dentistry) when such programs are not available to qualified students in their own states. Other services/activities include: (1) maintaining an Information Clearinghouse; (2) several health services efforts including one designed to develop linkages between policymakers and health research; and (3) sponsorship of an internship program to help students gain practical experience in their fields of study.

WICHE's main office is in Boulder, Colorado.

Reference: Western Interstate Commission for Higher Education, *Improving Education in the West: Annual Report 1979,* Boulder, CO: The Commission, 1979.

WET CARREL—See CARREL

WHITE ACADEMIES, racially segregated private schools, located in border and southern states, that experienced significant enrollment increases following the 1954 U.S. Supreme Court decision (*Brown v. Board of Education*) outlawing the separate-but-equal doctrine for education. White academies, many of which were established after 1954, were viewed by many white parents as being, for them, a viable alternative to desegregated public schools. Some unofficial estimates, in 1969–70, placed enrollments in the increasingly popular academies at close to 500,000 (See *BROWN v. BOARD OF EDUCATION OF TOPEKA.*)

References: Anthony M. Champagne, "The Segregation Academy and the Law," *The Journal of Negro Education,* Winter 1973; Thomas J. Flygare, "Schools and the Law: The Supreme Court Ruling on Exclusion by Private Schools," *Phi Delta Kappan,* November 1976; *Runyon v. McCrary,* 96 S.Ct. 2586 (1976).

WHITE FLIGHT, the outmigration of white residents from central cities to suburban and rural communities. This exodus, coupled with migration of blacks and other minorities into the cities, has resulted in significantly high minority enrollment ratios in many city school districts.

In 1975, James S. Coleman published a report in which he concluded that the white flight phenomenon was causally related to school desegregation efforts. This conclusion precipitated considerable negative reaction by Robert Green, Thomas Pettigrew, and other critics who were inclined to attribute these demographic changes to factors other than court-ordered desegregation.

References: James S. Coleman, "Racial Segregation in the Schools: New Research with New Policy Implications," *Phi Delta Kappan,* October 1975; James S. Coleman, et al., *Trends in School Segregation, 1968–73,* Washington, DC: Urban Institute, 1975; Robert L. Green and Thomas F. Pettigrew, "Urban Desegregation and White Flight: A Response to Coleman," *Phi Delta Kappan,* February 1976; Robert G. Wegmann, "White Flight and School Resegregation: Some Hypotheses," *Phi Delta Kappan,* January 1977.

WHOLE LANGUAGE, a theoretical premise that language is acquired through use. Anyone using language, regardless of the level of language facility, uses all language cueing systems interactively to get meaning. These cueing systems are phonology, orthography, morphology, syntax, semantics, and pragmatics. Whole Language proponents believe that language is acquired through actual use and not through isolated practicing of the separate components. Translation of the theory into practice involves the learner in experiences with original oral and written materials as opposed to interaction with the separate components of language via practice exercises.

Whole Language classrooms are stocked with a variety of print material. There is a heavy reliance on literature as well as purposeful print such as maps, recipes, and directions. Writing is conducted for specific purposes as well. There is little use for materials designed specifically to teach separate reading or writing subskills. Since the theory views the learner as a social being, Whole Language strategies would include activities such as a small-group literature study, small-group social studies projects, and peer evaluation of writing. The teacher serves as facilitator, resource person, and director to a collaborative learning experience.

References: Kenneth Goodman, *What's Whole in Whole Language?* Exeter, NH: Heinemann, 1986; Judith Lindfords, *Children's Language and Learning* (Second Edition), Englewood Cliffs, NJ: Prentice-Hall, 1987; Judith Newman, *Whole Language: Theory in Use,* Portsmouth, NH: Heinemann, 1985.

WHOLE-TONE SCALE—See SCALE, MUSICAL

WHO'S WHO IN AMERICAN EDUCATION, a biennial biographic dictionary of living educators of the United States and Canada that was first published in 1928. The 23rd and last edition was published in 1968. Many university and college professors, librarians, superintendents, and school principals were listed in these reference works. Professional experiences, education, accomplishments, and some personal activities were included in each biography. The volumes were published by Who's Who in American Education, Inc., Hattiesburg, Mississippi. (See LEADERS IN EDUCATION.)
References: Robert C. Cook and Margie McDuff (Editors), *Who's Who in American Education,* Hattiesburg, MS: Who's Who in American Education, Inc., 1968; Eugene P. Sheehy (Compiler), *Guide to Reference Books,* Chicago: American Library Association, 1976.

WILES, KIMBALL (October 17, 1913–February 2, 1968), noted author and teacher of educational curriculum and supervision. He taught at the University of Alabama and New York University and, for a time, worked for the National Safety Council. Wiles's last university position was as Professor and Dean of Education at the University of Florida. Of his numerous books and articles, his widely read *Supervision for Better Schools* (1955) and *The Changing Curriculum of the American High School* (1963) did much to influence the teaching of educational supervision and curriculum in the United States. Wiles served as President of the Association for Supervision and Curriculum Development in 1963–64.
References: Jesse M. Hansen, *Kimball Wiles' Contributions to Curriculum and Instruction: An Analysis Within an Historical Context,* University of Texas at Austin: Ph.D. Dissertation, 1971; Gerald A. Ponder, "Wiles, Kimball" in John F. Ohles (Editor), *Biographical Dictionary of American Educators* (Volume 3), Westport, CT: Greenwood Press, 1978.

WILLARD, EMMA H. (February 3, 1787–April 15, 1870), early champion of improved and equal education for American women. In 1819, she authored a "plan" designed to make postelementary schooling available to women and on a par with educational programs then available to men. The significance of her pioneering effort is better appreciated when one realizes that, at the time her "plan" was written, public high schools had yet to be established; Latin Grammar schools were catering to male students only; and no American college would admit female students.

In 1821, at the invitation of some leading citizens, she opened her Troy School (Seminary) for girls in Troy, New York. Ninety girls enrolled. In time, the school became well known for its high academic standards and succeeded in attracting young women students from all social strata. Willard directed the Troy School until 1838. It was later renamed the Emma Willard School.

In 1840, she was elected Superintendent of the Kensington, Connecticut, school district, one of the first women to achieve the superintendency.
References: Mildred S. Fenner and Eleanor C. Fishburn, *Pioneer American Educators,* Port Washington, NY: Kennikat Press, Inc., 1968; Alma Lutz, *Emma Willard: Pioneer Educator of American Women,* Boston: Beacon Press, 1964.

WING STANDARDIZED TESTS OF MUSICAL INTELLIGENCE, a test that purports to measure acuity of musical hearing and sensitivity to musical performance. The test itself is made up of seven subtests, with each subtest providing a score. Chord Analysis, Pitch Change, and Memory are considered measures of *acuity;* Rhythmic Accent, Harmony, Intensity, and Phrasing are measures of *sensitivity.* The test provides a total score as well. The test is published by the National Foundation for Educational Research in England and Wales and was first developed by H. D. Wing, in 1939, for children eight years of age and older. The latest edition of the test was published in 1961. Musical traits, rather than musical factual knowledges, are the major discriminators in the test. (See MUSICAL APTITUDE.)
References: Oscar K. Buros (Editor), *Tests in Print II,* Highland Park, NJ: The Gryphon Press, 1974; Oscar K. Buros (Editor), *The Sixth Mental Measurements Yearbook,* Highland Park, NJ: The Gryphon Press, 1965; Paul R. Lehman, *Tests and Measurements in Music,* Englewood Cliffs, NJ: Prentice-Hall, Inc., 1968; Herbert Wing, *Tests of Musical Ability and Appreciation* (Second Edition), Cambridge, England: Cambridge University Press, 1968.

WINNETKA PLAN, introduced in 1919 by Winnetka, Illinois, Superintendent Carleton Washburne as a way to individualize instruction in the elementary school. Curriculum was divided into two components. The first part consisted of the "common knowledges or skills" (reading, writing, language usage, and spelling) that the plan's author believed all students needed to master. These subjects were taught on an individualized basis; pupils progressed through the programs at their own rate. Each student was required to record his/her progress on worksheets developed for the program. The second part of the curriculum consisted of cultural and creative experiences that were taught in group settings.

References: Elwood P. Cubberly, *Public Education in the United States: A Study and Interpretation of American Educational History,* Cambridge, MA: The Riverside Press, 1962 (Printed originally by Houghton Mifflin Company, 1919); Carleton W. Washburne, *Adjusting the School to the Child,* New York: World Book Company, 1932; Carleton W. Washburne and Sidney P. Marland, Jr., *Winnetka: The History and Significance of an Educational Experiment,* Englewood Cliffs, NJ: Prentice-Hall, Inc., 1963.

WISC—See WECHSLER INTELLIGENCE SCALE FOR CHILDREN

WITHDRAWAL, a term that has two major meanings. Behaviorists use the term to describe lack of interaction (voluntary or involuntary) with others. Withdrawal is sometimes a form of adaptive reaction to constant frustration or failure. Compromising or substitution may be a form of withdrawal, although not all compromises or substitutions are necessarily withdrawal symptoms. Autism is an extreme example of social withdrawal. In some cases, withdrawal is one of the primary symptoms of schizophrenia.

When used in the context of drugs, the term *withdrawal* is identified with the symptoms one experiences when the use of drugs is discontinued. These symptoms may be physical (e.g. pain, vomiting, cramps, diarrhea) and/or psychological (e.g. irritability, depression, restlessness, inability to sleep, inability to concentrate). Withdrawal symptoms may occur whenever one has established a physical dependence on something (whether it be drugs, coffee, cigarettes) and then discontinues its use. Under some conditions, sudden cessation of a drug may produce withdrawal symptoms so severe as to cause death.

The physical symptoms of withdrawal are easier to identify than are the social/psychological (until they become extreme).

References: James Geiwitz, *Looking at Ourselves,* Boston: Little, Brown and Company, 1976; Barbara Gordon, *I'm Dancing As Fast As I Can,* New York: Harper and Row, Publishers, 1979; Kurt Schlesinger, et al., *Psychology,* Dubuque, IA: Wm. C. Brown Company, Publishers, 1976; James O. Whittaker, *Introduction to Psychology* (Second Edition), Philadelphia: W. B. Saunders Company, 1970.

W. K. KELLOGG FOUNDATION—See KELLOGG FOUNDATION

WOODSON, CARTER G.—See BLACK HISTORY MONTH

WORD-ASSOCIATION PROCEDURES, those psychological tests (procedures) in which stimulus words are read to an individual; the individual, in turn, responds with a word that he or she associates with each stimulus presented. There are generally two types of word-association tests: (1) *free-association tests,* in which the individual may select any word that comes to mind, and (2) *controlled-association tests,* in which an individual can only select responses falling within certain prescribed areas. In psychology, word-association tests are used to assess the personality, perceptions, attitudes and/or feelings of individuals. Jung and Freud were psychologists who used word association in their work. The semantic differential scale is a special case of word association.

Word-association procedures can be employed in the teaching of reading as well. When used for this purpose, they serve to develop vocabulary and to promote language learning. For example, pictures and words (associated with the picture) are placed next to each other. In this way, children learn the meaning of a particular word by associating it with a picture. Word-association procedures can include the association of words with words (similar or opposites), a procedure normally reserved for use with the more mature and developed reader. (See SEMANTIC DIFFERENTIAL TECHNIQUE.)

References: Donald C. Cushenbery, *Guide to Meeting Competency Requirements: Effective Diagnosis and Correction of Reading Difficulties,* West Nyack, NY: Parker Publishing Company, Inc., 1981; C. G. Jung, *Studies in Word Association,* New York: Moffat Yard, 1919; Donald E. P. Smith, *Learning to Read and Write,* New York: Academic Press, 1976; Lorand B. Szalay and James Deese, *Subjective Meaning and Culture: An Assessment Through Word Associations,* Hillsdale, NJ: Lawrence Erlbaum Associates, Publishers, 1978.

WORD-ATTACK SKILLS, specific skills taught to students for use when they encounter new and unfamiliar words. Most reading authorities agree that there are two principal word recognition methods that students need to understand: structural analysis and phonic analysis. *Structural analysis* involves the breaking down of new words by seeking out their meaningful parts (e.g. roots, prefixes, suffixes). *Phonic analysis* is the method that involves the association of particular sounds with specific letters and blending them to form words. Some authorities also list *context analysis* as a third word recognition method, one in which readers are taught to use word and picture clues to infer the meaning of an unfamiliar word. (See CLUES, READING; PHONICS; and STRUCTURAL ANALYSIS.)

References: Daniel R. Hittleman, *Developmental Reading, K–8* (Third Edition), Columbus, OH: Merrill Publishing Company, 1988; William H. Rupley and Timothy R. Blair, *Reading Diagnosis and Remediation: A Primer for Classroom and Clinic*, Chicago: Rand McNally College Publishing Company, 1979; Ellen L. Thomas and H. Alan Robinson, *Improving Reading in Every Class: A Sourcebook for Teachers* (Second Edition), Boston: Allyn and Bacon, Inc., 1977; Robert M. Wilson and Craig J. Cleland, *Diagnostic and Remedial Reading for Classroom and Clinic* (Sixth Edition), Columbus, OH: Merrill Publishing Company, 1989.

WORD-BY-WORD READING—See WORD CALLING

WORD CALLING, or word-by-word reading, in reading, a term used to describe those individuals who read and pronounce one word at a time, usually without regard for the word's relationship to other words in the sentence. Word calling may be a result of poor word-attack skills, poor sight vocabulary, or a habit acquired during early reading instruction. Word calling affects both comprehension and reading rate. This problem can be corrected through exercises and techniques geared to improve speed, phrasing, rhythmic use of the eyes, sight vocabulary, and word-attack skills.

References: Emerald Dechant (Editor), *Detection and Correction of Reading Difficulties*, New York: Appleton-Century-Crofts, Inc., 1971; Eddie C. Kennedy, *Classroom Approaches to Remedial Reading* (Second Edition), Itasca, IL: F. E. Peacock Publishers, Inc., 1977; Miles V. Zintz, *The Reading Process: The Teacher and the Learner* (Second Edition), Dubuque, IA: Wm. C. Brown Company, Publishers, 1975.

WORD CONFIGURATION, an aid to teaching word recognition that calls the word's shape to the attention of the learner. The configuration of a word is shown by outlining it (e.g. grandfather, play). The technique is not without limitation, primarily because the outlining system does little to help with the discrimination of words having identical or similar shapes (e.g. saw, was; funny, fancy). (See SIGHT WORD.)

References: Dolores Durkin, *Teaching Them to Read* (Third Edition), Boston: Allyn and Bacon, Inc., 1978; Diane Lapp and James Flood, *Teaching Reading to Every Child*, New York: Macmillan Publishing Company, Inc., 1978.

WORD DEAFNESS—See CENTRAL DEAFNESS

WORD FAMILY, groups of words that rhyme, because they have a like element. The word family method of teaching reading (also known as the linguistic method) is recommended for students possessing limited phonics ability. Different initial consonants are placed before each word family (e.g. *f, c, b* before *at;* or *g, l, n* before *ame*) to create different words. The method requires the teacher to emphasize the symbol-sound associations of each initial consonant.

References: Albert J. Harris and Edward R. Sipay, *How to Increase Reading Ability: A Guide to Developmental and Remedial Methods* (Sixth Edition), New York: David McKay Company, Inc., 1975; Dale R. Jordan, *Dyslexia in the Classroom* (Second Edition), Columbus, OH: Charles E. Merrill Publishing Company, 1977.

WORD LISTS, or vocabulary lists that report frequently used words. Edward Thorndike's *A Teacher's Wordbook of 20,000 Words* was published in 1926 and later expanded to 30,000 words. Other wisely used word lists were prepared by Arthur Gates and Edward Dolch. The latter are designed for use with primary grade children. Other word lists are: *High Frequency Words* by A. J. Moe; *Harris-Jacobson Core Words; Great Atlantic and Pacific Word List* by W. Otto and R. Chester; *80 Most Frequently Occurring Words* by H. Kucere and W. Francis; and *Instant Words* by E. B. Fry. Word lists help to standardize vocabulary among reading textbook series with so-called *overlap* words (e.g. "come," "and," "here") appearing in many of these textbooks. Although teachers and publishers find word lists to be useful, some concern has been voiced that undue dependence on them can result in an unnecessarily controlled vocabulary.

References: Edward L. Dolch, *Methods in Reading*, Champaign, IL: The Garrard Publishing Company, 1955; Arthur I. Gates, *A Reading Vocabulary for the Primary Grades*, New York: Bureau of Publications, Teachers College, Columbia University, 1935; Joan P. Gipe, *Corrective Reading Techniques for the Classroom Teacher*, Scottsdale, AZ: Gorsuch Scarisbrick Publishers, 1987; Robert L. Hillerich, *A Writing Vocabulary of Elementary Children*, Springfield, IL: Charles C. Thomas, Publisher, 1978; Edward L. Thorndike, *A Teacher's Wordbook of 20,000 Words*, New York: Bureau of Publications, Teachers College, Columbia University, 1926.

WORD-RECOGNITION SKILL, the ability of a student to read a word on sight (from recall), to pronounce it correctly, and to know its meaning. Flash cards, simple teacher-made tachistoscopes, and word lists are materials used in the classroom to measure and to improve the student's word-recognition skills. (See TACHISTOSCOPE.)

References: Albert J. Harris and Edward R. Sipay, *How to Increase Reading Ability: A Guide to Developmental and Remedial Methods* (Sixth Edition), New York: David McKay Company, Inc., 1977; John F. Savage and Jean F. Mooney, *Teaching Reading to Children with Special Needs*, Boston: Allyn and Bacon, Inc., 1979.

WORDS-IN-COLOR, a linguistic-phonic system for the teaching of beginning reading, developed by Caleb Gattegno in 1957. Shades of colors (39) are used for the 47 sounds of English. These color cues are used to help a student learn letter-sound correspondences. Each vowel sound has its own color regardless of the letters of the word that represent the sound. Children may have difficulty with visual discrimination when the colors are not significantly different. Words-in-color can be classified as an artificial orthographic approach to reading. It has been found to be effective in teaching English as a second language. (See COLOR PHONICS SYSTEM.)
References: Verna D. Anderson, *Reading and Young Children*, New York: The Macmillan Company, 1968; Jeanne S. Chall, *Learning to Read: The Great Debate*, New York: McGraw-Hill Book Company, 1967; Diane Lapp and James Flood, *Teaching Reading to Every Child*, New York: Macmillan Publishing Company, Inc., 1978; Bernard Spodek, *Teaching in the Early Years*, Englewood Cliffs, NJ: Prentice-Hall, Inc., 1972.

WORD WHEEL, a simple aid for improving students' reading skills. The aid consists of one large wheel cut from cardboard on which, like numbers on a clock, are printed selected consonants. An inner (and smaller) wheel, superimposed over the first, contains a given phonogram (e.g. "at," "am," "ap"). By rotating one of the wheels, different alignments of consonants and phonograms occur that children are then asked to read. The word wheel may also be used to practice blends, prefixes, and suffixes. (See PHONOGRAMS.)
References: Pose Lamb and Richard Arnold (Editors), *Reading: Foundations and Instructional Strategies*, Belmont, CA: Wadsworth Publishing Company, Inc., 1976; Miles V. Zintz, *Corrective Reading* (Third Edition), Dubuque, IA: Wm. C. Brown Company, Publishers, 1977.

WORKBOOK, an exercise book, sometimes a supplement to a basic text, that is used to provide students with extra drills and/or training in a particular subject (e.g. reading, arithmetic, social studies). Several include inventory tests that help the teacher interested in individualizing instruction. Many workbooks are consumable soft-bound materials.

Workbooks had their origin in the change of reading instruction from oral to silent reading (about 1910). Children needed independent seatwork activities. Consequently, work-exercise materials were developed, first as single activity sheets, later bound into a workbook format.

Paul Burns and Betty Broman pointed out that workbooks can be used effectively, or abused in the instructional program, with the determinant of effectiveness being teacher use and not the material itself. They presented several usage suggestions for teachers of language, suggestions that are equally applicable to teachers of other subjects: (1) determine what the material assigned is to accomplish; (2) check work completed by students as soon as possible; (3) use inventory tests to ascertain student needs; (4) record pupil progress; and (5) refrain from excessive use of whole-class workbook assignments.
References: Walter R. Borg, et al., *Student Workbook in Educational Research* (to accompany *Educational Research: An Introduction,* Second Edition), New York: David McKay Company, Inc., 1974; Paul C. Burns and Betty L. Broman, *The Language Arts in Childhood Education* (Fourth Edition), Chicago: Rand McNally College Publishing Company, 1979; Douglas E. Cruikshank, et al., *Young Children Learning Mathematics*, Boston: Allyn and Bacon, Inc., 1980; Albert J. Harris and Edward R. Sipay, *How to Increase Reading Ability: A Guide to Developmental and Remedial Methods* (Sixth Edition), New York: David McKay Company, Inc., 1975.

WORK ORDER, a written instruction authorizing/ directing the performance of a specified task. Work orders are normally prepared by a supervisory person and are sent to those who are to direct and/or perform the work. They detail information such as: (1) task to be performed (e.g. installation of a classroom door); (2) work location; (3) specifications; and (4) job number. Work orders serve as a source of control, are usually arranged in some priority order, and serve as a basis for determining labor, supply, and equipment costs.
References: Combined Glossary: Terms and Definitions from the Handbooks of the State Educational Records and Reports Series, Washington, DC: National Center for Education Statistics, U.S. Department of Health, Education, and Welfare, 1974; Sheldon J. Fuchs, "Maintenance Management" in Lester R. Bittel (Editor), *Encyclopedia of Professional Management,* New York: McGraw-Hill Book Company, 1978; John Greenhalgh, *Practitioner's Guide to School Business Management,* Boston: Allyn and Bacon, Inc., 1978.

WORKSHOP, a mode of instruction that brings

together individuals with a common education concern, interest, or problem to work and learn together, in a specific place, for a short period. Workshops normally provide participants with new knowledges and skills. The emphasis of most workshops is skill development (as opposed to theory development); consequently, active "hands-on" participation and group planning are elements common to this type of instruction.

Workshops are usually shorter than regular courses, are oriented to practical use, are also solution oriented, and can be designed and/or sponsored by a variety of people, organizations, or groups. They may be designed by the participants themselves. Some carry college credit, continuing education unit credit, inservice credit, or credit for professional growth. The structures of workshops vary. Some make use of specialists who serve as leaders or consultants; others do not. Design, too, is flexible.

Workshops have been used by many groups, in and out of education. Businesses, artists, and social organizations, for example, use the workshop approach to teach a variety of topics, examples of which follow: How to Use Silver, Citizenship Obligations, Career Opportunities, Taxes and the Single Man/Woman, and How to Raise Money for Political Candidates.

Workshops in vocational rehabilitation provide handicapped individuals with special skills before entering the full labor market. (See CONTINUING EDUCATION UNIT.)

References: Charles R. Ashbee, *A Few Chapters in Workshop Reconstruction and Citizenship*, New York: Garland Publishing, Inc., 1978; Larry N. Davis and Earl McCallon, *Planning, Conducting, Evaluating Workshops: A Practitioner's Guide to Adult Education*, Austin, TX: Learning Concepts, 1974; Albert Nissman and Jack Lutz, *Organizing and Developing a Summer Professional Workshop*, Hamden, CT: Linnet Books, 1971.

WORK STUDY—See COLLEGE WORK-STUDY PROGRAM

WORLD CONFEDERATION OF ORGANIZATIONS OF THE TEACHING PROFESSION (WCOTP), international body made up of teachers' organizations from all parts of the world. WCOTP was formed in 1952 when three international federations of teachers agreed to merge. They were: (1) World Organization of the Teaching Profession; (2) International Federation of Teachers' Associations; and (3) International Federation of Secondary Teachers.

WCOTP's constitution, included in the organization's *1979 Annual Report,* sets forth the organization's four aims: "(1) to foster a conception of education directed towards the promotion of international understanding and good will....; (2) to improve teaching methods, educational organization and the academic and professional training of teachers....' (3) to defend the rights and the material and moral interests of the teaching profession; and (4) to promote closer relationship between teachers in different countries" (pp. 30-31). Approximately 120 national teachers' organizations enjoy full member status including the National Union of Teachers of England and Wales, the Canadian Teachers' Federation, and the National Education Association. (Associate memberships, open to state, provincial, or other regional organizations, account for an additional 40 to 50 organizations.)

WCOTP's organizational structure consists of the Assembly of Delegates (with numerous votes granted to each delegation based on the individual unit's membership size), the Executive Committee, and the Secretariat. The Assembly of Delegates meets at least every two years, with meetings rotated among the continents. Each meeting is devoted to a particular theme topic (e.g. rural education, 1971; teachers and the political process, 1975; education and development, 1980). Additional conferences and seminars are also held to study special problems of education and the teaching profession.

WCOTP publishes: *Echo,* a quarterly newsletter; an *Annual Report;* a *WCOTP Directory;* and numerous reports and service publications. The confederation is headquartered in Geneva, Switzerland.

References: World Confederation of Organizations of the Teaching Profession, *Annual Report, 1979,* Geneva, Switzerland: The Confederation, 1979; World Confederation of Organizations of the Teaching Profession, *World Confederation of Organizations of the Teaching Profession,* Geneva, Switzerland: The Confederation, Undated Brochure.

WORLD ORGANIZATION OF THE TEACHING PROFESSION—See WORLD CONFEDERATION OF ORGANIZATIONS OF THE TEACHING PROFESSION

WORLD YEARBOOK OF EDUCATION, a reference book of interest to comparative educators that first appeared in 1932 as the *Year Book of Education.* It was published from 1932-74 (except for the 1941-47 period) by Evans Brothers, United

Kingdom, and was concerned principally with educational issues in the United Kingdom and the Commonwealth. Considerable statistical information was included in each volume. In 1965, the yearbook's title was changed to *World Year Book of Education* (sometimes listed as *World Yearbook of Education*). Since 1953, the *Yearbook* has been prepared under the joint auspices of the University of London Institute of Education and Teachers College, Columbia University.

Published in English, this monographic-type work contains lengthy articles on varying subjects, these authored by authorities from different countries who represent a cross-section of educational disciplines.

References: John W. Best, *Research in Education* (Third Edition), Englewood Cliffs, NJ: Prentice-Hall, Inc., 1977; Tom Schuller and Jacquetta Megarry (Editors), *World Yearbook of Education 1979: Recurrent Education and Lifelong Learning*, London, England: Kogan Page Ltd., 1979; Eugene P. Sheehy, *Guide to Reference Books* (Ninth Edition), Chicago: American Library Association, 1976; Marda Woodbury, *A Guide to Sources of Educational Information*, Washington, DC: Information Resources Press, 1976.

WRITING CENTER, a section of an elementary school classroom set aside for the display and storage of writing materials. Such centers are designed to motivate individual or small groups of children to do original writing. The nature of the writing activities engaged in by the children is variable, ranging from personal letters to completion of reports on special topics. Included in writing centers are numerous resource materials such as personalized stationery, dictionaries, encyclopedias, and selected audio-visual equipment.

Reference: Duane R. Tovey, *Writing Centers in the Elementary Schools* (PDK Fastback 127), Bloomington, IN: The Phi Delta Kappa Educational Foundation, 1979.

WRITING SYSTEMS, methods for using written symbols to communicate words and ideas. Three writing systems have been developed: *pictographic*, *ideographic*, and *alphabetic*. In the first of these systems, pictures are used as symbols. During prehistoric times, cave drawings were used to record events. Currently, pictographic charts and graphs, with picture symbols, depict numbers, productivity, and so on. Ideographic systems (e.g. Chinese writing) have one symbol for each word. The alphabetic system, a phonetic one, consists of symbols that represent specific speech sounds. English, although phonetically imperfect, and other written languages, make use of the alphabetic system.

References: Leonard Bloomfield, "Linguistics and Reading" in *Elementary English Review*, April 1942; Dolores Durkin, *Teaching Them to Read* (Third Edition), Boston: Allyn and Bacon, Inc., 1978; Leonard R. Palmer, *Descriptive and Comparative Linguistics: A Critical Introduction*, London, England: Faber and Faber, 1972.

WRITING TO READ, a reading instruction system designed for use with primary grade children. The technique uses the language experience approach (LEA) to develop early reading and writing skills. The program is designed to be used in a laboratory setting with approximately 10 children. Phoneme mastery is accomplished via computerized instruction. Student workbooks and language development exercises are built on the premise that writing is an important activity prior to reading instruction. The approach was developed by John Henry Martin. Beginning with the natural language of children, Writing to Read provides a variety of ways for the children to express themselves. Martin believes that the freedom to experiment with language results in power over language. Children begin with the activity of writing rather than the passivity of reading. The program stresses creation first and correctness later. Hardware and software for piloting the program were provided by IBM. (See LANGUAGE EXPERIENCE APPROACH.)

References: Ron Brandt, "On Reading, Writing and Computers: A Conversation with John Henry Martin," *Educational Leadership*, Volume 39, October 1981; Kathie Durbin, "Writing to Read Program Teaches Reading through the Hands," *Oregonian*, May 30, 1983, p. B2; Susan Ohanian, "IBM's 'Writing to Read' Program: Hot New Item or Same Old Stew?" *Classroom Computer Learning*, March 1984.

YALE–NEW HAVEN TEACHERS INSTITUTE, founded in 1978 by Yale University and New Haven Public Schools, was initiated to strengthen teaching and learning in the New Haven middle and high schools. It was one of the first university-school collaboratives in the nation.

Faculty from Yale University and teachers work in a collegial relationship on school curriculum. Those teachers who become fellows in the institute must attend talks and seminars and must be involved in reading periods, curriculum unit writing, workshops and technical assistance on unit development, and meetings with their seminar leaders once or twice a week. The institute organization includes school representatives, institute coordinators, a university advisory council, a national advisory committee, and individual fellows (for 1988, in English, history, languages, art, science, and mathematics). The institute is funded by the Carnegie Corporation of New York, the College Board, a bank, the Ford Foundation, the National Endowment for the Humanities, and the New Haven Foundation.

Reference: Yale–New Haven Teachers Institute, *Yale–New Haven Teachers Institute, 1988*, New Haven, CT: The Institute, 1988.

YEARBOOK, STUDENT, a student publication designed to record the events of one academic year in a given school. Sometimes referred to as an "annual," the yearbook is most commonly published at the high school and college levels. One of the earliest known publications of this type was developed by a group of students in 1845.

Yearbooks are customarily prepared by groups of graduating seniors working closely with a faculty adviser. The book itself is divided into sections that feature academic, athletic, and club highlights of the year; pictures and commentaries about the school's administration, academic departments, and faculty members; and an expanded section consisting of student portraits with accompanying statements describing each student's school accomplishments. Paid advertising is frequently used to help defray publication costs.

References: Jim Nelson Black, *Managing the Student Yearbook*, Dallas, TX: Taylor Publishing Co., 1983; N. S. Patterson, *Yearbook Planning, Editing, and Production*, Ames, IA: Iowa State University Press, 1976.

YEARBOOK OF HIGHER EDUCATION, annual publication that provides information about all degree-granting institutions of higher education in the United States and Canada. Institutions are listed by state and province. Brief descriptive information about each college/university is furnished along with names of central office administrators, deans, and department chairpersons. The yearbook also includes current statistics relating to higher education in general (e.g. enrollments, degrees, faculty, expenditures). Finally, a section titled "Resource Information in Higher Education" lists American and Canadian higher education associations and consortia.

Reference: Yearbook of Higher Education: 1979–80 (Eleventh Edition), Chicago: Marquis Academic Media, Marquis Who's Who, 1979.

YEAR OF THE CHILD—See INTERNATIONAL YEAR OF THE CHILD

YEAR-ROUND SCHOOL, a generic term used to describe school programs that operate on a 12-months-a-year basis. Such programs are often motivated by economic factors (i.e. saving money by using school facilities and other resources during the summer months). Proponents argue that year-round schooling makes it possible for able students to graduate early through program acceleration. They also point out that teachers desiring to do so can oftentimes increase their salaries by working 12 rather than 9 months. Several year-round school plans have been developed, including: (1) the *four-quarter plan,* which divides students into four groups and requires each to be in school for three assigned (and staggered) quarters each year; (2) the *45-15 plan,* which, like the four-quarter plan, reduces enrollment at any one time to three-fourths of the total student body (in this case by scheduling 45 days of classes followed by 15 days of vacation); and (3) the *quinmester plan,* which divides the year into five nine-week sessions and requires students to attend four of the five. (See QUINMESTER PLAN.)

References: American Association of School Administrators, *9 + The Year-Round School*, Washington, DC: The Association, 1970; National Education Association, *What Research Says About: Year-Round Schools*, Washington, DC: National Education Association, 1987; Mossie J. Richmond, Jr., *Issues in Year-Round Education*, North Quincy, MA: Christopher Publishing House, 1977.

YESHIVAH, plural is Yeshivot, originally a Jewish educational institution devoted exclusively to the study of the Talmud. Students at the Yeshivot became masters of the Talmud and could, if they desired to pursue further studies, become rabbis. Later, rabbinical seminaries developed in Europe to train rabbis. They had broader curricula than the single-focus programs of the Yeshivot. Bible, Talmud, Midrash, history, and rabbinical literature were included in these curricula. From these two institutional models developed the major rabbinical institutions of today.

In the United States, these institutions are: (1) Yeshiva University; (2) the Jewish Theological Seminary of America; and (3) the Hebrew Union College-Jewish Institute of Religion. The last two are more like rabbinical seminaries than Yeshivot.

Yeshiva University in New York City had its origins in the Yeshivot Etz Chaim School (for young boys), founded in 1886, and the Rabbi Isaac Elchanan Theological Seminary (RIETS), founded in 1897. Today, it is a multipurpose urban university offering secular as well as religious programs.

In the United States, Yeshivah also refers to Jewish elementary day schools sponsored by orthodox Jewish organizations. (See JEWISH EDUCATION and PAROCHIAL SCHOOLS.)
References: Alexander Guttmann, *Rabbinic Judaism in the Making*, Detroit: Wayne State University Press, 1970; Charles S. Liebman, *Aspects of Religious Behavior of American Jews*, New York: Ktav Publishing House, 1974.

YOUNG MEN'S CHRISTIAN ASSOCIATION (YMCA), a worldwide movement founded (1844) in England by George Williams and introduced in the United States in 1851. In its early years, the English YMCA was basically concerned with improving the "spiritual condition of young men in the drapery and other trades by the introduction of religious services among them" (Romanofsky, p. 758).

In the United States, the YMCA movement took hold immediately and expanded considerably during the 19th and early 20th centuries. Today, the American organization consists of 1,800 independent YMCA's with a total membership of approximately 10,000,000 (including girls and women as well as boys and men). Local leadership is provided by 6,000 professional directors and 700,000 volunteers. The work of the organization is coordinated by the National Council. Elected delegates (approximately 350) represent local and regional groups at biennial National Council meetings. National Council is headquartered in New York City.

Throughout its existence, YMCA has been associated with physical education and recreation activities. In recent years, the association has diversified its program, addressing national problems such as juvenile delinquency, drug addiction, and urban problems in general.

In 1963, seven goals were established for local YMCAs. In accordance with them, each unit works to help its individual members: (1) to develop self-confidence and self-respect; (2) to develop faith for daily living based on the teachings of Jesus Christ; (3) to grow as responsible members of their families and communities; (4) to appreciate health of mind and body; (5) to recognize the worth of all persons and work for interracial and intergroup understanding; (6) to develop worldwide understanding; and (7) to develop capacities for leadership.

YMCA is found in 90 countries and includes a total of 12,000 centers. The World Alliance of YMCA's is headquartered in Geneva, Switzerland.
References: National Board of YMCA's, *Odyssey Through a Decade: Report of the National Board of YMCA's to the National Council of Young Men's Christian Association of the United States of America*, New York: The Board, May 1979; National Board of YMCA's, *People Service People*, New York: The Board, 1975; Peter Romanofsky (Editor), *Social Service Organizations* (Volume 2), Westport, CT: Greenwood Press, 1978.

YOUNG MEN'S/YOUNG WOMEN'S HEBREW ASSOCIATION (YM-YWHA), local organizations (also known as Jewish Community Centers) that serve the needs of Jewish people of all ages. Programs are offered to meet members' educational, cultural, recreation, health, social, and physical needs.

The first YMHA unit was established in Baltimore (1854). In 1888, the world famous New York YMHA (92nd Street Y) organized the first YWHA. These early Y's were generally modelled after YMCA units, with program emphasis placed on gymnastic activities and sports. During and after World War I, the Jewish Welfare Board began working to consolidate Jewish groups. It merged with YMHA in 1921, later with YWHA. Gradually, the formerly separate YMHA and YWHA units were replaced by the more broadly based *Jewish Community Centers*. The Jewish Community Center idea spread to other parts of the world, including countries such as India, Australia, Argentina, Mexico, Canada, and Israel.

There are over 400 Jewish Community Centers in the United States today with a combined membership of over 700,000. The work of the centers is carried out by local volunteers and professionals with some centralized planning and coordination provided by the National Jewish Welfare Board. The Jewish Welfare Board is in New York City.

References: Lionel Koppman, "Little Known Interesting Items About Jewish Community Centers and JWB," New York: National Jewish Welfare Board (Mimeographed) 1974; Lionel Koppman, *Made in America: The Story of a Unique Institution,* New York: National Jewish Welfare Board, Undated Booklet.

YOUNG WOMEN'S CHRISTIAN ASSOCIATION OF THE U.S.A. (YWCA), an organization founded in 1866 for the purpose of fostering "the temporal, moral, and religious welfare of young women who are dependent on their own exertions for support" (Romanofsky, p. 765). The YWCA of the U.S.A. had a forerunner in England, a YWCA formed but a few years earlier when the Prayer Union and the General Female Training Institute, two organizations working to improve the plight of English working women, were merged. The American and British YWCA's were pretty much modelled after the existing American and British YMCA's.

Currently, YWCA has almost 5,000 locations in over 400 American communities. They serve over 2,500,000 members/participants. A national board carries out policies that delegates from local associations develop. Financial support is derived from membership dues, donations, fees, and United Way support. Basic services include direct service to women and girls and action programs designed to improve their environment and working conditions. Special programs for the foreign born, students, the elimination of racism, and some overseas projects constitute a part of the association's total effort.

YWCA's main office is in New York City.

References: Communications, National Board, YWCA, *The Story of the YWCA* (Mimeographed), New York: The Association, August 1977; Peter Romanofsky (Editor), *Social Service Organizations* (Volume 2), Westport, CT: Greenwood Press, 1978.

YOUTH CONSERVATION CORPS, first enacted in 1970 (Public Law 91-378) and amended in 1977 by the 95th Congress of the United States, a program that provides funds for unemployed young adults to work on conservation projects such as timber stand improvement, reforestation, trail and campground improvement, and soil erosion projects. The Departments of the Interior and Agriculture operate the program.

Initially, young people could not be employed in the corps on a year-round basis, but in 1977 the amendments allowed for up to 12 months' employment. Unemployed high school graduates, ages 19 to 24, and unemployed high school dropouts, ages 16 to 19, were able to participate in the program. Hiring of such youth was tied to the unemployment rate, with those in areas of unemployment over 6 percent having preference.

Although many of the projects required housing away from home, each corps member was paid at least federal minimum wage. Not all projects had to be on federal lands; many state conservation projects were included. Under the 1977 amendments, 100,000 youth were to be served during the first year and up to 500,000 were to be served by the program's fifth year of operation. The Youth Conservation Corps was funded in 1979–80 for $60,000,000. It is similar, in several respects, to the Civilian Conservation Corps of the Great Depression. (See CIVILIAN CONSERVATION CORPS.)

References: Public Law 91-378, *United States Statutes at Large, 1970–1971* (Volume 84, Part 1), Washington, DC: Government Printing Office, 1971; *Youth Employment and Training Legislation* (Hearing before the Subcommittee on Employment Opportunities), Washington, DC: U.S. Government Printing Office, 1977.

ZERO-BASE BUDGETING, a form of budgeting that requires the administrator to assume that no dollars are available; from this "zero" starting position, every program item (unit) is described with accompanying justifications and cost estimates. Items requested are then listed in order of priority and evaluated on a regular basis.

The zero-base budgeting approach was developed at Texas Instruments in the 1960s and later adopted by numerous corporations and governmental agencies. Paul J. Stonich and his colleagues describe zero-base planning and budgeting as a six-step process: (1) developing planning assumptions; (2) identifying "decision units" (activity units that can be analyzed individually); (3) analysis of each decision unit; (4) ranking, or the establishment of priorities; (5) preparation of detailed budgets; and (6) evaluation.

John Greenhalgh, authority on school business management, advises those interested in introducing zero-base budgeting to apply this approach to noninstructional activities first, principally because application is easier; furthermore, results are more readily measured there.

References: Percy E. Burrup, Vern Brimsley, Jr., and Rulon R. Garfield, *Financing Education in a Climate of Change* (Fourth Edition), Boston: Allyn and Bacon, Inc., 1988; John Greenhalgh, *Practitioner's Guide to School Business Management,* Boston: Allyn and Bacon, Inc., 1978; Paul J. Stonich, et al., *Zero-Base Planning and Budgeting: Improved Cost Control and Resource Allocation,* Homewood, IL: Dow Jones-Irwin, 1977.

ZERO REJECTION—See *MILLS v. DISTRICT OF COLUMBIA BOARD OF EDUCATION; PARC DECISION*

z-SCORE, a standard score used in statistics that allows comparison of a score or scores by reporting distance from the mean. Distance is expressed as the number of standard deviations from the mean to a particular score.

A z-score is found by calculating the mean ($\bar{X}$) and standard deviation (S) of a set of scores. These figures are then substituted in the following formula:

$$z = \frac{X - \bar{X}}{S} \text{ (where } X \text{ is the score itself).}$$

If a student received a score of 40 on a test, for example, the mean for the class was 30, and the standard deviation for the class was 10, the z-score would be 1.00, calculated as follows:

$$z = \frac{40 - 30}{10} = +1.00$$

If another student received a score of 25 on the same test, the z-score for the second student would be −0.50, calculated as follows:

$$z = \frac{25 - 30}{10} = -0.50$$

In these illustrations, the first student's score is +1 standard deviations above the mean while the second student's score falls one half of a standard deviation below the mean. These facts enable an investigator to compare one individual's position with that of another. It also allows comparisons of positions on other tests. (See STANDARD DEVIATION and STANDARD SCORES.)

References: L. R. Gay, *Educational Evaluation and Measurement: Competencies for Analysis and Application* (Third Edition), Columbus, OH: Charles E. Merrill Publishing Company, 1987; Charles D. Hopkins, *Understanding Educational Research: An Inquiry Approach,* Columbus, OH: Charles E. Merrill Publishing Company, 1980.

Appendixes

APPENDIX I
Code of Ethics of the Education Profession

The educator, believing in the worth and dignity of each human being, recognizes the supreme importance of the pursuit of truth, devotion to excellence, and the nurture of democratic principles. Essential to these goals is the protection of freedom to learn and to teach and the guarantee of equal educational opportunity for all. The educator accepts the responsibility to adhere to the highest ethical standards.

The educator recognizes the magnitude of the responsibility inherent in the teaching process. The desire for the respect and confidence of one's colleagues, of students, of parents, and of the members of the community provides the incentive to attain and maintain the highest possible degree of ethical conduct. The Code of Ethics of the Education Profession indicates the aspiration of all educators and provides standards by which to judge conduct.

The remedies specified by the NEA and/or its affiliates for the violation of any provision of this Code shall be exclusive and no such provision shall be enforceable in any form other than one specifically designated by the NEA or its affiliates.

PRINCIPLE 1
Commitment to the Student

The educator strives to help each student realize his or her potential as a worthy and effective member of society. The educator therefore works to stimulate the spirit of inquiry, the acquisition of knowledge and understanding, and the thoughtful formulation of worthy goals.

In fulfillment of the obligation to the student, the educator—

1. Shall not unreasonably restrain the student from independent action in the pursuit of learning.
2. Shall not unreasonably deny the student access to varying points of view.
3. Shall not deliberately suppress or distort subject matter relevant to the student's progress.
4. Shall make reasonable effort to protect the student from conditions harmful to learning or to health and safety.
5. Shall not intentionally expose the student to embarrassment or disparagement.
6. Shall not on the basis of race, color, creed, sex, national origin, marital status, political or religious beliefs, family, social or cultural background, or sexual orientation, unfairly:
   a. Exclude any student from participation in any program;
   b. Deny benefits to any student;
   c. Grant any advantage to any student.
7. Shall not use professional relationships with students for private advantage.
8. Shall not disclose information about students obtained in the course of professional service, unless disclosure serves a compelling professional purpose or is required by law.

PRINCIPLE II
Commitment to the Profession

The education profession is vested by the public with a trust and responsibility requiring the highest ideals of professional service.

In the belief that the quality of the services of the education profession directly influences the nation and its citizens, the educator shall exert every effort to raise professional standards, to promote a climate that encourages the exercise of professional judgment, to achieve conditions which attract persons worthy of the trust to careers in education, and to assist in preventing the practice of the profession by unqualified persons.

In fullfillment of the obligations to the profession, the educator—

1. Shall not in an application for a professional position deliberately make a false statement or fail to disclose a material fact related to competency and qualifications.
2. Shall not misrepresent his/her professional qualifications.
3. Shall not assist entry into the profession of a person known to be unqualified in respect to character, education, or other relevant attribute.
4. Shall not knowingly make a false statement concerning the qualifications of a candidate for a professional position.
5. Shall not assist a noneducator in the unauthorized practice of teaching.
6. Shall not disclose information about colleagues obtained in the course of professional service unless disclosure serves a compelling professional purpose or is required by law.
7. Shall not knowingly make false or malicious statements about a colleague.
8. Shall not accept any gratuity, gift, or favor that might impair or appear to influence professional decisions or actions.

Source: NEA Handbook, 1988–89. Washington, DC: National Education Association, 1988; with permission.

Declaration of the Rights of the Child (Approved unanimously by the U.N. General Assembly, November 20, 1959)

PREAMBLE

Whereas the peoples of the United Nations have, in the Charter, reaffirmed their faith in fundamental human rights and in the dignity and worth of the human person, and have determined to promote social progress and better standards of life in larger freedom,

Whereas the United Nations has, in the Universal Declaration of Human Rights, proclaimed that everyone is entitled to all the rights and freedoms set forth therein, without distinction of any kind, such as race, colour, sex, language, religion, political or other opinion, national or social origin, property, birth or other status,

Whereas the child by reason of his physical and mental immaturity, needs special safeguards and care, including appropriate legal protection, before as well as after birth,

Whereas the need for such special safeguards has been stated in the Geneva Declaration of the Rights of the Child of 1924, and recognized in the Universal Declaration of Human Rights and in the statutes of specialized agencies and international organizations concerned with the welfare of children,

Whereas mankind owes to the child the best it has to give,

Now therefore,

The General Assembly

Proclaims this Declaration of the Rights of the Child to the end that he may have a happy childhood and enjoy for his own good and for the good of society the rights and freedoms herein set forth, and calls upon parents, upon men and women as individuals, and upon voluntary organizations, local authorities and national Governments to recognize these rights and strive for their observance by legislative and other measures progressively taken in accordance with the following principles:

PRINCIPLE 1

The child shall enjoy all the rights set forth in this Declaration. Every child, without any exception whatsoever, shall be entitled to these rights, without distinction or discrimination on account of race, colour, sex, language, religion, political or other opinion, national or social origin, property, birth or other status, whether of himself or of his family.

PRINCIPLE 2

The child shall enjoy special protection, and shall be given opportunities and facilities, by law and by other means, to enable him to develop physically, mentally, morally, spiritually and socially in a healthy and normal manner and in conditions of freedom and dignity. In the enactment of laws for this purpose, the best interests of the child shall be the paramount considerations.

PRINCIPLE 3

The child shall be entitled from his birth to a name and a nationality.

PRINCIPLE 4

The child shall enjoy the benefits of social security. He shall be entitled to grow and develop in health; to this end, special care and protection shall be provided both to him and to his mother, including adequate pre-natal and post-natal care. The child shall have the right to adequate nutrition, housing, recreation and medical services.

PRINCIPLE 5

The child who is physically, mentally or socially handicapped shall be given the special treatment, education and care required by his particular condition.

PRINCIPLE 6

The child, for the full and harmonious development of his personality, needs love and understanding. He shall, wherever possible, grow up in the care and under the responsibility of his parents, and, in any case, in an atmosphere of affection and of moral and material security; a child of tender years shall not, save in exceptional circumstances, be separated from his mother. Society and the public authorities shall have the duty to extend particular care to children without a family and to those without adequate means of support. Payment of State and other assistance towards the maintenance of children of large families is desirable.

PRINCIPLE 7

The child is entitled to receive education, which shall be free and compulsory, at least in the elementary stages.

He shall be given an education which will promote his general culture, and enable him, on a basis of equal opportunity, to develop his abilities, his individual judgement, and his sense of moral and social responsibility, and to become a useful member of society.

The best interests of the child shall be the guiding principle of those responsible for his education and guidance; that responsibility lies in the first place with his parents.

The child shall have full opportunity for play and recreation, which should be directed to the same purpose as education; society and the public authorities shall endeavor to promote the enjoyment of this right.

PRINCIPLE 8

The child shall in all circumstances be among the first to receive protection and relief.

PRINCIPLE 9

The child shall be protected against all forms of neglect, cruelty and exploitation. He shall not be the subject of traffic, in any form.

The child shall not be admitted to employment before an appropriate minimum age; he shall in no case be caused or permitted to engage in any occupation or employment which would prejudice his health or education, or interfere with his physical, mental or moral development.

The child shall be protected from practices which may foster racial, religious and any other form of discrimination. He shall be brought up in a spirit of understanding, tolerance, friendship among peoples, peace and universal brotherhood, and in full consciousness that his energy and talents should be devoted to the service of his fellow man.

Ethical Standards of the American Association for Counseling and Development

(Approved by Executive Committee upon referral of the Board of Directors, January 17, 1981, and revised by the AACD Governing Council, March, 1988.

PREAMBLE

The Association is an educational, scientific, and professional organization whose members are dedicated to the enhancement of the worth, dignity, potential, and uniqueness of each individual and thus to the service of society.

The Association recognizes that the role definitions and work settings of its members include a wide variety of academic disciplines, levels of academic preparation, and agency services. This diversity reflects the breadth of the Association's interest and influence. It also poses challenging complexities in efforts to set standards for the performance of members, desired requisite preparation or practice, and supporting social, legal, and ethical controls.

The specification of ethical standards enables the Association to clarify to present and future members and to those served by members, the nature of ethical responsibilities held in common by its members.

The existence of such standards serves to stimulate greater concern by members for their own professional functioning and for the conduct of fellow professionals such as counselors, guidance and student personnel workers, and others in the helping professions. As the ethical code of the Association, this document establishes principles that define the ethical behavior of Association members. Additional ethical guidelines developed by the Association's Divisions for their specialty areas may further define a member's ethical behavior.

Section A: General

1. The member influences the development of the profession by continuous efforts to improve professional practices, teaching, services, and research. Professional growth is continuous throughout the member's career and is exemplified by the development of a philosophy that explains why and how a member functions in the helping relationship. Members must gather data on their effectiveness and be guided by the findings. Members recognize the need for continuing education to ensure competent service.

2. The member has a responsibility both to the individual who is served and to the institution within which the service is performed to maintain high standards of professional conduct. The member strives to maintain the highest levels of professional services offered to the individuals to be served. The member also strives to assist the agency, organization, or institution in providing the highest caliber of professional services. The acceptance of employment in an institution implies that the member is in agreement with the general policies and principles of the institution. Therefore the professional activities of the member are also in accord with the objectives of the institution. If, despite concerted efforts, the member cannot reach agreement with the employer as to acceptable standards of conduct that allow for changes in institutional policy conducive to the positive growth and development of clients, then terminating the affiliation should be seriously considered.

3. Ethical behavior among professional associates, both members and nonmembers, must be expected at all times. When information is possessed that raises doubt as to the ethical behavior of professional colleagues, whether Association members or not, the member must take action to attempt to rectify such a condition. Such action shall use the institution's channels first and then use procedures established by the Association.

4. The member neither claims nor implies professional qualifications exceeding those possessed and is responsible for correcting any misrepresentations of these qualifications by others.

5. In establishing fees for professional counseling services, members must consider the financial status of clients and locality. In the event that the established fee structure is inappropriate for a client, assistance must be provided in finding comparable services of acceptable cost.

6. When members provide information to the public or to subordinates, peers or supervisors, they have a responsibility to ensure that the content is general, unidentified client information that is accurate, unbiased, and consists of objective, factual data.

7. Members recognize their boundaries of competence and provide only those services and use only those techniques for which they are qualified by training or experience. Members should accept only those positions for which they are professionally qualified.

8. In the counseling relationship the counselor is aware of the intimacy of the relationship and maintains respect for the client and avoids engaging in activities that seek to meet the counselor's personal needs at the expense of the client.

9. Members do not condone or engage in sexual harassment which is defined as deliberate or repeated comments, gestures, or physical contacts of a sexual nature.

10. The member avoids bringing personal issues into the counseling relationship, especially if the potential for harm is present. Through awareness of the negative impact of both racial and sexual stereotyping and discrimination, the counselor guards the individual rights and personal dignity of the client in the counseling relationship.

11. Products or services provided by the member by means of classroom instruction, public lectures, demonstrations, written articles, radio or television programs, or other types of media must meet the criteria cited in these standards.

Section B: Counseling Relationship

This section refers to practices and procedures of individual and/or group counseling relationships.

The member must recognize the need for client freedom of choice. Under those circumstances where this is not possible, the member must apprise clients of restrictions that may limit their freedom of choice.

1. The member's primary obligation is to respect the integrity and promote the welfare of the client(s), whether the client(s) is (are) assisted individually or in a group relationship. In a group setting, the member is also responsible for taking reasonable precautions to protect individuals from physical and/or psychological trauma resulting from interaction within the group.

2. Members make provisions for maintaining confidentiality in the storage and disposal of records and follow an established record retention and disposition policy. The counseling relationship and information resulting therefrom must be kept confidential, consistent with the obligations of the member as a professional person. In a group counseling setting, the counselor must set a norm of confidentiality regarding all group participants' disclosures.

3. If an individual is already in a counseling relationship with another professional person, the member does not enter into a counseling relationship without first contacting and receiving the approval of that other professional. If the member discovers that the client is in another counseling relationship after the counseling relationship begins, the member must gain the consent of the other

professional or terminate the relationship, unless the client elects to terminate the other relationship.

4. When the client's condition indicates that there is clear and imminent danger to the client or others, the members must take reasonable personal action or inform responsible authorities. Consultation with other professionals must be used where possible. The assumption of responsibility for the client(s) behavior must be taken only after careful deliberation. The client must be involved in the resumption of responsibility as quickly as possible.

5. Records of the counseling relationship, including interview notes, test data, correspondence, tape recordings, electronic data storage, and other documents, are to be considered professional information for use in counseling, and they should not be considered a part of the records of the institution or agency in which the counselor is employed unless specified by state statute or regulation. Revelation to others of counseling material must occur only upon the expressed consent of the client.

6. In view of the extensive data storage and processing capacities of the computer, the member must ensure that data maintained on a computer is: (a) limited to information that is appropriate and necessary for the services being provided; (b) destroyed after it is determined that the information is no longer of any value in providing services; and (c) restricted in terms of access to appropriate staff members involved in the provision of services by using the best computer security methods available.

7. Use of data derived from a counseling relationship for purposes of counselor training or research shall be confined to content that can be disguised to ensure full protection of the identity of the subject client.

8. The member must inform the client of the purposes, goals, techniques, rules of procedure and limitations that may affect the relationship at or before the time that the counseling relationship is entered. When working with minors or persons who are unable to give consent, the member protects these clients' best interests.

9. In view of common misconceptions related to the perceived inherent validity of computer-generated data and narrative reports, the member must ensure that the client is provided with information as part of the counseling relationship that adequately explains the limitations of computer technology.

10. The member must screen prospective group participants, especially when the emphasis is on self-understanding and growth through self-disclosure. The member must maintain an awareness of the group participants' compatability throughout the life of the group.

11. The member may choose to consult with any other professionally competent person about a client. In choosing a consultant, the member must avoid placing the consultant in a conflict of interest situation that would preclude the consultant's being a proper party to the member's efforts to help the client.

12. If the member determines an inability to be of professional assistance to the client, the member must either avoid initiating the counseling relationship or immediately terminate that relationship. In either event, the member must suggest appropriate alternatives. (The member must be knowledgeable about referral resources

so that a satisfactory referral can be initiated.) In the event the client declines the suggested referral, the member is not obligated to continue the relationship.

13. When the member has other relationships, particularly of an administrative, supervisory and/or evaluative nature with an individual seeking counseling services, the member must not serve as the counselor but should refer the individual to another professional. Only in instances where such an alternative is unavailable and where the individual's situation warrants counseling intervention should the member enter into and/or maintain a counseling relationship. Dual relationships with clients that might impair the member's objectivity and professional judgment (e.g., as with close friends or relatives) must be avoided and/or the counseling relationship terminated through referral to another competent professional.

14. The member will avoid any type of sexual intimacies with clients. Sexual relationships with clients are unethical.

15. All experimental methods of treatment must be clearly indicated to prospective recipients, and safety precautions are to be adhered to by the member.

16. When computer applications are used as a component of counseling services, the member must ensure that: (a) the client is intellectually, emotionally, and physically capable of using the computer application; (b) the computer application is appropriate for the needs of the client; (c) the client understands the purpose and operation of the computer application; and (d) a follow-up of client use of a computer application is provided to both correct possible problems (misconceptions or inappropriate use) and assess subsequent needs.

17. When the member is engaged in short-term group treatment/training programs (e.g., marathons and other encounter-type or growth groups), the member ensures that there is professional assistance available during and following the group experience.

18. Should the member be engaged in a work setting that calls for any variation from the above statements, the member is obligated to consult with other professionals whenever possible to consider justifiable alternatives.

19. The member must ensure that members of various ethnic, racial, religious, disability, and socioeconomic groups have equal access to computer applications used to support counseling services and that the content of available computer applications does not discriminate against the groups described above.

20. When computer applications are developed by the member for use by the general public as self-help/stand-alone computer software, the member must ensure that: (a) self-help computer applications are designed from the beginning to function in a stand-alone manner, as opposed to modifying software that was originally designed to require support from a counselor; (b) self-help computer applications will include within the program statements regarding intended user outcomes, suggestions for using the software, a description of the conditions under which self-help computer applications might not be appropriate, and a description of when and how counseling services might be beneficial; and (c) the manual for such applications will include the qualifications of the developer, the

development process, validation data, and operating procedures.

Section C: Measurement and Evaluation

The primary purpose of educational and psychological testing is to provide descriptive measures that are objective and interpretable in either comparative or absolute terms. The member must recognize the need to interpret the statements that follow as applying to the whole range of appraisal techniques including test and nontest data. Test results constitute only one of a variety of pertinent sources of information for personnel, guidance, and counseling decisions.

1. The member must provide specific orientation or information to the examinee(s) prior to and following the test administration so that the results of testing may be placed in proper perspective with other relevant factors. In so doing, the member must recognize the effects of socioeconomic, ethnic and cultural factors on test scores. It is the member's professional responsibility to use additional unvalidated information carefully in modifying interpretation of the test results.

2. In selecting tests for use in a given situation or with a particular client, the member must consider carefully the specific validity, reliability, and appropriateness of the test(s). General validity, reliability and the like may be questioned legally as well as ethically when tests are used for vocational and educational selection, placement, or counseling.

3. When making any statement to the public about tests and testing, the member must give accurate information and avoid false claims or misconceptions. Special efforts are often required to avoid unwarranted connotations of such terms as IQ and grade equivalent scores.

4. Different tests demand different levels of competence for administration, scoring, and interpretation. Members must recognize the limits of their competence and perform only those functions for which they are prepared. In particular, members using computer-based test interpretations must be trained in the construct being measured and the specific instrument being used prior to using this type of computer application.

5. In situations where a computer is used for test administration and scoring, the member is responsible for ensuring that administration and scoring programs function properly to provide clients with accurate test results.

6. Tests must be administered under the same conditions that were established in their standardization. When tests are not administered under standard conditions or when unusual behavior or irregularities occur during the testing session, those conditions must be noted and the results designated as invalid or of questionable validity. Unsupervised or inadequately supervised test-taking, such as the use of tests through the mails, is considered unethical. On the other hand, the use of instruments that are so designed or standardized to be self-administered and self-scored, such as interest inventories, is to be encouraged.

7. The meaningfulness of test results used in personnel, guidance, and counseling functions generally depends

on the examinee's unfamiliarity with the specific items on the test. Any prior coaching or dissemination of the test materials can invalidate test results. Therefore, test security is one of the professional obligations of the member. Conditions that produce most favorable test results must be made known to the examinee.

8. The purpose of testing and the explicit use of the results must be made known to the examinee prior to testing. The counselor must ensure that instrument limitations are not exceeded and that periodic review and/or retesting are made to prevent client stereotyping.

9. The examinee's welfare and explicit prior understanding must be the criteria for determining the recipients of the test results. The member must see that specific interpretation accompanies any release of individual or group test data. The interpretation of test data must be related to the examinee's particular concerns.

10. Members responsible for making decisions based on test results have an understanding of educational and psychological measurement, validation criteria, and test research.

11. The member must be cautious when interpreting the results of research instruments possessing insufficient technical data. The specific purposes for the use of such instruments must be stated explicitly to examinees.

12. The member must proceed with caution when attempting to evaluate and interpret the performance of minority group members or other persons who are not represented in the norm group on which the instrument was standardized.

13. When computer-based test interpretations are developed by the member to support the assessment process, the member must ensure that the validity of such interpretations is established prior to the commercial distribution of such a computer application.

14. The member recognizes that test results may become obsolete. The member will avoid and prevent the misuse of obsolete test results.

15. The member must guard against the appropriation, reproduction, or modifications of published tests or parts thereof without acknowledgment and permission from the previous publisher.

16. Regarding the preparation, publication and distribution of tests, reference should be made to:

  a. *Standards for Educational and Psychological Tests and Manuals*, revised edition, 1985, published by the American Psychological Association on behalf of itself, the American Educational Research Association and the National Council on Measurement in Education.

  b. "The Responsible Use of Tests: A Position Paper" of AMEG, APGA, and NCME. *Measurement and Evaluation in Guidance*, 1972, 5, 385-388.

  c. "Responsibilities of Users of Standardized Tests," APGA, *Guidepost*, October 5, 1978, pp. 5-8.

Section D: Research and Publication

1. Guidelines on research with human subjects shall be adhered to, such as:

  a. *Ethical Principles in the Conduct of Research with Human Participants*, Washington, D.C.: American Psychological Association, Inc., 1982.

  b. Code of Federal Regulations, Title 45, Subtitle A, Part 46, as currently issued.

  c. *Ethical Principles of Psychologists*, American Psychological Association, Principle #9: Research with Human Participants.

  d. Family Educational Rights and Privacy Act (the Buckley Amendment).

  e. Current federal regulations and various state rights privacy acts.

2. In planning any research activity dealing with human subjects, the member must be aware of and responsive to all pertinent ethical principles and ensure that the research problem, design, and execution are in full compliance with them.

3. Responsibility for ethical research practice lies with the principal researcher, while others involved in the research activities share ethical obligation and full responsibility for their own actions.

4. In research with human subjects, researchers are responsible for the subjects' welfare throughout the experiment, and they must take all reasonable precautions to avoid causing injurious psychological, physical, or social effects on their subjects.

5. All research subjects must be informed of the purpose of the study except when withholding information or providing misinformation to them is essential to the investigation. In such research the member must be responsible for corrective action as soon as possible following completion of the research.

6. Participation in research must be voluntary. Involuntary participation is appropriate only when it can be demonstrated that participation will have no harmful effects on subjects and is essential to the investigation.

7. When reporting research results, explicit mention must be made of all variable and conditions known to the investigator that might affect the outcome of the investigation or the interpretation of the data.

8. The member must be responsible for conducting and reporting investigations in a manner that minimizes the possibility that results will be misleading.

9. The member has an obligation to make available sufficient original research data to qualified others who may wish to replicate the study.

10. When supplying data, aiding in the research of another person, reporting research results, or in making original data available, due care must be taken to disguise the identity of the subjects in the absence of specific authorization from such subjects to do otherwise.

11. When conducting and reporting research, the member must be familiar with, and give recognition to, previous work on the topic, as well as observe all copyright laws and follow the principles of giving full credit to all to whom credit is due.

12. The member must give due credit through joint authorship, acknowledgment, footnote statements, or other appropriate means to those who have contributed

significantly to the research and/or publication, in accordance with such contributions.

13. The member must communicate to other members the results of any research judged to be of professional or scientific value. Results reflecting unfavorably on institutions, programs, services, or vested interests must not be withheld for such reasons.

14. If members agree to cooperate with another individual in research and/or publication, they incur an obligation to cooperate as promised in terms of punctuality of performance and with full regard to the completeness and accuracy of the information required.

15. Ethical practice requires that authors not submit the same manuscript or one essentially similar in content, for simultaneous publication consideration by two or more journals. In addition, manuscripts published in whole or in substantial part, in another journal or published work should not be submitted for publication without acknowledgment and permission from the previous publication.

Section E: Consulting

Consultation refers to a voluntary relationship between a professional helper and help-needing individual, group or social unit in which the consultant is providing help to the client(s) in defining and solving a work-related problem or potential problem with a client or client system.

1. The member acting as consultant must have a high degree of self-awareness of his/her own values, knowledge, skills, limitations, and needs in entering a helping relationship that involves human and/or organizational change and that the focus of the relationship be on the issues to be resolved and not on the person(s) presenting the problem.

2. There must be understanding and agreement between member and client for the problem definition, change goals and predicated consequences of interventions selected.

3. The member must be reasonably certain that she/he or the organization represented has the necessary competencies and resources for giving the kind of help that is needed now or may be needed later and that appropriate referral resources are available to the consultant.

4. The consulting relationship must be one in which client adaptability and growth toward self-direction are encouraged and cultivated. The member must maintain this role consistently and not become a decision maker for the client or create a future dependency on the consultant.

5. When announcing consultant availability for services, the member conscientiously adheres to the Association's *Ethical Standards*.

6. The member must refuse a private fee or other remuneration for consultation with persons who are entitled to these services through the member's employing institution or agency. The policies of a particular agency may make explicit provisions for private practice with agency clients by members of its staff. In such instances, the clients must be apprised of other options open to them should they seek private counseling services.

Section F: Private Practice

1. The member should assist the profession by facilitating the availability of counseling services in private as well as public settings.

2. In advertising services as a private practitioner, the member must advertise the services in such a manner that accurately informs the public of professional services, expertise, and techniques of counseling available. A member who assumes an executive leadership role in the organization shall not permit his/her name to be used in professional notices during periods when he/she is not actively engaged in the private practice of counseling.

3. The member may list the following: highest relevant degree, type and level of certification and/or license, address, telephone number, office hours, type and/or description of services, and other relevant information. Such information must not contain false, inaccurate, misleading, partial, out-of-context, or deceptive material or statements.

4. Members do not present their affiliation with any organization in such a way that would imply inaccurate sponsorship or certification by that organization.

5. Members may join in partnership/corporation with other members and/or other professionals provided that each member of the partnership or corporation makes clear the separate specialties by name in compliance with the regulations of the locality.

6. A member has an obligation to withdraw from a counseling relationship if it is believed that employment will result in violation of the *Ethical Standards*. If the mental or physical condition of the member renders it difficult to carry out an effective professional relationship or if the member is discharged by the client because the counseling relationship is no longer productive for the client, then the member is obligated to terminate the counseling relationship.

7. A member must adhere to the regulations for private practice of the locality where the services are offered.

8. It is unethical to use one's institutional affiliation to recruit clients for one's private practice.

Section G: Personnel Administration

It is recognized that most members are employed in public or quasi-public institutions. The functioning of a member within an institution must contribute to the goals of the institution and vice versa if either is to accomplish their respective goals or objectives. It is therefore essential that the member and the institution function in ways to (a) make the institution's goals explicit and public; (b) make the member's contribution to institutional goals specific; and (c) foster mutual accountability for goal achievement.

To accomplish these objectives, it is recognized that the member and the employer must share responsibilities in the formulation and implementation of personnel policies.

1. Members must define and describe the parameters and levels of their professional competency.

2. Members must establish interpersonal relations and working agreements with supervisors and subordinate regarding counseling or clinical relationships, confidentiality, distinction between public and private material, maintenance, and dissemination of recorded information, work load and accountability. Working agreements in each instance must be specified and made known to those concerned.

3. Members must alert their employers to conditions that may be potentially disruptive or damaging.

4. Members must inform employers of conditions that may limit their effectiveness.

5. Members must submit regularly to professional review and evaluation.

6. Members must be responsible for inservice development of self and/or staff.

7. Members must inform their staff of goals and programs.

8. Members must provide personnel practices that guarantee and enhance the rights and welfare of each recipient of their service.

9. Members must select competent persons and assign responsibilities compatible with their skills and experiences.

10. The member, at the onset of a counseling relationship, will inform the client of the member's intended use of supervisors regarding the disclosure of information concerning the case. The member will clearly inform the client of the limits of confidentiality in the relationship.

11. Members, as either employers or employees, do not engage in or condone practices that are inhumane, illegal, or unjustifiable (such as considerations based on sex, handicap, age, race) in hiring, promotion, or training.

Section H: Preparation Standards

Members who are responsible for training others must be guided by the preparation standards of the Association and relevant Divisions(s). The member who functions in the capacity of trainer assumes unique ethical responsibilities that frequently go beyond that of the member who does not function in a training capacity. These ethical responsibilities are outlined as follows:

1. Members must orient students to program expectations, basic skills development, and employment prospects prior to admission to the program.

2. Members in charge of learning experiences must establish programs that integrate academic study and supervised practice.

3. Members must establish a program directed toward developing students' skills, knowledge, and self-under-standing, stated whenever possible in competency of performance terms.

4. Members must identify the levels of competencies of their students in compliance with relevant Division standards. These competencies must accommodate the para-professional as well as the professional.

5. Members, through continual student evaluation and appraisal, must be aware of the personal limitations of the learner that might impede future performance. The instructor must not only assist the learner in securing remedial assistance but also screen from the program those individuals who are unable to provide competent services.

6. Members must provide a program that includes training in research commensurate with levels of role functioning. Para-professional and technician-level personnel must be trained as consumers of research. In addition, these personnel must learn how to evaluate their own and their program's effectiveness. Graduate training, especially at the doctoral level, would include preparation for original research by the member.

7. Members must make students aware of the ethical responsibilities and standards of the profession.

8. Preparatory programs must encourage students to value the ideals of service to individuals and to society. In this regard, direct financial remuneration or lack thereof must not influence the quality of service rendered. Monetary considerations must not be allowed to overshadow professional and humanitarian needs.

9. Members responsible for educational programs must be skilled as teachers and practitioners.

10. Members must present thoroughly varied theoretical positions so that students may make comparisons and have the opportunity to select a position.

11. Members must develop clear policies within their educational institutions regarding field placement and the roles of the student and the instructor in such placements.

12. Members must ensure that forms of learning focusing on self-understanding or growth are voluntary, or if required as part of the educational program, are made known to prospective students prior to entering the program. When the educational program offers a growth experience with an emphasis on self-disclosure or other relatively intimate or personal involvement, the member must have no administrative, supervisory, or evaluating authority regarding the participant.

13. The member will at all times provide students with clear and equally acceptable alternatives for self-understanding or growth experiences. The member will assure students that they have a right to accept these alternatives without prejudice or penalty.

14. Members must conduct an educational program in keeping with the current relevant guidelines of the Association and its Divisions.

Source: Reprinted by permission from the American Association for Counseling and Development.

APPENDIX IV
Randolph Caldecott
Medal Award Winners

(For Children's Picture Book Illustrations)

Year	Book	Author	Illustrator	Publisher
1938	*Animals of the Bible*	H. D. Fish	D. P. Lathrop	Lippincott
1939	*Mei Li*	T. Handforth	Same	Doubleday
1940	*Abraham Lincoln*	I. & E. Parin d'Aulaire	Same	Doubleday
1941	*They Were Strong and Good*	R. Lawson	Same	Viking
1942	*Make Way for Ducklings*	R. McCloskey	Same	Viking
1943	*The Little House*	V. L. Burton	Same	Houghton
1944	*Many Moons*	J. Thurber	L. Slobodkin	Harcourt
1945	*Prayer for a Child*	R. Field	E. O. Jones	Macmillan
1946	*The Rooster Crows*	(Mother Goose)	M. & M. Petersham	Macmillan
1947	*The Little Island*	G. MacDonald	L. Weisgard	Doubleday
1948	*White Snow, Bright Snow*	A. Tresselt	R. Duvoisin	Lothrop
1949	*The Big Snow*	B. & E. Hader	Same	Macmillan
1950	*Song of the Swallows*	L. Politi	Same	Scribner
1951	*The Egg Tree*	K. Milhous	Same	Scribner
1952	*Finders Keepers*	Will	Nicolas	Harcourt
1953	*The Biggest Bear*	L. Ward	Same	Houghton
1954	*Madeline's Rescue*	L. Bemelmans	Same	Viking
1955	*Cinderella, Or the Little Glass Slipper*	C. Perrault	M. Brown	Scribner
1956	*Frog Went A-Courtin*	J. Langstaff	F. Rojankovsky	Harcourt
1957	*A Tree Is Nice*	J. A. Udry	M. Simont	Harper
1958	*Time of Wonder*	R. McCloskey	Same	Viking
1959	*Chanticleer and the Fox*	Chaucer	B. Cooney	Crowell
1960	*Nine Days to Christmas*	M. Hall Ets & A. Labastida	M. Hall Ets	Viking
1961	*Baboushka and the Three Kings*	R. Robbins	N. Sidjakov	Parnassus
1962	*Once a Mouse*	M. Brown	Same	Scribner
1963	*The Snowy Day*	E. J. Keats	Same	Viking
1964	*Where the Wild Things Are*	M. Sendak	Same	Harper
1965	*May I Bring a Friend?*	B. Schenk de Regniers	B. Montresor	Atheneum
1966	*Always Room for One More*	S. Nic Leodhas	N. Hogrogian	Holt
1967	*Sam, Bangs and Moonshine*	E. Ness	Same	Holt
1968	*Drummer Hoff*	B. Emberley	E. Emberley	Prentice
1969	*The Fool of the World and the Flying Ship*	A. Ransome	U. Shulevitz	Farrar
1970	*Sylvester and the Magic Pebble*	W. Steig	Same	Windmill/Simon & Schuster
1971	*A Story-A Story*	G. E. Haley	Same	Atheneum
1972	*One Fine Day*	N. Hogrogian	Same	Macmillan
1973	*The Funny Little Woman*	A. Mosel	B. Lent	Dutton
1974	*Duffy and the Devil*	H. Zemach	M. Zemach	Farrar
1975	*Arrow to the Sun*	G. McDermott	Same	Viking
1976	*Why Mosquitoes Buzz in People's Ears*	V. Aardema	L. & D. Dillon	Dial

Year	Book	Author	Illustrator	Publisher
1977	*Ashanti to Zulu: African Traditions*	M. Musgrove	L. & D. Dillon	Dial
1978	*Noah's Ark*	——	P. Spier	Doubleday
1979	*The Girl Who Loved Wild Horses*	P. Goble	Same	Bradbury
1980	*Ox-Cart Man*	D. Hall	B. Cooney	Viking
1981	*Fables*	A. Lobel	Same	Harper
1982	*Jumanji*	C. Allsburg	Same	Houghton Mifflin
1983	*Shadow*	B. Cendrars	M. Brown	Scribner
1984	*Glorious Flight: Across the Channel with Louis Bleriot*	A. Provenson & M. Provenson	Same	Viking
1985	*St. George and the Dragon*	Retold by M. Hodges	T. S. Hyman	Little, Brown
1986	*Polar Express*	C. Van Allsburg	Same	Houghton
1987	*Hey Al*	A. Yorinks	R. Egielski	Farrar, Straus, and Giroux
1988	*Owl Moon*	J. Yolen	J. Schoenherr	Philomel
1989	*Song and Dance Man*	K. Ackerman	S. Gammel	Knopf
1990	*Lon PoPo: A Red Riding Hood Story from China*	E. Young	Same	Philomel

APPENDIX V
ERIC Clearinghouses

ADULT, CAREER, AND
VOCATIONAL EDUCATION
Ohio State University
National Center for Research in Vocational
Education
1900 Kenny Road
Columbus, Ohio 43210–1090
(614) 292–4353; (800) 848–4815

COUNSELING AND PERSONNEL
SERVICES
University of Michigan
School of Education, Room 2108
Ann Arbor, Michigan 48109–1259
(313) 764–9492

EDUCATIONAL MANAGEMENT
University of Oregon
1787 Agate Street
Eugene, Oregon 97403–5207
(503) 686–5043

ELEMENTARY AND EARLY CHILD-
HOOD EDUCATION
University of Illinois
College of Education
805 West Pennsylvania Avenue
Urbana, Illinois 61801–4897
(217) 333–1386

HANDICAPPED AND GIFTED
CHILDREN
Council for Exceptional Children
1920 Association Drive
Reston, Virginia 22091–1589
(703) 620–3660

HIGHER EDUCATION
The George Washington University
One Dupont Circle, N.W., Suite 630
Washington, D.C. 20036–1183
(202) 296–2597

INFORMATION RESOURCES
Syracuse University
School of Education
Huntington Hall, Room 030
Syracuse, New York 13244–2340
(315) 443–3640

JUNIOR COLLEGES
University of California at Los Angeles
Mathematical Science Building, Room 8118
Los Angeles, California 90024–1564
(213) 825–3931

LANGUAGES AND LINGUISTICS
Center for Applied Linguistics
1118 22nd St., N.W.
Washington, D.C. 20037–0037
(202) 429–9551

READING AND COMMUNICATION
SKILLS
Indiana University, Smith Research Ctr.
2805 East 10th St., Suite 150
Bloomington, Indiana 47408–2373
(812) 855–5847

RURAL EDUCATION AND SMALL
SCHOOLS
Appalachia Educational Laboratory
1031 Quarrier Street, P.O. Box 1348
Charleston, WV 25325
(304) 347–0400

SCIENCE, MATHEMATICS, AND
ENVIRONMENTAL EDUCATION
Ohio State University
1200 Chambers Road, Room 310
Columbus, Ohio 43212–1792
(614) 292–6717

Sources: Educational Network Division, *Directory of Institutional Projects Funded by OERI*, Washington, DC: Office of Educational Research and Improvement, January 1986; Educational Resources Information Center, *Current Index to Journals in Education*, Volume 22, No. 8, August 1990.

APPENDIX VI
Friend of Education
Award Winners

(Conferred Annually by the National Education Association)

Year	Recipient	Position
1972	Lyndon B. Johnson	President of the U.S.
1973	Abraham Ribicoff	U.S. Senator (Connecticut)
1974	Carl D. Perkins	U.S. Representative (Kentucky)
1975	Terry Sanford	Former Governor (North Carolina)
1976	Roy Wilkins	Executive Director, National Association for the Advancement of Colored People
1977	Hubert Humphrey	U.S. Senator (Minnesota)
1978	Joan Ganz Cooney	President, Children's Television Workshop and creator of "Sesame Street"
1979	Thurgood Marshall	Associate Justice, U.S. Supreme Court
1980	Jimmy Carter	President of the U.S.
1981	George McGovern	Former U.S. Senator (South Dakota)
1982	Arthur S. Flemming	Civil Rights Leader
1983	Frosty B. Troy	Newspaper Publisher (Oklahoma)
1984	Robert T. Stafford	U.S. Senator (Vermont)
1985	Barbara Parker	Director, Freedom to Learn Project (Washington, D.C.)
1986	Christa McAuliffe	Astronaut/Teacher (New Hampshire)
1987	Ernest Boyer	President, Carnegie Foundation for the Advancement of Teaching
1988	Augustus F. Hawkins	U.S. Representative (California)

Land Grant Colleges and Universities

Institution	Date State Accepted Morrill Act	Date College Was Authorized	Date College Opened to Students
Alabama A & M University	1891	1873	1875
Auburn University	1867	1872	1872
University of Alaska	1929	1922	1922
University of Arizona	1910	1885	1891
University of Arkansas	1864	1871	1872
University of Arkansas, Pine Bluff	1891	1873	1882
University of California	1866	1868	1869
Colorado State University	1879	1877	1879
University of Connecticut	1862	1881	1881
Delaware State College	1891	1891	1892
University of Delaware	1867	1867	1869
Federal City College	—	1966	1968
Florida A & M University	1891	1887	1887
University of Florida	1870	1870	1884
Fort Valley State College	1890	1891	1891
University of Georgia	1886	1785	1801
University of Guam	1972	1952	—
University of Hawaii	—	1907	1908
University of Idaho	1890	1889	1892
University of Illinois	1867	1867	1868
Purdue University	1865	1869	1874
Iowa State University	1862	1858	1859
Kansas State University	1863	1863	1863
Kentucky State University	1893	1866	1887
University of Kentucky	1863	1879	1880
Louisiana State University	1869	1874	1874
Southern University	1892	1880	1881
University of Maine	1863	1865	1868
University of Maryland	1864	1856	1859
University of Massachusetts	1863	1863	1867
Massachusetts Institute of Technology	1863	1861	1865
Michigan State University	1863	1855	1857
University of Minnesota	1863	1851	1851
Alcorn A & M College	1892	1871	1872
Mississippi State University	1866	1878	1880
Lincoln University	1891	1866	1866
University of Missouri	1863	1839	1841
Montana State College	1889	1839	1893
University of Nebraska	1867	1869	1871
University of Nevada, Reno	1866	1873	1874
University of New Hampshire	1863	1866	1868
Rutgers, the State University	1863	1766	1771
New Mexico State University	1898	1889	1890
Cornell University	1863	1865	1868
N. Carolina A & T State University	1891	1891	1891
N. Carolina State University	1866	1887	1889
N. Dakota State University	1889	1890	1891

Institution	Date State Accepted Morrill Act	Date College Was Authorized	Date College Opened to Students
Ohio State University	1864	1870	1873
Langston University	1890	1897	1898
Oklahoma State University	1890	1890	1891
Oregon State University	1868	1865	1865
Pennsylvania State University	1863	1855	1859
University of Puerto Rico	—	1903	1903
University of Rhode Island	1863	1888	1890
Clemson University	1868	1869	1893
S. Carolina State College	1868	1895	1896
S. Dakota State University	1889	1881	1884
Tennessee State University	1868	1912	1912
University of Tennessee	1868	1794	1794
Texas A & M University	1866	1871	1876
Prairie View A & M University	1891	1876	1876
Utah State University	1888	1888	1890
University of Vermont	1862	1791	1801
College of the Virgin Islands	1972	1962	—
Virginia State College	1870	1867	1868
Virginia Polytechnic Institute and State University	1870	1872	1872
Washington State University	1889	1890	1892
West Virginia University	1863	1867	1868
University of Wisconsin	1863	1848	1849
University of Wyoming	1889	1886	1887

Source: Reprinted by permission·from G. Lester Anderson (Editor), *Land-Grant Universities and Their Continuing Challenge,* copyright 1976, Michigan State University Press.

APPENDIX VIII
John Newbery Medal
Award Winners

(For Most Distinguished Contributions to Children's Literature)

Year	Book	Author	Publisher
1922	*The Story of Mankind*	H. W. van Loon	Liveright
1923	*The Voyages of Doctor Doolittle*	H. Lofting	Lippincott
1924	*The Dark Frigate*	C. Hawes	Atlantic-Little
1925	*Tales from Silver Lands*	C. Finger	Doubleday
1926	*Shen of the Sea*	A. B. Chrisman	Dutton
1927	*Smoky, The Cowhorse*	W. James	Scribner
1928	*Gayneck, The Story of a Pigeon*	D. G. Mukerji	Dutton
1929	*The Trumpeter of Krakow*	E. P. Kelly	Macmillan
1930	*Hitty, Her First Hundred Years*	R. Field	Macmillan
1931	*The Cat Who Went to Heaven*	E. Coatsworth	Macmillan
1932	*Waterless Mountain*	L. Armer	Longmans
1933	*Young Fu of the Upper Yangtze*	E. Lewis	Winston
1934	*Invincible Louisa*	C. Meigs	Little
1935	*Dobry*	M. Shannon	Viking
1936	*Caddie Woodlawn*	C. R. Brink	Macmillan
1937	*Roller Skates*	R. Sawyer	Viking
1938	*The White Stag*	K. Seredy	Viking
1939	*Thimble Summer*	E. Enright	Rinehart
1940	*Daniel Boone*	J. Daugherty	Viking
1941	*Call it Courage*	A. Sperry	Macmillan
1942	*The Matchlock Gun*	W. Edmonds	Dodd
1943	*Adam of the Road*	E. J. Gray	Viking
1944	*Johnny Tremain*	E. Forbes	Houghton
1945	*Rabbit Hill*	R. Lawson	Viking
1946	*Strawberry Girl*	L. Lenski	Lippincott
1947	*Miss Hickory*	C. Bailey	Viking
1948	*The Twenty-One Balloons*	W. P. du Bois	Viking
1949	*King of the Wind*	M. Henry	Rand
1950	*The Door in the Wall*	M. de Angeli	Doubleday
1951	*Amos Fortune, Free Man*	E. Yates	Aladdin
1952	*Ginger Pye*	E. Estes	Harcourt
1953	*Secret of the Andes*	A. N. Clark	Viking
1954	*. . . And Now Miguel*	J. Krumgold	Crowell
1955	*The Wheel on the School*	M. Dejong	Harper
1956	*Carry On, Mr. Bowditch*	J. Latham	Houghton
1957	*Miracles on Maple Hill*	V. Sorensen	Harcourt
1958	*Rifles for Watie*	H. Keith	Crowell
1959	*The Witch of Blackbird Pond*	E. Speare	Houghton
1960	*Onion John*	J. Krumgold	Crowell
1961	*Island of the Blue Dolphins*	S. O'Dell	Houghton
1962	*The Bronze Bow*	E. Speare	Houghton
1963	*A Wrinkle in Time*	M. L'Engle	Farrar
1964	*It's Like This, Cat*	E. Neville	Harper
1965	*Shadow of a Bull*	M. Wojciechowska	Atheneum
1966	*I, Juan de Pareja*	E. B. Trevino	Farrar
1967	*Up a Road Slowly*	I. Hunt	Follett

Year	Book	Author	Publisher
1968	*From the Mixed-up Files of Mrs. Basil E. Frankweiler*	E. L. Konigsburg	Atheneum
1969	*The High King*	L. Alexander	Holt
1970	*Sounder*	W. Armstrong	Harper
1971	*Summer of the Swans*	B. Byars	Viking
1972	*Mrs. Frisby and the Rats of Nimh*	R. O'Brien	Atheneum
1973	*Julie of the Wolves*	J. George	Harper
1974	*The Slave Dancer*	P. Fox	Bradbury
1975	*M. C. Higgins, The Great*	V. Hamilton	Macmillan
1976	*The Grey King*	S. Cooper	McElderry/Atheneum
1977	*Roll of Thunder, Hear My Cry*	M. Taylor	Dial
1978	*Bridge to Terabithia*	K. Paterson	Crowell
1979	*The Westing Game*	E. Raskin	Dutton
1980	*A Gathering of Days: A New England Girl's Journal, 1830-32*	J. Blos	Scribner
1981	*Jacob Have I Loved*	K. Paterson	Crowell
1982	*Visit to William Blake's Inn: Poems for Innocent and Experienced Travelers*	N. Willard	Harcourt, Brace and Jovanovich
1983	*Dicey's Song*	Cynthia Voight	Atheneum
1984	*Dear Ms. Henshaw*	Beverly Cleary	Morrow
1985	*The Hero and the Crown*	Robin McKinley	Greenwillow
1986	*Sarah, Plain and Tall*	Patricia MacLacklan	Harper
1987	*The Whipping Boy*	Sid Fleischmann	Greenwillow
1988	*Lincoln: A Photobiography*	Russell Freedman	Clarion
1989	*Joyful Noise: Poems for Two Voices*	Paul Fleischman	Harper & Row
1990	*Number the Stars*	Lois Lowry	Mifflin

APPENDIX IX
Past Presidents of the American Association of Colleges for Teacher Education

Year	President	Professional Position	Institutional Affiliation
1948–49	Walter E. Hager	President	Wilson Teachers College
1949–50	Wesley N. Peik	Dean	School of Education, University of Minnesota
1950–51	John G. Flowers	President	Southwest Texas State University
1951–52	Waldo E. Lessenger	Dean	School of Education, Wayne State University
1952–53	Robert E. McConnell	President	Central Washington State College
1953–54	Marion R. Trabue	Dean	School of Education, Pennsylvania State University
1954–55	Herbert D. Welte	President	Central Connecticut State College
1955–56	L. D. Haskew	Dean	School of Education, University of Texas
1956–57	Rees H. Hughes	President	Pittsburg State College
1957–58	Donald P. Cottrell	Dean	School of Education, Ohio State University
1958–59	Harvey M. Rice	President	Buffalo State College
1959–60	Wendell W. Wright	Dean	School of Education, Indiana University
1960–61	Henry H. Hill	President	George Peabody College for Teachers
1961–62	J. Ralph Rackley	Dean	School of Education, University of Oklahoma
1962–63	J. W. Maucker	President	Iowa State Teachers College
1963–64	Warren C. Lovinger	President	Central Missouri State College
1964–65	Walter Anderson	Dean	School of Education, New York University
1965–66	Evan R. Collins	President	University of New York, Albany
1966–67	John E. King	President	Kansas State Teachers College
1967–68	John R. Emens	President	Ball State University
1968–69	William E. Engebretson	Professor of Higher Education	Temple University
1969–70	J. Lawrence Walkup	President	Northern Arizona University
1970–71	Paul H. Masoner	Dean	School of Education, University of Pittsburgh
1971–72	Nathaniel H. Evers	Dean	Graduate School of Arts and Science, University of Denver
1972–73	George W. Denemark	Dean	School of Education, University of Kentucky
1973–74	William A. Hunter	Dean	School of Education, Tuskegee University
1974–75	Sam P. Wiggins	Dean	School of Education, Ohio University
1975–76	John Dunworth	President	George Peabody College for Teachers
1976–77	Frederick R. Cyphert	Dean	School of Education, Ohio State University
1977–78	Henry J. Hermanowicz	Dean	School of Education, Pennsylvania State Univ.
1978–79	J. T. Sandefur	Dean	School of Education, Western Kentucky University
1979–80	Bert L. Sharp	Professor of Education	University of Florida
1980–81	Robert L. Egbert	Dean	Teachers College, University of Nebraska—Lincoln
1981–82	Dean C. Corrigan	Dean	College of Education, Texas A and M University
1982–83	Jack L. Gant	Dean	College of Education, Florida State University
1983–84	Anne Flowers	Dean	School of Education, Georgia Southern College
1984–85	David C. Smith	Dean	College of Education, University of Florida
1985–86	Robert L. Saunders	Dean	College of Education, Memphis State University

Year	President	Professional Position	Institutional Affiliation
1986–87	Norene Daly	Dean	College of Education, Florida Atlantic University
1987–88	William Gardner	Dean	College of Education, University of Minnesota
1988–89	Eugene E. Eubank	Dean	School of Education, University of Missouri–Kansas City
1989–90	John I. Goodlad	Professor	Center for Educational Renewal, University of Washington
1990–91	Janice F. Weaver	Dean	College of Education, Murray State University

Source: Information furnished by American Association of Colleges for Teacher Education.

APPENDIX X
Past Presidents of the American Association of School Administrators

Year	President	Year	President
1865	Birdsey G. Northrop (Chairman)	1912	Charles E. Chadsey
1866	Birdsey G. Northrop	1913	Franklin B. Dyer
1867	N.A.	1914	Ben Blewett
1868	Emerson E. White	1915	Henry Snyder
1869	J. W. Bulkley	1916	M. P. Shawkey
1870	James P. Wickersham	1917	John D. Shoop
1871	W. D. Henkle	1918	Thomas E. Finegan
1872	John Hancock	1919	Ernest C. Hartwell
1873	William T. Harris	1920	E. U. Graff
1874	J. H. Binford	1921	Calvin N. Kendall
1875	J. Ormond Wilson	1922	Robinson G. Jones
1876	Charles S. Smart	1923	John H. Beveridge
1877	Charles S. Smart	1924	Payson Smith
1878	N.A.	1925	William McAndrew
1879	James P. Wickersham	1926	Frank W. Ballou
1880	M. A. Newell	1927	Randall J. Condon
1881	A. P. Marble	1928	Joseph M. Gwinn
1882	W. H. Ruffner	1929	Frank D. Boynton
1883	N. A. Calkins	1930	Frank Cody
1884	B. L. Butcher	1931	Norman R. Crozier
1885	Leroy D. Brown	1932	Edwin C. Broome
1886	Warren Easton	1933	Milton C. Potter
1887	Charles S. Young	1934	Paul C. Stetson
1888	N. C. Dougherty	1935	E. E. Oberholtzer
1889	Fred M. Campbell	1936	A. J. Stoddard
1890	Andrew S. Draper	1937	A. L. Threlkeld
1891	Andrew S. Draper	1938	C. B. Glenn
1892	Henry Sabin	1939	John A. Sexson
1893	Edward Brooks	1940	Ben G. Graham
1894	D. L. Kiehle	1941	Carroll R. Reed
1895	William H. Maxwell	1942	W. Howard Pillsbury
1896	Lewis H. Jones	1943	Homer W. Anderson
1897	C. B. Gilbert	1944	Worth McClure
1898	Nathan C. Schaeffer	1945	N. L. Engelhardt
1899	Edgar H. Mark	1946	Charles H. Lake
1900	Augustus S. Downing	1947	Henry H. Hill
1901	Lorenzo D. Harvey	1948	Herold C. Hunt
1902	G. R. Glenn	1949	Willard E. Goslin
1903	Charles M. Jordan	1950	John L. Bracken
1904	Henry P. Emerson	1951	Warren Travis White
1905	Edwin G. Cooley	1952	Kenneth E. Oberholtzer
1906	John W. Carr	1953	Virgil M. Rogers
1907	W. W. Stetson	1954	Lawrence G. Derthick
1908	Frank B. Cooper	1955	Jordan L. Larson
1909	William H. Elson	1956	Henry I. Willett
1910	Stratton D. Brooks	1957	Paul J. Misner
1911	William M. Davidson	1958	Philip J. Hickey

Year	President
1959	C. C. Trillingham
1960	Martin Essex
1961	Forrest E. Conner
1962	Benjamin C. Willis
1963	Irby B. Carruth
1964	Natt B. Burbank
1965	J. Win Payne
1966	George B. Brain
1967	Harold Spears
1968	William H. Curtis
1969	John L. Miller
1970	Arnold W. Salisbury
1971	Harold H. Eibling
1972	John B. Geissinger
1973	Paul A. Miller
1974	William L. Austin
1975	Norman B. Scharer
1976	H. Vaughn Phelps
1977	Frank Dick
1978	Dana P. Whitmer
1979	Norman R. Hall
1980	Olin W. Stratton
1981	Richard D. Miller
1982	William G. Stevenson
1983	Lloyd Nielsen
1984	Gale T. Bartow
1985	William B. Royster
1986	Dwight M. Davis
1987	Earl E. Ferguson
1988	June Gabler
1989	Raymond O. Shelton

Source: Information furnished by the American Association of School Administrators. The organization changed names several times during its history: 1865–70, National Association of School Superintendents; 1871–1907, Department of School Superintendence of the National Education Association; 1908–37, Department of Superintendence of the National Education Association; 1938–69, American Association of School Administrators: A Department of the National Education Association of the United States; 1970–Present, American Association of School Administrators: An Associated Organization with the National Education Association of the United States.

APPENDIX XI
Past Presidents of the American Teachers Association

Year	President	State	Year	President	
1904	J. R. E. Lee	Alabama	1951	George W. Gore, Jr.	Tennessee
1905	J. R. E. Lee	Alabama	1952	Robert C. Hatch	Alabama
1906	J. R. E. Lee	Alabama	1953	Robert C. Hatch	Alabama
1907	J. R. E. Lee	Alabama	1954	Gerard Anderson	South Carolina
1908	J. R. E. Lee	Alabama	1955	Lillian Rogers Johnson	Mississippi
1909	R. R. Wright, Sr.	Georgia	1956	Elmer T. Hawkins	Maryland
1910	R. R. Wright, Sr.	Georgia	1957	Theodore R. Speigner	North Carolina
1911	W. T. B. Williams	Virginia	1958	Charles W. Orr	Alabama
1912	W. T. B. Williams	Virginia	1959	Lucius T. Bacote	Georgia
1913	M. W. Dogan	Texas	1960	George W. Brooks	Tennessee
1914	M. W. Dogan	Texas	1961	Lelia A. Bradby	South Carolina
1915	Nathan B. Young	Florida	1962	Lucius H. Pitts	Georgia
1916	John Hope	Georgia	1963	Richard V. Moore	Florida
1917	W. H. Singleton	Tennessee	1964	J. Rupert Picott	Virginia
1918	J. S. Clark	Louisiana	1965	C. J. Duckworth	Mississippi
1919	S. G. Atkins	North Carolina	1966	R. J. Martin	Georgia
1920	John M. Gandy	Virginia			
1921	Levi J. Rowan	Mississippi			
1922	H. L. McCrorey	North Carolina			
1923	J. A. Gregg	Ohio			
1924	Mary McLeod Bethune	Florida			
1925	William W. Saunders	West Virginia			
1926	R. S. Grosley	Delaware			
1927	William A. Robinson	North Carolina			
1928	William J. Hale	Tennessee			
1929	John W. Davis	West Virginia			
1930	Mordecai W. Johnson	Dist. of Columbia			
1931	Fannie C. Williams	Louisiana			
1932	H. Councill Trenholm	Alabama			
1933	Francis W. Wood	Maryland			
1934	J. W. Scott	Ohio			
1935	Garnet C. Wilkinson	Dist. of Columbia			
1936	Rufus E. Clement	Georgia			
1937	Willa Carter Burch	Dist. of Columbia			
1938	Alphonse Heningburg	North Carolina			
1939	Carrington Davis	Maryland			
1940	Carrington Davis	Maryland			
1941	Mary L. Williams	West Virginia			
1942	Mary L. Williams	West Virginia			
1943	Mary L. Williams	West Virginia			
1944	Mary L. Williams	West Virginia			
1945	Walter N. Ridley	Virginia			
1946	Walter N. Ridley	Virginia			
1947	Walter N. Ridley	Virginia			
1948	John Brodhead	Pennsylvania			
1949	John Brodhead	Pennsylvania			
1950	George W. Gore, Jr.	Tennessee			

Source: A.T.A. Journal; June 1966; NEA Handbook, 1988-89, Washington, DC: National Education Association, 1988.
Note: ATE; national black teachers' organization; merged with National Education Association in 1966.

APPENDIX XII
Past Presidents of Association for Student Teaching (1921-69) and Association of Teacher Educators (1970-present)

Year	President	Institutional Affiliation
1921	Arthur R. Mead	Ohio Wesleyan University, Delaware, Ohio
1922	Arthur R. Mead	Ohio Wesleyan University, Delaware, Ohio
1923	W. P. Burris	University of Cincinnati, Ohio
1924	W. F. Tidyman	Virginia State Normal School for Women, Farmville, Virginia
1925	W. F. Tidyman	Virginia State Normal School for Women, Farmville, Virginia
1926	Frank E. Ellsworth	Western State Normal School, Kalamazoo, Michigan
1927	Frank E. Ellsworth	Western State Normal School, Kalamazoo, Michigan
1928	Ned H. Dearborn	New York State Department of Education, Albany, New York
1929	W. D. Armentrout	Colorado State College of Education, Greeley, Colorado
1930	W. D. Armentrout	Colorado State College of Education, Greeley, Colorado
1931	Lida Lee Tall	Maryland State Normal School, Maryland
1932	Earl C. Bowman	DePaul University, Greencastle, Indiana
1933	Florence B. Stratemeyer	Teachers College, Columbia University, New York, New York
1934	Raleigh Schorling	University of Michigan, Ann Arbor, Michigan
1935	W. D. Armentrout	Colorado State College of Education, Greeley, Colorado
1936	Alonzo F. Myers	New York University, New York City, New York
1937	Charles W. Sanford	University of Illinois, Urbana, Illinois
1938	Clara G. Stratemeyer	New York State Teachers College, Brockport, New York
1939	Edith E. Beechel	Ohio University, Athens, Ohio
1940	Edith E. Beechel	Ohio University, Athens, Ohio
1941	Verna A. Carley	Stanford University, Stanford, California
1942	Verna A. Carley	Stanford University, Stanford, California
1943	J. W. Carrington	Illinois State Normal University, Normal Illinois
1944	J. W. Carrington	Illinois State Normal University, Normal, Illinois
1945	Camilla M. Low	University of Wisconsin, Madison, Wisconsin
1946	L. O. Andrews	Indiana University, Bloomington, Indiana
1947	F. G. Borgeson	New York University, New York City, New York
1948	Louise Wilson Worthington	University of Kentucky, Lexington, Kentucky
1949	Edgar M. Tanruther	Miami University, Oxford, Ohio
1950	Margaret Lindsey	Teachers College, Columbia University, New York, New York
1951	Max Huebner	Northern Illinois State College, DeKalb, Illinois

Year	President	Institutional Affiliation
1952	Edna Heilbronn	Central Michigan University, Mt. Pleasant, Michigan
1953	Paul R. Grim	University of Minnesota, Minneapolis, Minnesota
1954	Pearl Merriman	Western Washington University, Bellingham, Washington
1955	Dwight K. Curtis	Iowa State Teachers College, Cedar Falls, Iowa
1956	Grace S. Nugent	St. Cloud State Teachers College, St. Cloud, Minnesota
1957	Thomas D. Horn	University of Texas, Austin, Texas
1958	Jessie Mae Halsted	University of Wyoming, Laramie, Wyoming
1959	Helen M. Reed	University of Kentucky, Lexington, Kentucky
1960	Lois C. Blair	Indiana University of Pennsylvania, Indiana, Pennsylvania
1961	Donald M. Sharpe	Indiana State University, Terre Haute, Indiana
1962	Lois Haynes Demille	Los Angeles Public Schools, Los Angeles, California
1963	Karl D. Edwards	University of Kansas, Lawrence, Kansas
1964	Randall R. Bebb	University of Northern Iowa, Cedar Falls, Iowa
1965	George R. Myers	Michigan State University, East Lansing, Michigan
1966	Dorothy M. McGeoch	Teachers College, Columbia University, New York, New York
1967	Alberta L. Lowe	University of Tennessee, Knoxville, Tennessee
1968	E. Brooks Smith	Wayne State University, Detroit, Michigan
1969	Curtis E. Nash	Central Michigan University, Mt. Pleasant, Michigan
1970	Mary Ellen Perkins	Georgia State University, Atlanta, Georgia
1971	Bernadene Schunk	University of Wyoming, Laramie, Wyoming
1972	Bill J. Fullerton	Arizona State University, Tempe, Arizona
1973	Hans C. Olsen	University of Missouri–St. Louis, St. Louis, Missouri
1974	Duaine C. Lang	Indiana University, Bloomington, Indiana
1975	Diane C. Sorenson	San Joaquin County Schools, Stockton, California
1976	Alan F. Quick	Central Michigan University, Mt. Pleasant, Michigan
1977	Marvin A. Henry	Indiana State University, Terre Haute, Indiana
1978	James F. Collins	Syracuse University, Syracuse, New York
1979	Charlotte Mendoza	Colorado College, Colorado Springs, Colorado
1980	F. M. (Mike) Shada	Kearney State College, Kearney, Nebraska
1981	Louis F. Dieterle	Northern Illinois University, DeKalb, Illinois
1982	Louis F. Dieterle	Northern Illinois University, DeKalb, Illinois
1983	Robert A. Roth	Michigan State Department of Education, Lansing, Michigan
1984	Peggy G. Elliott	Indiana University Northwest, Gary, Indiana
1985	W. Robert Houston	University of Houston, Houston, Texas
1986	Robert F. Schuck	Mississippi State University, Starkville, Mississippi
1987	Janet Towslee Collier	Georgia State University, Atlanta, Georgia
1988	Billy G. Dixon	Southern Illinois University, Carbondale, Illinois
1989	John Sikula	California State University, Long Beach, California
1990	Shirley Robards	University of Tulsa, Tulsa, Oklahoma
1991	Dora Scott-Nichols	Special Education Teacher, Houston Independent Schools, Houston, Texas

Note: Association for Student Teaching changed its name to Association for Teacher Educators in 1970.

Past Presidents of the Association for Supervision and Curriculum Development

Term	President	State
1944–46	Hollis L. Caswell	New York
1946–48	Bess Goodykoontz	District of Columbia
1948–50	Walter A. Anderson	New York
1950–52	Gladys Potter	California
1952–53	Maurice Ahrens	Texas
1953–54	Alice Miel	New York
1954–55	Prudence Bostwick	Colorado
1955–56	Gordon N. Mackenzie	New York
1956–57	Robert S. Gilchrist	Missouri
1957–58	G. Robert Koopman	Michigan
1958–59	Jane Franseth	District of Columbia
1959–60	William Alexander	Tennessee
1960–61	Arthur W. Foshay	New York
1961–62	William Van Til	New York
1962–63	Chester D. Babcock	Washington
1963–64	Kimball Wiles	Florida
1964–65	Harold D. Drummond	New Mexico
1965–66	Galen Saylor	Nebraska
1966–67	Arthur W. Combs	Florida
1967–68	J. Harlan Shores	Illinois
1968–69	Muriel Crosby	Delaware
1969–70	Alexander Frazier	Ohio
1970–71	John D. Greene	Louisiana
1971–72	Alvin D. Loving, Sr.	Michigan
1972–73	Jack R. Frymier	Ohio
1973–74	Harold G. Shane	Indiana
1974–75	Glenys Unruh	Missouri
1975–76	Delmo Della-Dora	California
1976–77	Philip L. Hosford	New Mexico
1977–78	Elizabeth S. Randolph	North Carolina
1978–79	Donald R. Frost	Illinois
1979–80	Benjamin Ebersole	Maryland
1980–81	Barbara Day	North Carolina
1981–82	Lucille Jordan	Georgia
1982–83	O. L. Davis, Jr.	Texas
1983–84	Lawrence S. Finkel	New York
1984–85	Phil C. Robinson	Michigan
1985–86	Carolyn S. Hughes	Ohio
1986–87	Gerald R. Firth	Georgia

Term	President	State
1987–88	Marcia Knoll	New York
1988–89	Arthur L. Costa	California
1989–90	Patricia Conran	Utah

Source: Information furnished by Association for Supervision and Curriculum Development.

APPENDIX XIV
Past Presidents of the National Association of Elementary School Principals

Term	President	State	Term	President	State
1921–22	Leonard Power	Texas	1965–66	James H. May	Oklahoma
1922–23	Worth McClure	Washington	1966–67	Maxine Hess	Colorado
1923–24	W. T. Longshore	Missouri	1967–68	Glen L. Hanks	Missouri
1924–25	Jessie M. Fink	Michigan	1968–69	Ruth Crossfield	Kansas
1925–26	Ida G. Sargeant	New Jersey	1969–70	Andrew J. Mitchell	Nevada
1926–27	E. Ruth Pyrtle	Nebraska	1970–71	Anna Rockhill	New York
1927–28	Arthur S. Gist	California	1971–72	William H. Forsberg	Minnesota
1928–29	Eva G. Pinkston	Texas	1972–73	Jack F. Dodds	Nebraska
1929–30	Herbert C. Hansen	Illinois	1973–74	John R. Tout	Missouri
1930–31	Cassie F. Roys	Nebraska	1974–75	Winston E. Turner	Dist. of Columbia
1931–32	Earl R. Laing	Michigan	1975–76	Ted E. Gary	Washington
1932–33	Elizabeth McCormick	Wisconsin	1976–77	Bertha G. Maguire	Georgia
1933–34	Aaron Kline	Illinois	1977–78	Bill M. Hambrick	Wyoming
1934–35	M. Emma Brookes	Ohio	1978–79	Nellie B. Quander	Virginia
1935–36	Harley W. Lyon	California	1979–80	Paul D. Collins	New Hampshire
1936–37	Edythe J. Brown	Indiana	1980–81	John Ourth	Illinois
1937–38	Mason A. Stratton	New Jersey	1981–82	Elaine M. Banks	Washington
1938–39	Maude A. Rhodes	Georgia	1982–83	Robert D. Anderson	Kansas
1939–40	Irvin A. Wilson	Illinois	1983–84	Gilmon W. Jenkins	Tennessee
1940–41	Isabel Tucker	Missouri	1984–85	James L. Doud	Iowa
1941–42	Robert H. Edgar	Pennsylvania	1985–86	Mildred L. Walton	Georgia
1942–43	Sarah L. Young	California	1986–87	Edna May Merson	Maryland
1943–44	Sarah L. Young	California	1987–88	Dolores B. Hardison	Florida
1944–45	Lester J. Nielson	Utah	1988–89	Alryn D. Gunderman	Minnesota
1945–46	Lester J. Nielson	Utah	1989–90	Gary D. Salyers	Oregon
1946–47	Marjorie Walters	Iowa			
1947–48	Eugene H. Herrington	Colorado			
1948–49	Raymon Eldridge	Massachusetts			
1949–50	Florence Gabriel	Ohio			
1950–51	Thomas E. Pierce	Texas			
1951–52	Blanche L. Schmidt	California			
1952–53	Edwon L. Riggs	Arizona			
1953–54	Mamie Reed	Missouri			
1954–55	Ethel Nash	Virginia			
1955–56	Robert W. Langerak	Iowa			
1956–57	Mathilda A. Gilles	Oregon			
1957–58	Robert N. Chenault	Tennessee			
1958–59	Margaret W. Efraemson	Pennsylvania			
1959–60	Vincent J. Dodge[a]	North Dakota			
1960–61	Roberta S. Barnes	Dist. of Columbia			
1961–62	Martin C. Tate	Arizona			
1962–63	Marion Cranmore	Michigan			
1963–64	Orville B. Aftreth	California			
1964–65	Helen L. Ferslev	Wisconsin			

Source: Information furnished by the National Association of Elementary School Principals.

[a]Acting President; replaced A. Raymond Ebaugh, Royal Oak, Michigan.

APPENDIX XV
Past Presidents of the National Association of Secondary School Principals

Term	President	State	Term	President	State
1916–17	B. F. Brown	Illinois	1963–64	Calloway Taulbee	New Mexico
1917–18	Jesse B. Davis	Michigan	1964–65	John M. Sexton	Florida
1918–19	William D. Davis	Pennsylvania	1965–66	Samuel M. Graves	Massachusetts
1919–20	William A. Bailey	Kansas	1966–67	G. Mason Hall	Washington
1920–21	Edmund D. Lyon	Ohio	1967–68	Robert L. Foose	New Jersey
1921–22	Merle C. Prunty	Oklahoma	1968–69	Delmas F. Miller	West Virginia
1922–23	Edward Rynearson	Pennsylvania	1969–70	Curtis Johnson	Minnesota
1923–24	Claude P. Briggs	Ohio	1970–71	J. Frank Malone	Oklahoma
1924–25	L. W. Brooks	Kansas	1971–72	W. Hobart Millsaps	Tennessee
1925–26	William E. Wing	Maine	1972–73	Edwin B. Keim	Pennsylvania
1926–27	M. R. McDaniel	Illinois	1973–74	Carey M. Pace, Jr.	Ohio
1927–28	Francis L. Bacon	Illinois	1974–75	W. D. Bruce, Jr.	Kentucky
1928–29	Joseph K. Stevens	Massachusetts	1975–76	Allan D. Walker	Connecticut
1929–30	Milo H. Stuart	Indiana	1976–77	Charles M. Fallstrom	Washington
1930–31	Louis E. Plummer	California	1977–78	LeRoy Amen	Missouri
1931–32	Curtis H. Threlkeld	New Jersey	1978–79	E. Eugene Miller	Nebraska
1932–33	William W. Haggard	Illinois	1979–80	George E. Melton	Illinois
1933–34	Robert B. Clem	Kentucky	1980–81	Larry G. Olsen	Nevada
1934–35	Charles F. Allen	Arizona	1981–82	John S. Yates	Georgia
1935–36	Harrison C. Lyseth	Maine	1982–83	J. Walter Potter	Maryland
1936–37	W. N. Van Slyck	Kansas	1983–84	Robert C. Howe	Missouri
1937–38	McClellan G. Jones	California	1984–85	Dale E. Graham	Indiana
1938–39	Paul E. Elicker	Massachusetts	1985–86	John E. Boie	Wisconsin
1939–40	K. J. Clark	Alabama	1986–87	Eugene R. Hawley	New Hampshire
1940–41	Oscar Granger	Pennsylvania	1987–88	Robert St. Clair	Minnesota
1941–42	John E. Wellwood	Michigan	1988–89	George W. Fowler	Oklahoma
1942–43	Virgil M. Hardin	Missouri	1989–90	Gerald Purdy	Utah
1943–44	Hugh H. Stewart	New York			
1944–45	E. R. Jobe	Mississippi			
1945–46	Wilfred H. Ringer	Massachusetts			
1946–47	E. W. Montgomery	Arizona			
1947–48	Galen Jones	New Jersey			
1948–49	Clarence E. Blume	Minnesota			
1949–50	William E. Buckey	West Virginia			
1950–51	W. L. Spencer	Alabama			
1951–52	Joseph B. Chaplin	Maine			
1952–53	Harold B. Brooks	California			
1953–54	Joseph C. McLain	New York			
1954–55	James E. Blue	Illinois			
1955–56	Leland N. Drake	Ohio			
1956–57	George L. Cleland	Kansas			
1957–58	R. B. Norman	Texas			
1958–59	George E. Shattuck	Connecticut			
1959–60	Cliff Robinson	Oregon			
1960–61	James E. Nancarrow	Pennsylvania			
1961–62	James D. Logsdon	Illinois			
1962–63	Eugene S. Thomas	Michigan			

Source: Information furnished by the National Association of Secondary School Principals.

APPENDIX XVI
Past Presidents of the National School Boards Association

Dates Served	President	State
1940–45	Florence C. Porter	California
1945–47	Arthur J. Crowley	New York
1947–49	David J. Rose	North Carolina
1949–50	J. Paul Elliott	California
1950–51	J. Paul Elliott	California
1951–52	Frank H. Trotter	Tennessee
1952–53	Frank H. Trotter	Tennessee
1953–54	Clifton B. Smith	New York
1954–55	J. G. Stratton	Oklahoma
1955–56	O. H. Roberts, Jr.	Indiana
1956–57	Taylor Hicks	Arizona
1957–58	Everett N. Luce	Michigan
1958–59	Carl B. Munck	California
1959–60	Robert E. Willis	Florida
1960–61	Roy O. Frantz	Colorado
1961–62	Theodore C. Sargent	Massachusetts
1962–63	Cyrus M. Higley	New York
1963–64	Fred A. Radke	Washington
1964–65	W. Leonard Robinson	Georgia
1965–66	Edna Paul	Minnesota
1966–67	Joseph Ackerman	Illinois
1967–68	Ruth Mancuso	New Jersey
1968–69	R. Winfield Smith	Pennsylvania
1969–70	Boardman W. Moore	California
1970–71	George Ewan	Wyoming
1971–72	Kenneth E. Buhrmaster	New York
1972–73	F. E. "Bud" Phillips	Iowa
1973–74	Barbara Reimers	Connecticut
1974–75	Philip B. Swain	Washington
1975–76	Cecil L. Gilliatt	North Carolina
1976–77	George W. Smith	California
1977–78	Will D. Davis	Texas
1978–79	Margaret S. Buvinger	Oklahoma
1979–80	Hiroshi Yamashita	Hawaii
1980–81	Jean S. Tufts	New Hampshire
1981–82	Robert V. Haderlein	Kansas
1982–83	Raym C. Page	Florida
1983–84	M. Joan Parent	Minnesota
1984–85	Ted J. Comstock	Idaho
1985–86	Mack J. Spears	Louisiana
1986–87	Nellie C. Weil	Alabama

Dates Served	President	State
1987–88	Jonathan T. Howe	Illinois
1988–89	Leonard Rovins	Connecticut
1989–90	James R. Oglesby	Missouri

Source: Information furnished by the National School Boards Association.

APPENDIX XVII
Past Presidents of the National Education Association

Year	President	State	Year	President	State
1857	James L. Enos	Iowa	1902	William M. Beardshear	Iowa
1858	Zalman Richards	Washington, DC	1903	Charles W. Eliot	Massachusetts
1859	Andrew J. Rickoff	Ohio	1904	John W. Cook	Illinois
1860	John W. Bulkley	New York	1905	William H. Maxwell	New York
1861	John W. Bulkley	New York	1906	William H. Maxwell	New York
1862	John W. Bulkley	New York	1907	Nathan C. Schaeffer	Pennsylvania
1863	John D. Philbrick	Massachusetts	1908	Edwin G. Cooley	Illinois
1864	William H. Wells	Illinois	1909	Lorenzo D. Harvey	Wisconsin
1865	Samuel S. Greene	Rhode Island	1910	James Y. Joyner	North Carolina
1866	James P. Wickersham	Pennsylvania	1911	Ella F. Young	Illinois
1867	James P. Wickersham	Pennsylvania	1912	Carroll G. Pearse	Wisconsin
1868	John M. Gregory	Michigan	1913	Edward T. Fairchild	Kansas
1869	Liberties Van Bokkelen	Maryland	1914	Joseph Swain	Pennsylvania
1870	Daniel B. Hagar	Massachusetts	1915	David S. Jordan	California
1871	Josiah L. Pickard	Illinois	1916	David B. Johnson	South Carolina
1872	Emerson E. White	Ohio	1917	Robert J. Aley	Maine
1873	Birdsey G. Northrop	Connecticut	1918	Mary C. Bradford	Colorado
1874	Samuel H. White	Illinois	1919	George D. Strayer	New York
1875	William T. Harris	Missouri	1920	Josephine C. Preston	Washington
1876	William F. Phelps	Minnesota	1921	Frederick M. Hunter	California
1877	McFadden A. Newell	Maryland	1922	Charl O. Williams	Tennessee
1878	McFadden A. Newell	Maryland	1923	William B. Owen	Illinois
1879	John Hancock	Ohio	1924	Olive M. Jones	New York
1880	James O. Wilson	Washington, DC	1925	Jesse H. Newlon	Colorado
1881	James H. Smart	Indiana	1926	Mary McSkimmon	Massachusetts
1882	Gustavus J. Orr	Georgia	1927	Francis G. Blair	Illinois
1883	Eli T. Tappan	Ohio	1928	Cornelia S. Adair	Virginia
1884	Thomas W. Bicknell	Massachusetts	1929	Vel W. Lamkin	Missouri
1885	Frank L. Soldan	Missouri	1930	E. Ruth Pyrtle	Nebraska
1886	Norman A. Calkins	New York	1931	Willis A. Sutton	Georgia
1887	William E. Sheldon	Massachusetts	1932	Florence Hale	Maine
1888	Aaron Gove	Colorado	1933	Joseph Rosier	West Virginia
1889	Albert P. Marble	Massachusetts	1934	Jessie Gray	Pennsylvania
1890	James H. Canfield	Kansas	1935	Henry L. Smith	Indiana
1891	William R. Garrett	Tennessee	1936	Agnes M. Samuelson	Iowa
1892	Ezekiel H. Cook	New York	1937	Orville C. Pratt	Washington
1893	Albert G. Lane	Illinois	1938	Caroline S. Woodruff	Vermont
1894	Albert G. Lane	Illinois	1939	Reuben T. Shaw	Pennsylvania
1895	Nicholas M. Butler	New Jersey	1940	Amy H. Hinricks	Louisiana
1896	Newton C. Dougherty	Illinois	1941	Donald DuShane	Indiana
1897	Charles R. Skinner	New York	1942	Myrtle H. Dahl	Minnesota
1898	James M. Greenwood	Missouri	1943	Abram C. Flora	South Carolina
1899	Eliphalet O. Lyte	Pennsylvania	1944	Edith B. Joynes	Virginia
1900	Oscar T. Corson	Ohio	1945	Edith B. Joynes	Virginia
1901	James M. Green	New Jersey	1946	Frank L. Schlagle	Kansas

Year	President	State
1947	Pearl A. Wanamaker	Washington
1948	Glen E. Snow	Utah
1949	Mabel Studebaker	Pennsylvania
1950	Andrew D. Holt	Tennessee
1951	Corma A. Mowrey	West Virginia
1952	J. Cloyd Miller	New Mexico
1953	Sarah C. Caldwell	Ohio
1954	William A. Early	Georgia
1955	Waurine E. Walker	Texas
1956	John L. Buford	Illinois
1957	Martha A. Shull	Oregon
1958	Lyman V. Ginger	Kentucky
1959	Ruth A. S. Wright	Kansas
1960	Walter W. Eshelman	Pennsylvania
1961	Clarice Kline	Wisconsin
1962	Ewald Turner	Oregon
1963	Hazel A. Blanchard	California
1964	Robert H. Wyatt	Indiana
1965	Lois V. Edinger	North Carolina
1966	Richard D. Batchelder	Massachusetts
1967	Irvamae Applegate	Minnesota
1968	Braulio Alonso	Florida
1969	Elizabeth D. Koontz (NC)/George D. Fischer (Iowa)	
1970	George D. Fischer	Iowa
1971	Helen P. Bain	Tennessee
1972	Donald E. Morrison	California
1973	Catharine Barrett	New York
1974	Helen D. Wise	Pennsylvania
1975	James A. Harris	Iowa
1976	John Ryor	Michigan
1977	John Ryor	Michigan
1978	John Ryor	Michigan
1979	John Ryor	Michigan
1980	Willard H. McGuire	Minnesota
1981	Willard H. McGuire	Minnesota
1982	Willard H. McGuire	Minnesota
1983	Willard H. McGuire	Minnesota
1984	Mary H. Futrell	Virginia
1985	Mary H. Futrell	Virginia
1986	Mary H. Futrell	Virginia
1987	Mary H. Futrell	Viginia
1988	Mary H. Futrell	Virginia
1989	Keith Geiger	Michigan

Source: *NEA Handbook, 1988–89*, Washington, DC: National Education Association, 1988.

APPENDIX XVIII
Regional Accrediting Associations

Association and Address	States Served
New England Association of Schools and Colleges 15 High St. Winchester, MA 01890	Connecticut, Maine, Massachusetts, New Hampshire, Rhode Island, Vermont
Southern Association of Colleges and Schools 795 Peachtree Street, NE Atlanta, GA 30308	Alabama, Florida, Georgia, Kentucky, Louisiana, Mississippi, North Carolina, South Carolina, Tennessee, Texas, Virginia
Northwest Association of Schools and Colleges 3700-B University Way, NE Seattle, WA 98105	Alaska, Idaho, Montana, Nevada, Oregon, Utah, Washington
North Central Association of Colleges and Schools P.O. Box 18 Boulder, CO 80306	Arizona, Arkansas, Colorado, Illinois, Indiana, Iowa, Kansas, Michigan, Minnesota, Missouri, Nebraska, New Mexico, North Dakota, Ohio, Oklahoma, South Dakota, West Virginia, Wisconsin, Wyoming
Western Association of Schools and Colleges 1614 Rollins Rd. Burlingame, CA 94010	California, Hawaii, Guam, and certain areas of the Pacific Trust Territories
Middle States Association of Colleges and Schools 3624 Market Street Philadelphia, PA 19104	Canal Zone, Delaware, District of Columbia, Maryland, New Jersey, New York, Pennsylvania, Puerto Rico, Virgin Islands

Sources: U.S. Office of Education, *Nationally Recognized Accrediting Agencies and Associations*, November 1978; Douglas Moody (Editor), *Patterson's American Education*, Volume LXXXVI, 1990 Edition, Mt. Prospect, IL: Educational Directories, Inc., 1989; Kenneth E. Young et al., *Understanding Accreditation*, San Francisco, CA: Jossey-Bass, Publishers, 1983.

Regional Educational Laboratories (funded by the U.S. Government)

Regional Educational Laboratories	Address	Regional Educational Laboratories	Address
Appalachia Educational Laboratory, Inc. (AEL)	1031 Quarrier St. P.O. Box 1348 Charleston, WV 25325 (304) 347–0400	Regional Laboratory for Educational Improvement of the Northeast and Islands	290 South Main St. Andover, MA 01810 (617) 470–1080
Far West Laboratory for Educational Research and Development (FWL)	1855 Folson St. San Francisco, CA 94103 (415) 565–3000/3125/3115	Research for Better Schools (RBS)	444North Third St. Philadelphia, PA 19123 (215) 574–9300
Mid Continent Regional Educational Laboratory (MCREL)	Denver Office—Suite 201 12500 East Iliff Aurora, CO 80014 (303) 337–0990	Southeastern Educational Improvement Laboratory (SEIL)	P.O. Box 12746 200 Park Offices, Suite 200 Research Triangle Park, NC 27709–2746 (919) 549–8216
North Central Regional Educational Laboratory (NCREL)	295 Emroy Avenue Elmhurst, IL 60126 (312) 941–7677	Southwestern Educational Development Laboratory (SEDL)	211 East Seventh St. Austin, TX 78701 (512) 476–6861
Northwest Regional Educational Laboratory (NWREL)	101 S.W. Main St., Suite 500 Portland, OR 97204 (503) 275–9500		

Source: Educational Network Division, *Directory of Institutional Projects Funded by OERI*, Washington, DC: Office of Educational Research and Improvement, January 1986; Department of Education Information Services, *Regiona Educational Laboratories*, Washington, DC: U.S. Department of Education, August 22, 1990.

Research and Development Centers (funded by the U.S. Government)

Research and Development Centers	Address	Research and Development Centers	Address
Center for Research on Elementary and Middle Schools	John Hopkins University 3505 North Charles Street Baltimore, Maryland 21218 (301) 338–7570		New Brunswick, New Jersey 08901 (201) 828–3872
National Center on Effective Secondary Schools	University of Wisconsin - Madison 1025 West Johnson Street Madison, Wisconsin 53706 (608) 263–7575	Center for Research on Evaluation, Standards, and Student Testing	Regents of the University of California Center for the Study of Evaluation 405 Hilgard Avenue University of California at Los Angeles Los Angeles, California 90024 (213) 825–4711
National Center on Education and Employment	Columbia University Teachers College Box 174 New York, New York 10027 (212) 678–3091		School of Education Campus Box 249 University of Colorado Boulder, Colorado 80309–0249 (303) 492–8280
National Center for Research to Improve Postsecondary Teaching and Learning	University of Michigan School of Education Ann Arbor, Michigan 48198–1259 (313) 936–2741	Center for the Study of Learning	University of Pittsburgh Learning, Research and Development Center 3939 O'Hara Street Pittsburgh, Pennsylvania 15260 (412) 624–7455
National Center for Postsecondary Governance and Finance	University of Maryland College of Education Room 4114 CSS Building College Park, Maryland 20742–2435 (301) 454–1568		
Center for Policy Research in Education	Rutgers, The State University of New Jersey The Eagleton Institute of Politics Wood Lawn - Neilson Campus	Center for the Study of Writing	University of California at Berkeley School of Education Berkeley, California 94720 (415) 643–7022

Research and Development Centers	Address	Research and Development Centers	Address
National Center for Research on Teacher Education	Michigan State University College of Education Erickson Hall East Lansing, Michigan 48824–1034 (517) 355–9302		School of Education l400 Washington Avenue Albany, New York 12222 (518) 442–5026
Reading Research and Education Center	University of Illinois 174 Children's Research Center 51 Gerty Drive Champaign, Illinois 61820 (217) 333–2552	National Center for Research in Mathematical Sciences Education	University of Wisconsin at Madison Wisconsin Center for Education Research 1025 West Johnson Street Madison, Wisconsin 53706 (608) 263–4285
Center for Research on the Context of Secondary School Teaching	Center for Research on the Context of Secondary School Teaching Stanford University School of Education CERAS Building Stanford, California 94305 (415) 723–4972	National Center for Improving Science Education	The Network, Inc. 290 South Main Street Andover, Massachusetts 01810 (508) 470–1080 Washington, D.C. Office 1920 L. Street, N.W. Suite 202 Washington, D.C. 20036 (202) 467–0652
National Arts Education Research Center	New York University School of Education, Health, Nursing, and Arts Profession 32 Washington Place, #31 New York, New York 10003 (212) 998–5050 University of Illinois at Urbana-Champaigne College of Applied and Fine Arts 105 Davenport House 809 South Wright Street Champaign, Illinois 61820–6219 (217) 333–2186	National Center for Educational Leadership	Graduate School of Education Harvard University Monroe C. Guttman Library 6 Appian Way Cambridge, Massachusetts 02138–3704 (617) 495–3575 George Peabody College of Education Vanderbilt University - Box 514 Nashville, Tennessee 37203 (615) 322–8014
Center for the Learning and Teaching of Elementary Subjects	Michigan State University College of Education East Lansing, Michigan 48824 (517) 353–6470	Center for Technology in Education	Bank Street College of Education 610 West 112th Street New York, New York 10025 (212) 222–6700
Center for the Learning and Teaching of Literature	State University of New York at Albany		

Research and Development Centers	Address
National Center for School Leadership	College of Education University of Illinois at Urbana-Champaign Urbana, Illinois 61801 (217) 333–2870, 244–1122
Center for Research on Effective Schooling for Disadvantaged Students	School of Arts and Sciences The John Hopkins University 3505 North Charles Street Baltimore, Maryland 21218 (301) 338–7570

Source: Office of Educational Research and Improvement, Office of Research, *Education Research and Development Centers Directory*, Washington, D.C.: U.S. Department of Education, January 1990

APPENDIX XXI
Secretaries and Executive Directors of the National Education Association of the United States*

Total Years Served	Secretary	Actual Years Served
6	William E. Sheldon	1857, 1865, 1882, 1883, 1885–86
2	John W. Bulkey	1858–59
1	Zalman Richards	1860
3	James Cruikshank	1861–63
1	David N. Camp	1864
3	Samuel Holmes White	1866, 1872, 1873
2	Libertus Van Bokkelen	1867–68
2	William Edward Crosby	1869, 1871
2	Albert Prescott Marble	1870, 1874
1	William R. Abbot	1875
6	William D. Henkle	1876–81
1	Horance Sumner Tarbell	1884
3	James Hulme Canfield	1887–89
1	William Robertson Garrett	1890
1	Ezekiel Hanson Cook	1891
1	Robert Wallace Stevenson	1892
20	Irwin Shepard	1893–1912
5	Durand William Springer	1912–17
17	James William Crabtree	1917–34
17	Willard Earl Givens	1935–52
15	William George Carr	1952–67
5	Sam M. Lambert	1967–72
10	Terry Herndon	1973–83
	Don Cameron	1983–

Source: Information furnished by the National Education Association.
*Secretaries become Executive Directors, starting in 1985.

Secretaries of Health, Education, and Welfare, and Secretaries of Education

Secretaries of Health, Education, and Welfare
(U.S. Department of Health, Education, and Welfare)

Appointed	Secretary	President
1953	Oveta Culp Hobby	Eisenhower
1955	Marion B. Folsom	Eisenhower
1958	Arthur S. Flemming	Eisenhower
1961	Abraham A. Ribicoff	Kennedy
1962	Anthony J. Celebrezze	Kennedy and L. B. Johnson (1963)
1965	John W. Gardner	L. B. Johnson
1968	Wilbur J. Cohen	
1969	Robert H. Finch	Nixon
1970	Elliot L. Richardson	Nixon
1973	Caspar W. Weinberger	Nixon and Ford (1974)
1975	Forrest D. Mathews	Ford
1977	Joseph A. Califano, Jr.	Carter
1979	Patricia R. Harris	Carter

Secretaries of Education
(U.S. Department of Education)

1979	Shirley M. Hufstedler	Carter
1981	Terrel H. Bell	Reagan
1985	William J. Bennett	Reagan
1988	Lauro F. Cavazos	Reagan/Bush

Note: A separate Department of Education, with its own secretary, was created in May 1980.

APPENDIX XXIII
Significant Federal Legislation for Education

Year	Legislation	Principal Provisions
1785	Northwest Ordinance	Aided territories by endowing Lot No. 16 of every township for public schools.
1787	Northwest Ordinance	Endowed public lands for public higher education institutions.
1802	Ohio Enabling Act	When Ohio became a state, reserved Lot No. 16 of every township for support of public schools.
1862	Morrill Act	Provided federal land grants for the establishment of agricultural-mechanical arts colleges.
1867	Office of Education	Created first federal agency for education (now U.S. Department of Education).
1887	Hatch Act	Provided funds for the establishment of experiment stations at land grant colleges.
1890	Second Morrill Act	Strengthened first Morrill Act by providing yearly endowments for agricultural-technical colleges and universities.
1914	Smith-Lever Act	Provided for extension services (home economics, agriculture) to be provided by land grant colleges.
1917	Smith-Hughes Act	Provided fiscal support for teaching of vocational education in public schools and for training of vocational education teachers.
1920	Smith-Bankhead Act	Introduced federal-state cooperation in the area of vocational rehabilitation. Included education.
1934	Johnson-O'Malley Act	Authorized contractual agreements with individual states for the education of Indian children.
1936	George-Deen Act	Increased dollar allocation to implement Smith-Hughes Act; amended Smith-Hughes to include distributive occupations.
1941	Lanham Act	Provided federal assistance for construction and operation of public schools in communities affected adversely by war-related federal activity.
1944	Serviceman's Readjustment Act (G.I. Bill of Rights)	Encouraged education of World War II veterans by providing training benefits. (Extended later to include Korean and Vietnam War veterans.)
1946	George-Barden Act	Increased dollar support of vocational education; also provided funds for practical nursing education.
1946	National School Lunch Act	Provided for distribution of funds and federally purchased foods to both public and private schools.
1946	Fulbright Act	Provided for international educational exchanges with support coming from foreign currencies acquired by the U.S. through sale of surplus property.
1950	Housing Act	Made loans available for college housing.
1950	National Science Foundation	Created NSF as a federally supported foundation; made scholarships and fellowships available for study and research in various areas of science.
1950	Public Laws 815 and 874	Also known as Impacted Area Aid legislation. Provided federal support for school construction and operation in districts where enrollments increased owing to federal activity (e.g. certain defense plants, military bases).
1956	Rural Libraries Act	Made federal funds available to the states for establishment of libraries in rural areas.
1958	National Defense Education Act	Sought to strengthen national defense by: increasing supply of competent teachers; improving education in areas of mathematics, expanded community schools program; replaced the National Reading Act with a basic skills program. Other new programs were also introduced.

Year	Legislation	Principal Provisions
1978	Middle-Income Student Assistance Act	Still guaranteeing aid to the most needy students, extended numbers of grants and loans (BEOG, Supplementary Opportunity Grants, College Work-Study, and Guaranteed Student Loans) to middle-income students.
1979	Department of Education	Established Department of Education as a cabinet-level agency; charged it with administration of over 150 existing educational programs.
1980	Refugee Education Assistance Act	Provides general assistance to local educational agencies for the education of Cuban, Haitian and Indo-Chinese refugee children and to provide assistance to State Education Agencies for the education of Cuban and Haitian refugee adults.
1981	Omnibus Budget Reconciliation Act	Replaced Title I, II, etc. of Elementary and Secondary Education Act of 1965 (ESEA) with chapters I, II, III, etc. and simplified the ESEA (1965) Act.
1982	Job Training Partnership Act	The act established programs to prepare youth and unskilled adults for entry into the labor market. Job Training programs were established for disadvantaged youth and adults. Private industry councils were established under this act.
1983	Emergency Veterans' Job Training Act	The act addressed the problem of severe and continuing unemployment among veterans (Korean Conflict, Vietnam era) by providing payments for training of these veterans and for incentives to employers to hire them. The act provides for employee job training (either at the site or through educational institutions) and counseling.
1984	Education for Economic Security Act	Provides assistance to improve elementary, secondary, and post-secondary education in mathematics and science and to provide assistance in engineering, technical and scientific personnel and in the creation of new jobs in the private sector. The law included teacher institutes and graduate fellowships.
1985	National Science Engineering and Mathematics Authorization Act	This act reauthorized the National Science Foundation (one billion dollars for FY86), the Education for Economic Security (1984), mathematics and science teacher institutes, mathematics and science in-service programs as well as the reauthorization of a variety of other educational programs (vocational, handicapped).
1986	Anti–Drug Abuse Act	Subtitle B of the act established programs for Drug-Free schools and communities. Programs include drug abuse education and prevention, with funds going to states (for use at the local level) and to institutions of higher education
1987	Stewart B. McKinney Homeless Assistance Act	The act provided funds to deal with the homeless. State literacy programs for adults and children/youth were established. Job training was provided under the act.
1989	Omnibus Trade and Competitiveness Act	Authorized almost two billion dollars (FY88, FY89) to reestablish U.S. competitiveness in the world market. Mathematics and science education, workplace literacy partnerships, English literacy, foreign language assistance, partnerships in elementary/secondary mathematics and science, and technology education are all part of the focus of the act.
1989	Jacob K. Javits Gifted and Talented Students Education Program	Authorized up to 20 million dollars per year for 1989–93 to fund programs for gifted and talented children/youth. Programs include: Pre- and In-Service Teacher Training, models and exemplary programs, technical assistance, and research under the National Center for Research and Development of Gifted and Talented Youth.
1989	Drug-Free Schools and Communities Act Amendments of 1989	For 1989, $14,700,000 was authorized for state and local programs, the training of teachers, counselors, and school personnel, grants to colleges and universities, and the development of early childhood education drug abuse prevention materials. About 25 million dollars per year was authorized for 1990–93.

Source: The principal (though not exclusive) sources for this table were: NEA's *Legislative Report*, March 1980 (used with permission); Congressional Research Service, *Major Legislation of the Congress*, Washington, DC: The Service (various volumes); US. Government Printing Office, *United States Statutes at Large*, Washington, DC; U.S. Government Printing Office (various volumes).

APPENDIX XXIV
The Teacher of the Year

Year	Teacher	Position	Community
1952	Geraldine Jones	Grade 1	Santa Barbara, CA
1953	Dorothy Hamilton	Social Studies	Milford, CT
1954	Willard Widerberg	Grade 7	Dekalb, IL
1955	Margaret Perry Teufel	Grade 4	Monmouth, OR
1956	Richard Nelson	Science	Kalispell, MT
1957	Eugene Guy Bizzell	Speech, English & Debate	Austin, TX
1958	Jean Listebarger Humphrey	Grade 2	Ames, IA
1959	Edna Donley	Math. & Speech	Alva, OK
1960	Hazel Bragg Davenport	Grade 1	Beckley, WV
1961	Helen Adams	Kindergarten	Cumberland, WI
1962	Marjorie French	Math	Topeka, KS
1963	Elmon Ousley	Speech, American Govt.& World Problems	Bellevue, WA
1964	Lawana Trout	English, Student Counselor	Sand Springs, OK
1965	Richard E. Klinck	Grade 6	Wheat Ridge, CO
1966	Mona Dayton	Grade 1	Tucson, AZ
1967	Roger Tenney	Music, Choral Director	Owatonna, MN
1968	David E. Graf	Vocational Ed. & Ind. Arts	Sandwich, IL
1969	Barbara Goleman	Language Arts & Eng. Dept. Head	Miami, FL
1970	Johnnie T. Dennis	Physics, Math, Analysis & Physics Dept. Head	Walla Walla, WA
1971	Marcha Marion Stringfellow	Grade 1	Chester County, SC
1972	James Marshall Rogers	Am. History & Black Studies	Raleigh, NC
1973	John A. Ensworth	Grade 6	Bend, OR
1974	Vivian Tom	Social Studies	Yonkers, NY
1975	Robert G. Heyer	Science	St. Paul, MN
1976	Ruby S. Murchison	Grade 7 Language Arts	Fayetteville, NC
1977	Myrra Lenore Lee	History & Social Studies	La Mesa, CA
1978	Elaine Barbour	Grade 6	Montrose, CO
1979	Marilyn W. Black	Art	Hanover, NH
1980	Beverly J. Bimes	English	St. Louis, MO
1981	Jay Sommers	Foreign Language	New Rochelle, NY
1982	Bruce E. Brombacher	Mathematics	Upper Arlington, OH
1983	LeRoy E. Hay	English	Manchester, CT
1984	Shirleen Sisney	History/Economics	Louisville, KY
1985	Therese Knecht Dozier	World History	Columbia, SC
1986	Guy R. Doud	Language/Arts	Brainerd, MN
1987	Donna H. Oliver	Biology	Burlington, NC
1988	Terry M. Weeks	Social Studies	Murfreesboro, TN
1989	Mary V. Bicouvaris	Government	Hampton, VA

Note: Sponsored by the Council of Chief State School Officers, Encyclopedia Britannica, Inc., and *Good Housekeeping* Magazine.

APPENDIX XXV
State Departments of Education

State Department of Education	Mailing Address of Chief State School Officer	State Department of Education	Mailing Address of Chief State School Officer
Alabama	50 N. Ripley Street Montgomery, Alabama 36130	Louisiana	626 North Fourth Street P.O. Box 94064 Baton Rouge, Louisiana 70804
Alaska	State Office Building P.O. Box F Juneau, Alaska 99811	Maine	Department of Education and Cultural Services Education Building State House Station #23 Augusta, Maine 04333
American Samoa	Education Building Pago Pago, American Samoa 96799		
Arizona	1535 West Jefferson Phoenix, Arizona 85007	Maryland	200 W. Baltimore Street Baltimore, Maryland 21201
Arkansas	State Education Building 4 State Capitol Mall Little Rock, Arkansas 72201	Massachusetts	Quincy Center Plaza 1385 Hancock Street Quincy, Massachusetts 02169
California	721 Capitol Mall Sacramento, California 95814	Michigan	Ottawa Street Office Building P.O. Box 30008 Lansing, Michigan 48902
Colorado	State Office Building 201 E. Colfax Denver, Colorado 80203	Minnesota	712 Capitol Square Building 550 Cedar Street St. Paul, Minnesota 55101
Connecticut	P.O. Box 2219 Hartford, Connecticut 06115	Mississippi	Sillers State Office Building P.O. Box 771 Jackson, Mississippi 39205
Delaware	Townsend Building P.O. Box 1402 Dover, Delaware 19903	Missouri	Jefferson State Office Building P.O. Box 480, 100 E. Capitol Jefferson City, Missouri 65102
District of Columbia	Public Schools of the District of Columbia 415 12th Street N.W. Washington, D.C. 20004	Montana	Office of Public Instruction Helena, Montana 59620
Florida	325 W. Gaines Street Tallahassee, Florida 32399	Nebraska	301 Centennial Mall South P.O. Box 94987 Lincoln, Nebraska 68509
Georgia	2066 Twin Towers East Atlanta, Georgia 30334	Nevada	Capitol Complex 400 West King Street Carson City, Nevada 89710
Guam	P.O. Box "D.E." Agana, Guam 96910		
Hawaii	Queen Lilluokalani Building P.O. Box 2360 Honolulu, Hawaii 96804	New Hampshire	State Office Park South 101 Pleasant Street Concord, New Hampshire 03301
Idaho	Len B. Jordan Office Building 650 W. State Street Boise, Idaho 83720	New Jersey	225 West State Street, CN500 Trenton, New Jersey 08625
Illinois	100 North First Street Springfield, Illinois 62777	New Mexico	State Department of Education Building 300 Don Gaspar Santa Fe, New Mexico 87501
Indiana	100 N. Capitol Street, #229 Room 227, State House Indianapolis, Indiana 46204	New York	111 Education Building Washington Avenue Albany, New York 12234
Iowa	State Department of Instruction E. 14th and Grand Street Des Moines, Iowa 50319	North Carolina	State Department of Public Instruction Education Building 116 W. Edenton Street Raleigh, North Carolina 27611
Kansas	Kansas State Education Building 120 East 10th Street Topeka, Kansas 66612		

State Department of Education	Mailing Address of Chief State School Officer	State Department of Education	Mailing Address of Chief State School Officer
North Dakota	Department of Public Instruction 600 Boulevard Avenue E. Bismarck, North Dakota 58505	Texas	Texas Education Agency 1701 N. Congress Avenue Austin, Texas 78701
Ohio	Ohio Departments Building 65 S. Front Street Columbus, Ohio 43215	Utah	250 East 5th South Salt Lake City, Utah 84111
Oklahoma	Oliver Hodge Memorial Education Building 2500 N. Lincoln Blvd. Oklahoma City, Oklahoma 73105	Vermont	State Department of Education 120 State Street Montpelier, Vermont 05602
Oregon	700 Pringle Parkway, S.E. Salem, Oregon 97310	Virginia	Box 6Q Richmond, Virginia 23216
Pennsylvania	Department of Education 333 Market Street Harrisburg, Pennsylvania 17126	Virgin Islands	Virgin Islands P.O. Box 630 Charlotte Amalie 00801
Puerto Rico	Education Building Apartado 759 Hato Rey, Puerto Rico 00919	Washington	Old Capitol Building Mail Stop FG–11 Olympia, Washington 98504
Rhode Island	22 Hayes Street Providence, Rhode Island 02908	West Virginia	1900 Washington Street, East Charleston, West Virginia 25305
South Carolina	Rutledge Building 1429 Senate Street Columbia, South Carolina 29201	Wisconsin	State Department of Public Instruction P.O. Box 7841 Madison, Wisconsin
South Dakota	Kneip Office Building 700 N. Illinois Street Pierre, South Dakota 57501	Wyoming	Hathaway Building Cheyenne, Wyoming 82002

Sources: Douglas Moody (Editor), *Patteson's American Education*, Volume LXXXVII, 1991 Edition, Mt. Prospect, IL: Educational Directories, Inc., 1989; Joanell Porter, *Education Directory: State Education Agency Officials 1978*, National Center for Education Statistics.

*All titles of departments are *Department of Education* unless indicated otherwise.

APPENDIX XXVI
United States Commissioners of Education

Dates of Service	Commissioner	Position Held Preceding Appointment	Appointed by President
1867–70	Henry Barnard	President, St. John College, MD	A. Johnson
1870–86	John Eaton	State Superintendent of Schools, TN	Grant
1886–89	Nathaniel H. R. Dawson	Chairman, Alabama State Executive Committee	Cleveland
1889–1906	William T. Harris	Co-founder, Concord School of Philosophy	Harrison
1906–11	Elmer E. Brown	Science Professor, Univ. of California	T. Roosevelt
1911–21	Philander P. Claxton	Education Professor, Univ. of Tennessee	Taft
1921–28	John J. Tigert	Psychology Professor, Univ. of Kentucky	Harding
1929–33	William J. Cooper	California Commissioner of Education	Coolidge
1933–34	George F. Zook	President, Univ. of Akron	F. Roosevelt
1934–48	John W. Studebaker	Superintendent, Des Moines, IA	F. Roosevelt
1949–53	Earl J. McGrath	Dean of Liberal Arts, Univ. of Iowa	Truman
1953	Lee Thurston	Dean of Education, Michigan St. College	Eisenhower
1953–56	Samuel M. Brownell	President, New Haven St. Teachers College	Eisenhower
1956–61	Lawrence G. Derthick	Superintendent, Chattanooga, TN	Eisenhower
1961–62	Sterling M. McMurrin	Vice-President, Univ. of Utah	Kennedy
1962–66	Francis Keppel	Dean of Education, Harvard Univ.	Kennedy
1966–68	Harold Howe II	Superintendent, Scarsdale, NY	L. Johnson
1969–70	James E. Allen, Jr.	N. Y. Commissioner of Education	Nixon
1970–72	Sidney P. Marland	President, Institute for Educational Development	Nixon
1973–74	John R. Ottina	Acting Commissioner	Nixon
1974–76	Terrel H. Bell	Superintendent, Salt Lake City, UT	Nixon
1976–77	Edward Aguirre	Director, U. S. Office of Education Regional Office, San Francisco	Ford
1977–79	Ernest L. Boyer	Vice-Chancellor, State Univ. of N.Y.	Carter
1980	William Smith	Director, National Teacher Corps	Carter

Note: A separate Department of Education, with its own secretary, was created in May 1980; refer to Appendix XXII for listing of secretaries of education.

APPENDIX XXVII
U.S. Department of Education (Washington, D.C.)

Major Offices	Executive Officer Title	Major Offices	Executive Officer Title
Office of the Secretary	Secretary of Education	Fund for the Improvement of Postsecondary Education	Director
Bilingual Education and Minority Languages Affairs	Director		
Legislation Office	Assistant Secretary	Higher Education	Deputy Assistant Secretary
General Counsel	General Counsel	Higher Education Management Services	Director
Inspector General	Inspector General		
Management Office	Deputy Undersecretary	Student Financial Assistance	Deputy Assistant Secretary
Intergovernmental and Interagency Affairs	Deputy Undersecretary	Vocational and Adult Education	Assistant Secretary
Planning, Budget and Evaluation	Deputy Undersecretary	Special Education and Rehabilitation Services	Assistant Secretary
Civil Rights	Assistant Secretary		
Educational Research and Improvement	Assistant Secretary	Special Education Programs	Director
Elementary and Secondary Education	Assistant Secretary	National Institute of Handicapped Research	Director
Indian Education Programs	Director	Rehabilitation Services Administration	Commissioner
Postsecondary Education	Assistant Secretary		

Approved: Deputy Undersecretary for Management, The Office of Management, September 1987.

About the Authors

The late EDWARD L. DEJNOZKA was Dean of the College of Education at the University of Nebraska-Omaha, and later Professor of Education at Florida Atlantic University.

DAVID E. KAPEL is Dean of the School of Education and Related Professional Studies at Glassboro State College, Glassboro, New Jersey. He has published over 60 articles and technical reports in his field. He was honored as one of 70 Leaders in Teacher Education by the Association of Teacher Educators at their annual meeting in Las Vegas, 1990. He published the original edition of the *American Educators' Encyclopedia* in 1982 with Edward L. Dejnozka. Dr. Kapel is the senior editor of the *Urban Review*.

CHARLES S. GIFFORD is Professor of Curriculum and Instruction at the University of New Orleans. He has published extensively in professional journals such as *Contemporary Education*, *The Clearing House*, and *Reading Improvement*. Dr. Gifford co-authored *Trends and Issues Affecting Curriculum* and *Test-Taking Made Easier*.

MARILYN B. KAPEL is Principal of Kellman Academy in Cherry Hill, New Jersey. She was an Associate Professor of Education at Our Lady of Holy Cross College, New Orleans. Her publications include "Case Study of a Teacher Effectiveness Based Reading Program" and "Improving Reading Competence of City Housing Authority Personnel: A Diversified Approach."